# WHEELOCK'S LATIN

# THE WHEELOCK'S LATIN SERIES

*Wheelock's Latin*
Frederic M. Wheelock, revised by Richard A. LaFleur

*Workbook for Wheelock's Latin*
Paul Comeau, revised by Richard A. LaFleur

*Wheelock's Latin Reader: Selections from Latin Literature*
Frederic M. Wheelock, revised by Richard A. LaFleur

*Scribblers, Scvlptors, and Scribes*
Richard A. LaFleur

# WHEELOCK'S LATIN

Frederic M. Wheelock

Revised by

Richard A. LaFleur

7th Edition

COLLINS REFERENCE
An Imprint of HarperCollins Publishers
www.harpercollins.com

Editorial consultant: Prof. Ward Briggs, University of South Carolina

WHEELOCK's™ is a trademark of Martha Wheelock and Deborah Wheelock Taylor.
WHEELOCK's LATIN (SEVENTH EDITION). Copyright © 2011 by Frederic M. Wheelock, Martha Wheelock, and Deborah Wheelock Taylor. Revision text copyright © 2011 by Richard A. LaFleur. All rights reserved. Printed in the United States of America. No part of this book may be used or reproduced in any manner whatsoever without written permission except in the case of brief quotations embodied in critical articles and reviews. For information, address HarperCollins Publishers, 195 Broadway, New York, NY 10007.

Answer keys for *Wheelock's Latin* are available only to instructors and homeschoolers; for access to these keys, please click on the Wheelock's Latin Guides link at http://harperacademic .blogspot.com/.

HarperCollins books may be purchased for educational, business, or sales promotional use. For information, please e-mail the Special Markets Department at SPsales@harpercollins.com.


SEVENTH EDITION

Library of Congress Cataloging-in-Publication data is available upon request.

ISBN 978-0-06-199722-8 (pbk.)
          17   GC/RRD   20   19   18   17   16   15   14   13

ISBN 978-0-06-199721-1
16   17   18   GC/RRD   10

# CONTENTS

Foreword . . . . . . . . . . . . . . . . . . . . . . . . . . . . . . . . . . . . . . . . . . . . ix

Preface . . . . . . . . . . . . . . . . . . . . . . . . . . . . . . . . . . . . . . . . . . . . . xiii

The Revised Edition . . . . . . . . . . . . . . . . . . . . . . . . . . . . . . . . . . . xix

*Intrōdvctiō* . . . . . . . . . . . . . . . . . . . . . . . . . . . . . . . . . . . . . . . . . . . xxv

    The Position of the Latin Language in Linguistic History . . . . . . xxv

    A Brief Survey of Latin Literature . . . . . . . . . . . . . . . . . . . . . . . . xxx

    The Alphabet and Pronunciation. . . . . . . . . . . . . . . . . . . . . . . . xxxv

Maps . . . . . . . . . . . . . . . . . . . . . . . . . . . . . . . . . . . . . . . . . . . . . . . . xlii

    I  Verbs; First and Second Conjugations; Adverbs;
       Reading and Translating . . . . . . . . . . . . . . . . . . . . . . . . . . . . . . . . 1

   II  First Declension Nouns and Adjectives; Prepositions,
       Conjunctions, Interjections. . . . . . . . . . . . . . . . . . . . . . . . . . . . . . 12

  III  Second Declension Masculine Nouns and Adjectives;
       Apposition; Word Order . . . . . . . . . . . . . . . . . . . . . . . . . . . . . . . . 23

  IV  Second Declension Neuters; Adjectives; Present of *Sum*;
       Predicate Nominatives; Substantives . . . . . . . . . . . . . . . . . . . . . . 32

   V  First and Second Conjugations: Future and Imperfect;
       Adjectives in *-er* . . . . . . . . . . . . . . . . . . . . . . . . . . . . . . . . . . . . . . 40

  VI  *Sum* and *Possum*; Complementary Infinitive . . . . . . . . . . . . . . . . 48

 VII  Third Declension Nouns . . . . . . . . . . . . . . . . . . . . . . . . . . . . . . . . 55

VIII  Third Conjugation: Present System . . . . . . . . . . . . . . . . . . . . . . . 63

  IX  Demonstratives *Hic, Ille, Iste*; Special *-īus* Adjectives . . . . . . . . . . . . . 71

   X  Fourth Conjugation and *-iō* Verbs of the Third . . . . . . . . . . . . . . . 80

  XI  Personal Pronouns *Ego, Tū,* and *Is*; Demonstratives *Is* and *Īdem*. . . . 87

 XII  The Perfect Active System; Synopsis . . . . . . . . . . . . . . . . . . . . . . . . 96

XIII  Reflexive Pronouns and Possessives; Intensive Pronoun . . . . . . . . 105

XIV    *I*-Stem Nouns of the Third Declension; Ablatives of Means, Accompaniment, and Manner ............................. 114

XV    Numerals; Genitive of the Whole; Ablative with Numerals and Ablative of Time ............................. 123

XVI    Third Declension Adjectives ................................. 131

XVII    The Relative Pronoun ..................................... 139

XVIII    First and Second Conjugations: Present System Passive; Ablative of Agent ........................................ 146

XIX    Perfect Passive System; Interrogative Pronouns and Adjectives ............................................ 153

XX    Fourth Declension; Ablatives of Place from Which and Separation ........................................... 162

XXI    Third and Fourth Conjugations: Present System Passive ......... 169

XXII    Fifth Declension; Ablative of Place Where and Summary of Ablative Uses ......................................... 176

XXIII    Participles ............................................. 184

XXIV    Ablative Absolute; Passive Periphrastic; Dative of Agent ......... 193

XXV    Infinitives; Indirect Statement ............................. 201

XXVI    Comparison of Adjectives; Ablative of Comparison ............ 210

XXVII    Irregular Comparison of Adjectives ......................... 218

XXVIII    Subjunctive Mood; Present Subjunctive; Jussive and Purpose Clauses .......................................... 227

XXIX    Imperfect Subjunctive; Present and Imperfect Subjunctive of *Sum* and *Possum*; Result Clauses .......................... 236

XXX    Perfect and Pluperfect Subjunctive; Indirect Questions; Sequence of Tenses ....................................... 245

XXXI    *Cum* Clauses; *Ferō* ..................................... 255

XXXII    Formation and Comparison of Adverbs; *Volō, Mālō, Nōlō*; Proviso Clauses .......................................... 264

XXXIII    Conditions .............................................. 273

XXXIV    Deponent Verbs; Ablative with Special Deponents .............. 282

XXXV    Dative with Adjectives, Special Verbs, and Compounds .......... 294

XXXVI    Jussive Noun Clauses; *Fīō* ................................ 303

XXXVII    Conjugation of *Eō*; Place and Time Constructions ............ 312

XXXVIII    Relative Clauses of Characteristic; Dative of Reference; Supines ................................................ 323

XXXIX    Gerund and Gerundive ................................... 332

XL  *-Ne, Num,* and *Nōnne* in Direct Questions; Fear Clauses;
Genitive and Ablative of Description. . . . . . . . . . . . . . . . . . . . . . . . . 341

*Locī Antīqvī* . . . . . . . . . . . . . . . . . . . . . . . . . . . . . . . . . . . . . . . . . . . 351

*Locī Immvtātī.* . . . . . . . . . . . . . . . . . . . . . . . . . . . . . . . . . . . . . . . . . 363

Self-Tutorial Exercises . . . . . . . . . . . . . . . . . . . . . . . . . . . . . . . . . . . 412

Key to Self-Tutorial Exercises . . . . . . . . . . . . . . . . . . . . . . . . . . . . . 446

Appendix . . . . . . . . . . . . . . . . . . . . . . . . . . . . . . . . . . . . . . . . . . . . . . 484

    Some Etymological Aids . . . . . . . . . . . . . . . . . . . . . . . . . . . . . 484

    Supplementary Syntax. . . . . . . . . . . . . . . . . . . . . . . . . . . . . . . 491

    *Svmmārivm Fōrmārvm* . . . . . . . . . . . . . . . . . . . . . . . . . . . . . 495

*Vocābvla:* English-Latin . . . . . . . . . . . . . . . . . . . . . . . . . . . . . . . . . 510

*Vocābvla:* Latin-English . . . . . . . . . . . . . . . . . . . . . . . . . . . . . . . . . 518

*Abbreviātiōnēs* . . . . . . . . . . . . . . . . . . . . . . . . . . . . . . . . . . . . . . . . 537

Index. . . . . . . . . . . . . . . . . . . . . . . . . . . . . . . . . . . . . . . . . . . . . . . . . 541

Location of the *Sententiae Antīqvae*. . . . . . . . . . . . . . . . . . . . . . . . 555

About the Authors . . . . . . . . . . . . . . . . . . . . . . . . . . . . . . . . . . . . . . 559

Credits . . . . . . . . . . . . . . . . . . . . . . . . . . . . . . . . . . . . . . . . . . . . . . . 561

# FOREWORD

The genesis of, and inspiration for, *Wheelock's Latin* was the 1946 G.I. Education bill which granted World War II veterans a college education upon their return from service. "Why would a vet, schooled on the battlefields of Europe and Asia, want to study Latin?" asked our father, then a Professor of Classics at Brooklyn College. What could this language say to those who had already seen so much reality? How could a teacher make a "dead" language become alive, pertinent, and viable? How could one teach Latin, not as an extinct vehicle, but as the reflection of a lively culture and philosophy? This was the challenge our father undertook.

Frederic Wheelock set about to create a Latin text that would give students something to think about, a humanistic diet to nurture them both linguistically and philosophically. The book began with lessons he designed especially for his Brooklyn College students. As children we smelled regularly the pungent hectograph ink which allowed him to painstakingly reproduce the chapters of a book he was designing, page by page on a gelatin pad, for one student at a time. In 1950, on Frederic's six-month sabbatical leave, the Wheelock family travelled to the remote village of San Miguel De Allende in Mexico, where Frederic conscientiously wrote his text, and our diligent mother, Dorothy, meticulously typed the manuscript on an old portable typewriter. We young children scampered irreverently underfoot or played with native children and burros.

Twelve years of refinement, revision, and actual usage in our father's classrooms resulted in the book's first edition. When students needed to learn grammar, they read lessons and literature from the great ancient writers who used the grammar in a meaningful context. Our father sought to graft the vital flesh and blood of Roman experience and thinking onto the basic bones of forms, syntax, and vocabulary; he wanted students to transcend mere gerund grinding by giving them literary and philosophical substance on which to sharpen their teeth.

As early as we can remember, classical heritage filled our house. The etymology of a word would trigger lengthy discussion, often tedious for us as adolescents but abiding as we became adults. Knowing Latin teaches us English, we were constantly reminded; at least 60% of English words are derived from Latin. Students who take Latin are more proficient and earn higher scores on the verbal SAT exam. The business world has long recognized the importance of a rich vocabulary and rates it high as evidence of executive potential and success. Understanding the etymological history of a word gives the user vividness, color, punch, and precision. It also seems that the clearer and more numerous our verbal images, the greater our intellectual power. *Wheelock's Latin* is profuse with the etymological study of English and vocabulary enrichment. Our own experiences have shown that students will not only remember vocabulary words longer and better when they understand their etymologies, but also will use them with a sharper sense of meaning and nuance.

Why, then, exercise ourselves in the actual translation of Latin? "Inexorably accurate translation from Latin provides a training in observation, analysis, judgment, evaluation, and a sense of linguistic form, clarity, and beauty which is excellent training in the shaping of one's own English expression," asserted Frederic Wheelock. There is a discipline and an accuracy learned in the translation process which is transferable to any thinking and reasoning process, such as that employed by mathematicians. In fact, our father's beloved editor at Barnes & Noble, Dr. Gladys Walterhouse, was the Math Editor there and yet an ardent appreciator of Latin and its precision.

Our father loved the humanistic tradition of the classical writers and thinkers. And he shared this love not only with his students through the *Sententiae Antīquae* sections of his Latin text, but also with his family and friends in his daily life. As young girls, we were peppered with phrases of philosophical power from the ancients, and our father would show how these truths and lessons were alive and valid today. Some of the philosophical jewels which students of Latin will find in this book are: *carpe diem,* "harvest the day"; *aurea mediocritās,* "the golden mean"; *summum bonum,* "the Highest Good"; and the derivation of "morality" from *mōrēs* ("good habits create good character," as our father used to tell us).

If learning the Latin language and the translation process are important, then getting to know the messages and art of Horace, Ovid, Vergil, and other Roman writers is equally important. Wheelock presents these classical authors' writings on such illuminating topics as living for the future, attaining excellence, aging, and friendship. The *summum bonum* of Latin studies, Frederic Wheelock wrote, "is the reading, analysis, and appreciation of genuine ancient literary humanistic Latin in which our civilization is so deeply rooted and which has much to say to us in our own century."

For the 45 years that Frederic Wheelock was a Professor of Latin, he instilled in his students the love of Latin as both language and literature, and he did so with humor and humility. He dearly loved teaching, because he was so enthusiastic about what he taught. He had a deep and abiding respect for his students and demanded discipline and high standards. He wished for Latin to be loved and learned as he lived it, as a torch passed down through the ages, to help light our way today.

In 1987, as Frederic Wheelock was dying at the end of 85 richly lived years, he recited Homer, Horace, and Emily Dickinson. He, like the ancients, leaves a legacy of the love of learning and a belief that we stand on the shoulders of the ancients. He would be delighted to know that there are still active and eager students participating in the excitement and enjoyment of his beloved Latin.

Martha Wheelock and Deborah Wheelock Taylor
*Fīliae amantissimae*

## FOR THE SEVENTH EDITION

Welcome to *Wheelock's Latin*, seventh edition! After almost a quarter of a century since our father's death, *Wheelock's Latin* and the classical tradition are current and alive. Frederic Wheelock's original intention for this textbook was the instruction of Latin in the context of Roman writers. To this design and classic text, revision author Richard A. LaFleur has brought modernity and invigoration through new but ancient and enlivening material; he has also shepherded *Wheelock's Latin* into contemporary media and arenas. We express our heartfelt gratitude to Rick LaFleur for his enterprise, his intelligence, and his loyalty.

*Wheelock's Latin* endures because Latin and the ancient Romans are universal and relevant. Philosophers, poets, and psychologists recognize the wisdom of the ancients: "*Ut amēris, amābilis estō!*" (Ovid, *Ars Amātōria,* II, 107), "In order to be loved, be lovable!" Ben Franklin then borrowed this truth, "If you would be loved, love, and be lovable." Self-help books, therapists, and even songwriters of today continue to offer this insight. In this way, *Wheelock's Latin* has become as timeless as the ancients it respects and is beloved by countless who have studied with it.

*Wheelock's Latin* is available to today's learners through modern developments which our father never could have foreseen, but about which, we imagine, he is smiling: the website, www.wheelockslatin.com, offering a rich array of interesting and useful ancillary materials; the proliferation of study aids, such as the audio CDs from Bolchazy-Carducci, where Latin is eloquently spoken; a Facebook page; smartphone apps for vocabulary and grammar; and finally, the arrival of an e-book. *Wheelock's Latin* is edifying, fun, and accessible, now more than ever with this 7th edition! *Gaudēte!*

Martha and Deborah, *semper amantissimae fīliae*

# PREFACE

Why a new beginners' Latin book when so many are already available? The question may rightly be asked, and a justification is in order.

Every year increasing numbers of students enter college without Latin; and consequently they have to begin the language as undergraduates, typically as an elective or to satisfy a foreign language requirement, if they are to have any Latin at all. Though some college beginners do manage to continue their study of Latin beyond the second year, an unfortunate number have to be satisfied with only two or three semesters. Included among these are Romance language majors, English majors, and undergraduates in a great many other fields who have been convinced of the cultural and the practical value of even a little Latin. Common too are graduate students who discover that they need some Latin and want to study it on their own—much as I taught myself Spanish from E. V. Greenfield's *Spanish Grammar* when I decided to make a trip to Mexico—and other adults who wish to learn some Latin independently of a formal academic course. Into the hands of such mature students it is a pity and a lost opportunity to put textbooks which in pace and in thought are graded to much younger learners. On the other hand, in the classical spirit of moderation, we should avoid the opposite extreme of a beginners' book so advanced and so severe that it is likely to break the spirit of even mature students in its attempt to cover practically everything in Latin.

Accordingly, the writer has striven to produce a beginners' book which is mature, humanistic, challenging, and instructive, and which, at the same time, is reasonable in its demands. Certainly it is not claimed that Latin can be made easy and effortless. However, the writer's experience with these chapters in preliminary form over a number of years shows that Latin can be made interesting despite its difficulty; it can give pleasure and profit even to the first-year student and to the student who takes only one year; it can be so presented as to afford a sense of progress and literary accomplishment more nearly commensurate with that achieved, for instance, by the student of Romance languages. The goal, then, has been a book which provides both the roots and at least some literary fruits of a sound Latin experience for those who will have only a year or so of Latin in their entire educational career, and a book which at the same time provides adequate introduction and encouragement for those who plan to continue their studies in the field. The distinctive methods and exercises employed in this book in order to attain this goal are here listed with commentary.

## 1. *SENTENTIAE ANTĪQVAE* AND *LOCĪ ANTĪQVĪ*

It can hardly be disputed that the most profitable and the most inspiring approach to ancient Latin is through original Latin sentences and passages derived from the ancient authors themselves. With this conviction the writer perused a number of likely ancient works, excerpting sentences and passages which could constitute material for the envisioned beginners' book. A prime desideratum was that the material be interesting per se and not chosen merely because it illustrated forms and syntax. These extensive excerpts provided a good cross section of Latin literature on which to base the choice of the forms, the syntax, and the vocabulary to be presented in the book. All the sentences which constitute the regular reading exercise in each chapter under the heading of *Sententiae Antīquae* ("Ancient Sentences") are derived from this body of original Latin, as is demonstrated by the citing of the ancient author's name after each sentence. The same holds for the continuous reading passages which appear both in the chapters and in the section entitled *Locī Antīquī* ("Ancient Passages"). Once the work of the formal chapters has been completed, one can go on to the crowning experience of the course, reading additional real Latin passages from ancient authors, texts that cover a wide range of interesting topics such as love, biography, philosophy, religion, morality, friendship, philanthropy, games, laws of war, anecdotes, wit, satirical comment. A few selections are drawn from late Latin and medieval authors, in order to illustrate, among other things, the continuity of Latin through the Middle Ages. The readings have in many instances been edited, omitting a word or phrase or simplifying the syntax in one way or another, but all reflect the ancient author's thought and fundamental expression and by the nature of their content constitute something of an introduction to the Roman experience; they are not "made-up" Latin composed simply to illustrate vocabulary, forms, and rules—though they are intended to do this too.

## 2. VOCABULARIES

Every chapter has a regular vocabulary list of new Latin words to be thoroughly learned. Each entry includes: the Latin word with one or more forms (e.g., with all principal parts, in the case of verbs); essential grammatical information (e.g., the gender of nouns, case governed by prepositions); English meanings (usually with the basic meaning first); and, in parentheses, representative English derivatives. The full vocabulary entry must be memorized for each item; in progressing from chapter to chapter, students will find it helpful to keep a running vocabulary list in their notebooks or a computer file, or to use vocabulary cards (with the Latin on one side, and the rest of the entry on the other). With an eye to the proverb *repetītiō est māter memoriae* ("repetition is the mother of memory"), words in the chapter vocabularies are regularly repeated in the sentences and reading passages of the immediately following chapters, as well as elsewhere in the book.

In order to avoid overloading the regular chapter vocabularies, words that are less common in Latin generally or which occur infrequently (sometimes only once) in this book are glossed in parentheses following the *Sententiae Antīquae* and the reading passages. These glosses are generally less complete than the regular vocabulary entries and are even more abbreviated in the later chapters than in the earlier ones, but they should provide sufficient information for translating the text at hand; for words whose meanings can be easily deduced from English derivatives, the English is usually not provided. The instructor's requirements regarding these vocabulary items may vary, but in general students should be expected to have at least a "passive" mastery of the words, i.e., they should be able to recognize the words if encountered in a similar context, in a later chapter, for example, or on a test; full entries for most of these "recognition" items will also be found in the end Vocabulary.

## 3. SYNTAX

Although the above-mentioned corpus of excerpts constituted the logical guide to the syntactical categories which should be introduced into the book, common sense dictated the mean between too little and too much. The categories which have been introduced should prove adequate for the reading of the mature passages of *Locī Antīquī* and also provide a firm foundation for those who wish to continue their study of Latin beyond the first year. In fact, with the skill acquired in handling this mature Latin and with a knowledge of the supplementary syntax provided in the Appendix, a student can move directly into reading a wide variety of classical and later authors. The syntax has been explained in as simple and unpedantic a manner as possible and illustrated by a large number of examples. Finally, in light of the sad reality that even English majors in college may have an inadequate knowledge of grammar, explanations of most grammatical terms have been added, usually with benefit of etymology; and these explanations have not been relegated to some general summarizing section (the kind that students usually avoid!) but have been worked in naturally as the terms first appear in the text.

## 4. FORMS AND THEIR PRESENTATION

The varieties of inflected and uninflected forms presented here are normal for a beginners' book. However, the general practice in this text has been to alternate lessons containing noun or adjective forms with lessons containing verb forms. This should help reduce the ennui which results from too much of one thing at a time. The same consideration prompted the postponement of the locative case, adverbs, and most irregular verbs to the latter part of the book, alternating with chapters that introduce subjunctives and other complex syntax.

Considerable effort has been made to place paradigms of more or less similar forms side by side for easy visual cross reference in the same chapter and also, as a rule, to have new forms follow familiar related ones in natural sequence (as when adjectives of the third declension follow the i-stem nouns).

The rate at which the syntax and the forms can be absorbed will obviously depend on the nature and the caliber of the class; the instructor will have to adjust the assignments to the situation. Though each chapter forms a logical unit, it has been found that at least two assignments have to be allotted to many of the longer chapters: the first covers discussion of the new grammar, the paradigms, the vocabularies, the "Practice and Review" sentences (renamed *Exercitātiōnēs* in the latest edition), and some of the *Sententiae Antīquae;* the second requires review, completion of the *Sententiae,* the reading passage(s), and the occasional section on etymology. Both these assignments are in themselves natural units, and this double approach contains the obvious gain of repetition.

## 5. PRACTICE AND REVIEW / *EXERCITĀTIŌNĒS*

The "Practice and Review" sentences (*Exercitātiōnēs*) were introduced to provide additional repetition of forms, syntax, and vocabulary, which is so essential in learning a language. If the author of a textbook can start with a predetermined sequence of vocabulary and syntax, for example, and is free to compose sentences based on that material, then it should be fairly simple to make the sentences of succeeding lessons repeat the items of the previous few lessons, especially if the intellectual content of the sentences is not a prime concern. But the challenge of providing readings based instead, and exclusively, on ancient texts is considerably greater; and so, while most of the items introduced in a given chapter do re-appear in the *Sententiae Antīquae* of the following chapters, the author frankly concocted the "Practice and Review" sentences (only a few of which were inspired by ancient sources) to fill in the lacunae, to guarantee further repetition than could otherwise have been secured, and to provide exercises for continuous review. The few English-to-Latin sentences in each chapter provide an entirely different approach to the language than Latin-to-English readings and should, therefore, be done regularly, but the others need not be assigned as part of the ordinary outside preparation. They are easy enough to be done at sight in class as time permits; or they can be used as a basis for review after every fourth or fifth chapter in lieu of formal review lessons.

## 6. ETYMOLOGIES

Lists of English derivatives are provided in parentheses after the words in the vocabularies to help impress the Latin words on the student, to demonstrate the direct or indirect indebtedness of English to Latin, and to enlarge the student's own vocabulary. Occasionally, English cognates have been added. At the end of some chapters an "Etymology" section (re-titled *Etymologia* in the seventh edition) introduces additional English and also Romance language derivatives, as well as other interesting points which could not be easily included in the vocabulary. From the beginning, students should consult the lists of prefixes and suffixes given in the Appendix under the heading of "Some Etymological Aids."

## 7. THE INTRODUCTION / *INTRŌDVCTIŌ*

In addition to discussing the Roman alphabet and pronunciation, the book's general *Intrōductiō* sketches the linguistic, literary, and palaeographical background of Latin. This background and the actual Latin of the *Sententiae Antīquae* and the *Locī Antīquī* give the student considerable insight into Roman literature, thought, expression, and experience, and evince the continuity of the Roman tradition down to our own times. It is hoped that the *Intrōductiō* and especially the nature of the chapters themselves will establish this book as not just another Latin grammar but rather as a humanistic introduction to the reading of genuine Latin.

The book had its inception as a group of typed lessons I designed and tried out in class as a result of the dissatisfaction expressed at the beginning of this Preface. Those initial lessons worked well, despite imperfections soon evident to myself and to colleagues who generously offered their critique. To Professor Lillian B. Lawler of Hunter College I am grateful for her perusal of the typescript and for her suggestions. I also wish to acknowledge the patience of my students and colleagues at Brooklyn College who worked with the typed material, and their helpfulness and encouragement in stating their reactions to the text. Subsequently these trial lessons were completely revised and rewritten in the light of experience. I am indebted to Professor Joseph Pearl of Brooklyn College for his kindness in scrutinizing the 40 chapters of the manuscript in their revised form and for many helpful suggestions. To the Reverend Joseph M.-F. Marique, S.J., of Boston College I herewith convey my appreciation for his encouraging and helpful review of the revised manuscript. Thomas S. Lester of Northeastern University, a man of parts and my *alter īdem amīcissimus* since classical undergraduate years, has my heartfelt thanks for so often and so patiently lending to my problems a sympathetic ear, a sound mind, and a sanguine spirit. To my dear wife, Dorothy, who so faithfully devoted herself to the typing of a very difficult manuscript, who was often asked for a judgment, and who, in the process, uttered many a salutary plea for clarity and for compassion toward the students, I dedicate my affectionate and abiding gratitude. My final thanks go to Dr. Gladys Walterhouse and her colleagues in the editorial department of Barnes & Noble for their friendly, efficient, and often crucial help in many matters. It need hardly be added that no one but the author is responsible for any infelicities which may remain.

# THE SECOND AND THIRD EDITIONS

Because of the requests of those who found they needed more reading material than that provided by the *Locī Antīquī*, the author prepared a second edition which enriched the book with a new section entitled *Locī Immūtātī* ("Unaltered Passages"). In these selections the original ancient Latin texts have been left unchanged except for omissions at certain points, and footnotes are provided comparable to those in the *Locī Antīquī*. It is hoped that these readings will prove sufficiently extensive to keep a class well supplied after completing the book's 40 chapters, will give an interesting additional challenge to the person who is self-tutored, and will provide a very direct approach to the use of the regular annotated texts of classical authors.

Because of the indisputable value of repetition for establishing linguistic reflexes, a new section of "Self-Tutorial Exercises," consisting of questions on morphology and syntax, and sentences for translation, was added to the third edition. A key provides answers to all the questions and translations of all the sentences.

The second and third editions would be incomplete without a word of deep gratitude to the many who in one way or another have given kind encouragement, who have made suggestions, who have indicated emendanda. I find myself particularly indebted to Professors Josephine Bree of Albertus Magnus College, Ben L. Charney of Oakland City College, Louis H. Feldman of Yeshiva College, Robert J. Leslie of Indiana University, Mr. Thomas S. Lester of Northeastern University, the Reverend James R. Murdock of Glenmary Home Missioners, Professors Paul Pascal of the University of Washington, Robert Renehan of Harvard University, John E. Rexine of Colgate University, George Tyler of Moravian College, Ralph L. Ward of Hunter College, Dr. Gladys Walterhouse of the Editorial Staff of Barnes & Noble, and most especially, once again, to my wife Dorothy.

Frederic M. Wheelock

# THE REVISED EDITION

When Professor Frederic Wheelock's *Latin* first appeared in 1956, the reviews extolled its thoroughness, organization, and concision; one reviewer predicted that the book "might well become the standard text" for introducing college students and other adult learners to elementary Latin. Now, more than half a century later, that prediction has certainly been proven accurate. A second edition was published in 1960, retitled *Latin: An Introductory Course Based on Ancient Authors* and including a rich array of additional reading passages drawn directly from Latin literature (the *Locī Immūtātī*); the third edition, published in 1963, added Self-Tutorial Exercises, with an answer key, for each of the 40 chapters and greatly enhanced the book's usefulness both for classroom students and for those wishing to study the language independently. In 1984, three years before the author's death, a list of passage citations for the *Sententiae Antīquae* was added, so that teachers and students could more easily locate and explore the context of selections they found especially interesting; and in 1992 a fourth edition appeared under the aegis of the book's new publisher, HarperCollins, in which the text was re-set and re-designed.

The fifth edition, published in 1995 and aptly retitled *Wheelock's Latin*, constituted the first truly substantive revision of the text in more than 30 years. The revisions which I introduced were intended, not to alter the basic concept of the text, but to enhance it; indeed, a number of the most significant changes were based on Professor Wheelock's own suggestions, contained in notes made available for the project by his family, and others reflected the experiences of colleagues around the country, many of whom (myself included) had used and admired the book for two decades or more and had in the process arrived at some consensus about certain basic ways in which it might be improved for a new generation of students.

The most obvious change in the fifth edition reflected Wheelock's own principal desideratum, shared by myself and doubtless by most who had used the book over the years, and that was the addition of passages of continuous Latin, based on ancient authors, to all 40 chapters. These are in the early chapters brief and highly adapted, but later on are more extensive and often excerpted verbatim from a variety of prose and verse writers; some had appeared in previous editions among the *Locī Antīquī* and the *Locī Immūtātī*, while many were included for the first time in the fifth edition. Some of the "Practice and Review" sentences (*Exercitātiōnēs*) were revised or replaced, as were a few of the *Sententiae Antīquae* (which in some instances were expanded into longer readings), again as suggested in part by Professor Wheelock himself.

The chapter vocabularies, generally regarded as too sparse, were expanded in most instances to about 20–25 words, a quite manageable list including new items as well as many found previously as glosses to the *Sententiae Antīquae*. Full principal parts were provided for all verbs from the beginning, as colleagues around the country had agreed should be done, so students would not be confronted with the somewhat daunting list previously presented in Chapter 12.

There was only minimal shifting of grammar, but in particular the imperfect tense was introduced along with the future in Chapters 5, 8, and 10, so that a past tense would be available for use in the readings at a much earlier stage. Numerals and the associated material originally in Chapter 40 were introduced in Chapter 15; and a half dozen or so important grammatical constructions previously presented in the Supplementary Syntax were instead introduced in Chapter 40 and a few of the earlier chapters. Many of the grammatical explanations were rewritten; essential information from the footnotes was incorporated into the text, while some less important notes were deleted.

Finally, I included at the end of each chapter a section titled *Latīna Est Gaudium—et Ūtilis,* which presents, in a deliberately informal style, a miscellany of Latin mottoes and well-known quotations, familiar abbreviations, interesting etymologies, classroom conversation items, occasional humorous asides, and even a few ghastly Latinate puns, all intended to demonstrate, on the lighter side, that Latin can indeed be pleasurable as well as edifying.

The success of the fifth edition encouraged all of us involved—Professor Wheelock's daughters, Martha Wheelock and Deborah Wheelock Taylor, our editor Greg Chaput and his associates at HarperCollins, and myself—to proceed with revisions I had proposed for a new sixth edition, published in 2000; these included: the handsome new cover art, a Roman mosaic from Tunisia depicting Vergil with a copy of the *Aeneid* in his lap and flanked by two Muses representing his work's inspiration; maps of ancient Italy, Greece and the Aegean area, and the Mediterranean, specially designed to include, inter alia, all the placenames mentioned in the book's readings and notes (except a few situated on the remotest fringes of the empire); numerous photographs selected primarily from classical and later European art to illustrate literary and historical figures and aspects of classical culture and mythology presented in the chapters; revision of chapter readings, for greater clarity and increased reinforcement of new and recently introduced chapter vocabulary items; expansion of derivatives lists in the chapter vocabularies and of cross-references to related words in other chapters; and enlargement of the English-Latin end vocabulary. The "sixth edition, revised" (2005) included revisions to the *Intrōductiō* and some of the readings and accompanying notes, as well as further expansion of the English-Latin vocabulary designed to better complement the *Workbook for Wheelock's Latin* (in its revised third edition by Paul Comeau and myself). The revised sixth edition was also the first in many years to appear in a hardbound version, along with the traditional paperback; audio files were produced and posted online, with an introduction to pronunciation and reading of all the chapter vocabularies; and, also for the first time, a teacher's guide was written and made available online for teachers, home-schoolers, and independent learners.

## THE NEW SEVENTH EDITION

This latest edition, the seventh, published in 2011, features a great many revisions intended to make *Wheelock's Latin* even more effective, more interesting, and more user-friendly. The text has been entirely re-keyed, providing the opportunity for formatting and design changes that help clarify each chapter's organization and, along with new photographs and drawings, make the book more visually appealing. SMALL BOLD CAPITALS are employed to call attention to important new grammatical and other technical terms. To encourage active use of the language in the classroom, Latin is employed in the chapter titles and for section heads (*Exercitātiōnēs* instead of "Practice and Review," *Vocābula* for "Vocabulary," etc.). Material in the footnotes has either been incorporated into the text or deleted. The maps have been updated, and more frequent references appear in the text to encourage their use; the Index has been expanded.

Significant revisions have been made in each chapter's grammar discussion section (newly titled *Grammatica*), including systematic introduction and definition of all parts of speech, earlier introduction of verb synopsis, and clarification of numerous grammatical points. The chapter *Vocābula* have been revised in several ways, including spelling out full nominatives for all adjectives, genitives for all nouns, and principal parts for all verbs, even regular first conjugation verbs—thus eliminating abbreviations potentially distracting to students trying to learn new vocabulary items for the first time. Each list is preceded by a brief discussion of new or exceptional types of words that will be encountered, as well as general suggestions on how to master vocabulary.

Similarly, each chapter's *Lēctiōnēs et Trānslātiōnēs* ("Readings and Translations") section opens with a variety of tips aimed at building reading and translating skills. English derivatives are provided for Latin words glossed in the *Sententiae Antīquae* and reading passages, as an aid to learning and recalling their meanings. Some of the existing readings have been slightly revised for improved reinforcement of new and recent vocabulary and grammar; and a few new authentic readings have been added to each chapter, in particular a selection of graffiti from Pompeii, titled *Scrīpta In Parietibus* ("Writings on Walls"), which are accompanied by drawings or photographs and designed to provide interesting insights into the lives, and literacy, of ancient Roman men and women. These inscriptions and the chapter's literary passages are provided with expanded introductions and a few *Quaestiōnēs,* reading comprehension and discussion questions designed to focus the reader's attention on important points of both subject and style.

The *Etymologia* sections have been in some instances shortened, in other instances expanded, particularly with the addition of more Romance language derivatives; and there are a few changes to the *Latīna Est Gaudium* sections as well.

Finally, the website at www.wheelockslatin.com, the online teacher's guide, vocabulary cards, and other ancillaries available from Bolchazy-Carducci Publishers (www.bolchazy.com) have been updated to reflect changes to the textbook.

## A FINAL NOTE TO STUDENTS AND INSTRUCTORS

The *Lēctiōnēs et Trānslātiōnēs* in this edition purposely provide more material for reading and translation than one would want to require for homework in the two or three days typically allotted to a chapter in a semester course or the week or so allotted in high school. Instructors are encouraged to be selective: my suggestion is to assign study of the new grammar, paradigms, and vocabulary for the first day or two, requiring for written homework only limited selections from the *Exercitātiōnēs* and *Sententiae Antīquae,* and reserving the others (or some of the others, carefully selected in advance) for in-class sight translation; assignments for the second or third day should include the reading passages and graffiti following the *Sententiae Antīquae,* which will give students the experience they need with continuous narrative. I like to assign one or two of the English-to-Latin *Exercitātiōnēs* each day, or will sometimes divide the students into small groups, giving them five minutes or so to work on one of the sentences together and having a member of each group put their sentence on the board for review. Students should regularly be encouraged to practice new material at home with the Self-Tutorial Exercises located at the back of the book, checking their accuracy with the answer key that follows, and sentences from these exercises, again pre-selected for the purpose, can be used to drill mastery of new concepts via sight translation in class.

The companion reader *Scribblers, Scvlptors, and Scribes* provides a broad array of entirely authentic, unadapted classical Latin texts whose vocabulary and grammar are correlated with the 40 chapters of *Wheelock's Latin.* These readings, including a wide range of graffiti and other inscriptions, proverbs, and literary texts, provide insights into not just the minds of Rome's movers and shakers—her politicians and generals, philosophers and poets—but also into the daily lives of the average Roman. Students should be assigned a selection from these readings for their final day on each chapter.

Most instructors will also want their students to use the *Workbook for Wheelock's Latin,* which contains a variety of additional exercises, including for each chapter a detailed set of *Intellegenda* (learner objectives), a series of questions designed to focus directly on the newly introduced grammar, a variety of transformation drills, word, phrase, and sentence translations, questions on etymologies, synonyms, antonyms, and analogies for new vocabulary items, and reading comprehension questions to test the student's understanding of the chapter's reading passages.

Those who may not have time to complete all of the many *Workbook* items provided for each chapter are advised at least to review the *Intellegenda,* answer all the *Grammatica* questions and then complete one or two items from each section of the *Exercitātiōnēs,* all the *Vīs Verbōrum* ("The Power of Words") etymology items, one or two of the Latin-to-English translations in section A of the *Lēctiōnēs* (readings), and all the items in *Lēctiōnēs* B (questions on the chapter's literary passages).

There are numerous other materials designed to complement *Wheelock's Latin,* the *Workbook for Wheelock's Latin,* and *Scribblers, Scvlptors, and Scribes,* including audio CDs, computer software, vocabulary cards, and a wealth of internet resources, most of which, along with further suggestions on teaching and learning Latin via Wheelock, are accessible at the official Wheelock's Latin Series Website, www.wheelockslatin.com, and described in my book *Latin for the 21st Century: From Concept to Classroom* (available from Pearson Publishers).

# MĪLLE GRĀTIĀS . . .

There are many whom I am eager to thank for their support of my work on *Wheelock's Latin:* first and foremost, my dear wife and steadfast companion, Alice, and my children, Jean-Paul, Laura Caroline, and Kimberley Ellen, for their constant affection; my colleague Jared Klein, a distinguished Indo-European linguist, for reading and offering his judicious advice on my revisions to both the *Intrōductiō* and the individual chapters; graduate assistants Derek Bast, David Driscoll, Cleve Fisher, Marshall Lloyd, Sean Mathis, Matthew Payne, and Jim Yavenditti, for their energetic and capable help with a variety of tasks; Mary Wells Ricks, long-time friend and former Senior Associate Editor for the *Classical Outlook,* for her expert counsel on a variety of editorial matters; our department secretaries, JoAnn Pulliam and Connie Russell, for their generous clerical assistance, and graphic designer Kay Stanton for her drawings of graffiti and general assistance with illustrations; my editors at HarperCollins, Erica Spaberg, Patricia Leasure, Greg Chaput, and Stephanie Meyers, each of whom enthusiastically supported my proposals for the revised editions; Tim McCarthy, Michael Slade, and Alison Strum of Art Resource in New York, as well as colleagues Jim Anderson, Bob Curtis, Timothy Gantz†, and Frances Van Keuren, for their assistance with the graphics, and Amélia Hutchinson, Mihai Spariosu, and Sallie Spence for consulting on Romance language derivatives; Tom Elliott and Brian Turner, with the Ancient World Mapping Center, for their expertise in designing the maps; students and associates at the University of Georgia who field-tested the new material or provided other helpful assistance, among them Bob Harris and Richard Shedenhelm; colleagues around the country who offered suggestions for specific revisions, especially Ward Briggs at the University of South Carolina (whose biographies of Professor Wheelock appear in his book, *A Biographical Dictionary of American Classicists,* Westport CT: Greenwood Press, 1994, and in the Winter, 2003, *Classical Outlook*), Marshall Joseph Becker, Rob Latousek, John Lautermilch, John McChesney-Young, Braden Mechley, Fred Mench, Betty Rose Nagle, Krzysztof Odyniec, John Ramsey, Joseph Riegsecker, Cliff Roti, Les Sheridan, David Sider, Alden Smith, Brad Tillery, Cliff Weber, Stephen Westergan, Stephen Wheeler, and David J. White; Dean Wyatt Anderson, for his encouragement of my own work and all our Classics Department's endeavors; Martha Wheelock and Deborah Wheelock Taylor, my "sisters-in-Latin," for their steadfast advocacy of my work on the revised editions and their generous sharing of their father's notes; and finally, Professor Frederic M. Wheelock himself, for producing a textbook that has truly become a classic in its own right and one whose revision, therefore, became for me a *labor amōris.*

Richard A. LaFleur
University of Georgia
Autumn, 2010

I love the language, that soft bastard Latin,
Which melts like kisses from a female mouth.
George Noel Gordon, Lord Byron
*Beppo* (where he was speaking of Italian, Latin's first-born)

I would make them all learn English: and then I would let the clever ones learn Latin as an honor, and Greek as a treat.
Sir Winston Churchill
*Roving Commission: My Early Life*

He studied Latin like the violin, because he liked it.
Robert Frost
*The Death of the Hired Man*

# INTRŌDVCTIŌ

*Wer fremde Sprachen nicht kennt, weiss nichts von seiner eigenen.* (Goethe)

*Apprendre une langue, c'est vivre de nouveau.* (French proverb)

Your appreciation of the Latin language can be considerably increased by even a limited awareness of the background sketched in this *Intrōdvctiō*. The paragraphs on the position of the Latin language in the Indo-European language family provide some linguistic perspective not only for Latin but also for the Romance languages and English. The brief survey of Latin literature introduces the authors whose works are excerpted in the book's *Sententiae Antīquae, Locī Antīquī,* and *Locī Immūtātī* and provides a literary perspective which the student may never otherwise gain. And, of course, no introduction to the language would be complete without a discussion of the Roman alphabet and pronunciation.

## THE POSITION OF THE LATIN LANGUAGE IN LINGUISTIC HISTORY

Say the words "I," "me," "is," "mother," "brother," and "ten," and you are speaking words which, in one form or another, men and women of Europe and Asia have used for thousands of years. In fact, we cannot tell how old these words actually are. If their spelling and pronunciation have changed somewhat from period to period and place to place, little wonder; what does pique the imagination is the fact that the basic elements of these symbols of human thought have had the vitality to traverse such spans of time and space down to this very moment on this continent. The point is demonstrated in this considerably abbreviated and simplified table:

| English | I | me | is | mother | brother | ten |
|---|---|---|---|---|---|---|
| Sanskrit[1] | aham | mā | asti | mātar- | bhrātar- | daśam |
| Greek | egō | me | esti | mētēr | phrātēr[2] | deka |
| Latin | ego | mē | est | māter | frāter | decem |
| Anglo-Saxon[3] | ic | mē | is | mōdor | brōthor | tīen |
| Old Irish[4] | | mé | is | máthir | bráthir | deich |
| Lithuanian[5] | aš | manè | esti | motė | broterėlis | dešimtis |
| Russian[6] | ja | menja | jest' | mat' | brat | desjat' |

You can see from these columns of words that the listed languages are related. And yet, with the exception of the ultimate derivation of English from Anglo-Saxon, none of these languages stems directly from another in the list. Rather, they all go back through intermediate stages to a common ancestor, which is now lost but which can be predicated on the evidence of the languages that do survive. Such languages the philologist calls COGNATES (Latin for "related" or, more literally, "born together," i.e., from the same ancestry). The name most commonly given to the now lost ancestor of all these "relatives," or cognate languages, is INDO-EUROPEAN, because its descendants are found both in or near India (Sanskrit, Iranian) and also in Europe (Greek and Latin and the Germanic, Celtic, Slavic, and Baltic languages).[7] The Indo-European languages for which we have the oldest surviving documents are Sanskrit, Iranian, Greek, and Latin, and these documents go back centuries before the time of Christ. In addition to the common vocabulary illustrated in the above chart, this large family of languages shares many INFLECTIONS, or word-endings, in common. An INFLECTED LANGUAGE is one in which the nouns, pronouns, adjectives, and verbs have variable endings that indicate the relationship of the words to each other in a sentence. In particular, note that Anglo-Saxon, like Latin, was an inflected language but that its descendant English has lost most of its inflections (though some survive, such as "who," "he," "she" for subjects, vs. "whom," "him," her" for objects, "she loves" for third person singular, vs. "I love," "you love," etc.).

[1] The language of the sacred writings of ancient India, parent of the modern Indo-European languages of India.

[2] Though cognate with the other words in this column, classical Greek **phrātēr** meant *member of a clan.*

[3] As an example of the Germanic languages; others are Gothic, German, Dutch, Danish, Norwegian, Swedish, Icelandic, English.

[4] As an example of the Celtic languages; others are Welsh, Gaulish, Breton, Scots (Gaelic). Old Irish **mé** in the chart is actually nominative case, equivalent to "I" in meaning and usage but to "me" in form.

[5] As an example of the Baltic group; others are Latvian and Old Prussian.

[6] As an example of the Slavic group; others are Polish, Bulgarian, Czech.

[7] Note that many world languages (e.g., the Semitic languages, Egyptian, Basque, Chinese, the native languages of Africa and the Americas) lie outside the Indo-European family.

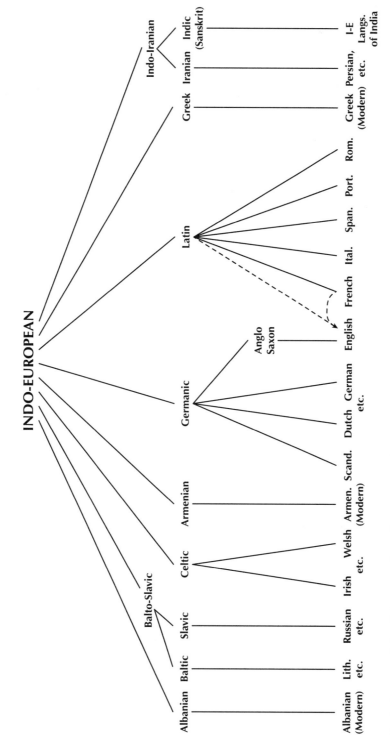

*In the interest of simplicity a number of languages and intermediate stages have been omitted. Latin, for example, was only one of a number of Italic dialects, including Oscan and Umbrian, which it eventually submerged; among the Greeks there were likewise several dialects (Aeolic, Attic, Ionic, Doric). Two branches of the Indo-European language family, Anatolian and Tocharian, are now extinct and not shown on the chart.*

The difference between **DERIVED** (from roots meaning "to flow downstream from" a source) and **COGNATE** languages can be demonstrated by the relationship of the Romance languages to Latin and to each other. Here we are in the realm of recorded history and can see that with the Roman political conquest of such districts as Gaul (France), Spain, and Dacia (Romania) there occurred also a Roman linguistic conquest. Out of this victorious ancient Latin as spoken by the common people (**vulgus**, hence "vulgar" Latin) grew the Romance languages, such as French, Spanish, Portuguese, Romanian, Occitan (or Provençal), and, of course, Italian. All these languages are "derived" from Latin and thus "cognate" with each other.

| Parent | Cognate Romance Derivatives | | | | |
|---|---|---|---|---|---|
| **Latin** | **Italian** | **Spanish** | **French** | **Portuguese** | **English Meaning** |
| amīcus | amico | amigo | ami | amigo | friend |
| liber | libro | libro | livre | livro | book |
| tempus | tempo | tiempo | temps | tempo | time |
| manus | mano | mano | main | mão | hand |
| bucca | bocca | boca | bouche | boca (mouth) | mouth (cheek *in classical Lat.*) |
| caballus | cavallo | caballo | cheval | cavalo | horse |
| filius | figlio | hijo | fils | filho | son |
| ille | il | el | le | o | the (that *in classical Lat.*) |
| illa | la | la | la | a | the (that *in classical Lat.*) |
| quattuor | quattro | cuatro | quatre | quatro | four |
| bonus | buono | bueno | bon | bom | good |
| bene | bene | bien | bien | bem | well (*adv.*) |
| facere | fare | hacer | faire | fazer | make, do |
| dīcere | dire | decir | dire | dizer | say |
| legere | leggere | leer | lire | ler | read |

Although English ultimately stems from Anglo-Saxon, which is cognate with Latin, there is much more than that to the story. Anglo-Saxon itself had early borrowed a few words from Latin; and then in the 7th century more Latin (including many Latinized Greek and Hebrew words drawn from Jerome's "Vulgate" translation of the Bible) entered the language as a result of the work of St. Augustine (the Lesser), who had been sent by Pope Gregory to Christianize the Angles. After the victory of William the Conqueror in 1066, Norman French became the polite language and Anglo-Saxon was held in low esteem as the tongue of vanquished men and serfs—no longer a literary language, but simply the speech of humble daily life. Some two centuries later, however, as the descendants of the Normans finally amalgamated with the English natives, the Anglo-Saxon language reasserted itself; but in its poverty it had to borrow hundreds of French words (literary, intellectual, and cultural) before it could become the language of literature. Borrow it did abundantly, and in the 13th and 14th centuries this development produced what is called Middle English, known especially from Chaucer, who died in 1400. Along with the adoption of these Latin-rooted French words there was also some borrowing directly from Latin itself, and the renewed interest in the classics which characterized the Renaissance naturally intensified this trend during the 16th and the 17th centuries.[8] From that time to the present Latin has continued to be a source of new words, particularly for the scientist but even for ad writers and those marketing folks who invent product names!

Consequently, since English through Anglo-Saxon is cognate with Latin and yet also has directly or indirectly borrowed so many words from the language, our own vocabulary contains thousands of Latin cognates and thousands of derivatives. English "brother," for example, is cognate with Latin **frāter,** while "fraternal" clearly is derived from it. An important linguistic principle of sound change in the evolution of the Germanic languages, known as GRIMM'S LAW, describes shifts in consonants such as **p** to **f,** hard **c** (**k**) to **h,** and **d** to **t,** which account for the fact that Latin-English cognates like **pēs/ped-**/"foot" and **cor/cord-**/"heart" have a common origin. Following are a variety of examples of English cognates and derivatives of Latin words:

| Latin | English Derivative | English Cognate |
|-------|-------------------|-----------------|
| māter | maternal | mother |
| duo | dual, duet | two |
| dēns, *stem* dent- | dental | tooth |
| pēs, *stem* ped- | pedal | foot |
| cor, *stem* cord- | cordial | heart |
| ferō | fertile | bear |

Here you see one of the reasons for the richness of our vocabulary, and the longer you study Latin the more keenly you will realize what a limited language ours would be without the Latin element. Despite the brevity of this survey you can comprehend the general position of Latin in European linguistic history and

---

[8] Thomas Wilson (16th century) says: "The unlearned or foolish fantastical, that smells but of learning (such fellows as have been learned men in their days), will so Latin their tongues, that the simple cannot but wonder at their talk, and think surely they speak by some revelation." Sir Thomas Browne (17th century) says: "If elegancy still proceedeth, and English pens maintain that stream we have of late observed to flow from many, we shall within a few years be fain to learn Latin to understand English, and a work will prove of equal facility in either." These statements are quoted by permission from the "Brief History of the English Language" by Hadley and Kittredge in Webster's *New International Dictionary,* Second Edition, copyright, 1934, 1939, 1945, 1950, 1953, 1954, by G. & C. Merriam Co.

something of its continuing importance to us today. It is the cognate of many languages and the parent of many, and can even be called the adoptive parent of English.

# A BRIEF SURVEY OF LATIN LITERATURE

Since throughout this entire book you will be reading sentences and passages excerpted from Latin literature, a brief outline is here sketched to provide an overview of both the nature and the extent of this great literary corpus. Following is a conventional chronology:

    I.   Archaic through Early Republican Period (down to ca. 80 B.C.)
   II.   Late Republican and Augustan Period (the "Golden Age": 80 B.C.–A.D. 14)
      A.   Ciceronian Period (80–43 B.C.)
      B.   Augustan Period (43 B.C.–A.D. 14)
  III.   Post-Augustan Period (the "Silver Age": A.D. 14–138)
  IV.   Patristic Period (late 2nd–5th cent.)
   V.   Medieval Period (6th–14th cent.)
  VI.   Renaissance (15th cent.) to the Present

## ARCHAIC THROUGH EARLY REPUBLICAN PERIOD (DOWN TO CA. 80 B.C.)

The apogee of Greek civilization, including the highest development of its magnificent literature and art, was reached during the 5th and the 4th centuries before Christ. In comparison, Rome during those centuries had little to offer. Our fragmentary evidence shows only a rough, accentual native meter called Saturnian, some native comic skits, and a simple, practical prose for records and speeches.

In the 3d century B.C., however, the expansion of Roman power brought the Romans into contact with Greek civilization. Somehow the hard-headed, politically and legally minded Romans were fascinated by what they found, and the writers among them went to school to learn Greek literature. From this time on, Greek literary forms, meters, rhetorical devices, subjects, and ideas had a tremendous and continuing influence on Roman literature, even as it developed its own character and originality in a great many ways.

In fact, the Romans themselves did not hesitate to admit as much. Although the Romans now composed epics, tragedies, satires, and speeches, the greatest extant accomplishments of this period of apprenticeship to Greek models are the comedies of Plautus (ca. 254–184 B.C.) and Terence (185–159 B.C.). These were based on Greek plays of the type known as New Comedy, the comedy of manners, and they make excellent reading today. Indeed, a number of these plays have influenced modern playwrights; Plautus' *Menaechmi,* for instance, inspired Shakespeare's *Comedy of Errors.*

## LATE REPUBLICAN AND AUGUSTAN PERIOD (80 B.C.–A.D. 14)

During the first century before Christ the Roman writers perfected their literary media and made Latin literature one of the world's greatest. It is particularly famous for its beautiful, disciplined form, which we think of as "classic," and for its real substance as well. If Lucretius complained about the poverty of the Latin vocabulary, Cicero so molded the vocabulary and the general usage that Latin remained a supple and a subtle linguistic tool for thirteen centuries and more.

*THE CICERONIAN PERIOD* (80–43 B.C.). The literary work of the Ciceronian Period was produced during the last years of the Roman Republic. This was a period of civil wars and dictators, of military might against constitutional right, of selfish interest, of brilliant pomp and power, of moral and religious laxity. Outstanding authors important for the book which you have in hand are:

*Lucretius* (Titus Lūcrētius Cārus, ca. 98–55 B.C.): author of *Dē Rērum Nātūrā,* a powerful didactic poem on happiness achieved through the Epicurean philosophy. This philosophy was based on pleasure, or rather the absence of pain and suffering, and was buttressed by an atomic theory which made the universe a realm of natural, not divine, law and thus eliminated fear of the gods and the tyranny of religion, which Lucretius believed had shattered men's happiness.

*Catullus* (Gāius Valerius Catullus, ca. 84–54 B.C.): lyric poet, the Robert Burns of Roman literature, an intense and impressionable young provincial from northern Italy who fell totally under the spell of an urban sophisticate, Lesbia (a literary pseudonym for her real name, Clodia), but finally escaped bitterly disillusioned; 113 of his poems have survived.

*Cicero* (Mārcus Tullius Cicerō, 106–43 B.C.): the greatest Roman orator, whose eloquence thwarted the conspiracy of the bankrupt aristocrat Catiline in 63 B.C. and 20 years later cost Cicero his own life in his patriotic opposition to Mark Antony's high-handed policies; admired also as an authority on Roman rhetoric, as an interpreter of Greek philosophy to his countrymen, as an essayist on friendship (*Dē Amīcitiā*) and on old age (*Dē Senectūte*), and, in a less formal style, as a writer of self-revealing letters. Cicero's vast contributions to the Latin language itself have already been mentioned.

*Caesar* (Gāius Iūlius Caesar, 102 or 100–44 B.C.): orator, politician, general, statesman, dictator, author; best known for his military memoirs, *Bellum Gallicum* and *Bellum Cīvīle.*

*Nepos* (Cornēlius Nepōs, 110–24 B.C.): friend of Catullus and Caesar and a writer of biographies noted rather for their relatively easy and popular style than for their importance as historical documents.

*Publilius Syrus* (fl. 43 B.C.): a slave who was taken to Rome and there became famous for his mimes, which today are represented only by a collection of epigrammatic sayings.

*THE AUGUSTAN PERIOD* (43 B.C.– A.D. 14). The first Roman Emperor gave his name to this period. Augustus wished to correct the evils of the times, to establish civil peace by stable government, and to win the Romans' support for his new regime. With this in mind he and Maecenas, his unofficial prime minister, sought to enlist literature in the service of the state. Under their patronage Vergil and Horace became what we should call poets laureate. Some modern critics feel that this fact vitiates the noble sentiments of these poets; others see in Horace a spirit of independence and of genuine moral concern, and maintain that Vergil, through the character of his epic hero Aeneas, is not simply glorifying Augustus but is actually suggesting to the emperor what is expected of him as head of the state.

*Vergil* (Pūblius Vergilius Marō, 70–19 B.C.): from humble origins in northern Italy; lover of nature; profoundly sympathetic student of humankind; Epicurean and mystic; severe and exacting self-critic, master craftsman, linguistic and literary architect, "lord of language"; famous as a writer of pastoral verse (the *Eclogues*) and of a beautiful didactic poem on farm life (the *Georgics*); best known as the author of one of the world's great epics, the *Aeneid,* a national epic with contemporary political resonances, to be sure, but one also with ample universal and human appeal to make it powerful reading for our own age.

*Horace* (Quīntus Horātius Flaccus, 65–8 B.C.): a freedman's son who, thanks to his father's vision and his own qualities, rose to the height of poet laureate; writer of genial and self-revealing satires; author of superb lyrics both light and serious; meticulous composer famed for the happy effects of his linguistic craftsmanship (**cūriōsa fēlīcitās,** *painstaking felicity*); synthesist of Epicurean **carpe diem** (*harvest the day*) and Stoic **virtūs** (*virtue*); preacher and practitioner of **aurea mediocritās** (*the golden mean*).

*Livy* (Titus Līvius, 59 B.C.– A.D. 17): friend of Augustus but an admirer of the Republic and of olden virtues; author of a monumental, epic-spirited history of Rome, and portrayer of Roman character at its best as he judged it.

*Propertius* (Sextus Propertius, ca. 50 B.C.–ca. A.D. 2): author of four books of romantic elegiac poems, much admired by Ovid.

*Ovid* (Pūblius Ovidius Nāsō, 43 B.C.– A.D.17): author of several volumes of love poetry which was hardly consonant with Augustus' plans; most famous today as the writer of the long and clever hexameter work on mythology entitled *Metamorphōsēs,* which has proved a thesaurus for subsequent poets. Ovid, like Pope, "lisped in numbers, for the numbers came."

# THE POST-AUGUSTAN PERIOD (A.D. 14–138)

In the post-Augustan age there was a great deal of excellent writing; but often there were also artificialities and conceits, a striving for effects and a passion for epigram, characteristics which often indicate a less sure literary sense and power—hence the conventional, though overstated, distinction between the "Golden Age" of the late Republic and Augustan era and this so-called "Silver Age." The temperaments of not a few emperors also had a limiting, even blighting effect on the literature of this period.

*Seneca* (Lūcius Annaeus Seneca, 4 B.C.–A.D. 65): Stoic philosopher from Spain; tutor of Nero; author of moral essays on the Stoic spirit, of tragedies (which, though marred by too much rhetoric and too many conceits, had considerable influence on the early modern drama of Europe), and of the *Apocolocyntōsis* ("Pumpkinification"), a brilliantly witty, though sometimes cruel, prosimetric satire on the death and deification of the emperor Claudius.

*Petronius* (exact identity and dates uncertain, but probably Titus Petrōnius Arbiter, died A.D. 66): Neronian consular and courtier; author of the *Satyricon,* a satiric, prosimetric novel of sorts, famous for its depiction of the nouveau-riche freedman Trimalchio and his extravagant dinner-parties.

*Quintilian* (Mārcus Fabius Quīntiliānus, ca. A.D. 35–95): teacher and author of the *Īnstitūtiō Ōrātōria,* a famous pedagogical work which discusses the entire education of a person who is to become an orator; a great admirer of Cicero's style and a critic of the rhetorical excesses of his own age.

*Martial* (Mārcus Valerius Mārtiālis, A.D. 45–104): famed for his more than 1,500 witty epigrams and for the satirical twist which he so often gave to them. As he himself says, his work may not be great literature but people do enjoy it.

*Pliny the Younger* (Gāius Plīnius Caecilius Secundus, ca. A.D. 62–113): a conscientious public figure, who is now best known for his *Epistulae,* letters which reveal both the bright and the seamy sides of Roman life during this imperial period.

*Tacitus* (Pūblius Cornēlius Tacitus, A.D. 55–117): most famous as a satirical, pro-senatorial historian of the period from the death of Augustus to the death of Domitian.

*Juvenal* (Decimus Iūnius Iuvenālis, ca. A.D. 55–post 127): a relentless, intensely rhetorical satirist of the evils of his times, who concludes that the only thing for which one can pray is a **mēns sāna in corpore sānō** (*a sound mind in a sound body*). His satires inspired Dr. Samuel Johnson's *London* and *The Vanity of Human Wishes* and the whole conception of caustic, "Juvenalian" satire.

*THE ARCHAISING PERIOD.* The mid- to late 2nd century may be distinguished as an archaizing period, in which a taste developed for the vocabulary and style of early Latin and for the incorporation of diction from vulgar Latin; characteristic authors of the period were the orator Fronto and the antiquarian Aulus Gellius, known for his miscellaneous essays *Noctēs Atticae* ("Nights in Attica").

## THE PATRISTIC PERIOD (Late 2nd Cent.–5th Cent.)

The name of the Patristic Period comes from the fact that so much of the vital literature was the work of the Christian leaders, or fathers (**patrēs**), among whom were Tertullian, Cyprian, Lactantius, Jerome, Ambrose, and Augustine. These men had been well educated; they were familiar with, and frequently fond of, the best classical authors; many of them had even been teachers or lawyers before going into service of the Church. At times the classical style was deliberately employed to impress the pagans, but more and more the concern was to reach the common people (**vulgus**) with the Christian message. Consequently, it is not surprising to see a re-emergence of in contemporary literature of vulgar Latin, the language of the common people whose linguistic roots date back to early Republican times. In fact, the language of Plautus has much in common with this later vulgar Latin, and we know that throughout the late Republican and post-Augustan periods vulgar Latin lived on as the colloquial idiom of the people while kept distinct from the literary idiom of the texts and the polished conversation of those ages. St. Jerome in his letters is essentially Ciceronian, but in his Latin edition of the Bible, the "Vulgate" (383–405 A.D.), he uses the language of the people. Similarly St. Augustine, though formerly a teacher and a great lover of the Roman classics, was willing to use any idiom that would reach the people and remarked that it did not matter if even the barbarians conquered Rome provided they were Christian.

## THE MEDIEVAL PERIOD (6th–14th Cents.)

During the first three centuries of the Medieval period, vulgar Latin underwent rapid changes—e.g., the loss of most declensional endings and the increased use of prepositions, extensive employment of auxiliary verbs, widely variable uses of the subjunctive and the indicative—and, reaching the point when it could no longer be called Latin, it became this or that Romance language according to the locality.

On the other hand, Latin, the literary idiom more or less modified by the Vulgate and other influences, continued throughout the Middle Ages as the living language of the Church and of the intellectual world. Though varying considerably in character and quality, it was an international language, and Medieval Latin literature is sometimes called "European" in contrast to the earlier "national Roman." In this Medieval Latin was written a varied and living literature (religious works, histories, anecdotes, romances, dramas, sacred and secular poetry), examples of which appear in this book, in the excerpt from the 7th century writer Isidore of Seville (in Capvt XXIX) and selections from other authors in the *Locī Antīquī*. The long life of Latin is attested in the early 14th century by the facts that Dante composed in Latin the political treatise *Dē Monarchiā*, that he wrote in Latin his *Dē Vulgārī Ēloquentiā* to justify his use of the vernacular Italian for literature, and that in Latin pastoral verses he rejected the exhortation to give up the vernacular, in which he was writing the *Divine Comedy,* and compose something in Latin. At the same time, by token of Dante's success and that of others in the use of the vernacular languages, it must be admitted that Latin had begun to wage a losing battle.

## THE PERIOD FROM THE RENAISSANCE (15th Cent.) TO THE PRESENT

Because of Petrarch's new-found admiration of Cicero, Renaissance scholars scorned Medieval Latin and turned to Cicero in particular as the canon of perfection. Although this return to the elegant Ciceronian idiom was prompted by great affection and produced brilliant effects, it was an artificial movement which made Latin somewhat imitative and static compared with the spontaneous, living language which it had been during the Middle Ages. However, Latin continued to be effectively employed well into the modern period—by Erasmus and Sir Thomas More in the 16th century, by Milton, Bacon, and Newton in the 17th century, and by botanists, classical scholars, and poets of the later centuries—and the ecclesiastical strain is still very much alive (despite its de-emphasis in the early 1960s) as the language of the Roman Catholic Church and seminaries. Furthermore, the rediscovery of the true, humanistic spirit of the ancient Latin and Greek literatures and the fresh attention to literary discipline and form as found in the classics proved very beneficial to the native literature of the new era.

The purpose of this abbreviated outline has been to provide some sense of the unbroken sweep of Latin literature from the 3rd century B.C. down to our own times. Besides enjoying its own long and venerable history, Latin literature has also inspired, schooled, and enriched our own English and other occidental literatures to a degree beyond easy assessment. Add to this the wide influence of the Latin language itself as outlined above and you can hardly escape the conclusion that Latin is dead only in the narrow technical sense of the word, and that even a limited knowledge of Latin is a great asset to anyone who works with or is interested in English and the Romance languages and literatures and, indeed, to any educated person determined to read, write, and think with precision and a broad cultural perspective.

# THE ALPHABET AND PRONUNCIATION

The forms of the letters which you see on this printed page are centuries old. They go back through the earliest Italian printed books of the 15th century[9] and

---

[9]Called "incunabula" because they were made in the "cradle days" of printing. The type is called "Roman" to distinguish it from the "black-letter" type which was used in northern

through the finest manuscripts of the 12th and 11th centuries to the firm, clear Carolingian bookhand of the 9th century as perfected under the inspiration of the Carolingian Renaissance by the monks of St. Martin's at Tours in France. These monks developed the small letters from beautiful clear semi-uncials, which in turn lead us back to the uncials and square capitals of the Roman Empire—uncials, developed from Roman cursive, resembled square capitals except that the sharp corners of the angular letters were rounded so that they could be written with greater rapidity. Today we are in the habit of distinguishing the Roman alphabet from the Greek, but the fact is that the Romans learned to write from the Etruscans, who in turn had learned to write from Greek colonists who had settled in the vicinity of Naples during the 8th century B.C.; thus the Roman alphabet is simply one form of the Greek alphabet. But the Greeks were themselves debtors in this matter, for, at an early date, they had adapted their alphabet from a Semitic source, the Phoenicians; while the 22 letters of the Phoenician script, itself influenced by Egyptian hieroglyphics, had represented only consonant sounds, however, the Greeks showed their originality in using some of these letters to designate vowel sounds. The history of the letter-forms you see in our books today provides one more illustration of our indebtedness to European, Near Eastern, and North African antiquity.

The Roman alphabet was like ours except that it lacked the letters **j** and **w.** Furthermore, the letter **v** originally stood for both the sound of the vowel **u** and the sound of the consonant **w** (originally a literal "double u," i.e., vv). Not until the second century of our era did the rounded **u**-form appear to distinguish vowel from consonant, but for convenience both **v** and **u** are employed in the Latin texts of most modern editions. The letter **k** was rarely used, and then only before **a,** in a very few words. The letters **y** (Greek upsilon, Y) and **z** (Greek zeta) were introduced toward the end of the Republic to be used in spelling words of Greek origin.

The following tables indicate approximately the sounds of Latin and how the letters were used by Romans of the classical period to represent those sounds (there are several differences of pronunciation in medieval and ecclesiastical Latin).

### Vowels

Vowels in Latin had essentially two possible pronunciations, long and short. Long vowels were generally held about twice as long as short vowels (cf. half notes to quarter notes in music) and are marked in this book, as in most beginning texts,

---

Europe (cp. the German type). The Italian printers based their Roman type on that of the finest manuscripts of the period, those written for the wealthy, artistic, exacting Renaissance patrons. The scribes of those manuscripts, seeking the most attractive kind of script with which to please such patrons, found it in manuscripts written in the best Carolingian book-hand.

with a MACRON or LONG MARK (e.g., ā); vowels without a macron are short. Students should regard macrons as part of the spelling of a word, since the differences of pronunciation they indicate are often crucial to meaning (e.g., **liber** is a noun meaning *book,* while **līber** is an adjective meaning *free*); the Romans themselves recognized the importance of such differences and (occasionally, not always) marked long vowels in a variety of ways, sometimes by writing them larger than short vowels (**LIBER**) or writing them twice (**LIIBER**) or, more commonly and even in personal letters and graffiti, by writing a mark called in Latin an APEX, resembling an acute accent, above the vowel (**LÍBER**). Though there were most certainly individual differences, the pronunciations of the long and short vowels were approximately as follows—be sure to listen to the pronunciation of these words and all the Latin in this *Intrōdvctiō* either on the audio CD set *Readings from Wheelock's Latin* or online at www.wheelockslatin.com):

| Long | Short |
|---|---|
| ā as in *father:* **dās, cārā** | a as in *Dinah:* **dat, casa** |
| ē as in *they:* **mē, sēdēs** | e as in *pet:* **et, sed** |
| ī as in *machine:* **hīc, sīca** | i as in *pin:* **hic, sicca** |
| ō as in *clover:* **ōs, mōrēs** | o as in *orb, off:* **os, mora** |
| ū as in *rude:* **tū, sūmō** | u as in *put:* **tum, sum** |

y, either short or long, a vowel with a sound intermediate between **u** and **i,** as in French **tu** or German **über**—one of only a few sounds in classical Latin that do not occur in modern English

## Diphthongs

Latin has the following six diphthongs, combinations of two vowel sounds that were collapsed together into a single syllable:

**ae** as *ai* in *aisle:* **cārae, saepe**

**au** as *ou* in *house:* **aut, laudō**

**ei** as in *reign:* **deinde**

**eu** as Latin **e** + **u**, pronounced rapidly as a single syllable: **seu.** The sound does not occur in English and is rare in Latin.

**oe** as *oi* in *oil:* **coepit, proelium**

**ui** as in Latin **u** + **i**, spoken as a single syllable like Spanish **muy** (or like English *gooey,* pronounced quickly as a single syllable). This diphthong occurs only in **huius, cuius, huic, cui, hui.** Elsewhere the two letters are spoken separately as in **fu-it, frūctu-ī.**

## Consonants

Latin consonants had essentially the same sounds as the English consonants with the following exceptions:

**bs** and **bt** were pronounced *ps* and *pt* (e.g., **urbs, obtineō**); otherwise Latin **b** had the same voiced sound as our letter (e.g., **bibēbant**).

**c** was always hard as in *can*, never soft as in *city*: **cum, cīvis, facilis.**

**g** was always hard as in *get*, never soft as in *gem*: **glōria, gerō.** When it appeared before **n**, the letter **g** represented a nasalized *ng* sound as in *hangnail*: **magnus.**

**h** was a breathing sound, an ASPIRATE, as in English, only less harshly pronounced: **hic, haec**

**i** (which also represented a vowel) usually functioned as a consonant with the sound of *y* as in *yes* when used before a vowel at the beginning of a word (**iūstus** = yustus); between two vowels within a word it served in double capacity: as the vowel *i* forming a diphthong with the preceding vowel, and as the consonant *y* (**reiectus** = rei-yectus; **maior** = mai-yor, with the *ai* pronounced like that in *aisle*; **cuius** = cui-yus); otherwise it was usually a vowel. This so-called CONSONANTAL **i** regularly appears in English derivatives as a *j* (a letter added to the alphabet in the Middle Ages); hence **maior** = *major*, **Iūlius** = *Julius*.

**m** had the sound it has in English, pronounced with the lips closed: **monet.** There is some evidence, however, that in at least certain instances final **-m** (i.e., **-m** at the end of a word), following a vowel, was pronounced with the lips open, producing a nasalization of the preceding vowel, another of the few sounds of classical Latin not occurring in English: **tum, etiam.**

**q**, as in English, is always followed by consonantal **u**, the combination having the sound *kw*: **quid, quoque.**

**r** was trilled; the Romans called it the **littera canīna**, because its sound suggested the snarling of a dog: **Rōma, cūrāre.**

**s** was always voiceless as in *see*, never voiced as in our word *ease*: **sed, posuissēs, mīsistis.**

**t** always had the sound of *t* as in *tired*, never of *sh* as in *nation* or *ch* as in *mention*: **taciturnitās, nātiōnem, mentiōnem.**

**v** had the sound of our *w*: **vīvō** = wīwō, **vīnum** = wīnum.

**x** had the sound of *ks* as in *axle*, not of *gz* as in *exert*: **mixtum, exerceō.**

**ch** represented Greek *chi* and had the sound of *ckh* in *blockhead*, not of *ch* in *church*: **chorus, Archilochus.**

**ph** represented Greek *phi* and had the sound of *ph* in *uphill*, not the *f* sound in our pronunciation of *philosophy*: **philosophia.**

**th** represented Greek *theta* and had the sound of *th* in *hothouse*, not of *th* in *thin* or *the*: **theātrum.**

The Romans quite appropriately pronounced double consonants as two separate consonants; we in our haste usually render them as a single consonant. For instance, the **rr** in the Latin word **currunt** sounded something like the two *r*'s in *watch the cur run* (except that in Latin each **r** was trilled); and the **tt** in **admittent** sounded like the two *t*'s in *admit ten.*

## Syllables

In Latin as in English, a word has as many syllables as it has vowels and diphthongs.

*Syllabification:* In dividing a word into syllables:

1. Two contiguous vowels or a vowel and a diphthong are separated: **dea, de-a; deae, de-ae.**
2. A single consonant between two vowels goes with (because pronounced with) the second vowel: **amīcus, a-mī-cus.**
3. When two or more consonants stand between two vowels, generally only the last consonant goes with the second vowel: **mittō, mit-tō; servāre, ser-vā-re; cōnsūmptus, cōn-sūmp-tus.** However, a stop (**p, b, t, d, c, g**) + a liquid (**l, r**) generally (with common exceptions in poetry) count as a single consonant and go with the following vowel: **patrem, pa-trem; castra, cas-tra.** Also counted as single consonants are **qu** and the aspirates **ch, ph, th,** which should never be separated in syllabification: **architectus, ar-chi-tec-tus; loquācem, lo-quā-cem.**

*Syllable quantity:* A syllable is LONG BY NATURE if it contains a long vowel or a diphthong; a syllable is LONG BY POSITION if it contains a short vowel followed by two or more consonants or by **x,** which is a double consonant (= *ks*). Otherwise a syllable is short; again, the difference is rather like that between a musical half-note and a quarter-note. In applying these rules, remember that a stop + a liquid as well as **qu** and the aspirates **ch, ph,** and **th** regularly count as a single consonant: e.g., **pa-trem, quo-que, phi-lo-so-phi-a.**

Syllables long by nature (here underlined): <u>lau</u>-<u>dō</u>, <u>Rō</u>-ma, a-<u>mī</u>-cus.
Syllables long by position (underlined): <u>ser</u>-vat, sa-pi-<u>en</u>-ti-a, <u>ax</u>-is (= ak-sis).
Examples with all long syllables, whether by nature or by position, underlined:
    <u>lau</u>-<u>dā</u>-te, mo-ne-<u>ō</u>, <u>sae</u>-pe, <u>cōn</u>-<u>ser</u>-<u>vā</u>-tis, pu-<u>el</u>-<u>lā</u>-rum.

Even in English, syllables have this sort of temporal quantity, i.e., some syllables take longer to pronounce than others (consider the word "enough," with its very short, clipped first syllable, and the much longer second syllable), but it is not a phenomenon we think much about. The matter is important in Latin, however, for at least two reasons: first, syllable quantity was a major determinant of the rhythm of Latin poetry, as you will learn later in your study of the language; and, of more immediate importance, syllable quantity determined the position of the stress accent in words of three or more syllables, as explained below.

### Accent

Words in Latin, like those in English, were pronounced with extra emphasis on one syllable (or more than one, in the case of very long words); the placement of this STRESS ACCENT in Latin (unlike English) followed these strict and simple rules:

1. In a word of two syllables the accent always falls on the first syllable: **sér-vō, saé-pe, ní-hil.**
2. In a word of three or more syllables (a) the accent falls on the next to last syllable (sometimes called the PENULT), if that syllable is long (**ser-vā́-re, cōn-sér-vat, for-tū́-na**); (b) otherwise, the accent falls on the syllable before that (the ANTEPENULT: **mó-ne-ō, pá-tri-a, pe-cū́-ni-a, vó-lu-cris**).

Because these rules for accentuation are so regular, accent marks (as opposed to macrons) are not ordinarily included when writing Latin; in this text, however, accents are provided in both the PARADIGMS (sample declensions and conjugations) and the chapter vocabularies, as an aid to correct pronunciation.

## LANGUAGE IS SPEECH: The Importance of Pronunciation and Reading Aloud

Although oral-aural communication and conversational skills are sometimes—and unfortunately—given little stress in the Latin classroom, nevertheless a reasonably correct and consistent pronunciation is essential to the mastery of Latin, as of any language. An ability to pronounce words and to read sentences and longer texts aloud according to the few, simple rules provided in this *Intrōdvctiō* will also enable you to "pronounce" correctly in your mind and, as you think of a word, to spell it correctly. Without that ability, you will confuse not only the sounds of the language, but also the spelling and often therefore the meaning of its words.

Fortunately, as you have seen in this discussion, **prōnūntiātiō Latīna est facilis,** *Latin pronunciation is easy,* far easier than that of English or any other language I know. Vowels have only two possible sounds; most consonants have only one; and the rules for accentuation are just that, rules that you can count on every time. Moreover, nearly every sound that existed in classical Latin occurs also in English (the chief exceptions being the vowel **y** and the diphthong **eu**, neither of which was very common, the trilled **r**, and final -**m**). And in Latin, "what you see is what you get" or rather "what you see is what you hear": there are no "silent e's" or other such oddities of correlating spelling with sound that have led to the familiar quip that in English "ghoti" can even be pronounced "fish" (gh- as in "enough," -o- as in "women," and -ti as in "nation")!

As you begin your study of Latin, remember that it did not merely consist of written texts to be read mutely from a printed page, but it was for a millennium and more a spoken language—a language learned and spoken by Roman boys and girls, in fact, just as your own native language was acquired and spoken by you in your childhood; it was a living language read and spoken by average Roman women and men, and not just by famous orators, poets, and politicians. And—a fact some may find startling—the Romans themselves never read silently, but always aloud; they regarded language as speaking and listening, and viewed writing as merely a convenient means of recording communications spoken and heard.

In your study of this classic and (because of its recurring inflections) highly sonorous tongue, you should apply all your language learning skills toward acquiring mastery, spending at least a few minutes every day listening and speaking, and not just silently reading and writing. In a classroom setting, you will have abundant opportunity to hear the language; but even so, or if you are studying independently, the *Readings from Wheelock's Latin* CDs and the online audio at www.wheelockslatin.com are indispensable resources. Always practice and review paradigms and vocabulary items by listening to and reading them aloud. Most especially, like a true Roman, *read aloud every Latin sentence or passage you encounter;* and, though this book will certainly help you develop your skills in translating Latin into English, you should first read every Latin text aloud *for comprehension,* reading and hearing and thinking what the text is saying, before ever attempting to translate into English.

**Carpe diem—carpe Latīnam!**

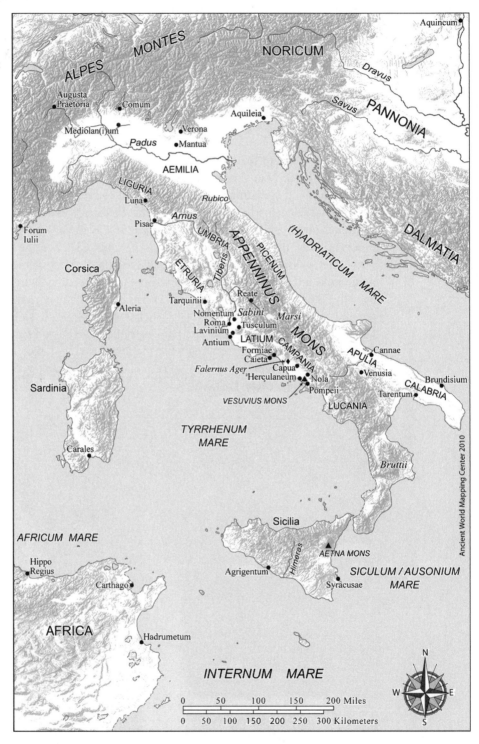

*Map 1: ANCIENT ITALY*

*Map by Richard A. LaFleur and Thomas R. Elliott, revised by Brian Turner, with materials
provided by the Ancient World Mapping Center, www.unc.edu/awmc*

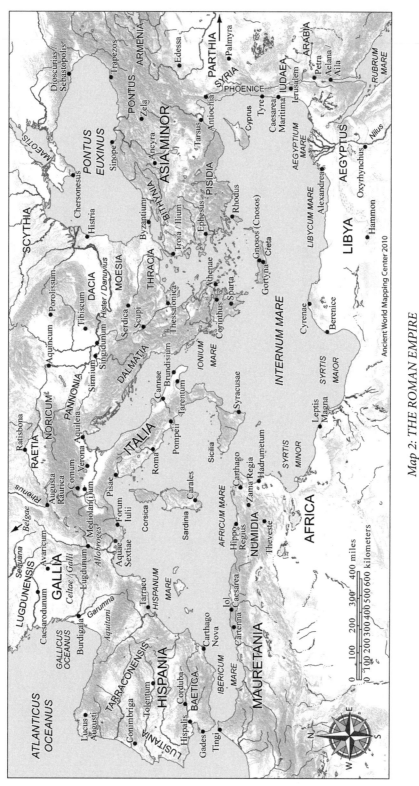

*Map 2: THE ROMAN EMPIRE*

*Map by Richard A. LaFleur and Thomas R. Elliott, revised by Brian Turner, with materials provided by the Ancient World Mapping Center,*
*www.unc.edu/awmc*

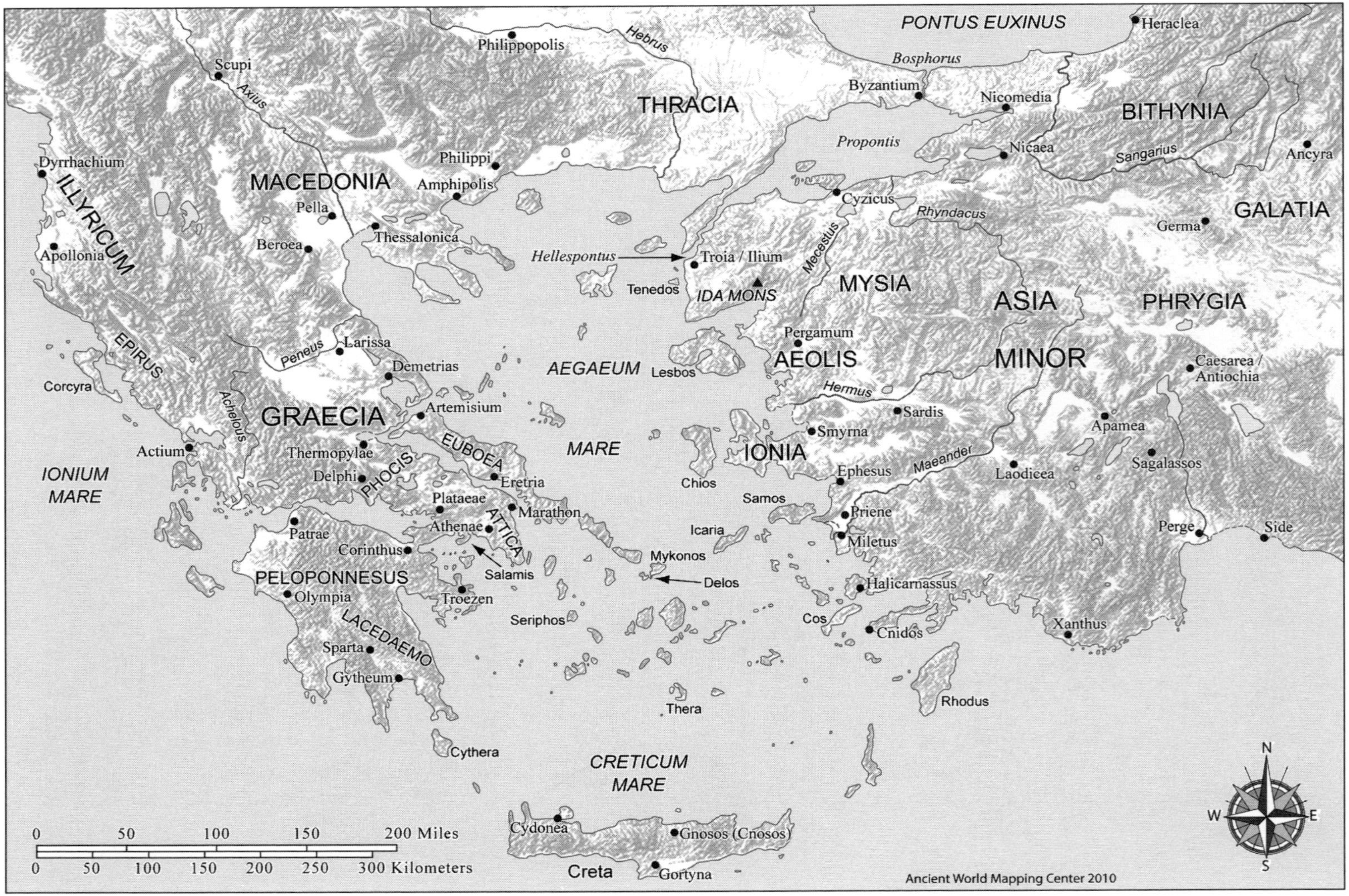

Map 3: ANCIENT GREECE AND THE AEGEAN

Map by Richard A. LaFleur and Thomas R. Elliott, revised by Brian Turner, with materials provided by the Ancient World Mapping Center, www.unc.edu/awmc

# CAPVT I &#x25A4;&#x25A4;&#x25A4;

# Verbs; First and Second Conjugations; Adverbs; Reading and Translating

**Salvē** ("Greetings!"), and *WELCOME* to the study of classical Latin, or what I affectionately call "The Mother Tongue"! You already know a great deal about the design and purposes of this book from reading the Preface and *Intrōductiō* and thus are aware you are embarking on a fascinating journey into, not only the language, but also the literature and culture of ancient Rome. The task will be challenging, but the rewards manifold, and so I bid you **bonam fortūnam**! (you can deduce the meaning of that phrase from the context and English derivatives, but, if not, look up both words in the Latin-English **Vocābula** at the back of the book....)

## GRAMMATICA ("GRAMMAR TOPICS")

Each of this book's chapters opens with a discussion of grammatical issues essential to the mastery of Latin, typically including both **MORPHOLOGY** (word forms) and **SYNTAX** (usage of those forms within a sentence). Throughout each chapter important new terms, like "morphology" and "syntax" here, are regularly printed in these **SMALL BOLD CAPITALS**, usually at their first few occurrences in the book, as a reminder that they are items you must be familiar with.

### VERBS (sg. *verbum,* pl. *verba*)

Since a **VERB** (from Latin **verbum,** whose basic meaning is *word*) describes its subject's activity or state of being, and is thus one of the most important words in a sentence, we may best begin our study of Latin with a look at that part of speech (the other **PARTS OF SPEECH** in Latin are the same as those in English: **NOUNS,**

**PRONOUNS, ADJECTIVES, ADVERBS, PREPOSITIONS, CONJUNCTIONS, INTERJECTIONS**, each of which is systematically introduced in this book).

In Latin as in English, verbs exhibit the following five characteristics:

**PERSON** (Lat. **persōna**): who is the subject, i.e., who performs (or, in the passive, receives) the action, from the speaker's point of view; 1st person = the speaker(s), *I, we;* 2nd = the person(s) spoken to, *you;* 3rd = the person(s) spoken about, *he, she, it, they.*

**NUMBER** (**numerus**): how many subjects, singular or plural.

**TENSE** (**tempus**, *time*): the time of the action; Latin has six tenses, present, future, imperfect, perfect, future perfect, and pluperfect.

**MOOD** (**modus**, *manner*): the manner of indicating the action or state of being of the verb; like English, Latin has the **INDICATIVE** (which "indicates" facts) and the **IMPERATIVE** (which orders actions), both introduced in this chapter, and the **SUBJUNCTIVE** (which describes, in particular, hypothetical or potential actions), introduced in Capvt XXVIII

**VOICE** (**vōx**): an indication, with transitive verbs (those that can take direct objects), of whether the subject performs the action (**ACTIVE VOICE**) or receives it (**PASSIVE VOICE**).

## Conjugation (*coniugātiō*)

To **CONJUGATE** (**coniugāre**, *join together*) a **FINITE VERB** (i.e., a verb that exhibits the above characteristics, as opposed to *in*finitives, which lack person and number) is to list all its forms, according to these variations of person, number, tense, mood, and voice. If asked to conjugate the English verb *to praise* in the present tense, active voice, of the indicative mood, you would say:

|  | Singular | Plural |
|---|---|---|
| *1st person* | I praise | we praise |
| *2nd person* | you praise | you praise |
| *3rd person* | he (she, it) praises | they praise |

The person and the number of five of these forms cannot be determined in English without the aid of pronouns *I, you, we, they.* Only in the third person singular can you omit the pronoun *he (she, it)* and still make clear by the special ending of the verb that *praises* is third person singular.

## Personal Endings

What English can accomplish in only one of the six forms, Latin can do in all six by means of **PERSONAL ENDINGS**, which indicate distinctly the person, the number, and the voice of the verb. Since these personal endings will be encountered in every Latin sentence, you need to memorize them now, and it's easily done. For the active voice they are:

**Singular**

| *1st person* | **-ō** or **-m**, which corresponds to *I*. |
| *2nd person* | **-s**, which corresponds to *you* (sg.). |
| *3rd person* | **-t**, which corresponds to *he, she, it*. |

**Plural**

| *1st person* | **-mus**, which corresponds to *we*. |
| *2nd person* | **-tis**, which corresponds to *you* (pl.). |
| *3rd person* | **-nt**, which corresponds to *they*. |

The next step is to find a verb **STEM** to which these endings can be added.

### Present Active Infinitive and Present Stem

An **INFINITIVE** is a common verbal form, usually preceded with "to" in English ("to err is human, to forgive divine"). The present active infinitives of the model verbs used in this book for the first and second conjugations are:

　　**laudāre**, *to praise*　　　　　　　　**monēre**, *to advise*

The **-āre** ending, with its **-ā-** **STEM VOWEL**, identifies a verb as first conjugation; **-ēre** and the **-ē-** characterize second conjugation verbs (Latin has four conjugations altogether, each marked by a different stem vowel—the third and fourth conjugations are introduced in later chapters). Drop the **-re**, the actual infinitive ending, and you have the **PRESENT STEM**, which ends in ā for first conjugation verbs, ē for second:

　　**laudā-**　　　　　　　　**monē-**

To this stem add the personal endings (with the few modifications noted below), and you are ready to read or to say something in Latin about the present: e.g., **laudā + s > laudās**, *you praise;* **monēmus**, *we advise*.

　　This leads us to the first of many paradigms presented in this book. **PARADIGMS** (from Greek **paradeigma**, *pattern, example*) are presented throughout the chapters and in the Appendix (see **Summārium Fōrmārum**, p. 495–509) to provide model summaries of forms. The ancient Romans learned the many **INFLECTIONS** (the changing endings of individual words) from their parents, teachers, and daily contact with other Latin speakers, just as we as children learned our own native language (and such inflections as "they" and "them," or "see" and "sees"). Since we lack this natural Latin-speaking environment and usually begin the study of Latin at a relatively late age under the exigencies of time, the analytical "grammar-translation" approach through paradigms (which even the Romans themselves had to learn) is widely regarded as a highly effective method for high-schoolers, college students, and other adult learners.

In the process of memorizing paradigms, be sure always to say them *aloud,* as speaking and listening to the language, to its basic sounds and rhythms, is essential to acquiring mastery; if you have the audio package, *Readings from Wheelock's Latin,* you can hear all the book's paradigms (as well as the 40 chapter vocabularies and Latin readings) pronounced there.

### Present Indicative Active of *laudō* and *moneō*

#### Singular

1. laúdō, *I praise, am praising, do praise*       móneō, *I advise,* etc.
2. laúdās, *you praise, are praising, do praise*       mónēs, *you advise,* etc.
3. laúdat, *he (she, it) praises, is praising, does praise*       mónet, *he (she, it) advises,* etc.

#### Plural

1. laudāmus, *we praise, are praising, do praise*       monḗmus, *we advise,* etc.
2. laudātis, *you praise, are praising, do praise*       monḗtis, *you advise,* etc.
3. laúdant, *they praise, are praising, do praise*       mónent, *they advise,* etc.

Note that Latin has only these present active indicative forms, and so the following English translations are possible, depending on context; e.g., **mē laudant,** *they praise me* (SIMPLE PRESENT) or *they are praising me* (PROGRESSIVE PRESENT) or *they do praise me* (EMPHATIC PRESENT).

ACCENT marks (as in **mónent**) are provided in the paradigms only for convenience; since they follow the strict rules for accentuation explained in the *Intrōductiō,* they need not, and should not, be included in your own conjugation of Latin verbs (unless you are asked to do so by your instructor).

The MACRONS, however, must be included (just as the Romans themselves frequently marked long vowels in a variety of ways), and the long vowel sounds they indicate must be taken into account in pronouncing and memorizing the paradigms and in conjugating other verbs. Note that the stem vowel has no macron in certain forms (e.g., **moneō, laudant**); learn the following rule, which will make it easier to account for macrons that seem to disappear and reappear arbitrarily:

> Vowels that are normally long are regularly shortened when they occur immediately before another vowel (hence **moneō** instead of *\*monēō**), before -m, -r, or -t at the end of a word (hence **laudat,** not *\*laudāt*), or before nt or nd in any position (**laudant,** not *\*laudānt*: the asterisks here and elsewhere in this book indicate a hypothetical form not actually occurring in classical Latin).

In the case of first conjugation, or -ā-, verbs (vs. second conjugation, -ē- verbs), the stem vowel is not merely shortened but disappears entirely in the first person singular, through contraction with final -ō (**laudō,** not *\*laudāō*).

**Present Active Imperative**

The IMPERATIVE MOOD is used for giving commands; the singular imperative is identical to the present stem, and the plural imperative (employed when addressing two or more persons) is formed by adding -**te** to that stem:

| | | |
|---|---|---|
| 2nd person singular | laúdā, *praise!* | mónē, *advise!* |
| 2nd person plural | laudáte, *praise!* | monéte, *advise!* |

E.g., **Monē mē!** *Advise me!* **Servāte mē!** *Save me!*

## ADVERBS (sg. *adverbium*, pl. *adverbia*)

In Latin and English, an ADVERB is a word that modifies a verb, an adjective, or another adverb, and is typically positioned before that word (**ad** + **verbum**, *next to/ near the verb*); **nōn** and **saepe** appear in the following **Vocābula**, and many others will be introduced in subsequent chapters.

> **Nōn valet.** *She* (or *he*) *is not well.* **Mē saepe laudant.** *They often praise me.* **Mē nōn saepe monēs.** *You do not often advise me.*

# VOCĀBVLA ("VOCABULARY")

In memorizing the **Vocābula** in every chapter, pronounce (**prōnūntiā!**) each Latin word carefully, with attention to macrons, according to the rules learned in the *Intrōductiō,* along with the English meanings; listen to each chapter's vocabulary on the *Readings from Wheelock's Latin* CDs or online at www.wheelockslatin.com. Thorough memorization of vocabulary is a sine qua non (**sine quā nōn,** *without which not*), an absolute essential to mastering a language, and there are no shortcuts; spend at least 5-10 minutes every single day studying a chapter's new vocabulary and reviewing words introduced in previous chapters.

Most vocabulary entries contain additional information that should be learned, often including an indication of the part of speech (adverb, conjunction, etc.) and a selection of English derivatives listed in parentheses at the end of the entry. Like an English verb, a Latin verb has PRINCIPAL PARTS (usually four, vs. three in English, as in "go, went, gone") which must be memorized in order to fully conjugate the verb. As you will see from the following list, the first principal part is the first person singular present active indicative, and the second principal part is the present active infinitive; the function of the remaining principal parts will be explained in later chapters. Try conjugating two or three of the verbs in this list, and give their singular and plural imperatives too.

**mē**, pron. (= pronoun, see p. 537–39 for a list of the abbreviations used in this book) *me, myself*

**quid**, pron., *what* (quid pro quo, quiddity)

**níhil**, noun, *nothing* (nil, nihilism, annihilate)

**nōn**, adv. (adverb), *not*

**saépe**, adv., *often*

**sī**, conj. (conjunction), *if*

**ámō, amā́re, amā́vī, amā́tum**, *to love, like;* **amā́bō tē**, idiom, *please* (lit., *I will love you*) (amorous, amatory, Amanda)

**cṓgitō, cōgitā́re, cōgitā́vī, cōgitā́tum**, *to think, ponder, consider, plan* (cogitate, cogitation, cogitative)

**dḗbeō, dēbḗre, dḗbuī, dḗbitum**, *to owe; ought, must, should* (debt, debit, due, duty)

**dō, dáre, dédī, dátum**, *to give, offer* (date, data, dative); unlike other first conj. verbs, the stem vowel of **dō** is long only in the 2nd pers. sg. indic. (**dās**) and sg. imperat. (**dā**).

**érrō, errā́re, errā́vī, errā́tum**, *to wander; err, go astray, make a mistake, be mistaken* (erratic, errant, erroneous, error, aberration)

**laúdō, laudā́re, laudā́vī, laudā́tum**, *to praise* (laud, laudable, laudatory)

**móneō, monḗre, mónuī, mónitum**, *to remind, advise, warn* (admonish, admonition, monitor, monument, monster, premonition)

**sálveō, salvḗre**, *to be well, be in good health;* **sálvē, salvḗte**, *hello, greetings!* (salvation, salver, salvage)

**sérvō, servā́re, servā́vī, servā́tum**, *to preserve, save, keep, guard* (observe, preserve, reserve, reservoir)

**cōnsérvō, cōnservā́re, cōnservā́vī, cōnservā́tum (con-servō)**, a stronger form of **servō**, *to preserve, conserve, maintain* (conservative, conservation, conservator)

**térreō, terrḗre, térruī, térritum**, *to frighten, terrify* (terrible, terrific, terrify, terror, terrorist, deter)

**váleō, valḗre, váluī, valitū́rum**, *to be strong, have power; be well;* **válē (valḗte)**, *good-bye, farewell!* (valedictorian, valid, invalidate, prevail, prevalent)

**vídeō, vidḗre, vī́dī, vī́sum**, *to see; observe, understand* (video, provide, evident, view, review, revise, revision, television)

**vócō, vocā́re, vocā́vī, vocā́tum**, *to call, summon* (vocation, advocate, vocabulary, convoke, evoke, invoke, provoke, revoke)

# LĒCTIŌ ET TRĀNSLĀTIŌ ("READING AND TRANSLATION")

Before attempting to read the following sentences and passage (all of which are based, however freely, on ancient sources), be sure you have memorized the paradigms and **Vocābula** and practiced conjugating some of the verbs in the list. You should also first assess your mastery of each chapter's grammatical material by using the Self-Tutorial Exercises at the back of the book (p. 412–45): write out your answers to the grammar questions and your translations of at least some of the sentences, and then check your responses against the Answer Key at p. 446–83; if you have made mistakes, analyze them and review accordingly, before proceeding to the chapter's readings.

The following simple rules will assist you with reading and translating. First, listen to the CDs, if you have them, and always read each sentence *aloud* (just as the Romans did!); read for comprehension, thinking about the meanings of words and phrases and the likely sense of the whole sentence. The verb often comes last in Latin: if its ending is either first or second person, you already know the subject ("I," "we," or "you") and can begin your translation there; if the verb is third person (i.e., ending with -t or -nt), look for a noun that might be the subject, frequently the first word in the sentence. Subject-object-verb (SOV) is a common word-order pattern in Latin (vs. SVO in English).

## SENTENTIAE ("Sentences")

1. Labor mē vocat. (Note the SOV word order.—**labor**; "laboratory," "elaborate"; a noun, and one of hundreds of Lat. words that come into Eng. with their spelling unchanged; such words are typically *not* defined in these notes, as you are expected to intuit their meaning, but usually they may be found in the end Vocab., p. 518–36 below. )
2. Monē mē, sī errō—amābō tē!
3. Festīnā lentē. (A favorite saying of the emperor Augustus.—**festīnō, festīnāre**, *to hasten, make haste;* "Festina," a brand of wristwatch.—**lentē**, adv., *slowly.*)
4. Laudās mē; culpant mē. (**culpō, culpāre**, *to blame, censure;* "culpable," "culprit.")
5. Saepe peccāmus. (**peccō, peccāre**, *to sin;* "peccadillo," "impeccable.")
6. Quid dēbēmus cōgitāre?
7. Cōnservāte mē!
8. Rūmor volat. (**volō, volāre**, *to fly;* "volatile," "volley.")
9. Mē nōn amat.
10. Nihil mē terret. (SOV again.)
11. Apollō mē saepe servat.
12. Salvēte!—quid vidētis? Nihil vidēmus.
13. Saepe nihil cōgitās.
14. Bis dās, sī citō dās. (**bis**, adv., *twice;* "bisect," "bicycle."—**citō**, adv., *quickly;* "citation," "incite."—What do you suppose this ancient proverb meant?)
15. Sī valēs, valeō. (A friendly sentiment with which Romans often commenced a letter.)

Each chapter contains a few sentences to translate from English into Latin; you will enjoy these composition exercises, which will soon have you thinking like an ancient Roman! You will need to carefully analyze the English sentence first, of course, thinking for example about the person and number of the verb; and use the few rules of word order you have learned in this chapter.

16.  What does he see?
17.  They are giving nothing.
18.  You ought not to praise me.
19.  If I err, he often warns me.
20.  If you love me, save me, please!

### The Poet Horace Contemplates an Invitation

Maecēnās et Vergilius mē hodiē vocant. Quid cōgitāre dēbeō? Quid dēbeō respondēre? Sī errō, mē saepe monent et culpant; sī nōn errō, mē laudant. Quid hodiē cōgitāre dēbeō?

Horace (Quintus Horatius Flaccus, 65–8 B.C.) is one of the best known and admired of all classical Lat. poets; as a young man he composed two volumes of satires, but he is perhaps even better known for his lyric poems, the *Odes* or *Carmina*, from which comes the

Horace, Virgil, and Varius at the House of Maecenas. *Oil on canvas.*
*Charles Francois Jalabert (1819–1901). Musée des Beaux-Artes, Nimes, France*

poet's urgent dictum to "harvest the day," **carpe diem**! For further particulars on Horace and the other authors cited in these chapter reading passages, review the Introd. above, p. xxxii. The wealthy literary patron Maecenas and the poet Vergil, author of Rome's great epic poem, the *Aeneid,* were both friends of Horace, and this brief passage is very freely adapted from autobiographical references in his poetry.—**et,** conj., *and.*—**hodiē,** adv., *today;* "hodiernal."—**respondeō, respondēre,** *to reply, respond;* "response," "correspond.")

*QVAESTIŌNĒS:* Why is Horace hesitant about the invitation he has received? In view of the shared interests of the three men, what do you suppose Horace may have done that Maecenas and Vergil might sometimes criticize?

## SCRĪPTA IN PARIETIBVS ("Writings on Walls")

Like modern Americans—and literate humans everywhere!—the ancient Romans loved scribbling on walls, and a vast number of their graffiti have been preserved in the ruins of Pompeii, the south Italian city near Naples that was at once both destroyed and, in an archaeological sense, preserved in the dreadful, catastrophic eruption of Mount Vesuvius in August of A.D. 79 (see Map 1, above). Examples of these graffiti are presented throughout book, for the interest and insights they provide into one aspect or another of life in ancient Italy; dozens more graffiti and other inscriptions from throughout the Roman empire are included in the companion reader, *Scribblers, Scvlptors, and Scribes,* also available from HarperCollins Publishers.

Many of the graffiti from Pompeii have been damaged, sometimes obscuring letters or entire words, and others contain—like those you have likely seen yourself on public bathroom walls!—spelling errors or other oddities of language that are interesting in themselves as reflections of varying levels of literacy, pronunciation variants, and other evidence of the general fluidity of language. You will learn lots of rules (**rēgulae**) of spelling and grammar as you proceed through this text (rules that Latin, as a highly "regular" language, tends to follow), but you should keep in mind that these reflect a limited, albeit important, segment of the population of ancient Italy, i.e., well educated, highly literate Romans of the 1st centuries B.C. and A.D.; many other Romans could read and write, however, and though they may not have produced any literary masterpieces, the "Writings on Walls" (**scrīpta in parietibus**) they have left us—in their own handwriting—are a valuable legacy from the ancient world. In editing these graffiti, the following conventional symbols are regularly employed to indicate the sorts of errors and omissions mentioned above, as well as abbreviations that were common in both formal and informal texts:

(abc)   an abbreviation expanded by the editor
[abc]   letters missing due to damage and supplied by the editor

{abc}    letters included by error
<abc>    letters omitted either by error, or as a reflection of the writer's
         pronunciation, and supplied by the editor

Av<ē>, pu<e>l<l>a!

*Corpus Inscriptionum Latinarum* (*CIL*) 4.10040: From the attic of a lodging in Pompeii,
Reg. II, Ins. 1, = Region II, Insula 1: archaeologists have divided the ancient city into re-
gions and blocks, **regiōnēs** and **īnsulae,** the numbers for which are generally provided
in this book; individual houses and shops within each insula were also typically num-
bered and sometimes named. The lad who scribbled this graffito to his sweetheart was
not highly literate: as you can see from the drawing, he actually wrote **AV,** a contraction
of **AVE,** = **avē,** which here had essentially the same meaning as **salvē;** and his **PVLA** was
a misspelling of **puella,** which as you will see in Capvt II means *girl* or *girlfriend.* The
above drawing, and those in subsequent chapters, are reproduced directly from the *CIL*
by graphic artist Kay Stanton.


## LATĪNA EST GAVDIVM—ET ŪTILIS! ("Latin Is Fun—and Useful!")

**Salvēte!** Here and at the close of each chapter, you will find a trove of Latin **miscellānea**
(you can easily deduce the meaning of that term—it became an English word too, spelled
exactly the same!) for your pleasure and edification! **Gaudium,** in the title of this section,
is the noun (**nōmen**) for *joy* or just plain *fun;* and **ūtilis,** an adjective (**adiectīvum**) meaning *useful,* is a reminder here of the amazing "utility" of the Latin language, whose careful study will provide you with invaluable knowledge that you can "utilize" every day! To
start with, here is some "first day" conversational Latin:

    **Salvē, discipula** or **discipule!** *Hello, student!* (The -**a**/-**e** variants distinguish between
female and male students.)
    **Salvēte, discipulae et discipulī!** *Hello, students!* (feminine and masculine plural)
    **Salvē, magister** or **magistra!** *Greetings, teacher!* (again, masculine or feminine)
    **Valēte, discipulī et discipulae! Valē, magister (magistra)!** *Good-bye, students . . . ,* etc.
    **Quid est nōmen tibi?** *What's your name?*
    **Nōmen mihi est "Mark."** *My name is Mark.* (Or, better yet, how about a **nōmen
Latīnum,** *Latin name:* **nōmen mihi est "Mārcus."**)

Your instructor may employ conversational "classroom Latin" in teaching grammar:
several Latin grammatical terms are introduced above, e.g., **adverbium, verbum,** and
**coniugāre;** would you know how to respond if your instructor said to you, **Coniugā verbum "amō, amāre"?** (She/he might add . . . **in tempore praesentī,** which you could likely
guess means *in the present tense*—most of our English grammar terms derive from Latin,
so this is easy!) In Capvt II you will learn that **est** = *is;* if your teacher asked, **Quid est**

"saepe"—**verbum aut** (*or*) **adverbium?**—how would you reply? You'll be speaking, and thinking, like a Roman before you know it!

Oh, and remember that **labor** in sentence 1 (**sententia I**) above is one of many Latin words that come directly into English without any alteration in spelling? Well, **rūmor** in **sententia VIII** is another, and so is **videō** in the **Vocābula**. On the other hand, **amō** does not mean "bullets" ("ammo"!!) nor is **amat** "a small rug," so, in this section of the book, beware of . . . **iocī terribilēs** (*terrible jokes*): **valēte!**

In Maecenas' Foyer
*Oil on canvas, 1890*
*Stefan Bakalowicz (1857–1947)*
*Tretyakov Gallery, Moscow, Russia*

# CAPVT II ᗡᗡᗡ

# First Declension Nouns and Adjectives; Prepositions, Conjunctions, Interjections

## GRAMMATICA

### NOUNS (sg. *nōmen*, pl. *nōmina*) AND CASES

A **NOUN** (nōmen *name*) "names" or identifies a person, place, or thing, either generally, **poēta**, *poet*, **urbs**, *city*, **liber**, *book* (so-called **COMMON NOUNS**), or specifically, **Vergilius**, *Vergil*, **Rōma**, *Rome*, **Aenēis**, *Aeneid* (**PROPER NOUNS**). Nouns are also categorized as **ABSTRACT** (**īra**, *anger*) or **CONCRETE** (**porta**, *gate*). As a Latin verb has various **INFLECTIONS** or endings that signal specifics of meaning, so a noun has various terminations to show whether it functions as a verb's subject or object, indicates possession, etc. The inflected forms of a noun are called **CASES**, the more common uses and meanings of which are catalogued below; you will encounter several other case uses in subsequent chapters, all of which you must be able to identify and name, so it is advisable to begin now keeping a list for each case, with definitions and examples, in your notebook or a computer file. For illustrative purposes, we will refer to the following simple English sentences, which have been limited to the material available in Capita I and II and later in the chapter will be translated into Latin for further analysis.

A. The poet is giving the girl large roses (*or* is giving large roses to the girl).
B. The girls are giving the poet's roses to the sailors.
C. Without money the girls' country (*or* the country of the girls) is not strong.

### Nominative Case

The Romans used the **NOMINATIVE CASE** most commonly to indicate the **SUBJECT** of a finite verb; e.g., "poet" in sentence A above and "girls" in B. As you will see in a later chapter, the nominative was also employed with forms of *to be* (**sum, esse**) and other linking verbs, as a PREDICATE NOMINATIVE: **Puella est poēta,** *the girl is a poet;* **Patria est antīqua,** *the country is ancient.*

## Genitive Case

When one noun was used to modify (from **modus,** *limit*) another, the Romans put the modifying/limiting noun, like *poet's* in sentence B and *girls'* in sentence C, in the GENITIVE CASE. One idea commonly conveyed by the genitive is POSSESSION and, although other uses are distinguished, the genitive can generally be translated with the preposition "of" or by using an apostrophe (*'s* or *s'*). A noun in the genitive case usually follows the noun it modifies.

## Dative Case

The Romans used the DATIVE to mark the person or thing indirectly affected by the action of the verb, as *(to) the girl* in sentence A and *to the sailors* in B; both of these nouns are INDIRECT OBJECTS, the most common use of the dative. "To" or "for" are most commonly supplied in translating a dative.

## Accusative Case

The Romans used the ACCUSATIVE CASE to indicate the DIRECT OBJECT of the verb, the person or thing directly affected by the verb's action. In sentences A and B, *roses* is the direct object of *is (are) giving.*

The accusative can also be used as OBJECT OF A PREPOSITION, with certain (not all) prepositions: e.g., **ad,** *toward/at;* **in,** *into;* **post,** *after, behind.* A PREPOSITION (**praepositiō,** *placing before;* pl. **praepositiōnēs**) is usually "positioned before" a noun or pronoun (its "object"), forming with that object a PREPOSITIONAL PHRASE that modifies either a noun (**agricola ad portam est vir bonus,** *the farmer at the gate is a good man*—**ad portam** is adjectival, answering the question "which farmer?"), or a verb (**agricola ad portam ambulat,** *the farmer is walking toward the gate*—**ad portam** is adverbial and answers the question "where?"), or some other word in the sentence. Most prepositions govern objects in either the ablative case or the accusative; a few can take both cases but with different shades of meaning.

## Ablative Case

The ABLATIVE CASE is sometimes called the "adverbial case" because it was used by the Romans to modify, or limit, the verb by such ideas as *means* ("by/with what," e.g., **pecūniā,** *with money*), *agent* ("by whom": **ab puellā,** *by the girl*), *accompaniment* ("with whom": **cum poētā,** *with the poet*), *manner* ("how": **cum īrā,** *with anger, angrily*), *place* ("where/from which": **in/ex patriā,** *in/from the country*), *time* ("when/within which": **ūnā hōrā**, *in one hour*). The ablative was often employed as object of a preposition; when a preposition was not used, typically "by," "with," or "from" should be supplied in translating to English.

### Vocative Case

The Romans used the **VOCATIVE CASE** to address or call on (**vocāre**, *to call*) a person or thing directly; e.g., **Salvē, nauta**, *Greetings, sailor.* Sometimes the **IN-TERJECTION Ō** was employed, **Ō puella, servā mē**, *O (oh) girl, save me!*—an interjection (**interiectiō**, *throwing into*; pl. **interiectiōnēs**) is an exclamatory word "thrown into" a sentence and expressing some emotion, e.g., "oh," "aha," "wow," "yikes!" In modern punctuation the vocative (or noun/pronoun of **DIRECT AD-DRESS**, as the usage is typically called) is separated from the rest of the sentence by commas. With one major exception to be studied in Capvt III, the vocative has the same form as that of the nominative, and so it is ordinarily not listed in the paradigms.

## FIRST DECLENSION NOUNS AND ADJECTIVES

The listing of all the cases of a noun or adjective is called a **DECLENSION** (from **dēclīnāre**, *to change the direction or form* of something). Just as we conjugate verbs by adding endings to a stem, so we **DECLINE** nouns and adjectives by adding endings to a **BASE**. The nominative and genitive singular forms of a noun are provided in the vocabulary entry, which must be completely memorized, and *the base is found by dropping the genitive ending*; the vocabulary entry for an adjective includes the masculine, feminine, and neuter nominative singular forms, and the surest way to determine its base is by *dropping the feminine ending*. The following paradigm, which should be memorized (and remember to practice *aloud!*), illustrates the declension of a noun/adjective phrase, **porta magna**, *the large gate;* note that since Latin lacked equivalents of the English **ARTICLES** "a," "an," and "the," they must be supplied in translation:

|  | **porta**, *gate* Base: port- | **magna**, *large* Base: magn- |  | Endings |
|---|---|---|---|---|
| **Singular** |  |  |  |  |
| *Nom.* | pórta | mágna | *the (a) large gate* | -a |
| *Gen.* | pórtae | mágnae | *of the large gate* | -ae |
| *Dat.* | pórtae | mágnae | *to/for the large gate* | -ae |
| *Acc.* | pórtam | mágnam | *the large gate* | -am |
| *Abl.* | pórtā | mágnā | *by/with/from*, etc., *the large gate* | -ā |
| *Voc.* | pórta | mágna | *O large gate* | -a |

**Plural**

| | | | | |
|---|---|---|---|---|
| *Nom.* | pórtae | mágnae | *the large gates* or *large gates* | **-ae** |
| *Gen.* | portārum | magnārum | *of the large gates* | **-ārum** |
| *Dat.* | pórtīs | mágnīs | *to/for the large gates* | **-īs** |
| *Acc.* | pórtās | mágnās | *the large gates* | **-ās** |
| *Abl.* | pórtīs | mágnīs | *by/with/from*, etc., *the large gates* | **-īs** |
| *Voc.* | pórtae | mágnae | *O large gates* | **-ae** |

### Gender

Like English, Latin distinguishes three GENDERS: masculine, feminine, and neuter. While Latin nouns indicating male beings are naturally masculine and those indicating female beings are feminine, the gender of most other nouns was a grammatical concept, not a natural one, and so a noun's gender must be memorized as part of the vocabulary entry.

Most first declension nouns are feminine; e.g., **puella**, *girl;* **pecūnia**, *money.* A few nouns denoting individuals engaged in what were among the Romans traditionally male occupations are masculine; e.g., **poēta**, *poet;* **nauta**, *sailor;* **agricola**, *farmer* (others not employed in this book are **aurīga**, *charioteer;* **incola**, *inhabitant;* **pīrāta**, *pirate*).

## ADJECTIVES, AGREEMENT, AND WORD ORDER

An ADJECTIVE (sg. **adiectīvum**, pl. **adiectīva**, *set next to, added*) "adds" information about, or "modifies," a noun or pronoun; e.g., **magna porta**, *the large gate;* **patria antīqua**, *the ancient country.* In these examples, "large" and "ancient" describe "attributes" of the nouns, and adjectives used as simple modifiers in this way are called ATTRIBUTIVE ADJECTIVES. Like nouns, adjectives are declined, and *an adjective agrees with its noun in gender, number, and case;* like nouns, adjectives can be singular or plural and they have the same cases, but an adjective has varying forms to agree with a particular noun's gender (an adjective that modifies more than one noun usually agrees in gender with the nearest one, though sometimes the masculine predominates). As its Latin root meaning suggests, an adjective was usually positioned next to its noun (except in poetry, where word order is much freer). Most often the adjective followed the noun; common exceptions were adjectives denoting size or number, as well as demonstratives (**hic**, *this;* **ille**, *that*), which normally precede, as do adjectives which the speaker or writer wishes to emphasize.

## GRAMMAR: MORPHOLOGY AND SYNTAX

Two major aspects of a language's GRAMMAR are its morphology and syntax. MORPHOLOGY refers to the forms of words, such as verb conjugations and noun-adjective declensions. SYNTAX, from the Greek verb **syntattein** meaning *to arrange,* refers to the arrangement and interrelation of words to form meaningful phrases, clauses, and sentences. To describe the syntax of a given noun or adjective, you should state its form, the word on which it most closely depends, and the reason for the form (i.e., its grammatical USE or FUNCTION in the sentence). The sentences presented at the beginning of the chapter, here translated into Latin, provide some examples. Notice in the subject and verb endings the rule that *a verb must agree with its subject in person and number;* note too that where a noun ending such as -ae can represent more than one case and thus result in AMBIGUOUS FORMS, word order and context provide essential clues to a sentence's meaning (hence **puellae** is the indirect object in A, subject in B).

A. **Poēta puellae magnās rosās dat.**
B. **Puellae nautīs rosās poētae dant.**
C. **Patria puellārum sine pecūniā nōn valet.**

The syntax of some of these words can be described as follows:

| Word | Form | Dependence | Use/Function |
|---|---|---|---|
| *Sentence A* | | | |
| poēta | nom. sg. | dat | subject |
| puellae | dat. sg. | dat | indirect object |
| magnās | acc. pl. | rosās | modifies and agrees with noun |
| *Sentence B* | | | |
| puellae | nom. pl. | dant | subject |
| nautīs | dat. pl. | dant | indirect object |
| rosās | acc. pl. | dant | direct object |
| poētae | gen. sg. | rosās | possession |
| *Sentence C* | | | |
| pecūniā | abl. sg. | sine | object of preposition |

Be sure you can explain the syntax of all nouns and adjectives in the sentences and reading passage below.

# VOCĀBVLA

This new vocabulary list includes, inter alia (**inter alia,** *among other things*), several nouns and adjectives. In addition to English meanings and (in parentheses) derivatives, each noun entry includes the nominative and genitive singular, so you can identify the noun's base, and its gender. Adjective entries include the nominative for all three genders, e.g., **magnus, magna, magnum** (often abbreviated **magnus, -a, -um** in this book's notes); the nominative form **magna** is recognizably first declension and feminine, and thus has the genitive singular form **magnae** and the base **magn-**; the full declensions of masculine (**magnus**) and neuter (**magnum**) adjectives are introduced in the next two chapters, but it will be easiest for you to learn the nominatives for all three genders now. As you learn the new first declension nouns and adjectives, try declining two or three of them.

Also in this list are two new CONJUNCTIONS (you learned **sī**, *if,* in Capvt I), **et** and **sed**: a conjunction (sg. **coniūnctiō**, pl. **coniūnctiōnēs**, *joining together*) connects two or more elements, such as two nouns (**fāma et fortūna**, *fame and fortune*) or two clauses (**puella mē laudat sed nauta mē monet**, *the girl praises me but the sailor warns me*); COORDINATING CONJUNCTIONS connect equivalent elements (**poētam amāmus et laudāmus**, *we love and praise the poet*), while SUBORDINATING CONJUNCTIONS introduce a subordinate (dependent) clause and connect it with a main (independent) clause (**sī errō, mē monēs**, *if I make a mistake, you advise me*).

In studying any language, ancient or modern, you must learn through *listening* and *speaking*, not just by reading silently from a printed page; as you study each chapter's vocabulary, use the CDs or the audio online at www.wheelocks latin.com (where you can also find vocabulary cards and cumulative lists), and listen to (**audī!**) and say aloud (**prōnūntiā!**) each Latin word and its meaning. Pay close attention to macrons, which indicate important differences of pronunciation and often of meaning. Latin pronunciation is easy—**prōnūntiātiō Latīna est facilis!**—and generally "what you see is what you get (i.e., what you say and hear)"; but recall that the consonant cluster -**gn**- is an exception, representing an -**ngn**- sound as in "ha*ngn*ail," so that **magna** sounds something like *mangna: listen carefully to this word on the website or CDs.

**fāma, fāmae**, f., *rumor, report; fame, reputation* (famous, defame, infamy)

**fōrma, fōrmae**, f., *form, shape; beauty* (formal, format, formula, formless, deform, inform, etc.; but not formic, formidable)

**fortūna, fortūnae**, f., *fortune, luck* (fortunate, misfortune, unfortunate)

**īra, īrae**, f., *ire, anger* (irate, irascible; but not irritate)

**nauta, nautae**, m., *sailor* (nautical, nautilus, argonaut)

**patria, patriae**, f., *fatherland, native land, (one's) country* (patriotic, expatriate, repatriate)

**pecūnia, pecūniae**, f., *money* (pecuniary, impecunious; cf. peculation)

**philosophia, philosophiae**, f. (Greek **philosophia**, *love of wisdom*), *philosophy*

**poena, poenae**, f., *penalty, punishment;* **poenās dare**, idiom, *to pay the penalty* (penal, penalize, penalty, pain, subpoena)

**poēta, poētae**, m., *poet* (poetry, poetic)

**porta, portae**, f., *gate, entrance* (portal, portico, porch, porthole)

**puella, puellae**, f., *girl*

**rosa, rosae**, f., *rose* (rosary, roseate, rosette)

**sententia, sententiae**, f., *feeling, thought, opinion, vote, sentence* (sententious, sentencing)

**vīta, vītae,** f., *life; mode of life* (vital, vitals, vitality, vitamin, vitalize, devitalize, revitalize)

**antíquus, antíqua, antíquum,** adj., *ancient, old-time* (antique, antiquities, antiquated, antiquarian)

**mágnus, mágna, mágnum,** adj., *large, great; important* (magnify, magnificent, magnate, magnitude, magnanimous)

**méus, méa, méum,** adj., *my*

**múltus, múlta, múltum** adj., *much, many* (multitude, multiply, multiple; multi-, a prefix as in multimillionaire)

**túus, túa, túum** adj., *your,* used when speaking to only one person

**et,** conj., *and; even;* **et . . . et,** *both . . . and*

**sed,** conj., *but*

**Ō,** interj. (interjection), *O!, Oh!,* commonly preceding a vocative

**síne,** prep. (preposition) + abl., *without* (sinecure, sans)

**est,** *is*

# LĒCTIŌ ET TRĀNSLĀTIŌ

As always, before attempting the following readings, be sure you have memorized the paradigms and **Vocābula,** and assessed your mastery by writing out your answers to the grammar questions and translations of some of the sentences in the Self-Tutorial Exercises for this chapter (p. 413–14), comparing your answers with the key (p. 446–47), and reviewing accordingly. Check your ability to recognize the new noun forms in the sentences below by identifying the case, number, gender, and use (function) of the first several that occur, e.g., **veniam** in the third sentence is: acc., sg., f., direct object. For adjectives, identify the nouns they modify.

Read each **Sententia** aloud, listening to the CDs if you have them, and think about its meaning, before translating. Likewise with the Catullus selection: read aloud and for comprehension, trying to get the sense of the entire passage. Remember that subject-object-verb (SOV) is a common pattern (as in S.A. 4)—but word order is quite variable in Latin, and so you must pay careful attention to word endings, which, for nouns, signal distinctions of number and case/use that are essential to meaning; watch the endings of adjectives too, for noun-adjective agreement, and of verbs for differences of person and number. Remember too that in translating you must routinely supply the ARTICLES "a," "an," or "the," as appropriate to the context. In translating from English to Latin, use SOV order, and analyze carefully the use of each word in the sentence; in S.A. 16, e.g., "life" is the direct object, and singular, so be sure to select the correct form of **vīta.**

All the book's **Sententiae Antīquae** and reading passages are drawn from ancient Roman sources, and the author is identified in parentheses; most of the readings in these early chapters are "adapted," i.e., simplified to accommodate the limited grammar and vocabulary you have learned, but an asterisk before an author's name means that the text is presented verbatim. The specific work from which each reading passage is drawn is cited in the notes, and citations for the individual **Sententiae** are provided at p. 553–55, for students who are interested in the context and wish to do further reading.

## SENTENTIAE ANTĪQVAE

1. Salvē, Ō patria! (Plautus.)
2. Fāma et sententia volant. (Vergil.—**volāre**, *to fly, move quickly;* "volatile.")
3. Dā veniam puellae, amābō tē. (Terence.—**venia, -ae,** f., *favor, pardon;* "venial," "veniality.")
4. Clēmentia tua multās vītās servat. (Cicero.—**clēmentia, -ae,** f., *clemency;* "clement," "inclement.")
5. Multam pecūniam dēportat. (Cicero.—**dēportāre,** *to carry away;* "deport," "deportation.")
6. Et fortūnam et vītam antīquae patriae saepe laudās sed recūsās. (Horace.—**recūsāre,** *to refuse, reject;* "recusation," "recuse.")
7. Mē vītāre turbam iubēs. (*Seneca.—**vītāre,** *to avoid;* do not confuse this verb with the noun **vīta**; "inevitable." —**turba, -ae,** f., *crowd, multitude;* "turbid," "turbulent."—**iubēre,** *to order;* "jussive.")
8. Mē philosophiae dō. (Seneca.)
9. Philosophia est ars vītae. (*Cicero.—**ars,** nom. sg., *art;* "artifice," "artistry.")
10. Sānam fōrmam vītae cōnservāte. (Seneca.—**sānus, -a, -um,** *sound, sane;* "sanitary," "sanatorium.")
11. Immodica īra creat īnsāniam. (Seneca.—**immodicus, -a, -um,** *immoderate, excessive.*—**creāre,** *to create;* "creation," "creature."—**īnsānia, -ae,** f., *unsoundness, insanity;* "insane.")
12. Quid cōgitās?—dēbēmus īram vītāre. (Seneca.)
13. Nūlla avāritia sine poenā est. (*Seneca.—**nūllus, -a, -um,** *no;* "nullify," "annul."—**avāritia, -ae,** f., *avarice;* "avaricious.")
14. Mē saevīs catēnīs onerat. (Horace.—**saevus, -a, -um,** *cruel.*—**catēna, -ae,** f., *chain;* "catenary."—**onerāre,** *to load, oppress;* "onerous," "exonerate.")
15. Rotam fortūnae nōn timent. (Cicero.—**rota, -ae,** f., *wheel;* "rotary," "rotate."—**timēre,** *to fear;* "timid," "intimidate.")
16. The girls save the poet's life.
17. Without philosophy we often go astray and pay the penalty.
18. If your land is strong, nothing terrifies the sailors and you (sg.) ought to praise your great fortune.
19. You (pl.) often see the penalty of my anger and warn me.
20. The ancient gate is large.

### Catullus Bids His Girlfriend Farewell

Puella mea mē nōn amat. Valē, puella! Catullus obdūrat: poēta puellam nōn amat, puellam nōn vocat, fōrmam puellae nōn laudat, puellae rosās nōn dat, et puellam nōn bāsiat! Īra mea est magna! Obdūrō, mea puella—sed sine tē nōn valeō.

Catullus *Carm.* 8, prose adaptation: We have surviving from Catullus (Gaius Valerius Catullus, ca. 84–54 B.C.) 113 finely crafted poems, at once scholarly but intensely emotional; several are satirical and brazenly targeted at contemporaries like Julius Caesar, Cicero, and Pompey the Great, but most are love poems. Of those amatory poems, some two dozen dramatically chronicle his relationship—from initial infatuation, to torrid romance, to the eventual devastating breakup—with the mistress whom he calls "Lesbia," but who we are confident was actually Clodia, wife of the Roman senator Quintus Caecilius Metellus Celer. For unadapted excerpts from the original poem, see Capvt XIX below.—**obdūrāre,** *to be firm, tough;* "durable," "endure."—**bāsiāre,** *to kiss.*—**tē,** *you.*)

*QUAESTIŌNĒS:* Think of this brief passage as a miniature "drama" with three scenes; where does each scene begin and end? It might be said that there are two Catulluses here, marked by the shift from first person to third and back to first: where does each shift occur, what is the intended effect, and how does the Catullus of the first and third scenes differ emotionally from the persona he imagines in the second? Which might one suppose, within this dramatic construct, is "the real" Catullus?

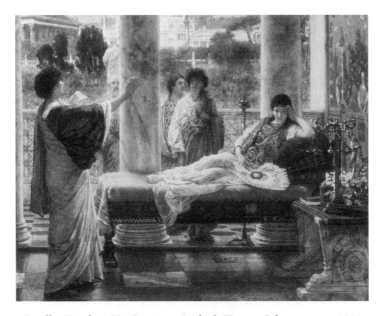

Catullus Reading His Poems at Lesbia's House. *Oil on canvas, 1870.*
*Sir Lawrence Alma-Tadema (1836–1912). Private collection.*

## SCRĪPTA IN PARIETIBVS

Fortūna.

*CIL* 4.5371 (Reg. IX, near Ins. 8): This scribbler roughly configured his single-word inscription in the form of a ship, with the T representing the mast and the tails of the F, R, and A representing oars—a whimsical jeu d'esprit seen elsewhere in Pompeian graffiti (cf. Capvt III, below); was the writer hoping for luck, or hailing the goddess Fortuna (to whom there were temples in Rome and who was often depicted holding a ship's rudder), or both?

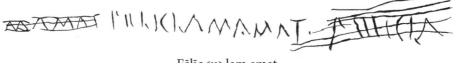

Fēlīc<u>lam amat.

*CIL* 4.8917: The Pompeian who scrawled this graffito near a doorway in an inn (Reg. III, Ins. 6) struggled with his handwriting: he tried writing the sentence three times, then marked out the first and last versions and saved his second attempt (have you ever had this problem in writing out a sentence yourself?). Spelling was an issue for this writer too; the name of the woman he had in mind was properly "Felicula" (a **DIMINUTIVE** from Lat. **fēlīx**, *lucky*), though we find this same variant form elsewhere in the city, a type of contraction known as **SYNCOPE**, which here reflects the common tendency in informal speech to drop a short, unaccented vowel occurring in a word's penultimate syllable.

## ETYMOLOGIA ("Etymology")

Note that the term **ETYMOLOGY** comes from the Gk. **etymos**, *true, real,* and **logos**, *word, meaning.* Consequently, the etymology of a word traces the derivation of the word back to its original meaning. Under this heading will be introduced various items not covered by the derivatives listed in the vocabularies, and often including derivatives in Italian, Spanish, and other Romance languages.

**Pecūnia** is connected with **pecus**, *cattle,* just as Eng. *fee* is related to Ger. **Vieh,** *cattle.* **Fortūna** derives from **fors**, *chance, accident.* Explain the meanings of the following Eng. words on the basis of the Lat. source words in the sentences indicated. Further aid, if needed, can be obtained from a good dictionary; *Webster's New World Dictionary* and the *American Heritage Dictionary* are especially helpful with etymologies, and other resources are available online.

| | | | |
|---|---|---|---|
| volatile (2) | insane (10) | concatenation (14) | rotary, rotate (15) |
| venial (3) | nullify (13) | onerous (14) | obdurate ("Catullus") |
| turbulent (7) | creature (11) | | |

## LATĪNA EST GAVDIVM—ET VTILIS!

**Salvēte, discipulī et discipulae!** From the **Vocābula:** To do something **sub rosā** is to do it secretly or in confidence (the rose was in antiquity a symbol of secrecy); **aqua vītae,** literally, *the water of life,* is an old Latin phrase for "whiskey"; and a "sinecure" (from **sine** + **cūra,** *care*) is an office or position that is largely *without responsibility.* And here's some more conversational Latin:

**Quid hodiē agis?** *How are you today?*

> **Optimē!** *Great!*     **Pessimē!** *Terrible!*     **Bene!** *Good!*
>
> **Satis bene.** *So-so* or *okay.*     **Nōn bene.** *Not well.*     **Et tū?** *And you?*

**Discipulae et discipulī, valēte!**

Pompeii: At the Walls
*Oil on canvas*
*Stefan Bakalowicz (1857–1947)*

# CAPVT III ⌐⌐⌐

# Second Declension Masculine Nouns and Adjectives; Apposition; Word Order

## GRAMMATICA

### THE SECOND DECLENSION

The second declension follows the rule you learned for the first: base + endings. The endings differ from those of the first declension, except in the dative and ablative plural, and second declension nouns are regularly either masculine or neuter; masculine nouns and adjectives are introduced below, neuters in Capvt IV. Most second declension masculines have a nominative singular ending in -**us**, while a few end in -**er**.

**Masculines in** *-us*

|  | amīcus, friend | magnus, great |  | Endings |
|---|---|---|---|---|
| **Base:** | amīc- | magn- |  |  |
| **Singular** |  |  |  |  |
| *Nom.* | amícus | mágnus | *a/the great friend* | **-us** |
| *Gen.* | amícī | mágnī | *of a great friend* | **-ī** |
| *Dat.* | amícō | mágnō | *to/for a great friend* | **-ō** |
| *Acc.* | amícum | mágnum | *a great friend* | **-um** |
| *Abl.* | amícō | mágnō | *by/with/from a great friend* | **-ō** |
| *Voc.* | amíce | mágne | *O great friend* | **-e** |

**Plural**

| Nom. | amīcī | mágnī | *great friends* | -ī |
|------|-------|-------|-----------------|-----|
| Gen. | amīcṓrum | magnṓrum | *of great friends* | -ṓrum |
| Dat. | amīcīs | mágnīs | *to/for great friends* | -īs |
| Acc. | amīcōs | mágnōs | *great friends* | -ōs |
| Abl. | amīcīs | mágnīs | *by/with/from great friends* | -īs |
| Voc. | amīcī | mágnī | *O great friends* | -ī |

### Masculines in -*er*

Some second declension -**er** masculines, like **puer,** retain the -e- in the base, while most, like **ager,** drop the -e-, hence the importance of learning the genitive as part of the vocabulary entry (though a knowledge of such English derivatives as "puerile" and "agriculture" will also help you remember the base). Similar is the unique -**ir** masculine, **vir, virī,** *man.* The underlined forms below are the ones that call for special attention; the adjective **magnus** is added for the sake of comparison: note, e.g., the combinations **puer magnus,** *a big boy,* and **Ō puer magne,** O *big boy.*

| | **puer,** *boy* | **ager,** *field* | | |
|------|------|------|------|------|
| **Base:** | **puer-** | **agr-** | | **Endings** |
| **Singular** | | | | |
| Nom. | púer | áger | mágnus | -er/-us |
| Gen. | púerī | ágrī | mágnī | -ī |
| Dat. | púerō | ágrō | mágnō | -ō |
| Acc. | púerum | ágrum | mágnum | -um |
| Abl. | púerō | ágrō | mágnō | -ō |
| Voc. | púer | áger | mágne | -er/-e |
| **Plural** | | | | |
| Nom. | púerī | ágrī | mágnī | -ī |
| Gen. | puerṓrum | agrṓrum | magnṓrum | -ṓrum |
| Dat. | púerīs | ágrīs | mágnīs | -īs |
| Acc. | púerōs | ágrōs | mágnōs | -ōs |
| Abl. | púerīs | ágrīs | mágnīs | -īs |
| Voc. | púerī | ágrī | mágnī | -ī |

### Comments on Vocatives and Other Case Endings

Note that some second declension endings are identical to those in the first (the dative/ablative plural in -īs) and others are similar (e.g., -am/-um accusative singular, -ārum/-ōrum genitive plural, and -ās/-ōs accusative plural). As in the first declension, some second declension endings are used for different cases (e.g., what different cases may the forms **amīcī, amīcō,** and **amīcīs** represent?); again, for these ambiguous forms word order and context are essential aids to reading comprehension and translation. You recall that an adjective must agree with the noun it modifies in number, gender, and case; but note from **ager magnus** and **puer magne** that their endings may not always be *spelled* the same, nor even must they be of the same declension, as seen, e.g., in **agricola Rōmānus**: since the noun for "farmer," although first declension, is masculine, a masculine (second declension) adjective is required.

It is also important to note that only in the singular of -**us** nouns and adjectives of the second declension does the vocative ever differ in spelling from the nominative: singular **amīcus, amīce**; but plural **amīcī, amīcī**. Nouns in -**ius** (e.g., **fīlius**, *son*, **Vergilius**, *Vergil*) and the adjective **meus**, *my*, have a single -**ī** in the vocative singular: **mī fīlī**, *my son*; **Ō Vergilī**, *O Vergil*.

## APPOSITION

An **APPOSITIVE** (from **ad**, *at/next to*, + **pōnō, positus**, *to set/position*) is a noun that is "positioned next to" another noun as an explanatory equivalent:

**Gāium, fīlium meum, in agrō videō.** *I see Gaius, my son, in the field.*

In this sentence **fīlium** is said to be "in apposition with" **Gāium**. Nouns in apposition always agree in case, usually in number, and often in gender as well, and an appositive is commonly separated from the preceding noun by commas.

## WORD ORDER

Typical word order in a simple Latin sentence or clause is: (1) the subject and its modifiers, (2) indirect object and modifiers, (3) direct object and modifiers, (4) adverbial words or phrases, (5) verb. Remember, too, that adjectives and genitive nouns commonly follow the words they modify. However, although these patterns should be kept in mind, exceptions to these rules, especially for purposes of variety and emphasis, were common in classical Latin. In fact, in highly inflected languages like Latin, the basic sense of a clause is somewhat independent of word order, thanks to the inflectional endings, which tell so much about the interrelationship of the words in a sentence.

On the other hand, in English, where inflections are relatively few, sense commonly depends on stricter conventions of word order. Compare the following English sentence and the four Latin versions, which all mean essentially the same despite the differences of word order:

(1) *The boy is giving the pretty girl a rose.*
(2) **Puer puellae bellae rosam dat.**
(3) **Bellae puellae puer rosam dat.**
(4) **Bellae puellae rosam dat puer.**
(5) **Rosam puer puellae bellae dat.**

Whatever the order of the words in the Latin sentence, the sense remains the same (though the emphasis does vary, the first and last words typically being the most emphatic). Note also that according to its ending, **bellae** must modify **puellae** no matter where these words stand. But if you rearrange the words in the English sentence, you alter the sense:

(1) *The boy is giving the pretty girl a rose.*
(2) *The pretty girl is giving the boy a rose.*
(3) *The girl is giving the boy a pretty rose.*
(4) *The girl is giving the pretty boy a rose.*
(5) *The rose is giving the boy a pretty girl.*

In all these sentences the same words are used with the same spellings, but the sense of each sentence differs in accordance with the conventions of English word order. Furthermore, where the fifth English sentence is nonsense, the final Latin sentence, in much the same order, makes perfectly good sense—and lends emphasis to the direct object, the gift the boy is giving, i.e., the rose.

# VOCĀBVLA

This chapter's **Vocābula** list introduces several second declension masculine nouns. As is clear from a word like **ager, agrī**, a noun's base is best determined by dropping its genitive ending, and the surest way to identify an adjective's base is by dropping the nominative ending from the feminine form. Remember that while the gender of a noun is fixed—i.e., nouns regularly have but a single gender (there are some obvious exceptions, like the Latin word for "citizen," which could be either masculine or feminine)—adjectives have all three genders. As you learn these new words, test your mastery by declining a noun-adjective pair such as **vir avārus** or **populus Rōmānus** and comparing your work with the paradigms.

Nouns and adjectives generally follow the patterns described in this book, but there are occasional exceptions, like these in the list below: **fīlia,** *daughter,* has the dative and ablative plural **fīliābus,** as distinct from **fīliīs,** the dative and ablative of **fīlius,** *son;* the adjective **paucī, paucae, pauca,** *few,* since it denotes plurality, has only plural forms.

As always, memorize the entire entry for each new word, and review words from the preceding two chapters as well; using vocabulary cards or cumulative vocabulary lists will help with comprehensive review, but ideally you should learn and review all chapter vocabularies by listening to the CDs or the audio lists at www.wheelockslatin.com. When using the online audio, look closely at the spelling of each word, including macrons, then click on it and listen to it, say the word aloud, read and think about its English meanings (which appear on the web-page with the full Latin entry), then look/click/listen and repeat aloud again. Learn

Latin as you did your native language, or any modern language you may have studied, i.e., through your eyes, your ears, and your mouth; and when studying vocabulary, **semper audī et prōnūntiā!**

**áger, ágrī,** m., *field, farm* (agrarian, agriculture, agronomy)

**agrícola, agrícolae,** m., *farmer* (cf. **ager**)

**amícus, amícī,** m., and **amíca, amícae,** f., *friend* (amicable, amiable, amity; cf. **amō**)

**fémina, féminae,** f., *woman* (female, feminine, femininity)

**fília, fíliae,** f., dat. and abl. pl. **filiábus,** *daughter* (filiation, affiliation, affiliate, filial)

**fílius, fíliī,** m., *son* (for derivatives, see **fília**)

**númerus, númerī,** m., *number* (numeral, innumerable, enumerate)

**pópulus, pópulī,** m., *the people, a people, a nation* (populace, population, popularity, popularize, populous)

**púer, púerī,** m., *boy;* pl. *boys, children* (puerile, puerility, puerperous)

**sapiéntia, sapiéntiae,** f., *wisdom* (sapience, sapient, sage, savant)

**vir, vírī,** m., *man, hero* (virtue, virile, triumvirate; *not* virulent)

**avárus, avára, avárum,** *greedy, avaricious* (avarice, avariciousness, avid)

**paúcī, paúcae, paúca,** usually pl., *few, a few* (paucity, pauciloquent, poco)

**Rōmánus, Rōmána, Rōmánum,** *Roman* (Romance, romance, romantic, romanticism, Romanesque, Romania)

**dē,** prep. + abl., *down from, from; concerning, about;* as a prefix **dē-** with such meanings as *down, away, aside, out, off* (demote, from **dē-moveō**; decline, descend)

**in,** prep. + abl., *in, on;* also as a prefix (induce, inscribe, invoke; for **dē-, in-,** and other prefixes, see App., p. 485–89)

**hódiē,** adv., *today* (hodiernal)

**sémper,** adv., *always* (sempiternal)

**hábeō, habére, hábuī, hábitum,** *to have, hold, possess; consider, regard* (in-habit and in-hibit, "hold in"; ex-hibit, "hold forth"; habit, habitat)

**sátiō, satiáre, satiávī, satiátum,** *to satisfy, sate* (satiate, insatiable, satiety, satisfaction)

# LĒCTIŌ ET TRĀNSLĀTIŌ

After memorizing the paradigms and **Vocābula** and checking your mastery with the Self-Tutorial Exercises, find each second declension noun in the following readings and identify its case, number, and function; in particular, identify any nouns used as appositives (easy to spot as they are set off by commas). Remember always to read aloud and for comprehension, before attempting a translation; let the chapter's observations on word order assist, and, as always, pay close attention to word endings. Since Latin often omits **possessives** where English would normally employ them, you should in translation *routinely supply them,* just as you do articles; e.g., for natural English idiom you should supply "his" with **fīliābus** in Ex. 7 and "your" with **amīcōs** in S.A. 10.

## EXERCITĀTIŌNĒS

1. Fīlium nautae Rōmānī in agrīs vidēmus.
2. Puerī puellās hodiē vocant.
3. Sapientiam amīcārum tuārum, Ō fīlia mea, semper laudat.
4. Multī virī et fēminae philosophiam antīquam cōnservant.
5. Sī īra valet, Ō mī fīlī, saepe errāmus et poenās damus.
6. Fortūna virōs magnōs amat.
7. Agricola fīliābus pecūniam dat.
8. Without a few friends life is not strong.
9. Today you have much fame in your country.
10. We see great fortune in your daughters' lives, my friend.
11. He always gives my daughters and sons roses.

## SENTENTIAE ANTĪQVAE

1. Dēbētis, amīcī, dē populō Rōmānō cōgitāre. (Cicero.)
2. Maecēnās, amīcus Augustī, mē in numerō amīcōrum habet. (Horace.— **Maecēnās,** a name in nom. sg.; see Capvt I reading passage.—**Augustus, -ī,** m.)
3. Libellus meus et sententiae meae vītās virōrum monent. (Phaedrus.—**libellus, -ī,** m., *little book;* "libel," "libelous.")

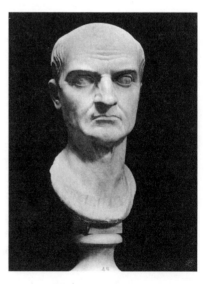

*Gaius Maecenas.*
*Palazzo dei Conservatori*
*Rome, Italy.*

4. Paucī virī sapientiae student. (Cicero.—**studēre** + dat., *to be eager for;* "student," "studious.")
5. Fortūna adversa virum magnae sapientiae nōn terret. (Horace.—**adversus, -a, -um,** = Eng.; "adversary," "adversity.")
6. Cimōn, vir magnae fāmae, magnam benevolentiam habet. (Nepos.—**Cimōn,** proper name nom. sg.—**benevolentia, -ae,** f. = Eng.)
7. Semper avārus eget. (*Horace.—**avārus** = **vir avārus.**—**egēre,** *to be in need.*)
8. Nūlla cōpia pecūniae avārum virum satiat. (Seneca.—**nūllus, -a, -um,** *no;* "null," "annulment."—**cōpia, -ae,** f., *abundance;* "copious," "cornucopia.")
9. Pecūnia avārum irrītat, nōn satiat. (Publilius Syrus.—**irrītāre,** *to excite, exasperate;* "irritable," "irritate.")
10. Sēcrētē amīcōs admonē; laudā palam. (*Publilius Syrus.—**sēcrētē,** adv., *in secret;* "secret," "discrete."—**admonē:** = **monē.**—**palam,** adv., *openly.*)
11. Modum tenēre dēbēmus. (*Seneca.—**modus, -ī,** m., *moderation;* "mode," "modify."—**tenēre,** *to hold, maintain;* "tenable," "tenant.")

### The Grass Is Always Greener

Agricola et vītam et fortūnam nautae saepe laudat; nauta magnam fortūnam et vītam poētae saepe laudat; et poēta vītam et agrōs agricolae laudat. Sine philosophiā avārī virī dē pecūniā semper cōgitant: multam pecūniam habent, sed nihil virum avārum satiat.

Horace *Sat.* 1.1: Freely adapted into prose from one of Horace's early satires (which he titled **Sermōnēs,** *Conversations*), this passage elaborates upon a theme sounded in several of the preceding **Sententiae Antīquae.—et . . . et:** you may be tempted to translate the first **et** as *and;* as a coordinating conjunction, however, **et** must connect parallel elements, and so it cannot join the nom. **agricola** with the acc. **vītam** but should instead be construed with the two dir. objs. **vītam** and **fortūnam.**

*QVAESTIŌNĒS:* Horace here comments on a common human failing. What is that flaw, and what does the satirist regard as its cause?—do you agree with his assessment of cause and effect?

## SCRĪPTA IN PARIETIBVS

G. Iūlius Trophimus

Venustus

*CIL* 4.7309b (Reg. I, Ins. 8, a **caupōna,** *inn, tavern*) and 8020 (Reg. I, Ins. 6): Ancient Romans, like modern Americans, loved to write or paint their own and others' names on walls, sometimes with "portraits." Gaius Julius Trophimus, to judge from the drawing seen here, was a handsome young man, one of several figures shown in a ritual procession; his full name typifies the nomenclature of male Roman citizens, consisting of a given name or PRAENOMEN (here "Gaius," regularly abbreviated "G" or even more commonly "C"), the family (**gēns**) name or NOMEN (here "Julius," which the scribe at first misspelled "Juliaus" and then corrected by marking out the superfluous **A**), and a COG-NOMEN, a sort of nickname, often referring to some physical or mental trait and sometimes identifying a branch of a family ("Trophimus" was a Greek word meaning "foster child," suggesting that the man here may have been a **lībertīnus,** or "freedman," of the Julius family). **Venustus** was a relatively common cognomen, related to the name of the goddess Venus and meaning "Charming" or "Attractive"; the ship motif is seen in several other Pompeian graffiti, including the Fortuna graffito in Capvt II above.


## ETYMOLOGIA

Following are some of the Romance words you can recognize based on your study of this chapter's **Vocābula:**

| Latin | Italian | Spanish | French | Portuguese |
|---|---|---|---|---|
| amīcus | amico | amigo | ami | amigo |
| fīlius | figlio | hijo | fils | filho |
| numerus | numero | número | numéro | número |
| populus | popolo | pueblo | peuple | povo |
| paucī | poco | poco | peu | pouco |
| semper | sempre | siempre | | sempre |
| habēre | avere | haber | avoir | haver |
| dē | di | de | de | de |

Occitan (Occ.) is another Romance language spoken, chiefly as a second language, only in the south of France (in a dialect known as Provençal), Monaco, and some districts of northern Spain and the Italian Alps; you too can read Occitan (!), or at least these words from Old Occ. (the language of the troubadour literature of the 11th–12th centuries): **amic, filh, nọmbre, pople, pauc, sẹmpre, avẹr** (loss of initial **h**- and the shift from **b** to **v** were common in the evolution of the Romance languages from Lat.), and **de.** And here are the Romanian (Rom.) derivatives for some of these same words; you can easily determine which is which: **amic, fiu, număr, popor, avea, de.**

## LATĪNA EST GAVDIVM—ET VTILIS!

**Salvēte, amīcae et amīcī! Quid hodiē agitis?** Well, if you are in the Coast Guard, you are **semper parātus,** *always prepared,* or if you're a U.S. Marine, it's **semper fidēlis,** *always faithful* (from the same Latin root as "Fido," your trusty hound). These are just two (suggested by this chapter's **Vocābula**) of countless Latin mottoes representing a wide range of modern institutions and organizations. **Valēte et habēte fortūnam bonam!**

*A* caupona *on the Via dell'Abbondanza, with its serving counter opening onto the street*
*Pompeii, Italy*

# CAPVT IV ⬚⬚⬚

# Second Declension Neuters; Adjectives; Present of *Sum*; Predicate Nominatives; Substantives

## GRAMMATICA

### SECOND DECLENSION NEUTERS

In the first declension there are no nouns of neuter gender but in the second declension there are many. They are declined as follows, again by adding endings to a base:

|  | dōnum, *gift* | cōnsilium, *plan* | magnum, *great* | Endings |
|---|---|---|---|---|
| Base: | dōn- | cōnsili- | magn- | |
| **Singular** | | | | |
| *Nom.* | dṓnum | cōnsílium | mágnum | -um |
| *Gen.* | dṓnī | cōnsíliī (cōnsilī) | mágnī | -ī |
| *Dat.* | dṓnō | cōnsíliō | mágnō | -ō |
| *Acc.* | dṓnum | cōnsílium | mágnum | -um |
| *Abl.* | dṓnō | cōnsíliō | mágnō | -ō |
| **Plural** | | | | |
| *Nom.* | dṓna | cōnsília | mágna | -a |
| *Gen.* | dōnṓrum | cōnsiliṓrum | magnṓrum | -ōrum |
| *Dat.* | dṓnīs | cōnsíliīs | mágnīs | -īs |
| *Acc.* | dṓna | cōnsília | mágna | -a |
| *Abl.* | dṓnīs | cōnsíliīs | mágnīs | -īs |

Second declension neuter endings are the same as the masculine, except that the nominative, accusative, and vocative are identical to one another (true of all neuters of all declensions): -**um** in the singular, -**a** in the plural. Word order and context will enable you to distinguish between a neuter noun used as a subject and one used as an object (vocatives are even more easily distinguished, of course, as they are regularly set off from the rest of the sentence by commas). The plural -**a** ending might be mistaken for a first declension nominative singular, so you can see again how important it is to memorize vocabulary entries completely, including the gender of nouns. In spelling the genitive singular of neuter (and masculine) nouns with a base ending in -**i**- the Romans sometimes dropped that vowel, e.g., **cōnsilī** for **cōnsiliī** (see above) and **fīlī** for **fīliī**; in this book, however, the stem vowel is regularly retained. Second declension neuter nouns will be abbreviated in the notes as follows: **dōnum, -ī** (= **dōnum, dōnī**), n.

## DECLENSION AND AGREEMENT OF ADJECTIVES

The paradigms of **magnus** presented in Capita II–IV illustrate the point that, while the base remains constant, the adjective has masculine, feminine, and neuter endings to match the gender of the noun it modifies, with which it likewise agrees in number and case. The full declension of **magnus** below provides an overview of the first two declensions.

|          | M.       | F.       | N.       |
|----------|----------|----------|----------|
| **Singular** |      |          |          |
| *Nom.*   | mágnus   | mágna    | mágnum   |
| *Gen.*   | mágnī    | mágnae   | mágnī    |
| *Dat.*   | mágnō    | mágnae   | mágnō    |
| *Acc.*   | mágnum   | mágnam   | mágnum   |
| *Abl.*   | mágnō    | mágnā    | mágnō    |
| *Voc.*   | mágne    | mágna    | mágnum   |
| **Plural** |        |          |          |
| *Nom.*   | mágnī    | mágnae   | mágna    |
| *Gen.*   | magnórum | magnárum | magnórum |
| *Dat.*   | mágnīs   | mágnīs   | mágnīs   |
| *Acc.*   | mágnōs   | mágnās   | mágna    |
| *Abl.*   | mágnīs   | mágnīs   | mágnīs   |
| *Voc.*   | mágnī    | mágnae   | mágna    |

Such first/second declension adjectives will be abbreviated in the notes as follows: **magnus, -a, -um, meus, -a, -um,** etc.

## PRESENT INFINITIVE AND INDICATIVE OF *Sum*

As the English verb "to be" is irregular, so is the important Latin verb **sum.** Although the personal endings are familiar, the stem varies so much in the present tense that the forms must be memorized. Note that, since **sum** is an INTRANSITIVE LINKING VERB (i.e., often connecting its subject with a predicate noun or adjective), we do not refer to its voice as either active or passive.

**Present infinitive:** esse, *to be*

**Present Indicative:**

| Singular | Plural |
|---|---|
| 1. sum, *I am* | súmus, *we are* |
| 2. es, *you are* | éstis, *you are* |
| 3. est, *he* (*she, it*) *is, there is* | sunt, *they are, there are* |

Some sample sentences: **Fīlia tua est bona,** *Your daughter is good.* **Amīcī meī estis,** *You are my friends.* **Sunt multī agricolae in agrīs,** *There are many farmers (many farmers are) in the fields.*

## PREDICATE NOUNS AND ADJECTIVES

As an intransitive verb, **sum** cannot take a direct object but instead, like other linking verbs to be introduced later, serves to connect the subject of a clause with a noun or adjective in the PREDICATE (the main divisions of a sentence are the subject, with its modifiers, and the predicate, which consists of the verb and all its dependent words and phrases). Such predicate nouns and adjectives—or PREDICATE NOMINATIVES, as they are often called—are connected or even equated with the subject by the linking verb, and so they naturally agree with the subject in number and case (usually the nominative, of course) and, wherever possible, in gender as well. In the case of compound subjects of different gender, a predicate adjective usually agrees in gender with the nearest, though the masculine often predominates. Study the following examples:

**Vergilius est amīcus Augustī.** *Vergil is the friend of Augustus.*
**Vergilius est poēta.** *Vergil is a poet.*
**Vergilius est magnus.** *Vergil is great.*
**Fāma Vergiliī est magna.** *The fame of Vergil is great.*
**Amīcae sunt bonae.** *The girlfriends are good.*
**Puerī dēbent esse bonī.** *The boys ought to be good.*
**Puer et puella sunt bonī.** *The boy and girl are good.*
**Dōnum est magnum.** *The gift is large.*
**Dōna sunt magna.** *The gifts are large.*
**Sumus Rōmānī.** *We are Romans (Roman men).*
**Sumus Rōmānae.** *We are Roman women.*

## SUBSTANTIVE ADJECTIVES

You learned about **ATTRIBUTIVE ADJECTIVES** (e.g., **vir Rōmānus** and **fēmina bona**) in Capvt II, and **PREDICATE ADJECTIVES** have just been introduced (**porta est antīqua**). The Romans also often used an adjective as a **SUBSTANTIVE**, i.e., in place of a noun, just as we do in English ("the meek shall inherit the earth"—i.e., "the meek *people*"). Such adjectives can sometimes be translated as English substantives, but for natural idiom you will often need to supply *man* or *men, woman* or *women, thing* or *things,* in accordance with the word's number and gender; compare the following examples:

> **Bonās saepe laudant.** *They often praise the good women.*
> **Multī sunt stultī.** *Many (men) are foolish.*
> **Puerī mala nōn amant.** *The boys do not love bad things.*
> **Paucī dē perīculō cōgitant.** *Few (men) are thinking about the danger.*

# VOCĀBVLA

The vocabulary for this chapter introduces several neuter nouns, easily identified by the nominative **-um** and of course by the gender abbreviation "n."; the neuter noun **nihil** (reintroduced from Capvt I, now that you understand the concepts of declension and gender) is identified as **INDECLINABLE,** meaning that the one form could be used as subject, direct object, etc. **Vocābula** itself, by the way, is the plural of **vocābulum,** a neuter noun originally meaning what we "call" (from **vocāre**) a person or thing and ultimately giving us our word "vocabulary." Practice your mastery of neuters by declining a noun-adjective pair from the list (e.g., **remedium bonum**) and checking your work against the paradigms provided above. Memorize the entire entry for each new word, and review words from the preceding three chapters as well, ideally by listening to the CDs or the audio lists at www.wheelockslatin.com.

**bắsium, bắsiī,** n., *kiss* (basiate)
**béllum, béllī,** n., *war* (bellicose, belligerent, rebel, rebellion, revel)
**cōnsílium, cōnsíliī,** n., *plan, purpose, counsel, advice, judgment, wisdom* (counsel, counselor, consiliate, reconcile)
**cúra, cúrae,** f., *care, attention, caution, anxiety* (cure, curator, curious, curiosity, curio, curettage, sinecure)
**dốnum, dốnī,** n., *gift, present* (donate, donation, condone; cf. **dō**)
**exítium, exítiī,** n., *destruction, ruin* (exit)
**magíster, magístrī,** m., and **magístra, magístrae,** f., *schoolmaster* or *schoolmistress,*

*teacher, master* or *mistress* (magistrate, magistracy, magisterial, maestro, mastery, mister, miss; cf. **magnus**)

**móra, mórae,** f., *delay* (moratorium, demur)

**níhil,** indeclinable, n., *nothing* (nihilist, annihilate)

**óculus, óculī,** m., *eye* (ocular, oculist, binoculars, monocle)

**offícium, offíciī,** n., *duty, service* (office, officer, official, officious)

**ótium, ótiī,** n., *leisure, peace* (otiose, negotiate)

**perículum, perículī,** n., *danger, risk* (peril, perilous, imperil, parlous)

**remédium, remédiī,** n., *cure, remedy* (remedial, irremediable, remediation)

**béllus, bélla, béllum,** *pretty, handsome, charming* (belle, beau, beauty, embellish, belladonna, belles-lettres). Do not confuse with **bellum,** *war.*

**bónus, bóna, bónum,** *good, kind* (bonus, bonanza, bonny, bounty, bona fide)

**hūmā́nus, hūmā́na, hūmā́num,** *pertaining to man, human; humane, kind; refined, cultivated* (humanity, humanitarian, humanism, the humanities, humanist, inhuman, superhuman)

**málus, mála, málum,** *bad, wicked, evil* (malice, malicious, malign, malignant, malaria, malady, malefactor, malfeasance, malevolent; mal-, a prefix as in maladjustment, malnutrition, maltreat, malapropos)

**párvus, párva, párvum,** *small, little* (parvovirus, parvule, parvicellular)

**stúltus, stúlta, stúltum,** *foolish;* **stúltus, stúltī,** m., *a fool* (stultify, stultification)

**vérus, véra, vérum,** *true, real, proper* (verify, verisimilitude, very, veracity)

**iúvō** (or **ádiuvō**), **iuvā́re, iū́vī, iū́tum,** *to help, aid, assist; please* (adjutant, coadjutant, aid, aide-de-camp)

**sum, ésse, fúī, futū́rum,** *to be, exist* (essence, essential, future, futurity)

# LĒCTIŌ ET TRĀNSLĀTIŌ

Be sure you have memorized the paradigms and **Vocābula,** practiced declining some of the new neuter nouns and adjectives, and completed some of the Self-Tutorial Exercises, before attempting the readings; find some second declension nouns in the sentences, and identify their case, number, gender, and function (and beware of neuters ending in -a: they're plural, of course, but students often confuse them with first declension singulars in -a); also identify all forms of **sum, esse** in the readings, and any predicate nominatives and substantives. Finally, as you read the sentences, the Cicero passage (listen to this on the CDs, if you have them), and the graffito, read aloud and for comprehension, before translating. And always choose meanings for words that best suit the context; e.g., *cares/worries/anxieties* would be a better choice than *attentions* or *cautions* for **cūrīs** in Ex. 5, and *plan* makes more sense than *wisdom* for **cōnsiliō** in Ex. 6.

## EXERCITĀTIŌNĒS

1. Ōtium est bonum, sed ōtium multōrum est parvum.
2. Bella (from **bellum, -ī, n.**) sunt mala et multa perīcula habent.
3. Officium nautam dē ōtiō hodiē vocat.
4. Paucī virī multās fōrmās perīculī in pecūniā vident—nōn dēbēmus esse avārī!.
5. Sī multam pecūniam habētis, saepe nōn estis sine cūrīs.
6. Puellae magistram dē cōnsiliō malō sine morā monent.
7. Ō magne poēta, sumus vērī amīcī; mē iuvā, amābō tē!
8. Fēmina et agrōs et portam agricolae videt.
9. You (sg.) are in great danger.
10. My son's opinions are often foolish.
11. The daughters and sons of great men and women are not always great.
12. Without wisdom the sailors' good fortune is nothing and they are paying the penalty.

## SENTENTIAE ANTĪQVAE

1. Fortūna caeca est. (*Cicero.—**caecus, -a, -um**, *blind;* "Cecil.")
2. Sī perīcula sunt vēra, īnfortūnātus es. (Terence.—**īnfortūnātus, -a, -um**, *unfortunate*.)
3. Salvē, Ō amīce; vir bonus es. (Terence.)
4. Nōn bella est fāma fīliī tuī. (Horace.)
5. Errāre est hūmānum. (Seneca.—As an indecl. n. verbal noun, an infin. can be the subj. of a verb.)
6. Nihil est omnīnō beātum. (Horace—**omnīnō**, adv., *wholly.*—**beātus, -a, -um**, *happy, fortunate;* "beatify," "beatitude.")
7. Remedium īrae est mora. (Seneca.)
8. Bonus Daphnis, amīcus meus, ōtium et vītam agricolae amat. (Vergil.—Daphnis is a pastoral character.)
9. Magistrī parvīs puerīs crūstula et dōna saepe dant. (Horace.—**crūstulum, -ī, n.**, *cookie;* "crouton," "crustacean.")
10. Amīcam meam magis quam oculōs meōs amō. (Terence.—**magis quam**, *more than*.)
11. Salvē, mea bella puella—dā mihi multa bāsia, amābō tē! (Catullus.—**mihi**, dat., *to me*.)
12. Īnfīnītus est numerus stultōrum. (Ecclesiastes.—**īnfīnītus, -a, -um** = Eng.; "infinity.")
13. Officium mē vocat. (Persius.)
14. Malī sunt in nostrō numerō et dē exitiō bonōrum virōrum cōgitant. Bonōs adiuvāte; cōnservāte patriam et populum Rōmānum. (Cicero.—**nostrō**, *our;* "nostrum," "paternoster.")

*Cicero*
*Musei Capitolini*
*Rome, Italy*

### The Rarity of Friendship

Paucī virī vērōs amīcōs habent, et paucī sunt dignī. Amīcitia vēra est praeclāra, et omnia praeclāra sunt rāra. Multī virī stultī dē pecūniā semper cōgitant, paucī dē amīcīs; sed errant: possumus valēre sine multā pecūniā, sed sine amīcitiā nōn valēmus et vīta est nihil.

Cicero *Amīc.* 21.79–80: The Roman lawyer and statesman Cicero (Marcus Tullius Cicero, 106–43 B.C.) is one of the best known figures from the ancient world, thanks in large measure to the enormous number of his writings that have survived, including hundreds of letters on both political and personal matters, dozens of political and courtroom speeches, and several philosophical treatises. Written in 45 B.C. when Cicero was in his early 60's, the **Dē Amīcitiā,** *On Friendship,* remains one of the most popular and influential of those philosophical works.—**dignus, -a, -um,** *worthy, deserving;* "deign," "dignify." **amīcitia, -ae,** f., *friendship.*—**omnia:** *all* [*things*]; "omnipotent," "omniscient."—**praeclārus, -a, -um,** *splendid, remarkable;* "clarity."—**rārus, -a, -um** = Eng.; "rarefy," "rarity."—**possumus:** *we are able;* "posse," "possible.")

*QVAESTIŌNĒS:* What observations does Cicero make here on the rarity of friendship, and how is his perspective similar to that of Horace in the passage from his satires which you read in the preceding chapter?

## SCRĪPTA IN PARIETIBVS

Prīme, av<ē>, valē.

*CIL* 4.8615: Salutation to a friend named "Primus," a common Roman cognomen, from a column in the colonnade around the Large Palaestra near the amphitheater in Pompeii's Region II; we have seen **avē** before, also in its contracted form **av'**, in the graffito in Capvt I; and **avē et valē** was a widely used expression of greeting and farewell, best known today from the poet Catullus' lament (in his poem 101) to his deceased brother: **frāter, avē atque** [= **et**] **valē**. Seen in the drawing is the common use of the letter form || for E.

## ETYMOLOGIA

Some Romance derivatives:

| Latin | Italian | Spanish | French | Portuguese |
|---|---|---|---|---|
| oculus | occhio | ojo | œil | olho |
| ōtium | ozio | ocio | oisiveté | ócio |
| perīculum | pericolo | peligro | péril | perigo |
| officium | officio | oficio | office | ofício |
| bonus | buono | bueno | bon | bom |
| vērus | vero | verdadero | vrai | vero |
| magister | maestro | maestro | maître | mestre |
| bellus | bello | bello | belle | belo |
| hūmānus | umano | humano | humain | humano |
| beātus | beato | beato | béat | beato |
| bāsium | bacio | beso | baiser | beijo |
| rārus | raro | raro | rare | raro |

Here are some of the Old Occ. derivatives: **perilh, ofíci, bos, vẹr, maïstre, bel, umaṇ, beat, bais, rar.** And cf. Rom.: **ochi, pericol, oficiu, bun, magistru, uman, beat** (in Rom. the word actually means "drunk"!), **rar.**

## LATĪNA EST GAVDIVM—ET ŪTILIS!

**Salvē, amīce** (or **amīca**)! There are countless Latin expressions in current English usage (remember **sub rosā**?); one of them, related to an adjective encountered in this chapter, is **rāra avis**, literally *a rare bird*, but used for an exceptional or unusual individual or a rarity. The student of Latin in the United States was becoming a **rāra avis** in the 1960s and early 70s, but there has been a remarkable resurgence of interest since then. "Oculus," an architectural term for a circular opening in the apex of a dome, or a round window, is one of thousands of English words that come directly from Latin with no spelling change at all—an imaginative derivation, since Latin **oculus**, as seen in this chapter's **Vocābula**, means *eye*. **Ergō**, *therefore*, is another Latin word that has come straight into English; ergo, you now know what Descartes meant in his *Discourse on Method* when he said **cōgitō ergō sum. Semper cōgitā, amīce, et valē!**

# CAPVT V ▣▣▣

# First and Second Conjugations: Future and Imperfect; Adjectives in *-er*

## GRAMMATICA

### THE FUTURE AND IMPERFECT TENSES

The Romans indicated future time in the first two conjugations by inserting the future **TENSE SIGN** (-**bi**- in most forms) between the present stem and the personal endings. The tense sign -**bā**- was similarly employed (in all four conjugations) for the imperfect tense, a past tense generally equivalent to the English past progressive. Along with the present tense, the future and imperfect make up the **PRESENT SYSTEM,** all of whose forms, as seen in the following paradigms, are based on the present stem:

#### Future and Imperfect Active of *Laudō* and *Moneō*

| Future | Imperfect |
|---|---|
| **Singular** | |
| 1. laudā́-bō, *I will /shall praise* | laudā́-ba-m, *I was praising, kept praising, used to praise, (often/always/usually) praised* |
| 2. laudā́-bi-s, *you will praise* | laudā́-bā-s, *you were praising*, etc. |
| 3. laudā́-bi-t, *he, she, it will praise* | laudā́-ba-t, *he was praising*, etc. |
| **Plural** | |
| 1. laudābímus, *we will /shall praise* | laudābā́mus, *we were praising*, etc. |
| 2. laudābítis, *you will praise* | laudābā́tis, *you were praising*, etc. |
| 3. laudā́bunt, *they will praise* | laudā́bant, *they were praising*, etc. |

## Singular

1.  moné-bō, *I will/shall advise*          moné-ba-m, *I was advising, kept advising, used to advise, (often/always/usually) advised*
2.  moné-bi-s, *you will advise*             moné-bā-s, *you were advising, etc.*
3.  moné-bi-t, *he, she, it will advise*     moné-ba-t, *he was advising, etc.*

## Plural

1.  monébimus, *we will/shall advise*        monēbámus, *we were advising, etc.*
2.  monébitis, *you will advise*             monēbátis, *you were advising, etc.*
3.  monébunt, *they will advise*             monébant, *they were advising, etc.*

Notice the vowel change in the first person singular and third plural future tense sign (chant out loud **bō/bi/bi/bi/bi/bu**—sounds like baby talk!), and the shortened -a- in the first and third singular and third plural of the imperfect (remember that vowels which are normally long are regularly shortened before -**m**, -**r**, and -**t** at the end of a word, and before **nt** or another vowel in any position).

The INFIXES -**bi**- and -**bā**- (with the distinctive -**i**- and -**ā**-) can be easily remembered as signs of the future and imperfect tenses by associating them with the English auxiliary verbs "will" and "was," which are also spelled with -*i*- and -*a*- and are generally used to translate those two tenses. Note that, where English requires three separate words for the ideas *he will praise* or *he was praising*, Latin requires only a single word with the three components of stem + tense sign + personal ending (**laudā** + **bi** + **t** = *praise-will-he* or **laudā-ba-t** = *praising-was-he*).

## Translation

Translation of the future tense, usually with *will* (*shall* is less common in current English), should present no difficulty: **dē amīcō cōgitābō**, *I will think about my friend;* **multam sapientiam habēbunt,** *they will have much wisdom.* The imperfect tense commonly indicates an action that was continuing or progressive in the past, as suggested by the term "imperfect" (from **imperfectum**, *not completed*), including actions that were *going on, repeated, habitual, attempted,* or *just beginning.* All the following translations are possible, depending upon the context in which the sentence appears:

> **Nautam monēbam.** *I was warning (kept warning, used to warn, tried to warn, was beginning to warn) the sailor.*
> **Poētae vītam agricolae laudābant.** *Poets used to praise the farmer's life.*
> **Magister puerōs vocābat.** *The teacher kept calling (was calling) the boys.*

Occasionally the imperfect may be translated as a simple past tense, especially with an adverb that in itself indicates continuing action: **nautam saepe monēbam,**

*I often warned (kept warning) the sailor;* **magister puellās semper laudābat,** *the teacher always praised (used to praise) the girls.*

## ADJECTIVES OF THE FIRST AND SECOND DECLENSION IN -er

There are several first/second declension adjectives whose masculine nominative singular ends with -**er** rather than -**us**; some, like the noun **puer** retain the -**e**- in the base, and others, like the noun **ager,** drop the -**e**-. This should present no difficulty, since, as with all adjectives, the base, whether with or without the -**e**-, appears in the feminine and the neuter nominative forms, as seen in the following examples; likewise, just as with the -**er** nouns, your familiarity with derivatives can assist in remembering the base ("liberal" from **līber,** "pulchritude" from **pulcher,** "miserable" from **miser,** etc.).

| | | | |
|---|---|---|---|
| līber | līber-a | līber-um | *free* |
| pulcher | pulchr-a | pulchr-um | *beautiful* |

The rest of the paradigm continues with the base and the regular endings:

| | **M.** | **F.** | **N.** | **M.** | **F.** | **N.** |
|---|---|---|---|---|---|---|
| *Nom.* | līber | lībera | līberum | púlcher | púlchra | púlchrum |
| *Gen.* | līberī | līberae | līberī | púlchrī | púlchrae | púlchrī |
| *Dat.* | līberō | līberae | līberō | púlchrō | púlchrae | púlchrō |
| | | (etc.) | | | (etc.) | |

For the singular of these samples fully declined, see the **Summārium Fōrmārum,** p. 496, and remember to refer to this section of the Appendix whenever reviewing declensions and conjugations.

# VOCĀBVLA

The **Vocābula** list for this chapter, as always, includes in parentheses at the end of most entries a number of English words derived from the Latin term; to boost your English Word Power (!), always take note of these derivatives—and see if you can think of others. Nearly all Latin nouns are declined on the principle of base + endings; a few, however, like **satis,** *enough,* in the list below, are indeclinable, a concept discussed in connection with **nihil** in the previous chapter's vocabulary. **Satis** is remarkably versatile, in fact, as it can function not only as a noun, when it is often construed with a genitive, as in **satis pecūniae,** *enough (of) money,* but also as an adjective, meaning *sufficient,* and even an adverb, *sufficiently.* The conjunction **igitur,** *therefore,* is identified below as **POSTPOSITIVE,** meaning that it ordinarily does not appear as the first word of a sentence, but instead is positioned (**positum**) after (**post**) the first word or phrase. **Tē**, like **mē** (Capvt I), is the form of the accusative and ablative cases; the other forms of these personal pronouns are introduced in Capvt XI. As you learn the newly introduced verbs, test your mastery by conjugating one or two of them in all three PRESENT SYSTEM tenses, then comparing your work with the paradigms; practice declining a noun-adjective pair too, such as **animus noster** or **caelum pulchrum**—or both!

**adulēscéntia, adulēscéntiae,** f., *youth, young manhood; youthfulness* (adolescence, adolescent)

**ánimus, ánimī,** m., *soul, spirit, mind;* **ánimī, ánimṓrum,** *high spirits, pride, courage* (animus, animosity, magnanimous, unanimous, pusillanimous)

**caélum, caélī,** n., *sky, heaven* (ceiling, celestial, Celeste, cerulean)

**cúlpa, cúlpae,** f., *fault, blame* (cf. **culpō** below; culpable, culprit, exculpate, inculpate)

**glṓria, glṓriae,** f., *glory, fame* (glorify, glorification, glorious, inglorious)

**vérbum, vérbī,** n., *word* (verb, adverb, verbal, verbiage, verbose, proverb)

**tē,** abl. and acc. sg., *you; yourself;* cf. **mē**

**líber, líbera, líberum,** *free* (liberal, liberality, libertine)

**nóster, nóstra, nóstrum,** *our, ours* (nostrum, paternoster)

**púlcher, púlchra, púlchrum,** *beautiful, handsome; fine* (pulchritude, pulchritudinous)

**sánus, sána, sánum,** *sound, healthy, sane* (sanity, sanitary, sanitation, sanitarium, insane)

**ígitur,** conj., postpositive, *therefore, consequently*

**-ne,** interrog. suffix attached to the first word of a sentence, typically the verb or another word on which the question hinges, to introduce a question whose answer is uncertain. (For other types of direct questions, see **nōnne** and **num** in Capvt XL.)

**própter,** prep. + acc., *on account of, because of* (post hoc, ergo propter hoc, "after this, therefore on account of this"—a type of fallacious argument in logic)

**crās,** adv., *tomorrow* (procrastinate, procrastination)

**heri,** adv., *yesterday*

**quándō,** interrog. and rel. adv. and conj., *when;* **sī quándō,** *if ever*

**sátis,** indecl. noun, adj., and adv., *enough, sufficient (-ly)* (cf. **satiō;** satisfy, satisfactory, satiate, insatiable, sate; assets, from **ad,** *up to* + **satis**)

**tum,** adv., *then, at that time; thereupon, in the next place*

**cḗnō, cēnā́re, cēnā́vī, cēnā́tum,** *to dine* (cenacle)

**cúlpō, culpā́re, culpā́vī, culpā́tum,** *to blame, censure* (cf. **culpa** above)

**mā́neō, manḗre, mā́nsī, mā́nsum** or **remā́neō, remanḗre, remā́nsī, remā́nsum,** *to remain, stay, stay behind, abide, continue* (mansion, manor, permanent, remnant, immanent—do not confuse with "imminent")

**súperō, superā́re, superā́vī, superā́tum,** *to be above* (cf. **super,** adv. and prep. +

abl. or acc., *above*), *have the upper hand, surpass; overcome, conquer* (super-able, insuperable)

# LĒCTIŌ ET TRĀNSLĀTIŌ

The essential activities for these **Lēctiō et Trānslātiō** sections are to read aloud, read for comprehension, and then translate (listening to the Latin too, if you have the CDs); but for practice identifying the newly introduced verb forms, you should scan the readings for all the verbs and identify the tense, person, number, voice, mood, and whether the verb is first or second conjugation. An important transla-tion tip is to always *choose the meaning for a word that best suits the context*: in the "Thermopylae" passage below, e.g., *courage* would be a better choice for **animīs**, in view of the military context, than *minds* or even *pride*. And don't forget the variety of options for translating the imperfect tense.

## EXERCITĀTIŌNĒS

1. Officium līberōs virōs semper vocābat.
2. Habēbimusne multōs virōs et fēminās magnōrum animōrum?
3. Perīcula bellī nōn sunt parva, sed patria tua tē vocābit et agricolae adiu-vābunt.
4. Propter culpās malōrum patria nostra nōn valēbit.
5. Mora animōs nostrōs superābat et remedium nōn habēbāmus.
6. Multī in agrīs herī manēbant et Rōmānōs iuvābant.
7. Paucī virī dē cūrā animī cōgitābant.
8. Propter īram in culpā estis et crās poenās dabitis.
9. Vērum ōtium nōn habēs, vir stulte!
10. Nihil est sine culpā; sumus bonī, sī paucās habēmus.
11. Poēta amīcae multās rosās, dōna pulchra, et bāsia dabat.
12. Will war and destruction always remain in our land?
13. Does money satisfy the greedy man?
14. Therefore, you (sg.) will save the reputation of our foolish boys.
15. Money and glory were conquering the soul of a good man.

## SENTENTIAE ANTĪQVAE

1. Invidiam populī Rōmānī crās nōn sustinēbis. (Cicero.—**invidia, -ae**, f., *dislike;* "invidious," "envious."—**sustinēre**, *to endure, sustain;* "sustenance.")
2. Perīculumne igitur herī remanēbat? (Cicero.)
3. Angustus animus pecūniam amat. (Cicero.—**angustus, -a, -um**, *narrow;* "an-guish," "anxious.")

4. Superā animōs et īram tuam. (Ovid.)
5. Culpa est mea, Ō amīcī. (Cicero.)
6. Dā veniam fīliō et fīliābus nostrīs. (Terence.—**venia, -ae,** f., *favor, pardon;* "venial," "veniality.")
7. Propter adulēscentiam, fīliī meī, mala vītae nōn vidēbātis. (Terence.)
8. Amābō tē, cūrā fīliam meam. (Cicero.—**cūrāre,** *to take care of;* "curative," "curator.")
9. Vīta hūmāna est supplicium. (Seneca.—**supplicium, -iī,** n., *punishment;* "suppliant," "supplicate.")
10. Satisne sānus es? (Terence.)
11. Sī quandō satis pecūniae habēbō, tum mē cōnsiliō et philosophiae dabō. (Seneca.—**pecūniae,** gen. case.)
12. Semper glōria et fāma tua manēbunt. (Vergil.)
13. Vir bonus et perītus aspera verba poētārum culpābit. (Horace.—**perītus, -a, -um,** *skillful;* "experiment," "expert."—**asper, aspera, asperum,** *rough, harsh;* "asperate," "exasperate.")

### His Only Guest Was a Real Boar!

> Nōn cēnat sine aprō noster, Tite, Caeciliānus:
>     bellum convīvam Caeciliānus habet!

*Martial *Epig.* 7.59: This is the first of several selections included in this book from the **Epigrammata** of Martial (Marcus Valerius Martialis, A.D. 45–104), who today remains one of the most popular of Roman writers. Most of Martial's 1500 epigrams are quite short, like this two-line elegiac couplet, with a satirical punch-line at the end, and targeted at specific, but usually fictitious, characters, here the glutton Caecilianus.—**Titus:** the poem's addressee, but not its target.—**aper, aprī,** m., *boar, pig.*—**convīva, -ae,** m., one of a few m. first decl. nouns, *dinner-guest;* "convive," "convivial.")

*QUAESTIŌNĒS:* What effect does Martial achieve by positioning the subject at the end of the sentence in the epigram's opening verse? Gluttony—one of the "seven deadly sins"—was a frequent target of Roman satire, as was stinginess; who (or what) seems to have been Caecilianus' only dinner-guest here, and what is the comic image?

### Thermopylae: A Soldier's Humor

"Exercitus noster est magnus," Persicus inquit, "et propter numerum sagittārum nostrārum caelum nōn vidēbitis!" Tum Lacedaemonius respondet: "In umbrā, igitur, pugnābimus!" Et Leōnidās, rēx Lacedaemoniōrum, exclāmat: "Pugnāte cum animīs, Lacedaemoniī; hodiē apud īnferōs fortasse cēnābimus!"

Cicero *Tusc.* 1.42.101: This passage adapted from the "Tusculan Disputations," another of Cicero's philosophical treatises, relates an anecdote about the battle of Thermopylae (see Map 3), 480 B.C., in which the invading Persian army under king Xerxes defeated a courageous band of 300 Spartans under the leadership of Leonidas; all 300 Spartans fell in battle, but not before slaying thousands of the enemy and delaying their advance long enough for other Greek forces to ready themselves for what proved to be a decisive victory at the Battle of Salamis (Map 3) later in the year.—**exercitus,** *army;* "exercise."—**Persicus, -ī,** m., *a Persian.*—**inquit,** *says.*—**sagitta, -ae,** f., *arrow;* "Sagittarius," "sagittate."—**Lacedaemonius, -ī,** m., *a Spartan.*—**respondēre:** = Eng.—**umbra, -ae,** f., *shade, shadow; ghost;* "umbrage" and "umbrella," which, with its DIMINUTIVE suffix "-ella," lit. means "little shade/shadow." —**pugnāre,** *to fight;* "pugilist," "pugnacious."—**rēx,** *king;* "regal," "regalia."—**exclāmāre,** *to shout;* "exclaim," "exclamation."—**cum** + abl., *with.*—**apud** + acc., *among.*—**īnferī, -ōrum,** m. pl., *those below, the dead;* "inferior," "inferiority."—**fortasse,** adv., *perhaps.*)

*QVAESTIŌ:* Both king Leonidas and his soldiers—the famed "300," who fought to the death to resist the Persian invasion of Greece—were apparently not only courageous but quick-witted as well; comment on the humor in their remarks, as Cicero reports them here.

*Spartan warrior (Leonidas?)*
*Ca. 490–480 B.C.*
*Found near the Sanctuary of*
*Athena Chalkiokos*
*Archaeological Museum*
*Sparta, Greece*

## SCRĪPTA IN PARIETIBVS

Aureus est, Danaē.

*CIL* 4.5303: Many graffiti from Pompeii echo literary texts or otherwise allude to Greco-Roman myths, some of them the work of school children (as we know, e.g., from the height at which they were written on walls), and all of them important to our understanding of the nature and extent of literacy in the Roman world. This graffito, found near a doorway in a house in Reg. IX, Ins. 8, alludes to the myth of Danaë, the legendary Greek princess who was impregnated by Jupiter in the form of a golden shower of rain, a mystical encounter that resulted in the birth of the hero Perseus; some scholars think the writer here had in mind a phrase from Ovid *Met.* 6.113.—**aureus, -a, -um,** *golden;* "Au" (symbol for the element gold, from the Lat. noun **aurum**), "auriferous."—**est:** sc. "Jupiter" as subject.—**Danaē:** a Gk. voc. form.

## LATĪNA EST GAVDIVM—ET VTILIS!

**Salvēte, et amīcī et amīcae meae! Quid hodiē agitis?** In fact, I hope you are **sānī et sānae,** both physically and spiritually; if so, you have attained what the 1st century A.D. Roman satirist Juvenal suggested was the highest good in life, **mēns sāna in corpore sānō,** *a healthy mind in a healthy body* (you'll encounter the two third declension nouns **mēns** and **corpus** later on, but in the meantime you can keep this famous quotation **in mente**). It's rumored, by the way, that the athletic gear brand-name ASICS is an acronym for **animus sānus in corpore sānō;** with a glance back at the **Vocābula** you can figure that one out too. NIKE, an ASICS competitor, takes its name from the Greek word for "victory," which in Latin is **victōria,** a winning name for a queen or any powerful lady (whose male counterpart might well be dubbed "Victor," from Latin **victor**).

You may have encountered the expressions **verbum sap** and **mea culpa** before; if not, you will. The former is an abbreviation of **verbum satis sapientī est: sapientī** is dative of the third declension adjective **sapiēns,** *wise,* used here as a noun (remember substantives from Capvt IV?), so you should already have deduced that the phrase means *a word to the wise is sufficient.* If you couldn't figure that out, just shout **"mea culpa!"** and (here's a **verbum sap**) go back and review the **Vocābula** in Capita I–V. **Valēte!**

# CAPVT VI 𐙮𐙮𐙮

# *Sum* and *Possum;*
# Complementary Infinitive

## GRAMMATICA

### FUTURE AND IMPERFECT INDICATIVE OF *Sum*

The best procedure for learning the future and imperfect tenses of **sum, esse,** as for the present tense introduced in Capvt IV, is simply to memorize the paradigms below (listening to the audio CDs, if you have them); these forms are more regular than those for the present, however, each formed on the stem **er-** and with the familiar present system personal endings (**-ō/-m, -s, -t, -mus, -tis, -nt**).

|      | Future Indicative | Imperfect Indicative |
|------|-------------------|----------------------|
|      | 1. érō, *I shall be* | éram, *I was* |
| Sg.  | 2. éris, *you will be* | érās, *you were* |
|      | 3. érit, *he (she, it, there) will be* | érat, *he (she, it, there) was* |
|      | 1. érimus, *we shall be* | erấmus, *we were* |
| Pl.  | 2. éritis, *you will be* | erấtis, *you were* |
|      | 3. érunt, *they (there) will be* | érant, *they (there) were* |

### IRREGULAR *Possum, posse, potuī,* to be able, can, could

The very common verb **possum, posse, potuī,** is simply a compound of **pot-,** from the irregular adjective **potis** (*able, capable;* cf. "potent," "potential") + **sum.** Before forms of **sum** beginning with s-, the -t- was altered or ASSIMILATED to -s- (hence **possum** from *\*potsum*); otherwise the -t- remained unchanged. The irregular present infinitive **posse** developed from an earlier, uncontracted form which followed this rule (**potesse**).

|      |                     | Present Indicative   | Future Indicative   | Imperfect Indicative |
| ---- | ------------------- | -------------------- | ------------------- | -------------------- |
|      |                     | *I am able, can*     | *I shall be able*   | *I was able, could*  |
|      |                     | 1. pós-sum           | pót-erō             | pót-eram             |
| Sg.  |                     | 2. pót-es            | pót-eris            | pót-erās             |
|      |                     | 3. pót-est           | pót-erit            | pót-erat             |
|      |                     | 1. póssumus          | potérimus           | poterāmus            |
| Pl.  |                     | 2. potéstis          | potéritis           | poterātis            |
|      |                     | 3. póssunt           | póterunt            | póterant             |

For both **sum** and **possum** it is helpful to note the similarity of the future and imperfect endings, **-ō/-is/-it,** etc., and **-am/-ās/-at,** etc., to the regular first and second conjugation future and imperfect endings, **-bō/-bis/-bit,** etc., and **-bam/-bās/-bat,** etc., which were introduced in the previous chapter.

## COMPLEMENTARY INFINITIVE

**Possum,** like English *to be able,* requires an infinitive to "complete" its meaning, hence the term COMPLEMENTARY (not "compl*i*mentary") INFINITIVE, which simply means "completing" infinitive. You have already seen the complementary infinitive used with **dēbeō,** and you will find it employed with **audeō, audēre,** *to dare,* and other verbs.

> *Our friends were able to overcome (could overcome) many dangers.*
> **Amīcī nostrī poterant superāre multa perīcula.**
> *My friend is not able to remain (cannot remain).*
> **Amīcus meus remanēre nōn potest.**
> *You ought to save your money.*
> **Dēbēs cōnservāre pecūniam tuam.**

Note that a complementary infinitive has no separate subject of its own; its subject is the same as that of the verb on which it depends.

# VOCĀBVLA

Most nouns follow the pattern of base + endings, but some few, like **dea** and **deus** in this list (and **fīlia** in Capvt III), have one or more irregular forms; **īnsidiae** is exceptional too in having plural forms with singular meanings. Pay careful attention to these and other sorts of irregularities when you encounter them in any of the chapter **Vocābula.** Some further caveats for this list: you will not confuse **ibi** and **ubi,** if you recall that *there* precedes *where* alphabetically, just as **ibi** precedes **ubi;** thinking "alphabetically" should also help you distinguish **noster/***our* from **vester/***your;* and note that **-que** suffixed to a word generally equates to **et** before the word. The importance of learning macrons as part of a word's spelling and pronunciation is again seen in the case of the noun **liber** (pronounced "LIH-ber"), meaning *book,* in this chapter's vocabulary, which you would not want to confuse with the adjective **līber** ("LEE-ber"), *free,* introduced in Capvt V—another reminder that you should study all new vocabulary, not silently, but by *listening to* and *pronouncing* each word aloud: **vocābula semper audī et prōnūntiā!**

**déus, -ī,** m., voc. sg. **deus,** nom. pl. **dī,** dat. and abl. pl. **dīs** (the plurals **deī** and **deīs** became common during the Augustan Period), *god,* and **déa, déae,** f., dat. and abl. pl. **deābus,** *goddess* (adieu, deify, deity)

**discípulus, discípulī,** m., and **discípula, discípulae,** f., *learner, pupil, student* (disciple, discipline, disciplinary)

**īnsídiae, īnsídiārum,** f. pl., *ambush, plot, treachery* (insidious)

**líber, líbrī,** m., *book* (library, librarian, libretto); not to be confused with **līber,** *free*

**tyránnus, tyránnī,** m., *absolute ruler, tyrant* (tyrannical, tyrannous, tyrannicide)

**vítium, vítiī,** n., *fault, crime, vice* (vitiate, vicious, vituperate; but not "vice versa")

**Graécus, Graéca, Graécum,** *Greek;* **Graécus, Graécī,** m., *a Greek*

**perpétuus, perpétua, perpétuum,** *perpetual, lasting, uninterrupted, continuous* (perpetuate, perpetuity)

**plḗnus, plḗna, plḗnum,** *full, abundant, generous* (plenary, plenteous, plentiful, plenitude, plenty, replenish, plenipotentiary)

**sálvus, sálva, sálvum,** *safe, sound* (cf. **salveō**)

**secúndus, secúnda, secúndum,** *second; favorable* (secondary)

**véster, véstra, véstrum,** *your* (pl., i.e., used in addressing more than one person, vs. **tuus, -a, -um**), *yours*

**-que,** ENCLITIC (essentially = "suffixed") conj., *and;* appended to the second of two words to be joined: **fāma glōriaque,** *fame and glory*

**úbi:** (1) rel. adv. and conj., *where, when;* (2) interrog. adv. and conj., *where?* (ubiquitous, ubiquity)

**íbi,** adv., *there* (ib. or ibid.)

**nunc,** adv., *now, at present* (quidnunc)

**quárē,** adv., lit. *because of which thing* (**quā rē**), but more commonly *therefore, wherefore, why*

**póssum, pósse, pótuī,** *to be able, can, could, have power* (posse, possible, potent, potentate, potential, omnipotent)

**tólerō, tolerāre, tolerāvī, tolerātum,** *to bear, endure* (tolerate, toleration, tolerable, intolerable, intolerance)

# LĒCTIŌ ET TRĀNSLĀTIŌ

By now, you know the ideal regimen: before attempting these readings, memorize paradigms and vocabulary, and assess your mastery with the Self-Tutorial Exercises. Listen to the readings, if you have the CDs, read them aloud once or twice for comprehension, and then write out your translations–which should always be reasonably literal but within the bounds of natural English idiom; for practice with the new grammar, scan the readings and identify (1) the tense, person, and number of all forms of **sum** and **possum** that occur, and (2) all complementary infinitives.

## EXERCITĀTIŌNĒS

1. Oculī nostrī nōn valēbant; quārē agrōs bellōs vidēre nōn poterāmus.
2. Sine multā pecūniā et multīs dōnīs tyrannus stultus satiāre populum Rōmānum nōn poterit.
3. Nōn poterant, igitur, tē dē poenā amīcōrum tuōrum heri monēre.
4. Parvus numerus Graecōrum crās ibi remanēre et amīcōs adiuvāre poterit.
5. Magister discipulōs malōs sine morā vocābit.
6. Discipulae vestrae dē librīs magnī poētae saepe cōgitābant.
7. Quandō satis sapientiae habēbimus?
8. Multī librī antīquī propter sapientiam cōnsiliumque erant magnī.
9. Glōria bonōrum librōrum semper manēbit.
10. Possuntne pecūnia ōtiumque cūrās vītae hūmānae superāre?
11. Therefore, we cannot always see the real vices of a tyrant.
12. Few free men will be able to tolerate an absolute ruler.
13. Many Romans used to praise the words of the ancient Greeks.
14. Where can glory and (use -**que**) fame be perpetual?

## SENTENTIAE ANTĪQVAE

1. Dionȳsius tum erat tyrannus Syrācūsānōrum. (Cicero.—**Dionȳsius, -iī,** m., a Greek name.—**Syrācūsānus, -ī,** *a Syracusan.*)
2. Optāsne meam vītam fortūnamque gustāre? (Cicero.—**optāre,** *to wish;* "optative," "adopt."—**gustāre,** *to taste;* "gustatory," "disgust.")
3. Possumusne, Ō dī, in malīs īnsidiīs et magnō exitiō esse salvī? (Cicero.—Can you explain why the nom. pl. **salvī** is used here?)
4. Propter cūram meam in perpetuō perīculō nōn eritis. (Cicero.)
5. Propter vitia tua multī tē culpant et nihil tē in patriā tuā dēlectāre nunc potest. (Cicero.—**dēlectāre,** *to delight;* "delectable," "delectation.")
6. Fortūna Pūnicī bellī secundī varia erat. (Livy.—**Pūnicus, -a, -um,** *Punic, Carthaginian.*—**varius, -a, -um,** *varied;* "variety," "various.")
7. Patria Rōmānōrum erat plēna Graecōrum librōrum statuārumque pulchrārum. (Cicero.—**statua, -ae,** f., Eng; "statuary," "statuesque.")
8. Sine dīs et deābus in caelō animus nōn potest sānus esse. (Seneca.)
9. Sī animus īnfīrmus est, nōn poterit bonam fortūnam tolerāre. (Publilius Syrus. —**īnfīrmus, -a, -um,** *not strong, weak;* "infirm," "infirmary.")

10. Ubi lēgēs valent, ibi populus līber potest valēre. (Publilius Syrus.—**lēgēs**, nom. pl., *laws;* "legal," "legislature.")

### "I Do Not Love Thee, Dr. Fell"

Nōn amo tē, Sabidī, nec possum dīcere quārē.
　　Hoc tantum possum dīcere: nōn amo tē.

*Martial *Epig.* 1.32: For Martial's *Epigrams,* see notes to "His Only Guest," in Capvt V. The "Dr. Fell" title here derives from an anecdote, perhaps apocryphal, about a 17th cent. Oxford University student named Tom Brown (who later gained some acclaim as a translator and satirist) and Dr. John Fell, a Latinist, Dean of Christ Church, and Bishop of Oxford, who had threatened the young man with expulsion. Fell told Brown he would give him a reprieve if he could properly translate this epigram, and Brown came up with the following version on the spot: "I do not love thee, Dr. Fell, the reason why I cannot tell; but this I know, and know full well: I do not love thee, Dr. Fell." Meter: elegiac couplet.—**amo:** final -ō was often shortened in Lat. poetry, for metrical reasons but also as a reflection of actual pronunciation habits.—**Sabidius, -iī:** the name of Martial's perhaps fictitious target.—**nec:** = **et nōn.**—**dīcere,** *to say;* "dictate," "diction."—**hoc,** *this;* "ad hoc;" acc. case.—**tantum,** adv., *only.*)

*QVAESTIŌNĒS:* Though quite brief, this little epigram makes its point and is neatly stylized. What seems to you most striking in terms of its **DICTION** (choice and use of words)? Next, look at the poem's structure—two lines, four clauses—and note that the clauses are set in a reverse ABBA order, an arrangement known as **CHIASMUS** that was commonly employed in Latin verse to achieve some sort of emphasis, often to underscore contrasting ideas; what do you see as its effect here?

### "The Historian Livy Laments the Decline of Roman Morals"

Populus Rōmānus magnōs animōs et paucās culpās habēbat. Dē officiīs nostrīs cōgitābāmus et glōriam bellī semper laudābāmus. Sed nunc multum ōtium habēmus, et multī sunt avārī. Nec vitia nostra nec remedia tolerāre possumus.

Livy *Urbe Cond.* Preface: The Augustan writer Livy (Titus Livius, 59 B.C.–A.D. 17) authored the monumental **Ab Urbe Conditā,** *From the Founding of the City,* a history of Rome from its legendary founding in 753 B.C. down to the reign of the emperor Augustus; only 35 of the original 142 volumes have survived. The passage excerpted here is drawn from his preface to the work.—**nec . . . nec,** conj., *neither . . . nor.*

*QVAESTIŌNĒS:* The author employs contrast to point out differences between early Rome and his own contemporary society; how many instances of this device can you identify? How would you characterize the overall tone of the passage?

*Manuscript page with preface of Livy's* Ab Urbe Condita *and miniature in four parts, including scenes of Lucretia and Rome's kings. Burney manuscript 198. Ca. 1400, border added 1471–1474. The British Library*

## SCRĪPTA IN PARIETIBVS

Amīculus

CIL 4.8269: This artfully etched graffito from Reg. I, Ins. 10, appeared above a crude drawing of two gladiators. **Amīculus, -ī,** m., is the DIMINUTIVE form of **amīcus,** *little . . .* or *dear . . .* ; diminutive suffixes in **-ulus/-olus/-ula/-ola,** etc., were commonly employed in Lat. both to indicate something small (**saxum,** *rock;* **saxulum,** *little rock*) and as terms of endearment (**fīlia > fīliola,** *dear [little] daughter*).

## ETYMOLOGIA

Eng. "library" is clearly connected with **liber.** Many European languages, however, derive their equivalent from **bibliothēca,** a Lat. word of Gk. origin meaning in essence the same thing as our word. What, then, do you suppose **biblos** meant in Greek?—cf. the *Bible.* Fr. **y** in the common phrase **il y a** (*there is*) derives from **ibi.** And the following Fr. words are also derived from Lat.: **êtes = estis; nôtre = noster; vôtre = vester; goûter = gustāre.** What, then, is one thing which the Fr. circumflex accent indicates?

## LATĪNA EST GAVDIVM—ET V̄TILIS!

**Salvēte, discipulī et discipulae! Quid hodiē agitis, Ō amīcī? Cōgitātisne dē linguā Latīnā?** Well, I assume by now that your etymological sense will tell you that **lingua Latīna** means. . . *the Latin language* or just "Latin," your favorite subject. Now that you've developed a taste for the language, I know that you study with great "gusto"! (If you missed that bit of etymologizing, see S.A. 2 above.) The new **Vocābula** item **deus** turns up in the expression **deus ex machinā,** *god from a machine,* which refers (in drama and other contexts) to any person or mechanism that performs an amazing rescue from some seemingly hopeless dilemma.

Do you know that **sub** is a preposition meaning *under,* as in "subterranean," under the **terra,** *earth;* if so, you can laugh at this old favorite: **semper ubi sub ubi!** (Good hygiene and prevents rash!) And speaking of **ubi,** it asks the question that **ibi** answers; a compound form of the latter constructed with the intensifying suffix **-dem,** *the same* (see Capvt XI for a similar use of **-dem**), **ibidem,** gives us **ibid.,** *in the same place cited,* just one of many Latin-based abbreviations commonly employed in English. Here are some others:

cf. = **cōnfer,** *compare*
cp. = **comparā,** *compare*
e.g. = **exemplī grātiā,** *for the sake of example*
et al. = **et aliī/aliae,** *and others* (of persons)
etc. = **et cētera,** *and others* (of things)
i.e. = **id est,** *that is*
n.b. = **nōtā bene,** *note carefully* (i.e., pay close attention)
v.i. and v.s. = **vidē īnfrā** and **vidē suprā,** *see below* and *see above*

**Semper ubi sub ubi** AND the scholarly **ibid.** both in the same lesson? Well, that's what the title means: **Latīna EST gaudium—ET ūtilis! Valēte!**

# CAPVT VII ⌐⌐⌐

# Third Declension Nouns

## GRAMMATICA

### THIRD DECLENSION NOUNS

The third of Latin's five declensions contains nouns of all three genders with a great variety of nominative singular endings, but all characterized by the genitive singular in **-is;** because of this variety of gender and nominative form, it is especially important to memorize the full vocabulary entry. The declension itself follows the same principles learned for first and second declension nouns: find the base (by dropping the genitive singular **-is**) and add the endings. Because the vocative is identical to the nominative (with the sole exception of second declension **-us/-ius** words), it will not appear in subsequent paradigms.

|  | rēx, m. *king* | virtūs, f. *merit* | homō, m. *man* | corpus, n. *body* | Case Endings M./F. | N. |
|---|---|---|---|---|---|---|
| **Base** | rēg- | virtūt- | homin- | corpor- |  |  |
| **Singular** |  |  |  |  |  |  |
| *Nom.* | rēx (rēg-s) | vírtūs | hómō | córpus | — | — |
| *Gen.* | rḗg-is | virtū́tis | hóminis | córporis | -is | -is |
| *Dat.* | rḗg-ī | virtū́tī | hóminī | córporī | -ī | -ī |
| *Acc.* | rḗg-em | virtū́tem | hóminem | córpus | -em | — |
| *Abl.* | rḗg-e | virtū́te | hómine | córpore | -e | -e |
| **Plural** |  |  |  |  |  |  |
| *Nom.* | rḗg-ēs | virtū́tēs | hóminēs | córpora | -ēs | -a |
| *Gen.* | rḗg-um | virtū́tum | hóminum | córporum | -um | -um |
| *Dat.* | rḗg-ibus | virtū́tibus | homínibus | corpóribus | -ibus | -ibus |
| *Acc.* | rḗg-ēs | virtū́tēs | hóminēs | córpora | -ēs | -a |
| *Abl.* | rḗg-ibus | virtū́tibus | homínibus | corpóribus | -ibus | -ibus |

### Gender

Since the third declension contains nouns of all three genders, memorizing gender as part of the vocabulary entry remains imperative. Nouns denoting human beings, however, are typically masculine or feminine according to sense (e.g., **rēx**, *king*, m., and **uxor**, *wife*, f.), and the following rules also have few or no exceptions:

<u>Masculine</u> (including a large group of AGENT NOUNS, i.e., for persons performing actions, such as: **actor**, *one who acts, actor;* **amātor**, *one who loves, lover*)

> **-or, -ōris** (amor, -mōris; labor, -bōris; victor, -tōris; scrīptor, -tōris; the long ō vowel of the base is short in the nominative, as usual before final **-r**)

<u>Feminine</u> (including a large group of ABSTRACT NOUNS, for abstract concepts)

> **-tās, -tātis** (vēritās, -tātis; lībertās, -tātis)
> **-tūs, -tūtis** (virtūs, -tūtis; senectūs, -tūtis)
> **-tūdō, -tūdinis** (multitūdō, -tūdinis; pulchritūdō, -tūdinis)
> **-tiō, -tiōnis** (nātiō, -tiōnis; ōrātiō, -tiōnis)

<u>Neuter</u>

> **-us** (genus, generis; corpus, corporis; tempus, temporis: in contrast to masculine nouns, for neuters with a base ending in **or** the o is short)
> **-e, -al, -ar** (mare, maris; animal, -mālis; exemplar, -plāris)
> **-men** (carmen, -minis; nōmen, -minis)

**Noun-Adjective Agreement**

In declining, note that a third declension noun may be modified by a first or second declension adjective; e.g., *great king* in Latin is **magnus rēx, magnī rēgis**, etc., *true peace* is **pāx vēra, pācis vērae**, etc. While an adjective and noun must agree in number, gender, and case, the spelling of their endings will not necessarily be identical—as seen before in such noun-adjective pairs as **agricola bonus.**

# VOCĀBVLA

In this list of new words you can see how essential it is to look at a noun's genitive ending, not the nominative, in order to identify its declension; otherwise, e.g., **-us** nouns like **corpus** and **tempus** might easily be mistaken as second declension. Likewise recall that a noun's base is best determined from its genitive form; this is especially true with third declension nouns, whose nominatives frequently do not reveal the base, as with the chapter's paradigm nouns, **rēx/rēgis, virtūs/virtūtis, homō/hominis, corpus, corporis.** English derivatives can be helpful in remembering a noun's base; e.g., **iter, itineris,** *journey:* itinerary; **cor, cordis,** *heart:* cordial; **custōs, custōdis,** *guard:* custodian. Since the third declension contains nouns of all genders, it remains imperative that you memorize gender as part of the entry; as you learn this list, practice declining some noun-adjective pairs, e.g., **amor novus, carmen nostrum, uxor bona.** You'll see that two nouns in this list (**mōs** and **littera**) have special, idiomatic meanings in the plural; we've seen this before, with **animus,** and it's something to note carefully.

As you learn this new vocabulary, you should also review words learned in Capita I–VI (**capita,** by the way, is from **caput, capitis,** n., *head; heading, chapter*); for review you can use vocabulary cards or cumulative vocabulary lists (available at www.wheelockslatin.com, or you can compile your own), but in memorizing this new list, be sure to use the CDs or the online audio, and . . . **audī prōnūntiāque**— the verb **prōnūntiō,** by the way, is an exception to the general rule, introduced in Capvt I, that vowels are generally short before **nt,** so be sure you are "pronouncing" it correctly!

ámor, amṓris, m., *love* (amorous, enamored; cf. **amō, amīcus** )

cármen, cárminis, n., *song, poem* (charm)

cīvitās, cīvitā́tis, f., *state, citizenship* (city)

córpus, córporis, n., *body* (corps, corpse, corpuscle, corpulent, corporal, corporeal, corporate, corporation, incorporate, corsage, corset)

hómō, hóminis, m., *human being, man* (homicide, homage; homo sapiens, but not the prefix homo-; cf. **hūmānus** and **vir** )

lábor, labṓris, m., *labor, work, toil; a work, production* (laboratory, belabor, laborious, collaborate, elaborate)

líttera, lítterae, f., *a letter of the alphabet;* líttera, litterā́rum, pl., *a letter* (*epistle*), *literature* (literal, letters, belles-lettres, illiterate, alliteration)

mōs, mṓris, m., *habit, custom, manner;* mṓrēs, mṓrum, pl., *habits, morals, character* (mores, moral, immoral, immorality, morale, morose)

nṓmen, nṓminis, n., *name* (nomenclature, nominate, nominative, nominal, noun, pronoun, renown, denomination, ignominy, misnomer)

pāx, pā́cis, f., *peace* (pacify, pacific, pacifist, appease, pay)

rēgína, rēgínae, f., *queen* (Regina, regina, reginal)

rēx, rḗgis, m., *king* (regal, regalia, regicide, royal; cf. rajah)

témpus, témporis, n., *time; occasion, opportunity* (tempo, temporary, contemporary, temporal, temporize, extempore, tense [of a verb])

térra, térrae, f., *earth, ground, land, country* (terrestrial, terrace, terrier, territory, inter [verb], parterre, subterranean, terra cotta)

úxor, uxṓris, f., *wife* (uxorial, uxorious, uxoricide)

vírgō, vírginis, f., *maiden, virgin* (virgin, virginal, virginity, Virginia)

vírtūs, virtū́tis, f., *manliness, courage; excellence, character, worth, virtue* (virtuoso, virtuosity, virtual; cf. **vir** )

nóvus, nóva, nóvum, *new; strange* (novel, novelty, novice, innovate)

post, prep. + acc., *after, behind* (posterity, posterior, posthumous, post mortem, P.M. = post meridiem, preposterous, post- as a prefix, postgraduate, postlude, postpositive, postwar, etc.)

**sub,** prep. + abl. with verbs of rest, + acc. with verbs of motion, *under, up under, close to; down to/into, to/at the foot of* (sub- or, by ASSIMILATION, suc-, suf-, sug-, sup-, sus-, in countless compounds: subterranean, suburb, succeed, suffix, suggest, support, sustain)

**aúdeō, audḗre, aúsus sum** (the unusual third principal part of this SEMI-DEPONENT verb is explained in Capvt XXXIV), *to dare* (audacious, audacity)

**nécō, necā́re, necā́vī , necā́tum,** *to murder, kill* (internecine; cf. **nocēre,** *to harm*)

# LĒCTIŌ ET TRĀNSLĀTIŌ

A new challenge to reading comprehension and translation is that some third declension endings resemble the endings of different cases in other declensions, e.g., -ī can be the ending for a third declension dative singular or a second declension genitive singular or masculine nominative/vocative plural; -**us** could be a second declension masculine nominative or a third declension neuter accusative; etc. The key is careful vocabulary study, first and foremost, though word order and context can also be a help when dealing with ambiguous endings. For practice, use the Self-Tutorial Exercises for this chapter, of course, but also scan through the following readings and identify number, case/use, and gender for all the third declension nouns. And don't forget, when translating, to supply articles and possessives, choose meanings for words that best suit the context, and strive for as accurate and reasonably literal a rendering as possible within the bounds of natural English idiom.

## EXERCITĀTIŌNĒS

1. Secundās litterās discipulae heri vidēbās et dē verbīs tum cōgitābās.
2. Fēminae sine morā cīvitātem dē īnsidiīs et exitiō malō monēbunt.
3. Rēx et rēgīna igitur crās nōn audēbunt ibi remanēre.
4. Mōrēs Graecōrum nōn erant sine culpīs vitiīsque.
5. Quandō hominēs satis virtūtis habēbunt?
6. Corpora vestra sunt sāna et animī sunt plēnī sapientiae.
7. Propter mōrēs hūmānōs pācem vēram nōn habēbimus.
8. Poteritne cīvitās perīcula temporum nostrōrum superāre?
9. Post bellum multōs librōs dē pāce et remediīs bellī vidēbant.
10. Officia sapientiamque oculīs animī poterāmus vidēre.
11. Without sound character we cannot have peace.
12. Many students used to have little time for Greek literature.
13. After bad times true virtue and much labor will help the state.
14. The daughters of your friends were dining there yesterday.

## SENTENTIAE ANTĪQVAE

1. Homō sum. (*Terence.)
2. Nihil sub sōle novum (*Ecclesiastes.—**sōl, sōlis,** m., *sun;* "solar," "solstice."—**novum: sc. est.**)
3. Carmina nova dē adulēscentiā virginibus puerīsque nunc cantō. (Horace.—**cantāre,** *to sing;* "canto," "chant," "recant.")
4. Laudās fortūnam et mōrēs antīquae plēbis. (*Horace.—**plēbs, plēbis,** f., *the common people;* "plebe," "plebeian," "plebiscite.")
5. Bonī propter amōrem virtūtis peccāre ōdērunt. (Horace.—**peccāre,** *to sin;* "peccadillo," "impeccable."—**ōdērunt:** *(they) hate;* "odious," "odium.")
6. Sub prīncipe dūrō temporibusque malīs audēs esse bonus. (Martial.—**prīnceps, -cipis,** m., *chief, prince;* "principal," "principality."—**dūrus, -a, -um,** *hard, harsh;* "durable," "endure," "obdurate.")
7. Populus stultus virīs indignīs honōrēs saepe dat. (Horace.—**honor, -nōris,** m., *honor, office;* "honorable," "honorary."—**indignus, -a, -um,** *unworthy;* "indignant," "indignation.")
8. Nōmina stultōrum in parietibus et portīs semper vidēmus. (Cicero.—Witness the graffiti in this book!—**pariēs, -etis,** m., *wall of a building;* "parietal.")
9. Ōtium sine litterīs mors est. (*Seneca.—**mors, mortis,** f., *death;* "mortal," "mortuary.")
10. Multae nātiōnēs servitūtem tolerāre possunt; nostra cīvitās nōn potest. Praeclāra est recuperātiō lībertātis. (Cicero.—**nātiō, -ōnis** f., = Eng.; "nationalism," "nationality."—**servitūs, -tūtis,** f., *servitude;* "service."—**praeclārus, -a, -um,** *noble, remarkable;* "clarity."—**recuperātiō, -ōnis,** f., *recovery;* "recuperate."—**lībertās, -tātis,** f. = Eng.; "liberate," "libertine.")
11. Nihil sine magnō labōre vīta mortālibus dat. (Horace.—**mortālis, -tālis,** *a mortal;* "mortality.")
12. Quōmodo in perpetuā pāce salvī et līberī esse poterimus? (Cicero.—**quōmodo,** *how.*)
13. Glōria in altissimīs Deō et in terrā pāx hominibus bonae voluntātis. (*Luke.—**altissimīs,** abl. pl., *the highest;* "altimeter," "altitude."—**voluntās, -tātis,** *will;* "voluntary," "volunteer.")

### The Rape of Lucretia

Tarquinius Superbus erat rēx Rōmānōrum, et Sextus Tarquinius erat fīlius malus tyrannī. Sextus Lucrētiam, uxōrem Collātīnī, rapuit, et fēmina bona, propter magnum amōrem virtūtis, sē necāvit. Rōmānī antīquī virtūtem animōsque Lucrētiae semper laudābant et Tarquiniōs culpābant.

Livy *Urbe Cond.* 1.58: For Livy's history of Rome, see "The Historian Livy Laments the Decline of Roman Morals," in Capvt VI above. Lucius Tarquinius Superbus was Rome's

The Rape of Lucretia. *Felice Ficherelli, 1605–1660. Oil on tinned copper.*
*The Wallace Collection, London, Great Britain*

last king and an Etruscan, Collatinus a Roman nobleman; according to legend, the rape of Lucretia was a precipitating factor that led to the overthrow of the Tarquin dynasty, the end of Etruscan rule and of the monarchy itself, and the establishment of the Roman Republic in 509 B.C.—**rapuit:** *raped;* "rapacious," "rapture."—**sē:** *herself.*—**necāvit:** a past tense form.—**Tarquiniōs:** i.e., the entire royal family.

*QVAESTIŌNĒS:* Livy's moralizing tone was evident in the passage adapted from his preface, which you read in the last chapter, and throughout his work it seems he was as interested in drawing moral lessons as he was in reporting facts. Based on this brief, adapted passage, what were some of the virtues Romans most admired? What is your personal view of Lucretia's suicide, and of the Roman response to it, as suggested in this passage? Compare Ficherelli's painting above with the manuscript illustration on p. 53.

### Catullus Dedicates His Poetry Book

Cornēliō, virō magnae sapientiae, dabō pulchrum librum novum. Cornēlī, mī amīce, librōs meōs semper laudābās, et es magister doctus litterārum! Quārē habē novum labōrem meum: fāma librī (et tua fāma) erit perpetua.

Catullus *Carm.* 1: For Catullus, Cornelius Nepos, and other Roman writers presented in these chapter readings, be sure to review the "Brief Survey of Latin Literature" in the Introd. (above, p. xxx–xxxv); and cf. "Catullus Bids His Girlfriend Farewell," in Capvt II. Catullus dedicated his poetry book, in the opening poem from which this prose passage is adapted, to the historian and biographer Cornelius Nepos; the entire, unadapted poem appears later in this text (**Locī Im.** I, p. 363–64).—**doctus, -a, -um,** *learned, scholarly;* "doctor," "indoctrinate."

*QVAESTIŌNĒS:* Cornelius Nepos (ca. 110–24 B.C.), the author of some 400 biographies of famous Greeks and Romans, is not today regarded as one of the great Roman classic writers, but he was nevertheless respected by Catullus. Based on this prose excerpt from his dedicatory poem, what qualities did the young poet most admire in Nepos?—and what else had the biographer done to earn this honor in Catullus' dedication?

## SCRĪPTA IN PARIETIBVS

Perārī, fūr es!

*CIL* 4.4764 (Reg. VII, Ins. 7): Personal insults like this one from the House of the Cissonii were common in ancient graffiti, just as they are today. What case must **Perārī** be?—and so, what was his name, i.e., was the nom. form?—**fūr, fūris,** m., *thief;* "furtive," "furtively."

Mulviu<s>

*CIL* 4.4885: The Pompeian responsible for this graffito found in a house in Reg. VIII, Ins. 2, was about as talented at drawing as he was at spelling: he tried twice, and failed, to write **MVLVIVS** (?), and while **Mulvius** was in fact a Lat. word—the name of a Roman **gēns** (family)—it seems more likely, in view of the drawing, that he was trying to label his bird **mīluus** or **mīlvus,** *kite,* a common bird of prey, proverbial in ancient Rome for its rapacity and the vast distances it could fly. Our artist's fine-feathered friend, alas, looks more like a coot, or a goose, than a kite!

## ETYMOLOGIA

What Lat. word do you suppose gives us It. **uomo,** Sp. **hombre,** Fr. **homme** and **on,** Port. **homem,** Rom. **om,** and Old Occ. **ome?**

"Tense" meaning the "time" of a verb comes from **tempus** through Old Fr.

tens; but "tense" meaning "stretched tight" goes back to **tendō, tendere, tetendī, tēnsum,** *to stretch.*

In late Lat., **cīvitās** came to mean *city* rather than *state,* and thus it became the parent of the Romance words for city: It. **città,** Sp. **ciudad,** Fr. **cité,** Port. **cidade,** and Occ. **ciutat.**

Here are the Romance and Eng. equivalents of three common Lat. suffixes introduced in this chapter:

| Latin | Italian | Spanish | French | English |
|---|---|---|---|---|
| -tās, -tātis | -tà | -dad | -té | -ty |
| vēritās | verità | verdad | vérité | verity (truth) |
| antīquitās | antichità | antigüedad | antiquité | antiquity |
| -tiō, -tiōnis | -zione | -ción | -tion | -tion |
| nātiō | nazione | nación | nation | nation |
| ratiō | razione | ración | ration | ration |
| -tor, -tōris | -tore | -tor | -teur | -tor |
| inventor | inventore | inventor | inventeur | inventor |
| actor | attore | actor | acteur | actor |

Cf. Port. **-dade (verdade, antiguidade), -ção/-zão (nação, razão), -tor (inventor, actor/ator);** Rom. **antichitate, naţie/naţiune, raţiune, inventator, actor;** Old Occ. **ver, antiquitat, nacion, razon, autor.**


## LATĪNA EST GAVDIVM—ET VTILIS!

**Salvēte, et discipulī et discipulae! Quid nunc agitis?** You are beginning to see by now that Latin is living everywhere in our language; in fact, it's a **rāra avis** these days who considers Latin a dead language. To anyone who does, you might quip, **quot hominēs, tot sententiae**—an old proverb from the 2nd century B.C. comic playwright Terence meaning, freely, *there are as many opinions as there are men.* Notice **terra** in the **Vocābula:** we met "subterranean" in the last chapter, now do you think of "ET"? In the 1980s the little guy was everybody's favorite *Extra-Terrestrial* (from **extrā,** prep. + acc., *beyond,* + **terra**). Until he became familiar with the terrain, he was in a **terra incognita;** but once he'd learned the territory he felt he was on **terra firma** (look up all these earth-words in your Funk and Wagnall's—if you need to!). And, speaking of movies, Stephen Spielberg's top-grossing *Jurassic Park* reminded us all that Tyrannosaurus rex was truly both a "tyrant" and a "king" (though Spielberg's "velociraptors" were certainly terrifying "swift-snatchers," from the Latin adjective **vēlōx,** *fast,* as in "velocity," + **raptor,** a third declension noun based on the verb **rapere,** *to seize, snatch, grab*). **Latīnam semper amābitis**—**valēte!**

# CAPVT VIII ▣▣▣

# Third Conjugation: Present System

## GRAMMATICA

### THIRD CONJUGATION VERBS

The third conjugation, in its present system tenses (present, future, and imperfect), is somewhat less regular than the other conjugations. Because the stem vowel was short (-e-), unlike those of the other three conjugations (-ā- in the first, -ē- in the second, and -ī- in the fourth, introduced in Capvt X—cf. laudā́re, monḗre, and audī́re with ā́gere), it had undergone a number of sound and spelling changes by the classical period. The surest procedure, as always, is to memorize the following paradigms (listening to the CDs, if you have them); note in particular the vowel alternation in the present tense endings, and the new future tense endings.

### Present Indicative Active

|      |                | |
|------|----------------|--------------------|
| Sg.  | 1. ág-ō        | (*I lead*) |
|      | 2. ág-is       | (*you lead*) |
|      | 3. ág-it       | (*he, she, it leads*) |
| Pl.  | 1. ágimus      | (*we lead*) |
|      | 2. ágitis      | (*you lead*) |
|      | 3. águnt       | (*they lead*) |

### Future Indicative Active

|      |                | |
|------|----------------|--------------------|
| Sg.  | 1. ág-am       | (*I will lead*) |
|      | 2. ág-ēs       | (*you will lead*) |
|      | 3. ág-et       | (*he, she, it will lead*) |
| Pl.  | 1. agḗmus      | (*we will lead*) |
|      | 2. agḗtis      | (*you will lead*) |
|      | 3. ágent       | (*they will lead*) |

## Imperfect Indicative Active

|      |                 |                                    |
|------|-----------------|------------------------------------|
|      | 1. ag-ébam      | (*I was leading, used to lead,* etc.) |
| Sg.  | 2. ag-ébās      | (*you were leading,* etc.)         |
|      | 3. ag-ébat      | (*he, she, it was leading,* etc.)  |
|      | 1. agēbámus     | (*we were leading,* etc.)          |
| Pl.  | 2. agēbátis     | (*you were leading,* etc.)         |
|      | 3. agébant      | (*they were leading,* etc.)        |

## Present Imperative Active

2. **Sg.** áge (*lead!*)          2. **Pl.** ágite (*lead!*)

## Present Infinitive

As the infinitive endings -**āre** and -**ēre** indicate the first and second conjugations respectively, so -**ere** indicates the third. Once again you can see the importance of meticulous vocabulary study, including attention to macrons: you must be especially careful to distinguish between second conjugation verbs in -**ēre** and third conjugation verbs in -**ere,** something you can practice right now by glancing ahead at this chapter's **Vocābula.**

## Present Stem and Present Indicative

According to the normal rule for finding the present stem, you would drop the infinitive ending -**re** from **agere** and have **age-** as the present stem. To this you would expect to add the personal endings to form the present indicative. But in fact the short, unaccented stem vowel disappears altogether in the first person singular, and it was altered to -**i-** in the second and third persons singular and the first and second persons plural, and appears as -**u-** in the third plural. The most practical procedure is to memorize the present tense paradigm, paying close attention to the altered stem vowel plus personal endings; it should be helpful to note that the vowel alternation **ō/is/it/imus/itis/unt** is exactly the same as that seen in the future endings of first and second conjugation verbs (-**bō,** -**bis,** -**bit,** -**bimus,** -**bitis,** -**bunt**).

## Future Indicative

Most striking in the future tense of the third conjugation (and the fourth, introduced in Capvt X) is the lack of the tense sign -**bi-**. Here -**ē-** is the sign of the future in all forms except the first singular, and by contraction the stem vowel itself has disappeared.

### Imperfect Indicative

The imperfect tense is formed precisely according to the rules learned for the first two conjugations (present stem + -**bam**, -**bās**, etc.), except that the stem vowel has been lengthened to -**ē**-, yielding forms analogous to those in the first and second conjugations.

### Present Imperative

Also in accordance with the rule already learned, the second person singular of the present imperative is simply the present stem; e.g., **mitte** (from **mittere**, *to send*), **pōne** (**pōnere**, *to put*). In the plural imperative, however, we see again the shift from short, unaccented -**e**- to -**i**-: hence, **mittite** and **pōnite** (not *mittete or *pōnete).

*Irregular forms:* The singular imperative of **dūcere** was originally **dūce**, a form seen in the early writer Plautus. Later, however, the -**e** was dropped from **dūce**, as it was from the singular imperatives of three other common third conjugation verbs: **dīc** (**dīcere**, *to say*), **fac** (**facere**, *to do*), and **fer** (**ferre**, *to bear*). The other verbs of this conjugation follow the rule as illustrated by **age**, **mitte**, and **pōne**; the four irregulars, **dīc**, **dūc**, **fac**, and **fer**, should simply be memorized.

# VOCĀBVLA

Macrons can be mighty important: an -**ēre** verb is second conjugation, while the new -**ere** verbs, with the short stem vowel, are third conjugation and therefore have a great many different forms. So as you memorize each new vocabulary entry, pay close attention to the macrons, as a part of the word's spelling, listen carefully to its pronunciation on the CDs or online audio, and then repeat the word correctly yourself from the very outset. When you carefully pronounce aloud first **docēre**, with its long, accented stem vowel, and then **dūcere**, with the short, unaccented vowel, it will be impossible not to notice which is the second conjugation verb, and which is third. All the more reason to remember, whenever you study or review vocabulary: **semper audī et prōnūntiā!** And be sure to practice conjugating a first, second, and third conjugation verb from this new list; write out the forms for all three tenses, check them against the paradigms in the **Summārium Fōrmārum**, p. 501, and recite them aloud.

**Cícerō, Cicerōnis**, m., (*Marcus Tullius*) *Cicero* (Ciceronian, cicerone)
**cōpia, cōpiae**, f., *abundance, supply;* **cōpiae, cōpiārum**, pl., *supplies, troops, forces*
(copious, copy, cornucopia)
**fráter, frátris**, m., *brother* (fraternal, fraternity, fraternize, fratricide)
**laus, laúdis**, f., *praise, glory, fame* (laud, laudable, laudation, laudatory, magna cum laude; cf. **laudō**)

lībértās, lībertâtis, f., *liberty* (cf. **līber**)

rátiō, ratiốnis, f., *reckoning, account; reason, judgment, consideration; system; manner, method* (ratio, ration, rational, irrational, ratiocination)

scrîptor, scrīptôris, m., *writer, author* (scriptorium; cf. **scrībō** below)

sóror, sorôris, f., *sister* (sororal, sororicide, sorority)

victôria, victôriae, f., *victory* (victorious, Victoria; see **Latīna Est Gaudium**, Capvt V, and cf. **vincō** below)

dum, conj., *while, as long as, at the same time that;* + subjunct., *until*

ad, prep. + acc., *to, up to, near to,* in the sense of "place to which" with verbs of motion; contrast the dat. of ind. obj., also translated with "to," but in a different sense (administer, ad hoc, ad hominem). In compounds the **d** is sometimes ASSIMILATED to the following consonant so that **ad** may appear, for instance, as ac- (**accipiō: ad-capiō**), ap- (**appellō: ad-pellō**), a- (**aspiciō: ad-spiciō**): see App., p. 485.

ex or ē, prep. + abl., *out of, from, from within; by reason of, on account of;* following cardinal numbers, *of* (exact, except, exhibit, evict). The Romans used **ex** before consonants or vowels; **ē** (like "a" vs. "an" in Eng.) before consonants only. Like **ad** and many other prepositions, **ex/ē** was often used as a prefix in compounds, sometimes with the **x** assimilated to the following consonant; e.g., **excipiō, ēdūcō, ēventus, efficiō** from **ex + faciō**, etc.; App., p. 486.

númquam, adv., *never*

támen, adv., *nevertheless, still*

ágō, ágere, êgī, âctum, *to drive, lead, do, act; pass, spend* (life or time); **grâtiās ágere** + dat. for the person being thanked, *to thank* (someone), lit., *to give thanks to* (agent, agenda, agile, agitate, active, actor, action, actual, actuate)

dēmônstrō, dēmōnstrâre, dēmōnstrâvī, dēmōnstrâtum, *to point out, show, demonstrate* (demonstrable, demonstration, demonstrative)

díscō, díscere, dídicī, *to learn* (disciple, disciplinary; cf. **discipulus, discipula**)

dóceō, docêre, dócuī, dóctum, *to teach* (docent, docile, document, doctor, doctrine, indoctrinate)

dûcō, dûcere, dûxī, dúctum, *to lead; consider, regard; prolong* (ductile, abduct, adduce, deduce, educe, induce, produce, reduce, seduce)

gérō, gérere, géssī, géstum, *to carry; carry on, manage, conduct, wage, accomplish, perform* (gerund, gesture, gesticulate, jest, belligerent, congeries, digest, suggest, exaggerate, register, registry)

scrîbō, scrîbere, scrîpsī, scrîptum, *to write, compose* (ascribe, circumscribe, conscript, describe, inscribe, proscribe, postscript, rescript, scripture, subscribe, transcribe, scribble, scrivener, shrive)

tráhō, tráhere, trâxī, tráctum, *to draw, drag; derive, acquire* (attract, contract, retract, subtract, tractor, etc.)

víncō, víncere, vîcī, víctum, *to conquer, overcome* (convince, convict, evince, evict, invincible, Vincent, victor, Victoria, vanquish)

# LĒCTIŌ ET TRĀNSLĀTIŌ

As always, before attempting these readings, memorize the paradigms and vocabulary, and check your mastery with the Self-Tutorial Exercises. Then listen to the readings, if you have the CDs, read them aloud for comprehension, and write out your translations; for practice with the new grammar, scan through the readings and identify the person, number, and tense of all third conjugation verbs. A common translation error involves misconstruing future tense third conjugation forms like **aget** in S.A. 1 below as present tense, since they resemble second conjugation forms like **monet, dēbet,** etc.; you can avoid such problems by carefully studying vocabulary. Another common mistake occurs in translating "to" in English-to-Latin exercises; with a verb of motion, use the newly introduced preposition **ad;** use the dative when "to" indicates an indirect object. The noun **error** in S.A. 6 is one of countless Latin words whose meanings are easily understood from English derivatives; here and in similar instances elsewhere in the notes, English definitions are omitted, sometimes with the note "= Eng.," and you'll be expected to deduce the meanings.

## EXERCITĀTIŌNĒS

1. Tempora nostra nunc sunt mala; vitia nostra, magna.
2. Quārē soror mea uxōrī tuae litterās scrībit (scrībet, scrībēbat)?
3. Tyrannus populum stultum ē terrā vestrā dūcet (dūcit, dūcēbat).
4. Ubi satis ratiōnis animōrumque in hominibus erit?
5. Cōpia vērae virtūtis multās culpās superāre poterat.
6. In līberā cīvitāte adulēscentiam agēbāmus.
7. Rēgem malum tolerāre numquam dēbēmus.
8. Post parvam moram multa verba dē īnsidiīs scrīptōrum stultōrum scrībēmus.
9. The body will remain there under the ground.
10. Write (sg. and pl.) many things in your (sg. and pl.) books about the glory of our state.
11. Does reason always lead your (pl.) queen to virtue?
12. We shall always see many Greek names there.

## SENTENTIAE ANTĪQVAE

1. Frāter meus vītam in ōtiō semper aget. (Terence.)
2. Age, age! Iuvā mē! Dūc mē ad secundum fīlium meum. (Terence.—**age, age** = *come on, come on/get moving!*)
3. Ō amīcī, lībertātem perdimus. (Laberius.—**perdere**, *to destroy;* "perdition.")

4. Nova perīcula populō Rōmānō expōnam sine morā. (Cicero.—**expōnere,** *to set forth, expose, explain;* "exponent," "exposition.")

5. Numquam perīculum sine perīculō vincēmus. (Publilius Syrus.)

6. Ex meīs errōribus hominibus rēctum iter dēmōnstrāre possum. (Seneca.— **error, -rōris,** m., = Eng.; "erroneous," "unerring."—**rēctus, -a, -um,** *right;* "rectangle," "rectify"; Eng. "right" is cognate.—**iter, itineris,** n., *road, way;* "itinerant," "itinerary.")

7. Catullus Mārcō Tulliō Cicerōnī magnās grātiās agit. (Catullus.—See "Thanks a Lot, Tully!" Capvt XXVII.)

8. Eximia fōrma virginis oculōs hominum convertit. (Livy.—**eximius, -a, -um,** *extraordinary;* "example," "exempt."—**convertere,** *to turn around, attract;* "converse," "convert.")

9. Agamemnon magnās cōpiās ē terrā Graecā ad Trōiam dūcet, ubi multōs virōs necābit. (Cicero.—**Agamemnon, -nonis,** m.)

*Gold funerary mask of "Agamemnon"*
*Mycenae, 16th cent. B.C.*
*National Archaeological Museum,*
*Athens, Greece*

10. Amor laudis hominēs trahit. (Cicero.)

11. Auctōrēs pācis Caesar cōnservābit. (Cicero.—**auctor, -tōris,** m., *author;* "authority," "authorize."—**Caesar, -saris,** m.; "kaiser," "czar.")

12. Inter multās cūrās labōrēsque carmina scrībere nōn possum. (Horace.—**inter,** prep. + acc., *among;* "interlude," "interval.")

13. Dum in magnā urbe dēclāmās, mī amīce, scrīptōrem Trōiānī bellī in ōtiō relegō. (Horace.—**urbs, urbis,** f., *city;* "urban," "urbane."—**dēclāmāre,** *to declaim;* "declamation," "declamatory."—**Trōiānus, -a, -um.**—**relegere,** *to re-read.*)

14. Nōn vītae, sed scholae, discimus. (*Seneca.—**vītae** and **scholae,** datives expressing purpose; see S.S., p. 492.—**schola, -ae,** f., *school;* "school" comes through Lat. **schola** from Gk. **scholē,** *leisure;* "scholar," "scholastic.")

15. Hominēs, dum docent, discunt. (*Seneca.)

16. Ratiō mē dūcet, nōn fortūna. (Livy.)

### Cicero on the Ethics of Waging War

Cīvitās bellum sine causā bonā aut propter īram gerere nōn dēbet. Sī fortūnās et agrōs vītāsque populī nostrī sine bellō dēfendere poterimus, tum pācem cōnservāre dēbēbimus; sī, autem, nōn poterimus esse salvī et servāre pātriam lībertātem-que nostram sine bellō, bellum erit necessārium. Semper dēbēmus dēmōnstrāre, tamen, magnum officium in bellō, et magnam clēmentiam post victōriam.

Cicero *Off.* 1.11.34–36 and *Rep.* 3.23.34–35 (see **Locī Ant.** VII for a fuller adaptation): The views expressed by Cicero here are adapted from his political treatise on the ideal state, the **Dē Rē Pūblicā** (*On the Republic*), written in the late 50s, before his governorship in Cilicia, and from another of his philosophical works, the **Dē Officiīs** (*On Moral Respon-sibilities*), written in 45–44 B.C., when he was semi-retired from politics and living in self-imposed exile during the dictatorship of Julius Caesar and its aftermath (the same pe-riod during which he composed the *Tusculan Disputations* and *On Friendship*, selections from which you read in Capita IV and V above).—**causa, -ae,** f.; "causal," "accuse."—**aut,** conj., *or.*—**dēfendere:** = Eng.; "defendant" "defensive."—**poterimus . . . dēbēbimus:** The fut. tense in the **PROTASIS**, or "if-clause," of a **CONDITIONAL SENTENCE** may be trans-lated as pres. tense, since Eng. typically employs the pres. in such conditions, the "if" it-self implying fut. action; similarly the auxiliary verb "ought" in Eng. often implies futu-rity and so the fut. of **dēbēre** can often be translated as a pres., though here **dēbēbimus** strictly has the fut. sense of *we will have an obligation (to).*—**autem,** conj., *however.*—**necessārius, -a, -um:** = Eng.; "necessity."—**clēmentia, -ae,** f., *mildness, gentleness, mercy;* "clemency," "inclement."

*QVAESTIŌNĒS:* What specific ethical views on waging war are set forth here, do you agree or disagree with them, and how do they compare with modern American attitudes and practices? Based on this reading, does Cicero seem to have been a hawk, a dove, or a pragmatist?

## SCRĪPTA IN PARIETIBVS

Crēscē<n>s Spatalō sal(ūtem)!

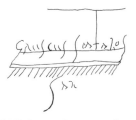

*CIL* 4.4742: From the House of the Cissonii, Reg. VII, Ins. 7. Romans often scribbled a "hello" to their friends—on any convenient wall, or in this case on a column, in a favor-ite hangout; for the nautical form, cf. the graffiti in Capita II–III above. "Crescens" (from **Crēscēns, Crēscentis,** m., but often spelled and doubtless therefore pronounced, as here, without the -n- ) and "Spatalus" are both cognomina.—**salūs, salūtis,** f., *health, safety;*

*greeting(s);* "salutation," "salute"; the word was commonly abbreviated in inscriptions, as here; **salūtem** = ACCUSATIVE OF EXCLAMATION, a grammatical construction indicating emotion and generally with some transitive verb understood, here, e.g., **dīcō.**

## LATĪNA EST GAVDIVM—ET VTILIS!

**Salvēte!** With this chapter's copious new vocabulary, you can see again what a veritable linguistic cornucopia (a "horn of plenty," from **cōpia** + **cornū,** *horn,* which is cognate with "cornet"!) you have in Latin. **Scrīptor** is one of a large group of masculine third declension nouns formed by replacing the -**um** of a verb's fourth principal part with -**or,** a suffix meaning essentially *one who performs the action of the verb.* So, a **monitor, -tōris,** is *one who advises,* i.e., *an advisor;* an **amātor** is *a lover;* etc. What would be the similarly formed nouns from **docēre** and **agō?** Look at the other verbs introduced in this chapter and at the vocabularies in the previous chapters; what other such -**or** nouns can you form and recognize? The point is that if you know one Latin root word, then you will often discover and be able to deduce the meanings of whole families of words: the verb **discere,** e.g., is related to **discipulus** and **discipula,** of course, and also to the noun **disciplīna.** I like to point out that "discipline" is *not* "punishment" but "learning." If you saw the popular 1993 film *Man Without a Face,* you heard lots of Latin, including a favorite old injunction and the motto of England's Winchester College, **aut disce aut discēde,** *either learn or leave* (I have this posted on my office door). You'll be learning, not leaving, I have no doubt, but for now, **valēte, discipulī et discipulae!**

# CAPVT IX ⊐⊐⊐

# Demonstratives *Hic, Ille, Iste;* Special *-īus* Adjectives

## GRAMMATICA

### DEMONSTRATIVE PRONOUNS (sg. *prōnōmen*, pl. *prōnōmina*) AND ADJECTIVES

DEMONSTRATIVES (from **dēmōnstrāre**, *to point out*) are adjectives and pronouns that in general "point" to persons or things that are relatively near to, or far from, a speaker or an addressee. The Latin demonstratives **hic, iste,** and **ille** are variously equivalent to English "this/these" and "that/those"; their declensions generally follow that of **magnus, -a, -um** (Capvt IV), with the exception of the forms underlined in the following paradigms (which, as always, should be memorized by repeating the forms aloud, from left to right, **hic, haec, hoc; huius, huius, huius;** etc.).

| | ille, *that, those* | | | hic, *this, these* | | |
|---|---|---|---|---|---|---|
| | **M.** | **F.** | **N.** | **M.** | **F.** | **N.** |
| **Singular** | | | | | | |
| *Nom.* | ílle | ílla | íllud | hic | haec | hoc |
| *Gen.* | illī́us | illī́us | illī́us | húius | húius | húius |
| *Dat.* | íllī | íllī | íllī | huic | huic | huic |
| *Acc.* | íllum | íllam | íllud | hunc | hanc | hoc |
| *Abl.* | íllō | íllā | íllō | hōc | hāc | hōc |
| **Plural** | | | | | | |
| *Nom.* | íllī | íllae | ílla | hī | hae | haec |
| *Gen.* | illṓrum | illā́rum | illṓrum | hṓrum | hā́rum | hṓrum |
| *Dat.* | íllīs | íllīs | íllīs | hīs | hīs | hīs |
| *Acc.* | íllōs | íllās | ílla | hōs | hās | haec |
| *Abl.* | íllīs | íllīs | íllīs | hīs | hīs | hīs |

Iste, *that (near you), that of yours,* follows the declension of **ille:**

|          | **M.**  | **F.**  | **N.**   |
|----------|---------|---------|----------|
| **Singular** |     |         |          |
| *Nom.*   | íste    | ísta    | ístud    |
| *Gen.*   | istíus  | istíus  | istíus   |
| *Dat.*   | ístī    | ístī    | ístī     |
| *Acc.*   | ístum   | ístam   | ístud    |
| *Abl.*   | ístō    | ístā    | ístō     |
| **Plural** |       |         |          |
| *Nom.*   | ístī    | ístae   | ísta     |
|          | etc.    |         |          |

## Declension

Again, all three demonstratives follow the pattern of **magnus, -a, -um** quite closely, entirely in the plural with the exception of the neuter **haec.** The most striking differences are the genitive and dative singular forms (shared by the nine other special adjectives discussed below) and the -c in several forms of **hic,** a shortened form of the demonstrative enclitic -**ce.** Note that **huius** and **huic** are among the few words in which **ui** functions as a diphthong; for the special pronunciation of **huius** (= **huí-yus**) see the *Intrōductiō* (p. xxxvii—and listen to the CDs, if you have them).

## Usage, Translation, and Word Order

In general the demonstratives point out persons or things either near the speaker (**hic liber,** *this book = this book of mine, this book here*) or near the addressee (**iste liber,** *that book, that book of yours, that book next to you*), or distant from both (**ille liber,** *that book = that book over there, that book of his or hers*). **Ille** and **hic** are sometimes equivalent to *the former* and *the latter,* respectively, and occasionally they have little more force than our personal pronouns, *he, she, it, they;* **ille** can also mean *the famous* (**ille rēx Philippus,** *that famous/well-known king Philip*); **iste** is sometimes best translated *such (as you speak of/refer to),* and occasionally has a disparaging sense, as in **ista īra,** *that awful anger of yours,* **iste tyrannus,** *that despicable tyrant.*

When demonstratives modify nouns, they function as adjectives; since they are by nature emphatic, they regularly precede the nouns they modify. The following examples provide practice with some of the various forms:

| | |
|---|---|
| **hic liber,** *this book* | **hanc cīvitātem,** *this state* |
| **ille liber,** *that book* | **huic cīvitātī,** *to this state* |

| | |
|---|---|
| **illīus librī,** *of that book* | **illī cīvitātī,** *to that state* |
| **illī librī,** *those books* | **illae cīvitātēs,** *those states* |
| **illī librō,** *to that book* | **haec cīvitās,** *this state* |
| **illō librō,** *by that book* | **haec cōnsilia,** *these plans* |
| **istīus amīcī,** *of that friend* (*of yours*) | **hoc cōnsilium,** *this plan* |
| **istī amīcī,** *those friends* (*of yours*) | **hōc cōnsiliō,** *by this plan* |
| **istī amīcō,** *to that friend* (*of yours*) | **huic cōnsiliō,** *to this plan* |

When used alone, demonstratives function as PRONOUNS (words used **prō nōmine,** "in place of a noun," and referring, less specifically than a noun, to a person, place, or thing) and are often best translated as *this man, that woman, these things,* etc., according to their gender, number, and context. (Generally the neuter was used as a pronoun only in the nominative and accusative; in the other cases the demonstrative was usually employed as an adjective agreeing with the noun for "thing," e.g., **huius reī,** *of this thing.*)

| | |
|---|---|
| **hic,** *this man* | **ille,** *that man* |
| **hanc,** *this woman* | **illa,** *that woman* |
| **hunc,** *this man* | **illa,** *those things* |
| **haec,** *this woman* | **huius,** *of this man or woman* |
| **haec,** *these things* | **illī,** *to that man or woman* |
| **istum,** *that man* | **illī,** *those men* |
| **istārum,** *of those women* | |

## SPECIAL -īus ADJECTIVES

Nine common first/second declension adjectives have the genitive singular ending -**īus** and dative singular ending -**ī,** following the pattern of **illīus** and **illī.** Elsewhere in the singular and throughout the plural these are regular adjectives, following the pattern of **magnus, -a, -um,** except for the neuter singular **aliud** (cf. **illud**) and the common use of **alterīus,** borrowed from **alter,** for the genitive singular of **alius, alia, aliud,** instead of the regular **alīus.**

|  | **sōlus, -a, -um,** *alone, only* | | | **alius, alia, aliud,** *another, other* | | |
|---|---|---|---|---|---|---|
| **Singular** | | | | | | |
| *Nom.* | sōlus | sōla | sōlum | álius | ália | áliud |
| *Gen.* | sōlíus | sōlíus | sōlíus | alteríus | alteríus | alteríus |
| *Dat.* | sōlī | sōlī | sōlī | áliī | áliī | áliī |
| *Acc.* | sōlum | sōlam | sōlum | álium | áliam | áliud |
| *Abl.* | sōlō | sōlā | sōlō | áliō | áliā | áliō |
| **Plural** | | | | | | |
| *Nom.* | sōlī | sōlae | sōla | áliī | áliae | ália |
| | etc. | | | etc. | | |

The nine adjectives in this group can be easily remembered via the acronym UNUS NAUTA, each letter of which represents the first letter of one of the adjectives (and which at the same time includes one of the nine words, **ūnus,** and even reminds you that **nauta,** though a first declension noun, is masculine, hence the masculine form **ūnus**). Note, too, that each of the nine words indicates some aspect of number:

| | |
|---|---|
| U | **ūnus, -a, -um (ūnīus,** etc.), *one* |
| N | **nūllus, -a, -um (nūllīus,** etc.), *no, none* |
| U | **ūllus, -a, -um,** *any* |
| S | **sōlus, -a, -um,** *alone, only* |
| N | **neuter, neutra, neutrum,** *neither* |
| A | **alius, -a, -ud,** *another, other* |
| U | **uter, utra, utrum,** *either, which* (*of two*) |
| T | **tōtus, -a, -um,** *whole, entire* |
| A | **alter, altera, alterum,** *the other* (*of two*) |

# VOCĀBVLA

We have seen a few Latin nouns that have irregularities, including variant endings or special meanings for the plural; **locus** in the list below has both masculine and neuter endings in the plural, with some different meanings for each gender, so take careful note. Note too the exceptional **-ud** neuter endings seen in **illud, istud, aliud.** The adverb **nimis** is also unusual in having two essentially opposite meanings, *excessively,* which has negative connotations, and—usually when modifying an adjective or another adverb—*exceedingly,* which can have a positive connotation: choose the one that suits the context. **In,** like **sub,** takes an accusative with verbs of motion (**virōs in hunc locum dūcēbās,** *you were leading the men into this place*), an ablative with verbs of rest (**illī in agrō sunt,** *those men are in the field*).

Remember, as always, to learn these new words by listening and saying them aloud—**audī et prōnūntiā!**—and continue reviewing vocabulary from prior chapters as well. Practice the new forms by declining some noun-adjective phrases of different genders, such as **ille rēx alius, ista soror sōla,** and **hoc studium tōtum.**

**lócus, lócī,** m., *place; passage in literature;* pl., **lóca, locṓrum,** n., *places, region;* **lócī, locṓrum,** m., *passages in literature* (allocate, dislocate, locality, locomotion)

**mórbus, mórbī,** m., *disease, sickness* (morbid, morbidity, morbidness, morbose)

**stúdium, stúdiī,** n. *eagerness, zeal, pursuit, study* (studio, studious; cf. **studēre,** *to be eager for, study* )

**hic, haec, hoc,** *this; the latter;* at times weakened to *he, she, it, they* (ad hoc)

**ílle, ílla, íllud,** *that; the former; the famous; he, she, it, they*

**íste, ísta, ístud,** *that of yours, that; such (as you have, as you speak of);* sometimes with contemptuous force, e.g., *that despicable, that wretched*

**álius, ália, áliud,** *other, another;* **áliī . . . áliī,** *some . . . others* (alias, alibi, alien)

**álter, áltera, álterum,** *the other (of two), second* (alter, alteration, alternate, alternative, altercation, altruism, adulterate, adultery)

**neúter, neútra, neútrum,** *not either, neither* (neutrality, neutralize, neutron)

**núllus, núlla, núllum,** *not any, no, none* (null, nullify, nullification, annul)

**sólus, sóla, sólum,** *alone, only, the only;* **nōn sólum . . . sed étiam,** *not only . . . but also* (sole, solitary, soliloquy, solo, desolate, sullen)

**tótus, tóta, tótum,** *whole, entire* (total, totality, factotum, in toto)

**úllus, úlla, úllum,** *any*

**únus, úna, únum,** *one, single, alone* (unit, unite, union, onion, unanimous, unicorn, uniform, unique, unison, universal, university)

**úter, útra, útrum,** *either, which (of two)*

**énim,** postpositive conj., *for, in fact, truly*

**in,** prep. + acc., *into, toward; against* (also **in** + abl., *in, on,* see Capvt III); in compounds **in-** may also appear as **il-, ir-, im-;** and it may have its literal meanings or have simply an intensive force (intend, invade, impugn): contrast the inseparable negative prefix **in-,** *not, un-, in-,* and for these and other prefixes, see the App., p. 485–89

**nímis** or **nímium,** adv., *too, too much, excessively;* in a positive sense, esp. with adjectives and adverbs, *exceedingly, very* (nimiety)

# LĒCTIŌ ET TRĀNSLĀTIŌ

After completing some of the Self-Tutorial Exercises, check your mastery of the newly introduced demonstratives and **-īus** adjectives by identifying the number, gender, case, and use of those in the chapter's readings. Reminder: when **hic, iste,** and **ille** have no noun to modify, it is often necessary, in order to avoid ambiguity, to supply "man/men," "woman/women," or "thing(s)," depending on the word's number and gender; thus **hic . . . dūcet** in S.A. 2 should be translated *this man will lead,* and not *this will lead.*

## EXERCITĀTIŌNĒS

1. Hic tōtus liber multōs locōs litterārum Rōmānārum laudat.
2. Hī igitur illīs deābus heri grātiās agēbant.
3. Illud dē vitiīs istīus rēgīnae nunc scrībam, et ista poenās dabit.
4. Neuter alterī plēnam cōpiam pecūniae tum dabit.
5. Potestne laus ūllīus terrae esse perpetua?
6. Labor ūnīus numquam poterit hās cōpiās vincere.

7. Mōrēs istīus scrīptōris erant nimis malī.
8. Nūllī magistrī, tamen, sub istō vēra docēre audēbant.
9. Valēbuntne pāx et lībertās in patriā nostrā post hanc victōriam?
10. Dum illī ibi remanent, aliī nihil agunt, aliī discunt.
11. Cicero was writing about the glory of the other man and his wife.
12. The whole state was thanking this man's brother alone.
13. On account of that courage of yours those (men) will lead no troops into these places tomorrow.
14. Will either new book be able to point out and overcome the faults of these times?

## SENTENTIAE ANTĪQVAE

1. Ubi illās nunc vidēre possum? (Terence.)
2. Hic illam virginem in mātrimōnium dūcet. (Terence.—**mātrimōnium, -iī,** n.)
3. Huic cōnsiliō palmam dō. (Terence.—**palma, -ae,** f., *palm branch of* victory; "palmetto," "impalm.")
4. Virtūtem enim illīus virī amāmus. (Cicero.)
5. Sōlus hunc iuvāre potes. (Terence.)
6. Poena istīus ūnīus hunc morbum cīvitātis relevābit sed perīculum semper remanēbit. (Cicero.—**relevāre,** *to relieve, diminish;* "relevant," "relief.")
7. Hī enim dē exitiō huius cīvitātis et tōtīus orbis terrārum cōgitant. (Cicero.—**orbis, -is,** m., *circle, orb;* "orbicular" "orbit." **orbis terrārum,** idiom, *the world.*)
8. Est nūllus locus utrī hominī in hāc terrā. (Martial.)
9. Nōn sōlum ēventus hoc docet—iste est magister stultōrum!—sed etiam ratiō. (Livy.—**ēventus,** *outcome;* "event," "eventual.")

### When I Have . . . Enough!

Habet Āfricānus mīliēns, tamen captat.
Fortūna multīs dat nimis, satis nūllī.

*Martial *Epig.* 12.10: This epigram targets one of those scoundrels known in ancient Rome as **captātōrēs,** lit. *grabbers,* men who practically made a career of kissing up to wealthy patrons—esp. those who were old or sick—with an eye to gaining a favorable place in their wills. The legacy-hunter satirized here, Africanus, is already a millionaire, but is still on the lookout for inheritances; Martial helps emphasize the paradox by FRAMING the first verse with the contrasting verbs—a rhetorical device common in Lat. poetry. Meter: choliambic.—**mīliēns:** from the Lat. word **mīlle,** *thousand,* but often used hyperbolically, as here; freely = *millions;* "millennium," "millipede."—**captāre,** *to hunt for legacies;* "captive," "captor."—**Fortūna:** here PERSONIFIED; like the Greek goddess Tyche, Fortuna was deified and worshiped in temples throughout the Roman empire.

*QVAESTIŌNĒS:* Identify the CHIASMUS in line 2 (if you do not recall the meaning of the term, see the notes on "Dr. Fell," in Capvt VI above); what is the intended effect?

Sī vīs studēre philosophiae animōque, hoc studium nōn potest valēre sine frūgāli-tāte. Haec frūgālitās est paupertās voluntāria. Tolle, igitur, istās excūsātiōnēs: "Nōn-dum satis pecūniae habeō. Sī quandō illud 'satis' habēbō, tum mē tōtum philoso-phiae dabō." Incipe nunc philosophiae, nōn pecūniae, studēre.

Seneca *Ep.* 17.5: Seneca "the Younger" (Lucius Annaeus Seneca, ca. 4 B.C.–A.D. 65), Stoic philosopher, tutor to the young Nero, and author of numerous moralizing essays, epistles, and tragedies, here urges his reader to pursue the life of the mind; accused of involvement in a conspiracy against Nero, he was forced by the emperor to commit suicide.—**vīs:** irreg. form, *you wish.*—**studēre:** one of several Lat. verbs that take a dat. "object" (formally introduced in Capvt XXXV), *to be eager (for), devote oneself (to), pursue;* related to **studium** in the above **Vocābula;** you will be happy to note that a "student" is one "eager" for learning!—**frūgālitās -tātis,** f.: recall that many Lat. third decl. -tās nouns become "-ty" nouns in Eng., like "liberty" from **lībertās.**—**paupertās, -tātis,** f., *small means, poverty;* "pauper," "impoverish"—**voluntārius, -a, -um:** = Eng.; "volunteer," "involuntary."—**tollere,** *to take away;* "extol," "extolment."—**excūsātiō, -ōnis,** f., *excuse;* "excusable."—**nōndum,** adv., *not yet.*— **tōtum:** Lat. often uses an adj. in the pred., where Eng. would employ an adv.; hence *entirely* is a good option here, but what would be a more lit. translation?—**incipe:** imperat., *begin;* "incipient," "inception."

*QVAESTIŌNĒS:* What, in Seneca's opinion, often stands in the way of living a philosophically sound lifestyle? What solution does he propose? What special force does **istās** have here?

*Seneca (the Younger)*
*Museo Archaeologico Nazionale*
*Naples, Italy*

## SCRĪPTA IN PARIETIBVS

P. Cornēlius Faventīnus, tōnsor

CIL 4.8741: Numerous graffiti from Pompeii, like this one scrawled on a column in the Large Palaestra, near the amphitheater (Reg. II), advertised a variety of services available, from architects to tailors, perfumers, and launderers. It was also common in graffiti (and other types of inscriptions as well), esp. when space was limited, to continue a word begun on one line onto the following line, as here with CORNELI/VS FAVENTI/NUS.—P. = **Pūblius;** praenomina, as noted before, were commonly abbreviated.—**tōnsor, -sōris,** m., *barber,* "tonsorial"; barbers were an essential profession in the Roman empire as they are today, and archaeologists have even found in Pompeii a painted campaign notice announcing the support of a barbers' guild for a favorite political candidate.

## ETYMOLOGIA

A few examples of **in-** as a prefix connected with the preposition: invoke, induce, induct, inscribe, inhibit, indebted. Some examples of **in-** as an inseparable negative prefix: invalid, innumerable, insane, insuperable, intolerant, inanimate, infamous, inglorious, impecunious, illiberal, irrational. For both prefixes, see Appendix, p. 487.

Lat. **ille** provided the Romance languages with the definite article ("the") and with pronouns of the third person; and Lat. **ūnus** provided these languages with the indefinite article ("a," "an"). Some of these forms and a few other derivatives are shown in the following table:

| Latin | It. | Sp.. | Port. | Fr. | Old Occ. | Rom. |
|---|---|---|---|---|---|---|
| ille, illa | il, la | el, la | o, a | le, la | lo, la | ăla, aia |
| ille, illa | egli, ella | él, ella | ele, ela | il, elle | el, ela | el, ea |
| ūnus, ūna | un(o), una | un(o), una | um, uma | un, une | uns, una | un |
| tōtus | tutto | todo | todo | tout | totz | tot |
| sōlus | solo | solo | só | seul | sols | solo |
| alter | altro | otro | outro | autre | autre | alt |

Fr. **là** (*there*) comes from **illāc** (**viā**), an adverbial form meaning *there* (*that way*); similarly, It. **là,** Sp. **allá,** Port. **lá/acolá/ali,** Old Occ. **lai/la,** Rom. **acolo.**

## LATĪNA EST GAVDIVM—ET VTILIS!

**Salvēte!** Here is a mysterious old inscription, found on a hitching post out west in Dodge City:

TOTI
EMUL
ESTO

Aha!—looks like the newly learned dat. of **tōtus** + **emul**, like **simul**, *simultaneously?* + some form of **sum, es, est,** the exotic future imperative, perhaps? (NOT!—that old post was just "to tie mules to"!)

Here are some more vocabulary items useful for Latin conversation and other classroom activities: **surgere**, *to rise, stand up* (surge, resurgence, insurgence); **cōnsīdere**, *to sit down* (sedentary); **ambulāre**, *to walk* (ambulatory, amble, ambulance); **aperīre** (fourth conjugation), *to open* (aperture); **claudere**, *to close* (clause, closet); **dēclīnāre; coniugāre; crēta, -ae,** *chalk* (cretaceous); **ērāsūra, -ae,** *eraser;* **stilus, -ī,** *pen* or *pencil* (actually a stylus); **tabula, -ae,** *chalkboard* (tabular, tabulate); **tabella, -ae,** the DIMINUTIVE form of **tabula,** *notebook, writing pad* (tablet); **iānua, -ae,** *door* (janitor, Janus, January); **fenestra, -ae,** *window;* **cella, -ae,** *room* (cell); **sella, -ae,** *chair;* **mēnsa, -ae,** *table;* **podium, -iī.** Now you'll know just what to do when your instructor says to you, **Salvē, discipula** (or **discipule**)! **Quid hodiē agis? Surge ex sellā tuā, ambulā ad tabulam, et dēclīnā** "hic, haec, hoc." Next thing you know, you'll be speaking Latin—not so difficult (even Roman toddlers did!): **semper valēte, amīcae amīcīque!**

*The Large Palaestra, Pompeii, Italy*

# CAPVT X ▨▨▨

# Fourth Conjugation and
# -*iō* Verbs of the Third

## GRAMMATICA

### FOURTH CONJUGATION AND
### THIRD CONJUGATION -*iō* VERBS

This chapter introduces the active voice of the last of the regular conjugations, the fourth conjugation (illustrated here by **audiō, audīre, audīvī, audītum,** *to hear*) and -**iō** verbs of the third (illustrated by **capiō, capere, cēpī, captum,** *to take, seize*). Like the first two conjugations, the fourth is characterized by a long stem vowel; as seen in the paradigm below, the -**ī**- is retained through all the present system tenses (present, future, imperfect), although it is shortened before vowels as well as before final -**t.** Certain third conjugation verbs are formed in the same way in the present system, except that the -**i**- is everywhere short and **e** appears as the stem vowel in the singular imperative (**cape**) and the present active infinitive (**capere**). **Agō** is presented alongside these new paradigms for comparison and review (see Capvt VIII).

### Present Active Indicative

|      |            |          |          |                             |
|------|------------|----------|----------|-----------------------------|
|      | 1. ágō     | aúdi-ō   | cápi-ō   | (*I hear, take*)            |
| Sg.  | 2. ágis    | aúdī-s   | cápi-s   | (*you hear, take*)         |
|      | 3. ágit    | aúdi-t   | cápi-t   | (*he, she, it hears, takes*) |
|      | 1. ágimus  | audī́mus | cápimus  | (*we hear, take*)          |
| Pl.  | 2. ágitis  | audī́tis | cápitis  | (*you hear, take*)         |
|      | 3. águnt   | aúdiunt  | cápiunt  | (*they hear, take*)        |

## Future Active Indicative

|     |            |             |            |                                  |
|-----|------------|-------------|------------|----------------------------------|
|     | 1. ágam    | aúdi-am     | cápi-am    | (*I will hear, take*)            |
| Sg. | 2. ágēs    | aúdi-ēs     | cápi-ēs    | (*you will hear, take*)          |
|     | 3. áget    | aúdi-et     | cápi-et    | (*he, she, it will hear, take*)  |
|     | 1. agḗmus  | audiḗmus    | capiḗmus   | (*we will hear, take*)           |
| Pl. | 2. agḗtis  | audiḗtis    | capiḗtis   | (*you will hear, take*)          |
|     | 3. ágent   | aúdient     | cápient    | (*they will hear, take*)         |

## Imperfect Active Indicative

|     |            |              |             |                                      |
|-----|------------|--------------|-------------|--------------------------------------|
|     | 1. agḗbam  | audi-ḗbam    | capi-ḗbam   | (*I was hearing, taking*)           |
| Sg. | 2. agḗbās  | audi-ḗbās    | capi-ḗbās   | (*you were hearing, taking*)        |
|     | 3. agḗbat  | audi-ḗbat    | capi-ḗbat   | (*he, she, it was hearing, taking*) |
|     | 1. agēbámus| audiēbámus   | capiēbámus  | (*we were hearing, taking*)         |
| Pl. | 2. agēbátis| audiēbátis   | capiēbátis  | (*you were hearing, taking*)        |
|     | 3. agḗbant | audiḗbant    | capiḗbant   | (*they were hearing, taking*)       |

## Present Active Imperative

|     |            |           |           |                  |
|-----|------------|-----------|-----------|------------------|
| Sg. | 2. áge     | aúdī      | cápe      | (*hear, take!*)  |
| Pl. | 2. ágite   | audī́-te   | cápi-te   | (*hear, take!*)  |

## Conjugation of *Audiō*

The **-īre** distinguishes the infinitive of the fourth conjugation from those of the other conjugations (**laud-áre, mon-ére, ág-ere, aud-íre, cáp-ere**).

As in the case of the first two conjugations, the rule for the formation of the present indicative is to add the personal endings to the present stem (**audī-**). In the third person plural this rule would give us *audi-nt but the actual form is **audi-unt,** an ending reminiscent of **águnt.**

For the future of **audiō** a good rule of thumb is this: shorten the ī of the present stem, **audi-,** and add the future endings of **agō**: -am, -ēs, -et, -ēmus, -ētis, -ent. Once again, as in the third conjugation, -ē- is the characteristic vowel of the future.

The imperfect is formed with -iē-, instead of simply the stem vowel -ī-, before the -bā- tense sign, so that the forms are **audiēbam, audiēbās,** etc. (rather than *audībam, etc., as might be expected).

The imperatives, however, follow exactly the pattern of the first and second conjugations, i.e., the singular is identical to the present stem (**audī**) and the plural adds -te (**audīte**).

### Conjugation of *Capiō*

As seen from its short **e** stem vowel, **capere** is clearly an infinitive of the third conjugation, not of the fourth. The imperative forms also show that this is a verb of the third conjugation.

The present, future, and imperfect indicative of **capiō** follow the pattern of **audiō**, except that **capiō**, like **agō**, has a short **-i-** in **cápis, cápimus, cápitis.**

Note carefully again that **-i-** appears in all present system active indicative forms for both fourth conjugation and third **-iō** verbs, and remember that two vowels, **-iē-**, appear before the **-bā-** in the imperfect.

# VOCĀBVLA

Without careful vocabulary study, third conjugation **-iō** verbs and fourth conjugation verbs may be easily confused; the second principal part is a sure indicator: when you see, and *hear* and *say* (**semper audī et prōnūntiā!**), the accented, long-ī stem vowel, you'll know the verb is fourth conjugation. Some other words you should beware of confusing: **via** and **vīta, dīcō** and **dūcō** (and don't forget those irregular imperatives, **dīc, dūc, fac, fer**).

You'll see from the list below that the preposition **cum,** *with,* frequently appears in one form or another as a prefix; for this, and numerous other prefixes and suffixes that appear commonly in both Latin words and their English derivatives, take a close look now at "Some Etymological Aids," in the App., p. 485–91. After memorizing this new vocabulary, practice with some of the new verbs by writing out conjugations of **vīvō, fugiō,** and **veniō** in the three tenses you have learned, plus the imperatives; compare your work with the paradigms in the **Summārium Fōrmārum**, p. 501, and recite all the forms aloud.

**amīcítia, amīcítiae,** f., *friendship* (amicable, amity; cf. **amō, amīca, amīcus**)
**cupíditās, cupiditấtis,** f., *desire, longing, passion; cupidity, avarice* (Cupid)
**hốra, hốrae,** f., *hour, time* (horoscope: from Lat., via Fr., but ultimately Gk.)
**nātū́ra, nātū́rae,** f., *nature* (natural, preternatural, supernatural)
**senéctūs, senectū́tis,** f., *old age* (senescent, senility)
**tímor, timốris,** m., *fear* (timorous, timid)
**vḗritās, vēritấtis,** f., *truth* (verify, veritable, verity)
**vía, víae,** f., *way, road, street* (via, viaduct, deviate, devious, obvious, pervious, impervious, previous, trivial, voyage, envoy)
**volúptās, voluptấtis,** f., *pleasure* (voluptuary, voluptuous, voluptuosity)
**beấtus, beấta, beấtum,** *happy, fortunate, blessed* (beatific, beatify, beatitude, Beatrice)
**quóniam,** conj., *since, inasmuch as*
**cum,** prep. + abl., *with.* As a prefix **cum** may appear as **com-, con-, cor-, col-, co-,**

and means *with, together, completely,* or simply has an intensive force (complete, connect, corroborate, collaborate; see App., p. 486)

**aúdiō, audíre, audívī, audítum,** *to hear, listen to* (audible, audience, audit, audition, auditory; obey, through Fr. **obéir** from Lat. **obēdīre** = ob + **audīre**)

**cápiō, cápere, cḗpī, cáptum,** *to take, capture, seize, get.* In compounds the -a- becomes -i-, -cipiō (see App., p. 484): **ac-cipiō, ex-cipiō, in-cipiō, re-cipiō,** etc. (capable, capacious, capsule, captious, captive, captor)

**dícō, dícere, díxī, díctum,** *to say, tell, speak; name, call* (dictate, dictum, diction, dictionary, dight, ditto, contradict, indict, edict, verdict)

**fáciō, fácere, fḗcī, fáctum,** *to make, do, accomplish.* In compounds the -a- becomes -i-, -ficiō (App., p. 484): **cōn-ficiō, per-ficiō,** etc. (facile, fact, faction, factotum, facsimile, faculty, fashion, feasible, feat, hacienda; cf. **officium**)

**fúgiō, fúgere, fū́gī, fúgitūrum,** *to flee, hurry away; escape; go into exile; avoid, shun* (fugitive, fugue, centrifugal, refuge, subterfuge)

**véniō, veníre, vḗnī, véntum,** *to come* (advent, adventure, avenue, convene, contravene, covenant, event, inconvenient, intervene, parvenu, prevent, provenience, venue)

**invéniō, inveníre, invḗnī, invéntum,** *to come upon, find* (invent, inventor, inventive, inventory)

**vívō, vívere, vīxī, víctum,** *to live* (convivial, revive, survive, vivacity, vivid, vivify, viviparous, vivisection, victual, vittle; cf. **vīta**)

# LĒCTIŌ ET TRĀNSLĀTIŌ

After memorizing the paradigms and vocabulary, and practicing with the Self-Tutorial Exercises, search for all **-iō** verbs in the chapter's readings, and identify their person, number, tense, mood (indicative or imperative), and whether they are third or fourth conjugation. Remember to read each sentence and passage aloud, think what the Latin is saying, and then write out translations that are at once accurate and idiomatic.

## EXERCITĀTIŌNĒS

1. Quid discipulae hodiē discere dēbent?
2. Frātrēs nihil cum ratiōne heri gerēbant.
3. Ille magnam virtūtem labōris et studiī docēre saepe audet.
4. Hic dē senectūte scrībēbat; ille, dē amōre; et alius, dē lībertāte.
5. Ex librīs ūnīus virī nātūram hārum īnsidiārum dēmōnstrābimus.
6. Istī sōlī victōriam nimis amant; neuter dē pāce cōgitat.
7. Ubi cīvitās ūllōs virōs magnae sapientiae audiet?
8. Ex illīs terrīs in haec loca cum amīcīs vestrīs venīte.

9. Tamen post paucās hōrās sorōrem illīus invenīre poterāmus.
10. Cōpiae vestrae utrum virum ibi numquam capient.
11. Alter Graecus remedium huius morbī inveniēbat.
12. Carmina illīus scrīptōris sunt plēna nōn sōlum vēritātis sed etiam virtūtis.
13. We shall then come to your land without any friends.
14. While he was living in that place, nevertheless, we were able to have no peace.
15. The whole state now shuns and will always shun these vices.
16. He will, therefore, thank the queen and the whole people.

## SENTENTIAE ANTĪQVAE

1. Cupiditātem pecūniae glōriaeque fugite. (Cicero.)
2. Officium meum faciam. (*Terence.)
3. Fāma tua et vīta fīliae tuae in perīculum crās venient. (Terence.)
4. Vīta nōn est vīvere sed valēre. (Martial.)
5. Semper magnō cum timōre incipiō dīcere. (Cicero.—**incipiō, -ere,** *to begin;* "incipient," "inception.")
6. Sī mē dūcēs, Mūsa, corōnam magnā cum laude capiam. (Lucretius.—**Mūsa, -ae,** f., *Muse;* "museum," "music."—**corōna, -ae,** f., *crown;* "coronation," "coronary.")

*Marble statue of Calliope,*
*muse of epic poetry. Hadrianic copy,*
*probably of a 2nd cent. B.C.*
*original by Philiskos of Rhodes*
*Museo Nazionale Romano*
*(Palazzo Altemps), Rome, Italy*

7. Vīve memor mortis; fugit hōra. (Persius.—**memor**, adj., nom. sg., *mindful;* "memorial," "commemorate."—**mors, mortis,** f., *death;* "mortify," "postmortem.")

8. Rapite, amīcī, occāsiōnem dē hōrā. (Horace.—**rapiō, -ere,** *to snatch, seize;* "rapid," "rapture," "ravage."—**occāsiō, -ōnis,** f., *opportunity;* "occasion," "occasional.")

9. Paucī veniunt ad senectūtem. (*Cicero.)

10. Sed fugit, intereā, fugit tempus. (Vergil.—**intereā**, adv., *meanwhile.*—Why is the verb repeated?)

11. Fāta viam invenient. (*Vergil.—**fātum, -ī,** n., *fate;* "fatal," "fateful.")

12. Bonum virum nātūra, nōn ōrdō, facit. (*Publilius Syrus.—**ōrdō, -dinis,** m., *rank;* "ordain," "ordinary.")

13. Obsequium parit amīcōs; vēritās parit odium. (Cicero.—**obsequium, -ī,** n., *compliance;* "obsequent," "obsequious."—**pariō, -ere,** *to produce;* "parent," "postpartum."—**odium, -ī,** n., *hate;* "odious," "annoy.")


## The Incomparable Value of Friendship

Nihil cum amīcitiā possum comparāre; dī hominibus nihil melius dant. Pecūniam aliī mālunt; aliī, corpora sāna; aliī, fāmam glōriamque; aliī, voluptātēs—sed hī virī nimium errant, quoniam illa sunt incerta et ex fortūnā veniunt, nōn ex sapientiā. Amīcitia enim ex sapientiā et amōre et mōribus bonīs et virtūte venit; sine virtūte amīcitia nōn potest esse. Sī nūllōs amīcōs habēs, habēs vītam tyrannī; sī inveniēs amīcum vērum, vīta tua erit beāta.

Cicero *Amīc.* (see **Locī Ant.** VI for more extensive excerpts): Before reading this selection, look back at the passage from "On Friendship" that was introduced in Capvt IV, and you will realize how much your Latin skills have improved over the course of just the past few chapters.—**comparāre:** = Eng.; "comparable," "comparison." A common mistranslation of the opening clause is "nothing can compare with . . .": before you make this mistake, look at the ending of **possum.**—**melius:** *better;* "ameliorate."—**mālunt:** *prefer.*—**incertus, -a, -um,** *uncertain;* "certitude."—**inveniēs:** as noted before, a fut. tense verb in the "if-clause," or PROTASIS, of a CONDITIONAL SENT. may be translated as pres. tense, in keeping with Eng. idiom.

*QVAESTIŌNĒS:* What major points is Cicero making here? What are the full implications of his remark about the personal attributes that form the basis of friendship (**amīcitia . . . venit**); do you agree, as an ancient Stoic would, that genuine friendship cannot truly exist in the absence of these traits? What does Cicero mean when he compares a friendless existence to a **vīta tyrannī**? Identify one or two of the most striking stylistic devices in the passage, and comment on their rhetorical effect.

## SCRĪPTA IN PARIETIBVS

Pompeiānīs ubique sal(ūtem)!

*CIL* 4.9143: The person who scribbled this graffito in the atrium of the House of Fabius Rufus (Reg. VII, Ins. 16) was quite generous in his good wishes for one and all! The mark between **POMPEIANIS** and **VBIQVE** seems to be a PUNCTUM, a mark of punctuation used only occasionally in graffiti, but often in other types of inscriptions, to indicate the separation between two words. The welcoming sentiment of this graffito inspired the title of a musical score for flute and voice, "Pompeianis Ubique Salutem," by the early 20th-century composer Wolfgang Hildemann.—**Pompeiānus, -a, -um,** *at/of Pompeii, Pompeian.*—**ubique,** adv., *anywhere; everywhere;* "ubiquitous."—**salūtem:** do you recall the meaning of **salūs,** and why the acc. is employed here, from the graffito in Capvt VIII? The word is related to **salveō.**

## LATĪNA EST GAVDIVM—ET VTILIS!

**Salvēte!** Do you remember being introduced in Capvt VIII to masculine **-or** nouns formed from the fourth principal parts of verbs? Well, there are lots of others related to the new verbs in this chapter: **audītor,** *auditor, listener,* is one; can you find others? Look at the section on Etymological Aids in the App., p. 489–90 below, and you'll learn a great deal more about word families, including another group of third declension nouns, mostly feminine, formed by adding the suffix **-iō (-iōnis, -iōnī,** etc.) to the same fourth principal part. Such nouns generally indicate the performance or result of an action, e.g., **audītiō, audītiōnis,** f., *listening, hearing,* and many have English derivatives in *-ion* (like "audition"). Another example from this chapter's **Vocābula** is **dictiō,** (*the act of*) *speaking, public speaking,* which gives us such derivatives as "diction" (the manner or style of one's speaking or writing), "dictionary," "benediction," "contradiction," etc. How many other Latin nouns and English derivatives can you identify from the new verbs in this chapter? Happy hunting, but in the meantime **tempus fugit,** so I'll have to say **valēte!**

# CAPVT XI 🮱🮱🮱

# Personal Pronouns *Ego, Tū,* and *Is*; Demonstratives *Is* and *Īdem*

## GRAMMATICA

### PERSONAL PRONOUNS

A **PERSONAL PRONOUN** is a word used "in place of a noun" (the literal meaning of **prōnōmen**) to designate a particular person, from the speaker's point of view: the first person pronoun indicates the speaker herself or himself (**ego/nōs,** *I/me, we/ us*), the second person pronoun indicates the person(s) addressed by the speaker (**tū/vōs,** *you*), and the third person indicates the person(s) or thing(s) the speaker is talking about (**is, ea, id,** and their plurals, *he/him, she/her, it, they/them*). You should keep a list of the types of pronouns you have learned, including the demonstratives **hic, iste, ille** introduced in Capvt IX.

### The First and Second Person Pronouns *Ego/Nōs, Tū/Vōs*

While the first and second person pronouns are irregular in form, their declensions are similar to one another and are easily memorized; note that there are two different forms for the genitive plural.

|  | **Singular** |  | **Plural** |  |
|---|---|---|---|---|
| **1st Person—Ego,** *I/we* |  |  |  |  |
| *Nom.* | égo | *(I)* | nōs | *(we)* |
| *Gen.* | méī | *(of me)* | nóstrum | *(of us)* |
|  |  |  | nóstrī | *(of us)* |
| *Dat.* | míhi | *(to/for me)* | nṓbīs | *(to/for us)* |
| *Acc.* | mē | *(me)* | nōs | *(us)* |
| *Abl.* | mē | *(by/with/from me)* | nṓbīs | *(by/with/from us)* |

**2nd Person—Tū,** *You*

| | | | | | |
|---|---|---|---|---|---|
| *Nom.* | tū | *(you)* | vōs | *(you)* | |
| *Gen.* | túī | *(of you)* | véstrum | *(of you)* | |
| | | | véstrī | *(of you)* | |
| *Dat.* | tíbi | *(to/for you)* | vōbīs | *(to/for you)* | |
| *Acc.* | tē | *(you)* | vōs | *(you)* | |
| *Abl.* | tē | *(by/with/from you)* | vōbīs | *(by/with/from you)* | |

### The Third Person Pronoun *Is, Ea, Id*

The declension of the pronoun **is, ea, id** is comparable to those of **hic** and **ille** (Capvt IX), i.e., the pattern is that of **magnus, -a, -um** (Capvt IV), with the exception of the ten forms underlined below; note that the base is **e-** in all but the four forms underlined and in bold below (including the alternate nominative plural **iī**). For the pronunciation of **eius**, something like "ei-yus," review the discussion of consonantal **i** in the *Intrōductiō* (and listen to the Capvt XI pronoun declensions on the CDs, if you have them).

| | **Masculine** | | **Feminine** | | **Neuter** | |
|---|---|---|---|---|---|---|
| **Singular** | | | | | | |
| *N.* | is | *(he, this man)* | éa | *(she, this woman)* | id | *(it, this thing)* |
| *G.* | éius | *(of him, his)* | éius | *(of her, her)* | éius | *(of it, its)* |
| *D.* | éī | *(to/for him)* | éī | *(to/for her)* | éī | *(to/for it)* |
| *A.* | éum | *(him)* | éam | *(her)* | id | *(it)* |
| *A.* | éō | *(by/with/from him)* | éā | *(by/with/from her)* | éō | *(by/with/from it)* |
| **Plural** | | | | | | |
| *N.* | éī, íī | *(they, m.)* | éae | *(they, f.)* | éa | *(they, n.)* |
| *G.* | eṓrum | *(of them, their)* | eā́rum | *(of them, their)* | eṓrum | *(of them, their)* |
| *D.* | éīs | *(to/for them)* | éīs | *(to/for them)* | éīs | *(to/for them)* |
| *A.* | éōs | *(them)* | éās | *(them)* | éa | *(them)* |
| *A.* | éīs | *(by/with/from them)* | éīs | *(by/with/from them)* | éīs | *(by/with/from them)* |

### Usage and Translation

Since these pronouns are employed as substitutes for nouns, they are in general used as their corresponding nouns would be: as subjects, direct objects, indirect objects, objects of prepositions, etc.:

**Ego tibi (vōbīs) librōs dabō.** *I shall give the books to you.*
**Ego eī (eīs) librōs dabō.** *I shall give the books to him* or *her (to them).*

**Tū mē (nōs) nōn capiēs.** *You will not capture me (us).*
**Eī id ad nōs mittent.** *They (m.) will send it (this thing) to us.*
**Vōs eōs (eās, ea) nōn capiētis.** *You will not seize them (those men/women/ things).*
**Eae ea ad tē mittent.** *They (f.) will send them (those things) to you.*

Note, however, that the Romans used the nominatives of the pronouns (**ego, tū,** etc.) *only* when they wished to *stress* the subject. Commonly, therefore, the pronominal subject of a Latin verb is not indicated except by the verb's ending.

**Eīs pecūniam dabō.** *I shall give them money.*
**Ego eīs pecūniam dabō; quid tū dabis?** *I shall give them money; what will **you** give?*

Another point of usage: when **cum** was employed with the ablative of the personal pronouns, it was generally suffixed to the pronoun, rather than preceding it as a separate preposition: **eōs nōbīscum ibi inveniēs,** *you will find them there with us.*

Note also that the genitives of **ego** and **tū** (namely **meī, nostrum, nostrī; tuī, vestrum, vestrī**) were employed in constructions to be introduced later in the book and were *not* used to indicate possession, for which the Romans preferred instead to employ the POSSESSIVE ADJECTIVES you have already learned:

| | |
|---|---|
| **meus, -a, -um,** *my* | **tuus, -a, -um,** *your* |
| **noster, -tra, -trum,** *our* | **vester, -tra, -trum,** *your* |

English usage is comparable: just as Latin says **liber meus,** not **liber meī,** so English says *my book,* not *the book of me.*

The genitives of **is, ea, id,** on the other hand, *were* quite commonly used to indicate possession. Hence, while **eius** can sometimes be translated *of him/of her/ of it,* it is very often best translated *his/her/its;* likewise **eōrum/eārum/eōrum** can be rendered *of them,* but its common possessive usage should be translated *their.* Study the possessives in the following examples, in which **mittam** governs all the nouns:

**Mittam** (*I shall send*)

| | |
|---|---|
| **pecūniam meam** (*my money*). | **amīcōs meōs** (*my friends*). |
| **pecūniam nostram** (*our money*). | **amīcōs nostrōs** (*our friends*). |
| **pecūniam tuam** (*your money*). | **amīcōs tuōs** (*your friends*). |
| **pecūniam vestram** (*your money*). | **amīcōs vestrōs** (*your friends*). |
| **pecūniam eius** (*his, her money*). | **amīcōs eius** (*his, her friends*). |
| **pecūniam eōrum** (*their money*). | **amīcōs eōrum** (*their friends*). |
| **pecūniam eārum** (*their money*). | **amīcōs eārum** (*their friends*). |

The possessive pronominal adjectives of the first and the second persons naturally agree with their noun in *gender, number,* and *case,* as all adjectives agree with their nouns. The possessive genitives **eius, eōrum,** and **eārum,** being pronouns, remain unchanged regardless of the gender, number, and case of the noun on which they depend.

A last important reminder regarding possessives is the fact that Latin routinely omits them, except for emphasis or to avoid ambiguity. English, on the other hand, employs possessives regularly, and so you will often need to supply them in translating from Latin (just as you do the articles "a," "an," and "the"), in order to produce an idiomatic translation; e.g., **patriam amāmus,** *we love our country.*

## *Is, ea, id* AS DEMONSTRATIVE

While commonly serving as Latin's third person pronoun, **is/ea/id** was also used as a demonstrative, somewhat weaker in force than **hic** or **ille** and translatable as either *this/these* or *that/those.* In general you should translate the word in this way when you find it immediately preceding and modifying a noun, i.e., in the same number, gender, and case; contrast the following:

> **Is est bonus.** *He is good.*
> **Is amīcus est vir bonus.** *This friend is a good man.*
> **Vidēsne eam.** *Do you see her?*
> **Vidēsne eam puellam.** *Do you see that girl?*

## THE DEMONSTRATIVE *Īdem, eadem, idem*

The common demonstrative **īdem, eadem, idem,** *the same* (*man, woman, thing*), is formed simply by adding **-dem** directly to the forms of **is, ea, id,** e.g., gen. **eiusdem,** dat. **eīdem,** etc.; besides the singular nominatives **īdem** (m., for \***isdem**) and **idem** (n., rather than \***iddem**), the only forms not following this pattern exactly are those shown below, where final **-m** changes to **-n-** before the **-dem** suffix (for the full declension of **īdem,** see the **Summārium Fōrmārum,** p. 498 below).

|  | Masculine | Feminine | Neuter |
|---|---|---|---|
| **Singular** |  |  |  |
| *Acc.* | eúndem | eándem | ídem |
| **Plural** |  |  |  |
| *Gen.* | eōrúndem | eārúndem | eōrúndem |

Like other demonstratives, **īdem** may function as an adjective or a pronoun: **eōsdem mittō,** *I am sending the same men;* **dē eādem ratiōne cōgitābāmus,** *we were thinking about the same plan.*

# VOCĀBVLA

One unusual item in this list is the noun **nēmō**, which–logically, since it means *no one*–occurs only in the singular. A further irregularity is that **nūllīus** and **nūllō** or **nūllā**, forms of **nūllus, -a, -um** (Capvt IX), were usually employed instead of the expected **nēminis** and **nēmine**, an example of a linguistic phenomenon called **SUP-PLETION**, the use of one word as part of the form set of another, though the two are not cognate; examples in English include the verb "go, went, gone" ("went" being originally past tense of "to wend") and irregular adjective comparisons such as "good, better, best." The conjunction **autem** is also exceptional in that (like **nimis**, discussed in the Capvt IX **Vocābula**) it has two quite opposite meanings, *however* and *moreover:* choose the former if the statement the word introduces seems contrary to what might be expected from the preceding statement, the latter if the second statement reinforces the first. Practice with some of the new words by writing out declensions of **id caput** and **īdem cōnsul** and comparing your work with the paradigms in the **Summārium Fōrmārum,** p. 498.

**cáput, cápitis,** n., *head; leader; beginning; life; heading; chapter* (cape = headland, capital, capitol, capitulate, captain, chief, chieftain, chef, cattle, chattels, cadet, cad, achieve, decapitate, recapitulate, precipice, occiput, sinciput, kerchief)

**cónsul, cónsulis,** m., *consul* (consular, consulate, consulship; cf. **cōnsilium**)

**nēmō, nūllíus, néminī, néminem, nū́llō** or **nū́llā,** m. or f., *no one, nobody* (Jules Verne's "Captain Nemo," nullify; cf. **nūllus**)

**égo, méī,** *I* (ego, egoism, egotism, egotistical; cf. **meus, noster**)

**tū, túī,** *you* (cf. **tuus, vester**)

**is, éa, id,** *this, that; he, she, it* (i.e. = **id est,** *that is*)

**ī́dem, éadem, ī́dem,** *the same* (the bibliographic abbreviation id. = **idem,** identical, identity, identify)

**amī́cus, amī́ca, amī́cum,** *friendly* (amicable, amiable, amiably—cf. **amō** and the nouns **amīcus, amīca,** and **amīcitia**).

**cā́rus, cā́ra, cā́rum,** *dear* (caress, charity, charitable, cherish)

**quod,** conj., *because*

**néque, nec,** conj. *and not, nor;* **néque . . . néque** or **nec . . . nec,** *neither . . . nor*

**aútem,** postpositive conj., *however; moreover*

**béne,** adv. of **bonus,** *well, satisfactorily, quite* (benediction, benefit, benefactor, beneficent, benevolent)

**étiam,** adv., *even, also*

**intéllegō, intéllegere, intélléxī, intelléctum,** *to understand* (intelligent, intellegentsia, intelligible, intellect, intellectual)

**míttō, míttere, mī́sī, míssum,** *to send, let go* (admit, commit, emit, omit, permit, promise, remit, submit, transmit, compromise, demise)

séntiō, sentíre, sḗnsī, sḗnsum, *to feel, perceive, think, experience* (assent, consent, dissent, presentiment, resent, sentient, sentimental, scent)

# LĒCTIŌ ET TRĀNSLĀTIŌ

Before translating, scan through the readings for the newly introduced personal pronouns and demonstratives and identify the number, gender, case, and use of each. Reminder: when a form of **is, ea, id** precedes a noun and agrees with it in number, gender, and case, it functions as a demonstrative and should be translated as "this" or "that," e.g., **eam discipulam** in Ex. 5; otherwise the word functions as a pronoun, as in Ex. 1. Remember that **tēcum, nōbīscum,** etc., were regularly employed instead of **cum tē** and **cum nōbīs.** And don't forget to read aloud and for comprehension, before attempting to translate.

## EXERCITĀTIŌNĒS

1. Eum ad eam cum aliō agricolā heri mittēbant.
2. Tū autem filiam beātam eius nunc amās.
3. Propter amīcitiam, ego hoc faciō. Quid tū faciēs, mī amīce?
4. Vōsne eāsdem litterās ad eum mittere crās audēbitis?
5. Venī, mī amīce, et dūc mē ad eius discipulam (ad eam discipulam), amābō tē.
6. Post labōrem eius grātiās magnās eī agēmus.
7. Tūne vēritātem in eō librō dēmōnstrās?
8. Audē, igitur, esse semper īdem.
9. Venitne nātūra mōrum nostrōrum ex nōbīs sōlīs?
10. Dum ratiō nōs dūcet, valēbimus et multa bene gerēmus.
11. Illum timōrem in hōc virō ūnō invenīmus.
12. Sine labōre enim nūlla pāx in cīvitātem eōrum veniet.
13. Studium nōn sōlum pecūniae sed etiam voluptātis hominēs nimium trahit; aliī eās cupiditātēs vincere possunt, aliī nōn possunt.
14. His life was always dear to the whole people.
15. You will often find them and their friends with me in the same place.
16. We, however, shall now capture their forces on this road.
17. Since I was saying the same things to him about you and his other sisters, your brother was not listening.

## SENTENTIAE ANTĪQVAE

1. Virtūs tua mē amīcum tibi facit. (Horace.)
2. Id sōlum est cārum mihi. (Terence.—**cārus** and other adjectives indicating relationship or attitude often take the dat., translated *to* or *for;* see Capvt XXXV).

3. Sī valēs, bene est; ego valeō. (Pliny.—**bene est,** idiom, *it's good/that's good.*)
4. Bene est mihi quod tibi bene est. (Pliny.)
5. "Valē." "Et tū bene valē." (Terence.)
6. Quid hī dē tē nunc sentiunt? (Cicero.)
7. Omnēs idem sentiunt. (*Cicero.—**omnēs,** *all men,* nom. pl.; "omnifarious," "omnivore.")
8. Videō nēminem ex eīs hodiē esse amīcum tibi. (Cicero.—The subject of an infin. is regularly in the acc., hence **nēminem;** add this to your list of acc. case uses, and see Capvt XXV.)
9. Hominēs vidēre caput Cicerōnis in Rōstrīs poterant. (Livy.—Antony proscribed Cicero and had the great orator's head cut off and displayed on the Rostra! —**rōstra, -ōrum;** see **Etymologia** below.)
10. Nōn omnēs eadem amant aut eāsdem cupiditātēs studiaque habent. (Horace.)
11. Nec tēcum possum vīvere nec sine tē (*Martial.)
12. Vērus amīcus est alter īdem. (Cicero.—Explain how **alter īdem** can mean "a second self.")

## Cicero Denounces Catiline in the Senate

Quid facis, Catilīna? Quid cōgitās? Sentīmus magna vitia īnsidiāsque tuās. Ō tempora! Ō mōrēs! Senātus haec intellegit, cōnsul videt. Hic tamen vīvit. Vīvit? Etiam in senātum venit; etiam nunc cōnsilia agere audet; oculīs dēsignat ad mortem nōs! Et nōs, bonī virī, nihil facimus! Ad mortem tē, Catilīna, cōnsul et senātus dūcere dēbent. Cōnsilium habēmus et agere dēbēmus; sī nunc nōn agimus, nōs, nōs— apertē dīcō—errāmus! Fuge nunc, Catilīna, et dūc tēcum amīcōs tuōs. Nōbīscum remanēre nōn potes; nōn tē, nōn istōs, nōn cōnsilia vestra tolerābō!

Cicero *Cat.* 1.1.ff: Lucius Sergius Catilina, "Catiline" as he is commonly called, masterminded a political conspiracy during Cicero's consulship; Catiline had raised an army and his plans involved a violent take-over of the government and assassination of Cicero himself; this excerpt is adapted from the **In Catilīnam** I, Cicero's first oration "Against Catiline," which he delivered, after uncovering the plot, in an emergency meeting of the senate, in October of 63 B.C. Catiline, as a Roman senator, was himself present, and the excerpt here is alternately addressed to him and to the other senators. You will read more excerpts from the Catilinarian orations—Cicero delivered four altogether—in Capita XIV and XX, below, and extensive unadapted excerpts appear in **Locī Im.** V–VI, p. 366–74.—**senātus:** *senate;* "senescence," "senility."—**dēsignāre:** = Eng.; "design," "designation."—**mors, mortis,** f., *death;* "postmortem," "rigor mortis."—**apertē,** adv., *openly;* "aperture," "overt.")

*QVAESTIŌNĒS:* What course of action does Cicero believe he and the senate should ultimately take? But what is he urging Catiline to do? What range of emotions does he attempt to arouse in his fellow senators? in Catiline? One device Cicero employs exten-

Cicero Denouncing Catiline in the Roman Senate. *Wall painting.*
*Cesare Maccari, 19th century. Palazzo Madama, Rome, Italy*

sively here is ANAPHORA, the emphatic repetition of words or phrases; identify several instances of this device and comment on their effect. What other rhetorical strategies does he employ here in order to arouse his audience?

## SCRĪPTA IN PARIETIBVS

Hecticē, pūpe, "va(lē)" Mercātor tibi dīcit.

*CIL* 4.4485 (Reg. VI, Ins. 13, House of Sextus Pompeius Axiochus): Mercator wrote this note carefully in tall, 4"-high letters, with puncta (see *CIL* 4.9143 in Capvt X) separating all the words, to his ladyfriend Hectice: both names are likely cognomina (unless **mercātor** is simply a common noun, = *merchant;* "mercantile," "merchandise"); **Hecticē** is Greek, suggesting the lady may have been a slave or a freedwoman, and voc. case. —**pūpe:** = **pūpa**, from **pūpa, -ae,** f., *girl, doll;* "pupa," "pupal."

## ETYMOLOGIA

**Cārus,** in this chapter's **Vocābula,** sometimes meant *expensive,* like Eng. "dear" and Fr. **cher.** The **rōstra** mentioned in S.A. 9 were in origin the ramming beaks of ships captured in a naval battle at Antium (Anzio) in 338 B.C. and affixed to the speakers' platform in the Roman Forum to attest the victory; the beaks ultimately gave their name to the platform, and both "rostrum" and "rostra" continue in Eng. usage today as terms for a dais or pulpit for public speakers.

Some Romance derivatives from the Lat. personal pronouns follow:

| Latin | Italian | Spanish | Portuguese | French |
|-------|---------|---------|------------|--------|
| ego, tū | io, tu | yo, tu | eu, tu | je, tu |
| mihi, tibi | mi, ti | | me/mim, te/ti | |
| mē, tē | me, te | me, te | me, te | me, moi, te, toi |
| nōs, vōs (nom.) | noi, voi | nosotros, vosotros | nós, vós | nous, vous |
| nōs, vōs (acc.) | | nos, os | nos, vos | nous, vous |

Fr. **moi, toi** came from accented Lat. **mē, tē,** and Fr. **me, te** came from unaccented Lat. **mē, tē;** the Sp. suffix -otros derived from **alterōs.** Cf. Old Occ. **eu; me; me; nos/nọs, vos/vọs; nos; vos;** and Rom. **eu, tu; mie; ţie; mie; ţie; noi, voi; noi, voi.**

## LATĪNA EST GAVDIVM—ET V̄TILIS!

**Salvēte, discipulī et discipulae cārae!** Notice the ending on that adjective **cārae?**—remember that when adjectives modify two nouns of different gender, one solution in classical Latin was to have it agree with the one closer to it in the sentence. By the way, now you know the source of Freud's **ego** and **id,** and the meaning of the salutation **pāx vōbīscum/pāx tēcum.** And, you Caesar fans, can you believe that all of the following phrases/sentences have the same translation (well. . .sort of!): **Caesar, Caesar! Caesar eam videt. Caesar, cape eam! Caesaris convulsiō** (that last one *is,* I'll admit, a bit of a stretch: *Caesar's seizure!*). According to tradition, Caesar's last words to the assassin Brutus were **et tū, Brūte?**—to which Brutus hungrily replied, according to the late great comedian Brother Dave Gardner, "Nah, I ain't even et *one* yet!" Did you notice in the **Vocābula** the origin of the abbreviations **i.e.** and **id.?** There are dozens of Latin abbreviations in current usage; for some others, besides those at the end of Capvt VI, scan through the list on p. 538–39. And remember those **-or/-iō** nouns? From the verbs in this **Vocābula** come **missor, missōris,** m., *a shooter* (of "missiles"—lit., *a sender*) and **missiō, missiōnis,** f., literally *a sending forth* and used in classical Latin for *release from captivity, liberation* (itself from **līberāre,** *to free*), *discharge* (from military service), *dismissal,* and, of course, *mission;* from compounds of **mittō** come a host of Latin nouns with further English derivatives such as "admission," "commission," "emission," "permission," etc. Can you think of others, both the Latin nouns and the English derivatives, from **mittō?** And how about **sentiō?** Well, **tempus fugit,** so **pāx vōbīscum et valēte!**

# CAPVT XII 𐫱𐫱𐫱

# The Perfect Active System; Synopsis

## GRAMMATICA

### THE PERFECT ACTIVE SYSTEM

You are already familiar with the formation and translation of the present, future, and imperfect tenses, the three tenses that constitute the present system, so-called because they are all formed on the present stem and all look at time from the absolute perspective of the present. In Latin, as in English, there are three other tenses, the perfect, the future perfect, and the pluperfect, which constitute the **PERFECT SYSTEM,** so-called because they are formed on a perfect (active or passive) stem and look at time from a somewhat different perspective.

Learning the forms for these three tenses in the active voice (the perfect passive system is taken up in Capvt XIX) is an easy matter, since verbs of all conjugations follow the same simple rule: perfect active stem + endings.

### Principal Parts

To identify the perfect active stem of a Latin verb you must know the verb's principal parts, just as you must know the principal parts of an English verb if you want to use English correctly. As you have seen from your vocabulary study, most regular Latin verbs have four principal parts, as illustrated by **laudō:**

1. Present Active Indicative: **laúdō,** *I praise*
2. Present Active Infinitive: **laudáre,** *to praise*
3. Perfect Active Indicative: **laudávī,** *I praised, have praised*
4. Perfect Passive Participle: **laudátum,** *praised, having been praised*

The principal parts of the other verbs that have appeared in the paradigms are as follows:

| Pres. Indic. | Pres. Infin. | Perf. Indic. | Perf. Pass. Partic. |
| --- | --- | --- | --- |
| móneō | monḗre | mónuī, *I advised* | mónitum, *(having been) advised* |
| ágō | ágere | ḗgī, *I led* | áctum, *(having been) led* |
| cápiō | cápere | cḗpī, *I took* | cáptum, *(having been) taken* |

| aúdiō | audîre | audîvī, *I heard* | audîtum, *(having been) heard* |
|---|---|---|---|
| sum | ésse | fúī, *I was* | futûrum, *about to be* |
| póssum | pósse | pótuī, *I was able* | ——— |

The first two principal parts, necessary for conjugating a verb in the present system, have been dealt with extensively already. As the first person singular of the perfect active indicative, which always ends in -ī, a verb's third principal part is analogous to its first (which is, of course, the first person singular of the present active indicative and regularly ends in -ō). The fourth principal part, while given in its neuter form in this book, is for regular transitive verbs the perfect passive participle, a fully declinable verbal adjective of the **-us/-a/-um** variety (**laudātus, -a, -um,** etc.—some uses of participles will be explained in Capita XIX and XXIII–XXIV). Verbs lacking a perfect passive participle substitute the accusative supine (see Capvt XXXVIII), and some verbs like **sum** and other intransitives substitute a future active participle (e.g., **futūrum = futūrus, -a, -um**), while others like **possum** have no fourth principal part at all.

While the first and second principal parts for regular verbs follow a very consistent pattern, there are no simple rules to cover the many variations in the third and fourth principal parts (though, as we have seen, most first conjugation verbs do follow the **-ō/-āre/-āvī/-ātum** pattern of **laudō**, and many second and fourth conjugation verbs follow the patterns of **moneō** and **audiō**); hence, as pointed out earlier, it is crucial to memorize all the principal parts in the vocabulary entry for each verb by both *saying them aloud* and *writing them out*. Your knowledge of English will help you in this memorization, since there are many derivatives from both the present stem and the perfect participial stem, as you have already discovered (e.g., "docile" and "doctor," "agent" and "action," etc.).

## The Perfect Active Stem

Once you know a verb's principal parts, finding the **PERFECT ACTIVE STEM** is easy: simply drop the final -ī which characterizes the third principal part of every verb. The stems for the sample verbs in the preceding list are: **laudāv-, monu-, ēg-, cēp-, audīv-, fu-,** and **potu-**. The following paradigms show you the endings for the three perfect system tenses.

## Perfect Active Indicative

| | | *I praised, have praised* | *I led, have led* | *I was, have been* | **Endings** |
|---|---|---|---|---|---|
| | 1. | laudấv-ī | ḗg-ī | fú-ī | -ī |
| Sg. | 2. | laudāv-ístī | ēg-ístī | fu-ístī | -istī |
| | 3. | laudấv-it | ḗg-it | fú-it | -it |
| | 1. | laudávimus | ḗgimus | fúimus | -imus |
| Pl. | 2. | laudāvístis | ēgístis | fuístis | -istis |
| | 3. | laudāvḗrunt | ēgḗrunt | fuḗrunt | -ērunt, -ēre |

| | | Pluperfect Active Indicative | | Future Perfect Active Indicative | |
|---|---|---|---|---|---|
| | | *I had praised* | *I had been* | *I shall have praised* | *I shall have been* |
| | 1. | laudáv-eram | fú-eram | laudáv-erō | fú-erō |
| Sg. | 2. | laudáv-erās | fú-erās | laudáv-eris | fú-eris |
| | 3. | laudáv-erat | fú-erat | laudáv-erit | fú-erit |
| | 1. | laudāverámus | fuerámus | laudāvérimus | fuérimus |
| Pl. | 2. | laudāverátis | fuerátis | laudāvéritis | fuéritis |
| | 3. | laudáverant | fúerant | laudáverint | fúerint |

The perfect endings (**-ī, -istī, -it,** etc.) are new and must be memorized; the alternate ending **-ēre** (**laudāvēre, ēgēre, fuēre**), while fairly common, especially in Latin poetry, appears only once or twice in this book. The pluperfect is in effect the perfect stem + **eram,** the imperfect of **sum.** The future perfect is in effect the perfect stem + **erō,** the future of **sum,** except that the third person plural is **-erint,** not **-erunt.**

## Usage, Translation, and Distinction from the Imperfect

One might ask why there are more than three tenses, since there are only three times, i.e., the past, the present, and the future. Simply put, the perfect system presents a different way of looking at time, focusing on actions that, at some given point, have been *completed* (**perfectum,** *perfect,* is from **perficiō, perficere, perfēcī, perfectum,** *to do thoroughly, complete*), and typically considering the *consequences* of the completed action. The following chart illustrates how this works in English, which employs the auxiliary verbs "had," "has," and "will have" (the past, present, and future tenses of "to have") to convey the sense of completed actions, and the concept in Latin is comparable:

| **Pluperfect** | **Perfect** | **Future Perfect** |
|---|---|---|
| *I had studied this* | *I have studied this* | *I will have studied (by* |
| *(previously)* | *(already)* | *tomorrow)* |
| \ | \ | \ |
| *and so I under-* | *and so I under-* | *and so I will* |
| *stood it* | *stand it* | *understand it* |
| **Past** | **Present** | **Future** |

The pluperfect (**plūperfectum = plūs quam perfectum,** *more than complete*), sometimes called the PAST PERFECT, describes an action completed in the distant past and with consequences on some action in the more recent past: "you *had studied* the material previously, and so by last Friday you already *understood* it well." The future perfect (**futūrum perfectum**) describes an act that will have been completed at some future point and its consequences on a more distant point in the future: "by this weekend you *will have studied* the material, and so you *will understand* it thoroughly for Monday's quiz." The perfect tense describes a completed act that has consequences for the *present* (and hence is sometimes called the "present perfect"): "by now you *have studied* this chapter thoughtfully, and so you *understand* the concepts." You can see from these examples how the three perfect system tenses parallel the three tenses of the present system; in the latter we simply look at events of the past, present, or future, while in the former we look at completed actions with an eye to their consequences on some subsequent time in the past, present, or future.

The perfect tense, though often functioning as a pure PRESENT PERFECT, sometimes serves as a SIMPLE PAST TENSE; thus **puer amīcum monuit** can in some contexts, when not thinking specifically of the action's consequences, mean simply *the boy warned his friend*. While the imperfect tense (**imperfectum,** *not completed,* i.e., continuing) is like a video of the past, the perfect tense is more like a still photograph: with the imperfect the action is viewed as going on, repeated, or habitual, so a more exact translation of **puer amīcum monēbat,** depending upon the context, might be *the boy was warning/kept warning/used to warn his friend*. The more static perfect tense looks back at an action as a single, completed event (*he warned his friend once*), or as an event that, although completed, has consequences for the present; in this latter case, you should translate with the auxiliary "has/have" (*he has warned his friend, and so his friend is now prepared*).

## SYNOPSIS

To test your ability to conjugate a Latin verb completely, you may be asked to provide a labeled SYNOPSIS of the verb in a specified person and number, in lieu of writing out all of the verb's forms. Following is a sample third person singular synopsis of **agō** in the indicative mood, active voice:

|  | Pres. | Fut. | Imperf. | Perf. | Fut. Perf. | Pluperf. |
|---|---|---|---|---|---|---|
| **Lat.** | ágit | áget | agḗbat | ḗgit | ḗgerit | ḗgerat |
| **Eng.** | he drives | he will drive | he was driving | he has driven | he will have driven | he had driven |

# VOCĀBVLA

Be sure to distinguish between **pater,** *father,* in this new list and **patria,** *fatherland,* learned previously; and don't give the **s** in **Caesar** the "z" sound it has in English. As you study this new vocabulary, you should also check your mastery of words learned in Capita I–XI; for review you can use vocabulary cards or cumulative vocabulary lists (available at www.wheelockslatin.com—or make your own), but in memorizing this new list, be sure to listen to the CDs or the online audio, and . . . **audī et prōnūntiā!** After memorizing this list, practice with its three new verbs by writing out a synopsis, each in a different person and number, then check your work by comparing the paradigms in the **Summārium Fōrmārum**, p. 501.

**adulḗscēns, adulēscéntis,** m. and f., *young man* or *woman* (adolescent, adolescence, adult; cf. **adulēscentia**)

**ánnus, ánnī,** m., *year* (annals, anniversary, annuity, annual, biennial, perennial, centennial, millennium, superannuated)

**Ásia, Ásiae,** f., *Asia,* commonly referring to Asia Minor (see Map 3)

**Caésar, Caésaris,** m., *Caesar* (Caesarian, Caesarism, kaiser, czar, tsar)

**máter, mātris,** f., *mother* (maternal, maternity, matriarchy, matrimony, matricide, matriculate, matrilineal, matrix, matron)

**médicus, médicī,** m., and **médica, médicae,** f., *doctor, physician* (medic, medical, medicate, medicine, medicinal)

**páter, pátris,** m., *father* (paternal, paternity, patrician, patrimony, patron, patronage, patronize, patter, padre, père; cf. **patria**)

**patiéntia, patiéntiae,** f., *suffering; patience, endurance* (patient, impatient)

**prīncípium, prīncípiī,** n., *beginning* (principal, principle)

**acérbus, acérba, acérbum,** *harsh, bitter, grievous* (acerbic, acerbity, exacerbate)

**prō,** prep. + abl., *in front of, before, on behalf of, for the sake of, in return for, instead of, for, as;* also as prefix (pros and cons; for pro- as a prefix, see App., p. 488)

**díū,** adv., *long, for a long time*

**nū́per,** adv., *recently*

**āmíttō, āmíttere, āmī́sī, āmíssum,** *to send away; lose, let go* (amissible; cf. omit, omission)

**cádō, cádere, cécidī, cāsū́rum,** *to fall* (cadence, case, casual, cascade, chance, accident, incident, decadence, decay, deciduous)

**créō, creā́re, creā́vī, creā́tum,** *to create* (creation, creativity, creature, procreate)

# LĒCTIŌ ET TRĀNSLĀTIŌ

After learning the new paradigms and vocabulary and testing yourself with some of the Self-Tutorial Exercises, scan through the following readings for examples of perfect system verbs, identifying the tense, number, and person of each. Listen to the CDs, if you have them, and read each sentence and passage aloud. In translating the perfect tense, remember the options: e.g., which is the better choice for **āmīsit** in the selection "Pliny Writes to Marcellinus" the simple past tense "lost" or the pure present perfect "has lost," and why?

## EXERCITĀTIŌNĒS

1. Vōs nōbīs dē voluptātibus adulēscentiae tum scrīpseritis.
2. Ratiōnēs alterīus fīliae herī nōn fuērunt eaedem.
3. Nēmō in hanc viam ex utrā portā fūgerat.
4. Illī autem ad nōs cum medicā eius nūper vēnērunt.
5. Illī adulēscentēs ad tē propter amīcitiam saepe veniēbant.
6. Eundem timōrem nec in istō cōnsule nec in amīcō eius sēnsimus.
7. Post paucās hōrās Caesar Asiam cēpit.
8. Illa fēmina beāta sōla magnam cupiditātem pācis sēnsit.
9. Potuistisne bonam vītam sine ūllā lībertāte agere?
10. Vēritās igitur fuit tōtī populō cāra.
11. Neuter medicus nōmen patris audīverat.
12. That friendly queen did not remain there a long time.
13. Our mothers had not understood the nature of that place.
14. However, we had found no fault in the head of our country.
15. They kept sending her to him with me.

## SENTENTIAE ANTĪQUAE

1. In prīncipiō Deus creāvit caelum et terram; et Deus creāvit hominem. (Genesis.)
2. In triumphō Caesar praetulit hunc titulum: "Vēnī, vīdī, vīcī." (Suetonius.—**triumphus, -ī**, m., *triumphal procession*, here celebrating his quick victory at Zela in Asia Minor in 47 B.C.—**praeferō, -ferre, -tulī, -lātum**, *to display*; "prefer," "prelate."—**titulus, -ī**, m., *placard*; "title," "titular.")
3. Vīxit, dum vīxit, bene. (*Terence.)
4. Adulēscēns vult diū vīvere; senex diū vīxit. (Cicero.—**vult**, irreg., *wishes*; "volition," "benevolent."—**senex, senis**, m., *old man*; "senator," "senior.")
5. Nōn ille diū vīxit, sed diū fuit. (*Seneca.)
6. Hui, dīxistī pulchrē! (*Terence.—**hui**, interj., comparable to Eng. "whee!"—**pulchrē**, adv. from **pulcher**; adverbs were commonly formed from adjectives in this way. See Capita XXVI–XXVII, and cf., e.g., **vērē** from **vērus**, **līberē** from **līber**, and the irreg. **bene** from **bonus**.)
7. Sophoclēs ad summam senectūtem tragoediās fēcit. (*Cicero.—**Sophoclēs, -clis**, m., the famous Athenian playwright.—**summus, -a, -um**, *extreme*; "summary," "summit."—**tragoedia, -ae**, f., *tragedy*; "tragedian," "tragic.")
8. Illī nōn sōlum pecūniam sed etiam vītam prō patriā prōfūdērunt. (Cicero.—**prōfundō, -ere, -fūdī, -fūsum**, *to pour forth*; "profuse," "refuse.")
9. Rēgēs Rōmam ā prīncipiō habuēre; lībertātem Lūcius Brūtus Rōmānīs dedit. (Tacitus.—**ā** + abl., *from*.—**habuēre**: though this may resemble an infin., it is one of the newly introduced perf. system forms.)

10. Sub Caesare autem lībertātem perdidimus. (Laberius.—**perdō, -ere, -didī, -ditum,** *to destroy, lose;* "perdition," "perdue.")

11. Quandō lībertās ceciderit, nēmō līberē dīcere audēbit. (Publilius Syrus.)

### Pliny Writes to Marcellinus about the Death of Fundanus' Daughter

Salvē, Marcellīne! Haec tibi scrībō dē Fundānō, amīcō nostrō, quod is fīliam cāram et bellam āmīsit. Illa puella nōn XIII annōs vīxerat, sed nātūra eī multam sapientiam dederat. Mātrem patremque, frātrem sorōremque, nōs et aliōs amīcōs, magistrōs magistrāsque semper amābat, et nōs eam amābāmus laudābāmusque. Medicī eam adiuvāre nōn poterant. Quoniam illa autem magnōs animōs habuit, morbum nimis malum cum patientiā tolerāvit. Nunc, mī amīce, mitte Fundānō nostrō litterās dē fortūnā acerbā fīliae eius. Valē.

Pliny *Ep.* 5.16 (for a longer, unadapted excerpt, see **Locī Im.** XL): Pliny the Younger (Gaius Plinius Caecilius Secundus, ca. A.D. 61–112) was a senator, consul, and provincial governor, and an important literary figure during the reigns of Domitian, Nerva, and Trajan. Among his surviving works are 10 volumes of letters that provide us with invaluable insights into the society and politics of the period.—**XIII annōs,** *for 13 years,* ACC. OF DURATION OF TIME (a construction formally introduced in Capvt XXXVII). Minicius Fundanus was a consul in A.D. 107; his daughter's funerary urn and the following epitaph were found in the family's tomb outside of Rome (the parentheses indicate words abbreviated in the original inscription): **D(īs) M(ānibus) Miniciae Marcellae Fundānī f(īliae); v(īxit) a(nnōs) XII m(ēnsēs) XI d(iēs) VII.** The **dī mānēs** to whom the epitaph is dedicated were the *spirits of the dead,* who protected the deceased.—**mēnsēs:** *months;* "semester," "trimester."—**diēs:** *days;* "diary," "meridian," "carpe diem."

*QVAESTIŌNĒS:* What are Pliny's specific objectives in writing to Marcellinus? What virtues did Pliny especially admire in Minicia, Fundanus' daughter?

### Diaulus Still Buries His Clients

Nūper erat medicus, nunc est vespillo Diaulus.
　　Quod vespillo facit, fēcerat et medicus.

*Martial *Epig.* 1.47: meter: elegiac couplet.—**vespillō, -lōnis,** m., *undertaker;* final -ō was often shortened in verse, for metrical purposes and as a reflection of actual pronunciation habits in conversational Latin.—**quod:** *what.*—**et:** here, as often, = **etiam.**

*QVAESTIŌNĒS:* What is (grimly) humorous about Diaulus' career change?—how were his two professions strikingly different, and yet alike? Comment on the different word order strategies employed in each verse; what is "suspenseful" in the arrangement of line 1? How is the arrangement of the second line, including the juxtaposition **facit/**

*Page from manuscript of*
*Pliny's* Epistulae
*(Ep. 3.4.8–9 and 3.5.1–3)*
*6th cent.* A.D., *Italy*
*The Pierpont Morgan Library*
*New York*

**fēcerat,** especially appropriate to the circumstance Martial describes? Do you see the chiasmus in the overall ordering of the four clauses in the two lines?

## SCRĪPTA IN PARIETIBVS

Lūcius pīnxit.

*CIL* 4.7535: Of the thousands of wall paintings in Pompeii, only those in the outside dining area of the large and richly decorated house of Octavius Quartio (Reg. II, Ins. 5.2, on the Via dell'Abbondanza) are signed by the artist; on a bench situated near his murals of Narcissus, in one panel, and of Pyramus and Thisbe, in another, Lucius painted his own signature about 5″ wide in bold white letters on a red background.—**pingō, -ere, pīnxī, pictum,** *to decorate with color, paint (a picture);* "picture," "depict."

## ETYMOLOGIA

Further examples of how your knowledge of Eng. words can assist in learning the principal parts of Lat. verbs, as well as vice-versa:

| Latin Verb | Pres. Stem in Eng. Word | Perf. Partic. Stem in Eng. Word |
|---|---|---|
| videō | provide (vidēre) | provision (vīsum) |
| maneō | permanent (manēre) | mansion (mānsum) |
| vīvō | revive (vīvere) | victuals (vīctum) |
| sentiō | sentiment (sentīre) | sense (sēnsum) |
| veniō | intervene (venīre) | intervention (ventum) |
| faciō | facile (facere) | fact (factum) |

The connection between Lat. **pater** and **patria** (*father-land*) is obvious. However, although Eng. "patriarch," "patriot," and "patronymic" contain the stem **patr-**, which is meaningful to one who knows the Lat. words, nevertheless these Eng. words are actually derived from Gk., in which the stem **patr-** is cognate with the Lat. stem; cf. Gk. **patḗr**, *father,* **pátrā** or **patrís**, *fatherland,* **patriá**, *lineage.*

And here are several other derivatives from **fundere**, the root verb of **prō-fundere** in S.A. 8: confound, confuse, effuse, effusive, fuse, fusion, refund, transfusion.

## LATĪNA EST GAVDIVM—ET VTILIS!

**Salvēte, discipulae discipulīque cārī!** As we saw in S. A. 2 above, Caesar is said to have proclaimed **vēnī, vīdī, vīcī** in propagandizing his victory at Zela—a good example of the perfect tense, a "snapshot" of the action whose rapid conclusion the general wanted to emphasize. There are now some 20th-cent. variants on this boast: from the mall-masters, **VENI, VIDI, VISA,** "I came, I saw, I shopped!" and from the vegetarians, **VENI, VIDI, VEGI,** "I came, I saw, I had a salad"; and how about **VENI, VIDI, VELCRO,** "I came, I saw, I stuck around"? Are you groaning?!!—but remember, **patientia est virtūs,** and there may yet be worse to come: meantime, **rīdēte** (from **rīdēre,** *to smile*) **et valēte!**

# CAPVT XIII 🔲🔲🔲

# Reflexive Pronouns and Possessives; Intensive Pronoun

## GRAMMATICA

### REFLEXIVE PRONOUNS

REFLEXIVE PRONOUNS differ from other pronouns in that they are used ordinarily only in the predicate and refer back to the subject. "Reflexive" derives from **reflectō, -ere, -flexī, -flexum,** *to bend back:* reflexive pronouns "bend back" to the subject, i.e., they "reflect" or refer to the subject. Here are some English examples, contrasted with personal pronouns:

| Reflexive Pronouns | Personal Pronouns |
|---|---|
| I praised *myself.* | You praised *me.* |
| Cicero praised *himself.* | Cicero praised *him* (Caesar). |

### Declension of Reflexives

Since reflexive pronouns *refer* to the subject, they cannot *be* the subject (except, as you will see in Capvt XXV, as accusative subject of an infinitive phrase, as in English "He considered *himself to be* a good student"), and hence they have no nominative case. Otherwise, the declension of the reflexives of the first and the second persons is the same as that of the corresponding personal pronouns.

The third person reflexive pronoun, however, has its own peculiar forms; these are easily recognizable because, as seen from the following chart, they are identical to the singular of **tū,** except that the nominative is lacking and the forms begin with s- rather than t-. Note also that the singular and plural are identical, or, to put it another way, singular and plural were not distinguished and did not need to be, since reflexives in fact "reflect" the number (as well as the gender) of the subject; e.g., **sē** is easily understood to mean *herself* in the sentence **fēmina dē sē cōgitābat** (*the woman was thinking about herself*) and *themselves* in the sentence **virī dē sē cōgitābant** (*the men were thinking about themselves*).

|  | 1st Pers. | 2nd Pers. | 3rd Pers. |
|---|---|---|---|
| **Singular** |  |  |  |
| *Nom.* | — | — | — |
| *Gen.* | méī (*of myself*) | túī | súī (*of himself, herself, itself*) |
| *Dat.* | míhi (*to/for myself*) | tíbi | síbi (*to/for himself,* etc.) |
| *Acc.* | mē (*myself*) | tē | sē (*himself, herself, itself*) |
| *Abl.* | mē (*by/with/from myself*) | tē | sē (*by/with/from himself,* etc.) |
| **Plural** |  |  |  |
| *Nom.* | — | — | — |
| *Gen.* | nóstrī (*of ourselves*) | véstrī | súī (*of themselves*) |
| *Dat.* | nṓbīs (*to/for ourselves*) | vṓbīs | síbi (*to/for themselves*) |
| *Acc.* | nōs (*ourselves*) | vōs | sē (*themselves*) |
| *Abl.* | nṓbīs (*by/with/from ourselves*) | vṓbīs | sē (*by/with/from themselves*) |

### Comparison of First and Second Person Reflexive and Personal Pronouns

1. Tū *tē* laudāvistī. *You praised* **yourself.**
2. Cicerō *tē* laudāvit. *Cicero praised* **you.**
3. Nōs laudāvimus *nōs*. *We praised* **ourselves.**
4. Cicerō *nōs* laudāvit. *Cicero praised* **us.**
5. Ego *mihi* litterās scrīpsī. *I wrote a letter to* **myself.**
6. Cicerō *mihi* litterās scrīpsit. *Cicero wrote a letter to* **me.**

### Comparison of Third Person Reflexive and Personal Pronouns

1. Cicerō *sē* laudāvit. *Cicero praised* **himself.**
2. Cicerō *eum* laudāvit. *Cicero praised* **him** (e.g., Caesar).
3. Rōmānī *sē* laudāvērunt. *The Romans praised* **themselves.**
4. Rōmānī *eōs* laudāvērunt. *The Romans praised* **them** (e.g., the Greeks).
5. Puella *sē* servāvit. *The girl saved* **herself.**
6. Puella *eam* servāvit. *The girl saved* **her** (i.e., another girl).

## REFLEXIVE POSSESSIVE ADJECTIVES

The **REFLEXIVE POSSESSIVE ADJECTIVES** of the first and the second persons are identical with the regular possessives already familiar to you: **meus, tuus, noster, vester** (i.e., *my, my own; your, your own;* etc.): **Meum librum habēs;** *you have my book.* **Meum librum habeō;** *I have my own book.*

The third person reflexive possessive, however, is a new word, **suus, sua, suum,** *his (own), her (own), its (own), their (own).* While easily declined (just like **tuus, -a, -um,** a regular first/second declension adjective), some important points must be kept in mind regarding the word's usage and translation. First, like any adjective, **suus, -a, -um,** must agree with the noun it modifies in number, gender, and case. Its English translation, however, like that of the reflexive pronoun, must naturally reflect the gender and number of the subject to which it refers; e.g., **vir fīlium suum laudat,** *the man praises his* (own) *son,* vs. **fēmina fīlium suum laudat,** *the woman praises her* (own) *son,* and **virī patriam suam laudant,** *the men praise their* (own) *country.* Finally, the reflexive possessive adjective **suus, -a, -um** must be carefully distinguished from the nonreflexive possessive genitives **eius, eōrum, eārum** (*his/her, their*: see Capvt XI), which refer to some person(s) other than the subject.

1. **Cicerō amīcum** *suum* **laudāvit.** *Cicero praised his (own) friend.*
2. **Cicerō amīcum** *eius* **laudāvit.** *Cicero praised his (Caesar's) friend.*
3. **Rōmānī amīcum** *suum* **laudāvērunt.** *The Romans praised their (own) friend.*
4. **Rōmānī amīcum** *eōrum* **laudāvērunt.** *The Romans praised their (the Greeks') friend.*
5. **Fēmina amīcīs** *suīs* **litterās scrīpsit.** *The woman wrote a letter to her (own) friends.*
6. **Fēmina amīcīs** *eius* **litterās scrīpsit.** *The woman wrote a letter to his (or her, i.e., someone else's) friends.*
7. **Fēmina amīcīs** *eōrum* **litterās scrīpsit.** *The woman wrote a letter to their (some other persons') friends.*

## THE INTENSIVE PRONOUN Ipse, ipsa, ipsum

The **INTENSIVE PRONOUN** **ipse, ipsa, ipsum** follows the declensional pattern of the demonstratives in the genitive and the dative singular (i.e., gen. **ipsīus, ipsīus, ipsīus,** dat. **ipsī, ipsī, ipsī**: see App., p. 497); otherwise, it is like **magnus, -a, -um.** The Romans used the intensive pronoun to emphasize any noun or pronoun in either the subject or the predicate of a sentence; consequently its possible translations include *myself/ourselves* (1st pers.), *yourself/yourselves* (2nd pers.), and *himself/herself/itself/themselves* (3rd pers.), as well as *the very* and *the actual,* as illustrated in the following examples:

**Cicerō** *ipse* **mē laudāvit.** *Cicero himself praised me.*
**Cicerō mē** *ipsum* **laudāvit.** *Cicero praised me myself* (i.e., *actually praised me*)
*Ipse* **amīcum eius laudāvī.** *I myself praised his friend.*
**Fīlia vōbīs** *ipsīs* **litterās scrīpsit.** *Your daughter wrote a letter to you yourselves.*
**Cicerō litterās** *ipsās* **Caesaris vīdit.** *Cicero saw Caesar's letter itself* (i.e., *Caesar's actual letter*).

# VOCĀBVLA

This chapter's vocabulary list introduces another noun, **dīvitiae,** which, like **īnsidiae** in Capvt VI and others you'll encounter later on, has plural forms with essentially singular meaning—though in this case the singular, *wealth,* is a "collective," implying amassed riches; language has lots of twists and turns like this, all of them intriguing. **Per,** as you will see, is another preposition that turns up frequently, in a variety of forms, as a prefix, both in Latin words and in such English derivatives as "perfect," "perspire," and "pellucid"; review again the several common Latin prefixes and suffixes listed in "Some Etymological Aids," in the App., p. 485–89. **Ōlim,** with its seemingly opposite meanings of *long ago* and *some day (in the future),* is related to **ille** and like it refers to something distant, i.e., a time in either the distant past or the distant future. Once you have memorized the new vocabulary, practice by writing out the declension of **ipsum factum** and doing a synopsis of one of the newly introduced verbs, then compare your work with the paradigms in the **Summārium Fōrmārum,** p. 497 and 501.

**dīvítiae, dīvítiárum,** f. pl., *riches, wealth*

**fáctum, fáctī,** n., *deed, act, achievement* (fact, factual, faction, feat; cf. **faciō**)

**sígnum, sígnī,** n., *sign, signal, indication; seal* (assign, consign, countersign, design, ensign, insignia, resign, seal, signet)

**ípse, ípsa, ípsum,** intensive pron., *myself, yourself, himself, herself, itself,* etc., *the very, the actual* (ipso facto, solipsistic)

**quísque, quídque** (gen. **cuiúsque;** dat. **cuíque**), indefinite pron., *each one, each person, each thing*

**súī,** reflexive pron. of 3rd pers., *himself, herself, itself, themselves* (suicide, per se)

**dóctus, dócta, dóctum,** *taught, learned, skilled* (doctor, doctorate, doctrine, indoctrinate; cf. **doceō**)

**fortūnátus, fortūnáta, fortūnátum,** *lucky, fortunate, happy* (unfortunate; cf. **fortūna**)

**súus, súa súum,** reflexive possessive adj. of 3rd pers., *his own, her own, its own, their own* (sui generis)

**nam,** conj., *for*

**ánte,** prep. + acc., *before* (in place or time), *in front of;* adv., *before, previously;* not to be confused with Greek **anti,** *against* (antebellum, antedate, ante-room, anterior, antediluvian, A.M. = **ante merīdiem**/"before midday," advance, advantage)

**per,** prep. + acc., *through;* with reflexive pron., *by;* **per-** (assimilated to **pel-** before forms beginning with **l**-), as a prefix, *through, through and through = thoroughly, completely, very* (perchance, perforce, perhaps, perceive, perfect, perspire, percolate, percussion, perchloride, pellucid)

**ólim,** adv., *once (upon a time), long ago, formerly; some day, in the future*

**álō, álere, áluī, áltum,** *to nourish, support, sustain, increase; cherish* (aliment, alimentary, alimony, coalesce, adolescence; the adj. **altus, -a, -um,** = *tall, high,* because what is "nourished" grows)

**dílígō, dīlígere, dīléxī, dīléctum,** *to esteem, love* (diligent, diligence)

**iúngō, iúngere, iúnxī, iúnctum,** *to join* (join, joint, junction, juncture, adjunct, conjunction, enjoin, injunction, subjunctive)

**stō, stáre, stétī, státum,** *to stand, stand still* or *firm* (stable, state, station, statue, stature, statute, establish, instant, instate, reinstate, stay)

# LĒCTIŌ ET TRĀNSLĀTIŌ

Before attempting these readings, remember to test your mastery of the new material by writing out your answers to several of the Self-Tutorial Exercises (p. 421–22), including some of the translations, and then checking your work against the Answer Key (p. 455). Next listen to the readings, if you have the CDs, read them aloud once or twice for comprehension, and then write out your translations; for practice with the new grammar, scan through the readings for all the reflexives and intensives and identify the number, gender, case, and use of each. Translation tips: when an intensive modifies a noun or pronoun, simply translate accordingly, e.g., **mē ipsum** in Ex. 3 means *me myself,* but when there is no modified noun/pronoun, you must supply "he, she, they," etc., e.g., in Ex. 6 **ipsī** is clearly masculine nominative plural and must be the subject, hence *they themselves* or *the men themselves.* In the case of a reflexive possessive, when the antecedent is clear from the context and no particular emphasis is intended, you may sometimes omit "own" for more natural English idiom; in Ex. 10, e.g., it is acceptable to translate **litterās suās** simply as *her letter,* understanding of course that the reference is to her own, not someone else's, letter.

## EXERCITĀTIŌNĒS

1. Cōnsulēs sē nec tēcum nec cum illīs aliīs iungēbant.
2. Tōtus populus Rōmānus lībertātem āmīsit.
3. Rēx malus enim mē ipsum capere numquam potuit.
4. Ad patrem mātremque eōrum per illum locum tum fūgistis.
5. Dī animōs creant et eōs in corpora hominum ē caelō mittunt.
6. Ipsī per sē eum in Asiā nūper vīcērunt.
7. In hāc viā Cicerō medicum eius vīdit, nōn suum.
8. Nēmō fīliam acerbam cōnsulis ipsīus diū dīligere potuit.
9. Hī Cicerōnem ipsum sēcum iūnxērunt, nam eum semper dīlēxerant.
10. Fēmina amīca vōbīs ante illam hōram litterās suās mīserit.

11. Ille bonam senectūtem habuit, nam per annōs bene vīxerat.
12. Māter fīlium bene intellēxit et īram sēnserat, et adulēscēns eī prō patientiā grātiās ēgit.
13. Mē cum istīs et capite eōrum nōn iungam, nec tū autem tē eīscum iungere dēbēs.
14. However, those young men came to Caesar himself yesterday.
15. Cicero, therefore, will never join his (Caesar's) name with his own.
16. Cicero always esteemed himself and even you esteem yourself.
17. Cicero used to praise his own books and I now praise my own books.
18. The consul Cicero himself had never seen his (Caesar's) book.

## SENTENTIAE ANTĪQVAE

1. Ipse ad eōs contendēbat equitēsque ante sē mīsit. (Caesar.—**contendō, -ere,** *to hasten;* "contender," "contention."—**eques, equitis,** m., *horseman;* "equestrian"; cf. **equus,** *horse.*)
2. Ipsī nihil per sē sine eō facere potuērunt. (Cicero.)
3. Ipse signum suum et litterās suās ā prīncipiō recognōvit. (Cicero.—**recognōscō, -ere, -cognōvī, -cognitum,** *to recognize;* "recognizance," "reconnaissance.")
4. Quisque ipse sē dīligit, quod quisque per sē sibi cārus est. (Cicero.)
5. Ex vitiō alterīus sapiēns ēmendat suum. (*Publilius Syrus.—**sapiēns, -entis,** m., *wise man, philosopher;* "savant," "homo sapiens."—**ēmendāre,** *to correct;* "amend," "emend," "mend.")
6. Recēde in tē ipsum. (*Seneca.—**recēdō, -ere,** *to withdraw;* "recede," "recess.")
7. Animus sē ipse alit. (*Seneca.)
8. Homō doctus in sē semper dīvitiās habet. (Phaedrus.)

### Alexander the Great and the Power of Literature

Magnus ille Alexander multōs scrīptōrēs factōrum suōrum sēcum semper habēbat. Is enim ante tumulum Achillis ōlim stetit et dīxit haec verba: "Fuistī fortūnātus, Ō adulēscēns, quod Homērum laudātōrem virtūtis tuae invēnistī." Et vērē! Nam, sine *Īliade* illā, īdem tumulus et corpus eius et nōmen obruere potuit. Nihil corpus hūmānum cōnservāre potest; sed litterae magnae nōmen virī magnī saepe cōnservāre possunt.

Cicero *Arch.* 10.24: The **Prō Archiā**, *In Defense of Archias,* is one of the best known of Cicero's dozens of surviving speeches; in it Cicero defended his friend, the Greek poet Archias, against legal challenges to his Roman citizenship status. As just one means of persuading the court, Cicero spoke eloquently on the benefits that poets and poetry could provide a society and its citizens, including its ruling class. Alexander the Great, son of Philip of Macedon, became king when his father died in 336 and by the time of his own premature death in 323 at the age of 33 had led his Macedonian army in the

*Alexander the Great. Detail of marble Roman statue, 1st cent. A.D.*
*Found in the Baths of Trajan at Cyrene. Museum, Cyrene, Libya*

conquest of Greece, much of the near east, and Egypt, marching even into India. He had been educated by Aristotle and himself clearly understood the power of poetry, and of the written word in general, as this anecdote makes clear. —**ille:** what special sense of the demonstrative is particularly apt here, and in the phrase *Īliade* **illā** below as well?— **tumulus, -ī,** m., *tomb, grave;* "tumulus," "tumular."—**sē:** here, as often, "-self" can be omitted, both for more natural Eng. idiom and because the reflexive force is sufficiently clear from the context.—**Achillēs, -lis,** m.—**Homērus, -ī.** m.—**laudātor, -tōris,** m., lit., *one who praises* (see Capvt VIII, **Latīna Est Gaudium,** for the basic sense of nouns ending in **-or**), *eulogist, chronicler;* "laud," "laudatory." —**vērē:** adv. of **vērus;** "verify," "verity."— **Īlias, -adis,** f., *Iliad.*—**et . . . et:** take careful note of what the conjunctions here must be linking; the potential for misconstruing derives from the fact that **corpus** is an ambiguous form, but the ambiguity is resolved with the sg. verb **potuit.**—**obruō, -ere,** *to overwhelm, bury;* "ruin," "ruination."

*QVAESTIŌNĒS:* Explain what Alexander felt had made Achilles so fortunate, despite his legendary early death. What point does Cicero draw from this anecdote, how was it appropriate to his own political position, and would a U.S. senator today likely agree?

### The Authority of a Teacher's Opinion

Magistrī bonī discipulīs sententiās suās nōn semper dīcere dēbent. Discipulī Pȳthagorae in disputātiōnibus saepe dīcēbant: "Ipse dīxit!" Pȳthagorās, eōrum magister philosophiae, erat "ipse": sententiae eius etiam sine ratiōne valuērunt. In philosophiā autem ratiō sōla, nōn sententia, valēre dēbet.

Cicero *Nat. D.* 1.5.10: The **Dē Nātūrā Deōrum** (whose Lat. title you can easily translate) was one of three religious treatises (the others being **Dē Fātō,** *On Fate,* and **Dē Dīvinātiōne,** *On Divination*) authored by Cicero in 45–44 B.C. and dealing with the major views then prevalent of the nature of the gods (Cicero himself believed in the existence of a divine being), the validity of divination (which he rejected), and the free will/determinism debate (in which he argued for the former). In this passage he comments on dogmatism and the fallacy of arguments based on an "expert's" authority.—**Pȳthagorās, -ae,** m.; Pythagoras was a 6th cent. B.C. Greek scientist, mathematician, philosopher, and religious leader known for his doctrine of the transmigration of souls into other humans, animals, and plants, as well as such discoveries as the Pythagorean theorem and theories of musical harmonies.—**disputātiō, -ōnis,** f., *argument, debate;* "disputable," "disputation."—**ipse dīxit:** sc. **id** as direct obj.

*QVAESTIŌNĒS:* On what basis does Cicero criticize Pythagoras and, less directly, his followers as well? Have you ever had a teacher yourself whose "authority" in a sense diminished the true effectiveness of his or her teaching?

## SCRĪPTA IN PARIETIBVS

"Vēnimus hōc cupidī!" Scrībit{t} Cornēlius Mārtiālis.

*CIL* 4.8891 (Reg. III, Ins. 5): The first sentence of this graffito, written near the entrance to a shop, is the opening of an amatory poem found in several other locations in Pompeii (e.g., *CIL* 4.1227 and 6697); the meter is ELEGIAC COUPLET, so we know the verb must be **vēnimus** and not **venimus:** what are the two different tenses? The scribbler was so pleased with recalling and writing out this half verse that he signed his work—unfortunately misspelling the verb **scrībit:** remember that the brackets {. . .} are conventionally employed to indicate letters added to a word's spelling in error.—**hōc** (more commonly **hūc**), adv., *to this place, hither* (related to **hic, haec, hoc**).—**cupidus, -a, -um,** *desirous, eager, fond;* "Cupid," "cupidity."

Aephēbus Successō patrī suō salūt(em).

*CIL* 4.4753: Inscribed by a lad to his dad, on a column in the house of L. Cissonius Se-cundus (Reg. VII, Ins. 7) ; both names are cognomina, or **aephēbus** (more often spelled **ephēbus**), -ī, m., may just be the common noun = *boy, young man.*—**Successō:** the end of the name is not quite legible and illustrates one sort of challenge faced by editors working with graffiti; *CIL*'s editors think the writer first wrote -**N** (an odd mistake), then corrected it to -**O;** but it has also been suggested that the correct reading, with the last three letters squeezed together, may be **SVCCESSORI,** dat. of **Successor** (also a Roman cognomen).—**salūtem:** if you do not recall the meaning, see *CIL* 4.4742 in Capvt VIII. Though a tad sloppy writing his father's name, the young fellow did embellish the tail of his **T** with a decorative flourish—ever do something like that when you were signing a greeting card, maybe even a Father's Day card?

## LATĪNA EST GAVDIVM—ET ŪTILIS!

**Salvēte!** If you've spent much time in court, or even reading John Grisham novels, you've doubtless encountered some legal Latin. **Ipse** turns up more than once in the lawyer's lexicon: there's **ipsō factō,** *by that very fact;* **ipsō jūre** (classical **iūre**), *by the law itself;* and **rēs ipsa loquitur,** *the matter speaks for itself.* And from the third person reflexive pos-sessive there's **suī jūris (iūris),** literally *of his own right,* i.e., legally competent to manage one's own affairs. Not a legal term, but from the reflexive and common in English is **suī generis,** literally *of his/her/its own kind* (from **genus, generis**), used of a person or thing that is unique. Another common English phrase, seen in the above reading on Pythago-ras, is **ipse dīxit,** used of any dogmatic or arbitrary statement; likewise from the inten-sive pronoun are the phrase **ipsissima verba,** *the very words* (of a person being quoted), the medical term "ipsilateral," meaning "on or affecting the same side of the body" (from **latus, lateris,** n., *side*), and the word "solipsism," for the philosophical theory that the self alone is the only reality or that it conditions our perception of reality. By now you've had all the vocabulary needed to translate the famous quotation from Constantine, **in hōc signō vincēs** (*under this standard*—i.e., the cross—*you shall prevail*), seen in more recent decades on a well-known brand of cigarettes, where, freely, it means, *You'll win with this brand* (but would the U.S. Surgeon General agree?). Well, **tempus iterum fūgit: valēte!**

# CAPVT XIV 𒀖𒀖𒀖

# *I*-Stem Nouns of the Third Declension; Ablatives of Means, Accompaniment, and Manner

## GRAMMATICA

### THIRD DECLENSION *i*-STEM NOUNS

Some third declension nouns have a characteristic **i** in certain case endings and are thus called **I-STEM NOUNS**, as distinct from those introduced in Capvt VII, which are sometimes called **CONSONANT STEMS**. As you will see from the following paradigms, the only new ending shared by all i-stems is the genitive plural in **-ium** rather than simply **-um**; neuters have, in addition, **-ī** instead of **-e** in the ablative singular and **-ia** instead of **-a** in the nominative, accusative, and vocative plural; **vīs** is a common irregular i-stem and should be memorized (its genitive and dative singular forms, given in parentheses, are rarely used).

| | Cons.-stem Reviewed | Parisyllabics | | Base in 2 Consonants | N. in -e, -al, -ar | Irregular |
|---|---|---|---|---|---|---|
| | rēx, rēgis, m., *king* | cīvis, -is, m., *citizen* | nūbēs, -is, f., *cloud* | urbs, -is, f., *city* | mare, -is, n., *sea* | vīs, vīs, f., *force;* pl. *strength* |
| *N.* | rēx | cívis | nū́bēs | úrbs | máre | vīs |
| *G.* | rḗgis | cívis | nū́bis | úrbis | máris | (vīs) |
| *D.* | rḗgī | cívī | nū́bī | úrbī | márī | (vī) |
| *A.* | rḗgem | cívem | nū́bem | úrbem | máre | vim |
| *A.* | rḗge | cíve | nū́be | úrbe | márī | vī |
| *N.* | rḗgēs | cívēs | nū́bēs | úrbēs | mária | vī́rēs |
| *G.* | rḗgum | cívium | nū́bium | úrbium | márium | vī́rium |
| *D.* | rḗgibus | cívibus | nū́bibus | úrbibus | máribus | vī́ribus |
| *A.* | rḗgēs | cívēs | nū́bēs | úrbēs | mária | vī́rēs |
| *A.* | rḗgibus | cívibus | nū́bibus | úrbibus | máribus | vī́ribus |

An alternate masculine and feminine accusative plural ending in -īs (e.g., cīvīs for cīvēs), though rarely appearing in this book, was frequently employed throughout Republican literature and into the Augustan period and should be remembered.

Besides learning these few new endings, it is also important to be able to recognize that a noun is an i-stem when you encounter it in a vocabulary list or a reading. The following three rules will enable you to do so and should be memorized.

### Masculine and Feminine *i*-Stems

1. Most masculine and feminine nouns that have a nominative singular in -is or -ēs and the same number of syllables in both the nominative and genitive (and hence called "parisyllabic," from **pār**, *equal*, + **syllaba**).

> **hostis, hostis,** m.; gen. pl. **hostium;** *enemy*
> **nāvis, nāvis,** f.; **nāvium;** *ship*
> **mōlēs, mōlis,** f.; **mōlium;** *mass, structure*
> **cīvis, cīvis,** and **nūbēs, nūbis,** above

2. Masculine and (chiefly) feminine nouns with a nominative singular in -s or -x which have a base ending in two consonants; most, like the following, have monosyllabic nominatives.

> **ars, art-is,** f.; **artium;** *art, skill*
> **dēns, dent-is,** m.; **dentium;** *tooth*
> **nox, noct-is,** f.; **noctium;** *night*
> **urbs, urb-is,** above

Again, the only ending ordinarily distinguishing these masculine and feminine nouns from consonant stems is the genitive plural in -ium.

### Neuter *i*-Stems

3. Neuter nouns with a nominative singular ending in -al, -ar, or -e have the characteristic i not only in the genitive plural -ium but also in the ablative singular -ī and the nominative/accusative/vocative plural -ia.

> **animal, animālis,** n., *animal*
> **exemplar, exemplāris,** n., *model, pattern, original*
> **mare, maris,** above

### Irregular Vīs

The common irregular i-stem **vīs** must be memorized and carefully distinguished from **vir**. Note that the characteristic long ī appears in most forms of **vīs**, vs. the short i of **vir**; contrast the following: **virī, virōs, vīrēs, virīs, vīrium, virum, vīribus.**

## ABLATIVE CASE USES

You have frequently encountered in the readings ablative nouns and pronouns employed simply as objects of prepositions; there are several more distinct uses of the ablative, some requiring a preposition and some not. Following are three of the most common, and others will be introduced in later chapters, so you may wish to maintain a list in your notebook or computer file, with the name, a definition, and examples for each (you should keep similar lists for all the other cases as well).

### Ablative of Means or Instrument

As you continue to learn new syntactical constructions, always keep in mind these three things: DEFINITION (what is it?), RECOGNITION (how do I recognize one when I see it in a sentence), TRANSLATION (how do I translate it into English?). For the **ABLATIVE OF MEANS/INSTRUMENT**, a usage you have actually already encountered a few times in the readings, it's as simple as this:

*Definition:* a noun or pronoun that answers the question "by means of what (instrument)?/by what?/with what?" is the action of the verb performed.

*Recognition:* a noun/pronoun in the ablative *without* a preposition.

**Translation:** Supply the English prepositions *by (means of), with.*

>  **Litterās stilō scrīpsit.** *He wrote the letter with a pencil* (**stilus, -ī**).
>  **Cīvēs pecūniā vīcit.** *He conquered the citizens with/by money.*
>  **Id meīs oculīs vīdī.** *I saw it with my own eyes.*
>  **Suīs labōribus urbem cōnservāvit.** *By his own labors he saved the city.*

### Ablatives of Accompaniment and Manner

You have also already encountered the **ABLATIVE OF ACCOMPANIMENT** (DEFINITION: an ablative noun/pronoun, usually a person, that answers the question "in whose company/with whom is the action performed"; RECOGNITION: an ablative with the preposition **cum**; TRANSLATION: translate **cum** as "with," followed by the noun/pronoun, e.g., **cum agricolā labōrat,** *he is working with the farmer*) and the **ABLATIVE OF MANNER** (DEF.: a noun that answers the question "how/in what manner" is the action performed; REC.: **cum** + an ablative noun, regularly an abstract noun; TRANS.: e.g., **cum cūrā labōrat,** *she works with care/carefully*).

>  **Cum amīcīs vēnērunt.** *They came with friends* (= with whom?).
>  **Cum celeritāte vēnērunt.** *They came with speed* (= how?; *speedily.*—celeritās, -tātis).
>  **Id cum eīs fēcit.** *He did it with them* (= with whom?).
>  **Id cum virtūte fēcit.** *He did it with courage* (= how?; *courageously*).

Each of these three constructions may be translated using the English preposition "with" (among other possibilities), but the three usages are conceptually different and must be distinguished. Recall that ablatives generally function adverbially, telling you something about the action of the verb; in these three instances they tell you, respectively, by what means the action was performed, with whom the action was performed, and in what manner the action was performed. The only challenge comes in translating from English to Latin: if *with* tells *with whom* or *in what manner*, use **cum** + ablative; if *with* tells *by what means/with what instrument*, use the ablative without a preposition.

# VOCĀBVLA

As you learn this chapter's vocabulary (by listening and repeating aloud, right?— **semper audī et prōnūntiā!**), keep in mind the rules for recognizing third declension i-stems and identify those you find in this list; practice by declining at least one of each gender—or, better yet, decline some noun-adjective phrases like **animal ipsum** and **urbs sōla**—and comparing with the paradigms. A few of the nouns require special attention: **cīvis,** *citizen,* is one of a small group of nouns that can, for obvious reasons, be either feminine or masculine (another is **canis,** *dog,* "canine"); and be careful not to confuse **mors** with **mora** or **mōs,** or **vīs** with **vir.** The new prepositions introduced here, **ā/ab** and **trāns,** also commonly function as prefixes: see "Some Etymological Aids," App., p. 485–89.

**ánimal, animális,** n., *a living creature, animal* (related to **anima,** *breath, air, spirit, soul,* and **animus;** animate, animation)

**áqua, áquae,** f., *water* (aquatic, aquarium, Aquarius, aqueduct, subaqueous, ewer, sewer, sewage, sewerage)

**ars, ártis,** f., *art, skill* (artifact, artifice, artificial, artisan, artist, inert)

**aúris, aúris,** f., *ear* (aural, auricle, auricular, auriform; not to be confused with "auric," "auriferous," from **aurum,** *gold*)

**cīvis, cīvis,** m. and f., *citizen* (civic, civil, civilian, civility, civilize; cf. **cīvitās**)

**iūs, iū́ris,** n., *right, justice, law* (jurisdiction, jurisprudence, juridical, jurist, juror, jury, just, justice, injury)

**máre, máris,** n., *sea* (marine, mariner, marinate, maritime, submarine, cormorant, rosemary, mere = Eng. cognate, archaic for "small lake")

**mors, mórtis,** f., *death* (mortal, immortal, mortify, mortgage; murder = Eng. cognate)

**nū́bēs, nū́bis,** f., *cloud* (nubilous, nubilose, nuance)

**ōs, óris,** n., *mouth, face* (oral, orifice, orator; cf. **ōrāre,** *to speak, plead* )

**pars, pártis,** f., *part, share; direction* (party, partial, partake, participate, participle, particle, particular, partisan, partition, apart, apartment, depart)

**Rṓma, Rṓmae,** f., *Rome* (romance, romantic, romanticism; cf. **Rōmānus**)

**túrba, túrbae,** f., *uproar, disturbance; mob, crowd, multitude* (cf. **turbāre,** *to disturb, throw into confusion;* turbid, turbulent, turbine, turbo, disturb, perturb, imperturbable, trouble)

**urbs, úrbis,** f., *city* (urban, urbane, urbanity, suburb, suburban)

**vīs, vīs,** f., *force, power, violence;* **vīrēs, vīrium,** pl., *strength* (vim, violate, violent; do not confuse with **vir**)

**ā** (before consonants, like Eng. "a," vs. "an"), **ab** (before vowels or consonants), prep. + abl., *away from, from; by* (personal agent); frequent in compounds (aberration, abject, abrasive, absolve, abstract, abundant, abuse)

**trāns,** prep. + acc., *across;* also a prefix (transport, transmit, transfer)

**appéllō, appellā́re, appellā́vī, appellā́tum,** *to speak to, address (as), call, name* (appellation, appellative, appeal, appellant, appellate)

**cúrrō, cúrrere, cucúrrī, cúrsum,** *to run, rush, move quickly* (current, cursive, cursory, course, coarse, discursive, incur, occur, recur)

**mū́tō, mūtā́re, mūtā́vī, mūtā́tum,** *to change, alter; exchange* (mutable, immutable, mutual, commute, permutation, transmutation, molt)

**téneō, tenḗre, ténuī, téntum,** *to hold, keep, possess; restrain;* **-tineō, -ēre, -tinuī, -tentum** in compounds, e.g., **contineō** (tenable, tenacious, tenant, tenet, tenure, tentacle, tenor, continue, content, continent, pertinent, pertinacity, lieutenant, appertain, detain, retain, sustain)

**vī́tō, vītā́re, vītā́vī, vītā́tum,** *to avoid, shun;* not to be confused with **vīvō** (inevitable)

# LĒCTIŌ ET TRĀNSLĀTIŌ

After memorizing the paradigms and vocabulary, and practicing with the Self-Tutorial Exercises, listen to the readings, if you have the CDs, read them aloud for comprehension, and then write out your translations. For practice with the new grammar, scan through the readings and, first, find all the i-stem nouns; next, find all the ablative nouns and pronouns and identify the specific usage of each (means, manner, accompaniment, or simply object of a preposition).

## EXERCITĀTIŌNĒS

1. Magnam partem illārum urbium post multōs annōs vī et cōnsiliō capiēbat.
2. Ante Caesaris ipsīus oculōs trāns viam cucurrimus et cum amīcīs fūgimus.
3. Nēmō vitia sua videt, sed quisque illa alterīus.
4. Monuitne nūper eōs dē vīribus illārum urbium in Asiā?
5. Ipsī autem lībertātem cīvium suōrum magnā cum cūrā aluerant.

6. Nōmina multārum urbium ab nōminibus urbium antīquārum trāximus.
7. Pars cīvium dīvitiās cēpit et per urbem ad mare cucurrit.
8. Hodiē multae nūbēs in caelō sunt signum īrae acerbae deōrum.
9. Illud animal heri ibi cecidit et sē trāns terram ab agrō trahēbat.
10. That wicked tyrant did not long preserve the rights of these citizens.
11. Great is the force of the arts.
12. His wife was standing there with her (own) friends and doing that with patience.
13. Cicero felt and said the same thing concerning his own life and the nature of death.

## SENTENTIAE ANTĪQVAE

1. Et Deus aquās "maria" in prīncipiō appellāvit. (Genesis; **aquās** is dir. obj.; **maria** is an OBJECTIVE COMPLEMENT, a construction common with such verbs as **appellō**, *to call*, as in "to call him a friend," and **faciō**, *to make*, as in "to make her the leader.")
2. Terra ipsa hominēs et animālia ōlim creāvit. (Lucretius.)
3. Pān servat ovēs et magistrōs fortūnātōs ovium. (Vergil.—Pan, the god of pastures and shepherds.—**ovis, ovis**, f., *sheep;* "ovine.")
4. Parva formīca onera magna ōre trahit. (Horace.—**formīca, -ae**, f., *ant;* "formic acid," "formaldehyde."—**onus, oneris**, n., *load;* "onerous," "exonerate.")
5. Auribus teneō lupum. (*Terence.—a picturesque, proverbial statement of a dilemma, like Eng. "to have a tiger by the tail."—**lupus, -ī**, m., *wolf;* "lupus," the disease, "lupine.")
6. Ille magnam turbam clientium sēcum habet. (Horace.—**cliēns, -entis**, m., *client, dependent;* "clientage," "clientele.")
7. Hunc nēmō vī neque pecūniā superāre potuit. (Ennius.)
8. Animus eius erat ignārus artium malārum. (Sallust.—**ignārus, -a, -um**, *ignorant;* "ignorance," "ignore.")
9. Magna pars meī mortem vītābit. (Horace.—**meī**, partitive gen., Capvt XV.)
10. Vōs, amīcī doctī, exemplāria Graeca semper cum cūrā versāte. (Horace.—**exemplar, -plāris**, n., *model, original;* "exemplary," "example."—**versāre**, *to turn; study;* "versatile," "verse.")
11. Nōn vīribus et celeritāte corporum magna gerimus, sed sapientiā et sententiā et arte. (Cicero.—**celeritās, -tātis**, *swiftness;* "celerity," "accelerate.")
12. Istī caelum, nōn animum suum, mūtant, sī trāns mare currunt. (Horace.)

### Store Teeth

Thāis habet nigrōs, niveōs Laecānia dentēs.
    Quae ratiō est? Ēmptōs haec habet, illa suōs.

*Ancient Roman
and Etruscan
dental appliances*

*Martial *Epig.* 5.43: Yes, the Romans DID have dentures—made of ivory, wood, or even their own teeth, with roots removed, of course! Meter: elegiac couplet.—**Thāis** and **Laecānia** are names of women; take **habet . . . dentēs** with both these subjects.—**niger, -gra, -grum,** *black,* here, i.e., discolored and decayed; "denigrate."—**niveus, -a, -um,** *snowy;* "nivation," "niveal."—**dēns, dentis,** m., *tooth;* "dental," "trident."—**quae** (interrog. adj. modifying **ratiō**), *what?*—**ēmptōs** [**dentēs**], perf. pass. partic., *bought, purchased;* "exempt," "preempt."

*QVAESTIŌNĒS:* Both verses of this two-liner contain an example of chiasmus—can you identify each, and comment on the intended effect? To which of the women do **haec** and **illa** refer?—if necessary, refer to the range of meanings for these demonstratives in the Capvt IX **Vocābula.**) If you judged your lady-friends by their teeth, which of these two would you prefer to hang out with?

### Cicero Imagines the State of Rome Itself Urging Him to Punish the Catilinarian Conspirators

M. Tullī Cicerō, quid agis? Istī prō multīs factīs malīs poenās dare nunc dēbent; eōs enim ad mortem dūcere dēbēs, quod Rōmam in multa perīcula trāxērunt. Saepe Rōmānī in hāc cīvitāte etiam cīvēs morte multāvērunt. Sed nōn dēbēs cōgitāre hōs malōs esse cīvēs, nam numquam in hāc urbe prōditōrēs patriae iūra cīvium tenuērunt; hī iūra sua āmīsērunt. Populus Rōmānus tibi magnās grātiās aget, M. Tullī, sī istōs cum virtūte nunc multābis.

Cicero *Cat.* 1.11.27–28: A continuation of Cicero's first Catilinarian oration (see notes on "Cicero Denounces Catiline," Capvt XI); in a particularly histrionic moment, Cicero here assumes the role of the personified city of Rome, urging action against the conspirators.—**M.:** the standard abbreviation for the praenomen **Mārcus** (for the Roman system of personal nomenclature, see notes on the graffito in Capvt III).—**multāre,** *to punish.*—**prōditor, -tōris,** m., *betrayer.*

*QVAESTIŌNĒS:* It was illegal to execute Roman citizens without a trial. Cicero here, in a moment of high rhetorical drama, imagines the state of Rome itself urging a rationale for immediately executing Catiline's supporters (as in fact Cicero ultimately did);

what exactly is that argument?–would it carry any weight in a modern American court-room?

## SCRĪPTA IN PARIETIBVS

Ars Urbicī ub(i)q(ue)!

*CIL* 4.4722-4723: From a wall in the courtyard of the House of the Cissonii (Reg. VII, Ins. 7: for another graffito from the same house, see *CIL* 4.4742 in Capvt VIII above); pre-sumably Urbicus himself etched these drawings of a deer and a boar (?) and the two ac-companying graffiti, the second of which is excerpted here—seemingly a self-gratulatory note on the ubiquitousness of his doodlings!—**Ars . . . ubique:** sc. **est.**—**ubique,** adv., *anywhere; everywhere;* often abbreviated in inscriptions, but usually as **ubiq.;** "ubiquity."

## ETYMOLOGIA

Pan (in S.A. 3), the Greek god of woods and countryside, was endowed with the power of engendering sudden fear in people; hence from Gk. comes our word "panic" (however, "pan-," as in "Pan-American," comes from a different Gk. word meaning *all.*) And here are some more derivatives from **dēns, dentis,** in "Store Teeth": dentist, dentifrice, dentil, indent, dandelion (from Fr. **dent de lion**); Eng. "tooth" is cognate, as is the Gk. root **dont-,** as in "orthodontist," a doctor who makes your teeth "straight" (Gk. **ortho-**).

Following are some more Romance derivatives:

| Latin | It. | Sp. | Port. | Fr. |
|---|---|---|---|---|
| ars, artis; artem | arte | arte | arte | art |
| mors, mortis; mortem | morte | muerte | morte | mort |
| pars, partis; partem | parte | parte | parte | parti |
| pēs, pedis; pedem | piede | pie | pé | pied |
| dēns, dentis; dentem | dente | diente | dente | dent |
| nāvis, nāvis; nāvem | nave | nave | nave | navire, nef (*nave*) |
| nox, noctis; noctem | notte | noche | noite | nuit |

Cf. Rom. **arta, moarte, parte, picior** (from **pediculus,** diminutive of **pes**), **dinte, nava, noapte;** and Old Occ. **art, mọrt, part, pẹ, dẹn, nau, nọch.** Clearly most of these Romance derivatives do not come from the nom. of the Lat. words. The rule is that Romance nouns and adjectives of Lat. origin generally derive from the acc.

form, often with the loss of some part of the final syllable; one exception thus far in this book has been Fr. **fils,** *son,* from Lat. **fīlius,** and cf. Old Fr. **fiz,** whence Eng. "Fitz-," *natural son,* e.g., Fitzgerald.


## LATĪNA EST GAVDIVM—ET VTILIS!

**Quid agitis, amīcī et amīcae!** Here's hoping yours is a **mēns sāna in corpore sānō,** in all of its **partēs.** You've now learned the Latin names for several body parts: **oculus, auris, ōs,** and **dēns** (remember Thais and Laecania?). Here are some others, from the **caput** up only, that can be easily remembered from their English derivatives: **collum, -ī,** *neck* ("collar"); **nāsus, -ī,** *nose* ("nasal"); **supercilium, -ī,** *eyebrow* (let's hope you've never raised an eyebrow superciliously at a friend); **coma, -ae,** *hair* (astronomy buffs know the constellation **Coma Berenīcēs,** *Berenice's lock*—sorry, no connection with "comb," but "comet" is related); **lingua, -ae,** *tongue* as well as *language* ("multilingual," "lingo," and even "linguine," which is long and flat like a tongue!). For more **partēs corporis,** see Capvt XX. Languages, by the way, should be learned with "oral-aural" techniques, and not just through reading and writing, so I hope you're remembering to practice your declensions and conjugations aloud, and to say **salvē** or **tē amō** to someone everyday. Looking back at the **Vocābula** and the new **i**-stems, I am reminded of **ars grātiā artis,** *art for the sake of art,* the motto of M.G.M. film studios, and **B.A.** and **M.A.** for **Baccalaureus Artium** and **Magister Artium,** academic degrees you may have or aspire to. Then there's the familiar Latin phrase, **mare nostrum,** which is either what the Romans used to call the Mediterranean (*our sea*) or, perhaps somewhat less likely, Caesar's critical comment on his unmusical equine ("my horse doesn't play the guitar"—groan!!!). **Valēte!**

# CAPVT XV ﹃﹄﹃﹄

# Numerals; Genitive of the Whole; Ablative with Numerals and Ablative of Time

## GRAMMATICA

### NUMERALS

The commonest numerals in Latin, as in English, are the **CARDINALS** (from **cardō, cardinis**, m., *hinge,* the "pivotal" numbers in counting, "one, two, three. . . ," etc.) and the **ORDINALS** (from **ōrdō, ōrdinis**, m., *rank, order,* the numerals indicating "order" of occurrence, "first, second. . . ," etc.).

### Cardinal Numerals

In Latin most cardinal numerals through 100 are indeclinable adjectives; one form is used for all cases and genders. The following, however, are declined as indicated.

**únus, úna, únum,** *one* (for declension, see Capvt IX)

|    | **duo,** *two* | | | **trēs,** *three* | | **mīlle,** *thousand* <br> **mīlia,** *thousands* | |
|----|----------|----------|----------|----------|----------|----------|----------|
|    | M.       | F.       | N.       | M.&F.    | N.       | M.F.N.   | N.       |
| *N.* | dúo    | dúae     | dúo      | trēs     | tría     | mílle    | mília    |
| *G.* | duórum | duárum   | duórum   | tríum    | tríum    | mílle    | mílium   |
| *D.* | duóbus | duábus   | duóbus   | tríbus   | tríbus   | mílle    | mílibus  |
| *A.* | dúōs   | dúās     | dúo      | trēs     | tría     | mílle    | mília    |
| *A.* | duóbus | duábus   | duóbus   | tríbus   | tríbus   | mílle    | mílibus  |

The cardinals indicating the hundreds from 200 through 900 are declined like plural adjectives of the first and second declensions; e.g., **ducentī, -ae, -a,** *two hundred.*

    **Mīlle,** 1,000, is an indeclinable *adjective* in the singular, but in the plural it functions as a neuter i-stem *noun* of the third declension (e.g., **mīlle virī**, *a thousand men;* **mīlia virōrum**, *thousands of men*).

The cardinals from **ūnus** through **vīgintī quīnque** should be memorized (see list in the App., p. 500) and with them **centum** (100) and **mīlle**. The following sentences illustrate these various forms and uses of cardinal numerals:

> **Trēs puerī duābus puellīs rosās dedērunt.** *Three boys gave roses to two girls.*
> **Octō puerī decem puellīs librōs dedērunt.** *Eight boys gave books to ten girls.*
> **Ūnus vir cum quattuor amīcīs vēnit.** *One man came with four friends.*
> **Cōnsul cum centum virīs vēnit.** *The consul came with 100 men.*
> **Cōnsul cum ducentīs virīs vēnit.** *The consul came with 200 men.*
> **Cōnsul cum mīlle virīs vēnit.** *The consul came with 1,000 men.*
> **Cōnsul cum sex mīlibus virōrum vēnit.** *The consul came with six thousand(s) (of) men.*

### Ordinal Numerals

The ordinal numerals, which indicate the order of sequence, are regular first/second declension adjectives (**prīmus, -a, -um; secundus, -a, -um;** etc.—see App., p. 500). The ordinals from **prīmus** through **duodecimus** should be learned.

## GENITIVE OF THE WHOLE

The genitive of a word indicating the whole of some thing or group is used after a word designating a part of that whole:

> **pars urbis,** *part of the city* (city = the whole)
>
> **nēmō amīcōrum meōrum,** *no one of my friends*

This **GENITIVE OF THE WHOLE** (sometimes called the **PARTITIVE GENITIVE**) is also used with **mīlia** and after the neuter nominative and accusative of certain pronouns and adjectives such as **aliquid, quid, multum, plūs, minus, satis, nihil, tantum, quantum:**

> **nihil temporis,** *no time (nothing of time)*
> **quid cōnsiliī?** *what plan?*
>
> **satis ēloquentiae,** *sufficient eloquence*
> **decem mīlia virōrum,** *10,000 men (but* **mīlle virī,** *1,000 men)*

The genitive of the whole may itself be the neuter singular of a *second* declension adjective:

> **multum bonī,** *much good* (lit. *of good*)
> **nihil certī,** *nothing certain*
>
> **Quid novī?** *What (is) new?*

## ABLATIVE WITH CARDINAL NUMERALS

With cardinal numerals (other than **mīlia**) and with **quīdam** (*a certain one*) and sometimes **paucī** the idea of the whole is expressed by **ex** or **dē** and the ablative:

**trēs ex amīcīs meīs,** *three of my friends* (*but* **trēs amīcī** = *three friends*)
**quīnque ex eīs,** *five of them*              **centum ex virīs,** *100 of the men*
**quīdam ex eīs,** *a certain one of them*       **paucī ex amīcīs,** *a few of the friends*

## ABLATIVE OF TIME WHEN OR WITHIN WHICH

The Romans indicated the TIME WHEN OR WITHIN WHICH an action occurred by using the ablative, without a preposition; in translating you usually must supply "at," "on," "in," or "within," depending upon English idiom ("for" is *not* an option, as it indicates DURATION OF TIME, an accusative construction introduced in Capvt XXXVII):

**Eō tempore nōn poteram id facere.** *At that time I could not do it.*
**Agricolae bonīs annīs valēbant.** *In good years the farmers flourished.*
**Eōdem diē vēnērunt.** *They came (on) the same day* (**diē,** abl. of **diēs,** *day*).
**Aestāte lūdēbant.** *In the summer they used to play.* (**aestāte,** abl. of **aestās,** *summer*)
**Paucīs hōrīs id faciet.** *In (within) a few hours he will do it.*

Since this construction always involves some noun indicating a unit of time, without a preposition, you can easily distinguish it from the other ablative uses you have learned (object of certain prepositions, means, manner, accompaniment, and ablative with cardinal numerals); you must be able to identify and translate these six ablative usages, so for each remember: DEFINITION, RECOGNITION, TRANSLATION.

# VOCĀBVLA

Numerous Latin nouns ending in -ia evolve into English nouns in *-y;* **Italia** and **memoria** are two examples in this chapter's list, as is **glōria** (Capvt V—for others, see "Some Etymological Aids," p. 490). Is **tempestās** an **i**-stem or not?—if you're uncertain, review the rules in Capvt XIV. Some verbs lack a fourth principal part; **timeō** in this chapter, and **discō** in Capvt VIII are examples. A special challenge in this chapter is learning to count from **ūnus** to **vīgintī quīnque,** *1–25,* and from **prīmus** to **duodecimus,** *1st–12th.* Listen to these numerals on the CDs or at www.wheelockslatin.com for correct pronunciation, then practice counting aloud, just as you did when you were learning as a young child to count in your native language: "one, two, three . . .," "**ūnus, duo, trēs** . . ." "first, second, third . . .," "**prīmus, secundus, tertius.**" Once you have worked at learning the list and new declensions, decline some noun-adjective phrases using the new vocabulary, such as **duae memoriae** and **trēs tempestātēs** (both plural only, of course).

**Itália, Itáliae,** f., *Italy* (italics, italicize)

**memória, memóriae,** f., *memory, recollection* (memoir, memorial, memorize, memorandum, commemorate)

**tempéstās, tempestátis,** f., *period of time, season; weather, storm* (tempest, tempestuous; cf. **tempus**)

Cardinal numerals from **únus** to **vīgíntī quínque** (App., p. 500)

Ordinal numerals from **prímus** to **duodécimus** (App., p. 500)

**céntum,** indecl. adj., *a hundred* (cent, centenary, centennial, centigrade, centimeter, centipede, centurion, century, bicentennial)

**mílle,** indecl. adj. in sg., *thousand;* **mília, mílium,** n. i-stem noun in pl., *thousands* (millennium, mile, milligram, millimeter, millipede, million, mill = 1/10 cent)

**míser, mísera, míserum,** *wretched, miserable, unfortunate* (misery, commiserate)

**ínter,** prep. + acc., *between, among* (intern, internal; common as Eng. prefix, App., p. 487, e.g., interact, intercept, interdict)

**ítaque,** adv., *and so, therefore*

**commíttō, commíttere, commísī, commíssum,** *to entrust, commit* (committee, commission, commissary, commitment, noncommissioned, noncom)

**exspéctō, exspectáre, exspectávī, exspectátum,** *to look for, expect, await* (expectant, expectation)

**iáciō, iácere, iécī, iáctum,** *to throw, hurl.* Appears in compounds as **-iciō, -icere, -iēcī, -iectum:** e.g., **ēiciō, ēicere, ēiēcī, ēiectum,** *to throw out, drive out* (abject, adjective, conjecture, dejected, eject, inject, interject, object, project, reject, subject, trajectory)

**tímeō, timére, tímuī,** *to fear, be afraid (of)* (timid, timorous, intimidate; cf. **timor**)

# LĒCTIŌ ET TRĀNSLĀTIŌ

After learning the new paradigms and vocabulary and testing your mastery with the Self-Tutorial Exercises, scan the readings to identify all ablative and genitive uses. The trick in translating ablative of time is that you usually must supply "at," "on," "in," or "within," based on English idiom; thus, for **ūnō annō** in Ex. 4, we would say *in* or *within one year,* not *at* or *on one year.* Listen to the CDs, if you have them, and read aloud before translating.

## EXERCITĀTIŌNĒS

1. Illae quīnque fēminae inter ea animālia mortem nōn timēbant.
2. Duo ex fīliīs ā portā per agrōs cum patre suō heri currēbant et in aquam cecidērunt.
3. Prīmus rēx dīvitiās in mare iēcit, nam magnam īram et vim turbae timuit.
4. Nēmō eandem partem Asiae ūnō annō vincet.
5. Rōmānī quattuor ex eīs urbibus prīmā viā iūnxērunt.
6. Itaque mīlia librōrum eius ab urbe trāns Italiam mīsistis.
7. Lībertātem et iūra hārum urbium artibus bellī cōnservāvimus.
8. Dī Graecī sē inter hominēs cum virtūte saepe nōn gerēbant.
9. Cicerō mīlia Rōmānōrum vī sententiārum suārum dūcēbat.
10. Sententiae medicī eum cārum mihi numquam fēcērunt.
11. The tyrant used to entrust his life to those three friends.
12. The greedy man never has enough wealth.
13. At that time we saved their mother with those six letters.
14. Through their friends they conquered the citizens of the ten cities.

## SENTENTIAE ANTĪQUAE

1. Diū in istā nāve fuī et propter tempestātem nūbēsque semper mortem exspectābam. (Terence.—**nāvis, -vis,** *f., ship;* "naval," "navigate.")
2. Septem hōrīs ad eam urbem vēnimus. (Cicero.)
3. Italia illīs temporibus erat plēna Graecārum artium, et multī Rōmānī ipsī hās artēs colēbant. (Cicero.—**artēs,** in the sense of studies, e.g., literature and philosophy.—**colō, -ere,** *to cultivate, pursue;* "culture," "agriculture.")
4. Inter bellum et pācem dubitābant. (Tacitus.—**dubitāre,** *to hesitate, waver;* "doubtful," "dubious.")
5. Eō tempore istum ex urbe ēiciēbam. (Cicero.)
6. Dīcēbat quisque miser: "Cīvis Rōmānus sum." (Cicero.)
7. Mea puella passerem suum amābat, et passer ad eam sōlam semper pīpiābat nec sē ex gremiō movēbat. (Catullus.—**passer, -seris,** m., *sparrow,* a pet bird; "passeriform," "passerine."—**pīpiāre,** *to chirp;* "peep," "piper."—**gremium, -iī,** n., *lap.*—**movēre;** "movement," "motor.")
8. Fīliī meī frātrem meum dīligēbant, mē vītābant; mē patrem acerbum appellābant et meam mortem exspectābant. Nunc autem mōrēs meōs mūtāvī et duōs fīliōs ad mē crās traham. (Terence.)
9. Dionȳsius tyrannus, quoniam tōnsōrī caput committere timēbat, fīliās suās barbam et capillum tondēre docuit; itaque virginēs tondēbant barbam et capillum patris. (Cicero.—**tōnsor, -sōris,** m., *barber;* "tonsorial," "tonsure."—**barba, -ae,** f., *beard;* "barb," "barber."—**capillus, -ī,** m., *hair;* "capillary."—**tondēre,** *to shave, cut.*)

*Mausoleum of Cyrus the Great*
*6th cent. B.C.*
*Pasargadae, Iran*

## Cyrus' Dying Words on Immortality

Ō meī fīliī trēs, nōn dēbētis esse miserī. Ad mortem enim nunc veniō, sed pars meī, animus meus, semper remanēbit. Dum eram vōbīscum, animum nōn vidēbātis, sed ex factīs meīs intellegēbātis eum esse in hōc corpore. Crēdite igitur animum esse eundem post mortem, etiam sī eum nōn vidēbitis, et semper cōnservāte mē in memoriā vestrā.

Cicero *Sen.* 22.79–81: This passage and the next are both drawn from Cicero's treatise **Dē Senectūte,** composed shortly before Julius Caesar's assassination. Cyrus the Great, whom Cicero quotes here, was a Persian king of the 6th cent. B.C. and founder of the Persian Achaemenid Empire.—**crēdō, -ere,** *to believe;* "credible," "credulity," "creed."

*QVAESTIŌNĒS:* What view of the afterlife is evidenced in this passage? Comment on Cyrus' argument for the existence of the soul.

## Fabian Tactics

Etiam in senectūte Quīntus Fabius Maximus erat vir vērae virtūtis et bella cum animīs adulēscentis gerēbat. Dē eō amīcus noster Ennius, doctus ille poēta, haec verba ōlim scrīpsit: "Ūnus homō cīvitātem fortūnātam nōbīs cūnctātiōne cōnservāvit. Rūmōrēs et fāmam nōn pōnēbat ante salūtem Rōmae. Glōria eius, igitur, nunc bene valet et semper valēbit."

Cicero *Sen.* 4.10: Quintus Fabius Maximus enjoyed considerable success against Hannibal in the Second Punic War (218–201 B.C.) through his delaying tactics, thus earning the cognomen **Cūnctātor,** *the Delayer.*—**Ennius:** Quintus Ennius (239–169 B.C.), an early Lat. poet sometimes called "the Father of Latin Literature," was author of numerous plays and an influential epic poem titled the **Annālēs.**—**cūnctātiō, -ōnis,** m., *delaying;* "cunctation."—**rūmor, -mōris,** m., *rumor, gossip.*—**pōnō, -ere,** *to put, place;* "posit," "exponent."—**salūs, -lūtis**, f., *safety;* "salutary," "salutation"; cf. **salvēre.**–**valet:** the sense here is to *prevail* (a derivative) or *endure, survive.*

*QVAESTIŌNĒS:* What did Cicero find especially praiseworthy in the character of Quintus Fabius Maximus? What one virtue in particular did Fabius' contemporary, the poet Ennius, single out?

## SCRĪPTA IN PARIETIBVS

*CIL* 4.5081 (Reg. XI, Ins. 5) and 6856 (Reg. VI, Ins. 16): The Pompeians who inscribed these ornate graffiti in their houses were clearly feeling patriotic at the time! I have not provided transcriptions here, because you can certainly read 6856, which was inscribed on the wall of one home's corridor leading from the atrium to the back of the house; and, given that the last six letters of 5081, inscribed near a kitchen door in another house, are **CAESAR,** you should easily decipher the four letters of the first word (two of which also appear in the second word) and thus determine the name of the notorious Roman emperor whom the writer here chose to memorialize.

## ETYMOLOGIA

Following are some Eng. derivatives from the Lat. cardinals and ordinals 2–12: (2) dual, duel, duet, double (cf. doubt, dubious), duplicity; second; (3) trio, triple, trivial; (4) quart, quarter, quartet, quatrain; (5) quinquennium, quintet, quintuplets, quincunx; (6) sextet, sextant; (7) September; (8) October, octave, octavo; (9) November, noon; (10) December, decimal, decimate, dime, dean; (12) duodecimal, dozen.

The following table lists some Romance cardinal numbers derived from Latin.

| Latin | It. | Sp. | Port. | Fr. | Old Occ. | Rom. |
|-------|-----|-----|-------|-----|----------|------|
| ūnus | un(o) | un(o) | um | un | un | unu |
| duo | due | dos | dois | deux | dọs | doi |
| trēs | tre | tres | três | trois | trẹs | trei |
| quattuor | quattro | cuatro | quatro | quatre | catre | patru |
| quīnque | cinque | cinco | cinco | cinq | cinc | cinci |
| sex | sei | seis | seis | six | sẹis | şase |
| septem | sette | siete | sete | sept | sẹt | sapte |
| octō | otto | ocho | oito | huit | ọch | opt |
| novem | nove | nueve | nove | neuf | nọu | nouă |
| decem | dieci | diez | dez | dix | dẹtz | zece |
| ūndecim | undici | once | onze | onze | ọnge | unsprezece |
| duodecim | dodici | doce | doze | douze | dọtze | doisprezece |
| centum | cento | ciento | cem | cent | cẹn | o sută |
| mīlle | mille | mil | mil | mille | mil | o mie |

## LATĪNA EST GAVDIVM—ET VTILIS!

**Salvēte! Quid novī, meī amīcī amīcaeque?** Latin has other types of numerals, besides the cardinals and ordinals, which you will encounter later in your study of the language and many of which are already familiar. "Roman numerals" developed from counting on the fingers: I = one finger, II = two, etc., V = five (the hand held outstretched with the thumb and index finger making a "V"), VI = a "handful of fingers" plus one, etc., X = two V's, one inverted on the other, and so on. There were also DISTRIBUTIVE numerals, **singulī, -ae, -a** (*one each*); **bīnī, -ae, -a** (*two each*), **ternī, -ae, -a**, etc., and MULTIPLICATIVES, **simplex, simplicis** (*single*), **duplex** (*double*), **triplex**, etc.; likewise numeral adverbs, **semel** (*once*), **bis** (*twice*), **ter** (*three times*), etc. All these words have numerous (pardon the pun) English derivatives! For practice, in or out of the classroom, try some math too: **duo et trēs sunt quīnque.** And with the interrogative **quot** (*how many?*), your instructor may ask you questions like **quot oculōs habēs?**—remember to reply in the correct gender and case, **duōs** or **duōs oculōs habeō**—or **quot discipulae hodiē sunt in classe** (*in class*)?—**quot discipulī in classe sunt?**—**quot discipulae et discipulī sunt?** Your family physician may write a prescription that includes the common medical abbreviation "t.i.d.," which stands for **ter in diē,** *three times (in a) day.* Well, *this* doctor's prescription, for your intellectual health, is "study your Latin, t.i.d."—**et valēte!**

# CAPVT XVI ⌐⌐⌐

# Third Declension Adjectives

## GRAMMATICA

### THIRD DECLENSION ADJECTIVES

Latin has two major categories of adjectives. You are already familiar with first/second declension adjectives like **magnus, -a, -um** (Capvt IV) and the small sub-set of that group with **-īus** in the genitive singular and **-ī** in the dative singular (Capvt IX). Adjectives of the second major group generally have third declension **i**-stem forms and are declined exactly like **i**-stem nouns, except that the ablative singular of all genders (not just the neuter) ends with **-ī.** Adjectives of this group fall into three categories that differ from each other in simply one respect. Some, called "adjectives of three endings," have distinct forms of the *nominative singular* that differentiate each of the three genders, just as **magnus, magna,** and **magnum** do (e.g., **ācer** M., **ācris** F., and **ācre** N.); those of "two endings" (the largest category of third declension adjectives) have a single nominative form for both masculine and feminine, and another for the neuter (e.g., **fortis** M. and F., **forte** N.); and those of "one ending" do not differentiate the genders at all in the nominative singular (e.g., **potēns** is the M., F., and N. nominative singular form). In all other respects the adjectives of all three categories are the same, with the masculine and feminine endings differing from the neuters only in the accusative singular and the nominative (= vocative) and accusative plural.

Paradigms are given below, with the distinctive **i**-stem endings in bold; the nouns **cīvis** and **mare** are provided for comparison (review Capvt XIV, if necessary) and to show that there is very little new to be learned in order to master third declension adjectives:

|  | **I-Stem Nouns Reviewed** | | **Adj. of 2 Endings** | |
|---|---|---|---|---|

**fortis, forte,** *strong, brave*

|  | M. or F. | N. | M. & F. | N. |
|---|---|---|---|---|
| *Nom.* | cívis | máre | fórtis | fórte |
| *Gen.* | cívis | máris | fórtis | fórtis |
| *Dat.* | cívī | márī | fórtī | fórtī |
| *Acc.* | cívem | máre | fórtem | fórte |
| *Abl.* | cíve | márī | fórtī | fórtī |
| *Nom.* | cívēs | **már**ia | fórtēs | fórtia |
| *Gen.* | cí**vium** | má**rium** | fór**tium** | fór**tium** |
| *Dat.* | cívibus | máribus | fórtibus | fórtibus |
| *Acc.* | cívēs | má**ria** | fórtēs | fór**tia** |
| *Abl.* | cívibus | máribus | fórtibus | fórtibus |

|  | **Adj. of 3 Endings** | | **Adj. of 1 Ending** | |
|---|---|---|---|---|

| **ācer, ācris, ācre,** | | | **potēns,** gen. **potentis,** | |
| *keen, severe, fierce* | | | *powerful* | |

|  | M. & F. | N. | M. & F. | N. |
|---|---|---|---|---|
| *Nom.* | ácer, ácris | ácre | pótēns | pótēns |
| *Gen.* | ácris | ácris | poténtis | poténtis |
| *Dat.* | ácrī | ácrī | poténtī | poténtī |
| *Acc.* | ácrem | ácre | poténtem | pótēns |
| *Abl.* | ácrī | ácrī | poténtī | poténtī |
| *Nom.* | ácrēs | ác**ria** | poténtēs | poténtia |
| *Gen.* | ác**rium** | ác**rium** | potén**tium** | potén**tium** |
| *Dat.* | ácribus | ácribus | poténtibus | poténtibus |
| *Acc.* | ácrēs | ác**ria** | poténtēs | potén**tia** |
| *Abl.* | ácribus | ácribus | poténtibus | poténtibus |

Note the forms in which the characteristic **i** appears, as indicated in the paradigms:

(1) **-ī** in the ablative singular of all genders.
(2) **-ium** in the genitive plural of all genders.
(3) **-ia** in the nominative and accusative plural of the neuter.

Like **i**-stem nouns, third declension adjectives have an alternate -**īs** ending in the accusative plural, but it will rarely be used in this book.

A third declension adjective can be used with a noun of any declension just as a first/second declension adjective can. Compare the following, where **omnis, -e,** *every, all,* is used as the example of an adjective of two endings:

| omnis amīcus *or* homō | ācer amīcus/homō | potēns amīcus/homō |
|---|---|---|
| omnis rēgīna *or* māter | ācris rēgīna/māter | potēns rēgīna/māter |
| omne bellum *or* animal | ācre bellum/animal | potēns bellum/animal |

Analyze the forms in the following phrases:

| omnī fōrmae | in omnī fōrmā | omnium fōrmārum |
|---|---|---|
| omnī animō | in omnī animō | omnium animōrum |
| omnī hominī | in omnī homine | omnium hominum |
| omnī urbī | in omnī urbe | omnium urbium |
| omnī marī | in omnī marī | omnium marium |

### Usage and Word Order

Third declension adjectives function in the following four ways (the first three of which have already been introduced), just like first/second declension adjectives:

**ATTRIBUTIVE ADJECTIVE: virī fortēs,** *the brave men* (simple modifier)

**PREDICATE ADJECTIVE: virī sunt fortēs,** *the men are brave* (describing the subject, with a form of **sum** or some other linking verb)

**SUBSTANTIVE ADJECTIVE: fortūna fortēs adiuvat,** *fortune helps the brave* (used in place of a noun)

**OBJECTIVE COMPLEMENT: virtūs fēcit virōs fortēs,** *virtue made the men brave* (describing the result of the action of the verb on the object; cf. "she painted the house yellow"—quite different from the attributive use in "she painted the yellow house")

Remember that attributive adjectives commonly follow the nouns they modify, except those that denote size or quantity, demonstratives, and those meant to be emphatic.

# VOCĀBVLA

Watch the third declension adjectives: it's easy to identify those of two endings and three endings; entries for those of one ending provide the genitive, so you can determine the base. These adjectives are regularly i-stem, but are any of the third declension nouns in this list i-stem?—if you are unsure, review Capvt XIV, then decline at least one or two noun-adjective pairs from this list, e.g., **satura ācris** or **mēns celeris,** and compare with the paradigms. And remember, as you learn these new words, to use the CDs or the online audio at www.wheelockslatin.com and **semper audī et prōnūntiā!**

aétās, aetåtis, f., *period of life, life, age, an age, time* (eternal, eternity, sempiternal)

audítor, audītóris, m., *hearer, listener, member of an audience* (auditor, auditory, auditorium; cf. **audiō**)

clēméntia, clēméntiae, f., *mildness, gentleness, mercy* (clement, clemency, inclement, Clementine)

mēns, méntis, f., *mind, thought, intention* (mental, mentality, mention, demented; "mind" is cognate)

sátura, sáturae, f., *satire* (satirist, satirical, satirize)

ácer, ácris, ácre, *sharp, keen, eager; severe, fierce* (acrid, acrimony, acrimonious, eager, vinegar)

brévis, bréve, *short, small, brief* (brevity, breviary, abbreviate, abridge)

céler, céleris, célere, *swift, quick, rapid* (celerity, accelerate, acceleration, decelerate)

difficilis, difficile, *hard, difficult, troublesome* (difficulty)

dúlcis, dúlce, *sweet; pleasant, agreeable* (dulcify, dulcet, dulcimer)

fácilis, fácile, *easy, agreeable* (facile, facility, facilitate; cf. **faciō**)

fórtis, fórte, *strong, brave* (fort, forte, fortify, fortitude, force, comfort)

íngēns, gen. ingéntis, *huge*

iūcúndus, iūcúnda, iūcúndum, *pleasant, delightful, agreeable, pleasing* (jocund)

lóngus, lónga, lóngum, *long* (longitude, longevity, elongate, oblong, prolong; Eng. "long" is cognate)

ómnis, ómne, *every, all* (omnibus, bus, omnipresent, omnipotent, omniscient, omnivorous)

pótēns, gen. poténtis, pres. partic. of **possum** as an adj., *able, powerful, mighty, strong* (potent, impotent, omnipotent, potentate, potential)

sénex, gen. sénis, adj. and noun, *old, aged; old man* (senate, senator, senescent, senile, senior, seniority, sir, sire; cf. **senectūs**)

quam, adv., *how*

régō, régere, rḗxī, réctum, *to rule, guide, direct* (regent, regime, regiment, regular, regulate, correct, direction, rectitude; cf. **rēx, rēgīna**)

# LĒCTIŌ ET TRĀNSLĀTIŌ

After learning the paradigms and vocabulary and doing some of the Self-Tutorial Exercises, scan through the following readings for examples of third declension adjectives and identify the form and use of each. As always, read aloud before translating.

## EXERCITĀTIŌNĒS

1. Fortēs virī et fēminae ante aetātem nostram vīvēbant.
2. Eōs centum senēs miserōs ab Italiā trāns maria difficilia heri mittēbat.

3. Illī duo virī omnēs cupiditātēs ex sē ēiēcērunt, nam nātūram corporis timuērunt.
4. Potēns rēgīna, quoniam sē dīlēxit, istōs trēs vītāvit et sē cum eīs numquam iūnxit.
5. Itaque inter eōs ibi stābam et signum cum animō fortī diū exspectābam.
6. Celer rūmor per ōra aurēsque omnium sine morā currēbat.
7. Vīs bellī acerbī autem vītam eius paucīs hōrīs mūtāvit.
8. Quīnque ex nautīs sē ex aquā trāxērunt sēque Caesarī potentī commīsērunt.
9. Caesar nōn poterat suās cōpiās cum celeribus cōpiīs rēgis iungere.
10. Themistoclēs omnēs cīvēs ōlim appellābat et nōmina eōrum ācrī memoriā tenēbat.
11. In caelō sunt multae nūbēs et animālia agricolae tempestāte malā nōn valent.
12. The father and mother often used to come to the city with their two sweet daughters.
13. The souls of brave men and women will never fear difficult times.
14. Does he now understand all the rights of these four men?
15. The doctor could not help the brave girl, for death was swift.

## SENTENTIAE ANTĪQVAE

1. Quam dulcis est lībertās! (Phaedrus.)
2. Labor omnia vīcit. (*Vergil.)
3. Fortūna fortēs adiuvat. (Terence.)
4. Quam celeris et ācris est mēns! (Cicero.)
5. Polyphēmus erat mōnstrum horrendum, īnfōrme, ingēns. (Vergil.—**mōnstrum, -ī,** n., = Eng.; "monstrosity," "monstrous."—**horrendus, -a, -um,** = Eng.; "horrid," "abhorrent."—**īnfōrmis, -e,** *formless, hideous;* "informal.")

*The blinding of Polyphemus*
*Hydria from Cerveteri, 525* B.C.
*Museo Nazionale di Villa Giulia, Rome, Italy*

6. Varium et mūtābile semper fēmina. (*Vergil.—Order: **fēmina semper [est] varium et mūtābile.—varius, -a, -um,** *varying, fickle;* "variegate," "variety."— **mūtābilis, -e,** *changeable;* "immutable," "transmute." The neuters **varium** and **mūtābile** are used to mean "a fickle and changeable *thing*.")

7. Facile est epigrammata bellē scrībere, sed librum scrībere difficile est. (*Martial.—**epigramma, -matis,** n., *short poem, epigram;* "epigrammatist."— **bellē,** adv. from **bellus, -a, -um.**)

8. Īra furor brevis est; animum rege. (*Horace.—**furor, -rōris,** m., *madness;* "furious," "infuriate.")

9. Ars poētica est nōn omnia dīcere. (*Servius.—**poēticus, -a, -um;** "poetaster," "poetical.")

10. Nihil est ab omnī parte beātum. (*Horace.)

11. Liber meus hominēs prūdentī cōnsiliō alit. (Phaedrus.—**prūdēns,** gen. **-dentis,** = Eng.; "prudence," "imprudent"; the word is a contraction of **prōvidēns,** *provident*)

12. Māter omnium bonārum artium sapientia est. (*Cicero.)

13. Clēmentia rēgem salvum facit; nam amor omnium cīvium est inexpugnābile mūnīmentum rēgis. (Seneca.—**inexpugnābilis, -e,** *impregnable.*—**mūnīmentum, -ī,** n., *fortification, defense;* "muniment.")

14. Vīta est brevis; ars, longa. (Hippocrates, quoted by Seneca.)

15. Breve tempus aetātis autem satis longum est ad bene vīvendum. (Cicero.— **vīvendum,** *living,* verbal noun obj. of **ad,** *for.*)

16. Vīvit et vīvet per omnium saeculōrum memoriam. (*Velleius Paterculus.— **saeculum, -ī,** n., *century, age;* "secular," "secularize.")

### Juvenal Explains His Impulse to Satire

Semper ego audītor erō? Est turba poētārum in hāc urbe—ego igitur erō poēta! Sunt mīlia vitiōrum in urbe—dē istīs vitiīs scrībam! Difficile est saturam nōn scrībere. Sī nātūra mē adiuvāre nōn potest, facit indignātiō versum. In librō meō erunt omnia facta hominum—timor, īra, voluptās, culpa, cupiditās, īnsidiae. Nunc est plēna cōpia vitiōrum in hāc miserā urbe Rōmae!

Juvenal *Sat.* 1.1ff: The satirist Juvenal (Decimus Junius Juvenalis, ca. A.D. 60–130) has been over the centuries one of the most widely read and influential of Roman writers. His 16 verse satires, published in six volumes, were largely characterized by a tone of anger and indignation that was in marked contrast to the more genial satires of his Augustan predecessor Horace (a selection from whose **Sermōnēs** you read in Capvt III). In this passage from the opening of his programmatic first satire, Juvenal announces his reasons for writing **satura,** a literary genre the Romans laid claim to inventing; Juvenal's contemporary, Quintilian, author of an important work on Roman education and rhetoric, asserted **satura quidem** (*indeed*) **tōta nostra est. —audītor:** a reminder that satire, like other verse genres in Rome, was composed for recitation as much as for a reading audience.—**turba poētārum:** an exaggeration, but similar complaints are heard from other writers of the day.—**nātūra:** i.e., any innate talent he might have for writing poetry.—**indignātiō, -ōnis,** f.; = Eng.; "indignant," "indignity."—**versus,** *verse, poetry;* "versify," "version."

*QVAESTIŌNĒS:* Juvenal here gives two reasons for his decision to write satire, the first facetious, the second quite serious–what are they? How does Juvenal's **difficile est saturam nōn scrībere** (his exact words) make an even more cynical point than if he had instead written **nōn difficile est saturam scrībere?** The satirist claims that his book will survey **omnia facta hominum:** what then is the implication of the list of behaviors and the concluding sentence that follow?

### On a Temperamental Friend

> Difficilis facilis, iūcundus acerbus—es īdem:
> nec tēcum possum vīvere nec sine tē.

*Martial *Epig.* 12.46: Martial was a friend of Juvenal's and a major influence on his writing; though not himself a satirist in the strictly formal sense—i.e., he wrote epigrams and not the long dactylic hexameter poems that characterized Roman satire—his writings, as we have seen, were nevertheless highly satirical. Meter: elegiac couplet.

*QVAESTIŌNĒS:* Is Martial's addressee here male or female?—how do you know? Elaborate on Martial's characterization of this person—have you ever been acquainted with someone like this? The most striking stylistic feature of the epigram is ANTITHESIS, which is deftly employed by the poet in three sets of contrasting words and phrases in the two verses; identify them. **Difficilis facilis, iūcundus acerbus** is an example, not only of chiasmus, but also of the rhetorical device known as ASYNDETON, the deliberate omission of conjunctions where typically expected; what is the intended effect of the two devices here? The second verse is structured in a series of three phrases: what are they, and how does their arrangement suit the line's meaning?

## SCRĪPTA IN PARIETIBVS

*CIL* 4.6787: Here's another graffito that should require no transcription; if you can't figure it out, try to find the word in this chapter's **Vocābula.** Have you ever written simply your name on a wall somewhere?—the Romans often did, and this graffito, not just an adjective but the writer's cognomen, is typical; the same writer in another graffito (4.6786) on the same wall (in the atrium of a house in Reg. V, Ins. 4) wrote his name again, followed by **Grāt<a>e salūtem,** a "hello" to his girlfriend Grata, whose name means "Pleasing" or "Agreeable." Both names are representative of hundreds of Roman cognomina that describe a person's positive character traits or attractive physical attributes; we saw **Venustus,** "Charming," in Capvt III above, and other common examples are **Audēns,** "Daring/Courageous," **Fēlīx,** "Fortunate," **Magnus,** as in "Pompey the Great," and **Caesar,** probably = "Long-/Luxuriant-haired." On the other hand, Romans were not bashful about drawing attention to what might be considered negative traits or physical anomalies, and so we find such equally common cognomina as **Paetus** and **Strabō,** both meaning "Squinty-eyed," **Scaurus,** "Swollen-Ankled," **Valgus,** "Bow-legged," and even **Cicerō,** "Chickpea," which the ancient Greek biographer Plutarch claimed was given to one of Marcus Tullius Cicero's ancestors (and then passed on to him) because he had a deformity on his nose resembling a garbanzo bean!

## LATĪNA EST GAVDIVM—ET VTILIS!

**Salvēte! Quid agitis? Quid hodiē est tempestās?** Here are some possible answers, many of which you can again recognize from derivatives: **frīgida** (**tempestās** is feminine, as you recall from Capvt XV, hence the feminine adjective, from **frīgidus, -a, -um**); **calida** ("scald" is a derivative); **nimbōsa** (from **nimbus,** which means the same as **nūbēs,** + the common suffix **-ōsus, -a, -um,** *full of,* hence "cloudy"—cf. "cumulonimbus clouds"); **ventōsa** (an identical formation from **ventus,** *wind*); **sōl lūcet,** *the sun is shining* (cf. "solar," "translucent"); **pluit,** *it's raining* ("pluvial," "pluviometer"); **ningit,** *it's snowing* (Eng. "niveous" from Lat. **niveus, -a, -um** is related).

Well, enough of the weather. Here's an omnibus of **omni-** words and phrases to delight you all: If you were "omnific" (from **facere**) and "omnipresent" (*-sent* from **sum**) and your appetite "omnivorous" (**vorāre,** *to eat,* cf. "carnivorous," "herbivorous") and your sight were "omnidirectional" (see **regō** in the **Vocābula** above), then you might potentially be "omnipotent" and even "omniscient" (**scīre,** *to know*). But as a proverbial saying from Vergil reminds us, **nōn omnia possumus omnēs.** Then there's the made-up word, "omnium-gatherum," a Latin-English hybrid that refers to a "miscellaneous collection" (of people or things)—it may seem silly but the word was used by British literati as early as the 16th cent., according to the *Oxford English Dictionary!* Well, speaking of silly, be aware that **regō,** mentioned above, does NOT mean "to go again," nor should **regit** be translated "leave, y'all, and this time I mean it!" Enough of that too: **Valēte, omnēs amīcī et amīcae meae, et semper amāte Latīnam!**

# CAPVT XVII 𓏤𓏤𓏤

# The Relative Pronoun

## GRAMMATICA

### THE RELATIVE PRONOUN

The **RELATIVE PRONOUN** **quī, quae, quod**, as common in Latin as its English equivalent *who/which/that*, ordinarily introduces a subordinate clause and refers back to some noun or pronoun known as its **ANTECEDENT**; the **RELATIVE CLAUSE** itself has an adjectival function, providing descriptive information about the antecedent (e.g., "the man who was from Italy" = "the Italian man").

The forms of the relative pronoun are so diverse that the only practical procedure is to memorize them. However, the genitive and dative endings **cuius** and **cui** resemble **huius/huic** and **illīus/illī**, and it is easy to identify the case, the number, and often the gender of most of the remaining forms, based on their similarity to various first, second, and third declension endings.

**Quī, Quae, Quod,** *who, which, that*

| Singular | | | Plural | | |
|---|---|---|---|---|---|
| **M.** | **F.** | **N.** | **M.** | **F.** | **N.** |
| quī | quae | quod | quī | quae | quae |
| cuíus | cuíus | cuíus | quórum | quárum | quórum |
| cui | cui | cui | quíbus | quíbus | quíbus |
| quem | quam | quod | quōs | quās | quae |
| quō | quā | quō | quíbus | quíbus | quíbus |

For the pronunciation of the **ui** in **cuius** (as if spelled *cui-yus*) and in **cui**, cf. **huius** and **huic** (Capvt IX) and see the *Intrōductiō*, p. xxxvii (listen to the CDs too, if you have them).

### Usage and Agreement

Since the relative pronoun (from **referō, referre, rettulī, relātum**) refers to and is essentially equivalent to its antecedent (from **antecēdere**, *to go before*, since the antecedent usually appears in a preceding clause), the two words naturally agree in number and gender; the case of the relative, however, like that of any noun or pronoun, is determined by its use within its own clause. The logic of this can be demonstrated by analyzing and translating the following sentence:

*The woman whom you are praising is wise.*

1. The main clause of the sentence reads: *The woman . . . is wise.* **Fēmina . . . est sapiēns.**
2. *Whom* introduces a subordinate, relative clause modifying *woman.*
3. *Woman* (**fēmina**) stands before the relative *whom* and is its antecedent.
4. *Whom* has a double loyalty: (1) to its antecedent, **fēmina,** and (2) to the subordinate clause in which it stands.

a. Since the antecedent, **fēmina,** is feminine and singular, *whom* in Latin will have to be feminine and singular.
b. Since in the subordinate clause *whom* is the direct object of (*you*) *are praising* (**laudās**), it must be in the accusative case in Latin.
c. Therefore, the Latin form must be *feminine* and *singular* and *accusative:* **quam.**

The complete sentence in Latin appears thus:

**Fēmina quam laudās est sapiēns.**

Again, succinctly, the rule is this: the *gender* and *number* of a relative are determined by its *antecedent*; its *case* is determined by its *use* in its own clause. Identify the gender, number, case, use, and antecedent of the relatives in the following sentences:

1. **Dīligō puellam** *quae* **ex Italiā vēnit.** *I admire the girl who came from Italy.*
2. **Homō dē** *quō* **dīcēbās est amīcus cārus.** *The man about whom you were speaking is a dear friend.*
3. **Puella** *cui* **librum dat est fortūnāta.** *The girl to whom he is giving the book is fortunate.*
4. **Puer** *cuius* **patrem iuvābāmus est fortis.** *The boy whose father we used to help is brave.*
5. **Vītam meam committam eīs virīs** *quōrum* **virtūtēs laudābās.** *I shall entrust my life to those men whose virtues you were praising.*
6. **Timeō idem perīculum** *quod* **timētis.** *I fear the same danger which you fear.*

In translating, be sure not to shift words from the relative clause into the main clause or vice versa; e.g., in the third sentence above, **puella** should not be mistaken as the subject of **dat.** Note that a relative clause is a self-contained unit, usually beginning with the relative pronoun and ending with the first verb you encounter (**cui . . . dat** in the third sample sentence); in complex sentences, like S.A. 3 below, you may find it helpful first to identify and actually even bracket the relative clause(s):

> **Multī cīvēs aut ea perīcula [quae imminent] nōn vident aut ea [quae vident] neglegunt.**

As you read and translate such a sentence, translate the relative clause as soon as you have translated the relative pronoun's antecedent (which very often, as here, precedes the relative pronoun immediately).

# VOCĀBVLA

This list includes several common verbs: note the conjugation of each and remember the rule for **-iō** verbs, i.e., that you'll find the characteristic **-i-** in every single form of the three present system active indicative tenses. **Coepī** is an example of a DEFECTIVE VERB, i.e., a verb many or most of whose conjugational forms were rarely employed. **Aut . . . aut** will remind you of **et . . . et:** both are examples of CORRELATIVE CONJUNCTIONS. Practice recently introduced grammar with some of the new words; e.g., decline **libellus levis** and write out a synopsis of **dēsīderō** or **dēleō,** checking your work with the paradigms in the **Summārium Fōrmārum,** p. 495–505.

**libéllus, libéllī,** m., *little book* (libel, libelous; diminutive of **liber**)

**quī, quae, quod,** rel. pron., *who, which, what, that* (qui vive, quorum)

**caécus, caéca, caécum,** *blind* (caecum, caecal, caecilian)

**lévis, léve,** *light; easy; slight, trivial* (levity, lever, levy, levee, Levant, leaven, legerdemain, alleviate, elevate, relevant, irrelevant, relieve)

**aut,** conj., *or;* **aut . . . aut,** *either . . . or*

**cíto,** adv., *quickly* (excite, incite, recite; cf. **recitō,** below)

**quóque,** adv., *also, too*

**admíttō, admíttere, admī́sī, admíssum,** *to admit, receive, let in* (admission, admissible, inadmissible, admittedly)

**coépī, coepísse, coéptum,** *began,* defective verb used in the perf. system only; the pres. system is supplied by **incipiō** (below).

**cúpiō, cúpere, cupī́vī, cupī́tum,** *to desire, wish, long for* (Cupid, cupidity, concupiscence, covet, covetous, Kewpie doll; cf. **cupiditās**)

**déleō, dēlḗre, dēlḗvī, dēlḗtum,** *to destroy, wipe out, erase* (delete, indelible)

**dēsī́derō, dēsīderáre, dēsīderávī, dēsīderátum,** *to desire, long for, miss* (desiderate, desideratum, desiderative, desire, desirous)

**incípiō, incípere, incépī, incéptum,** *to begin* (incipient, inception; cf. **capiō**)

**nāvigō, nāvigāre, nāvigāvī, nāvigātum,** *to sail, navigate* (navigation, navigable; cf. **nauta**)

**néglegō, neglégere, neglḗxī, neglḗctum,** *to neglect, disregard* (negligent, negligee, negligible)

**récitō, recitāre, recitāvī, recitātum,** *to read aloud, recite* (recital, recitation, recitative)

# LĒCTIŌ ET TRĀNSLĀTIŌ

Reading and translating sentences that contain relative clauses (like the one you just this moment read: "that contain relative clauses") need not be difficult. Bracketing the clause as suggested in the preceding discussion of S.A. 3 below can help you avoid jumbling words from the subordinate clause into the main clause; practice with a few sentences in the Self-Tutorial Exercises. Watch out for look-alike **qu-** words like the adverb **quam** in Ex. 5 (which cannot be a relative pronoun because it has no antecedent), and the conjunction **quod,** *because:* when **quod** immediately follows a neuter singular word, it is nearly always the relative pronoun; when there is no apparent antecedent, it is more likely the conjunction. And, beware: as you'll see in the Martial epigram below, the antecedent does not always *ante*cede!

## EXERCITĀTIŌNĒS

1. Potēns quoque est vīs artium, quae nōs semper alunt.
2. Miserōs hominēs, autem, sēcum iungere coeperant.
3. Nam illā aetāte pars populī in Italiā iūra cīvium numquam tenuit.
4. Incipimus vēritātem intellegere, quae mentēs nostrās semper regere dēbet et sine quā valēre nōn possumus.
5. Quam difficile est bona aut dulcia ex bellō trahere!
6. Centum ex virīs mortem diū timēbant et nihil clēmentiae exspectābant.
7. Puer mātrem timēbat, quae eum saepe neglegēbat.
8. Inter omnia perīcula fēmina fortis sē cum sapientiā gessit.
9. Itaque celer rūmor mortis ācris per ingentēs urbēs cucurrit.
10. Quoniam memoria factōrum nostrōrum dulcis est, beātī nunc sumus et senectūtem facilem agēmus.
11. Multī audītōrēs saturās ācrēs timēbant quās poēta recitābat.
12. They feared the powerful men whose city they were ruling by force.
13. We began to help those three pleasant women to whom we had given our friendship.
14. We fear that book with which he is beginning to destroy our liberty.

## SENTENTIAE ANTĪQVAE

1. Salvē, bone amīce, cui fīlium meum herī commīsī. (Terence.)
2. Dionȳsius, dē quō ante dīxī, ā Graeciā ad Siciliam per tempestātem brevem sed potentem nāvigābat. (Cicero.—**Sicilia, -ae,** f., *Sicily.*)
3. Multī cīvēs aut ea perīcula quae imminent nōn vident aut ea quae vident neglegunt. (Cicero.—**imminēre,** *to impend, threaten;* "imminence," "imminent.")
4. Bis dat quī cito dat. (Publilius Syrus.—**bis,** adv., *twice;* "biped," "bipolar.")
5. Quī coepit, dīmidium factī habet. Incipe! (Horace.—**dīmidium, -ī,** n., *half;* "dimidiate.")
6. Levis est fortūna: id cito reposcit quod dedit. (Publilius Syrus.—**reposcō, -ere,** *to demand back.*)
7. Fortūna eum stultum facit quem nimium amat. (Publilius Syrus.)
8. Nōn sōlum fortūna ipsa est caeca sed etiam eōs caecōs facit quōs semper adiuvat. (Cicero.)
9. Bis vincit quī sē vincit in victōriā. (*Publilius Syrus.)
10. Simulātiō dēlet vēritātem, sine quā nōmen amīcitiae valēre nōn potest. (Cicero.—**simulātiō, -ōnis,** f., *pretense, insincerity;* "simulate," "simulation.")
11. Virtūtem enim illīus virī amāvī, quae cum corpore nōn periit. (Cicero.—**pereō, -īre, -iī, -itum,** *to perish;* "perish," "perishable.")
12. Turbam vītā. Cum hīs vīve quī tē meliōrem facere possunt; illōs admitte quōs tū potes facere meliōrēs. (Seneca.—**melior,** *better;* "meliorate," "ameliorate.")

### On the Pleasures of Love in Old Age

Estne amor in senectūte? Voluptās enim minor est, sed minor quoque est cupiditās. Nihil autem est cūra nōbīs, sī nōn cupimus, et nōn caret is quī nōn dēsīderat. Adulēscentēs nimis dēsīderant; senēs satis amōris saepe habent et multum sapientiae. Cōgitō, igitur, hoc tempus vītae esse iūcundum.

Cicero *Sen.* 14.47–48: For Cicero's **Dē Senectūte,** see the notes to the two passages in Capvt XV.—**minor:** *less;* "minority," "minus."—**carēre,** *to lack, want;* "caret."—**is quī:** a rel. pron. is often immediately preceded by a form of **is, ea, id** as antecedent; another common example is **id quod,** *that which.*

*QVAESTIŌNĒS:* What reason does Cicero offer for his view that the lessening of romantic passion that can accompany old age need not be a source of concern? Comment on the word order of the second sentence and how it neatly suits the nature of the argument.

### It's All in the Delivery

Quem recitās meus est, ō Fīdentīne, libellus;
    sed male cum recitās, incipit esse tuus!

A Reading from Homer, *Sir Lawrence Alma-Tadema, 1885*
*Philadelphia Museum of Art: The George W. Elkins Collection*

*Martial *Epig.* 1.38: In ancient Rome, poetry was performance and was meant first and foremost for a listening audience; proper delivery (**āctiō**) and recitation (**recitātiō**) were skills taught in school, and **recitātiōnēs** were a favorite entertainment among educated Romans. Poets recited their own poetry, and sometimes their work was recited by others—not always to good effect, however. Juvenal complains about the city's **turba poētārum,** as we read in the previous chapter, and Martial here expresses his displeasure with Fidentinus, who has been reciting some of his epigrams, and **nōn bene!** Meter: elegiac couplet.—**libellus:** the delayed antecedent of **quem;** in prose the order might be **libellus quem recitās est meus.**—**male,** adv. of **malus.**—**cum,** conj., *when.*

*QVAESTIŌNĒS:* What does this epigram tell us about the consequences of poorly reciting a text?—what are some specific ways in which delivery can affect meaning? Comment specifically on the effect of positioning **meus** before the subject to which it refers in line 1 and then delaying **tuus** to the the poem's end.

## SCRĪPTA IN PARIETIBVS

Omnēs lūserō: sum Max(imus)!

*CIL* 4.9008: Inscribed on a column in a Pompeian house (Reg. VII, Ins. 6). The context is not entirely certain, but quite possibly Maximus was an actor in mimes, a popular form of Roman comedy characterized by satiric, lively, and often obscene dance and miming routines in which a single actor, using a variety of masks, played all the roles. Certainly the writer here had a sense of humor, as his "self-portrait" in the role of a soldier incorporates the **S-** of **sum** into the nose-piece of his helmet and the **-SERO** of **lūserō** into its crest.—**omnēs:** i.e., parts or characters in a performance?—**lūdō, lūdere, lūsī, lūsum,** *to play, sport; play the role of, mime;* "ludicrous, delude, illusion."

## ETYMOLOGIA

The Lat. rel. pron. was the parent of the following Romance forms: It. **chi, che;** Sp. **que;** Port. **que** or, if referring to people, **quem;** Fr. **qui, que;** Old Occ. **qui;** Rom. **care, ce.** To Lat. **aut** can be traced It. **o;** Sp. **o;** Port. **ou;** Fr. **ou;** Old Occ. **ǫ;** Rom. **ou** (now obsolete).

If the suffix **-scō** shows a Lat. verb to be an "inceptive" verb, what force or meaning does this ending impart to the verb?—**tremō,** *tremble;* **tremēscō** = ? In medieval manuscripts many texts begin with an "incipit"; e.g., **liber prīmus Epistulārum Plīniī incipit.**

## LATĪNA EST GAVDIVM—ET VTILIS!

**Iterum salvēte!** There are a couple of English abbreviations from **quī, quae, quod** which you may have seen: **q.v.** = **quod vidē,** *which see* (i.e., "see this item"), and **Q.E.D.** = **quod erat dēmōnstrandum,** *that which was to be proved* (used, e.g., in mathematical proofs—for the verbal form, a "passive periphrastic," see Capvt XXIV). Less common are **q.e.** = **quod est,** *which is,* and **Q.E.F.** = **quod erat faciendum,** *which was/had to be done.* You are beginning to see that for a truly literate person Latin is **sine quā nōn** (*indispensable,* lit. something *without which* one can *not* manage), and that's a point we needn't "quibble" over (a diminutive derived from the frequent use of **quibus** in legal documents). The root meaning of **recitāre,** by the way, is *to arouse again* (cf. "excite," "incite"); when we "recite" a text, we are quite literally "reviving" or bringing it back to life, which is why we—just like the Romans—should always read literature, especially poetry, aloud! And here's some good advice on doing your translations: **semper scrībe sententiās in tabellā tuā** (*your notebook*). An old proverb tells you why: **quī scrībit, bis discit!** And here's a proverb with the **Vocābula** item **cito: cito matūrum, cito putridum,** *quickly ripe, quickly rotten.* So let's not go too fast: **valēte!**

# CAPVT XVIII 回回回

# First and Second Conjugations: Present System Passive; Ablative of Agent

## GRAMMATICA

### FIRST AND SECOND CONJUGATIONS: PRESENT SYSTEM PASSIVE VOICE

In Latin as in English there are **PASSIVE VOICE** verb forms and passive sentence types, in which the subject is *passive recipient* of the action (rather than *actively performing* the action, as in the active voice). The rule for forming the passive of first and second conjugation present system passives (i.e., passives of the present, future, and imperfect tenses) is an easy one: simply substitute the new passive endings (-**r**, -**ris**, -**tur**; -**mur**, -**minī**, -**ntur**) for the active ones learned in Capvt I (-ō/-m, -s, -t; -mus, -tis, -nt). The few exceptions to this rule are highlighted in bold in the following paradigms.

### Present Indicative Passive *Laudō* and *Moneō*

*Passive Endings*

| | | | |
|---|---|---|---|
| 1. -r | laúd-**or** | móneor | *I am (being) praised, warned* |
| 2. -ris | laudắ-ris | monếris | *you are (being) praised, warned* |
| 3. -tur | laudắ-tur | monétur | *he is (being) praised, warned* |
| 1. -mur | laudắ-mur | monếmur | *we are (being) praised, warned* |
| 2. -minī | laudắ-minī | monéminī | *you are (being) praised, warned* |
| 3. -ntur | laudá-ntur | monéntur | *they are (being) praised, warned* |

## Imperfect Indicative Passive

| *I was (being) praised, used to be praised*, etc. | *I was (being) warned, used to be warned*, etc. |
|---|---|
| 1. laudā́-ba-r | monḗbar |
| 2. laudā-bā́-ris | monēbā́ris |
| 3. laudā-bā́-tur | monēbā́tur |
| 1. laudā-bā́-mur | monēbā́mur |
| 2. laudā-bā́-minī | monēbā́minī |
| 3. laudā-bá-ntur | monēbántur |

## Future Indicative Passive

| *I will be praised* | *I will be warned* |
|---|---|
| 1. laudā́-**b-or** | monḗ**bor** |
| 2. laudā́-**be**-ris | monḗ**be**ris |
| 3. laudā-bi-tur | monḗbitur |
| 1. laudā́-bi-mur | monēbimur |
| 2. laudā-bí-minī | monēbíminī |
| 3. laudā-bú-ntur | monēbúntur |

The exceptional forms, highlighted in bold above, are few: in the first person singular, present and future, the active ending -ō is shortened and -r is added directly to it, instead of being substituted for it; -**bi**- is changed to -**be**- in the future second person singular. Notice, too, that the stem vowel remains short in **laudantur/monentur** but is long in **laudātur/monētur** (review the rule in Capvt I: vowels are generally shortened before **nt** in any position but only before a *final* -**m**, -**r**, or -**t**, hence **laudat** but **laudātur**). Latin had an alternate second person singular passive ending in -**re** (e.g., **laudābere** for **laudāberis**); this ending is not employed in this book, but you will likely encounter it in your later readings.

## Present Passive Infinitive

The present passive infinitive of first and second conjugation verbs is formed by changing final -**e** of the active to -**ī**.

| **laudāre**, *to praise* | **monēre**, *to warn* |
|---|---|
| **laudārī**, *to be praised* | **monērī**, *to be warned* |

## Usage

When a verb is active voice (from **agō, agere, ēgī, āctum,** *to act*), the subject performs the action; with a verb in passive voice (from **patior, patī, passus sum,** *to undergo, experience*) the subject is passively acted upon. As a rule, only transitive verbs are used in the passive; and what had been the object of the transitive verb (receiving the action of the verb) now becomes the subject of the passive verb (still receiving the action of the verb). To make verbs passive in English, we use a form of the verb "to be":

**Caesarem admonet.** *He warns Caesar.*
**Caesar admonētur.** *Caesar is (being) warned.*

**Urbem dēlēbant.** *They were destroying the city.*
**Urbs dēlēbātur.** *The city was being destroyed.*

**Patriam cōnservābit.** *He will save the country.*
**Patria cōnservābitur.** *The country will be saved.*

## ABLATIVE OF PERSONAL AGENT

The personal *agent by whom* the action of a passive verb is performed is indicated by **ā/ab** and the **ABLATIVE OF AGENT**; the *means by which* the action is accomplished is indicated by the **ABLATIVE OF MEANS**, without a preposition, as you have already learned in Capvt XIV. Both constructions are common with passive verbs, as seen in the following examples:

**Dī Caesarem admonent.** *The gods are warning Caesar.*
**Caesar ā dīs admonētur.** *Caesar is warned by the gods.* (Agent)
**Caesar hīs prōdigiīs admonētur.** *Caesar is warned by these omens* (**prōdigium**). (Means)
**Malī virī urbem dēlēbant.** *Evil men were destroying the city.*
**Urbs ab malīs virīs dēlēbātur.** *The city was being destroyed by evil men.* (Agent)
**Urbs flammīs dēlēbātur.** *The city was being destroyed by flames* (**flamma**). (Means)
**Hī cīvēs patriam cōnservābunt.** *These citizens will save the country.*
**Patria ab hīs cīvibus cōnservābitur.** *The country will be saved by these citizens.* (Agent)
**Patria armīs et vēritāte cōnservābitur.** *The country will be saved by arms and truth.* (**Means**)

As seen in these examples, an active sentence construction can be transformed to a passive construction in this way: what was the direct object becomes the subject; what was the subject becomes in Latin an ablative of agent, if a person, or an ablative of means, if a thing; and a passive verb form, in the appropriate person, number, and tense, is substituted for the active.

# VOCĀBVLA

**Genus** is one of thousands of Latin words (like **oculus** and **corpus**) that have come into English without any change in spelling. **Hostis,** *enemy* (of the state) is another noun with a special sense in the plural, equivalent to our COLLECTIVE NOUN, *the enemy* (as opposed to an individual enemy). Don't confuse **clārus** with **cārus,** or **moveō** with **moneō.** Note carefully also that the passive **videor, vidērī,** while it can certainly mean *to be seen,* very often means *to seem, appear;* for practice, conjugate this verb in the six active tenses and three passive tenses you have now learned, and cf. with the full conjugation of **moneō** in the **Summārium Fōrmārum.**

**flū́men, flū́minis,** n., *river* (flume, fluminous; cf. **fluō,** below)

**génus, géneris,** n., *origin; kind, type, sort, class* (genus, generic, genitive, gender, general, generous, genuine, degenerate, genre, congenial)

**hóstis, hóstis,** m., *an enemy* (of the state); **hóstēs, -ium,** *the enemy* (hostile, hostility, host)

**lúdus, lúdī,** m., *game, sport; school* (ludicrous, delude, elude, elusive, allude, allusion, illusion, collusion, interlude, prelude, postlude)

**próbitās, probitátis,** f., *uprightness, honesty* (probity, probation)

**sciéntia, sciéntiae,** f., *knowledge* (science, scientific, scientist, prescience; cf. **scīre,** *to know*)

**clā́rus, clā́ra, clā́rum,** *clear, bright; renowned, famous, illustrious* (clarify, clarity, claret, clarinet, clarion, declare, Clara, Clarissa, Claribel)

**mortā́lis, mortā́le,** *mortal* (mortality, immortal, immortality; cf. **mors**)

**cūr,** adv., *why*

**deínde,** adv., *thereupon, next, then*

**flúō, flúere, flúxī, flúxum,** *to flow* (fluid, fluent, flux, influx, affluence, influence, confluence, influenza, flu, mellifluous, superfluous)

**légō, légere, légī, léctum,** *to pick out, choose; read* (elect, elegant, eligible, lecture, legend, legible, intellect; cf. **dīligō, intellegō, neglegō**)

**mísceō, miscére, míscuī, míxtum,** *to mix, stir up, disturb* (miscellaneous, miscible, meddle, medley, melee, promiscuous)

**móveō, movḗre, móvī, mótum,** *to move; arouse, affect* (mobile, motion, motive, motor, commotion, emotion, remote, locomotive, mutiny)

**vídeor, vidḗrī, vī́sus sum,** pass. of **video,** *to be seen, seem, appear*

# LĒCTIŌ ET TRĀNSLĀTIŌ

As always, practice first with the Self-Tutorial Exercises, then read the following sentences and passage aloud, listening to the CDs, if you have them, and reading initially for comprehension. Look for all occurrences of the ablatives of agent and means, and for all passive verb forms, identifying the person, number, and tense of each.

## EXERCITĀTIŌNĒS

1. Multī morte etiam facilī nimis terrentur.
2. Beāta memoria amīcitiārum dulcium numquam dēlēbitur.
3. Illa fēmina caeca omnia genera artium quoque intellēxit et ab amīcīs iūcundīs semper laudābātur.
4. Pater senex vester, ā quō saepe iuvābāmur, multa dē celeribus perīculīs ingentis maris herī dīcere coepit.
5. Mentēs nostrae memoriā potentī illōrum duōrum factōrum cito moventur.
6. Cōnsilia hostium illō tertiō bellō longō et difficilī dēlēbantur.
7. Itaque māter mortem quārtī fīliī exspectābat, quī nōn valēbat et cuius aetās erat brevis.
8. Bella difficilia sine cōnsiliō et clēmentiā numquam gerēbāmus.
9. Tē cum novem ex aliīs miserīs ad Caesarem crās trahent.
10. Rēgem ācrem, quī officia neglegere incēperat, ex urbe suā ēiēcērunt.
11. Ille poēta in tertiō libellō saturārum scrīpsit dē hominibus avārīs quī ad centum terrās aliās nāvigāre cupiunt quod pecūniam nimis dēsīderant.
12. Mercy will be given by them even to the citizens of other cities which they rule.
13. Many are moved too often by money but not by truth.
14. The state will be destroyed by the powerful king, whom they are beginning to fear.
15. Those ten women were not frightened by plans of that trivial sort.

## SENTENTIAE ANTĪQVAE

1. Possunt quia posse videntur. (*Vergil.—**quia**, conj., *because.*)
2. Etiam fortēs virī subitīs perīculīs saepe terrentur. (Tacitus.—**subitus, -a, -um**, *sudden.*)
3. Tua cōnsilia sunt clāra nōbīs; tenēris scientiā hōrum cīvium omnium. (Cicero.)
4. Malum est cōnsilium quod mūtārī nōn potest. (*Publilius Syrus.)
5. Fās est ab hoste docērī. (Ovid.—**fās est**, *it is right.*)
6. Eō tempore erant circēnsēs lūdī, quō genere levī spectāculī numquam teneor. (Pliny.—**circēnsēs lūdī**, *contests in the Circus;* "circa," "circle"; "ludicrous," "interlude."—**quō genere:** *by which kind = a kind . . . by which;* occasionally, as here, the antecedent is incorporated into the rel. clause.—**spectāculum, -ī**, n.; "spectacular," "spectator.")
7. Haec est nunc vīta mea: admittō et salūtō bonōs virōs quī ad mē veniunt; deinde aut scrībō aut legō; post haec omne tempus corporī datur. (Cicero.—**salutāre**, *to greet* at the early morning reception; "salutation," "salutatorian.")

*Marble funerary relief of circus scene, 1st–2nd cent.* A.D.
*Museo Gregoriano Profano, Vatican Museums, Vatican State*

8. Nihil igitur mors est, quoniam nātūra animī habētur mortālis. (Lucretius.)
9. Amor miscērī cum timōre nōn potest. (*Publilius Syrus.)
10. Numquam enim temeritās cum sapientiā commiscētur. (*Cicero.—**temeritās,
    -tātis,** f., *rashness;* "temerarious," "temerity."–**commiscētur:** = **miscētur** + the
    prefix **com-** with its common intensifying force.)
11. Dīligēmus eum quī pecūniā nōn movētur. (Cicero.)
12. Laudātur ab hīs; culpātur ab illīs. (*Horace.)
13. Probitās laudātur—et alget. (*Juvenal.—**algēre,** *to be cold, be neglected;* "algid.")

### On Death and Metamorphosis

Ō genus hūmānum, quod mortem nimium timet! Cūr perīcula mortis timētis?
Omnia mūtantur, omnia fluunt, nihil ad vēram mortem venit. Animus errat et in
alia corpora miscētur; nec manet, nec eāsdem fōrmās servat, sed in fōrmās novās
mūtātur. Vīta est flūmen; tempora nostra fugiunt et nova sunt semper. Nostra corpora semper mūtantur; id quod fuimus aut sumus, nōn crās erimus.

Ovid *Met.* 15.153–216: Ovid (Publius Ovidius Naso, 43 B.C.–A.D. 17) has remained for 2000
years enormously popular, both for his several books of erotic poetry (including his racy
**Ars Amātōria,** *The Art of Love,* which seems to have been one of the reasons Augustus
exiled him from Rome in A.D. 8 at the height of his career) and for his **Metamorphōsēs,**
his most influential work, a quasi-epic collection of 250 interconnected transformation
myths in 15 volumes. The passage presented here, a prose adaptation from that poem's
closing book, presents some imaginative views on the transmigration of souls in the context of an argument on why men should not fear death (with which you might compare
Lucretius' remark in S. A. 8 above).

*QVAESTIŌNĒS:* What specific arguments are presented here to allay the fear of death? Would readers ancient or modern (yourself included) find them persuasive and consoling, or unsettling?

## SCRĪPTA IN PARIETIBVS

M. Lucrētius Frontō, vir fortis et ho<nestus>

*CIL* 4.6796: Graffito from a wall in the courtyard of a house in Reg. V, Ins. 4. Whoever wrote this, whether Fronto himself or an admirer, began to add in a second line **ET** and (probably) **HONESTVS** (*honorable,* a common epithet in such inscriptions), then stopped and, caught in the act or for whatever other reason, attempted to erase the incomplete phrase. Do you recall the term for the dot used to separate the words?—if not, see the graffiti in Capita X–XI.—**M.:** if you do not recall this abbreviation, see "Cicero Imagines," Capvt XIV.

## LATĪNA EST GAVDIVM—ET VTILIS!

**Salvēte!** Wondering how the same verb, **legere,** can mean both *to pick out* and *to read?* Because the process of reading was likened to gathering and collecting the words of a text. What a splendid metaphor: we are all of us (especially Latin students) "word collectors"! "Gather ye rosebuds while ye may" . . . and also the delights of language. Remember the special passive meaning of **videor** introduced in this **Vocābula;** here it is in the present passive infinitive form, also newly introduced in this chapter: **esse quam vidērī,** *to be rather than to seem,* the state motto of North Carolina. **Scientia** also turns up in several mottoes: **scientia est potentia,** *knowledge is power,* is one favorite, and another is **scientia sōl mentis est,** *knowledge is the sun of the mind* (motto of the University of Delaware). **Valēte, discipulae discipulīque!**

# CAPVT XIX ⌐⌐⌐

# Perfect Passive System; Interrogative Pronouns and Adjectives

## GRAMMATICA

### THE PERFECT PASSIVE SYSTEM

The construction of the forms of the **PERFECT PASSIVE SYSTEM** is quite simple: a verb's **PERFECT PASSIVE PARTICIPLE** (the fourth principal part) is combined with **sum, erō,** and **eram** to form the perfect, future perfect, and pluperfect passive, respectively. The same pattern is employed for verbs of all conjugations; thus, in the following paradigms, **monitus, āctus, audītus, captus,** or any other perfect passive participle could be substituted for **laudātus**.

**Perfect Indicative Passive**

|  |  |
|---|---|
| 1. laudātus, -a, -um sum | *I was praised, have been praised* |
| 2. laudātus, -a, -um es | *you were praised, have been praised* |
| 3. laudātus, -a, -um est | *he, she, it was praised, has been praised* |
| 1. laudātī, -ae, -a súmus | *we were praised, have been praised* |
| 2. laudātī, -ae, -a éstis | *you were praised, have been praised* |
| 3. laudātī, -ae, -a sunt | *they were praised, have been praised* |

**Future Perfect Indicative Passive**

*I will have been praised, etc.*
1. laudātus, -a, -um érō
2. laudātus, -a, -um éris
3. laudātus, -a, -um érit

1. laudātī, -ae, -a érimus
2. laudātī, -ae, -a éritis
3. laudātī, -ae, -a érunt

**Pluperfect Indicative Passive**

*I had been praised, etc.*
1. laudātus, -a, -um éram
2. laudātus, -a, -um érās
3. laudātus, -a, -um érat

1. laudātī, -ae, -a erámus
2. laudātī, -ae, -a erátis
3. laudātī, -ae, -a érant

### Usage and Translation

Although **sum** + the participle function together in Latin as a verbal unit, the participle in essence is a type of predicate adjective; i.e., **puella laudāta est** = **puella est laudāta**, cf. **puella est bona**. Consequently, and logically, the participle agrees with the subject in gender, number, and case.

Just as Latin uses the present, future, and imperfect of **sum, esse** to form these perfect system passive verbs, so English uses the present, future, and past tenses of the verb *to have* as perfect system (active and passive) auxiliaries: **laudātus est,** *he has been praised* (or, simple past, *was praised*); **laudātus erit,** *he will have been praised;* **laudātus erat,** *he had been praised.* Be careful to avoid such common mistranslations as *is praised* for **laudātus est** and *was praised* for **laudātus erat** (caused by looking at the forms of **esse** and the participle separately, rather than viewing them as a unit). The following examples illustrate these rules of form, usage, and translation:

> **Puella laudāta est.** *The girl has been* (or *was*) *praised.*
> **Puellae laudātae erant.** *The girls had been praised.*
> **Puellae laudātae erunt.** *The girls will have been praised.*
> **Puerī monitī sunt.** *The boys have been* (*were*) *warned.*
> **Perīculum nōn vīsum erat.** *The danger had not been seen.*
> **Perīcula nōn vīsa sunt.** *The dangers were not seen.*
> **Litterae scrīptae erunt.** *The letter will have been written.*

### Synopsis

You can now do a synopsis of first and second conjugation verbs in all six tenses of the indicative, active and passive; here is an example:

| **Pres.** | **Fut.** | **Imperf.** | **Perf.** | **Fut. Perf.** | **Pluperf.** |
|---|---|---|---|---|---|
| **Active** | | | | | |
| amat | amābit | amābat | amāvit | amāverit | amāverat |
| **Passive** | | | | | |
| amātur | amābitur | amābātur | amātus est | amātus erit | amātus erat |

## THE INTERROGATIVE PRONOUN

As with the English interrogative pronoun ("who?"/"whose?"/"whom?"/"what?"/"which?"), the Latin **INTERROGATIVE PRONOUN** quis, quid asks for the identity of a person or thing: e.g., **quid vidēs?** *what do you see?* and **quis cōnsilium habet?** *who has a plan?* In the plural the forms of the Latin interrogative pronoun are identical to those of the relative pronoun; in the singular it follows the pattern of the relative with two exceptions: (1) the masculine and the feminine have the same forms, (2) the nominative forms are **quis, quid** (and **quid** is also, of course, the n. acc. form).

|  | Singular | | Plural | | |
|---|---|---|---|---|---|
|  | M. & F. | N. | M. | F. | N. |
| *Nom.* | quis | quid | quī | quae | quae |
| *Gen.* | cuíus | cuíus | quórum | quárum | quórum |
| *Dat.* | cui | cui | quíbus | quíbus | quíbus |
| *Acc.* | quem | quid | quōs | quās | quae |
| *Abl.* | quō | quō | quíbus | quíbus | quíbus |

## THE INTERROGATIVE ADJECTIVE

Like the English interrogative adjective ("which . . . ?"/"what . . . ?"/"what kind of . . . ?"), the Latin **INTERROGATIVE ADJECTIVE** quī, quae, quod asks for *more specific* identification of a person or thing: e.g., **quod signum vidēs?** *what sign do you see?* **quae fēmina cōnsilium habet?** *which woman has a plan?* **in quā urbe vīvimus?** *in what kind of city are we living?* The word sometimes has exclamatory force: **quōs mōrēs malōs istī habent!** *what terrible morals those men have!* The forms of the interrogative adjective are identical to those of the relative pronoun, in both the singular and the plural.

### The Interrogatives and Relative Distinguished

The forms **quis** and **quid** are easily recognized as interrogative pronouns, but otherwise the interrogative pronoun, the interrogative adjective, and the relative pronoun can only be distinguished by their function and context, not by their forms. The following points will make the distinction simple:

- the *interrogative pronoun* asks a question about the identity of a person or thing, has no antecedent, and often introduces a sentence with a question mark at the end (an exception is the "indirect question," introduced in Capvt XXX): **quid legis?** *what are you reading?*
- the *interrogative adjective* asks for more specific identification of a person or thing and both precedes and agrees in gender, number, and case with the noun it is asking about: **quem librum legis?** *which book are you reading?*
- the *relative pronoun* usually introduces a subordinate clause, has an antecedent, and does not ask a question (in fact, relative clauses *answer* questions, in the sense that they are adjectival and provide further information about their antecedents: **liber quem legis est meus,** *the book which you are reading is mine.*

Determine whether a relative pronoun, an interrogative pronoun, or an interrogative adjective is used in the following examples:

*Quis* librum tibi dedit? *Who gave the book to you?*
Vir *quī* librum tibi dedit tē laudāvit. *The man who gave you the book praised you.*
*Quem* librum tibi dedit? *Which book did he give you?*

*Cuius* librum Cicerō tibi dedit? *Whose book did Cicero give to you?*
*Cuius* librī fuit Cicerō auctor? *Of which book was Cicero the author?*
Vir *cuius* librum Cicerō tibi dedit tē laudāvit. *The man whose book Cicero gave to you praised you.*

*Cui* amīcō librum dedistī? *To which friend did you give the book?*
*Cui* librum Cicerō dedit? *To whom did Cicero give the book?*
Vir *cui* Cicerō librum dedit tē laudāvit. *The man to whom Cicero gave the book praised you.*

*Quid* dedit? *What did he give?*
*Quod* praemium dedit? *What reward did he give?* (**praemium, -iī.**)
Praemium *quod* dedit erat magnum. *The reward which he gave was large.*

Ā *quō* praemium datum est? *By whom was the reward given?*
Vir ā *quō* praemium datum est tē laudāvit. *The man by whom the reward was given praised you.*
*Quō* praemiō ille mōtus est? *By which reward was that man motivated?*

# VOCĀBVLA

Be careful not to confuse look-alike words such as **iūdex** and **iūdicium** in this **Vocābula,** and the conjunctions **at,** in the list below, and **et,** learned previously. As you study this new vocabulary, do a synopsis of one of the three new verbs and compare your work with the full conjugation of **laudāre** in the **Summārium Fōrmārum,** p. 501–03; decline the interrogative adjective with one of the new nouns in this list too, e.g., **quī auctor,** *which author?* or **quod scelus,** *what crime?*

**argūméntum, argūméntī,** n., *proof, evidence, argument* (argumentation, argumentative)
**aúctor, auctóris,** m., *increaser; author, originator* (authority, authorize)
**benefícium, benefíciī,** n., *benefit, kindness; favor* (beneficence, beneficial, beneficiary; cf. **faciō**)
**família, famíliae,** f., *household, family* (familial, familiar, familiarity)
**Graécia, Graéciae,** f., *Greece*
**iúdex, iúdicis,** m., *judge, juror* (judge, judgment; cf. **iūdicium** below, and **iūs**)

iūdícium, iūdíciī, n., *judgment, decision, opinion; trial* (adjudge, adjudicate, judicial, judicious, injudicious, misjudge, prejudge, prejudice)

scélus, scéleris, n., *evil deed, crime, sin, wickedness*

quis? quid?, interrog. pron., *who? whose? whom? what? which?* (quiddity, quidnunc, quip; cf. **quisque**)

quī? quae? quod? interrog. adj., *what? which? what kind of?;* sometimes with exclamatory force, *what (a)! what sort of!* (quo jure)

cértus, cérta, cértum, *definite, sure, certain, reliable* (ascertain, certify, certificate)

grávis, gráve, *heavy, weighty; serious, important; severe, grievous* (aggravate, grief, grievance, grieve, grave, gravity)

immortális, immortále, *not subject to death, immortal* (cf. **mors**)

at, conj. *but; but, mind you; but, you say;* typically a stronger adversative than **sed**

nísi, conj., *if . . . not, unless; except* (nisi prius)

cóntrā, prep. + acc., *against* ("contra-" in compounds such as contradict, contrast, contravene, contrapuntal, and see "Some Etymological Aids," p. 486; contrary, counter, encounter, country, pro and con)

iam, adv., *now, already, soon*

dēléctō, dēlectáre, dēlectávī, dēlectátum, *to delight, charm, please* (delectable, delectation)

líberō, līberáre, līberávī, līberátum, (1), *to free, liberate* (liberate, liberation, liberal, deliver; cf. **līber, lībertās**)

párō, paráre, parávī, parátum, (1), *to prepare, provide; get, obtain* (apparatus, compare, parachute, parapet, parasol, pare, parry, repair, reparation, separate, several)

# LĒCTIŌ ET TRĀNSLĀTIŌ

Scan the readings for perfect system passives and interrogative pronouns and adjectives. To avoid confusing the **qu-** words you've recently learned, be sure to review "The Interrogatives and Relative Distinguished" above; and be careful not to translate perfect system passives as simple present, future, and imperfect by mistakenly focusing on the forms of **esse:** e.g., **dēlēta est** in Ex. 2 means *has been/was destroyed,* not *is destroyed.*

## EXERCITĀTIŌNĒS

1. Quis lībertātem eōrum eō tempore dēlēre coepit?
2. Cuius lībertās ab istō auctōre deinde dēlēta est?
3. Quōs librōs bonōs poēta caecus heri recitāvit?
4. Fēminae librōs difficilēs crās legent quōs mīsistī.
5. Omnia flūmina in mare fluunt et cum eō miscentur.

6. Itaque id genus lūdōrum levium, quod ā multīs familiīs laudābātur, nōs ipsī numquam cupimus.
7. Puerī et puellae propter facta bona ā mātribus patribusque quoque laudātae erunt.
8. Cūr istī vēritātem timēbant, quā multī adiūtī erant?
9. Hostēs trāns ingēns flūmen in Graeciā deinde cito nāvigāre incēpērunt.
10. Quī vir fortis clārusque, dē quō lēgistī, aetātem brevem mortemque celerem exspectābat?
11. Quae studia gravia tē semper dēlectant, aut quae nunc dēsīderās?
12. Who saw the six men who had prepared this?
13. What was neglected by the second student yesterday?
14. We were helped by the knowledge which had been neglected by him.
15. Whose plans did the old men of all those cities fear? Which plans did they esteem?

## SENTENTIAE ANTĪQVAE

1. Quae est nātūra animī? Est mortālis. (Lucretius.)
2. Illa argūmenta vīsa sunt et gravia et certa. (Cicero.)
3. Quid nōs facere contrā istōs et scelera eōrum dēbēmus? (Cicero.)
4. Quid ego ēgī? In quod perīculum iactus sum? (Terence.)
5. Ō dī immortālēs! In quā urbe vīvimus? Quam cīvitātem habēmus? Quae scelera vidēmus? (Cicero.)
6. Quī sunt bonī cīvēs nisi eī quī officiō moventur et beneficia patriae memoriā tenent? (Cicero.)
7. Alia, quae pecūniā parantur, ab eō stultō parāta sunt; at mōrēs eius vērōs amīcōs parāre nōn potuērunt. (Cicero.)

### The Aged Playwright Sophocles Holds His Own

Quam multa senēs in mentibus tenent! Sī studium grave et labor et probitās in senectūte remanent, saepe manent etiam memoria, scientia, sapientiaque. Sophoclēs, scrīptor ille Graecus, ad summam senectūtem tragoediās fēcit; sed propter hoc studium familiam neglegere vidēbātur et ā fīliīs in iūdicium vocātus est. Tum auctor eam tragoediam quam sēcum habuit et quam proximē scrīpserat, "Oedipum Colōnēum," iūdicibus recitāvit. Ubi haec tragoedia recitāta est, senex sententiīs iūdicum est līberātus.

Cicero *Sen.* 7.22: In this selection from "On Old Age" (you should re-read the others in Capita XV and XVII), Cicero relates an anecdote about the Greek tragedian Sophocles (ca. 496–406 B.C.), who during his long career authored more than 120 plays, many of them prize-winning. —**summam,** *extreme;* "summary," "summit."—**tragoedia, -ae,** f.; the diphthong **oe** has become **e** in the Eng. word; "tragedian," "tragic."—**proximē,** adv., *shortly before;* "proximity," "approximate."—**Oedipum Colōnēum:** Sophocles composed his last play, "Oedipus at Colonus," near the end of his life, and it won first place in the theatrical competitions at which it was produced posthumously, by his grandson, in 401 B.C.

*QVAESTIŌNĒS:* What is Cicero's purpose in relating this anecdote about Sophocles in his treatise **Dē Senectūte?** Why did the court acquit Sophocles of the charges his sons had brought against him?

*Marble statue of Sophocles*
*Roman copy of a 4th cent. B.C. Greek original*
*Museo Gregoriano Profano*
*Vatican Museums, Vatican State*

### Catullus Bids a Bitter Farewell to Lesbia

Valē, puella—iam Catullus obdūrat.

. . .

15 Scelesta, vae tē! Quae tibī manet vīta?
Quis nunc tē adībit? Cui vidēberis bella?
Quem nunc amābis? Cuius esse dīcēris?
Quem bāsiābis? Cui labella mordēbis?
At tū, Catulle, dēstinātus obdūrā.

*Catullus *Carm.* 8.12, 15–19: Lines excerpted directly from the Catullus poem which you read in a much simplified prose adaptation in Capvt II (and which is presented in nearly complete form in **Locī Ant.** I, below, p. 351–52); meter: choliambic.—**obdūrāre,** *to be hard, be tough, endure;* "obdurate."—**scelestus, -a, -um,** *wicked, accursed;* "scelerat."—**vae tē,** *woe to you.*—**quae:** with **vīta.**—**tibī:** just as final long vowels were sometimes shortened in verse, for metrical reasons, final short vowels were sometimes lengthened.—**adībit:** *will visit.*—**dīcēris:** *will you be said.*—**bāsiāre,** *to kiss.*—**cui:** here = **cuius,** as the dat. often has possessive force.—**labellum, -ī,** n., *lip;* "labial."—**mordēre,** *to bite;* "mordant," "morsel," "remorse."—**dēstinātus, -a, -um,** *resolved, firm;* "destination," "destiny.")

*QVAESTIŌNĒS:* What are the most striking stylistic features of this excerpt?—think even of rhythms and sound effects. How does Catullus' language resemble that of a prosecuting attorney?—how do his questions become progressively more intense? What psychology does Catullus play upon in describing himself in third person, and then addressing and lecturing himself in the poem's closing line?

### Message from a Bookcase

> Sēlectōs nisi dās mihī libellōs,
> admittam tineās trucēsque blattās!

*Martial *Epig.* 14.37: One of the first books Martial wrote, though appearing in manuscripts as Liber XIV, was separately titled **Apophorēta,** a Greek word lit. meaning "things (for guests) to take away," like our "party favors." Each of these little gift poems was labeled with the name of the object it accompanied (here a **scrīnium,** a cylindrical container for holding books), and in many the gift itself addresses the reader—in this instance with a threat! Meter: hendecasyllabic.—**sēlectus, -a, -um,** *select, carefully chosen;* "selection," "selective."—**tinea, -ae,** f., *maggot, bookworm;* "tineal."—**trux,** gen. **trucis,** *fierce, savage;* "truculent."—**blatta, -ae,** f., *cockroach.*

*QVAESTIŌNĒS:* As we have seen, word order in verse is much freer than that of prose; how might you here re-arrange the words of the first line into standard prose order? Which word in particular adds mock intensity to the bookcase's threat?

## SCRĪPTA IN PARIETIBVS

Casta sum māter, et omnīnō alō quod mercās.

*CIL* 4.8842: This graffito was found in a structure in Reg. III, Ins. 3, identified by the editors of *CIL* as a school for Pompeian youth (**schola iūventūtis**). The building seems to have had an association with Flora, Roman goddess of spring and flowering and the renewal of life, whose name appears twice in a nearby graffito (4.8840) and who was perhaps the school's tutelary deity; the editors of *CIL* take this graffito to be from a hymn in which the goddess addresses the young worshiper.—**castus, -a, -um,** *unstained, holy, pure;* "chaste," "chastity."—**casta . . . māter:** the designation suits Flora, as a major fertility goddess; her yearly festival, the Floralia, was regarded by prostitutes as their own special holiday.—**omnīnō,** adv., *wholly, entirely, altogether;* "omnipotent," "omniscient."— **mercāre,** *to buy, trade; deal in, traffic in* (for the likely sense here, cf. the Eng. idiom, "in all your dealings" = "all that you deal with"); "mercantile," "merchant."

## LATĪNA EST GAVDIVM—ET V̄TILIS!

**Salvēte!**—**quid agitis?** We've been seeing **quid** in that idiom (*how are you doing?* not *what are you doing?*) ever since Capvt II, and do you recall **quid novī,** *what's new?,* from the discussion of the genitive of the whole in Capvt XV? Even before beginning your study of Latin you'd likely encountered the common phrase **quid prō quō,** *one thing in return for another* (= "tit for tat"—**quid** was often equivalent to the indefinite *something*) and you may even have run into **quidnunc,** a "busybody" (lit., *what-now?!*). The interrogative adjective has also come into English: **quō jūre** (= classical **iūre**), *by what (legal) right,* **quō animō,** *with what intention,* and **quō modō,** *in what manner.* You learned **iaciō, iacere, iēcī, iactum** in Capvt XV: you can now recognize the perfect passive form in Julius Caesar's famous dictum, **alea iacta est,** *the die has been cast,* a remark he made in 49 B.C. when crossing the Rubicon river in northern Italy (see Map 1) and embarking upon civil war with Pompey the Great. **Discipulī discipulaeque, valēte!**

# Fourth Declension; Ablatives of Place from Which and Separation

## GRAMMATICA

### FOURTH DECLENSION

The fourth declension is easily learned and contains relatively few nouns; most are masculine, with the nominative singular in -**us,** but there are some feminines, also in -**us,** and a few neuters, with the nominative singular in -**ū.** To decline, simply add the new endings presented below to the base; note that the character-istic vowel **u** appears in all endings except the dative and ablative plural (and even there a few nouns have -**ubus** for -**ibus**) and that, of all the -**us** endings, only the masculine and feminine nominative singular has a short -**u**-.

|       | frūctus, -ūs, m. | cornū, -ūs, n. | Endings |       |
|-------|------------------|----------------|---------|-------|
|       | *fruit*          | *horn*         | M. & F. | N.    |
| Nom.  | frúctus          | córnū          | -us     | -ū    |
| Gen.  | frúctūs          | córnūs         | -ūs     | -ūs   |
| Dat.  | frúctuī          | córnū          | -uī     | -ū    |
| Acc.  | frúctum          | córnū          | -um     | -ū    |
| Abl.  | frúctū           | córnū          | -ū      | -ū    |
|       |                  |                |         |       |
| Nom.  | frúctūs          | córnua         | -ūs     | -ua   |
| Gen.  | frúctuum         | córnuum        | -uum    | -uum  |
| Dat.  | frúctibus        | córnibus       | -ibus   | -ibus |
| Acc.  | frúctūs          | córnua         | -ūs     | -ua   |
| Abl.  | frúctibus        | córnibus       | -ibus   | -ibus |

Remember that there are also -**us** nouns in the second and third declensions, e.g., **amīcus** and **corpus;** it is a noun's genitive ending, not the nominative, that deter-mines its declension, so it is imperative that you memorize the full vocabulary entry for every new noun you encounter. Recall, too, that a noun and modifying adjective, though they must agree in number, gender, and case, will not necessarily have the same endings, hence **frūctus dulcis, frūctūs dulcis,** etc., *sweet fruit;* **manus mea, manūs meae,** etc., *my hand;* **cornū longum, cornūs longī,** etc., *a long horn;* etc.

## ABLATIVES OF PLACE FROM WHICH AND SEPARATION

The ablatives of place from which and separation are common and closely related constructions (which you should add to your list of ablative uses). The principal difference is that the ABLATIVE OF PLACE FROM WHICH, already encountered in your readings, regularly involves a *verb of active motion* from one place to another; nearly always, too, the ablative is governed by one of the prepositions **ab, dē,** or **ex** (*away from, down from, out of*):

> **Graecī ā patriā suā ad Italiam nāvigāvērunt.** *The Greeks sailed from their (own) country to Italy.*
> **Flūmen dē montibus in mare flūxit.** *The river flowed down from the mountains into the sea.*
> **Multī ex agrīs in urbem venient.** *Many will come from the country into the city.*
> **Cicerō hostēs ab urbe mīsit.** *Cicero sent the enemy away from the city.*

The ABLATIVE OF SEPARATION, as the terminology suggests, implies only that some person or thing is separate from another; there is no movement from one place to another; and sometimes there is no preposition, particularly with certain verbs meaning "to free," "to lack," and "to deprive," which commonly take an ablative of separation:

> **Cicerō hostēs ab urbe prohibuit,** *Cicero kept the enemy away from the city* (cf. the similar example above).
> **Eōs timōre līberāvit.** *He freed them from fear.*
> **Agricolae pecūniā saepe carēbant.** *The farmers were often lacking money.*

# VOCĀBVLA

Recall that there are **-us** nouns, not just in the fourth declension, but in the second and third as well, e.g., **amīcus** and **corpus;** it is a noun's genitive ending, not the nominative, that identifies its declension, so it is imperative to memorize the full vocabulary entry for every new noun. **Coniūrātī** is found only in the plural, and logically so—can you explain why? Comparing such forms as **frūctus** and **frūctūs** provides a reminder that macrons often signal important differences of meaning and usage and so must be learned as part of a word's spelling and pronunciation; always practice new paradigms and vocabulary by listening (to your instructor and/or the online audio, and the CDs too, if you have them) and repeating them aloud: **semper audī prōnūntiāque!** As you learn the new vocabulary, decline some noun-adjective pairs such as **sēnsus commūnis, manus dextra,** and **genū sinistrum.**

**coniūrā́tī, coniūrātṓrum,** m. pl., *conspirators* (conjure, conjurer; cf. **coniūrātiō,** *conspiracy,* conjuration)

**có̆rnū, có̆rnūs,** n., *horn* (corn—not the grain, but a thick growth of skin; cornea, corner, cornet, cornucopia, unicorn)

**frū́ctus, frū́ctūs,** m., *fruit; profit, benefit, enjoyment* (fructify, fructose, frugal)

**gé̆nū, gé̆nūs,** n., *knee* (genuflect, genuflection, genual; "knee" is cognate)

**má̆nus, má̆nūs,** f., *hand; handwriting; band* (manual, manufacture, manumit, manuscript, emancipate, manacle, manage, manicle, maneuver)

**mé̆tus, mé̆tūs,** m., *fear, dread, anxiety* (meticulous; cf. **metuere,** *to fear, dread*)

**mōns, mó̆ntis,** m., *mountain* (mount, mountainous, Montana, amount, catamount, paramount, surmount, tantamount)

**senā́tus, senā́tūs,** m., *senate* (senator, senatorial; related to **senex,** as the senate was a council of "elders")

**sḗnsus, sḗnsūs,** m., *feeling, sense* (sensation, sensory, sensual, sensuous, senseless, insensate, sensible, sensitive; cf. **sentiō**)

**sé̆rvitūs, servitū́tis,** f., *servitude, slavery* (service; cf. **servō**)

**spí̆ritus, spí̆ritūs,** m., *breath, breathing; spirit, soul* (spiritual, spiritous, conspire, inspire, expire, respiratory, transpire; cf. **spīrāre,** *to breathe*)

**vé̆rsus, vé̆rsūs,** m., *line of verse* (versify, versification)

**commū́nis, commū́ne,** *common, general, of/for the community* (communal, commune, communicate, communicable, communion, communism, community, excommunicate)

**dé̆xter, dé̆xtra, dé̆xtrum,** *right, right-hand* (dexterity, dextrous, ambidextrous)

**siní̆ster, siní̆stra, siní̆strum,** *left, left-hand; harmful, ill-omened* (sinister, sinistral, sinistrodextral)

**cá̆reō, caré̆re, cá̆ruī, caritū́rum** + abl. of separation, *to be without, be deprived of, want, lack; be free from* (caret—not carat)

**dēfé̆ndō, dēfé̆ndere, dēfé̆ndī, dēfḗnsum,** *to ward off; defend, protect* (defendant, defense, defensible, defensive, fence, fencing, fend, fender, offend)

**discḗdō, discḗdere, discḗssī, discḗssum,** *to go away, depart* (proceed, secede; do not confuse with **discō**)

**ṓdī, ōdí̆sse, ṓsum,** a DEFECTIVE VERB (see comments on **coepī,** Capvt XVII), having chiefly perf. system forms with pres. force, *to hate* (odium, odious)

**prohí̆beō, prohibḗre, prohí̆buī, prohí̆bitum,** *to keep (back), prevent, hinder, restrain, prohibit* (prohibitive, prohibition, prohibitory; cf. **habeō**)

**prōnū́ntiō, prōnūntiā́re, prōnūntiā́vī, prōnūntiā́tum,** *to proclaim, announce; declaim; pronounce* (pronouncement, pronunciation; cf. **nūntius,** *messenger, message*)

# LĒCTIŌ ET TRĀNSLĀTIŌ

Scan through the readings for all fourth declension nouns, identifying the gender, number, case, and use of each, as well as for all occurrences of the ablative of place from which and ablative of separation constructions. Listen to the CDs, if you have them, and read aloud, and for comprehension, before translating.

## EXERCITĀTIŌNĒS

1. Etiam senēs frūctibus sapientiae et cōnsiliīs argūmentīsque certīs saepe carēre videntur.
2. Aut ingentēs montēs aut flūmina celeria quae dē montibus fluēbant hostēs ab urbe prohibēbant.
3. Quoniam nimis fortia facta faciēbat, aetās eius erat brevis.
4. Illa medica facere poterat multa manū dextrā sed sinistrā manū pauca.
5. At vēritās nōs metū gravī iam līberābit quō diū territī sumus.
6. Quibus generibus scelerum sinistrōrum illae duae cīvitātēs dēlētae erunt?
7. Quī mortālis sine amīcitiā et probitāte et beneficiō in aliōs potest esse beātus?
8. Pater pecūniam ex Graeciā in suam patriam movēre coeperat, nam familia discēdere cupīvit.
9. Ā quibus studium difficilium artium eō tempore neglēctum est?
10. Ubi versūs illīus auctōris clārī lēctī sunt, audītōrēs dēlectātī sunt.
11. Sē cito iēcērunt ad genua iūdicum, quī autem nūllam clēmentiam dēmōnstrāvērunt.
12. Istī coniūrātī ab urbe prohibērī nōn possunt.
13. We cannot have the fruits of peace, unless we ourselves free our families from heavy dread.
14. Those bands of unfortunate men and women will come to us from other countries in which they are deprived of the benefits of citizenship.
15. The old men lacked neither games nor serious pursuits.
16. Who began to perceive our common fears of serious crime?

## SENTENTIAE ANTĪQVAE

1. Cornua cervum ā perīculīs dēfendunt. (Martial.—**cervus, -ī,** m., *stag.*)
2. Oedipūs duōbus oculīs sē prīvāvit. (Cicero.—**prīvāre,** *to deprive;* "privation," privative.")
3. Themistoclēs bellō Persicō Graeciam servitūte līberāvit. (Cicero.—**Persicus, -a, -um,** *Persian;* "peach," from **Persica,** *peachtree,* and **Persicum mālum,** *Persian apple,* what the Romans called the peach.)
4. Dēmosthenēs multōs versūs ūnō spīritū prōnūntiābat. (Cicero.)
5. Persicōs apparātūs ōdī. (Horace.—**apparātus, -ūs,** m., *equipment, display*)

6. Iste commūnī sēnsū caret. (Horace.—**commūnī**, here *social,* referring to the man's tact.)

7. Senectūs nōs prīvat omnibus voluptātibus neque longē abest ā morte. (Cicero.—**longē**, adv. of **longus.—absum**, *to be away;* "absence," "absentee.")

8. Nūllus accūsātor caret culpā; omnēs peccāvimus. (Seneca.—**accūsātor, -tōris**, m., "accusative," "accusatory."—**peccāre**, *to sin;* "peccant," "impeccable.")

9. Nūlla pars vītae vacāre officiō potest. (Cicero.—**vacāre**, *to be free from;* "vacate," "evacuate.")

10. Prīma virtūs est vitiō carēre. (Quintilian.)

11. Vir scelere vacuus nōn eget iaculīs neque arcū. (Horace.—**vacuus, -a, -um**, *free from;* "vacuum," "vacant."—**egēre**, *to need;* "indigence," "indigent."—**iaculum, -ī**, n., *javelin;* "projectile."—**arcus, -ūs**, m., *bow;* "arc," "archer.")

12. Magnī tumultūs urbem eō tempore miscēbant. (Cicero.—**tumultus, -ūs**, m.; "tumult," "tumultuous.")

13. Litterae senātuī populōque Allobrogum manibus coniūrātōrum ipsōrum erant scrīptae. (Cicero.—**Allobrogēs, -gum**, m. pl., a Gallic tribe the Catilinarian conspirators tried to recruit against Rome.)

## Cicero Urges Catiline's Departure from Rome

Habēmus senātūs cōnsultum contrā tē, Catilīna, vehemēns et grave; ācre iūdicium habēmus, et vīrēs et cōnsilium cīvitās nostra habet. Quid est, Catilīna? Cūr remanēs? Ō dī immortālēs! Discēde nunc ex hāc urbe cum malā manū scelerātōrum; magnō metū mē līberābis, sī omnēs istōs coniūrātōs tēcum ēdūcēs. Nisi nunc discēdēs, tē cito ēiciēmus. Nihil in cīvitāte nostrā tē dēlectāre potest. Age, age! Deinde curre ad Manlium, istum amīcum malum; tē diū dēsīderāvit. Incipe nunc; parā cōpiās et gere bellum in cīvitātem! Brevī tempore tē omnēsque tuōs, hostēs patriae, vincēmus, et omnēs vōs poenās gravēs semper dabitis.

Lucius Sergius Catilina
*Bronze sculpture, 1889*
*Thomas Vincotte (1850–1925)*
*Nationalgalerie, Staatliche Museen*
*Berlin, Germany*

Cicero *Cat.* 1.1.3ff: Another passage adapted from Cicero's first oration against Catiline; be sure to read again the other excerpts, and accompanying notes, in Capita XI and XIV (the selection presented here comes shortly after the passage of the speech excerpted in Capvt XI).—**cōnsultum, -ī,** n., *decree;* "consult," "consultant."—**vehemēns,** gen. **vehementis,** = Eng.; "vehemence."—**scelerātus, -a, -um,** *wicked, criminal, defiled;* adj. from **scelus.**—**Manlium:** Manlius was one of Catiline's principal fellow conspirators.

*QVAESTIŌNĒS:* What several reasons does Cicero give Catiline to encourage his departure from the city? Which are most compelling, which somewhat less so or even facetious? What is unusual, and effective, in the positioning of the adjectives in the opening sentence?

## SCRĪPTA IN PARIETIBVS

Habitus Issae sal(ūtem)!

*CIL* 4.8954: Habitus scribbled this note to a lady friend near the entrance to a shop in Reg. III, Ins. 7. What was her name, i.e., in the nom. form, and what case is it here?—**salūtem:** if you do not recall the meaning and case usage of this word, see the graffiti in Capita VIII and X; here, as often in graffiti, the word was abbreviated, but you can practice a bit of "forgery" by writing out the full word, replicating as nearly as possible Habitus' handwriting: you'll have to be creative with the final **-m,** but specimens of the other three letters appear in the first two words. By the way, actual forgeries of "ancient" graffiti are not uncommon; folks prowling through Pompeii in relatively modern times have scrawled their own Lat. messages on the walls of ruins throughout the city or added words or phrases next to or beneath genuine ancient graffiti, many of them published separately in *CIL* 4 and labeled as **Falsae vel (= aut) Suspectae.**

## LATĪNA EST GAVDIVM—ET VTILIS!

**Salvēte!** This chapter's **Vocābula** provides some "handy" items: can you explain the etymologies of "manumit," "manuscript," and "manufacture"? A "manual" is the Latin equivalent of the Germanic "handbook." Then there's the old Roman proverb **manus manum lavat** (**lavāre,** *to bathe,* gives us "lavatory"), *one hand washes the other.* You can see the right-handed bias in the etymologies of "dexterity" and "sinister" (from the ancient superstition that bad signs and omens appeared to one's left) and even "ambidextrous" (from **ambō,** *both, two:* is having "two right hands" better than having two left hands?).

And speaking of hands, how about fingers? The Latin word is **digitus, -ī,** which gives us "digit," "digital," "prestidigitation" (for a magician's quick fingers), and even "digitalis," a heart medication from a plant whose flowers are finger-shaped. These appendages are also handy for counting (**numerāre**): **prīmus digitus, secundus digitus, tertius** . . . etc. (**Potestisne numerāre omnēs digitōs vestrōs, discipulī et discipulae?** If not, look back at Capvt XV and review your **numerī!**) The Romans had special names for each of the fingers, beginning with the thumb, **pollex,** then **index** (from **indicāre,** *to point*), **medius** (*middle*) or **īnfāmis** (*infamous, evil*—not all our body language is new!), **quārtus** or **ānulārius** (where they often wore **ānulī,** *rings:* see "Ringo," Capvt XXXI), and **minimus** (*the smallest*) or **auriculārius** (the **parvus digitus,** and so handy for scratching or cleaning one's **aurēs!**). **Valēte!**

# CAPVT XXI ᗏᗏᗏ

# Third and Fourth Conjugations: Present System Passive

## GRAMMATICA

### THIRD AND FOURTH CONJUGATION PRESENT SYSTEM PASSIVE

The pattern of substituting passive endings for active endings, which you learned in Capvt XVIII for the present system passives of first and second conjugation verbs, generally applies to third and fourth conjugation verbs as well; the only exceptions are in the second person singular present tense (set in bold in the following paradigms) and the present infinitive of third conjugation verbs.

**Present Indicative Passive**

| | | |
|---|---|---|
| 1. ágor | aúdior | cápior |
| 2. ág**eris** | audī́ris | cáp**eris** |
| 3. ágitur | audī́tur | cápitur |
| 1. ágimur | audī́mur | cápimur |
| 2. agíminī | audī́minī | capíminī |
| 3. agúntur | audiúntur | capiúntur |

**Future Indicative Passive**

| | | |
|---|---|---|
| 1. ágar | aúdiar | cápiar |
| 2. agḗris | audiḗris | capiḗris |
| 3. agḗtur | audiḗtur | capiḗtur |
| 1. agḗmur | audiḗmur | capiḗmur |
| 2. agḗminī | audiḗminī | capiḗminī |
| 3. agéntur | audiéntur | capiéntur |

## Imperfect Indicative Passive

| | | |
|---|---|---|
| 1. agḗbar | audiḗbar | capiḗbar |
| 2. agēbā́ris | audiēbā́ris | capiēbā́ris |
| 3. agēbā́tur | audiēbā́tur | capiēbā́tur |
| 1. agēbā́mur | audiēbā́mur | capiēbā́mur |
| 2. agēbā́minī | audiēbā́minī | capiēbā́minī |
| 3. agēbā́ntur | audiēbā́ntur | capiēbā́ntur |

Be careful not to confuse the second person singular present and future third conjugation forms, which are distinguished only by the vowel quantity (**ageris** vs. **agēris**). Note that **capiō** and **audiō** are identical throughout the present system active and passive, except for variations in -i- vs. -ī- (in the present tense only) and the second singular passive **caperis** vs. **audīris**. Remember that the perfect passive system for third and fourth conjugation verbs follows the universal pattern introduced in Capvt XIX.

## Present Passive Infinitive

The present infinitive passive of the fourth conjugation is formed by changing the final -**e** to -**ī**, as in the first two conjugations; but in the third conjugation, including -**iō** verbs, the whole -**ere** is changed to -**ī**.

| | |
|---|---|
| audī́re, *to hear* | audī́rī, *to be heard* (cf. laudā́rī, monḗrī) |
| ágere, *to drive* | ágī, *to be driven* |
| cápere, *to take* | cápī, *to be taken* |

## Synopsis

You can now provide a synopsis of regular verbs of all four conjugations in the indicative mood; following is a sample third person plural synopsis of **agō**:

| | Pres. | Fut. | Imperf. | Perf. | Fut. Perf. | Pluperf. |
|---|---|---|---|---|---|---|
| **Act.** | águnt | ágent | agḗbant | ēgḗrunt | ḗgerint | ḗgerant |
| **Pass.** | agúntur | agéntur | agēbántur | ā́ctī sunt | ā́ctī ḗrunt | ā́ctī ḗrant |

# VOCĀBVLA

**Āh** (English *ah* or *aha*)!—more look-alikes in this list: **casa** and **causa**. But say them aloud—**prōnūntiā**—and you'll hear and learn the difference. N.B. the common use of ablative **causā** with a preceding genitive, e.g., **pecūniae causā**, *for the sake of money,* or **virtūtis causā**, *on account of virtue*. There are several new third declension nouns here; if you don't recognize which are **i**-stems, review Capvt XIV. And practice synopses of some third and fourth conjugation verbs—then compare your work with the paradigms in the **Summārium Fōrmārum**.

**cása, cásae,** f., *house, cottage, hut* (casino)

**caúsa, caúsae,** f., *cause, reason; case, situation;* **caúsā,** abl. with a preceding gen., *for the sake of, on account of* (accuse, because, excuse)

**fenéstra, fenéstrae,** f., *window* (fenestrated, fenestration, fenestella, defenestration)

**fínis, fínis,** m., *end, limit, boundary; purpose;* **fínēs, fínium,** *boundaries, territory* (affinity, confine, define, final, finale, finance, fine, finesse, finial, finicky, finish, finite, infinite, paraffin, refine)

**gēns, géntis,** f., *clan, race, nation, people* (gentile, gentle, genteel, gentry; cf. **genus**)

**múndus, múndī,** m., *world, universe* (mundane, extramundane, demimonde)

**nāvis, nāvis,** f., *ship, boat* (naval, navy, navigate, nave; cf. **nāvigāre, nauta**)

**sálūs, salútis,** f., *health, safety; greeting* (salubrious, salutary, salutation, salute, salutatorian, salutatory; cf. **salveō, salvus**)

**Trôia, Trôiae,** f., *Troy* (Trojan)

**vīcînus, vīcînī,** m., and **vīcîna, vīcînae,** f., *neighbor* (vicinity, vicinal, vicinage)

**vúlgus, vúlgī,** n. (sometimes m.), *the common people, mob, rabble* (vulgar, vulgarity, vulgarize, vulgate, divulge)

**ásper, áspera, ásperum,** *rough, harsh* (asperity, exasperate, exasperation)

**átque** or **ac** (both forms used before consonants, **atque** regularly before vowels or **h**), conj., *and also, and even, and in fact*

**íterum,** adv., *again, a second time* (iterate, iterative, reiterate, reiteration)

**contíneō, continére, contínuī, conténtum,** *to hold together, contain, keep, enclose, restrain* (content, discontent, malcontent, continual; cf. **teneō**)

**iúbeō, iubére, iússī, iússum,** *to bid, order, command* (jussive)

**labôrō, labōráre, labōrávī, labōrátum,** *to labor; be in distress* (laboratory, laborer, belabor; cf. **labor**)

**rápiō, rápere, rápuī, ráptum,** *to seize, snatch, carry away* (rapacious, rapid, rapine, rapture, ravage, ravish; cf. **ēripere,** *to snatch away*)

**relínquō, relínquere, relíquī, relíctum,** *to leave behind, leave, abandon, desert* (relinquish, reliquary, relict, relic, delinquent, dereliction)

**scíō, scíre, scívī, scítum,** *to know* (science, scientific, conscience, conscious, prescience, scilicet; cf. **scientia, nescīre,** *to not know, be ignorant of*)

**tángō, tángere, tétigī, táctum,** *to touch* (tangent, tangible, tact, tactile, contact, contagious, contiguous, contingent, integer, taste, tax)

# LĒCTIŌ ET TRĀNSLĀTIŌ

After learning the new paradigms and vocabulary and testing yourself with some of the Self-Tutorial Exercises, scan through the following readings for examples of third and fourth conjugation present system passive verbs, identifying the tense, number, and person of each.

## EXERCITĀTIŌNĒS

1. Laus autem nimis saepe est neque certa neque magna.
2. Senēs in gente nostrā ab fīliīs numquam neglegēbantur.
3. Quis tum iussus erat Graeciam metū gravī līberāre, familiās dēfendere, atque hostēs ā fīnibus prohibēre?
4. Salūtis commūnis causā eōs coniūrātōs ex urbe discēdere ac trāns flūmen ad montēs dūcī iussit.
5. Aliī auctōrēs coepērunt spīritūs nostrōs contrā iūdicium atque argūmenta senātūs iterum movēre, quod omnēs metū novō territī erant.
6. Omnia genera servitūtis nōbīs videntur aspera.
7. Rapiēturne igitur Cicerō ex manibus istōrum?
8. Quī fīnis metūs atque servitūtis in eā cīvitāte nunc potest vidērī?
9. At senectūtis bonae causā iam bene vīvere dēbēmus.
10. In familiā eōrum erant duae fīliae atque quattuor fīliī.
11. Casa vīcīnae nostrae habuit paucās fenestrās per quās vidēre potuit.
12. Quandō cornū audīvit, senex in genua cecidit et deīs immortālibus grātiās prōnūntiābat.
13. Propter beneficia et sēnsum commūnem tyrannī, paucī eum ōdērunt.
14. The truth will not be found without great labor.
15. Many nations which lack true peace are being destroyed by wars.
16. Their fears can now be conquered because our deeds are understood by all.
17. Unless serious pursuits delight us, they are often neglected for the sake of money or praise.

## SENTENTIAE ANTĪQVAE

1. Numquam perīculum sine perīculō vincitur. (Publilius Syrus.)
2. Novius est vīcīnus meus et manū dextrā tangī dē fenestrīs meīs potest. (Martial.—**Novius:** a personal name.)
3. Nōnne iūdicēs iubēbunt hunc propter scelera in vincula dūcī et ad mortem rapī? (Cicero.—**nōnne** introduces a question which anticipates the answer "yes"; see Capvt XL.—**vinculum, -ī,** n., *chain;* "vinculum.")
4. Altera aetās bellīs cīvīlibus teritur et Rōma ipsa suīs vīribus dēlētur. (Horace.—**cīvīlis, -e,** = Eng.; cf. **cīvis, cīvitās;** "civilian," "civilize."—**terō, -ere, trīvī, trītum,** *to wear out;* "trite," "contrite," "detriment.")
5. At amīcitia nūllō locō exclūditur; numquam est intempestīva aut sinistra; multa beneficia continet. (Cicero.—**exclūdō, -ere,** *to shut out;* "exclude," "exclusion."—**intempestīvus, -a, -um,** *untimely.*)
6. Futūra scīrī nōn possunt. (Cicero.—**futūrus, -a, -um,** = Eng.; "futuristic.")

7. Prīncipiō ipse mundus deōrum hominumque causā factus est, et quae in eō sunt, ea parāta sunt ad frūctum hominum. (Cicero.)

8. Quam cōpiōsē ā Xenophonte agrīcultūra laudātur in eō librō quī "Oeconomicus" īnscrībitur. (Cicero.—**cōpiōsē**, adv., *fully, copiously;* cf. **cōpia.**—**Xenophōn, -phontis,** m., name of a famous Greek historian.—**agrīcultūra, -ae,** f.; "agriculture."—**īnscrībō, -ere,** *to entitle;* "inscribe," "inscription.")

9. Vulgus vult dēcipī. (*Phaedrus.—**vult:** *wants;* "volition," "volunteer."—**dēcipiō, -ere,** *to deceive;* "deceiver," "deception.")

10. Ubi scientia ac sapientia inveniuntur? (Job.)

11. Vēritās nimis saepe labōrat; exstinguitur numquam. (Livy.—**exstinguō, -ere;** "extinguish," "extinct.")

## Vergil's Messianic Eclogue

Venit iam magna aetās nova; dē caelō mittitur puer, quī vītam deōrum habēbit deōsque vidēbit et ipse vidēbitur ab illīs. Hic puer reget mundum cui virtūtēs patris pācem dedērunt. Pauca mala, autem, remanēbunt, quae hominēs iubēbunt labōrāre atque bellum asperum gerere. Erunt etiam altera bella atque iterum ad Trōiam magnus mittētur Achillēs. Tum, puer, ubi iam longa aetās tē virum fēcerit, erunt nūllī labōrēs, nūlla bella; nautae ex nāvibus discēdent, agricolae quoque iam agrōs relinquent, terra ipsa omnibus hominibus omnia parābit. Currite, aetātēs; incipe, parve puer, scīre mātrem, et erit satis spīritūs mihi tua dīcere facta.

Vergil *Ecl.* 4: Vergil (Publius Vergilius Maro, 70–19 B.C.) is best known for his epic poem, the *Aeneid,* but other, earlier works included his quasi-didactic poem, the *Georgics,* a

*Marble portrait bust of Vergil*
*Imperial Roman*
*Museo Gregoriano Profano*
*Vatican Museums, Vatican State*

glorification of farming, and the *Eclogues,* a collection of 10 short pastoral poems extolling the shepherd's life. The fourth *Eclogue,* composed ca. 40 B.C., stood apart from the others, as it heralded the world's rebirth and a new Golden Age of peace and freedom from toil that would be ushered in with the birth of a divine boy child; readers ancient and modern have speculated over the child's identity, some supposing reference to the families of Octavian and/or Mark Antony, but the poem's hopeful, messianic message, taken by many early Christians as a prophecy of the birth of Christ, may have been intended more generally to reflect contemporary longing for an end to Roman civil war.—**altera bella:** here = *the same wars over again.*—**scīre mātrem:** i.e., to be born, but what is the lit. meaning?—**spīritūs:** here, as often, in the sense of *inspiration.*)

*QVAESTIŌNĒS:* Which aspects of this prophecy strike you as especially mystical? Where does the narrator address the boy, and what do you sense is the intended effect?

## SCRĪPTA IN PARIETIBVS

Crēscēns Crȳsērōtī salūtem! Quid agit tibi dexter ocellus?

*CIL* 4.8347: Graffito found near the entrance to the kitchen of the House of Menander (Reg. I, Ins. 10). We have seen the cognomen **Crēscēns** before; this is likely a different fellow (the name was common), and the editors of *CIL* speculate that he might have been the family's doorman (**ōstiārius**), as his name was also found in the house's entranceway (**vestibulum**). The exact context is unclear, but Crescens seems to be asking Cryseros about a friend or lover; the second sentence is in dactylic meter (˘˘/¯˘˘/¯˘˘/¯¯) and may be a quotation from an amatory poem.—**Crȳsērōs** (or **Chrȳsērōs**), **Crȳsērōtis,** m., *C(h)ryseros,* a Greek cognomen, probably a slave's or a freedman's, meaning "golden."—**salūtem:** cf. the graffiti in Capita VIII, X, and XIX.—**quid:** with agis/agit commonly = *how?,* as in the conversational **quid agis,** *how are you (doing)?*—**tibi:** here, as often, the dat. has possessive force.—**ocellus:** diminutive of **oculus,** lit. *little eye,* but in an amatory context = *darling,* comparable to the Eng. expression "apple of my eye"; with **ocellus** in this sense **dexter** essentially = **cārus** (the expression survives in modern It. **occhio destro**). A less artful interpretation would be simply opthalmological!—in that case, what would Crescens quite literally be asking?

*The House of Menander, view through the atrium into the peristyle garden, Pompeii, Italy*

## ETYMOLOGIA

Romance derivatives from some of the words in the **Vocābula:**

| Latin | It. | Sp. | Port. | Fr. |
|-------|-----|-----|-------|-----|
| causa | cosa | cosa | causa | chose |
| fīnis | fine | fin | fim | fin |
| gēns | gente | gente | gente | gent; gens (pl.) |
| continēre | continere | contener | conter | contenir |
| mundus | mondo | mundo | mundo | monde |

Cf. Rom. **cauza, fine, ginte** (obsolete), **conţine;** Old Occ. **cauza, fin, gen, contener, mon.**

## LATĪNA EST GAVDIVM—ET V̄TILIS!

**Salvēte, discipulae atque discipulī! Quid novī?** Well, how about some more well-known Latin phrases and mottoes related to the **verba nova** in this chapter's **Vocābula?** First, for you *Godfather* fans, there's Italian **cosa nostra,** from **causa nostra. Vestra causa tōta nostra est** is the motto of the American Classical League, a national organization for teachers of Latin, Greek, and classical humanities. The University of Georgia's motto is **et docēre et rērum exquīrere causās,** *both to teach and to seek out the causes of things* (i.e., to conduct research—for **rērum,** see the next chapter). Here are some others: **finis corōnat opus,** *the end crowns the work;* **gēns togāta,** *the toga-clad nation* (a phrase Vergil applies to Rome, where the toga was a man's formal attire); **tangere ulcus,** *to touch a sore spot* (lit., *ulcer*); **sīc trānsit glōria mundī,** *so passes the glory of the world* (Thomas à Kempis, on the transitory nature of worldly things—some comedian who shall forever remain nameless has offered an alternate translation, to wit, "Gloria always gets sick on the subway at the beginning of the week"!!!); and the abbreviation **sc.,** meaning *supply* (something omitted from a text but readily understood), comes from **scīlicet,** short for **scīre licet,** literally *it is permitted for you to understand.* **Hic est fīnis: valēte!**

# CAPVT XXII 𝄢𝄢𝄢

# Fifth Declension; Ablative of Place Where and Summary of Ablative Uses

## GRAMMATICA

### THE FIFTH DECLENSION

This chapter introduces the fifth and last of the Latin noun declensions. The characteristic vowel is -ē-, and -ēī or -eī is the genitive and dative ending (the gen./dat. -e- is long when preceded by a vowel, short when preceded by a consonant; cf. **diēī** and **reī** below). Nouns of this declension are all feminine, except **diēs** (*day*) and its compound **merīdiēs** (*midday*), which are masculine. To decline, follow the usual pattern of base plus endings:

|      | **rēs, reī, f.** *thing* | **diēs, diēī, m.** *day* | **Case Endings** |
|------|------|------|------|
| *Nom.* | rēs    | díēs   | -ēs       |
| *Gen.* | réī    | diéī   | -eī, -ēī  |
| *Dat.* | réī    | diéī   | -eī, -ēī  |
| *Acc.* | rem    | díem   | -em       |
| *Abl.* | rē     | díē    | -ē        |
|        |        |        |           |
| *Nom.* | rēs    | díēs   | -ēs       |
| *Gen.* | rérum  | diérum | -ērum     |
| *Dat.* | rébus  | diébus | -ēbus     |
| *Acc.* | rēs    | díēs   | -ēs       |
| *Abl.* | rébus  | diébus | -ēbus     |

Note that the genitive and dative singular are identical (true of the first declension also), as are the nominative singular and the nominative and accusative plural (the vocatives, too, of course), and the dative and ablative plural (true of all declensions); word order, context, and such cues as subject-verb and noun-adjective agreement will help you distinguish among those ambiguous forms in a sentence.

## ABLATIVE OF PLACE WHERE AND SUMMARY OF ABLATIVE USES

You have thus far been introduced to these ablative uses: object of a preposition (Capvt II), means, manner, accompaniment (Capvt XIV), ablative with cardinal numerals and ablative of time (Capvt XV), agent (Capvt XVIII), place from which and separation (Capvt XX). You have also encountered the **ABLATIVE OF PLACE WHERE** construction, a noun in the ablative, typically with **in**, *in/on*, or **sub**, *under*, describing where someone or something is located or an action is occurring:

**In magnā casā vīvunt.** *They live in a large house.*

**Nāvis sub aquā fuit.** *The ship was under water.*

Some ablative case uses require a preposition in Latin, others do not, and in some instances the practice was variable. Notably, in the ablative of manner construction, when the noun is modified by an adjective, **cum** is frequently omitted; if **cum** is used, it is usually preceded by the adjective (e.g., **id magnā cūrā fēcit** and **id magnā cum cūrā fēcit**, both meaning *he did it with great care*). The following summary reviews each of the ablative uses studied thus far:

### Ablatives with a Preposition

The ablative is used as a simple object of a preposition and specifically with:

1. cum to indicate **ACCOMPANIMENT**:
   **Cum amīcō id scrīpsit.** *He wrote it with his friend.*
2. cum to indicate **MANNER** (whether or not an adjective is used):
   **Cum cūrā id scrīpsit.** *He wrote it with care.*
   **Magnā cum cūrā id scrīpsit.** *He wrote it with great care.*
3. in and sub to indicate **PLACE WHERE**:
   **In urbe id scrīpsit.** *He wrote it in the city.*
4. ab, dē, ex to indicate **PLACE FROM WHICH**:
   **Ex urbe id mīsit.** *He sent it from the city.*
5. ab, dē, ex to indicate **SEPARATION**:
   **Ab urbe eōs prohibuit.** *He kept them from the city.*
6. ab to indicate **PERSONAL AGENT**:
   **Ab amīcō id scrīptum est.** *It was written by his friend.*
7. ex or dē following certain **CARDINAL NUMERALS** to indicate a group of which some part is specified:
   **Trēs ex nāvibus discessērunt.** *Three of the ships departed.*

### Ablatives without a Preposition

The ablative is used without a preposition to indicate:

1. MEANS/INSTRUMENT:
   **Suā manū id scrīpsit.** *He wrote it with his own hand.*
2. MANNER, when an adjective is used:
   **Magnā cūrā id scrīpsit.** *He wrote it with great care.*
3. TIME WHEN/WITHIN WHICH:
   **Eō tempore** *or* **ūnā hōrā id scrīpsit.** *He wrote it at that time* or *in one hour.*
4. SEPARATION, especially with ideas of freeing, lacking, depriving:
   **Metū eōs līberāvit.** *He freed them from fear.*

## VOCĀBVLA

Remember that for some fifth declension nouns the genitive/dative singular ending is -ēī and for others -eī; learn these new nouns, like all vocabulary, by looking carefully at their spelling, macrons included, listening to them at www.wheelockslatin.com (or on the CDs), and then repeating each aloud correctly. Do not confuse **diēs** and **deus**—though the two, *day/daylight* and *god,* derive from the same Indo-European root, which is also reflected in the names of the sky god **Zeus** and **Iuppiter** (a form later reconfigured as **diēs pater**). And don't forget to nasalize the -gn- in **ignis**, i.e., **prōnūntiā** as if it were spelled *ingnis. Practice with some of the new words by declining **fidēs incerta** and **fēlīx spēs**; compare your work with the paradigms in the **Summārium Fōrmārum**, p. 495–96.

**diēs, diḗī**, m., *day* (diary, dial, dismal, diurnal, journal, adjourn, journey, meridian, sojourn)

**ferrum, férrī**, n., *iron; sword* (ferric, ferrite, ferro-; Fe, the chemical symbol for iron)

**fidēs, fídeī**, f., *faith, trust, trustworthiness, fidelity; promise, guarantee, protection* (confide, diffident, infidel, perfidy, fealty)

**ígnis, ígnis**, m., *fire* (igneous, ignite, ignition)

**módus, módī**, m., *measure, bound, limit; manner, method, mode, way* (model, moderate, modern, modest, modicum, modify, mood)

**rēs, réī**, f., *thing, matter, property, business, affair* (real, realistic, realize, reality, real estate, rebus)

**rēs pública, réī públicae** (often seen as a single word, **rēspública**), f., *state, commonwealth, republic* (Republican)

**spēs, spéī**, f., *hope* (despair, desperate; cf. **spērāre**, *to hope*)

**aéquus, aéqua, aéquum**, *level, even; calm; equal, just; favorable* (equable, equanimity, equation, equator, equilateral, equilibrium, equinox, equity, equivalent, equivocal, inequity, iniquity, adequate, coequal)

**félīx**, gen. **fēlícis**, *lucky, fortunate, happy* (felicitation, felicitous, infelicitous, felicity, infelicity, Felix)

**incértus, incérta, incértum** (**in-certus**), *uncertain, unsure, doubtful* (incertitude)

**Latínus, Latína, Latínum,** *Latin* (Latinate, Latinist, Latinity, Latinize, Latino)

**médius, média, médium,** *middle;* used partitively, *middle of:* **media urbs,** *middle of the city* (Mediterranean, medium, median, mediate, mean, medieval, meridian, immediate, intermediary)

**quóndam,** adv., *formerly, once* (quondam)

**últrā,** adv. and prep. + acc., *on the other side of, beyond* (ultra, ultrasonic, ultrasound, ultraviolet, outrage, outrageous)

**prótinus,** adv., *immediately*

**cérnō, cérnere, crḗvī, crḗtum,** *to distinguish, discern, perceive* (discernible, discreet, discrete, discretion)

**ērípiō, erípere, ērípuī, ēréptum** (**ē+rapiō**), *to snatch away, take away; rescue* (for the **VOWEL WEAKENING** seen in the compound form **-ripiō** from **rapiō,** see "Two Rules of Phonetic Change," p. 484–85)

**ínquit,** defective verb, *he says* or *said,* placed after one or more words of a direct quotation but usually translated before the quote

**tóllō, tóllere, sústulī, sublātum,** *to raise, lift up; take away, remove, destroy* (extol, sublate, sublation; cf. **tolerō;** the principal parts are another example of **SUPPLETION:** see above, p. 91)

# LĒCTIŌ ET TRĀNSLĀTIŌ

Before translating, practice with the new grammar by scanning the readings and identifying the number, gender, case, and use of all fifth declension nouns, as well as the use of each ablative noun and pronoun.

## EXERCITĀTIŌNĒS

1. Vīcīnī nostrī sē in genua prōtinus iēcērunt et omnēs deōs in mundō laudāvērunt.
2. Gentēs Graeciae ingentibus montibus et parvīs fīnibus continēbantur.
3. Quis iussit illam rem pūblicam servitūte asperā līberārī?
4. "Iste," inquit, "sceleribus suīs brevī tempore tollētur."
5. Contrā aliās manūs malōrum cīvium eaedem rēs iterum parābuntur; senātus rem pūblicam dēfendet et istī ex fīnibus nostrīs citō discēdent.
6. Senectūs senēs ā mediīs rēbus saepe prohibet.
7. At rēs gravēs neque vī neque spē geruntur sed cōnsiliō.

8. Sī versūs hōrum duōrum poētārum neglegētis, magnā parte Rōmānārum litterārum carēbitis.

9. Eōdem tempore nostrae spēs salūtis commūnis vestrā fidē altae sunt, spīritūs
sublātī sunt, et timōrēs relictī sunt.

10. Nova genera scelerum in hāc urbe inveniuntur quod multī etiam nunc bonīs
mōribus et sēnsū commūnī carent ac nātūram sinistram habent.

11. Vulgus multa ex fenestrīs casārum ēiciēbat.

12. Great fidelity can now be found in this commonwealth.

13. His new hopes had been destroyed by the common fear (what would the correct forms be of both **metus** and **timor**?) of uncertain things.

14. On that day the courage and the faith of the brave Roman men and women
were seen by all.

15. The tyrant knew the enemy's plans, and with great hope he ordered those ships
to be destroyed.

16. He could not defend himself with his left hand or his right.

## SENTENTIAE ANTĪQVAE

1. Dum vīta est, spēs est. (Cicero.)

2. Aequum animum in rēbus difficilibus servā. (Horace.)

3. Ubi tyrannus est, ibi plānē est nūlla rēs pūblica. (*Cicero.—**plānē**, adv., *clearly;*
"plain," "explain.")

4. Fuērunt quondam in hāc rē pūblicā virī magnae virtūtis et antīquae fideī.
(Cicero.)

5. Hanc rem pūblicam salvam esse volumus. (*Cicero.—**volumus:** *we wish;* "volition," "malevolent.")

6. Spēs coniūrātōrum mollibus sententiīs multōrum cīvium alitur. (Cicero.—
**mollis, -e,** *soft, mild;* "mollify," "emollient.")

7. Rēs pūblica cōnsiliīs meīs eō diē ex igne atque ferrō ērepta est. (Cicero.)

8. Quod bellum ōdērunt, prō pāce cum fidē labōrābant. (Livy.)

9. Dīc mihi bonā fidē: tū eam pecūniam ex eius manū dextrā nōn ēripuistī?
(Plautus.)

10. Amīcus certus in rē incertā cernitur. (Ennius.)

11. Homērus audītōrem in mediās rēs rapit. (Horace.)

12. Fēlīx est quī potest causās rērum intellegere; et fortūnātus ille quī deōs antīquōs
dīligit. (Vergil.)

13. Stōicus noster, "Vitium," inquit, "nōn est in rēbus sed in animō ipsō." (Seneca.—
**Stōicus, -ī,** m., *a Stoic philosopher;* "stoic," "stoical.")

14. Et mihi rēs subiungam, nōn mē rēbus. (Horace.—**subiungō, -ere,** *to subject;*
"subjoin," "subjunctive.")

15. Est modus in rēbus; sunt certī fīnēs ultrā quōs virtūs invenīrī nōn potest.
(Horace.)

16. Hoc, Fortūna, tibi vidētur aequum? (*Martial.)

### A Visit from the Young Interns

> Languēbam: sed tū comitātus prōtinus ad mē
>   vēnistī centum, Symmache, discipulīs.
> Centum mē tetigēre manūs aquilōne gelātae:
>   nōn habuī febrem, Symmache, nunc habeō!

Martial *Epig.* 5.9: Anyone who has ever visited the health center of a university that has a medical school can fully sympathize with this complaint!—if you weren't sick when you GOT there, you might well be when you LEFT! Meter: elegiac couplet.—**languēre**, *to be weak, sick;* "languid," "languish."—**comitātus, -a, -um,** *accompanied (by);* "concomitance," "concomitant."—**Symmachus:** the name of this doctor, a med school "professor," is Greek, which adds an ethnic slur to the piece, not uncommon in Roman satire.— **centum . . . discipulīs:** abl. of agent with **comitātus;** the prep. was often omitted in poetry.—**tetigēre:** = **tetigērunt;** for this alternate ending, see Capvt XII.—**aquilō, -lōnis,** m., *the north wind.*—**gelātus, -a, -um,** *chilled,* here modifying **centum . . . manūs;** "gel," "gelatin."—**febris, febris,** f., *fever;* "febrile," "feverish."

*QVAESTIŌNĒS:* The disjointedness of the phrases **comitātus . . . centum . . . discipulīs** and **centum . . . manūs . . . gelātae** is deliberate; which pairs of words are emphasized and what is the purpose? Comment on the arrangement of the two adverb-verb phrases in the last verse and how the word order helps underscore the punch-line (Martial's epigrams, as you have seen, nearly always have a zinger in the closing verse!).

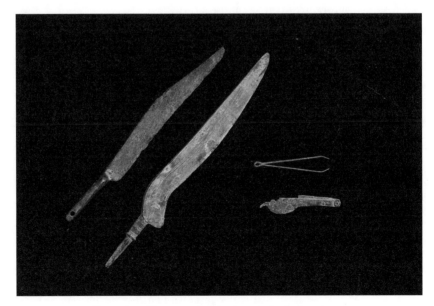

*Bronze and iron surgical instruments. 3rd cent. A.D.*
*Private collection*

**On Ambition and Literature, Both Latin and Greek**

Poētae per litterās hominibus magnam perpetuamque fāmam dare possunt; multī virī, igitur, litterās dē suīs rēbus scrībī cupiunt. Trahimur omnēs studiō laudis et multī glōriā dūcuntur, quae aut in litterīs Graecīs aut Latīnīs invenīrī potest. Quī, autem, videt multum frūctum glōriae in versibus Latīnīs sed nōn in Graecīs, nimium errat, quod litterae Graecae leguntur in omnibus ferē gentibus, sed Latīnae in fīnibus suīs continentur.

Cicero *Arch.* 11.26, 10.23: Review the passage about Alexander the Great from this same speech which you read in Capvt XIII, and recall that the speech was in defense of the Greek poet Archias.—**ferē**, adv., *almost.*

*QVAESTIŌNĒS:* What is Cicero's initial observation regarding the benefits that literature can provide an ambitious man?—how does this compare with the anecdote he relates about Alexander elsewhere in the speech? Explain the author's point in comparing the advantages of Greek and Latin literature: is his position surprising to you?—why or why not? Identify the device of word order seen in both **trahimur omnēs . . . multī . . . dūcuntur** and **leguntur in omnibus ferē gentibus . . . in fīnibus suīs continentur;** what is the writer's purpose in employing this arrangement?

## SCRĪPTA IN PARIETIBVS

C. Iūlium Polybium
duumvir(um) [Cuculla] rog(at).

*CIL* 4.7841: An example of the hundreds of electoral notices (**programmata**, sg. **programma**) found on the walls of buildings lining the streets of Pompeii; most of these programmata were dipinti (sg. dipinto) rather than graffiti, i.e., they were painted not incised. In this notice (the top two lines in the photo), which appears immediately above another one painted on the street-front wall of a wool processing shop on the Via dell'Abbondanza (Reg. IX, Ins. 7), the name of the woman lobbying for Polybius' election, Cuculla, has been painted over, perhaps because the candidate, or another of his supporters, did not welcome the endorsement.—**duumvir, -ī, m.,**

*Storefront with programma for*
*Gaius Julius Polybius (CIL 4.7841)*
*Via dell'Abbondanza. 1st cent.* A.D. *Pompeii, Italy*

frequently, as here, abbreviated **IIVIR,** *duumvir;* the duumvirs were Pompeii's two chief magistrates, sharing authority, like the two consuls in Rome.—**rogō** (1), *to ask, ask for;* in electoral campaigning, *ask to elect, ask approval for;* "interrogate," "prerogative."

## ETYMOLOGIA

Connected with **diēs** is the adj. **diurnus,** *daily,* whence come the words for "day" in It. and Fr.: It. **giorno,** Fr. **jour, journée;** cf. Sp. **día;** Port. **dia, diurno;** Old Occ. **jorn;** Rom. **ziua.** In late Lat. there was a form **diurnālis,** from which derive It. **giornale,** Fr. **journal,** Port. **diurnal,** Old Occ. **jornal,** Eng. "journal"; cf. Sp. **diario,** Rom. **zilnic.** Eng. "dismal" stems ultimately from **diēs malus.** The stem of **fidēs** can be found in the following words even though it may not be immediately obvious: affidavit, defy, affiance, fiancé. Eng. "faith" is from early Old Fr. **feit, feid,** from Lat. **fidem.** Other words connected with **modus** are: modulate, accommodate, commodious, discommode, incommode, à la mode, modus operandi.

## LATĪNA EST GAVDIVM—ET VTILIS!

**Salvēte!** Now that you've encountered **merīdiēs,** you understand **a.m.** and **p.m.,** from **ante** and **post merīdiem.** Your physician might prescribe a medication **diēbus alternīs,** *every other day,* or **diēbus tertiīs,** *every third day,* or even **b.i.d.** or **t.i.d., bis in diē** or **ter in diē** (if you've thought about those last two twice or thrice and still can't figure them out, look back at Capvt XV!). Other items you might encounter one of these days: **diem ex diē,** *day by day;* **diēs fēlīx,** *a lucky day;* the legal terms **diēs jūridicus** and **nōn jūridicus,** days when court is and is not in session; and the **Diēs Īrae,** a medieval hymn about the Day of Judgment, part of the requiem mass. And surely you follow Horace's advice every day and **carpe diem** (an agricultural metaphor, since **carpō, carpere** really means *to harvest* or *pluck* from the vine or stalk—so your days, once seized, should be a bountiful cornucopia). Now you know, too, what is meant by the phrase **amīcus certus in rē incertā;** a **bonā fidē** agreement is made *with good faith* (recognize the ablative usage?); and if your "friend indeed" is your trusty dog, you should consider dubbing him "Fido." **Carpite omnēs diēs, discipulī discipulaeque, et valēte!**

# CAPVT XXIII ⌐⌐⌐

# Participles

## GRAMMATICA

### PARTICIPLES (*participium, -ī, n.*)

Like English, Latin has a set of verbal adjectives, i.e., adjectives formed from a verb stem, called **PARTICIPLES**. Regular transitive verbs in Latin have four participles, two of them active voice (the present and future), and two passive (future and perfect). The present active and future passive participles are formed on a verb's present stem, while the perfect passive and future active are formed on the **PARTICIPIAL STEM**, found by dropping the endings from the perfect passive participle, which is itself usually a verb's fourth principal part: i.e., **laudāt-** from **laudātus, -a, -um**:

|        | Active                                   | Passive                          |
| ------ | ---------------------------------------- | -------------------------------- |
| *Pres.* | present stem + **-ns** (gen. **-ntis**)  | ——————                           |
| *Perf.* | ——————                                   | partic. stem + **-us, -a, -um**  |
| *Fut.*  | participial stem + **-ūrus, -ūra, -ūrum** | pres. stem + **-ndus, -nda, -ndum** |

This pattern can perhaps best be recalled by memorizing the participles of **agō**, in which the difference between the present stem and the participial stem is sufficient to eliminate any confusion. It is also helpful to note that the base of the prese*nt* participle is marked by **-nt-**, the fut*ur*e active by **-ūr-**, and the future passive, often called the "geru*nd*ive," by **-nd-**.

**agō, agere, ēgi, āctum,** *to drive, do, lead, act*

|        | Active                                          | Passive                                                        |
| ------ | ----------------------------------------------- | -------------------------------------------------------------- |
| *Pres.* | ágēns, agéntis, *doing*                         | ——————                                                         |
| *Perf.* | ——————                                          | ắctus, -a, -um, *done, having been done*                       |
| *Fut.*  | āctū́rus, -a, -um, *about to do,* *going to do* | agéndus, -a, -um, *(about) to be done,* *deserving to be done* |

English derivatives neatly illustrate the sense of three of these participles: "agent" (from **agēns**), *a person doing something;* "act" (**āctus, -a, -um**), *something done;*

"agenda" (**agendus, -a, -um**), *something to be done.* The participles of three of the model verbs follow:

|  | Act. | Pass. | Act. | Pass. | Act. | Pass. |
|---|---|---|---|---|---|---|
| *Pres.* | laúdāns | —— | aúdiēns | —— | cápiēns | —— |
| *Perf.* | —— | laudấtus | —— | audítus | —— | cáptus |
| *Fut.* | laudātū́rus | laudándus | audītū́rus | audiéndus | captū́rus | capiéndus |

Note that fourth conjugation and third conjugation -**iō** verbs have -**ie**- in both the present active participle (-**iēns, -ientis**) and the future passive (-**iendus, -a, -um**). Notice too that while Latin has present active, perfect passive, and future active and passive participles, the equivalents of *praising, having been praised, about to praise,* and (*about*) *to be praised,* it lacks both a present passive participle (*being praised*) and a perfect active participle (*having praised*).

## Declension of Participles

Three of the four participles are declined on the pattern of **magnus, -a, -um.** Only the present participle has third declension forms, following the model of **potēns** (Capvt XVI), except that the ablative singular sometimes ends in -**e**, sometimes (especially when used strictly as an attributive adjective) in -**ī**; the vowel before -**ns** in the nominative singular is always long, but before -**nt**- (according to the rule learned earlier) it is always short.

|  | M. & F. | N. |
|---|---|---|
| *Nom.* | ágēns | ágēns |
| *Gen.* | agéntis | agéntis |
| *Dat.* | agéntī | agéntī |
| *Acc.* | agéntem | ágēns |
| *Abl.* | agéntī, agénte | agéntī, agénte |
| *Nom.* | agéntēs | agéntia |
| *Gen.* | agéntium | agéntium |
| *Dat.* | agéntibus | agéntibus |
| *Acc.* | agéntēs | agéntia |
| *Abl.* | agéntibus | agéntibus |

## Participles as Verbal Adjectives

The etymology of the term "participle," from **pars** + **capere**, *to take part/share in,* reflects the fact that participles share in the characteristics of both adjectives and verbs. As *adjectives,* participles agree in gender, number, and case with the words they modify. Sometimes also, like adjectives, they modify no expressed noun but function as nouns themselves: **amāns,** *a lover;* **sapiēns,** *a wise man, philosopher;*

**venientēs,** *those coming.* As *verbs,* participles have tense and voice; they may take direct objects or other constructions used with the particular verb; and they may be modified by an adverb or an adverbial phrase:

> **Patrem in casā videntēs, puella et puer ad eum cucurrērunt.** *Seeing their father in the house, the boy and girl ran up to him.*

In Latin as in English, the time of the action indicated by a participle is not absolute but relative to that of the main verb. For example, the action of a present participle is contemporaneous with the action of the verb of its clause, no matter whether that verb is a present, past, or future tense; in the above sentence it was at some past time that the children first saw and then ran toward their father (seeing him, i.e., when they saw him, they ran up to him). The time indicated by perfect and future participles is also relative, as can be seen in the following table:

1. Present participle = action *contemporaneous* with that of the verb (same time)
2. Perfect participle = action *prior* to that of the verb (time before)
3. Future participle = action *subsequent* to that of the verb (time after)

> **Graecī nautae, videntēs Polyphēmum, timent, timuērunt, timēbunt.**
> *The Greek sailors, seeing Polyphemus, are afraid, were afraid, will be afraid.*

> **Graecī nautae, vīsī ā Polyphēmō, timent, timuērunt, timēbunt.**
> *The Greek sailors, (having been) seen by P., are afraid, were afraid, will be afraid.*

> **Graecī nautae, vīsūrī Polyphēmum, timent, timuērunt, timēbunt.**
> *The Greek sailors, about to see Polyphemus, are afraid, were afraid, will be afraid.*

### Translating Participial Phrases as Clauses

Participial phrases are used more frequently in Latin than in English, which prefers clauses with regular verbs. In translating Latin into idiomatic English, therefore, it is often preferable to transform a participial phrase into a subordinate clause. In doing so you need to consider (1) the relationship between the action in the phrase and the action in the clause to which it is attached, so you can choose an appropriate subordinating conjunction (usually "when," "since," or "although"), and (2) the relativity of tenses, so you can transform the participle into the appropriate verb tense.

Thus the example given earlier, **patrem in casā videntēs, puella et puer ad eum cucurrērunt,** can be translated *seeing their father in the house, the girl and boy ran up to him* or, more idiomatically, *when they saw their father in the house, the girl and boy ran up to him.* Likewise **Graecī nautae, vīsī ā Polyphēmō, timuērunt** is better translated *when/since they had been seen* [time prior to main verb] *by*

*Polyphemus, the Greek sailors were afraid* than the more literal *having been seen by Polyphemus, the Greek sailors were afraid*. Consider these further examples:

> **Māter, fīlium amāns, auxilium dat.** *Since she loves her son* [lit., *loving her son*], *the mother gives him assistance.*
>
> **Pater, fīliam vīsūrus, casam parābat.** *Since he was about to see his daughter, the father was preparing the house.*
>
> **Puella, in casam veniēns, gaudēbat.** *When she came into the house* [lit., *coming into the house*], *the girl was happy.*

# VOCĀBVLA

This chapter's new word-list contains, in **opprimō** from **premō**, another example of the sort of VOWEL WEAKENING common in compounds (see note on **ēripiō** in Capvt XXIII, and App., p. 484–85). The list also introduces another SEMI-DEPONENT verb, **gaudeō**, which, like **audeō, audēre, ausus sum** (Capvt VII), has only three principal parts and perfect system forms that are passive but have active meanings (you'll learn more about such verbs in Capvt XXXIV). For practice with the new grammar, write out the four participles for one or two of the verbs in this list, such as **ēducō** and **vertō**, include the English translations, then compare with the above paradigms.

**arx, árcis,** f., *citadel, stronghold* (possibly related to **arca**, *box, chest,* from which we get "ark")

**dux, dúcis,** m., *leader, guide; commander, general* (duke, ducal, ducat, duchess, duchy, doge; cf. **dūcō**)

**équus, équī,** m., *horse* (equestrian, equine; cf. **equa**, *mare*)

**hásta, hástae,** f., *spear* (hastate)

**ínsula, ínsulae,** f., *island* (insular, insulate, isolate, peninsula)

**lítus, lítoris,** n., *shore, coast* (littoral, sublittoral)

**míles, mílitis,** m., *soldier* (military, militaristic, militate, militant, militia)

**ōrátor, ōrātóris,** m., *orator, speaker* (oratory, oratorio; cf. **ōs** and **ōrāre**, *to speak, plead*)

**sacérdōs, sacerdótis,** m., *priest* (sacerdotal; cf. **sacer**, *sacred*)

**áliquis, áliquid** (gen. alicuíus, dat. álicui, etc.; cf. decl. of **quis, quid;** nom. and acc. n. pl., **áliqua**), indef. pron., *someone, somebody, something*

**quísquis, quídquid** (**quis** repeated; cases other than nom. rare), indef. pron., *whoever, whatever*

**magnánimus, magnánima, magnánimum,** *great-hearted, brave, magnanimous* (magnanimity)

**úmquam,** adv., in questions or negative clauses, *ever, at any time* (**numquam** = **ne** + **umquam**)

**édūcō, ēdūcāre, ēdūcāvī, ēdūcātum,** *to bring up, educate* (education, educator, educable; do not confuse with **ēdūcere,** *to lead out*)

**gaúdeō, gaudēre, gāvīsus sum,** *to be glad, rejoice* (gaudy, gaudeamus; cf. **gaudium,** *joy,* as in **Latīna est gaudium!**)

**osténdō, osténdere, osténdī, osténtum,** *to exhibit, show, display* (ostentation, ostentatious, ostensible; cf. **tendere,** *to stretch, extend*)

**pétō, pétere, petīvī, petītum,** *to seek, aim at, beg, beseech* (appetite, compete, competent, impetuous, petition, petulant, repeat; cf. **perpetuus**)

**prémō, prémere, préssī, préssum,** *to press; press hard, pursue;* spelled **-primō, -primere** in compounds such as **opprimō** below (compress, depress, express, impress, imprint, print, repress, reprimand, suppress)

**ópprimō, opprímere, oppréssī, oppréssum,** *to suppress, overwhelm, overpower, check* (oppress, oppression, oppressive, oppressor)

**vértō, vértere, vértī, vérsum,** *to turn; change;* so **āvertō,** *turn away, avert,* **revertō,** *turn back,* etc. (adverse, advertise, averse, convert, controversy, diverse, divorce, invert, pervert, revert, subvert; cf. **versus**)

# LĒCTIŌ ET TRĀNSLĀTIŌ

After learning the new paradigms and vocabulary and testing your mastery with the Self-Tutorial Exercises, scan through the following readings for all the participles, identifying the tense, voice, number, gender, case, and the noun modified. Listen to the CDs, if you have them, and read aloud before translating.

## EXERCITĀTIŌNĒS

1. Aliquid numquam ante audītum in hāc rē pūblicā cernō.
2. Illum ōrātōrem in mediō senātū iterum petentem fīnem bellōrum ac scelerum nōn adiūvistis.
3. Certī frūctūs pācis ab territō vulgō atque senātū cupiēbantur.
4. Quī vir magnanimus aliās gentēs gravī metū servitūtis līberābit?
5. Nēmō fidem neglegēns timōre umquam carēbit.
6. Illa fēmina fortūnāta haec cōnsilia contrā eōs malōs quondam aluit et salūtis commūnis causā semper labōrābat.
7. Illam gentem Latīnam oppressūrī et dīvitiās raptūrī, omnēs virōs magnae probitātis premere ac dēlēre prōtinus coepērunt.
8. Tollēturne fāma huius medicī istīs versibus novīs?
9. At vīta illīus modī aequī aliquid iūcundī atque fēlīcis continet.
10. Quō diē ex igne et ferrō atque morte certā ēreptus es?
11. We gave many things to nations lacking hope.

12. Those ten men, (when) called, will come again into this territory with great eagerness.
13. Through the window they saw the second old man running out of his neighbor's house and away from the city.
14. He himself was overpowered by uncertain fear because he desired neither truth nor liberty.

## SENTENTIAE ANTĪQVAE

1. Vīvēs meīs praesidiīs oppressus. (Cicero.—**praesidium, -iī**, n., *guard;* "preside," "president.")
2. Illī autem, tendentēs manūs dextrās, salūtem petēbant. (Livy.—**tendō, -ere,** *to stretch, extend;* "tend," "distend," "tension.")
3. Tantalus sitiēns flūmina ab ōre fugientia tangere dēsīderābat. (Horace.—**Tantalus:** From Tantalus' name and the myth of his offense against the gods comes the word "tantalizing."—**sitīre,** *to be thirsty.*)
4. Signa rērum futūrārum mundō ā dīs ostenduntur. (Cicero.)
5. Graecia capta asperum victōrem cēpit. (Horace.—**victor, -tōris,** m., here = Rome.)
6. Atticus Cicerōnī ex patriā fugientī multam pecūniam dedit. (Nepos.—**Atticus,** a friend of Cicero.)
7. Sī mihi eum ēducandum committēs, studia eius fōrmāre ab īnfantiā incipiam. (Quintilian.—**fōrmāre;** "reform," "transform."—**īnfantia, -ae,** f.; "infantile," "infanticide.")
8. Saepe stilum verte, bonum libellum scrīptūrus. (Horace.—**stilum vertere,** *to invert the stilus* = to use the eraser; "stiletto," "style.")
9. Cūra ōrātōris dictūrī eōs audītūrōs dēlectat. (Quintilian.)
10. Mortī Sōcratis semper illacrimō, legēns Platōnem. (Cicero.—**Sōcratēs, -cratis,** m.—**illacrīmāre,** *to weep over;* "lachrymose," "lacrimal."—**Platō, -tōnis,** m.)
11. Memoria vītae bene āctae multōrumque bene factōrum iūcunda est. (Cicero.)
12. Quī timēns vīvet, līber nōn erit umquam. (Horace.—**quī,** as often, = **is quī.**)
13. Nōn is est miser quī iussus aliquid facit, sed is quī invītus facit. (Seneca.—**invītus, -a, -um,** *unwilling;* the adj. here has adverbial force, as it commonly does in Latin.)
14. Verbum semel ēmissum volat irrevocābile. (Horace.—**semel,** adv., *once.*—**ē-mittere;** "emissary," "emission."—**volāre,** *to fly;* "volatile," "volley."—**irrevocābilis, -e.**)

### Laocoon Speaks Out Against the Trojan Horse

Oppressī bellō longō et ā deīs āversī, ducēs Graecōrum, iam post decem annōs, magnum equum ligneum arte Minervae faciunt. Uterum multīs mīlitibus complent, equum in lītore relinquunt, et ultrā īnsulam proximam nāvigant. Trōiānī nūllās cōpiās aut nāvēs vident; omnis Trōia gaudet; panduntur portae. Dē equō, autem, Trōiānī sunt incertī. Aliī eum in urbem dūcī cupiunt; aliī eum Graecās īnsidiās appellant. Prīmus ibi ante omnēs, dē arce currēns, Lāocoōn, sacerdōs Trōiānus, haec verba dīcit: "Ō miserī cīvēs, nōn estis sānī! Quid cōgitātis? Nōnne intellegitis Graecōs et scītis īnsidiās eōrum? Aut inveniētis in istō equō multōs mīlitēs ācrēs, aut equus est machina bellī, facta contrā nōs, ventūra in urbem, vīsūra casās nostrās et populum. Aut aliquid latet. Equō nē crēdite, Trōiānī: quidquid id est, timeō Danaōs et dōna ferentēs!" Dīxit, et potentem hastam magnīs vīribus manūs sinistrae in uterum equī iēcit; stetit illa, tremēns.

Vergil *Aen.* 2.13–52: You read a passage adapted from Vergil's Fourth *Eclogue* in Capvt XXI; here, and in Capvt XXV, you will read dramatic selections, also in prose adaptation, from Book Two of his 12-volume epic poem, the *Aeneid* (Capvt XL presents a long, un-adapted passage in its original dactylic hexameter form). In this scene the Trojan prince Aeneas tells Carthage's queen Dido of the Greeks' ruse of "the Trojan horse," a huge wooden horse they have left outside Troy's walls after seemingly abandoning their 10-year effort to sack the city and sailing home; as seen in the accompanying photograph of an

*Trojan Horse with Greek soldiers. Relief from neck of an earthenware amphora*
*Ca. 640 B.C. Mykonos, Greece. Archaeological Museum, Mykonos, Greece*

archaic Greek amphora (storage jug), a squadron of Greek soldiers have been concealed within the horse's belly (which Vergil purposefully calls its "womb," **uterus**). The Trojans are divided over what to do with the horse, when in the midst of their debate the priest Laocoön rushes forth to deliver a stern warning that the device must be a Greek trick, designed for their destruction —**ligneus, -a, -um,** *wooden, of wood;* "ligneous," "lignite."—**Minerva, -ae,** f., *Minerva,* goddess of war and protectress of the Greeks.—**uterus, -ī,** m.; "uterine," "in utero."—**complēre,** *to fill up, make pregnant;* "complete," "complement."—**proximus, -a, -um,** *nearby;* "proximity," "approximate."—**Trōiānus, -a, -um,** *Trojan.*—**pandō, -ere,** *to open;* "expand," "expansive."—**Lāocoön, -ontis,** m.—**nōnne:** the word introduces a question anticipating an affirmative answer, *Don't you . . . ?*—**machina, -ae,** f.; = Eng.; "machination," "machinery"; Aeneas, later in his narration of Troy's doomsday (lines 237–38), calls the horse a **fātālis machina . . . fēta armīs,** *a deadly machine, pregnant with weapons.*—**vīsūra:** here *to spy on.*—**latēre,** *to be hidden, be concealed;* "latency," "latent."—**equō:** dat. "object" of **crēdite** (a construction we have seen before, formally introduced in Capvt XXXV).—**nē:** = **nōn.**—**Danaōs:** = **Graecōs.**—**et** (with **ferentēs**): = **etiam.**—**ferentēs:** pres. partic. of the irreg. verb **ferō,** *to carry, bear;* "fertile," "conference." **Quidquid . . . ferentēs** is a hexameter line drawn verbatim from the poem (Book Two, verse 49); read it aloud and listen to the dactylic rhythms.—**tremō, -ere,** *to tremble, shake, vibrate;* "tremor," "tremulous."

*QVAESTIŌNĒS:* Vergil's poetry is highly cinematographic; what details even in this prose adaptation are especially visual, and how might you, as a motion picture director, advise your camera-man to film them? What striking poetic sound-effects do you hear in the verse **quidquid id est, timeō Danaōs et dōna ferentēs?**

## SCRĪPTA IN PARIETIBVS

Paule ed Petre, petite prō Victōre.

This graffito is one of hundreds found in a 3rd-cent. A.D. Christian burial area in the catacombs beneath the basilica of St. Sebastian on Rome's Via Appia. Family members inscribed prayers for the deceased such as this one to the apostles Paul and Peter.—**ed:** = **et.**—**Paule . . . Petre:** what case are these nouns, and what would their nom. forms be?—**petite:** here = *pray.*

## LATĪNA EST GAVDIVM—ET VTILIS!

**Salvēte!** This chapter's **Vocābula** list suggests a couple of literary titles from ancient Rome: among Cicero's dozens of books was a rhetorical treatise titled **Dē Ōrātōre,** and one of Plautus' most popular plays was the **Mīles Glōriōsus,** usually translated *The Brag-gart Soldier.* Then there's the medieval student song with the famous line (quite apt for college Latin students) **gaudeāmus, igitur, iuvenēs dum sumus,** *so let us rejoice, while we are young!* From **vertere** is **verte** for *turn the page* and **versō** for the left-hand page in a book (i.e., the side you see when you have just *turned* the page); printers call the right-hand page the **rectō.** And from the reading passage: the expression "a Trojan horse" is used of any person, group, or device that tries to subvert a government or any orga-nization from within. Also from Vergil's story of Aeneas' sojourn in Carthage is the fa-mous quotation regarding the country's queen, Dido: **dux fēmina factī,** *a woman (was) leader of the action!* **Gaudēte atque valēte!**

*Athena (Minerva) constructing the Trojan horse*
*Red-figure Greek kylix (drinking cup)*
*The "Sabouroff Painter," 470–460 B.C.*
*Museo Archeologico, Florence, Italy*

# Ablative Absolute; Passive Periphrastic; Dative of Agent

## GRAMMATICA

### ABLATIVE ABSOLUTE

The **ABLATIVE ABSOLUTE** is a type of participial phrase generally consisting of a noun (or pronoun) and a modifying participle in the ablative case; loosely connected to the rest of the sentence (hence the term, from **absolūtum,** *loosened from, separated*) and usually set off by commas, the phrase describes some general circumstance under which the action of the sentence occurs:

> **Rōmā vīsā, virī gaudēbant.** *Rome having been seen, the men were rejoicing.*

As typified by this example, the ablative absolute always is self-contained, i.e., the participle and the noun it modifies are in the same phrase and the noun of the ablative absolute phrase is not referred to at all in the attached clause. In other types of participial phrases (such as those seen in Capvt XXIII), the participles modify some noun or pronoun in the attached clause; compare the following example, which has an ordinary participial phrase, with the previous example:

> **Rōmam videntēs, virī gaudēbant.** *Seeing Rome, the men were rejoicing.*

In this instance the participle modifies the subject of the main clause, and so an ablative absolute is not used.

Like other participial phrases, the ablative absolute can be translated literally, as in **Rōmā vīsā,** *(with) Rome having been seen.* For more natural idiom, however, it is generally better to transform the phrase to a clause, converting the participle to a verb in the appropriate tense, treating the ablative noun as its subject, and supplying the most logical conjunction (usually "when," "since," or "although"), as explained in the last chapter; thus, a more idiomatic translation of **Rōmā vīsā, virī gaudēbant** would be *since Rome was (had been) seen, the men were rejoicing.* Compare the following additional examples:

*Hīs rēbus audītīs,* coepit timēre.
> *These things having been heard, he began to be afraid.*

Or in more natural English:
> When (*since, after,* etc., depending on the context) *these things had been heard, he began . . .*
> When (*since, after,* etc.) *he had heard these things, he began . . .*

*Eō imperium tenente,* ēventum timeō.
> *With him holding the power,*
> *Since he holds the power,*
> *When he holds the power,*    ⎫
> *If he holds the power,*    ⎬ *I fear the outcome.*
> *Although he holds the power,*    ⎭

In the ablative absolute, the ablative noun/pronoun regularly comes first, the participle last; when the phrase contains additional words, like the participle's direct object (**imperium**) in the preceding example, they are usually enclosed within the noun/participle frame.

As seen in the following examples, even two nouns, or a noun and an adjective, can function as an ablative absolute, with the present participle of **sum** (lacking in classical Latin) to be understood:

*Caesare duce,* nihil timēbimus.
> *Caesar (being) the commander,*
> *Under Caesar's command,*    ⎫
> *With Caesar in command,*    ⎬ *we shall fear nothing.*
> *Since (when, if,* etc.) *Caesar is the commander,*    ⎭

*Caesare incertō,* bellum timēbāmus.
> *Since Caesar was uncertain (with Caesar uncertain), we were afraid of war.*

## THE PASSIVE PERIPHRASTIC

The **PASSIVE PERIPHRASTIC** is a passive verb form consisting of the **GERUNDIVE**, a common term for the future passive participle, along with a form of **sum** (the term "periphrastic" means literally a "roundabout way of speaking" and refers simply to such combinatory forms). The gerundive, as essentially a predicate adjective, agrees with the subject of **sum** in gender, number, and case, e.g., **haec fēmina laudanda est,** *this woman is to be praised.*

The gerundive often conveys an idea of necessary, obligatory, or appropriate action, rather than simple futurity, and this is the case in the passive periphrastic construction. Hence **id faciendum est** means not simply *this is (about) to be done,* but rather *this has to be (must/should be) done;* cf. **id faciendum erat,** *this had to be done;* **id faciendum erit,** *this will have to be done.* Just as Latin uses the auxiliary **sum** in its various tenses in this construction, English commonly uses the expressions "has to be," "had to be," and "will have to be," as seen in these examples; "should," "ought," and "must" are also commonly employed (cf. **dēbeō**, which, as you have already learned, is also used to indicate obligatory action).

## DATIVE OF AGENT

Instead of the ablative of agent, the **DATIVE OF AGENT** is used with the passive periphrastic. A literal translation of the passive periphrastic + dative of agent often sounds awkward, and so it is generally best to transform such clauses into active constructions:

> **Hic liber mihi cum cūrā legendus erit.** *This book will have to be read by me with care* or (better) *I will have to (ought to, must, should) read this book with care.*

> **Illa fēmina omnibus laudanda est.** *That woman should be praised by all* or *everyone should praise that woman.*

> **Pāx ducibus nostrīs petenda erat.** *Peace had to be sought by our leaders* or *our leaders had to seek peace.*

# VOCĀBVLA

Among this chapter's new words are several **COMPOUND VERBS**, including **accipiō**, **excipiō**, and **recipiō**, all formed from **capiō** and exhibiting the sort of vowel weakening you have seen before. **Re-** is an **INSEPARABLE PREFIX**, meaning that it does not stand alone as a separate word, as do **ad, ex**, etc.; other examples are: **sē-**, *apart, aside,* as in **sēdūcō**, *to lead aside,* the negative **in-** (**im-, il-, ir-**), *not, un-,* as in **incertus**, *uncertain;* and **dis-** (**dif-, dī-**), *apart, away, not,* as in **discēdō**, *to go away,* and **difficilis**, *not easy.* **Difficilis** (**dis- + facilis**) and **accipiō** (**ad + capiō**), by the way, illustrate another common type of phonetic change known as **ASSIMILATION**, where the final consonant of a prefix was, for ease of pronunciation, altered to match the initial consonant of the base word (App., p. 485).

**Carthágō, Cartháginis,** f., *Carthage* (city in North Africa)
**fábula, fábulae,** f., *story, tale; play* (fable, fabulous, confabulate; cf. **fāma**)
**imperátor, imperātóris,** m., *general, commander-in-chief, emperor* (cf. **imperium**, below, and **imperāre**, *to command*)
**impérium, impériī,** n., *power to command, supreme power, authority, command, control* (imperial, imperialism, imperious, empire)
**perfúgium, perfúgiī,** n., *refuge, shelter* (cf. **fugiō**)
**sérvus, sérvī,** m., and **sérva, sérvae,** f., *slave* (serf, servant, servile, service)

sōlācium, sōlāciī, n., *comfort, relief* (solace, consolation, inconsolable)

vúlnus, vúlneris, n., *wound* (vulnerable, vulnerability, invulnerable)

re- or (before words beginning with d) red-, inseparable prefix (see above), *again, back* (recede, receive, remit, repeat, repel, revert)

ut, conj. + indic., *as, just as, when*

póstea, adv., *afterwards* (cf. post)

accípiō, accípere, accḗpī, accéptum, *to take* (to one's self), *receive, accept* (acceptable, acceptance)

excípiō, excípere, excḗpī, excéptum, *to take out, except; take, receive, capture* (exception, exceptionable)

recípiō, recípere, recḗpī, recéptum, *to take back, regain; admit, receive* (recipe, R$_x$, receipt, recipient, receptacle, reception)

péllō, péllere, pépulī, púlsum, *to strike, push; drive out, banish* (compel, compulsion, dispel, impel, propel, repel, pulsate, pulse)

expéllō, expéllere, éxpulī, expúlsum, *to drive out, expel, banish* (expulsion)

nā́rrō, nārrā́re, nārrā́vī, nārrā́tum, *to tell, report, narrate* (narration, narrative, narrator)

quaérō, quaérere, quaesī́vī, quaesī́tum, *to seek, look for, strive for; ask, inquire, inquire into* (acquire, conquer, exquisite, inquire, inquest, inquisition, perquisite, query, quest, question, request, require)

rī́deō, rīdḗre, rī́sī, rī́sum, *to laugh, laugh at* (deride, derisive, ridicule, ridiculous, risible; cf. rīdiculus, *laughable*)

# LĒCTIŌ ET TRĀNSLĀTIŌ

Identify each ablative absolute, passive periphrastic, and dative of agent in the following readings; the challenge in translating these constructions is to strive for natural, idiomatic English, which generally requires transforming ablative absolute phrases into "when/since/although" clauses, and passive periphrastic/dative of agent clauses into active voice constructions.

## EXERCITĀTIŌNĒS

1. Igne vīsō, omnēs virī et uxōrēs territae sunt et ultrā urbem ad lītus īnsulae nāvigāvērunt, ubi perfugium inventum est.
2. Populō metū oppressō, iste imperātor nōbīs ex urbe pellendus est.
3. Ōrātor, signō ā sacerdōte datō, eō diē revēnit et nunc tōtus populus Latīnus gaudet.
4. Gēns Rōmāna versūs illīus scrīptōris magnā laude quondam recēpit.
5. Laudēs atque dōna huius modī ab ōrātōribus dēsīderābantur.

6. Imperiō acceptō, dux aequus magnanimusque fidem suam reī pūblicae ostendit.
7. Aliquis eōs quīnque equōs ex igne ēripī posteā iusserat.
8. Cernisne umquam omnia quae tibi scienda sunt?
9. Ille, ab arce urbis reventūrus, ab istīs hominibus premī coepit.
10. Cupiō tangere manum illīus mīlitis quī metū caruit atque gravia scelera contrā rem pūblicam oppressit.
11. Iste dux prōtinus expulsus est, ut imperium excipiēbat.
12. Illae servae, autem, perfugium sōlāciumque ab amīcīs quaerēbant.
13. Cornū audītō, ille mīles, incertus cōnsiliī, cōpiās ad mediam īnsulam vertit.
14. When the common danger had been averted, two of our sons and all our daughters came back from Asia.
15. Our hopes must not be destroyed (use **tollō**) by those three evil men.
16. Since the people of all nations are seeking peace, all leaders must conquer the passion for (= of) power. (Use an ablative absolute and a passive periphrastic.)
17. The leader, having been driven out by both the free men and the slaves, could not regain his command.

## SENTENTIAE ANTĪQVAE

1. Carthāgō dēlenda est. (Cato.)
2. Asiā victā, dux Rōmānus fēlīx multōs servōs in Italiam mīsit. (Pliny the Elder.)
3. Omnibus ferrō mīlitis perterritīs, quisque sē servāre cupiēbat. (Caesar.)
4. Quidquid dīcendum est, līberē dīcam. (Cicero.—**līberē**, adv. of **līber**.)
5. Haec omnia vulnera bellī tibi nunc sānanda sunt. (Cicero.—**sānāre**, *to heal;* "sanatorium," "sane.")
6. Nec tumultum nec hastam mīlitis nec mortem violentam timēbō, Augustō terrās tenente. (Horace.—**tumultus -ūs,** m., *disturbance, civil war;* "tumult," "tumultuous."—**violentus, -a, -um;** related to **vīs;** "violence," "nonviolent."—**Augustus, -ī,** m.)
7. Tarquiniō expulsō, nōmen rēgis audīre nōn poterat populus Rōmānus. (Cicero.)
8. Ad ūtilitātem vītae omnia cōnsilia factaque nōbīs regenda sunt. (Tacitus.—**ūtilitās, -tātis,** f., *benefit, advantage;* "utility," "utilitarian.")
9. Caesarī omnia ūnō tempore erant agenda. (*Caesar.)

### Dē Cupiditāte

Homō stultus, "Ō cīvēs, cīvēs," inquit, "pecūnia ante omnia quaerenda est; virtūs et probitās post pecūniam."

Pecūniae autem cupiditās fugienda est. Fugienda etiam est cupiditās glōriae; ēripit enim lībertātem. Neque imperia semper petenda sunt neque semper accipienda; etiam dēpōnenda nōn numquam.

Horace *Epist.* 1.1.53 and Cicero *Off.* 1.20.68: Horace turned to writing verse *Epistles* (**Epistulae**), as well as lyric poetry, after publishing his two volumes of satire (see above, Capvt III); like his satires, many of the **Epistulae** dealt with moralizing themes, including the poem from which the above excerpt, along with a brief passage from Cicero's "On Moral Responsibilities" (introduced in Capvt VIII above), has been adapted.—**imperia:** i.e., military commands, which some contemporaries, Caesar notably, had not resigned, when, in Cicero's opinion, they should have.—**dēpōnō, -ere,** *to put down, resign;* "depose," "deposition.")—**nōn numquam:** the double-negative was a common Lat. idiom for *sometimes.*

Caelō receptus propter virtūtem, Herculēs multōs deōs salūtāvit; sed Plūtō veniente, quī Fortūnae est fīlius, āvertit oculōs. Tum, causā quaesītā, "Ōdī," inquit, "illum, quod malīs amīcus est atque omnia corrumpit lucrī causā."

Phaedrus *Fab.* 4.12: Gaius Julius Phaedrus (ca. 15 B.C.–A.D. 50), a freedman of the emperor Augustus, composed five volumes of moralizing fables in verse, many of them animal fables based on the early, semi-legendary Greek fabulist Aesop. Here he imagines the entry of Hercules into heaven, following his deification, and his encounter with Plutus.—**Herculēs, -lis,** m.; "Herculean."—**salūtāre,** *to greet;* "salutation," "salutatorian."—**Plūtus, -ī,** m., god of wealth; "plutocracy" (originally from Gk., not Lat.)—**Fortūnae:** here personified, as in Martial's "When I Have Enough" (Capvt IX).—**corrumpō, -ere,** *to corrupt;* "corruptible," "corruption."—**lucrum, -ī,** n., *gain, profit;* "lucrative," "lucre."

*QVAESTIŌNĒS:* What, according to these three writers, are some of the negative moral consequences of the lust for wealth, and in Cicero's opinion, ambition for glory as well? What do you suppose Cicero meant by **ēripit . . . lībertātem?** Plutus was generally said to be the son of the grain goddess Demeter and the mortal or demi-god Iasion; in what sense, though, does Phaedrus logically call him **fīlius Fortūnae?**

*Heracles (Hercules) fighting the Nemean lion, one of his 12 labors Attic black-figure kalpis, early 5th cent. B.C. Kunsthistorisches Museum, Vienna, Austria*

## The Satirist's Modus Operandi

Rīdēns saturās meās percurram, et cūr nōn? Quid vetat mē rīdentem dīcere vērum, ut puerīs ēducandīs saepe dant crūstula magistrī? Quaerō rēs gravēs iūcundō lūdō et, nōminibus fictīs, dē multīs culpīs vitiīsque nārrō. Sed quid rīdēs? Mūtātō nōmine, dē tē fābula nārrātur!

Horace *Sat.* 1.1.23–27, 69–70: In this prose adaptation from his programmatic first satire (from which "The Grass Is Always Greener," in Capvt III, was also adapted), Horace tells us something about his modus operandi as a satirist.—**per + currō.**—**vetāre,** *to forbid;* "veto."—**puerīs . . . magistrī:** the order of the nouns is varied for effect: ind. obj., dir. obj., subject.—**crūstulum, -ī,** n., *cookie, pastry;* "crouton," "crust."—**fingō, -ere, fīnxī, fictum,** *to form, invent, make up;* "feign," "fiction."

*QVAESTIŌNĒS:* Naming names was a signal characteristic of Roman satire from the genre's beginnings; the second cent. B.C. satirist, Lucilius, recognized as the genre's founder, was known for his naming attacks on persons alive, powerful, and proud: what is Horace's accommodation to that tradition?—but then what is the point of his closing admonition to his audience? How, specifically, does he engage his audience in his closing remarks? What differences of purpose and tone do you detect between Horace's programmatic remarks here and those of Juvenal adapted from his program poem in Capvt XVI above?—support your answer with references to specific words and phrases in both texts. Which satirist seems more interested in education, which in condemnation?

## SCRĪPTA IN PARIETIBVS

Vīnum acceptum ab dominō VII Īdūs Aprīlēs

*CIL* 4.10565: Dated notice of receipt of goods, possibly recorded by a slave; from a wall in the courtyard of the House of Neptune and Amphitrite, one of the best preserved houses in Herculaneum, named for its splendid mosaic of the sea god and his Nereid wife (Ins. 5).—**vīnum, -ī,** n., *wine;* "vineyard," "viniferous."—**dominus, -ī,** m., *master, lord;* "dominate," "dominion."—**Īdūs, Īduum,** f. pl., *the Ides:* the 12 months in the imperial Roman calendar each had three named days, the "Kalends," which was the 1st day of the month, the "Nones," which was the 7th in March, May, July, and October, and the 5th in the others, and the "Ides," which was the 15th in March, May, July, and October, the

13th in others. The remaining days were identified as so many days before the Ides, the Nones, or the Kalends; the Roman counting system was "inclusive," meaning that **VII Īdūs Aprīlēs,** *seven (days) before the Ides of April* = April 7 (7–8–9–10–11–12–13 = seven days, counting inclusively).—**Aprīlis, -lis,** m., *(month of) April.*

*Courtyard of the House of Neptune and Amphitrite, Herculaneum, Italy*

## LATĪNA EST GAVDIVM—ET VTILIS!

**Salvēte, amīcae amīcīque! Quid agitis hodiē?** Bet you didn't know that R$_x$ and "recipe" came from the same word (see **recipiō** in the Vocab.), but now, thanks to Latin, you do! There are countless derivatives from the **capiō** family, as you have seen already; and from **excipere** there are some "exceptionally" familiar phrases: **exceptiō probat regulam,** *the exception proves the rule,* and **exceptīs excipiendīs,** *with all the necessary exceptions* (lit., *with things excepted that should be excepted:* recognize the gerundive?). And, by analogy with this last, what are the idiomatic and the literal meanings of the very common phrase **mūtātīs mūtandīs?** (If you can't figure that out, it's in your Webster's, along with hundreds of other Latin phrases, mottoes, words, and abbreviations in current English usage!) Some other gerundives that pop up in English: **agenda** (*things to be done*), **corrigenda** (*things to be corrected,* i.e., an **errāta** list), and even the passive periphrastics **dē gustibus nōn disputandum est,** sometimes shortened simply to **dē gustibus** (*you shouldn't argue about taste*), and **quod erat dēmōnstrandum** (which we've seen before), abbreviated **Q.E.D.** at the end of a mathematical proof. **Servus,** also in the new **Vocābula** gives us one of the Pope's titles, **servus servōrum deī** (another is **pontifex,** the name of an ancient Roman priestly office, which may originally have meant *bridge-builder*—because priests bridge the gap between men and gods?); and **quaere** is used in English as a note to request further information. **Nunc est satis: valēte atque semper rīdēte!**

# CAPVT XXV 🢒🢒🢒

# Infinitives; Indirect Statement

## GRAMMATICA

### INFINITIVES

Having surveyed the forms and uses of the verbal adjectives known as participles in the last two chapters, we turn now to the INFINITIVE, a common verbal noun used in a variety of ways. Most transitive verbs have six infinitives, present, future, and perfect, active and passive; intransitive verbs usually lack the passive. You are already familiar with the present active and passive infinitives, whose forms vary with each of the four conjugations; the perfect and future infinitives are all formed according to the following patterns, regardless of conjugation:

|  | Active | Passive |
|---|---|---|
| *Pres.* | -āre, -ēre, -ere, -īre | -ārī, -ērī, -ī, -īrī |
| *Perf.* | perfect stem + -isse | perfect passive participle + esse |
| *Fut.* | future active participle + esse | [supine in -um + īrī] |

The future passive infinitive is bracketed because it is rare and does not occur in this book; the SUPINE in -um (formally introduced in Capvt XXXVIII) has the same spelling as the perfect passive participle in the nominative neuter singular. Following are the infinitives of **agō, agere, ēgī, āctum,** *to drive, do, lead, act:*

|  | Active | Passive |
|---|---|---|
| *Pres.* | ágere, *to lead* | ágī, *to be led* |
| *Perf.* | ēgísse, *to have led* | ắctus, -a, -um ésse, *to have been led* |
| *Fut.* | āctū́rus, -a, -um ésse, *to be about to lead, to be going to lead* | ắctum ī́rī, *to be about to be led, to be going to be led* |

The participles employed as components of three of these infinitives are essentially predicate adjectives (e.g., cf. "to be active" and "to be" + "about to act") and in usage agree with the subject of **esse.** The literal translations given above are conventional; in actual use (especially in indirect statement, as explained below) the perfect and particularly the future infinitives are rarely translated literally.

The infinitives of the other model verbs are as follows:

## Active

| | | | | |
|---|---|---|---|---|
| *Pres.* | laudā́re | monḗre | audī́re | cápere |
| *Perf.* | laudāvísse | monuísse | audīvísse | cēpísse |
| *Fut.* | laudātū́rus, -a, -um, ésse | monitū́rus, -a, -um, ésse | audītū́rus, -a, -um, ésse | captū́rus, -a, -um, ésse |

## Passive

| | | | | |
|---|---|---|---|---|
| *Pres.* | laudā́rī | monḗrī | audī́rī | cápī |
| *Perf.* | laudā́tus, -a, -um, ésse | mónitus, -a, -um, ésse | audī́tus, -a, -um, ésse | cáptus, -a, -um, ésse |
| *Fut.* | laudā́tum ī́rī | mónitum ī́rī | audī́tum ī́rī | cáptum ī́rī |

## Usage

As a verbal noun, an infinitive can function in a variety of ways. We have seen its use as a subject (**errāre est humānum,** *to err is human*) and as a complement with such verbs as **possum** and **dēbeō** (**discēdere nunc possunt,** *they can leave now*—Capvt VI); and the infinitive, with its own accusative subject, can also serve as a direct object (**iussit eōs venīre,** *he ordered them to come:* see S.S., p. 494). One of the commonest uses of the infinitive, however, is in a construction known as indirect statement.

## INDIRECT STATEMENT

An **INDIRECT STATEMENT** simply reports indirectly (i.e., not in direct quotation) what someone has said, thought, felt, etc. The following is a *direct* statement, made by a teacher:

Julia is a good student.

Here the teacher's comment is *directly* reported or quoted:

"Julia is a good student," says the teacher.
The teacher said, "Julia is a good student."

Latin also uses direct quotations with certain verbs of speaking, etc., including **inquit:**

"Iūlia," magister inquit, "est discipula bona."

Often, however, both Latin and English will report someone's remarks (or thoughts or feelings) indirectly. In English we regularly put such indirect statements into a subordinate clause introduced by "that":

The teacher says that Julia is a good student.
The teacher said that Julia was a good student.

Latin, on the other hand, uses no introductory word for "that" and employs an infinitive phrase with an accusative subject, instead of a clause:

**Magister dīcit Iūliam esse discipulam bonam.**
**Magister dīxit Iūliam esse discipulam bonam.**

This construction is regularly employed in Latin after verbs of speech, mental activity, or sense perception–sometimes called "head verbs"—i.e., verbs of saying, thinking, knowing, perceiving, feeling, seeing, hearing, etc. (a list of such Latin verbs follows the **Vocābula**). English uses a similar objective case + infinitive construction after a few verbs of this type (e.g., "the teacher considers *her to be* a good student"), but in classical Latin this pattern is always followed and the accusative subject is always expressed, even when it is the same as the subject of the verb of *saying*, etc., in which case the subject is ordinarily a reflexive pronoun:

**Iūlia putat sē esse bonam discipulam.** *Julia thinks that she (herself) is a good student.*

Recognizing indirect statements is easy: look for the main verb of speech, mental activity, or sense perception with an accusative + infinitive phrase following. The greater challenge is in translation, since you must usually supply "that" and convert the infinitive phrase into a regular clause, as in the above examples, where literal translations (e.g., *the teacher says Julia to be a good student* or *Julia thinks herself to be a good student*) would not produce idiomatic English. After supplying *that* and translating the accusative subject as if it were a nominative, you must then transform the infinitive into a regular finite verb *in the correct tense,* noting that tenses of the infinitive, like those of the participle, are relative not absolute.

## Translating Infinitive Tenses in Indirect Statement

Study carefully the tenses in the following groups of sentences:

1. Dīcunt—*They say*
   A. **eum** *iuvāre* **eam.**              *that he **is helping** her.*
   B. **eum** *iūvisse* **eam.**             *that he **helped/was helping** her.*
   C. **eum** *iūtūrum esse* **eam.**        *that he **will help** her.*

2. Dīxērunt—*They said*
   A. eum *iuvāre* eam.    *that he was helping her.*
   B. eum *iūvisse* eam.    *that he had helped her.*
   C. eum *iūtūrum esse* eam.    *that he would help her.*

3. Dīcent—*They will say*
   A. eum *iuvāre* eam.    *that he is helping her.*
   B. eum *iūvisse* eam.    *that he helped/was helping her.*
   C. eum *iūtūrum esse* eam.    *that he will help her.*

Note that after any tense of the main verb (*dīcunt, dīxērunt, dīcent*) the present, the perfect, or the future tense of the infinitive may be used. As with participles, the tenses of the infinitive are relative, not absolute:

the *present infinitive* indicates the *same time as* that of the main verb.
the *perfect infinitive* indicates *time before* that of the main verb.
the *future infinitive* indicates *time after* that of the main verb.

In the following examples note the translation of tenses, the use of reflexives, the agreement of participial endings with the accusative subjects, and the use in one instance of the passive periphrastic infinitive (gerundive + **esse,** to indicate obligatory action):

Gāius dīcit *sē* iūvisse eam.
  *Gaius says that he* (Gaius) **helped** *her.*

Gāius dīxit *eum* iūvisse eam.
  *Gaius said that he* (e.g., Marcus) **had helped** *her.*

Gāius dīcit litterās ā sē scrīptās esse.
  *Gaius says that the letter was written by him* (Gaius).

Gāius dīcit litterās tibi scrībendās esse.
  *Gaius says that the letter ought to be written by you* (or, better: *that you ought to write the letter*).

Discipulī putant *sē* linguam Latīnam amātūrōs esse.
  *The (male) students think that they will love the Latin language.*

Magistra scīvit discipulās Latīnam amātūrās esse.
  *The teacher knew that the (female) students would love Latin.*

# VOCĀBVLA

**Āit** and **āiunt** are two of the most frequently used forms of **āiō,** a common defective verb; the first person form **āiō** itself occasionally had the sense, *I say so, I agree,* *yes.* For practice with the new grammar, write out the six infinitives for some of the verbs in this list, e.g. **crēdō** and **nūntiō**, include the English translations, then compare with the above paradigms.

**língua, línguae,** f., *tongue; language* (linguist, linguistics, bilingual, lingo, linguine: see **Latīna Est Gaudium,** Capvt XIV)

**férōx,** gen. **ferócis,** *fierce, savage* (ferocious, ferocity; cf. **ferus, -ī,** *beast*)

**fidélis, fidéle,** *faithful, loyal* (fidelity, infidelity, infidel; cf. **fidēs**)

**géminus, gémina, géminum,** *twin* (geminate, gemination, Gemini)

**sápiēns,** gen. **sapiéntis,** as adj., *wise, judicious;* as noun, *a wise man/woman, philosopher* (homo sapiens, sapience, insipience, insipid, verbum sapienti, savant, sage; cf. **sapientia**)

**últimus, última, últimum,** *farthest, extreme; last, final* (ultimate, ultimatum, penultimate, antepenult)

**déhinc,** adv., *then, next*

**hīc,** adv., *here* (cf. **hic, haec, hoc**)

**áit, áiunt,** defective verb, *he says, they say, assert,* commonly used in connection with proverbs and anecdotes (adage)

**crédō, crédere, crédidī, créditum** + acc. or (Capvt XXXV) dat., *to believe, trust* (credence, credentials, credible, incredible, credulity, credulous, creed, credo, credit, creditable, accreditation)

**iáceō, iacére, iácuī,** *to lie; lie prostrate; lie dead* (adjacent, adjacency, interjacent, subjacent, gist, joist; do not confuse with **iaciō, iacere**)

**négō, negáre, negávī, negátum,** *to deny, say that . . . not* (negate, negative, abnegate, renegade, renege, denial)

**nésciō, nescíre, nescívī, nescítum,** *to not know, be ignorant* (nice, nescient; cf. **sciō**)

**núntiō, nūntiáre, nūntiávī nūntiátum,** *to announce, report, relate* (denounce, enunciate, pronounce, renounce, nuncio; cf. **prōnūntiō, nūntius,** *messenger*)

**patefáciō, patefácere, patefécī, patefáctum,** *to make open, open; disclose, expose* (patent; cf. **patēre,** *to be open*)

**pútō, putáre, putávī, putátum,** *to reckon, suppose, judge, think, imagine* (compute, count, account, dispute, impute, putative, repute)

**spérō, spēráre, spērávī, spērátum,** *to hope for, hope (that)* (despair, desperado, desperate, desperation, prosper; cf. **spēs**)

**suscípiō, suscípere, suscépī, suscéptum** (**sub + capiō**), *to undertake* (susceptible)

## Verbs That May Introduce Indirect Statement

1. *saying:* dícō, négō, áit, núntiō, prōnúntiō, nárrō, scríbō, dóceō, osténdō, dēmónstrō, móneō, pétō
2. *knowing:* scíō, nésciō, intéllegō, memóriā téneō, díscō
3. *thinking:* cérnō, cógitō, crédō, hábeō, pútō, spérō
4. *perceiving and feeling:* aúdiō, vídeō, séntiō, gaúdeō

Others to be introduced later are **respondeō,** *answer;* **cognōscō,** *learn, know;* **arbitror,** *think;* **opīnor,** *think, suppose;* **prōmittō,** *promise;* **dēcernō,** *decide;* **doleō,** *grieve.*

# LĒCTIŌ ET TRĀNSLĀTIŌ

As with ablative absolutes, the challenge in translating indirect statements is that, for natural English idiom, a transformation is usually required, turning the accusative + infinitive phrase into a subordinate clause introduced by "that" and with a normal subject + finite verb in the correct tense; review the examples on p. 203–04 above and practice some translations in the Self-Tutorial Exercises. To test your ability to recognize indirect statements, scan through all the following readings looking for a "head verb" followed by accusative + infinitive.

## EXERCITĀTIŌNĒS

1. "Quisque," inquit, "semper putat suās rēs esse magnās."
2. Posteā audīvimus servōs dōnōrum causā labōrāvisse, ut mīlitēs fidēlēs heri nārrāverant.
3. Vīcīnī nostrī vim ignis magnā virtūte dehinc āvertērunt, quod laudem atque dōna cupīvērunt.
4. Hoc signum perīculī tōtam gentem nostram tanget, nisi hostem ex urbe excipere ac ab Italiā pellere poterimus.
5. Duce ferōcī Carthāginis expulsō, spēs fidēsque virōrum magnanimōrum rem pūblicam continēbunt.
6. Cūr iūcundus Horātius culpās hūmānās in saturīs semper ostendēbat atque rīdēbat?
7. Crēdimus fidem antīquam omnibus gentibus iterum alendam esse.
8. Dux, officium susceptūrus, imperium accēpit et imperātor factus est.
9. Rēs pūblica, ut āit, libellīs huius modī tollī potest.
10. Aliquī negant hostēs victōs servitūte umquam opprimendōs esse.
11. Crēdunt magistram sapientem vēritātem patefactūram esse.
12. Quisquis vēritātem quaeret atque recipiet bene ēducābitur.
13. We thought that your sisters were writing the letter.
14. They will show that the letter was written by the brave slavegirl.
15. The orator said that the book had never been written.
16. We hope that the judge's wife will write those two letters tomorrow.

## SENTENTIAE ANTĪQVAE

1. Id factum esse tum nōn negāvit. (Terence.)
2. Hīs rēbus prōnūntiātīs, igitur, eum esse hostem scīvistī. (Cicero.)

3. Eum ab hostibus exspectārī nunc sentīs. (Cicero.)
4. Vīdī eōs in urbe remānsisse et nōbīscum esse. (Cicero.)
5. Itaque aeternum bellum cum malīs cīvibus ā mē susceptum esse cernō. (Cicero.)
6. Idem crēdō tibi faciendum esse. (Cicero.)
7. Tē enim esse fidēlem mihi sciēbam. (Terence.)
8. Hostibus sē in cīvitātem vertentibus, senātus Cincinnātō nūntiāvit eum factum esse dictātōrem. (Cicero.—**Cincinnātus, -ī,** m.; "Cincinnati."—**dictātor, -tōris,** m.; "dictation," "dictatorship.")
9. Dīcō tē, Pyrrhe, Rōmānōs posse vincere. (Ennius.—**Pyrrhus, -ī,** m.; the Greek general Pyrrhus defeated the Romans twice, but the victories cost him so many men he lost the war; hence the term "Pyrrhic victory.")
10. Dīc, hospes, Spartae tē nōs hīc iacentēs vīdisse, patriae fidēlēs. (Cicero; epigram on the Spartans who died at Thermopylae.—**hospes, -pitis,** m., *stranger;* "hospice," "hospital."—**Sparta, -ae,** f., *the city of Sparta.*)
11. Sōcratēs putābat sē esse cīvem tōtīus mundī. (Cicero.)
12. Illī magistrī negant quemquam virum esse bonum nisi sapientem. (Cicero.—**quisquam, quidquam,** *anyone, anything; any.*)
13. Negāvī, autem, mortem timendam esse. (Cicero.)
14. Crēdō deōs immortālēs sparsisse spīritūs in corpora hūmāna. (Cicero.—**spargō, -ere, sparsī, sparsum,** *to scatter, sow;* "sparse," "intersperse.")
15. Adulēscēns spērat sē diū vīctūrum esse; senex potest dīcere sē diū vīxisse. (Cicero.—Do not confuse **vīctūrum,** from **vīvō,** with **victūrum,** from **vincō**).
16. Āiunt enim multum legendum esse, nōn multa. (\*Pliny.)

### The Death of Laocoön . . . and Troy

Hīc alius magnus timor (Ō fābula misera!) animōs caecōs nostrōs terret. Lāocoön, sacerdōs Neptūnī fortūnā factus, ācrem taurum ad āram in lītore mactābat. Tum geminī serpentēs potentēs, mare prementēs, ab īnsulā ad lītora currunt. Iamque agrōs tenēbant et, oculīs igne ardentibus, ōra linguīs sībilīs lambēbant.

Nōs omnēs fugimus; illī viā certā Lāocoonta filiōsque eius petunt. Prīmum parva corpora duōrum puerōrum capiunt et lacerant necantque dēvorantque. Tum patrem fortem, ad filiōs miserōs currentem, rapiunt et magnīs spīrīs tenent et superant. Nec sē ā vulneribus dēfendere nec fugere potest, et ipse, ut taurus saucius ad āram, clāmōrēs horrendōs ad caelum tollit. Eōdem tempore serpentēs fugiunt, petuntque perfugium in arce Minervae ācris.

Quod Lāocoön in equum Minervae hastam iēcerat, nōs putāvimus eum errāvisse et poenās dedisse; vēritātem acerbam nescīvimus. Portās patefacimus et admittimus istum equum in urbem; ac puerī puellaeque—Ō patria, Ō dī magnī, Ō Trōia!—eum tangere gaudent. Et quoque gaudēmus nōs miserī, quibus ille diēs fuit ultimus ac quibus numquam erit ūllum sōlācium.

*The Laocoön group
Roman copy, perhaps after
Agesander, Athenodorus,
and Polydorus of Rhodes
1st cent. B.C.
Museo Pio Clementino,
Vatican Museums, Vatican State*

Vergil *Aen.* 2.199–249: A continuation, in prose adaptation, of the Laocoön passage from *Aeneid* Book Two read in Capvt XXIII. After the priest's warning to his fellow countrymen in that scene, a Greek spy named Sinon allows himself to be captured and fabricates a tale that nearly persuades the Trojans that they should bring the colossal wooden horse into the city, in order to assure the favor of Minerva and their protection from the Greeks. Just as the Trojans are wavering over the right course of action, two giant serpents course over the sea from the direction of Tenedos (the island where the Greek forces are secretly hiding: Map 3), glide onto the shore, and attack Laocoön and his sons, in the process sealing Troy's fate.—**Lāocoön, -ontis,** m.—**Neptūnus, -ī,** m.: Neptune, god of the sea, took the Greek side in the Trojan war.—**fortūnā factus:** Neptune's former priest had been slain, and Laocoön was hastily chosen by lot to make offerings to the god.—**taurus, -ī,** m., *bull;* "taurine," "toreador."—**āra, -ae,** f., *altar.*—**mactāre,** *to sacrifice, sacrificially slaughter.*—**serpēns, -pentis,** m., = Eng.; "serpentine."—**ardēre,** *to blaze;* "ardent," "arson."—**sībilus, -a, -um,** *hissing;* "sibilant," "sibilate."—**lambō, -ere,** *to lick;* "lambent," "lap."—**Lāocoonta:** Gk. acc.—**prīmum,** adv. of **prīmus.**—**lacerāre,** *to tear to pieces, mangle;* "lacerate," "laceration."—**dēvōrāre,** *to devour;* "carnivore," "voracious."—**spīra, -ae,** f., *coil;* "spire," "spiral."—**saucius, -a, -um,** *wounded.*—**clāmor, -mōris,** m., *shout, scream;* "clamor," "exclaim."—**horrendus, -a, -um,** = Eng.; "horrid," "abhorrent."

*QVAESTIŌNĒS:* You have already discussed the cinematographic aspects of the earlier Laocoön passage in Capvt XXIII; comment on the several highly visual elements in this passage. Identify the SIMILE Vergil employs to describe the priest's screams, and explain its irony. What are the moments of greatest pathos in the passage, and what key words, phrases, and images does Vergil employ to evoke our emotional response?

## SCRĪPTA IN PARIETIBVS

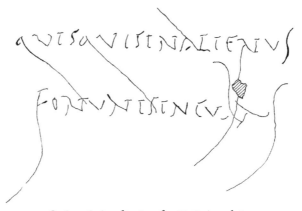

Quisquis in alterīus fortūnīs incubās.

*CIL* 4.5087: Graffito found near the kitchen door of a Pompeian house (Reg. IX, Ins. 5); a reprimand to the covetous, with a proverbial ring.—**quisquis:** with the 2nd-pers. verb, = *you, who(ever). . . .*—**incubāre,** *to lie upon, recline on; jealously watch (over), obsess (on);* "incubate," "incubus."

## LATĪNA EST GAVDIVM—ET VTILIS!

**Quid agitis hodiē, amīcī et amīcae?** Also from **iacēre** in the new **Vocābula** is the phrase **hīc iacet,** *here lies . . . ,* often inscribed on tombstones (sometimes spelled **hic jacket** and mistaken to mean *a country boy's sportcoat!*). And here are some other well-known mottoes and phrases: **dum spīrō, spērō,** *while I breathe, I hope* (South Carolina's state motto—the verb **spīrāre** is related to **spīritus,** Capvt XX, and gives us "conspire," "expire," "inspire," "perspire," "respiratory," "transpire," etc.); **crēde Deō,** *trust in God;* and Italian (ultimately from Latin and Arabic!) **lingua franca,** literally *Frankish language,* used of any hybrid language that is employed for communication among different cultures. **Spīrāte, spērāte, rīdēte, atque valēte!**

# CAPVT XXVI ⌐⌐⌐

# Comparison of Adjectives; Ablative of Comparison

## GRAMMATICA

### COMPARISON OF ADJECTIVES

The adjective forms you have learned thus far indicate a basic characteristic (a quality or quantity) associated with the modified noun, e.g., **vir beātus,** *a happy man.* This is called the **POSITIVE DEGREE** of the adjective.

In Latin, as in English, an adjective may be "compared" in order to indicate whether a person or thing being described has a greater degree of a particular characteristic than some other person(s) or thing(s), or more than is usual or customary. When comparing a person/thing with just one other, the **COMPARATIVE DEGREE** is used: **vir beātior,** *the happier man.* When comparing a person/thing with two or more others, the **SUPERLATIVE DEGREE** is employed: **vir beātissimus,** *the happiest man.*

#### Formation of Comparatives and Superlatives

The form of the positive degree is learned from the vocabulary. The comparative and superlative forms of regular adjectives add suffixes to base of the positive:

**Comparative:** base of positive + **-ior** (m. & f.), **-ius** (n.); **-iōris,** gen.
**Superlative:** base of positive + **-issimus, -issima, -issimum**

| Positive | Comparative | Superlative |
|---|---|---|
| cárus, -a, -um | cárior, -ius | cāríssimus, -a, -um |
| (*dear*) | (*dearer*) | (*dearest*) |
| lóngus, -a, -um | lóngior, -ius | longíssimus, -a, -um |
| (*long*) | (*longer*) | (*longest*) |
| fórtis, -e | fórtior, -ius | fortíssimus, -a, -um |
| (*brave*) | (*braver*) | (*bravest*) |

| | | |
|---|---|---|
| fēlīx, *gen.* fēlícis (*happy*) | fēlícior, -ius (*happier*) | fēlīcíssimus, -a, -um (*happiest*) |
| pótēns, *gen.* poténtis (*powerful*) | poténtior, -ius (*more powerful*) | potentíssimus, -a, -um (*most powerful*) |
| sápiēns, *gen.* sapiéntis (*wise*) | sapiéntior, -ius (*wiser*) | sapientíssimus, -a, -um (*wisest*) |

Some adjectives are compared by adding **magis** (*more*) and **maximē** (*most*) to the positive, especially those like **idōneus, -a, -um** (*suitable*) whose base ends in a vowel: **magis idōneus, maximē idōneus.**

## Declension of Comparatives

The declension of superlatives simply follows the pattern of **magnus, -a, -um.** Comparatives, however, are two-ending adjectives of the third declension, but are not i-stems (i.e., they do not have the -ī abl. sg., -**ium** gen. pl., or -**ia** n. nom./acc. pl. endings that characterize other third declension adjectives, as seen in Capvt XVI). Memorize the following paradigm, taking special note of the endings printed in bold:

| | Singular M. & F. | N. | Plural M. & F. | N. |
|---|---|---|---|---|
| *Nom.* | fórtior | fórtius | fortiórēs | fortióra |
| *Gen.* | fortióris | fortióris | fortió**rum** | fortió**rum** |
| *Dat.* | fortiórī | fortiórī | fortióribus | fortióribus |
| *Acc.* | fortiórem | fórtius | fortiórēs | fortióra |
| *Abl.* | fortió**re** | fortió**re** | fortióribus | fortióribus |

## Usage and Translation

Comparative degree adjectives are commonly translated with *more* or the suffix *-er* and superlatives with *most* or *-est,* depending on the context and English idiom, e.g.: **fēmina sapientior,** *the wiser woman;* **urbs antīquior,** *a more ancient city;* **tempus incertissimum,** *a most uncertain time;* **lūx clārissima,** *the brightest light.* Though there is no direct connection between the forms, it may be helpful for mnemonic purposes to associate the Latin comparative marker -ōr- with English "more"/"-er" and the superlative marker -ss- with English "most/-est."

The comparative sometimes has the force of "rather," indicating a greater degree of some quality than *usual* (**lūx clārior,** *a rather bright light*), or "too," indicating a greater degree than *desirable* (**vīta eius erat brevior,** *his/her life was too short*). The superlative is sometimes translated with "very," especially when comparing a person/thing to what is *usual* or *ideal:* **vīta eius erat brevissima,** *his/her life was very short.*

### *Quam* with Comparatives and Superlatives

When **quam** *follows* a *comparative* degree adjective it functions as a coordinating conjunction meaning "than," linking two items that are being compared; the same case or construction follows **quam** as precedes:

> **Hī librī sunt clāriōrēs quam illī.** *These books are more famous than those.*
> **Dīcit hōs librōs esse clāriōrēs quam illōs.** *He says that these books are more famous than those.*

When **quam** *precedes* a *superlative,* it functions adverbially and indicates that the person/thing modified has the greatest possible degree of a particular quality:

> **Amīcus meus erat vir quam iūcundissimus.** *My friend was the pleasantest man possible* or *as pleasant as can be.*

## ABLATIVE OF COMPARISON

When the first element being compared was nominative or accusative, **quam** was often omitted and the second element followed in the ablative case, the so-called **ABLATIVE OF COMPARISON** (which should be added to your now extensive list of ablative case uses):

> **Cōnsilia tua sunt clāriōra lūce.** *Your plans are clearer than light.* (Cf. **cōnsilia tua sunt clāriōra quam lūx,** which means the same.)
> **Quis in Italiā erat clārior Cicerōne?** *Who in Italy was more famous than Cicero?*
> **Paucōs fēlīciōrēs patre tuō vīdī.** *I have seen few men happier than your father.*

# VOCĀBVLA

As you review this list, practice the new grammar by writing out the comparative and superlative forms, including the nominative singular for all genders and the English meanings, for a few of the adjectives, such as **superbus** and **trīstis,** then check your work by comparing with the samples in the chart on p. 210–11. As always—**ut semper**—learn all these new items by focusing on their spelling, listening to them online (or on the CDs), and repeating them aloud: **audī atque prōnūntiā!**

**cḗna, cḗnae,** f., *dinner* (cenacle; cf. **cēnō**)
**fórum, fórī,** n., *marketplace, forum* (forensic)
**lēx, lḗgis,** f., *law, statute;* cf. **iūs,** which emphasizes *right, justice* (legal, legislator, legitimate, loyal, colleague, college, privilege)
**līmen, līminis,** n., *threshold* (liminality, subliminal, eliminate, preliminary)

**lūx, lúcis,** f., *light* (lucid, elucidate, translucent, illustrate, illuminate)

**mēnsa, mḗnsae,** f., *table; dining; dish, course;* **mēnsa secúnda,** *dessert* (the constellation Mensa)

**nox, nóctis,** f., *night* (nocturnal, nocturne, equinox, noctiluca, noctuid)

**sómnus, sómnī,** m., *sleep* (somnambulate, somnambulist, somniferous, somniloquist, somnolent, insomnia, Sominex)

**quídam, quaédam, quíddam** (pron.) or **quóddam** (adj.), indef. pron. and adj.; as pron., *a certain one* or *thing, someone, something;* as adj., *a certain, some* (gen. **cuiúsdam,** dat. **cuídam,** etc.)

**pudícus, pudíca, pudícum,** *modest, chaste* (impudent, pudency, pudendum; cf. **pudīcitia,** *modesty, chastity*)

**supérbus, supérba, supérbum,** *arrogant, overbearing, haughty, proud* (superb; cf. **superāre**)

**trīstis, trīste,** *sad, sorrowful; joyless, grim, severe* (tristful; cf. **trīstitia,** *sorrow*)

**túrpis, túrpe,** *ugly; shameful, base, disgraceful* (turpitude, turpitudinous)

**urbānus, urbāna, urbānum,** *of the city, urban; urbane, elegant* (urbanity, urbanization, suburban; cf. **urbs**)

**prae,** prep. + abl., *in front of, before* (frequent as a prefix, App. p. 488, e.g., **praepōnere,** *to put before, prefer;* sometimes intensifying, e.g., **praeclārus, praeclāra, praeclārum,** *especially famous, remarkable;* precede, prepare, preposition)

**quam,** conj. after comparatives, *than;* adv. before superlatives, *as . . . as possible:* **quam fortissimus,** *as brave as possible* (do not confuse with **quam,** adv., *how,* or with the f. acc. sg. of the rel. pron. or interrog. adj.)

**tántum,** adv., *only* (tantamount)

**invītō, invītāre, invītāvī, invītātum,** *to entertain, invite, summon* (invitation, invitational, vie)

# LĒCTIŌ ET TRĀNSLĀTIŌ

After careful study of the new grammar and vocabulary, search through the following readings for all the comparative and superlative degree adjectives and occurrences of the ablative of comparison construction. Listen to the CDs, if you have them, and read aloud before translating.

## EXERCITĀTIŌNĒS

1. Ille dux nescīvit cōnsilium nūntiātum esse et sē imperium prōtinus susceptūrum esse.
2. "Quīdam," inquit, "imperium quondam petēbant et līberōs virōs opprimere cupiēbant."

3. Eōdem diē decem mīlia hostium ab duce fidēlissimō āversa ac pulsa sunt; multī mīlitēs vulnera recēperant et in agrīs iacēbant.

4. Morte tyrannī ferōcis nūntiātā, quisque sē ad ōrātōrem potentissimum magnā spē vertit.

5. Rīdēns, scrīptor illīus fābulae sapiēns aliquid iūcundius dehinc nārrāvit.

6. Hīs rēbus audītīs, adulēscentēs geminī propter pecūniae cupiditātem studium litterārum relinquent.

7. Rēgīna fortissima Carthāginis posteā ostendit fidem semper esse sibi cāriōrem dīvitiīs.

8. Negāvit sē umquam vīdisse servam fidēliōrem quam hanc.

9. Iūcundior modus vītae hominibus nunc quaerendus est.

10. Crēdimus illōs vīgintī līberōs virōs fēmināsque vītam quam iūcundissimam agere.

11. Imperātor centum mīlitēs fortissimōs prae sē herī mīsit.

12. Lūx in illā casā nōn fuit clārissima, quod familia paucās fenestrās patefēcerat.

13. Amīcōs trīstēs excēpit, ad mēnsam invītāvit, et eīs perfugium ac sōlācium hīc dedit.

14. What is sweeter than a very pleasant life?

15. Certain men, however, say that death is sweeter than life.

16. When these three very sure signs had been reported, we sought advice and comfort from the most powerful leader.

17. In that story the author says that all men seek as happy lives as possible.

18. This light is always brighter than the other.

## SENTENTIAE ANTĪQVAE

1. Senectūs est loquācior. (Cicero.—**loquāx,** gen. **loquācis,** *garrulous;* "loquacious," "loquacity.")

2. Tua cōnsilia omnia nōbīs clāriōra sunt quam lūx. (Cicero.)

3. Quaedam remedia graviōra sunt quam ipsa perīcula. (Seneca.)

4. Eō diē virōs fortissimōs atque amantissimōs reī pūblicae ad mē vocāvī. (Cicero.—**amāns reī pūblicae,** i.e., *patriotic.*)

5. Quī imperia libēns accēpit, partem acerbissimam servitūtis vītat. (Seneca.—**libēns,** gen. **libentis,** *willing;* "ad lib."; here, as often, the adj. has adverbial force.)

6. Iūcundissima dōna, ut āiunt, semper sunt ea quae auctor ipse cāra facit. (Ovid.)

7. Beātus sapiēnsque vir forum vītat et superba līmina potentiōrum cīvium. (Horace.)

8. Quid est turpius quam ab aliquō illūdī? (Cicero.—**illūdō, -ere,** *to deceive;* "illude," "illusion.")

9. Quid enim est stultius quam incerta prō certīs habēre, falsa prō vērīs? (*Cicero.—**falsus, -a, -um;** "falsify," "fault.")

10. Saepe mihi dīcis, cārissime amīce: "Scrībe aliquid magnum; dēsidiōsissimus homō es." (Martial.—**dēsidiōsus, -a, -um,** *lazy;* "desidiose.")

11. Verba currunt; at manus notāriī est vēlōcior illīs; nōn lingua mea, sed manus eius, labōrem perfēcit. (Martial.—**notārius, -ī,** m., *stenographer;* "notary," "note."—**vēlōx,** gen. **vēlōcis,** *swift;* "velocity."—**perficiō, -ere, -fēcī, -fectum,** *to complete;* "perfect," "perfection.")

12. Multī putant rēs bellicās graviōrēs esse quam rēs urbānās; sed haec sententia mūtanda est, nam multae rēs urbānae sunt graviōrēs clāriōrēsque quam bellicae. (Cicero.—**bellicus, -a, -um,** adj. of **bellum;** "bellicose.")

13. Invītātus ad cēnam, manū sinistrā lintea neglegentiōrum sustulistī. Hoc salsum esse putās? Rēs sordidissima est! Itaque mihi linteum remitte. (Catullus.—**linteum, -ī,** n., *linen, napkin;* "lint."—**neglegēns,** gen. **-gentis,** *careless;* "neglect," "negligent."—**salsus, -a, -um,** *salty; witty;* "sauce," "saucy," "sausage."—**sordidus, -a, -um,** *dirty, mean;* "sordid.")

### The Nations of Gaul

Gallia est omnis dīvīsa in partēs trēs, quārum ūnam incolunt Belgae, aliam Aquītānī, tertiam quī ipsōrum linguā Celtae, nostrā Gallī appellantur. Hī omnēs linguā, īnstitūtīs, lēgibus inter sē differunt. Gallōs ab Aquītānīs Garumna flūmen, ā Belgīs Matrona et Sequana dīvidit. Hōrum omnium fortissimī sunt Belgae.

*Caesar *B. Gall.* 1.1: Gaius Julius Caesar (100–44 B.C.), politician, author, military commander, and ultimately dictator, remains one of the best known of all ancient Romans—not least because of the extensive memoirs he wrote on his military campaigns as gover-

*Bust of Julius Caesar*
*Museo Pio Clementino,*
*Vatican Museums, Vatican State*

nor of the Roman province of Gaul, titled the **Bellum Gallicum,** and on his subsequent conflict with Pompey and his supporters in Rome's civil wars, the **Bellum Cīvīle.** The passage included here is drawn directly from the opening of the earlier work, which he begins by describing something of the geography and ethnography of the tribes of Gaul.—The places and peoples mentioned: Gaul, the Belgae, the Aquitani, the Celts or Gauls, and the rivers Garonne, Marne, and Seine (see Map 2).—**dīvidō, -ere, -vīsī, -vīsum,** *to divide, separate;* "dividend," "divisible."—**incolō, -ere,** *to inhabit;* **Belgae, Aquītānī,** and (**eī**) **quī** are all subjects of **incolunt.**—**ipsōrum linguā:** = **linguā suā.**—**nostrā:** sc. **linguā.**—**īnstitūtum, -ī,** n., *custom, institution;* "institute," "institutionalize."–**linguā, īnstitūtīs, lēgibus:** ABL. OF RESPECT OR SPECIFICATION, *in (respect to their) language,* . . . . —**differō:** = Eng.; "difference," "differential."

*QVAESTIŌ:* Caesar's writing was often characterized by its direct language and succinctness; how does this excerpt typify those aspects of his style?

### The Good Life

Haec sunt, amīce iūcundissime, quae vītam faciunt beātiōrem: rēs nōn facta labōre sed ā patre relicta, ager fēlīx, parvum forī et satis ōtiī, mēns aequa, vīrēs et corpus sānum, sapientia, amīcī vērī, sine arte mēnsa, nox nōn ebria sed solūta cūrīs, nōn trīstis torus et tamen pudīcus, somnus facilis. Dēsīderā tantum quod habēs, cupe nihil; nōlī timēre ultimum diem aut spērāre.

Martial *Epig.* 10.47: In this prose adaptation from one of his longer *Epigrams,* Martial shares with a friend his views of what makes for a happy life. —**rēs:** here *property, wealth.*—**ā patre relicta:** i.e., inherited.—**forī:** i.e., the hustle-bustle of the business world (the same sense of the word seen in S.A. 7 above); here gen. of the whole with **parvum.**—**arte:** here = *ostentation, pretentiousness.*—**ebrius, -a, -um,** *drunken;* "inebriated."—**solvō, -ere, solvī, solūtum,** *to loosen, free ( from);* "solve," "absolve."—**torus, -ī,** m., *bed;* "torus."—**nōlī:** imperat. regularly used with an infin. for a negative command, *do not.* . . .

*QVAESTIŌNĒS:* Literal translations often do not convey a writer's intent; how might you paraphrase this list of desiderata, in order to clarify Martial's meaning? Which one of his objectives is inconsonant with America's conventional "work ethic"?

## SCRĪPTA IN PARIETIBVS

Prīma, domina

*CIL* 4.8241: Proprietors' names were often posted on their shops, as in the case of this inn or tavern (**caupōna**), situated adjacent to a small house in Reg. I, Ins. 10.—**Prīma:** ordinal numerals, often indicating birth order, were used both as praenomina and cognomina, esp. in women's names, e.g., **Secunda, Tertia, Quārta,** etc.—**domina, -ae,** f., *mistress* (female head of a household), *owner;* "dominate," "prima donna."

## ETYMOLOGIA

Just a few more of the numerous Eng. derivatives from **solvō** (in "The Good Life," above) are: absolution, dissolve, dissolute, resolve, resolution, solution, ablative absolute.

In Sp. the compar. degree of an adj. is regularly formed by putting **más,** from Lat. **magis,** *more,* before the adj.: **más caro, más alto;** Port. similarly employs **mais,** as in **mais caro.** It., Sp., and Port. retain vestiges of the Lat. superl. ending **-issimus,** but generally in the intensive sense of *very, exceedingly:*

| Latin | Italian | Spanish | Portuguese | |
|-------|---------|---------|------------|---|
| cārissimus | carissimo | carisimo | caríssimo | *very dear* |
| clārissimus | chiarissimo | clarisimo | claríssimo | *very clear* |
| altissimus | altissimo | altisimo | altíssimo | *very high* |

For further discussion of comparison of adjectives in the Romance languages, including Fr., Occ., and Rom., see the next chapter's **Etymologia.**

## LATĪNA EST GAVDIVM—ET VTILIS!

**Salvēte!** Here are some more familiar mottoes, phrases, famous quotations, and etymological tidbits **ex vocābulīs huius capitis** (**vocābula,** by the way, are lit. "what you call things," from **vocāre**): **auctor ignōtus** means *author unknown,* i.e., "anonymous"; **cēna Dominī** is the *Lord's Supper;* **dūra lēx sed lēx,** *a harsh law, but the law nevertheless;* **lēx nōn scrīpta,** *customary law* (as opposed to **lēx scrīpta**—what are the lit. meanings?—you can also figure out **lēx locī**); then there's Ovid's admonition to loners, **trīstis eris sī sōlus eris,** and the hope of one of Plautus' characters for **lēx eadem uxōrī et virō;** a legal decree of **ā mēnsā et torō,** *from table and bed* (**torus, -ī**), is a separation prohibiting husband and wife from cohabiting. Knowing the noun **lūx** and the related verb **lūceō, lūcēre,** *to shine brightly,* can shed some light on these items: **lūx et vēritās** is the motto of Yale University, **lūx et lēx** is the motto of the University of North Carolina at Chapel Hill, pellucid explanations are perfectly clear (**per + lūc-**), translucent materials let the light shine through, and Lux soap will make you shine like light! **Lūcēte, discipulae discipulīque, et valēte!**

# CAPVT XXVII ⌐⌐⌐

# Irregular Comparison of Adjectives

## GRAMMATICA

### IRREGULAR COMPARISON OF ADJECTIVES

Some adjectives have comparisons that do not follow the regular patterns introduced in Capvt XXVI.

### Superlatives of *-er* and *-lis* Adjectives

Two groups of adjectives, which are otherwise regular, have peculiar forms in the superlative. Six adjectives ending in **-lis** form the superlative by adding **-limus, -lima, -limum** to the base:

| Positive | Comparative | Superlative |
|---|---|---|
| fácilis, -e (*easy*) | facílior, -ius (*easier*) | facíl-limus, -a, -um (*easiest*) |
| diffícilis, -e (*difficult*) | difficílior, -ius (*more difficult*) | difficíllimus, -a, -um (*most difficult*) |
| símilis, -e (*like*) | simílior, -ius (*more l.*) | simíllimus, -a, -um (*most l.*) |

**Dissimilis** (*unlike, dissimilar*), **gracilis** (*slender, thin*), and **humilis** (*low, humble*) follow this same pattern; all other **-lis** adjectives have regular superlatives (e.g., **fidēlissimus, ūtilissimus,** etc.).

Adjectives with a masculine in **-er,** regardless of declension, form the superlative by adding **-rimus,** not to the base, but directly to this masculine **-er;** the comparatives of such adjectives are formed regularly, by adding **-ior, -ius** to the base (which, as you know, in some cases retains the **-e-** and sometimes drops it):

| Positive | Comparative | Superlative |
|---|---|---|
| līber, -bera, -berum (*free*) | lībérior, -ius (*freer*) | lībér-rimus, -a, -um (*freest*) |
| púlcher, -chra, -chrum (*beautiful*) | púlchrior, -ius (*more beautiful*) | pulchérrimus, -a, -um (*most beautiful*) |
| ácer, ácris, ácre (*keen*) | ácrior, ácrius (*keener*) | ācérrimus, -a, -um (*keenest*) |

## Other Irregular Adjective Comparisons

A few common adjective comparisons are so irregular that their comparatives and superlatives must simply be memorized; many of the irregularities are examples of SUPPLETION (see Capvt XI), just like English "good, better, best" and "bad, worse, worst," whose comparatives and superlatives derive from words not cognate with the positive forms. Following are some of the most important, which you will need to memorize (English derivatives can help with this: see the **Etymologia** section below):

| Positive | Comparative | Superlative |
|---|---|---|
| bónus, -a, -um (*good*) | mélior, -ius (*better*) | óptimus, -a, -um (*best*) |
| mágnus, -a, -um (*great*) | máior, -ius (*greater*) | máximus, -a, -um (*greatest*) |
| málus, -a, -um (*bad*) | péior, -ius (*worse*) | péssimus, -a, -um (*worst*) |
| múltus, -a, -um (*much*) | ——, plūs (*more*) | plúrimus, -a, -um (*most*) |
| párvus, -a, -um (*small*) | mínor, mínus (*smaller*) | mínimus, -a, -um (*smallest*) |
| (prae, prō) (*in front of, before*) | príor, -ius (*former*) | prímus, -a, -um (*first*) |
| súperus, -a, -um (*that above*) | supérior, -ius (*higher*) | $\left\{\begin{array}{l}\text{súmmus, -a, -um}\\ \quad(\textit{highest, furthest})\\ \text{suprémus, -a, -um}\\ \quad(\textit{highest, last})\end{array}\right.$ |

There is no positive degree adjective corresponding to **prior** and **prīmus,** since those words, by the very definition of "priority" and "primacy," imply comparison with one or more persons or things; the prepositions **prae** and **prō,** however, are related.

## Declension of *Plūs*

None of the irregular forms offers any declensional difficulty except **plūs.** In the plural **plūs** functions as an adjective (e.g., **plūrēs amīcī**), but has mixed i-stem and consonant-stem forms (**-ium** in the genitive plural but **-a,** not **-ia,** in the neuter nominative and accusative); in the singular it functions not as an adjective at all, but as a neuter noun which is commonly followed by a genitive of the whole (e.g., **plūs pecūniae,** *more money,* lit. *more of money*—see Capvt XV).

| | Singular M. & F. | N. | Plural M. & F. | N. |
|---|---|---|---|---|
| *Nom.* | —— | plūs | plúrēs | plúra |
| *Gen.* | —— | plúris | plúrium | plúrium |
| *Dat.* | —— | —— | plúribus | plúribus |
| *Acc.* | —— | plūs | plúrēs | plúra |
| *Abl.* | —— | plúre | plúribus | plúribus |

# VOCĀBVLA

Some tips for the new vocabulary: don't confuse forms of **sōl** and **sōlus, -a, -um;** review the discussion of consonantal **i** in the *Intrōductiō,* p. xxxviii, and listen carefully online to the pronunciation of **maior, maius,** something like "mai-yor," "maiyus," etc.; note the special meanings of the plurals **superī** and **maiōrēs** (which the Romans often employed in a phrase invoking ancestral custom, the **mōs maiōrum**); and note that you must learn all the irregular comparative and superlative adjective forms listed in the table above.

**dēlectātiō, dēlectātiốnis,** f., *delight, pleasure, enjoyment* (delectation, delectable, delicious, dilettante; cf. **dēlectō**)

**népōs, nepốtis,** m., *grandson, descendant* (nephew, nepotism, niece)

**sōl, sốlis,** m., *sun* (solar, solarium, solstice, parasol)

**dīligēns,** gen. **dīligéntis,** *diligent, careful* (diligence, diligently)

**dissímilis, dissímile,** *unlike, different* (dissimilar, dissimilarity, dissemble)

**grácilis, grácile,** *slender, thin* (gracile, gracility)

**húmilis, húmile,** *lowly, humble* (humility, humiliate, humiliation)

**máior, máius,** compar. adj., *greater; older;* **maiốrēs, maiốrum,** m. pl., *ancestors* (i.e., *the older ones;* major, majority, etc.—see **Etymologia** below)

**prīmus, prīma, prīmum,** *first, foremost, chief, principal* (primary, primate, prime, primeval, primer, premier, primitive, prim, primo-geniture, prima facie, primordial, primrose)

**quot,** indecl. adj., *how many, as many as* (quota, quotation, quotient)

**símilis, símile,** + gen. or dat., *similar (to), like, resembling* (simile, assimilate, simulate, dissimulate, verisimilitude, assemble, resemble, simultaneous; "same" is cognate)

**súperus, súpera, súperum,** *above, upper;* **súperī, superốrum,** m. pl., *the gods* (superior, etc.; cf. **superō** and see **Etymologia** below)

**ūtilis, ūtile,** *useful, advantageous* (what Latin is to YOU!—utility, from **ūtilitās, -tātis;** utilitarian, utilization, utilize)

All the irregular adjectival forms listed above, p. 218–19

**pốnō, pốnere, pósuī, pósitum,** *to put, place, set* (see **Etymologia** below)

**próbō, probấre, probấvī, probấtum,** *to approve, recommend; test* (probe, probate, probable, approbation, proof, prove, approval, improve, reprobate; cf. **probitās**)

# LĒCTIŌ ET TRĀNSLĀTIŌ

The most important activities for the **Lēctiō et Trānslātiō** section are to read aloud, read for comprehension, and then translate (listen to the Latin too, if you have the CDs); but for practice with the new grammar, you should scan through the readings for all comparative and superlative adjectives, noting which are regular and which are irregular.

## EXERCITĀTIŌNĒS

1. Quisque cupit quam pulcherrima atque ūtilissima dōna dare.
2. Quīdam turpēs habent plūrima sed etiam plūra petunt.
3. Ille ōrātor, ab tyrannō superbissimō expulsus, ducem iūcundiōrem et lēgēs aequiōrēs dehinc quaesīvit.
4. Summum imperium optimīs virīs semper petendum est.
5. Senex nepōtibus trīstibus casam patefēcit et eōs trāns līmen invītāvit.
6. Ostendit ultimum signum lūce clārissimā ab hostibus illā nocte datum esse.
7. Iste tyrannus pessimus negāvit sē virōs līberōs umquam oppressisse.
8. Fidēlissimus servus plūs cēnae ad mēnsam accipiēbat quam trēs peiōrēs.
9. Āiunt hunc auctōrem vītam humillimam hīc agere.
10. Cūr dī superī oculōs ā rēbus hūmānīs eō tempore āvertērunt?
11. Habēsne pecūniam et rēs tuās prae rē pūblicā?
12. Sōlem post paucās nūbēs gracillimās in caelō hodiē vidēre possumus.
13. Some believe that very large cities are worse than very small ones.
14. In return for the three rather small gifts, the young man gave even more and prettier ones to his very sad mother.
15. Those very large mountains were higher than these.

## SENTENTIAE ANTĪQVAE

1. Trahit mē nova vīs: videō meliōra probōque, sed peiōra tantum faciō et nesciō cūr. (Ovid.)
2. Quaedam carmina sunt bona; plūra sunt mala. (Martial.)
3. Optimum est. Nihil melius, nihil pulchrius hōc vīdī. (Terence.)
4. Spērō tē et hunc nātālem et plūrimōs aliōs quam fēlīcissimōs āctūrum esse. (Pliny.—**nātālis [diēs]**, *birthday;* "natal," "Natalie.")
5. Quoniam cōnsilium et ratiō sunt in senibus, maiōrēs nostrī summum concilium appellāvērunt "senātum." (Cicero.—**concilium, -ī,** n., *council;* "conciliate," "reconcile"; be careful to distinguish **concilium, cōnsilium,** and **cōnsul.**)
6. Plūs operae studiīque in rēbus domesticīs nōbīs nunc pōnendum est etiam quam in rēbus mīlitāribus. (Cicero.—**opera, -ae,** f., *work, effort;* "opera," "operation," "cooperate."—**domesticus, -a, -um;** "domesticate," "domesticity."—**mīlitāris, -e;** "militarism," "demilitarize"; cf. **mīles.**)
7. Neque enim perīculum in rē pūblicā fuit gravius umquam neque ōtium maius. (Cicero.)

8. Sumus sapientiōrēs illīs, quod nōs nātūram esse optimam ducem scīmus. (Cicero.—**optimam:** f. by attraction to the gender of **nātūram.**)

9. Nātūra minimum petit; nātūrae autem sē sapiēns accommodat. (*Seneca.—**accommodāre,** *to adapt;* "accommodation.")

10. Maximum remedium īrae mora est. (*Seneca.)

11. Quī animum vincit et īram continet, eum cum summīs virīs nōn comparō sed eum esse simillimum deō dīcō. (Cicero.—**comparāre,** *to compare;* "comparable," "comparison.")

12. Dionȳsius, tyrannus urbis pulcherrimae, erat vir summae in vīctū temperantiae et in omnibus rēbus dīligentissimus et ācerrimus. Īdem tamen erat ferōx ac iniūstus. Quā ex rē, sī vērum dīcimus, vidēbātur miserrimus. (Cicero.—Dionysius, ruler of Syracuse in the 4th cent. B.C.—**vīctus, -ūs,** m., *mode of life;* "victual," "vittles."—**temperantia, -ae,** f.; "temperate," "intemperance."—**iniūstus, -a, -um,** *unjust;* "injustice."—**quā ex rē:** = **ex illā rē.**)

13. Nisi superōs vertere possum, Acheronta movēbō. (Vergil.—**Acheronta:** Gk. acc., *Acheron,* a river in the underworld, here by metonymy *the land of the dead.*)


## Alley Cat

> Caelī, Lesbia nostra, Lesbia illa,
> illa Lesbia, quam Catullus ūnam
> plūs quam sē atque suōs amāvit omnēs,
> nunc in quadriviīs et angiportīs
> 5  glūbit magnanimī Remī nepōtēs.

*Catullus *Carm.* 58: This poem, a single sent. sardonically addressed to Caelius, a former rival for Lesbia's favors, clearly was composed at an even lower point of Catullus' relationship with Lesbia than his **Carmen** 8, which you read (and may wish to re-read now) in Capvt XIX; meter: hendecasyllabic.—**quadrivium, -iī,** n., *crossroads.*—**angiportum, -ī,** n., *alley.*—**glūbō, -ere,** *to peel* (*back*), *strip* (*off*); used of stripping the bark off trees or the skin off an animal, here in an obscene sense.—**Remus:** Remus was slain by his brother, Romulus, who became legendary founder of Rome and the city's first king; his **nepōtēs** are his imagined descendants—Rome's nobility—in Catullus' day.

*QVAESTIŌNĒS:* Marcus Caelius Rufus, a dissolute young senator, had earned Catullus' resentment for his own affair with Lesbia (a pseudonym, you may recall from Capvt II, for Clodia, wife of another senator: this was a true Roman soap opera!); comment on the irony in Catullus' use of **nostra** in addressing him. Recalling that demonstratives are "pointing words," what do you sense as the effect of **illa** here, and in what ways does Catullus emphasize the word?—comment too on the arrangement of **Lesbia illa, illa Lesbia.** Why do you suppose Catullus chose to imagine Lesbia's dallying in alleyways with Remus' descendants, rather than Romulus'?

## Thanks a Lot, Tully!

Dīsertissime Rōmulī nepōtum,
quot sunt quotque fuēre, Mārce Tullī,
quotque post aliīs erunt in annīs,
grātiās tibi maximās Catullus
5　agit, pessimus omnium poēta,
tantō pessimus omnium poēta
quantō tū optimus omnium patrōnus.

*Catullus *Carm.* 49: The poet sends "thanks" to the orator and statesman, Marcus Tullius Cicero; whether or not the tone is ironic is a matter much debated by scholars, but it is worth noting here that Cicero had not only on occasion expressed his disdain for romantic poetry, but also had defended the Caelius Rufus of Catullus 58 on charges the orator claimed were instigated by Clodia/Lesbia. Like Catullus 58 above, this poem is structured as a single, long sent., and its meter is hendecasyllabic.—**dīsertus, -a, -um,** *eloquent, learned;* "dissertation."—**fuēre:** = **fuērunt,** see Capvt XII.—**post:** = **posteā.**— **tantō . . . quantō,** *just as much . . . as.*—**tū:** sc. **es.**

*QVAESTIŌNĒS:* Irony can often be detected by the intonation of a speaker, or a poet reciting his verse, but is sometimes difficult to discern in a written text; what do you see as this poem's most striking stylistic feature (occurring in virtually every line) and how might its exuberance suggest that Catullus' "thank you" here is in fact sarcastic? INTER-TEXTUALITY, i.e., resonances between one literary text and another, can often be a clue to an author's intent; what connection do you see between this poem's opening line, and the closing verse of poem 58, and, if deliberate, what might its purpose be?

## An Uncle's Love for His Nephew and Adopted Son

Adulēscēns est cārior mihi quam ego ipse! Atque hic nōn est fīlius meus sed ex frātre meō. Studia frātris iam diū sunt dissimillima meīs. Ego vītam urbānam ēgī et ōtium petīvī et, id quod quīdam fortūnātius putant, uxōrem numquam habuī. Ille, autem, haec omnia fēcit: nōn in forō sed in agrīs vītam ēgit, parvum pecūniae accēpit, uxōrem pudīcam dūxit, duōs fīliōs habuit. Ex illō ego hunc maiōrem adoptāvī mihi, ēdūxī ā parvō puerō, amāvī prō meō. In eō adulēscente est dēlectātiō mea; sōlum id est cārum mihi.

Terence *Ad.* 39–49: Terence (Publius Terentius Afer, ca. 185–159 B.C.), brought to Rome from Carthage as a slave, was subsequently freed and went on to a career as comic playwright and producer. The **Adelphoe,** *Brothers,* last of his six plays, is a comedy of manners, something like a modern "sitcom," about two fathers with quite different philosophies about raising their adolescent sons; Micio, the more lenient father, speaks here about his affection for his son, whom he has adopted from his brother.—**iam diū:** commonly used with a pres. tense verb for an action begun in the past but continuing in

*Scene from Terence's comedy,* The Andria. *Marble bas-relief, 1st cent.* A.D.
*Museo Archeologico Nazionale, Naples, Italy*

the pres., where in Eng., and thus in translation, we would use perf. tense.—**dūxit:** here,
*married.*—**adoptāre,** = Eng.; "adoption," "adoptive."—**ēdūxī:** *raised.*–**id:** *this thing,* i.e.,
their relationship.

*QVAESTIŌNĒS:* It was a matter of great importance in the Greco-Roman world for a
man to have a male heir; why did Micio resort to adoption? Marriage humor was standard fodder for comics in antiquity as it is today; what is the joke here?

## SCRĪPTA IN PARIETIBVS

Liquāmen optimum!

*CIL* 4.9415: Not exactly a graffito, but another example of Roman script: just as manu-
facturers label jars and cans of processed foods today, ancient food producers incised or

painted labels on their storage and shipping containers, which were usually ceramic ware, like the jug (**urceus**) that bore this inscription; from the atrium of a house in Reg. I, Ins. 8.—**liquāmen, -minis,** n., *liquid, fluid, sauce; liquamen;* liquamen and another popular fish-sauce called **garum** were widely used for seasoning—this jar was also inscribed, in a second hand, **SCOMBR,** a common abbreviation for **scomber,** *mackerel,* the fish typically used to produce these sauces.—**optimum:** a bit of advertising hype, another aspect of marketing familiar to us today!

## ETYMOLOGIA

In many instances the irregular comparison of a Lat. adj. can easily be remembered by Eng. derivatives:

| | |
|---|---|
| **bonus** | **melior:** ameliorate |
| | **optimus:** optimist, optimum, optimal |
| **magnus** | **maior:** major, majority, mayor |
| | **maximus:** maximum |
| **malus** | **peior:** pejorative |
| | **pessimus:** pessimist |
| **multus** | **plūs:** plus, plural, plurality, nonplus |
| **parvus** | **minor:** minor, minority, minus, minute, minuet, minister, minstrel |
| | **minimus:** minimum, minimize |
| (**prō**) | **prior:** prior, priority |
| | **prīmus:** prime, primacy, primary, primeval, primitive |
| **superus** | **superior:** superior, superiority |
| | **summus:** summit, sum, consummate |
| | **suprēmus:** supreme, supremacy |

Lat. **plūs** is the parent of Fr. **plus,** It. **più,** and Old Occ. **plus** or **pus,** words which are placed before adjectives to form the compar. degree in those Romance languages. In Fr. and It. adding the definite article to these comparatives converts them into superlatives:

| Latin | French | Italian |
|---|---|---|
| longior | plus long | più lungo |
| longissimus | le plus long | il più lungo |
| cārior | plus cher | più caro |
| cārissimus | le plus cher | il più caro |

For comparatives Rom. uses **mai,** like Port. **mais** and Sp. **más** (all from Lat. **magis**), before an adj., e.g., **mai lung,** *longer;* then, like Fr., It., and Port., it adds the definite article for superlatives, **cel mai lung,** *longest.* For the intensive sense often conveyed by Lat. superlatives, Rom. employs **foarte,** *very,* from Lat. **forte,** before an adj.; e.g., **foarte clar,** *very clear.* The practice for forming superlatives in Occ. is variable; but cf., e.g., **carisme.**

From **pōnō** come innumerable derivatives: apposite, apposition, component, composite, compost, compound, deponent, deposit, deposition, depot, exponent, exposition, expound, imposition, impost, impostor, juxtaposition, opponent, opposite, positive, post, postpone, preposition, proposition, propound, repository, supposition, transposition. However, note that some Eng. compounds ending in "-pose," e.g., "repose," derive through Fr. **poser** from late Lat. **pausāre,** which stems from Gk. **pausis,** *a pause,* and **pauein,** *to stop.*

## LATĪNA EST GAVDIVM—ET VTILIS!

**Salvē! Quid hodiē agis? Spīrāsne? Spērāsne? Rīdēsne? Valēsne? Sī tū valēs, ego valeō!** And here are some more **rēs Latīnae** to give you a **mēns sāna:** first, an old Latin maxim which you should now be able to read, **sapiēns nihil affirmat quod nōn probat.** Likewise this quote from Horace (*Epist.* 1.1.106), **sapiēns ūnō minor est Iove,** and the motto of the Jesuit order, **ad maiōrem glōriam Deī.** Now, **quid est tempestās? Pluitne? Estne frīgida? Nimbōsa?** Well, it really won't matter, if you remember this proverb: **sōl lūcet omnibus!** (Remember **lūcēre** from last chapter?) Birds of a feather flock together and, according to another old Latin proverb, **similis in similī gaudet.** Here are some more from the irregular comparatives and superlatives you've just learned: **meliōrēs priōrēs,** freely, *the better have priority;* **maximā cum laude** and **summā cum laude** (what you should have on your next diploma, **sī es dīligēns in studiō Latīnae!**); **peior bellō est timor ipse bellī** (note the ablative of comparison); **ē plūribus ūnum,** motto of the United States, *one from several,* i.e., one union from many states; **nē plūs ultrā,** *no more beyond* (this point), i.e., the ultimate; **prīmus inter parēs,** *first among equals;* **prīmā faciē,** *at first sight;* and, finally, **summum bonum,** *the highest good,* which can come from studying Latin, of course: **valē!**

# CAPVT XXVIII ▱▱▱

# Subjunctive Mood; Present Subjunctive; Jussive and Purpose Clauses

## GRAMMATICA

### THE SUBJUNCTIVE MOOD

You will recall from Capvt. I that MOOD (from **modus**) is the "manner" of expressing a verbal action or state of being, and you are already familiar with two of the three Latin moods, the INDICATIVE and the IMPERATIVE: an imperative (from **imperāre**, *to command*) emphatically commands someone to undertake an action that is not yet going on, while indicatives (from **indicāre**, *to point out*) "indicate" real actions, i.e., actions that definitely have (or have not) occurred in the past, that are (or are not) occurring in the present, or that likely will (or will not) occur in the future.

In contrast to the indicative, the mood of actuality and factuality, the SUBJUNCTIVE is in general (though not always) the mood of potential, tentative, hypothetical, ideal, or even unreal action. An example in English is, "If the other student were here, he would be taking notes"; in this conditional sentence, which imagines actions that are contrary to the actual facts, English employs the auxiliaries "were" and "would" to indicate that the action described is only hypothetical. Among the other auxiliaries used in English to describe potential or ideal actions are "may," "might," "should," "would," "may have," "would have," etc.

Latin employs the subjunctive much more frequently than English, in a wide variety of clause types, and it uses special subjunctive verb forms rather than auxiliaries. There are two tasks involved in mastering the subjunctive: first, the morphology, i.e., learning the new forms, a relatively simple matter; second, the syntax, i.e., learning to recognize and translate the various subjunctive clause types, which is also quite easily done if your approach is systematic.

## PRESENT SUBJUNCTIVE

There are only four tenses in the subjunctive mood. The present subjunctive is introduced in this chapter and has rules for formation that vary slightly among the four conjugations; rules for forming the imperfect, perfect, and pluperfect (Capita XXIX–XXX) are the same for all conjugations, even for irregular verbs.

| | | | | |
|---|---|---|---|---|
| 1. laúdem | móneam | ágam | aúdiam | cápiam |
| 2. laúdēs | mónēas | ágās | aúdiās | cápiās |
| 3. laúdet | móneat | ágat | aúdiat | cápiat |
| | | | | |
| 1. laudḗmus | moneámus | agámus | audiámus | capiámus |
| 2. laudḗtis | moneátis | agátis | audiátis | capiátis |
| 3. laúdent | móneant | ágant | aúdiant | cápiant |

Note that in the first conjugation the characteristic stem vowel changes from -ā- in the present indicative to -ē- in the present subjunctive. In the other conjugations -ā- is consistently the sign of the present subjunctive, but with variations in the handling of the actual stem vowel (shortened in the second, replaced in the third, altered to short -i- in the fourth/third -iō); the mnemonic **"we fear a liar"** will help you remember that the vowels preceding the personal endings are -ē-, -eā-, -ā-, and -iā- for the first, second, third, and fourth/third -iō conjugations, respectively. Note that a subjunctive may be mistaken for an indicative, if you neglect to recognize a verb's conjugation (e.g., cf. **agat** with **amat,** and **amet** with **monet**), so remember your vocabulary.

The present passive subjunctive follows the usual pattern of substituting passive endings:

> laúder, laudḗris (and remember the alternate -**re** ending, Capvt XVIII), laudḗtur; laudḗmur, laudḗminī, laudéntur
> mónear, moneáris, moneátur; moneámur, moneáminī, moneántur
> ágar, agáris, agátur; agámur, agáminī, agántur
> aúdiar, audiáris, audiátur; audiámur, audiáminī, audiántur
> cápiar, capiáris, capiátur; capiámur, capiáminī, capiántur

### Translation

While "may" is sometimes used to translate the present subjunctive (e.g., in purpose clauses), the translation of all subjunctive tenses, in fact, varies with the type of clause, as you will see when each is introduced.

## THE JUSSIVE SUBJUNCTIVE

In this and subsequent chapters you will be introduced to a series of subjunctive clause types: the jussive subjunctive and purpose clauses (Capvt XXVIII), result clauses (XXIX), indirect questions (XXX), **cum** clauses (XXXI), proviso clauses (XXXII), conditions (XXXIII), jussive noun clauses (XXXVI), relative clauses of characteristic (XXXVIII), and fear clauses (XL). You should catalog these clause types in your notebook or computer file and systematically learn three details for each: (1) its definition, (2) how to recognize it in a Latin sentence, and (3) how to translate it into English.

As suggested by the term "subjunctive" itself (from **subiungere,** *to subjoin, subordinate*), subjunctive verbs were used chiefly in SUBORDINATE (dependent) CLAUSES. However, the subjunctive was also employed in certain types of INDE-PENDENT (main) CLAUSES. The JUSSIVE SUBJUNCTIVE (from **iubēre,** *to order*) is among the most important of these independent uses, and the only one formally introduced in this book. *Definition:* as the term implies, the JUSSIVE SUBJUNC-TIVE expresses a command or exhortation, especially in the first or third person (the imperative is generally used for the second person). *Recognition:* The clause type is easily recognized, since the sentence's main verb (often its only verb) is sub-junctive; negative commands are introduced by **nē.** *Translation:* while "may" and "should" are sometimes employed in translating jussives (particularly in second person: **semper spērēs,** *you should always hope*), "let" is the auxiliary most often used, followed by the subject noun or pronoun (in the objective case, i.e., "me," "us," "him," "her," "them"):

> **Cōgitem nunc dē hāc rē, et tum nōn errābō.** *Let me now think about this mat-ter, and then I will not make a mistake.*
>
> **Discipulus discat aut discēdat.** *Let the student either learn or leave.*
>
> **Doceāmus magnā cum dēlectātiōne linguam Latīnam.** *Let us teach the Latin language with great delight.*
>
> **Nē id faciāmus.** *Let us ("let's") not do this.*
>
> **Audeant illī virī et fēminae esse fortēs.** *Let those men and women dare to be brave.*

## PURPOSE CLAUSES

*Definition:* A PURPOSE CLAUSE is a subordinate clause indicating the objective of the action in the main clause; e.g., "we study Latin *so that we may learn more about ancient Rome*" or "we study Latin *to improve our English.*" As seen in this second example, English often employs an infinitive to express purpose, but that use of the infinitive is rare in classical Latin prose, which instead employed a subordinate clause with a subjunctive verb. *Recognition:* Look for a subjunctive clause intro-duced by **ut** or, for a negative purpose, **nē,** and stating the purpose of the action in the main clause. *Translation:* The auxiliary "may" is often used in translating the present tense in a purpose clause, but it is generally more idiomatic to trans-late with an infinitive ("to" or "in order to"), so long as the purpose clause and the main clause have the same subject. Study the following examples:

Hoc dīcit *ut* eōs *iuvet.*
*He says this to help them.*
    *in order to help them.*
    *that he may help them.*
    *so that he may help them.*
    *in order that he may help them.*

The first two translations above are more colloquial, the others more formal.

Discēdit *nē* id *audiat.*
*He is leaving in order not to hear this.*
    *so that he may not hear this.*

Cum cūrā docet *ut* discipulī bene *discant.*
*He teaches with care so (that) his students may learn well.*

Hoc facit *nē capiātur.*
*He does this in order not to be captured.*

Librōs legimus *ut* multa *discāmus.*
*We read books (in order) to learn many things.*

Bonōs librōs nōbīs dent *nē* malōs *legāmus.*
*Let them give us good books so that we may not read bad ones.*

# VOCĀBVLA

As you learn the new verbs in this list, conjugate a few in the present subjunctive. **Parēns/parentis** (originally present participle of a verb meaning *to give birth to*) is another noun that, for obvious reasons, can be feminine or masculine; it serves as a reminder that vowels before **ns** are regularly long, those before **nt** are regularly short. The Romans variously treated **vesper** as second or third declension (even **vespera**, first declension, is attested); so expect a variety of endings.

árma, armṓrum, n. pl., *arms, weapons* (army, armament, armada, armistice, armadillo, gendarme, alarm–from It. **all'arme,** *to arms,* Lat. **ad illa arma**)

cúrsus, cúrsūs, m., *running, race; course* (courser, cursor, cursory, cursive, concourse, discourse, recourse, precursor, excursion; cf. **currō**)

lúna, lúnae, f., *moon* (lunar, lunacy, lunate, lunatic, interlunar)

occāsiō, occāsiṓnis, f., *occasion, opportunity* (occasional)

párēns, paréntis, m./f., *parent* (parental, parenting; cf. **pariō, parere,** *give birth to*)

stḗlla, stḗllae, f., *star, planet* (stellar, constellation, interstellar)

vésper, vésperis or vésperī, m., *evening; evening star* (vesper, vesperal)

mórtuus, mórtua, mórtuum, *dead* (mortuary)

**prínceps,** gen. **príncipis,** *chief, foremost;* m./f. noun, *leader, emperor* (prince, principal, principality; cf. **prímus, prīncipium**)

**ut,** conj. + subjunct., *in order that, so that, that, in order to, so as to, to;* + indic., *as, when*

**nē,** adv. and conj. with subjunct. of command and purpose, *not; in order that . . . not, that . . . not, in order not to*

**cḗdō, cḗdere, céssī, céssum,** *to go, withdraw; yield to, grant, submit* (accede, access, antecedent, ancestor, cede, concede, deceased, exceed, intercede, precede, proceed, recede, secede; cf. **discēdō**)

**dḗdicō, dēdicā́re, dēdicā́vī, dēdicā́tum,** *to dedicate* (dedication, dedicatory)

**égeō, egḗre, éguī** + abl. or gen., *to need, lack, want* (indigence, indigent; do not confuse with **ēgī,** from **agō**)

**éxpleō, explḗre, explḗvī, explḗtum,** *to fill, fill up, complete* (expletive, deplete, replete; cf. **plēnus, pleō,** *to fill*)

**praéstō, praestā́re, praéstitī, praéstitum,** *to excel; exhibit, show, offer, supply, furnish* (presto; **prae + stō,** lit. "to stand in front of")

**táceō, tacḗre, tácuī, tácitum,** *to be silent, leave unmentioned* (tacit, taciturn, taciturnity, reticence, reticent)

# LĒCTIŌ ET TRĀNSLĀTIŌ

After memorizing the new paradigms and vocabulary and testing your mastery with some of the Self-Tutorial Exercises, scan the following readings for all present subjunctive verbs, identifying which are jussive and which are in purpose clauses. Before translating each sentence and passage, read aloud for comprehension.

## EXERCITĀTIŌNĒS

1. Auctor sapiēns et dīligēns turpia vītet et tantum plūra bona probet.
2. Itaque prō patriā etiam maiōra meliōraque nunc faciāmus.
3. Nepōs tuus ā mēnsā discēdat nē ista verba acerba audiat.
4. Nē imperātor superbus crēdat sē esse fēlīciōrem quam virum humillimum.
5. Quisque petit quam fēlīcissimum et urbānissimum modum vītae.
6. Quīdam dēlectātiōnēs et beneficia aliīs praestant ut beneficia similia recipiant.
7. Multī medicī lūcem sōlis fuisse prīmum remedium putant.
8. Imperium ducī potentiōrī dabunt ut hostēs ācerrimōs āvertat.
9. Hīs verbīs trīstibus nūntiātīs, pars hostium duōs prīncipēs suōs relīquit.
10. Maiōrēs putābant deōs superōs habēre corpora hūmāna pulcherrima et fortissima.
11. Uxor pudīca eius haec decem ūtilissima tum probāvit.

12. Let him not think that those dissimilar laws are worse than the others (translate with and without **quam**).
13. They will send only twenty men to do this very easy thing in the forum.
14. They said: "Let us call the arrogant emperor a most illustrious man in order not to be expelled from the country."
15. Therefore, let them not order this very wise and very good woman to depart from the dinner.

## SENTENTIAE ANTĪQVAE

1. Ratiō dūcat, nōn fortūna. (*Livy.)
2. Arma togae cēdant. (Cicero.—**toga, -ae,** f., *toga,* the garment of peace and civil, in contrast to military, activity.)
3. Ex urbe nunc discēde nē metū et armīs opprimar. (Cicero.)
4. Nunc ūna rēs mihi prōtinus est facienda ut maximum ōtium et sōlācium habeam. (Terence.)
5. Rapiāmus, amīcī, occāsiōnem dē diē. (*Horace.)
6. Corpus enim somnō et multīs aliīs rēbus eget ut valeat; animus ipse sē alit. (Seneca.)
7. Quī beneficium dedit, taceat; nārret quī accēpit. (*Seneca.)
8. Dē mortuīs nihil nisi bonum dīcāmus. (Diogenes Laertius.)
9. Parēns ipse nec habeat vitia nec toleret. (Quintilian.)
10. In hāc rē ratiō habenda est ut monitiō acerbitāte careat. (Cicero.—**monitiō, -ōnis,** f., *admonition;* "admonish."—**acerbitās, -tātis,** f., noun of **acerbus;** "acerbity.")
11. Fēminae ad lūdōs semper veniunt ut videant—et ut ipsae videantur. (Ovid.)
12. Arma virumque canō quī prīmus ā lītoribus Trōiae ad Italiam vēnit. (Vergil.—**canō, -ere,** *to sing about;* "cantor," "accent.")

**Please Remove My Name from Your Mailing List!**

Cūr nōn mitto meōs tibi, Pontiliāne, libellōs?—
    nē mihi tū mittās, Pontiliāne, tuōs!

*Martial *Epig.* 7.3: Roman poets, just like American writers, would often exchange copies of their works with one another; but Pontilianus' poems are not Martial's cup of tea! Meter: elegiac couplet.—**mitto:** as you have seen before, final -ō was often shortened in verse.—**nē . . . mittās:** not jussive, but purpose, following the implied statement, "I don't send mine to you. . . .")

*QVAESTIŌ:* How do word order and the use of pronouns underscore the insult in line 2?

## To Have Friends One Must Be Friendly

> Ut praestem Pyladēn, aliquis mihi praestet Orestēn.
> Hoc nōn fit verbīs, Mārce; ut amēris, amā.

*Martial *Epig.* 6.11.9–10: Orestes, son of Agamemon, and Pylades, son of King Strophius of Phocis and Agamemnon's sister Anaxibia, were in Greek myth exemplars of close friendship; meter: elegiac couplet. —**Pyladēn . . . Orestēn:** both are Gk. acc. sg. forms.—**fit:** *is accomplished;* "fiat.")

*QVAESTIŌ:* Explain how the second line's **ut**-clause + imperat. parallels both the thought and the syntax of the first line.

## The Days of the Week

Diēs dictī sunt ā deīs quōrum nōmina Rōmānī quibusdam stēllīs dēdicāvērunt. Prīmum enim diem ā Sōle appellāvērunt, quī prīnceps est omnium stēllārum ut īdem diēs est prae omnibus diēbus aliīs. Secundum diem ā Lūnā appellāvērunt, quae ex Sōle lūcem accēpit. Tertium ab stēllā Mārtis, quae Vesper appellātur. Quārtum ab stēllā Mercuriī. Quīntum ab stēllā Iovis. Sextum ā Veneris stēllā, quam Lūciferum appellāvērunt, quae inter omnēs stēllās plūrimum lūcis habet. Septimum ab stēllā Sāturnī, quae dīcitur cursum suum trīgintā annīs explēre. Apud Hebraeōs autem diēs prīmus dīcitur ūnus diēs sabbatī, quī inter nōs diēs dominicus est, quem pāgānī Sōlī dēdicāvērunt. Sabbatum autem septimus diēs ā dominicō est, quem pāgānī Sāturnō dēdicāvērunt.

Isidore *Orig.* 5.30: The Spanish writer (Saint) Isidore, Bishop of Seville (ca. A.D. 560–636), was a polymath best known for his 20-volume work, the **Orīginēs** or **Etymologiae,** which he intended to be an encyclopedia of all that was worth knowing about classical antiquity; in this passage, which you should compare with the graffito from 1st-cent. Pompeii below, he discusses the Greco-Roman names for the days of the weeks, briefly comparing the Judaeo-Christian system. The early Germanic calendar adopted the Roman system but substituted the names of Germanic deities (including Tiu, Woden, Thor, and Freya) for all but Saturday.—**Mārs, Mārtis,** m.; "March," "martial."—**Mercurius, -ī,** m.; "mercury," "mercurial."—**Iuppiter, Iovis,** m.; "jovial," "Jovian."—**Venus, Veneris,** f.; "Venusian," "venereal."—**Lūciferus, -ī,** m., *Lucifer, light-bringer, the morning star;* "luciferous."—**Sāturnus, -ī,** m.; "Saturday," "saturnine."—**trīgintā:** *30.*—**Hebraeus, -ī,** m., *Hebrew.*—**sabbatum, -ī,** n., *the Sabbath;* **ūnus diēs sabbatī:** i.e., *the first day after the Sabbath.*—**dominicus, -a, -um,** *of the Lord, the Lord's;* "Dominic," "dominican."—**pāgānus, -ī,** m., *rustic, peasant; heathen, pagan;* "paganism."

*QVAESTIŌNĒS:* What three types of celestial bodies does the word **stēlla** refer to here? To what group specifically does Isidore refer in the phrase **inter nōs**?

## SCRĪPTA IN PARIETIBVS

Diēs:
Sat(urnī)
Sōl(is)
Lūn(ae)
Mār(tis)
Mer(curiī)
Iov(is)
Ven(eris)

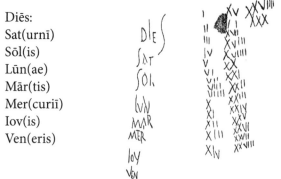

*CIL* 4.8863: The columns reproduced in this drawing of a graffito from a Pompeian shop in Reg. III, Ins. 4, are four from a total of eight in which the writer included the different weekly market-days (**nūndinae**) for several neighboring towns along with some other specific dates, listing the names of the days of the week, as seen here, and numbering the days of the month from 1–30 (I–XXX). The Romans typically abbreviated the days of the week (and the months), just as we do; the numerals employed here include the common variants VIIII for IX, XVIIII for XIX, and XXVIIII for XXIX (see the table of numerals in the **Summārium Fōrmārum**).

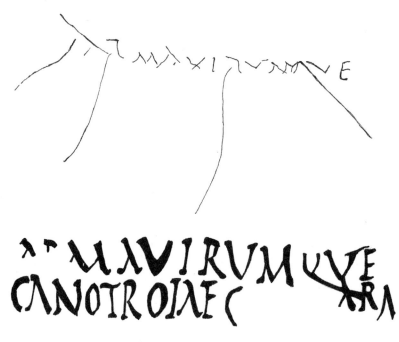

*CIL* 4.5002 and 7131: A wonderful testimony to the literacy, and literary interests, of ancient Pompeians, snippets from some of the already "classic" Roman poets were often written on walls by enthusiasts or students, including these two excerpts from the opening verse of Vergil's *Aeneid* (cf. **S.A.** 12 above), a line that appears, in whole or part, in more than a dozen other graffiti throughout the city. The graffito above (top), from the atrium of the House of Marcus Casellius Marcellus (in Reg. IX, Ins. 2), has only the first two words of the verse, **ARMA VIRVMQVE,** while the other inscription, a dipinto painted in the middle of an electoral programma on the front of the shop of the black-smith (**ferrārius**) Tyrsus on the Via dell'Abbondanza (Reg. I, Ins. 6), continues with **CANO TROIAE** and a curving stroke that formed the beginning of the **Q** in the line's next word, **QVI** (a stray **ARM** also appears beneath the **-QVE**—another, aborted attempt at beginning the verse?); the original poetic word order seen in the dipinto, **Arma virumque canō Trōiae quī . . . ,** has been simplified in **S.A.** 12, where **Trōiae** is repositioned within the rel. clause to which it belongs syntactically.


## LATĪNA EST GAVDIVM—ET ŪTILIS!

**Salvēte!** Here are some nuggets from the new **Vocābula:** teachers and guardians can serve **in locō parentis; mortuī nōn mordent,** "dead men tell no tales" (lit., *the dead don't bite!*); **occāsiō fūrem facit,** *opportunity makes a thief;* those who know about Watergate will now recognize the etymology of the "expletives deleted" (four-letter words that "fill out" the sentences of vulgar and illiterate folk!); an **ēditiō prīnceps** is a *first edition;* **tacet,** a musical notation calling for a vocalist or instrumentalist to be silent; related to **cursus** is **curriculum,** *running, course, course of action,* hence a résumé provides your **curriculum vītae;** and the motto of New York University (**fīliō meō grātiās!**), a good one for Latin students, is **perstāre et praestāre,** *to persevere and to excel.*

Now let's focus on jussives: first off, I hope that all my students in Wyoming recognized **arma togae cēdant** as their state motto; another motto, with this new verb **cēdere** and an imperative rather than a jussive, is Vergil's **nē cēde malīs,** *yield not to evils;* and Vegetius, an ancient military analyst, has advised us, **quī dēsīderat pācem, praeparet bellum.** Before bidding you farewell, here's a proverb—with both a purpose clause and a jussive—that makes the same point as the Pylades reading above: **ut amīcum habeās, sīs amīcus** (**sīs,** as you'll see in the next chapter, is the subjunctive for **es**), *in order to have a friend, you should be a friend.* By the way, I call first person plural jussives the "salad subjunctives" (remember VENI, VIDI, VEGI?) because they always contain "let us"—a reminder of the salad most ordered by honeymooners, "lettuce alone!" On that note, let us just say: **amīcī amīcaeque meae, semper valeātis!**

# CAPVT XXIX 𝖹𝖹𝖹

# Imperfect Subjunctive; Present and Imperfect Subjunctive of *Sum* and *Possum*; Result Clauses

## GRAMMATICA

### THE IMPERFECT SUBJUNCTIVE

The imperfect subjunctive is easy to recognize and form, consisting of the present active infinitive + the present system personal endings, active and passive, with the -ē- long (except, as usual, before final -**m**, -**r**, and -**t**, and both final and medial -**nt**/-**nt**-). Samples are given in the following paradigms; for complete conjugations, see the **Summārium Fōrmārum**, p. 502–03:

| | | | | |
|---|---|---|---|---|
| 1. laudā́re-m | laudā́re-r | ágerer | audī́rem | cáperem |
| 2. laudā́rē-s | laudā́rē-ris | agerḗris | audī́rēs | cáperēs |
| 3. laudā́re-t | laudā́rḗ-tur | agerḗtur | audī́ret | cáperet |
| 1. laudārḗ-mus | laudārḗ-mur | agerḗmur | audīrḗmus | caperḗmus |
| 2. laudārḗ-tis | laudārḗ-minī | agerḗminī | audīrḗtis | caperḗtis |
| 3. laudā́re-nt | laudārḗ-ntur | ageréntur | audī́rent | cáperent |

### PRESENT AND IMPERFECT SUBJUNCTIVE OF *Sum* AND *Possum*

The present subjunctives of **sum** and **possum** are irregular but follow a consistent pattern; the imperfect subjunctives, however, follow the rule given above:

| Present Subjunctive | | Imperfect Subjunctive | |
|---|---|---|---|
| 1. sim | póssim | éssem | póssem |
| 2. sīs | póssīs | éssēs | póssēs |
| 3. sit | póssit | ésset | pósset |
| 1. sĩmus | possĩmus | essẽmus | possẽmus |
| 2. sĩtis | possĩtis | essẽtis | possẽtis |
| 3. sint | póssint | éssent | póssent |

### Usage and Translation of the Imperfect Subjunctive

The imperfect subjunctive is used in a variety of clause types, when the main verb is a past tense. As for all subjunctives, the translation depends upon the type of clause, but auxiliaries sometimes used with the imperfect include "were," "would," and, in purpose clauses, "might" (vs. "may" for the present tense). Study these sample sentences containing purpose clauses:

> **Hoc dīcit *ut* eōs *iuvet*.**
> *He says this (in order) to help them.*
> *so that he **may** help them.*

> **Hoc dīxit (dīcēbat) *ut* eōs *iuvāret*.**
> *He said (kept saying) this (in order) to help them.*
> *so that he **might** help them.*

> **Hoc facit *nē* urbs *capiātur*.**
> *He does this so that the city **may** not be captured.*

> **Hoc fēcit (faciēbat) *nē* urbs *caperētur*.**
> *He did (was doing) this so that the city **might** not be captured.*

Remember that in order to master the subjunctive (notice the purpose clause?) you must (1) learn a definition for each clause type, (2) be able to recognize each, and (3) know the proper translation for the subjunctive verb in each type. Keep these three points in mind—*definition, recognition, translation*—as you proceed to the following discussion of result clauses and to the subsequent chapters in this book.

## RESULT CLAUSES

*Definition:* A RESULT CLAUSE is a subordinate clause that shows the result of the action in the main clause; the purpose clause answers the question "*why* is (was) it being done?", while the result clause answers the question "what is (was) the *outcome?*" Examples in English are: "it is raining so hard *that the streets are flooding*" and "she studied Latin so diligently *that she knew it like a Roman*." Notice that English introduces such clauses with "that" and uses the indicative mood, generally with *no auxiliary* (i.e., neither *may* nor *might*).

*Recognition:* Latin result clauses begin with **ut** and contain (usually at the end) a subjunctive verb. The result clause can be easily recognized, and distinguished from a purpose clause, by the sense and context and also by the fact that the main clause usually contains an adverb (**ita, tam, sīc,** *so*) or adjective (**tantus,** *so much, so great*) indicating degree and signaling that a result clause is to follow. Moreover, if the clause describes a negative result, it is still introduced by **ut** but contains a negative word such as **nōn, nihil, nēmō, numquam** or **nūllus** (vs. a negative purpose clause, which is introduced by **nē**).

*Translation:* In result clauses (vs. purpose clauses) the subjunctive verb is regularly translated *as an indicative,* without an auxiliary; "may" or "might" are used only in those instances where a potential or ideal result, rather than an actual result, is being described. Analyze these examples:

> *Tanta* fēcit *ut* urbem *servāret.* He did **such great** things **that** he **saved** the city. (Result)
> *Haec* fēcit *ut* urbem *servāret.* He did these things **so that** he **might save** the city. (Purpose)

> *Tam* strēnuē labōrat *ut* multa *perficiat.* He works **so** energetically **that** he **accomplishes** many things. (Result)
> Strēnuē labōrat *ut* multa *perficiat.* He works energetically **so that** he **may accomplish** many things. (Purpose)

> Hoc *tantā* benevolentiā dīxit *ut* eōs *nōn offenderet.* He said this with **such great** kindness **that** he **did not offend** them. (Result)
> Hoc magnā benevolentiā dīxit *nē* eōs *offenderet.* He said this with great kindness **in order that** he **might not offend** them. (Purpose)

> Saltus erat angustus, *ut* paucī Graecī multōs mīlitēs prohibēre *possent.* The pass was narrow, **so that** a few Greeks **were able** to stop many soldiers. (Result)

Note that in this last example there is no "signal word" such as **ita** or **tam** in the main clause, but it is clear from the context that the **ut** clause indicates the result, not the purpose, of the narrowness of the pass.

# VOCĀBVLA

Nothing too unusual in this new list: **moenia** was regularly employed only in the plural, just as when speaking in English of defensive fortifications, we refer to a city's "walls" not "wall"; one word for a wall of a house, by the way, is **mūrus,** which gives us "mural." Practice conjugating a few of the verbs in this list in the newly in-troduced imperfect subjunctive–and why not the present subjunctive too!

**fắtum, fắtī,** n., *fate; death* (fatal, fatalism, fatality, fateful, fairy; **fābula** and **fāma** are from the same stem)

**ingénium, ingéniī,** n., *nature, innate talent* (ingenuity, genius, genial, congenial; cf. **genus, gēns,** and **gignere,** *to create, give birth to*)

**moénia, moénium,** n. pl., *walls of a city* (munitions, ammunition; cf. **mūnīre,** *to fortify*)

**nắta, nắtae,** f., *daughter* (prenatal, postnatal, Natalie; cf. **nātūra**)

**ōsculum, ōsculī,** n., *kiss* (osculate, osculation; cf. **ōs**)

**sīdus, sīderis,** n., *constellation, star* (sidereal, consider, desire)

**dígnus, dígna, dígnum** + abl., *worthy, worthy of* (dignify, dignity from **dignitās,** indignation from **indignātiō,** deign, disdain, dainty)

**dūrus, dūra, dūrum,** *hard, harsh, rough, stern, unfeeling, hardy, difficult* (dour, du-rable, duration, during, duress, endure, obdurate)

**tántus, tánta, tántum,** *so large, so great, of such a size* (tantamount; do not confuse with the adv. **tantum,** *only*)

**dēnique,** adv., *at last, finally, lastly*

**íta,** adv. used with adjs., verbs, and advs., *so, thus*

**quídem,** postpositive adv., *indeed, certainly, at least, even;* **nē . . . quídem,** *not . . . even* (do not confuse with **quīdam,** *certain*)

**sīc,** adv. most commonly with verbs, *so, thus* (sic)

**tam,** adv. with adjs. and advs., *so, to such a degree;* **tam . . . quam,** *so . . . as;* **tam-quam,** *as it were, as if, so to speak*

**vḗrō,** adv., *in truth, indeed, to be sure, however* (very, verily, etc.; cf. **vērus, vēritās**)

**cóndō, cóndere, cóndidī, cónditum,** *to put together* or *into, store; found, establish* (= **con-** + **dō, dare;** condiment, abscond, recondite)

**conténdō, conténdere, conténdī, conténtum,** *to strive, struggle, contend; hasten* (contender, contentious; cf. **tendō,** *to stretch, extend*)

**móliō, mollīre, mollīvī, mollītum,** *to soften; make calm* or *less hostile* (mollescent, mollify, mollusk, emollient; cf. **mollis,** *soft, mild*)

**púgnō, pugnắre, pugnắvī, pugnắtum,** *to fight* (pugnacious, impugn, pugilist)

**respóndeō, respondḗre, respóndī, respōnsum,** *to answer* (respond, response, re-sponsive, responsibility, correspond)

**súrgō, súrgere, surrḗxī, surrḗctum,** *to get up, arise* (surge, resurgent, resurrection, insurgent, insurrection, source, resource)

# LĒCTIŌ ET TRĀNSLĀTIŌ

The challenge in these readings is to distinguish between purpose and result clauses, both of which may be introduced by **ut:** if you see **tam, tantus, ita,** or **sīc** in the main clause, the **ut**-clause indicates result; likewise an **ut**-clause that contains **nōn, numquam,** or **nēmō** is a negative result clause, whereas negative purpose clauses are introduced by **nē**. Remember that the verb in a result clause is generally translated without "may" or "might," which are commonly used in English to signal purpose rather than result.

## EXERCITĀTIŌNĒS

1. Prīnceps arma meliōra in manibus mīlitum posuit, ut hostēs terrērent.
2. Hostēs quidem negāvērunt sē arma dissimilia habēre.
3. Pars mīlitum lūcem diēī vītāvit nē hīc vidērentur.
4. Sōlem prīmam lūcem caelī superī, lūnam prīmam lūcem vesperī, et stēllās oculōs noctis appellābant.
5. Illī adulēscentēs sapientiae dēnique cēdant ut fēlīciōrēs hīs sint.
6. Sapientēs putant beneficia esse potentiōra quam verba acerba et turpia.
7. Quīdam magister verba tam dūra discipulīs dīxit ut essent trīstēs atque discēderent.
8. Respondērunt auctōrem hōrum novem remediōrum esse medicam potentissimam.
9. Nihil vērō tam facile est ut sine labōre id facere possīmus.
10. Prō labōre studiōque patria nostra nōbīs plūrimās occāsiōnēs bonās praestat.
11. Parentēs plūrima ōscula dedērunt nātae pulcherrimae gracilīque, in quā maximam dēlectātiōnem semper inveniēbant.
12. The words of the philosopher were very difficult, so that those listening were unable to learn them.
13. The two women wished to understand these things so that they might not live base lives.
14. Those four wives were so pleasant that they received very many kindnesses.
15. He said that the writer's third poem was so beautiful that it delighted the minds of thousands of citizens.

## SENTENTIAE ANTĪQUAE

1. Omnia vincit Amor; et nōs cēdāmus Amōrī. (Vergil.)
2. Urbem clārissimam condidī; mea moenia vīdī; explēvī cursum quem Fāta dederant. (Vergil.)
3. Ita dūrus erās ut neque amōre neque precibus mollīrī possēs. (Terence.—**prex, precis,** f., *prayer;* "precarious," "imprecation," "pray.")
4. Nēmō quidem tam ferōx est ut nōn mollīrī possit, cultūrā datā. (Horace.—**cultūra, -ae,** f.; "agriculture," "horticulture.")
5. Difficile est saturam nōn scrībere; nam quis est tam patiēns malae urbis ut sē teneat? (Juvenal.—**patiēns,** gen. **-entis,** *tolerant of;* "patience.")

6. Fuit quondam in hāc rē pūblicā tanta virtūs ut virī fortēs cīvem perniciōsum ācriōribus poenīs quam acerbissimum hostem reprimerent. (Cicero.—**perniciōsus, -a, -um,** *pernicious.*—**re-primō,** cf. **opprimō;** "repress," "reprimand.")

7. Ita praeclāra est recuperātiō lībertātis ut nē mors quidem in hāc rē sit fugienda. (Cicero.—**recuperātiō, -ōnis,** f., *recovery;* "recuperate.")

8. Nē ratiōnēs meōrum perīculōrum ūtilitātem reī pūblicae vincant. (Cicero.—**ūtilitās, -tātis,** f., *advantage;* cf. **ūtilis;** "utilitarian," "utility.")

9. Eō tempore Athēniēnsēs tantam virtūtem praestitērunt ut decemplicem numerum hostium superārent, et hōs sīc perterruērunt ut in Asiam refugerent. (Nepos.—**Athēniēnsēs, -ium,** *Athenians.*—**decemplex, -plicis,** *tenfold.*—**per +** **terreō.**)

10. Ōrātor exemplum dignum petat ab Dēmosthene illō, in quō tantum studium tantusque labor fuisse dīcuntur ut impedīmenta nātūrae dīligentiā industriāque superāret. (Cicero.—**exemplum, -ī,** n., *example;* "exemplify," "sample."— **Dēmosthenēs, -thenis,** m., a famous Greek orator.—**impedīmentum, -ī,** n.; "impede."—**dīligentia, -ae,** f.; "diligently."—**industria, -ae,** f.; "industrious.")

*Marble head of Demosthenes*
*Roman copy of a 3rd cent.* B.C. *bronze*
*statue by Polyeuktos*
*Louvre, Paris, France*

11. Praecepta tua sint brevia ut cito mentēs plūrium discipulōrum ea discant teneantque memoriā fidēlī. (Horace.—**praeceptum, -ī,** n., *precept;* "preceptor.")

12. Nihil tam difficile est ut nōn possit studiō invēstīgārī. (Terence.—**invēstīgāre,** *to track down, investigate;* "investigation," "vestige.")

13. Bellum autem ita suscipiātur ut nihil nisi pāx quaesīta esse videātur. (Cicero.)

14. Tanta est vīs probitātis ut eam etiam in hoste dīligāmus. (Cicero.)

### How Many Kisses Are Enough?

Quaeris, Lesbia, quot bāsia tua sint mihi satis? Tam multa bāsia quam magnus numerus Libyssae harēnae aut quam sīdera multa quae, ubi tacet nox, furtīvōs amōrēs hominum vident—tam bāsia multa (nēmō numerum scīre potest) sunt satis Catullō īnsānō!

Catullus *Carm.* 7: In an earlier poem (*Carm.* 5, which you will read in its entirety in Capvt XXXI) Catullus had begged Lesbia for hundreds and thousands of kisses and a life immersed in love; in this prose adaptation of *Carm.* 7 (for verse excerpts from the poem, see **Locī Im.** II) the poet imagines his mistress cooly asking just *exactly* how many kisses he wants.—**quot . . . sint:** an IND. QUEST., a construction formally introduced in Capvt XXX but easily understood here.—**Libyssus, -a, -um,** *Libyan, African.*—**harēna, -ae,** f., *sand,* here = *grains of sand;* "arena."—**furtīvus, -a, -um,** *stolen, secret;* "furtive."—**īnsānus, -a, -um:** = Eng.; "insanity."

*QVAESTIŌNĒS:* Catullus' response is as calculated as Lesbia's question; how are his analogies alike and yet different?—try to visualize them both—how do they look different and, in a sense, even "feel" different?

### The Nervousness of Even a Great Orator

Ego dehinc ut respondērem surrēxī. Quā sollicitūdine animī surgēbam—dī immortālēs—et quō timōre! Semper quidem magnō cum metū incipiō dīcere. Quotiēnscumque dīcō, mihi videor in iūdicium venīre nōn sōlum ingeniī sed etiam virtūtis atque officiī. Tum vērō ita sum perturbātus ut omnia timērem. Dēnique mē collēgī et sīc pugnāvī, sīc omnī ratiōne contendī ut nēmō mē neglēxisse illam causam putāret.

Cicero *Cluent.* 51: Cicero's speech **Prō Cluentiō,** *In Defense of Cluentius,* resulted in the acquittal of a man accused by his mother of poisoning his step-father; this passage is interesting, as it shows the trepidation that can plague even the greatest of public speakers.—**sollicitūdō, -dinis,** f., *anxiety;* "solicit," "solicitous."—**quotiēnscumque,** adv., *as often as, whenever.*—**ingeniī . . . virtūtis . . . officiī:** all modify **iūdicium.**—**perturbāre,** *to disturb, confuse;* "perturbation," "imperturbable."—**colligō, -ere, -lēgī, -lēctum,** *to gather, collect, control;* "collection," "recollect."

*QVAESTIŌNĒS:* Cicero's concern over public opinion was a great source of anxiety; explain in your own words the three areas in which he feared he might be judged lacking. By what multiple means did he overcome his concerns on this occasion and win his case?

### You're All Just Wonderful!

Nē laudet dignōs, laudat Callistratus omnēs:
cui malus est nēmō, quis bonus esse potest?

*Martial *Epig.* 12.80: meter: elegiac couplet.—**dignōs:** i.e., *only the deserving.*—**Callistratus:** a Greek name, meant to suggest perhaps a former slave.—**quis . . . potest:** supply **eī,** antecedent of **cui,** *to a man to whom.*

*QVAESTIŌNĒS:* Explain the ethical implications of the question Martial poses in line 2; why would befriending someone like Callistratus ultimately be meaningless?—have you ever known such a person?

## SCRĪPTA IN PARIETIBVS

Fēlīcem Aufidium, fēlīcem, semper deus faciat!

*CIL* 4.6815: If this prayer, written with a flourish between two doors of an apartment house (Reg. VI, Ins. 16), achieved its purpose, Aufidius was a very lucky guy!—**Fēlīcem:** repeated for emphasis, a rhetorical device known as ANAPHORA; or, as some editors suppose, the second occurrence of the word may be the man's cognomen, i.e., his name was Aufidius Felix and the writer is engaging in a bit of name-play, a favorite type of Roman humor.

## ETYMOLOGIA

The adverbial ending -**mente** or -**ment** so common in Romance languages derives from Lat. **mente** (abl. of **mēns**) used originally as an abl. of manner but reduced to an adverbial suffix. The following examples are based on Lat. adjectives which have already appeared in the vocabularies:

| Latin Words | It. Adverb | Sp. Adverb | Fr. Adverb |
|---|---|---|---|
| dūrā mente | duramente | duramente | durement |
| clārā mente | chiaramente | claramente | clairement |
| sōlā mente | solamente | solamente | seulement |
| certā mente | certamente | certamente | certainement |
| dulcī mente | dolcemente | dulcemente | doucement |
| brevī mente | brevemente | brevemente | brèvement |
| facilī mente | facilmente | fácilmente | facilement |

Cf. Port. **duramente, claramente, somente, certamente, docemente, brevemente, facilmente;** Old Occ. **solamęn, certamęn, breumęn.**

## LATĪNA EST GAVDIVM—ET V̄TILIS!

**Salvē! Sunt multae dēlectātiōnēs in novō vocābulāriō nostrō:** e.g., there's Virginia's state motto, **sīc semper tyrannīs,** *thus always to tyrants* (i.e., death!); and **ingenium,** which really means *something inborn,* like a Roman man's **genius** (his inborn guardian spirit, counterpart to the woman's **iūnō,** magnified and deified in the goddess Juno); the connection of **moenia** and **mūnīre** reminds us that fortification walls were the ancients' best munitions, and there's the old proverb **praemonitus, praemūnītus,** *forewarned (is) fore-armed;* **sīc** is an editor's annotation, meaning *thus (it was written),* and used to identify an error or peculiarity in a text being quoted, and it's also the parent of It. **sì,** Sp. **sí,** Port. **sim,** Fr. **si,** Old Occ. **si,** all meaning *yes.* And here's a brief "kissertation" on the nicest word in this new list: **ōsculum** was the native word for *kiss* (vs. **bāsium,** which the poet Catullus seems to have introduced into the language from the north); it is actually the diminutive of **ōs, ōris** and so means literally *little mouth*—which perhaps proves the Romans "puckered up" when they smooched! Catullus, by the way, loved to invent words, and one was **bāsiātiō,** *kissification* or *smooch-making* ("smooch," by the way, is not Latinate, alas, but Germanic and related to "smack," as in "to smack one's lips," which one might do before enjoying either a kiss or a slice of toast with "Smucker's"!). **Rīdēte et valēte!**

# Perfect and Pluperfect Subjunctive; Indirect Questions; Sequence of Tenses

## GRAMMATICA

### PERFECT AND PLUPERFECT SUBJUNCTIVE

Perfect system subjunctives, like perfect system indicatives, all follow the same basic rules of formation, regardless of the conjugation to which they belong. For the perfect subjunctive active, add -erī- + the personal endings to the perfect stem (shortening the -i- before -m, -t, and -nt); for the pluperfect active, add -issē- + the personal endings to the perfect stem (shortening the -e- before -m, etc.). For the passives, substitute the subjunctives **sim** and **essem** for the equivalent indicatives **sum** and **eram**. The forms of **laudō** are shown below; those for the other model verbs (which follow the very same pattern) are provided in the Appendix (p. 502–04).

### Perfect Subjunctive Active

Sg. laudáv-erim, laudáverīs, laudáverit
Pl. laudāverímus, laudāverítis, laudáverint

Note that these forms are identical to those of the future perfect indicative except for the first person singular and the long -ī- in certain of the subjunctive forms; the identical forms can be distinguished as indicative or subjunctive by sentence context.

### Pluperfect Subjunctive Active

Sg. laudáv-íssem, laudavíssēs, laudavísset
Pl. laudāvissḗmus, laudāvissḗtis, laudavíssent

These forms resemble the perfect active infinitive, **laudāvisse**, + the endings (with the -ē- long except before -**m**, etc.; cf. the imperfect subjunctive, which resembles the present active infinitive + endings).

### Perfect Subjunctive Passive

Sg.    laudātus, -a, -um sim, laudātus sīs, laudātus sit
Pl.    laudātī, -ae, -a sīmus, laudātī sītis, laudātī sint

### Pluperfect Subjunctive Passive

Sg.    laudātus, -a, -um éssem, laudātus éssēs, laudātus ésset
Pl.    laudātī, -ae, -a essēmus, laudātī essētis, laudātī éssent

### Translation and Usage

As with the present and imperfect subjunctives, the perfect and pluperfect are employed in a variety of clauses (in accordance with the sequence of tenses discussed below) and with a variety of translations. Just as "may" and "might/would" are *sometimes* used in translating the present and imperfect, respectively, so "may have" and "might have/would have" are *sometimes* employed with the perfect and pluperfect; likewise, they are often translated as simple indicatives: the best procedure is to learn the rules for translation of each clause type.

### Synopsis

You can now conjugate a verb fully in all of its finite forms; following is a complete third person singular synopsis of **agō, agere, ēgī, āctum**:

### Indicative Mood

|       | Pres.   | Fut.    | Imperf.   | Perf.      | Fut.Perf.   | Pluperf.    |
|-------|---------|---------|-----------|------------|-------------|-------------|
| Act.  | ágit    | áget    | agḗbat    | ḗgit       | ḗgerit      | ḗgerat      |
| Pass. | ágitur  | agḗtur  | agēbātur  | áctus est  | áctus érit  | áctus érat  |

### Subjunctive Mood

|       | Pres.   | Fut.    | Imperf.   | Perf.      | Fut.Perf.   | Pluperf.    |
|-------|---------|---------|-----------|------------|-------------|-------------|
| Act.  | ágat    | ——      | ágeret    | ḗgerit     | ——          | ēgísset     |
| Pass. | agátur  | ——      | agerétur  | áctus sit  | ——          | áctus ésset |

## INDIRECT QUESTIONS

*Definition:* An **INDIRECT QUESTION** is a subordinate clause which reports a question indirectly, not via a direct quotation (e.g., "they asked what Gaius was doing" vs. "they asked, 'What is Gaius doing?'"); as such, it is comparable in concept to an indirect statement, which reports indirectly, not a question, but a statement (Capvt XXV). *Recognition:* The indirect question uses a subjunctive verb (not an infinitive, like an indirect statement) and is distinguished from other subjunctive clauses as it is introduced by an interrogative word such as **quis/quid, quī/quae/quod** (the interrogative adjective), **quam, quandō, cūr, ubi, unde, uter, utrum . . . an** (*whether . . . or*), **-ne** (attached to the clause's first word, = *whether*), etc.; the verb in the main clause is ordinarily a verb of speech, mental activity, or sense perception (including many of the same verbs that introduce indirect statements, listed in Capvt XXV). *Translation:* The subjunctive verb in an indirect question is usually translated as an indicative in the same tense, i.e., without any auxiliary such as "may" or "might." Compare the first three examples below, which are direct questions, with the next three, which contain indirect questions:

| | |
|---|---|
| **Quid Gāius facit?** | *What is Gaius doing?* |
| **Quid Gāius fēcit?** | *What did Gaius do?* |
| **Quid Gāius faciet?** | *What will Gaius do?* |
| | |
| **Rogant quid Gāius faciat.** | *They ask what Gaius is doing.* |
| **Rogant quid Gāius fēcerit.** | *They ask what Gaius did.* |
| **Rogant quid Gāius factūrus sit.** | *They ask what Gaius will do* (lit., *is about to do*). |

**Factūrus sit** in this last example is a form sometimes called the **FUTURE ACTIVE PERIPHRASTIC**; in the absence of an actual future subjunctive, this combination of a form of **sum** + the future active participle (cf. the passive periphrastic, consisting of **sum** + the future passive participle, Capvt XXIV) was occasionally employed to indicate future time unambiguously in certain types of clauses, including the indirect question. In this last example, if the main verb were a past tense, then (in accordance with the rules for sequence of tenses) the sentence would be **rogāvērunt quid Gaius factūrus esset,** *they asked what Gaius would do (was about to do, was going to do).*

## SEQUENCE OF TENSES

In Latin as in English there is a logical sequence of tenses as the speaker or writer proceeds from a main clause to a subordinate clause. The rule in Latin is simple: a **PRIMARY TENSE** of the indicative must be followed by a primary tense of the subjunctive, and an indicative **HISTORICAL** (or **SECONDARY**) **TENSE** must be followed by a historical subjunctive tense, as illustrated in the following chart:

| Group | Main Verb | Subordinate Subjunctive |
|-------|-----------|-------------------------|
| Primary | Pres. or Fut. | { Present (= action *at same time* or *after*) <br> { Perfect (= action *before*) |
| Historical | Past Tenses | { Imperfect (= action *at same time* or *after*) <br> { Pluperfect (= action *before*) |

After a primary main verb the *present* subjunctive indicates action occurring *at the same time* as that of the main verb or *after* that of the main verb; the *perfect* subjunctive indicates action which occurred *before* that of the main verb. Similarly after a historical main verb the *imperfect* subjunctive indicates action occurring *at the same time* as that of the main verb or *after* that of the main verb, and the *pluperfect* subjunctive indicates action *before* that of the main verb. The primary tenses of the indicative, the present and future, both indicate *incomplete* actions (i.e., actions now going on, in the present, or only to be begun in the future), while the historical tenses, as the term implies, refer to past actions.

The rules for the sequence of tenses operate in purpose clauses, result clauses, indirect questions, and similar constructions to be introduced in subsequent chapters; analyze carefully the sequencing in each of the following examples:

Id *facit* (faciet) ut mē iuvet. *He does (will do) it to help me.*
Id *fēcit* (faciēbat) ut mē iuvāret. *He did (kept doing) it to help me.*

Tam dūrus *est* ut eum vītem. *He is so harsh that I avoid him.*
Tam dūrus *fuit* (erat) ut eum vītārem. *He was so harsh that I avoided him.*

Rogant, rogābunt—*They ask, will ask*
   quid faciat. *what he is doing.*
   quid fēcerit. *what he did.*
   quid factūrus sit. *what he will (is about to) do.*
Rogāvērunt, rogābant—*They asked, kept asking*
   quid faceret. *what he was doing.*
   quid fēcisset. *what he had done.*
   quid factūrus esset. *what he would (was about to) do.*

There are two common exceptions to the rules for sequence of tenses: a HISTORICAL PRESENT main verb (a present tense used for the vivid narration of past events: "I'm sitting in my room last night, when suddenly I hear a knock at the door") often takes a historical sequence subjunctive, and a perfect tense main verb, when focusing on the present consequences of the past action, may be followed by a primary sequence subjunctive (see Exerc. 8 below). Note, too, that since purpose and result clauses logically describe actions that *follow* the actions of the main verb, they do not ordinarily contain perfect or pluperfect tense verbs, which indicate *prior* action.

# VOCĀBVLA

A few unusual items: **cēterī** has only plural forms for the same reason as **paucī**, i.e., because the meaning essentially connotes plurality; **tantus . . . quantus,** when employed together, are known as CORRELATIVE ADJECTIVES, comparable to the correlative conjunctions **et . . . et** and **aut . . . aut;** the verb **cognōscō/nōscō** in the perfect means *I have learned,* and since, once you have learned something, you "know" it, the word's perfect tense is often translated with present force, e.g., **cognōvit** = *she has learned* or *she knows,* and similarly **nōverant** = *they had learned/they knew.* As you learn the verbs in this list, practice conjugating a few of them in the perfect and pluperfect subjunctive, and do a synopsis of one or two as well, then compare your work with the paradigms.

**hónor, honóris,** m., *honor, esteem; public office* (honorable, honorary, honorific, dishonor, honest)

**cēterī, cēterae, cētera,** pl., *the remaining, the rest, the other, all the others;* cf. **alius,** *another, other* (etc. = et cetera)

**quántus, quánta, quántum,** *how large, how great, how much* (quantify, quantity, quantitative, quantum); **tántus . . . quántus,** *just as much (many) . . . as*

**rīdículus, rīdícula, rīdículum,** *laughable, ridiculous* (ridicule; cf. **rīdeō**)

**vívus, víva, vívum,** *alive, living* (vivid, vivify, convivial; cf. **vīvō, vīta**)

**fúrtim,** adv., *stealthily, secretly* (furtively, ferret; cf. **fūrtīvus, -a, -um,** *secret, furtive;* **fūr, fūris,** m./f., *thief* )

**mox,** adv., *soon*

**prímō,** adv., *at first, at the beginning* (cf. **prīmus, -a, -um**)

**repénte,** adv., *suddenly*

**únde,** adv., *whence, from what* or *which place, from which, from whom*

**útrum . . . an,** conj., *whether . . . or*

**bíbō, bíbere, bíbī,** *to drink* (bib, bibulous, imbibe, wine-bibber, beverage)

**cognóscō, cognóscere, cognóvī, cognitum** and (its base form) **nóscō, nóscere, nóvī, nótum,** *to become acquainted with, learn, recognize;* in perf. tenses, *know* (cognizance, cognition, connoisseur, incognito, reconnaissance, reconnoiter, notice, notify, notion, notorious)

**comprehéndō, comprehéndere, comprehéndī, comprehénsum,** *to grasp, seize, arrest; comprehend, understand* (comprehensive, comprehensible)

**cōnsúmō, cōnsúmere, cōnsúmpsī, cōnsúmptum,** *to consume, use up* (consumer, consumption, assume, assumption, presume, presumption, presumptuous, resume, resumption; cf. **sūmere,** *to take*)

**dúbitō, dubitáre, dubitávī, dubitátum,** *to doubt, hesitate* (dubious, dubitable, doubtful, doubtless, indubitable, undoubtedly)

**expónō, expónere, expósuī, expósitum,** *to set forth, explain, expose* (exponent, exposition, expository, expound) mínuō, minúere, mínuī, minútum, *to lessen, diminish* (cf. **minor, minus, minimus;** diminish, diminutive, minuet, minute, minutiae, menu)

rógō, rogáre, rogávī, rogátum, *to ask* (interrogate, abrogate, arrogant, derogatory, prerogative, surrogate)

# LĒCTIŌ ET TRĀNSLĀTIŌ

Before reading the following selections, be sure you have memorized the paradigms and **Vocābula** and assessed your mastery by answering the grammar questions and translating some of the sentences in the Self-Tutorial Exercises for this chapter (p. 436–37); check your answers to the Exercises against the key (p. 471–72), analyze any errors, and review accordingly. Scan through the readings below for all subjunctives verbs and identify the clause type in which each appears; recall that "may" or "might" are commonly employed when translating verbs in purpose clauses into English, but subjunctives in result clauses or indirect questions are usually translated simply as indicatives, without any auxiliary.

## EXERCITĀTIŌNĒS

1. Rogāvit ubi illae duae discipulae dignae haec didicissent.
2. Vidēbit quanta fuerit vīs illōrum verbōrum fēlīcium.
3. Hās īnsidiās repente exposuit nē rēs pūblica opprimerētur.
4. Hī taceant et trēs cēterī expellantur nē occāsiōnem similem habeant.
5. Ita dūrus erat ut beneficia nē parentum quidem comprehendere posset.
6. Cēterī quidem nesciēbant quam ācris esset mēns nātae eōrum.
7. Dēnique prīnceps cognōscet cūr potentior pars mīlitum nōs vītet.
8. Iam cognōvī cūr clāra facta vērō nōn sint facillima.
9. Quīdam auctōrēs appellābant arma optimum remedium malōrum.
10. Mortuīs haec arma mox dēdicēmus nē honōre egeant.
11. Fātō duce, Rōmulus Remusque Rōmam condidērunt; et, Remō necātō, moenia urbis novae cito surrēxērunt.
12. Tell me in what lands liberty is found.
13. We did not know where the sword had finally been put.
14. He does not understand the first book which they wrote about the moon, stars, and constellations.
15. They asked why you could not learn what the rest had done.
16. Let all men now seek better things than money or supreme power so that their souls may be happier.

## SENTENTIAE ANTĪQVAE

1. Nunc vidētis quantum scelus contrā rem pūblicam et lēgēs nostrās vōbīs prōnūntiātum sit. (Cicero.)
2. Quam dulcis sit lībertās vōbīs prōtinus dīcam. (Phaedrus.)
3. Rogābat dēnique cūr umquam ex urbe cessissent. (Horace.)
4. Nunc sciō quid sit amor. (*Vergil.)
5. Videāmus uter hīc in mediō forō plūs scrībere possit. (Horace.)
6. Multī dubitābant quid optimum esset. (*Cicero.)
7. Incipiam expōnere unde nātūra omnēs rēs creet alatque. (Lucretius.)
8. Dulce est vidēre quibus malīs ipse careās. (Lucretius.)
9. Auctōrem Trōiānī bellī relēgī, quī dīcit quid sit pulchrum, quid turpe, quid ūtile, quid nōn. (Horace.—**Trōiānus, -a, -um,** *Trojan.*)
10. Doctōs rogābis quā ratiōne bene agere cursum vītae possīs, utrum virtūtem doctrīna paret an nātūra ingeniumque dent, quid minuat cūrās, quid tē amīcum tibi faciat. (Horace.—**doctrīna, -ae,** f., *teaching;* "doctrine," "indoctrinate.")
11. Istī autem rogant tantum quid habeās, nōn cūr et unde. (Seneca.)
12. Errat, quī fīnem vēsānī quaerit amōris: vērus amor nūllum nōvit habēre modum. (*Propertius.—**vēsānus, -a, -um,** *insane.*)
13. Sed tempus est iam mē discēdere ut cicūtam bibam, et vōs discēdere ut vītam agātis. Utrum autem sit melius, dī immortālēs sciunt; hominem quidem nēminem scīre crēdō. (Cicero.—Socrates' parting words to the jury which had condemned him to death.—**cicūta, -ae,** f., *hemlock;* "cicutoxin."—**nēminem:** = **nūllum.**)

The Death of Socrates. *Charles Alphonse Dufresnoy. Oil on canvas, 17th cent. Galleria Palatina, Palazzo Pitti, Florence, Italy*

### Evidence and Confession

Sit dēnique scrīptum in fronte ūnīus cuiusque quid dē rē pūblicā sentiat; nam rem pūblicam labōribus cōnsiliīsque meīs ex igne atque ferrō ēreptam esse vidētis. Haec iam expōnam breviter ut scīre possītis quā ratiōne comprehēnsa sint. Semper prōvīdī quō modō in tantīs īnsidiīs salvī esse possēmus. Omnēs diēs cōnsūmpsī ut vidērem quid coniūrātī āctūrī essent. Dēnique litterās intercipere potuī quae ad Catilīnam ā Lentulō aliīsque coniūrātīs missae erant. Tum, coniūrātīs comprehēnsīs et senātū convocātō, contendī in senātum, ostendī litterās Lentulō, quaesīvī cognōsceretne signum. Dīxit sē cognōscere; sed prīmō dubitāvit et negāvit sē dē hīs rēbus respōnsūrum esse. Mox autem ostendit quanta esset vīs cōnscientiae; nam repente mollītus est atque omnem rem nārrāvit. Tum cēterī coniūrātī tam fūrtim inter sē aspiciēbant ut nōn ab aliīs indicārī sed indicāre sē ipsī vidērentur.

Cicero *Cat.* 1 and 3: Cicero finally succeeded in forcing Catiline to leave Rome, but some of his henchmen remained in the city and tangible evidence was still needed to prove their guilt; in this selection, adapted from passages in his first and third Catilinarian orations, Cicero shows how he finally obtained that evidence and even extracted a confession from Publius Cornelius Lentulus Sura, a disgraced former consul and Catiline's second in command. Be sure to review the readings and notes on the Catilinarian conspiracy in Capita XI, XIV, and XX; a final reading, "Testimony Against the Conspirators," appears in Capvt XXXVI.—**frōns, frontis,** f., *brow, face;* "frontal," "affront."—**breviter:** adv. of **brevis.**—**prō-videō,** *to fore-see, give attention to;* "provide," "provident."—**intercipiō, -ere, -cēpī, -ceptum,** = Eng.; "interception," "interceptor."—**convocāre,** *to convene;* "convoke," "convocation."—**cognōsceretne:** when introducing an ind. quest., **-ne** = *whether.*—**cōnscientia, -ae,** f., *conscience;* "conscientious," "unconscionable."—**inter sē aspiciō, -ere,** *to glance at each other;* "aspect."—**indicāre,** *to accuse;* "indication," "indicative."—**sē ipsī:** a lit. Eng. translation might produce the unfortunate redundancy *themselves . . . themselves,* but in Lat. of course the words are identical in neither form nor function and would in no way sound odd.

*QVAESTIŌNĒS:* What incriminating evidence had Cicero obtained against the conspirators, and how did it lead to Lentulus' confession?

### A Covered Dish Dinner!

> Mēnsās, Ōle, bonās pōnis, sed pōnis opertās.
> Rīdiculum est: possum sīc ego habēre bonās.

*Martial *Epig.* 10.54: Olus was the sort of stingy host often targeted in Roman satire—one might as well dine at home! Meter: elegiac couplet.—**mēnsās:** here, as often, the word refers not to *tables* but to the *dishes,* i.e., the platters of food, set out on them at dinner.—**opertus, -a, -um,** *concealed, covered;* "coverlet," "covert."—**sīc:** here better rendered *(in) that way,* rather than simply "so" or "thus."—**ego:** i.e., even a "poor" fellow like the speaker could host fancy dinner parties!

*QVAESTIŌNĒS:* Explain exactly what tantalizing circumstance the speaker is complaining about in line 1; how does word order underscore the point in that line, and echo it in the following verse as well?

### A Legacy-hunter's Wish

Nīl mihi dās vīvus; dīcis post fāta datūrum:
    sī nōn es stultus, scīs, Maro, quid cupiam!

*Martial *Epig.* 11.67: The speaker wants something Maro is just dying to give him! For Rome's **captātōrēs,**, see "When I Have . . . Enough," Capvt IX above. Meter: elegiac couplet.—**nīl:** a common variant for **nihil.**—**fāta:** poetic pl. for sg., = **mortem.**—**datūrum:** = **tē datūrum esse.**

*QVAESTIŌNĒS:* What does the speaker want, so that he can get, well, what he wants? Identify the chiasmus in line 1, and explain its purpose.

### Note on a Copy of Catullus' *Carmina*

Tantum magna suō dēbet Vērōna Catullō
    quantum parva suō Mantua Vergiliō.

*Martial *Epig.* 14.195: A gift-note from the **Apophorēta** (see "Message from a Bookcase," in Capvt XIX), and a high compliment to Catullus, who was a favorite of Martial's and a major influence on his epigrams. Meter: elegiac couplet.—**Vērōna . . . Mantua:** Verona and Mantua, both towns in northern Italy (see Map 1), were the birthplaces of Catullus and Vergil respectively.—**magna suō . . . Vērōna Catullō:** this kind of ABAB arrangement (adj. A . . . adj. B . . . noun A . . . noun B), known as **INTERLOCKED WORD ORDER,** is common in Lat. verse.

*QVAESTIŌNĒS:* Comment on the word order in the second verse, and on the parallel structure of the two lines; how is the parallelism suited to the point Martial is making?

## SCRĪPTA IN PARIETIBVS

Sīc [t]i[b]i contingat semper flōrēre, Sabīna,
    contingat fōrmae, sīsque puella diū.

*CIL* 4.9171: This verse graffito, found outside Pompeii's Porta Vesuviana, seems to have been an original composition, addressed by the writer to his girlfriend Sabina (though some scholars see a reference to Poppaea Sabina, wife of the emperor Nero); meter: elegiac couplet.—**contingō, -tingere, -tigī, -tāctum,** *to touch;* + dat. + infin., *fall to one's lot, be granted* (to someone to do something); "contingent," "contact"; **tibi contingat . . . contingat fōrmae** = chiasmus (dative^A-verb^B=verb^B-dative^A).—**flōrēre,** *to flower, blossom; shine, excel;* "floral," "fluorish."

*QVAESTIŌNĒS:* What, specifically, are the writer's wishes for Sabina? What does he mean by **puella** here? The editors of *CIL* considered **fōrmae** an error for **fōrma,** nom.; but, besides the fact that the nom. with its short final syllable would not fit the meter, what other arguments favor the reading **fōrmae**?


## LATĪNA EST GAVDIVM—ET VTILIS!

**Salvēte, amīcī!** This chapter's **Vocābula** list brings a veritable **cēna verbōrum** for your **mēnsa Latīna;** let's start with the main course: the **cursus honōrum,** a familiar phrase in English, was the traditional course of political office-holding in Rome; ordinarily one served first as **quaestor** (a treasury official), then as **praetor** (judge), and only later as **cōnsul.** The consulship was something like our presidency, but the term was one year, and there were two consuls, each with veto power over the other (Cicero, as you recall, was one of the consuls in 63 B.C., when he uncovered the Catilinarian conspiracy).

Now for the **mēnsa secunda:** first, an old proverb that will serve you near as well as **carpe diem: occāsiōnem cognōsce!** And here's another that may save you from temptation to even the slightest of crimes: **nēmō repente fuit turpissimus,** *no one was ever suddenly most vicious* (Juvenal 2.83: the satirist meant that even the worst criminals attained that status through the gradual accumulation of guilty acts). An honorary degree is granted **honōris causā; honōrēs mūtant mōrēs** is an ancient truism; from **cēterī,** besides **et cētera**/*etc.,* is **cētera dēsunt,** *the rest is lacking,* an editorial notation for missing sections of a text; from **quantus** comes a large quantity of phrases, one of which should be sufficient here, **quantum satis,** *as much as suffices* (if you are not satisfied, you'll find more **quantum** phrases in Capita XXXII and XXXIV); and when day is done you can shout **mox nox, in rem,** *soon ('twill be) night, (let's get down) to business.* **Valēte!**

# CAPVT XXXI ▣▣▣

# *Cum* Clauses; *Ferō*

## GRAMMATICA

### *Cum* CLAUSES

You are already familiar with the use of **cum** as a preposition meaning "with." The word can also serve as a conjunction, meaning *when, since,* or *although* and introducing a subordinate CUM CLAUSE that describes an action connected in one way or another with the main clause. Sometimes the verb employed is indicative, especially when describing the precise time of an action. In these so-called CUM TEMPORAL CLAUSES, **cum** is translated "when" (or "while"); **tum** is occasionally found in the main clause, and **cum . . . tum** together may be translated "not only . . . but also":

> **Cum eum vidēbis, eum cognōscēs.** *When you (will) see him* [i.e., at that very moment], *you will recognize him.*

> **Cum vincimus, tum pācem spērās.** *When (while) we are winning, you are (at the same time) hoping for peace.*

> **Cum ad illum locum vēnerant, tum amīcōs contulerant.** *When they had come to that place, they had brought their friends* or *not only had they come to that place, but they had also brought their friends.*

Often, however, the verb of the **cum** clause is subjunctive, especially when it describes the general circumstances (rather than the exact time) when the main action occurred (often called a CUM CIRCUMSTANTIAL CLAUSE), or explains the cause of the main action (CUM CAUSAL CLAUSE), or describes a circumstance that might have obstructed the main action or is in some other way opposed to it (CUM ADVERSATIVE or CONCESSIVE CLAUSE):

> **Cum hoc fēcisset, ad tē fūgit.**
> *When he had done this, he fled to you.* (circumstantial)

> **Cum hoc scīret, potuit eōs iuvāre.**
> *Since he knew this, he was able to help them.* (causal)

Cum hoc scīret, *tamen* mīlitēs mīsit.
*Although he knew this, **nevertheless** he sent the soldiers.* (adversative)

Cum Gāium dīligerēmus, nōn poterāmus eum iuvāre.
*Although we loved Gaius, we could not help him.* (adversative)

*Recognition:* You should have little difficulty distinguishing among the four basic types of **cum** clauses: the temporal has an indicative verb, and the three subjunctive types can generally be recognized by analyzing the relationship between the actions in the main and subordinate clauses; in the case of adversative clauses the adverb **tamen** often appears in the main clause. *Translation:* Remember that when **cum** is followed immediately by a noun or pronoun in the ablative case, you should translate it *with.* When instead it introduces a subordinate clause, translate it *when, since, although,* etc. As seen in the above examples, the verb in a **cum** clause, whatever its type, is regularly translated *as an indicative,* i.e., without an auxiliary such as *may* or *might.*

## IRREGULAR *Ferō, ferre, tulī, lātum,* to bear, carry

**Ferō** is one of a series of irregular verbs to be introduced in the closing chapters of this text (the others being **volō, nōlō, mālō, fīō,** and **eō**); they are all commonly used and must be learned thoroughly. The English verb "to bear" is cognate with Latin **ferō, ferre** and has generally the same basic and metaphorical meanings, *to carry* and *to endure.* In the present system **ferō** is simply a third conjugation verb, formed exactly like **agō** except that the stem vowel does not appear in a few places, including the infinitive **ferre.** The only irregular forms, all in the present tense (indicative, imperative, and infinitive), are highlighted below in bold; the imperfect subjunctive, while formed on the irregular infinitive **ferre,** nevertheless follows the usual pattern of present infinitive + endings. Although **tulī** (originally **tetulī**) and **lātum** (originally *tlātum) derive ultimately, by suppletion, from a different verb related to **tollō,** the conjugation follows the regular pattern of the perfect system and should cause no difficulty. The singular imperative lacks the -**e,** like **dīc, dūc,** and **fac** (Capvt VIII).

### Present Indicative

| Active | Passive |
|---|---|
| **Active** | **Passive** |
| 1. férō | féror |
| 2. **fers** (cf. ágis) | **férris** (ágeris) |
| 3. **fert** (cf. ágit) | **fértur** (ágitur) |
| 1. férimus | férimur |
| 2. **fértis** (cf. ágitis) | feríminī |
| 3. férunt | ferúntur |

**Present Active Imperative:**   fer (áge), férte (ágite)

**Infinitives**

| Active | Passive |
|---|---|
| Pres. **férre** (ágere) | **férrī** (ágī) |
| Perf. tulísse | lấtus ésse |
| Fut. lātū́rus ésse | lấtum ī́rī |

### Synopsis

The following synopsis, showing irregular forms in bold, provides an overview of the conjugation of **ferō**; for the complete conjugation, see the App. (p. 508–09).

**Indicative Mood**

|  | Pres. | Fut. | Imperf. | Perf. | Fut.Perf. | Pluperf. |
|---|---|---|---|---|---|---|
| Act. | **fert** | féret | ferḗbat | túlit | túlerit | túlerat |
| Pass. | **fértur** | ferḗtur | ferēbā́tur | lấtus est | lấtus érit | lấtus érat |

**Subjunctive Mood**

|  | Pres. | Fut. | Imperf. | Perf. | Fut.Perf. | Pluperf. |
|---|---|---|---|---|---|---|
| Act. | férat | — | **férret** | túlerit | — | tulísset |
| Pass. | ferấtur | — | **ferrḗtur** | lấtus sit | — | lấtus ésset |

# VOCĀBVLA

As always, learn the entire entry for each word in the following list, and review vocabulary from preceding chapters as well, ideally by listening to the CDs or the audio lists at www.wheelockslatin.com. When using the online audio, look carefully at each word's spelling, including macrons, then click on the word and listen to it, say the word and its meaning aloud, then look/click/listen and repeat aloud again. **Semper audiās ac prōnūntiēs!**

**as, ássis,** m., *an as,* a small copper coin, comparable to a penny (ace)

**auxílium, auxíliī,** n., *aid, help* (auxiliary; cf. **auctor** and **augēre,** *to increase, augment*)

**dígitus, dígitī,** m., *finger, toe* (digit, digital, digitalis, digitalize, digitize, prestidigitation; see **Latīna Est Gaudium,** Capvt XX)

**elephántus, elephántī,** m. and f., *elephant* (elephantiasis, elephantine)

**exsílium, exsíliī,** n., *exile, banishment* (often without the -s-, **exilium;** exilic)

**invídia, invídiae,** f., *envy, jealousy, hatred* (invidious, envious)

**rūmor, rūmṓris,** m., *rumor, gossip* (rumormonger)

**vínum, vínī,** n., *wine* (vine, vinegar, viniferous, vintage, vinyl)

**medíocris, medíocre,** *ordinary, moderate, mediocre* (mediocrity; cf. **medius**)

**cum,** conj. + subjunct., *when, since, although;* conj. + indic., *when*

**ápud,** prep. + acc., *among, in the presence of, at the house of*

**sémel,** adv., *a single time, once, once and for all, simultaneously*

**úsque,** adv., *all the way, up (to), even (to), continuously, always*

**dóleō, dolḗre, dóluī, dolitū́rum,** *to grieve, suffer; hurt, give pain* (doleful, dolor, dolorous, Dolores, condole, condolences, indolent)

**dórmiō, dormī́re, dormī́vī, dormī́tum,** *to sleep* (dormitory, dormer, dormancy, dormant, dormouse)

**férō, férre, túlī, lātum,** *to bear, carry, bring; suffer, endure, tolerate; say, report* (fertile, circumference, defer, differ, infer, prefer, proffer, suffer, transfer; cf. **tolerō, tollō**)

**ádferō, adférre, áttulī, allā́tum,** *to bring to* (afferent, allative)

**cṓnferō, cōnférre, cóntulī, collā́tum,** *to bring together, compare; confer, bestow;* **sē cōnférre,** idiom, *to go,* lit., *to take/betake oneself* (conference, collate, collation; the abbreviation "cf." = **cōnfer,** "compare")

**ófferō, offérre, óbtulī, oblā́tum,** *to offer* (offertory, oblation)

**réferō, reférre, réttulī, relā́tum,** *to carry back, bring back; repeat, answer, report* (refer, reference, referent, referral, relate, relation, relative)

**invídeō, invidḗre, invī́dī, invī́sum,** *to be envious;* + dat. (see Capvt XXXV), *to look at with envy, envy, be jealous of* (invidious, invidiousness)

**óccidō, occídere, occidī, occā́sum,** *to fall down; die; set* (occident, occidental, occasion, occasional; cf. **cadō, occāsiō**)

# LĒCTIŌ ET TRĀNSLĀTIŌ

Scan the following readings for (a) all forms of **ferō,** identifying the person, number, tense, mood, and voice of each, and (b) all **cum** clauses, determining for each the specific type and whether "when," "since," or "although" conveys the intended sense. Before translating, read each sentence and passage aloud for comprehension, and listen to the CDs if you have them.

## EXERCITĀTIŌNĒS

1. Iam vērō cognōvimus istās mentēs dūrās ferrum prō pāce offerre.
2. Nē nātae geminae discant verba tam acerba et tam dūra.
3. Cum hī decem virī dignī ex moenibus semel discessissent, alia occāsiō pācis numquam oblāta est.
4. Tantum auxilium nōbīs referet ut nē ācerrimī quidem mīlitēs aut pugnāre aut hīc remanēre possint.
5. Rogābat cūr cēterae tantam fidem apud nōs praestārent et nōbīs tantam spem adferrent.

6. Cum patria nostra tanta beneficia offerat, tamen quīdam sē in īnsidiās fūrtim cōnferunt et contrā bonōs mox pugnābunt.
7. Dēnique audiāmus quantae sint hae īnsidiae ac quot coniūrātī contrā cīvitātem surgant.
8. Haec scelera repente exposuī nē alia et similia ferrētis.
9. Respondērunt plūrima arma ā mīlitibus ad lītus allāta esse et in nāvibus condita esse.
10. Cum parentēs essent vīvī, fēlīcēs erant; mortuī quoque sunt beātī.
11. Nesciō utrum trēs coniūrātī maneant an in exsilium contenderint.
12. Nōs cōnferāmus ad cēnam, meī amīcī, bibāmus multum vīnī, cōnsūmāmus noctem, atque omnēs cūrās nostrās minuāmus!
13. When the soldiers had been arrested, they soon offered us money.
14. Although life brings very difficult things, let us endure them all and dedicate ourselves to philosophy.
15. Since you know what help is being brought by our six friends, these evils can be endured with courage.
16. Although his eyes could not see the light of the sun, nevertheless that humble man used to do very many and very difficult things.

## SENTENTIAE ANTĪQVAE

1. Potestne haec lūx esse tibi iūcunda, cum sciās hōs omnēs cōnsilia tua cognōvisse? (Cicero.)
2. Themistoclēs, cum Graeciam servitūte Persicā līberāvisset et propter invidiam in exsilium expulsus esset, ingrātae patriae iniūriam nōn tulit quam ferre dēbuit. (Cicero.—**Persicus, -a, -um.—ingrātus, -a, -um,** *ungrateful;* "ingrate," "ingratitude."—**iniūria, -ae,** f., *injury;* "injurious," "injuriously;" cf. **iūs.**)
3. Quae cum ita sint, Catilīna, cōnfer tē in exsilium. (Cicero.—**quae cum: = et cum haec.**)
4. Ō nāvis, novī flūctūs bellī tē in mare referent! Ō quid agis? Unde erit ūllum perfugium? (Horace.—**nāvis:** *ship [of state].*—**flūctus, -ūs,** m., *wave, billow;* "fluctuate," "fluctuation.")
5. Cum rēs pūblica immortālis esse dēbeat, doleō eam salūtis egēre ac in vītā ūnīus mortālis cōnsistere. (Cicero.—**cōnsistō, -ere + in,** *to depend on;* "consist," "consistency.")
6. Cum illum hominem esse servum nōvisset, eum comprehendere nōn dubitāvit. (Cicero.)
7. Ille comprehēnsus, cum prīmō impudenter respondēre coepisset, dēnique tamen nihil negāvit. (Cicero.—**impudenter,** adv.; "impudence," "impudent.")
8. Milō dīcitur per stadium vēnisse cum bovem umerīs ferret. (Cicero.—**Milō, -lōnis,** m., a famous Greek athlete.—**stadium, -iī,** n.—**bōs, bovis,** m./f., *ox;* "bovine," "beef."—**umerus, -ī,** m., *shoulder;* "humerus," "humeral.")
9. Quid vesper et somnus ferant, incertum est. (Livy.)

10. Ferte miserō tantum auxilium quantum potestis. (Terence.)
11. Hoc ūnum sciō: quod fāta ferunt, id ferēmus aequō animō. (Terence.)
12. Lēgum dēnique idcircō omnēs servī sumus, ut līberī esse possīmus. (*Cicero.—
    **idcircō,** adv., *for this reason.*)

### Give Me a Thousand Kisses!

Vīvāmus, mea Lesbia, atque amēmus,
rūmōrēsque senum sevēriōrum
omnēs ūnius aestimēmus assis!
Sōlēs occidere et redīre possunt;
5   nōbīs cum semel occidit brevis lūx,
nox est perpetua ūna dormienda.
Dā mī bāsia mīlle, deinde centum;
dein mīlle altera, dein secunda centum;
deinde usque altera mīlle, deinde centum.
10  Dein, cum mīlia multa fēcerīmus—
conturbābimus illa, nē sciāmus,
aut nē quis malus invidēre possit,
cum tantum sciat esse bāsiōrum.

*Catullus *Carm.* 5: In one of his most popular **carmina,** Catullus here exhorts Lesbia to live, and love, and ignore the gossip of grumpy old men who envy young lovers and curse their passion.—**rūmōrēs:** with **omnēs;** adj. and noun were often widely separated in poetry, so it is essential to pay close attention to the endings.—**sevērus, -a, -um,** = Eng.; "persevere."—**ūnius . . . assis:** GEN. OF INDEF. VALUE; we would say *at* (rather than *of*) *one. . . .*—**aestimāre,** *to value, estimate;* "esteem," "estimate."–**sōlēs:** pl., as, in the poetic imagination, each day's sun is a new one.—**redīre,** *to return.*—**nōbīs:** DAT. OF REFERENCE, a usage formally introduced in Capvt XXXVIII, but whose sense is easily understood here.—**mī:** = mihi.—**dein:** = deinde.— **conturbāre,** *to throw into confusion, mix up;* "disturb," "perturbation"; here possibly an allusion to jumbling the counters on an abacus.—**nē sciāmus:** sc. **numerum;** if the number is unknown, then, in a sense, it is

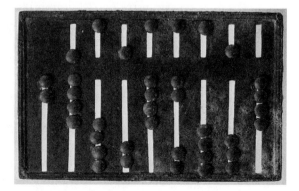

*Roman abacus*
*Museo Nazionale Romano*
*(Terme di Diocleziano)*
*Rome, Italy*

limitless; in ancient views of black magic, knowing the exact number of, say, a neighbor's sheep made a curse upon them more efficacious.—**quis:** here indef., *someone.*—**invidēre:** with **malus,** the word means both *to envy* and *to cast an evil eye upon,* i.e., to hex.—**tantum:** with **bāsiōrum,** gen. of the whole, = *so many kisses.*

*QVAESTIŌNĒS:* The poem is about living—and dying—as much as about loving, as announced in the equation set forth in the opening verse; what opposing images does Catullus employ for life and death, and how does he manipulate word order, and even sound effects, to draw our attention to the antitheses? How, in the vision of this poem, might one seemingly escape death? How are the **senēs** and the **quis malus** associated, and what do they represent? How does the poet employ numbers here–and not just the hundreds and thousands, but also the number "one"?

## Ringo

> Sēnōs Charīnus omnibus digitīs gerit
> > nec nocte pōnit ānulōs,
> nec cum lavātur. Causa quae sit quaeritis?
> > Dactyliothēcam nōn habet!

*Martial *Epig.* 11.59: Charinus–his Greek name suggests servile origins—was an ostentatious chap who liked to show off his many rings; meter: alternating iambic trimeter and dimeter.—**sēnī, -ae, -a,** a DISTRIBUTIVE NUMERAL, *six each, six apiece;* "senarii" (a verse form with six iambic feet per line).—**ānulus, -ī,** m., *ring;* "annelid" (a type of ringworm) and "annular eclipse," both spelled with *nn,* perhaps by analogy with **annus,** *year,* though **ānulus,** to get down to "fundamentals," is actually the diminutive of **ānus,** *ring, circle, anus*); and for the **digitus ānulārius,** see **Latīna Est Gaudium,** Capvt XX.—**pōnit:** = **dēpōnit,** *put away;* use of a simple verb form, where a compound might be expected,

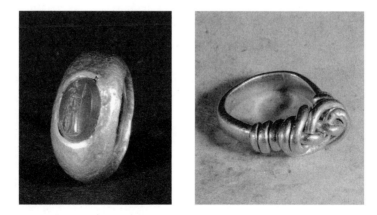

*Roman gold rings, one with a red carnelian intaglio of Minerva, one with a twisted knot. 1st–3rd cent.* A.D. *Kunsthistorisches Museum, Vienna, Austria*

was common in Lat. verse.—**lavāre**, *to bathe;* "laundry," "lavatory."—**causa . . . quaeritis:** the usual order would be **quaeritisne quae sit causa.**—**dactyliothēca, -ae,** f., *ring-box, jewelry chest;* a Gk. word, as befits Charinus; "dactylic," "pterodactyl" (both originally derive from Gk., not Lat.).

*QVAESTIŌNĒS:* What noun must **sēnōs** modify? What effect was the poet hoping to achieve by so widely separating noun and adj.? You can do the math: how many rings did Charinus own? How many ring-boxes? So, what's the joke?

### Facētiae (Witticisms)

Cum Cicerō apud Damasippum cēnāret et ille, mediocrī vīnō in mēnsā positō, dīceret, "Bibe hoc Falernum; hoc est vīnum quadrāgintā annōrum," Cicerō sīc respondit, "Bene aetātem fert!"

Augustus, cum quīdam rīdiculus eī libellum trepidē adferret, et modo prōferret manum et modo retraheret, "Putās," inquit, "tē assem elephantō dare?"

Macrobius *Sat.* 2.3–4: Macrobius Ambrosius Theodosius was a 5th-cent. A.D. scholar whose writings reflected a keen interest in Rome's pagan past; his **Saturnālia** was a collection of dramatized dialogues set during the December festival of Saturnalia in the year A.D. 383 and featuring discussions among important figures of the period: among more serious topics the interlocutors shared a series of jokes told by famous persons from earlier times.—**Falernum, -ī,** n., *Falernian (wine),* the most revered of ancient Roman wines, from vineyards in northern Campania; Cicero's host Damasippus has substituted an inferior vintage.—**quadrāgintā,** indecl., *40;* "quarantine."—**trepidē,** adv., *in confusion;* "trepidation," "intrepid."—**modo . . . modo,** *now . . . now.*—**prō** + **ferō** and **re** + **trahō:** you can easily deduce the meanings of these two compound verbs, which give us such derivatives as "profer" and "retract."—**elephantō:** one thinks of a child offering a peanut to a circus elephant.

*QVAESTIŌNĒS:* Can you explain the humor in each of these two jokes? Which do you regard as more clever, which as unkind?

## SCRĪPTA IN PARIETIBVS

Quī vītam spernit facile contemnet deī. . . .

*CIL* 4.5370: The person who wrote this graffito on a wall in Reg. IX (near Ins. 7) offered passers-by a religious admonition.—**spernō, -ere, sprēvī, sprētum,** *to scorn, despise, spurn* (which, by the way, is not a derivative).—**facile:** adv. from **facilis.—contemnō, -temnere, -tempsī, -temptum,** *to despise, scorn;* "contemn," "contempt"; the line following is unintelligible, but must have contained an acc. noun modified by **deī** and dir. obj. of this verb, e.g., **cōnsilium;** cf., e.g., *Luke* 7.30: **cōnsilium Deī sprēvērunt.**

## LATĪNA EST GAVDIVM—ET ŪTILIS!

**Iterum salvēte, doctae doctīque!** Having made it this far, you've certainly earned that appellation, and, as a further reward, here are more tidbits **ex vocābulīs novīs huius capitis,** all focused on that villainous Catiline: to start with, there's that famous **cum** temporal clause from Cicero's indictment of Catiline: **cum tacent, clāmant,** *when they are silent, they are shouting,* i.e., "by their silence they condemn you." Poor Catiline, perhaps he had too much to drink, **usque ad nauseam,** and spilled the beans, ignoring the warning, **in vīnō vēritās;** if only he had observed Horace's **aurea mediocritās,** *the golden mean,* he might have received **auxilium ab altō,** *help from on high,* but the gods, it appears, were against him. And so he soon met his end, **semel et simul,** *once and for all:* **valē, miser Catilīna, et valeātis, vōs omnēs, amīcī vēritātis honōrisque!**

# CAPVT XXXII 卍卍卍

# Formation and Comparison of Adverbs; *Volō, Mālō, Nōlō;* Proviso Clauses

## GRAMMATICA

### FORMATION AND COMPARISON OF ADVERBS

You are by now familiar with a wide range of Latin adverbs, words that are employed (as in English) to modify verbs, adjectives, or other adverbs, and that usually precede the words they modify. Many have their own peculiar forms and endings and must simply be memorized when first introduced in the **Vocābula** (often without benefit of English derivatives to aid in the memorization): among these are **cūr, etiam, ita, tam,** etc.

#### Positive Degree

A great many adverbs, however, are formed directly from adjectives and are easily recognized. Many first/second declension adjectives form positive degree adverbs by adding -ē to the base:

| | |
|---|---|
| lóng-ē | (*far;* longus, -a, -um) |
| líber-ē | (*freely;* līber, lībera, līberum) |
| púlchr-ē | (*beautifully;* pulcher, -chra, -chrum) |

Adverbs are often formed from third declension adjectives by adding -iter to the base; if the base ends in -nt- only -er is added:

| | |
|---|---|
| fórt-iter | (*bravely;* fortis, -e) |
| celér-iter | (*quickly,* celer, celeris, celere) |
| ácr-iter | (*keenly;* ācer, ācris, ācre) |
| fēlíc-iter | (*happily;* fēlīx, gen. fēlīcis) |
| sapiént-er | (*wisely;* sapiēns, gen. sapientis) |

## Comparative and Superlative Degree

Many Latin adverbs have comparative and superlative forms, just as they do in English, and their English translations correspond to those of comparative and superlative adjectives; e.g., positive degree "quickly"; comparative "more (rather, too) quickly"; superlative "most (very) quickly," etc.

The comparative degree of adverbs is with few exceptions identical to the **-ius** form which you have already learned as the neuter of the comparative degree of the adjective: **dīligentius,** *more/rather diligently.*

The superlative degree of adverbs, being normally derived from the superlative degree of adjectives, regularly ends in **-ē** according to the rule given above for converting adjectives of the first and the second declensions into adverbs: **iūcundissimē,** *most/very pleasantly.*

## *Quam* with Comparative and Superlative Adverbs

**Quam** is used with adverbs in the same ways as with adjectives: **hic puer celerius cucurrit quam ille,** *this boy ran more quickly than that one;* **illa puella quam celerrimē cucurrit,** *that girl ran as quickly as possible.* The ablative of comparison is not ordinarily employed after comparative adverbs (except in poetry).

## Comparison of Irregular Adverbs

When the comparison of an adjective is irregular (see Capvt XXVII), the comparison of the adverb derived from it normally follows the irregularities of the adjective but has adverbial endings. Study carefully the following list of representative adverbs; those that do not follow the standard rules stated above for forming adverbs from adjectives are highlighted in bold (be prepared to point out how they do not conform). Note the alternate superlatives **prīmō,** which usually means *first (in time)* vs. **prīmum,** usually *first (in a series);* **quam prīmum** has the idiomatic meaning *as soon as possible.*

| Positive | Comparative | Superlative |
|---|---|---|
| lóngē (*far*) | lóngius (*farther, too f.*) | longíssimē (*farthest, very f.*) |
| líberē (*freely*) | lībérius (*more f.*) | lībérrimē (*most, very f.*) |
| púlchrē (*beautifully*) | púlchrius (*more b.*) | pulchérrimē (*most b.*) |
| fórtiter (*bravely*) | fórtius (*more b.*) | fortíssimē (*most b.*) |
| celériter (*quickly*) | celérius (*more q.*) | celérrimē (*most q.*) |
| ácriter (*keenly*) | ácrius (*more k.*) | ācérrimē (*most k.*) |
| fēlíciter (*happily*) | fēlícius (*more h.*) | fēlīcíssimē (*most h.*) |
| sapiénter (*wisely*) | sapiéntius (*more w.*) | sapientíssimē (*most w.*) |
| **fácile** (*easily*) | facílius (*more e.*) | facíllimē (*most e.*) |
| **béne** (*well*) | mélius (*better*) | óptimē (*best*) |

| mále (*badly*) | peíus (*worse*) | péssimē (*worst*) |
|---|---|---|
| múltum (*much*) | plūs (*more*, quantity) | plúrimum (*most, very much*) |
| magnópere (*greatly*) | mágis (*more*, quality) | máximē (*most, especially*) |
| párum (*little, not very* [*much*]) | mínus (*less*) | mínimē (*least*) |

| (prō) | príus (*before, earlier*) | prímō (*first, at first*) <br> prímum (*in the first place*) |
|---|---|---|
| díū (*for a long time*) | diútius (*longer*) | diūtíssimē (*very long*) |

## IRREGULAR *Volō, velle, voluī,* to wish

Like **ferō** (Capvt XXXI), **volō** is another common third conjugation verb which, though regular for the most part, does have several irregular forms, including the present infinitive **velle.** Remember these points:

—**volō** has no passive forms at all, no future active infinitive or participle, and no imperatives;
—the perfect system is entirely regular;
—the only irregular forms are in the present indicative (which must be memorized) and the present subjunctive (which is comparable to **sim, sīs, sit**);
—the imperfect subjunctive resembles that of **ferō**; while formed from the irregular infinitive **velle,** it nevertheless follows the usual pattern of present infinitive + personal endings;
—**vol-** is the base in the present system indicatives, **vel-** in the subjunctives.

| Pres. Ind. | Pres. Subjunct. | Imperf. Subjunct. | Infinitives |
|---|---|---|---|
| 1. vólō | vélim | véllem | *Pres.* vélle |
| 2. vīs | vélīs | véllēs | *Perf.* voluísse |
| 3. vult | vélit | véllet | *Fut.*——— |
| 1. vólumus | velímus | vellémus | **Participle** |
| 2. vúltis | velítis | vellétis | *Pres.* vólēns |
| 3. vólunt | vélint | véllent | |

### Synopsis

The following synopsis, with irregular forms in bold, provides an overview of the conjugation of **volō;** for the full conjugation, see the App. (p. 507–08):

**Indicative Mood**

| | Pres. | Fut. | Imperf. | Perf. | Fut.Perf. | Pluperf. |
|---|---|---|---|---|---|---|
| Act. | **vult** | vólet | volébat | vóluit | volúerit | volúerat |

**Subjunctive Mood**

| | | | | | | |
|---|---|---|---|---|---|---|
| Act. | **vélit** | — | **véllet** | volúerit | — | voluísset |

## *Nōlō* AND *Mālō*

The compounds **nōlō, nōlle, nōluī** (**nē + volō**), *not to wish, to be unwilling,* and **mālō, mālle, māluī** (**magis + volō**), *to want (something) more* or *instead, prefer,* follow **volō** closely, but have long vowels in their stems (**nō-, mā-**) and some other striking peculiarities, especially in the present indicative.

### Present Indicative of *Nōlō*

> **Sg.** nōlō, nōn vīs, nōn vult **Pl.** nōlumus, nōn vúltis, nōlunt

### Present Indicative of *Mālō*

> **Sg.** málō, mávīs, mávult **Pl.** málumus, māvúltis, málunt

The following synopses provide overviews of both verbs, with irregular forms in bold; see the App. (p. 507–08) for full conjugations:

**Indicative Mood**

|  | Pres. | Fut. | Imperf. | Perf. | Fut.Perf. | Pluperf. |
|---|---|---|---|---|---|---|
| Act. | **nōn vult** | nōlet | nōlébat | nōluit | nōlúerit | nōlúerat |

**Subjunctive Mood**

|  | Pres. | Fut. | Imperf. | Perf. | Fut.Perf. | Pluperf. |
|---|---|---|---|---|---|---|
| Act. | **nōlit** | — | **nōllet** | nōlúerit | — | nōluísset |

**Indicative Mood**

|  | Pres. | Fut. | Imperf. | Perf. | Fut.Perf. | Pluperf. |
|---|---|---|---|---|---|---|
| Act. | **mávult** | mālet | mālébat | máluit | mālúerit | mālúerat |

**Subjunctive Mood**

|  | Pres. | Fut. | Imperf. | Perf. | Fut.Perf. | Pluperf. |
|---|---|---|---|---|---|---|
| Act. | **málit** | — | **mállet** | mālúerit | — | māluísset |

### *Nōlō* and Negative Commands

While **volō** and **mālō** lack imperatives, **nōlō** has singular and plural imperatives that were commonly employed with complementary infinitives to express NEGA-TIVE COMMANDS:

> **Nōlī manēre, Catilīna!** *Do not remain, Catiline!*
> **Nōlīte discēdere, amīcī meī!** *Do not leave, my friends!*

## PROVISO CLAUSES

The subjunctive is used in a subordinate clause introduced by **dummodo,** *provided that, so long as,* and certain other words that express a provisional circumstance or "proviso"; **nē** is used as the negative in such clauses. The verb in such clauses is simply translated as an indicative:

Nōn timēbō, dummodo hīc remaneās. *I shall not be afraid, provided that you remain here.*

Erimus fēlīcēs, dummodo nē discēdās. *We shall be happy, so long as (provided that) you do not leave.*

## VOCĀBVLA

You must learn all the irregular adverbs in the chart on p. 265–66—not a daunting task if you have mastered the irregular adjective comparisons presented in Capvt XXVII. To reinforce learning **volō**, **nōlō**, and **mālō**, do a synopsis of each in a different person and number and then check your work against the full conjugations in the **Summārium Fōrmārum**, p. 507–08.

**custṓdia, custṓdiae,** f., *protection, custody;* pl., *guards* (custodian)

**exércitus, exércitūs,** m., *army* (exercise)

**paupértās, paupertấtis,** f., *poverty, humble circumstances* (cf. **pauper** below)

**dîves,** gen. **dîvitis** or **dîtis,** *rich, wealthy* (Dives; cf. **dīvitiae**)

**pār,** gen. **páris** + dat., *equal, like* (par, pair, parity, peer, peerless, disparage, disparity, umpire, nonpareil)

**paúper,** gen. **paúperis,** *of small means, poor* (pauper, poverty, impoverished)

**dúmmodo,** conj. + subjunct., *provided that, so long as*

All adverbs in the list above, p. 265–66

**mấlō, mấlle, mấluī,** *to want (something) more, instead; prefer*

**nṓlō, nṓlle, nṓluī,** *to not . . . wish, be unwilling* (nolo contendere, nol. pros., nolens volens)

**páteō, patḗre, pátuī,** *to be open, lie open; be accessible; be evident* (patent, pātent, patency; cf. **patefacere**)

**praébeō, praebḗre, praébuī, praébitum,** *to offer, provide* (provender)

**prōmíttō, prōmíttere, prōmîsī, prōmíssum,** *to send forth; promise* (promissory, compromise)

**vólō, vélle, vóluī,** *to wish, want, be willing, will* (volition, voluntary, volunteer, volitive, voluptuous, benevolent, malevolent)

## LĒCTIŌ ET TRĀNSLĀTIŌ

Test your mastery of the new material by writing out your answers to some of the Self-Tutorial Exercises and then checking the Answer Key. Next, scan the following selections to find (a) all forms of **volō**, **nōlō**, and **mālō**, identifying the person, number, tense, mood, and voice of each, and (b) all proviso clauses. Finally, before translating, read each sentence and passage aloud once or twice, reading for comprehension, and listen to the CDs if you have them.

## EXERCITĀTIŌNĒS

1. Prīmō illī trēs rīdiculī nē mediocria quidem perīcula fortiter ferre poterant et ūllum auxilium offerre nōlēbant.
2. Maximē rogāvimus quantum auxilium septem fēminae adferrent et utrum dubitārent an nōs mox adiūtūrae essent.
3. Dēnique armīs collātīs, imperātor prōmīsit decem mīlia mīlitum celerrimē discessūra esse, dummodo satis cōpiārum reciperent.
4. Paria beneficia, igitur, in omnēs dignōs cōnferre māvultis.
5. Haec mala melius expōnant nē dīvitiās minuant aut honōrēs suōs āmittant.
6. At volumus cognōscere cūr sīc invīderit et cūr verba eius tam dūra fuerint.
7. Cum cēterī hās īnsidiās cognōverint, vult in exsilium fūrtim ac quam celerrimē sē cōnferre ut rūmōrēs et invidiam vītet.
8. Multīne discipulī tantum studium usque praestant ut hās sententiās facillimē ūnō annō legere possint?
9. Cum dīvitiās āmīsisset et ūnum assem nōn habēret, tamen omnēs cīvēs ingenium mōrēsque eius maximē laudābant.
10. Plūra meliōraque lēgibus aequīs quam ferrō certē faciēmus.
11. Oculī tuī sunt pulchriōrēs sīderibus caelī, mea puella; es gracilis et bella, ac ōscula sunt dulciōra vīnō: amēmus sub lūce lūnae!
12. Iste hostis, in Italiam cum multīs elephantīs veniēns, prīmō pugnāre nōluit et plūrimōs diēs in montibus cōnsūmpsit.
13. Sī nepōs tē ad cēnam semel invītābit, mēnsam explēbit et tibi tantum vīnī offeret quantum vīs; nōlī, autem, nimium bibere.
14. Do you wish to live longer and better?
15. He wishes to speak as wisely as possible so that they may yield to him very quickly.
16. When these plans had been learned, we asked why he had been unwilling to prepare the army with the greatest possible care.
17. That man, who used to be very humble, now so keenly wishes to have wealth that he is willing to lose his two best friends.

## SENTENTIAE ANTĪQVAE

1. Occāsiō nōn facile praebētur sed facile ac repente āmittitur. (Publilius Syrus.)
2. Nōbīscum vīvere iam diūtius nōn potes; nōlī remanēre; id nōn ferēmus. (Cicero.)
3. Vīs rēctē vīvere? Quis nōn? (*Horace.—**rēctus, -a, -um,** straight, right;* "rectify," "rectilinear.")

4. Plūs nōvistī quid faciendum sit. (Terence.)

5. Mihi vērē dīxit quid vellet. (Terence.)

6. Parēs cum paribus facillimē congregantur. (*Cicero.—**congregāre**, *to gather into a flock;* "congregate," "gregarious," "segregation.")

7. Tē magis quam oculōs meōs amō. (Terence.)

8. Hominēs libenter id crēdunt quod volunt. (Caesar.—**libenter**, adv., *with pleasure, gladly, willingly;* "ad lib.")

9. Multa ēveniunt hominibus quae volunt et quae nōlunt. (Plautus.—**ē** + **venīre**, lit. "come out," *to happen;* "event," "eventual.")

10. Cōnsiliō melius contendere atque vincere possumus quam īrā. (Publilius Syrus.)

11. Optimus quisque facere māvult quam dīcere. (Sallust.—**māvult quam:** = **magis vult quam.**)

12. Omnēs sapientēs fēlīciter, perfectē, fortūnātē vīvunt. (Cicero.—**perfectē**, adv., *completely, fully;* "perfect," "perfectly.")

13. Maximē eum laudant quī pecūniā nōn movētur. (Cicero.)

14. Sī vīs scīre quam nihil malī in paupertāte sit, cōnfer pauperem et dīvitem: pauper saepius et fidēlius rīdet. (Seneca.)

15. Magistrī puerīs crūstula dant ut prīma elementa discere velint. (Horace.—**crūstulum, -ī,** n., *cookie;* "crust."—**elementum, -ī,** n.; "elemental," "elementary.")

16. Sī vīs mē flēre, dolendum est prīmum ipsī tibi. (*Horace.—**flēre**, to weep; "feeble.")


## The Character of Cimon

Cimōn celeriter ad summōs honōrēs pervēnit. Habēbat enim satis ēloquentiae, summam līberālitātem, magnam scientiam lēgum et reī mīlitāris, quod cum patre ā puerō in exercitibus fuerat. Itaque hic populum urbānum in suā potestāte facillimē tenuit et apud exercitum valuit plūrimum auctōritāte.

Cum ille occidisset, Athēniēnsēs dē eō diū doluērunt; nōn sōlum in bellō, autem, sed etiam in pāce eum graviter dēsīderāvērunt. Fuit enim vir tantae līberālitātis ut, cum multōs hortōs habēret, numquam in hīs custōdiās pōneret; nam hortōs līberrimē patēre voluit nē populus ab hīs frūctibus prohibērētur. Saepe autem, cum aliquem minus bene vestītum vidēret, eī suum amiculum dedit. Multōs locuplētāvit; multōs pauperēs vīvōs iūvit atque mortuōs suō sūmptū extulit. Sīc minimē mīrum est sī, propter mōrēs Cimōnis, vīta eius fuit sēcūra et mors eius fuit omnibus tam acerba quam mors cuiusdam ex familiā.

Nepos *Cim.* (adapted excerpts): Cornelius Nepos, as you may recall from the notes to "Catullus Dedicates His Poetry Book" in Capvt II above, was author of hundreds of brief biographies of famous Greeks and Romans. Two dozen or so of Nepos' biographies survive, including his life of the 5th-cent. Athenian statesman Cimon, whose career, while distinguished, did have its low points, including a 10-year ostracism (exile) from Athens.—**per** + **venīre:** another compound verb whose meaning you can easily deduce; "parvenu."—**ēloquentia, -ae,** f., = Eng.; "eloquent."—**līberālitās, -tātis,** f., = Eng.; "liberal," "liberalism."—**mīlitāris, -e,** = Eng.; "militarism," "demilitarize."—**ā puerō:** *from his boyhood.*—**potestās, -tātis,** f., *power;* "potent"; cf. **possum.**—**auctōritās, -tātis,** f., *authority;* "authoritative"; cf. **auctor;** here ABL. OF RESPECT OR SPECIFICATION, *in (respect to his).* . . .—**Athēniēnsis, -is,** m./f., *an Athenian.*—**hortus, -ī,** m., *garden;* "horticulture," "cohort."—**vestītus, -a, -um,** *clothed;* "vest," "vestment," "divest."—**amiculum, -ī,** n., *cloak.*—**locuplētāre,** *to enrich;* "complete," "replete."—**sūmptus, -ūs,** m., *expense;* "sumptuous," "consumption."—**extulit:** from **ex** + **ferō (efferō),** here = *bury,* but what is the lit. meaning? "efferent," "elation."—**mīrus, -a, -um,** *surprising;* "miracle," "admiration."—**sēcūrus, -a, -um:** from **sē-,** *without,* + **cūra;** "secure," "security."

*QVAESTIŌNĒS:* Nepos, never regarded as a critical historian (one modern scholar has ungently termed him "an intellectual pygmy"), tended to eulogize his subjects and reshape the facts when useful to his moralizing purposes; what are the principal virtues Nepos here attributes to Cimon, and in what two different arenas of Athenian life?

## A Vacation . . . from You!

> Quid mihi reddat ager quaeris, Line, Nōmentānus?
>
> Hoc mihi reddit ager: tē, Line, nōn videō!

*Martial *Epig.* 2.38: Does Linus really wonder why Martial takes so many country vacations?! Meter: elegiac couplet.—**reddō, -ere,** *to give back, return (in profit);* "render," "rent."—**ager:** here, *farm,* i.e., Martial's rustic retreat.—**Nōmentānus, -a, -um,** *in Nomentum,* a town of Latium known for its wine industry.

*QVAESTIŌNĒS:* What is most striking stylistically in this epigram, and what is the comic effect?—though not so funny to poor Linus!

## Please . . . Don't!

> Nīl recitās et vīs, Māmerce, poēta vidērī.
>
> Quidquid vīs estō, dummodo nīl recitēs!

*Martial *Epig.* 2.88: Mamercus was a wannabe poet—there were plenty of those in Rome (cf. "Juvenal Explains," Capvt XVI)! Meter: elegiac couplet.—**nīl:** = **nihil.**—**estō:** fut. imperat. of **esse,** which often had the stern tone of a religious or legal dictum, "*Thou shalt be . . . !*"

*QVAESTIŌNĒS:* Compare this poem with *Epig.* 1.38 in Capvt XVII; how were Fidentinus and Mamercus at once alike, and unalike? Which, in Martial's view, was the greater pest? What do the two epigrams tell you about the importance of **recitātiō** in Roman literary culture?

## SCRĪPTA IN PARIETIBVS

M. Salāriō fēlīciter!

*CIL* 4.6811: Scribbled on the wall of a house in Reg. V by some well-wisher of Salarius. A Manius Salarius Crocus is known from two graffiti in a nearby house, and this Salarius may be the same: the Romans usually abbreviated the praenomen **Mārcus** with an **M** and **Mānius** with **M'**, but the distinction was not always observed in graffiti.—**fēlīciter:** an example of the sort of 3rd-decl. adj.-based adverbs newly introduced in this chapter; sc. **sit** or something such, in the sense of "may things go well for . . . !"

## LATĪNA EST GAVDIVM—ET VTILIS!

**Salvēte!** The modern Olympic games have as their motto three comparative adverbs, **citius, altius** (from **altus, -a, -um,** *high*), **fortius.** The new irregular verbs in this chapter, especially **volō** and **nōlō** are extremely common in Latin and you'll find them, willy-nilly, all through English. You know very well, for example, the legal plea of **nōlō,** short for **nōlō contendere,** *I am unwilling to contest* (the accusation); there's also **nol. pros.** = **nōlle prōsequī,** *to be unwilling to pursue* (the matter), meaning to drop a lawsuit; **nōlēns, volēns,** *unwilling (or) willing,* i.e., whether or not one wishes, like "willy-nilly" (a contraction of "will ye, nill ye"); the abbreviation "d.v.," for **deō volente;** also **volō, nōn valeō,** *I am willing but not able;* **nōlī mē tangere,** a warning against tampering as well as Latin for the jewel-weed flower or "touch-me-not"; **quantum vīs,** *as much as you wish* (which may be more than just **quantum satis,** Capvt XXX!); **Deus vult,** the call to arms of the First Crusade; and **mālō morī quam foedārī,** freely "death before dishonor" (lit., *I prefer to die than to be dishonored:* for the deponent verb **morior,** see Capvt XXXIV). Years ago some pundit wrote (demonstrating the importance of macrons), **mālō malō malō mālō,** *I'd rather be in an apple tree than a bad man in adversity;* the first **mālō** is from **mālum, -ī,** *apple, fruit-tree,* which calls to mind Horace's characterization of a Roman **cēna,** from the hors d'oeuvres to the dessert, as **ab ovō** (**ovum, -ī,** *egg*) **usque ad māla,** a phrase, very like the expression "from soup to nuts," that became proverbial for "from start to finish." **Et cētera ex vocābulīs novīs: cēterīs pāribus,** *all else being equal;* **custōdia** is related to **custōs, custōdis,** *guard,* and **custōdīre,** *to guard,* hence Juvenal's satiric query, **sed quis custōdiet ipsōs custōdēs; exercitus** is connected with **exerceō, exercēre,** *to practice, exercise,* and the noun **exercitātiō,** which gives us the proverb, most salutary for Latin students: **exercitātiō est optimus magister.** And so, **valēte, discipulī/ae, et exercēte, exercēte, exercēte!**

# CAPVT XXXIII 🔳🔳🔳

# Conditions

## GRAMMATICA

### CONDITIONAL SENTENCES

**CONDITIONS** are among the most common sentence types, others being **DECLAR-ATIVE**, **INTERROGATIVE**, and **EXCLAMATORY**. You have encountered numerous conditional sentences in your Latin readings already, and are likely aware that they consist of two clauses: (1) the condition or **PROTASIS** (Greek for "proposition" or "premise"), a subordinate clause usually introduced by **sī**, *if*, or **nisi**, *if not* or *unless*, and stating a hypothetical action or circumstance, and (2) the conclusion or **APODOSIS** (Greek for "outcome" or "result"), the main clause, which expresses the anticipated outcome if the premise turns out to be true.

There are six basic conditional types; three have their verbs in the indicative, three in the subjunctive, and the reason is simple. While all conditional sentences, by their very nature, describe actions in the past, present, or future that are to one extent or another hypothetical, the indicative was employed in those where the condition was more likely to be realized, the subjunctive in those where the premise was either less likely to be realized or where both the condition and the conclusion were absolutely contrary to the actual facts of a situation. Study the following summary, learning the names of each of the six conditional types, how to recognize them, and the standard formulae for translation:

### Indicative Conditions

1. **SIMPLE FACT PRESENT: Sī id facit, prūdēns est.** *If he is doing this* [*and it is quite possible that he is*], *he is wise.* Present indicative in both clauses; translate verbs as present indicatives.
2. **SIMPLE FACT PAST: Sī id fēcit, prūdēns fuit.** *If he did this* [*and quite possibly he did*], *he was wise.* Past tense (perfect or imperfect) indicative in both clauses; translate verbs as past indicatives.
3. **SIMPLE FACT FUTURE** (sometimes called **FUTURE MORE VIVID**): **Sī id faciet, prūdēns erit.** *If he does (will do) this* [*and quite possibly he will*], *he*

*will be wise.* Future indicative in both clauses; translate the verb in the protasis as a *present* tense (here English "if" + the present has a future sense), the verb in the apodosis as a future. (Occasionally the future perfect is used, in either or both clauses, with virtually the same sense as the simple future: see S.A. 8 and "B.Y.O.B." line 3, p. 277.)

### Subjunctive Conditions

The indicative conditions deal with potential facts; the subjunctive conditions are ideal rather than factual, describing circumstances that are either, in the case of the "future less vivid," somewhat less likely to be realized or less vividly imagined or, in the case of the two "contrary to fact" types, opposite to what actually is happening or has happened in the past.

1. CONTRARY TO FACT PRESENT: **Sī id faceret, prūdēns esset.** *If he were doing this [but in fact he is not], he would be wise [but he is not].* Imperfect subjunctive in both clauses; translate with auxiliaries *were (. . . ing)* and *would (be).*
2. CONTRARY TO FACT PAST: **Sī id fēcisset, prūdēns fuisset.** *If he had done this [but he did not], he would have been wise [but he was not].* Pluperfect subjunctive in both clauses; translate with auxiliaries *had* and *would have.*
3. FUTURE LESS VIVID (sometimes called SHOULD-WOULD): **Sī id faciat, prūdēns sit.** *If he should do this [and he may, or he may not], he would be wise.* Present subjunctive in both clauses; translate with auxiliaries *should* and *would.*

There are occasional variants on these six basic types, e.g., use of the imperative in the apodosis, MIXED CONDITIONS with different tenses or moods in the protasis and apodosis, different introductory words (e.g., **dum**), etc., but those are easily dealt with in context. For practice, identify the type of each of the following conditions:

1. **Sī hoc dīcet, errābit.** *If he says this, he will be wrong.*
2. **Sī hoc dīcit, errat.** *If he says this, he is wrong.*
3. **Sī hoc dīxisset, errāvisset.** *If he had said this, he would have been wrong.*
4. **Sī hoc dīcat, erret.** *If he should say this, he would be wrong.*
5. **Sī hoc dīxit, errāvit.** *If he said this, he was wrong.*
6. **Sī hoc dīceret, errāret.** *If he were saying this, he would be wrong.*
7. **Sī veniat, hoc videat.** *If he should come, he would see this.*
8. **Sī vēnit, hoc vīdit.** *If he came, he saw this.*
9. **Sī venīret, hoc vidēret.** *If he were coming, he would see this.*
10. **Sī veniet, hoc vidēbit.** *If he comes, he will see this.*
11. **Sī vēnisset, hoc vīdisset.** *If he had come, he would have seen this.*

# VOCĀBVLA

Note that **ops** (like a few other nouns you've learned, e.g., **animus** and **fīnis**) has some different meanings in the plural; and be aware that **quis, quid,** as you'll see below, is often indefinite and not interrogative; finally, the **eu** diphthong in **heu** is one of the very few sounds in classical Latin (the sound represented by the letter **y** is another) that we do not have in English: as always, listen carefully to this chapter's vocabulary either on the CDs or at www.wheelockslatin.com.

**inítium, inítiī,** n., *beginning, commencement* (initial, initiate, initiation)
**ops, ópis,** f., *help, aid;* **ópēs, ópum,** pl., *power, resources, wealth* (opulent, opulence; cf. **cōpia,** from **con-** + **ops**)
**philósophus, philósophī,** m., and **philósopha, philósophae,** f., *philosopher* (philosophical; cf. **philosophia**)
**plēbs, plḗbis,** f., *the common people, populace, plebeians* (plebs, plebe, plebeian, plebiscite)
**sāl, sális,** m., *salt; wit* (salad, salami, salary, saline, salinometer, sauce, sausage)
**spéculum, spéculī,** n., *mirror* (speculate, speculation; cf. **spectāre,** *to watch, look at*)
**quis, quid,** after **sī, nisi, nē, num,** indef. pron., *anyone, anything, someone, something* (cf. **quis? quid? quisque, quisquis**)
**cándidus, cándida, cándidum,** *shining, bright, white; beautiful* (candid, candidate, candor, incandescent, candle, chandelier)
**mérus, méra, mérum,** *pure, undiluted* (mere, merely)
**suávis, suáve,** *sweet* (suave, suaveness, suasion, dissuade, persuade)
**-ve,** conj. suffixed to a word = **aut** before the word (cf. **-que**), *or*
**heu,** interj., *ah!, alas!* (a sound of grief or pain; cf. "woe")
**súbitō,** adv., *suddenly* (sudden, suddenness)
**recū́sō, recūsā́re, recūsā́vī, recūsā́tum,** *to refuse* (recuse, recusant, recusative; cf. **causa**)
**trā́dō, trā́dere, trā́didī, trā́ditum** (**trāns** + **dō**), *to give over, surrender; hand down, transmit, teach* (tradition, traitor, treason)

# LĒCTIŌ ET TRĀNSLĀTIŌ

Read each sentence and passage aloud, and read for comprehension, before attempting a translation. As you read, identify the specific type of each conditional sentence and translate according to the rules introduced above.

## EXERCITĀTIŌNĒS

1. Dummodo exercitus opem mox ferat, moenia urbis celeriter cōnservāre poterimus.
2. Cum cōnsilia hostium ab initiō cognōvissēs, prīmō tamen ūllum auxilium offerre aut etiam centum mīlitēs prōmittere nōluistī.
3. Sī dīvitiae et invidia nōs ab amōre et honōre usque prohibent, dīvitēsne vērē sumus?
4. Pauper quidem nōn erit pār cēterīs nisi scientiam ingeniumve habēbit; sī autem haec habeat, multī magnopere invideant.
5. Nisi īnsidiae patērent, ferrum eius maximē timērēmus.
6. Sī quis rogābit quid nunc discās, nōlī dubitāre: refer tē artem nōn mediocrem sed ūtilissimam ac difficillimam discere.
7. Lēgēs ita scrībantur ut dīvitēs et plēbs—etiam pauper sine asse—sint parēs.
8. Sī custōdiae dūriōrēs fortiōrēsque ad casam tuam contendissent, heu, numquam tanta scelera suscēpissēs et hī omnēs nōn occidissent.
9. Illa philosopha sapientissima, cum id semel cognōvisset, ad eōs celerrimē sē contulit et omnēs opēs suās praebuit.
10. Dūrum exsilium tam ācrem mentem ūnō annō mollīre nōn poterit.
11. Propter omnēs rūmōrēs pessimōs (quī nōn erant vērī), nātae suāvēs eius magnopere dolēbant et dormīre nōn poterant.
12. If those philosophers should come soon, you would be happier.
13. If you had not answered very wisely, they would have hesitated to offer us peace.
14. If anyone does these three things well, he will live better.
15. If you were willing to read better books, you would most certainly learn more.

## SENTENTIAE ANTĪQVAE

1. Sī vīs pācem, parā bellum. (Flavius Vegetius.—**parā:** *prepare for.*)
2. Arma sunt parvī pretiī, nisi vērō cōnsilium est in patriā. (Cicero.—**pretium, -ī,** n., *value;* "precious," "price," "appraise.")
3. Salūs omnium ūnā nocte certē āmissa esset, nisi illa sevēritās contrā istōs suscepta esset. (Cicero.—**sevēritās, -tātis,** f., = Eng.; "severe," "persevere.")
4. Sī quid dē mē posse agī putābis, id agēs—sī tū ipse ab istō perīculō eris līber. (Cicero.)
5. Sī essem mihi cōnscius ūllīus culpae, aequō animō hoc malum ferrem. (Phaedrus.—**cōnscius, -a, -um,** *conscious;* "conscience," "unconscious.")
6. Dīcis tē vērē mālle fortūnam et mōrēs antīquae plēbis; sed sī quis ad illa subitō tē agat, illum modum vītae recūsēs. (Horace.)
7. Minus saepe errēs, sī sciās quid nesciās. (Publilius Syrus.)

8. Dīcēs "heu" sī tē in speculō vīderis. (Horace.)

9. Nīl habet īnfēlīx paupertās dūrius in sē quam quod rīdiculōs hominēs facit. (*Juvenal.—nīl: = nihil.—īnfēlīx: = īn-, *not*, + fēlīx.–quod, *the fact that.*)

10. Magnō mē metū līberābis, dummodo inter mē atque tē mūrus intersit. (*Cicero.–mūrus, -ī, m., *wall, city-wall*; "mural."–intersum, -esse, -fuī, *to be between, lie between*; "interest.")

11. Sī occīdī, rēctē fēcī; sed nōn occīdī. (*Quintilian.–occīdō, -ere, -cīdī, -cīsum, *to kill*; "homicide."–rēctē, adv., *rightly, justly*; "rectitude.")


## B.Y.O.B., etc., etc.

Cēnābis bene, mī Fabulle, apud mē
paucīs (sī tibi dī favent) diēbus—
sī tēcum attuleris bonam atque magnam
cēnam, nōn sine candidā puellā
5    et vīnō et sale et omnibus cachinnīs;
haec sī, inquam, attuleris, venuste noster,
cēnābis bene; nam tuī Catullī
plēnus sacculus est arāneārum.
Sed contrā accipiēs merōs amōrēs,
10    seu quid suāvius ēlegantiusve est:
nam unguentum dabo, quod meae puellae
dōnārunt Venerēs Cupīdinēsque;
quod tū cum olfaciēs, deōs rogābis
tōtum ut tē faciant, Fabulle, nāsum.

*Catullus *Carm.* 13: The perfect reading selection for a chapter on conditions; this dinner invitation, one of Catullus' most popular poems, was *highly* conditional, but if Fabullus accepts, he's in for an unusual treat! Meter: hendecasyllabic.—favēre: + dat., *to be favorable toward, favor*; "favorite."—cachinna, -ae, f., *laugh, laughter*; "cachinnate"; probably in origin ONOMATOPOETIC, like Eng. "cackle."—venustus, -a, -um, from venus/Venus, *attractive* (in appearance or manner), *charming*; "venereal."—sacculus, -ī, m., *money-bag, wallet*; "sack," "satchel."—arānea, -ae, f., *spiderweb*; "araneid," cognate with "arachnid."— contrā, here adv., *on the other hand, in return*; "contrary."—seu, conj., *or if, or perhaps.*— ēlegāns, gen. -gantis; "elegance," "elegantly."—unguentum, -ī, n., *salve, perfume*; "unguent," "ointment."—dabo: -ō was often shortened in verse.—dōnārunt: = dōnāvērunt (such contractions, dropping v and the following vowel, were common in perf. system forms), from dōnāre, *to give*; "donation," "donor."—Venus, -neris, f., and Cupīdō, -dinis, m.; *Venus* and *Cupid*, pl. here to represent all the fostering powers of Love; "venerate," "cupidity;" cf. cupiō; cupiditās.—quod . . . olfaciēs: = cum tū id olfaciēs.—olfaciō, -ere, *to smell*; "olfactory," "olfactant."—deōs rogābis . . . ut . . . faciant: JUSSIVE NOUN CLAUSE, a construction formally introduced in Capvt XXXVI, but easily translated here.—nāsus,

-ī, m., *nose;* "nasal" and "nasalize" are derivatives, "nostril" and "nozzle" are cognate; obj. complement with **tē;** the wide separation of adj. and noun suggests the cartoon-like enormity of the imagined schnoz!

*QVAESTIŌNĒS:* The poem neatly falls into two parts, the first describing what Fabullus will *not* receive at this **cēna,** and what therefore he must bring, and why; the second describing what he *will* receive, and why. Comment on Catullus' use of **cēnābis/cēna** and **nam** as structural markers, and on how effectively the poet produces a surprise ending at the close of each of the poem's halves. What other thematic connections do you see between the two sections?

## The Rich Get Richer

Semper pauper eris, sī pauper es, Aemiliāne:
  dantur opēs nūllī nunc nisi dīvitibus.

*Martial *Epig.* 5.81: Aemilianus, like most of Martial's addresses, is doubtless fictitious but represents a type. Meter: elegiac couplet.

*QUAESTIŌ:* Comment on the poet's use of anaphora, word order, and **ALLITERATION** (repetition of consonant sounds) to help make his point.

## Aristotle, Tutor of Alexander the Great

An Philippus, rēx Macedonum, voluisset Alexandrō, fīliō suō, prīma elementa litterārum trādī ab Aristotele, summō eius aetātis philosophō, aut hic suscēpisset illud maximum officium, nisi initia studiōrum pertinēre ad summam sapientissimē crēdidisset?

Quintilian *Inst.* 1.1.23: Quintilian (Marcus Fabius Quintilianus, ca. A.D. 35–95) is best known for his 12-volume work on oratory and education, the **Īnstitūtiōnēs Ōrātōriae;** he has given us the well known phrase defining the teacher's role of serving **in locō parentis,** and you read his dictum on Roman satire in the notes to "Juvenal Explains" in Capvt XVI. Philip hired Aristotle to tutor Alexander when the boy was 13; for another reflection on the intellectual interests of Alexander the Great, review the passage you read from Cicero's **Prō Archiā** in Capvt XIII.—**an,** interrog. conj., *or, can it be that.*—**Macedonēs, -num,** m./f. pl., *Macedonians.*—**Aristotelēs, -lis,** m.—**pertinēre ad:** *to relate to, affect;* "pertain," "pertinent."—**summa, -ae,** f., *highest part, whole;* "sum," "summary."

*QVAESTIŌNĒS:* Explain in your own words the view Quintilian expresses here regarding teachers and the education of the young. Did Philip and Aristotle agree? Do you?

*Aristotle*
*Roman copy of a Greek original*
*Galleria Spada, Rome, Italy*

### Your Loss, My Gain!

Cum Quīntus Fabius Maximus magnō cōnsiliō Tarentum fortissimē recēpisset et
Salīnātor (quī in arce fuerat, urbe āmissā) dīxisset, "Meā operā, Quīnte Fabī, Tarentum recēpistī," Fabius, mē audiente, "Certē," inquit rīdēns, "nam nisi tū urbem
āmīsissēs, numquam eam recēpissem."

Cicero *Sen.* 4.11: Another example of Roman wit, from Cicero's treatise *On Old Age* (take
a few minutes now to review the other selections you have read from that same work, in
Capita XV, XVII, and XIX). During the second Punic War, the inhabitants of Tarentum,
in southeastern Italy (Map 1), revolted from the Romans to Hannibal, though the Romans under Marcus Livius Salinator managed to hold the citadel. In 209 B.C. the city was
recaptured by Quintus Fabius Maximus (Fabius "the Delayer," about whose accomplishments you read in Capvt XV).— **opera, -ae,** f., *work, help, effort;* **meā operā** is rather like
our idiom, "thanks to me."—**mē audiente:** like our idiom "in my presence," but what is
the lit. meaning? Like Cicero's other philosophical treatises, the **Dē Senectūte** was written in the form of a dialogue; the "me" speaking here was Cato the Elder, a contemporary of Fabius.

*QVAESTIŌ:* Explain Salinator's hubris, and Fabius' wit.

## SCRĪPTA IN PARIETIBVS

Mūnus Nōlae dē quādrīdu[ō] M(ārcī) Cōminiī Hērēdi[s]:
Prī<n>ceps Ner(ōniānus), XII, c(orōnae) X[?]; v(īcit).
Hilārus Ner(ōniānus), XIV, c(orōnae) XII; v(īcit).
Creunus, VII, c(orōnae) V; m(issus est).

CIL 4.10237: One of several illustrated gladiatorial graffiti from a tomb in the necropolis outside Pompeii's Porta di Nocera; the games whose results are recorded here were sponsored by Marcus Cominius Heres (**Hērēs, -rēdis**), apparently a local magistrate. The three named gladiators, Princeps (whose name is misspelled) and the two depicted in the drawing, Hilarus and Creunus, all of them slaves, had impressive winning records: the first Roman numeral after each gladiator's name stands for the number of **pugnae,** *fights,* in which he had competed, the second for the number of **corōnae** (here, as often, abbreviated as a reverse **C**), *crowns* or *victory garlands,* which he had won; someone, perhaps the fan of a rival, marked out the number of Hilarus' victories with two lines; the meaning of the letters (**TAAV?**) written beneath Creunus' name is unclear. Pictured to the right are musicians (gladiatorial games had bands just like football games today!); the figures to the far left are probably spectators.—**mūnus, -neris,** n., *service, function, duty; public show, game; offering, gift;* "munificence," "munificent."—**Nōlae:** LOCATIVE case (see Capvt XXXVII) of the place name **Nōla,** = *at Nola,* a town northeast of Pompeii.—**quādrīduum, -ī,** n., *(a period of) four days;* with **dē,** *for a . . . ;* gladiatorial games were often scheduled for several consecutive days.—**Nerōniānus, -a, -m,** *of (the emperor) Nero, Neronian;* the epithet indicates that these fighters were from the imperial gladiatorial camp at Capua.—**missus est:** i.e., he was defeated but spared ("sent home to fight another day").

## LATĪNA EST GAVDIVM—ET VTILIS!

**Salvēte!** Here are some well known conditions: **sī nātūra negat, facit indignātiō versum,** *if nature denies* (i.e., if my talent is lacking), *indignation creates my verse* (so said the satirist Juvenal, who had plenty of both!—see "Juvenal Explains," Capvt XVI); **sī fēcistī, negā!** (a lawyer's advice); **sī Deus nōbīscum, quis contrā nōs** (the verbs are left out, but the meaning is clear); **sī post fāta venit glōria, nōn properō,** *if glory comes* (*only*) *after death, I'm in no hurry!* (Martial); **sī sīc omnēs,** freely, a wistful "if only everything were like this" (or does it really mean "all on the boat became ill"?!!). **Ex vocābulīs novīs quoque:** well, to start "from the beginning," the phrase **ab initiō** is quite common in English; those running for political office in Rome wore the **toga candida,** *white toga,* hence English "candidate." The Romans called undiluted wine **merum** (which the bibulous merely imbibed!); **ope et cōnsiliō** is a good way to manage life. The expression "with a grain of salt" comes from Latin **cum grānō salis;** "salary" is also from **sāl,** a package of which was part of a Roman soldier's pay (we "bring home the salty bacon," Romans brought home the salt!); and **sāl Atticum** is dry *Athenian wit.* Art is a **speculum vītae.** If you remember how to form adverbs from adjectives, then you can decipher the proverb **suāviter in modō, fortiter in rē,** a good mode for the Latin teacher; and if you read music, you may have seen **subitō,** a musical annotation meaning *quickly.*

Hope you enjoy these closing **miscellānea** (from **miscellāneus, -a, -um,** *varied, mixed*), and here's one reason why: **sī fīnis bonus est, tōtum bonum erit,** an old proverb, a "mixed condition," and familiar vocabulary, so I'll give you the free version, "All's well that ends well (including this chapter)!": **et vōs omnēs, quoque valeātis!**

*Necropolis outside the Porta di Nocera, Pompeii, Italy*

# CAPVT XXXIV 🏛🏛🏛

# Deponent Verbs; Ablative with Special Deponents

## GRAMMATICA

### DEPONENT VERBS

Latin has a number of common **DEPONENT VERBS,** verbs that have passive endings but active meanings. There are few new forms to be learned (only the imperatives); the most crucial matter is simply to recall *which verbs are deponent,* so that you remember to translate them in the active voice, and that can be managed through careful vocabulary study. There are a few exceptions to the rule of passive forms/active meanings, and those will also need to be carefully noted.

#### Principal Parts and Conjugation

As you will see from the following examples, deponents have only three principal parts, the passive equivalents of the first three principal parts of regular verbs (1. first pers. sg. pres. indic., 2. pres. infin., 3. first pers. sg. perf. indic.).

| Present Indic. | Present Infin. | Perfect Indic. |
|---|---|---|
| hórtor, *I urge* | hortárī, *to urge* | hortátus (-a, -um) sum, *I urged* |
| fáteor, *I confess* | fatérī, *to confess* | fássus (-a, -um) sum, *I confessed* |
| séquor, *I follow* | séquī, *to follow* | secútus (-a, -um) sum, *I followed* |
| mólior, *I work at* | mōlírī, *to work at* | mōlítus (-a, -um) sum, *I worked at* |
| pátior, *I suffer* | pátī, *to suffer* | pássus (-a, -um) sum, *I suffered* |

Deponents are conjugated according to the same rules as regular verbs in the passive voice; the following representative forms are provided for review, and full conjugations for each of the five examples given above are included in the App. (p. 504–06).

*Indicative*
**Present**

| | |
|---|---|
| 1. hórtor, *I urge* | séquor, *I follow* |
| 2. hortåris (-re), *you urge* | séqueris (-re), *you follow* |
| 3. hortåtur, *he urges* | séquitur, *he follows* |
| 1. hortåmur, *we urge* | séquimur, *we follow* |
| 2. hortåminī, *you urge* | sequíminī, *you follow* |
| 3. hortántur, *they urge* | sequúntur, *they follow* |

**Imperfect**

| | |
|---|---|
| 1. hortåbar, *I was urging* | sequêbar, *I was following* |
| 2. hortābåris (-re), *you were urging*, etc. | sequēbåris (-re), *you were following*, etc. |

**Future**

| | |
|---|---|
| 1. hortåbor, *I shall urge* | séquar, *I shall follow* |
| 2. hortåberis (-re), *you will urge* | sequêris (-re), *you will follow* |
| 3. hortåbitur, *he will urge*, etc. | sequêtur, *he will follow*, etc. |

**Perfect**

| | |
|---|---|
| hortåtus, -a, -um sum, *I urged*, etc. | secútus, -a, -um sum, *I followed*, etc. |

**Pluperfect**

| | |
|---|---|
| hortåtus, -a, -um éram, *I had urged*, etc. | secútus, -a, -um éram, *I had followed*, etc. |

**Future Perfect**

| | |
|---|---|
| hortåtus, -a, -um érō, *I shall have urged*, etc. | secútus, -a, -um érō, *I shall have followed*, etc. |

*Subjunctive*
**Present**

| | |
|---|---|
| hórter, hortêris, hortêtur, etc. | séquar, sequåris, sequåtur, etc. |

**Imperfect**

| | |
|---|---|
| hortårer, hortārêris, hortārêtur, etc. | séquerer, sequerêris, sequerêtur, etc. |

**Perfect**

| | |
|---|---|
| hortåtus, -a, -um sim, sīs, etc. | secútus, -a, -um sim, sīs, etc. |

**Pluperfect**

| | |
|---|---|
| hortåtus, -a, -um éssem, etc. | secútus, -a, -um éssem, etc. |

## Synopsis

The following synopsis of **fateor, fatērī, fassus sum** provides a useful overview of the conjugation of deponents; remember that all English equivalents are active, i.e., *he confesses, he will confess,* etc.

**Indicative Mood**

| Pres. | Fut. | Imperf. | Perf. | Fut. Perf. | Pluperf. |
|-------|------|---------|-------|------------|----------|
| fatétur | fatébitur | fatēbâtur | fássus est | fássus érit | fássus érat |

**Subjunctive Mood**

| fateâtur | —— | fatērétur | fássus sit | —— | fássus ésset |
|----------|----|-----------|-----------|----|--------------|

## Participles, Infinitives, and Imperatives

The participles and infinitives of typical deponent verbs are here given in full not because of any new forms but because of certain discrepancies in the general rule of passive forms with active meanings:

### Participles

*Pres.* hórtāns, *urging*           séquēns, *following*
*Perf.* hortâtus, -a, -um, *having urged*    secûtus, -a, -um, *having followed*
*Fut.* hortātûrus, -a, -um, *about to urge*   secūtûrus, -a, -um, *about to follow*
*Ger.* hortándus, -a, -um, *to be urged*    sequéndus, -a, -um, *to be followed*

### Infinitives

*Pres.* hortârī, *to urge*             séquī, *to follow*
*Perf.* hortâtus, -a, -um ésse, *to have urged*   secûtus, -a, -um ésse, *to have followed*
*Fut.* hortātûrus, -a, -um ésse, *to be about*   secūtûrus, -a, -um ésse, *to be about to*
    *to urge*                       *follow*

*Exceptions:* Deponents have the same four participles as regular verbs, but only three infinitives, one for each tense. Three of the participles and one of the infinitives present exceptions to the rule that deponents are passive in form but active in meaning:

1. Present and future participles: active forms with active meanings.
2. Gerundive (future passive participle): passive form with passive meaning.
3. Future infinitive: active form with active meaning.

### Imperatives

The present imperative of deponents would naturally have the forms of the present passive imperative. These forms have not been given before because they are found chiefly in deponent verbs, but they are easy to learn: the second person singular has the same spelling as that of the *alternate* second person singular passive of the present *indicative*, e.g., **sequere**, *follow!* Note that, coincidentally, this form is also identical to the (non-existent) present active *infinitive:* be careful not to mistake this deponent imperative for an infinitive. The plural imperative is spelled the same as the second person plural passive of the present indicative, e.g., **sequiminī**, *follow!* Compare the following examples:

| hortā́re, *urge!* | fatḗre, *confess!* | mōlī́re, *work at!* | pátere, *endure!* |
| hortā́minī, *urge!* | fatḗminī, *confess!* | mōlī́minī, *work at!* | patíminī, *endure!* |

## Semi-Deponent Verbs

Latin has a few SEMI-DEPONENT VERBS, which are normal in the present system but deponent in the perfect system, as seen in their principal parts:

| aúdeō, *I dare* | audḗre, *to dare* | aúsus sum, *I dared* |
| gaúdeō, *I rejoice* | gaudḗre, *to rejoice* | gāvī́sus sum, *I rejoiced* |

Study the following sentences, containing both deponent and semi-deponent verbs:

1. **Eum patientem haec mala hortātī sunt.**
   *They encouraged him (as he was) suffering these evils.*
2. **Eum passūrum haec mala hortātī sunt.**
   *They encouraged him (as he was) about to suffer these evils.*
3. **Is, haec mala passus, hortandus est.**
   *This man, having suffered these evils, ought to be encouraged.*
4. **Is haec mala fortiter patiētur.**
   *He will suffer these evils bravely.*
5. **Eum sequere et haec mōlīre.**
   *Follow him and work at these things.*
6. **Eum sequī et haec mōlīrī nōn ausus es.**
   *You did not dare to follow him and work at these things.*
7. **Eum sequeris/sequḗris.**
   *You are following/will follow him.*
8. **Eum hortēmur et sequāmur.**
   *Let us encourage and follow him.*

## ABLATIVE WITH SPECIAL DEPONENTS

The ablative is used as object of a few deponent verbs, of which **ūtor** (and its compounds) is the most common (others, including **fruor**, *to enjoy,* **fungor**, *to perform,* **potior**, *to possess,* and **vēscor**, *to eat,* are not employed in this book, but may be encountered in your later reading). Ūtor, *to use, enjoy,* may originally have meant *I am benefitted/I benefit myself (by),* so that this ABLATIVE WITH SPECIAL DEPONENTS may in origin have been an ablative of means:

Ūtitur stilō. *He is using a pencil* (lit., *He is benefitted/benefits himself by means of a pencil*).

Cicerō Graecīs litterīs ūtēbātur. *Cicero used to enjoy Greek literature.*

Nōn audent ūtī nāvibus. *They do not dare to use the ships.*

Nōn ausī sunt ūtī nāvibus. *They did not dare to use the ships.*

# VOCĀBVLA

The basic sense of **anima,** introduced below, was *life-breath,* whereas **animus,** as you have already learned, refers fundamentally to *mind,* as opposed to body; but there came to be some overlap in meaning, and both words could mean *soul.* As you learn the principal parts of the deponent verbs introduced here, practice by doing a synopsis, with English translation, of two or three of them from different conjugations, each in a different person and number; and be careful not to confuse **patior** with **pateō,** learned earlier.

**ánima, ánimae,** f., *air* (breathed by an animal), *breath; soul, spirit* (anima, animism, animation, animated, inanimate; cf. **animal, animus**)

**remíssiō, remissiṓnis,** f., *letting go, release; relaxation* (remiss, remission; from **re + mittō**)

**vōx, vṓcis,** f., *voice, word* (vocal, vocalic, vocalize, vociferous, vowel; vox angelica, vox humana, vox populi; cf. **vocō**)

**advérsus, advérsa, advérsum,** *opposite, adverse* (adversary, adversative, adversity; cf. **vertō**)

**tális, tále,** *such, of such a sort* (cf. **quālis,** *of what sort, what kind of* )

**vae,** interj., often + dat. or acc., *alas, woe to*

**árbitror, arbitrā́rī, arbitrā́tus sum,** *to judge, think* (arbiter, arbitress, arbitration, arbitrator, arbitrary, arbitrarily)

**cṓnor, cōnā́rī, cōnā́tus sum,** *to try, attempt* (conation, conative)

**crḗscō, crḗscere, crḗvī, crḗtum,** *to increase* (crescent, crescendo, concrete, decrease, excrescence, increment, accretion, accrue, crew, recruit)

**ēgrédior, ḗgredī, ēgréssus sum,** *to go out* (egress; cf. aggression, congress, digress, ingredient, ingress, progress, regress, retrogress, transgress)

**fáteor, fatḗrī, fássus sum,** *to confess, admit* (confession, profess, profession, professor; cf. **fābula, fāma, fātum**)

**hórtor, hortā́rī, hortā́tus sum,** *to encourage, urge* (hortatory, exhortation)

**lóquor, lóquī, locū́tus sum,** *to say, speak, tell* (loquacious, circumlocution, colloquial, elocution, eloquent, obloquy, soliloquy, ventriloquist)

**mṓlior, mōlī́rī, mōlī́tus sum,** *to work at, build, undertake, plan* (demolish, demolition; cf. **mōlēs,** *a large mass, massive structure*)

**mórior, mórī, mórtuus sum,** fut. act. partic. **moritū́rus,** *to die* (moribund, mortuary; cf. **mors, mortālis, mortuus, immortālis**)

**nā́scor, nā́scī, nā́tus sum,** *to be born; spring forth, arise* (agnate, cognate, innate, nascent, natal, nation, nature, naive; cf. **nāta, nātūra**)

**pátior, pátī, pássus sum,** *to suffer, endure; permit* (passion, passive, compassion, compatible, impassioned, dispassionate; cf. **patientia**)

**proficī́scor, proficī́scī, profḗctus sum,** *to set out, start* (profit and proficient from the related **prōficiō,** *to make headway, gain results*)

**rū́sticor, rūsticā́rī, rūsticā́tus sum,** *to live in the country* (rusticate, rustic, rural, cf. **rūsticus,** *rural*)

**sédeō, sedḗre, sḗdī, séssum,** *to sit* (sedan, sedate, sedentary, sediment, sessile, session, assess, assiduous, president, siege, subsidy)

**séquor, séquī, secū́tus sum,** *to follow* (consequent, consecutive, obsequious, persecute, sequence, sequel, subsequent; cf. **secundus**)

**spéctō, spectā́re, spectā́vī, spectā́tum,** *to look at, see* (spectator, spectacle, speculate, aspect, circumspect, inspect; cf. **speculum**)

**ū́tor, ū́tī, ū́sus sum** + abl., *to use; enjoy, experience* (abuse, disuse, peruse, usual, usurp, usury, utensil, utilize, utility, utilitarian; cf. **ūtilis**)

# LĒCTIŌ ET TRĀNSLĀTIŌ

After studying the new grammar, memorizing the vocabulary, and testing your mastery with the Self-Tutorial Exercises, scan the following readings for all (a) deponent verbs, identifying the tense, number, person, and mood of each, and (b) ablatives with special deponents. Listen to the CDs, if you have them, and read aloud for comprehension before translating.

## EXERCITĀTIŌNĒS

1. Nisi quis plēbī opem celeriter referet auxiliumve prōmissum praebēbit, mīlia pauperum morientur.
2. Cum urbs plēna custōdiārum esset, nōn ausī estis suscipere scelera tam gravia quam voluerātis.
3. Dīc nunc cūr velīs tē ad istam dīvitem et candidam cōnferre. Vērē ac līberē loquere; nōlī recūsāre!
4. Dīvitiīs opibusque trāditīs, heu, illī philosophī eādem nocte subitō profectī sunt in exsilium, unde numquam ēgredī potuērunt.
5. Nē patiāmur hanc antīquissimam scientiam āmittī.
6. Fateor mē vīnō merō apud mē ūsūrum esse.
7. Ab initiō nōn comprehendistī quantus exercitus nōs sequerētur et quot elephantōs istī mīlitēs sēcum dūcerent.
8. Prīmō respondit sē nōlle sequī ducem mediocris virtūtis sapientiaeve, cum cīvitās in līmine bellī stāret.
9. Ex urbe subitō ēgressus, ferrō suō morī semel cōnātus est.
10. Cum Aristotelēs hortārētur hominēs ad virtūtem, tamen arbitrābātur virtūtem in hominibus nōn nāscī.
11. Māter paterque nunc rūsticārī plūrimum mālunt, ut ā labōribus remissiōne suāvī fēlīcius ūtantur.
12. Dā mihi, amābō tē, multum salis et vīnum aquamve, ut cēnā maximē ūtar.

13. They did not permit me to speak with him at that time.

14. We kept thinking (**arbitror**) that, on account of the plebeians' poverty, he would use the office more wisely.

15. If any one should use this water even once, he would die.

16. If those four soldiers had followed us, we would not have dared to put the weapons on the ships.

17. This dinner will be good, provided that you use salt.

## SENTENTIAE ANTĪQVAE

1. Cēdāmus Phoebō et, monitī, meliōra sequāmur. (*Vergil.—Phoebus Apollo was god of prophecy.)

2. Nam nēmō sine vitiīs nāscitur; optimus ille est quī minima habet. (Horace.)

3. Mundus est commūnis urbs deōrum atque hominum; hī enim sōlī, ratiōne ūtentēs, iūre ac lēge vīvunt. (Cicero.)

4. Tardē sed graviter vir sapiēns īrāscitur. (*Publilius Syrus.—**tardē**, adv., *slowly;* "tardy," "retard."—**īrāscor, īrāscī, īrātus sum,** *to become angry;* "irascible," "irate.")

5. Quae cum ita sint, Catilīna, ēgredere ex urbe; patent portae; proficīscere; nōbīscum versārī iam diūtius nōn potes; id nōn feram, nōn patiar. (Cicero.— **Quae cum: = Cum haec.—versor, -sārī, -sātus sum,** lit. *to be turned, turn* [*oneself*] *around;* idiom = *to spend one's time* [in a place], *remain;* "versatile," "converse.")

6. Cūra pecūniam crēscentem sequitur et dīves male dormit. (Horace.)

7. Sī in Britanniam profectus essēs, nēmō in illā tantā īnsulā iūre perītior fuisset. (Cicero.—**Britannia, -ae,** f., *Britain.*—**perītus, -a, -um** + abl., *skilled in;* "expert," "experience.")

8. Nisi laus nova nāscitur etiam vetus laus in incertō iacet ac saepe āmittitur. (Publilius Syrus.)—**vetus,** gen. **veteris,** *old;* "veteran," "inveterate.")

9. Spērō autem mē secūtum esse in libellīs meīs tālem temperantiam ut nēmō bonus dē illīs querī possit. (Martial.—**temperantia, -ae,** f.; "temperate," "intemperance."—**queror, querī, questus sum,** *to complain;* "querulous," "quarrel.")

10. Hōrae quidem et diēs et annī discēdunt; nec praeteritum tempus umquam revertitur, nec quid sequātur potest scīrī. (Cicero.—**praeteritus, -a, -um,** *past;* "preterit," "praeteritio."—**revertor, -vertī, -versus sum,** *to return;* "reverse," "revert.")

11. Nōvistī mōrēs mulierum: dum mōliuntur, dum cōnantur, dum in speculum spectant, annus lābitur. (Terence.—**mulier, -eris,** f., *woman;* "muliebrity."— **lābor, lābī, lāpsus sum,** *to slip, glide;* "lapse," "collapse.")

12. Amīcitia rēs plūrimās continet; nōn aquā, nōn igne in plūribus locīs ūtimur quam amīcitiā. (Cicero.)

13. Homō stultus! Postquam dīvitiās habēre coepit, mortuus est! (Cicero.—**postquam**, conj., *after;* "postscript.")
14. Ō passī graviōra, dabit deus hīs quoque fīnem. (*Vergil.—**Ō passī**, voc. pl., *O you who have. . . .*—**hīs:** = **hīs rēbus gravibus.**)

## Claudius' Excremental Expiration

Et ille quidem animam ēbulliit, et ex eō dēsiit vīvere vidērī. Exspīrāvit autem dum comoedōs audit, ut sciās mē nōn sine causā illōs timēre. Ultima vōx eius haec inter hominēs audīta est, cum maiōrem sonitum ēmisisset illā parte quā facilius loquēbātur: "Vae mē, putō, concacāvī!" Quod an fēcerit, nesciō—omnia certē concacāvit!

*Seneca *Apoc.* 4: The 1st-cent. A.D. philosopher Seneca the Younger, whose views on frugality you read in Capvt IX ("When I Have . . . Enough!"), is also credited with authoring a satirical and occasionally cruel farce on the emperor Claudius' death and deification; the work's Greek title, **Apocolocyntōsis,** seems to have meant "Pumpkinification" or "Deification of a Pumpkin-Head."—**ēbulliō, -īre, ēbulliī,** *to bubble out,* + **animam,** comic for "he died"; "ebullient."—**ex eō:** sc. **tempore.**—**dēsinō, -sinere, -siī, -situm,** *to cease.*—**exspīrāre,** *to breathe out, die;* "expiration," "expire."—**comoedus, -ī,** m., *comic actor, comedian.*—**audit:** use of the pres. instead of the expected perf. was a colloquialism.—**vōx:** i.e., *utterance.*—**sonitus, -ūs,** m., *sound;* "sonic," "resonate."—**ē/ex + mittere:** = Eng.; "emission," "emissary."—**illā parte:** sc. **corporis,** i.e., his bottom; the suggestion that Claudius spoke from his anus with greater ease than from his mouth was an indelicate slur on the emperor's affliction with stuttering.—**concacāre,** *to defecate upon.*—**quod:** = id.—**an,** *whether,* introducing an ind. question.

*The emperor Claudius*
*Head from a life-size bronze statue*
*Saxmundham, Suffolk, England*
*1st cent. A.D.*
*British Museum, London, Great Britain*

*QVAESTIŌNĒS:* What is the satiric implication of the remark **dēsiit vīvere vidērī**? At the outset of the satire, the narrator assumes the persona of a historian trying to report the facts of an actual event according to the limited sources available to him; where in this excerpt does that persona humorously appear?

## And Vice Is Not Nice!

Mentītur quī tē vitiōsum, Zōile, dīcit:
    nōn vitiōsus homō es, Zōile, sed vitium!

*Martial *Epig.* 11.92: meter: elegiac couplet.—**mentior, -tīrī, -tītus sum,** *to lie, deceive.*—**vitiōsus:** adj. from **vitium;** "viciousness"; for the suffix **-ōsus, -a, -um,** = Eng. "-ous" or "-ose," see S.S., p. 490; —**tē vitiōsum:** sc. **esse;** remember that the verb **sum, esse** is often omitted when readily understood from the context, a type of omission known as ELLIPSIS.—**Zōilus:** a Greek name.

*QVAESTIŌNĒS:* What do we initially think the narrator's attitude toward Zoilus is? Comment specifically on the epigram's word-play and how anaphora and word order accentuate the surprise ending.

## Pretty Is as Pretty Does

Bella es, nōvimus, et puella, vērum est,
et dīves—quis enim potest negāre?
Sed cum tē nimium, Fabulla, laudās,
nec dīves neque bella nec puella es!

*Martial *Epig.* 1.64: Fabulla boasteth too much! Meter: hendecasyllabic.

*QVAESTIŌNĒS:* Fabulla either is **bella,** a **puella,** and **dīves,** or . . . she isn't! Comment on the poet's use of word order, alliteration, and POLYSYNDETON (use of more conjunctions than usual or necessary) to make his point; and what are the multiple ramifications of telling this lady she is **nec puella?**

## On Lesbia's Husband

Ille mī pār esse deō vidētur,
ille, sī fās est, superāre dīvōs,
quī, sedēns adversus, identidem tē
        spectat et audit
5    dulce rīdentem, miserō quod omnīs
ēripit sēnsūs mihi: nam simul tē,
Lesbia, aspexī, nihil est super mī,

[Lesbia, vōcis,]
lingua sed torpet, tenuis sub artūs
10 flamma dēmānat, sonitū suōpte
tintinant aurēs, geminā teguntur
lūmina nocte.
Ōtium, Catulle, tibi molestum est;
ōtiō exsultās nimiumque gestīs;
15 ōtium et rēgēs prius et beātās
perdidit urbēs.

*Catullus *Carm.* 51: One of the most admired of Catullus' poems, **Carmen** 51 is generally regarded as dramatically at least, if not in its actual order of composition, first of the Lesbia cycle; in part an imitation of an erotic poem by the 7th cent. B.C. Greek poetess Sappho of Lesbos (whose home and literary milieu inspired the pseudonym Catullus gave his mistress), the poet recalls an occasion when, gazing upon Lesbia and a man sitting opposite her (likely her husband), he becomes emotionally and even physiologically overwhelmed by her beauty and the sweet sound of her laughter. Meter: Sapphic stanza.—**mī**: = **mihi.**— **fās est**: *it is right;* read the two opening verses aloud and listen to the rhyming of the first four words in each.—**dīvōs**: = **deōs.**—**identidem**, adv., *again and again;* "identical."—**dulce**: adv. of **dulcis.**—**miserō . . . mihi**: DATIVE OF SEPARATION, essentially the same as the abl. usage; the prose order would be **quod omnīs** (= **omnēs**) **sēnsūs mihi miserō ēripit.**—**quod**: *a circumstance which;* the entire preceding clause is the antecedent.—**simul**, adv., *as soon as;* "simultaneous," "ensemble."—**aspexī**: = **spectāvī;** "aspect."—**nihil**: with **vōcis,** gen. of the whole, *no. . . .*—**est super**: = **superest,** *remains.*—**Lesbia, vōcis**: an editorial suggestion for a verse missing in the manuscripts.—**torpēre**, *to grow numb;* "torpedo," "torpid."—**tenuis**: with **flamma,** from **tenuis, -e,** *thin, slender;* "tenuous," "extenuate."—**artus, -ūs,** m., *joint, limb* (of the body); "article," "articulation."—**flamma, -ae,** f., *flame;* "flammable," "inflammation."—**dēmānāre**, *to flow through.*—**suōpte**: intensive for **suō.**—**tintināre**, *to ring;* "tintinnabulation."—**tegō, -ere,** *to cover;* "protect," "detect."—**lūmen, -minis,** n., *light; eye;* "luminary," "luminous."—**molestus, -a, -um,** *troublesome;* "molest."—**exsultāre**, *to celebrate, exult* (*in*), + **ōtiō;** "exultant," "exultation."—**gestīre**, *to act without restraint, be elated* or *triumphant.*—**perdō, -ere, -didī, -ditum,** *to destroy;* "perdition."

*QUAESTIŌNĒS:* What makes the man sitting with Lesbia godlike?—i.e., what can he endure that, by contrast, overpowers Catullus? Describe as exactly as possible what happens to Catullus in the second and third stanzas, esp. in lines 11–12. **Geminā** is an example of a TRANSFERRED EPITHET, modifying **nocte** grammatically when logically it should apply to Catullus' **lūmina;** what effect does the resultant image exert on the reader? Some scholars have questioned whether the fourth stanza, with its abrupt transition and self reprimand, was even a part of the original poem or if instead it was somehow misplaced here by scribal error during the transmission of the manuscript from antiquity into the middle ages and beyond; review your other readings from Catullus, including poem 5 (Capvt XXXI) and esp. the excerpt from poem 7 (Capvt XIX), and argue your own position on this issue.

## SCRĪPTA IN PARIETIBVS

Pittacius cum Prīmigeniā hīc. Prīma, sequere! Volumnius

*CIL* 4.8769: Pittacius Volumnius scribbled this note on a column of Pompeii's Large Palaestra (Reg. II, Ins. 7), recording a liaison with his girlfriend, then urging another lady (or was "Prima" just his shortened, pet name for Primigenia?) to follow him.—**sequere:** watch out—this form is not what it may seem to be, as you know if you've studied this chapter carefully. Because he was writing on a fluted column (#106: archaeologists have assigned identifying numbers to all these columns), Volumnius could fit only a few letters on each line and after writing **SEQ** on one line continued with **VERE** on the next, a common practice seen again in his signature **VOLV/MNIVS**; to help the reader avoid confusion on the one line that contained more than one word, he placed a punctum between **PRIMA** and **SEQ**.

## LATĪNA EST GAVDIVM—ET VTILIS!

**Salvēte, meī discipulī discipulaeque! Quid agitis? (Spērō vōs valēre.)** Now that you've begun to read more real, unadapted Latin literature (like the above selections from Martial, Seneca, and Catullus), you might appreciate the following remark: "Looking back on school, I really liked Latin. In my case, a little bit stuck: I ended up with a feeling for literature."—Paul McCartney. So, how much Latin is enough?—**quantum placeat,** *as much as gives one pleasure* (close to **quantum vīs,** Capvt XXXII, and more, one hopes, than **quantum satis,** Capvt XXX!).

Here are some Latin phrases that are by no means moribund: first, an unfortunate (and fortunately overstated!) old proverb, **quem dī dīligunt, adulēscēns moritur;** a reminder of one's mortality is a **mementō morī,** freely "remember that you must die" (the **-tō** form is a relatively rare FUTURE IMPERATIVE not formally introduced in this book but often employed in ancient legal and religious texts); on sacrificing one's life for one's country, Horace wrote **dulce et decōrum** (from **decōrus, -a, -um,** *fitting, proper*) **est prō patriā morī;** another bleak proverb (but essential here, as it offers two deponents!) is the astronomer Manilius' dictum, **nascentēs morimur** (*even as we are*) *being born, we* (*begin to*) *die;* and then there is Seneca's version of "eat, drink, and be merry," complete with a passive periphrastic, **bibāmus, moriendum est,** and the words addressed to the emperor by gladiators preparing to fight, **Avē, Imperātor: moritūrī tē salūtant,** *hail, Emperor, they* (*who are*) *about to die salute you!* To any who have suffered, not death, but defeat, one might proclaim **vae, victīs,** *woe to the conquered,* a famous line from Livy's account of the Gallic sack of Rome in 390 B.C.

Well, enough morbidity. **Hīc sunt alia miscellānea ex vocābulīs novīs: vōx populī; vōx clamantis in dēsertō,** *the voice of one calling out in the wilderness* (from the gospel of Matthew); **crēscit amor nummī quantum ipsa pecūnia crēvit,** *love of the coin grows as much as one's wealth itself has grown* (Juvenal 14.139); **sedente animō,** *with a calm mind.* And here are some other deponents: Maryland's state motto is **crēscite et multiplicāminī** (can you figure that one out?); **loquitur** is a note in a dramatic text; and the legal phrase **rēs ipsa loquitur,** *the matter speaks for itself,* we have seen before, but now you understand the verb form. And how about this sequence: **seq.** is an abbreviation for **sequēns/ sequentēs,** *the following,* once common in footnotes; a **nōn sequitur** is a remark that *does not follow* logically from a prior statement (a **sequitur,** of course, does!); **sequor nōn īnferior,** *I follow* (*but am*) *not inferior.* Will this exciting chapter have a sequel in the subsequent chapter? And, if not, what will be the consequences? Stay tuned . . . **et valēte!**

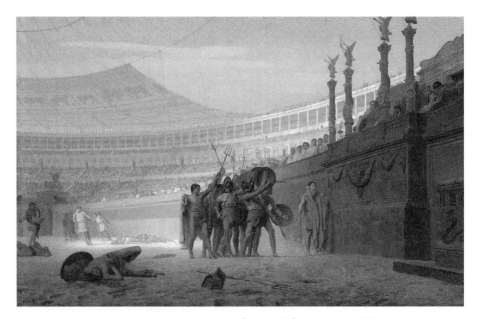

Ave Caesar—Morituri te salutant! *Oil on canvas, 1859.*
*Jean-Léon Gérôme (1824–1904)*
*Yale University Art Gallery, New Haven, Connecticut*

# CAPVT XXXV ▨▨▨

# Dative with Adjectives, Special Verbs, and Compounds

## GRAMMATICA

### THE DATIVE CASE

The dative case is in general employed to indicate a person or thing that some act or circumstance applies to or refers to "indirectly," as opposed to the accusative, which indicates the more immediate recipient or object of an action. The indirect object, e.g., is the person/thing toward which a direct object is "referred" by the subject + verb: "I am giving the book [direct object] to you [indirect object]" = "I am giving the book, not just to anyone anywhere, but in your direction, i.e., to you." Even in the passive periphrastic construction, the dative of agent indicates the person for whom a certain action is obligatory. A number of other dative usages are distinguished by grammarians, but most are variants on this basic notion of reference or direction.

### DATIVE WITH ADJECTIVES

The **DATIVE WITH ADJECTIVES** construction is one you have already encountered in your readings, though it has not yet been formally introduced. Simply stated, a noun in the dative case is employed with many Latin adjectives—particularly those indicating attitude, quality, or relation—to indicate the direction (literally or metaphorically) in which the adjective applies; such adjectives are normally followed by "to," "toward," or "for" in English (e.g., "friendly to/toward," "hostile to/toward," "suitable to/for," "useful to," "similar to," "equal to," etc.).

> **Mors est similis *somnō*.** *Death is similar to sleep.*
> **Sciēbam tē *mihi* fidēlem esse.** *I knew that you were loyal to me.*
> ***Nōbīs* est vir amīcus.** *He is a man friendly toward us.*
> **Quisque *sibi* cārus est.** *Each person is dear to himself.*
> **Ille vidētur pār esse *deō*.** *That man seems to be equal to a god.*

## DATIVE WITH SPECIAL VERBS

Conceptually similar is the **DATIVE WITH SPECIAL VERBS** construction. Many of these verbs (the most important of which are listed below) are actually intransitive and, like adjectives that take a dative, indicate attitude or relationship, e.g., **nocēre,** *to be injurious to,* **parcō,** *to be lenient toward,* etc. Although these verbs are often translated into English as if they were transitive and the dative nouns they govern as though they were direct objects (e.g., **tibi parcit,** *he spares you;* lit., *he is lenient toward you*), the datives again indicate the person/thing toward whom the attitude or quality applies.

Although a common rule for the dative with special verbs lists those meaning to "favor," "help/harm," "please/displease," "trust/distrust," "believe," "persuade," "command," "obey," "serve," "resist," "envy," "threaten," "pardon," and "spare," the list is cumbersome and involves some important exceptions (including **iuvō,** *to help,* and **iubeō,** *to command, order,* which take accusatives). More useful is simply to understand the concept and recognize some of the commonest Latin verbs that take this construction. In learning the following list, note that the more literal translation, given first for each verb, includes English *to* and thus reminds you of the required dative; note as well that each verb conveys some notion of *attitude toward* a person or thing, again suggesting a dative.

> **crēdō** + dat., *entrust to; trust, believe* (**crēdō tibi,** *I believe you*)
> **ignōscō** + dat., *grant pardon to; pardon, forgive* (**ignōscō virīs,** *I forgive the men*)
> **imperō** + dat., *give orders to; command* (**imperō mīlitibus,** *I command the soldiers*)
> **noceō** + dat., *do harm to; harm* (**noceō hostibus,** *I harm the enemy*)
> **nūbō** + dat., *be married to; marry* (**nūbō illī virō,** *I am marrying that man*)
> **parcō** + dat., *be lenient to; spare* (**parcō vōbīs,** *I spare you*)
> **pāreō** + dat., *be obedient to; obey* (**pāreō ducī,** *I obey the leader*)
> **persuādeō** + dat., *make sweet to, make agreeable to; persuade* (**persuādeō mihi,** *I persuade myself*)
> **placeō** + dat., *be pleasing to; please* (**placeō patrī,** *I please my father*)
> **serviō** + dat., *be a slave to; serve* (**serviō patriae,** *I serve my country*)
> **studeō** + dat., *direct one's zeal to; study* (**studeō litterīs,** *I study literature*)

**Crēde amīcīs.** *Believe (trust) your friends.*
**Ignōsce mihi.** *Pardon me (forgive me).*
**Magistra discipulīs parcit.** *The teacher spares (is lenient toward) her pupils.*
**Hoc eīs nōn placet.** *This does not please them.*
**Nōn possum eī persuādēre.** *I cannot persuade him.*
**Variae rēs hominibus nocent.** *Various things harm men.*
**Cicerō philosophiae studēbat.** *Cicero used to study philosophy.*
**Philosophiae servīre est lībertās.** *To serve philosophy is liberty.*

Some of these verbs, it should be noted, can also take a direct object (e.g., **crēdō** takes a dative for a person believed, **mātrī crēdit,** *he believes his mother,* but an accusative for a thing, **id crēdit,** *he believes it*); and some, like **imperō** and **persuādeo,** take a noun clause as an object, as we shall see in the next chapter.

## DATIVE WITH COMPOUND VERBS

A very similar dative usage occurs with certain verbs compounded with **ad, ante, con-** (=**cum**), **in, inter, ob, post, prae, prō, sub, super,** and sometimes **circum** and **re-** (in the sense of *against*). This DATIVE WITH COMPOUNDS is especially common when the meaning of a compound verb is significantly different from its simple form, whether transitive or intransitive; conversely, if the meaning of the compound is not essentially different from that of the simple verb, then the dative is ordinarily not employed:

> **Eum sequor.** *I follow him.*
> **Eī obsequor.** *I obey him* (lit., *I follow in the direction of,* i.e., in his path)
> **Sum amīcus eius.** *I am his friend.*
> **Amīcō adsum.** *I support my friend* (lit., *I am next to my friend,* i.e., at his side).
> **Ad nōs vēnit.** *He came to us.*
> **Ad nōs advēnit.** *He came to us.*

Often the dative functions essentially as object of the prepositional prefix, though the preposition would take another case if separate from the verb; thus **adsum amīcō** above and the following examples:

> **Aliīs praestant.** *They surpass the others* (lit., *they stand before the others*).
> **Exercituī praeerat.** *He was in charge of the army* (lit., *he was in front of/before the army*).

If the simple verb is transitive, then the compound may take an accusative as object of the root verb as well as a dative dependent on the prefix:

> **Exercituī eum praeposuī.** *I put him in charge of the army* (lit., *I put him* [**posuī eum**] *in front of the army* [**prae-** + **exercituī**]).
> **Amīcitiae pecūniam praeposuī.** *I preferred money to friendship* (lit., *I put money* [**posuī pecūniam**] *before friendship* [**prae-** + **amīcitiae**]).

Since there is such variability in the rules for dative with special verbs and compounds, the best procedure is to *understand the concepts involved* and then, when encountering a dative in a sentence, to be aware of these possible functions; just as with the other cases, you should be maintaining a list of the dative uses you have learned (there have been five thus far) in your notebook or computer file, including definitions and representative examples.

# VOCĀBVLA

Be careful not to confuse **aestās** below with **aetās**, nor **parcō** and **pāreo** below with **parō**, nor **serviō** with **servō**. And remember to learn all these new words, as always, by listening to them on the CDs or at www.wheelockslatin.com and repeating them aloud.

**aéstās, aestātis,** f., *summer* (estival, estivate, estivation; cf. **aestus, -ūs,** *heat,* **aestuāre,** *to be hot, seethe, boil*)

**iānua, iānuae,** f., *door* (janitor, Janus, January)

**péctus, péctoris,** n., *breast, heart* (pectoral, expectorate, parapet)

**praémium, praémiī,** n., *reward, prize* (premium)

**īrātus, īrāta, īrātum,** *angry* (irate; cf. **īra, īrāscor,** *to be angry*)

**antepōnō, antepōnere, antepósuī, antepósitum,** *to put before, prefer*

**fóveō, fovēre, fōvī, fōtum,** *to comfort, nurture, cherish* (foment)

**ignōscō, ignōscere, ignōvī, ignōtum** + dat., *to grant pardon to, forgive*

**ímperō, imperāre, imperāvī, imperātum** + dat., *to give orders to, command* (imperative, emperor; cf. **imperātor, imperium**)

**míror, mīrārī, mīrātus sum,** *to marvel at, admire, wonder* (admire, marvel, miracle, mirage, mirror; cf. **mīrāculum,** *a marvel*)

**nóceō, nocēre, nócuī, nócitum** + dat., *to do harm to, harm, injure* (innocent, innocuous, nuisance, obnoxious; cognate with **necō**)

**nūbō, nūbere, nūpsī, nūptum,** *to cover, veil;* + dat. (of a bride) *to be married to, marry* (nubile, connubial, nuptials; cf. **nūptiae,** *marriage*)

**párcō, párcere, pepércī, parsūrum** + dat., *to be lenient to, spare* (parsimonious, parsimony)

**pāreō, pārēre, pāruī** + dat., *to be obedient to, obey* (apparent, appear, apparition)

**persuádeō, persuādēre, persuāsī, persuāsum** + dat., *to succeed in urging, persuade, convince* (assuage, dissuade, suasion; cf. **suāvis**)

**pláceō, placēre, plácuī, plácitum** + dat., *to be pleasing to, please* (complacent, placable, implacable, placate, placid, plea, plead, pleasure)

**sápiō, sápere, sapīvī,** *to have good taste; have good sense, be wise* (sapient, sapid, insipid, sage, savor; cf. **sapiēns, sapientia**)

**sérviō, servīre, servīvī, servītum** + dat., *to be a slave to, serve* (service, disservice, subservient, servile, servility, deserve, desert = reward, dessert; cf. **servus, servitūs**)

**stúdeō, studēre, stúduī** + dat., *to direct one's zeal to, be eager for, study* (student; cf. **studium, studiōsus,** *eager, diligent, scholarly*)

**subrīdeō, subrīdēre, subrīsī, subrīsum,** *to smile (down) upon* (cf. **rīdeō, rīdiculus**)

# LĒCTIŌ ET TRĀNSLĀTIŌ

After thorough study of the new grammar and vocabulary, scan the following readings for all dative nouns and pronouns, identifying the specific usage of each. Then read each sentence and passage aloud, listening to the CDs if you have them, and translate into idiomatic English.

## EXERCITĀTIŌNĒS

1. Minerva, fīlia Iovis, nāta est plēna scientiae et ingeniī.
2. Custōdiae sī cum duce nostrō līberē loquantur et huic tyrannum trādere cōnentur, sine perīculō ex moenibus urbis prōtinus ēgredī possint.
3. Pārēre lēgibus aequīs melius est quam tyrannō servīre.
4. Cum optimē honōribus ūsus esset et sibi cīvitātem semper antepōneret, etiam plēbs eī crēdēbat et nōn invidēbat.
5. Diū passa, māter vestra fēlīciter, sedēns apud amīcōs, mortua est.
6. Philosophī cōnsilium spectāvērunt et recūsāvērunt tālem rem suscipere mōlīrīve.
7. Cum dīves sīs atque dīvitiae crēscant, tamen opibus tuīs parcere vīs et nēminī assem offerēs.
8. Ab illā īnsulā subitō profectus, eādem nocte ad patriam nāve advēnit; tum, quaerēns remissiōnem animae, diū rūsticābātur.
9. Hic mīles, cum imperātōrī vestrō nōn placēret, heu, illa praemia prōmissa āmīsit.
10. Nisi mōrēs parēs scientiae sunt—id nōbīs fatendum est—scientia nōbīs magnopere nocēre potest.
11. Magistra tum rogāvit duōs parvōs puerōs quot digitōs habērent.
12. Māter candida nātae cārissimae subrīdet, quam maximē fovet, et eī plūrima ōscula suāvia dat.
13. Why does he now wish to hurt his two friends?
14. If he does not spare the plebeians, alas, we shall neither trust him nor follow him.
15. Since you are studying Roman literature, you are serving a very difficult but a very great master.
16. If they were truly willing to please us, they would not be using their wealth thus against the state.

## SENTENTIAE ANTĪQVAE

1. Nēmō līber est quī corporī servit. (Seneca.)
2. Imperium habēre vīs magnum? Imperā tibi! (Publilius Syrus.)
3. Bonīs nocet quisquis pepercit malīs. (*Id.)

4. Cum tū omnia pecūniae postpōnās, mīrāris sī nēmō tibi amōrem praestat? (Horace.—**post-pōnō**; "postponement," "postpositive.")

5. Frūstrā aut pecūniae aut imperiīs aut opibus aut glōriae student; potius studeant virtūtī et honōrī et scientiae et alicui artī. (Cicero.—**frūstrā**, adv., *in vain*; "frustrate," "frustration."—**potius**, adv., *rather.*)

6. Virtūtī melius quam Fortūnae crēdāmus; virtūs nōn nōvit calamitātī cēdere. (Publilius Syrus.—**calamitās, -tātis**; "calamitous.")

7. Et Deus āit: "Faciāmus hominem ad imāginem nostram et praesit piscibus maris bēstiīsque terrae." (*Genesis.*—**imāgō, -ginis**, f.; "imagery," "imagination."—**prae-sum.**—**piscis, -is**, m., *fish*; "Pisces," "piscine."—**bēstia, -ae**, f., *beast*; "bestial," "bestiary.")

8. Omnēs arbitrātī sunt tē dēbēre mihi parcere. (Cicero.)

9. Quid facere vellet, ostendit, et illī servō spē lībertātis magnīsque praemiīs persuāsit. (Caesar.)

10. Sī cui librī Cicerōnis placent, ille sciat sē prōfēcisse. (Quintilian.—**prōficiō:** = **prō + faciō**, *to progress, benefit*; "proficiency," "profit.")

11. In urbe nostrā mihi contigit docērī quantum īrātus Achillēs Graecīs nocuisset. (Horace.—**contingō, -ere, -tigī, -tāctum**, *to touch closely, fall to the lot of*; "contingent," "contiguous," "contact.")

12. Alicui rogantī melius quam iubentī pārēmus. (Publilius Syrus.)

13. Vīvite fortiter fortiaque pectora rēbus adversīs oppōnite. (Horace.—**oppōnō:** = **ob + pōnō**, *to set against*; "opponent," "opposite.")

14. Nōn ignāra malī, miserīs succurrere discō. (*Vergil.—**ignārus, -a, -um**, *ignorant*; "ignorance," "ignore;" **ignāra** is f. because it agrees with Dido, exiled queen, who speaks these words to the shipwrecked Aeneas.—**succurrō:** = **sub + currō**, *to help*; "succor.")

15. Ignōsce saepe alterī, numquam tibi. (Publilius Syrus.)

16. Cum enim tē, deum meum, quaerō, vītam beātam quaerō; quaeram tē ut vīvat anima mea. (*St. Augustine.)

17. Sequere hāc, mea gnāta, mē, cum dīs volentibus. (*Plautus.–**hāc**, adv., *in this direction, this way.*—**gnāta:** = **nāta.**)

### Ovid Asks the Gods to Inspire His Work

In nova fert animus mūtātās dīcere fōrmās
corpora: dī, coeptīs—nam vōs mūtāstis et illās—
adspīrāte meīs prīmāque ab orīgine mundī
ad mea perpetuum dēdūcite tempora carmen!

*Ovid *Met.* 1.1–4: Ovid invokes the gods to inspire his work in these opening verses of his **Metamorphōsēs** (review "On Death and Metamorphosis," and the accompanying notes, in Capvt XVIII); the challenge in translating this excerpt, as with much of Lat. verse, is to connect the adjectives with the nouns they modify, so watch the endings!—**nova:** of the three nouns in this sent., which does this adj. agree with?—**fert**: here, *compels (me)*.—**coeptum, -ī**, n., usually pl., *beginning, undertaking, enterprise;* "inception."—**mūtāstis**: = **mūtāvistis**; such contractions, with **v** and the following vowel dropped, are common in perf. system forms; cf. **dōnārunt** for **dōnāvērunt** in Catullus 13 (Capvt XXXIII).—**et**: = **etiam**.—**adspīrāre**, *to breathe upon, inspire;* "aspire," "aspirant."—**orīgō, -ginis**, f., = Eng.; "originator," "aboriginal."—**mea perpetuum . . . tempora carmen**: if you do not recall the technical term for this common poetic word order device, see "Note on a Copy of Catullus' **Carmina**," Capvt XXX. —**dē + dūcō**: derivatives include "deduce" and "deduction," but the verb has a more lit. meaning here.

*QVAESTIŌNĒS:* What range of time is spanned by the transformation tales Ovid's poem will relate? What are the theological implications of Ovid's prologue?

## Sorry, Nobody's Home!

Nāsīca ad poētam Ennium vēnit. Cum ad iānuam Ennium quaesīvisset et serva respondisset eum in casā nōn esse, sēnsit illam dominī iussū id dīxisse et Ennium vērō esse in casā. Post paucōs diēs, cum Ennius ad Nāsīcam vēnisset et eum ad iānuam quaereret, Nāsīca ipse exclāmāvit sē in casā nōn esse. Tum Ennius "Quid?" inquit, "Ego nōn cognōscō vōcem tuam?" Hīc Nāsīca merō cum sale respondit: "Vae, homō es impudēns! Ego, cum tē quaererem, servae tuae crēdidī tē nōn in casā esse; nōnne tū mihi ipsī nunc crēdis?"

Cicero *De Or.* 2.276.—Cicero's **Dē Ōrātōre**, published in 55 B.C., was one of several treatises he wrote on oratory and rhetoric, important subjects for the Roman ruling class; in this passage he relates a humorous anecdote about Publius Cornelius Scipio Nasica, a celebrated jurist, and his friend the poet Quintus Ennius, as an example of the potential value of using jokes in speeches.—**iussū**, *at the command of;* cf. **iubeō**.—**exclāmāre**, *to shout out;* "exclaim," "exclamation."—**impudēns**, gen. **-dentis**; "impudence."

*QVAESTIŌ:* Explain the joke—and if you laughed out loud when you read it, that means your Latin is getting better and better!

## "I Do." "I Don't!"

> Nūbere vīs Prīscō. Nōn mīror, Paula; sapīstī.
>     Dūcere tē nōn vult Prīscus: et ille sapit!

*Martial *Epig.* 9.10: Priscus was an eligible bachelor, maybe a rich one; Paula was apparently not his type! Meter: elegiac couplet.—**sapīstī**: = **sapīvistī**; for the form, see on **mūtāstis** above.—**dūcere**: i.e., **in mātrimōnium**.

*QVAESTIŌNĒS:* Which of these two players was smart, and how does Martial use word order to underscore the point?

### Maronilla Has a Cough

Petit Gemellus nūptiās Marōnillae
et cupit et īnstat et precātur et dōnat.
Adeōne pulchra est? Immo, foedius nīl est.
Quid ergō in illā petitur et placet? Tussit!

*Martial *Epig.* 1.10: meter: choliambic.—**nūptiāe, -ārum,** f. pl., *marriage;* "nuptial," "pre-nuptial"; cf. **nūbere.—īnstāre,** *to press, insist;* "instance," "instant."—**precor, -cārī, -cātus sum,** *to beg, entreat;* "deprecation," "imprecate."—**dōnat:** = dat; "donation."—**adeō:** = **tam.—immō,** adv., *on the contrary;* the -**o** is shortened here for metrical purposes.—**foe-dius:** = **turpius.—nīl:** = **nihil.—ergō:** = **igitur.—tussīre,** *to cough;* "tussive," "pertussis."

*QVAESTIŌNĒS:* Identify the **POLYSYNDETON** and comment on its effect (if you don't recall the term, see "Pretty Is" in the last chapter). Explain Gemellus' interest in Maro-nilla (if you can't, recall what you've learned about Rome's **captātōrēs**)–and where is his motivation revealed?

### Summer Vacation

Ludī magister, parce simplicī turbae:
. . .
aestāte puerī sī valent, satis discunt.

*Martial *Epig.* 10.62.1, 12: Even in ancient Rome students got a summer vacation and were "spared the rod" during harvest time, from July to October. Meter: choliambic.—**simplex,** gen. **-plicis,** *simple, unaffected,* here *youthful;* "simplicity," "simplistic."

## SCRĪPTA IN PARIETIBVS

[A]mōre tuō moreor. . . . Pereō, vīta, in am[ōre]. . . . Vīt{i}a, amō tē!

*CIL* 4.9054: From one of several stucco fragments found in the Building of Eumachia (Reg. VII, Ins. 9); only these three sentences can be confidently restored, but it seems from the few other legible words (**amantem, Venus:** can you find them in the drawing?) that perhaps all or most of what was inscribed here was amatory in nature.—**amōre:** ABLATIVE OF CAUSE, a common abl. case construction whose sense is easily understood here.—**moreor:** = **morior;** the lovestruck writer was not a great speller, but at least he recalled that the verb is deponent. In a curious illustration of the continuity of classical Lat., however coincidental it may be, the exclamatory **Amōre tuō morior** is uttered both by Helen to Paris, as she implores him to take her to be his lover in Troy, in the 13th cent. **Excidium Troie** (*The Destruction of Troy*), a narrative ultimately dating back to ancient sources, and by Mary Magdalene, crying out to the crucified Christ, in the 17th-cent. hymn "Maria Magdalene Stabat," composed by the Benedictine nun Chiara Margarita Cozzolani.—**pereō, -īre, -iī, -itum,** *to pass away, be destroyed, perish;* "perishable."—**vīta:** a common term of endearment, esp. among lovers, often **mea vīta;** why was the scribbler's misspelling VITIA, instead of VITA, somewhat comically unfortunate?

## LATĪNA EST GAVDIVM—ET ŪTILIS!

**Salvēte, discipulī discipulaeque!** Or perhaps now that you have learned the meaning of **studēre** you should be termed **studentēs,** since it is clearly your zeal for learning that has brought you this far in your study of Latin! So, **studentēs,** here is your **praemium,** more delectables for your **cēna Latīna,** once more **ex novīs grammaticīs atque vocābulīs:** if you remember that verbs signifying "favor . . . etc." govern the dative, you can understand this first, fortuitously alliterative motto, **fortūna favet fortibus;** the command **favēte linguīs,** lit. *be favorable with your tongues,* was used in religious rituals to call for silence and the avoidance of any ill-omened speech; **imperō** obviously gives us "imperative," but also the expression **dīvide** (from **dīvidere,** *to separate, divide*) **et imperā;** a **placet** is an affirmative vote, a **placitum** a judicial decision, and a "placebo" is an unmedicated preparation meant to humor a patient (what, literally, does the "medicine" promise to do?); secret meetings are held **iānuīs clausīs** (from **claudō, claudere, clausī, clausum,** *to close,* as in "recluse," "closet," etc.), but **iānuae mentis** are the ones studying Latin will help you to open (**aperiō, aperīre, aperuī, apertum** is *to open,* as in "aperture"). Also from **iānua** we have: "janitor," lit. a "doorman"; "Janus," the two-faced god of doors, of entrances and exits, of beginnings and ending; and "January," the doorway into the new year. **Studēte Latīnae, aperīte mentēs, et semper valēte, studentēs!**

# CAPVT XXXVI 🗗🗗🗗

# Jussive Noun Clauses; *Fīō*

## GRAMMATICA

### JUSSIVE NOUN CLAUSES

The JUSSIVE NOUN CLAUSE is a kind of indirect command: as with indirect statements (Capvt XXV) and indirect questions (Capvt XXX), the actual command (or request, entreaty, etc.) is not quoted verbatim, via an imperative or a jussive subjunctive (Capvt XXVIII) in a main clause, but is reported indirectly in a subordinate clause, i.e., not "he ordered them, 'Do this!'" but "he ordered them to do this." In Latin such clauses are introduced by **ut** or **nē** and employ a subjunctive verb, usually present or imperfect tense, whereas in English, and therefore in translation, we ordinarily employ a present infinitive with no introductory word and no auxiliary such as "may" or "might":

1. **Hoc facite.** *Do this!* (imperative, direct command)
2. **Hoc faciant.** *Let them do this.* (jussive subjunctive, direct command)
3. **Imperat vōbīs ut hoc faciātis.** *He commands you to do this.*
4. **Imperāvit eīs ut hoc facerent.** *He commanded them to do this.*
5. **Persuādet eīs ut hoc faciant.** *He persuades them to do this.*
6. **Petīvit ab eīs nē hoc facerent.** *He begged (from) them not to do this.*
7. **Monuit eōs nē hoc facerent.** *He warned them not to do this.*
8. **Hortātus est eōs ut hoc facerent.** *He urged them to do this.*

These clauses are often confused with purpose clauses because in appearance they are identical, but a study of the examples given above reveals their jussive nature. In contrast to purpose clauses, which function adverbially (answering the question "why?"), jussive noun clauses function as objects of the main verbs which introduce them (answering the question "what . . . was ordered, requested, advised, etc.?"). The following list includes some of the more common verbs that can introduce jussive noun clauses and indicates the case employed for the person being ordered or requested to act:

> **hortor eum ut,** *I urge him to . . .*
> **imperō eī ut,** *I order him to . . .*

**moneō eum ut,** *I advise him to . . .*
**ōrō eam ut,** *I beg her to . . .*
**persuādeō eī ut,** *I persuade him to . . .* (or *I persuade him that . . .*)
**petō ab eō ut,** *I beg (from) him to . . .*
**quaerō ab eā ut,** *I request (from/of) her to . . .*
**rogō eum ut,** *I ask him to . . .*

**Volō, nōlō,** and **mālō** (Capvt XXXII) sometimes introduce such clauses (e.g., **mālō ut,** *I prefer that. . .*), although they also commonly are followed by infinitives; **iubeō** nearly always takes the infinitive construction.

## IRREGULAR *Fīō, fierī, factus sum,* to occur, happen; be done, be made

The common irregular verb **fīō, fierī,** meaning *to occur, happen,* was used by the Romans in place of the passive of the present system of **faciō** and so, although active in form, also has the passive meanings *to be done, be made;* e.g., **fit** was used instead of **facitur** for *it is done, is made* (the practice with compounds of **faciō** varied: **perficitur,** *is completed,* but **calefit** instead of **calefacitur** for *is heated*). Conversely, the perfect system of **fīō** was lacking and was supplied by the perfect passive system of **faciō,** the same sort of suppletion seen earlier in the use of **tulī** and **lātum** for the perfect system of **ferō, ferre.**

In effect, we have a composite verb with the principal parts **fīō, fierī, factus sum** and with the range of related meanings *occur, happen, become, be made, be done.* In translating, when you see the active present system forms of **fīō** remember the passive force options *be done, be made,* and when you see the passive perfect system forms **factus est, factus erat, factus sit,** etc., remember the options *has become, had occurred,* etc.

The only new forms to be learned are those listed below; note that: the stem vowel -ī- is long in all places except **fit, fierī,** and the imperfect subjunctive; otherwise, the forms of the present, future, and imperfect indicative and the present subjunctive follow the pattern of **audiō;** the imperfect subjunctive follows a predictable pattern, given the infinitive **fierī.**

| Indicative | | | Subjunctive | |
|---|---|---|---|---|
| **Pres.** | **Imperf.** | **Fut.** | **Pres.** | **Imperf.** |
| 1. fīō | fīēbam | fīam | fīam | fíerem |
| 2. fīs | fīēbās | fīēs | fīās | fíerēs |
| 3. fit | fīēbat | fíet | fíat | fíeret |
| 1. fīmus | fīēbámus | fīēmus | fīámus | fierémus |
| 2. fītis | fīēbátis | fīētis | fīátis | fierétis |
| 3. fīunt | fīēbant | fíent | fíant | fíerent |

Infinitive                                    Imperatives

fíerī                                         **Sg.** fī **Pl.** fíte

Study carefully the following examples:

Hoc facit (faciet). *He is doing* or *making this* (*will do* or *make*).
Hoc fit (fíet). *This is done* or *made* (*will be done* or *made*).
Hoc faciat. *Let him do* or *make this*.
Hoc fīat. *Let this be done* or *made*.
Dīcunt eum hoc facere. *They say that he is doing this*.
Dīcunt hoc fierī. *They say that this is being done* (*is happening*).
Perīculum fit gravius. *The danger is becoming graver*.
Mox factī sunt fēlīces. *They soon became happy*.

# VOCĀBVLA

As a check on your mastery of **fīō**, do a synopsis in all six tenses with the book closed, then compare your work with the full conjugation on p. 509. And remember: as you memorize this new list, **audī ac prōnūntiā!**

cupídō, cupídinis, f., *desire, passion* (cupidity, Cupid; cf. **cupiō, cupiditās**)
léctor, lēctṓris, m., and lḗctrīx, lēctrī́cis, f., *reader* (lector; cf. **legō**, lectern, lecture)
vínculum, vínculī, n., *bond, chain, fetter* (vinculum; cf. **vinciō**, to bind)
cōtī́diē, adv., *daily, every day* (**quot + diēs**; cotidian)
fortásse, adv., *perhaps* (cf. **fortūna**)
accḗdō, accḗdere, accéssī, accéssum (**ad + cēdō**), *to come* (*to*), *approach* (accede, access, accessible, accession, accessory; cf. **discēdō**)
cárpō, cárpere, cárpsī, cárptum, *to harvest, pluck; seize* (carp at, excerpt, carpet, scarce; **carpe diem**: see *Latīna Est Gaudium*, Capvt XXII)
cṓgō, cṓgere, coḗgī, coáctum (**cum + agō**), *to drive* or *bring together, force, compel* (cogent, coaction, coactive, coagulate; cf. **cōgitō**)
contémnō, contémnere, contémpsī, contémptum, *to despise, scorn* (contemn, contempt, contemptible, contemptuous)
contúndō, contúndere, cóntudī, contúsum, *to beat, crush, bruise, destroy* (contuse, contusion; obtuse, from **obtundō**, *to beat, make blunt*)
cū́rō, cūrā́re, cūrā́vī, cūrā́tum, *to care for, attend to; heal, cure; take care* (cure, curator, procure, proctor, accurate; cf. **cūra**)
dēcérnō, dēcérnere, dēcrḗvī, dēcrḗtum, *to decide, settle, decree* (decretal, decretory; cf. **cernō**)
éxigō, exígere, exḗgī, exáctum (**ex + agō**), *to drive out, force out, exact; drive through, complete, perfect* (exactitude, exigent, exigency)

**fīō, fíerī, fáctus sum,** *to occur, happen; become; be made, be done* (fiat)
**obléctō, oblectáre, oblectávī, oblectátum,** *to please, amuse, delight; pass time pleasantly* (oblectation; cf. **dēlectō, dēlectātiō**)
**ốrō, ōráre, ōrávī, ōrátum,** *to speak, plead; beg, beseech, entreat, pray* (orator, oration, oracle, adore, inexorable, peroration; cf. **ōrátor**)
**récreō, recreáre, recreávī, recreátum** (**re + creō**), *to restore, revive; refresh, cheer* (recreate, recreation)
**requírō, requírere, requīsívī, requīsítum** (**re + quaerō**), *to seek, ask for; miss, need, require* (requisite, requisition, prerequisite, request)
**serénō, serēnáre, serēnávī, serēnátum,** *to make clear, brighten; cheer up, soothe* (serene, serenity, serenade)

# LĒCTIŌ ET TRĀNSLĀTIŌ

After studying the new grammar and vocabulary, check your mastery with the Self-Tutorial Exercises and Answer Key, and then scan the readings to identify (a) the tense, person, number, and mood of all forms of **fīō,** and (b) all jussive noun clauses; be careful not to confuse jussive noun and purpose clauses, and remember to translate the subjunctive verbs in the former (and often the latter) simply as infinitives. Listen to each sentence and passage, if you have the CDs, read them aloud for comprehension, and write out your translations.

## EXERCITĀTIŌNĒS

1. Poterāsne etiam centum virīs persuādēre ut viam virtūtis sine praemiīs sequerentur?
2. Haec fēmina vult ex urbe ēgredī et ad illam īnsulam proficīscī ut sine morā illī agricolae nūbat et semper rūsticētur.
3. Petēbant ā nōbīs ut etiam in adversīs rēbus huic ducī pārērēmus et servīrēmus.
4. Haec ab fēminīs facta sunt nē tantam occāsiōnem āmitterent.
5. Rogāmus tē ut honōre et opibus sapientius ūtāris et hōs quīnque amīcōs semper foveās.
6. Nisi quis hoc suscipere audēbit, nōlent nōbīs crēdere et fīent īrātī.
7. Rogāvit nōs cūr neque dīvitibus neque pauperibus placēre cōnātī essēmus.
8. Arbitrābātur tālem vītam nōn ex dīvitiīs sed ex animō plēnō virtūtis nāscī.
9. Scientiam et ingenium magis quam magnās dīvitiās mīrēmur.
10. Senātus ducī imperāvit nē hostibus victīs nocēret sed eīs parceret et remissiōnem poenae daret.
11. Ille ōrātor vulgum īrātissimum vōce potentī serēnāvit atque, ut omnibus spectantibus subrīsit, eōs oblectāvit.

12. Ut parva puella per iānuam currēbat, subitō occidit et genua male contudit.
13. Dummodo sīs aequus hīs virīs, fīent tibi fidēlēs.
14. That summer they urged that this be done better.
15. Provided that this is done, they will beg us to spare him.
16. That teacher wants to persuade her twenty pupils to study more good literature.
17. Since his hope is becoming very small, let him confess that he commanded (use **imperō**) those two men not to do it.

## SENTENTIAE ANTĪQVAE

1. Dīxitque Deus: "Fīat lūx." Et facta est lūx. (*Genesis.)
2. Fatendum est nihil dē nihilō posse fierī. (Lucretius.—**nihilum, -ī,** n.: = **nihil.**)
3. Magnae rēs nōn fīunt sine perīculō. (Terence.)
4. Hīs rēbus cognitīs, ille suōs hortātus est nē timērent. (Caesar.)
5. Omnia fīent quae fierī aequum est. (Terence.)
6. "Pater, ōrō tē ut mihi ignōscās." "Fīat." (Terence.)
7. Dum loquimur, fūgerit invida aetās: carpe diem! (*Horace.—**invidus, -a, -um,** *envious;* "invidious," "envy.")
8. Carpāmus dulcia; post enim mortem cinis et fābula fiēs. (Persius.—**cinis, -neris,** m., *ashes;* "cinerary," "incinerate.")
9. Ante senectūtem cūrāvī ut bene vīverem; in senectūte cūrō ut bene moriar. (Seneca.)
10. Solōn dīxit sē senem fierī cotīdiē aliquid addiscentem. (Cicero.—**Solōn, -lōnis,** m., *Solon,* great 6th cent. B.C. Athenian legislator.—**ad** + **discō, -ere.**)
11. Caret pectus tuum inānī ambitiōne? Caret īrā et timōre mortis? Ignōscis amīcīs? Fīs lēnior et melior, accēdente senectūte? (Horace.—**inānis, -e,** *empty, vain;* "inane," "inanity."—**ambitiō, -ōnis,** f.; "ambitious"; from **ambi-,** *around,* + **īre,** *to go,* the word was applied to political candidates who "went around" canvassing for votes.—**lēnis, -e,** *gentle, kind;* "lenience," "lenient.")
12. Hoc dūrum est; sed levius fit patientiā quidquid corrigere est nefās. (Horace.—**corrigō, -ere;** "incorrigible," "correct."—**est nefās,** *it is wrong, contrary to divine law.*)
13. Sapiāmus et cēdāmus! Leve fit onus quod bene fertur. (Ovid.—**onus, oneris,** n., *burden;* "onerous," "exonerate.")
14. Ego vōs hortor ut amīcitiam omnibus rēbus hūmānīs antepōnātis—vae illīs quī nūllōs amīcōs habent! (Cicero.)
15. Petō ā vōbīs ut patiāminī mē dē studiīs hūmānitātis ac litterārum loquī. (Cicero.—**hūmānitās, -tātis,** f., *culture;* "humanity," "the humanities"; cf. **homō, hūmānus.**)
16. Auribus frequentius quam linguā ūtere! (*Seneca.—**frequenter,** adv., *often, frequently.*)

17. Citius venit perīclum cum contemnitur. (*Publilius Syrus.—**perīclum:** = **perīculum;** for another example of this type of contraction, known as SYN-COPE, see the **Fēlīc<u>lam** graffito in Capvt II.)

## The Quality of Martial's Book

Sunt bona, sunt quaedam mediocria, sunt mala plūra
    quae legis hīc; aliter nōn fit, Avīte, liber.

*Martial *Epig.* 1.16: Anyone who has ever written a book will be grateful for this defense Martial offers to Avitus; meter, elegiac couplet.—**aliter,** adv., *otherwise.*

## I Don't Cook for Cooks!

Lēctor et audītor nostrōs probat, Aule, libellōs,
    sed quīdam exāctōs esse poēta negat.
Nōn nimium cūrō, nam cēnae fercula nostrae
    mālim convīvīs quam placuisse cocīs!

*Martial *Epig.* 9.81; meter: elegiac couplet.—**probat:** it was common for a verb to agree in number with the nearer of two subjects, though here the hypothetical **lēctor** and **audītor** are perhaps thought of as one and the same person.—**esse:** sc. **eōs,** = **libellōs,** as subject.—**ferculum, -ī,** n., *course* (of a meal).—**mālim:** POTENTIAL SUBJUNCTIVE, a common usage employed for hypothetical action, *I would prefer that.*—**cēnae . . . cocīs:** more usual order might be **mālim fercula cēnae nostrae placuisse convīvīs quam cocīs.**—**quam:** i.e., **magis quam.**—**convīva, -ae,** m., *dinner-guest;* "convivial."—**cocus, -ī,** m., *cook;* "concoction."

*QVAESTIŌNĒS:* In both epigrams the poet offers a defense of his work, proving the obvious point that literary critics existed then as now; comment on the issues Martial raises in both poems, and on the effectiveness of the culinary metaphor employed in the second.

## Oh, I'd Love to Read You My Poems . . . Not!

Ut recitem tibi nostra rogās epigrammata. Nōlō—
    nōn audīre, Celer, sed recitāre cupis!

*Martial *Epig.* 1.63: Unlike the implied critics in the preceding epigrams, Celer was a fan of Martial's—or at least pretended to be! Meter: elegiac couplet.—**epigramma, -matis,** n.; "epigrammatic," "epigrammatist."

*QVAESTIŌNĒS:* Compare Martial's response to Celer with his response to Pontilianus in "Please Remove My Name from Your Mailing List" (Capvt XXVIII); how are they alike, how different, and what do they tell you about Roman literary culture of the 1st cent. A.D.? What several additional selections have you read in this book, from Martial and other authors as well, in which writers talk about writing?—what range of issues do they raise?

## I Love Her . . . I Love Her Not

> Ōdī et amō! Quārē id faciam fortasse requīris.
> Nesciō, sed fierī sentiō et excrucior.

*Catullus *Carm.* 85: Brief, but intense, and one of Catullus' most admired poems; meter: elegiac couplet.—**excruciāre,** *to crucify, torment;* "excruciate," "crux"; from **crux, crucis,** f., *cross;* crucifixion, a form of punishment borrowed by the Romans from the Carthaginians, was largely reserved for slaves.

*QVAESTIŌNĒS:* The poem is largely about antitheses, but not just love and hate; 8 of the 14 words are verbs: which, on the one hand, are about asking and knowing and acting, and which, conversely, are about feeling, and suffering, and being acted upon? What is the effect of these oppositions?

## Who Is Truly Free?

Quis igitur vērō līber est? Tantum vir sapiēns, quī sibi imperat, quem neque fortūna adversa neque paupertās neque mors neque vincula terrent, quī potest cupīdinibus fortiter respondēre honōrēsque contemnere, cuius virtūs cōtīdiē crēscit, quī in sē ipsō tōtus est.

Horace *Sat.* 2.7.83ff: In this prose adaptation from one of his later satires, Horace comments on what was a central topic in ancient philosophy, following essentially the views of Stoicism; review the other selections you have read from the **Sermōnēs,** in Capita III and XXIV.

*QVAESTIŌNĒS:* Summarize these requisites of intellectual and moral freedom, and explain how they are encapsulated, in a sense, in the final clause; do you agree with them all, including Horace's privileging of the **vir sapiēns,** which reflects Stoic dogma that all but the wise are slaves?

## Testimony Against the Conspirators

Senātum coēgī. Intrōdūxī Volturcium sine Gallīs. Fidem pūblicam eī dedī. Hortātus sum ut ea quae scīret sine timōre nūntiāret. Tum ille, cum sē ex magnō timōre recreāvisset, dīxit sē ab Lentulō habēre ad Catilīnam mandāta ut auxiliō servōrum ūterētur et ad urbem quam prīmum cum exercitū accēderet. Intrōductī autem Gallī dīxērunt sibi litterās ad suam gentem ab Lentulō datās esse et hunc imperāvisse ut equitātum in Italiam quam prīmum mitterent. Dēnique, omnibus rēbus expositīs, senātus dēcrēvit ut coniūrātī, quī hās īnsidiās mōlītī essent, in custōdiam trāderentur.

Cicero *Cat.* 3, excerpts: In this adaptation from his third oration against Catiline, Cicero informs the Roman citizenry of the evidence against the conspirators and of actions taken by the senate; be sure to review all the earlier readings on the Catilinarian conspiracy in Capita XI, XIV, XX, and XXX.—**intrō + dūcō, -ere,** = Eng.; "introduction," "introductory."—**Volturcium:** Titus Volturcius, a minor figure among the conspirators, had been arrested in possession of the incriminating letters you read about in Capvt XXX; he was given immunity, **fidem pūblicam,** in return for his testimony here.—**Gallus, -ī,** m. *a Gaul;* Lentulus, the leading conspirator at Rome in Catiline's absence, had been seeking support from the Gallic Allobroges (Map 2), who had a delegation at Rome. The ambassadors pretended to go along, but instead reported what they knew to Cicero and assisted him in trapping Volturcius and seizing Lentulus' letters.—**scīret:** a subordinate clause that would ordinarily have an indic. verb often has instead a subjunct. when the clause occurs either within an ind. state. or, as here, within another subjunct. clause; in this latter instance the verb is often termed SUBJUNCTIVE BY ATTRACTION.—**mandātum, -ī,** n., *order;* "mandate," "command," "demand."—**quam prīmum:** see Capvt XXXII.—**equitātus, -ūs,** m., *cavalry;* "equitation," "equestrian."

*QVAESTIŌ:* Summarize what you have learned about the Catilinarian conspiracy, and the role Cicero played in its suppression, from the several passages you have read in this book.

## SCRĪPTA IN PARIETIBVS

Satrium quīnq(uennālem) ō(rō) v(ōs) f(aciātis).

*CIL* 4.7620: Another electoral **programma** like the one presented in Capvt XXII above, painted on the front wall of the House of Trebius Valens, facing onto Pompeii's Via dell'Abbondanza (Reg. III, Ins. 2). This notice advocated election of Satrius to the post of **duumvir quīnquennālis,** the title given to duumvirs (see Capvt XXII) who were elected in a census year (usually every five years, hence the title, from **quīnque**); from other programmata we know the candidate was Marcus Satrius Valens, member of a prominent Pompeian family, who ran for this office along with Quintus Postumius Modestus in A.D. 75. Abbreviations were common in these dipinti, as was the punctum, the raised dot seen in the photo following QVINQ, which was often employed to mark the ending of a word or an abbreviation.—**ōrō vōs:** sc. **ut;** the conj. was frequently omitted in a jussive noun clause.

## LATĪNA EST GAVDIVM—ET VTILIS!

**Salvēte, studentēs!** Here are some **fīō** items: if you've found it easier to write a speech than a poem, you'll believe the old saying **nāscimur poētae, fīmus ōrātōrēs;** a **fiat** (*not the car*) is a magisterial command, *let it be done!* From Publilius Syrus (the source of many of this book's **sententiae**) comes **repente dīvēs nēmō factus est bonus** (like Juvenal's **nēmō repente fuit turpissimus,** Capvt XXX); also the legal expression regarding "consenting adults," **volentī nōn fit iniūria,** *injury is not done to a willing person,* and **fiat ut petitur,** *let it be done as requested,* the phrase used for granting a legal petition. Et **cētera ex vocābulīs novīs in hōc capite:** an **accessit** (lit., *he/she approached, came close*) is a recognition for second place or honorable mention in a competition; **vinculum mātrimōniī** is *the bond of matrimony,* and **ā vinculō mātrimōniī** is legal Latin for an annulment; **dē minimīs nōn cūrat lēx,** *the law does not concern itself with trivialities,* is another familiar legal maxim; there are numerous mottoes and familiar sayings from **ōrāre,** including **ōrāre et spērāre** and **ōrā et labōrā;** besides **carpe diem,** there is **carpent tua pōma nepōtēs,** *your descendants will harvest your fruits.* **Carpāmus omnēs diēs, lēctōrēs et lēctrīcēs!**

*Front wall of the House of Trebius Valens*
*with the electoral notice for Satrius and adjacent* programmata
*Via dell'Abbondanza, Pompeii, Italy*

# CAPVT XXXVII 🏛🏛🏛

# Conjugation of *Eō;*
# Place and Time Constructions

## GRAMMATICA

### IRREGULAR *Eō, īre, iī, itum,* to go

The irregular fourth conjugation verb **eō, īre, iī, itum,** *to go,* is fully conjugated below; the verb is as common in Latin as "go" is in English, and so the conjugation should be learned thoroughly.

### Indicative

| Pres. | Imperf. | Fut. | Perf. | Pluperf. | Fut. Perf. |
|-------|---------|------|-------|----------|------------|
| 1. éō | íbam | íbō | íī | íeram | íerō |
| 2. īs | íbās | íbis | ístī | íerās | íeris |
| 3. it | íbat | íbit | íit | íerat | íerit |
| 1. ímus | ībámus | íbimus | íimus | ierámus | iérimus |
| 2. ítis | ībátis | íbitis | ístis | ierátis | iéritis |
| 3. éunt | íbant | íbunt | iérunt | íerant | íerint |

### Subjunctive

| Pres. | Imperf. | Perf. | Pluperf. |
|-------|---------|-------|----------|
| 1. éam | írem | íerim | íssem |
| 2. éās | írēs | íerīs | íssēs |
| 3. éat | íret | íerit | ísset |
| 1. eámus | īrémus | ierímus | īssémus |
| 2. eátis | īrétis | ierítis | īssétis |
| 3. éant | írent | íerint | íssent |

**Imperatives:**   Sg. ī Pl. îte   **Gerund:** eúndī

**Participles (in common use):**   Pres. íēns (eúntis, eúntī, etc.)   Fut. itúrus, -a, -um

**Infinitives:**   Pres. îre Fut. itúrus ésse Perf. îsse

A few irregularities in the present system of **eō** merit particular attention. First, the normal stem, **ī-**, seen in the present infinitive, becomes **e-** before **a, o,** and **u** in the present indicative and subjunctive (e.g., **eō, eunt, eam, eundī**), as well as in all forms of the present participle, except the nominative singular, and in the gerund (a form explained in Capvt XXXIX). Second, the future has the tense sign and endings of a first or second conjugation verb, i.e., **-bō, -bis,** etc., not **-am, -ēs,** etc. The perfect system is regular except that **ii-** before **s** usually contracts to **ī-**; e.g., **īstī, īsse.** Forms with **-v-**, such as **īvī**, are rare and do not appear in this book.

Only the active forms are presented here; the rare impersonal passive (e.g., **ītur, ībātur**) and the future and perfect passive participles (**eundum, itum**) do not appear in this book. Transitive compounds such as **adeō,** *to approach,* commonly have passive endings (e.g., **adeor, adībātur,** etc.), but those forms likewise are not employed in this book.

## PLACE CONSTRUCTIONS

You have already learned the prepositions and cases employed in the following regular place constructions:

(1) PLACE WHERE: **in** or **sub** + ablative
   **In illā urbe vīsus est.** *He was seen in that city.*
   **Nihil sub sōle est novum.** *There is nothing new under the sun.*

(2) PLACE TO WHICH: **in, ad,** or **sub** + accusative
   **In illam urbem ībit.** *He will go into that city.*
   **Sub hastam hostis occidit.** *He fell under the enemy's spear.*

(3) PLACE FROM WHICH: **ab, dē,** or **ex** + ablative
   **Ex illā urbe iit.** *He went out of that city.*

### Special Place Constructions

With the actual names of cities, towns, and small islands, as well as the nouns **domus, humus,** and **rūs,** no prepositions were employed in Latin, though they usually must be supplied in English translation (cf., however, English "he ran home" for "he ran *to* his home").

(1) For **PLACE WHERE** with these words a special case was used in Latin, the **LOCATIVE**. The locative is identical to the *genitive* for the singular of first and second declension nouns; elsewhere the locative is usually identical to the *ablative*.

> **Vīsus est Rōmae, Ephesī, Athēnīs, et Carthāgine.**
> *He was seen at Rome, Ephesus, Athens, and Carthage.*

(2) **PLACE TO WHICH**: accusative without a preposition
> **Ībit Rōmam, Ephesum, Athēnās, et Carthāginem.**
> *He will go to Rome, Ephesus, Athens, and Carthage.*

(3) **PLACE FROM WHICH**: ablative without a preposition
> **Iit Rōmā, Ephesō, Athēnīs, et Carthāgine.**
> *He went from Rome, Ephesus, Athens, and Carthage.*

**Domus,** as seen in the **Vocābula** below, is an irregular feminine noun, having some second declension endings and some fourth. In place constructions the commonest forms are as follows:

**domī** (locative), *at home*      **Domī vīsus est.** *He was seen at home.*
**domum** (acc.), *home* (= *to home*)      **Domum ībit.** *He will go home.*
**domō** (abl.), *from home*      **Domō iit.** *He went from home.*

The locative of **humus,** a feminine second declension noun, follows the rule: **humī,** *on the ground.* The locative of **rūs** is either **rūrī** or **rūre,** *in the country.*

## TIME CONSTRUCTIONS

You are familiar with the **ABLATIVE OF TIME WHEN OR WITHIN WHICH** (Capvt XV); no preposition is used in Latin, but in English translation you must supply "in," "within," "at," "on," etc., depending on the particular noun:

> **Eōdem diē iit.** *He went on the same day.*
> **Paucīs hōrīs domum ībit.** *He will go home in/within a few hours.*

Newly introduced here is the **ACCUSATIVE OF DURATION OF TIME,** which indicates, not the time at or within which an action occurs, but *for how long a period of time* the action occurs. No preposition is employed in Latin; in English translation, the preposition "for" is sometimes used, sometimes omitted. The construction also commonly occurs with **nātus** to indicate a person's age.

> **Multōs annōs vīxit.** *He lived (for) many years.*
> **Paucās hōrās domī manēbit.** *He will stay at home (for) a few hours.*
> **Quīnque et vīgintī annōs nātus, imperātor factus est.** *At the age of 25 (lit., having been born for 25 years), he became commander.*

# VOCĀBVLA

You'll find a few exceptional forms in this list: the toponyms **Athēnae** and **Syrā-cūsae** are nouns that (like **īnsidiae**) have plural forms with singular meanings; the Romans treated **domus** sometimes as second declension, sometimes fourth, and so you'll see a variety of endings. **Licet** is one of several common IMPERSONAL VERBS, which have only third person (and infinitive) forms because they have as their subject, not a person, but a phrase or clause or an indefinite "it" or "one"; e.g., **licet tibi abīre** literally means *to leave is permitted for you,* though the idiomatic translation is *it is permissible for you to leave* or, simply, *you may leave.* As an aid to mastering **eō,** try a synopsis with your book closed, then check your work by referring to the full conjugation above; the new noun **iter,** by the way, is related and literally means "a going."

**Athḗnae, Athēnā́rum,** f. pl., *Athens* (cf. athenaeum)
**dómus, dómūs (dómī),** f., *house, home* (domain, domicile, domestic, domesticate, dome, major-domo)
**húmus, húmī,** f., *ground, earth; soil* (humus, exhume, inhumation, posthumous; cf. humiliate, humility, from **humilis,** lit. = *on the earth, down-to-earth*)
**íter, itíneris,** n., *journey; route, road* (itinerant, itinerary; cf. **eō**)
**rūs, rū́ris,** n., *the country, countryside* (rustic, rusticity; cf. **rūsticor**)
**Syrācū́sae, Syrācūsā́rum,** f. pl., *Syracuse*
**ábsēns,** gen. **abséntis,** *absent, away* (absence, absentee, absenteeism, in absentia; from **absum, abesse**)
**grátus, gráta, grátum,** *pleasing, agreeable; grateful* (gracious, gratify, gratis, gratuity, ingrate, ingratiate, congratulate)
**idṓneus, idṓnea, idṓneum,** *suitable, fit, appropriate*
**immṓtus, immṓta, immṓtum,** *unmoved; unchanged; unrelenting* (immotile; cf. **moveō**)
**fórīs,** adv., *out of doors, outside* (foreclose, foreign, forest, forfeit)
**éō, íre, íī, ítum,** *to go* (ambition, circuit, concomitant, preterit, sedition, transient)
**ábeō, abī́re, ábiī, ábitum,** *to go away, depart, leave*
**ádeō, adī́re, ádiī, áditum,** *to go to, approach* (adit)
**éxeō, exī́re, éxiī, éxitum,** *to go out, exit* (cf. **exitium**)
**íneō, inī́re, íniī, ínitum,** *to go in, enter; enter into, begin* (initial, initiate, initiative)
**óbeō, obī́re, óbiī, óbitum,** *to go up against, meet; die* (obiter dictum, obituary)
**péreō, perī́re, périī, péritum,** *to pass away, be destroyed* (perish)
**rédeō, redī́re, rédiī, réditum,** *to go back, return*
**interfíciō, interfícere, interfḗcī, interféctum,** *to kill, murder*
**lícet, licḗre, lícuit,** impers., + dat. + infin., *it is permitted* (to someone to do something), *one may* (license, licentious, illicit, leisure; the abbreviations "viz." and "sc.": see **Latīna Est Gaudium** below)

peregrĭnor, peregrīnắrī, peregrīnắtus sum, *to travel abroad, wander* (peregrine, peregrinate, pilgrim, pilgrimage; from **per** + **ager**)

requiḗscō, requiḗscere, requiḗvī, requiḗtum, *to rest* (requiescat, requiem)

sóleō, solḗre, sólitus sum, *to be accustomed* (insolent, obsolete)

# LĒCTIŌ ET TRĀNSLĀTIŌ

After studying the new grammar, memorizing the vocabulary, and checking your mastery with the Self-Tutorial Exercises and key, scan the following readings for (a) forms of **eō** and its compounds, identifying tense, number, person, and mood of each, and (b) occurrences of place and time constructions, identifying the case and use of each. Listen to the CDs, if you have them, and read aloud for comprehension before translating.

## EXERCITĀTIŌNĒS

1. Dehinc petet ā frātre meō et sorōre ut occāsiōnem carpant et in urbem quam celerrimē ineant.
2. Nisi domum hāc aestāte redīssēs, in longō itinere Athēnās fortasse peregrīnātī essēmus et nōs ibi oblectāvissēmus.
3. Nē levēs quidem timōrēs ferre poterātis; rūrī, igitur, nōn in urbe semper vīvēbātis.
4. Haec locūtī, lēctōribus et lēctrīcibus persuādēbunt nē opēs cupīdinēsque prae-miīs bonae vītae antepōnant.
5. Multōs annōs eōs cīvitātī servīre coēgit, sed animōs numquam contudit.
6. At nōs, ipsī multa mala passī, cōnātī sumus eīs īrātīs persuādēre ut servōs vinculīs līberārent et nē cui nocērent.
7. Sī quis vult aliōs iuvāre, cūret ut ad eōs adeat plēnus sapientiae.
8. Philosophī cōtīdiē requīrēbant utrum illī discipulī nātūrae pārērent.
9. Contemnāmus omnia perīcula, ea ex pectoribus exigāmus, et fateāmur haec difficillima Rōmae suscipienda esse.
10. Omnēs solent mīrārī ea pulcherrima quae Athēnīs vident.
11. Nisi māvīs morī, exī Syrācūsīs, sequere alium ducem, et accēde Athēnās.
12. Fēmina candida ante speculum immōta stetit, sed sē spectāre recūsāvit et animōs recreāre nōn potuit.
13. Paucās hōrās duodecim puerī puellaeque humī sedēbant, ut magistra, su-brīdēns et eōs serēnāns, plūrimās fābulās nārrābat.
14. Sī sapiēs et tibi imperāre poteris, fīēs grātior iūstiorque, parcēs miserīs ac amīcōs fovēbis.
15. They commanded that this be done in Rome for three days.

16. Unless he goes to Syracuse within five days, his father's fear will become greater.
17. He thought that his brother would perhaps not go away from home that summer.
18. Nobody may (use **licet**) speak freely in that country, as we all know.

## SENTENTIAE ANTĪQVAE

1. Mortālia facta perībunt. (*Horace.)
2. Noctēs atque diēs patet ātrī iānua Dītis. (*Vergil.—**āter, ātra, ātrum,** *dark, gloomy;* "atrocious," "atrocity."—**Dīs, Dītis,** m., *Dis,* another name for Pluto, god of the dead.)
3. Annī eunt mōre modōque fluentis aquae. Numquam hōra quae praeteriit potest redīre; ūtāmur aetāte. (Ovid.—**praeterīre,** *to go by, pass;* "preterit," "praeteritio.")
4. Heu, obiī! Quid ego ēgī! Fīlius nōn rediit ā cēnā hāc nocte. (Terence.)
5. Frāter meus ōrat nē abeās domō. (Terence.)
6. Dīcit patrem ab urbe abīsse sed frātrem esse domī. (Terence.)
7. Tertiā hōrā forīs ībam Sacrā Viā, ut meus mōs est. (Horace.—**Sacrā Viā: ABLATIVE OF ROUTE,** a common construction, usually translated *by way of. . . .* The Sacred Way was the main street through the Roman Forum; another famous street in Rome was **Via Lāta,** from **lātus, -a, -um,** *broad:* how would you translate the street's name?)

*The Roman Forum with remains of the temple of Castor and Pollux in the foreground and beyond it the Sacra Via Rome, Italy*

8. Dēnique Dāmoclēs, cum sīc beātus esse nōn posset, ōrāvit Dionȳsium tyrannum ut abīre ā cēnā licēret. (Cicero.)

9. Eō tempore, Syrācūsīs captīs, Mārcellus multa Rōmam mīsit; Syrācūsīs autem multa atque pulcherrima relīquit. (Cicero.)

10. Diēs multōs in eā nāve fuī; ita adversā tempestāte ūsī sumus. (Terence.)

11. Īram populī ferre nōn poterō, sī in exsilium ieris. (Cicero.)

12. Caesare interfectō, Brūtus Rōmā Athēnās fūgit. (Cicero.)

13. Ipse Rōmam redīrem, sī satis cōnsiliī dē hāc rē habērem. (Cicero.)

14. Nēmō est tam senex ut nōn putet sē ūnum annum posse vīvere. (Cicero.)

15. Dum nōs fāta sinunt, oculōs satiēmus amōre; nox tibi longa venit, nec reditūra diēs. (*Propertius.—**sinō, -ere,** *to allow;* "site," "desinence."—**reditūra:** sc. **est,** fut. act. periphrastic for **redībit; diēs** is sometimes f.)

16. Adversus nēminī, numquam praepōnit sē aliīs. (Terence.—**praepōnō, -ere, -posuī, -positum,** *to place before;* "preposition.")

### Thanks . . . But No Thanks!

Candidius nihil est tē, Caeciliāne. Notāvī:
    sī quandō ex nostrīs disticha pauca legō,
prōtinus aut Mārsī recitās aut scrīpta Catullī.
    Hoc mihi dās, tamquam dēteriōra legās,
5   ut collāta magis placeant mea? Crēdimus istud:
    mālo tamen recitēs, Caeciliāne, tua!

*Martial *Epig.* 2.71: Caecilianus is yet another contemporary reciter on Martial's "don't go there" list! Meter: elegiac couplet. —**candidius:** here, *kinder, more generous.*—**notāre,** *to note, notice;* "notary," "annotate."—**nostrīs:** sc. **libellīs.**—**disticha:** Gk. acc., *couplets, verses.*—**Mārsī:** Domitius Marsus, a popular Augustan poet, who, like Catullus, was a favorite of Martial's; only fragments of his work survive.—**scrīptum, -ī,** n., *writing, written works;* from the fourth principal part of **scrībō;** "manuscript," "prescription."—**hoc . . . dās,** i.e., as a favor.—**tamquam:** here introduces an imagined comparison, something like a condition, hence the verb is subjunctive.—**dēteriōra:** sc. **scrīpta,** *worse poetry;* "deteriorate."—**collāta:** with **mea,** *compared, in comparison;* "collate," "collation."—**mālo . . . (ut) recitēs:** as we have seen before, the conj. is often omitted before a jussive noun clause.

*QVAESTIŌNĒS:* Explain the joke—i.e., how can Caecilianus *really* make Martial's poetry look good? The punch-line, as so often, comes down to one, strategically placed word: what is that word?

### Trimalchio's Epitaph

"Īnscrīptiō quoque vidē dīligenter sī haec satis idōnea tibi vidētur: 'C. Pompeius Trimalchiō Maecēnātiānus hīc requiēscit. Huic sēvirātus absentī dēcrētus est. Cum posset in omnibus decuriīs Rōmae esse, tamen nōluit. Pius, fortis, fidēlis, ex parvō crēvit; sestertium relīquit trecentiēs, nec umquam philosophum audīvit. Valē. Et tū.'" Haec ut dīxit Trimalchiō, flēre coepit ūbertim. Flēbat et Fortūnāta; flēbat et Habinnas; tōta dēnique familia, tamquam in fūnus rogāta, lāmentātiōne triclīnium implēvit.

*Petronius *Sat.* 71–72: Petronius (his exact identity and dates are uncertain, but probably Titus Petronius Arbiter, forced by Nero to commit suicide in A.D. 66) was author of the **Satyricon,** a picaresque novel whose antiheroes in one episode arrive at the home of Trimalchiō, a freedman known for his lavish but utterly gauche dinner-parties; in this scene Trimalchio asks his guests their opinion of his proposed epitaph.—**īnscrīptiō, -ōnis,** f., = Eng. ; the more usual order would be **quoque vidē dīligenter sī haec īnscrīptiō. . . .**— **C.:** = **Gāius.**—**Maecēnātiānus:** Trimalchio takes this name to associate himself with the famous Maecenas, a powerful and wealthy associate of Augustus.—**huic . . . absentī:** i.e., in absentia from Rome.—**sēvirātus, -ūs,** m., *the post of* sēvir *Augustālis,* a member of the six-man commission that supervised the cult of the emperor.—**decūria, -ae,** f., *club;* these were groups of ten men organized for both business and social purposes.—**pius, -a, -um,** *devoted, dedicated;* "pious," "expiate."—**ex parvō:** i.e., from humble beginnings.— **sestertium . . . trecentiēs:** *30 million sesterces,* a hefty sum!—**nec . . . audīvit:** i.e., he "never even went to college!"—**et tū:** sc. **valē**; epitaphs typically represented such "conversations": the deceased wishes the passerby "*Farewell,*" and the passerby, reading the inscription, replies, "*And you (likewise farewell).*"—**haec ut:** = **ut haec.**—**flēre,** *to weep;* from the related adj. **flēbilis,** *lamentable, tearful,* we have "feeble."—**ūbertim,** adv., *profusely.*—**et:** = **etiam.**—Fortunata ("Lucky") and Habinnas were Trimalchio's wife and a guest.—**fūnus, -neris,** n., *funeral;* "funereal," "funerary."—**lāmentātiō, -ōnis,** f.; "lament," "lamentable."— **triclīnium, -iī,** n., *dining room.*—**impleō, -plēre, -plēvī, -plētum,** *to fill;* "implement," "implementation."

*QVAESTIŌ:* Elsewhere during the banquet, Trimalchio joyfully mis-tells the Trojan War story, confusing all the characters and events; in what specific ways does his epitaph reflect his anti-intellectualism, and other aspects of his arrogance?

## Mārcus Quīntō Frātrī S.

Licinius, servus Aesōpī nostrī, Rōmā Athēnās fūgit. Is Athēnīs apud Patrōnem prō līberō virō fuit. Deinde in Asiam abiit. Posteā Platō, quīdam quī Athēnīs solet esse multum et quī tum Athēnīs fuerat cum Licinius Athēnās vēnisset, litterīs Aesōpī dē Liciniō acceptīs, hunc Ephesī comprehendit et in custōdiam trādidit. Petō ā tē, frāter, ut Ephesō exiēns servum Rōmam tēcum redūcās. Aesōpus enim ita īrāscitur propter servī scelus ut nihil eī grātius possit esse quam recuperātiō fugitīvī. Valē.

Cicero *Q Fr.* 1.2.14: As noted earlier, hundreds of Cicero's letters survive, on both personal and political matters; this one he wrote to his brother Quintus, then governor of the Roman province of Asia (Asia Minor), regarding a friend's fugitive slave.—**S.:** =

**salūtem dīcit,** *says greetings,* a standard opening in Roman letters.—**Aesōpus:** the leading tragic actor in Rome and a friend of Cicero, to whom he gave elocution lessons.—**Patrō, -trōnis,** m., identified by Cicero only as an Epicurean.—**Platō:** another Epicurean, from Sardis.—**multum,** adv.—**Ephesus, -ī,** m., a city in Asia Minor.—**re + dūcō;** "reduce," "reduction."—**īrāscor, -cī, īrātus sum,** *to be angry;* "irascible," "irate"; cf. **īra** and **īrātus.**—**recuperātiō, -ōnis,** f., *recovery;* "recuperate" and "recover" are cognates, both derived from **recuperō,** *to regain.*—**fugitīvus, -ī,** m.; = Eng.; cf. **fugere.**

*QVAESTIŌ:* Just to be sure you understand the geography, trace Licinius' itinerary, referring to the maps of the Roman Empire and Greece (Maps 1 and 2).

## SCRĪPTA IN PARIETIBVS

Ō utinam liceat collō complexa tenēre
brāciola et tenerīs ōscula ferre labellīs.
Ī nunc, ventīs tua gaudia, pūpula, crēde;
crēde mihī, levis est nātūra virōrum.
Saepe ego, cu<m> mediā vigilāre<m> perdita nocte,                    5
haec mēcum meditā<n>s—multōs Fortūna quōs supstulit altē,
hōs modo prōiectōs subitō praecipitēsque premit;
sīc Venus ut subitō co<n>iūnxit corpora amantum,
dīvidit lūx, et sē pariies quid aam. . . .

*CIL* 4.5296: This elaborate graffito found near a doorway in a house in Reg. IX, Ins. 7, is an erotic poem in dactylic hexameter, though the meter, as well as some of the syntax, is irregular—due either to compositional flaws or to the failure of the person inscribing it on the wall to recall the text perfectly from memory. The lovesick soliloquy is clearly delivered, and the poem itself most likely authored, by a woman; the piece is a variation on the **PARACLAUSITHYRON** form, a verse lament spoken by a lover shut out at his or her paramour's door. Though echos from the republican poets Catullus and Lucretius have been detected, the poem is clearly an original composition and further testimony to the level of literacy found in Pompeii.—**utinam,** conj. + subjunct., introducing wishes, *how I wish that, if only.*—**collum, -ī,** n., *neck;* "collar"; **collō:** with **tenēre brāciola,** sc.

"around (my). . . ."—**complector, -plectī, -plexus sum**, *to hold in the arms, hug, embrace;* "complection," "complex"; **complexa:** this partic. is commonly employed in combination with **tenēre**, in the sense of "holding in an embrace."—**brāciolum:** = **brācchiolum, -ī**, n., dimin. of **brācchium**, *little arm;* "brace," "bracelet."—**tener, -nera, -nerum,** *soft, tender;* "tenderness."—**labellum, -ī**, n., diminutive of **labrum,** *(little) lip;* "labellum," "labroid."—**ventus, -ī**, m., *wind;* "vent," "ventilate."—**gaudium, -ī**, n., *joy, delight;* "gaudy," "gaudiness."—**pūpula, -ae**, f., diminutive of **pūpa** (see *CIL* 4.4485 in Capvt XI above), *little girl, little doll;* "pupa," "pupal."—**levis:** *fickle* would be a good choice here; what are some others?—**virōrum:** i.e., as opposed to **fēminārum.**—**vigilāre,** *to be awake, watch;* "vigil," "vigilant"; a vowel before final **-m** was often nasalized and, as the **-m** itself was barely pronounced, it was frequently dropped in spelling, as the writer has done here with both **cum** (influenced in part by the initial **m-** of **mediā** following) and **vigilārem.**—**perditus, -a, -um,** *ruined, lost* (emotionally), *hopeless;* "perdition."—**meditor, -tārī, -tātus sum,** *to think about constantly, contemplate, ponder;* "meditate," "meditation"; the writer again dropped the nasal **-n-** from the ending of **meditāns.** We would expect a finite verb here, but the sense breaks off, either in error or as a dramatic APOSIOPESIS.—**Fortūna quōs:** in prose **Fortūna,** as subj. of the rel. clause, would follow **quōs,** but word order in poetry, as you have seen, is much freer; Fortuna was widely worshiped as a deity throughout the Roman empire.—**supstulit:** = **sustulit** (**substulit**), from **tollō.**—**altē,** adv. from **altus, -a, -um,** *high, up;* "altitude," "altimeter."—**modo,** adv., *now, just now; just, only.*— **prōiciō, -icere, -iēcī, -iectum,** *to throw forward, cast out;* "project," "projectile."—**praeceps,** gen. **-cipitis,** *plunging head-first, headlong, in an uncontrolled fall;* "precipitous(ly)."—**sīc . . . ut:** = **sīcut,** conj., *just as.*—**coniungō, -ere, -iūnxī, -iūnctum,** *to join together, connect;* "conjoin," "conjunction"; in **coiūnxit** the writer has again dropped medial **-n-,** likely an-

*"Poetess of Pompeii"*
*Fresco from Insula*
*Occidentale, Pompeii*
*Museo Archaeologico*
*Nazionale, Naples, Italy*

other reflection of her pronunciation.—**dīvidō, -ere, -vīsī, -vīsum,** *to separate into two parts; divide;* "division."—**lūx:** i.e., the dawn of a new day, after a love affair has ended; the remainder of the verse is unintelligible, and one or more additional lines may have been lost.

*QVAESTIŌNĒS:* In what one or two places do you see the clearest evidence that the speaker is female? What do you see as the intended effect of the diminutives in lines 2–3? What apparently has the addressee done to upset the speaker, and what is the speaker's admonition to her in verses 3–4? What are the writer's closing observations on the power of the goddesses Fortuna and Venus? What do you imagine the poem's closing verse(s) may have said—i.e., how would you have concluded the poem? Verse 2, with its repeated **la/la/la/llīs** syllables is highly alliterative; which other lines are marked by alliteration?

## LATĪNA EST GAVDIVM—ET VTILIS!

**Salvēte!** These familiar words and phrases from **eō** are certainly *going to* interest you (notice how colloquial English employs "go" as an auxiliary verb to indicate futurity, and cf. Latin's use of **īrī** in those rare future passive infinitive forms): **exit** and **exeunt omnēs** are stage directions; to "perish" is to be "thoroughly gone" (from **per + eō**), i.e., to make one's final "exit" from life's stage, an exodus often marked by **obiit** on old tombstones or by the abbreviation **O.S.P.** for **obiit sine prōle** (*he/she died without offspring,* from **prōlēs, prōlis,** f., the source of "proletariate"); **pereant quī ante nōs nostra dīxērunt** is a proverbial curse on folks who had all our best ideas before we had them ourselves (!); **iter** (lit. *a going*) is related to **eō** and also to the adverb **obiter,** which gives us **obiter dictum,** something *said along the way* (or "in passing"), and likewise **obiter scrīptum;** Monty Python fans will recall the **Rōmānī, īte domum** routine from the "Life of Brian"; and finally **aut bibat aut abeat,** *let him either drink or go away,* is an old Roman proverb and the motto of our local pub!

    Et cētera: **grātus** is related to **grātia,** *favor, kindness, gratitude,* as in **grātiās agere,** *to give thanks,* **Deī grātiā,** *by the grace of God,* and also English "gratis," something done "for thanks" (**grātīs**), i.e., without a fee. **R.I.P.,** also found on tombstones (though not Trimalchio's!), stands for **requiēscat in pāce** (remember the jussive subjunctive?); **rūs in urbe,** a phrase from Martial, refers to a city park or garden or some other rustic setting or view that reminds one of the countryside. **Vidēlicet,** *namely,* derives from **vidēre licet,** lit., *it is permitted to see,* i.e., *it is plain to see.* In medieval manuscripts the word was often contracted to **vi-et,** and one abbreviation for **et** resembled a **z;** hence the abbreviation **viz.** From another compound of **licet** is the much more common abbreviation **sc.** for **scīlicet,** *namely, clearly* (from **scīre licet,** *you may understand*), which we use as an instruction to supply some word or idea that has been omitted from a text but is readily understood (see the example above in the notes on "Trimalchio"). Well, enough for today: **nunc domum eāmus!**

# CAPVT XXXVIII 𓂀𓂀𓂀

# Relative Clauses of Characteristic; Dative of Reference; Supines

## GRAMMATICA

### RELATIVE CLAUSES OF CHARACTERISTIC

The type of relative clause you have encountered thus far provides some factual description of its antecedent, an actual person or thing, and thus has an indicative verb (Capvt XVII); e.g., **haec est discipula quae Latīnam amat,** *this is the student who loves Latin.* The **RELATIVE CLAUSE OF CHARACTERISTIC,** by contrast, describes some general quality of an antecedent that is itself either general, indefinite, interrogative, or negative, and accordingly has its verb in the subjunctive; e.g., **haec est discipula quae Latīnam amet,** *this is a student* (or *the sort of student*) *who would love Latin.*

*Recognition:* The relative clause of characteristic is easily recognized, since its verb is subjunctive and its antecedent is often obviously general, negative, etc. (typical examples are **sunt quī,** *there are people who;* **quis est quī,** *who is there who;* **nēmō est quī,** *there is no one who*). *Translation:* the auxiliary "would" is sometimes used in translating the subjunctive verb, and sometimes a phrase like "the sort of" or "the kind of" is employed in the main clause to make it clear that the antecedent is indefinite:

> **Quis est quī huic crēdat?** *Who is there who trusts this man (of such a sort that he would trust this man)?*
> **Nēmō erat quī hoc scīret.** *There was no one who knew this.*
> **Sunt quī hoc faciant.** *There are some who do this (of such a sort as to do this).*
> **Is nōn est quī hoc faciat.** *He is not a person who does (would do) this.*
> **Hic est liber quem omnēs legant.** *This is the kind of book that all read (a book that all would read).*
> **Hic est liber quem omnēs legunt.** *This is the book that all are reading (= a fact, hence the indicative).*

Some relative clauses have the force of result (e.g., S.A. 4 below), purpose (see "More Examples of Roman Wit" below), causal, or adversative clauses (i.e., clauses otherwise generally introduced by **ut, cum,** etc.) and so also have subjunctive verbs.

## DATIVE OF REFERENCE OR INTEREST

The dative case is often used to indicate a person (or a thing) to whom some statement refers, or from whose perspective it is true, or to whom it is of special interest. This **DATIVE OF REFERENCE OR INTEREST** (which should be compared to the dative uses discussed in Capvt XXXV) can sometimes be translated with "to" or "for," but often some more elaborate phrase is required, depending upon the context, as you will see from the following examples; occasionally the function seems to be simply possessive (as in the second example below), but the intended force is generally more emotional.

> **Sī quis metuēns vīvet, līber *mihi* nōn erit umquam.**
> *If anyone lives in fear, he will not ever be free—as I see it* (**mihi**) *or to my way of thinking or in my opinion.*
> **Caret *tibi* pectus inānī ambitiōne?**
> *Is your breast free from vain ambition—are you sure* (**tibi**)?
> **Nūllīus culpae *mihi* cōnscius sum.**
> *In my own heart* (**mihi**), *I am conscious of no fault.*
> **Claudia est sapiēns *multīs*.**
> *To many people Claudia is wise.*

Remember to add this usage to your list of other dative case constructions (indirect object, dative of agent, dative with adjectives, dative with special verbs and compounds).

## SUPINES

The **SUPINE** is a defective fourth declension verbal noun, based on the same stem as the perfect passive participle; only two forms were in common use, the accusative and ablative singular. The supines for our model verbs are: acc. **laudắtum,** abl. **laudắtū; mónitum, mónitū; ắctum, ắctū; audītum, audītū; cáptum, cáptū.**

The ablative is used with the neuter of certain adjectives to indicate in what respect a particular quality is applicable: e.g., **mīrābile dictū,** *amazing to say* (lit., *amazing in respect to saying*); **facile factū,** *easy to do.* The accusative (which must not be confused with the perfect passive participle) is employed with verbs of motion to indicate purpose: e.g., **ībant Rōmam rogātum pecūniam,** *they were going to Rome to ask for money;* **persuāsum amīcīs vēnērunt,** *they came to persuade their friends* (note that the supine can take a direct object, a dative, or any other construction the basic verb can govern).

# VOCĀBVLA

Not only is **arbor,** *tree,* feminine, but so regularly are the names of individual trees, regardless of declension, e.g.: **betulla, -ae,** *birch;* **fīcus, -ī,** *fig;* **abies, -etis,** *fir;* **quercus, -ūs,** *oak.* Some more look-alikes to beware of: **opus/ops, queror/quaerō, odium/ōtium.** As you learn the verbs in this list, see if you can form the supines for the four regular ones (excluding **metuō,** which lacks a fourth principal part, and the deponent **queror**); your instructor can check your answers, or you can simply compare the supines of the five model verbs presented above. Finally, don't forget the sound of **gn** in **dignitās:** listen to this, and all new words, online or on the CDs, and practice saying each aloud several times.

**árbor, árboris,** f., *tree* (arbor, Arbor Day, arboretum, arboriculture)

**dígnitās, dignitā́tis,** f., *merit, prestige, dignity* (indignity, deign, dignify, indignant, indignation; cf. **dignus**)

**dólor, dolṓris,** m., *pain, grief* (doleful, dolorous, condolences; cf. **doleō**)

**ódium, ódiī,** n., *hatred* (odium, odious, annoy, ennui, noisome; cf. **ōdī**)

**ópus, óperis,** n., *a work, task; deed, accomplishment* (opus, opera, operate, operative, inoperative, co-operate, hors d'oeuvre, maneuver, manure)

**ōrā́tiō, ōrātiṓnis,** f., *speech* (oration, oratory; cf. **ōrō, ōrātor**)

**pēs, pédis,** m., *lower leg, foot* (pedal, pedate, pedestal, pedestrian, pedicel, pedigree, piedmont, pawn, peon, pioneer, biped, quadruped, impede, impediment, expedite, expedition, expeditious)

**sátor, satṓris,** m., *sower, planter; begetter, father; founder* (cf. **serere,** *to plant, sow;* serial, series, assert, desert, exert, insert)

**fírmus, fírma, fírmum,** *firm, strong; reliable* (firmament, affirm, affirmation, affirmative, confirm, confirmation, farm, farmer)

**īnfírmus, īnfírma, īnfírmum,** *not strong, weak, feeble* (infirm, infirmary, infirmity)

**mīrā́bilis, mīrā́bile,** *amazing, wondrous, remarkable* (mirabilia, admirable, marvel, miracle, mirador, mirage, mirror; cf. **mīror**)

**prístinus, prístina, prístinum,** *ancient; former, previous* (pristine)

**sublī́mis, sublī́me,** *elevated, lofty; heroic, noble* (sublimate, sublime, sublimity; not subliminal)

**étsī (et + sī),** conj. with indic. or subjunct. according to rules for **sī,** *even if, although*

**érgā,** prep. + acc., *toward*

**libénter,** adv., *with pleasure, gladly* (ad lib.; cf. the IMPERSONAL VERB libet, *it pleases, is pleasing;* cognate with "love")

**impédiō, impedī́re, impedī́vī, impedī́tum,** *to impede, hinder, prevent* (impediment, impedance, impeach; cf. **pēs** above and see **Lātina Est Gaudium**)

**métuō, metúere, métuī,** *to fear, dread; be afraid for* + dat. (meticulous; cf. **metus**)

**quéror, quérī, quéstus sum,** *to complain, lament* (querulous; cf. quarrel, from **querēla, -ae,** *complaint*)

**recognóscō, recognóscere, recognóvī, recognitum,** *to recognize, recollect* (recognition, recognizance, reconnaisance, reconnoitre; cf. **nóscō, cognóscō**)

**suspéndō, suspéndere, suspéndī, suspênsum,** *to hang up, suspend; interrupt* (suspense, suspension; cf. **pendere,** *to hang,* pendant, pendulum)

**vêndō, vêndere, vêndidī, vênditum,** *to sell* (vend, vendor)

# LĒCTIŌ ET TRĀNSLĀTIŌ

After testing your mastery of the chapter's new material with the Self-Tutorial Exercises, scan the readings for each (a) relative clause of characteristic, (b) dative of reference, and (c) supine; remember that in translating the relative clause of characteristic you often must supply some word/phrase indicating the indefinite nature of the antecedent or action, e.g., "a book that all *would* enjoy," "the *sort of* book that all enjoy." Listen to the CDs, if you have them, and read aloud for comprehension before translating.

## EXERCITĀTIŌNĒS

1. Rēgī persuāsī ut sorōrī frātrīque tuō grātiōra praemia libenter daret.
2. Deinde, ab eā īnsulā nāve profecta, vīsum amīcōs Athēnās iniit.
3. Eum hortātī sumus ut ad Caesarem sine timōre accēdere cōnārētur.
4. Solitī sunt eī crēdere quī philosophiae servīret, virtūtem sequerētur, et cupīdinēs superāret.
5. Sapiēns nōs ōrat nē virīs sententiārum adversārum noceāmus.
6. In illīs terrīs nōn licet litterīs bonīs vērīsque studēre, ut sub tyrannō saepe fit; dēbēs, igitur, exīre et peregrīnārī.
7. Cūrēmus nē cīvitātem eīs trādāmus quī sē patriae antepōnant.
8. Sunt īnfirmī quī levia opera mīrentur et semper sibi ignōscant.
9. Iste dux, diū absēns, tam stultīs cōnsiliīs cīvitātī ūtēbātur ut mīlia cīvium adversa patī cōgerentur atque multī bonī perīrent.
10. Haec locūtus, fassus est illōs, quī odium immōtum ergā cīvitātem multōs annōs habēbant, Rōmae interfectōs esse.
11. Initium operis nōs saepe impedit–inīte opus nunc!
12. Sator sublīmis hominum atque animālium omnibus nōbīs animās dedit; cum corpora obeant, animae numquam morientur.
13. Cum rūs rediimus, tum domī invēnimus—mīrābile vīsū!—plūrimōs amīcōs.

14. Cicero, who was the greatest Roman orator, was a consul who would obey the senate.
15. I shall persuade him to become a better student and to return to Syracuse soon, I assure you.
16. We begged them not to trust a man whom a tyrant pleased.
17. Wherefore, let that man who hesitates to defend our country depart (use **abeō**) to another land.

## SENTENTIAE ANTĪQVAE

1. Sē omnēs Caesarī ad pedēs prōiēcērunt. (Caesar.—**prō-iaciō;** "project," "projectile.")
2. Hīc in nostrō numerō sunt quī lēgēs contemnant ac dē exitiō huius urbis cōtīdiē cōgitent. (Cicero.)
3. Quis est cui haec rēs pūblica atque possessiō lībertātis nōn sint cārae et dulcēs? (Id.—**possessiō, -ōnis,** f.; "possess," "possessive.")
4. Quae domus tam stabilis est, quae cīvitās tam firma est quae nōn odiīs, invidiā, atque īnsidiīs possit contundī? (Id.—**stabilis, -e;** "stability," "establish."—**quae . . . contundī:** here the characteristic clause has the force of result.)
5. Quārē, quid est quod tibi iam in hāc urbe placēre possit, in quā nēmō est quī tē nōn metuat? (Id.)
6. Quis enim aut eum dīligere potest quem metuat aut eum ā quō sē metuī putet? (Id.)
7. Tibi sōlī necēs multōrum cīvium impūnītae ac līberae fuērunt. (Id.—**nex, necis,** f., *murder;* "internecine," "pernicious;" cf. **necō.—impūnītus, -a, -um,** *unpunished;* "impune," "impunity," "punitive"; cf. **poena.**)
8. Habētis autem eum cōnsulem quī exigere officium et pārēre vestrīs dēcrētīs nōn dubitet atque vōs dēfendere possit. (Id.—**dēcrētum, -ī,** n., *decree;* "decretal.")
9. Ille mihi semper deus erit. (Vergil.)
10. Nūllus dolor est quem nōn longinquitās temporis minuat ac molliat. (*Cicero.—**longinquitās, -tātis,** n., *length;* "longinquity.")
11. Parāvisse dīvitiās fuit multīs hominibus nōn fīnis sed mūtātiō malōrum. (Epicurus quoted by Seneca.—**mūtātiō, -ōnis,** f., *change;* "mutation," "permutation.")
12. Nihil est opere et manū factum quod tempus nōn cōnsūmat. (Cicero.)
13. Vīribus corporis dēficientibus, vigor tamen animī dūrāvit illī ad vītae fīnem. (Pliny.—**dēficiō, -ere,** *to fail;* "defect," "deficient," "deficit."—**vigor, -gōris,** m.—**dūrāre,** *to last;* "durable," "duration.")
14. Nunc est bibendum; nunc pede līberō pulsanda tellus. (*Horace; from his ode celebrating the death of the Egyptian queen Cleopatra.—sc. **nōbīs** as dat. of agent with both pass. periphrastics.—**pulsāre,** *to strike, beat;* with **pulsanda,**

sc. **est**, *should be struck,* i.e., *danced upon;* "pulse," "pulsar."—**tellūs, -lūris,** f., = **terra;** "tellurian," "tellurium.")

15. Ē tacitō vultū scīre futūra licet. (*Ovid.–**tacitus, -a, -um,** *silent;* "tacit," "taciturn."-**vultus, -ūs,** m., *countenance, face.*)

16. Stultitiast, pater, vēnātum dūcere invītās canēs. (*Plautus.–**stultitia, -ae,** f., noun from **stultus, -a, -um;** "stultifying."-**stultitiast:** a common type of contraction known as PRODELISION, = **stultitia est.**-**vēnor, -ārī, -ātus sum,** *to go hunting, hunt.*-**invītus, -a, -um,** *unwilling, against one's will;* cf. **volō.**-**canis, -is,** m./f., *dog;* "canine." )

## Note on a Book by Lucan

> Sunt quīdam quī mē dīcant nōn esse poētam;
> sed quī mē vēndit bibliopōla putat.

*Martial *Epig.* 14.194: In this note from a gift copy of Lucan's poetry (compare the note from a copy of Catullus in Capvt XXX), the author is himself imagined as speaking; meter: elegiac couplet.—**bibliopōla, -ae,** m., *book-dealer,* antecedent of **quī;** "bibliopole," "bibliopolist," and cf. "bibliography" and "bibliophile," all Gk. in origin.

*QVAESTIŌNĒS:* Is the accusation in line 1 real or hypothetical?—how do you know? The language of verse, as of daily speech, is often elliptical; what must be understood following **putat?**

## More Examples of Roman Wit

Cum quīdam, querēns, dīxisset uxōrem suam dē ficū suspendisse sē, amīcus illīus "Amābō tē," inquit, "dā mihi ex istā arbore surculōs quōs seram!"

Cum quīdam ōrātor sē misericordiam ōrātiōne fortasse mōvisse putāret, rogāvit Catulum vidērēturne misericordiam mōvisse. "Ac magnam quidem, mihi," inquit, "putō enim nēminem esse tam dūrum cui ōrātiō tua nōn vīsa sit digna misericordiā!"

Cicero *De Or.* 2.278: You read another joke ("Sorry, Nobody's Home!") from the same section of **Dē Ōrātōre** in Capvt XXXV; the first one here you ought not tell your wife, but the second just might get a laugh in a class on public speaking!—**ficus, -ūs,** f., *fig tree;* "ficus."—**surculus, -ī,** m., *shoot, sprig;* "surculose."—**quōs:** = **ut eōs,** RELATIVE CLAUSE OF PURPOSE, a common alternative, introducing the purp. clause with a rel. pron. instead of **ut.**—**serō, -ere,** *to plant, sow;* "season."—**misericordia, -ae,** f., *pity;* "misericord"; cf. **miser;** an important objective for the ancient orator, and one for which he was trained, was to arouse the audience's emotions.—**Catulus, -ī,** m.; Quintus Lutatius Catulus, orator, author, and statesman, consul in 102 B.C.—**vidērēturne:** the **-ne,** *whether,* signals an ind. question.—**magnam:** sc. **misericordiam mōvistī!**—**cui:** = **ut eī,** RELATIVE CLAUSE

OF RESULT; like the rel. clause of purp., this construction is a common variant in which the clause is introduced by a rel. pron., rather than by **ut.**

*QVAESTIŌ:* The first of these jokes, albeit unkind, is clear enough, but how about the second: "pitiful" in contemporary American English can carry a double entendre identical to the one intended here—can you explain the joke?

## Two Letters to Cicero

### Cn. Magnus Prōcōnsul Salūtem Dīcit Cicerōnī Imperātōrī

Sī valēs, bene est. Tuās litterās libenter lēgī; recognōvī enim tuam prīstinam virtūtem etiam in salūte commūnī. Cōnsulēs, Rōmā abientēs, ad eum exercitum vēnērunt quem in Āpūliā habuī. Magnopere tē hortor ut occāsiōnem carpās et tē ad nōs cōnferās, ut commūnī cōnsiliō reī publicae miserae opem atque auxilium ferāmus. Moneō ut Rōmā exeās, viā Appiā iter faciās, et quam celerrimē Brundisium veniās.

### Caesar Imperātor Salūtem Dīcit Cicerōnī Imperātōrī

Cum Brundisium celerius adeam atque sim in itinere, exercitū iam praemissō, dēbeō tamen ad tē scrībere et grātiās idōneās tibi agere, etsī hoc fēcī saepe et saepius factūrus videor; ita dignus es. Imprīmīs, quoniam crēdō mē celeriter ad urbem ventūrum esse, ā tē petō ut tē ibi videam ut tuō cōnsiliō, dignitāte, ope ūtī possim. Festīnātiōnī meae brevitātīque litterārum ignōscēs; cētera ex Furniō cognōscēs.

Cicero *Atticum* 8.11c and 9.6a: Among the hundreds of letters surviving from Cicero's correspondence, several were written, not by him, but to him, including these two adapted from the collection of his epistles to his friend Atticus, **Epistulae ad Atticum;** one is from Gnaeus Pompeius Magnus, "Pompey the Great," written on February 20, 49 B.C., and the other was sent about two weeks later, on March 5, by Julius Caesar, both of whom were

*Marble bust of Pompey the Great*
*1st cent. B.C.*
*Museo Archeologico, Venice, Italy*

at this point bidding for the statesman's support in the civil war that broke out between them after Caesar's crossing of the Rubicon on January 10.—**prōcōnsul, -sulis,** m., *proconsul, governor* (of a province).—**salūte commūnī:** here *the public welfare.*—**Āpūliā:** Apulia was a district in southeastern Italy.—**viā Appiā:** ABLATIVE OF ROUTE (see S.A. 7, Capvt XXVII); the Via Appia, or "Appian Way," built in the 4th cent. B.C., was the highway leading south from Rome and, ultimately, to Brundisium (see Map 1), the port of departure for Greece, where Pompey was fleeing with his army, in order to regroup and then take a stand against Caesar's forces.—**commūnī:** with **cōnsiliō**, *mutual, collaborative.*—**prae + mittō, -ere;** "premise."—**imprīmīs,** adv., *especially.*—**festīnātiō, -ōnis,** f., *haste, rush;* "festination."—**brevitās, -tātis,** f.; cf. **brevis;** "abbreviate."—**Furnius:** Gaius Furnius was tribune of the plebs and a friend of both Cicero and Caesar.

*QVAESTIŌNĒS:* What one thing in particular (look for a repeated noun) are both generals seeking from Cicero? Do you detect any difference of tone between the two letters that might suggest one of the two men was on better terms with Cicero?

### Ask Me If I Care

> Nīl nimium studeō, Caesar, tibi velle placēre,
>     nec scīre utrum sīs albus an āter homō!

*Catullus *Carm.* 93:* As noted earlier, Catullus wrote not only love poems, but also satiric zingers aimed at the high and mighty. Here he deals Julius Caesar the ultimate insult, pretending to know nothing of the man—not even the color of his skin!—this is not a racial slur, as the Romans were largely without color prejudice, but rather a barb aimed at Caesar's pride in being a **nōbilis** or "known man." Meter: elegiac couplet.—**nīl:** = **nōn.**—**albus, -a, -um,** *white;* "albino," "album," "albumen."—**āter, ātra, ātrum,** *black;* "atrabilious," "atrous."

*QVAESTIŌNĒS:* What is the effect of using **nīl nimium** instead of simply **nōn?** How does Catullus' use of **homō** vs. **vir** contribute to the intended tone?

## SCRĪPTA IN PARIETIBVS

Nunc est īra recēns, nunc est disc[ēdere tempus.]
Sī dolor āfuerit, crēde: redībit [amor]!

*CIL* 4.4491: An elegiac couplet inscribed—after a lovers' spat?—at the entrance to the House of Sextus Pompeius Axiochus (Reg. VI, Ins. 13). The text of the two damaged verses is easily restored, as the writer was copying out lines from the elegist Propertius (*El.* 2.5.9–10), lines perhaps memorized in school.—**recēns,** gen. -**centis,** *of recent origin, recent; fresh in the mind/memory.*—**absum, -esse, āfuī, āfutūrum,** *to be away, be absent; be removed, be distant;* "absence."

## ETYMOLOGIA

Here are Romance derivatives from a few of the new **vocābula:**

| Latin | It. | Sp. | Port. | Fr. | Old Occ. | Rom. |
|-------|-----|-----|-------|-----|----------|------|
| dolor | dolore | dolor | dor | douleur | dolọr | durere |
| odium | odio | odio | ódio | odieux | ọdi | odiu |
| pēs, pedis | piede | pie | pé | pied | pẹs | picior |

## LATĪNA EST GAVDIVM—ET VTILIS!

**Salvēte!** Have you noticed that we like to **ad lib.** in this section of each chapter? **Ad libitum,** *at one's pleasure,* is connected with **libenter,** which is how Latin should be both taught and learned: *gladly!* So, **libenter carpite diem et hās rēs novās:** first, note that **impediō** is from **in** + **pēs;** when you're "impeded," you've got something *on your feet* (like "fetters," from the same base as "foot"), so perhaps you should consult a podiatrist (**pod-** is the Greek cognate of Latin **ped-**) and ask him to "expedite" your treatment (**expedīre** is essentially "to de-fetter," the opposite of **impedīre;** cf. "implicate" and "explicate" from **implicāre/explicāre**); otherwise, just give up your pedestrian ways and start pedaling. **Odium** means *rivalry* as well as *hatred;* guess who the rivals are in **odium medicum, odium scholasticum,** and **odium theologicum?** And speaking of odious types, the emperor Tiberius (A.D. 14–37) is said to have remarked of his subjects, **ōderint dum metuant,** *let them hate (me), so long as they fear (me)!* The abbreviation **op. cit.** is from **opere citātō,** *in the work cited;* and **opera omnia** are an author's *complete works.* The use of **opus** in the titles of musical works is well known, e.g., Beethoven's "Symphony No. 5 in C Minor, Opus 67"; "opera" comes to us through It. from **opera, -ae,** *effort, pains, work,* which clearly has the same root as **opus.** The term **magnum opus,** on the other hand, is commonly used in the literary field. An old legal prescript provides that **vēndēns eandem rem duōbus est falsārius** (*fraudulent*); such a swindle would be **īnfrā dignitātem,** *beneath one's dignity,* so remember the familiar admonition **caveat ēmptor,** *let the buyer beware!* **Iterum tempus fūgit: valeātis, amīcī et amīcae!**

# CAPVT XXXIX ▨▨▨

# Gerund and Gerundive

## GRAMMATICA

### THE GERUNDIVE

You are already familiar with the GERUNDIVE, or future passive participle, a verbal adjective formed with the endings -**ndus, -nda, -ndum** (Capvt XXIII). Besides functioning occasionally as a simple adjective (**liber legendus,** *a book to be read*), the gerundive is commonly employed in the passive periphrastic conjugation (Capvt XXIV: **hic liber legendus est,** *this book should be read*); some further uses are examined in this chapter.

### THE GERUND

The GERUND is a verbal *noun* resembling the gerundive, except that it has only four forms, the neuter singular of the genitive, dative, accusative, and ablative. These forms are identical to the corresponding cases of the gerundive, but are *active* in meaning and correspond to the English gerund in "-ing" (**legendī,** *of reading,* as in **magnum amōrem legendī habet,** *he has a great love of reading*). Following are the complete gerund declensions for some representative Latin verbs:

| | | | | |
|---|---|---|---|---|
| *Gen.* | laudándī | dūcéndī | sequéndī | audiéndī |
| | (*of praising, leading, following, hearing*) | | | |
| *Dat.* | laudándō | dūcéndō | sequéndō | audiéndō |
| | (*to/for praising,* etc.) | | | |
| *Acc.* | laudándum | dūcéndum | sequéndum | audiéndum |
| | (*praising,* etc.) | | | |
| *Abl.* | laudándō | dūcéndō | sequéndō | audiéndō |
| | (*by praising,* etc.) | | | |

Since the gerund is a verbal noun, it can be modified as a verb and used as a noun in the various cases. The gerund had no nominative case, however, and was not used as a subject, a function performed instead by the infinitive, another of Latin's verbal nouns (i.e., Latin could say **errāre est humānum,** *to err is human,* but not *err-*

*ing is human*); the accusative was ordinarily employed as an object of **ad** and certain other prepositions, but not as a direct object (a function again performed by the infinitive, e.g., **iussit eōs venīre**, *he ordered them to come:* see App., p. 494). The following sentences illustrate typical uses of the gerund in its four cases:

> **Studium** *vīvendī* **cum amīcīs habet.** *She has a fondness of (for) living with friends.*
> **Bene** *vīvendō* **operam dat.** *He gives attention to living well.*
> **Ad bene** *vīvendum* **Athēnās iit.** *She went to Athens to live well.*
> **Bene** *vīvendō* **fēlīciōrēs fīmus.** *We become happier by living well.*

### Differences between Gerund and Gerundive

Remember these distinctions between gerund and gerundive: (1) the gerund*ive* is a verbal adjec*tive* (**liber legendus**, *a book to be read*), the gerund a verbal noun (**amor legendī**, *love of reading*); (2) as an adjective, the gerundive has a full set of masculine, feminine, and neuter endings, singular and plural, for all cases, whereas the gerund has only neuter singular forms and only in the genitive, dative, accusative, and ablative, i.e., a total of four forms altogether; (3) the gerundive is passive in meaning, the gerund active.

### Gerund and Gerundive Phrases

As a verbal noun, the gerund may take the case construction required by its verb:

> **Studium legendī librōs habet.** *She has a fondness of reading books.*
> **Librōs legendō discimus.** *We learn by reading books.*

In actual practice, however, when the gerund would take a noun in the accusative as direct object, the Romans preferred to put this noun in the case in which the gerund would otherwise appear and to use instead a gerundive in agreement with the noun. The translation is the same no matter which construction is used, since English requires the gerund construction rather than the unidiomatic gerundive. In the following examples, those marked "A" are what we would expect on the basis of English idiom; those marked "B" are the gerundive phrases more common in Latin:

A. **studium legendī librōs** (acceptable)
B. **studium librōrum legendōrum** (preferred)
   *fondness of reading books* (not *fondness of books to be read*, which is unidiomatic)

A. **Librōs legendō operam dat.**
B. **Librīs legendīs operam dat.**
   *He gives attention to reading books.*

A. **Librōs legendō discimus.**
B. **Librīs legendīs discimus.**
   *We learn by reading books.*

A. **Dē legendō librōs hoc locūta est.**
B. **Dē librīs legendīs hoc locūta est.**
   *She said this about reading books.*

The preposition **ad** + an accusative gerundive (or gerund) phrase and postpositive **causā** + a genitive phrase were often employed to indicate *purpose:*

A. **Ad legendum librōs vēnit.**
B. **Ad librōs legendōs vēnit.**
   *He came to read books.*

A. **Legendī librōs causā ōtium petit.**
B. **Librōrum legendōrum causā ōtium petit.**
   *She seeks leisure for the sake of reading books.*

Remember that purpose can be expressed in Latin, not only with gerundive/gerund phrases, but also with **ut/nē** + the subjunctive and, after a main verb of motion, the accusative supine: **venit ut hōs librōs legat** and **hōs librōs lēctum venit** both mean *she is coming to read these books.*

# VOCĀBVLA

Knowing that diphthongs in Latin often drop their first vowel in English derivatives will help you recall the meanings of some words like **aedificium**, *edifice, building,* in the list below. Whereas **fēmina** means *woman* or *female* in its most basic sense, the new noun **mulier** (which gives us Spanish **mujer**) more often connotes an experienced woman, a wife, a lover (as opposed to a **virgō**). As you learn the new verbs in this list, you might practice with a synopsis or two; and can you identify the gerund and gerundive forms of, e.g., **ōrnō?**

**aedifícium, aedifíciī,** n., *building, structure* (edification, edifice, edify, aedile)
**iniū́ria, iniū́riae,** f., *injustice, injury, wrong* (injurious; cf. **iūdex, iūdicium, iūs**)
**múlier, mulíeris,** f., *woman* (muliebrity)
**trā́nsitus, trā́nsitūs,** m., *passing over, transit; transition*
**véntus, véntī,** m., *wind* (vent, ventilate, ventilation, ventilator)
**cúpidus, cúpida, cúpidum,** *desirous, eager, fond;* + gen., *desirous of, eager for* (cf. **cupiō, cupiditās, cupīdō**)
**līberā́lis, līberā́le,** *of, relating to a free person; worthy of a free man, decent, liberal; generous* (liberal arts, liberality; cf. **līber, līberō, lībertās**)

**necésse,** indecl. adj. used as nom. or acc., *necessary, inevitable;* often **necesse est** + infin., *it is necessary (to)* (necessitate, necessitous; from **nec** + **cēdō,** in the sense of a requirement that is "not going away")

**vétus,** gen. **véteris,** *old* (veteran, inveterate, veterinary, veterinarian)

**quási,** adv. or conj., *as if, as it were* (quasi; = **quam** + **sī**)

**ámbulō, ambuláre, ambulávī, ambulátum,** *to walk* (amble, ambulance, ambulate, ambulatory, preamble, somnambulist)

**expérior, experírī, expértus sum,** *to try, test; experience* (experiment, expert, inexpert, inexperience; cf. **perīculum**)

**lībō, lībáre, lībávī, lībátum,** *to pour a libation of, on; pour ritually; sip; touch gently* (libation)

**opórtet, oportére, opórtuit,** impers., + infin., *it is proper, right, necessary*

**oppúgnō, oppugnáre, oppugnávī, oppugnátum,** *to fight against, attack, assault, assail* (oppugn, impugn, pugnacious; cf. **pugnō**)

**órnō, ōrnáre, ōrnávī, ōrnátum,** *to equip, furnish, adorn* (adornment, ornate, ornament, ornamental, suborn)

**pernóctō, pernoctáre, pernoctávī, pernoctátum,** *to spend* or *occupy the night* (nocturnal, nocturne; cf. **nox**)

**tránseō, trānsíre, tránsiī, tránsitum,** *to go across, cross; pass over, ignore* (transition, transitive, transitory, trance; cf. **trānsitus** above)

# LĒCTIŌ ET TRĀNSLĀTIŌ

After thorough study of the new grammar and vocabulary, identify all gerunds and gerundives in the following readings. Then read each sentence and passage aloud, listening to the CDs if you have them, and translate; remember that, for natural English idiom, gerundive phrases generally must be translated as active constructions, e.g., in Ex. 7 below, **in rē pūblicā gerendā** = *in governing the republic,* not *in the republic to be governed.*

## EXERCITĀTIŌNĒS

1. Caesar, bellum inītūrus, eōs cōtīdiē ōrābat nē fāta adversa metuerent.
2. Etsī hoc fīat, illī mīlitēs urbem oppugnātum fortasse accēdant et multī cīvēs obeant.
3. Sī licēbit, septem diēbus domum ībimus ad nostrōs amīcōs videndōs.
4. Amīcus līberālissimus noster, quōcum pernoctābāmus, dīs vīnum ante cēnam lībāvit, et deinde mēnsam ōrnāvit.
5. Cōnsul, vir maximae dignitātis, ōtium cōnsūmere solet in operibus sublīmibus scrībendīs.

6. Sunt autem quī dolōrum vītandōrum causā, ut āiunt, semper levia opera faciant, labōrem contemnant, et dē officiīs querantur.

7. In rē pūblicā gerendā istī nōn dubitant praemia grāta sibi requīrere, officia suspendere, atque honōrem suum vēndere.

8. Lēctrīx doctissima mox surget ad tria carmina recitanda, quae omnēs audītōrēs oblectābunt atque animōs serēnābunt.

9. Nēmō est cui iniūria placeat, ut nōs omnēs recognōscimus.

10. Nisi vincula patī ac sub pedibus tyrannōrum humī contundī volumus, lībertātī semper studeāmus et eam numquam impediāmus.

11. Pauca opera mihi sedendō fīunt, multa agendō et experiendō.

12. Illa mulier mīrābilis frūctūs amōris libenter carpsit et virō grātissimō nūpsit.

13. They are returning to Rome to talk about conquering the Greeks.

14. By remaining at Rome he persuaded them to become braver.

15. Who is there who has hope of doing great works without pain?

16. We urged the consul to serve the state and preserve our dignity by attacking these injustices.

## SENTENTIAE ANTĪQVAE

1. Coniūrātiōnem nāscentem nōn crēdendō corrōborāvērunt. (*Cicero.—coniūrātiō, -ōnis, f., *conspiracy;* "conjure," "conjurer"; cf. coniūrātī. —corrōborāre, *to strengthen;* "corroborate," "corroboration"; cf. rōbur, rōboris, n., *oak tree; hard wood.*)

2. Malī dēsinant īnsidiās reī pūblicae cōnsulīque parāre et ignēs ad īnflammandam urbem. (Cicero.—dēsinō, -ere, *to cease.*—īnflammāre, *to set on fire;* "inflame," "inflammatory.")

3. Multī autem propter glōriae cupiditātem sunt cupidī bellōrum gerendōrum. (Cicero.)

4. Veterem iniūriam ferendō invītāmus novam. (Publilius Syrus.)

5. Cūrēmus nē poena maior sit quam culpa; prohibenda autem maximē est īra in pūniendō. (Cicero.—pūnīre, *to punish;* "punitive," "impunity"; cf. poena)

6. Syrācūsīs captīs, Mārcellus aedificiīs omnibus sīc pepercit—mīrābile dictū—quasi ad ea dēfendenda, nōn oppugnanda vēnisset. (Cicero.)

7. Rēgulus laudandus est in cōnservandō iūre iūrandō. (*Cicero.—Regulus, prisoner of the Carthaginians, swore to them that he would return to Carthage after a mission to Rome.—iūs iūrandum, iūris iūrandī, n., *oath.*)

8. In ōrātiōne meā dīcam dē mōribus firmīs Sēstiī et dē studiō cōnservandae salūtis commūnis. (Cicero.—Sēstius, -iī, m.)

9. Trānsitus ad senectūtem nōs āvocat ā rēbus gerendīs et corpus facit īnfīrmius. (Cicero.)

10. Cum recreandae vōcis īnfīrmae causā necesse esset mihi ambulāre, hās litterās dictāvī forīs ambulāns. (Cicero.—dictāre, *to dictate;* "dictation," "dictator.")

11. Semper metuendō sapiēns vītat malum. (Publilius Syrus.)

12. Haec virtūs ex prōvidendō est appellāta "prūdentia." (Cicero.—**prōvidēre;** "provident," "provision."—**prūdentia:** = **prō-videntia;** "prudence," "jurisprudent.")

13. Fāma vīrēs acquīrit eundō. (Vergil.—**acquīrō,** from **ad-quaerō,** *to acquire;* "acquirable," "acquisition.")

14. Hae vicissitūdinēs fortūnae, etsī nōbīs iūcundae in experiendō nōn fuērunt, in legendō tamen erunt iūcundae. Recordātiō enim praeteritī dolōris dēlectātiōnem nōbīs habet. (Cicero.—**vicissitūdō, -dinis,** f.; "vicissitude," "vicissitudinous."—**recordātiō, -ōnis,** f., *recollection;* "record," "recorder."—**praeteritus, -a, -um,** *past;* "preterit," "preteritive.")

15. Ācerrimus ex omnibus nostrīs sēnsibus est sēnsus videndī. (Cicero.)

### Promises, Promises!

> Nūllī sē dīcit mulier mea nūbere mālle
>     quam mihi, nōn sī sē Iuppiter ipse petat.
> Dīcit: sed mulier cupidō quod dīcit amantī,
>     in ventō et rapidā scrībere oportet aquā.

*Catullus *Carm.* 70: No mention of Lesbia here, but doubtless the woman Catullus had in mind; no longer **puella,** Lesbia is now **mulier . . . mulier:** as distinct from **virgō** and even **fēmina,** the word here, as often, denotes a woman with sexual experience, a wife or a mistress. Meter: elegiac couplet.—**Nūllī . . . mihi:** both are dat. with **nūbere,** and **quam** = **magis quam;** the prose order might be **mulier mea dīcit sē nūllī quam mihi nūbere mālle.**—**amantī:** *lover.*—**rapidus, -a, -um,** = Eng.; "rapidity," "rapacious"; cf. **rapiō.**

*QVAESTIŌNĒS:* What is the poem's one key word, and in what ways does Catullus emphasize it? Read the opening verse aloud and comment on the multiple sound effects. What makes the imagery in the last line so remarkable; how does word order underscore its impact?

### Paete, Nōn Dolet

> Casta suō gladium cum trāderet Arria Paetō,
>     quem dē vīsceribus strīnxerat ipsa suīs,
> "Sī qua fidēs, vulnus quod fēcī nōn dolet," inquit,
>     "sed quod tū faciēs, hoc mihi, Paete, dolet."

*Martial *Epig.* 1.13: Caecina Paetus was compelled to commit suicide in A.D. 42, because of the role he had played in a conspiracy against the emperor Claudius; his courageous and devoted wife Arria, choosing to die with him, stabbed herself before passing the sword to her husband, and assured him that the pain would be slight. Pliny the Younger relates the story in one of his letters, excerpted below in **Locī Im. XXXIX.** Meter: elegiac couplet.—**castus, -a, -um,** *loyal, chaste;* "caste," "chastity."—**gladius, -ī,** m., *sword;* "gladi-

Arria and Paetus. *Pierre Lepautre (1659–1744)*
*Louvre, Paris, France*

ator," "gladiola."—**vīscera, -rum,** n. pl., *vital organs, abdomen;* "visceral," "eviscerate."—
**stringō, -ere, strīnxī, strictum,** *to draw tight, tie; pull, draw out;* "stringent," "restrict."—**sī
qua** (=**quae,** indef.) **fidēs:** i.e., *if you have any faith in me, if you will trust me.*

*QVAESTIŌNĒS:* What common device of verse word order is seen in line 1, and what is
its particular effect here? How does Martial's use of pronouns and the parallel word order
and repetitions add to the pathos in verses 3-4?

### Hannibal and the Beginnings of the Second Punic War

Hannibal, fīlius Hamilcaris, Carthāgine nātus est. In adulēscentiā prīstinum
odium patris ergā Rōmānōs sīc firmē cōnservāvit ut numquam id dēpōneret.
Cum patre exiit Carthāgine et in Hispāniam longō itinere profectus est; et post
multōs annōs, Hamilcare interfectō, exercitus eī imperium trādidit. Sīc Hannibal,
quīnque et vīgintī annōs nātus, imperātor factus est. Tribus annīs nōn requiēvit,
sed omnēs gentēs Hispāniae superāvit et trēs exercitūs maximōs parāvit. Ex hīs
ūnum in Āfricam mīsit, alterum cum frātre in Hispāniā relīquit, tertium in Italiam sēcum dūxit.

Ad Alpēs adiit, quās nēmō umquam ante eum cum exercitū trānsierat.
Populōs cōnantēs prohibēre eum trānsitū necāvit; loca patefēcit; et cum multīs
elephantīs mīlitibusque in Italiam iniit. In hōc itinere tam gravī morbō oculōrum

adfectus est ut posteā numquam dextrō oculō bene ūtī posset. Multōs ducēs, tamen, exercitūsque Rōmānōs vīcit, et propter illum imperātōrem mīlia mīlitum Rōmānōrum periērunt.

Nepos *Hann.*, excerpts: In this passage adapted from his life of Hannibal, Nepos summarizes some major events in the life of the Carthaginian general who led the Carthaginians against the Romans in the Second Punic War, 218–202 B.C.; for longer excerpts, see **Locī Ant.** VIII, and cf. the reading from Nepos' biography of Cimon in Capvt XXXII above.—**Hamilcar, -caris,** m.; Hamilcar Barca had commanded Carthage's army in the First Punic War (264–241 B.C.).—**dē + pōnō;** "deponent," "depose."—**Hispānia, -ae,** f., *Spain;* "Hispanic"; see Maps 1–2 for the locations mentioned in this passage.–**quīnque . . . nātus:** the phrase **annōs nātus** was a common idiom for indicating a person's age; we would say "at the age of . . . ," but what is the lit. translation? For the case usage of **annōs** here, see Capvt XXXVII.—**Āfrica, -ae,** f.—**Alpēs, -pium,** f. pl., *the Alps.*—**adficiō, -ere, -fēcī, -fectum,** *to affect, afflict, weaken;* "affection," "affectionate."

*QVAESTIŌ:* Though Hannibal was viewed by Romans for many generations after his death as one of their nation's bitterest and most terrifying enemies—he had very nearly brought his invading forces to the gates of Rome—nevertheless Nepos attributes to him qualities that even Romans would admire; what are some of those traits seen in this brief passage?

## SCRĪPTA IN PARIETIBVS

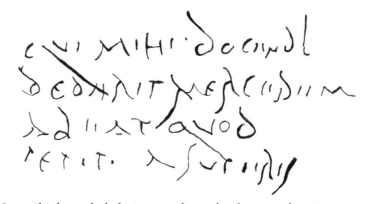

Quī mihi docendī dederit mercēdem, <h>abeat quod petit ā superīs!

*CIL* 4.8562: Graffito from a column in the colonnade around the Large Palaestra near the amphitheater in Pompeii (Reg. II); here, among many other activities, teachers instructed schoolboys for a fee, a common practice in Pompeii as in Rome, and this pedagogue prayed the gods would bless his paying customers!—**mercēs, -cēdis,** f., *wage, fee; payment (for),* + gen. for the service rendered.—**<h>abeat:** the letter **h** in the Roman alphabet represented a weak aspirate that was often dropped in speech and sometimes, even by teachers (!), in spelling.

## ETYMOLOGIA

In **recordātiō** (S.A. 14) you see the stem of **cor, cordis,** n., *heart:* in antiquity the heart was regarded as the seat not only of the emotions, but also of the intellect and memory, a belief reflected in the Eng. expression "learn by heart"; derivatives, besides "record" and "recorder," include: accord, concord, discord, cordial, courage.

The terms "gerund" and "gerundive" derive ultimately from **gerundum,** variant of **gerendum,** fom **gerō,** *to carry on, do.* The gerund indicates "doing" (action); the gerundive indicates what is "to be done." In late Lat. the abl. of the gerund was used increasingly as the equivalent of a pres. participle; from this usage derive the following Romance language participles:

| Lat. | It. | Sp. | Port. | Rom. |
|------|-----|-----|-------|------|
| dandō | dando | dando | dando | dând |
| faciendō | facendo | haciendo | fazendo | făcând |
| dīcendō | dicendo | diciendo | dizendo | zicând |
| pōnendō | ponendo | poniendo | pondo | punând |
| scrībendō | scrivendo | escribiendo | escrevendo | scriind |

## LATĪNA EST GAVDIVM—ET VTILIS!

**Salvēte, discipulī discipulaeque; haec sunt discenda:** Cato's definition of an orator, as quoted by the 1st cent. A.D. educator Quintilian (*Īnstitūtiō Ōrātōria* 12.1.1), is quite well known, and you can easily translate it now that you've studied gerunds (and with the explanation that **perītus, -a, -um** + gen. = *experienced in*): **ōrātor est vir bonus dīcendī perītus.** Here are some more familiar items with gerunds and gerundives: New Mexico's state motto, **crēscit eundō** (review Capvt XXXVII, if you have trouble with that one!); **docendō discimus,** something all teachers know; **spectēmur agendō,** *let us be judged by what we do* (lit., *by our doing*); **modus vīvendī** and **modus operandī** ("m.o." to you detective show buffs!); **onus probandī,** *the burden of proof* (lit., *of proving*); then, of course, there are these many "things to be done": **agenda, addenda, corrigenda, memorandum, referendum.**

Et duo cētera ex vocābulīs novīs huius capitis: iniūria nōn excūsat iniūriam, (*one*) *injury does not excuse (another) injury,* is an old legal tenet, and **expertō crēdite** is still good advice. **Habēte fēlīcem modum vīvendī, studentēs, et valēte!**

# CAPVT XL 🏛

## -*Ne, Num,* and *Nōnne* in Direct Questions; Fear Clauses; Genitive and Ablative of Description

## GRAMMATICA

### -*Ne, Num,* AND *Nōnne* IN DIRECT QUESTIONS

As we have already seen, a Roman could ask a direct question in a variety of ways, by beginning a sentence with an interrogative pronoun (**quis, quid**) or such other interrogatives as **ubi** or **cūr,** or by suffixing **-ne** to the first word of the sentence (often the verb, or some other word on which the question hinged). But "leading questions" can also be asked in Latin: if the speaker expected "yes" as an answer, the question was introduced with **nōnne** (a construction already encountered, though not formally discussed); if a negative reply was anticipated, **num** was the introductory word:

> **Quis venit?** *Who is coming?*
> **Cūr venit?** *Why is he coming?*
> **Venitne?** *Is he coming?*
> **Nōnne venit?** *He is coming, isn't he?* or *Isn't he coming?*
> **Num venit?** *He isn't coming, is he?*
> **Scrīpsistīne illās litterās?** *Did you write that letter?*
> **Nōnne illās litterās scrīpsistī?** *You wrote that letter, didn't you?* or *Didn't you write that letter?*
> **Num illās litterās scrīpsistī?** *You didn't write that letter, did you?*

### FEAR CLAUSES

Verbs denoting fear or apprehension often take subjunctive noun clauses introduced by **nē** (*that*) or **ut** (*that . . . not*; occasionally **nē nōn** was employed instead of **ut**); the conjunctions in these **FEAR CLAUSES** are the opposite of what might be expected, because in origin the clauses they introduced were essentially independent jussive clauses (i.e., **timeō nē abeās**, *I fear that you may go away*, = **Timeō. Nē abeās!**, *I'm afraid—Don't go away!*). Auxiliaries commonly employed in translating include "will" or "may" (in primary sequence) and "would" or "might" (in secondary sequence):

> **Timeō nē id crēdant.** *I fear that they will (may) believe this.*
> **Vereor ut id crēdant.** *I am afraid that they will (may) not believe this.*
> **Timuērunt nē amīcōs āmitterent.** *They feared that they might (would) lose their friends.*
> **Metuistī ut mulierēs ex casā exīssent.** *You were afraid that the women had not left the house.*

## GENITIVE AND ABLATIVE OF DESCRIPTION

A noun in either the ablative or genitive case plus a modifying adjective may be employed to modify another noun; both the **ABLATIVE OF DESCRIPTION** and the **GENITIVE OF DESCRIPTION** (already encountered in the readings) might describe a noun by indicating its character, quality, or size, although the ablative usage was especially common in describing physical traits. Like adjectives, these descriptive phrases usually follow the nouns they modify:

> fēmina *magnae sapientiae, a woman of great intellect*
> pāx in hominibus *bonae voluntātis, peace among men of good will*
> cōnsilium *eius modī, a plan of this kind*
> Dīligō hominem *antīquā virtūte, I esteem a man of old-fashioned morality.*
> mīles *firmā manū, the soldier with the strong hand*
> Es *mōribus bonīs. You are a person of good character.*

# VOCĀBVLA

Welcome to your final Wheelock **Vocābula**! While fewer than a thousand words have been formally introduced in these 40 chapter lists, you have actually been introduced to nearly a thousand more through the glosses in the hundreds of **Sententiae Antīquae**, reading passages, and graffiti, and there are countless others whose meanings you can now easily intuit based on English derivatives and your knowledge of compounding, prefixes, suffixes, assimilation, and vowel shortening, and of the interrelations of word families like **regō, rēx, rēgina**, and **cupiō, cupidus, cupiditās**, etc.; from **dominus** and **domina** below, e.g., you should be able to guess the meanings of **domināre** and **dominātiō**, from **lacrima** you should know

**lacrimāre** and **lacrimōsus,** etc. So in your future readings, when you encounter some word you've not formally learned, take a closer look, both at the word itself and at its context, and very often you will find one or more secure clues to its meaning. Watch out for these last few look-alikes: **metus/mēta, vultus/vulgus/ vulnus.** And be sure this one final time to use the CDs or online audio, in order to learn this new vocabulary by listening to and pronouncing each word aloud and not just by reading mutely from the written page.

**aes, aéris,** n., *bronze* (era; cf. **aerārium, -ī,** *treasury;* **aereus, -a, -um,** *made of bronze*)

**dóminus, dóminī,** m., *master (of a household), lord,* and **dómina, dóminae,** f., *mistress, lady* (dominate, domineer, dominion, domain, domino, don, dungeon, belladonna, madonna, dame, damsel; cf. **domus**)

**lácrima, lácrimae,** f., *tear* (lacrimal, lacrimation, lachrymose, lacrimoso)

**mēta, mētae,** f., *turning point, goal; limit, boundary*

**monuméntum, monuméntī,** n., *monument* (monumental; cf. **moneō**)

**nāsus, nāsī,** m., *nose* (nasal, nasalize, nasogastric; cognates: nostril, nozzle)

**sáxum, sáxī,** n., *rock, stone* (saxifrage, saxicolous; cf. **secō,** *to cut,* saw)

**vúltus, vúltūs,** m., *countenance, face*

**iūstus, iūsta, iūstum,** *just, right* (justice, unjust, justify, justification, adjust; cf. **iūs, iūdex, iniūria**)

**tot,** indecl. adj., *so many, as many;* **tot . . . quot,** *as many . . . as;* cf. **totidem,** indecl. adj., *the same number;* **totiēns,** adv., *that number of times, so often*

**praéter,** prep. + acc., *besides, except; beyond, past* (preterit, preterition, pretermit, preternatural; cf. **prae**)

**nōnne,** interrog. adv. which introduces questions expecting the answer "yes"

**num,** interrog. adv.: (1) introduces direct questions which expect the answer "no"; (2) introduces indirect questions and means *whether*

**omnínō,** adv., *wholly, entirely, altogether;* with negatives, *at all* (cf. **omnis**)

**postrēmum,** adv., *after all, finally; for the last time* (cf. **post**)

**quīn,** adv., *indeed, in fact, furthermore*

**éxplicō, explicāre, explicāvī, explicātum,** *to unfold; explain; spread out, deploy* (explicate, inexplicable; implicate, from **implicō,** *to enfold, interweave*)

**fatīgō, fatīgāre, fatīgāvī, fatīgātum,** *to weary, tire out* (fatigue, indefatigable)

**for, fārī, fātus sum,** *to speak (prophetically), talk, foretell* (affable, ineffable, infant, infantry, preface; cf. **fābula, fāma, fateor, fātum:** what is "foretold" is one's "fate")

**opínor, opīnārī, opīnātus sum,** *to suppose* (opine, opinion)

**repériō, reperīre, répperī, repértum,** *to find, discover, learn; get* (repertoire, repertory; cf. **parēns** and **pariō,** *to give birth to*)

**véreor, verērī, véritus sum,** *to show reverence for, respect; be afraid of, fear* (revere, reverend, reverent, reverential, irreverent)

# LĒCTIŌ ET TRĀNSLĀTIŌ

One last reminder, for the following selections and your future readings, always to read aloud and for comprehension, before attempting to translate. Test your mastery of the new grammar with the Self-Tutorial Exercises, then scan the sentences and passages below for all occurrences of fear clauses, the genitive and ablative of description, and -**ne**, **num**, and **nōnne** questions. In your translations of fear clauses, recall the seeming anomaly that **ut** = "that not" and **nē** = "that"; and whenever translating, always choose meanings that best suit the context—e.g., in the Vergil passage below *will receive/take over* is a better choice than *will capture* for **excipiet**, and *will call/name* makes better sense for **dīcet** than *will say.*

## EXERCITĀTIŌNĒS

1. Nōnne Rōmulus, sator huius urbis, fuit vir mīrābilis virtūtis et fideī prīstinae atque quī deōs semper vereātur?
2. At postrēmum vereor, heu, ut ā virīs parvae sapientiae hoc studium vetus intellegī possit.
3. Nōn oportet nōs trānsīre haec līberālia hūmānaque studia, nam praemia eōrum certē sunt maxima.
4. Dignitās illīus ōrātiōnis fuit omnīnō idōnea occāsiōnī.
5. Equī eius, cum fatīgātī essent et ventus esset eīs adversus, ad mētam tamen quam celerrimē currēbant.
6. Vir corpore īnfirmō id nōn facere poterat.
7. Etsī trēs fīliī sunt cupidī magnōrum operum faciendōrum, eīs nōn licet domō abīre.
8. Domina firma acerbē querēbātur plūrimōs servōs fuisse absentēs—vae illīs miserīs!
9. Mīrābile rogātū, num istam mulierem amās, mī amīce?
10. Nōnne timent nē et Rōmae et rūrī magnī tumultūs sint?
11. Num opīnāris tot hominēs iūstōs omnīnō errāre?
12. Recognōvistīne, ut illa aedificia vīsum ambulābās, mulierem sub arbore humī requiēscentem?
13. I am afraid, in my heart, that few things can be accomplished now even by trying.
14. You do not hesitate to say this, do you?
15. They supposed that, after all, he was a man of very little faith.
16. You do recognize how great the danger is, do you not?

## SENTENTIAE ANTĪQVAE

1. Quattuor causās reperiō cūr senectūs misera videātur. Videāmus quam iūsta quaeque eārum sit. (Cicero.)
2. Verērī videntur ut habeam satis praesidī. (*Cicero.—**praesidium**, -iī, n., *guard;* "preside," "president.")
3. Necesse est enim sit alterum dē duōbus: aut mors sēnsūs omnīnō aufert aut animus in alium locum morte abit. Sī mors somnō similis est sēnsūsque exstinguuntur, dī bonī, quid lucrī est morī! (Cicero.—**necesse est:** here + subjunct. rather than infinitive.—**aufert:** = ab + fert; "ablate," "ablative."—**exstinguō,** -ere; "extinct," "extinction."—**lucrum,** -ī, m., *gain, profit;* "lucrative," "lucre.")
4. Aetās semper trānsitum et aliquid novī adfert. (Terence.)
5. Nōnne ūnum exemplum luxuriae aut cupiditātis multum malī facit? (Seneca.—**luxuria,** -ae, f.; "luxury," "luxuriant.")
6. Mīror tot mīlia virōrum tam puerīliter identidem cupere currentēs equōs vidēre. (Pliny.—**puerīliter,** adv., based on **puer,** *childishly;* "puerile," "puerility."—**identidem,** adv., *again and again.*—**currentēs:** i.e., in the races.)
7. Nōnne vidēs etiam guttās, in saxa cadendō, pertundere illa saxa? (Lucretius.—**gutta,** -ae, f., *drop* [*of water*]; "gout," "gutter," "gtt.," medical abbreviation for "drops."—**pertundō,** -ere, *to bore a hole through, erode.*)
8. Metuō nē id cōnsilī cēperīmus quod nōn facile explicāre possīmus. (*Cicero.—**cōnsilī:** gen. of the whole with **id.**)
9. Antōnius, ūnus ex inimīcīs et vir minimae clēmentiae, iussit Cicerōnem interficī et caput eius inter duās manūs in Rōstrīs pōnī. (Livy.—**inimīcus,** -ī, m., from **in** + **amīcus,** *personal enemy;* "inimical," "enemy."—**Rōstra,** -ōrum, n., *the Rostra,* the speaker's stand in the Roman Forum; "rostrum.")
10. Omnēs quī habent aliquid nōn sōlum sapientiae sed etiam sānitātis volunt hanc rem pūblicam salvam esse. (*Cicero.—**sānitās,** -tātis, f.; "sanitary," "sanity.")
11. Salvē, nec minimō puella nāsō nec bellō pede nec nigrīs ocellīs nec longīs digitīs nec ōre siccō! (*Catullus.—**niger,** -gra, -grum, *black, dark;* "denigrate."—**ocellus:** diminutive of **oculus.**—**siccus,** -a, -um, *dry;* "desiccate," "desiccation.")
12. Homō sum; nihil hūmānī aliēnum ā mē putō. (Terence.—**aliēnus,** -a, -um, *of/belonging to another;* + **ā/ab,** idiom, *foreign to;* cf. **alius;** "alien," "alienate.")
13. Amīcus animum amīcī ita cum suō miscet quasi facit ūnum ex duōbus. (Cicero.)
14. Sex diēbus fēcit Dominus caelum et terram et mare et omnia quae in eīs sunt, et requiēvit diē septimō. (Exodus.)
15. Mīsit legātum Valerium Procillum, summā virtūte et hūmānitāte adulēscentem, cum imperātōre hostium colloquendī causā. (Caesar.—**legātus,** -ī, m., *ambassador;* "legate," "legation."—Valerius Procillus.—**hūmānitās,** -tātis, f.; "humanitarian"; cf. **hūmānus, homō.**—**colloquor,** -loquī, -locūtus sum, *to talk to, hold discussions/parley with;* "colloquy," "colloquium.")

16. Num negāre audēs? Quid tacēs? Convincam, sī negās; videō enim esse hīc in senātū quōsdam quī tēcum ūnā fuērunt. Ō dī immortālēs! (*Cicero.—**quid:** here = *why?*—**con + vincō,** *to prove wrong;* sc. **tē;** "convince," "convict."—**ūnā,** adv., *together, in concert.*)

17. Nunc timeō nē nihil tibi praeter lacrimās queam reddere. (*Cicero—**queam:** = **possim.**—**reddō, -dere,** *to give back, return;* "render," "rent.")

## Jupiter Prophesies to Venus the Future Glory of Rome

Ollī subrīdēns hominum sator atque deōrum
255 vultū, quō caelum tempestātēsque serēnat,
ōscula lībāvit nātae, dehinc tālia fātur:
"Parce metū, Cytherēa; manent immōta tuōrum
fāta tibī. Cernēs urbem et prōmissa Lavīnī
moenia sublīmemque ferēs ad sīdera caelī
260 magnanimum Aenēan; neque mē sententia vertit.

. . .

263 Bellum ingēns geret Ītaliā populōsque ferōcīs
contundet mōrēsque virīs et moenia pōnet.

. . .

Rōmulus excipiet gentem et Māvortia condet
moenia Rōmānōsque suō dē nōmine dīcet.
Hīs ego nec mētās rērum nec tempora pōnō:
imperium sine fīne dedī. Quīn aspera Iūnō,
280 quae mare nunc terrāsque metū caelumque fatīgat,
cōnsilia in melius referet, mēcumque fovēbit
Rōmānōs, rērum dominōs gentemque togātam."

*Vergil *Aen.* 1.254ff: At this point in *Aeneid* Book One, the Trojan prince Aeneas and his followers have been shipwrecked in a storm caused by the ever hostile Juno. The hero's divine mother, Venus, has come to her father (and Juno's husband) Jupiter to ask whether his intentions toward the Trojans have changed, or if Aeneas is still destined to found a new Trojan nation in Italy; the passage here, in its original dactylic hexameter verse form, is part of Jupiter's reply.—**Ollī:** = **illī,** i.e., Venus.—**vultū:** abl. of means with **subrīdēns.**—**ōscula lībāvit:** i.e., he kissed her in ritual fashion.—**nātae:** ind. object.—**dehinc:** if you have been studying Latin metrics, you will need to know that this word is here scanned as a monosyllable.—**metū:** an alternate form of the dat. **metuī.**—**Cytherēa, -ae,** f., *the Cytherean,* i.e., Venus, so-called for the Aegean island of Cythera, her birthplace and a cult center.—**immōta:** pred. adj., after **manent.**—**tuōrum:** i.e., Aeneas and his Trojan followers.—**Lavīnium, -iī,** n., *Lavinium,* the town Aeneas was destined to found in Latium, near the future city of Rome.—**sublīmem:** in the pred. with **Aenēan** (a Gk. acc. form), *you will carry Aeneas on high.*—**neque . . . vertit:,** i.e., "I have not changed my mind," but what is the lit. translation?—**geret . . . pōnet:** Aeneas is subj. of all three verbs.—

*Vergil flanked by two Muses*
*Mosaic, Hadrumetum (modern Sousse), Tunisia. 3rd cent. A.D.*
*Musée National du Bardo, Tunis, Tunisia*

**Ītaliā:** sc. **in;** prepositions usual in prose were commonly omitted in verse.—**ferōcīs:** = ferōcēs, acc. pl.—**pōnet:** through a device known as ZEUGMA, the verb has different senses with its two objects, *institute* with **mōrēs** and *build* with **moenia.**—**Māvortius, -a, -um,** *of Mars,* the walls were so called from the legend that Mars was father of Romulus, Rome's first king.—**rērum:** *of their affairs,* i.e., *for their empire.*—**tempora:** here = *time limits.*—**terrāsque . . . caelumque:** this use of the double -**que,** rather like the use of **et . . . et . . .** you have often seen, is common in epic.—**in melius:** cf. the Eng. idiom "to change for the better"; Juno had sided with the Greeks in the Trojan war and had continued to resist Aeneas' fated mission.—**togātus, -a, -um,** *togaed, toga-clad;* the toga was the formal woolen outer garment worn by freeborn Roman men, particularly in the conduct of civic enterprise, whether in the forum, the courts, or legislative bodies.

*QVAESTIŌNĒS:* Jupiter's speech—the first of several major prophecies in the *Aeneid*—not only briefly foretells the fulfillment of Aeneas' mission, and Romulus', but also alludes to the destiny of the Roman empire; how specifically does he characterize the future nation in verses 278–282, and to what different realms of activity does he seem to allude in the two distinct phrases **rērum dominōs** and **gentem . . . togātam** ?

## The Value of Literature

Sī ex hīs studiīs dēlectātiō sōla peterētur, tamen, ut opīnor, hanc animī remissiōnem hūmānissimam ac līberālissimam iūdicārētis. Nam cēterae neque temporum sunt neque aetātum omnium neque locōrum; at haec studia adulēscentiam alunt, senectūtem oblectant, rēs secundās ōrnant, adversīs perfugium ac sōlācium praebent, dēlectant domī, nōn impediunt forīs, pernoctant nōbīscum, peregrīnantur, rūsticantur.

*Cicero *Arch.* 7.16: Along with this passage you should review the selections you have read previously from Cicero's **Prō Archiā**, including his anecdote on Alexander the Great in Capvt XIII and his remarks on ambition and literature in Capvt XXII; this speech has remained over the centuries one of the orator's most admired, particularly for its eloquent defense of the value of the humanities.—**studiīs . . . studia:** i.e., literary pursuits; Cicero has in his preceding remarks discussed their "practical" benefits, and here turns to their value as a **remissiō animī.—hanc:** sc. **esse.—iūdicāre,** *to judge, consider;* "judicious," "adjudicate."—**cēterae:** sc. **remissiōnēs.—omnium:** modifies all three nouns, **temporum, aetātum,** and **locōrum;** this construction, a gen. following a verb (often **sum, esse**) and in one way or another describing the subj., is often termed a PREDICATE GENITIVE.—**nōbīscum:** construe with each of the three verbs.

*QVAESTIŌNĒS:* What are the multiple implications of the adjs. **hūmānissimam** and **līberālissimam?**–think of the root meanings of both words, which certainly Cicero himself had in mind. Looking back at the passages from this speech read earlier, compare specifically the benefits of literature he recounts there with those he describes here.

## A Monument More Lasting than Bronze

Exēgī monumentum aere perennius.

. . .

Nōn omnis moriar, multaque pars meī
vītābit Libitīnam.

*Horace *Carm.* 3.30.1, 6–7: In the closing poem of his third volume of *Odes* (a longer excerpt from which appears below in **Locī Im.** XXVIII), Horace proudly lays claim to a degree of immortality; meter: first Asclepiadean.—**perennis, -e,** *lasting (throughout the years,* **per annōs);** "perennial."—**multa:** here = **magna.—Libitīna, -ae,** f., *Libitina,* ancient Italic goddess of funerals and here a symbol of death.

*QVAESTIŌ:* Likely it is too obvious to ask, but as a fitting final **quaestiō** for this book, what do you understand to be Horace's **monumentum,** though he does not explicitly identify it, and that **multa . . . pars meī** which he here proclaims will be deathless?

## SCRĪPTA IN PARIETIBVS

Catus valeat—et vōs!

*CIL* 4.5200: This graffito was etched on the wall of a house in Reg. IX, Ins. 6; nearby was a painting of the Athenian hero Theseus and Ariadne, princess of Crete. The inscription seemed an apt one with which to conclude this final chapter's readings, as the writer here bids farewell not only to Catus, presumably a friend, but to you as well, and to all who would read this message inscribed so graciously by its anonymous scribbler nearly two thousand years ago. . . .

## LATĪNA EST GAVDIVM—ET V̄TILIS!

**Salvēte postrēmum, discipulī et discipulae!** Here are some **rēs novae ex hōc capite ultimō: dominus illūminātiō mea,** *the Lord is my light,* is the motto of Oxford University; **lacrima Christī** is a well known Latin phrase for *the tear of Christ* (and also the name of a sweet Italian wine). An oft quoted line from Vergil's *Aeneid* comes as the hero Aeneas, shipwrecked in North Africa, gazes upon a Carthaginian mural that depicts the suffering of both his own people and the Greeks in the Trojan war: **hīc etiam . . . sunt lacrimae rērum et mentem mortālia tangunt.** The Latin works better than a literal English translation (which you can now easily provide for yourself), but a free rendering would be: *even here there are tears for the ways of the world, and man's mortality touches the heart.*

Not to be so lacrimose (or "lachrymose," an alternate spelling), let's move to some more upbeat items: remember how to make masculine agent nouns from verbs?—e.g., from **reperiō** is **repertor,** *discover.* Well, the feminine agentive suffix is **-trīx, -trīcis** (cf. Eng. "aviator" and "aviatrix," and **lēctor/lēctrīx,** which we've seen before), hence this proverb: **paupertās omnium artium repertrīx,** something like our "necessity is the mother of invention" (but what is the literal meaning?). **Vultus est index animī,** *the face is an indication of the soul,* it has often been said. And speaking of faces, to "stick your nose up in the air" and to "look down your nose" on someone are not wholly modern idioms for viewing others critically or with disdain; the Neronian satirist Persius says of his predecessor Horace, in a brilliant and not wholly complimentary metaphor, that he *hung the people from his well-blown nose* (**excussō populum suspendere nāsō**). And finally, the Augustan poet Ovid's cognomen was **Nāsō**, a less than flattering appellation often given someone with a big snub nose—a reminder of Cicero's poor wart-nosed ancestor, as you may recall from the notes to Capvt XVI's **Scrīpta in Parietibus!**

May your love of Latin be **aere perennius: rīdēte, gaudēte, carpite omnēs diēs vestrōs, atque postrēmum, lēctōrēs et lēctrīcēs dulcēs, valēte!**

*Fresco from Pompeii, depicting a woman and a man with writing implements*
*Museo Archeologico Nazionale, Naples, Italy*

# LOCĪ ANTĪQVĪ

Although these passages selected from ancient authors have been adapted to accommodate the limited experience you have had with Latin thus far, they have been edited as little as possible; the language and thoughts are those of the ancient writers. In the case of poetry, one or more verses have been omitted from each excerpt, but the lines actually presented here have not been altered at all. In the case of a prose passage, some words or sentences may have been omitted or the wording may have been somewhat simplified at one point or another.

Not only will you find reading these varied **Locī Antīquī** interesting per se, but you should also gain considerable satisfaction and a sense of accomplishment in being able to read and translate passages of such complexity at this early stage in your study of "The Mother Tongue." As always, you should begin each passage by reading it aloud, at least once or twice, and reading for comprehension—attempting to gain a good sense of what the author is saying, before you attempt a translation into English.

Words appearing in these selections that have not been introduced in the 40 chapter **Vocābula** lists are glossed at their first one or two occurrences at least, and especially important words are listed in the **Vocābula** following the glosses to each passage; most are also included in the Latin-English **Vocābula** at the end of the book for easy reference.

## I. DISILLUSIONMENT

Miser Catulle, dēsinās[1] ineptīre,[2]
et quod vidēs perīsse perditum[3] dūcās.
Fulsēre[4] quondam candidī tibī[5] sōlēs,
cum ventitābās[6] quō[7] puella dūcēbat,

---

**I**
METER: choliambic.
[1] **dēsinō, -ere, -siī, -situm,** cease (dēsinās = *juss. subjunct. for* dēsine)
[2] **ineptiō** (4), play the fool

[3] **perdō, -ere, -didī, -ditum,** destroy, lose
[4] **fulgeō, -ēre, fulsī,** shine (fulsēre = fulsērunt)
[5] *final -ī is long here because of meter.*
[6] **ventitō** (1), *frequentative form of* **veniō,** come often
[7] **quō,** *adv.,* whither, where

> 5 amāta nōbīs quantum amābitur nūlla.
> Fulsēre vērē candidī tibī sōlēs.
> Nunc iam illa nōn vult; tū quoque, impotēns,[8] nōlī;
> nec quae fugit sectāre[9] nec miser vīve,
> sed obstinātā[10] mente perfer,[11] obdūrā.[12]
> 10 Valē, puella, iam Catullus obdūrat,
> nec tē requīret nec rogābit invītam[13];
> at tū dolēbis, cum rogāberis nūlla.
> Scelesta, vae tē! Quae tibī manet vīta![14]
> Quis nunc tē adībit? Cui vidēberis bella?
> 15 Quem nunc amābis? Cuius esse dīcēris?
> At tū, Catulle, dēstinātus obdūrā. (**Catullus** 8)

## II. HOW DEMOSTHENES OVERCAME HIS HANDICAPS

Ōrātor imitētur[1] illum cui summa vīs dīcendī concēditur,[2] Dēmosthenem, in quō tantum studium fuisse dīcitur ut impedīmenta[3] nātūrae dīligentiā[4] industriāque[5] superāret. Nam cum ita balbus[6] esset ut illīus ipsīus artis[7] cui studēret prīmam litteram nōn posset dīcere, perfēcit[8] meditandō[9] ut nēmō plānius[10] loquerētur.
5 Deinde, cum spīritus eius esset angustior,[11] spīritū continendō multum perfēcit in dīcendō; et coniectīs[12] in ōs calculīs,[13] summā vōce versūs multōs ūnō spīritū prōnūntiāre cōnsuēscēbat[14]; neque id faciēbat stāns ūnō in locō sed ambulāns. (**Cicero**, *Dē Ōrātōre* 1.61.260–61)

## III. THE TYRANT CAN TRUST NO ONE

Multōs annōs tyrannus Syrācūsānōrum[1] fuit Dionȳsius. Pulcherrimam urbem servitūte oppressam tenuit. At ā bonīs auctōribus cognōvimus eum fuisse hominem summae temperantiae[2] in vīctū[3] et in rēbus gerendīs ācrem et industrium,[4]

---

[8]**im-potēns**, *gen.* **-tentis**, powerless, weak, hopelessly in love
[9]**sectāre**, *imperat. of* **sector** (1), follow eagerly, pursue; *word order:* **sectāre (eam) quae fugit**
[10]**obstinātus, -a, -um**, firm
[11]**per-ferō**, endure
[12]**obdūrō** (1), *verb of adj.* **dūrus**
[13]**invītus, -a, -um**, unwilling
[14]*see notes on excerpt in Capvt XIX.*
VOCĀBVLA: **perdō, quō, invītus.**

**II**
[1]**imitor, -ārī, -ātus sum**
[2]**con-cēdō**
[3]**impedīmentum, -ī**
[4]**dīligentia, -ae**
[5]**industria, -ae**

[6]**balbus, -a, -um**, stuttering
[7]**illīus . . . artis**, *i.e.,* rhetoric
[8]**per-ficiō**, do thoroughly, bring about, accomplish
[9]**meditor** (1), practice
[10]**plānius**, *compar. of adv.* **plānē**
[11]**angustus, -a, -um**, narrow, short
[12]**con-iciō (iaciō)**
[13]**calculus, -ī**, pebble
[14]**cōnsuēscō, -ere, -suēvī, -suētum**, become accustomed
VOCĀBVLA: **concēdō, perficiō, angustus, coniciō, cōnsuēscō.**

**III**
[1]**Syrācūsānī, -ōrum**, Syracusans
[2]**temperantia, -ae**
[3]**vīctus, -ūs**, mode of life
[4]**industrius, -a, -um**

eundem tamen malum et iniūstum.[5] Quārē, omnibus virīs bene vēritātem quaer-
5 entibus hunc vidērī miserrimum necesse est, nam nēminī crēdere audēbat. Itaque
propter iniūstam cupiditātem dominātūs[6] quasi in carcerem[7] ipse sē inclūserat.[8]
Quīn etiam,[9] nē tōnsōrī[10] collum[11] committeret, filiās suās artem tōnsōriam docuit.[12] Ita hae virginēs tondēbant[13] barbam[14] et capillum[15] patris. Et tamen ab hīs
ipsīs, cum iam essent adultae,[16] ferrum remōvit, eīsque imperāvit ut carbōnibus[17]
10 barbam et capillum sibi adūrerent.[18] (**Cicero,** *Tusculānae Disputātiōnēs* 5.20.57–58)

## IV. THE SWORD OF DAMOCLES

Hic tyrannus ipse dēmōnstrāvit quam beātus esset. Nam cum quīdam ex eius
assentātōribus,[1] Dāmoclēs,[2] commemorāret[3] cōpiās eius, maiestātem[4] dominātūs,
rērum abundantiam,[5] negāretque quemquam[6] umquam beātiōrem fuisse, Dionȳsius "Vīsne igitur," inquit, "Ō Dāmocle, ipse hanc vītam dēgustāre[7] et fortūnam
5 meam experīrī?" Cum ille sē cupere dīxisset, hominem in aureō[8] lectō[9] collocārī[10]
iussit mēnsāsque ōrnāvit argentō[11] aurōque.[12] Tum puerōs bellōs iussit cēnam
exquīsītissimam[13] īnferre. Fortūnātus sibi Dāmoclēs vidēbātur. Eōdem autem tempore Dionȳsius gladium suprā[14] caput eius saetā equīnā[15] dēmittī[16] iussit. Dāmoclēs,
cum gladium vīdisset, timēns ōrāvit tyrannum ut abīre licēret, quod iam "beātus"
10 nōllet esse. Satisne Dionȳsius vidētur dēmōnstrāvisse nihil esse eī beātum cui semper aliquī[17] metus impendeat?[18] (**Cicero,** *Tusculānae Disputātiōnēs* 5.20.61–62)

[5]**in-iūstus, -a, -um**
[6]**dominātus, -ūs,** absolute rule or power
[7]**carcer, -eris,** *m.,* prison
[8]**inclūdō, -ere, -clūsī, -clūsum,** shut in
[9]**quīn etiam,** moreover
[10]**tōnsor, -ōris,** *m.,* barber
[11]**collum, -ī,** neck
[12]**doceō** *may take two objects.*
[13]**tondeō, -ēre, totondī, tōnsum,** shear, clip
[14]**barba, -ae,** beard
[15]**capillus, -ī,** hair
[16]**adultus, -a, -um**
[17]**carbō, -ōnis,** *m.,* glowing coal
[18]**adūrō, -ere, -ussī, -ustum,** singe
VOCĀBVLA: **temperantia, iniūstus, inclūdō.**

**IV**
[1]**assentātor, -ōris,** *m.,* flatterer, "yes-man"
[2]**Dāmoclēs, -is,** *m.*

[3]**commemorō** (1), mention, recount
[4]**maiestās, -tātis,** *f.,* greatness
[5]**abundantia, -ae**
[6]**quisquam, quidquam,** anyone, anything
[7]**dēgustō** (1), taste, try
[8]**aureus, -a, -um,** golden
[9]**lectus, -ī,** couch
[10]**col-locō,** place
[11]**argentum, -ī,** silver
[12]**aurum, -ī,** gold
[13]**exquīsītus, -a, -um: ex-quaesītus**
[14]**suprā,** *adv. and prep. + acc.,* above
[15]**saetā equīnā,** by a horsehair
[16]**dēmittō,** let down
[17]**aliquī, -qua, -quod,** *adj. of aliquis*
[18]**impendeō, -ēre,** hang over, threaten
VOCĀBVLA: **quisquam, collocō, aurum, suprā.**

## V. DERIVATION OF "PHILOSOPHUS" AND SUBJECTS OF PHILOSOPHY

Eī quī studia in contemplātiōne[1] rērum pōnēbant "sapientēs" appellābantur, et id nōmen usque ad Pȳthagorae[2] aetātem mānāvit.[3] Hunc aiunt doctē et cōpiōsē[4] quaedam cum Leonte[5] disputāvisse[6]; et Leōn, cum illīus ingenium et ēloquentiam[7] admīrātus esset,[8] quaesīvit ex eō quā arte maximē ūterētur. At ille dīxit sē artem
5 nūllam scīre sed esse philosophum. Tum Leōn, admīrātus novum nōmen, quaesīvit quī essent philosophī. Pȳthagorās respondit multōs hominēs glōriae aut pecūniae servīre sed paucōs quōsdam esse quī cētera prō nihilō[9] habērent sed nātūram rērum cognōscere cuperent; hōs sē appellāre "studiōsōs[10] sapientiae," id est enim "philosophōs."[11] Sīc Pȳthagorās huius nōminis inventor[12] fuit.
10    Ab antīquā philosophiā usque ad Sōcratem[13] philosophī numerōs et sīdera tractābant[14] et unde omnia orīrentur[15] et quō[16] discēderent. Sōcratēs autem prīmus philosophiam dēvocāvit ē caelō et in urbibus hominibusque collocāvit et coēgit eam dē vītā et mōribus rēbusque bonīs et malīs quaerere. (**Cicero,** *Tusculānae Disputātiōnēs* 5.3.8–9; 5.4.10)

## VI. CICERO ON THE VALUE AND THE NATURE OF FRIENDSHIP

Ego vōs hortor ut amīcitiam omnibus rēbus hūmānīs antepōnātis. Sentiō equidem,[1] exceptā[2] sapientiā, nihil melius hominī ā deīs immortālibus datum esse. Dīvitiās aliī antepōnunt; aliī, salūtem; aliī, potestātem[3]; aliī, honōrēs; multī, etiam voluptātēs. Illa autem incerta sunt, posita nōn tam in cōnsiliīs nostrīs quam in fortūnae
5 vicissitūdinibus.[4] Quī autem in virtūte summum bonum pōnunt, bene illī quidem faciunt; sed ex ipsā virtūte amīcitia nāscitur nec sine virtūte amīcitia esse potest.

Dēnique cēterae rēs, quae petuntur, opportūnae[5] sunt rēbus singulīs[6]: dīvitiae, ut eīs ūtāris; honōrēs, ut laudēris; salūs, ut dolōre careās et rēbus corporis ūtāris. Amīcitia rēs plūrimās continet; nūllō locō exclūditur[7]; numquam intempestīva,[8]

**V**

[1]contemplātiō, -ōnis, *f.*

[2]Pȳthagorās, -ae, *m.*

[3]mānō (1), flow, extend

[4]cōpiōsē, *adv.,* fully

[5]Leōn, -ontis, *m.,* ruler of Phlius

[6]disputō (1), discuss

[7]ēloquentia, -ae

[8]admīror (1), wonder at, admire

[9]nihilum, -ī, = nihil

[10]studiōsus, -a, -um, fond of

[11]philosophus: *Gk.* philos, fond of, + sophia, wisdom

[12]inventor, -ōris, *m., cf.* inveniō

[13]Sōcratēs, -is

[14]tractō (1), handle, investigate, treat

[15]orior, -īrī, ortus sum, arise, proceed, originate

[16]quō, *adv.,* where

VOCĀBVLA: **admīror, orior, quō.**

**VI**

[1]equidem, *adv.,* indeed

[2]excipiō, -ere, -cēpi, -ceptum, except

[3]potestās, -tātis, *f.,* power

[4]vicissitūdō, -inis, *f.*

[5]opportūnus, -a, -um, suitable

[6]singulus, -a, -um, single, separate

[7]exclūdō, -ere, -clūsī, -clūsum

[8]intempestīvus, -a, -um, unseasonable

10    numquam molesta[9] est. Itaque nōn aquā, nōn igne in locīs plūribus ūtimur quam
amīcitiā; nam amīcitia secundās rēs clāriōrēs facit et adversās rēs leviōrēs.

    Quis est quī velit in omnium rērum abundantiā ita[10] vīvere ut neque dīligat
quemquam[11] neque ipse ab ūllō dīligātur? Haec enim est tyrannōrum vīta, in quā
nūlla fidēs, nūlla cāritās,[12] nūlla benevolentia[13] potest esse; omnia semper metuun-
15    tur, nūllus locus est amīcitiae. Quis enim aut eum dīligat[14] quem metuat aut eum ā
quō sē metuī putet? Multī autem sī cecidērunt, ut saepe fit, tum intellegunt quam
inopēs[15] amīcōrum fuerint. Quid vērō stultius quam cētera parāre quae parantur
pecūniā sed amīcōs nōn parāre, optimam et pulcherrimam quasi supellectilem[16]
vītae?

20    Quisque ipse sē dīligit nōn ut aliam mercēdem[17] ā sē ipse petat sed quod
per sē quisque sibi cārus est. Nisi idem in amīcitiam trānsferētur,[18] vērus amīcus
numquam reperiētur. Amīcus enim est is quī est tamquam alter īdem. Ipse sē
dīligit et alterum quaerit cuius animum ita cum suō misceat ut faciat ūnum ex
duōbus. Quid enim dulcius quam habēre quīcum[19] audeās sīc loquī ut tēcum? (**Ci-**
25    **cero**, *Dē Amīcitiā*, excerpts from Chs. 5, 6, 15, 21)

## VII. CICERO ON WAR

Quaedam officia sunt servanda etiam adversus[1] eōs ā quibus iniūriam accēpimus.
Atque in rē pūblicā maximē cōnservanda sunt iūra bellī. Nam sunt duo genera
dēcertandī[2]: ūnum per disputātiōnem,[3] alterum per vim. Illud est proprium[4] hominis, hoc bēluārum[5]; sed bellum vī gerendum est sī disputātiōne ūtī nōn licet.
5    Quārē suscipienda quidem bella sunt ut sine iniūriā in pāce vīvāmus; post autem
victōriam eī cōnservandī sunt quī nōn crūdēlēs,[6] nōn dūrī in bellō fuērunt, ut
maiōrēs nostrī Sabīnōs[7] in cīvitātem etiam accēpērunt. At Carthāginem omnīnō
sustulērunt; etiam Corinthum sustulērunt—quod nōn approbō[8]; sed crēdō eōs hoc
fēcisse nē locus ipse ad bellum faciendum hortārī posset. Meā quidem sententiā,[9]
10    pāx quae nihil īnsidiārum habeat semper quaerenda est. Ac aequitās[10] bellī fētiālī[11]

---

[9]**molestus, -a, -um**, troublesome

[10]**abundantia, -ae**

[11]**quemquam**, *Locī Ant.* IV, n. 6

[12]**cāritās, -tātis,** *f.,* affection

[13]**bene-volentia, -ae**, goodwill

[14]**dīligat**, *deliberative subjunct.,* would esteem

[15]**inops, -opis**, bereft of

[16]**supellex, -lectilis,** *f.,* furniture

[17]**mercēs, -ēdis,** *f.,* pay, reward

[18]**trāns-ferō**, transfer, direct

[19]**habēre quīcum = habēre eum cum quō**

VOCĀBVLA: **equidem, potestās, trānsferō.**

### VII

[1]**adversus**, *prep. + acc.,* toward

[2]**dēcertō** (1), fight (to a decision)

[3]**disputātiō, -ōnis,** *f.,* discussion

[4]**proprius, -a, -um**, characteristic of

[5]**bēlua, -ae**, wild beast

[6]**crūdēlis, -e**, cruel

[7]**Sabīnī, -ōrum**

[8]**approbō** (1), approve

[9]**sententiā**: *abl. here expressing accordance*

[10]**aequitās, -tātis,** *f.,* fairness, justice

[11]**fētiālis, -e**, fetial, *referring to a college of priests who were con-
cerned with treaties and the ritual of declaring war*

iūre populī Rōmānī perscrīpta est.[12] Quārē potest intellegī nūllum bellum esse iūstum nisi quod aut rēbus repetītīs[13] gerātur aut ante dēnūntiātum sit.[14]

Nūllum bellum dēbet suscipī ā cīvitāte optimā nisi aut prō fidē aut prō salūte. Illa bella sunt iniūsta quae sine causā sunt suscepta. Nam extrā[15] ulcīscendī[16] aut
15   prōpulsandōrum[17] hostium causam nūllum bellum cum aequitāte gerī potest. Noster autem populus sociīs[18] dēfendendīs terrārum[19] omnium potītus est.[20] (**Cicero, Dē Officiīs** 1.11.34–36 and **Dē Rē Pūblicā** 3.23.34–35)

## VIII. HANNIBAL; THE SECOND PUNIC WAR

Hannibal,[1] fīlius Hamilcaris,[2] Carthāgine nātus est. Odium patris ergā Rōmānōs sīc cōnservāvit ut numquam id dēpōneret.[3] Nam post bellum Pūnicum,[4] cum ex patriā in exsilium expulsus esset, nōn relīquit studium bellī Rōmānīs īnferendī.[5] Quārē, cum in Syriam[6] vēnisset, Antiochō[7] rēgī haec locūtus est ut hunc quoque
5   ad bellum cum Rōmānīs indūcere[8] posset:

"Mē novem annōs nātō, pater meus Hamilcar, in Hispāniam[9] imperātor proficīscēns Carthāgine, sacrificium[10] dīs fēcit. Eōdem tempore quaesīvit ā mē vellemne sēcum proficīscī. Cum id libenter audīvissem et ab eō petere coepissem nē dubitāret mē dūcere, tum ille 'Faciam,' inquit, 'sī mihi fidem quam quaerō de-
10   deris.' Tum mē ad āram[11] dūxit et mē iūrāre[12] iussit mē numquam in amīcitiā cum Rōmānīs futūrum esse. Id iūs iūrandum[13] patrī datum usque ad hanc aetātem ita cōnservāvī ut nēmō sit quī plūs odiī ergā Rōmānōs habeat."

Hāc igitur aetāte Hannibal cum patre in Hispāniam profectus est. Post multōs annōs, Hamilcare et Hasdrubale[14] interfectīs, exercitus eī imperium trādidit. Sīc
15   Hannibal, quīnque et vīgintī annōs nātus, imperātor factus est. Tribus annīs omnēs gentēs Hispāniae superāvit et trēs exercitūs maximōs parāvit. Ex hīs ūnum in Āfricam[15] mīsit, alterum cum frātre in Hispāniā relīquit, tertium in Italiam sēcum dūxit.

Ad Alpēs[16] vēnit, quās nēmō umquam ante eum cum exercitū trānsierat.

---

[12] **per-scrībō,** write out, place on record
[13] **re-petō,** seek again
[14] **dēnūntiō** (1), declare officially
[15] **extrā,** *prep. + acc.,* beyond
[16] **ulcīscor, -ī, ultus sum,** avenge, punish
[17] **prōpulsō** (1), repel
[18] **socius, -iī,** ally
[19] **terrārum:** *depends on* **potītus est**
[20] **potior, -īrī, potītus sum,** + *gen. (or abl.),* get possession of
VOCĀBVLA: **dēcertō, proprius, crūdēlis, potior.**

### VIII
[1] **Hannibal, -alis,** *m., illustrious general who led the Carthaginian forces against the Romans in the Second Punic (= Carthaginian) War, 218–202* B.C.

[2] **Hamilcar, -aris,** *m.*
[3] **dē-pōnō**
[4] **Pūnicus, -a, -um**
[5] **bellum īn-ferō,** make war on
[6] **Syria, -ae**
[7] **Antiochus, -ī**
[8] **in-dūcō**
[9] **Hispānia, -ae,** Spain
[10] **sacrificium, -iī**
[11] **āra, -ae,** altar
[12] **iūrō** (1), swear
[13] **iūs iūrandum, iūris iūrandī,** *n.,* oath
[14] **Hasdrubal, -alis,** *m., next in command after Hamilcar*
[15] **Āfrica, -ae**
[16] **Alpēs, -ium,** *f. pl.,* the Alps

20 Alpicōs[17] cōnantēs prohibēre eum trānsitū occīdit[18]; loca patefēcit; itinera mūnīvit[19]; effēcit[20] ut[21] elephantus īre posset quā[22] anteā[23] ūnus homō vix[24] poterat rēpere.[25] Sīc in Italiam pervēnit et, Scīpiōne[26] superātō, Etrūriam[27] petīvit. Hōc in itinere tam gravī morbō[28] oculōrum adfectus est[29] ut posteā numquam dextrō oculō bene ūterētur.

25 Multōs ducēs exercitūsque Rōmānōs superāvit; longum est omnia proelia[30] ēnumerāre.[31] Post Cannēnsem[32] autem pugnam nēmō eī in aciē[33] in Italiā restitit.[34] Cum autem P. Scīpiō tandem[35] in Āfricam invāsisset,[36] Hannibal, ad patriam dēfendendam revocātus, Zamae[37] victus est. Sīc post tot annōs Rōmānī sē perīculō Pūnicō līberāvērunt. (**Nepos,** *Hannibal,* excerpts)

## IX. AUTOBIOGRAPHICAL NOTES BY HORACE

Nūlla fors[1] mihi tē, Maecēnās,[2] obtulit: optimus Vergilius et post hunc Varius[3] dīxērunt quid essem. Ut ad tē vēnī, singultim[4] pauca locūtus (nam pudor[5] prohibēbat plūra profārī[6]), ego nōn dīxī mē clārō patre nātum esse sed nārrāvī quod eram. Respondēs,[7] ut tuus mōs est, pauca. Abeō et post nōnum mēnsem[8] mē
5 revocās iubēsque esse in amīcōrum numerō. Hoc magnum esse dūcō, quod[9] placuī tibi, quī bonōs ā turpibus sēcernis[10] nōn patre clārō sed vītā et pectore pūrō.[11]

Atquī[12] sī mea nātūra est mendōsa[13] vitiīs mediocribus ac paucīs sed aliōquī[14] rēcta,[15] sī neque avāritiam neque sordēs[16] quisquam[17] mihi obiciet,[18] sī pūrus sum et īnsōns[19] (ut mē laudem!) et vīvō cārus amīcīs, causa fuit pater meus. Hic enim,
10 cum pauper in parvō agrō esset, tamen nōluit mē puerum in lūdum Flāviī[20] mit-

[17]**Alpicī, -ōrum,** men of the Alps
[18]**occīdō, -ere, -cīdī, -cīsum,** cut down
[19]**mūniō (4),** fortify, build
[20]**efficiō,** bring it about, cause
[21]**ut . . . posset:** *noun clause of result, obj. of* **effēcit**
[22]**quā,** *adv.,* where
[23]**anteā,** *adv.,* before, formerly
[24]**vix,** *adv.,* scarcely
[25]**rēpō, -ere, rēpsī, rēptum,** crawl
[26]**Scīpiō, -ōnis,** *m., father of the Scipio mentioned below*
[27]**Etrūria, -ae,** *district north of Rome, Tuscany*
[28]**morbus, -ī,** disease
[29]**adficiō,** afflict
[30]**proelium, -iī,** battle
[31]**ēnumerō (1)**
[32]**Cannēnsis pugna,** battle at Cannae, *where in 216 B.C. Hannibal cut the Roman army to shreds*
[33]**aciēs, -ēī,** battle line
[34]**resistō, -ere, -stitī,** + *dat.,* resist
[35]**tandem,** *adv.,* at last, finally
[36]**invādō, -ere, -vāsī, -vāsum,** go into, invade
[37]**Zama, -ae,** *city south of Carthage in North Africa*
VOCĀBVLA: **occīdō, efficiō, quā, anteā, vix, proelium, tandem.**

**IX**
[1]**fors, fortis,** *f.,* chance, accident
[2]**Maecēnās, -ātis,** *m., Augustus' unofficial prime minister and Horace's patron*
[3]**Varius, -iī,** *an epic poet*
[4]**singultim,** *adv.,* stammeringly
[5]**pudor, -ōris,** *m.,* bashfulness, modesty
[6]**profor (1),** speak out
[7]**respondēs, abeō, revocās, iubēs:** *in vivid narration the pres. tense was often used by the Romans with the force of the perf. This is called the "historical pres."*
[8]**mēnsis, -is,** *m.,* month
[9]**quod,** the fact that
[10]**sēcernō, -ere, -crēvī, -crētum,** separate
[11]**pūrus, -a, -um**
[12]**atquī,** *conj.,* and yet
[13]**mendōsus, -a, -um,** faulty
[14]**aliōquī,** *adv.,* otherwise
[15]**rēctus, -a, -um,** straight, right
[16]**sordēs, -ium,** *f. pl.,* filth
[17]**quisquam,** anyone
[18]**ob-iciō,** cast in one's teeth
[19]**īnsōns,** *gen.* **-ontis,** guiltless
[20]**Flāvius, -iī,** *teacher in Horace's small home town of Venusia*

tere sed ausus est mē Rōmam ferre ad artēs discendās quās senātōrēs[21] suōs filiōs docent. Ipse mihi paedagōgus[22] incorruptissimus[23] erat. Mē līberum servāvit nōn sōlum ab omnī factō sed etiam ab turpī opprobriō.[24] Quārē laus illī ā mē dēbētur et grātia[25] magna.

15    Sīc Rōmae nūtrītus sum[26] atque doctus sum quantum[27] īrātus Achillēs Graecīs nocuisset. Deinde bonae Athēnae mihi plūs artis adiēcērunt,[28] scīlicet[29] ut vellem rēctum ā curvō[30] distinguere[31] atque inter silvās[32] Acadēmī[33] quaerere vēritātem. Sed dūra tempora mē illō locō grātō ēmōvērunt et aestus[34] cīvīlis[35] bellī mē tulit in arma Brūtī.[36] Tum post bellum Philippēnse[37] dīmissus sum[38] et audāx[39] paupertās

20    mē humilem et pauperem coēgit versūs facere. (**Horace,** *Saturae* 1.6 and *Epistulae* 2.2; excerpts in prose form)

## X. HORACE LONGS FOR THE SIMPLE, PEACEFUL COUNTRY LIFE ON HIS SABINE FARM

Ō rūs, quandō tē aspiciam?[1] Quandō mihi licēbit nunc librīs veterum auctōrum, nunc somnō et ōtiō ūtī sine cūrīs sollicitae[2] vītae? Ō noctēs cēnaeque deōrum! Sermō[3] oritur[4] nōn dē vīllīs[5] et domibus aliēnīs[6]; sed id quaerimus quod magis ad nōs pertinet[7] et nescīre malum est: utrum dīvitiīs an virtūte hominēs fiant beātī;

5    quid nōs ad amīcitiam trahat, ūsus[8] an rēctum[9]; et quae sit nātūra bonī[10] et quid sit summum bonum.

Inter haec Cervius[11] fābulam nārrat. Mūs[12] rūsticus,[13] impulsus[14] ab urbānō mūre, domō rūsticā ad urbem abiit ut, dūrā vītā relictā, in rēbus iūcundīs cum illō vīveret beātus. Mox, autem, multa perīcula urbāna expertus, rūsticus "Haec vīta,"

---

[21] senātor, -ōris, *m.*

[22] paedagōgus, -ī, *slave who attended a boy at school*

[23] in-corruptus, -a, -um, uncorrupted

[24] opprobrium, -iī, reproach

[25] grātia, -ae, gratitude

[26] nūtriō (4), nourish, bring up

[27] quantum, *acc. as adv.*

[28] ad-iciō, add

[29] scīlicet (scīre-licet), *adv.,* naturally, of course, clearly, namely

[30] curvus, -a, -um, curved, wrong

[31] distinguō, -ere, -stīnxī, -stīnctum, distinguish

[32] silva, -ae, wood, forest

[33] Acadēmus, -ī; *Plato used to teach in the grove of Academus.*

[34] aestus, -ūs, tide

[35] cīvīlis, -e; *after the assassination of Julius Caesar on the Ides of March,* 44 B.C., *civil war ensued between the Caesarians, led by Antony and Octavian, and the "Republicans," led by Brutus and Cassius.*

[36] Brūtus, -ī

[37] Philippēnsis, -e, at Philippi, *where in 42* B.C. *Brutus was defeated*

[38] dī-mittō, discharge

[39] audāx, -ācis, daring, bold

VOCĀBVLA: sēcernō, quisquam, grātia, silva, audāx.

## X

[1] aspiciō, -ere, -spexī, -spectum, look at, see

[2] sollicitus, -a, -um, troubled, anxious

[3] sermō, -ōnis, *m.,* conversation

[4] orior, *Locī Ant. V n. 15*

[5] vīlla, -ae

[6] aliēnus, -a, -um, belonging to another

[7] per-tineō, pertain

[8] ūsus, -ūs, advantage

[9] rēctum, -ī, the right

[10] bonum, -ī, the good

[11] Cervius, -iī, *a rustic friend*

[12] mūs, mūris, *m/f.,* mouse

[13] rūsticus, -a, -um, rustic, country

[14] im-pellō, urge, persuade

10     inquit, "nōn est mihi necessāria.[15] Valē; mihi silva cavusque[16] tūtus[17] ab īnsidiīs
placēbit." (**Horace**, *Saturae* 2.6, excerpts in prose form)

## XI. WHY NO LETTERS?

C.[1] Plīnius Fabiō[2] Suō S.[3]

      Mihi nūllās epistulās[4] mittis. "Nihil est," inquis, "quod scrībam." At hoc ipsum
scrībe: nihil esse quod scrībās; vel[5] illa verba sōla ā quibus maiōrēs nostrī incipere
solēbant: "Sī valēs, bene est; ego valeō." Hoc mihi sufficit[6]; est enim maximum. Mē
5    lūdere[7] putās? Sēriō[8] petō. Fac ut sciam quid agās. Valē. (**Pliny**, *Epistulae* 1.11)

## XII. WHAT PLINY THINKS OF THE RACES

C. Plīnius Calvisiō[1] Suō S.

      Hoc omne tempus inter tabellās[2] ac libellōs iūcundissimā quiēte[3] cōnsūmpsī.
"Quemadmodum,[4]" inquis, "in urbe potuistī?" Circēnsēs[5] erant quō genere spectāculī[6] nē levissimē quidem teneor. Nihil novum, nihil varium,[7] nihil quod semel
5    spectāvisse nōn sufficiat. Quārē mīror tot mīlia virōrum tam puerīliter[8] identidem[9]
cupere currentēs equōs vidēre. Valē. (**Pliny**, *Epistulae* 9.6)

## XIII. PLINY ENDOWS A SCHOOL

Nūper cum Cōmī[1] fuī, vēnit ad mē salūtandum[2] fīlius amīcī cuiusdam. Huic ego
"Studēs?" inquam. Respondit: "Etiam." "Ubi?" "Mediolānī.[3]" "Cūr nōn hīc?" Et
pater eius, quī ipse puerum ad mē addūxerat, respondit: "Quod nūllōs magistrōs
hīc habēmus." Huic aliīsque patribus quī audiēbant ego: "Quārē nūllōs?" inquam.
5   "Nam ubi iūcundius līberī[4] vestrī discere possunt quam hīc in urbe vestrā et sub
oculīs patrum? Atque ego, quī nōndum[5] līberōs habeō, prō rē pūblicā nostrā quasi
prō parente tertiam partem eius pecūniae dabō quam cōnferre vōbīs placēbit.

---

[15]**necessārius, -a, -um**
[16]**cavus, -ī**, hole
[17]**tūtus, -a, -um**, safe
VOCĀBVLA: **aspiciō, orior, tūtus.**

### XI
[1]**C. = Gāius**
[2]**Fabius, -iī**
[3]**S. = salūtem (dīcit)**
[4]**epistula, -ae**, letter
[5]**vel**, or, *an optional alternative;* **aut** *means* or *without any option*
[6]**sufficiō**, suffice, be sufficient
[7]**lūdō, -ere, lūsī, lūsum**, play, jest
[8]**sēriō**, *adv.,* seriously
VOCĀBVLA: **vel, sufficiō.**

### XII
[1]**Calvisius, -ī**
[2]**tabella, -ae**, writing pad

[3]**quiēs, -ētis**, *f.,* quiet
[4]**quem-ad-modum**, *adv.,* how
[5]**Circēnsēs (lūdī)**, games, *races in the Circus Maximus*
[6]**spectāculum, -ī**
[7]**varius, -a, -um**, different
[8]**puerīliter**, *adv., based on* **puer**
[9]**identidem**, *adv.,* repeatedly
VOCĀBVLA: **quiēs, quemadmodum, varius.**

### XIII
[1]**Cōmum, -ī**, Como, *Pliny's birthplace in N. Italy*
[2]**salūtō (1)**, greet
[3]**Mediolānum, -ī**, Milan
[4]**līberī, -ōrum**, children
[5]**nōndum**, *adv.,* not yet
VOCĀBVLA: **līberī, nōndum.**

Nihil enim melius praestāre līberīs vestrīs, nihil grātius patriae potestis." (**Pliny,** *Epistulae* 4.13)

## XIV.  LARGE GIFTS—YES, BUT ONLY BAIT

"Mūnera[1] magna tamen mīsit." Sed mīsit in hāmō[2];
   et piscātōrem[3] piscis[4] amāre potest? (**Martial** 6.63.5–6)

## XV.  THE LORD'S PRAYER

Et cum ōrātis nōn eritis sīcut[1] hypocritae,[2] quī amant in synagōgīs[3] et in angulīs[4] plateārum[5] stantēs ōrāre ut videantur ab hominibus: āmēn[6] dīcō vōbīs, recēpērunt mercēdem[7] suam. Tū autem cum ōrābis, intrā[8] in cubiculum[9] tuum et, clausō[10] ōstiō[11] tuō, ōrā Patrem tuum in abscondītō[12]; et Pater tuus quī videt in abscondītō

5  reddet[13] tibi. . . . Sīc ergō[14] vōs ōrābitis: Pater noster quī es in caelīs, sānctificētur[15] nōmen tuum; adveniat rēgnum[16] tuum; fiat voluntās[17] tua sīcut in caelō et[18] in terrā. Pānem[19] nostrum supersubstantiālem[20] dā nōbīs hodiē, et dīmitte[21] nōbīs dēbita[22] nostra, sīcut et nōs dīmittimus dēbitōribus[23] nostrīs; et nē indūcās nōs in temptātiōnem[24]: sed līberā nōs ā malō. (*Vulgate, Matthew* 6.5–6, 9–13)

## XVI.  CAEDMON'S ANGLO-SAXON VERSES AND THE DIFFICULTIES OF TRANSLATION

Cum Caedmon[1] corpus somnō dedisset, angelus[2] Dominī eī dormientī "Caedmon," inquit, "cantā[3] mihi prīncipium creātūrārum.[4]" Et statim[5] coepit cantāre in laudem Deī creātōris[6] versūs quōs numquam audīverat, quōrum hic est sēnsus:

**XIV**
METER: elegiac couplet.
[1]**mūnus, mūneris,** *n.,* gift
[2]**hāmus, -ī,** hook
[3]**piscātor, -ōris,** *m.,* fisherman
[4]**piscis, -is,** *m.,* fish
VOCĀBVLA: **mūnus.**

**XV**
[1]**sīcut,** *adv. and conj.,* just as
[2]**hypocrita, -ae,** *m.,* hypocrite
[3]**synagōga, -ae,** synagogue
[4]**angulus, -ī,** corner
[5]**platea, -ae,** street
[6]**āmēn,** *adv.,* truly, verily
[7]**mercēs, -ēdis,** *f.,* wages, reward
[8]**intrō** (1), enter
[9]**cubiculum, -ī,** bedroom, room
[10]**claudō, -ere, clausī, clausum,** close
[11]**ōstium, -iī,** door
[12]**in abscondītō,** in (a) secret (place)
[13]**red-dō, -dere, -didī, -ditum,** give back, answer, requite

[14]**ergō,** *adv.,* therefore
[15]**sānctificō** (1), treat as holy
[16]**rēgnum, -ī,** kingdom
[17]**voluntās, -tātis,** *f.,* will, wish
[18]**et,** also
[19]**pānis, -is,** *m.,* bread
[20]**supersubstantiālis, -e,** necessary to the support of life
[21]**dī-mittō,** send away, dismiss
[22]**dēbitum, -ī,** that which is owing, debt (*figuratively*) = sin
[23]**dēbitor, -ōris,** *m.,* one who owes something, one who has not yet fulfilled his duty
[24]**temptātiō, -ōnis,** *f.*
VOCĀBVLA: **sīcut, claudō, reddō, ergō, rēgnum, voluntās.**

**XVI**
[1]**Caedmon,** *Anglo-Saxon poet of the 7th cent.*
[2]**angelus, -ī,** angel
[3]**cantō** (1), sing
[4]**creātūra, -ae,** creature
[5]**statim,** *adv.,* immediately
[6]**creātor, -ōris,** *m.*

"Nunc laudāre dēbēmus auctōrem rēgnī[7] caelestis,[8] potestātem[9] creatōris et cōnsilium illīus, facta Patris glōriae, quī, omnipotēns[10] custōs[11] hūmānī generis, fīliīs
hominum caelum et terram creāvit." Hic est sēnsus, nōn autem ōrdō[12] ipse verbōrum quae dormiēns ille cantāvit; neque enim possunt carmina, quamvīs[13]
optimē composita,[14] ex aliā in aliam linguam ad verbum[15] sine dētrīmentō[16] suī
decōris[17] ac dignitātis trānsferrī.[18] (**Bede,** *Historia Ecclēsiastica Gentis Anglōrum*
4.24; 8th cent.)

## XVII. WHO WILL PUT THE BELL ON THE CAT'S NECK?

Mūrēs[1] iniērunt cōnsilium quō modō sē ā cattō[2] dēfendere possent et quaedam sapientior quam cēterae āit: "Ligētur[3] campāna[4] in collō[5] cattī. Sīc poterimus eum
eiusque īnsidiās vītāre." Placuit omnibus hoc cōnsilium, sed alia mūs "Quis igitur,"
inquit, "est inter nōs tam audāx[6] ut campānam in collō cattī ligāre audeat?" Respondit ūna mūs: "Certē nōn ego." Respondit alia: "Certē nōn ego audeō prō tōtō
mundō cattō ipsī appropinquāre.[7]" Et idem cēterae dīxērunt.

Sīc saepe hominēs, cum quendam āmovendum esse arbitrantur et contrā eum
insurgere[8] volunt, inter sē dīcunt: "Quis appōnet sē contrā eum? Quis accūsābit[9]
eum?" Tum omnēs, sibi timentēs, dīcunt: "Nōn ego certē! Nec ego!" Sīc illum
vīvere patiuntur. (**Odo de Cerinton,** *Nārrātiōnēs,* 12th cent.)

## XVIII. THE DEVIL AND A THIRTEENTH-CENTURY SCHOOLBOY

In illā ecclēsiā[1] erat scholāris[2] parvus. Cum hic diē quādam[3] versūs compōnere ex
eā māteriā[4] ā magistrō datā nōn posset et trīstis sedēret, diabolus[5] in fōrmā hominis vēnit. Cum dīxisset: "Quid est, puer? Cūr sīc trīstis sedēs?" respondit puer:
"Magistrum meum timeō quod versūs compōnere nōn possum dē themate[6] quod
ab eō recēpī." Et ille: "Vīsne mihi servīre sī ego versūs tibi compōnam?" Puer, nōn

[7]**rēgnum, -ī,** kingdom
[8]**caelestis, -e,** *adj. of* **caelum**
[9]**potestās, -tātis,** *f.,* power
[10]**omni-potēns**
[11]**custōs, -tōdis,** *m.,* guardian
[12]**ōrdō, -inis,** *m.,* order
[13]**quamvīs,** *adv. and conj.,* although
[14]**com-pōnō,** put together, compose
[15]**ad verbum,** to a word, literally
[16]**dētrīmentum, -ī,** loss
[17]**decor, -ōris,** *m.,* beauty
[18]**trāns-ferō**
VOCĀBVLA: **statim, rēgnum, potestās, custōs, ōrdō, compōnō.**

**XVII**
[1]**mūs, mūris,** *m./f.,* mouse
[2]**cattus, -ī** (*late Lat. for* **fēles, -is**), cat

[3]**ligō** (1), bind
[4]**campāna, -ae** (*late Lat. for* **tintinnābulum**), bell
[5]**collum, -ī,** neck
[6]**audāx, -ācis,** daring, bold
[7]**appropinquō** (1), + *dat.,* approach
[8]**īnsurgō, -ere, -surrēxī, -surrēctum,** rise up
[9]**accūsō** (1)
VOCĀBVLA: **audāx, appropinquō.**

**XVIII**
[1]**ecclēsia, -ae,** church
[2]**scholāris, -is,** *m.,* scholar
[3]**diē quādam: diēs** *is sometimes f., esp. when referring to a specific day.*
[4]**māteria, -ae,** material
[5]**diabolus, -ī,** devil
[6]**thema, -atis,** *n.,* theme, subject

intellegēns quod[7] ille esset diabolus, respondit: "Etiam, domine, parātus sum facere quidquid iusseris—dummodo versūs habeam et verbera[8] vītem." Tum, versibus statim[9] dictātīs,[10] diabolus abiit. Cum puer autem hōs versūs magistrō suō dedisset, hic, excellentiam[11] versuum mīrātus, timuit, dūcēns scientiam in illīs dīvīnam,[12]

10    nōn hūmānam. Et ait: "Dīc mihi, quis tibi hōs versūs dictāvit?" Prīmum puer respondit: "Ego, magister!" Magistrō autem nōn crēdente et verbum interrogātiōnis[13] saepius repetente, puer omnia tandem[14] cōnfessus est.[15] Tum magister "Fīlī," inquit, "ille versificātor[16] fuit diabolus. Cārissime, semper illum sēductōrem[17] et eius opera cavē.[18]" Et puer diabolum eiusque opera relīquit. (**Caesar of Heisterbach,** *Mīrācula* 2.14; 13th cent.)

---

[7] **quod,** that, *introducing an ind. state., common in Medieval Lat.*
[8] **verbera, -um,** *n.,* blows, a beating
[9] **statim,** *adv.,* immediately
[10] **dictō** (1), dictate
[11] **excellentia, -ae**
[12] **dīvīnus, -a, -um; dīvīnam** *is pred. acc.*
[13] **interrogātiō, -ōnis,** *f.*

[14] **tandem,** *adv.,* at last
[15] **cōnfiteor, -ērī, -fessus sum**
[16] **versificātor, -ōris,** *m.,* versifier
[17] **sēductor, -ōris,** *m.,* seducer
[18] **caveō, -ēre, cāvī, cautum,** beware, avoid
VOCĀBVLA: **statim, tandem, cōnfiteor, caveō.**

# LOCĪ IMMŪTĀTĪ

The **Locī Immūtātī** are offered for those who may finish reading all the **Locī Antīquī** and wish to try their wits on some unaltered classical Latin. These passages are straight Latin, unchanged except for occasional omissions, which have been regularly indicated by three dots. Naturally this unadapted literary material had to be rather heavily annotated, but more in the matter of vocabulary than in other respects. As in the case of the **Locī Antīquī,** words appearing here that have not been introduced in the regular chapter **Vocābula** are glossed at their first one or two occurrences, and most are also included in the Latin-English **Vocābula** at the back of the book for quick reference, if needed. New grammatical principles have been treated as they occur, either by a brief statement in the notes or by reference to the Appendix.

Take the time, as always, to begin each passage by reading it aloud, once or twice at least, and always read first for comprehension—attempting to gain a clear sense of what the author is saying, before you attempt a translation into English.

## I.  A DEDICATION

Cui dōnō[1] lepidum[2] novum libellum
āridō[3] modo[4] pūmice[5] expolītum[6]?
Cornēlī,[7] tibi, namque[8] tū solēbās
meās esse aliquid putāre nūgās,[9]
5    iam tum cum ausus es ūnus Ītalōrum[10]
omne aevum[11] tribus explicāre[12] chartīs,[13]

---

**I**
METER: Phalaecean, or hendecasyllabic.
[1]**dōnō** (1), (= **dō**), present, dedicate
[2]**lepidus, -a, -um,** pleasant, neat
[3]**āridus, -a, -um,** dry, arid
[4]**modo,** *adv.,* just now
[5]**pūmex, -icis,** *m.,* pumice stone. *The ends of a volume were smoothed with pumice.*
[6]**expoliō** (4), smooth, polish

[7]*Cornelius Nepos, biographer and historian;* see Introd.
[8]*strong form of* **nam** = for (indeed, surely)
[9]**nūgae, -ārum,** trifles, nonsense
[10]**Ītalī, -ōrum,** the Italians; *initial* i- *long here for meter. This work, now lost, was apparently less annalistic than most histories by Romans.*
[11]**aevum, -ī,** time
[12]**explicō** (1), unfold, explain
[13]**charta, -ae,** leaf of (papyrus) paper; *here* = volume

doctīs—Iupitter!—et labōriōsīs.[14]
Quārē habē tibi quidquid hoc libellī[15]
quālecumque,[15] quod, Ō patrōna[16] virgō,
10    plūs ūnō maneat[17] perenne[18] saeclō.[19] (**Catullus 1**)

## II. HOW MANY KISSES[1]

Quaeris quot mihi bāsiātiōnēs[2]
tuae, Lesbia, sint satis superque.[3]
Quam magnus numerus Libyssae[4] harēnae[5]
laserpīciferīs[6] iacet Cyrēnīs,[7]

. . .

5    aut quam sīdera multa, cum tacet nox,
fūrtīvōs[8] hominum vident amōrēs,
tam tē[9] bāsia multa bāsiāre[10]
vēsānō[11] satis et super Catullō est. (**Catullus 7.1–4, 7–10**)

## III.  DEATH OF A PET SPARROW

Lūgēte,[1] Ō Venerēs[2] Cupīdinēsque[3]
et quantum est hominum[4] venustiōrum[5]!
Passer[6] mortuus est meae puellae,
passer, dēliciae[7] meae puellae,
5    quem plūs illa oculīs suīs amābat.
Nam mellītus[8] erat, suamque nōrat[9]
ipsam[10] tam bene quam puella mātrem;

---

[14] **labōriōsus, -a, -um,** laborious
[15] **libellī,** *gen. of whole; lit.* whatever kind of book this is of what-soever sort; *i.e.,* this book such as it is. **quāliscumque, quālecumque,** of whatever sort *or* kind
[16] **patrōna, -ae,** protectress; protectress maiden (**virgō**) = Muse
[17] let *or* may it remain
[18] **perennis, -e,** lasting, perennial
[19] **saeclum,** *syncopated form of* **saeculum, -ī,** age, century

## II
METER: Phalaecean.
[1] *This poem is obviously a companion piece to Catullus 5 (see Capvt XXXI).*
[2] **bāsiātiō, -ōnis,** *f.,* kiss
[3] and to spare, and more
[4] **Libyssus, -a, -um,** Libyan
[5] **harēna, -ae,** sand (*cf.* arena)
[6] **laserpīcifer, -a, -um,** bearing laserpicium, *a medicinal plant*
[7] **Cȳrēnae, -ārum,** Cyrene, *city of North Africa; short* y *here for meter.*
[8] **fūrtīvus, -a, -um,** stealthy, furtive (**fūr,** thief)

[9] *subj. of* **bāsiāre**
[10] **bāsiō** (1), to kiss kisses = to give kisses; **bāsiāre** *is subj. of* **est satis.**
[11] **vēsānus, -a, -um,** mad, insane

## III
METER: Phalaecean.
[1] **lūgeō, -ēre, lūxī, lūctum,** mourn, grieve
[2] **Venus, -eris,** *f.,* Venus; *here pl. as* **Cupīdinēs** *is.*
[3] **Cupīdō, -inis,** *m.,* Cupid, *often in the pl. as is Gk. Eros and as we see in art.*
[4] *gen. of whole with* **quantum:** how much of people there is = all the people there are
[5] **venustus, -a, -um,** charming, graceful; **venustiōrum** = more charming (*than ordinary men*)
[6] **passer, -eris,** *m.,* sparrow (*a bird which, incidentally, was sacred to Venus*)
[7] **dēliciae, -ārum,** delight, darling, pet
[8] **mellītus, -a, -um,** sweet as honey
[9] *contracted form* = **nōverat** (*from* **nōscō**)
[10] **suam . . . ipsam,** its very own (mistress)

nec sēsē[11] ā gremiō[12] illius movēbat,
    sed circumsiliēns[13] modo hūc[14] modo illūc[15]
10  ad sōlam dominam usque pīpiābat.[16]
    Quī[17] nunc it per iter tenebricōsum[18]
    illūc unde negant redīre quemquam.[19]
    At vōbīs male sit, malae tenebrae[20]
    Orcī,[21] quae omnia bella dēvorātis;[22]
15  tam bellum mihi[23] passerem abstulistis.[24]
    Ō factum male! Iō[25] miselle[26] passer!
    Tuā nunc operā[27] meae puellae
    flendō[28] turgidulī[29] rubent[30] ocellī.[31] (**Catullus 3**)

## IV. FRĀTER AVĒ, ATQUE VALĒ[1]

Multās per gentēs et multa per aequora[2] vectus[3]
    adveniō hās miserās, frāter, ad īnferiās,[4]
ut tē postrēmō[5] dōnārem[6] mūnere[7] mortis
    et mūtam[8] nēquīquam[9] adloquerer[10] cinerem,[11]
5  quandoquidem[12] fortūna mihī[13] tētē[14] abstulit[15] ipsum,
    heu miser indignē[16] frāter adempte[17] mihī.
Nunc tamen intereā[18] haec,[19] prīscō[20] quae mōre parentum

---

[11]**sēsē** = **sē** (*acc.*)
[12]**gremium, -iī,** lap
[13]**circumsiliō** (4), jump around
[14]**hūc,** *adv.,* hither, to this place
[15]**illūc,** *adv.,* thither, to that place
[16]**pīpiō** (1), chirp
[17]**quī** = **et hic,** *conjunctive use of the rel. at the beginning of a sent.*
[18]**tenebricōsus, -a, -um,** dark, gloomy
[19]*Locī Ant. IV n. 6.*
[20]**tenebrae, -ārum,** darkness
[21]**Orcus, -ī,** Orcus, the underworld
[22]**dēvorō** (1), devour, consume
[23]*dat. of separation*
[24]**auferō, auferre, abstulī, ablātum,** take away
[25]**iō,** *exclamation of pain,* oh!, *or of joy,* hurrah!
[26]**misellus, -a, -um,** *diminutive of* **miser,** wretched, poor, unhappy; *a colloquial word*
[27]**tuā operā,** thanks to you: **opera, -ae,** work, pains, effort
[28]**fleō, -ēre, flēvī, flētum,** weep
[29]**turgidulus, -a, -um,** (somewhat) swollen
[30]**rubeō, -ēre,** be red
[31]**ocellus, -ī,** *diminutive of* **oculus**

## IV

METER: elegiac couplet.
[1]*Catullus journeyed to Bithynia on the staff of Memmius, the governor, apparently for two prime reasons. He undoubtedly*

*wanted to get away from Rome in order to regain his equilibrium and fortitude after his final break with the notorious Lesbia. The present poem shows that he also deeply desired to carry out the final funeral rites for his dearly beloved brother, who had died in a foreign land far from his loved ones.*

[2]**aequor, -oris,** *n.,* flat surface, the sea
[3]**vehō, -ere, vexī, vectum,** carry
[4]**īnferiae, -ārum,** offerings in honor of the dead
[5]**postrēmus, -a, -um,** last
[6]**dōnō** (1), present you with; *cf. the idiom in Locī Im. I line 1.*
[7]**mūnus, -eris,** *n.,* service, gift
[8]**mūtus, -a, -um,** mute, silent
[9]**nequīquam,** *adv.,* in vain
[10]**ad-loquor,** address
[11]**cinis, -eris,** *m. but occasionally f. as here,* ashes (*cf.* incinerator)
[12]**quandoquidem,** *conj.,* since
[13]*dat. of separation. Final -ī is long here because of meter.*
[14]= **tē**
[15]*Locī Im. III n. 24*
[16]**indignē,** *adv.,* undeservedly
[17]**adimō, -ere, -ēmī, -ēmptum,** take away; **adēmpte,** *voc. agreeing with* **frāter**
[18]**intereā,** *adv.,* meanwhile
[19]*n. acc. pl., obj. of* **accipe**
[20]**prīscus, -a, -um,** ancient

trādita sunt trīstī mūnere ad īnferiās,
accipe frāternō[21] multum[22] mānantia[23] flētū,[24]
10      atque in perpetuum,[25] frāter, avē[26] atque valē. (**Catullus** 101)

## V. VITRIOLIC DENUNCIATION[1] OF THE LEADER OF A CONSPIRACY AGAINST THE ROMAN STATE

Quō usque[2] tandem abūtēre,[3] Catilīna, patientiā nostrā? Quam diū etiam furor[4] iste tuus nōs ēlūdet[5]? Quem ad fīnem sēsē[6] effrēnāta[7] iactābit[8] audācia[9]? Nihilne[10] tē nocturnum[11] praesidium[12] Palātī,[13] nihil urbis vigiliae,[14] nihil timor populī, nihil concursus[15] bonōrum omnium, nihil hic mūnītissimus[16] habendī senātūs locus, nihil
5    hōrum ōra[17] vultūsque mōvērunt? Patēre tua cōnsilia nōn sentīs? Cōnstrictam[18] iam omnium hōrum scientiā tenērī coniūrātiōnem[19] tuam nōn vidēs? Quid proximā,[20] quid superiōre[21] nocte ēgerīs, ubi fuerīs, quōs convocāverīs,[22] quid cōnsilī cēperīs, quem nostrum[23] ignōrāre[24] arbitrāris?

Ō tempora[25]! Ō mōrēs! Senātus haec intelligit, cōnsul videt; hic tamen vīvit.
10    Vīvit? Immō[26] vērō[27] etiam in senātum venit, fit pūblicī cōnsilī particeps,[28] notat[29] et dēsignat[30] oculīs ad caedem[31] ūnum quemque nostrum. Nōs, autem, fortēs virī, satis facere reī pūblicae vidēmur sī istīus furōrem ac tēla[32] vītāmus. Ad mortem tē, Catilīna, dūcī iussū[33] cōnsulis iam prīdem[34] oportēbat, in tē cōnferrī pestem[35] quam tū in nōs māchināris[36] . . .

---

[21]**frāternus, -a, -um,** fraternal, of a brother, a brother's
[22]**multum,** *adv. with* **mānantia**
[23]**mānō** (1), flow, drip with; **mānantia** *modifies* **haec** *in line 7.*
[24]**flētus, -ūs,** weeping, tears
[25]**in perpetuum,** forever
[26]**avē = salvē**

**V**

[1]*For the general situation of this speech see the introductory note to the reading passage in Capvt XXX. Since Cicero as yet lacked evidence that would stand in court, this speech is a magnificent example of bluff; but it worked to the extent of forcing Catiline (though not the other leaders of the conspiracy) to leave Rome for his army encamped at Fiesole near Florence.*
[2]**quō usque,** how far
[3]= **abūtēris; ab-ūtor** + *abl.,* abuse
[4]**furor, -ōris,** *m.,* madness
[5]**ēlūdō, -ere, -lūsī, -lūsum,** mock, elude
[6]**quem ad fīnem = ad quem fīnem; sēsē = sē**
[7]**effrēnātus, -a, -um,** unbridled; *cf.* **frēnum,** bridle, *and the* **frēnum** *of the upper lip*
[8]**iactō** (1), *frequentative form of* **iaciō,** toss about, vaunt
[9]**audācia, -ae,** boldness, audacity
[10]**nihil =** *strong* **nōn;** not at all
[11]**nocturnus, -a, -um,** *adj. of* **nox**
[12]**praesidium, -iī,** guard

[13]**Palātium, -ī,** the Palatine hill. *From the sumptuous dwellings on the Palatine comes our word "palace."*
[14]**vigilia, -ae,** watch; *pl.,* watchmen, sentinels
[15]**concursus, -ūs,** gathering
[16]**mūnītus, -a, -um,** fortified
[17]*here* = expression
[18]**cōnstringō, -ere, -strīnxī, -strictum,** bind, curb
[19]**coniūrātiō, -ōnis,** *f.,* conspiracy (a swearing together)
[20]**proximus, -a, -um,** nearest, last (*sc.* **nocte**)
[21]**superiōre** (*sc.* **nocte**) = the night before
[22]**con-vocō**
[23]*gen. of* **nōs** (*Capvt XI*)
[24]**ignōrō** (1), be ignorant, not know
[25]*The acc. was used in exclamatory expressions.*
[26]**immō,** *adv.,* on the contrary; nay more
[27]**vērō,** *adv.,* in fact
[28]**particeps, -cipis,** *m.,* participant
[29]**notō** (1), mark out, note
[30]**dēsignō** (1), mark out, designate, choose
[31]**caedēs, -is,** *f.,* slaughter
[32]**tēlum, -ī,** weapon
[33]**iussū,** *chiefly in abl.,* by *or* at the command of
[34]**iam prīdem,** *adv.,* long ago
[35]**pestis, -is,** *f.,* plague, destruction
[36]**māchinor** (1), contrive (*cf. "machine"*); **in nōs, in** + *acc. sometimes means* against (**contrā**)

15      Habēmus senātūs cōnsultum[37] in tē, Catilīna, vehemēns[38] et grave. Nōn deest[39] reī pūblicae cōnsilium, neque auctōritās[40] huius ōrdinis[41]; nōs, nōs, dīcō apertē,[42] cōnsulēs dēsumus . . . At nōs vīcēsimum[43] iam diem patimur hebēscere[44] aciem[45] hōrum auctōritātis. Habēmus enim eius modī[46] senātūs cōnsultum, . . . quō ex[47] senātūs cōnsultō cōnfestim[48] tē interfectum esse, Catilīna, convēnit.[49] Vīvis, et

20    vīvis nōn ad dēpōnendam,[50] sed ad cōnfirmandam[51] audāciam. Cupiō, patrēs cōnscrīptī,[52] mē esse clēmentem[53]; cupiō in tantīs reī pūblicae perīculīs mē nōn dissolūtum[54] vidērī, sed iam mē ipse inertiae[55] nēquitiaeque[56] condemnō.[57]

      Castra[58] sunt in Italiā contrā populum Rōmānum in Etrūriae[59] faucibus[60] collocāta[61]; crēscit in diēs singulōs[62] hostium numerus; eōrum autem castrōrum

25    imperātōrem ducemque hostium intrā[63] moenia atque adeō[64] in senātū vidēmus, intestīnam[65] aliquam cotīdiē perniciem[66] reī pūblicae mōlientem[67] . . .

      Quae[68] cum ita sint, Catilīna, perge[69] quō[70] coepistī. Ēgredere[71] aliquandō[72] ex urbe; patent portae; proficīscere. Nimium diū tē imperātōrem tua illa Mānliāna[73] castra dēsīderant. Ēdūc tēcum etiam omnēs tuōs; sī minus,[74] quam plūrimōs;

30    pūrgā[75] urbem. Magnō mē metū līberāveris dum modo inter mē atque tē mūrus[76] intersit.[77] Nōbīscum versārī[78] iam diūtius nōn potes; nōn feram, nōn patiar, nōn sinam[79] . . .

      Quamquam[80] nōn nūllī[81] sunt in hōc ōrdine quī aut ea quae imminent[82] nōn videant, aut ea quae vident dissimulent[83]; quī[84] spem Catilīnae mollibus[85] sententiīs

---

[37]**cōnsultum, -ī,** decree

[38]**vehemēns,** *gen.* **-entis,** emphatic, vehement

[39]**dē + sum,** be wanting, fail + *dat.*

[40]**auctōritās, -tātis,** *f.,* authority

[41]**ōrdō, -dinis,** *m.,* class, order

[42]*adv.,* openly

[43]**vīcēsimus, -a, -um,** twentieth

[44]**hebēscō, -ere,** grow dull

[45]**aciēs, -ēī,** sharp edge

[46]**eius modī,** of this sort; *modifies* **cōnsultum**

[47]*here* = in accordance with; *with* **quō . . . cōnsultō**

[48]**cōnfestim,** *adv.,* at once

[49]**convenit, -īre, -vēnit,** *impers.,* it is fitting

[50]**dē + pōnō,** put aside

[51]**cōnfirmō** (1), strengthen

[52]**patrēs cōnscrīptī,** senators

[53]**clēmēns,** *gen.* **-entis,** merciful, gentle

[54]**dissolūtus, -a, -um,** lax

[55]**inertia, -ae,** inactivity; *example of gen. of thing charged:* "I condemn myself *on a charge of inactivity,* find myself guilty of inactivity."

[56]**nēquitia, -ae,** worthlessness; *gen. of charge*

[57]**condemnō** (1), find guilty, condemn

[58]**castra, -ōrum,** a camp (*n. pl. form but sg. meaning*)

[59]**Etrūria, -ae,** Etruria

[60]**faucēs, -ium,** *f. pl.,* jaws, narrow pass

[61]**collocō** (1), to position

[62]**in diēs singulōs,** from day to day

[63]**intrā,** *prep. + acc.,* within

[64]**adeō,** *adv.,* so even

[65]**intestīnus, -a, -um,** internal

[66]**perniciēs, -ēī,** slaughter, destruction

[67]**mōlientem** *modifies* **ducem** *and has* **perniciem** *as its obj.*

[68]= **et haec,** *conjunctive use of the rel. pron.*

[69]**pergō, -ere, -rēxī, -rēctum,** proceed, continue

[70]**quō,** *adv.,* where. *A few lines before these words Cicero said:* **cōnfirmāstī** (you asserted) **tē ipsum iam esse exitūrum** (*from* **ex-eō**).

[71]**ēgredior, -ī, -gressus sum,** go out, depart. *What is the form of* **ēgredere**?

[72]**quandō,** *adv.,* at some time, at last

[73]*Manlius was in charge of Catiline's army at Fiesole.*

[74]**minus = nōn omnēs**

[75]**pūrgō** (1), cleanse

[76]**mūrus, -ī,** wall

[77]**inter-sum**

[78]**versor** (1), dwell, remain

[79]**sinō, -ere, sīvī, situm,** allow

[80]**quamquam,** *conj.,* and yet

[81]**nōn nūllī,** not none = some, several

[82]**immineō, -ēre,** overhang, threaten

[83]**dissimulō** (1), conceal

[84]**quī = et hī**

[85]**mollis, -e,** soft, weak

35  aluērunt coniūrātiōnemque nāscentem nōn crēdendō corrōborāvērunt[86]; quōrum[87] auctōritātem secūtī,[88] multī nōn sōlum improbī,[89] vērum[90] etiam imperītī,[91] sī in hunc animadvertissem,[92] crūdēliter[93] et rēgiē[94] factum esse[95] dīcerent. Nunc intellegō, sī iste, quō intendit,[96] in Mānliāna castra pervēnerit,[97] nēminem tam stultum fore[98] quī nōn videat coniūrātiōnem esse factam, nēminem tam improbum quī
40  nōn fateātur.

Hōc autem ūnō interfectō, intellegō hanc reī pūblicae pestem paulīsper[99] reprimī,[100] nōn in perpetuum[101] comprimī[102] posse. Quod sī[103] sē ēiēcerit,[104] sēcumque suōs[105] ēdūxerit, et eōdem[106] cēterōs undique[107] collēctōs[108] naufragōs[109] adgregārit,[110] exstinguētur[111] atque dēlēbitur nōn modo haec tam adulta[112] reī pūblicae pestis, vērum
45  etiam stirps[113] ac sēmen[114] malōrum omnium . . . Quod sī[103] ex tantō latrōciniō[115] iste ūnus tollētur, vidēbimur fortasse ad[116] breve quoddam tempus cūrā et metū esse relevātī;[117] perīculum autem residēbit[118] . . .

Quārē sēcēdant[119] improbī; sēcernant[120] sē ā bonīs; ūnum in locum congregentur[121]; mūrō dēnique (id quod saepe iam dīxī) sēcernantur ā nōbīs; dēsinant[122]
50  īnsidiārī[123] domī suae[124] cōnsulī, circumstāre[125] tribūnal[126] praetōris urbānī,[127] obsidēre[128] cum gladiīs cūriam,[129] malleolōs[130] et facēs[131] ad īnflammandam[132] urbem comparāre[133]; sit dēnique īnscrīptum[134] in fronte[135] ūnīus cuiusque quid dē rē pūblicā sentiat. Polliceor[136] hoc vōbīs, patrēs cōnscrīptī,[52] tantam in nōbīs cōnsulibus fore[98]

---

[86] corrōborō (1), strengthen; *cf. corroborate*
[87] quōrum = et eōrum
[88] secūtī, *partic. going with* multī
[89] improbus, -a, -um, wicked, depraved
[90] vērum etiam = sed etiam
[91] imperītus, -a, -um, inexperienced
[92] animadvertō, -ere, -vertī, -versum, notice; *with* in *+ acc.* = inflict punishment on. *This is a mixed condition of what general category?*
[93] crūdēliter, *adv. of* crūdēlis
[94] rēgiē, *adv.,* in the fashion of a king, tyrannically
[95] *Sc.* id *as subject.*
[96] intendō, -ere, -tendī, -tēnsum, intend; *parenthetical clause*
[97] per-veniō ad *or in + acc.,* arrive at, reach; pervēnerit = *perf. subjunct. for a fut. perf. indic. in a more vivid condition. For the subjunct. in a subordinate clause in ind. state., see App.*
[98] fore = futūrus, -a, -um, esse
[99] paulīsper, *adv.,* for a little while
[100] re-primō, press back, check
[101] = semper
[102] comprimō, -ere, -pressī, -pressum, suppress
[103] quod sī, but if
[104] *fut. perf. indic. What kind of condition?*
[105] suōs (virōs)
[106] eōdem, *adv.,* to the same place
[107] undique, *adv.,* from all sides
[108] colligō, -ligere, -lēgī, -lēctum, gather together
[109] naufragus, -ī, (shipwrecked) ruined man

[110] adgregō (1), gather; adgregārit = adgregāverit
[111] exstinguō, -ere, -stīnxī, -stīnctum, extinguish
[112] adultus, -a, -um, mature
[113] stirps, stirpis, *f.,* stem, stock
[114] sēmen, -inis, *n.,* seed
[115] latrōcinium, -iī, brigandage; band of brigands
[116] *here* = for
[117] relevō (1), relieve
[118] re-sideō (= sedeō), -ēre, -sēdī, -sessum, (sit down), remain
[119] sē-cēdō (sē = apart, away). *Why subjunct.?*
[120] sēcernō, -ere, -crēvī, -cretum, separate
[121] congregō (1), gather together
[122] dēsinō, -ere, -sīvī, -situm, cease
[123] īnsidior (1), plot against *+ dat.*
[124] domī suae, *loc. Catiline had tried to have Cicero assassinated.*
[125] circum-stō, -āre, -stetī, stand around, surround
[126] tribūnal, -ālis, *n.*
[127] praetor urbānus, *judicial magistrate who had charge of civil cases between Roman citizens*
[128] obsideō, -ere, -sēdī, -sessum, besiege, beset
[129] cūria, -ae, senate house
[130] malleolus, -ī, firebrand
[131] fax, facis, *f.,* torch
[132] īnflammō (1), set on fire
[133] = parāre
[134] īn-scrībō
[135] frōns, frontis, *f.,* forehead
[136] polliceor, -ērī, -licitus sum, promise

55   dīligentiam,[137] tantam in vōbīs auctōritātem,[40] tantam in equitibus[138] Rōmānīs
virtūtem, tantam in omnibus bonīs cōnsēnsiōnem,[139] ut Catilīnae profectiōne[140]
omnia patefacta, illūstrāta,[141] oppressa, vindicāta[142] esse videātis.

Hīsce[143] ōminibus,[144] Catilīna, cum summā reī pūblicae salūte,[145] cum tuā peste
ac perniciē,[146] cumque eōrum exitiō quī sē tēcum omnī scelere parricīdiōque[147]
iūnxērunt, proficīscere ad impium[148] bellum ac nefārium.[149] Tū, Iuppiter, quī
60   eīsdem[150] quibus haec urbs auspiciīs ā Rōmulō[151] es cōnstitūtus,[152] quem Statōrem[153]
huius urbis atque imperiī vērē nōmināmus,[154] hunc et huius sociōs ā tuīs cēterīsque
templīs,[155] ā tēctīs[156] urbis ac moenibus, ā vītā fortūnīsque cīvium arcēbis,[157] et
hominēs bonōrum inimīcōs,[158] hostēs patriae, latrōnēs[159] Italiae, scelerum foedere[160]
inter sē ac nefāriā societāte[161] coniūnctōs,[162] aeternīs[163] suppliciīs[164] vīvōs mortuōsque
65   mactābis.[165] (**Cicero,** *In Catilīnam Ōrātiō I,* excerpts)

## VI.  THE ARREST AND TRIAL OF THE CONSPIRATORS[1]

Rem pūblicam, Quirītēs,[2] vītamque[3] omnium vestrum, bona,[4] fortūnās, coniugēs[5]
līberōsque[6] vestrōs, atque hoc domicilium[7] clārissimī imperī, fortūnātissimam
pulcherrimamque urbem, hodiernō[8] diē deōrum immortālium summō ergā vōs
amōre, labōribus, cōnsiliīs, perīculīs meīs, ē flammā[9] atque ferrō ac paene[10] ex fau-

---

[137] dīligentia, -ae

[138] eques, equitis, *m.,* horseman, knight. *Here the* equitēs *are the wealthy business class in Rome.*

[139] cōnsēnsiō, -ōnis, *f.,* agreement, harmony

[140] profectiō, -ōnis, *f.,* departure; *cf.* profiscīscor

[141] illūstrō (1), bring to light

[142] vindicō (1), avenge, punish

[143] hīs-ce = hīs + *intensive enclitic* -ce; *abl. case with* ōminibus

[144] ōmen, ōminis, *n.,* omen: with these omens *or* with these words which I have uttered as omens, *abl. of attendant circumstance without* cum.

[145] cum . . . salūte (peste, exitiō) *abl. of attendant circumstance with* cum, *here indicating the result:* to the safety of state, to your own destruction. . . .

[146] perniciēs, -ēī, disaster, calamity

[147] parricīdium, -iī, murder

[148] impius, -a, -um, wicked, disloyal

[149] nefārius, -a, -um, infamous, nefarious

[150] eīsdem auspiciīs quibus haec urbs (cōnstitūta est); auspicia, -ōrum, auspices

[151] Rōmulus, -ī, *the founder of Rome*

[152] cōnstituō, -ere, -stituī, -stitūtum, establish

[153] Stator, -ōris, *m.,* the Stayer (of flight), the Supporter, Jupitor Stator

[154] nōminō (1), name, call (*cf.* nōmen)

[155] templum, -ī, temple

[156] tēctum, -ī, roof, house

[157] arceō, -ēre, -uī, ward off

[158] inimīcus, -ī, personal enemy; inimīcōs, hostēs, *etc. are in apposition with* hominēs.

[159] latrō, -ōnis, *m.,* robber, bandit

[160] foedus, -eris, *n.,* treaty, bond

[161] societās, -tātis, *f.,* fellowship, alliance (*cf.* socius)

[162] con (together) + iungō: coniūnctōs *modifies* latrōnēs, *etc.*

[163] aeternus, -a, -um, eternal

[164] supplicium, -iī, punishment

[165] mactō (1), punish, pursue. *The basic structure of the sent. is this:*
Tū (quī . . . es cōnstitūtus, quem . . . nōmināmus) hunc et sociōs ā templīs . . . fortūnīsque cīvium arcebis; et hominēs (inimīcōs . . . coniūnctōs) suppliciīs vīvōs mortuōsque mactābis.

### VI

[1] *Cicero here tells how, shortly after his first speech against Catiline, he secured the written evidence necessary for the trial and conviction of the conspirators.*

[2] fellow-citizens, *an old word of uncertain origin*

[3] *The Romans regularly used the sg. even when referring to a number of people; we use the pl.,* "lives."

[4] *n. pl., good things* = goods

[5] coniūnx, -iugis, *f.,* wife (*cf.* coniungō)

[6] līberī, -ōrum, children

[7] domicilium, -iī, home (*cf.* domus)

[8] hodiernus diēs, this day, today (*cf.* hodiē)

[9] flamma, -ae, flame

[10] paene, *adv.,* almost

5    cibus[11] fātī ēreptam et vōbīs cōnservātam ac restitūtam[12] vidētis[13] . . . Quae[14] quoniam in senātū illūstrāta, patefacta, comperta[15] sunt per mē, vōbīs iam expōnam breviter, Quirītēs, ut[16] et[17] quanta[18] et quā ratiōne investīgāta[19] et comprehēnsa sint, vōs, quī ignōrātis et exspectātis, scīre possītis.

     Prīncipiō, ut[20] Catilīna paucīs ante diēbus[21] ērūpit[22] ex urbe, cum sceleris suī

10    sociōs, huiusce[23] nefāriī bellī ācerrimōs ducēs, Rōmae relīquisset, semper vigilāvī[24] et prōvīdī,[25] Quirītēs, quem ad modum[26] in tantīs et tam absconditīs[27] īnsidiīs salvī esse possēmus. Nam tum cum ex urbe Catilīnam ēiciēbam (nōn enim iam vereor huius verbī invidiam, cum illa[28] magis[29] sit timenda, quod[30] vīvus exierit)—sed tum cum[31] illum exterminārī[32] volēbam, aut[33] reliquam[34] coniūrātōrum manum simul[35]

15    exitūram[36] aut eōs quī restitissent[37] īnfirmōs sine illō ac dēbilēs[38] fore[39] putābam. Atque ego, ut vīdī, quōs maximō furōre et scelere esse īnflammātōs sciēbam, eōs nōbīscum esse et Rōmae remānsisse, in eō[40] omnēs diēs noctēsque cōnsūmpsī ut quid agerent, quid mōlīrentur, sentīrem ac vidērem . . . Itaque, ut comperī lēgātōs[41] Allobrogum[42] bellī Trānsalpīnī[43] et tumultūs[44] Gallicī[45] excitandī[46] causā, ā

20    P. Lentulō[47] esse sollicitātōs,[48] eōsque in Galliam[49] ad suōs cīvēs eōdemque itinere cum litterīs mandātīsque[50] ad Catilīnam esse missōs, comitemque[51] eīs adiūnctum esse[52] T. Volturcium,[53] atque huic esse ad Catilīnam datās litterās, facultātem[54] mihi

---

[11] faucēs, -ium, *f. pl.,* jaws; a narrow passage

[12] restituō, -ere, -stituī, -stitūtum, restore

[13] *The outline of the sent. is this:* Rem pūblicam (. . . urbem) amōre deōrum (. . . perīculīs meīs) ē flammā (. . . faucibus fātī) ēreptam (. . . restitūtam) vidētis.

[14] *conjunctive use of the rel.; n. nom. pl.*

[15] comperiō, -īre, -perī, -pertum, find out

[16] *introduces* possītis

[17] et . . . et

[18] *nom. n. pl., subj. of* comprehēnsa sint

[19] investīgō (1), track out, investigate

[20] ut + *indic., here =* ever since

[21] before by a few days (*abl. of degree of difference, see S.S.*) = a few days ago; *actually some three weeks before*

[22] ērumpō, -ere, -rūpī, -ruptum, burst forth

[23] huius + ce, an intensifying suffix

[24] vigilō (1), watch, be vigilant

[25] prō-videō, foresee, make provision

[26] quem ad modum, how

[27] absconditus, -a, -um, hidden

[28] illa (invidia)

[29] *compar. of* magnopere

[30] *This clause is a noun clause in apposition with* illa (invidia). *The perf. subjunct.* (exierit) *is used in informal ind. state. indicating what people may say:* he went out alive (vīvus).

[31] tum cum, *mere repetition of* tum cum *above as Cicero starts the sent. over again.*

[32] exterminō (1), banish (ex + terminus, boundary)

[33] aut . . . exitūram (esse) aut . . . fore putābam

[34] reliquus, -a, -um, remaining, the rest of

[35] simul, *adv.,* at the same time

[36] ex-eō; exitūram (esse)

[37] restō, -āre, -stitī, stay behind, remain

[38] dēbilis, -e, helpless, weak

[39] = futūrōs esse

[40] in eō ut sentīrem et vidērem quid . . . mōlīrentur: in this that I might see . . . ; *the* ut-*clause of purpose is in apposition with* eō.

[41] lēgātus, -ī, ambassador

[42] Allobrogēs, -um, *m. pl.,* the Allobroges, *a Gallic tribe whose ambassadors had come to Rome to make complaints about certain Roman magistrates.*

[43] Trānsalpīnus, -a, -um, Transalpine

[44] tumultus, -ūs, *m.,* uprising

[45] Gallicus, -a, -um, Gallic

[46] excitō (1), excite, arouse

[47] *Publius Lentulus after having been consul in 71* B.C. *was removed from the Senate on grounds of moral turpitude. He was now one of the leading conspirators and at the same time he was holding the office of praetor.*

[48] sollicitō (1), stir up

[49] Gallia, -ae, Gaul

[50] mandātum, -ī, order, instruction

[51] comes, -itis, *m.,* companion

[52] ad-iungō

[53] Titus Volturcius, *an errand-boy for Lentulus*

[54] facultās, -tātis, *f.,* opportunity

oblātam putāvī ut—quod[55] erat difficillimum quodque ego semper optābam[56] ab dīs immortālibus—tōta rēs nōn sōlum ā mē sed etiam ā senātū et ā vōbis manifestō[57]

25  dēprehenderētur.[58]

Itaque hesternō[59] diē L. Flaccum et C. Pomptīnum praetōrēs,[60] fortissimōs atque amantissimōs[61] reī pūblicae[62] virōs, ad mē vocāvī, rem exposuī, quid fierī[63] placēret ostendī. Illī autem, quī omnia dē rē pūblicā praeclāra[64] atque ēgregia[65] sentīrent,[66] sine recūsātiōne[67] ac sine ūllā morā negōtium[68] suscēpērunt et, cum

30  advesperāsceret,[69] occultē[70] ad pontem[71] Mulvium pervēnērunt atque ibi in proximīs vīllīs[72] ita bipertītō[73] fuērunt ut Tiberis[74] inter eōs et pōns interesset.[75] Eōdem[76] autem et ipsī sine cuiusquam suspīciōne[77] multōs fortēs virōs ēdūxerant, et ego ex praefectūrā[78] Reātīnā[79] complūrēs[80] dēlēctōs[81] adulēscentēs, quōrum operā[82] ūtor assiduē[83] in rē pūblicā, praesidiō[84] cum gladiīs mīseram. Interim,[85] tertiā ferē[86]

35  vigiliā[87] exāctā, cum iam pontem Mulvium magnō comitātū[88] lēgātī Allobrogum ingredī[89] inciperent ūnāque[90] Volturcius, fit in eōs impetus[91]; ēdūcuntur[92] et ab illīs gladiī et ā nostrīs.[93] Rēs praetōribus erat nōta sōlīs, ignōrābātur ā cēterīs. Tum interventū[94] Pomptīnī atque Flaccī pugna[95] sēdātur.[96] Litterae, quaecumque[97] erant in eō comitātū, integrīs[98] signīs praetōribus trāduntur; ipsī, comprehēnsī, ad mē,

40  cum iam dīlūcēsceret,[99] dēdūcuntur. Atque hōrum omnium scelerum improbis-simum[100] māchinātōrem,[101] Cimbrum Gabīnium,[102] statim[103] ad mē nihildum[104]

---

[55] **quod**, a thing which. *The antecedent of* **quod** *is the general idea in the* **ut**-*clause*
[56] **optō** (1), desire
[57] **manifestō**, *adv.*, clearly
[58] **dēprehendō** (cf. **comprehendō**), detect, comprehend
[59] **hesternō diē**, yesterday
[60] *Though praetors were judicial magistrates, they did possess the imperium by which they could command troops.*
[61] most loving of the state = very patriotic
[62] *obj. gen.; see App.*
[63] **fierī**, *subj. of* **placēret** (it was pleasing) *used impersonally*
[64] **praeclārus, -a, -um**, noble
[65] **ēgregius, -a, -um**, excellent, distinguished
[66] *subjunct. in a characteristic clause*
[67] **recūsātiō, -ōnis**, *f.*, refusal
[68] **negōtium, -iī**, business, matter
[69] **advesperāscit, -ere, -perāvit**, *impers. inceptive*, it is approaching evening (*cf.* vespers)
[70] **occultē**, *adv.*, secretly
[71] **pōns, pontis**, *m.*, bridge; *the Mulvian bridge across the Tiber near Rome*
[72] **vīlla, -ae**, country house
[73] **bipertītō**, *adv.*, in two divisions
[74] **Tiberis, -is**, *m.*, the Tiber
[75] **inter-sum**, be between
[76] **eōdem**, *adv.*, to the same place
[77] **suspīciō, -ōnis**, *f.*, suspicion
[78] **praefectūra, -ae**, prefecture, *a city of the Roman allies governed by a Roman prefect*

[79] **Reātīnus, -a, -um**, of Reate, *a Sabine town about forty miles from Rome.*
[80] **complūrēs, -a**, *pl. adj.*, very many
[81] **dēligō, -ere, -lēgī, -lēctum**, choose, select
[82] **opera, -ae**, help; *why abl.?*
[83] **assiduē**, *adv.*, constantly
[84] **praesidiō**, as a guard, *dat. of purpose (S.S.)*
[85] **interim**, *adv.*, meanwhile
[86] **ferē**, *adv.*, about, almost; *usually follows the word it modifies*
[87] **vigilia, -ae**, watch. *The night was divided into four watches.*
[88] **comitātus, -ūs**, company, retinue. *The abl. of accompaniment may be used without* **cum** *in military expressions.*
[89] **ingredior, -gredī, -gressus sum**, enter on
[90] and together with (them)
[91] **impetus, -ūs**, attack
[92] **ēdūcuntur . . . gladiī**, swords were drawn
[93] **nostrīs** (virīs)
[94] **interventus, -ūs**, intervention
[95] **pugna, -ae**, fight
[96] **sēdō** (1), settle, stop (*not to be confused with* **sedeō**, sit)
[97] **quīcumque, quaecumque, quodcumque**, whoever, whatever
[98] **integer, -gra, -grum**, untouched, whole
[99] **dīlūcēscit, -ere, -lūxit**, it grows light, dawn comes
[100] **improbus, -a, -um**, wicked
[101] **māchinātor, -ōris**, *m.*, contriver, plotter
[102] **Cimber Gabīnius**
[103] **statim**, *adv.*, immediately
[104] **nihil-dum**, nothing yet

suspicantem,[105] vocāvī. Deinde item[106] arcessītus est[107] L. Statilius, et post eum C. Cethēgus. Tardissimē[108] autem Lentulus vēnit . . .

    Senātum frequentem[109] celeriter, ut vīdistis, coēgī. Atque intereā[110] statim ad-
45   monitū[111] Allobrogum C. Sulpicium praetōrem, fortem virum, mīsī quī ex aedibus[112] Cethēgī, sī quid tēlōrum[113] esset, efferret[114]; ex quibus[115] ille maximum sīcārum[116] numerum et gladiōrum extulit.[117]

    Intrōdūxī[118] Volturcium sine Gallīs; fidem pūblicam[119] iussū[120] senātūs dedī; hortātus sum ut ea quae scīret sine timōre indicāret.[121] Tum ille dīxit, cum vix[122]
50   sē ex magnō timōre recreāsset,[123] ā P. Lentulō sē habēre ad Catilīnam mandāta et litterās ut servōrum praesidiō ūterētur,[124] ut ad urbem quam prīmum[125] cum exercitū accēderet; id[126] autem eō cōnsiliō ut,[127] cum urbem ex[128] omnibus partibus, quem ad modum[129] discrīptum distribūtumque erat,[130] incendissent[131] caedemque[132] īnfīnītam[133] cīvium fēcissent, praestō[134] esset ille[135] quī et fugientēs exciperet[136] et sē
55   cum hīs urbānīs ducibus coniungeret.[137]

    Intrōductī autem Gallī iūs iūrandum[138] sibi et litterās ab Lentulō, Cethēgō, Statiliō ad suam gentem datās esse dīxērunt atque ita sibi ab hīs et ā L. Cassiō esse praescrīptum[139] ut equitātum[140] in Italiam quam prīmum mitterent[141] . . .

    Ac nē longum sit,[142] Quirītēs, tabellās[143] prōferrī[144] iussimus quae ā quōque

---

[105]suspicor (1), suspect

[106]item, *adv.,* likewise

[107]arcessō, -ere, -īvī, -ītum, summon

[108]tardē, *adv.,* slowly

[109]frequēns, *gen.* -entis, crowded, full

[110]intereā, *adv.,* meanwhile

[111]admonitus, -ūs, warning, suggestion

[112]aedēs, -ium, *f. pl.,* house

[113]tēlum, -ī, weapon; **tēlōrum** *is gen. of whole with* **quid:** anything of weapons = any weapons

[114]*rel. clause of purp.:* **quī = ut is**

[115]*Antecedent is* **aedibus.**

[116]sīca, -ae, dagger

[117]efferō: ex-ferō

[118]intrō-dūcō = *Eng.* introduce

[119]promise of protection in the name of the state

[120]iussus, -ūs, command

[121]indīcō (1), indicate, make known

[122]vix, *adv.,* hardly

[123]*The perf. endings in* -āvi-, -ēvi-, -ōvi- *often contract to* -ā-, -ē-, -ō-, *respectively. So here* **rēcreāvīsset** *has contracted to* **recreāsset.** *Perfs. in* -īvi- *may lose the* v *but the two resultant vowels rarely contract to* ī *except before* ss *and* st: **audīverat, audierat; audīvisse, audīsse; quaesīssent**

[124]*jussive noun clause with* **mandāta et litterās**

[125]quam prīmum, as soon as possible

[126](that he should do) this (**id**) with this plan (in mind) that . . .

[127]*The rest of the sentence can be outlined thus:* **ut (cum . . . par-**

tibus [**quem ad modum . . . distributum erat**] **incendissent et . . . fēcissent**) **praestō esset ille (quī et . . . exciperet et . . . coniungeret**)

[128]*here* in

[129]quem ad modum, as

[130]*impers. pass. verbs:* as had been marked out and assigned

[131]incendō, -ere, -cendī, -cēnsum, set fire to

[132]caedēs, -is, *f.,* slaughter

[133]īnfīnītus, -a, -um, unlimited

[134]praestō, *adv.,* on hand, ready

[135]ille = Catiline

[136]ex-cipiō, pick up, capture

[137]con + iungō. *Why are* **exciperet** *and* **coniungeret** *in the subjunct.?*

[138]iūs, iūrandum, iūris iūrandī, *n.,* oath

[139]prae-scrībō, order, direct; **esse praescrīptum,** *impers. pass.* (it had been commanded to themselves, **sibi**) *but translate as personal:* they had been directed.

[140]equitātus, -ūs, cavalry

[141]*jussive noun clause depending on* **esse praescrīptum**

[142]to be brief

[143]tabella, -ae, tablet: *very shallow trays, not unlike the modern slate, filled with wax on which writing was done with a sharp-pointed stilus. Two of these closed face to face, tied together with a string, and sealed with wax and the impression of a signet ring, were the equivalent of a modern letter in an envelope.*

[144]prō-ferō

60 dīcēbantur datae.[145] Prīmum ostendimus Cethēgō signum; cognōvit. Nōs līnum[146]
incīdimus[147]; lēgimus. Erat scrīptum ipsīus[148] manū Allobrogum senātuī et populō
sēsē[149] quae eōrum lēgātīs cōnfirmāsset[150] factūrum esse; ōrāre ut item illī facerent quae sibi eōrum lēgātī recēpissent. Tum Cethēgus (quī paulō[151] ante aliquid
tamen dē gladiīs ac sīcīs, quae apud ipsum erant dēprehēnsa,[152] respondisset dīx-
65 issetque[153] sē semper bonōrum ferrāmentōrum[154] studiōsum[155] fuisse) recitātīs litterīs dēbilitātus[156] atque abiectus[157] cōnscientiā,[158] repente conticuit.[159]

Intrōductus est Statilius; cognōvit et signum et manum suam. Recitātae sunt
tabellae in eandem ferē sententiam; cōnfessus est.

Tum ostendī tabellās Lentulō, et quaesīvī cognōsceretne signum. Adnuit[160] . . .
70 Leguntur eādem ratiōne ad senātum Allobrogum populumque litterae. Sī quid dē
hīs rēbus dīcere vellet,[161] fēcī potestātem.[162] Atque ille prīmō quidem negāvit. Post[163]
autem aliquantō,[164] tōtō iam indiciō[165] expositō atque ēditō,[166] surrēxit; quaesīvit ā
Gallīs quid sibi esset cum eīs, quam ob rem[167] domum suam vēnissent, itemque ā
Volturciō. Quī cum illī breviter cōnstanterque[168] respondissent per quem ad eum
75 quotiēnsque[169] vēnissent, quaesīssentque[170] ab eō nihilne sēcum[171] esset dē fātīs
Sibyllīnīs[172] locūtus, tum ille subitō, scelere dēmēns,[173] quanta cōnscientiae vīs esset
ostendit. Nam cum id posset īnfitiārī,[174] repente praeter opīniōnem[175] omnium
cōnfessus est . . .

Gabīnius deinde intrōductus, cum prīmō impudenter[176] respondēre coepisset,
80 ad extrēmum[177] nihil ex eīs[178] quae Gallī īnsimulābant[179] negāvit.

---

[145] datae (esse); datae *is nom. f. pl. to agree with* quae (tabellae), *the subj. of* dīcēbantur.

[146] līnum, -ī, string

[147] incīdō, -ere, -cīdī, -cīsum, cut

[148] (Cethēgī) ipsīus: *emphatic because letters were often written by an amanuensis, a slave to whom the letter was dictated.*

[149] sēsē = sē (*i.e.,* Cethegus), *subj. of* factūrum esse *and also of* ōrāre

[150] cōnfirmō (1), assert, declare; *subjunct. in ind. state.* (*see S.S.*)

[151] a little before (before by a little), *abl. of degree of difference* (*see S.S.*)

[152] dēprehendō, -ere, -hendī, -hēnsum, seize

[153] respondisset dīxissetque, *subjs. in rel. clause of characteristic, which have the force of a concessive clause* (= although)

[154] ferrāmentum, -ī, weapon

[155] studiōsus, -a, -um, fond of (*i.e.,* he was a collector.)

[156] dēbilitō (1), weaken

[157] abiectus, -a, -um, downcast

[158] cōnscientia, -ae, knowledge, conscience

[159] conticēscō, -ere, -ticuī, become silent

[160] adnuō, -ere, -nuī, nod assent

[161] vellet, *subjunct. because it is a subordinate clause in an implied ind. state. for Cicero's original words:* sī quid . . . dīcere vīs

[162] potestās, -tātis, *f.,* power, opportunity

[163] = posteā

[164] aliquantō, *abl. of degree of difference* (by somewhat) *equivalent to an adv.:* somewhat, a little

[165] indicium, -iī, evidence, information

[166] ē-dō, -ere, -didī, -ditum, give forth, publish

[167] quam ob rem = quārē

[168] constanter, *adv.,* consistently, steadily

[169] quotiēns, *adv.,* how often

[170] *contracted form, n. 122 above*

[171] sēcum: *an ind. reflexive referring to the subj. of* quaesīssent; *translate* to them.

[172] fāta Sibyllīna, *a collection of ancient prophecies for which the Romans had very high respect. By these Lentulus had sought to prove to the Allobroges that he was destined to hold the regnum and imperium at Rome.*

[173] dē-mēns, *gen.* -mentis, out of one's mind

[174] īnfitior (1), deny

[175] opīniō, -ōnis, *f.,* expectation

[176] impudenter, *adv.,* impudently

[177] ad extrēmum, at the last, finally

[178] eīs = *n. pl.,* those things

[179] īnsimulō (1), charge

Ac mihi[180] quidem, Quirītēs, cum[181] illa[182] certissima vīsa sunt argūmenta atque indicia sceleris, tabellae, signa, manūs, dēnique ūnīus cuiusque cōnfessiō,[183] tum multō[184] certiōra illa, color,[185] oculī, vultūs, taciturnitās.[186] Sīc enim obstupuerant,[187] sīc terram intuēbantur,[188] sīc fūrtim nōn numquam inter sēsē aspiciēbant ut nōn

85    iam ab aliīs indicārī[189] sed indicāre sē ipsī vidērentur.

Indiciīs expositīs atque ēditīs, Quirītēs, senātum cōnsuluī[190] dē summā rē pūblicā[191] quid fierī placēret. Dictae sunt ā prīncipibus ācerrimae ac fortissimae sententiae, quās senātus sine ūllā varietāte[192] est secūtus . . .

Quibus prō tantīs rēbus, Quirītēs, nūllum ego ā vōbīs praemium virtūtis,

90    nūllum īnsigne[193] honōris, nūllum monumentum laudis postulō[194] praeterquam[195] huius diēī memoriam sempiternam[196] . . .

Vōs, Quirītēs, quoniam iam est nox, venerātī[197] Iovem illum custōdem huius urbis ac vestrum, in vestra tēcta[198] discēdite; et ea, quamquam[199] iam est perīculum dēpulsum,[200] tamen aequē ac[201] priōre nocte custōdiīs vigiliīsque dēfendite. Id

95    nē vōbīs diūtius faciendum sit atque ut in perpetuā pāce esse possītis prōvidēbō. (**Cicero,** *In Catilīnam Ōrātiō III,* excerpts)

## DĒ VĪTĀ ET MORTE (VII–IX)

### VII.  SOCRATES' "EITHER-OR" BELIEF[1]

Quae est igitur eius ōrātiō quā[2] facit eum Platō ūsum apud iūdicēs iam morte multātum[3]?

"Magna mē," inquit "spēs tenet iūdicēs, bene mihi ēvenīre[4] quod mittar[5] ad mortem. Necesse[6] est enim sit[7] alterum dē duōbus, ut aut[8] sēnsūs omnīnō omnēs

5    mors auferat aut in alium quendam locum ex hīs locīs morte migrētur.[9] Quam ob

---

[180] *depends on* **vīsa sunt**

[181] **cum . . . tum,** not only . . . but also (*cf.* **nōn sōlum . . . sed etiam**)

[182] **illa argūmenta atque indicia** (*i.e.,* **tabellae . . . confessiō**) **certissima vīsa sunt**

[183] **cōnfessiō, -ōnis,** *f. = Eng.*

[184] *lit.* more certain by much. *What kind of abl. is* **multō?** (*see S.S.*)

[185] **color . . . taciturnitās,** *in apposition with* **illa,** *which is nom. n. pl.* **color, -ōris,** *m., = Eng.*

[186] **taciturnitās, -tātis,** *f.,* silence (*cf.* taciturn)

[187] **obstupēscō, -ere, -stupuī,** become stupefied, be thunderstruck

[188] **intueor, -ērī, -tuitus sum,** look at

[189] **indicō** (1), accuse (*cf.* **indicium,** *n. 165 above*)

[190] **cōnsulō, -ere, -suluī, -sultum,** consult, ask advice of

[191] highest interest of the state

[192] **varietās, -tātis,** *f.,* variation

[193] **īnsigne, -is,** *n.,* sign, symbol

[194] **postulō** (1), request, demand

[195] except

[196] **sempiternus, -a, -um,** eternal

[197] **veneror** (1), worship

[198] **tēctum, -ī,** roof; house

[199] **quamquam,** *conj.,* although

[200] **dēpellō,** drive off, avert

[201] equally as = just as

## VII

[1] *As part of his demonstration that death is not an evil, Cicero cites Socrates' views as given in Plato's "Apology," Socrates' defense of his life before the jury that finally condemned him to death.*

[2] **quā . . . ūsum,** which Plato represents him as using; **quā,** *abl. with the partic.* **ūsum**

[3] **multō,** (1), punish, sentence

[4] **ē-veniō,** turn out; *impers. infin. in ind. state.*

[5] *subordinate clause in ind. state.*

[6] **necesse,** *indecl. adj.,* (it is) necessary

[7] *Supply* **ut** *before* **sit:** that there be one of two possibilities, *with the* **ut . . . migrētur** *clause in apposition with* **duōbus**

[8] **aut . . . aut**

[9] **migrō** (1), depart, migrate; **migrātur** *as impers. pass.,* one departs

rem,[10] sīve[11] sēnsus exstinguitur morsque eī somnō similis est quī nōn numquam
etiam sine vīsīs[12] somniōrum[13] plācātissimam[14] quiētem adfert, dī bonī, quid lucrī
est ēmorī[15]! Aut quam multī diēs reperīrī possunt quī tālī noctī antepōnantur?
Cui sī similis futūra est[16] perpetuitās[17] omnis cōnsequentis[18] temporis, quis[19] mē
10   beātior?

"Sin[20] vēra[21] sunt quae dīcuntur, migrātiōnem[22] esse mortem in eās ōrās[23] quās
quī[24] ē vītā excessērunt[25] incolunt,[26] id multō[27] iam beātius est . . . Haec peregrīnātiō[28] mediocris vōbīs vidērī potest? Ut vērō colloquī[29] cum Orpheō, Mūsaeō,[30]
Homērō, Hēsiodō[31] liceat, quantī[32] tandem aestimātis[33]? . . . Nec enim cuiquam[34]
15   bonō malī[35] quicquam ēvenīre potest nec vīvō nec mortuō[36] . . .

"Sed tempus est iam hinc[37] abīre mē, ut moriar, vōs, ut vītam agātis. Utrum
autem sit melius, dī immortālēs sciunt; hominem quidem scīre arbitror nēminem."[38]
(**Cicero**, *Tusculānae Disputātiōnēs* 1.40.97–1.41.99, excerpts)

## VIII. A MORE POSITIVE VIEW ABOUT IMMORTALITY[1]

Artior[2] quam solēbat[3] somnus (mē) complexus est[4] . . . (et) Āfricānus sē ostendit
eā fōrmā[5] quae mihi ex imāgine[6] eius quam ex ipsō erat nōtior.[7] Quem ubi agnōvī,[8]
equidem cohorruī[9], . . . quaesīvī tamen vīveretne ipse et Paulus[10] pater et aliī quōs
nōs exstīnctōs[11] arbitrārēmur.
5   "Immō vērō," inquit, "hī vīvunt quī ē corporum vinclīs tamquam ē carcere[12]

[10] = **quārē**

[11] = **sī**

[12] **vīsum, -ī,** vision

[13] **somnium, -iī,** dream

[14] **plācātus, -a, -um,** peaceful

[15] **ē-morior,** die (off)

[16] **futūra est,** is going to be

[17] **perpetuitās, -tātis,** *f.,* perpetuity

[18] **cōn-sequor**

[19] **quis (est)**

[20] **sīn,** *conj.,* but if

[21] **(ea) sunt vēra**

[22] **migrātiō, -ōnis,** *f.,* the noun of **migrō,** *n. 9 above*

[23] **ōra, -ae,** shore, region

[24] **(eī) quī**

[25] **ex-cēdō = discēdō**

[26] **incolō, -ere, -uī,** inhabit

[27] *abl. of degree of difference (S.S.)*

[28] **peregrīnātiō, -ōnis,** *f.,* travel abroad

[29] **col-loquor,** talk with, converse (*cf.* colloquial)

[30] *Orpheus and Musaeus were famous poets and musicians before the time of Homer*

[31] *Hesiod, a Gk. epic poet chronologically next after Homer.*

[32] **quantī (pretiī),** of how much (value), *gen. of indef. value.* **quantī . . . aestimātis,** how valuable, pray, do you estimate this is?

[33] **aestimō** (1), estimate, value

[34] **quisquam, quidquam (quicquam),** anyone, anything; **cuiquam** *modified by* **bonō:** to any good man

[35] **malī** (*gen.*) *depends on* **quicquam:** anything of evil = any evil

[36] **vīvō** *and* **mortuō** *modify* **cuiquam bonō.**

[37] **hinc,** *adv.,* from this place

[38] **hominem . . . nēminem,** no man

## VIII

[1] *In these excerpts Scipio Africanus Minor (the Younger, hero of the Third Punic War in 146 B.C.) tells how the deceased Scipio Africanus Maior (the Elder, hero of the Second Punic War who defeated Hannibal in 202 B.C.) appeared to him in a dream and discoursed on the nature of life here and hereafter.*

[2] **artus, -a, -um,** deep (sleep); narrow

[3] **solēbat (esse)**

[4] **complector, -ī, -plexus sum,** embrace

[5] *abl. of description*

[6] **imāgō, -inis,** *f.,* image; *here* = portrait mask of an ancestor. *The* **imāginēs** *of a Roman patrician's ancestors were displayed in the atrium of the house.*

[7] **nōtus, -a, -um,** known, familiar

[8] **agnōscō** (*cf.* **cognōscō**), recognize

[9] **cohorrēscō, -ere, -horruī,** shudder

[10] L. Aemilius Paulus, *father of Africanus Minor*

[11] **exstīnctōs (esse): exstinguō**

[12] **carcer, -eris,** *n.,* prison

ēvolāvērunt[13]; vestra vērō quae dīcitur vīta mors est. Quīn[14] tū aspicis ad tē ve-
nientem Paulum patrem?"

Quem ut vīdī, equidem vim[15] lacrimārum prōfūdī. Ille autem mē complexus[4]
atque ōsculāns[16] flēre[17] prohibēbat. Atque ego ut prīmum[18] flētū[19] repressō[20] loquī
10  posse coepī, "Quaesō,[21]" inquam, "pater sānctissime[22] atque optime, quoniam haec
est vīta, ut Āfricānum audiō dīcere, quid moror[23] in terrīs? Quīn[24] hūc[25] ad vōs
venīre properō[26]?

"Nōn est ita,[27]" inquit ille. "Nisi enim deus is,[28] cuius hoc templum[29] est omne
quod cōnspicis,[30] istīs tē corporis custōdiīs līberāverit, hūc tibi aditus[31] patēre nōn
15  potest. Hominēs enim sunt hāc lēge[32] generātī,[33] quī tuērentur[34] illum globum[35]
quem in hōc templō medium vidēs, quae terra dīcitur, iīsque[36] animus datus est
ex illīs sempiternīs ignibus quae sīdera et stēllās vocātis . . . Quārē et tibi, Pūblī,[37]
et piīs omnibus retinendus[38] est animus in custōdiā corporis, nec iniussū[39] eius ā
quō ille[40] est vōbīs datus ex hominum vītā migrandum est, nē mūnus[41] hūmānum
20  adsignātum[42] ā deō dēfūgisse[43] videāminī . . . Iūstitiam[44] cole[45] et pietātem,[46] quae
cum sit magna[47] in parentibus et propinquīs,[48] tum[49] in patriā maxima est. Ea
vīta via est in caelum et in hunc coetum[50] eōrum quī iam vīxērunt et corpore
laxātī[51] illum incolunt locum . . . quem vōs, ut ā Grāīs accēpistis, orbem lacteum,[52]
nuncupātis.[53]" . . .

---

[13]ē-volō (1), fly away; *not to be confused with* volō, velle

[14]quīn aspicis: why, don't you see?

[15]vim = cōpiam

[16]ōsculor (1), kiss

[17]fleō, -ēre, flēvī, flētum, weep

[18]ut prīmum, as soon as

[19]flētus, -ūs, *noun of* fleō, *n. 17 above*

[20]re-primō (premō)

[21]quaesō, -ere, *commonly exclamatory:* I beg you!, pray tell!, please

[22]sānctus, -a, -um, holy

[23]moror (1), delay, wait

[24]why not?

[25]hūc, *adv.,* to this place, here

[26]properō (1), hasten

[27]= that is not the way

[28]*order* = is deus

[29]templum, -ī, sacred area, temple

[30]cuius . . . cōnspicis: whose this temple is *or* to whom belongs this temple—everything which you behold. *Apparently, as he says* hoc templum, *he makes a sweeping gesture with his arm to indicate the universe and then adds* omne quod cōnspicis *to make this even clearer.* cōnspiciō = aspiciō

[31]aditus, -ūs, approach, entrance

[32]*abl. of accordance:* in accordance with this law, on this condition

[33]generō (1), create

[34]tueor, -ērī, tūtus sum, watch, protect. *Why subjunct.?*

[35]globus, -ī, sphere, globe

[36]*i.e.,* hominibus

[37]Pūblius, praenomen ( *first name*) *of Africanus Minor*

[38]re-tineō, retain, preserve

[39]iniussū, *abl. as adv.,* without the command (of); *cf.* iussū

[40]ille (animus)

[41]mūnus, -eris, *n.,* duty, service

[42]adsignō (1), assign

[43]dē-fūgiō, flee from, avoid

[44]iūstitia, -ae, justice (*cf.* iūstus)

[45]colō, -ere, -uī, cultum, cultivate, cherish

[46]pietās, -tātis, *f.,* loyalty, devotion

[47]important

[48]propinquus, -ī, relative

[49]*here* = surely

[50]coetus, -ūs, gathering, company

[51]laxō (1), set free

[52]orbis (-is) lacteus (-ī), *m.,* the Milky Way (orb), *which Cicero here says is a term received from the Greeks (* ut ā Grāīs, *i.e.* Graecīs, accēpistis), *who called it* galaxias kyklos (= lacteus orbis); *cf. our word* galaxy.

[53]nuncupō (1) = appellō

25       Et ille, "Tū vērō . . . sīc habētō[54] nōn esse tē mortālem, sed corpus hoc[55]; nec enim tuīs[56] es quem fōrma ista dēclārat,[57] sed mēns cuiusque is est quisque, nōn ea figūra[58] quae digitō dēmōnstrārī potest. Deum tē igitur scītō[59] esse; sīquidem[60] deus est quī viget,[61] quī sentit, quī meminit,[62] quī prōvidet, quī tam regit et moderātur[63] et movet id corpus cui praepositus est[64] quam[65] hunc mundum ille prīnceps deus."[66] (**Cicero**, excerpts from *Somnium Scīpiōnis* 2ff. = *Dē Rē Pūblicā* 6.10 ff.)

## IX. ON CONTEMPT OF DEATH[1]

Sed quid[2] ducēs et prīncipēs nōminem[3] cum legiōnēs[4] scrībat Catō[5] saepe alacrēs[6] in eum locum profectās[7] unde reditūrās sē nōn arbitrārentur? Parī animō Lacedaemoniī[8] in Thermopylīs[9] occidērunt, in quōs[10] Simōnidēs:

      Dīc, hospes,[11] Spartae[12] nōs tē[13] hīc vīdisse iacentīs,[14]
5       dum sānctīs patriae lēgibus obsequimur.[15]

      Virōs commemorō.[16] Quālis[17] tandem Lacaena? Quae, cum fīlium in proelium mīsisset et interfectum[18] audīsset, "Idcircō,[19]" inquit, "genueram[20] ut esset quī[21] prō patriā mortem nōn dubitāret occumbere.[22]"

      . . . Admoneor[23] ut aliquid etiam dē humātiōne[24] et sepultūrā[25] dīcendum[26]
10 exīstimem[27] . . . Sōcratēs, rogātus ā Critōne[28] quem ad modum sepelīrī[29] vellet, "Multam vērō," inquit, "operam,[30] amīcī, frūstrā[31] cōnsūmpsī. Critōnī enim nostrō

---

[54]**habētō**, *fut. imperat.*, you shall consider; consider
[55]*sc.* esse **mortāle**
[56]**tuīs**, to your (friends), *dat. depending on* **dēclārat**
[57]**dēclārō** (1) = *Eng.*
[58]= **fōrma**
[59]**scītō**, *another fut. imperat.*, you shall know; know
[60]**sīquidem**, *conj.*, since
[61]**vigeō** -**ēre**, -**uī** be strong, be active
[62]**meminī, meminisse**, *defective, found only in perf. system*, remember
[63]**moderor** (1), control
[64]**prae-pōnō**, put in charge of
[65]as
[66]*From the preceding clause sc.* **regit**, *etc. as verbs*

## IX
[1]*If death is such a great evil, how can the following attitudes be explained?*
[2]**quid**, *as adv.*, why? (= **cūr**?)
[3]**nōminō** (1), name, mention (*cf.* **nōmen**)
[4]**legiō**, -**ōnis**, *f.*, legion
[5]**Catō**, -**ōnis**, *m.*, Cato, *the famous censor, who wrote a now-lost history of Rome called the Origines.*
[6]**alacer**, -**cris**, -**cre**, eager, happy. *We should use an adv. instead of a pred. adj.*: eagerly
[7]**profectās** (esse); **reditūrās** (esse)

[8]**Lacedaemoniī**, -**ōrum**, *m.*, Spartans
[9]**Thermopylae**, -**ārum**; *480* B.C.
[10]on whom Simonides (wrote); *Simonides a 6th-cent. Gk. poet famous esp. for his poems and epigrams in the elegiac couplet.*
[11]**hospes**, -**itis**, *m.*, stranger
[12]**Sparta**, -**ae**, *f.*, **Spartae**, *dat. depending on* **dīc**
[13]**tē vīdisse nōs**
[14]= **iacentēs**
[15]**ob-sequor** + *dat.*, obey
[16]**commemorō** (1), call to mind mention (*cf.* **memoria**)
[17]What kind of person, then, was the Spartan woman? **quālis**, -**e**, what kind of
[18](eum) interfectum (esse)
[19]**idcircō**, *adv.*, for that reason
[20]**gignō**, -**ere**, **genuī**, **genitum**, beget (*cf.* generate), bear
[21](the kind of person) who
[22]**occumbō**, -**ere**, -**cubuī**, -**cubitum**, meet
[23]**ad-moneō** = **moneō**, remind
[24]**humātiō**, -**ōnis**, *f.*, burial (*cf.* **humus**, earth)
[25]**sepultūra**, -**ae**, funeral (*cf.* sepulchre)
[26]**dīcendum** (esse)
[27]**exīstimō** (1), think
[28]**Critō**, -**ōnis**, *m.*, Crito, *a friend of Socrates*
[29]**sepeliō**, -**īre**, -**īvī**, -**pultum**, bury
[30]**opera**, -**ae**, effort, pains
[31]**frūstrā**, *adv.*, in vain (*cf.* frustrate)

nōn persuāsī mē hinc āvolātūrum,[32] neque meī[33] quicquam relictūrum[34] . . . Sed, mihi crēde, (Critō), nēmō mē vestrum,[35] cum hinc excesserō,[36] cōnsequētur.[37] . . .

Dūrior Diogenēs[38] Cynicus prōicī[39] sē iussit inhumātum.[40] Tum amīcī, "Vo-
15 lucribusne[41] et ferīs[42]?" "Minimē[43] vērō," inquit; "sed bacillum[44] propter[45] mē, quō abigam,[46] pōnitōte.[47]" "Quī[48] poteris?" illī; "nōn enim sentiēs." "Quid igitur mihi ferārum laniātus[49] oberit[50] nihil sentientī[51]?" (**Cicero,** *Tusculānae Disputātiōnēs* 1.42.101–43.104, excerpts)

## X. LITERATURE: ITS VALUE AND DELIGHT[1]

Quaerēs ā nōbīs, Grattī, cūr tantō opere[2] hōc homine dēlectēmur.[3] Quia[4] suppe-
ditat[5] nōbīs ubi[6] et animus ex hōc forēnsī[7] strepitū[8] reficiātur[9] et aurēs convīciō[10] dēfessae[11] conquiēscant[12] . . . Quārē quis tandem mē reprehendat,[13] aut quis mihi iūre[14] suscēnseat,[15] sī,[16] quantum[17] cēterīs ad suās rēs obeundās[18] quantum ad fēstōs[19]
5 diēs lūdōrum celebrandōs,[20] quantum ad aliās voluptātēs et ad ipsam requiem[21] animī et corporis concēditur[22] temporum, quantum aliī tribuunt[23] tempestīvīs[24]

---

[32]ā-volō (1); avolātūrum (esse), *infin. in ind. state. with* **persuāsī**
[33]meī, *gen. of* ego, *depending on* **quicquam**.
[34]relictūrum (esse)
[35]*gen. of* vōs
[36]ex-cēdō, *cf.* discēdō
[37]cōnsequor, -ī, -secūtus sum, overtake, catch
[38]*Diogenes, the Cynic philosopher, famed for his asceticism and in-dependence*
[39]prō-iciō (iaciō), throw out
[40]inhumātus, -a, -um, unburied
[41]volucris, -is, *f.,* bird
[42]fera, -ae, wild beast; *dat. with* prōicī *understood*
[43]minimē, *adv.,* no, not at all
[44]bacillum, -ī, staff (*cf.* bacillus, *a New Latin form*)
[45]*here* = near
[46]abigō, -ere, -ēgī, -āctum, drive away; *sc.* volucrēs et ferās. *Why subjunct.?*
[47]*fut. imperat.* = you shall put
[48]quī, *adv.,* how?
[49]laniātus, -ūs, lacerating
[50]obsum, -esse, -fuī, -futūrus, be against, hurt. *Why does* oberit *have the dat.* mihi?
[51]sentientī *modifies* mihi *and has* nihil *as its obj.*

## X
[1]*In the course of a speech defending the citizenship of the poet Archias against the charges of a certain Grattius, Cicero pronounced one of the world's finest encomiums on the inestimable value and delight of literature.*
[2]**tantō opere,** so greatly (*cf.* **magnopere**)
[3]**homine,** *the poet Archias.*
[4]**quia,** *conj.,* because
[5]**suppeditō** (1), supply

[6]the means by which
[7]forēnsis, -e, of the forum. *By Cicero's time the Forum was primarily the political and legal center of Rome.*
[8]strepitus, -ūs, din
[9]re-ficiō, refresh, revive
[10]convīcium, -iī, wrangling
[11]dēfessus, -a, -um, exhausted
[12]conquiēscō, -ere, -quiēvī, -quiētum, find rest
[13]reprehendō, -ere, -hendī, -hēnsum, censure; reprehendat, *deliberative, or dubitative, subjunct. The deliberative subjunct. is used in questions implying doubt, indignation, or impossibility.* **Quis mē reprehendat:** who is to blame me (I wonder)?
[14]iūre = cum iūre, *abl. of manner that has virtually become an adv.:* rightly
[15]suscēnseō, -ēre, -uī, be incensed, + *dat.*
[16]sī *introduces* sūmpserō. *The only real difficulty with this complex clause is the involvement of the* quantum *clauses. Although these clauses should be read and understood in the order in which they stand, the following outline may prove a welcome guide.* **Quis mē reprehendat . . . sī ego tantum temporum ad haec studia sūmpserō quantum temporum cēterīs ad suās rēs (fēstōs diēs, voluptātēs, etc.) concēditur, quantum temporum aliī tribuunt convīviīs (alveolō pilae)?**
[17]quantum (temporum)
[18]ob-eō, attend to
[19]fēstus, -a, -um, festive
[20]celebrō (1), celebrate
[21]requiēs, -ētis, *acc.* requiētem *or* requiem, rest
[22]concēdō, grant, concede
[23]tribuō, -ere, -uī, -ūtum, allot
[24]tempestīvus, -a, -um, timely; *here* = early, *beginning in the afternoon so as to be conveniently prolonged.*

convīviīs,[25] quantum dēnique alveolō,[26] quantum pilae,[27] tantum[28] mihi egomet[29] ad haec studia recolenda[30] sūmpserō[31]? Atque hoc ideō[32] mihi concēdendum est magis quod ex hīs studiīs haec quoque crēscit ōrātiō et facultās,[33] quae, quantacumque[34]
10   est in mē, numquam amīcōrum perīculīs dēfuit[35] . . .

Plēnī omnēs sunt librī, plēnae sapientium vōcēs, plēna exemplōrum[36] vetustās[37]; quae iacērent in tenebrīs[38] omnia, nisi litterārum lūmen[39] accēderet. Quam multās nōbīs imāginēs[40]—nōn sōlum ad intuendum,[41] vērum[42] etiam ad imitandum[43]— fortissimōrum virōrum expressās[44] scrīptōrēs et Graecī et Latīnī reliquērunt! Quās
15   ego mihi semper in admīnistrandā[45] rē pūblicā prōpōnēns[46] animum et mentem meam ipsā cōgitātiōne[47] hominum excellentium[48] cōnfōrmābam.[49]

Quaeret quispiam,[50] "Quid? illī ipsī summī virī quōrum virtūtēs litterīs prōditae sunt,[51] istāne doctrīnā[52] quam tū effers[53] laudibus ērudītī fuērunt[54]?" Difficile est hoc dē omnibus cōnfirmāre,[55] sed tamen est certum quid respondeam . . . : sae-
20   pius ad laudem atque virtūtem nātūram sine doctrīnā quam sine nātūrā valuisse[56] doctrīnam. Atque īdem[57] ego contendō,[58] cum ad nātūram eximiam[59] et illūstrem[60] accesserit[61] ratiō quaedam cōnfōrmātiōque[62] doctrīnae, tum illud nesciō quid[63] praeclārum ac singulāre[64] solēre exsistere[65] . . .

Quod sī nōn hic tantus frūctus ostenderētur, et sī ex hīs studiīs dēlectātiō
25   sōla peterētur, tamen, ut opīnor, hanc animī remissiōnem hūmānissimam ac līberālissimam iūdicārētis. Nam cēterae[66] neque temporum[67] sunt neque aetātum omnium neque locōrum; at haec studia adulēscentiam alunt, senectūtem oblectant,

---

[25]**convīvium, -iī,** banquet

[26]**alveolus, -ī,** gaming board

[27]**pila, -ae,** ball (*cf.* pill)

[28]**tantum (temporum) . . . quantum,** as much . . . as

[29]**ego-met,** *an emphatic form of* **ego**

[30]**re-colō, -ere, -uī, -cultum,** renew

[31]**sūmō, -ere, sūmpsī, sūmptum,** take

[32]**ideō,** *adv.,* for this reason, therefore

[33]**facultās, -tātis,** *f.,* skill. *Combine with* **ōrātiō** *and translate:* this oratorical skill.

[34]**quantuscumque, -acumque, -umcumque,** however great

[35]**dē-sum,** be lacking

[36]**exemplum, -ī,** example; **exemplōrum** *also goes with* **plēnī** *and* **plēnae.**

[37]**vetustās, -tātis,** *f.,* antiquity

[38]**tenebrae, -ārum,** darkness

[39]**lūmen, -inis,** *n.,* light

[40]**imāgō, -ginis,** *f.,* portrait, picture

[41]**intueor,** gaze on, contemplate

[42]**vērum,** *conj.,* but

[43]**imitor (1),** imitate

[44]**ex-primō (premō),** describe, portray

[45]**administrō (1),** manage

[46]**prō-pōnō,** put forward, set before; **prōpōnēns** *has* **quās** *as dir. obj. and* **mihi** *as ind. obj.*

[47]**cōgitātiō, -ōnis,** *f.,* thought; *cf.* **cōgitō**

[48]**excellēns,** *gen.* **-entis,** superior, remarkable

[49]**cōnfōrmō (1),** mold

[50]**quispiam, quaepiam, quidpiam,** someone

[51]**prōdō, -ere, -didī, -ditum,** transmit, reveal

[52]**doctrīna, -ae,** instruction

[53]**efferō, -ferre, extulī, ēlātum,** lift up, extol

[54]**ērudiō (4),** educate, train

[55]**cōnfirmō (1),** assert

[56]**valuisse ad laudem,** to be powerful toward praise = to have led to praise; *infin. in ind. state.*

[57]**idem ego,** I the same person = I also

[58]maintain

[59]**eximius, -a, -um,** extraordinary

[60]**illustris, -e,** noble, brilliant

[61]**accēdō** *here* = be added

[62]**cōnfōrmātiō, -ōnis,** *f.,* molding, shaping

[63]**nesciō quis, nesciō quid,** *indef. pron., lit.* I know not who/what = some (uncertain) person *or* thing; *the* **nesciō** *remains unchanged in this phrase.*

[64]**singulāris, -e,** unique, extraordinary

[65]**exsistō, -ere, -stitī,** arise, appear, exist

[66]**cēterae (remissiōnēs** *or* **dēlectātiōnēs)**

[67]*gen. of possession used in pred. = pred. gen.; sc.* **omnium** *with each gen.: the other delights do not belong to all times . . .*

rēs secundās ōrnant, adversīs perfugium ac sōlācium praebent, dēlectant domī, nōn impediunt forīs, pernoctant nōbīscum, peregrīnantur, rūsticantur. (**Cicero,** *Prō Archiā* 6.12–7.16, excerpts).

## ANECDOTES FROM CICERO (11–15)

### XI. DEATH OF A PUPPY (EXAMPLE OF AN OMEN)

L. Paulus[1] cōnsul iterum, cum eī[2] bellum[3] ut cum rēge Perse[4] gereret[5] obtigisset,[6] ut eā ipsā diē domum ad vesperum rediit, fīliolam[7] suam Tertiam,[8] quae tum erat admodum[9] parva, ōsculāns[10] animadvertit[11] trīsticulam.[12] "Quid est,[13]" inquit, "mea Tertia? Quid[14] trīstis es?" "Mī pater," inquit, "Persa[15] periit." Tum ille artius[16] puel-
5 lam complexus,[17] "Accipiō," inquit, "mea fīlia, ōmen.[18]" Erat autem mortuus catel-lus[19] eō nōmine. (**Cicero,** *Dē Dīvīnātiōne* 1.46.103)

### XII. TOO CONSCIENTIOUS (AN EXAMPLE OF IRONY)

Est huic fīnitimum[1] dissimulātiōnī[2] cum honestō[3] verbō vitiōsa[4] rēs appellātur: ut cum Āfricānus cēnsor[5] tribū[6] movēbat eum centuriōnem[7] quī in Paulī pugnā[8] nōn adfuerat,[9] cum ille sē custōdiae causā dīceret in castrīs[10] remānsisse quaereretque cūr ab eō notārētur[11]: "Nōn amō," inquit, "nimium dīligentēs." (**Cicero,** *Dē Ōrātōre* 2.67.272)

---

**XI**

[1] *L. Aemilius Paulus Macedonicus was the father of Scipio Afri-canus Minor. As consul in 168 B.C. he brought the war with Macedonia to a successful conclusion by the defeat of the Mac-edonian King, Perseus. This explains why, before setting out against Perseus, he interpreted the chance words* **Persa periit** *as a favorable omen. The Romans believed seriously in the im-portance of omens.*

[2] *dat. with* **obtigisset**

[3] *obj. of* **gereret**

[4] **Perseus, -eī; Perse** *abl.*

[5] **ut . . . gereret,** *noun clause subj. of* **obtigisset**

[6] **obtingō, -ere, -tigī,** touch, fall to one's lot

[7] **fīli (a)** *with the diminutive ending* **-ola,** little daughter

[8] **Tertia,** *a name meaning* third. *The Romans often used ordinal numerals as names, though commonly without strict regard to the number of children they had; e.g.,* **Secundus, Quīntus, Sextus, Decimus.**

[9] **admodum,** *adv.,* very

[10] **ōsculor (1),** kiss

[11] **anim-ad-vertō,** turn the mind to, notice, observe

[12] **trīsticulus, -a, -um,** rather sad, *diminutive of* **tristis**

[13] What is it? What is the matter?

[14] **quid = cūr**

[15] **Persa,** *the name of her pet*

[16] **artius,** *adv.,* closely

[17] **complector, -ī, -plexus sum,** embrace

[18] **ōmen, -inis,** *n.,* omen, sign; *i.e., the omen of his victory over Perseus*

[19] **catellus, -ī,** puppy

**XII**

[1] **fīnitimus, -a, -um,** neighboring; akin to: **est fīnitinum,** it is akin to

[2] **dissimulātiō, -ōnis,** *f.,* irony

[3] **honestus, -a, -um,** honorable, fine

[4] **vitiōsus, -a, -um,** faulty, bad

[5] **cēnsor, -ōris,** *m.,* censor, *Roman magistrate among whose duties was the assigning of citizens to their proper rank according to their property and service and the removal of names from the census rolls when citizens proved unworthy of citizenship.*

[6] **tribus, -ūs,** *f.,* tribe, *a political division of the Roman people*

[7] **centuriō, -ōnis,** *m.,* centurion

[8] **pugna, -ae,** battle

[9] **ad-sum,** be present

[10] **castra, -ōrum,** camp

[11] **notō (1),** mark, *here with the* **nota cēnsōria** *placed opposite a citizen's name to indicate his removal from the citizen list in disgrace.*

## XIII. QUAM MULTA NŌN DĒSĪDERŌ!

Sōcratēs, in pompā[1] cum magna vīs[2] aurī[3] argentīque[4] ferrētur, "Quam multa nōn dēsīderō!" inquit.

Xenocratēs,[5] cum lēgātī ab Alexandrō[6] quīnquāgintā[7] eī talenta[8] attulissent (quae erat pecūnia temporibus illīs, Athēnīs praesertim,[9] maxima), abdūxit lēgātōs
5   ad cēnam in Acadēmīam[10]; iīs apposuit[11] tantum quod satis esset, nūllō apparātū.[12] Cum postrīdiē[13] rogārent eum cui numerārī[14] iubēret, "Quid? Vōs hesternā,[15]" inquit, "cēnulā[16] nōn intellēxistis mē pecūniā nōn egēre?" Quōs cum trīstiōrēs vīdisset, trīgintā[17] minās[18] accēpit nē aspernārī[19] rēgis līberālitātem[20] vidērētur.

At vērō Diogenēs[21] līberius,[22] ut[23] Cynicus, Alexandrō rogantī ut dīceret sī quid
10   opus[24] esset: "Nunc quidem paululum,[25]" inquit, "ā sōle.[26]" Offēcerat[27] vidēlicet[28] aprīcantī.[29] (**Cicero**, *Tusculānae Disputātiōnēs* 5.32.91–92)

## XIV. WHAT MAKES A GOOD APPETITE

Dārēus[1] in fugā[2] cum aquam turbidam[3] et cadāveribus[4] inquinātam[5] bibisset, negāvit umquam sē bibisse iūcundius. Numquam vidēlicet sitiēns[6] biberat. Nec ēsuriēns[7] Ptolemaeus[8] ēderat,[9] cui cum peragrantī[10] Aegyptum,[11] comitibus[12] nōn cōnsecūtīs[13] cibārius[14] in casā pānis datus esset, nihil vīsum est illō pāne iūcundius.
5   Sōcratem ferunt,[15] cum usque ad vesperum contentius[16] ambulāret quaesītumque

**XIII**

[1]**pompa, -ae,** parade
[2]**vīs** here = quantity (*cf.* **cōpia**)
[3]**aurum, -ī,** gold
[4]**argentum, -ī,** silver
[5]**Xenocratēs, -is,** *pupil of Plato and later head of the Academy*
[6]**Alexander, -drī**
[7]*indecl. adj.,* fifty
[8]**talentum, -ī,** a talent, a large sum of money
[9]**praesertim,** *adv.,* especially
[10]**Acadēmīa, -ae,** the Academy, *a gymnasium in a grove just outside of Athens. Here Plato established his school, which might be called the first European university.*
[11]**ap-pōnō,** place near, serve
[12]**apparātus, -ūs,** equipment, splendor
[13]**postrīdiē,** *adv.,* on the next day
[14]**numerō** (1), count, pay out; *sc.* **pecūniam** *as subj. of* **numerārī**
[15]**hesternus, -a, -um,** of yesterday
[16]**cēnula, -ae,** diminutive of **cēna**
[17]*indecl. adj.,* thirty
[18]**mina, -ae,** a Greek coin
[19]**aspernor** (1), spurn, despise
[20]**līberālitās, -tātis,** *f.,* generosity
[21]*Locī Im. IX n. 38*
[22]**līberius,** *adv.,* freely, boldly
[23]as a Cynic, being a Cynic

[24]**opus** (*indecl.*) **est,** is necessary: if he needed anything
[25]**paululum,** *adv.,* a little
[26]*i.e.,* you are blocking my sunlight
[27]**officiō, -ere, -fēcī, -fectum** + *dat.,* be in the way, obstruct
[28]**vidē-licet,** *adv.* (you may see), clearly, evidently
[29]**aprīcor** (1), sun oneself

**XIV**

[1]*Darius III, defeated by Alexander the Great in 331 B.C. The spelling* **Dārīus** *reflects later Gk. pronunciation.*
[2]**fuga, -ae,** flight
[3]**turbidus, -a, -um,** turbid, roiled
[4]**cadāver, -eris,** *n.,* corpse (*cf.* cadaverous)
[5]**inquinātus, -a, -um,** polluted
[6]**sitiō** (4), be thirsty
[7]**ēsuriō** (4), be hungry
[8]*Which Egyptian king of this name is unknown.*
[9]**edō, -ere, ēdī, ēsum,** eat (*cf.* edible)
[10]**per-agrō** (1), wander through
[11]**Aegyptus, -ī,** *f.,* Egypt
[12]**comes, -itis,** *m.,* companion
[13]**cōn-sequor**
[14]**cibārius . . . pānis,** ordinary (coarse) bread; **pānis, -is,** *m.*
[15]**ferō** *here* = report, say
[16]**contentē,** strenuously, *adv. from* **contendō,** struggle

esset[17] ex eō quārē id faceret, respondisse sē, quō[18] melius cēnāret, obsōnāre[19] ambulandō famem.[20]

Quid? Vīctum[21] Lacedaemoniōrum in philitiīs[22] nōnne vidēmus? Ubi[23] cum tyrannus cēnāvisset Dionȳsius, negāvit sē iūre[24] illō nigrō quod cēnae[25] caput erat
10  dēlectātum.[26] Tum is quī illa coxerat,[27] "Minimē mīrum[28]; condīmenta[29] enim dēfuērunt.[30]" "Quae tandem?" inquit ille. "Labor in vēnātū,[31] sūdor,[32] cursus ad Eurōtam,[33] famēs, sitis.[34] Hīs enim rēbus Lacedaemoniōrum epulae[35] condiuntur.[36]"

Cōnfer sūdantēs,[37] ructantēs,[38] refertōs[39] epulīs tamquam opīmōs bovēs.[40] Tum intellegēs quī voluptātem maximē sequantur, eōs minimē cōnsequī[41]; iūcundi-
15  tātemque[42] vīctūs[43] esse in dēsīderiō,[44] nōn in satietāte.[45] (**Cicero,** *Tusculānae Disputātiōnēs* 5.34.97–98 and 100, excerpts)

## XV. THEMISTOCLES; FAME AND EXPEDIENCY

Themistoclēs fertur[1] Serīphiō[2] cuidam in iūrgiō[3] respondisse, cum ille dīxisset nōn eum suā sed patriae glōriā splendōrem[4] assecūtum[5]: "Nec hercule,[6]" inquit, "sī ego Serīphius essem, nec tū, sī Athēniēnsis[7] essēs, clārus umquam fuissēs." (**Cicero,** *Dē Senectūte,* 3.8)
5  Themistoclēs, post victōriam eius bellī quod cum Persīs[8] fuit, dīxit in cōntiōne[9] sē habēre cōnsilium reī pūblicae salūtāre,[10] sed id scīrī nōn opus esse.[11] Postulāvit[12] ut aliquem populus daret quīcum[13] commūnicāret.[14] Datus est Aristīdēs.

---

[17] it had been asked of him, he had been asked
[18] **quō,** *regularly used instead of* **ut** *to introduce a purp. containing a compar.*
[19] **obsōnō** (1), buy provisions, *here* = provide (an appetite)
[20] **famēs, -is,** *f.,* hunger
[21] **vīctus, -ūs,** living, mode of living, food
[22] **philitia, -ōrum,** public meals (*for Spartan citizens of military age*)
[23] **ubi** = *among the Lacedaemonians*
[24] **iūs, iūris,** *n.,* soup
[25] *dat. of purp.* (S.S.)
[26] **dēlectātum (esse)**
[27] **coquō, -ere, coxī, coctum,** cook (*cf.* concoct)
[28] **mīrus, -a, -um,** wonderful, surprising
[29] **condīmentum, -ī,** seasoning, condiment
[30] **dē-sum,** be lacking
[31] **vēnātus, -ūs,** hunting
[32] **sūdor, -ōris,** *m.,* sweat
[33] at the Eurotas (**Eurōtās, -ae,** *m., river on which Sparta was located*)
[34] **sitis, -is,** *f.,* thirst
[35] **epulae, -ārum,** banquet
[36] **condiō** (4), season, spice
[37] **sūdō** (1), sweat
[38] **ructō** (1), belch
[39] **refertus, -a, -um,** stuffed, crammed, + *abl.*

[40] **opīmus, -a, -um,** fertile, fat; **bōs, bovis,** *m.,* ox
[41] **cōn-sequor,** follow up, gain
[42] **iūcunditās, -tātis,** *f.,* pleasure, charm
[43] *n. 21 above; here* = food
[44] **dēsīderium, -iī,** desire
[45] **satietās, -tātis,** *f.,* abundance, satisfy

### XV

(*For more about Themistocles and Aristides see selections 19 and 20 below.*)
[1] is said, is reported
[2] **Serīphius, -iī,** *inhabitant of Seriphos, a small island in the Aegean Sea.*
[3] **iūrgium, -iī,** quarrel
[4] **splendor, -ōris,** *m.,* distinction, honor
[5] **as-sequor** = **ad-sequor,** gain, attain
[6] **hercule,** *a mild oath,* by Hercules
[7] **Athēniēnsis, -e,** Athenian
[8] **Persae, -ārum,** *m.,* the Persians
[9] **cōntiō, -ōnis,** *f.,* assembly
[10] **salūtāris, -e,** salutary, advantageous; *modifies* **cōnsilium**
[11] **opus est,** it is necessary
[12] **postulō** (1), demand, request
[13] **quīcum, quī** = *old abl. form* + **cum,** with whom
[14] **commūnicō** (1), communicate, share

Huic[15] ille (dixit) classem[16] Lacedaemoniōrum, quae subducta esset[17] ad Gythēum,[18] clam[19] incendī[20] posse, quō factō frangī[21] Lacedaemoniōrum opēs necesse esset.[22]

10  Quod Aristīdēs cum audīsset, in cōntiōnem magnā exspectātiōne[23] vēnit dīxitque perūtile[24] esse cōnsilium quod Themistoclēs adferret, sed minimē honestum. Itaque Athēniēnsēs, quod honestum nōn esset, id nē ūtile quidem putāvērunt, tōtamque eam rem, quam nē audierant quidem, auctōre Aristīde[25] repudiāvērunt.[26] (**Cicero,** *Dē Officiīs* 3.11.48–49)

## XVI.  GET THE TUSCULAN COUNTRY HOUSE READY[1]

Tullius[2] S.D.[3] Terentiae[4] Suae

In Tusculānum[5] nōs ventūrōs[6] putāmus aut Nōnīs[7] aut postrīdiē.[8] Ibi ut[9] sint omnia parāta. Plūrēs[10] enim fortasse[11] nōbīscum erunt et, ut arbitror, diūtius ibi commorābimur.[12] Lābrum[13] sī in balneō[14] nōn est, ut[15] sit; item[16] cētera quae sunt

5  ad vīctum et ad valētūdinem[17] necessāria.[18] Valē. Kal. Oct.[19] dē Venusīnō.[20] (**Cicero,** *Epistulae ad Familiārēs* 14.20)

## XVII.  LIVY ON THE DEATH OF CICERO[1]

M. Cicerō sub adventum[2] triumvirōrum[3] cesserat urbe . . . Prīmō in Tusculānum[4] fūgit; inde trānsversīs[5] itineribus in Formiānum,[6] ut ab Caiētā[7] nāvem cōnscēn-

---

[15]**huic** = *the last mentioned, Aristides*
[16]**classis, -is,** *f.,* fleet
[17]**sub-dūcō,** beach; *subjunct. because subordinate clause in ind. state. (see S.S.). Because of their shallow draft and small size, ancient ships were more often beached than anchored.*
[18]**Gythēum, -ī,** *the port of Sparta*
[19]**clam,** *adv.,* secretly
[20]**incendō, -ere, -cendī, -cēnsum,** set on fire, burn
[21]**frangō, -ere, frēgī, frāctum,** break, crush
[22]**necesse** (*indecl. adj.*) **est,** it is necessary
[23]**exspectātiō, -ōnis,** *f.,* expectation, *abl. of attendant circumstance*
[24]**per-ūtilis, -e,** very useful, advantageous
[25]**auctōre Aristīde,** *abl. abs.*
[26]**repudiō** (1), reject

[8]**postrīdiē,** *adv.,* the day after
[9](**cūrā**) **ut,** take care that
[10]**plūrēs,** several people
[11]**fortasse,** *adv.,* perhaps
[12]**com-moror** (1), remain
[13]**lābrum, -ī,** a wash basin or a bath
[14]**balneum, -ī,** bathroom
[15](**cūrā**) **ut**
[16]**item,** *adv.,* likewise
[17]**valētūdō, -inis,** *f.,* health
[18]**necessārius, -a, -um** = *Eng.*
[19]**Kalendīs Octōbribus,** on the Kalends of October = October 1st
[20]*Sent from his estate at Venusia, in Apulia. The year is said to be 47* B.C.

### XVI
[1]*A homely little letter which serves as an antidote to Cicero's usually lofty concerns.*
[2](**Mārcus**) **Tullius** (**Cicerō**)
[3]**salūtem dīcit**
[4]**Terentia, -ae,** wife of Cicero
[5]**Tusculānum, -ī,** Tusculan estate (**praedium**) *southeast of Rome in Latium*
[6]**ventūrōs** (**esse**)
[7]**Nōnae, -ārum,** the Nones *were the seventh day in March, May, July, October; the fifth day in other months.*

### XVII
[1]*In 43* B.C.
[2]**adventus, -ūs,** arrival
[3]**triumvirī, -ōrum,** commission of three men, *the second triumvirate composed of Antony, Octavian, and Lepidus*
[4]his Tusculan villa
[5]**trānsversus, -a, -um,** transverse, crosswise
[6]**Formiānum, -ī,** estate near Formiae, *which was nearly 100 miles south of Rome on the Appian Way near the sea*
[7]**Caiēta, -ae,** *a sea-coast town not far from Formiae*

sūrus,[8] proficīscitur. Unde aliquotiēns[9] in altum[10] provectum,[11] cum modo ventī adversī rettulissent, modo ipse iactātiōnem[12] nāvis ... patī nōn posset, taedium[13]

5      tandem eum et fugae[14] et vītae cēpit, regressusque[15] ad superiōrem vīllam ... "Moriar," inquit, "in patriā saepe servātā." Satis cōnstat[16] servōs fortiter fidēliterque parātōs fuisse ad dīmicandum,[17] ipsum dēpōnī lectīcam[18] et quiētōs[19] patī quod sors[20] inīqua[21] cōgeret iussisse. Prōminentī[22] ex lectīcā praebentīque immōtam cervīcem[23] caput praecīsum est.[24]

10         Manūs quoque, scrīpsisse in Antōnium aliquid exprobrantēs,[25] praecīdērunt. Ita relātum caput ad Antōnium, iussūque eius inter duās manūs in Rōstrīs positum,[26] ubi ille cōnsul, ubi saepe cōnsulāris,[27] ubi eō ipsō annō adversus[28] Antōnium ... (quanta nūlla umquam hūmāna vōx[29]!) cum admīrātiōne[30] ēloquentiae[31] audītus fuerat. Vix attollentēs[32] prae lacrimīs oculōs, hominēs intuērī[33] trucīdāta[34] membra[35]

15      eius poterant. Vīxit trēs et sexāgintā[36] annōs ... Vir magnus, ācer, memorābilis[37] fuit, et in cuius laudēs persequendās[38] Cicerōne laudātōre opus[39] fuerit.[40] (**Livy** 120.50)

## XVIII. MILTIADES AND THE BATTLE OF MARATHON[1]

Eīsdem temporibus Persārum rēx Dārēus, ex Asiā in Eurōpam[2] exercitū trāiectō,[3] Scythīs[4] bellum īnferre[5] dēcrēvit. Pontem fēcit in Histrō[6] flūmine, quā[7] cōpiās

[8]as he was going to board ship (**cōnscendō, -ere, -scendī, -scēnsum,** ascend)

[9]**aliquotiēns,** *adv.,* several times

[10]**altum, -ī,** the deep, the sea

[11]**prō-vehō, -ere, -vexī, -vectum,** carry forward; **provectum** (having sailed out) *goes with* **eum** *below*

[12]**iactātiō, -ōnis,** *f.,* tossing

[13]**taedium, -iī,** weariness, disgust

[14]**fuga, -ae,** flight; **fugae** *depends on* **taedium**

[15]**regredior, -ī, -gressus sum,** go back

[16]**cōnstat,** it is agreed

[17]**dīmicō** (1), fight (to the finish)

[18]**lectīca, -ae,** litter

[19](**eōs**) **quiētōs,** them quiet, *subj. of* **patī;** *but we say:* them quietly. (**quiētus, -a, -um**)

[20]**sors, sortis,** *f.,* lot

[21]**inīquus, -a, -um,** unfavorable, unjust (**in-aequus**)

[22]**prōmineō, -ēre, -uī,** jut out, step forth: (**eī**) **prōminentī,** for him stepping forth = as he stepped forth, *dat. of ref. or interest*

[23]**cervīx, -vīcis,** *f.,* neck

[24]**praecīdō, -ere, -cīdī, cīsum** (**prae-caedō,** cut), cut off—*by the soldiers whom Antony had sent to execute Cicero in reprisal for Cicero's "Philippics" denouncing Antony. Such were the horrors of the proscriptions.*

[25]**exprobrō** (1), reproach, charge: (**militēs**), **exprobrantēs** (**manūs**) **scrīpsisse aliquid, manūs praecīdērunt**

[26]**positum,** *sc.* **est**

[27]**cōnsulāris, -is,** *m.,* ex-consul

[28]**adversus,** *prep. + acc.,* against

[29]**quanta ... vōx** (**fuerat**), how great no voice had been = greater than any voice had been

[30]**admīrātiō, -ōnis,** *f. = Eng.*

[31]**ēloquentia, -ae,** *f.;* **ēloquentiae,** *obj. gen.* (S.S.)

[32]**attollō, -ere,** raise, lift

[33]**intueor, -ērī, -tuitus sum,** look at

[34]**trucīdō** (1), cut to pieces, butcher

[35]**membrum, -ī,** member (of the body), limb

[36]*indecl. adj.,* sixty

[37]**memorābilis, -e,** remarkable, memorable

[38]**per-sequor,** follow up, set forth

[39]**opus est + abl. =** there is need of (Cicero)

[40]**fuerit,** *perf. subjunct., potential subjunct.,* there would be need of

### XVIII

[1]*490 B.C., the first major battle of the Persian wars and one of the most illustrious victories in the apparently unending conflict between democracies and autocracies (despotisms): the relatively few Athenians, practically alone, against the hordes of the Persian autocracy.*

[2]**Eurōpa, -ae,** Europe

[3]**trāiciō, -ere, -iēcī, -iectus,** transfer

[4]**Scythae, -ārum,** *m.,* the Scythians, *a nomadic people of southeastern Europe;* **Scythīs,** *dat. with compound verbs*

[5]**bellum īn-ferō** (**-ferre, -tulī, -lātus**), make war upon, + *dat.*

[6]**Hister, -trī,** the Danube

[7]**quā,** *rel. adv. instead of rel. pron.,* where, by which, *referring to* **pontem**

trādūceret.[8] Eius pontis, dum ipse abesset,[9] custōdēs[10] relīquit prīncipēs quōs sēcum ex Iōniā et Aeolide[11] dūxerat; quibus singulārum[12] urbium perpetua dederat
5 imperia. Sīc enim facillimē putāvit sē[13] Graecā linguā loquentēs[14] quī Asiam incolerent[15] sub suā retentūrum[16] potestāte, sī amīcīs suīs oppida[17] tuenda[18] trādidisset.[19] In hōc[20] fuit tum numerō Miltiadēs.[21] Hic, cum crēbrī[22] adferrent nūntiī[23] male rem gerere Dārēum premīque ā Scythīs, hortātus est pontis custōdēs nē ā Fortūnā[24] datam occāsiōnem līberandae Graeciae dīmitterent.[25]

10 Nam sī cum eīs cōpiīs, quās sēcum trānsportārat,[26] interīsset Dārēus, nōn sōlum Eurōpam fore[27] tūtam,[28] sed etiam eōs quī Asiam incolerent Graecī genere[29] līberōs ā Persārum futūrōs dominātiōne[30] et perīculō. Id facile efficī[31] posse;[32] ponte enim rescissō[33] rēgem vel[34] hostium ferrō vel inopiā[35] paucīs diēbus interitūrum. Ad hoc cōnsilium cum plērīque[36] accēderent, Histiaeus[37] Mīlēsius . . . [dīxit] adeō[38]
15 sē abhorrēre[39] ā cēterōrum cōnsiliō ut nihil putet ipsīs ūtilius quam cōnfirmārī[40] rēgnum[41] Persārum. Huius cum sententiam plūrimī essent secūtī, Miltiadēs . . . Chersonēsum relīquit ac rūrsus[42] Athēnās dēmigrāvit.[43] Cuius[44] ratiō etsī nōn valuit, tamen magnopere est laudanda cum amīcior omnium libertātī quam suae fuerit dominātiōnī.

20 Dārēus autem, cum ex Eurōpā in Asiam redīsset, hortantibus amīcīs ut Graeciam redigeret[45] in suam potestātem, classem quīngentārum[46] nāvium comparāvit[47]

---

[8]**trā** (= **trāns**)-**dūcō**. *Why the subjunct. in the rel. clause?*

[9]**ab-sum**, be away, be absent; **abesset**, *subjunct. of implied ind. state., the thought in his mind being:* "while I shall be away"

[10]as guards

[11]Ionia and Aeolis, *Gk. sections of Asia Minor*

[12]**singulī, -ae, -a** (*pl.*), separate, one each

[13]**sē**, *acc., subj. of* **retentūrum** (**esse**)

[14]the Greek-speaking peoples, *obj. of* **retentūrum**

[15]**incolō, -ere, -uī,** inhabit

[16]**retentūrum** (**esse**); **re-tineō**

[17]**oppidum, -ī,** town; *occasionally* city

[18]**tuenda,** (the towns) to be protected = the protection of the towns (**tueor, -ērī, tūtus sum,** look at, protect)

[19]*fut. more vivid condition in ind. state.:* **eōs retinēbō sī amīcīs oppida trādiderō.**

[20]**hōc** *modifies* **numerō.** *Note carefully that a characteristic of Nepos' style is the fondness for separating modifiers from the words which they modify. Be sure to match up such separated words accurately according to the rules of agreement.*

[21]**Miltiadēs, -is,** *m.*, Miltiades, *Athenian general, hero of Marathon, who many years before the Battle of Marathon had been sent by the Athenians to rule over the Thracian Chersonesus, a peninsula west of the Hellespont.*

[22]**crēber, -bra, -brum,** numerous

[23]**nūntius, -iī,** messenger

[24]**Fortūna** *is here regarded as a person* (*deity*). *Why is* **ā** *used?*

[25]**dī-mittō,** let go, lose

[26]**trānsportō** (1), transport, take across; **trānsportārat** = **trānsportāverat**

[27]*ind. state. depending on the idea of saying in* **hortātus est** *of the preceding sent.; direct form:* **sī Dārēus interierit, Eurōpa erit tūta. inter-eō,** perish

[28]**tūtus, -a, -um**

[29]*abl. of specification* (*S.S.*), Greek in race *or* by race

[30]**dominātiō, -ōnis, f.** = *Eng.*

[31]**ef-ficiō,** accomplish

[32]*still ind. state.*

[33]**rescindō, -ere, rescidī, rescissum,** cut down

[34]**vel . . . vel,** either . . . or

[35]**inopia, -ae,** need, privation

[36]**plērīque, -ōrumque,** most people, very many (**plērusque, -aque, -umque,** the greater part, very many)

[37]**Histiaeus, -ī,** *tyrant of Miletus in Asia Minor*

[38]**adeō,** *adv.*, so, to such a degree

[39]**ab-horreō, -ēre, -uī,** shrink from, be averse to

[40]**cōnfirmō** (1), strengthen

[41]*subj. of* **cōnfirmārī**

[42]**rūrsus,** *adv.*, again

[43]**dēmigrō** (1), depart (*cf.* migrate)

[44]*conjunctive use of rel.*

[45]**redigō, -ere, -ēgī, -āctum,** reduce

[46]**quīngentī, -ae, -a,** 500

[47]**comparāvit** *here* = *strong form of* **parāvit**

eīque[48] Dātim praefēcit[49] et Artaphernem,[50] eīsque ducenta[51] (mīlia) peditum,[52] decem equitum[53] mīlia dedit—causam interserēns[54] sē hostem esse Athēniēnsibus quod eōrum auxiliō Iōnes[55] Sardīs[56] expugnāssent[57] suaque[58] praesidia interfēcissent.

25 Illī praefectī[59] rēgiī,[60] classe ad Euboeam[61] appulsā[62] celeriter Eretriam[63] cēpērunt, omnēsque eius gentis cīvēs abreptōs[64] in Asiam ad rēgem mīsērunt. Inde[65] ad Atticam[66] accessērunt ac suās cōpiās in campum[67] Marathōna[68] dēdūxērunt. Is abest ab oppidō circiter[69] mīlia passuum[70] decem.

Hōc tumultū[71] Athēniēnsēs tam propinquō[72] tamque magnō permōtī[73] auxilium nūsquam[74] nisi ā Lacedaemoniīs petīvērunt Phīdippumque,[75] cursōrem eius

30 generis quī hēmerodromoe[76] vocantur, Lacedaemonem[77] mīsērunt ut nūntiāret quam celerrimō opus esse[78] auxiliō. Domī autem creant[79] decem praetōrēs,[80] quī exercituī praeessent,[81] in eīs Miltiadem; inter quōs magna fuit contentiō[82] utrum moenibus sē dēfenderent an obviam[83] īrent hostibus aciēque[84] dēcernerent. Ūnus[85]

35 Miltiadēs maximē nītēbātur[86] ut prīmō tempore castra fierent[87] . . .

Hōc tempore nūlla cīvitās Athēniēnsibus auxiliō[88] fuit praeter Plataeēnsēs[89]; ea

---

[48]eī (= classī), *dat. with compounds*

[49]prae-ficiō, + *dat.*, put in charge *or* command of

[50]Dātis, -tidis, *acc.* Dātim, Datis, *a general;* Artaphernēs, -is, Artaphernes, *nephew of Darius*

[51]ducentī, -ae, -a, 200

[52]pedes, -itis, *m.*, foot-soldier

[53]eques, -itis, *m.*, horseman

[54]interserō, -ere, allege

[55]Iōnes, -um, *m.*, the Ionians, *a Gk. people inhabiting the central western coast of Asia Minor;* -es, *Gk. ending*

[56]Sardēs, -ium, *acc.* Sardīs, Sardis, *capital of the Persian province of Lydia in western Asia Minor*

[57]expugnō (1), take by storm

[58]sua, *refers to Sardis*

[59]praefectus, -ī, commander, deputy

[60]rēgius, -a, -um, royal

[61]Euboea, -ae, Euboea, *a large island off the eastern shore of central Greece*

[62]appellō, -ere, -pulī, -pulsum, drive, bring to land

[63]Eretria, -ae, Eretria, *a city of the western central coast of Euboea*

[64]ab-ripiō = ēripiō; abreptōs . . . mīsērunt, they carried away and sent to

[65]inde, *adv.*, from that place

[66]Attica, -ae, Attica, *district in central Greece of which the capital was Athens (somewhat unusually called an* oppidum *in the next sentence)*

[67]campus, -ī, field, plain

[68]Marathōn, -ōnis, *acc.* -ōna, *f.*, Marathon

[69]circiter, *adv.*, about

[70]passus, -ūs, pace (ca. 5'); mīlia passuum, thousands of paces = miles

[71]tumultus, -ūs, disturbance, uprising

[72]propinquus, -a, -um, near, neighboring

[73]per-moveō, move thoroughly, trouble

[74]nūsquam, *adv.*, nowhere

[75]Phīdippus, -ī, Phidippus, *an Athenian courier* (cursor, -ōris, *m.*, runner)

[76]hēmerodromus, -ī (-dromoe, *Gk. nom. pl.*), day runner (*Gk. word*), *professional runner. Herodotus says that Phidippus (or Phidippides) covered the 140 miles between Athens and Sparta in two days.* Quī agrees with hēmerodromoe *rather than generis since a rel. pron. agrees with a pred. noun rather than with the antecedent.*

[77]Lacedaemōn, -onis, *f.*, Lacedaemonia, Sparta

[78]opus est + *abl.* (*of means*), there is need of, *an impers. construction in which* opus *remains indecl.;* opus esse, *infin. in ind. state. with* auxiliō *in abl.*

[79]creant, *historical pres.*

[80]praetor, -ōris, *m.*, called stratēgoi, generals, *by the Athenians*

[81]prae-sum + *dat.*, be in charge of; *why subjunct.?*

[82]contentiō, -ōnis, *f.*, controversy

[83]obviam (*adv.*) īre + *dat.*, go to meet

[84]aciēs, -ēī, line of battle

[85]alone, *i.e., of the ten generals*

[86]nītor, -ī, nīxus sum, strive labor

[87]that a camp should be made = to take the field

[88]dat. of purp. (S.S.)

[89]Plataeēnsēs, -ium, *m. pl.*, the men of Plataea, *a city in Boeotia just over the border from Attica*

mīlle mīsit mīlitum.[90] Itaque hōrum adventū[91] decem mīlia armātōrum[92] complēta sunt,[93] quae manus mīrābilī[94] flagrābat[95] pugnandī cupiditāte; quō[96] factum est[97] ut plūs quam collēgae[98] Miltiadēs valēret.[99]

40      Eius ergō auctōritāte impulsī[100] Athēniēnsēs cōpiās ex urbe ēdūxērunt locōque[101] idōneō castra fēcērunt. Dein[102] posterō[103] diē sub montis rādīcibus[104] aciē regiōne[105] īnstrūctā[106] nōn apertissimā[107]—namque[108] arborēs multīs locīs erant rārae[109]—proelium commīsērunt[110] hōc cōnsiliō ut et montium altitūdine[111] tegerentur[112] et arborum tractū[113] equitātus[114] hostium impedīrētur, nē multitūdine[115] cla-

45 derentur.[116] Dātis, etsī nōn aequum locum[117] vidēbat suīs, tamen frētus[118] numerō cōpiārum suārum cōnflīgere[119] cupiēbat, eōque[120] magis quod, priusquam[121] Lacedaemoniī subsidiō[122] venīrent, dīmicāre ūtile arbitrābātur.

Itaque in aciem peditum centum (mīlia), equitum decem mīlia prōdūxit proeliumque commīsit. In quō[123] tantō[124] plūs[125] virtūte valuērunt Athēniēnsēs ut decem-

50 plicem[126] numerum hostium prōflīgārint,[127] adeōque eōs perterruērunt ut Persae nōn castra sed nāvēs petierint. Quā pugnā nihil adhūc[128] exsistit[129] nōbilius[130]; nūlla enim umquam tam exigua[131] manus tantās opēs prōstrāvit.[132] (**Nepos,** *Miltiadēs* 3–5, excerpts)

---

[90]**mīlle** *here* = *a noun with gen. of whole* **mīlitum.** *This is regular with* **mīlia** *but uncommon with* **mīlle.**

[91]**adventus, -ūs,** approach

[92]**armātī, -ōrum,** armed men

[93]**compleō, -ēre, -plēvī, -plētum,** fill out, complete

[94]**mīrābilis, -e,** wonderful, extraordinary; *modifies* **cupiditāte**

[95]**flagrō (1),** burn, be excited

[96]because of which = and because of this

[97]it happened that

[98]**collēga, -ae,** *m.,* colleague

[99]**plūs . . . valēret,** he had power more than = he had more power or influence than, he prevailed over. **valēret,** *why subjunct.?*

[100]**impellō, -ere, -pulī, -pulsum,** impel

[101]**locō,** *place where, no prep. necessary with* **locō**

[102]**dein** = **deinde**

[103]**posterus, -a, -um,** next following

[104]**rādīx, -īcis,** *f.,* root, base

[105]**regiō, -ōnis,** *f.,* region

[106]**īnstruō, -ere, -strūxī, -strūctum,** draw up (battle line)

[107]*interlocked word order:* **aciē īnstrūctā** (in) **regiōne nōn apertissimā; apertus, -a, -um,** open

[108]**namque,** *conj., more emphatic form of* **nam**

[109]**rārus, -a, -um,** scattered: there were scattered trees

[110]**proelium committere,** join battle

[111]**altitūdō, -inis,** *f.,* height

[112]**tegō, -ere, tēxī, tēctum,** cover, protect

[113]**tractus, -ūs,** dragging

[114]**equitātus, -ūs,** cavalry

[115]**multitūdō, -inis,** *f.,* large number

[116]**claudō,** *here* enclose, surround

[117]**locum (esse) nōn aequum suīs**

[118]**frētus, -a, -um,** + *abl.,* relying on

[119]**cōnflīgō, -ere, -flīxī, -flīctum,** fight (*cf.* conflict)

[120]**eō,** *adv.,* on that account

[121]**priusquam** *and* **antequam,** before, + *indic. denote an actual fact;* + *subjunct. denote anticipation as here:* before they could come

[122]*dat.*

[123]**in quō (proeliō)**

[124]*abl. of degree of difference (S.S.)*

[125]they were strong by so much more (strength) in respect to courage = they were so much more powerful in the matter of courage

[126]**decemplex,** *gen.* **-plicis,** tenfold

[127]**prōflīgō (1),** overthrow; **prōflīgārint** = **-gāverint.** *Why subjunct.?*

[128]**ad-hūc,** *adv.,* thus far, hitherto

[129]**exsistō, -ere, -stitī,** arise, exist, be

[130]**nōbilis, -e,** famous

[131]**exiguus, -a, -um,** small, scanty. "Never did so many owe so much to so few."

[132]**prōsternō, -ere, -strāvī, -strātum,** overthrow, throw down

## XIX.  THEMISTOCLES AND THE BATTLE OF SALAMIS[1]

Themistoclēs[2] ad (bellum Corcȳraeum[3]) gerendum praetor ā populō factus, nōn
sōlum praesentī[4] bellō sed etiam reliquō[5] tempore ferōciōrem reddidit cīvitātem.
Nam cum pecūnia pūblica, quae ex metallīs[6] redībat, largītiōne[7] magistrātuum[8]
quotannīs[9] interīret,[10] ille persuāsit populō ut eā pecūniā classis centum nāvium
5      aedificārētur.[11] Quā[12] celeriter effectā, prīmum Corcȳraeōs frēgit,[13] deinde maritimōs
praedōnēs[14] cōnsectandō[15] mare tūtum reddidit. In quō[16] . . . perītissimōs[17] bellī
nāvālis[18] fēcit Athēniēnsēs. Id quantae salūtī[19] fuerit ūniversae[20] Graeciae, bellō cognitum est Persicō.[21] Nam cum Xerxēs[22] et marī et terrā[23] bellum ūniversae īnferret
Eurōpae, cum tantīs cōpiīs eam invāsit[24] quantās neque ante nec posteā habuit
10     quisquam. Huius enim classis mīlle et ducentārum nāvium longārum[25] fuit, quam
duo mīlia onerāriārum[26] sequēbantur. Terrestris[27] autem exercitus septingenta[28]
(mīlia) peditum, equitum quadringenta[29] mīlia fuērunt.[30]
        Cuius dē adventū[31] cum fāma in Graeciam esset perlāta[32] et maximē Athēni-
ēnsēs petī dīcerentur propter pugnam Marathōniam, mīsērunt Delphōs[33] cōn-
15     sultum[34] quidnam[35] facerent[36] dē rēbus suīs. Dēlīberantibus[37] Pȳthia[38] respondit
ut moenibus līgneīs[39] sē mūnīrent.[40] Id respōnsum[41] quō[42] valēret cum intellegeret

**XIX**

[1] *480 B.C. The Battle of Salamis was the naval counterpart of Marathon, except that this time Athens had the help of Sparta.*
[2] **Themistoclēs, -is**, *or* **-ī**, Themistocles, *a talented Athenian politician.*
[3] **Corcȳraeus, -a, -um**, Corcyraen; *Corcyra, a large island off the
northwest coast of Greece. Actually Nepos is in error about
Themistocles' command in the Corcyraean affair but he is correct about the tremendous importance of Themistocles' big-
navy policy.*
[4] **praesēns**, *gen.* **-entis**, present
[5] **reliquus, -a, -um**, remaining, rest of
[6] **metallum, -ī**, a mine, *silver mines at Laurium in Attica south
of Athens*
[7] **largītiō, -ōnis**, *f.*, generosity, liberality
[8] **magistrātus, -ūs**, civil office; civil officer, magistrate
[9] **quotannīs**, *adv.*, annually
[10] **inter-eō**, be lost, perish (*cf.* **pereō**): **interīret**, *subjunct. introduced by* **cum**; *the subj. is* **pecūnia**.
[11] **aedificō** (1), build (*cf.* edifice)
[12] **quā** (classe)
[13] **frangō, -ere, frēgī, frāctum**, break, overcome
[14] **maritimus (-a, -um** = *Eng.; cf.* **mare**) **praedō** (**-ōnis**, *m.*, robber)
= pirate; *obj. of* **cōnsectandō**
[15] **cōnsector** (1), pursue, hound (*cf.* **cōnsequor**)
[16] in (doing) which
[17] **perītus, -a, -um**, + *gen.*, skilled in; *obj. complement*
[18] **nāvālis, -e**; *cf.* **nāvis**
[19] **quantae salūtī**, *dat. of purp. with a dat. of ref.,* **Graeciae** (*S.S.*)

[20] **ūniversus, -a, -um**, entire, whole, as a whole
[21] **Persicus, -a, -um**, Persian; *the Second Persian War*
[22] **Xerxēs, -is** *or* **-ī**, *m.*, Xerxes, *son of Darius and king of the Persians, 485–465 B.C.*
[23] **marī et terrā** (*or* **terrā marīque**) *abl. of place where, without a
prep., regular in this formula*
[24] **invādō, -ere, -vāsī, -vāsum**, move against, invade
[25] **nāvium longārum**, of 1,200 men-of-war; his fleet was of 1,200
ships = his fleet consisted of . . .
[26] **onerāria, -ae** (**nāvis**), transport
[27] **terrestris exercitus**, land army
[28] **septingentī, -ae, -a**, seven hundred
[29] **quadringentī, -ae, -a**, four hundred
[30] *Though the subj.,* **exercitus**, *is sg.,* **fuērunt** *is pl. according to the
idea of plurality which precedes it.*
[31] **adventus, -ūs**, approach, arrival
[32] **per-ferō**
[33] *acc. of place to which. At Delphi was the famous oracle of Apollo.*
[34] *acc. supine of* **cōnsulō** *to express purp.* = to consult
[35] **quisnam, quidnam**, who *or* what in the world
[36] *both ind. quest. and deliberative subjunct.*
[37] **dēlīberō** (1), deliberate; (**eīs**) **dēlīberantibus**, *dat.*
[38] **Pȳthia, -ae**, the Pythian priestess, *who gave the response of
Apollo*
[39] **ligneus, -a, -um**, wooden
[40] **mūniō** (4), fortify, defend
[41] **respōnsum, -ī**, *the noun of* **respondeō**, *subj. of* **valēret**
[42] **quō** (*adv.*) **valēret**, *lit.* in what direction this was strong or valid
= in what way this applied *or* what this meant

nēmō, Themistoclēs persuāsit cōnsilium esse[43] Apollinis ut in nāvēs sē suaque[44] cōnferrent: eum[45] enim ā deō significārī[46] mūrum ligneum. Tālī cōnsiliō probātō, addunt[47] ad superiōrēs (nāvēs) totidem[48] nāvēs trirēmēs,[49] suaque omnia quae
20  moverī poterant partim[50] Salamīna,[51] partim Troezēna[52] dēportant.[53] Arcem[54] sacerdōtibus paucīsque maiōribus nātū[55] ad sacra[56] prōcūranda[57] trādunt; reliquum[5] oppidum relinquunt.

Huius[58] cōnsilium plērīsque cīvitātibus[59] displicēbat[60] et in terrā dīmicārī[61] magis placēbat. Itaque missī sunt dēlēctī[62] cum Leōnidā,[63] Lacedaemoniōrum rēge,
25  quī Thermopylās[64] occupārent[65] longiusque barbarōs[66] prōgredī nōn paterentur. Iī vim hostium nōn sustinuērunt,[67] eōque locō omnēs interiērunt.[10]

At classis commūnis Graeciae trecentārum[68] nāvium, in quā ducentae[68] erant Athēniēnsium,[69] prīmum apud Artemīsium[70] inter Euboeam continentemque[71] terram cum classiāriīs[72] rēgiīs[73] cōnflīxit.[74] Angustiās[75] enim Themistoclēs
30  quaerēbat, nē multitūdine[76] circumīrētur.[77] Hinc etsī parī proeliō[78] discesserant, tamen eōdem locō nōn sunt ausī manēre, quod erat perīculum nē,[79] sī pars nāvium adversāriōrum[80] Euboeam superāsset,[81] ancipitī[82] premerentur perīculō. Quō[83] fac-

---

[43]**esse.** *The infin. shows that this is ind. state. with* **persuādeō** *and not the more common jussive noun clause introduced by* **ut:** he persuaded (them) that it was the advice of Apollo that they should betake* . . .

[44]**sua,** their things = their possessions

[45]**eum mūrum ligneum,** that wooden wall (= the ships)

[46]**significō** (1), signify, mean; **significārī,** *ind. state, depending on a verb of saying understood*

[47]**ad-dō, -dere, -didī, -ditum,** add

[48]**totidem,** *indecl. adj.,* just as many

[49]**trirēmis, -e,** having three banks of oars

[50]**partim,** *adv.,* partly

[51]**Salamīs, -īnis,** *acc.* **Salamīna,** *f.,* Salamis, *island on west coast of Attica; acc. of place to which (islands as well as cities and towns)*

[52]**Troezēn, -ēnis,** *acc.* **Troezēna,** *f.,* Troezen, *southeastern part of Argolis, across the Saronic Gulf from Athens.*

[53]**dēportō** (1), carry off

[54]*the acropolis of the city of Athens.*

[55]**maiōrēs nātū,** those greater in respect to birth = old men, elders

[56]**sacer, -cra, -crum,** sacred; **sacra,** *n. pl.* sacred vessels, *or* rites

[57]**prōcūrō** (1), take care of

[58]*i.e.,* Themistocles'

[59]**plērīsque cīvitātibus,** *i.e., the allies of the Athenians; dat. with* **displicēbat**

[60]**dis-placeō**

[61]**dīmicārī,** *impers. pass., lit.* that it be fought, *but translate* that the war be fought. *The infin.* **dīmicārī** *is subj. of* **placēbat.**

[62]**dēlēctus, -a, -um,** chosen, picked; chosen men

[63]**Leōnidās, -ae,** *m.,* Leonidas

[64]**Thermopylae, -ārum,** Thermopylae, *a mountain pass near the southern border of Thessaly*

[65]**occupō** (1), seize

[66]**barbarus, -a, -um,** foreign, uncivilized, barbarian (*commonly applied by a kind of ethnocentrism to those not of the Gk. and Roman civilization*)

[67]**sustineō, -ēre, -tinuī, -tentum,** sustain; *the subj. is* **iī** (= **eī**).

[68]*See App. under Numerals (cardinals 200 and 300);* **ducentae** (**nāvēs**)

[69]*pred. gen. of possession:* were of the Athenians = belonged to the Athenians

[70]**apud Artemīsium,** near Artemisium, *promontory at northern tip of Euboea*

[71]**continēns terra, continentis terrae,** the mainland

[72]**classiārius, -iī,** a marine (*lit.* a soldier of the fleet)

[73]**rēgius, -a, -um,** royal

[74]**cōnflīgō, -ere, -flīxī, -flīctum,** to fight

[75]**angustiae, -ārum,** narrow place

[76]**multitūdō, -inis,** *f.,* large number, multitude

[77]**circum-eō,** surround

[78]**parī proeliō,** the battle was a draw

[79]**nē** = lest, *similar to the construction after verbs of fearing*

[80]**adversārius, -a, -um,** hostile; **adversārius, -iī,** opponent, enemy

[81]*a simple fut. condition in a* **nē**- *clause* The original thought was **sī pars superāverit,** . . . **premēmur;** *the fut. perf. indic.* **superāverit** *becomes pluperf. subjunct.* **superāsset.**

[82]**anceps,** *gen.* **ancipitis,** two-headed, double

[83]**quō** = **quārē**

tum est ut[84] ab Artemīsiō discēderent et exadversum[85] Athēnās apud Salamīna classem suam cōnstituerent.[86]

35     At Xerxēs, Thermopylīs expugnātīs, prōtinus accessit astū,[87] idque, nūllīs dēfendentibus, interfectīs sacerdōtibus quōs in arce invēnerat, incendiō[88] dēlēvit. Cuius flammā perterritī[89] classiāriī cum manēre nōn audērent et plūrimī hortārentur ut domōs[90] suās discēderent moenibusque sē dēfenderent, Themistoclēs ūnus restitit[91] et ūniversōs parēs esse posse[92] aiēbat,[93] dispersōs[94] testābātur[95] peritūrōs;

40 idque Eurybiadī,[96] rēgī Lacedaemoniōrum, quī tum summae[97] imperiī praeerat,[98] fore[99] adfīrmābat.[100]

    Quem cum minus quam vellet movēret, noctū[101] dē servīs suīs[102] quem habuit[103] fidēlissimum ad rēgem mīsit ut eī nūntiāret suīs verbīs[104] adversāriōs eius[105] in fugā[106] esse; quī[107] sī discessissent,[108] maiōre cum labōre . . . (eum) bellum

45 cōnfectūrum, cum singulōs[109] cōnsectārī cōgerētur; quōs sī statim aggrederētur,[110] brevī (tempore) ūniversōs oppressūrum . . . Hāc rē audītā barbarus, nihil dolī[111] subesse[112] crēdēns, postrīdiē aliēnissimō[113] sibi locō, contrā[114] opportūnissimō[115] hostibus, adeō angusto marī[116] cōnflīxit ut eius multitūdō nāvium explicārī nōn potuerit[117] . . . Victus ergō est magis etiam cōnsiliō Themistoclī quam armīs Graeciae . . .

50 Sīc ūnīus virī prūdentiā[118] Graecia līberāta est Eurōpaeque succubuit[119] Asia.

    Haec (est) altera victōria quae cum Marathōniō possit comparārī tropaeō.[120] Nam parī modō apud Salamīna parvō numerō nāvium maxima post hominum memoriam classis est dēvicta.[121] (**Nepos,** *Themistoclēs* 2–4, excerpts)

---

[84] *result clause, subj. of* **factum est:** = the result was that

[85] **exadversum,** *prep. + acc.,* opposite

[86] **cōnstituō, -ere, -stituī, -stitūtum,** draw up, establish

[87] **astū,** *n. indecl.,* the city (= Athens), *obj. of* **accessit**

[88] **incendium, -iī,** burning, fire. *The marks of this fire can still be seen on some of the marble pieces later built into the wall of the Acropolis.*

[89] **per-terreō**

[90] *place to which without a prep. as in the sg.* **domum**

[91] **resistō, -ere, -stitī,** make a stand, resist

[92] **universōs . . . posse,** all together (united) they could be equal (*to the Persians*)

[93] *imperf. of* **ait**

[94] **di-spergō, -ere, -spersī, -spersum,** scatter

[95] **testor** (1), testify, declare

[96] **Eurybiadēs, -is,** *m.,* Eurybiades; **Eurybiadī** *depends on* **adfīrmābat.**

[97] **summa, -ae,** highest place

[98] **summae imperiī** (*gen. of whole*) **praeerat,** he was in charge of the highest part of the command = he was commander-in-chief

[99] *Subj. of* **fore** (= **futūrum esse**) *is* **id.**

[100] **adfīrmō** (1), assert, declare

[101] **noctū,** *adv.,* at night

[102] **(illum) dē servīs suīs,** that one of his slaves

[103] considered

[104] in his (Themistocles') own words, *i.e.,* in his own name

[105] **adversāriōs** (= **hostēs**) **eius** (= **rēgis**)

[106] **fuga, -ae,** flight

[107] **quī** = **et eī**

[108] **sī discessissent . . . (eum) bellum cōnfectūrum (esse),** *another simple fut. condition in ind. state.:* **sī discesserint** (*fut. perf.*), **tū bellum cōnficiēs . . .**; **cōnficiō, -ere, -fēcī, -fectum,** finish, accomplish.

[109] one at a time

[110] **aggredior, -gredī, -gressus sum,** attack

[111] **dolus, -ī,** deceit, trick. *What kind of gen. is* **dolī?**

[112] **sub-sum,** be under, be concealed

[113] **aliēnus, -a, -um,** foreign, unfavorable

[114] **contrā,** *adv.,* on the contrary

[115] **opportūnus, -a, -um,** advantageous, *referring to* **locō**

[116] *abl. of place where without a prep.*

[117] *The perf. subjunct. is not uncommon in result clause in historical sequence.*

[118] **prūdentia, -ae,** foresight, discretion

[119] **succumbō, -ere, -cubuī,** submit, succumb

[120] **Marathōniō tropaeō,** trophy *or* victory at Marathon

[121] **dē-vincō,** conquer completely

## XX. ARISTIDES THE JUST

Aristīdēs,[1] Lȳsimachī[2] fīlius, Athēniēnsis, aequālis[3] ferē fuit Themistoclī[4] atque cum eō dē prīncipātū[5] contendit . . . In hīs autem cognitum est quantō[6] antistāret[7] ēloquentia innocentiae.[8] Quamquam enim adeō excellēbat[9] Aristīdēs abstinentiā[10] ut ūnus post hominum memoriam . . . cognōmine[11] "Iūstus" sit appellātus, tamen ā
5    Themistocle collabefactus[12] testulā[13] illā[14] exsiliō[15] decem annōrum[16] multātus est.[17]

Quī quidem cum intellegeret reprimī[18] concitātam[19] multitūdinem nōn posse, cēdēnsque animadvertisset quendam scrībentem ut patriā pellerētur,[20] quaesīsse ab eō[21] dīcitur quārē id faceret aut quid Aristīdēs commīsisset cūr[22] tantā poenā dignus dūcerētur. Cui ille respondit sē ignōrāre[23] Aristīdēn, sed sibi nōn placēre[24]
10    quod tam cupidē labōrāsset ut praeter cēterōs "Iūstus" appellārētur. Hic decem annōrum lēgitimam[25] poenam nōn pertulit. Nam postquam[26] Xerxēs in Graeciam dēscendit,[27] sextō ferē annō quam[28] erat expulsus, populī scītō[29] in patriam restitūtus est.[30]

Interfuit[31] autem pugnae nāvālī apud Salamīna quae facta est priusquam[32]
15    poenā līberārētur. Īdem[33] praetor fuit Athēniēnsium apud Plataeās[34] in proeliō quō fūsus[35] (est) barbarōrum exercitus Mardoniusque[36] interfectus est . . . Huius aequitāte[37] factum est,[38] cum in commūnī classe esset Graeciae simul cum Pau-

---

## XX

[1] **Aristīdēs, -is,** *m.,* Aristides, *Athenian statesman and general*

[2] **Lȳsimachus, -ī,** Lysimachus

[3] **aequālis, -is,** *m.,* an equal in age, a contemporary

[4] **Themistoclī,** *here gen. of possession*

[5] **prīncipātus, -ūs,** first place, leadership

[6] *abl. of degree of difference (S.S.) depending on the idea of comparison in* **antistāret:** how much

[7] **anti-stō, -āre, -stetī,** stand before = excel

[8] **innocentia, -ae,** harmlessness; integrity. *Why dat.?*

[9] **excellō, -ere, -uī, -celsum,** excel; **excellēbat:** *note that* **quamquam** (although) *is used with the indic.*

[10] **abstinentia, -ae,** self-restraint, *esp. in matters involving public funds,* uprightness; **abstinentiā,** *abl. of specification (S.S.).*

[11] **cognōmen, -minis,** *n., here* = epithet, appellative. *Of the three regular Roman names* (**praenōmen, nōmen, cognōmen**) *the* **cognōmen** (*cf.* **cognōscō**) *seems to have originated as a kind of nickname.*

[12] **collabefiō, -fierī, -factus sum,** be overthrown, be ruined

[13] **testula, -ae,** little potsherd; ostracism; **testulā** *abl. of accordance or perhaps means. Look up the interesting history of ostracism, a political safety valve against tyranny.*

[14] **illā,** *in the unusual position of following its noun* = that famous

[15] **exsiliō,** *abl. of penalty* (= *a form of abl. of means*)

[16] **decem annōrum,** *gen. of description*

[17] **multō** (1), punish

[18] **re-primō, -ere, -pressī, -pressum,** press back, check

[19] **concitō** (1), arouse, excite

[20] *jussive noun clause,* writing that he should be driven out

[21] **eō,** *i.e., the* **quendam** *above*

[22] (what he had committed) that

[23] **ignōrō** (1), not know, be unacquainted with

[24] **sibi nōn placēre** (*impers.*), it was not pleasing to him = he was displeased (because . . .)

[25] **lēgitimus, -a, -um,** fixed by law, legal

[26] **postquam,** *conj.* + *perf. indic.,* after

[27] **dēscendō, -ere, -scendī, -scēnsum,** descend, march on

[28] **quam = postquam;** **post** *sometimes omitted after an ordinal number in the abl. of time construction*

[29] **scītum, -ī,** decree (*cf. plebiscite*)

[30] **restituō, -ere, -stituī, -stitūtum,** restore

[31] **inter-sum** + *dat.,* be present at, take part in

[32] **priusquam** + *subjunct.*

[33] the same man = he also

[34] **Plataeae, -ārum,** Plataea

[35] **fundō, -ere, fūdī, fūsum,** pour out, rout

[36] **Mardonius, -iī,** Mardonius, *Persian general under Xerxes in command of the "barbarians"*

[37] **aequitās, -tātis,** *f.,* equity, fairness; **aequitāte,** *abl. of cause (S.S.)*

[38] **factum est . . . ut summa imperiī trānsferrētur,** it happened that the chief command was transferred; **ut . . . trānsferrētur,** *noun clause of result used as subj. of* **factum est**

saniā[39] (quō duce[40] Mardonius erat fugātus[41]), ut summa imperiī[42] maritimī ab Lacedaemoniīs trānsferrētur ad Athēniēnsēs; namque ante id tempus et marī et
20    terrā ducēs erant Lacedaemoniī. Tum autem et intemperantiā[43] Pausaniae et iūstitiā factum est Aristīdis ut omnēs ferē cīvitātēs Graeciae ad Athēniēnsium societātem[44] sē applicārent[45] et adversus barbarōs hōs ducēs dēligerent[46] sibi.

Quōs[47] quō[48] facilius repellerent,[49] sī forte[50] bellum renovāre[51] cōnārentur, ad classēs aedificandās exercitūsque comparandōs[52] quantum pecūniae quaeque[53] cīvi-
25    tās daret, Aristīdēs dēlēctus est quī cōnstitueret,[54] eiusque arbitriō[55] quadringēna[56] et sexāgēna talenta quotannīs Dēlum[57] sunt conlāta; id enim commūne aerārium[58] esse voluērunt. Quae omnis pecūnia posterō[59] tempore Athēnās trānslāta est. Hic quā[60] fuerit[61] abstinentiā, nūllum est certius indicium[62] quam quod,[63] cum tantīs rēbus praefuisset,[64] in tantā paupertāte dēcessit,[65] ut quī[66] efferrētur vix relīquerit.
30    Quō[67] factum est ut fīliae eius pūblicē[68] alerentur et dē commūnī aerāriō dōtibus[69] datīs collocārentur.[70] (**Nepos**, *Aristīdēs*, excerpts)

## XXI. TIMOLEON[1]

Diōne[2] Syrācūsīs interfectō, Dionȳsius[3] rūrsus Syrācūsārum potītus est.[4] Cuius adversāriī opem ā Corinthiīs[5] petiērunt ducemque, quō in bellō ūterentur, pos-

---

[39]**Pausaniās, -ae,** *m.,* Pausanias, *a Spartan, victor over the Persians at Plataea in 479 b.c. but a person whose selfish ambition was too great to permit his continuing long as commander-in-chief of the united Gk. forces*

[40]*abl. abs.*

[41]**fugō** (1), put to flight, rout; *not to be confused with* **fugiō**

[42]*Locī Im. XIX n. 97–98*

[43]**intemperantia, -ae,** intemperance, arrogance

[44]**societās, -tātis,** *f.,* confederacy, alliance

[45]**applicō** (1), attach

[46]**dēligō, -ere, -lēgī, -lēctum = legō**

[47]= **barbarōs**

[48]*Locī Im. XIV n. 18*

[49]**re-pellō**

[50]**forte,** *adv.,* by chance

[51]*If* **novus** *is new, what must the verb* **re-novō** (1) *mean?*

[52]*Both gerundive phrases belong in the* **quantum** *clause*

[53]**quaeque cīvitās: quaeque,** *f. adj. form of* **quisque**

[54]**cōnstituō, -ere, -stituī, -stitūtum,** establish, decide; **quī cōnstitueret,** *rel. clause of purp., which has as its obj. the* **quantum . . . daret** *clause*

[55]**arbitrium, -ī,** judgment, decision; **arbitriō,** *what kind of abl.?*

[56]**quadringēna et sexāgēna** (*distributive numerals*) **talenta quotannīs,** 460 talents each year

[57]**Dēlos, -ī,** *f.,* Delos, *small island in the center of the Cyclades in the Aegean*

[58]**aerārium, -iī,** treasury

[59]**posterus, -a, -um,** coming after (post), later

[60]**quā abstinentiā,** *abl. of description,* of what integrity he was = how great was his integrity

[61]*perf. subjunct., ind. quest. depending on* **indicium**

[62]**indicium, -iī,** indication, proof

[63]the fact that

[64]**prae-sum** + *dat.,* be in charge of

[65]**dē-cēdō,** depart, die

[66]**quī** = *old form of abl.: with* **efferrētur** = by which he might be buried = enough to bury him

[67]**quō,** *adv.,* wherefore

[68]**pūblicē,** *adv.,* at public expense

[69]**dōs, dōtis,** *f.,* dowry

[70]**collocō** (1), place, settle in marriage

## XXI

[1]*Timoleon, who came from a noble family at Corinth, was a great champion of liberty against tyranny. By 334 b.c. he was in Sicily fighting the Carthaginians, expelling tyrants, and establishing democracies.*

[2]**Diōn, Diōnis,** *m.,* Dion, *relative and friend of the tyrant Dionysius the Elder. With the aid of Plato he tried—but in vain—to give a noble pattern to the life of Dionysius the Younger, who followed his father in tyranny. After finally exiling Dionysius the Younger from Syracuse, he himself ruled tyrannically and was assassinated in 353 b.c.*

[3]**Dionȳsius, -iī,** Dionysius the Younger

[4]**potior** + *gen. or abl.*

[5]**Corinthiī, -ōrum,** Corinthians

tulārunt. Hūc Tīmoleōn[6] missus incrēdibilī[7] fēlīcitāte[8] Dionȳsium tōtā Siciliā dē-
pulit.[9] Cum (eum) interficere posset, nōluit, tūtōque[10] ut Corinthum[11] pervenīret
5 effēcit,[12] quod utrōrumque[13] Dionȳsiōrum opibus Corinthiī saepe adiūtī fuerant . . .
eamque praeclāram victōriam dūcēbat in quā plūs esset clēmentiae quam crūdē-
litātis[14] . . .

Quibus rēbus cōnfectīs,[15] cum propter diūturnitātem[16] bellī nōn sōlum regiōnēs[17] sed etiam urbēs dēsertās[18] vidēret, conquīsīvit[19] . . . colōnōs.[20] Cīvibus ve-
10 teribus sua[21] restituit, novīs[22] bellō vacuēfactās[23] possessiōnēs[24] dīvīsit[25]; urbium
moenia disiecta[26] fānaque[27] dētēcta[28] refēcit[29]; cīvitātibus lēgēs lībertātemque reddidit . . . Cum tantīs esset opibus[30] ut etiam invītīs[31] imperāre posset, tantum[32]
autem amōrem habēret omnium Siculōrum[33] ut nūllō recūsante rēgnum obtinēre[34]
licēret, māluit sē dīligī quam metuī. Itaque, cum prīmum[35] potuit, imperium
15 dēposuit ac prīvātus[36] Syrācūsīs . . . vīxit. Neque vērō id imperītē[37] fēcit, nam quod
cēterī rēgēs imperiō potuērunt, hic benevolentiā[38] tenuit . . .

Hic cum aetāte iam prōvectus esset,[39] sine ūllō morbō lūmina[40] oculōrum
āmīsit. Quam calamitātem[41] ita moderātē[42] tulit ut . . . (nēmō) eum querentem
audierit[43] . . . Nihil umquam neque īnsolēns[44] neque glōriōsum[45] ex ōre eius exiit.
20 Quī quidem, cum suās laudēs audīret praedicārī,[46] numquam aliud dīxit quam[47] sē
in eā rē maximē dīs agere grātiās . . . quod, cum Siciliam recreāre cōnstituissent,
tum sē potissimum[48] ducem esse voluissent. Nihil enim rērum hūmānārum sine
deōrum nūmine[49] gerī putābat . . .

[6]**Tīmoleōn, -ontis,** *m.,* Timoleon
[7]**incrēdibilis, -e,** incredible
[8]**fēlīcitās, -tātis,** *f.,* happiness, good fortune
[9]**dē-pellō**
[10]**tūtō,** *adv.,* safely
[11]**Corinthus, -ī,** *f.,* Corinth, *on the Isthmus of Corinth*
[12]*Locī Ant. VIII n. 20–21*
[13]**uterque, utraque, utrumque,** each; *here* = both
[14]**crūdēlitās, -tātis,** *f.,* cruelty
[15]*These words refer not only to the expulsion of Dionysius, but also to a great victory over the Carthaginians in Sicily as recounted in the omitted passages.*
[16]**diūturnitās, -tātis,** *f.,* long duration
[17]**regiō, -ōnis,** *f.,* region; *here* = country districts
[18]**dēsertus, -a, -um,** deserted
[19]**con-quīrō, -ere, -quīsīvī, -quīsītum (quaerō),** seek out, gather together
[20]**colōnus, -ī,** settler, colonist
[21]**sua,** *n. pl.*
[22]**novīs (colōnīs)**
[23]**vacuē-faciō,** make empty
[24]**possessiō, -ōnis,** *f.,* possession, property
[25]**dīvidō, -ere, dīvīsī, dīvīsum,** divide, distribute
[26]**dis-iciō,** throw apart, scatter

[27]**fānum, -ī,** shrine, temple (*cf. profane, fanatic, fan = devotee*)
[28]**dē-tegō, -ere, -tēxī, -tēctum,** unroof, uncover (*cf. detect*)
[29]**re-ficiō**
[30]**tantīs . . . opibus:** *abl. of description*
[31]**(Siculīs) etiam invītīs,** (the Sicilians) even against their will
[32]**tantum . . . licēret: cum,** although, *introduces this clause as well as the preceding one.*
[33]**Siculī, -ōrum,** the Sicilians
[34]**obtineō, -ēre, -tinuī, -tentum,** occupy, hold
[35]**cum prīmum,** as soon as
[36]**prīvātus, -ī,** private citizen; as a private citizen, he . . .
[37]**imperītē,** *adv.,* unskillfully, ignorantly
[38]**benevolentia, -ae,** good-will, kindness
[39]**prō-vehō, -ere, -vexī, -vectum,** carry forward
[40]**lūmen, -minis,** *n.,* light; sight
[41]**calamitās, -tātis,** *f.,* misfortune
[42]**moderātē,** *adv.,* with moderation
[43]*perf. subjunct. in historical sequence*
[44]**īnsolēns,** *gen.* **-entis,** arrogant, insolent
[45]**glōriōsus, -a, -um,** *here* = boastful
[46]**praedicō (1),** declare, relate
[47]**aliud quam,** other than
[48]**potissimum,** *adv.,* especially, above all
[49]**nūmen, -minis,** *n.,* divine power, command

Proelia maxima nātālī[50] suō diē fēcit omnia; quō factum est ut[51] eius diem
25    nātālem fēstum[52] habēret ūniversa Sicilia . . .

Cum quīdam Dēmaenetus[53] in cōntiōne[54] populī dē rēbus gestīs[55] eius dētra-
here[56] coepisset ac nōnnūlla inveherētur[57] in Timoleonta, dīxit nunc dēmum[58] sē
vōtī esse damnātum[59]; namque hoc ā dīs immortālibus semper precātum[60] ut tālem
lībertātem restitueret Syrācūsānīs in quā cuivīs[61] licēret dē quō vellet impūne[62]
30    dīcere.[63]

Hic cum diem suprēmum obīsset, pūblicē[64] ā Syrācūsānīs in gymnasiō,[65] quod
Tīmoleontēum[66] appellātur, tōtā celebrante[67] Siciliā, sepultus est.[68] (**Nepos**, *Tīmoleōn* 2–5, excerpts)

## XXII.  HORACE'S "CARPE DIEM"

Tū nē quaesierīs[1]—scīre nefās[2]—quem mihi, quem[3] tibi
fīnem dī dederint, Leuconoē,[4] nec Babylōniōs
temptārīs[5] numerōs.[6] Ut melius,[7] quidquid erit, patī.

. . .

Spem longam[8] resecēs.[9] Dum loquimur, fūgerit invida[10]
5    aetās. Carpe diem, quam minimum[11] crēdula[12] posterō.[13] (**Horace**, *Odes* 1.11,
excerpts)

---

[50] nātālis diēs, nātālis diēī, *m.,* birthday
[51] quō . . . ut, *Locī Im. XX n. 38, 67*
[52] fēstus, -a, -um, festive
[53] Dēmaenetus, -ī, Demaenetus, *an enemy of Timoleon*
[54] cōntiō, -ōnis, *f.,* assembly
[55] rēs gestae, rērum gestārum (*lit.* things done), exploits, deeds
[56] dē-trahō, detract, disparage
[57] nōnnūlla *is n. acc. pl.*—invehor, -ī, -vectus sum (*deponent form of* in-vehō), + in + *acc.,* make an attack on, inveigh against: nōnnūlla inveherētur in, he made some attacks on
[58] dēmum, *adv.,* at last
[59] damnō (1) + *gen.,* condemn on the charge of; vōtī damnārī, to be condemned to pay a vow = to have a vow *or* prayer granted
[60] precor (1), beseech
[61] *dat. of* quī-vīs, quae-vīs, quid-vīs (quod-vīs), *indef.,* anyone at all, anything at all
[62] impūne, *adv.,* with impunity
[63] dīcere, *subj. of* licēret
[64] pūblicē, *adv. of* pūblicus
[65] gymnasium, -iī, gymnasium, *which in Gk. had a much broader meaning than it does in Eng.*
[66] Tīmoleontēum, the Timoleonteum (gymnasium)
[67] celebrō (1), celebrate
[68] sepeliō, -īre, -pelīvī, -pultum, bury

**XXII**
METER: Greater Asclepiad.
[1] nē quaesierīs (= quaesīverīs): nē + *perf. subjunct.* = *a colloquial prohibition* (*negative command*), do not seek
[2] nefās, *n., indecl.,* wrong, sin; nefās (est), it is wrong
[3] quem . . . quem, *modifies* fīnem
[4] Leuconoē, -es, *f.,* Leuconoë, *a Gk. name*
[5] temptō (1), try; temptārīs = temptāverīs, *another neg. command*
[6] numerōs, *calculations employed by astrologers in casting horoscopes; "Babylonian" because astrology was associated with the East. With the decay of belief in the old-time religion in Rome during the 1st cent.* B.C., *astrology and superstitions prospered. Apparently Leuconoë had visited a fortune teller.*
[7] ut melius (est), how (much) better it is
[8] *i.e., projected too far into the future*
[9] resecō, -āre, -secuī, -sectum, cut off, prune back; resecēs, *poetic use of the pres. subjunct.* (*jussive*) *for the pres. imperat.*
[10] invidus, -a, -um, envious
[11] minimum, *adv.* = minimē
[12] crēdulus, -a, -um, believing in, trusting + *dat.;* crēdula, *nom. f. sg. agreeing with the subj. of* carpe, *i.e.* Leuconoë
[13] posterō (diēī), *dat.*

## XXIII.  INTEGER VĪTAE

Integer[1] vītae scelerisque pūrus[2]
nōn eget Maurīs[3] iaculīs[4] neque arcū[5]
nec venēnātīs[6] gravidā[7] sagittīs,[8]
    Fusce,[9] pharetrā.[10]

. . .

5   Namque mē silvā lupus[11] in Sabīnā[12]
dum meam cantō[13] Lalagēn[14] et ultrā
terminum[15] cūrīs vagor[16] expedītīs[17]
    fūgit[18] inermem.[19]

. . .

    Pōne mē pigrīs[20] ubi nūlla campīs
10  arbor aestīvā[21] recreātur aurā,[22]
quod[23] latus mundī nebulae[24] malusque[25]
    Iuppiter urget[26];

pōne sub currū[27] nimium propinquī
sōlis in terrā domibus negāta:
15  dulce[28] rīdentem Lalagēn amābō
    dulce loquentem. (**Horace**, *Odes* 1.22.1–4, 9–12, 17–24)

## XXIII

METER: Sapphic stanza.

[1]**integer, -gra, -grum**, untouched, blameless; (**vir**) **integer vītae** (*poetic gen. of specification*), the person blameless in his life

[2]**pūrus, -a, -um**, pure, free from; **sceleris**, *poetic gen. of separation or specification*

[3]**Maurus, -a, -um**, Moorish (= Mauritanian)

[4]**iaculum, -ī**, missile, javelin (*cf.* **iaciō**)

[5]**arcus, -ūs**, bow

[6]**venēnātus, -a, -um**, poisonous, dipped in poison

[7]**gravidus, -a, -um**, laden (with); *cf.* **gravis**

[8]**sagitta, -ae**, arrow

[9]**Fuscus, -ī**, Fuscus, *a literary man and a close, sometimes waggish, friend of Horace*

[10]**pharetra, -ae**, quiver

[11]**lupus, -ī**, wolf

[12]**Sabīnus, -a, -um**, Sabine; *cf. Locī Ant. X*

[13]**cantō** (1), sing about; **dum** + *historical pres. to denote continued action in past time:* while I was singing about

[14]**Lalagē, -ēs**, *acc.* **Lalagēn** (*Gk. noun*), *f.*, Lalage, *name of a girl— a most mellifluous name!*

[15]**terminus, -ī**, boundary (*cf.* **terminus, term, terminate**)

[16]**vagor** (1), wander, ramble (*cf. vagary, vagabond*)

[17]**expediō** (4), disentangle, set free; **cūrīs expedītīs**, *abl. abs.*

[18]*Note the interlocked word order of this stanza, which is so characteristic of Lat. poetry:* **mē** (*obj. of* **fūgit**) *at the beginning modified by* **inermem** *at the end;* **silvā in Sabīnā**, *place where phrase interrupted by* **lupus** *subj. of* **fūgit**; *all this separated from the main verb by a double* **dum** *clause*

[19]**inermis, -e**, unarmed; *cf.* **integer vītae . . . nōn eget iaculīs.**

[20]**piger, -gra, -grum**, lazy, sluggish, torpid (*because frozen*), *modifying* **campīs** (**campus, -ī**, field) *in a place-where phrase without a prep.* (*the omission of a prep. is common in poetry*). *The order of the thought is:* **pōne mē** (**in**) **pigrīs campīs ubi . . .**

[21]**aestīvus, -a, -um**, summer (*cf.* **aestās**)

[22]**aura, -ae**, breeze

[23]= (*or put me*) **in eō latere mundī quod . . .** ; **latus, -eris**, *n.*, side, region

[24]**nebula, -ae**, mist, fog

[25]**malus** = inclement, *because Jupiter is here god of the weather*

[26]**urgeō, -ēre, ursī**, urge, press, oppress

[27]**currus, -ūs**, chariot

[28]**dulce**, *poetic for* **dulciter**. *These exquisitely mellifluous last lines somewhat onomatopoetically suggest the dulcet timbre of Lalage's voice and laugh.*

## XXIV. AUREA MEDIOCRITĀS—THE GOLDEN MEAN

Rēctius[1] vīvēs, Licinī,[2] neque altum[3]
semper urgendō[4] neque, dum procellās[5]
cautus[6] horrēscis,[7] nimium premendō
    lītus[8] inīquum.[9]
5  Auream[10] quisquis mediocritātem[11]
dīligit, tūtus[12] caret obsolētī[13]
sordibus[14] tēctī, caret invidendā[15]
    sōbrius[16] aulā.[17]
Saepius ventīs agitātur[18] ingēns
10  pīnus[19] et celsae[20] graviōre cāsū[21]
dēcidunt[22] turrēs[23] feriuntque[24] summōs
    fulgura[25] montēs.
Spērat[26] īnfestīs,[27] metuit secundīs[28]
alteram[29] sortem[30] bene praeparātum[31]
15  pectus.[32] Īnfōrmēs[33] hiemēs[34] redūcit
    Iuppiter[35]; īdem[36]
summovet.[37] Nōn, sī male[38] nunc, et ōlim[39]
sīc erit: quondam[40] citharā[41] tacentem

## XXIV

METER: Sapphic stanza.

[1] **rēctius,** *adv.,* rightly, well, suitably
[2] **Licinī,** *voc. of* **Licinius,** *a person who seems to have been wanting in the virtue of moderation*
[3] the deep (sea)
[4] *i.e.,* heading out to the deep
[5] **procella, -ae,** storm, gale
[6] **cautus, -a, -um,** cautious, circumspect; *with* **dum . . . horrēscis,** while you in your caution . . .
[7] **horrēscō, -ere, horruī,** begin to shudder at, begin to dread
[8] **altum** *and* **lītus** = *extremes*
[9] **inīquus, -a, -um,** unequal; *here* = treacherous
[10] **aureus, -a, -um,** golden
[11] **mediocritās, -tātis,** *f.,* moderation, the mean between extremes. Note that Horace does not say that "mediocrity" is golden! The idea of **(aurea) mediocritās** was common in Gk. ethical thought, and Aristotle made it a cardinal virtue in his "Ethics."
[12] **tūtus caret,** secure (*in his philosophy of the "golden mean"*) he is free from . . .
[13] **obsolētus, -a, -um,** worn out, dilapidated
[14] **sordēs, -ium,** *f. pl.,* dirt, filth; **sordibus,** *what kind of abl.?*
[15] **invidendā,** sure to be envied
[16] **sōbrius, -a, -um,** sober-minded, moderate, in his sobriety
[17] **aula, -ae,** palace
[18] **agitō (1),** agitate, toss
[19] **pīnus, -ī,** *f.,* pine

[20] **celsus, -a, -um,** high, lofty
[21] **cāsus, -ūs,** fall, destruction
[22] **dēcidō, -ere, -cidī,** fall down (*cf.* **cadō**)
[23] **turris, -is,** *f.,* tower
[24] **feriō (4),** strike
[25] **fulgur, -uris,** *n.,* lightning, thunderbolt
[26] anticipates, expects
[27] **īnfestus, -a, -um,** unsafe, dangerous, adverse; **īnfestīs (rēbus)** *dat., lit.:* for his adverse circumstances (= in adversity) he anticipates the other (= the opposite) fortune (**sortem**)
[28] **secundīs (rēbus)** *balances* **īnfestīs:** for his favorable circumstances (= in prosperity) he apprehends the opposite fortune.
[29] **alter,** the other of two; *here* = the opposite
[30] **sors, sortis,** *f.,* lot, fortune; **sortem,** *obj. of* **spērat** *and* **metuit**
[31] **prae-parō (1),** make ready in advance, prepare: well prepared (by the philosophy of life which Horace is here enunciating)
[32] *subj. of* **spērat** *and* **metuit**
[33] **īnfōrmis, -e,** shapeless, hideous, horrid
[34] **hiems, hiemis,** *f.,* stormy weather, winter
[35] Jupiter *as god of sky and weather*
[36] **īdem,** the same god = he also
[37] **sum-moveō,** remove, drive away, *sc.* **hiemēs**
[38] **male (est),** it is bad, things are bad
[39] **et ōlim,** also in the future
[40] *here* = sometimes
[41] **cithara, -ae,** lyre

suscitat[42] Mūsam,[43] neque semper arcum
20    tendit[44] Apollō.[45]
Rēbus angustīs[46] animōsus[47] atque
fortis appārē[48]; sapienter[49] īdem[50]
contrahēs[51] ventō nimium secundō
turgida[52] vēla.[53] (**Horace,** *Odes* 2.10)

## XXV. LĀBUNTUR ANNĪ

Ēheu![1] fugācēs,[2] Postume, Postume,
lābuntur[3] annī; nec pietās[4] moram
rūgīs[5] et īnstantī[6] senectae[7]
adferet indomitaeque[8] mortī.

. . .

5    Frūstrā[9] cruentō[10] Mārte[11] carēbimus
frāctīsque[12] raucī[13] flūctibus[14] Hadriae[15];
frūstrā[9] per autumnōs[16] nocentem
corporibus[17] metuēmus Austrum.[18]
Vīsendus[19] āter[20] flūmine languidō[21]
10    Cōcȳtos[22] errāns et Danaī genus[23]
īnfāme[24] damnātusque[25] longī

---

[42]suscitō (1), arouse; **suscitat,** *subj. is* **Apollō**

[43]**Mūsa, -ae,** a Muse

[44]**tendō, -ere, tetendī, tēnsum,** stretch

[45]**Apollō, -inis,** *m.,* Apollo, *god of the sun, prophecy, poetry, and music; also god of archery, pestilence, and medicine. Apollo has two aspects: happy and constructive (***Mūsam***); unhappy and destructive (***arcum***).*

[46]**rēbus angustīs,** *abl. abs.,* when things are narrow (= **difficult**), *i.e.,* in adversity

[47]**anim-ōsus, -a, -um (-ōsus,** *suffix* = full of), spirited

[48]**appāreō, -ēre, -uī, -itum,** show one's self; **appārē,** *analyze the form carefully.*

[49]*here* = if you are wise

[50]*see n. 36 above*

[51]**con-trahō,** draw in, shorten

[52]**turgidus, -a, -um,** swollen

[53]**vēlum, -ī,** sail

### XXV

METER: Alcaic stanza.

[1]**ēheu,** *cf.* **heu.** *This sigh is emphasized by the repetition of Postumus' name.*

[2]**fugāx,** *gen.* **-ācis,** fleeting

[3]**lābor, -ī, lāpsus sum,** slip, glide

[4]**pietās, -tātis,** *f.,* loyalty, devotion, piety

[5]**rūga, -ae,** wrinkle (*cf. corrugated*)

[6]**īnstāns,** *gen.* **-antis,** pressing, urgent

[7]**senecta, -ae** = **senectūs**

[8]**indomitus, -a, -um,** untamable, invincible

[9]**frūstrā,** *adv.,* in vain. *What is the significance of its emphatic position?*

[10]**cruentus, -a, -um,** bloody

[11]**Mārs, Mārtis,** *m.,* Mars, *god of war;* **Mārte,** *what abl.?*

[12]**frangō, -ere, frēgī, frāctum,** break

[13]**raucus, -a, -um,** hoarse, noisy

[14]**flūctus, -ūs,** wave; **frāctīs flūctibus,** broken waves = breakers

[15]**Hadria, -ae,** *m.,* Adriatic Sea

[16]**autumnus, -ī,** autumn, *unhealthy part of the year because of the Sirocco*

[17]*depends on* **nocentem**

[18]**auster, -trī,** the south wind, *the Sirocco blowing from the Sahara*

[19]**vīsō, -ere, vīsī, vīsum,** visit; **vīsendus (est)**

[20]**āter, ātra, ātrum,** dark, *modifying* **Cōcȳtos**

[21]**languidus, -a, -um,** sluggish, weak

[22]**Cōcȳtos, -ī,** *m.,* Cocytus, the river of wailing, *one of the rivers surrounding Hades;* **Cōcȳtos,** *Gk. nom.*

[23]**Danaī genus,** *the offspring of* **Danaüs,** *whose 49 daughters murdered their husbands and in Hades were punished by having to pour water eternally into a sieve*

[24]**īnfāmis, -e,** infamous

[25]**damnō** (1) condemn

Sīsyphus²⁶ Aeolidēs²⁷ labōris.²⁸

Linquenda²⁹ tellūs³⁰ et domus et placēns

uxor, neque hārum, quās colis, arborum

15     tē praeter invīsās³¹ cupressōs³²

ūlla³³ brevem dominum³⁴ sequētur. (**Horace,** *Odes* 2.14.1–4, 13–24)

## XXVI.  A SENSE OF BALANCE IN LIFE

Vīvitur¹ parvō bene cui² paternum³

splendet⁴ in mēnsā tenuī⁵ salīnum,

nec levēs⁶ somnōs timor aut cupīdō

sordidus⁷ aufert.⁸

5     Quid⁹ brevī fortēs¹⁰ iaculāmur¹¹ aevō

multa? Quid¹² terrās aliō calentēs

sōle mūtāmus? Patriae quis exsul¹³

sē quoque fūgit?¹⁴

Scandit¹⁵ aerātās¹⁶ vitiōsa nāvēs

10    cūra nec turmās¹⁷ equitum relinquit,

ōcior¹⁸ cervīs¹⁹ et agente nimbōs²⁰

ōcior Eurō.²¹

Laetus²² in praesēns²³ animus quod ultrā est

---

²⁶**Sīsyphus, -ī,** Sisyphus, *who was condemned eternally to roll up a hill a stone which rolled down again—an exquisite nightmare*

²⁷**Aeolidēs, -ae,** *m.,* son of Aeolus

²⁸*After verbs of accusing, condemning, and acquitting the gen. can be used to express the charge or the penalty involved.*

²⁹**linquenda (est),** *balancing* **vīsendus** in contrast; **linquō** = re-linquō

³⁰**tellūs, -ūris,** *f.,* earth, land

³¹**invīsus, -a, -um,** hated, hateful

³²**cupressus, -ī,** *f.,* cypress (tree); **invīsās** *because they were used at funerals and were planted near tombs*

³³**neque ūlla hārum arborum,** nor any = and none . . .

³⁴**brevem dominum,** *in apposition with* **tē; brevem,** *implying that life is brief*

## XXVI

METER: Sapphic stanza.

¹**vīvitur parvō bene (ab eō) cui,** it is lived on little well by him for whom: **vīvitur,** *impers. pass.* = he lives well on little (*i.e., not in abject poverty and not in the lap of luxury*).

²**cui,** *dat. of ref. but most easily translated by* whose

³**paternum salīnum (salīnum, -ī),** paternal salt-cellar; *the long list of words derived from* **sāl** *provides some idea of the importance of salt and the salt-cellar.*

⁴**splendeō, -ēre,** shine

⁵**tenuis, -e,** plain, simple

⁶**levis, -e,** *here* = gentle

⁷**sordidus, -a, -um,** sordid (*cf.* **sordēs** *Locī Im. XXIV n. 14*); **cupīdō** *is m. in Horace.*

⁸**auferō (ab-ferō)**

⁹= **cūr**

¹⁰**fortēs (virī) brevī aevō (aevum, -ī,** time, life)

¹¹**iaculor (1),** aim at

¹²**Quid . . . mūtāmus,** *lit.* why do we exchange lands warmed by another sun? *The expression is poetic and in part illogical but the sense is clear:* why do we exchange our lands for those warmed by another sun? "The pasture is always greener . . ."

¹³**exsul, exsulis,** *m.,* exile; *with* **patriae quis,** who an exile of (from) his native land

¹⁴**fūgit,** *perf.,* has ever fled

¹⁵**scandō, -ere, scandī, scānsum,** climb up

¹⁶**aerātus, -a, -um,** fitted with bronze, *probably referring to the bronze beaks of the men-of-war* (**longae nāvēs**), *which were faster than the ordinary ships—though even these cannot outstrip anxiety.*

¹⁷**turma, -ae,** a troop of cavalry (**equitum,** *Locī Im. XVIII n. 53*). *A person cannot ride fast enough to escape care.*

¹⁸**ōcior, -ius,** *adj. in compar. degree,* swifter, *agreeing with* **cūra**

¹⁹**cervus, -ī,** stag

²⁰**nimbus, -ī,** rain cloud

²¹**Eurus, -ī,** wind (from the southeast)

²²**laetus, -a, -um,** happy, joyful

²³**praesēns,** *gen.* **-entis,** present; **in praesēns (tempus)** for the present (*cf. the* **carpe diem** *philosophy*)

ōderit[24] cūrāre et amāra[25] lentō[26]
15 temperet[27] rīsū[28]: nihil est ab omnī
    parte[29] beātum. (**Horace**, *Odes* 2.16.13–28)

## XXVII. DIĒS FĒSTUS

Hic diēs[1] vērē mihi fēstus ātrās
eximet[2] cūrās: ego nec tumultum
nec morī per vim metuam tenente
    Caesare[3] terrās.
5 Ī, pete unguentum,[4] puer,[5] et corōnās,[6]
et cadum[7] Mārsī[8] memorem[9] duellī,
Spartacum[10] sī quā[11] potuit vagantem
    fallere[12] testa.[13] (**Horace**, *Odes* 3.14.13–20)

## XXVIII. A MONUMENT MORE LASTING THAN BRONZE

Exēgī monumentum aere perennius[1]
rēgālīque[2] sitū[3] pȳramidum[4] altius,[5]
quod nōn imber[6] edāx,[7] nōn Aquilō[8] impotēns[9]
possit dīruere[10] aut innumerābilis[11]
5 annōrum seriēs[12] et fuga temporum.
Nōn omnis moriar, multaque pars meī
    vītābit Libitīnam[13] . . . (**Horace**, *Odes* 3.30.1–7)

---

[24]**ōderit**, *perf. subjunct., jussive,* let (the **laetus animus**) refuse to (hate to) be anxious about (**cūrāre**)

[25]**amārus, -a, -um**, bitter, disagreeable; **amāra**, *n. pl.*

[26]**lentus, -a, -um**, pliant, tenacious, slow, lingering; *here* = tolerant, quiet

[27]**temperō** (1), control, temper

[28]**rīsus, -ūs**, laughter (*cf.* **rīdeō**)

[29]**ab omnī parte**, from every part = in every respect, completely

*the* **sociī** (*allies*) *of Rome in Italy gained full citizenship; i.e., a 65-year-old wine*

[9]**memor**, *gen.* **-oris**, mindful

[10]**Spartacus, -ī**, Spartacus, *the gladiator who led the slaves in revolt against Rome, 73–71 B.C.*

[11]**quā**, *adv.*, anywhere *or* in any way

[12]**fallō, -ere, fefellī, falsum**, deceive, escape the notice of

[13]**testa, -ae**, jug

## XXVII

METER: Sapphic stanza.

[1]**Hic diēs**, *referring to Augustus' return from the campaign of 27–25 B.C. in Spain*

[2]**eximō, -ere, -ēmī, -ēmptum**, take away

[3]**Caesar** = Augustus. *When C. Octavius was adopted by his great-uncle, C. Iulius Caesar, his name became C. Iulius Caesar Octavianus, to which the senate added the title of Augustus in 27 B.C.*

[4]**unguentum, -ī**, ointment, perfume

[5]**puer** = slave; *cf. Fr.* **garçon**

[6]**corōna, -ae**, crown, wreath

[7]**cadus, -ī**, wine jar

[8]**Mārsus, -a, -um**, Marsian; **duellum** = *old form of* **bellum: Mārsī duellī**, *of the Marsian, or Social, War of 91–88 B.C., by which*

## XXVIII

METER: Lesser Asclepiad.

[1]**perennis, -e**, lasting (throughout the year)

[2]**rēgālis, -e**, royal

[3]**situs, -ūs**, site, situation; *here* = structure

[4]**pȳramis, -idis, f.**, pyramid

[5]**altus, -a, -um**, high; **altius** *agrees with* **monumentum**.

[6]**imber, -bris, m.**, storm

[7]**edāx**, *gen.* **edacis**, greedy, destructive

[8]**aquilō, -ōnis, m.**, north wind

[9]**impotēns**, *gen.* **-ntis**, powerless (*to injure my monument*)

[10]**dīruō, -ere, -ruī, -rutum**, raze, destroy

[11]**in-numerābilis, -e** = *Eng.*

[12]**seriēs, -ēī**, succession

[13]**Libitīna, -ae**, Libitina, *goddess of funerals;* death

## XXIX.  THE OTHER PERSON'S FAULTS AND OUR OWN

Pērās[1] imposuit[2] Iuppiter nōbīs duās:
propriīs[3] replētam[4] vitiīs post tergum[5] dedit,[6]
aliēnīs[7] ante pectus[8] suspendit[9] gravem.
Hāc rē vidēre nostra mala nōn possumus;
5    aliī simul[10] dēlinquunt,[11] cēnsōrēs[12] sumus. (**Phaedrus**, *Fābulae* 4.10)

## XXX.  SOUR GRAPES

Famē[1] coācta vulpēs[2] altā in vīneā[3]
ūvam[4] appetēbat,[5] summīs saliēns[6] vīribus.
Quam[7] tangere ut nōn potuit, discēdēns ait:
"Nōndum mātūra[8] est; nōlō acerbam sūmere.[9]"
5    Quī facere[10] quae nōn possunt verbīs ēlevant,[11]
adscrībere[12] hoc dēbēbunt exemplum sibī. (**Phaedrus**, *Fābulae* 4.3)

## XXXI.  THE FOX AND THE TRAGIC MASK

Persōnam[1] tragicam[2] forte[3] vulpēs vīderat.
"Ō quanta speciēs,[4]" inquit, "cerebrum[5] nōn habet!"
Hoc illīs dictum est quibus honōrem et glōriam
Fortūna tribuit,[6] sēnsum commūnem abstulit. (**Phaedrus**, *Fābulae* 1.7)

### XXIX
METER: Iambic trimeter.
**Phaedrus:** freedman of Augustus, who made extensive use of Aesop's fables.
[1]**pēra, -ae,** wallet
[2]**im-pōnō,** + *dat.,* put on
[3]**proprius, -a, -um,** one's own, *here* = our own
[4]**repleō, -ēre, -plēvī, -plētum,** fill; (**pēram**) **replētam**
[5]**tergum, -ī,** back
[6]**dedit,** *here* = put
[7]**aliēnus, -a, -um,** belonging to another; **aliēnīs (vitiīs),** *abl. with* **gravem**
[8]*sc.* **nostrum**
[9](**alteram pēram**) **gravem . . . suspendit**
[10]**simul** = **simul ac,** as soon as
[11]**dēlinquō, -ere, -līquī, -lictum,** fail, commit a crime
[12]**cēnsor, -ōris,** *m.,* censor; censurer, severe judge

### XXX
METER: Iambic trimeter.
[1]**famēs, -is,** *abl.* **-e,** appetite, hunger

[2]**vulpēs, -is,** *f.,* fox
[3]**vīnea, -ae,** vineyard
[4]**ūva, -ae,** bunch of grapes
[5]**ap-petō** (= **ad-petō**), reach toward, desire (*cf. appetite*); **appetēbat,** *note the force of the imperf.*
[6]**saliō, -īre, -uī, saltum,** jump
[7]**quam** = **ūvam**
[8]**mātūrus, -a, -um,** ripe
[9]**sūmō, -ere, sūmpsī, sūmptum,** take
[10]*complem. infin. with* **possunt**
[11]**ēlevō** (1), disparage, weaken
[12]**ad-scrībō,** assign

### XXXI
METER: Iambic trimeter.
[1]**persōna, -ae,** mask *worn by actors*
[2]**tragicus, -a, -um,** tragic
[3]**forte,** *adv.,* by chance
[4]**speciēs, -ēī,** appearance, form
[5]**cerebrum, -ī,** brain
[6]**tribuō, -ere, -uī, -ūtum,** allot, assign, give

## XXXII. THE STAG AT THE SPRING

Ad fontem[1] cervus, cum bibisset, restitit,[2]
et in liquōre[3] vīdit effigiem[4] suam.
Ibi dum rāmōsa[5] mīrāns[6] laudat cornua,
crūrumque[7] nimiam[8] tenuitātem[9] vituperat,[10]
5  vēnantum[11] subitō vōcibus conterritus,[12]
per campum fugere coepit, et cursū levī
canēs[13] ēlūsit.[14] Silva tum excēpit ferum,[15]
in quā retentīs[16] impedītus cornibus,
lacerārī[17] coepit morsibus[18] saevīs[19] canum.
10  Tunc moriēns vōcem hanc ēdidisse[20] dīcitur:
"Ō mē īnfēlīcem[21]! quī nunc dēmum[22] intellegō
ūtilia mihi quam[23] fuerint quae[24] dēspexeram,[25]
et quae laudāram,[26] quantum lūctūs[27] habuerint." (**Phaedrus**, *Fābulae* 1.12)

## XXXIII. THE FOX GETS THE RAVEN'S CHEESE

Quī sē laudārī gaudet verbīs subdolīs,[1]
ferē dat poenās turpī paenitentiā.[2]
Cum dē fenestrā corvus[3] raptum cāseum[4]
comēsse[5] vellet, celsā residēns[6] arbore,
5  hunc vīdit vulpēs; deinde sīc coepit loquī:
"Ō quī tuārum, corve, pennārum[7] est nitor[8]!

## XXXII

METER: Iambic trimeter.

[1]**fōns, fontis,** *m.,* spring
[2]**restō, -āre, restitī,** remain (standing)
[3]**liquor, -ōris,** *m.,* liquid
[4]**effigiēs, -ēī,** image, likeness
[5]**rāmōsus, -a, -um,** branching
[6]**mīror** (1), marvel at, wonder
[7]**crūs, crūris,** *n.,* leg
[8]**nimius, -a, -um,** excessive
[9]**tenuitās, -tātis,** *f.,* thinness
[10]**vituperō** (1), blame, find fault with
[11]**vēnor** (1), hunt; **vēnantum,** *gen. pl. of pres. partic.*
[12]**con-territus**
[13]**canis, -is,** *m./f.,* dog
[14]**ēlūdō, -ere, -lūsī, -lūsum,** evade
[15]**ferus, -ī,** wild animal
[16]**re-tentus, -a, -um,** held back, held fast
[17]**lacerō** (1), tear to pieces (*cf.* lacerate)
[18]**morsus, -ūs,** bite
[19]**saevus, -a, -um,** fierce, savage

[20]**ēdō, -ere, -didī, -ditum,** give out, utter
[21]**mē īnfēlīcem,** *acc. of exclamation*
[22]**dēmum,** *adv.,* at last
[23]**ūtilia . . . quam = quam ūtilia**
[24]**(ea, those things) quae**
[25]**dēspiciō, -ere, -spexī, -spectum,** look down on, despise
[26]**= laudāveram**
[27]**lūctus, -ūs,** grief, sorrow

## XXXIII

METER: Iambic trimeter.

[1]**subdolus, -a, -um,** deceitful
[2]**paenitentia, -ae,** repentance
[3]**corvus, -ī,** raven
[4]**cāseus, -ī,** cheese
[5]**comedō, comedere** or **comēsse, -ēdī, -ēsum,** eat up
[6]**resideō, -ēre, -sēdī, -sessum,** sit, be sitting
[7]**penna, -ae,** feather
[8]**nitor, -ōris,** *m.,* brightness, beauty; **quī est nitor,** what (= how great) is the beauty

Quantum decōris[9] corpore et vultū geris![10]
Sī vōcem habērēs, nūlla prior[11] āles[12] foret."[13]
At ille stultus, dum vult vōcem ostendere,
10   ēmīsit[14] ōre cāseum, quem celeriter
dolōsa[15] vulpēs avidīs[16] rapuit dentibus.[17] (**Phaedrus**, *Fābulae* 1.13.1–10)

## XXXIV.  THE ASS AND THE OLD SHEPHERD

In prīncipātū[1] commūtandō[2] cīvium
nīl praeter dominī nōmen mūtant pauperēs.
Id esse vērum parva haec fābella[3] indicat.
Asellum[4] in prātō[5] timidus[6] pāscēbat[7] senex.
5    Is, hostium clamōre[8] subitō[9] territus,
suādēbat[10] asinō fugere nē possent capī.
At ille lentus:[11] "Quaesō,[12] num bīnās[13] mihī
clītellās[14] impositūrum[15] victōrem[16] putās?"
Senex negāvit. "Ergō quid rēfert meā[17]
10   cui serviam clītellās dum portem[18] meās?" (**Phaedrus**, *Fābulae* 1.15)

## XXXV.  THE TWO MULES AND THE ROBBERS

Mūlī[1] gravātī[2] sarcinīs[3] ībant duō.
Ūnus ferēbat fiscōs[4] cum pecūniā;
alter tumentēs[5] multō saccōs[6] hordeō.[7]
Ille onere[8] dīves, celsā cervīce[9] ēminēns[10]

---

[9] **decor, decōris**, *m.*, grace, beauty
[10] you bear, *i.e.,* have in your body and face; (**in**) **corpore**, *preps. often omitted in poetry*
[11] **prior**, *pred. adj. after* **foret**, better, finer
[12] **āles, ālitis**, *f.*, bird
[13] **foret** = **esset**
[14] **ē-mittō**
[15] **dolōsus, -a, -um**, crafty, cunning
[16] **avidus, -a, -um**, greedy, eager
[17] **dēns, dentis**, *m.*, tooth

[11] **lentus, -a, -um**, slow, motionless, apathetic
[12] **quaesō, -ere**, beg, beseech, = **quaerō**
[13] **bīnās clītellās**, two pairs of panniers (*i.e., instead of the present single pair*); **bīnī, -ae, -a**, *distributive numeral used with a regularly pl. noun*
[14] **clītellae, -ārum**, a pair of panniers, baskets
[15] **im-pōnō** = **in** + **pōnō**
[16] **victor, -ōris** = *Eng.*
[17] what difference does it make to me, *highly idiomatic*
[18] **portō** (1), bear, carry

## XXXIV
METER: Iambic trimeter.
[1] **prīncipātus, -ūs**, rule, dominion
[2] **com-mūtō** (1), change
[3] **fābella, -ae**, fable
[4] **asellus, -ī**, a little ass, *diminutive of* **asinus, -ī**, an ass (*verse 6*)
[5] **prātum, -ī**, meadow
[6] **timidus, -a, -um**, timid
[7] **pāscō, -ere, pāvī, pāstum**, pasture
[8] **clāmor, -ōris**, *m.*, shouting
[9] **subitus, -a, -um**, sudden
[10] **suādeō, -ēre, suāsī, suāsum**, urge

## XXXV
METER: Iambic trimeter.
[1] **mūlus, -ī**, mule
[2] **gravō** (1), load, burden
[3] **sarcina, -ae**, bundle, pack
[4] **fiscus, -ī**, basket
[5] **tumeō, -ēre**, swell, be swollen
[6] **saccus, -ī**, sack
[7] **hordeum, -ī**, barley
[8] **onus, -eris**, *n.*, burden, load
[9] **cervīx, -vīcis**, *f.*, neck
[10] **ēmineō, -ēre, -minuī**, stand out, be conspicuous

5  clārumque collō[11] iactāns[12] tintinnābulum[13];
   comes[14] quiētō[15] sequitur et placidō[16] gradū.[17]
   Subitō latrōnēs[18] ex īnsidiīs advolant,[19]
   interque caedem ferrō mūlum lancinant[20];
   dīripiunt[21] nummōs,[22] neglegunt vīle[23] hordeum.
10 Spoliātus[24] igitur cāsūs[25] cum flēret suōs,
   "Equidem," inquit alter, "mē contemptum gaudeō.
   Nam nihil āmīsī, nec sum laesus[26] vulnere."
   Hōc argūmentō tūta est hominum tenuitās[27];
   magnae perīclō[28] sunt opēs obnoxiae.[29] (**Phaedrus,** *Fābulae* 2.7)

## XXXVI. DELIGHTS OF THE COUNTRY

C.[1] Plīnius Calpurniō Macrō[2] Suō S.[1]

   Bene est[3] mihi quia[4] tibi est bene. Habēs uxōrem tēcum, habēs fīlium; fru-
eris[5] marī, fontibus, viridibus,[6] agrō, vīllā amoenissimā.[7] Neque enim dubitō esse
amoenissimam,[8] in quā sē composuerat[9] homō[10] fēlīcior antequam[11] "fēlīcissimus"
fieret. Ego in Tuscīs[12] et vēnor[13] et studeō, quae[14] interdum[15] alternīs,[16] interdum
5 simul[17] faciō; nec tamen adhūc[18] possum prōnūntiāre utrum sit difficilius capere
aliquid an scrībere. Valē. (**Pliny,** *Epistulae* 5.18)

---

[11]**collum, -ī,** neck
[12]**iactō** (1), toss
[13]**tintinnābulum, -ī,** bell, *a delightfully onomatopoetic word*
[14]**comes, comitis,** *m./f.,* companion
[15]**quiētus, -a, -um,** quiet
[16]**placidus, -a, -um,** placid, gentle
[17]**gradus, -ūs,** step
[18]**latrō, -ōnis,** *m.,* bandit, robber
[19]**advolō** (1), fly, hasten
[20]**lancinō** (1), mangle
[21]**dīripiō, -ere, -ripuī, -reptum,** plunder
[22]**nummus, -ī,** currency, money
[23]**vīlis, -e,** cheap
[24]**spoliō** (1), rob
[25]**cāsus, -ūs,** accident
[26]**laedō, -ere, laesī, laesum,** injure
[27]**tenuitās, -tātis,** *f.,* poverty
[28]**perīclum, -ī,** *early Lat. form, used instead of* **perīculum** *in clas-*
   *sical Lat. poetry whenever it was metrically convenient*
[29]**obnoxius, -a, -um,** subject to, exposed to

## XXXVI

[1]*Locī Ant. XI n. 1 and 3*
[2]**Calpurnius Macer**

[3]*it is*
[4]**quia,** *conj.,* because
[5]**fruor, -ī, frūctus sum** + *abl.,* enjoy (*cf.* **frūctus, -ūs**)
[6]**viridis, -e,** green; **viridia,** *gen.* **viridium,** *n. pl. as a noun,* green
   things, greenery
[7]**amoenus, -a, -um,** pleasant
[8]**amoenissimam,** *agreeing with* **vīllam** *understood as subj. of* **esse**
[9]**sē compōnere,** to compose oneself, to rest
[10]the man, *apparently referring to a former owner who had been
   happier* (**fēlīcior**) *on this estate as an ordinary person* (**homō**)
   *before he could realize his ambition of becoming* "most happy"
   (**fēlīcissimus**), *i.e., before he could achieve some very high position which did not give him supreme happiness after all.*
[11]**antequam** + *subjunct.*
[12]*lit.* in the Tuscans = on my Tuscan estate
[13]**vēnor** (1), hunt
[14]**quae,** *n. pl. referring to* **vēnor** *and* **studeō** *as antecedents*
[15]**interdum,** *adv.,* sometimes, at times
16**alternīs,** *adv.,* alternately, by turns
[17]**simul,** *adv.,* at the same time, simultaneously. *In another letter* (1.6), *Pliny tells how he combined hunting and studying in
   one operation.*
[18]**adhūc,** *adv.,* thus far, till now

## XXXVII.  MORE COUNTRY PLEASURES

C. Plīnius Canīniō[1] Suō S.

Studēs an[2] piscāris[3] an vēnāris an simul omnia? Possunt enim omnia simul fierī ad Lārium[4] nostrum. Nam lacus[5] piscem,[6] ferās[7] silvae quibus lacus cingitur,[8] studia altissimus iste sēcessus[9] adfatim[10] suggerunt.[11] Sed sīve[12] omnia simul sīve
5    aliquid facis, nōn possum dīcere "invideō"; angor[13] tamen . . . Numquamne hōs artissimōs laqueōs[14] . . . abrumpam?[15] Numquam, putō. Nam veteribus negōtiīs[16] nova accrēscunt,[17] nec tamen priōra peraguntur[18]; tot nexibus,[19] tot quasi catēnīs[20] maius in diēs[21] occupātiōnum[22] agmen[23] extenditur.[24] Valē. (**Pliny,** *Epistulae* 2.8, excerpts)

## XXXVIII.  HAPPY MARRIED LIFE

C. Plīnius Geminō Suō S.

Grave vulnus Macrinus noster accēpit: āmīsit[1] uxōrem singulāris[2] exemplī . . . Vīxit cum hāc trīgintā novem annīs[3] sine iūrgiō,[4] sine offēnsā.[5] Quam illa reverentiam[6] marītō[7] suō praestitit, cum ipsa summam merērētur![8] Quot quantāsque
5    virtūtēs ex dīversīs[9] aetātibus sūmptās collēgit et miscuit! Habet quidem Macrinus grande[10] sōlācium, quod tantum bonum tam diū tenuit; sed hinc[11] magis exacerbātur[12] quod āmīsit. Nam fruendīs voluptātibus crēscit carendī dolor. Erō ergō

### XXXVII

[1] *Pliny and Caninius were fellow townsmen from Comum (Como) at the south end of beautiful Lake Larius (Como) in northern Italy.*
[2] **an,** *in questions,* or
[3] **piscor** (1), to fish
[4] **Lārius, -iī,** Lake Larius (now Lake Como)
[5] **lacus, -ūs,** lake
[6] **piscis, -is,** *m.,* fish
[7] **fera** (*sc.* **bēstia**), **-ae,** wild animal
[8] **cingō, -ere, cīnxī, cīnctum,** surround, gird
[9] **sēcessus, -ūs,** retreat, summer place
[10] **adfatim,** *adv.,* sufficiently, abundantly
[11] **sug-gerō, -ere, -gessī, -gestum,** furnish, afford, supply
[12] **sīve . . . sīve, (sī-ve),** if . . . or if, whether . . . or
[13] **angō, -ere,** torment
[14] **artus, -a, -um,** close, narrow; **laqueus, -ī,** noose, cord
[15] **ab-rumpō, -ere, -rūpī, -ruptum,** break off, sever. *Pliny is tied up in Rome.*
[16] **negōtium, -iī,** business; duty
[17] **accrēscō, -ere, -crēvī, -crētum,** increase; **nova (negōtia) accrēscunt (veteribus negōtiīs)** new duties increase by . . . *or* are added to . . .

[18] **per-agō,** complete
[19] **nexus, -ūs,** coils, obligations
[20] **catēna, -ae,** chain
[21] **in diēs,** from day to day
[22] **occupātiō, -ōnis,** *f.,* occupation, employment
[23] **agmen, -minis,** *n.,* line of march, column
[24] **ex-tendō, -ere, -tendī, -tentum,** extend, increase

### XXXVIII

[1] he lost (*not* sent away)
[2] **singulāris, -e,** extraordinary
[3] *The abl. is sometimes used instead of the acc. to express the idea of extent of time.*
[4] **iūrgium, -iī,** quarrel
[5] **offēnsa, -ae,** hatred, affront
[6] **reverentia, -ae,** respect
[7] **marītus, -ī,** husband
[8] **mereor, -ērī, meritus sum,** deserve
[9] **dīversus, -a, -um,** diverse, different
[10] **grandis, -e,** great
[11] **hinc,** *here* = from this cause
[12] **exacerbō** (1), exasperate; embitter

suspēnsus[13] prō homine amīcissimō dum[14] admittere[15] āvocāmenta[16] et cicātrīcem[17] patī possit, quam nihil aequē ac[18] necessitās[19] ipsa et diēs[20] longa et satietās[21] dolōris indūcit.[22] Valē. (**Pliny,** *Epistulae* 8.5, excerpts)

10

## XXXIX. FAITHFUL IN SICKNESS AND IN DEATH

C. Plīnius Nepōtī Suō S.

(. . . Fannia[1]) neptis[2] Arriae[3] illīus[4] quae marītō[5] et sōlācium mortis et exemplum fuit. Multa referēbat[6] aviae[7] suae nōn minōra hōc,[8] sed obscūriōra,[9] quae tibi exīstimō tam mīrābilia legentī[10] fore[11] quam mihi audientī fuērunt.

5 Aegrōtābat[12] Caecīna Paetus, marītus eius, aegrōtābat et fīlius, uterque mortiferē,[13] ut vidēbātur. Fīlius dēcessit[14] eximiā[15] pulchritūdine,[16] parī verēcundiā,[17] et parentibus nōn minus ob[18] alia cārus quam quod fīlius erat. Huic illa ita fūnus[19] parāvit . . . ut ignōrāret marītus. Quīn immō,[20] quotiēns[21] cubiculum[22] eius intrāret,[23] vīvere fīlium atque etiam commodiōrem[24] esse simulābat[25]; ac persaepe[26]

10 interrogantī[27] quid ageret puer respondēbat, "Bene quiēvit,[28] libenter cibum[29] sūmpsit." Deinde, cum diū cohibitae[30] lacrimae vincerent prōrumperentque,[31] ēgrediēbātur; tunc sē dolōrī dabat. Satiāta, siccīs[32] oculīs, compositō vultū redībat,

---

[13]**suspēnsus, -a, -um,** in suspense, anxious

[14]**dum,** *conj.,* until, *used with the subjunct. to imply intention or expectancy*

[15]**ad-mittō,** admit, receive

[16]**āvocāmentum, -ī,** diversion

[17]**cicātrīx, -trīcis,** *f.,* scar, *which implies healing*

[18]**aequē ac,** equally as, quite so well as

[19]**necessitās (-tātis,** *f.)* **ipsa,** necessity itself, sheer necessity

[20]*here* = time

[21]**satietās, -tātis,** *f.,* satiety

[22]**in-dūcō,** bring on, induce

## XXXIX

[1]**Fannia (est)**

[2]**neptis, -is,** *f.,* granddaughter

[3]**Arria, -ae,** Arria (Maior), *brave wife of Caecina Paetus. When, because of his part in a conspiracy against the emperor Claudius, he had to commit suicide in 42 A.D., Arria committed suicide with him, actually setting him an example as indicated at the end of the letter. (Cf.* **"Paete, Nōn Dolet,"** *Capvt XXXIX).*

[4]**ille,** the famous, *when immediately following its noun*

[5]**marītō,** *dat.*

[6]**referēbat,** *subj. = Fannia, who related these episodes during a conversation with Pliny on the preceding day.*

[7]**avia, -ae,** grandmother; **aviae,** *gen. case*

[8]**hōc,** *abl. of comparison, referring to the rel. clause of the preceding sent.*

[9]**obscūrus, -a, -um,** obscure, unknown

[10]**legentī,** to be construed with **tibi**

[11]**fore = futūra esse,** *fut. infin. in ind. state. depending on* **exīstimō** (1), think

[12]**aegrōtō** (1), be sick

[13]**mortiferē,** *adv.* (**mors-ferō**), fatally

[14]**dē-cēdō,** go away, die (*cf.* deceased)

[15]**eximius, -a, -um,** extraordinary

[16]**pulchritūdō, -dinis,** *f.,* beauty; **eximiā pulchritūdine,** *abl. describing* **fīlius** *but more easily translated if we supply a word like* **puer:** *fīlius dēcessit—(puer) eximiā pulchritūdine, etc.*

[17]**verecūndia, -ae,** modesty

[18]**ob,** *prep. + acc.,* on account of; toward

[19]**fūnus, -eris,** *n.,* funeral

[20]**quīn immō,** why, on the contrary

[21]**quotiēns,** *adv.,* as often as

[22]**cubiculum, -ī,** bedroom

[23]**intrō** (1), enter; **intrāret:** *in Silver Lat. the imperf. subjunct. of customary action is often found in place of the indic.*

[24]**commodus, -a, -um,** suitable, satisfactory; *here* = better

[25]**simulō** (1) pretend

[26]**per-saepe,** *adv.,* very often

[27]**interrogō** (1), ask, inquire (*cf.* **rogō**); (**marītō**) **interrogantī**

[28]**quiēscō, -ere, -ēvī, -ētus,** rest, be quiet

[29]**cibus, -ī,** food

[30]**cohibeō, -ere, -uī, -itum,** hold together, hold back, restrain

[31]**prōrumpō, -ere, -rūpī, -ruptum,** burst forth

[32]**siccus, -a, -um,** dry; **siccīs oculīs** *abl. abs.*

tamquam orbitātem[33] forīs relīquisset.[34] Praeclārum quidem illud[35] eiusdem: ferrum stringere,[36] perfodere[37] pectus, extrahere[38] pugiōnem,[39] porrigere[40] marītō, ad-
15    dere[41] vōcem immortālem ac paene[42] dīvīnam,[43] "Paete, nōn dolet." ... Valē. (**Pliny,**
*Epistulae* 3.16, excerpts)

## XL.  A SWEET, BRAVE GIRL

C. Plīnius Marcellīnō Suō S.

Trīstissimus haec tibi scrībō, Fundānī nostrī fīliā minōre dēfūnctā,[1] quā puellā[2]
nihil umquam fēstīvius,[3] amābilius,[4] nec longiōre vītā ... dignius vīdī. Nōndum
annōs trēdecim implēverat,[5] et iam illī[6] anīlis[7] prūdentia, mātrōnālis[8] gravitās[9]
5    erat, et tamen suāvitās[10] puellāris[11] ... Ut[12] illa patris cervīcibus[13] inhaerēbat![14] Ut
nōs, amīcōs paternōs,[15] et amanter[16] et modestē[17] complectēbātur![18] Ut nūtrīcēs,[19]
ut paedagōgōs,[20] ut praeceptōrēs[21] prō suō quemque officiō dīligēbat! Quam
studiōsē,[22] quam intelligenter[23] lēctitābat![24] ...

Quā illa temperantiā,[25] quā patientiā, quā etiam cōnstantiā[26] novissimam va-
10    lētūdinem[27] tulit! Medicīs obsequēbātur;[28] sorōrem, patrem adhortābātur[29]; ip-
samque sē dēstitūtam[30] corporis vīribus vigōre[31] animī sustinēbat.[32] Dūrāvit[33] hic[34]
illī usque ad extrēmum,[35] nec aut spatiō[36] valētūdinis aut metū mortis īnfrāctus
est[37] ... Ō trīste plānē[38] acerbumque fūnus[39] ... Iam dēstināta erat[40] ēgregiō[41]

---

[33]**orbitās, -tātis,** *f.,* bereavement, loss
[34]*What kind of condition in the* **tamquam** *clause?*
[35]that deed; *sc.* **fuit**
[36]**stringō, -ere, -strīnxī, strictus,** draw; **stringere,** *infin. in apposition with* **illud**
[37]**perfodiō, -ere, -fōdī, -fossum,** pierce (*lit.* dig through)
[38]**ex-trahō**
[39]**pugiō, -ōnis,** *m.,* dagger
[40]**porrigō, -ere, -rēxī, -rēctum,** hold out, extend
[41]**ad-dō, -ere, -didī, -ditum,** add
[42]**paene,** *adv.,* almost
[43]**dīvīnus, -a, -um** = *Eng.*

## XL
[1]**dēfungor, -ī, -fūnctus sum,** finish *or* complete life, die
[2]**puellā,** *abl. of comparison*
[3]**fēstīvus, -a, -um,** pleasant, agreeable
[4]**amābilis, -e,** lovable, lovely
[5]**impleō, -ēre, -plēvī, -plētum,** fill up, complete
[6]*dat. of possession* (S.S.)
[7]**anīlis, -e,** of an old woman
[8]**mātrōnālis, -e,** of a matron, matronly
[9]**gravitās, -tātis,** *f.,* seriousness, dignity
[10]**suāvitās, -tātis,** *f.,* sweetness
[11]**puellāris, -e,** girlish
[12]how
[13]**cervīx, -īcis,** *f., usually pl.* (**cervīcēs**) *as here,* neck
[14]**inhaereō, -ēre, -haesī, -haesum,** cling

[15]**paternus, -a, -um,** paternal, of a father
[16]**amanter,** *adv. of* **amāns**
[17]**modestē,** *adv.,* modestly
[18]**complector, -ī, -plexus sum,** hold in the arms, embrace
[19]**nūtrīx, -īcis,** *f.,* nurse
[20]**paedagōgus, -ī,** tutor (*slave who escorted children*)
[21]**praeceptor, -ōris,** *m.,* teacher (*in a school, not a private tutor*)
[22]**studiōsē,** *adv. of* **studiōsus,** full of **studium**
[23]**intellegenter,** *adv. of* **intelligēns**
[24]**lēctitō** (1), read (eagerly)
[25]**temperantia, -ae,** self-control
[26]**cōnstantia, -ae,** firmness
[27]**valētūdō, -dinis,** *f., here* = bad health, illness
[28]**ob** + **sequor,** obey
[29]**adhortor** = **hortor**
[30]**dēstituō, -ere, -stituī, -stitūtum,** desert, abandon
[31]**vigor, -ōris,** *m.,* vigor; **vigōre,** *abl. of means with* **sustinēbat**
[32](**puella**) sustinēbat sē ipsam
[33]**dūrō** (1), endure
[34]**hic** (**vigor animī**)
[35]**extrēmum, -ī** = **fīnis**
[36]**spatium, -iī,** space, duration
[37]**īnfringō, -ere, -frēgī, -frāctum,** break
[38]**plānē,** *adv.,* clearly
[39]*here* = **mors**
[40]**dēstinō** (1), bind, engage
[41]**ēgregius, -a, -um,** excellent, distinguished

iuvenī,[42] iam ēlēctus[43] nūptiārum[44] diēs, iam nōs vocātī. Quod gaudium quō
15 maerōre[45] mūtātum est!

Nōn possum exprimere[46] verbīs quantum animō vulnus accēperim cum audīvī Fundānum ipsum praecipientem,[47] quod[48] in vestēs,[49] margarīta,[50] gemmās[51]
fuerat ērogātūrus,[52] hoc in tūs[53] et unguenta et odōrēs[54] impenderētur[55] . . . Sī quās
ad eum dē dolōre tam iūstō litterās mittēs, mementō[56] adhibēre[57] sōlācium . . .
20 molle[58] et hūmānum. (**Pliny,** *Epistulae* 5.16, excerpts)

## XLI. PLINY'S CONCERN ABOUT A SICK FREEDMAN

C. Plīnius Valeriō Paulīnō Suō S.

Videō quam molliter[1] tuōs[2] habeās[3]; quō simplicius[4] tibi cōnfitēbor quā indul-
gentiā[5] meōs tractem.[6] Quod sī essem nātūrā asperior et dūrior, frangeret mē tamen
īnfirmitās[7] lībertī[8] meī Zōsimī,[9] cui tantō maior hūmānitās[10] exhibenda[11] est, quantō
5 nunc illā magis eget. Homō probus,[12] officiōsus,[13] litterātus[14]; et ars quidem eius et
quasi īnscrīptiō[15]—cōmoedus . . . Ūtitur et cithārā perītē.[16] Īdem tam commodē[17]
ōrātiōnēs et historiās[18] et carmina legit ut hoc sōlum didicisse videātur.

Haec tibi sēdulō[19] exposuī quō magis scīrēs quam multa ūnus mihi et quam
iūcunda ministeria[20] praestāret. Accēdit longa iam cāritās[21] hominis, quam ipsa

---

[42] iuvenis, -is, *m.,* young man

[43] ē-ligō = legō

[44] nūptiae, -ārum, wedding

[45] maeror, -ōris, *m.,* grief

[46] ex-primō (= premō), express

[47] praecipiō, -ere, -cēpī, -ceptum, direct

[48] *The antecedent is* hoc *in the following line.*

[49] vestis, -is, *f.,* garment, clothes

[50] margarītum, -ī, pearl

[51] gemma, -ae, jewel

[52] ērogō (1), *pay out, spend;* fuerat ērogātūrus (*act. periphrastic*), he had been about to spend, had intended to spend (*on clothes, jewels, etc., for the wedding*)

[53] tūs, tūris, *n.,* incense

[54] odor, -ōris, *m.,* perfume

[55] impendō, -ere, -pendī, -pēnsum, expend; impenderētur, *subjunct. in a jussive noun clause*

[56] meminī, meminisse, *defective verb,* remember; mementō, *fut. imperat.,* remember

[57] adhibeō, -ere, -hibuī, -hibitum, use, furnish

[58] mollis, -e, soft, gentle

## XLI

[1] molliter, *adv. of* mollis

[2] tuōs (servōs et lībertōs); *so* meōs *below*

[3] treat

[4] simpliciter, *adv.,* frankly, candidly; quō simplicius by which (*degree of difference*) more frankly = the more frankly

[5] indulgentia, -ae, kindness

[6] tractō (1), handle, treat

[7] īnfirmitās, -tātis, *f.,* illness, weakness

[8] lībertus, -ī, freedman (*a slave who had somehow secured his freedom*) *in contrast to a* līber vir (*one who was born free*). *A freedman commonly remained closely attached to his former master.*

[9] Zōsimus, -ī, Zosimus, apparently a Greek

[10] hūmānitās, -tātis, *f.,* kindness

[11] ex-hibeō, show, exhibit

[12] probus, -a, -um, honorable, fine

[13] officiōsus, -a, -um, obliging, courteous

[14] litterātus, -a, -um, well-educated; *Gk. slaves esp. were often well educated.*

[15] īnscrīptiō, -ōnis, *f., here* = label, *a placard hung around a slave's neck in the slave market to indicate his special abilities.*— cōmoedus, -ī, comic actor, *often a slave trained to read at dinners scenes from famous comedies. Although this was Zosimus' specialty, we find him in the next two sents. surprisingly versatile and talented.*

[16] perītē, *adv.,* skillfully

[17] commodē, *adv.,* fitly, satisfactorily

[18] historia, -ae = *Eng.*

[19] sēdulō, *adv.,* carefully

[20] ministerium, -iī, service

[21] cāritās, -tātis, *f.,* dearness, affection (*cf.* cārus)

10    perīcula auxērunt[22] . . . Ante aliquot[23] annōs,[24] dum intentē instanterque[25] prō-
nūntiat, sanguinem[26] reiēcit[27]; atque ob hoc in Aegyptum[28] missus ā mē, post longam peregrīnātiōnem[29] cōnfirmātus[30] rediit nūper. Deinde . . . veteris īnfirmitātis[31]
tussiculā[32] admonitus,[33] rūrsus sanguinem reddidit.[34]

Quā ex causā dēstināvī[35] eum mittere in praedia[36] tua quae Forō Iūliī[37] pos-
15    sidēs.[38] Audīvī enim tē referentem esse ibi āera[39] salūbrem[40] et lac[41] eius modī
cūrātiōnibus[42] accommodātissimum.[43] Rogō ergō scrībās[44] tuīs[45] ut illī vīlla, ut
domus[46] pateat . . . Valē. (**Pliny**, *Epistulae* 5.19, excerpts)

## XLII.  ON BEHALF OF A PENITENT FREEDMAN (42–43)

C. Plīnius Sabīniānō Suō S.

Lībertus tuus, cui suscēnsēre[1] tē dīxerās, vēnit ad mē . . . Flēvit multum, multum rogāvit, multum etiam tacuit; in summā,[2] fēcit mihi fidem paenitentiae.[3]
Vērē crēdō ēmendātum[4] quia dēlīquisse[5] sē sentit. Īrāsceris, sciō; et īrāsceris me-
5    ritō,[6] id quoque sciō; sed tunc praecipua[7] mānsuētūdinis[8] laus cum īrae causa
iūstissima est. Amāstī[9] hominem et, spērō, amābis; interim[10] sufficit[11] ut exōrārī[12] tē
sinās[13] . . . Nē torserīs[14] illum, nē torserīs etiam tē; torquēris[15] enim, cum tam lēnis[16]
īrāsceris. Vereor nē videar nōn rogāre sed cōgere, sī precibus[17] eius meās iūnxerō.

[22]**augeō, -ēre, auxī, auctum**, increase
[23]**aliquot**, *indecl. adj.*, several, some
[24]**ante . . . annōs**, several years ago
[25]earnestly and emphatically
[26]**sanguis, -inis**, *m.*, blood
[27]**re-iciō**, reject, spit out
[28]**Aegyptus, -ī**, *f.*, Egypt
[29]**peregrīnātiō, -ōnis**, *f.*, travel *or* sojourn abroad
[30]**cōnfirmō** (1), strengthen
[31]**īnfirmitās, -tātis**, *f.*, weakness, sickness
[32]**tussicula, -ae**, slight cough
[33]**ad-monitus = monitus**
[34]**reddidit = reiēcit**
[35]**dēstinō** (1), intend, resolve
[36]**praedium, -iī**, country seat
[37]**Forum Iūliī, Forī Iūliī**, Forum of Julius, *modern* Fréjus, *a coastal town of southern France*; **Forō**, *place where*
[38]**possideō, -ēre, -sēdī, -sessum**, possess, own
[39]**āēr, āeris**, *m.*, air; **āera** = *Gk. acc. sg.*
[40]**salūbris, -e**, healthful; *still so regarded*
[41]**lac, lactis**, *n.*, milk; *i.e., for the milk cure*
[42]**cūrātiō, -ōnis**, *f.*, cure
[43]**accommodātus, -a, -um**, suited
[44]**(ut) scrībās: ut** *is sometimes omitted in such clauses*
[45]**tuīs**, your servants

[46]**ut vīlla (pateat), ut domus pateat**: *i.e., he is to have access to the great house itself as well as to the estate.*

### XLII

[1]**suscēnseō, -ēre, -cēnsuī, -cēnsum**, + *dat.*, be angry with
[2]**summa, -ae**, sum
[3]**paenitentia, -ae**, repentance
[4]**ēmendō** (1), correct; **(eum) ēmendātum (esse)**
[5]**dēlinquō, -ere, -līquī, -lictum**, fail (in duty), commit a crime
[6]**meritō**, *adv.*, rightly (with merit)
[7]**praecipuus, -a, -um**, special; *sc. est*
[8]**mānsuētūdō, -inis**, *f.*, gentleness, mildness
[9]*contracted form* = **amāvistī**
[10]**interim**, *adv.*, meanwhile (*cf. intereā*)
[11]**sufficit**, *subj.* = **ut**-*clause*
[12]**ex-ōrō**, *stronger form of* **ōrō**
[13]**sinō, -ere, sīvī, situm**, allow, permit
[14]**torqueō, -ēre, torsī, tortum**, twist, torture; **nē torserīs**, *Locī Im.* XXII n. 1
[15]**torquēris**, you are tormented = you torment yourself (*reflexive use of the pass.*)
[16]**lēnis, -e**, gentle, kind; *agreeing with subj. of* **īrāsceris**: you, such a gentle person
[17]**prex, precis**, *f.*, prayer

Iungam tamen tantō plēnius[18] et effūsius,[19] quantō[20] ipsum[21] ācrius sevēriusque[22]
10  corripuī[23] . . . Valē. (**Pliny,** *Epistulae* 9.21, excerpts)

## XLIII.  THANKS FOR A FRIEND'S CLEMENCY

C. Plīnius Sabīniānō Suō S.

Bene fēcistī[1] quod lībertum[2] aliquandō[3] tibi cārum redūcentibus[4] epistulīs[5] meīs
in domum,[6] in animum recēpistī. Iuvābit hoc tē, mē certē iuvat; prīmum,[7] quod tē
tam tractābilem[8] videō ut in īrā regī possīs; deinde, quod tantum mihi tribuis[9] ut
5  vel[10] auctōritātī meae pāreās vel precibus indulgeās.[11] Igitur laudō et grātiās agō . . .
Valē. (**Pliny,** *Epistulae* 9.24, excerpts)

## XLIV.  SELECTION OF A TEACHER

C. Plīnius Mauricō Suō S.

Quid ā tē mihi iūcundius potuit iniungī[1] quam ut praeceptōrem frātris tuī
līberīs quaererem? Nam beneficiō[2] tuō in scholam[3] redeō et illam dulcissimam
aetātem quasi resūmō.[4] Sedeō inter iuvenēs, ut solēbam, atque etiam experior quan-
5  tum apud illōs auctōritātis[5] ex studiīs habeam. Nam proximē[6] frequentī[7] audītōriō[8]
inter sē cōram[9] multīs ōrdinis[10] nostrī clārē[11] loquēbantur: intrāvī, conticuērunt[12];
quod[13] nōn referrem, nisi ad illōrum magis laudem quam ad meam pertinēret[14] . . .
Cum omnēs quī profitentur[15] audierō, quid dē quōque sentiam scrībam efficiamque,[16]
quantum tamen epistulā cōnsequī[17] poterō, ut ipse omnēs audīsse videāris. Dēbeō
10  enim tibi, dēbeō memoriae frātris tuī hanc fidem, hoc studium, praesertim[18] super[19]

---

[18]**plēnē,** *adv. of* **plēnus**
[19]**effūsē,** *adv., profusely, unrestrainedly*
[20]**tantō . . . quantō,** the more . . . the more, *abl. of degree of difference (S.S.)*
[21](**lībertum**) **ipsum**
[22]**sevērē,** *adv., seriously, severely*
[23]**cor-ripiō, -ere, -ripuī, -reptum,** seize, accuse, blame

## XLIII

[1]you did well because = thank you for
[2]**lībertum,** *in thought, the obj. of both* **redūcentibus** *and* **recēpistī**
[3]**aliquandō,** *adv.,* once
[4]**re-dūcō**
[5]**epistulīs,** *here pl. of a single letter (the preceding one) on the analogy of* **litterae, -ārum**
[6]*Both prepositional phrases, connected by* **et** *understood, depend
on* **recēpistī**
[7]**prīmum,** *adv.,* first
[8]**tractābilis, -ē,** tractable, compliant
[9]**tribuō, -ere, -buī, -būtum,** attribute, ascribe
[10]**vel . . . vel,** either . . . or
[11]**indulgeō, -ēre, -dulsī, -dultum,** yield to, gratify

## XLIV

[1]**in-iungō,** enjoin, impose
[2]**beneficiō tuō,** thanks to you
[3]**schola, -ae,** school
[4]**re-sūmō, -ere, -sūmpsī, -sūmptum,** resume
[5]*gen. with* **quantum**
[6]**proximē,** *adv.,* very recently
[7]**frequēns,** *gen.* **-entis,** crowded
[8]**audītōrium, -iī,** lecture room, school; **audītōriō,** *place where
without a prep.*
[9]**cōram,** *prep. + abl.,* in the presence of
[10]*i.e., the senatorial order*
[11]**clārē** (*adv. of* **clārus**), here = loudly
[12]**conticēscō, -ere, -ticuī,** become silent
[13]**quod,** *having as antecedent the whole preceding idea*
[14]**pertineō, -ēre, -uī, -tentum,** pertain to
[15]**profiteor, -ērī, -fessus sum,** teach, *a late meaning of the word*
[16]**efficiō . . . ut,** *Locī Ant. VIII n. 20–21*
[17]**cōn-sequor,** accomplish
[18]**praesertim,** *adv.,* especially
[19]**super,** *prep. + abl.,* about

tantā rē. Nam quid magis interest vestrā[20] quam ut līberī . . . dignī illō patre, tē patruō[21] reperiantur? . . . Valē. (**Pliny,** *Epistulae* 2.8 excerpts)

### XLV.  THE OLD BOY DYED HIS HAIR

Mentīris[1] iuvenem tīnctīs,[2] Laetīne,[3] capillīs,[4]
　　tam subitō corvus quī modo cycnus[5] erās.
Nōn omnēs fallis[6]; scit tē Prōserpina[7] cānum[8]:
　　persōnam capitī dētrahet[9] illa[10] tuō. (**Martial** 3.43)

### XLVI.  FAKE TEARS

Āmissum[1] nōn flet cum sōla est Gellia[2] patrem;
　　sī quis adest, iussae[3] prōsiliunt[4] lacrimae.
Nōn lūget[5] quisquis laudārī, Gellia, quaerit;
　　ille dolet vērē quī sine teste[6] dolet. (**Martial** 1.33)

### XLVII.  EVEN THOUGH YOU DO INVITE ME—I'LL COME!

Quod convīvāris[1] sine mē tam saepe, Luperce,[2]
　　invēnī noceam quā ratiōne tibi.
Īrāscor: licet[3] usque vocēs mittāsque[4] rogēsque—
　　"Quid faciēs?" inquis. Quid faciam? Veniam! (**Martial** 6.51)

### XLVIII.  PRO-*CRAS*-TINATION

Crās tē vīctūrum,[1] crās dīcis, Postume,[2] semper.
　　Dīc mihi, crās istud,[3] Postume, quandō venit?

---

[20]**interest vestrā**, interests you (*highly idiomatic*)
[21]**patruus, -ī**, (paternal) uncle; **tē patruō** *is in the same construction as* **illō patre**.

### XLV
METER: Elegiac couplet.
[1]**mentior, -īrī, -ītus sum**, lie, declare falsely, *here* = imitate
[2]**tingō, -ere, tīnxī, tīnctus**, wet, dye
[3]**Laetīnus, -ī**, Laetinus
[4]**capillī, -ōrum**, hair
[5]**cycnus, -ī**, swan
[6]**nōn ōmnēs (fallis)** *seems to imply that the hair dyes were good enough to deceive at least some people.*
[7]**Prōserpina, -ae**, Proserpina, *goddess of the underworld, and so of death*
[8]**cānus, -a, -um**, gray; **tē (esse) cānum**
[9]**dē-trahō**
[10]**illa** = Proserpina

### XLVI
METER: Elegiac couplet.
[1]**āmissum patrem**
[2]**Gellia, -ae**, Gellia

[3]*at her bidding; how literally?*
[4]**prōsiliō** (4), leap forth
[5]**lūgeō, -ēre, lūxī, lūctum**, mourn
[6]**testis, -is**, *m.*, witness

### XLVII
METER: Elegiac couplet.
[1]**convīvor** (1), to feast
[2]**Lupercus, -ī**, Lupercus
[3]**licet usque (ut) vocēs** (it is even permitted that you call), you may even invite me, *or even though you invite me*
[4]*i.e., send a slave as a special messenger*

### XLVIII
METER: Elegiac couplet.
[1]**vīctūrum**, *sc.* esse
[2]*No doubt Martial intended to have us think of Horace's Postumus in Locī Im. XXV above.*
[3]**crās istud**, that "tomorrow" of yours, *subj. of* **venit**
[4]**petendum (est)**

> Quam longē est crās istud? ubi est? aut unde petendum[4]?
> Numquid[5] apud Parthōs Armeniōsque[6] latet[7]?
> 5 Iam crās istud habet Priamī[8] vel Nestoris[9] annōs.
> Crās istud quantī[10] dīc mihi possit emī[11]?
> Crās vīvēs? Hodiē iam vīvere, Postume, sērum[12] est.
> Ille sapit quisquis, Postume, vīxit herī. (**Martial** 5.58)

## XLIX. ISSA

> Issa[1] est passere[2] nēquior[3] Catullī:
> Issa est pūrior ōsculō columbae;[4]
> Issa est blandior[5] omnibus puellīs;
> Issa est cārior Indicīs[6] lapillīs[7];
> 5 Issa est dēliciae[8] catella[9] Pūblī.[10]
>
> Hanc tū, sī queritur,[11] loquī putābis.
> Sentit trīstitiamque[12] gaudiumque.
> . . .
> Hanc nē lūx rapiat suprēma[13] tōtam,
> pictā[14] Pūblius exprimit[15] tabellā
> 10 in quā tam similem vidēbis Issam[16]
> ut sit tam similis sibī nec[17] ipsa.
> Issam dēnique pōne cum tabellā:
> aut utramque putābis esse vēram
> aut utramque putābis esse pictam. (**Martial** 1.109)

[5]**numquid latet**, it does not lie hidden, does it?
[6]among the Parthians and Armenians, *i.e., at land's end in the East*
[7]**lateō, -ēre, -uī**, lie hidden
[8]**Priamus, -ī**, Priam, *aged king of Troy*
[9]**Nestōr, -oris**, Nestor, *Gk. leader famed for his years and wisdom*
[10]**quantī**, *gen. of indef. value:* at what price, for how much can that tomorrow be bought
[11]**emō, -ere, ēmī, ēmptum**, buy
[12]**sērus, -a, -um**, late; **sērum**, *pred. adj. in n. to agree with* **hodiē vīvere**, *which is subj. of* **est**

### XLIX
METER: Hendecasyllabic.
[1]**Issa**, *colloquial and affectionate form for* **Ipsa** *and here used as the name of a pet dog*
[2]**passer Catullī**, *see Locī Im. III*
[3]**nēquam**, *indecl. adj.; compar.* **nēquior, -ius**, worthless, good for nothing, mischievous
[4]**columba, -ae**, dove

[5]**blandus, -a, -um**, flattering, caressing, coaxing
[6]**Indicus, -a, -um**, of India
[7]**lapillus, -ī**, precious stone, gem
[8]*see Locī Im. III*
[9]**catella, -ae**, little dog
[10]**Pūblī** = **Pūbliī**, *gen. sg. of* **Pūblius**
[11]*here* = whimper
[12]**trīstitia, -ae**, sadness
[13]**lūx (diēs) suprēma** = **mors**
[14]**pingō, -ere, pīnxī, pictum**, paint; **pictā tabellā**, by a painted tablet = in a painting
[15]**exprimō, -ere, -pressī, pressum**, express, portray
[16]**tam similem . . . Issam**: an Issa (*of the painting*) so similar (*to the real Issa*)
[17]**nec** *here* = not even

# SELF-TUTORIAL EXERCISES

These exercises have been included in the hope of enriching the potential of this book for its various types of users.

1. **Repetītiō est māter memoriae.** In language study the value of repetition is indisputable. To the already large amount of repetition achieved in the regular chapters these exercises add even more practice. The phrases and sentences have deliberately been made simple so that the immediate points in forms and syntax may stand out strikingly. The words are purposely limited to those of the formal lesson vocabularies, which obviously should be memorized before turning to these self-tutorial exercises. As a result of their very nature and purpose, such sentences can make no claim to inspiration. Some hints of the worthwhile reading matter for which one studies Latin are to be found in the **Sententiae Antīquae** and the reading passages from the ancient authors, which are the heart of this book; but if one wants additional repetitious drill by which to establish linguistic reflexes, one can find it here in these exercises. As has been suggested elsewhere, be sure always to read aloud every Latin word and sentence—carefully, for such a practice enables one to learn through the ear as well as the eye and can provide many of the benefits of a language laboratory.

2. To students enrolled in a regular Latin course these exercises with their keys can prove valuable for review and self-testing and can be helpful in preparation for examinations.

3. Also to the private individual who wishes to learn or review Latin independently, these exercises are certain to be valuable, since they can be used as self-tests which can be corrected via the key. Likewise, completing these practice exercises with benefit of key will provide greater confidence in tackling the regular exercises of the book.

4. All students can test themselves in simple Latin composition by translating the English sentences of the key back into Latin and checking this work via the corresponding Latin sentences of the exercises.

5. In the translations ordinarily only one of the various meanings of a word given in the vocabulary will be used in any specific instance. If at times the translations are somewhat formal, the reason is that they can in this way follow the Latin more closely; and certainly these particular sentences are intended to provide practice in understanding Latin rather than practice in literary expression. Polished literary expression in translation is most desirable and should be practiced in connection with the other exercises in this book.

6. The answer keys have been placed by themselves after the exercises to facilitate

self-testing and so that the exercises may be used for practice in class when the instructor wishes. It hardly need be added that the surest way to test oneself is to write out the answers before turning to the key.

7. Finally, let it be emphasized once again that for maximum value you must read aloud all the Latin words, phrases, and sentences, and that you must have studied the text of each lesson carefully through the vocabulary before turning to these exercises.

## EXERCISES FOR Capvt I

1. Give the English pronouns equivalent to each of the following Latin personal endings: (1) -t, (2) -mus, (3) -ō, (4) -nt, (5) -s, (6) -tis.
2. Name the following forms and translate each: (1) monēre, (2) vidēre, (3) valēre, (4) dēbēre.
3. Name the following forms and translate each: (1) vocāre, (2) servāre, (3) dare, (4) cōgitāre, (5) laudāre, (6) amāre, (7) errāre.
4. Name the following forms and translate each: (1) vocā, (2) servā, (3) dā, (4) cōgitā, (5) laudā, (6) amā, (7) monē, (8) vidē, (9) valē.
5. Name the following forms and translate each: (1) vocāte, (2) servāte, (3) date, (4) cōgitāte, (5) laudāte, (6) amāte, (7) monēte, (8) vidēte, (9) valēte.
6. Translate the following words: (1) vocat, (2) cōgitāmus, (3) amant, (4) dēbēs, (5) videt, (6) vident, (7) dēbēmus, (8) valēs, (9) errātis, (10) vidēmus, (11) amat, (12) vidētis, (13) errās, (14) dant, (15) servāmus, (16) dat, (17) amant, (18) vidēs.

7. Monent mē sī errō. 8. Monet mē sī errant. 9. Monēte mē sī errat. 10. Dēbēs monēre mē. 11. Dēbētis servāre mē. 12. Nōn dēbent laudāre mē. 13. "Quid dat?" "Saepe nihil dat." 14. Mē saepe vocant et (*and*) monent. 15. Nihil videō. Quid vidēs? 16. Mē laudā sī nōn errō, amābō tē. 17. Sī valētis, valēmus. 18. Sī valet, valeō. 19. Sī mē amat, dēbet mē laudāre. 20. Cōnservāte mē. 21. Nōn dēbeō errāre. 22. Quid dēbēmus laudāre? 23. Videt; cōgitat; monet.

## EXERCISES FOR Capvt II

1. Give the Latin for the definite article "the" and the indefinite article "a."
2. Name the Latin case for each of the following constructions or ideas: (1) direct object of a verb; (2) possession; (3) subject of a verb; (4) means; (5) direct address; (6) indirect object of a verb.
3. Name the case, number, and syntactical usage indicated by each of the following endings of the 1st declension: (1) -ās; (2) -a; (3) -am; (4) -ae (pl.).
4. Name the case(s) and number indicated by the following endings, and wherever possible name the English preposition(s) which can be associated with them: (1) -ārum; (2) -ā; (3) -ae; (4) -īs.
5. Translate the following nouns and state the syntactical usage of each as indicated by its ending: (1) puellam; (2) puella; (3) puellās; (4) puellae (plural form); (5) patriās; (6) patriam; (7) patria; (8) patriae (pl.); (9) pecūniam; (10) pecūnia; (11) poenās; (12) poenam.
6. Translate the following nouns in accordance with their case endings: (1) puellae (sg.); (2) puellārum; (3) Ō patria; (4) patriae (sg.); (5) pecūniā; (6) pecūniae (sg.); (7) poenīs; (8) poenā; (9) poenārum.

7. Given the following nominative singular forms, write the Latin forms requested in each instance: (1) **multa pecūnia** in the genitive and the accusative singular; (2) **magna fāma** in dat. and abl. sg.; (3) **vīta mea** in gen. sg. and nom. pl.; (4) **fortūna tua** in acc. sg. and pl.; (5) **magna patria** in gen. sg. and pl.; (6) **fortūna mea** in abl. sg. and pl.; (7) **magna poena** in dat. sg. and pl.; (8) **multa philosophia** in dat. and abl. pl.

8. Translate each of the following phrases into Latin according to the case either named or indicated by the English preposition in each instance: (1) by much money; (2) of many girls; (3) to/for my country; (4) great life (as direct object of a verb); (5) by your penalties; (6) many countries (subject of a verb); (7) to/for many girls; (8) of my life; (9) O fortune; (10) girl's; (11) girls'; (12) girls (direct address); (13) the girls (direct object of a verb); (14) the girls (subject of a verb).

9. Valē, patria mea. 10. Fortūna puellae est magna. 11. Puella fortūnam patriae tuae laudat. 12. Ō puella, patriam tuam servā. 13. Multae puellae pecūniam amant. 14. Puellae nihil datis. 15. Pecūniam puellae videt. 16. Pecūniam puellārum nōn vidēs. 17. Monēre puellās dēbēmus. 18. Laudāre puellam dēbent. 19. Vīta multīs puellīs fortūnam dat. 20. Vītam meam pecūniā tuā cōnservās. 21. Fāma est nihil sine fortūnā. 22. Vītam sine pecūniā nōn amātis. 23. Sine fāmā et fortūnā patria nōn valet. 24. Īram puellārum laudāre nōn dēbēs. 25. Vītam sine poenīs amāmus. 26. Sine philosophiā nōn valēmus. 27. Quid est vīta sine philosophiā?

## EXERCISES FOR Capvt III

1. Name the case, number, and syntactical usage indicated by each of the following endings of masculines of the 2nd declension: (1) -um; (2) -ī (pl.); (3) -us; (4) -ōs; (5) -e.

2. Name the case(s) and number of the following endings, and name the English preposition which can be associated with each: (1) -ō; (2) -ōrum; (3) -ī (sg.); (4) -īs.

3. Translate the following nouns and state the syntactical usage of each as indicated by its ending: (1) fīliōs; (2) fīliī (pl.); (3) fīlium; (4) populum; (5) popule; (6) populus; (7) vir; (8) virōs; (9) virī (pl.); (10) virum; (11) amīce; (12) amīcī (pl.); (13) amīcōs; (14) amīcum.

4. Translate the following in accordance with their case endings: (1) fīliōrum meōrum; (2) fīliō meō; (3) populī Rōmānī (sg.); (4) populō Rōmānō; (5) virīs; (6) virī (sg.); (7) virōrum; (8) amīcōrum paucōrum; (9) amīcīs paucīs; (10) amīcō meō; (11) amīcī meī (sg.); (12) multīs puerīs.

5. Given the following nom. sg. forms, write the Latin forms requested in each instance: (1) **populus Rōmānus** in gen. and abl. sg.; (2) **magnus vir** in acc. and abl. pl.; (3) **puer meus** in dat. and abl. pl.; (4) **magnus numerus** in dat. and abl. sg.; (5) **magnus vir** in voc. sg. and pl.; (6) **fīlius meus** in gen. sg. and pl.

6. Translate the following phrases into Latin according to the case named or indicated by the English preposition in each instance: (1) of many boys; (2) to/for the Roman people; (3) my sons (object of verb); (4) O my sons; (5) a great number (obj. of verb); (6) by the great number; (7) O great man; (8) to/for many boys; (9) the great man (subj. of verb); (10) of the Roman people.

7. Valē, mī amīce. 8. Populus Rōmānus sapientiam fīliī tuī laudat. 9. Ō vir magne, populum Rōmānum servā. 10. Numerus populī Rōmānī est magnus. 11. Multī puerī puellās amant. 12. Fīliō meō nihil datis. 13. Virōs in agrō videō. 14. Amīcum fīliī meī vidēs.

15. Amīcum fīliōrum tuōrum nōn videt. 16. Dēbēmus fīliōs meōs monēre. 17. Dēbent fīlium tuum laudāre. 18. Vīta paucīs virīs fāmam dat. 19. Mē in numerō amīcōrum tuōrum habēs. 20. Virī magnī paucōs amīcōs saepe habent. 21. Amīcus meus semper cōgitat. 22. Fīlius magnī virī nōn semper est magnus vir. 23. Sapientiam magnōrum virōrum nōn semper vidēmus. 24. Philosophiam, sapientiam magnōrum virōrum, laudāre dēbētis.

## EXERCISES FOR Capvt IV

1. A 2nd-declension neuter has the same forms as the regular 2nd-declension masculine except in three instances. Name these three instances and give their neuter endings.
2. Name the case(s), number, and syntactical usage indicated by each of the following endings of the 2nd-declension neuter nouns: (1) -a; (2) -um.
3. Name the case(s) and number of the following 2nd-declension neuter endings and name the English preposition(s) which can be associated with each: (1) -ō; (2) -ōrum; (3) -ī; (4) -īs.
4. Translate the following neuter nouns and state the syntactical usage of each as indicated by its ending: (1) bella; (2) bellum; (3) officium; (4) officia; (5) perīcula.
5. Translate the following phrases in accordance with their case endings: (1) bellōrum malōrum; (2) bellō malō; (3) bellī malī; (4) bellīs malīs; (5) officiī magnī; (6) officiīs magnīs; (7) perīculō parvō.
6. Given the following nom. sg. forms, write the Latin forms requested in each instance: (1) **bellum parvum** in nom. and acc. pl.; (2) **ōtium bonum** in acc. sg. and pl.; (3) **perīculum magnum** in gen. sg. and pl.; (4) **officium vērum** in acc. and abl. sg.
7. Translate the following phrases into Latin in accordance with the case named or indicated by the English preposition in each instance: (1) O evil war; (2) to/for great duty; (3) by the great danger; (4) good leisure (object of verb); (5) by many wars; (6) of good leisure; (7) by the dangers of many wars; (8) small wars (subject of verb); (9) small wars (obj. of verb); (10) O foolish wars; (11) the small war (subj.)

8. Ōtium est bonum. 9. Multa bella ōtium nōn cōnservant. 10. Perīculum est magnum. 11. In magnō perīculō sumus. 12. Et ōtium perīcula saepe habet. 13. Vīta nōn est sine multīs perīculīs. 14. Bonī virī ōtium amant. 15. Stultus vir perīcula bellī laudat. 16. Ōtium bellō saepe nōn cōnservāmus. 17. Populus Rōmānus ōtium bonum nōn semper habet. 18. Patriam et ōtium bellīs parvīs saepe servant. 19. Multae puellae sunt bellae. 20. Vērī amīcī sunt paucī. 21. Amīcus meus est vir magnī officiī. 22. Officia magistrī sunt multa et magna. 23. Vir parvī ōtiī es. 24. Virī magnae cūrae estis. 25. Sine morā cūram officiō dare dēbēmus. 26. Sine oculīs vīta est nihil.

## EXERCISES FOR Capvt V

1. Identify the *personal* endings of the future and imperfect tenses of the first two conjugations.
2. Are these the same as the endings of the present tense? If not, point out the differences.
3. Identify the future and imperfect tense signs in the first two conjugations.
4. How, in effect, can the following verb endings be translated: (1) -bāmus; (2) -bit; (3) -bitis; (4) -bō; (5) -bunt; (6) -bat?
5. When an adjective of the 1st and 2nd declensions has the masculine ending in -*er*, how can you tell whether the *e* survives in the other forms or is lost?

6. How do English words like *liberty, pulchritude,* and *nostrum* help with the declension of Latin adjectives?

7. Translate the following forms: (1) manēbant; (2) manēbit; (3) manēbimus; (4) dabam; (5) dabitis; (6) dabit; (7) vidēbis; (8) vidēbimus; (9) vocābant; (10) vocābis; (11) habē-bis; (12) habēbant.

8. Translate into Latin: (1) we shall give; (2) you (sg.) were remaining; (3) they will see; (4) we shall call; (5) he was calling; (6) you (pl.) will see; (7) I shall see; (8) they were saving; (9) we shall have; (10) we were having; (11) he will have; (12) he has.

9. Magister noster mē laudat et tē crās laudābit. 10. Līberī virī perīcula nostra superābant. 11. Fīliī nostrī puellās pulchrās amant. 12. Amīcus noster in numerō stultōrum nōn remanēbit. 13. Culpās multās habēbāmus et semper habēbimus. 14. Perīcula magna animōs nostrōs nōn superant. 15. Pulchra patria nostra est lībera. 16. Līberī virī estis; patriam pulchram habēbitis. 17. Magistrī līberī officiō cūram dabant. 18. Malōs igitur in patriā nostrā superābimus. 19. Sī īram tuam superābis, tē superābis. 20. Propter nostrōs animōs multī sunt līberī. 21. Tē, Ō patria lībera, semper amābāmus et semper amābimus. 22. Sapientiam pecūniā nōn cōnservābitis. 23. Habetne animus tuus satis sapientiae?

## EXERCISES FOR Capvt VI

1. What connection can be traced between the spelling of *complementary* in the term *complementary infinitive* and the syntactical principle?

2. In the verb **sum** and its compounds what do the following personal endings mean: (1) -mus; (2) -nt; (3) -s; (4) -t; (5) -ō; (6) -m; (7) -tis?

3. If the verb **possum** is composed of **pot + sum,** where among the various forms is the **t** changed to **s** and where does it remain unchanged?

4. Translate the following random forms: (1) erat; (2) poterat; (3) erit; (4) poterit; (5) sumus; (6) possumus; (7) poterāmus; (8) poterimus; (9) poteram; (10) eram; (11) erō; (12) poterō; (13) erunt; (14) poterunt; (15) poterant; (16) esse; (17) posse.

5. Translate into Latin: (1) we are; (2) we were; (3) we shall be; (4) we shall be able; (5) he is able; (6) he will be able; (7) he was able; (8) to be able; (9) they were able; (10) they are able; (11) they will be able; (12) they are; (13) to be; (14) I was able.

6. Patria vestra erat lībera. 7. Poteram esse tyrannus. 8. Amīcus vester erit tyrannus. 9. Ubi tyrannus est, ibi virī nōn possunt esse līberī. 10. In patriā nostrā heri nōn po-terat remanēre. 11. Tyrannī multa vitia semper habēbunt. 12. Tyrannōs superāre nōn poterāmus. 13. Tyrannum nostrum superāre dēbēmus. 14. Tyrannus bonōs superāre poterat; sed ibi remanēre nōn poterit. 15. Poteritis perīcula tyrannī vidēre. 16. Vitia tyrannōrum tolerāre nōn possumus. 17. Īnsidiās tyrannī nōn tolerābās. 18. Ōtium in patriā vestrā nōn potest esse perpetuum. 19. Dēbēs virōs līberōs dē tyrannīs monēre. 20. Magister vester librōs pulchrōs semper amābat. 21. Librī bonī vērīque poterant pa-triam cōnservāre. 22. Librīs bonīs patriam vestram cōnservāre poteritis. 23. Tyrannī sa-pientiam bonōrum librōrum superāre nōn poterunt. 24. Malī librōs bonōs nōn possunt tolerāre.

## EXERCISES FOR Capvt VII

1. In the 3rd declension do the case endings of feminine nouns differ from those of masculine nouns as they do in the 1st and 2nd declensions already learned?

2. Do neuter nouns of the 3rd declension have any case endings which are identical with those of neuter nouns of the 2nd declension? If so, name them.

3. Name the gender(s) and case(s) indicated by each of the following endings in the 3rd declension: (1) -ēs; (2) -a; (3) -em.

4. Name the case(s) and number of the following 3rd-declensional endings: (1) -ibus; (2) -ī; (3) -e; (4) -em; (5) -um; (6) -is; (7) -ēs.

5. To indicate the gender of the following nouns give the proper nominative singular form of **magnus, -a, -um** with each: (1) tempus; (2) virtūs; (3) labor; (4) cīvitās; (5) mōs; (6) pāx; (7) rēx; (8) corpus; (9) vēritās; (10) amor.

6. Translate the following phrases in accordance with their case endings wherever possible; where they are nominative or accusative so state: (1) labōre multō; (2) labōrī multō; (3) labōris multī; (4) labōrēs multī; (5) pācis perpetuae; (6) pāce perpetuā; (7) pācī perpetuae; (8) cīvitātum parvārum; (9) cīvitātem parvam; (10) cīvitātēs parvās; (11) cīvitātēs parvae; (12) cīvitāte parvā; (13) tempora mala; (14) tempus malum; (15) temporī malō; (16) temporum malōrum; (17) temporis malī; (18) mōrī tuō; (19) mōre tuō; (20) mōris tuī; (21) mōrēs tuī; (22) mōrēs tuōs; (23) mōrum tuōrum.

7. Translate the following phrases into Latin in accordance with the case named or indicated by the English preposition: (1) to/for great virtue; (2) great virtue (subject); (3) great virtues (object of verb); (4) of great virtues; (5) with great courage; (6) our time (obj. of verb); (7) our times (subj.); (8) our times (obj.); (9) to/for our times; (10) to/for our time; (11) of our time; (12) of our times; (13) my love (obj.); (14) my loves (obj.); (15) to/for my love; (16) by my love; (17) of my love; (18) of my loves.

8. Meum tempus ōtiō est parvum. 9. Virtūs tua est magna. 10. Pecūnia est nihil sine mōribus bonīs. 11. Virtūtēs hominum multōrum sunt magnae. 12. Mōrēs hominis bonī erunt bonī. 13. Hominī litterās dabunt. 14. Hominēs multōs in cīvitāte magnā vidēre poterāmus. 15. Magnum amōrem pecūniae in multīs hominibus vidēbāmus. 16. Paucī hominēs virtūtī cūram dant. 17. Cīvitās nostra pācem hominibus multīs dabit. 18. Pāx nōn potest esse perpetua. 19. Sine bonā pāce cīvitātēs temporum nostrōrum nōn valēbunt. 20. Post multa bella tempora sunt mala. 21. In multīs cīvitātibus terrīsque pāx nōn poterat valēre. 22. Sine magnō labōre homō nihil habēbit. 23. Virgō pulchra amīcōs mōrum bonōrum amat. 24. Hominēs magnae virtūtis tyrannōs superāre audēbant. 25. Amor patriae in cīvitāte nostrā valēbat.

## EXERCISES FOR Capvt VIII

1. (1) In the 3d conjugation what tense is indicated by the stem vowel ē? (2) Can you think of some mnemonic device to help you remember this important point?

2. (1) In the 3d conjugation what tense is indicated by the vowels **i, ō, u**? (2) What mnemonic device may help here?

3. State the person, number, and tense indicated by the following 3d conjugation endings: (1) -imus; (2) -ēs; (3) -unt; (4) -et; (5) -itis; (6) -ēmus; (7) -ō; (8) -ent; (9) -it; (10) -ētis; (11) -is; (12) -am; (13) -ēbant.

4. What form of the verb does each of the following endings indicate: (1) -e; (2) -ere; (3) -ite?

5. Given the verbs **mittō, mittere,** *send;* **agō, agere,** *do;* **scrībō, scrībere,** *write,* translate each of the following forms according to its ending: (1) mittēbant; (2) mittit;

(3) mittunt; (4) mittam; (5) mitte; (6) mittimus; (7) mittēbātis; (8) mittis; (9) mittite; (10) mittitis; (11) mittet; (12) mittēmus; (13) agit; (14) agent; (15) agunt; (16) agētis; (17) agēbāmus; (18) agam; (19) agēmus; (20) agis; (21) agitis; (22) scrībet; (23) scrībunt; (24) scrībam; (25) scrībēbam; (26) scrībitis; (27) scrībēmus; (28) scrībit; (29) scrībis; (30) scrībent; (31) scrībe.

6. Given **pōnō, pōnere,** *put,* translate the following phrases into Latin: (1) they were putting; (2) we shall put; (3) put (imperative sg.); (4) he puts; (5) they will put; (6) I shall put; (7) you (sg.) were putting; (8) you (pl.) will put; (9) put (imperat. pl.); (10) we put; (11) you (pl.) are putting; (12) he will put.

7. Quid agunt? Quid agētis? 8. Hominem ad mē dūcēbant. 9. Dūc hominem ad mē, et hominī grātiās agam. 10. Dum tyrannus cōpiās dūcit, possumus nihil agere. 11. Litterās ad virginem scrībit. 12. Librum magnum scrībēbās. 13. Librōs bonōs scrībēs. 14. Librōs dē pāce scrībēmus. 15. Cōpiamne librōrum bonōrum habētis? 16. Magister multōs puerōs docet. 17. Puerī magistrō grātiās nōn agunt. 18. Paucī cīvitātī nostrae grātiās agēbant. 19. Tyrannus magnās cōpiās ex cīvitāte nostrā dūcet. 20. Magna cōpia pecūniae hominēs ad sapientiam nōn dūcit. 21. Librīne bonī multōs ad ratiōnem dūcent? 22. Dūcimusne saepe hominēs ad ratiōnem? 23. Ratiō hominēs ad bonam vītam dūcere potest. 24. Agitisne bonam vītam? 25. Amīcō bonō grātiās semper agite.

## EXERCISES FOR Capvt IX

1. Explain the term *demonstrative* pronoun and adjective.
2. Translate each of the following according to case(s) and number, indicating also the gender(s) in each instance:

| | | | |
|---|---|---|---|
| (1) illī | (10) illīs | (19) huius | (28) ūnā |
| (2) illa | (11) illō | (20) hunc | (29) tōtī |
| (3) illīus | (12) illārum | (21) hōs | (30) tōtīus |
| (4) ille | (13) hōc | (22) huic | (31) tōta |
| (5) illā | (14) hoc | (23) hōrum | (32) tōtum |
| (6) illud | (15) haec | (24) hās | (33) nūllīus |
| (7) illōrum | (16) hae | (25) hīs | (34) nūllī |
| (8) illae | (17) hāc | (26) ūnīus | (35) nūlla |
| (9) illōs | (18) hanc | (27) ūnī | (36) nūllōs |

3. How can the presence of a noun be helpful in determining the form of a modifying demonstrative?
4. Translate the following phrases into Latin in the declensional forms indicated:

| | |
|---|---|
| (1) this girl (nom.) | (10) that girl (nom.) |
| (2) these girls (nom.) | (11) those times (nom.) |
| (3) these times (acc. pl.) | (12) those times (acc.) |
| (4) to/for this time | (13) that time (nom.) |
| (5) to/for this boy | (14) to/for this state alone |
| (6) of this time | (15) of this state alone |
| (7) of that time | (16) to/for that boy alone |
| (8) by this book | (17) to/for that girl alone |
| (9) by that book | (18) of that girl alone |

(19) of tyrants alone
(20) the whole state (acc.)
(21) of the whole country
(22) to/for the whole country
(23) of no reason
(24) no reason (acc.)
(25) no girls (nom.)
(26) to/for no book

(27) no books (acc.)
(28) to/for one state
(29) to/for one girl
(30) of one time
(31) of one war
(32) to/for the other book
(33) by another book

5. Hī tōtam cīvitātem dūcent (dūcunt, dūcēbant). 6. Ille haec in illā terrā vidēbit (videt, vidēbat). 7. In illō librō illa dē hōc homine scrībō (scrībam, scrībēbam). 8. Ūnus vir istās cōpiās in hanc terram dūcit (dūcet). 9. Magister haec alterī puerō dat. 10. Hunc librum dē aliō bellō scrībimus (scrībēmus). 11. Tōta patria huic sōlī grātiās agit (aget, agēbat). 12. Tōtam cūram illī cōnsiliō nunc dant. 13. Amīcus huius hanc cīvitātem illō cōnsiliō cōnservābit. 14. Alter amīcus tōtam vītam in aliā terrā aget. 15. Hic vir sōlus mē dē vitiīs huius tyrannī monēre poterat. 16. Nūllās cōpiās in alterā terrā habēbātis. 17. Illī sōlī nūlla perīcula in hōc cōnsiliō vident. 18. Nōn sōlum mōrēs sed etiam īnsidiās illīus laudāre audēs. 19. Propter īnsidiās enim ūnīus hominis haec cīvitās nōn valēbat.

## EXERCISES FOR Capvt X

1. Name the conjugation indicated by each of the following endings: (1) -ere; (2) -ēre; (3) -īre; (4) -āre.
2. State the person, number, and tense indicated by the following endings from the 4th conjugation and the -**iō** 3d: (1) -iunt; (2) -iēs; (3) -īs; (4) -iēbāmus; (5) -īmus; (6) -ī; (7) -iētis; (8) -īte; (9) -ītis; (10) -iō; (11) -it; (12) -e; (13) -iēbās.
3. State three points at which -**iō** verbs of the 3d conjugation differ from verbs of the 4th conjugation.
4. Translate the following in accordance with their specific forms:

| | | | |
|---|---|---|---|
| (1) veniet | (6) audiētis | (11) venīre | (16) faciunt |
| (2) venit | (7) audītis | (12) facit | (17) facis |
| (3) veniunt | (8) venīte | (13) faciet | (18) faciam |
| (4) venient | (9) veniēs | (14) faciēmus | (19) faciēs |
| (5) audīs | (10) venī | (15) facimus | (20) facere |

5. Given **sentiō, sentīre,** *feel,* and **iaciō, iacere,** *throw,* translate the following phrases into Latin:

| | | |
|---|---|---|
| (1) I shall feel | (8) feel (imperat. sg.) | (15) throw (imperat. sg.) |
| (2) we shall feel | (9) he will feel | (16) you (pl.) are throwing |
| (3) he feels | (10) we feel | (17) we shall throw |
| (4) you (pl.) feel | (11) he is throwing | (18) throw (imperat. pl.) |
| (5) they will feel | (12) he will throw | (19) to throw |
| (6) they do feel | (13) I shall throw | (20) you (sg.) are throwing |
| (7) to feel | (14) we are throwing | |

6. Ex hāc terrā fugiēbāmus. 7. Cum fīliā tuā fuge. 8. In illum locum fugient. 9. Tempus fugit; hōrae fugiunt; senectūs venit. 10. Venīte cum amīcīs vestrīs. 11. In patriam

vestram veniēbant. 12. Ō vir magne, in cīvitātem nostram venī. 13. Fīliam tuam in illā cīvitāte inveniēs. 14. Parvam pecūniam in viīs invenīre possunt. 15. Tyrannus viam in hanc cīvitātem invenit. 16. Illōs cum amīcīs ibi capiētis. 17. Ad tē cum magnīs cōpiīs venīmus. 18. Invenietne multam fāmam glōriamque ibi? 19. Iste bellum semper faciēbat. 20. Istī hominēs pācem nōn facient. 21. Multī hominēs illa faciunt sed haec nōn faciunt. 22. Officium nostrum facimus et faciēmus. 23. Magnam cōpiam librōrum faciam. 24. Puerī cum illō virō bonō vīvēbant. 25. In librīs virōrum antīquōrum multam philosophiam et sapientiam inveniētis.

## EXERCISES FOR Capvt XI

1. Name the nominative singular and plural of the following: (1) 3d personal pronoun; (2) 1st per. pron.; (3) 2nd per. pron.
2. Translate the following pronouns in accordance with case(s) and number; where a form is nom. or acc. so specify.
   (1) vōbīs; (2) nōbīs; (3) nōs; (4) vōs; (5) tuī; (6) meī; (7) mihi; (8) tibi; (9) tē; (10) mē.
3. Translate the following third-person pronouns in accordance with their gender(s), number(s), and case(s): (1) eōs; (2) eās; (3) eōrum; (4) eārum; (5) eius; (6) eā; (7) ea; (8) eō; (9) eī; (10) eīs; (11) eae; (12) id.
4. Give the Latin for the following:

| | | |
|---|---|---|
| (1) his | (10) to her | (19) it (n. acc.) |
| (2) her (possess.) | (11) by/with/from her | (20) you (emphatic nom. pl.) |
| (3) their (m.) | (12) by/withfrom him | (21) you (emphatic nom. sg.) |
| (4) their (f.) | (13) to/for you (pl.) | (22) you (acc. pl.) |
| (5) them (f.) | (14) to/for you (sg.) | (23) us |
| (6) them (m.) | (15) they (m.) | (24) we |
| (7) them (n.) | (16) they (n.) | (25) to/for us |
| (8) its | (17) they (f.) | (26) I (emphatic form) |
| (9) to him | (18) to/for it | (27) to/for me |

5. Hī tibi id dabunt. 6. Ego vōbīs id dabam. 7. Vōs eīs id dōnum dabitis. 8. Eī idem dabō. 9. Nōs eī ea dabimus. 10. Ille mihi id dabit. 11. Vōbīs librōs eius dabimus. 12. Nōbīs librōs eōrum dabis. 13. Pecūniam eōrum tibi dabimus. 14. Pecūniam eius mihi dabunt. 15. Eōs librōs ad eam mittēmus. 16. Librum eius ad tē mittam. 17. Ille autem pecūniam eōrum ad nōs mittēbat. 18. Eās cum eā mittimus. 19. Eum cum eīs mittō. 20. Eōs cum amīcīs eius mittēmus. 21. Tū mē cum amīcō eōrum mittēs. 22. Vōs mēcum ad amīcum eius mittēbant. 23. Nōs tēcum in terram eōrum mittit. 24. Eās nōbīscum ad amīcōs eōrum mittent. 25. Eum vōbīscum ad amīcōs eōrum mittam. 26. Tē cum eō ad mē mittent.

## EXERCISES FOR Capvt XII

1. Name the principal parts of a Latin verb in their regular sequence.
2. Give the principal parts of **mittō**, labeling and translating each one.
3. What is the major difference between the perfect and imperfect tenses?
4. You must be able to tell from what verb any specific verb form comes. Practice on the following list by naming the first principal part of each of the verbs in the list.

| | | | |
|---|---|---|---|
| (1) mīsērunt | (6) āctum | (11) remānserant | (16) dīxērunt |
| (2) laudāveram | (7) est | (12) scrīpsimus | (17) erat |
| (3) vincēbāmus | (8) dedimus | (13) fuit | (18) vīxī |
| (4) dictum | (9) futūrum | (14) fēcit | (19) faciēbās |
| (5) fēcistī | (10) ēgimus | (15) fugere | (20) vīsum |

5. Translate the following endings of the perfect system according to person, number, and tense in each instance, using these conventions: -ī = I (perfect) ...; **-eram** = I had ...; **-erō** = I shall have ...; (1) -istis; (2) -it; (3) -ērunt; (4) -istī; (5) -imus; (6) -erat; (7) -erimus; (8) -erāmus; (9) -erās; (10) -erint; (11) -erant; (12) -erit; (13) -erātis.

6. Translate the following in accordance with the person, number, and tense of each:

| | | | |
|---|---|---|---|
| (1) vidēbant | (10) vīxistī | (19) fugit | (28) remānsimus |
| (2) vīderant | (11) vīxērunt | (20) fūgit | (29) remānserāmus |
| (3) vīdistī | (12) vincet | (21) fugiunt | (30) vēnit |
| (4) fēcit | (13) vīcit | (22) fūgērunt | (31) venit |
| (5) faciēbat | (14) vīcimus | (23) servāvit | (32) veniēbātis |
| (6) fēcerāmus | (15) vincimus | (24) servāvērunt | (33) vēnistī |
| (7) fēcimus | (16) dedistī | (25) servāvistis | (34) vēnērunt |
| (8) faciēmus | (17) dederātis | (26) servāverat | (35) veniunt |
| (9) fēcērunt | (18) dedimus | (27) servāverit | (36) vēnerant |

7. Illī fūgerant (fugient; fugiunt; fugiēbant; fūgērunt). 8. Hī remānsērunt (remanent; remanēbunt; remanēbant; remānserant). 9. Rēx Asiam vīcerat (vincit; vīcit; vincet). 10. Rēgēs Asiam vīcērunt (vincent; vincunt; vīcerant). 11. Rēgēs Asiam habuērunt (habent; habēbunt; habuerant). 12. Caesar in eandem terram vēnerat (vēnit; venit; veniet). 13. Caesar eadem dīxit (dīcit; dīxerat; dīcet). 14. Vōs nōbīs pācem dedistis (dabitis; dabātis; dederātis). 15. Tū litterās ad eam mīsistī (mittēs; mittis; mīserās). 16. Eōs in eādem viā vīdimus (vidēmus; vīderāmus). 17. Diū vīxerat (vīxit; vīvet). 18. Id bene fēcerās (faciēs; fēcistī; facis). 19. Cīvitātem eōrum (eius) servāvī (servābō; servābam; servāveram). 20. Eum in eōdem locō invēnērunt (invēnerant; invenient). 21. Deus hominibus lībertātem dederat (dedit; dat; dabit). 22. Mihi grātiās ēgērunt (agent; agēbant; ēgerant; agunt). 23. Vōs fuistis (erātis; estis; eritis; fuerātis) virī līberī.

## EXERCISES FOR Capvt XIII

1. State the essential nature of reflexive pronouns, showing how, as a logical consequence, they differ from other pronouns.
2. Explain why the declension of reflexive pronouns begins with the genitive rather than with the nominative.
3. In what reflexive pronouns is the spelling the same as that of the corresponding simple pronoun?
4. Translate the following reflexive forms in accordance with their case(s) and number(s): (1) mihi; (2) tē; (3) nōbīs; (4) sibi; (5) vōs; (6) sē; (7) vōbīs.
5. Explain why the singular of **suus** can mean *their own* as well as *his own*, and the plural can mean *his own* as well as *their own*.

6. Explain why **eōrum** always means *their* and **eius** always means *his* (*her, its*) regardless of whether the nouns on which they depend are singular or plural.
7. Although **sē** and **ipse** can both be translated into English by *himself,* explain the basic difference between the Latin words.

8. Caesar eōs servāvit. 9. Caesar eum servābat. 10. Caesar sē servāvit. 11. Rōmānī sē servāvērunt. 12. Rōmānī eōs servāvērunt. 13. Rōmānī eum servāvērunt. 14. Caesar amīcum suum servāvit. 15. Caesar amīcōs suōs servāvit. 16. Caesar amīcum eius servāvit. 17. Caesar amīcōs eius servāvit. 18. Caesar amīcum eōrum servāvit. 19. Caesar amīcōs eōrum servāvit. 20. Rōmānī amīcum suum servāvērunt. 21. Rōmānī amīcōs suōs servāvērunt. 22. Rōmānī amīcum eōrum servāvērunt. 23. Rōmānī amīcōs eōrum servāvērunt. 24. Rōmānī amīcum eius servāvērunt. 25. Rōmānī amīcōs eius servāvērunt. 26. Caesar ipse eum servāvit. 27. Caesar ipse sē servāvit. 28. Caesarem ipsum servāvērunt. 29. Amīcum Caesaris ipsīus servābant. 30. Amīcum Rōmānōrum ipsōrum servāvērunt. 31. Amīcus Caesaris ipsīus sē servāvit. 32. Amīcī Caesaris ipsīus sē servāvērunt. 33. Amīcus Caesaris ipsīus eum servāvit. 34. Ipsī amīcī Caesaris eum servāvērunt. 35. Nōs nōn servāvērunt. 36. Nōs servāvimus. 37. Rōmānōs ipsōs servāvimus. 38. Rōmānī ipsī tē nōn servāvērunt. 39. Tū tē servāvistī. 40. Tū Rōmānōs ipsōs servāvistī. 41. Mihi nihil dabat. 42. Mihi nihil dedī. 43. Sibi nihil dedit. 44. Sibi nihil dedērunt. 45. Eīs nihil dedērunt. 46. Eī nihil dedērunt. 47. Mē vīcī. 48. Mē vīcērunt. 49. Īram eōrum vīcērunt. 50. Īram suam vīcērunt. 51. Īram suam vīcit. 52. Fīliōs suōs vīcit. 53. Fīliōs suōs vīcērunt.

### EXERCISES FOR Capvt XIV

1. In what specific case ending of all **i**-stem nouns does the characteristic **i** appear?
2. What are the other **i**-stem peculiarities of neuters in **-e, -al,** and **-ar**?
3. Translate each of the following according to its case(s) and number; when a form is nom. or acc. label it as such.

| | | | |
|---|---|---|---|
| (1) arte | (9) corporum | (17) rēgum | (25) virōs |
| (2) artium | (10) partis | (18) rēgī | (26) virī |
| (3) artēs | (11) partibus | (19) nōmina | (27) vīrēs |
| (4) marī | (12) partium | (20) animālia | (28) virīs |
| (5) maribus | (13) urbe | (21) animālī | (29) vīs |
| (6) mare | (14) urbī | (22) animālis | (30) vim |
| (7) maria | (15) urbium | (23) animālium | (31) vīribus |
| (8) corpora | (16) urbēs | (24) vīrium | (32) vī |

4. Of the forms in #3 above, list those which are **i-** stem forms.
5. Translate the following phrases into Latin:

(1) by/with/from great force
(2) great man (acc.)
(3) of great strength
(4) to/for great force
(5) of many citizens
(6) by/with/from a good citizen
(7) to/for many citizens
(8) many seas (nom.)
(9) by/with/from a great sea
(10) a great sea (acc.)
(11) great force (acc.)
(12) of many men (vir)
(13) by/with/from great strength
(14) great strength (acc.)

6. What kind of idea is expressed by each of the following ablatives? (1) cum rēge; (2) oculīs meīs; (3) cum cūrā; (4) labōre meō.

7. Translate each of the following verb forms and name the verb from which each comes: (1) cucurrērunt; (2) currēbāmus; (3) cucurristī; (4) trāxerāmus; (5) trahet; (6) trahunt; (7) gerēbat; (8) gerit; (9) gerunt; (10) gerēmus; (11) tenent; (12) tenēbunt; (13) tenuērunt; (14) tenuimus.

8. Multa bella cum Rōmānīs gessit. 9. Cīvitātem magnā cum sapientiā gerēbant. 10. Ipse cīvitātem vī cōpiārum tenuit. 11. Illa animālia multōs hominēs in mare trāxērunt. 12. Hoc magnā cum arte dīxistī. 13. Cum cūrā trāns urbem cucurrimus. 14. Magnā cum parte cīvium ad nōs veniēbat. 15. Iūra cīvium vī vincet. 16. Eum ad mortem trāns terram eius trāxistis. 17. Nōs cum cīvibus multārum urbium iungēmus. 18. Rēgī ipsī hās litterās cum virtūte scrīpsit. 19. Vīs illōrum marium erat magna. 20. Artem Graecōrum oculīs meīs vīdī. 21. Sententiās multās pulchrāsque ex virīs antīquīs trāximus.

22. Name the type of ablative found in each of the following sentences above: 8, 9, 10, 12, 13, 14, 15, 17, 18, 20.

## EXERCISES FOR Capvt XV

1. State the difference between cardinal and ordinal numerals.
2. What cardinals are declined?
3. What ordinals are declined?
4. State the form or possible forms of each of the following: (1) duōbus; (2) mīlle; (3) tria; (4) duo; (5) quīnque; (6) mīlia; (7) decem; (8) duābus; (9) centum; (10) trium; (11) vīgintī; (12) octō.
5. Why is the genitive of the whole so called?
6. What construction did the Romans use after cardinal numerals?
7. Translate each of the following phrases.

| | |
|---|---|
| (1) ūnus cīvis | (9) centum ex cīvibus |
| (2) decem cīvēs | (10) mīlle cīvēs |
| (3) pars cīvium | (11) tria mīlia cīvium |
| (4) trēs cīvēs | (12) quid novī |
| (5) trēs ex sex cīvibus | (13) multum laudis |
| (6) quīnque ex cīvibus | (14) satis pecūniae |
| (7) quīnque cīvēs | (15) nihil aquae |
| (8) centum cīvēs | |

8. When the Romans put a word of time in the ablative case without a preposition, what kind of ideas did they express?
9. Study the ablatives in the following sentences. Then translate the sentences and name the type of ablative found in each one.

| | |
|---|---|
| (1) Cum amīcīs veniēbat. | (4) Paucīs hōrīs librum scrīpsit. |
| (2) Ūnā hōrā veniet. | (5) Illō tempore librum scrīpsit. |
| (3) Eōdem tempore vēnit. | (6) Cum cūrā librum scrībēbat. |

10. Illō tempore sōlō illa tria perīcula timuit; sed mortem semper timēbat. 11. Istī duo rēgēs pecūniam inter mīlia cīvium iaciēbant. 12. Iste ūnus tyrannus sē semper laudābat. 13. Cīvēs illārum quīnque urbium lībertātem exspectābant. 14. Urbem duābus hōrīs

sapientiā suā cōnservāvērunt. 15. In urbem cum tribus ex amīcīs meīs veniēbam. 16. Bella magna cum virtūte gerēbātis. 17. Itaque centum Rōmānī mīlle Graecōs vīcērunt. 18. Patrēs fīliōs suōs saepe timēbant—et nunc multum timōris habent. 19. Vīdistīne duōs patrēs nostrōs eō tempore? 20. Ubi satis lībertātis invēnistis? 21. Tribus hōrīs vēnērunt, et idem nōbīs dīcēbat. 22. Parvum argūmentī intellegēbam. 23. Nūllam partem vītārum nostrārum mūtāvimus. 24. Cīvitās nostra lībertātem et iūra cīvium cōnservābat. 25. Rōmānī mōrēs temporum antīquōrum laudābant. 26. Duo patrēs quattuor ex fīliīs mīsērunt. 27. Decem virī satis sapientiae et multum virtūtis habuērunt. 28. Quid novī, mī amīce?

## EXERCISES FOR Capvt XVI

1. If one has carefully learned the declension of **cīvis** and **mare** one can easily decline the 3d-declension adjective **fortis, forte** with the exception of one form. What is that form?
2. (1) Adjectives of the 3d declension may be classified as adjectives of 3 endings, 2 endings, or 1 ending. Which type is by far the most common? (2) In what one case do adjectives of 1 and 3 endings differ from those of 2 endings?
3. Cite and label three endings in which adjectives of the 3d declension show themselves to be **i**-stems.
4. Of the endings of the 3d-declension adjectives none is likely to cause recognition difficulty except perhaps the ablative singular. What is the normal ending of the ablative singular in all genders?
5. Can 3d-declension adjectives be used with nouns of the 1st or the 2nd declension?
6. Translate the following phrases in accordance with their case(s) and number. When they are nom. or acc., so indicate.

| | | |
|---|---|---|
| (1) dulcī puellae | (8) omnia nōmina | (15) beātō hominī |
| (2) dulcī puellā | (9) omnia maria | (16) omnī marī |
| (3) dulcī mātre | (10) omnī parte | (17) omnī bonae artī |
| (4) dulcī mātrī | (11) omnium partium | (18) omnī bonā arte |
| (5) beātae mātrī | (12) omnium rēgum | (19) omnis bonae artis |
| (6) beātā mātre | (13) omnium bellōrum | (20) vī celerī |
| (7) omnia bella | (14) beātō homine | |

7. Aetās longa saepe est difficilis. 8. Aetās difficilis potest esse beāta. 9. Quam brevis erat dulcis vīta eius! 10. Memoria dulcis aetātis mīlia hominum adiuvat. 11. Librum brevem centum hōrīs scrīpsistī. 12. In omnī marī haec duo animālia potentia inveniēbāmus. 13. In omnī terrā multa mīlia virōrum fortium vidēbitis. 14. Celer rūmor (celeris fāma) per omnem terram cucurrit. 15. Illud bellum breve erat difficile. 16. Omnia perīcula sex hōrīs superāvimus. 17. Tyrannus potēns patriam eōrum vī celerī vincet. 18. Brevī tempore omnia iūra cīvium mūtābit. 19. Difficilem artem lībertātis dulcis nōn intellēxērunt, nam parvum sapientiae habuērunt. 20. Hominēs officia difficilia in omnibus terrīs timent.

## EXERCISES FOR Capvt XVII

1. Define the terms "antecedent" and "relative pronoun."
2. (1) What determines the *case* of the Latin relative pronoun? (2) What determines the *gender* and the *number* of the relative pronoun?

3. State in what ways a relative agrees with its antecedent.
4. Name (1) the English relative pronoun which refers to persons and (2) the one which refers to anything else. (3) Since in Latin the one relative pronoun serves both purposes, what two English meanings does it have?
5. Translate the following in accordance with their case(s) and number(s). When a form is nom. or acc., so indicate if the translation does not make the point clear.

| | | | |
|---|---|---|---|
| (1) cui | (4) cuius | (7) quā | (10) quās |
| (2) quōs | (5) quibus | (8) quī | (11) quōrum |
| (3) quae | (6) quod | (9) quem | (12) quam |

6. Cīvem laudāvērunt quem mīserātis. 7. Decem cīvēs laudāvērunt quōs mīserātis. 8. Cīvem laudāvērunt quī patriam servāverat. 9. Centum cīvēs laudāvērunt quī patriam servāverant. 10. Cīvem laudāvērunt cuius fīlius patriam servāverat. 11. Cīvēs laudāvērunt quōrum septem fīliī patriam servāverant. 12. Cīvem laudāvērunt cui patriam commīserant. 13. Multōs ex cīvibus laudāvērunt quibus patriam commīserant. 14. Cīvem laudāvērunt quōcum vēnerant. 15. Cīvēs laudāvērunt quibuscum vēnerant. 16. Cum cīve vēnit cui vītam suam commīserat. 17. Tyrannī iūra cīvium dēlent quōs capiunt. 18. Tyrannus urbem dēlēvit ex quā mīlia cīvium fūgerant. 19. Tyrannus urbem dēlēvit in quam illī novem cīvēs fūgerant. 20. Tyrannus urbēs dēlēvit ex quibus cīvēs fūgerant. 21. Tyrannus urbēs dēlēvit in quās cīvēs fūgerant. 22. Perīculum superāvit quod timuimus. 23. Perīcula superāvit quae timuimus. 24. Puellīs quās laudābat librōs dedit. 25. Vir cuius fīliam amās in urbem veniēbat. 26. Virō cuius fīliam amās vītam suam commīsit. 27. Mātrem adiuvābat, quae multum virtūtis habuit. 28. Mātribus quae multōs fīliōs habuērunt rēx pecūniam dabat.

## EXERCISES FOR Capvt XVIII

1. Define the term "passive voice" by explaining the etymology of "passive."
2. What is the difference between the ablative of means and the ablative of agent in both meaning and construction?
3. (1) What one letter occurs in 5 of the 6 passive personal endings and can thus be regarded as the peculiar sign of the passive?
   (2) Does this characteristically passive letter occur in any of the corresponding active personal endings?
4. Give the English pronoun by which each of the following passive endings can be translated: (1) -mur; (2) -tur; (3) -r; (4) -ntur; (5) -ris; (6) -minī.
5. (1) Name the tense signs of the imperfect and the future in the passive voice of the 1st and 2nd conjugations.
   (2) Are these the same as the tense signs in the active voice?
6. If -**bar** can be translated "I was being . . ." and -**bor,** "I shall be . . .," translate each of the following: (1) -bimur; (2) -bāminī; (3) -bātur; (4) -beris; (5) -buntur; (6) -bāmur; (7) -bitur; (8) -bāris; (9) -biminī; (10) -bantur.

7. Mē terrent; ab eīs terreor; vī eōrum terreor. 8. Tyrannus hanc urbem dēlēbat. 9. Haec urbs ā tyrannō dēlēbātur; īnsidiīs dēlēbitur. 10. Ab amīcīs movēbātur; cōnsiliīs eōrum movēbātur. 11. Vīribus hominum nōn dēlēmur, sed possumus īnsidiīs dēlērī. 12. Nōn bellō dēlēbiminī, sed amōre ōtiī et cōnsiliīs hominum malōrum. 13. Tū ipse nōn mūtāris, sed nōmen tuum mūtātur. 14. Mīlia hominum amōre pecūniae tenentur. 15. Aliī ab

tyrannīs tenēbantur. 16. Paucī amōre vēritātis amīcitiaeque tenēbuntur. 17. Puer ab amīcīs cōnservābitur. 18. Librī huius generis puerīs ā magistrō dabantur. 19. Lībertās populō ab rēge tertiō brevī tempore dabitur. 20. Patria nostra ā cīvibus fortibus etiam nunc servārī potest. 21. Fortūnā aliōrum monērī dēbēmus. 22. Cōnsiliīs istīus tyrannī quī trāns mare vīvit terrēmur; sed lībertātem amāmus et bellum magnā cum virtūte gerēmus. 23. Ab amīcīs potentibus adiuvābimur. 24. Omnēs virōs nostrōs laudāmus, quī virtūte et vēritāte moventur, nōn amōre suī.

### EXERCISES FOR Capvt XIX

1. Name the two basic verbal elements (1) of which the perfect passive indicative of all verbs is composed, and (2) of which the pluperfect passive indicative is composed.
2. In translation how does (1) **vir missus est** differ from **vir mittitur**, and (2) **vir missus erat,** from **vir mittēbātur?**
3. What is the use of the interrogative pronoun?
4. In what forms does the interrogative pronoun differ conspicuously in spelling from the relative?
5. By what two syntactical criteria can the interrogative pronoun be distinguished from the relative even when both have the same spelling?
6. Translate the following in accordance with their forms:

| | | |
|---|---|---|
| (1) movētur | (6) dēlēbantur | (11) tenēbāmur |
| (2) mōtus est | (7) dēlētī sunt | (12) mūtātus erat |
| (3) mōtum erat | (8) tenēmur | (13) mūtātus est |
| (4) movēbātur | (9) tentī sumus | (14) mūtātur |
| (5) dēlētī erant | (10) tentī erāmus | (15) mūtābātur |

7. Translate the following forms of the interrogative pronoun: (1) cuius?; (2) quem?; (3) quī?; (4) quid?; (5) quōrum?; (6) cui?; (7) quās?; (8) quis?; (9) quae?

8. Ā quō liber parātus est (parātus erat, parābātur)? 9. Magister ā quō liber parātus est labōre superātur. 10. Cui liber datus est (dabātur, datus erat)? 11. Quī puer servātus est? 12. Puerum quī servātus est ego ipse vīdī. 13. Cuius duo fīliī servātī sunt? 14. Senem cuius fīliī servātī sunt numquam vīdī. 15. Quis missus est? 16. Ā cīve quī missus erat pāx et lībertās laudātae sunt. 17. Quī missī sunt? 18. Ā decem cīvibus quī missī erant amīcitia laudāta est. 19. Quōs in urbe vīdistī? 20. Ubi sunt trēs novī amīcī quōs in urbe vīdistī? 21. Quae ā tē ibi inventa sunt? 22. Ubi sunt tria corpora quae ā tē ibi inventa sunt? 23. Ā quibus hoc dictum est? 24. Quibus hoc dictum est? 25. Octō hominēs miserī quibus haec dicta sunt ex urbe fūgērunt. 26. Quōrum fīliī ab eō laudātī sunt? 27. Patrēs quōrum fīliī laudātī sunt eī grātiās agent. 28. Quid vōs terret? 29. Quod perīculum vōs terret? 30. At perīculum quod vōs terret ā cīvibus fortibus victum est.

### EXERCISES FOR Capvt XX

1. Indicate the force of the following masculine and feminine endings of the 4th declension: (1) -um; (2) -uum; (3) -ū; (4) -us; (5) -ūs; (6) -uī.
2. Translate the following nouns in accordance with their case forms:

| | | |
|---|---|---|
| (1) manuī | (3) manuum | (5) manūs |
| (2) manus | (4) manū | (6) frūctibus |

| | | |
|---|---|---|
| (7) frūctum | (10) frūctū | (13) senātus |
| (8) frūctūs | (11) senātūs (sg.) | (14) senātū |
| (9) frūctuum | (12) senātuī | |

3. (1) What gender predominates in the 4th declension?
   (2) Name the noun which is the most common exception to this rule.
4. (1) Explain the difference of idea between the ablative of place from which and the ablative of separation.
   (2) Which of the two is regular with verbs of freeing, lacking, and depriving?
   (3) Which of the two is regular with verbs of motion?
5. State any differences of construction between them.

6. Quis ad nōs eō tempore vēnit? 7. Senex magnae fāmae ex patriā suā ad senātum nostrum fūgit. 8. Quid novī ab eō dictum est? 9. Hoc ab illō virō dictum est: "Lībertāte carēmus." 10. Nōs servitūte et gravī metū līberāte. 11. Cōpiae nostrae bellum longum contrā ācrēs manūs tyrannī gessērunt. 12. Illae manūs ācrēs quās tyrannus contrā nōs illā ex terrā mīsit ā nōbīs victae sunt. 13. Post haec cīvēs quī tyrannum timuērunt ex patriā suā in cīvitātem nostram ductī sunt. 14. Eōs sceleribus istīus tyrannī līberāvimus. 15. Nunc omnī metū carent. 16. Fīliī eōrum bonōs librōs in lūdīs nostrīs cum studiō legunt. 17. Itaque mīlle versūs manibus suīs scrīpsērunt. 18. Hī centum versūs nōbīs grātiās magnās agunt. 19. In hīs versibus senātus populusque Rōmānus laudantur. 20. Nam illī miserī nunc frūctūs pācis et multum lībertātis sine metū habent. 21. Quoniam aliōs adiūvimus, etiam nōs ipsī frūctum magnum habēmus. 22. Virī bonī cōpiā hōrum frūctuum numquam carēbunt. 23. Aetāte nostrā multī hominēs vītam in metū et servitūte agunt. 24. Dēbēmus illōs miserōs metū līberāre. 25. Nam quis potest beātus esse sī aliī hominēs frūctibus pācis lībertātisque carent?

26 What idea is expressed by each of the following ablatives, respectively? tempore (6), patriā (7), eō (8), virō (9), metū (10), nōbīs (12), patriā (13), sceleribus (14), metū (15), studiō (16), manibus (17), cōpiā (22), aetāte (23), metū (24).

## EXERCISES FOR Capvt XXI

1. Give the passive personal endings of the present and future tenses.
2. Repeat *aloud* the present and future passive of the model verbs **agō, audiō**, and **capiō**.
3. How can the present passive infinitive be distinguished from the active in the 1st, 2nd, and 4th conjugations? Illustrate by changing the following active infinitives into passive ones: (1) sentīre; (2) movēre; (3) servāre; (4) scīre; (5) tenēre. Translate each.
4. What is exceptional about the form of the present passive infinitive of the 3d conjugation? Illustrate by changing the following active infinitives into passive ones: (1) mittere; (2) iacere; (3) tangere; (4) trahere. Translate each.
5. Translate each of the following in accordance with its form:

| | | | |
|---|---|---|---|
| (1) mittar | (7) rapitur | (13) raperis | (19) tangēminī |
| (2) mitteris | (8) rapiētur | (14) rapiēris | (20) sciēris |
| (3) mittēris | (9) rapī | (15) tanguntur | (21) scīris |
| (4) mittī | (10) rapimur | (16) tangentur | (22) sciētur |
| (5) mittuntur | (11) rapientur | (17) tangī | (23) scītur |
| (6) mittor | (12) rapiuntur | (18) tangeris | (24) scīrī |

6. Quis mittitur (mittētur, mittēbātur, missus est)? 7. Ā quō hae litterae mittentur (missae sunt, mittuntur)? 8. Cuius manū illae litterae scrīptae sunt (scrībentur)? 9. Quid dictum est (dīcēbātur, dīcētur, dīcitur)? 10. "Quis rapiētur?" "Tū rapiēris." 11. "Quī rapientur?" "Vōs rapiēminī." 12. Diū neglegēris/neglegēminī (neglēctus es/neglēctī estis). 13. Post multās hōrās līberātī sumus (līberābimur). 14. Cīvitātis causā eum rapī iussērunt. 15. Lībertātis causā cīvitās nostra ab alterō virō gerī dēbet. 16. Animus eius pecūniā tangī nōn poterat. 17. Amor patriae in omnī animō sentiēbātur (sentiētur, sentītur, sēnsus est). 18. Amōre patriae cum aliīs cīvibus iungimur (iungēbāmur, iungēmur). 19. Amīcitia nōn semper intellegitur, sed sentītur. 20. Sapientia et vēritās in illīs duōbus hominibus nōn invenientur (inveniuntur, inventae sunt). 21. Sapientia etiam multā pecūniā nōn parātur (parābitur, parāta est). 22. Vēritās saepe nōn scītur (sciētur, scīta est), quod studium eius est difficile. 23. Nōn sine magnō labōre vēritās inveniētur (inventa est, potest invenīrī). 24. Aliī studiō pecūniae atque laudis trahuntur; nōs dēbēmus amōre vēritātis sapientiaeque trahī.

## EXERCISES FOR Capvt XXII

1. As **u** is characteristic of the 4th declension, what vowel is characteristic of the 5th declension?
2. List the case endings of the 5th declension which are enough like the corresponding endings of the 3rd declension that they can be immediately recognized without difficulty.
3. (1) What is the gender of most nouns of the 5th declension?
   (2) Name the chief exception.
4. Translate each of the following in accordance with its case(s) and number(s). Where a form is nom. or acc., so state.

| | | | |
|---|---|---|---|
| (1) speī | (6) fidē | (11) diēbus | (16) reī |
| (2) spērum | (7) fidem | (12) rem | (17) ignium |
| (3) spem | (8) fideī | (13) rērum | (18) ignem |
| (4) spēbus | (9) diērum | (14) rē | (19) ignibus |
| (5) spēs | (10) diēs | (15) rēbus | (20) ignēs |

5. Name the type of adverbial idea in each of the following, and then translate the sentence.

| | | |
|---|---|---|
| (1) In urbe remānsit. | (4) Cum eīs vēnit. | (7) Illud igne factum est. |
| (2) Ūnā hōrā veniet. | (5) Ex urbe vēnit. | (8) Id ab eīs factum est. |
| (3) Eō tempore vēnit. | (6) Igne carent. | (9) Id cum fidē factum est. |

6. Concerning each of the following adverbial ideas, state whether in Latin the ablative alone expresses the idea, or whether the Romans used a preposition with the ablative, or whether a preposition was sometimes used and sometimes not. Base your answers on the rules learned thus far.

| | |
|---|---|
| (1) personal agent | (5) means |
| (2) accompaniment | (6) manner |
| (3) separation | (7) place from which |
| (4) place where | (8) time when or within when |

7. Eō tempore lībertātem illōrum decem cīvium cum fidē cōnservāvit. 8. Rem pūblicam magnā cum cūrā gessit. 9. Rēs pūblica magnā cūrā ab eō gesta est. 10. Multae rēs bonae in mediā urbe vīsae sunt. 11. Eō diē multās rēs cum spē parāvērunt. 12. Ignem ex manibus puerī ēripuimus. 13. Quīnque diēbus Cicerō rem pūblicam ē perīculō ēripiet. 14. Duās rēs pūblicās metū līberāvistī. 15. Terra hominēs frūctibus bonīs alit. 16. Incertās spēs eōrum virtūte suā aluit. 17. Hāc aetāte spēs nostrae ā hīs tribus tyrannīs tolluntur. 18. Septem ex amīcīs nostrīs ex illā rē pūblicā magnō cum metū vēnērunt. 19. Tōta gēns in fīnēs huius reī pūblicae magnā cum manū amīcōrum ūnō diē vēnit. 20. Nōn omnēs virī līberī audent sē cum hāc rē pūblicā iungere. 21. Sī illī fidē carent, nūlla spēs est amīcitiae et pācis. 22. Bona fidēs et amor huius reī pūblicae possunt nōs cōnservāre. 23. Tōtam vītam huic reī pūblicae dedistī.

24. What idea is expressed by each of the following ablatives? (The numbers refer to the sentences.) (7) tempore, fidē; (8) cūrā; (9) cūrā; (10) urbe; (11) diē, spē; (13) diēbus, perīculō; (14) metū; (15) frūctibus; (16) virtūte; (17) aetāte, tyrannīs; (18) rē pūblicā, metū; (19) manū, diē; (21) fidē.

## EXERCISES FOR Capvt XXIII

1. State what Latin participle is indicated by each of the following endings and give the English suffix or phrase which can be used as an approximate equivalent in each instance: (1) -tus; (2) -ns; (3) -sūrus; (4) -ntem; (5) -tūrus; (6) -ndus; (7) -sus; (8) -ntēs; (9) -sī; (10) -tīs. Such forms should be practiced aloud until you have an immediate linguistic reflex to each one. These reflexes can be tested in the following exercise.

2. Translate the following participles in accordance with their tense and voice.

| | | | |
|---|---|---|---|
| (1) futūrus | (7) versus | (13) faciendus | (19) datī |
| (2) pressūrus | (8) versūrus | (14) rapientēs | (20) datūrōs |
| (3) premēns | (9) dictus | (15) raptūrōs | (21) dantem |
| (4) pressus | (10) dīcēns | (16) cupīta | (22) mōtus |
| (5) premendus | (11) dictūrus | (17) cupientēs | (23) moventem |
| (6) vertēns | (12) factus | (18) dandum | (24) mōtūrī |

3. Translate the following participles or participial phrases into Latin in their nom. sg. m. form.

| | |
|---|---|
| (1) (having been) seen | (10) (having been) conquered |
| (2) seeing | (11) about to conquer |
| (3) about to see | (12) conquering |
| (4) to be written | (13) about to join |
| (5) about to write | (14) joining |
| (6) (having been) written | (15) (having been) dragged |
| (7) sending | (16) dragging |
| (8) (having been) sent | (17) about to throw |
| (9) about to send | (18) (having been) thrown |

4. Captus nihil dīxit. 5. Servitūte līberātus, vītam iūcundam aget. 6. Dōna dantibus grātiās ēgit. 7. Aliquem dōna petentem nōn amō. 8. Hominī multam pecūniam cupientī pauca dōna sōla dabat. 9. Ad lūdum tuum fīlium meum docendum mīsī. 10. Iste, aliam

gentem victūrus, magistrōs librōsque dēlēre cupiēbat. 11. Hīs īnsidiīs territī, vītam miseram vīvēmus. 12. Diū oppressī, sē contrā opprimentem tyrannum vertere coepērunt. 13. Illī quattuor virī miserī, ā tyrannō vīsī, trāns fīnem cucurrērunt. 14. Ōrātor, tyrannum timēns, iūcunda semper dīcēbat. 15. Aliquem nōs timentem timēmus. 16. Hī vincentēs omnia iūra cīvium victōrum tollent. 17. Ille miser fugitūrus cōnsilium trium amīcōrum petēbat. 18. Senex, ab duōbus ex amīcīs monitus, ad nōs fūgit. 19. Ipse, ā sene secundō adiūtus, pecūniā carentibus multās rēs dabat. 20. Quis, hīs perīculīs līberātus, deīs grātiās nōn dabit? 21. Iūnctī vōbīscum, rem pūblicam cōnservābimus. 22. Fidem habentibus nihil est incertum.

### EXERCISES FOR Capvt XXIV

1. (1) What are the two essential parts of a regular ablative absolute in Latin?
   (2) Can the noun or pronoun of an ablative absolute also appear as the subject or the object of the verb?
2. (1) Explain the term "absolute."
   (2) Guided by the examples in Capvt XXIV, p. 194, tell what punctuation usually indicates an ablative absolute, and show how this harmonizes with the term "absolute."
3. Should the ablative absolute always be translated literally? Explain.
4. Name five subordinating conjunctions in English which may be used to translate the ablative absolute depending on the requirements of the context.
5. State whether the Romans would have regarded any or all of the following sentences as incorrect, and explain why. (Examples in Capvt XXIV will help you.)
   (1) Urbe captā, Caesar eam dēlēvit.
   (2) Caesar, urbem captus, eam dēlēvit.
   (3) Caesar urbem captam dēlēvit.
   (4) Urbe captā, Caesar multās gentēs dēlēvit.
6. (1) What idea is expressed by the -ndus participle (gerundive) + **sum?**
   (2) Explain the agreement of the -ndus, -nda, -ndum participle.
   (3) What Latin verb + the infinitive expresses a similar idea?
7. (1) Explain the syntax of **mihi** in the following sentence: Cīvitās mihi cōnservanda est.
   (2) Fill out the blank in the following sentence with the Latin for "by me" and explain the construction: Cīvitās—cōnservāta est.

8. Hīs duōbus virīs imperium tenentibus, rēs pūblica valēbit. 9. Hāc fāmā nārrātā, dux urbem sine morā relīquit. 10. Omnī cupiditāte pecūniae glōriaeque ex animō expulsā, ille dux sē vīcit. 11. Omnis cupiditās rērum malārum nōbīs vincenda est sī bonam vītam agere cupimus. 12. Cīvibus patriam amantibus, possumus habēre magnās spēs. 13. Omnēs cīvēs istum tyrannum timēbant, quī expellendus erat. 14. Tyrannō superātō, cīvēs lībertātem et iūra recēpērunt. 15. At tyrannō expulsō, alius tyrannus imperium saepe accipit. 16. Quis imperium accipiēns adiuvāre cīvitātem sōlam, nōn sē, cupit? 17. Multīs gentibus victīs, tōtum mundum tenēre cupīvistī. 18. Servitūs omnis generis per tōtum mundum opprimenda est. 19. Sī rēs pūblica nostra valet, nihil tibi timendum est. 20. Patria nostra cuique adiuvanda est quī nostrum modum vītae amat. 21. Omnia igitur iūra cīvibus magnā cūrā cōnservanda sunt. 22. Officiīs ā cīvibus relictīs,

rēs pūblica in magnō perīculō erit. 23. Hīs rēbus gravibus dictīs, ōrātor ā nōbīs laudātus est. 24. Vēritās et virtūs omnibus virīs semper quaerendae sunt. 25. Vēritāte et virtūte quaesītīs, rēs pūblica cōnservāta est.

26. From the above sentences list:
    A. 10 instances of the ablative absolute.
    B. 7 instances of the -**ndus sum** construction (passive periphrastic).
    C. 5 instances of the dative of agent.
    D. 2 instances of the ablative of agent.

## EXERCISES FOR Capvt XXV

1. Review the present active and passive infinitives of all four conjugations.
2. If -**tūrus** (-**sūrus**) marks the future active participle, what form logically is -**tūrus** (-**sūrus**) **esse?**
3. If -**tus** (-**sus**) marks the perfect passive participle, what form logically is -**tus** (-**sus**) **esse?**
4. With what do the participial elements of the above infinitives (the -**tūrus**, -**tūra**, -**tūrum** and the -**tus**, -**a**, -**um**) agree?
5. To what English verb phrase is the Latin ending -**isse** equivalent? Repeat this sufficiently so that when you see -**isse** your linguistic reflex automatically and instantly gives you the proper tense and voice of the infinitive.
6. Now try your reflexes by translating the following forms in accordance with their tense and voice.

| | | |
|---|---|---|
| (1) mōvisse | (11) sustulisse | (21) quaesītum esse |
| (2) mōtus esse | (12) trāxisse | (22) expulsum esse |
| (3) mōtūrus esse | (13) tetigisse | (23) relictōs esse |
| (4) movērī | (14) amāvisse | (24) data esse |
| (5) dīcī | (15) vīcisse | (25) datūra esse |
| (6) scīrī | (16) vīxisse | (26) versūrum esse |
| (7) servārī | (17) trāctōs esse | (27) pressūrōs esse |
| (8) rapī | (18) vīsam esse | (28) raptūrōs esse |
| (9) mittī | (19) raptum esse | (29) iussūrum esse |
| (10) crēdidisse | (20) missōs esse | (30) tāctūrōs esse |

7. Explain the difference between a direct and an indirect statement.
8. Indicate what verbs in the following list may introduce an indirect statement and give their meanings.

| | | | |
|---|---|---|---|
| (1) mittō | (7) videō | (13) audiō | (19) ostendō |
| (2) nūntiō | (8) nesciō | (14) sentiō | (20) spērō |
| (3) rīdeō | (9) parō | (15) agō | (21) iungō |
| (4) intellegō | (10) crēdō | (16) scrībō | (22) putō |
| (5) accipiō | (11) terreō | (17) audeō | (23) amō |
| (6) cupiō | (12) neglegō | (18) gerō | (24) negō |

9. In what main categories can we list most verbs which frequently introduce indirect statements?

10. In English the indirect statement most often appears as a "that" clause, though an infinitive with subject accusative is sometimes used ("I believe that he is brave"; "I believe him to be brave"). What is the form of the indirect statement in classical Latin?
11. In what case did the Romans put the subject of an infinitive?
12. In Latin indirect statement does the tense of the infinitive depend on the tense of the verb of saying? In other words, must a present infinitive be used only with a present main verb, a perfect only with a perfect main verb, etc.?
13. What time relative to that of the main verb does each of the following infinitive tenses indicate: (1) perfect; (2) future; (3) present?

14. Sciō tē hoc fēcisse (factūrum esse, facere). 15. Scīvī tē hoc fēcisse (factūrum esse, facere). 16. Crēdidimus eōs ventūrōs esse (vēnisse, venīre). 17. Crēdimus eōs ventūrōs esse (vēnisse, venīre). 18. Crās audiet (A) eōs venīre (i.e., crās); (B) eōs vēnisse (e.g., heri); (C) eōs ventūrōs esse (e.g., paucīs diēbus). 19. Hodiē audit (A) eōs venīre (hodiē); (B) eōs vēnisse (heri); (C) eōs ventūrōs esse (mox, *soon*). 20. Heri audīvit (A) eōs venīre (heri); (B) eōs vēnisse (e.g., prīdiē, *the day before yesterday*); (C) eōs ventūrōs (paucīs diēbus). 21. Spērant vōs eum vīsūrōs esse. 22. Sciō hoc ā tē factum esse. 23. Nescīvī illa ab eō facta esse. 24. Negāvērunt urbem ab hostibus capī (captam esse). 25. Scītis illōs esse (futūrōs esse, fuisse) semper fidēlēs. 26. Scīvistis illōs esse (futūrōs esse, fuisse) semper fidēlēs. 27. Putābant tyrannum sibi expellendum esse. 28. Crēdimus pācem omnibus ducibus quaerendam esse. 29. Dīcit pācem ab decem ducibus quaerī (quaesītam esse). 30. Dīxit duōs ducēs pācem quaesītūrōs esse (quaerere, quaesīvisse). 31. Hostēs spērant sē omnēs rēs pūblicās victūrōs esse. 32. Bene sciō mē multa nescīre; nēmō enim potest omnia scīre.

33. All infinitives except one in the above sentences are infinitives in indirect statement. Name that one exception.
34. Explain the syntax of the following words by stating in each instance (A) the form and (B) the reason for the form: (14) tē; fēcisse; (16) eōs; (17) ventūrōs esse; (21) eum; (22) hoc; (23) eō; (24) hostibus; (25) fidēlēs; (27) sibi; (28) pācem; ducibus; (29) ducibus; (30) pācem; (31) rēs pūblicās.

## EXERCISES FOR Capvt XXVI

1. (1) In the comparison of adjectives, to what English ending does the Latin -**ior** correspond?
   (2) What mnemonic aid can be found in their superficial similarity?
2. (1) To what English adjectival ending does -**issimus** correspond?
   (2) Can any mnemonic device be found here?
3. (1) To what part of an adjective are -**ior** and -**issimus** normally added?
   (2) Illustrate by adding these endings to the following adjectives: **turpis**; **vēlōx**, gen. **vēlōcis**, *swift;* **prūdēns**, gen. **prūdentis**, *prudent.*
4. If **acerbus** means *harsh* give (1) three possible forces of the comparative **acerbior** and (2) two possible forces of the superlative **acerbissimus.**
5. Give the meaning of **quam** (1) with the comparative degree (e.g., hic erat acerbior quam ille) and (2) with the superlative (e.g., hic erat quam acerbissimus).
6. What case follows **quam**, *than?*

7. (1) Do most adjectives of the 3rd declension have consonant stems or i-stems?
   (2) Do comparatives have consonant stems or i-stems?

8. Nūntiāvērunt ducem quam fortissimum vēnisse. 9. Lūce clārissimā ab quattuor virīs vīsā, cōpiae fortissimae contrā hostēs missae sunt. 10. Istō homine turpissimō expulsō, senātus cīvibus fidēliōribus dōna dedit. 11. Beātiōrēs cīvēs prō cīvibus miseriōribus haec dulcia faciēbant. 12. Hic auctor est clārior quam ille. 13. Quīdam dīxērunt hunc auctōrem esse clāriōrem quam illum. 14. Librōs sapientiōrum auctōrum legite, sī vītam sapientissimam agere cupitis. 15. Sex auctōrēs quōrum librōs lēgī sunt acerbiōrēs. 16. Quibusdam librīs sapientissimīs lēctīs, illa vitia turpiōra vītāvimus. 17. Hic vir, quī turpia vitia sua superāvit, fortior est quam dux fortissimus. 18. Quis est vir fēlīcissimus? Is quī vītam sapientissimam agit fēlīcior est quam tyrannus potentissimus. 19. Remedium vitiōrum vestrōrum vidētur difficilius. 20. Ille dux putāvit patriam esse sibi cāriōrem quam vītam. 21. Manus adulēscentium quam fidēlissimōrum senātuī quaerenda est.

## EXERCISES FOR Capvt XXVII

1. (1) What is peculiar about the comparison of adjectives in which the masculine of the positive degree ends in -**er**?
   (2) Does this hold for adjectives of any declension or only for those of the 1st and 2nd declension?
2. (1) What is peculiar about the comparison of **facilis**?
   (2) Do all adjectives in -**lis** follow this rule? Be specific.
3. Some of the most common adjectives are the most irregular in their comparison. To illustrate how helpful English can be in learning these irregular forms, write each of the following Latin words on a separate line:

   parvus, malus, bonus, (prō), magnus, superus, multus;

   and then, choosing from the following list, write opposite each of them the English words which suggest the comparative and the superlative respectively:

   pessimist, prime, minus, ameliorate, summit, maximum, supreme, optimist, plus, superior, pejorative, prior, major, minimum.

4. Translate the following:

| | | |
|---|---|---|
| (1) bellum minus | (13) fidēs minima | (25) plūrēs labōrēs |
| (2) bellum pessimum | (14) mare minus | (26) ducēs optimī |
| (3) bellum maius | (15) in marī minōre | (27) ducēs maiōrēs |
| (4) bella priōra | (16) maria maiōra | (28) ducēs meliōrēs |
| (5) liber simillimus | (17) frūctūs optimī | (29) dōna minima |
| (6) liber difficilior | (18) frūctus peior | (30) dōna plūra |
| (7) puer minimus | (19) hominēs ācerrimī | (31) dōna prīma |
| (8) puer melior | (20) hominēs ācriōrēs | (32) plūs laudis |
| (9) puella pulcherrima | (21) hominēs plūrēs | (33) plūrēs laudēs |
| (10) puella pulchrior | (22) labor difficillimus | (34) cīvēs pessimī |
| (11) puellae plūrimae | (23) labor suprēmus | (35) cīvēs meliōrēs |
| (12) fidēs maior | (24) plūs labōris | (36) cīvēs līberrimī |

5. Facillima saepe nōn sunt optima. 6. Difficilia saepe sunt maxima. 7. Meliōra studia sunt difficiliōra. 8. Pessimī auctōrēs librōs plūrimōs scrībunt. 9. Hī librī peiōrēs sunt quam librī auctōrum meliōrum. 10. Puer minor maius dōnum accēpit. 11. Illa rēs pūblica minima maximās spēs habuit. 12. Plūrēs virī crēdunt hoc bellum esse peius quam prīmum bellum. 13. Dux melior cum cōpiīs maiōribus veniet. 14. Ācrēs ducēs ācriōrēs cōpiās ācerrimōrum hostium saepe laudābant. 15. Tyrannō pessimō expulsō, cīvēs ducem meliōrem et sapientiōrem quaesivērunt. 16. Meliōrī ducī maius imperium et plūs pecūniae dedērunt. 17. Cīvēs urbium minōrum nōn sunt meliōrēs quam eī urbium maximārum. 18. Nōs nōn meliōrēs sumus quam plūrimī virī priōrum aetātum. 19. Maiōrēs nostrī Apollinem (Apollō, acc.) deum sōlis appellābant.

## EXERCISES FOR Capvt XXVIII

1. What does the subjunctive usually indicate in Latin—a fact or something other than a fact?
2. Is the subjunctive more or less common in Latin than it is in English?
3. What vowel is the sign of the present subjunctive (1) in the 1st conjugation and (2) in the other conjugations?
4. When the verb of the *main clause* is in the subjunctive, what is the force of this subjunctive?
5. What idea is expressed by the subjunctive in a *subordinate clause* introduced by **ut** or **nē?**
6. In this chapter when **nē** is used with a *main verb* in the subjunctive, what kind of subjunctive is it?
7. Did the Roman prose-writers of the classical period use the infinitive to express purpose as we do in English?
8. Whenever in the following list a form is subjunctive, so label it, indicating also its person and number. The indicative forms are to be translated in accordance with their person, number, and tense.

| | | |
|---|---|---|
| (1) mittet | (11) audiēmur | (21) līberēminī |
| (2) mittat | (12) audiāmur | (22) līberābiminī |
| (3) mittit | (13) audīmur | (23) dēlentur |
| (4) det | (14) ēripiās | (24) dēleantur |
| (5) dat | (15) ēripis | (25) vincēris |
| (6) crēdant | (16) ēripiēs | (26) vinceris |
| (7) crēdunt | (17) sciuntur | (27) vincāris |
| (8) crēdent | (18) scientur | (28) dīcimus |
| (9) movent | (19) sciantur | (29) dīcēmus |
| (10) moveant | (20) līberāminī | (30) dīcāmus |

9. Ille dux veniat. Eum exspectāmus. 10. Cīvēs turpēs ex rē pūblicā discēdant ut in pāce vīvāmus. 11. Sī illī duo amīcōs cupiunt, vēra beneficia faciant. 12. Beneficia aliīs praestat ut amētur. 13. Haec verba fēlīcia vōbīs dīcō nē discēdātis. 14. Patriae causā haec difficillima faciāmus. 15. Illīs miserīs plūs pecūniae date nē armīs contrā hostēs careant. 16. Putat eōs id factūrōs esse ut īram meam vītent. 17. Arma parēmus nē lībertās nostra tollātur. 18. Armīsne sōlīs lībertās nostra ē perīculō ēripiētur? 19. Nē sapientēs librōs difficiliōrēs scrībant. 20. Satis sapientiae enim ā librīs difficiliōribus nōn accipiēmus.

21. Meliōra et maiōra faciat nē vītam miserrimam agat. 22. Haec illī auctōrī clārissimō nārrā ut in librō eius scrībantur. 23. Vēritātem semper quaerāmus, sine quā maximī animī nōn possunt esse fēlīcēs.

24. Explain the syntax of the following words (i.e., copy the words each on a new line, state the form, and give the reason for that form): (9) veniat; (10) discēdant, vīvāmus; (11) faciant; (12) praestat, amētur; (13) discēdātis; (14) faciāmus; (15) date, armīs, careant; (16) eōs, factūrōs esse, vītent; (17) parēmus, tollātur; (18) armīs, ēripiētur; (19) scrībant; (20) accipiēmus; (21) faciat, agat; (22) nārrā, scrībantur; (23) quaerāmus.

## EXERCISES FOR Capvt XXIX

1. What is the easy rule for the recognition and the formation of the imperfect subjunctive active and passive?
2. Does this rule apply to such irregular verbs as **sum** and **possum?**
3. The indicatives in the following list are to be translated according to their forms. The subjunctives are to be so labeled, with indication also of their tense, person, and number.

| | | |
|---|---|---|
| (1) vocāret | (11) dīcat | (21) possīmus |
| (2) invenīrent | (12) dīcet | (22) essent |
| (3) vidērēmus | (13) dīcit | (23) accipiās |
| (4) dīcerem | (14) sint | (24) accipiēs |
| (5) ēriperēs | (15) posset | (25) acciperēs |
| (6) servet | (16) possit | (26) expellēminī |
| (7) servārētis | (17) discēderent | (27) expellerēminī |
| (8) videat | (18) discēdent | (28) expellāminī |
| (9) inveniēs | (19) discēdant | (29) movērentur |
| (10) inveniās | (20) dēmus | (30) moventur |

4. How can the idea of result be expressed in Latin?
5. How can result clauses be distinguished from purpose clauses?
6. When and where is the imperfect subjunctive used?

7. Optimōs librōs tantā cum cūrā lēgērunt ut multum sapientiae discerent. 8. Bonōs librōs cum cūrā legēbāmus ut sapientiam discerēmus. 9. Optimī librī discipulīs legendī sunt ut vēritātem et mōrēs bonōs discant. 10. Sapientissimī auctōrēs plūrēs librōs scrībant ut omnēs gentēs adiuvāre possint. 11. Animī plūrimōrum hominum tam stultī sunt ut discere nōn cupiant. 12. At multae mentēs ita ācrēs sunt ut bene discere possint. 13. Quīdam magistrī discipulōs tantā cum arte docēbant ut ipsī discipulī quidem discere cuperent. 14. Imperium istīus tyrannī tantum erat ut senātus eum expellere nōn posset. 15. Omnēs cīvēs sē patriae dent nē hostēs lībertātem tollant. 16. Caesar tam ācer dux erat ut hostēs mīlitēs Rōmānōs nōn vincerent. 17. Dūcimusne aliās gentēs tantā cum sapientiā et virtūte ut lībertās cōnservētur? 18. Tanta beneficia faciēbātis ut omnēs vōs amārent. 19. Tam dūrus erat ut nēmō eum amāret. 20. Mīlia cīvium ex eā terrā fugiēbant nē ā tyrannō opprimerentur. 21. Lībertātem sīc amāvērunt ut numquam ab hostibus vincerentur.

22. Explain the syntax of the following words: (7) discerent; (8) discerēmus; (9) discant; (10) scrībant, possint; (11) cupiant; (12) possint; (13) cuperent; (14) posset; (15) dent,

tollant; (16) vincerent; (17) cōnservētur; (18) amārent; (19) amāret; (20) opprimerentur; (21) vincerentur.

### EXERCISES FOR Capvt XXX

1. As the form of the imperfect subjunctive active is the present active infinitive plus personal endings, how can the pluperfect subjunctive active be easily recognized?
2. As the pluperfect indicative passive is the perfect passive particle + **eram** (i.e., the imperfect indicative of **sum**), what parallel rule holds for the pluperfect subjunctive passive?
3. If **positus est** is the perfect indicative passive, what most naturally is **positus sit?**
4. What forms of the active indicative do the forms of the perfect subjunctive active resemble in most instances?
5. State the tense, voice, person, and number of each of the following subjunctives:

| | | | |
|---|---|---|---|
| (1) ponerētur | (5) posuerint | (9) darent | (13) dedissēs |
| (2) posuissem | (6) ponerēmus | (10) datī essēmus | (14) darētur |
| (3) positī sint | (7) posuissētis | (11) det | (15) dederīmus |
| (4) ponāmur | (8) positus esset | (12) datus sīs | (16) dedissent |

6. (1) Name the primary tenses of the indicative.
   (2) Name the primary tenses of the subjunctive.
   (3) Name the historical tenses of the indicative.
   (4) Name the historical tenses of the subjunctive.
7. (1) What time does the present subjunctive indicate relative to that of a primary main verb?
   (2) What time does the imperfect subjunctive indicate relative to that of a historical main verb?
   (3) What time does the perfect subjunctive indicate relative to that of a primary main verb?
   (4) What time does the pluperfect subjunctive indicate relative to that of a secondary main verb?

8. Ubi dux est (fuit)? 9. Rogant ubi dux sit (fuerit). 10. Rogābant ubi dux esset (fuisset). 11. Rogābunt ubi dux sit (fuerit). 12. Nesciō ubi pecūnia posita sit. 13. Scīsne ubi pecūnia ponātur? 14. Scīvērunt ubi pecūnia ponerētur. 15. Nescīvit ubi pecūnia posita esset. 16. Vōbīs dīcēmus cūr mīles hoc fēcerit (faciat). 17. Mihi dīxērunt cūr mīles hoc fēcisset (faceret). 18. Dīc mihi quis vēnerit (veniat). 19. Ōrātor rogāvit cūr cēterī cīvēs haec cōnsilia nōn cognōvissent. 20. Ducī nūntiāvimus cēterōs mīlitēs in illam terram fugere (fūgisse). 21. Ducī nūntiāvimus in quam terram cēterī mīlitēs fugerent (fūgissent). 22. Audīvimus cīvēs tam fidēlēs esse ut rem pūblicam cōnservārent. 23. Audīvimus quid cīvēs fēcissent ut rem pūblicam cōnservārent. 24. Quaerēbant quōrum in rē pūblicā pāx invenīrī posset. 25. Cognōvimus pācem in patriā eōrum nōn inventam esse. 26. Illī stultī semper rogant quid sit melius quam imperium aut pecūnia. 27. Nōs quidem putāmus pecūniam ipsam nōn esse malam; sed crēdimus vēritātem et lībertātem et amīcitiam esse meliōrēs et maiōrēs. 28. Haec cupimus ut vītam pulchriōrem agāmus; nam pecūnia sōla et imperium possunt hominēs dūrōs facere, ut fēlīcēs nōn sint. 29. Dēnique omnia expōnat ut iam comprehendātis quanta scelera contrā rem pūblicam commissa sint.

30. Explain the syntax of the following: (15) posita esset; (16) fēcerit; (17) fēcisset; (18) vēnerit; (20) fugere; (21) fugerent; (22) esse, cōnservārent; (23) fēcissent, cōnservārent; (24) posset; (25) inventam esse; (26) sit; (27) esse; (28) agāmus, sint; (29) expōnat, comprehendātis, commissa sint.

## EXERCISES FOR Capvt XXXI

1. Name the three possible meanings of **cum** + the subjunctive.
2. When **tamen** follows a **cum**-clause, what does **cum** regularly mean?
3. (1) To what conjugation does **ferō** belong?
   (2) State the irregularity which the following forms of **ferō** have in common: ferre, fers, fert, fertis, ferris, fertur.
4. In the following list label the subjunctives and translate the rest according to their forms.

| | | | |
|---|---|---|---|
| (1) ferat | (6) ferunt | (11) fertis | (16) tulisse |
| (2) fert | (7) ferent | (12) ferēris | (17) lātūrus esse |
| (3) ferret | (8) ferant | (13) ferris | (18) ferendus |
| (4) feret | (9) fertur | (14) fer | (19) lātus esse |
| (5) ferre | (10) ferte | (15) ferrī | (20) tulisset |

5. Cum hoc dīxissēmus, illī vīgintī respondērunt sē pācem aequam oblātūrōs esse. 6. Cum sē in aliam terram contulisset, tamen amīcōs novōs invēnit. 7. Cum amīcitiam nōbīs offerant, eīs auxilium offerēmus. 8. Cum perīculum magnum esset, omnēs cōpiās et arma brevī tempore contulērunt. 9. Quid tū fers? Quid ille fert? Dīc mihi cūr haec dōna offerantur. 10. Cum exposuisset quid peteret, negāvistī tantum auxilium posse offerrī. 11. Cum dōna iūcunda tulissent, potuī tamen īnsidiās eōrum cognōscere. 12. Cum cōnsilia tua nunc comprehendāmus, īnsidiās tuās nōn ferēmus. 13. Tanta mala nōn ferenda sunt. Cōnfer tē in exsilium. 14. Dēnique hī centum cīvēs reī pūblicae auxilium ferant. 15. Putābam eōs vīnum nāvibus lātūrōs esse. 16. Cum mīlitēs nostrī hostēs vīcissent, tamen eīs multa beneficia obtulērunt. 17. Cum cognōvisset quanta beneficia cēterī trēs offerrent, ipse aequa beneficia obtulit. 18. Cīvibus miserīs gentium parvārum satis auxiliī dēbēmus offerre. 19. Cum cōnsul haec verba dīxisset, senātus respondit pecūniam ad hanc rem collātam esse.

20. Explain the syntax of the following words: (5) dīxissēmus, oblātūrōs esse; (6) contulisset; (7) offerant; (8) esset; (9) offerantur; (10) exposuisset, peteret; (11) tulissent; (12) comprehendāmus; (13) cōnfer; (14) ferant; (15) nāvibus, lātūrōs esse; (16) vīcissent; (17) offerrent; (19) dīxisset.

## EXERCISES FOR Capvt XXXII

1. What is the regular positive ending (1) of adverbs made from adjectives of the 1st and the 2nd declensions and (2) of adverbs made from adjectives of the 3rd declension?
2. In English what adverbial ending is equivalent to the Latin adverbial **-ē** or **-iter**?
3. Do all Latin adverbs of the positive degree end in **-ē** or **-iter**?
4. (1) What is the ending of the comparative degree of an adverb in Latin?
   (2) With what form of the adjective is this identical?
   (3) In English how is the comparative degree of the adverb usually formed?

5. How does the base of the superlative degree of a Latin adverb compare with that of the corresponding adjective?
6. Translate each of the following adverbs in two ways: (1) līberius; (2) līberrimē.
7. Translate each of the following adverbs in accordance with its form.

| | | | |
|---|---|---|---|
| (1) iūcundē | (6) breviter | (11) minimē | (16) minus |
| (2) iūcundius | (7) celerrimē | (12) magis | (17) facile |
| (3) iūcundissimē | (8) peius | (13) diūtius | (18) maximē |
| (4) melius | (9) fidēlius | (14) male | (19) gravissimē |
| (5) fidēlissimē | (10) facilius | (15) miserius | (20) celerius |

8. (1) What is the stem of **volō** in the indicative?
   (2) What is the stem of **volō** in the present and the imperfect subjunctive?
9. To what other irregular verb is **volō** similar in the present subjunctive?
10. Label the subjunctives in the following list and translate the other forms.

| | | | |
|---|---|---|---|
| (1) volēs | (7) māllēmus | (13) voluisse | (19) voluistī |
| (2) velīs | (8) voluissēs | (14) volunt | (20) vellet |
| (3) vīs | (9) volam | (15) voluimus | (21) nōlunt |
| (4) vellēs | (10) volēbant | (16) velle | (22) nōllet |
| (5) māvult | (11) volet | (17) voluerat | (23) mālit |
| (6) velīmus | (12) vultis | (18) voluērunt | (24) nōlet |

11. Quīdam mālunt crēdere omnēs esse parēs. 12. Quīdam negant mentēs quidem omnium hominum esse parēs. 13. Hī dīvitiās celerrimē invēnērunt; illī diūtissimē erunt pauperēs. 14. Hic plūrimōs honōrēs quam facillimē accipere vult. 15. Nōlīte hanc scientiam āmittere. 16. Cīvēs ipsī rem pūblicam melius gessērunt quam ille dux. 17. Ibi terra est aequior et plūs patet. 18. Nōs ā scientiā prohibēre nōlent virī līberī; sed tyrannī maximē sīc volunt. 19. Tyrannus cīvēs suōs ita male opprimēbat ut semper līberī esse vellent. 20. Plūrima dōna līberrimē offeret ut exercitus istum tyrannum adiuvāre velit. 21. Cum auxilium offerre minimē vellent, nōluimus eīs beneficia multa praestāre. 22. Cum hostēs contrā nōs celeriter veniant, volumus nostrōs ad arma quam celerrimē vocāre. 23. Cum lībertātem lēgēsque cōnservāre vērē vellent, tamen scelera tyrannī diūtissimē ferenda erant. 24. Māvult haec sapientius facere nē hanc quidem occāsiōnem āmittat. 25. Nōlī discēdere, mī amīce.

## EXERCISES FOR Capvt XXXIII

1. (1) What form of the verb is found in both clauses of a future less vivid condition?
   (2) Explain why this construction is called "less vivid" as compared with the simple future (or "future more vivid")
2. (1) Name the specific type of condition (A) that has the imperfect subjunctive in both clauses and (B) that has the pluperfect subjunctive in both clauses.
   (2) In each of these conditions which part of the sentence is essentially the same in both Latin and English?
3. What is the regular negative of the conditional clause in Latin?
4. What type of Latin condition is translated by "should . . . would" and hence can be called a "should-would condition"?
5. What is the meaning of **quis, quid** after **sī, nisi, nē,** and **num?**

6. Sī ratiō dūcit, fēlīx es. 7. Sī ratiō dūcet, fēlīx eris. 8. Sī ratiō dūcat, fēlīx sīs. 9. Sī ratiō dūceret, fēlīx essēs. 10. Sī ratiō dūxisset, fēlīx fuissēs. 11. Sī pecūniam amās, sapientiā carēs. 12. Sī pecūniam amābis, sapientiā carēbis. 13. Sī pecūniam amēs, sapientiā careās. 14. Sī pecūniam amārēs, sapientiā carērēs. 15. Sī pecūniam amāvissēs, sapientiā caruissēs. 16. Sī vēritātem quaerimus, scientiam invenīmus. 17. Sī vēritātem quaerēmus, scientiam inveniēmus. 18. Sī vēritātem quaerāmus, scientiam inveniāmus. 19. Sī vēritātem quaererēmus, scientiam invenīrēmus. 20. Sī vēritātem quaesīvissēmus, scientiam invēnissēmus. 21. Nisi īram vītābitis, duōs amīcōs āmittētis. 22. Nisi īram vītāvissētis, quīnque amīcōs āmīsissētis. 23. Nisi īram vītētis, multōs amīcōs āmittātis. 24. Nisi īram vītārētis, multōs amīcōs āmitterētis. 25. Nisi īram vītātis, multōs amīcōs āmittitis. 26. Nisi īram vītāvistis, multōs amīcōs āmīsistis. 27. Sī quis bonōs mōrēs habet, eum laudāmus. 28. Sī quis bonōs mōrēs habuisset, eum laudāvissēmus. 29. Sī quis bonōs mōrēs habeat, eum laudēmus. 30. Sī quis bonōs mōrēs habuit, eum laudāvimus (laudābāmus). 31. Sī quis bonōs mōrēs habēret, eum laudārēmus. 32. Sī quis bonōs mōrēs habēbit, eum laudābimus. 33. Sī istī vincent, discēdēmus. 34. Sī istī vincant, discēdāmus. 35. Sī istī vīcissent, discessissēmus. 36. Sī librōs bene lēgissēs, melius scrīpsissēs. 37. Sī librōs bene legēs, melius scrībēs. 38. Sī librōs bene legās, melius scrībās.

39. Name in sequence the types of conditions found in sentences 6–10 and 21–26.

## EXERCISES FOR Capvt XXXIV

1. State the chief peculiarity of deponent verbs.
2. Write a synopsis of the following verbs in the 6 tenses of the indicative and the 4 tenses of the subjunctive as indicated:
   (1) **cōnor** in the 1st person plural.
   (2) **loquor** in the 3d person singular.
3. (1) Write, label, and translate all the participles of **patior**.
   (2) Write, label, and translate all the infinitives of **patior**.
4. Using the proper form of **illud cōnsilium** fill in the following blanks to complete the idea suggested by the English sentence in each instance.
   (1) He will not follow that plan: nōn sequētur _____.
   (2) He will not use that plan: nōn ūtētur _____.
   (3) He will not permit that plan: nōn patiētur _____.
5. Explain the proper form of **illud cōnsilium** in #4 (2) above.
6. Name the *active forms* found in deponent verbs.
7. Give the imperative forms of (1) **cōnor** and (2) **loquor,** and translate each one.
8. Translate the following participles: (1) locūtus; (2) mortuus; (3) cōnātus; (4) passus; (5) secūtus; (6) ēgressus; (7) profectus.
9. In the following list label any subjunctive forms and translate the rest:

| | | | |
|---|---|---|---|
| (1) ūtētur | (6) ūsus esset | (11) patī | (16) patitur |
| (2) ūtātur | (7) ūsūrum esse | (12) passī sunt | (17) patiēmur |
| (3) ūtitur | (8) patiēris | (13) passum esse | (18) arbitrētur |
| (4) ūterētur | (9) pateris | (14) patientēs | (19) arbitrārētur |
| (5) ūsus | (10) patere | (15) patiātur | (20) patiendum est |

10. Arbitrātur haec mala patienda esse. 11. Cōnābimur haec mala patī. 12. Nisi morī vīs, patere haec mala. 13. Maxima mala passus, homō miser mortuus est. 14. Tyrannus

arbitrātus est eōs duōs haec mala diū passūrōs esse. 15. Cum tria bella passī essent, istum tyrannum in exsilium expellere ausī sunt. 16. Sī hunc ducem novum sequēminī, lībertāte et ōtiō ūtēminī. 17. Hīs verbīs dictīs, eum sequī ausī sumus. 18. Haec verba locūtī, profectī sumus nē in eō locō miserō morerēmur. 19. Cum vōs cōnsiliō malō ūsōs esse arbitrārētur, tamen vōbīscum līberē locūtus est. 20. Sī quis vīnō eius generis ūtī audeat, celeriter moriātur. 21. Eōdem diē fīlius eius nātus est et mortuus est. 22. Omnibus opibus nostrīs ūtāmur ut patria nostra servētur. 23. Cum in aliam terram proficīscī cōnārētur, ā mīlitibus captus est. 24. Arbitrābar eum ex urbe cum decem amīcīs ēgressūrum esse. 25. Eā nocte profectus, Caesar ad quandam īnsulam clārissimam vēnit. 26. Sī meliōribus librīs ūsī essent, plūra didicissent. 27. Sī multōs amīcōs habēre vīs, nōlī esse superbus.

28. Name the type of condition found above in each of the following sentences: 12, 16, 20, 26.
29. Explain the syntax of the following: (14) passūrōs esse; (17) verbīs; (18) locūtī, morerēmur; (19) cōnsiliō, arbitrārētur; (21) diē; (22) ūtāmur; (25) nocte; (26) librīs.

## EXERCISES FOR Capvt XXXV

1. A certain number of verbs, which in English apparently take a direct object, in Latin take a dative. In lieu of a good rule to cover such verbs, what procedures can prove helpful?
2. Some other verbs also, when compounded with certain prepositions, may take a dative.
   (1) What is the concept that underlies this?
   (2) Do all compound verbs take the dative?
3. Copy each of the following verbs on a new line; after it write that one of the three forms **eī, eum, eō** which is in the case required by the verb; and then translate the whole expression, using the pronoun to mean "him" generally and "it" where necessary.

| | | | |
|---|---|---|---|
| (1) cognōscunt | (7) patiuntur | (13) superant | (19) persuādent |
| (2) ignōscunt | (8) invenient | (14) crēdunt | (20) ūtuntur |
| (3) serviunt | (9) nocent | (15) carent | (21) pellunt |
| (4) servant | (10) iuvant | (16) student | (22) parcunt |
| (5) parāvī | (11) placent | (17) hortantur | (23) imperant |
| (6) pāruī | (12) iaciunt | (18) sequuntur | (24) iubent |

4. Ducem servāvit. 5. Ducī servīvit. 6. Servī aliīs hominibus serviunt. 7. Virī fortēs aliōs servant. 8. Ille servus fīliō meō servīvit et eum servāvit. 9. Sī quis sibi sōlī serviet, rem pūblicam numquam servābit. 10. Sī quis hunc labōrem suscēpisset, mīlle virōs servāvisset. 11. Deī mihi ignōscent; vōs, ō cīvēs, tōtī exercituī ignōscite. 12. Sī Deum nōbīs ignōscere volumus, nōs dēbēmus aliīs hominibus ignōscere. 13. Mihi nunc nōn crēdunt, neque umquam duōbus fīliīs meīs crēdere volent. 14. Illī amīcī sunt mihi cārissimī. 15. Cum bonā fidē carērēs, tibi crēdere nōn poterant. 16. Huic ducī pāreāmus ut nōbīs parcat et urbem servet. 17. Nisi Caesar cīvibus placēbit, vītae eius nōn parcent. 18. Litterīs Latīnīs studeō, quae mihi placent etiam sī amīcīs meīs persuādēre nōn possum. 19. Vēritātī et sapientiae semper studeāmus et pāreāmus. 20. Optimīs rēbus semper studēte sī vērē esse fēlīcēs vultis. 21. Hīs rēbus studentēs, et librīs et vītā ūtāmur. 22. Vir

bonus nēminī nocēre vult: omnibus parcit, omnēs iuvat. 23. Praemia mea sunt simillima tuīs.

24. Explain the syntax of the following: (5) ducī; (8) eum; (9) sibi; (11) exercituī; (12) hominibus; (13) fīliīs; (14) mihi; (15) fidē; (16) ducī, pāreāmus, servet; (17) cīvibus, vītae; (18) litterīs, amīcīs; (21) rēbus, librīs, ūtāmur; (22) omnibus; (23) tuīs.

## EXERCISES FOR Capvt XXXVI

1. We have already learned how the Romans expressed indirect statements (Capvt XXV) and indirect questions (Capvt XXX). Now after a verb having the connotation of command, how did the Romans express an indirect command?
2. List some common Latin verbs which can take an indirect command.
3. In the following list label the subjunctives and translate the other forms.

| | | | |
|---|---|---|---|
| (1) fīet | (6) fīunt | (10) fīerent | (14) fīerem |
| (2) fit | (7) fīēbant | (11) fīmus | (15) fīant |
| (3) fīat | (8) fīēs | (12) fīent | (16) faciendus |
| (4) fīeret | (9) factus esse | (13) fīs | (17) fīāmus |
| (5) fīerī | | | |

4. Dīxit eōs litterīs Latīnīs studēre. 5. Dīxit cūr litterīs Latīnīs studērent. 6. Dīxit ut litterīs Latīnīs studērent. 7. Ab eīs quaesīvimus cūr philosophiae Graecae studērent. 8. Quaerisne ut nātūram omnium rērum cognōscāmus? 9. Tē moneō ut hīs sapientibus parcās. 10. Mīlitēs monuit nē eīs pācem petentibus nocērent. 11. Nōbīs imperābit nē hostibus crēdāmus. 12. Tibi imperāvit ut ducī pārēris. 13. Tē rogō cūr hoc fēceris. 14. Tē rogō ut hoc faciās. 15. Ā tē petō ut pāx fīat. 16. Ā mē petēbant nē bellum facerem. 17. Eum ōrāvī nē rēgī turpī pārēret. 18. Vōs ōrāmus ut discipulī ācerrimī fīatis. 19. Nōlī esse similis istī tyrannō dūrō. 20. Caesar cūrāvit ut imperium suum maximum in cīvitāte fieret. 21. Ōrātor nōs hortātus est ut līberae patriae nostrae cum studiō servīrēmus. 22. Nōbīs persuāsit ut aequīs lēgibus semper ūterēmur. 23. Cōnāmur ducī persuādēre nē artibus et lēgibus patriae noceat. 24. Tyrannus imperat ut pecūnia fīat; et pecūnia fit. At ille stultus nōn sentit hanc pecūniam sine bonā fidē futūram esse nihil. 25. Plūrēs quidem discipulōs hortēmur ut linguae Latīnae studeant.

26. Explain the syntax of the following: (4) studēre; (5) studērent; (6) studērent; (7) studērent; (8) cognōscāmus; (9) parcās; (10) eīs, pācem; (11) hostibus; (13) fēceris; (14) faciās; (16) facerem; (18) fīātis; (22) lēgibus; (23) lēgibus; (24) futūram esse; (25) hortēmur.

## EXERCISES FOR Capvt XXXVII

1. (1) Name the tenses and moods in which the stem of **īre** is changed to **e** before **a, o,** and **u.**
   (2) Otherwise, what is the stem of **eō** in the indicative, subjunctive, imperative, and infinitives?
2. State the nominative singular and the nominative plural of the present participle of **eō.**
3. Write a synopsis of **eō** in the 2nd singular and the 3d plural indicative and subjunctive active.

4. In the following list label the subjectives and translate the other forms.

| | | | |
|---|---|---|---|
| (1) iimus | (7) itūrus esse | (13) iī | (19) euntēs |
| (2) īmus | (8) euntem | (14) ībat | (20) ībō |
| (3) īrēmus | (9) iērunt | (15) ierant | (21) iit |
| (4) ībimus | (10) eunt | (16) ierim | (22) ībāmus |
| (5) īssēmus | (11) eant | (17) īret | (23) īsset |
| (6) eāmus | (12) ībunt | (18) īsse | (24) eat |

5. State how the Romans regularly expressed the following place concepts and translate the English example into Latin:
   (1) place from which: from (out of) that land.
   (2) place where: in that land; on that island.
   (3) place to which: into (to) that land.
6. State the general rules for these place constructions when the name of a city is involved.
7. Define the locative case, and state the nature of the locative forms.
8. State how the Romans expressed each of the following time concepts and translate the English example:
   (1) time when: on the same day.
   (2) time how long: for many days.
   (3) time within which: in one day.
9. What is peculiar about the principal parts of **licet?** Explain. Translate into Latin "You may go."
10. Translate each of the following words or phrases in accordance with the principles of this chapter.

| | | |
|---|---|---|
| (1) ūnum diem | (7) paucīs diēbus | (13) domum |
| (2) ūnō diē | (8) eādem nocte | (14) Athēnīs |
| (3) illō diē | (9) multōs diēs | (15) domī |
| (4) Rōmā | (10) in nāvem | (16) Athēnās |
| (5) Rōmae | (11) in nāve | (17) domō |
| (6) Rōmam | (12) ex nāve | (18) paucās hōrās |

11. Paucīs hōrīs Rōmam ībimus. 12. Nōs ad urbem īmus; illī domum eunt. 13. Ut saepe fassī sumus, tibi nōn licet Rōmā Athēnās īre. 14. Cūr domō tam celeriter abīstī? 15. Rōmam veniunt ut cum frātre meō Athēnās eant. 16. Nōlīte abīre Rōmā. 17. Frātre tuō Rōmae interfectō, hortābāmur tē ut Athēnās redīrēs. 18. Sī in fīnēs hostium hōc tempore eat, paucīs hōrīs pereat. 19. Negāvit sē velle in istā terrā multōs diēs remanēre. 20. Dīxistī tē domum Athēnīs ūnā hōrā reditūrum esse. 21. Ā tē petō ut ex nāve ad īnsulam brevī tempore redeās. 22. Eīs diēbus solitī sumus Athēnīs esse. 23. Sī amīcīs eius Rōmae nocuissent, Rōmam brevissimō tempore redīsset. 24. Cum frāter meus domī remanēret, ego tamen in novās terrās domō abiī. 25. Rōmānī, sī quid malī loquī volēbant, saepe dīcēbant: "Abī in malam rem." 26. Eīs persuādet ut Latīnae studeant.

27. Explain the syntax of the following words: (11) hōrīs, Rōmam; (12) domum; (13) Rōmā, Athēnās, īre; (14) domō; (15) Rōmam; (17) frātre; (18) tempore, eat, hōrīs; (19) velle, diēs; (20) domum, Athēnīs, hōrā, reditūrum esse; (21) tempore,

redeās; (22) diēbus, Athēnīs; (23) amīcīs, Rōmae, redīsset; (24) domī, terrās, domō; (26) studeant.

## EXERCISES FOR Capvt XXXVIII

1. What does a relative clause with the indicative tell about the antecedent?
2. What does a relative clause with the subjunctive tell about its antecedent, and what is the nature of the antecedent?
3. What is the basic difference between the dative of indirect object and the dative of reference?
4. How are supines formed and what are their functions?

5. Amīcus meus quī cōnsulem dēfendit ipse erat vir clārissimus. 6. At nēmō erat quī istum hominem turpem dēfenderet. 7. Quid est quod virī plūs metuant quam tyrannum? 8. Quis est quī inter lībertātem et imperium tyrannī dubitet? 9. Rōmae antīquae erant quī pecūniam plūs quam rem pūblicam amārent. 10. Abeat ā patriā iste homō malus quī odium omnium cīvium bonōrum passus est. 11. Catilīna (= Catiline), quī tantās īnsidiās contrā rem pūblicam fēcerat, ex urbe ā Cicerōne expulsus est. 12. Istī ducī in exsilium abeuntī quae vīta potest esse iūcunda? 13. Quis est quī tantum dolōrem ferre possit? 14. Nisi quis iūcundus bonusque erit, vītam vērē fēlīcem mihi nōn vīvet. 15. Cōnsulī nōn crēdent quī opera turpia faciat. 16. Nōlī crēdere eī quī sit acerbus amīcīs. 17. Cicerō erat cōnsul quī rem pūblicam salūtī suae antepōneret. 18. Scīvērunt quārē cōnsulem tam fortem sequī vellēmus. 19. Nihil sciō quod mihi facilius esse possit. 20. Ducem quaerō quem omnēs laudent. 21. Rōmam ībant rogātum lībertātem. 22. Rōmānī, quī decem rēs pūblicās Graecās exercitibus suīs cēperant, ipsī—mīrābile dictū—Graecīs artibus captī sunt! 23. Virīs antīquīs nihil erat quod melius esset quam virtūs et sapientia. 24. Nihil metuendum est quod animō nocēre nōn possit.

25. Analyze the relative clauses in the following pair of sentences, showing how they differ in their force: 5 and 6.
26. Explain the syntax of the following words: (7) metuant; (8) dubitet; (9) Rōmae, amārent; (10) abeat, passus est; (11) fēcerat; (12) ducī, potest; (13) possit; (14) erit, mihi; (15) cōnsulī; (16) amīcīs; (17) salūtī, antepōneret; (18) vellēmus; (19) mihi, possit; (21) rogātum; (22) cēperant, dictū; (23) virīs; (24) animō, possit.

## EXERCISES FOR Capvt XXXIX

1. (1) Define the term *gerund.*
   (2) What is the ending of the gerund in English?
   (3) How is the gerund declined in Latin?
   (4) As a noun, what is the syntax of the gerund in Latin?
   (5) What serves in place of the nominative of the gerund in Latin?
2. (1) What part of speech is the Latin gerundive?
   (2) What mnemonic device may help you to remember this?
   (3) As an adjective, what is the syntax of the gerundive?
   (4) How is the gerundive declined?
   (5) How can the gerundive be distinguished from the gerund in Latin usage (though not in English translation)?

3. (1) How is the Latin gerund to be translated?
   (2) How is a noun-gerundive phrase usually best translated?
   (3) For example, translate:
      (A) Discimus legendō cum cūrā (gerund).
      (B) Discimus librīs legendīs cum cūrā (gerundive).

4. Experiendō discimus. 5. Ad discendum vēnērunt. 6. Sē discendō dedit. 7. Discendī causā ad lūdum tuum vēnērunt. 8. Puer cupidus discendī ad lūdum iit. 9. Metus moriendī eum terrēbat. 10. Spēs vīvendī post mortem multōs hortātur. 11. Cōgitandō eōs superāvit. 12. Sē dedit—

| | |
|---|---|
| (1) glōriae quaerendae. | (9) iniūriīs oppugnandīs. |
| (2) bellō gerendō. | (10) librīs scrībendīs. |
| (3) pecūniae faciendae. | (11) librīs legendīs. |
| (4) imperiō accipiendō. | (12) philosophiae discendae. |
| (5) cīvitātibus delendīs. | (13) litterīs Latīnīs discendīs. |
| (6) huic ducī sequendō. | (14) vēritātī intellegendae. |
| (7) patriae servandae. | (15) sapientiae quaerendae. |
| (8) pācī petendae. | (16) hominibus adiuvandīs. |

13. Rōmam vēnit—

| | |
|---|---|
| (1) ad hoc opus suscipiendum. | (5) huius operis suscipiendī causā. |
| (2) ad lūdōs Rōmānōs videndōs. | (6) philosophiae discendae causā. |
| (3) ad aedificia vetera videnda. | (7) novōrum librōrum legendōrum causā. |
| (4) ad pācem petendam. | (8) lūdōs vīsum. |

14. Librum scrīpsit—

| | |
|---|---|
| (1) dē dolōre ferendō. | (5) dē bellō gerendō. |
| (2) dē metū superandō. | (6) dē lībertāte dēfendendā. |
| (3) dē bonā vītā vīvendā. | (7) dē hostibus vincendīs. |
| (4) dē rē pūblicā gerendā. | (8) dē dōnīs dandīs. |

15. Sapientiōrēs fīmus—

| | |
|---|---|
| (1) Latīnīs litterīs legendīs. | (4) metū vincendō. |
| (2) philosophiā discendā. | (5) vēritāte sequendā. |
| (3) vītā experiendā. | |

16. Nōs ipsōs adiuvāmus—

| | |
|---|---|
| (1) bonīs librīs semper legendīs. | (3) auxiliō offerendō. |
| (2) virīs miserīs metū līberandīs. | (4) aliīs adiuvandīs. |

17. Multum tempus cōnsūmpsit—

| | |
|---|---|
| (1) in cōgitandō (loquendō, currendō). | (4) in exercitū parandō. |
| (2) in hīs operibus faciendīs. | (5) in cōpiīs parandīs. |
| (3) in viā inveniendā. | |

18. Tempus huic librō sōlī scrībendō habuit.

### EXERCISES FOR Capvt XL

1. Explain the essential differences involved in introducing questions with **-ne, nōnne,** and **num.**
2. What word is used to introduce a positive fear clause? a negative fear clause? Can you explain why this is the opposite of what one might expect?
3. In order for a noun to function as either a descriptive genitive or a descriptive ablative, what condition must be met?

4. Magnopere vereor ut imperātor nōbīs satis auxiliī mittat. 5. Fuit fēmina maximā virtūte et fidē atque simillima mātrī. 6. Nōlī timēre nē omnēs virī et fēminae magnōrum animōrum Rōmā discēdant. 7. Id quidem est facile dictū sed difficile factū! 8. Parentibus placitum domum vēnērunt. 9. Nōnne vīs audīre aliquid bonī? 10. Vīsne habēre multum sapientiae? Studē Latīnae! 11. Imperāvit tribus mīlitibus ut pācem petītum Rōmam adīrent. 12. Num dubitās hoc dīcere, mī amīce? 13. Tū mē hortāris ut sim animō magnō et spem salūtis habeam, sed timeō nē sim īnfirmior. 14. Ego dīvitiās sapientiae antepōnō. Nōn enim arbitror hominēs vītam fēlīcem sine cōpiā pecūniae reperīre posse. 15. Plūrimī autem virī dīvitēs multum metūs sentiunt. 16. Pauperēs saepe sunt fēlīciōrēs et minus metūs habent. 17. Pecūnia ipsa nōn est mala: sed rēs mentis animīque plūs opis ad fēlīciter vīvendum offerunt. 18. Novem ex ducibus nōs hortātī sunt ut plūs auxiliī praestārēmus. 19. Quīnque ex custōdiīs interfectīs, pater meus cum duōbus ex fīliīs et cum magnō numerō amīcōrum in illam terram līberam fūgit. 20. Numquam satis ōtiī habēbit; at aliquid ōtiī melius est quam nihil. 21. Nostrīs temporibus omnēs plūs metūs et minus speī habēmus. 22. Magna fidēs et virtūs omnibus virīs reperiendae sunt.

# KEY TO SELF-TUTORIAL EXERCISES

## KEY FOR Capvt I

1. (1) he, she, it; (2) we; (3) I; (4) they; (5) you (sg.); (6) you (pl.)
2. The forms are present active infinitives of the 2nd conjugation. (1) to advise/warn; (2) to see; (3) to be strong; (4) to owe.
3. The forms are present active infinitives of the 1st conjugation. (1) to call; (2) to save; (3) to give; (4) to think; (5) to praise; (6) to love; (7) to err.
4. The forms are present active imperatives 2nd person singular of the 1st or the 2nd conjugations. (1) call; (2) save; (3) give; (4) think; (5) praise; (6) love; (7) advise/warn; (8) see; (9) be strong/good-bye.
5. The forms are present active imperatives 2nd person plural of the 1st or the 2nd conjugations. (1) call; (2) save; (3) give; (4) think; (5) praise; (6) love; (7) advise/warn; (8) see; (9) be strong/good-bye.
6. (1) he/she/it calls, is calling, does call; (2) we think; (3) they love; (4) you (sg.) owe/ought; (5) he sees; (6) they see; (7) we owe/ought; (8) you (sg.) are strong; (9) you (pl.) err/are mistaken; (10) we see; (11) he/she/it loves; (12) you (pl.) see; (13) you (sg.) err; (14) they give; (15) we save; (16) he gives; (17) they love; (18) you (sg.) see.

7. They warn me if I err. 8. He warns me if they err. 9. Warn me if he errs. 10. You (sg.) ought to warn me. 11. You (pl.) ought to save me. 12. They ought not to praise me. 13. "What does he give?" "He often gives nothing." 14. They often call me and advise me. 15. I see nothing. What do you see? 16. Praise me, please, if I do not make a mistake. 17. If you (pl.) are well, we are well. 18. If he is well, I am well. 19. If he (she) loves me, he (she) ought to praise me. 20. Save me. 21. I ought not to err. 22. What ought we to praise? 23. He sees; he ponders; he advises.

## KEY FOR Capvt II

1. In classical Latin there was no regular definite or indefinite article. The words *the* and *a* have to be added in the English translation according to the sense of a Latin passage. Thus **puella** may mean *the girl* or *a girl,* and **puellae** may mean *the girls* or *girls* according to the Latin context. Often in an isolated sentence *the* and *a* can be used interchangeably, or perhaps no article at all need be used.
2. (1) acc. case; (2) gen. case; (3) nom. case; (4) abl.; (5) voc.; (6) dat.
3. (1) acc. pl. as direct object of a verb; (2) nom. sg. as subject of a verb or voc. sg. for direct address; (3) acc. sg. as direct object; (4) nom. pl. subject, or voc. for direct address.

4. (1) gen. pl., of; (2) abl. sg., by/with/from, etc.; (3) gen. sg., of; dat. sg., to/for; nom. pl.; voc. pl.; (4) dat. pl., to/for; abl. pl., by/with/from, etc.

5. (1) girl, direct obj. of verb; (2) girl, subject or vocative; (3) girls, object; (4) girls, subj. or voc.; (5) countries, obj.; (6) country, obj.; (7) country, subj. or voc.; (8) countries, subj. or voc.; (9) money, obj.; (10) money, subj. or voc.; (11) penalties, obj.; (12) penalty, obj.

6. (1) of the girl, girl's, or to/for the girl; (2) of the girls, girls'; (3) O fatherland; (4) of or to/for the fatherland; (5) by/with, etc., money; (6) of or to/for money; (7) to/for or by/with, etc., penalties; (8) by/with etc., a penalty; (9) of penalties.

7. (1) multae pecūniae, multam pecūniam; (2) magnae fāmae, magnā fāmā; (3) vītae meae, vītae meae; (4) fortūnam tuam, fortūnās tuās; (5) magnae patriae, magnārum patriārum; (6) fortūnā meā, fortūnīs meīs; (7) magnae poenae, magnīs poenīs; (8) multīs philosophiīs, multīs philosophiīs.

8. (1) multā pecūniā; (2) multārum puellārum; (3) meae patriae; (4) magnam vītam; (5) tuīs poenīs; (6) multae patriae; (7) multīs puellīs; (8) meae vītae; (9) Ō fortūna; (10) puellae; (11) puellārum; (12) puellae; (13) puellās; (14) puellae.

9. Farewell (goodbye), my native land. 10. The fortune of the girl (the girl's fortune) is great. 11. The girl is praising the fortune of your (sg.) country. 12. O girl, save your country. 13. Many girls love money. 14. You (pl.) are giving nothing to the girl, *or* you give nothing to a girl. 15. He sees the money of the girl, *or* the girl's money. 16. You (sg.) do not see the girls' money. 17. We ought to warn the girls. 18. They ought to praise the girl. 19. Life gives (good) fortune to many girls. 20. You (sg.) are saving my life by *or* with your money. 21. Fame is nothing without fortune. 22. You (pl.) do not like life without money. 23. A country is not strong without fame and fortune. 24. You (sg.) ought not to praise the anger of the girls. 25. We like a life without punishments. 26. We are not strong without philosophy. 27. What is life without philosophy?

## KEY FOR Capvt III

1. (1) acc. sg., obj.; (2) nom. pl. as subj., voc. pl. for direct address; (3) nom. sg., subj.; (4) acc. pl. obj.; (5) voc. sg., direct address.

2. (1) dat. sg., to/for; abl. sg., by/with, etc.; (2) gen. pl., of; (3) gen. sg., of; (4) dat. pl., to/for; abl. pl., by/with, etc.

3. (1) sons, obj.; (2) sons, subj. or direct address; (3) son, obj.; (4) people, obj.; (5) people, direct address; (6) people, subj.; (7) man, subj. or direct address; (8) men, obj.; (9) men, subj. or direct address; (10) man, obj.; (11) friend, direct address; (12) friends, subj. or direct address; (13) friends, obj.; (14) friend, obj.

4. (1) of my sons; (2) to/for my son, by/with, etc., my son; (3) of the Roman people; (4) to/for the Roman people, by/with, etc., the Roman people; (5) to/for the men, by/with, etc., the men; (6) of the man; (7) of the men; (8) of a few friends; (9) to/for or by/with, etc., a few friends; (10) to/for or by/with, etc., my friend; (11) of my friend; (12) to/for or by/with, etc., many boys.

5. (1) populī Rōmānī, populō Rōmānō; (2) magnōs virōs, magnīs virīs; (3) puerīs meīs, puerīs meīs; (4) magnō numerō, magnō numerō; (5) magne vir, magnī virī; (6) fīliī meī, fīliōrum meōrum.

6. (1) multōrum puerōrum; (2) populō Rōmānō; (3) fīliōs meōs; (4) Ō fīliī meī; (5) mag-

num numerum; (6) magnō numerō; (7) Ō vir magne; (8) multīs puerīs; (9) vir magnus; (10) populī Rōmānī.

7. Good-bye, my friend. 8. The Roman people praise your (sg.) son's wisdom. 9. O great man, save the Roman people. 10. The number of the Roman people is great. 11. Many boys love girls. 12. You (pl.) are giving nothing to my son. 13. I see men in the field. 14. You (sg.) see the friend of my son. 15. He does not see your (sg.) sons' friend. 16. We ought to warn my sons. 17. They ought to praise your (sg.) son. 18. Life gives fame to few men. 19. You (sg.) consider me in the number (circle) of your friends. 20. Great men often have few friends. 21. My friend is always thinking. 22. The son of a great man is not always a great man. 23. We do not always see (understand) the wisdom of great men. 24. You (pl.) ought to praise philosophy, the wisdom of great men.

## KEY FOR Capvt IV

1. Nom. sg. in -**um**; nom. and acc. pl. in -**a**. Actually the vocative should also be added here; but henceforth, since aside from the singular of 2nd-declension masculines in -**us** the vocatives follow the rule of having the same form as the nominative, little specific mention is made of the vocative.
2. (1) nom. pl. as subject; acc. pl. as obj.; (2) nom. sg. as subj.; acc. sg. as obj.
3. (1) dat. sg., to/for; abl. sg., by/with, etc.; (2) gen. pl., of; (3) gen. sg., of; (4) dat. pl., to/for; abl. pl., by/with, etc.
4. (1) wars, subj. or obj.; (2) war, subj. or obj.; (3) duty, subj. or obj.; (4) duties, subj. or obj.; (5) dangers, subj. or obj. Of course any of these forms could also be vocative.
5. (1) of evil wars; (2) to/for evil war, by/with, etc., evil war; (3) of evil war; (4) to/for evil wars, by/with, etc., evil wars; (5) of great duty or service; (6) to/for great duties, by/with, etc., great duties; (7) to/for small danger, by/with, etc., small danger.
6. (1) bella parva, bella parva; (2) ōtium bonum, ōtia bona; (3) perīculī magnī, perīculōrum magnōrum; (4) officium vērum, officiō vērō.
7. (1) Ō bellum malum; (2) officiō magnō; (3) perīculō magnō; (4) ōtium bonum; (5) multīs bellīs; (6) ōtiī bonī; (7) perīculīs multōrum bellōrum; (8) bella parva; (9) bella parva; (10) Ō bella stulta; (11) bellum parvum.

8. Peace (leisure) is good. 9. Many wars do not preserve peace. 10. The danger is great. 11. We are in great danger. 12. And leisure often has dangers. 13. Life is not without many dangers. 14. Good men love peace. 15. The foolish man praises the dangers of war. 16. Often we do not preserve the peace by war. 17. The Roman people do not always have good peace. 18. They often save the fatherland and peace by small wars. 19. Many girls are pretty. 20. True friends are few. 21. My friend is a man of great service. 22. The duties of a teacher are many and great. 23. You (sg.) are a man of little leisure. 24. You (pl.) are men of great care. 25. We ought to give attention to duty without delay. 26. Life is nothing without eyes.

## KEY FOR Capvt V

1. future: -**ō**, -**s**, -**t**, -**mus**, -**tis**, -**nt**; imperfect: -**m**, -**s**, -**t**, -**mus**, -**tis**, -**nt**.
2. They are the same in the future, but the imperfect has -**m** instead of -**ō** in the first pers. sg.

3. future: -**bi**- (-**b**- in 1st pers. sg.; -**bu**- in 3d pers. pl.); imperfect: -**bā**- (with the -**a**- shortened before -**m**, -**t**, and -**nt**).

4. (1) we were; (2) he will; (3) you (pl.) will; (4) I shall; (5) they will; (6) he was.

5. By learning the vocabulary form of the adjective: **līber, lībera, līberum, pulcher, pulchra, pulchrum**; and often by learning English derivatives.

6. They show whether the **e** of a masculine in -**er** survives throughout the rest of the paradigm; liberty, **līber, lībera, līberum**; pulchritude, **pulcher, pulchra, pulchrum.**

7. (1) they were remaining, remained; (2) he will remain; (3) we shall remain; (4) I was giving, I gave; (5) you (pl.) will give; (6) he will give; (7) you (sg.) will see; (8) we shall see; (9) they were calling, called; (10) you (sg.) will call; (11) you (sg.) will have; (12) they were having, had.

8. (1) dabimus; (2) manēbās; (3) vidēbunt; (4) vocābimus; (5) vocābat; (6) vidēbitis; (7) vidēbō; (8) servābant; (9) habēbimus; (10) habēbāmus; (11) habēbit; (12) habet.

9. Our teacher praises me and he will praise you tomorrow (sg.). 10. Free men were overcoming our dangers. 11. Our sons love pretty girls. 12. Our friend will not stay in the company (number) of fools. 13. We used to have many faults and always shall have. 14. Great dangers do not overcome our courage. 15. Our beautiful country is free. 16. You (pl.) are free men; you will have a beautiful country. 17. Free teachers were giving attention to duty. 18. Therefore, we shall overcome evil men in our country. 19. If you (sg.) overcome (lit., will overcome) your anger, you will overcome yourself. 20. Because of our courage many men are free. 21. Free fatherland, we always used to love you and we always shall love (you). 22. You (pl.) will not preserve wisdom by means of money. 23. Does your (sg.) soul possess enough wisdom?

## KEY FOR Capvt VI

1. See Capvt VI, p. 49, s.v. "Complementary Infinitive."

2. (1) we; (2) they; (3) you (sg.); (4) he, she, it; (5) I; (6) I; (7) you (pl.).

3. See p. 48–49.

4. (1) he, she, it was; (2) he, etc., was able; (3) he will be; (4) he will be able; (5) we are; (6) we are able; (7) we were able; (8) we shall be able; (9) I was able; (10) I was; (11) I shall be; (12) I shall be able; (13) they will be; (14) they will be able; (15) they were able; (16) to be; (17) to be able.

5. (1) sumus; (2) erāmus; (3) erimus; (4) poterimus; (5) potest; (6) poterit; (7) poterat; (8) posse; (9) poterant; (10) possunt; (11) poterunt; (12) sunt; (13) esse; (14) poteram.

6. Your (pl.) country was free. 7. I was able to be a tyrant. 8. Your friend will be a tyrant. 9. Where (there) is a tyrant, there men cannot be free. 10. He could not remain in our country yesterday. 11. Tyrants will always have many faults. 12. We were not able to overcome the tyrants. 13. We ought to overcome our tyrant. 14. The tyrant was able to overcome (the) good men; but he will not be able to remain there. 15. You (pl.) will be able to see the dangers of a tyrant. 16. We cannot tolerate the faults of tyrants. 17. You (sg.) were not tolerating (did not tolerate) the treachery of the tyrant. 18. The peace in your (pl.) country cannot be perpetual. 19. You (sg.) ought to warn free men about tyrants. 20. Your (pl.) teacher always used to like (liked) fine books. 21. Good and true books were able to save the country. 22. You (pl.) will be able to save your country with good

books. 23. Tyrants will not be able to overcome the wisdom of good books. 24. Bad men cannot tolerate good books.

## KEY FOR Capvt VII

1. No.
2. Yes: nom. and acc. pl.
3. (1) nom. and acc. pl. of m. and f.; (2) nom. and acc. pl. n.; (3) acc. sg. m. and f.
4. (1) dat. and abl. pl.; (2) dat. sg.; (3) abl. sg.; (4) acc. sg. m. and f.; (5) gen. pl.; (6) gen. sg.; (7) nom. and acc. pl. m. and f.
5. (1) magnum tempus; (2) magna virtūs; (3) magnus labor; (4) magna cīvitās; (5) magnus mōs; (6) magna pāx; (7) magnus rēx; (8) magnum corpus; (9) magna vēritās; (10) magnus amor.
6. (1) by/with much labor; (2) to/for much labor; (3) of much labor; (4) many labors (nom.); (5) of perpetual peace; (6) by/with perpetual peace; (7) to/for perpetual peace; (8) of small states; (9) a small state (acc.); (10) small states (acc.); (11) small states (nom.); (12) by a small state; (13) bad times (nom. or acc. pl.); (14) bad time (nom. or acc. sg.); (15) to/for a bad time; (16) of bad times; (17) of a bad time; (18) to/for your habit; (19) by your habit; (20) of your habit; (21) your character (nom.); (22) your character (acc.); (23) of your character.
7. (1) magnae virtūtī; (2) magna virtūs; (3) magnās virtūtēs; (4) magnārum virtūtum; (5) magnā virtūte; (6) tempus nostrum; (7) tempora nostra; (8) tempora nostra; (9) temporibus nostrīs; (10) temporī nostrō; (11) temporis nostrī; (12) temporum nostrōrum; (13) amōrem meum; (14) amōrēs meōs; (15) amōrī meō; (16) amōre meō; (17) amōris meī; (18) amōrum meōrum.

8. My time for leisure is small. 9. Your (sg.) courage is great. 10. Money is nothing without good character. 11. The virtues of many human beings are great. 12. The character of a good man will be good. 13. They will give a letter to the man. 14. We were able to see many men in the great state. 15. We used to see (saw, were seeing) a great love of money in many men. 16. Few men give attention to excellence. 17. Our state will give peace to many men. 18. Peace cannot be perpetual. 19. Without good peace the states of our times will not be strong. 20. Times are bad after many wars. 21. In many states and lands peace could not be strong. 22. Without great labor the man will have nothing. 23. The beautiful maiden loves friends of good character. 24. Men of great courage were daring to overcome tyrants. 25. Love of country was strong in our state.

## KEY FOR Capvt VIII

1. (1) Future. (2) It may be helpful to note that our word "future" ends in -e. The -a- in the 1st sg. is the only exception among six forms.
2. (1) Present. (2) The vowel alternation is the same seen in the future of 1st–2nd conjugation verbs.
3. (1) 1st pers. pl. pres.; (2) 2nd sg. fut.; (3) 3d pl. pres.; (4) 3d sg. fut.; (5) 2nd pl. pres.; (6) 1st pl. fut.; (7) 1st sg. pres.; (8) 3d pl. fut.; (9) 3d sg. pres.; (10) 2nd pl. fut.; (11) 2nd sg. pres.; (12) 1st sg. fut.; (13) 3d pl. impf.
4. (1) imper. sg.; (2) pres. infin.; (3) imper. pl.
5. (1) they were sending; (2) he is sending; (3) they are sending; (4) I shall send; (5) send (sg.); (6) we are sending; (7) you (pl.) were sending; (8) you (sg.) are sending; (9) send

(pl.); (10) you (pl.) send; (11) he will send; (12) we shall send; (13) he does; (14) they will do; (15) they are doing; (16) you (pl.) will do; (17) we were doing; (18) I shall do; (19) we shall do; (20) you (sg.) are doing; (21) you (pl.) are doing; (22) he will write; (23) they are writing; (24) I shall write; (25) I was writing; (26) you (pl.) are writing; (27) we shall write; (28) he is writing; (29) you (sg.) are writing; (30) they will write; (31) write!

6. (1) pōnēbant; (2) pōnēmus; (3) pōne; (4) pōnit; (5) pōnent; (6) pōnam; (7) pōnēbās; (8) pōnētis; (9) pōnite; (10) pōnimus; (11) pōnitis; (12) pōnet.

7. What are they doing? What will you (pl.) do? 8. They were leading the man to me. 9. Lead (sg.) the man to me, and I shall thank the man. 10. While the tyrant leads the troops, we can do nothing. 11. He is writing a letter to the maiden. 12. You (sg.) were writing a great book. 13. You (sg.) will write good books. 14. We shall write books about peace. 15. Do you (pl.) have an abundance of good books? 16. The teacher teaches many boys. 17. The boys do not thank the teacher. 18. Few men were thanking our state. 19. The tyrant will lead great forces out of our state. 20. A great abundance of money does not lead men to wisdom. 21. Will good books lead many men to reason? 22. Do we often lead men to reason? 23. Reason can lead men to a good life. 24. Are you (pl.) leading a good life? 25. Always thank (pl.) a good friend.

## KEY FOR Capvt IX

1. See p. 71.
2. 
   (1) to/for that (m., f., n.); those (nom. m.)
   (2) that (nom. f.); those (nom./acc. n.)
   (3) of that (m., f., n.)
   (4) that (nom. m.)
   (5) by that (f.)
   (6) that (nom./acc. n.)
   (7) of those (m., n.)
   (8) those (nom. f.)
   (9) those (acc. m.)
   (10) to/for by/with/from those (m., f., n.)
   (11) by that (m., n.)
   (12) of those (f.)
   (13) by this (m., n.)
   (14) this (nom./acc. n.)
   (15) this (nom. f.); these (nom./acc. n.)
   (16) these (nom. f.)
   (17) by this (f.)
   (18) this (acc. f.)
   (19) of this (m., f., n.)
   (20) this (acc. m.)
   (21) these (acc. m.)
   (22) to this (m., f., n.)
   (23) of these (m., n.)
   (24) these (acc. f.)
   (25) to/for these; by these (m., f., n.)
   (26) of one (m., f., n.)
   (27) to/for one (m., f., n.)
   (28) by one (f.)
   (29) to/for the whole (m., f., n.); whole (nom. pl. m.)
   (30) of the whole (m., f., n.)
   (31) the whole (nom. f.); whole (nom./acc. pl. n.)
   (32) the whole (acc. m.; nom./acc. n.)
   (33) of no (sg. m., f., n.)
   (34) to/for no (sg. m., f., n.); no (nom. pl. m.)
   (35) no (nom. sg. f.; nom./acc. pl. n.)
   (36) no (acc. pl. m.)

3. See text and examples on p. 72–73.
4. 
   (1) haec puella
   (2) hae puellae
   (3) haec tempora
   (4) huic temporī
   (5) huic puerō
   (6) huius temporis
   (7) illīus temporis
   (8) hōc librō
   (9) illō librō

|  |  |  |
|---|---|---|
| (10) illa puella | (18) illīus puellae sōlīus | (26) nūllī librō |
| (11) illa tempora | (19) tyrannōrum sōlōrum | (27) nūllōs librōs |
| (12) illa tempora | (20) tōtam cīvitātem | (28) ūnī cīvitātī |
| (13) illud tempus | (21) tōtīus patriae | (29) ūnī puellae |
| (14) huic cīvitātī sōlī | (22) tōtī patriae | (30) ūnīus temporis |
| (15) huius cīvitātis sōlīus | (23) nūllīus ratiōnis | (31) ūnīus bellī |
| (16) illī puerō sōlī | (24) nūllam ratiōnem | (32) alterī librō |
| (17) illī puellae sōlī | (25) nūllae puellae | (33) aliō librō |

5. These men will lead (lead, were leading) the whole state. 6. That man will see (sees, was seeing/saw) these things in that land. 7. In that book I am writing (I shall write, I was writing) those things about this man. 8. One man is leading (will lead) those forces into this land. 9. The teacher gives these things to the other boy. 10. We are writing (shall write) this book about another war. 11. The whole country thanks (will thank, was thanking) this man alone. 12. They are now giving their entire attention to that plan. 13. This man's friend will save this state by that plan. 14. The other friend will lead (his) entire life in another land. 15. This man alone was able to warn me about the faults of this tyrant. 16. You (pl.) had no forces in the other land. 17. Those men alone see no dangers in this plan. 18. You (sg.) dare to praise not only the character but also the treachery of that man. 19. In fact, on account of the treachery of one man this state was not strong.

## KEY FOR Capvt X

1. (1) 3d; (2) 2nd; (3) 4th; (4) 1st.
2. (1) 3d pl. pres.; (2) 2nd sg. fut.; (3) 2nd sg. pres.; (4) 1st pl. impf.; (5) 1st pl. pres.; (6) imper. sg.; (7) 2nd pl. fut.; (8) imper. pl.; (9) 2nd pl. pres.; (10) 1st sg. pres.; (11) 3d sg. pres.; (12) imper. sg. (13) 2nd sg. impf. Note: nos. 3, 5, 6, 8, 9 are 4th only; 12 is 3d only. The chief difference is the -ī- of the 4th and the -i- of the 3d. See p. 82.
3. (1) pres. infin.; (2) imper. sg.; (3) short stem vowels in 2nd sg. and 1st and 2nd pl. of pres. indic. and in the imper. pl.

4.
| (1) he will come | (11) to come |
|---|---|
| (2) he is coming | (12) he makes/does |
| (3) they are coming | (13) he will make/do |
| (4) they will come | (14) we shall make |
| (5) you (sg.) hear | (15) we are making |
| (6) you (pl.) will hear | (16) they make |
| (7) you (pl.) hear | (17) you (sg.) make |
| (8) come (pl.) | (18) I shall make |
| (9) you (sg.) will come | (19) you (sg.) will make |
| (10) come (sg.) | (20) to make |

5.
| (1) sentiam | (6) sentiunt | (11) iacit | (16) iacitis |
|---|---|---|---|
| (2) sentiēmus | (7) sentīre | (12) iaciet | (17) iaciēmus |
| (3) sentit | (8) sentī | (13) iaciam | (18) iacite |
| (4) sentītis | (9) sentiet | (14) iacimus | (19) iacere |
| (5) sentient | (10) sentīmus | (15) iace | (20) iacis |

6. We were fleeing from this land. 7. Flee (sg.) with your daughter. 8. They will flee into that place. 9. Time flees; the hours flee; old age is coming. 10. Come (pl.) with your

friends. 11. They were coming into your country. 12. O great man, come into our state. 13. You (sg.) will find your daughter in that state. 14. They can find little money in the streets. 15. The tyrant is finding a way into this state. 16. You (pl.) will capture those men there with (their) friends. 17. We are coming to you with great forces. 18. Will he find much fame and glory there? 19. That man was always making war. 20. Those men (of yours *or* such men) will not make peace. 21. Many men do those things but do not do these things. 22. We are doing and will do our duty. 23. I shall make a great supply of books. 24. The boys were living with that good man. 25. In the books of ancient men you (pl.) will find much philosophy and wisdom.

### KEY FOR Capvt XI

1. (1) **is, ea, id** and **eī, eae, ea**; (2) **ego** and **nōs**; (3) **tū** and **vōs.**
2. (1) to/for you (pl.); by/with/from you; (2) to/for us; by/w/from us; (3) we (nom.); us (acc.); (4) you (nom. pl.); you (acc. pl.); (5) of you (sg.); (6) of me; (7) to/for me; (8) to/for you (sg.); (9) you (acc. sg.); by/w/from you; (10) me (acc.); by/w/from me.
3. (1) them (m.); (2) them (f.); (3) their (m., n.); (4) their (f.); (5) his, her, its; (6) by/with/from her; (7) she (nom.); they (nom. and acc. pl. n.); (8) by/with/from him, it; (9) to/for him, her, it; they (m. nom.); (10) to/for them (m., f., n.); by/with/from them; (11) they (nom. f.); (12) it (nom. or acc. sg.). N.B. in the sg. any one of the three Latin genders of **is, ea, id** may be translated by *it* when the antecedent of the pronoun is a word which in English is neuter. For instance, suppose that in a preceding sentence the word **pāx** appears. Then we read: **Sine eā nūlla cīvitās valet.** The Latin feminine **eā** becomes English *it* because in English *peace* is regarded as neuter.
4. (1) eius       (8) eius       (15) eī        (22) vōs
   (2) eius       (9) eī         (16) ea        (23) nōs
   (3) eōrum      (10) eī        (17) eae       (24) nōs
   (4) eārum      (11) eā        (18) eī        (25) nōbīs
   (5) eās        (12) eō        (19) id        (26) ego
   (6) eōs        (13) vōbīs     (20) vōs       (27) mihi
   (7) ea         (14) tibi      (21) tū

5. These men will give it to you (sg.). 6. *I* was giving it to you (pl.). 7. *You* (pl.) will give this gift to them. 8. I shall give the same thing to him (her, it). 9. We shall give them (= those things) to him (her). 10. That man will give it to me. 11. We shall give you (pl.) his books. 12. You (sg.) will give us their (m.) books. 13. We shall give their money to you (sg.). 14. They will give his (her) money to me. 15. We shall send these/those books to her. 16. I shall send his (her) book to you (sg.). 17. That man, however, was sending their money to us. 18. We are sending them (f.) with her. 19. I am sending him with them. 20. We shall send them with his (her) friends. 21. *You* (sg.) will send me with their friend. 22. They were sending you (pl.) with me to his friend. 23. He is sending us with you (sg.) into their land. 24. They will send them (f.) with us to their friends. 25. I shall send him with you (pl.) to their friends. 26. They will send you (sg.) with him to me.

### KEY FOR Capvt XII

1. (1) pres. act. indic.; (2) pres. act. infin.; (3) perf. act. indic.; (4) perf. pass. partic.
2. (1) **mittō,** pres. act. indic., *I send*
   (2) **mittere,** pres. act. infin., *to send*

      (3) **mīsī**, perf. act. indic., *I sent*

      (4) **missum**, perf. pass. partic., *having been sent, sent*

3. The perfect is like a "snapshot" of a past, completed action; the imperfect looks at continuing or progressive past action, like a video.

4. | | | | |
|---|---|---|---|
| (1) mittō | (6) agō | (11) remaneō | (16) dīcō |
| (2) laudō | (7) sum | (12) scrībō | (17) sum |
| (3) vincō | (8) dō | (13) sum | (18) vīvō |
| (4) dīcō | (9) sum | (14) faciō | (19) faciō |
| (5) faciō | (10) agō | (15) fugiō | (20) video |

5. (1) you (pl. perf.) . . . ; (2) he (perf.) . . . ; (3) they (perf.) . . . ; (4) you (sg. perf.) . . . ; (5) we (perf.) . . . ; (6) he had . . . ; (7) we shall have . . . ; (8) we had . . . ; (9) you (sg.) had . . . ; (10) they will havev (11) they had . . . ; (12) he will have . . . ; (13) you (pl.) had. . . .

6. | | |
|---|---|
| (1) they saw, were seeing | (19) he flees |
| (2) they had seen | (20) he fled |
| (3) you (sg.) saw | (21) they flee |
| (4) he did | (22) they fled |
| (5) he was doing | (23) he saved |
| (6) we had done | (24) they saved |
| (7) we did | (25) you (pl.) saved |
| (8) we shall do | (26) he had saved |
| (9) they did | (27) he will have saved |
| (10) you (sg.) lived | (28) we remained |
| (11) they lived | (29) we had remained |
| (12) he will conquer | (30) he came |
| (13) he conquered | (31) he comes |
| (14) we conquered | (32) you (pl.) were coming |
| (15) we conquer | (33) you (pl.) came |
| (16) you (sg.) gave | (34) they came |
| (17) you (pl.) had given | (35) they come |
| (18) we gave | (36) they had come |

7. Those men had fled (will flee; are fleeing; were fleeing; fled). 8. These men remained (remain; will remain; were remaining; had remained). 9. The king had conquered (is conquering; conquered; will conquer) Asia. 10. The kings conquered (will conquer; are conquering; had conquered) Asia. 11. Kings possessed (possess; will possess; had possessed) Asia. 12. Caesar had come (came; is coming; will come) into the same land. 13. Caesar said (says; had said; will say) the same things. 14. *You* (pl.) gave (will give; were giving; had given) us peace. 15. *You* (sg.) sent (will send; are sending; had sent) a letter to her. 16. We saw (see; had seen) them in the same street. 17. He had lived (lived; will live) a long time. 18. You (sg.) had done (will do; did; are doing) it well. 19. I saved (shall save; was saving; had saved) their (his) state. 20. They found (had found; will find) him in the same place. 21. God had given (gave; gives; will give) liberty to men. 22. They thanked (will thank; were thanking; had thanked; thank) me. 23. *You* (pl.) were (were; are; will be; had been) free men.

## KEY FOR Capvt XIII

1. See p. 105, s.v. "Reflexive Pronouns."
2. See p. 105, s.v. "Declension of Reflexive Pronouns."
3. In pronouns of the first and the second persons.
4. (1) to/for myself.
   (2) yourself (sg. acc.); by/with/from yourself.
   (3) to/for ourselves; by/with/from ourselves.
   (4) to/for himself (herself, itself); to/for themselves.
   (5) yourselves (acc.).
   (6) himself (acc.); by/with/from himself; themselves (acc.); by/with/from themselves.
   (7) to/for yourselves; by/with/from yourselves.
5. Since **suus, -a, -um** is an adjective, it must agree in number with the noun which it modifies. Since **suus** is a reflexive, it means *his own* or *their own* according to whether the subject of the verb is singular or plural. See, for example, sentences 15 and 20 below.
6. **Eōrum** and **eius** are fixed genitives of possession; and therefore, they do not, like **suus,** agree with the nouns on which they depend. See, for example, sentences 16–19 below.
7. See p. 107, s.v. "The Intensive Pronoun." **Sē**, being reflexive, is used in the predicate and refers to the subject. **Ipse** can be used to emphasize a noun or pronoun in any part of a sentence. See, for example, sentences 27, 28, and 31 below.

8. Caesar saved them. 9. Caesar was saving him (= another person). 10. Caesar saved himself. 11. The Romans saved themselves. 12. The Romans saved them (= others). 13. The Romans saved him. 14. Caesar saved his own friend. 15. Caesar saved his own friends. 16. Caesar saved his (= another's) friend. 17. Caesar saved his (= another's) friends. 18. Caesar saved their friend. 19. Caesar saved their friends. 20. The Romans saved their (own) friend. 21. The Romans saved their (own) friends. 22. The Romans saved their (= others') friend. 23. The Romans saved their (= others') friends. 24. The Romans saved his friend. 25. The Romans saved his friends. 26. Caesar himself saved him. 27. Caesar himself saved himself. 28. They saved Caesar himself. 29. They were saving the friend of Caesar himself. 30. They saved the friend of the Romans themselves. 31. The friend of Caesar himself saved himself. 32. The friends of Caesar himself saved themselves. 33. The friend of Caesar himself saved him. 34. Caesar's friends themselves saved him. 35. They did not save us. 36. We saved ourselves. 37. We saved the Romans themselves. 38. The Romans themselves did not save you. 39. *You* (sg.) saved yourself. 40. *You* (sg.) saved the Romans themselves. 41. He was giving nothing to me. 42. I gave nothing to myself. 43. He gave nothing to himself. 44. They gave nothing to themselves. 45. They gave nothing to them (= others). 46. They gave nothing to him. 47. I conquered myself. 48. They conquered me. 49. They conquered their (= others') anger. 50. They conquered their own anger. 51. He conquered his own anger. 52. He conquered his own sons. 53. They conquered their own sons.

## KEY FOR Capvt XIV

1. In the gen. pl.
2. -ī in abl. sg.; -ia in nom. and acc. pl.

3. (1) by/with/from art
   (2) of the arts
   (3) arts (nom. or acc.)
   (4) to/for the sea; by/with/from the sea
   (5) to/for the seas; by/with/from the seas
   (6) the sea (nom. or acc.)
   (7) the seas (nom. or acc.)
   (8) bodies (nom. or acc.)
   (9) of bodies
   (10) of a part
   (11) to/for parts; by/with/from parts
   (12) of parts
   (13) by/with/from/the city
   (14) to/for the city
   (15) of cities
   (16) cities (nom. or acc.)
   (17) of the kings
   (18) to/for the king
   (19) names (nom. or acc.)
   (20) animals (nom. or acc.)
   (21) to/for an animal; by/with/from an animal
   (22) of an animal
   (23) of animals
   (24) of strength
   (25) men (acc.)
   (26) of the man; men (nom.)
   (27) strength (nom. or acc. pl.)
   (28) to/for men; by/with/from men
   (29) force (nom.); of force
   (30) force (acc.)
   (31) to/for strength; by/with/from strength
   (32) to/for force; by/with/from force

4. (2); (4) as abl.; (7); (12); (15); (20); (21) as abl; (23); (24); (30); (32) as abl.

5. (1) vī magnā
   (2) virum magnum
   (3) vīrium magnārum
   (4) vī magnae
   (5) cīvium multōrum
   (6) cīve bonō
   (7) cīvibus multīs
   (8) maria multa
   (9) marī magnō
   (10) mare magnum
   (11) vim magnam
   (12) virōrum multōrum
   (13) vīribus magnīs
   (14) vīrēs magnās

6. (1) accompaniment; (2) means; (3) manner; (4) means

7. (1) they ran (currō); (2) we were running (currō); (3) you (sg.) ran (currō); (4) we had dragged (trahō); (5) he will drag (trahō); (6) they are dragging (trahō); (7) he was managing (gerō); (8) he manages (gerō); (9) they manage (gerō); (10) we shall manage (gerō); (11) they hold (teneō); (12) they will hold (teneō); (13) they held (teneō); (14) we held (teneō).

8. He waged many wars with the Romans. 9. They were managing the state with great wisdom. 10. He himself held the state by the power of troops. 11. Those animals dragged many men into the sea. 12. You (sg.) said this with great skill. 13. We ran with care (carefully) across the city. 14. He was coming to us with a large part of the citizens. 15. He will conquer the rights of the citizens by force. 16. You (pl.) dragged him to death across his land. 17. We shall join ourselves with the citizens of many cities. 18. He wrote this letter to the king himself with courage (courageously). 19. The violence of those seas was great. 20. I have seen the art of the Greeks with my own eyes. 21. We have drawn many beautiful thoughts from the ancients.

22. 8, accompaniment; 9, manner; 10, means; 12, manner; 13, manner; 14, accompaniment; 15, means; 17, accompaniment; 18, manner; 20, means.

## KEY FOR Capvt XV

1. See p. 123.
2. See p. 123–24.

3. See p. 124.
4. (1) dat./abl. pl. m. and n.; (2) indecl. adj. agreeing with noun in any case; (3) nom./ acc. pl. n.; (4) nom. pl. m. and n., acc. pl. n.; (5) any form in pl.; (6) nom./acc. pl. n.; (7) any form in pl.; (8) dat./abl. pl. f.; (9) any form in pl.; (10) gen. pl. any gender; (11) any form in pl.; (12) any form in pl.
5. The word which indicates the whole number or amount out of which a part is taken is normally put in the genitive case. See p. 124 s.v. "Genitive of the Whole."
6. **Ex** or **dē** + abl.
7. (1) one citizen                    (6) 5 of the citizens          (11) 3000 citizens
   (2) ten citizens                   (7) 5 citizens                 (12) what (is) new?
   (3) part of the citizens           (8) 100 citizens               (13) much praise
   (4) three citizens                 (9) 100 of the citizens        (14) enough money
   (5) 3 of the 6 citizens            (10) 1000 citizens             (15) no water
8. Time when, at which, within which.
9. (1) He used to come (was coming, kept coming) with his friends. Ablative of accompaniment.
   (2) He will come in one hour. Abl. of time within which.
   (3) He came at the same time. Abl. of time when.
   (4) He wrote the book in a few hours. Time within which.
   (5) At that time he wrote a book. Time when.
   (6) He was writing the book with care. Manner.

10. At that time alone he feared those three dangers; but he always used to fear (was afraid of) death. 11. Those two kings used to throw money among the thousands of citizens. 12. That one tyrant (of yours) always used to praise himself. 13. The citizens of those five cities kept expecting liberty. 14. They saved the city in two hours by their own wisdom. 15. I used to come into the city with three of my friends. 16. You (pl.) used to wage great wars with courage (= courageously). 17. Therefore a hundred Romans conquered a thousand Greeks. 18. Fathers often used to fear their own sons—and now they have much (of) fear. 19. Did you (sg.) see our two fathers at that time? 20. Where did you (pl.) find enough freedom? 21. They came in three hours, and he kept saying the same thing to us. 22. I understood little of the argument. 23. We have changed no part of our lives. 24. Our state used to preserve the liberty and rights of the citizens. 25. The Romans used to praise the customs of ancient times. 26. The two fathers sent four of their sons. 27. The ten men had enough wisdom and much virtue. 28. What's new, my friend?

### KEY FOR Capvt XVI
1. Abl. sg. m. and f.: **fortī** as compared with **cīve.**
2. (1) The adjective of 2 endings.
   (2) Nom. sg. m. and f.: fortis, fortis; ācer, ācris; potēns, potēns.
3. -ī, in the abl. sg. of all genders; -**ium**, in the gen. pl. of all genders; -**ia**, in the nom. and acc. n. pl.
4. -ī.
5. Yes.
6. (1) to/for a sweet girl                    (4) to/for a sweet mother
   (2) by/with/from a sweet girl              (5) to/for a happy mother
   (3) by/with/from a sweet mother            (6) by/with/from a happy mother

(7) all wars, nom. or acc. pl.

(8) all names, nom. or acc. pl.

(9) all seas, nom. or acc. pl.

(10) by/with/from every part

(11) of all parts

(12) of all kings

(13) of all wars

(14) by/with/from a happy man

(15) to/for a happy man

(16) to/for or by/with/from every sea

(17) to/for every good art

(18) by/with/from every good art

(19) of every good art

(20) to/for, by/with/from swift force

7. A long life is often difficult. 8. A difficult life can be happy. 9. How brief was his sweet life! 10. The memory of a sweet period of life helps thousands of men. 11. You (sg.) wrote a short book in a hundred hours. 12. In every sea we kept finding these two powerful animals. 13. In every land you (pl.) will see many thousands of brave men. 14. Swift rumor ran through every land. 15. That short war was difficult. 16. We overcame all dangers in six hours. 17. The powerful tyrant will conquer their country with swift violence. 18. In a short time he will change all the rights of the citizens. 19. They did not understand the difficult art of sweet liberty, for they had little wisdom. 20. Men fear difficult duties in all lands.

## KEY FOR Capvt XVII

1. See Capvt XVII, p. 139–40, s.v. "Usage and Agreement."
2. (1) Its use in its own clause. (2) The antecedent.
3. In gender and number.
4. (1) who. (2) which. (3) who, which.
5. (1) to/for whom or which, m. sg.
   (2) whom or which, m. pl.
   (3) who/which, nom. sg. f.
       who/which, nom. pl. f.
       which, nom. or acc. pl. n.
   (4) of whom/which, whose, sg.
   (5) to/for or by/with/from whom/which, pl.
   (6) which, nom. or acc. n. sg.
   (7) by/with/from whom/which, f. sg.
   (8) who/which, m. sg. and pl.
   (9) whom/which, m. sg.
   (10) whom/which, f. pl.
   (11) of whom/which, whose, m. and n. pl.
   (12) whom/which, f. sg.

6. They praised the citizen whom you (pl.) had sent. 7. They praised the ten citizens whom you (pl.) had sent. 8. They praised the citizen who had saved the country. 9. They praised the hundred citizens who had saved the country. 10. They praised the citizen whose son had saved the country. 11. They praised the citizens whose seven sons had saved the country. 12. They praised the citizen to whom they had entrusted the country. 13. They praised many of the citizens to whom they had entrusted the country. 14. They praised the citizen with whom they had come. 15. They praised the citizens with whom they had come. 16. He came with the citizen to whom he had entrusted his own life. 17. Tyrants destroy the rights of the citizens whom they capture. 18. The tyrant destroyed

the city from which thousands of citizens had fled. 19. The tyrant destroyed the city into which those nine citizens had fled. 20. The tyrant destroyed the cities from which the citizens had fled. 21. The tyrant destroyed the cities into which the citizens had fled. 22. He overcame the danger which we feared. 23. He overcame the dangers which we feared. 24. He gave books to the girls whom he was praising. 25. The man whose daughter you (sg.) love kept coming into the city. 26. He entrusted his own life to the man whose daughter you (sg.) love. 27. He used to help the mother, who had much courage. 28. The king used to give money to the mothers who had many sons.

### KEY FOR Capvt XVIII
1. See p. 147–48 s.v. "The Passive Voice."
2. See p. 148 s.v. "Ablative of Personal Agent." Note that "agent" is a person; "means" is something other than a person.
3. (1) The letter **r.**
   (2) No.
4. (1) we; (2) he; (3) I; (4) they; (5) you (sg.); (6) you (pl.).
5. (1) **-bā-**, imperf.; **-bi-** (**-bō-**, **-be-**, **-bu-**), fut.
   (2) Yes, with the minor exception of **-be-** in the 2nd pers. sg.
6. (1) we shall be . . . ; (2) you (pl.) were being . . . ; (3) he was being . . . ; (4) you (sg.) will be . . . ; (5) they will be . . . ; (6) we were being . . . ; (7) he will be . . . ; (8) you (sg.) were being . . . ; (9) you (pl.) will be . . . ; (10) they were being. . . .

7. They terrify me; I am terrified by them; I am terrified by their violence. 8. The tyrant was destroying this city. 9. This city was being destroyed by the tyrant; it will be destroyed by a plot. 10. He used to be aroused (moved) by his friends; he used to be aroused by their plans. 11. We are not being destroyed by the strength of men, but we can be destroyed by a plot. 12. You (pl.) will be destroyed not by war but by love of leisure and by the plans of evil men. 13. You yourself (sg.) are not being changed, but your name is being changed. 14. Thousands of men are possessed by the love of money. 15. Others used to be held by tyrants. 16. A few will be possessed by love of truth and friendship. 17. The boy will be saved by his friends. 18. Books of this sort used to be given to the boys by the teacher. 19. Liberty will be given to the people by the third king in a short time. 20. Our country can even now be saved by brave citizens. 21. We ought to be warned by the fortune of other men (others). 22. We are terrified by the plans of that tyrant who lives across the sea; but we love liberty, and we shall wage war with great courage. 23. We shall be helped by powerful friends. 24. We praise all our men, who are moved by courage and truth, not by love of themselves.

### KEY FOR Capvt XIX
1. (1) The perfect passive participle plus the present of **sum.**
   (2) The perfect passive participle plus the imperfect of **sum.**
2. (1) **Vir missus est** = *a man was (has been) sent;* **vir mittitur** = *a man is (is being) sent.*
   (2) **Vir missus erat** = *a man had been sent;* **vir mittēbātur** = *a man was being (used to be) sent.*
3. An interrogative pronoun introduces a question.
4. **quis** (nom. sg. m. and f.); **quid** (nom. and acc. sg. n.).

5. See p. 155.

6. (1) he is (is being) moved
   (2) he was (has been) moved
   (3) it had been moved
   (4) he was being moved
   (5) they had been destroyed
   (6) they were being destroyed
   (7) they were destroyed
   (8) we are held

   (9) we were held
   (10) we had been held
   (11) we were being held
   (12) he had been changed
   (13) he was (has been) changed
   (14) he is (is being) changed
   (15) he was being changed

7. (1) whose (sg.)?
   (2) whom (sg.)?
   (3) who (pl.)?
   (4) what (nom. and acc. sg.)?
   (5) whose (pl.)?

   (6) to whom (sg.)?
   (7) whom (f. pl.)?
   (8) who (sg.)?
   (9) who (f. pl.)?; what (n. nom. and acc. pl.)?

8. By whom was the book prepared (had been prepared; was being prepared)? 9. The teacher by whom the book was prepared is overcome with work. 10. To whom was the book given (was being given, had been given)? 11. What boy was saved? 12. I myself saw the boy who was saved. 13. Whose (sg.) two sons were saved? 14. I never saw the old man whose sons were saved. 15. Who (sg.) was sent? 16. Peace and liberty were praised by the citizen who had been sent. 17. Who (pl.) were sent? 18. Friendship was praised by the ten citizens who had been sent. 19. Whom (pl.) did you (sg.) see in the city? 20. Where are the three new friends whom you (sg.) saw in the city? 21. What things were found by you (sg.) there? 22. Where are the three bodies which were found there by you (sg.)? 23. By whom was this (thing) said? 24. To whom was this said? 25. The eight wretched men to whom these things were said fled from the city. 26. Whose sons were praised by him? 27. The fathers whose sons were praised will thank him. 28. What terrifies you? 29. What danger terrifies you? 30. But the danger which terrifies you has been conquered by brave citizens.

## KEY FOR Capvt XX

1. (1) object, acc. sg.; (2) of, pl.; (3) by/with/from, sg.; (4) subject, sg.; (5) of (sg.); subject or object (pl.); (6) to/for, sg.

2. (1) to/for a hand (band)
   (2) a hand (subj.)
   (3) of hands
   (4) by/with/from a hand
   (5) of a hand; hands (subj./obj.)
   (6) to/for or by/with/from fruits
   (7) fruit (obj.)

   (8) of fruit; fruits (subj./obj.)
   (9) of fruits
   (10) by/with/from fruit
   (11) of the senate
   (12) to/for the senate
   (13) the senate (subj.)
   (14) by/with/from the senate

3. (1) Masculine; (2) **manus.**

4. (1) The ablative of place from which = motion apart; the ablative of separation = distance apart.
   (2) The ablative of separation.
   (3) The ablative of place from which.

5. Place from which regularly has a preposition (**ab, dē, ex**); for separation, see p. 163.

6. Who came to us at that time? 7. An old man of great fame fled from his country to our senate. 8. What new was said by him? 9. This (thing) was said by that man: "We lack liberty." 10. Free us from slavery and heavy fear. 11. Our forces waged long war against the tyrant's fierce bands. 12. Those fierce bands which the tyrant sent against us from that land were conquered by us. 13. After this (*lit.* these things) the citizens who feared the tyrant were led from their own country into our state. 14. We freed them from the crimes of that tyrant. 15. Now they lack (are free from) every fear (anxiety). 16. Their sons eagerly (with zeal) read good books in our schools. 17. And so they have written a thousand verses with their own hands. 18. These one hundred verses give great thanks to us. 19. In these verses the senate and the Roman people are praised. 20. For those unfortunate men now have the fruits of peace and much liberty without fear. 21. Since we have helped others, even we ourselves have great enjoyment. 22. Good men will never lack an abundance of these fruits. 23. In our age many human beings pass their life in fear and slavery. 24. We ought to free those unfortunate men from fear. 25. For who can be happy if other human beings lack the enjoyments of peace and liberty?

26. (6) time when; (7) place from which; (8) agent; (9) agent; (10) separation; (12) agent; (13) place from which; (14) separation; (15) separation; (16) manner; (17) means; (22) separation; (23) time when; (24) separation.

## KEY FOR Capvt XXI

1. See p. 169–70.
2. Check with paradigms on p. 169–70 and repeat them until you can say them without hesitation; listen to the CDs if you have them.
3. In the passive infinitive the final -e of the active infinitive has been changed to -ī: (1) **sentīrī**, *to be felt;* (2) **movērī**, *to be moved;* (3) **servārī**, *to be saved;* (4) **scīrī**, *to be known;* (5) **tenērī**, *to be held.*
4. The whole active ending -**ere** is changed to -ī: (1) **mittī**, *to be sent;* (2) **iacī**, *to be thrown;* (3) **tangī**, *to be touched;* **trahī**, *to be drawn.*
5.  (1) I shall be sent
    (2) you (sg.) are sent
    (3) you (sg.) will be sent
    (4) to be sent
    (5) they are sent
    (6) I am sent
    (7) he is seized
    (8) he will be seized
    (9) to be seized
    (10) we are seized
    (11) they will be seized
    (12) they are seized
    (13) you (sg.) are seized
    (14) you (sg.) will be seized
    (15) they are touched
    (16) they will be touched
    (17) to be touched
    (18) you (sg.) are touched
    (19) you (pl.) will be touched
    (20) you (sg.) will be known
    (21) you (sg.) are known
    (22) he will be known
    (23) he is known
    (24) to be known

6. Who is being sent (will be sent, used to be sent, was sent)? 7. By whom will this letter be sent (was sent, is sent)? 8. By whose hand was that letter written (will be written)? 9. What was said (was being said, will be said, is said)? 10. "Who (sg.) will be seized?" "You (sg.) will be seized." 11. "Who (pl.) will be seized?" "You (pl.) will be seized." 12. For a long time you (sg./pl.) will be neglected (were neglected). 13. After many hours we

were freed (shall be freed). 14. For the sake of the state they ordered him to be seized. 15. For the sake of liberty our state ought to be managed by the other man. 16. His soul could not be touched by money. 17. In every soul the love of country used to be felt (will be felt, is felt, was felt). 18. We are joined (used to be joined, will be joined) to (*lit.,* with) other citizens by love of country. 19. Friendship is not always understood, but it is felt. 20. Wisdom and truth will not be found (are not found, were not found) in those two men. 21. Wisdom is not obtained (will not be obtained, was not obtained) by even a great deal of (= much) money. 22. Truth often is not known (will not be known, was not known), because the study of it is difficult. 23. Not without great labor will truth be found (was found, can be found). 24. Others are drawn by eagerness for (*lit.,* of) money and fame; we ought to be drawn by love of truth and wisdom.

### KEY FOR Capvt XXII

1. ē.
2. -em, -ē; -ēs, -ēbus, -ēs, -ēbus (also -eī, dat., and -ērum, gen.)
3. (1) Feminine. (2) **Diēs.**
4. 

| | |
|---|---|
| (1) of hope; to/for hope | (11) to/for or by/with/from days |
| (2) of hopes | (12) thing (acc.) |
| (3) hope (acc.) | (13) of things |
| (4) to/for or by/with/from hopes | (14) by/with/from a thing |
| (5) hope (nom.); hopes (nom., acc.) | (15) to/for or by/with/from things |
| (6) by/with/from faith | (16) of or to/for a thing |
| (7) faith (acc.) | (17) of fires |
| (8) of or to/for faith | (18) fire (acc.) |
| (9) of days | (19) to/for or by/with/from fires |
| (10) day (nom.); days (nom., acc.) | (20) fires (nom., acc.) |

5. (1) place where; he remained in the city.
   (2) time within which; he will come in one hour.
   (3) time when; he came at that time.
   (4) accompaniment; he came with them.
   (5) place from which; he came from the city.
   (6) separation; they lack fire.
   (7) means; that was done by fire.
   (8) agent; it was done by them.
   (9) manner; it was done faithfully (with faith).
6. (1) **ab** + abl.
   (2) **cum** + abl.
   (3) abl. alone after verbs of freeing, lacking, and depriving; with other verbs **ab, dē, ex** is often used.
   (4) **in** + abl.
   (5) abl. alone
   (6) **cum** + abl.; **cum** may be omitted when the noun is modified by an adj.
   (7) **ab, dē, ex** + abl.
   (8) abl. alone.

7. At that time he faithfully preserved the liberty of those ten citizens. 8. He managed the state with great care (= very carefully). 9. The state was managed by him with great

care. 10. Many good things were seen in the middle of the city. 11. On that day they prepared many things hopefully. 12. We snatched the fire from the hands of the boy. 13. In five days Cicero will rescue the republic from danger. 14. You (sg.) freed the two republics from fear. 15. The earth nourishes human beings with good fruits. 16. He nourished their uncertain hopes by his own courage. 17. In this age our hopes are being destroyed by these three tyrants. 18. Seven of our friends came from that state with great fear. 19. The whole clan came into the territory of this state with a large band of friends in one day. 20. Not all free men dare to join themselves with this republic. 21. If those men lack faith, there is no hope of friendship and peace. 22. Good faith and the love of this republic can save us. 23. You (sg.) have given (your) whole life to this state.

24. (7) time when; manner; (8) manner; (9) manner; (10) place where; (11) time when; manner; (13) time within which; separation; (14) separation; (15) means; (16) means; (17) time when; agent; (18) place from which; manner; (19) accompaniment; time within which; (21) separation.

## KEY FOR Capvt XXIII

1.   (1) perf. pass. = having been . . . or Eng. perf. partic.
    (2) pres. act. = -īng
    (3) fut. act. = about to . . .
    (4) pres. act. = -ing
    (5) fut. act. = about to . . .
    (6) fut. pass. = (about) to be . . .
    (7) perf. pass. = having been . . .
    (8) pres. act. = -ing.
    (9) perf. pass. = having been (e.g., nom. pl.)
    (10) perf. pass. = having been (dat. or abl. pl.)

2. 

| | |
|---|---|
| (1) about to be | (13) (about) to be done |
| (2) about to press | (14) seizing |
| (3) pressing | (15) about to seize |
| (4) (having been) pressed | (16) (having been) desired |
| (5) (about) to be pressed | (17) desiring |
| (6) turning | (18) (about) to be given |
| (7) (having been) turned | (19) (having been) given |
| (8) about to turn | (20) about to give |
| (9) (having been) said | (21) giving |
| (10) saying | (22) (having been) moved |
| (11) about to say | (23) moving |
| (12) (having been) done | (24) about to move |

3. 

| | | | |
|---|---|---|---|
| (1) vīsus | (6) scrīptus | (11) victūrus | (15) tractus |
| (2) vidēns | (7) mittēns | (12) vincēns | (16) trahēns |
| (3) vīsūrus | (8) missus | (13) iūnctūrus | (17) iactūrus |
| (4) scrībendus | (9) missūrus | (14) iungēns | (18) iactus |
| (5) scrīptūrus | (10) victus | | |

4. When captured (*lit.*, having been captured) he said nothing. 5. Freed from slavery he will lead a pleasant life. 6. He thanked those giving the gifts. 7. I do not like some-

one seeking gifts. 8. To a man desiring much money he used to give only a few gifts. 9. I sent my son to your school to be taught. 10. That man, when about to conquer another people, kept wishing to destroy (their) teachers and books. 11. Terrified by this plot we shall live a wretched life. 12. Long oppressed, they began to turn themselves against the oppressing tyrant. 13. Those four unfortunate men, when seen by the tyrant, ran across the border. 14. The orator, because he feared the tyrant, always used to say pleasing things. 15. We fear someone fearing us. (= who fears us). 16. These men, if they conquer, will take away all the rights of the conquered citizens. 17. That wretched man on the point of fleeing kept seeking the advice of his three friends. 18. The old man, warned by two of his friends, fled to us. 19. Having himself been helped by the second old man, he kept giving many things to those lacking money. 20. Who, when freed from these dangers, will not thank the gods? 21. Joined with you (pl.), we shall save the republic. 22. To those having faith nothing is uncertain.

## KEY FOR Capvt XXIV

1. (1) A noun (pronoun) + participle in abl.
   (2) No. (See p. 193.)
2. (1) See p. 193.
   (2) As a rule commas separate an abl. abs. from the rest of the sentence. This makes it appear somewhat apart from the rest of the sentence.
3. No. Since this "absolute" construction is not too commonly favored in English, the literal translation if regularly adhered to would make rather clumsy English.
4. When, since, after, although, if. (See p. 193–94.)
5. (1) Incorrect because the noun (**urbe**) of the abl. abs. is used (through its pronoun **eam**) as the object.
   (2) Incorrect because **captus** means *having been* captured, not *having* captured.
   (3) Correct because **urbem captam** (*the captured city*) stands as the natural object of **dēlēvit**.
   (4) Correct because **urbe captā** is a normal abl. abs., the noun of which is not used elsewhere as subject or object.
6. (1) Obligation or necessity.
   (2) It is really a predicate adjective; and so it naturally agrees with the subject of **sum**.
   (3) **Dēbeō** + infin., though **dēbeō** more often expresses the idea of moral obligation.
7. (1) **Mihi** is dat. of agent.
   (2) **Ā mē**; abl. of agent.

8. If (since, etc.) these two men hold the power, the republic will be strong. 9. When (since, etc.) this rumor had been reported, the leader left the city without delay. 10. When every desire for (*lit.,* of) money and glory had been banished from his soul, that leader conquered himself. 11. Every desire for evil things ought to be conquered by us (= we ought to conquer . . .) if we wish to lead a good life. 12. If (since, etc.) the citizens love (their) country, we can have great hopes. 13. All citizens kept fearing that tyrant (of yours), who had to be banished. 14. When the tyrant had been overcome, the citizens regained their liberty and rights. 15. But after a tyrant has been expelled, another tyrant often gets the power. 16. Who in taking the power desires to help the state alone, not himself? 17. When many peoples had been conquered, you (sg.) desired to possess

the whole world. 18. Slavery of every sort must be checked throughout the whole world. 19. If our republic is strong, nothing is to be feared by you (sg.). 20. Our country ought to be helped by each one who likes our mode of life. 21. All rights, therefore, ought to be preserved by the citizens with great care. 22. When duties have been deserted by the citizens, the state will be in great danger. 23. When these important things had been said, the orator was praised by us. 24. Truth and virtue ought always to be sought by all men. 25. When (since) truth and virtue had been sought, the republic was saved.

26. A. (8) virīs tenentibus; (9) fāmā nārrātā; (10) cupiditāte expulsā; (12) cīvibus amantibus; (14) tyrannō superātō; (15) tyrannō expulsō; (17) gentibus victīs; (22) officiīs relictīs; (23) rēbus dictīs; (25) vēritāte . . . quaesītīs.
B. (11) vincenda est; (13) expellendus erat; (18) opprimenda est; (19) timendum est; (20) adiuvanda est; (21) cōnservanda sunt; (24) quaerendae sunt.
C. (11) nōbīs; (19) tibi; (20) cuique; (21) cīvibus; (24) virīs.
D. (22) ā cīvibus; (23) ā nōbīs.

## KEY FOR Capvt XXV
1. See p. 201–02, 504.
2. Future active infinitive.
3. Perfect passive infinitive.
4. They agree with the subject of the infinitive. See p. 201.
5. Since it is the ending of the perfect active infinitive, **-isse** in effect means "to have. . . ."
6. 

| | |
|---|---|
| (1) to have moved | (16) to have lived |
| (2) to have been moved | (17) to have been drawn |
| (3) to be about to move | (18) to have been seen |
| (4) to be moved | (19) to have been seized |
| (5) to be said | (20) to have been sent |
| (6) to be known | (21) to have been sought |
| (7) to be saved | (22) to have been expelled |
| (8) to be seized | (23) to have been left |
| (9) to be sent | (24) to have been given |
| (10) to have believed | (25) to be about to give |
| (11) to have destroyed | (26) to be about to turn |
| (12) to have drawn | (27) to be about to press |
| (13) to have touched | (28) to be about to seize |
| (14) to have loved | (29) to be about to order |
| (15) to have conquered | (30) to be about to touch |

7. See p. 202–03.
8. 

| | |
|---|---|
| (2) nūntiō, I announce | (14) sentiō, I feel, think |
| (4) intellegō, I understand | (16) scrībō, I write |
| (7) videō, I see | (19) ostendō, I show |
| (8) nesciō, I do not know | (20) spērō, I hope |
| (10) crēdō, I believe | (22) putō, I think |
| (13) audiō, I hear | (24) negō, I say that . . . not, deny |

9. Saying, knowing, thinking, perceiving, etc. See p. 203.
10. The infinitive with subject accusative; not a "that" clause.
11. The accusative.

12. No.

13. (1) The perfect infinitive = time *before* that of the main verb.

   (2) The future infinitive = time *after* that of the main verb.

   (3) The present infinitive = the *same time* as that of the main verb. See p. 204.

14. I know that you did (will do, are doing) this (thing). 15. I knew that you had done (would do, were doing) this. 16. We believed that they would come (had come, were coming). 17. We believe that they will come (came, are coming). 18. Tomorrow he will hear (A) that they are coming (i.e., tomorrow); (B) that they came (e.g., yesterday) *or* that they have come; (C) that they will come (e.g., in a few days). 19. Today he hears (A) that they are coming (today); (B) that they came (yesterday); (C) that they will come (soon). 20. Yesterday he heard (A) that they were coming (yesterday); (B) that they had come (e.g., the day before yesterday); (C) that they would come (in a few days). 21. They hope that you (pl.) will see him. 22. I know that this was done by you. 23. I did not know that those things had been done by him. 24. They said that the city was not being captured by the enemy (had not been captured). 25. You (pl.) know that those men are (will be, were/have been) always faithful. 26. You (pl.) knew that those men were (would be, had been) always faithful. 27. They kept thinking that the tyrant ought to be driven out by them (by themselves). 28. We believe that peace ought to be sought by all leaders. 29. He says that peace is being sought (was sought) by the ten leaders. 30. He said that the two leaders would seek (were seeking, had sought) peace. 31. The enemy hope that they will conquer all states. 32. I well know that I do not know many things, for no one can know all things.

33. **Scīre** (sentence 32) is a complementary infinitive depending on **potest.**

34. 

| *Word* | *Form* | *Reason* |
|---|---|---|
| (14) tē | acc. | subj. of infin. (fēcisse) |
| (14) fēcisse | perf. act. infin. | indir. state. |
| (16) eōs | acc. | subj. of infin. (ventūrōs esse) |
| (17) ventūrōs esse | fut. act. infin. | indir. state. |
| (21) eum | acc. | obj. of infin. (vīsūrōs esse) |
| (22) hoc | acc. | subj. of infin. (factum esse) |
| (23) eō | abl. | agent |
| (24) hostibus | abl. | agent |
| (25) fidēlēs | acc. | pred. adj. agreeing with illōs |
| (27) sibi | dat. | agent with pass. periphrastic |
| (28) pācem | acc. | subj. of infin. (quaerendam esse) |
| (28) ducibus | dat. | agent with pass. periphr. |
| (29) ducibus | abl. | agent |
| (30) pācem | acc. | obj. of infin. (quaesitūrōs esse) |
| (31) rēs pūblicās | acc. | obj. of infin. |

## KEY FOR Capvt XXVI

1. (1) Latin -**ior** corresponds to English -*er*.

   (2) They have a slight similarity in sound and they both have a final -**r** as a sign of the comparative.

2. (1) Latin -**issimus** corresponds to English -*est*.

(2) The **s**'s which they have in common suggest **s** as a sign of the superlative.

3. (1) They are added to the *base* of the adjective. (See p. 210–11.)

(2) turpior, turpissimus; vēlōcior, vēlōcissimus; prūdentior, prūdentissimus

4. (1) **Acerbior** = harsher, rather harsh, too harsh.

(2) **Acerbissimus** = harshest, very harsh.

5. (1) **Quam** with the comparative = *than* (this man was harsher than that one).

(2) **Quam** with the superlative = *as . . . as possible, -st possible* (this man was as harsh as possible, the harshest possible).

6. There is no fixed case after **quam,** which is an adverb or conjunction of comparison. The second word of a comparison, which comes after **quam,** is put in the same case as that of the first of the two words compared. (See p. 212.)

7. (1) Most have **i**-stems.

(2) Comparatives have consonant stems. (Note, incidentally, that *comparative* and *consonant* both begin with the same sound.)

8. They announced that the bravest possible leader had come. 9. After a very clear light had been seen by the four men, the bravest troops were sent against the enemy. 10. When that very base man had been banished, the senate gave gifts to the more faithful citizens. 11. The more fortunate citizens used to do these pleasant things on behalf of the more unfortunate citizens. 12. This author is more famous than that one. 13. Certain men said that this author was more famous than that one. 14. Read the books of wiser authors if you wish to lead the wisest (a very wise) life. 15. The six authors whose books I have read are too (rather) harsh. 16. After certain very wise books had been read, we avoided those baser faults. 17. This man, who has overcome his base faults, is braver than the very brave leader. 18. Who is the happiest man? He who leads the wisest life is happier than the most powerful tyrant. 19. The cure of your vices seems rather (too) difficult. 20. That leader thought that his country was dearer to him than life. 21. A band of the most faithful young men possible ought to be sought by the senate.

## KEY FOR Capvt XXVII

1. (1) and (2)—see p. 218.

2. (1) and (2)—see p. 218.

3.

| *Positive* | *Comparative* | *Superlative* |
|---|---|---|
| parvus | minus (minor, minus) | minimum (minimus) |
| malus | pejorative (peior) | pessimist (pessimus) |
| bonus | ameliorate (melior) | optimist (optimus) |
| (prō) | prior (prior) | prime (prīmus) |
| magnus | major (maior) | maximum (maximus) |
| superus | superior (superior) | supreme (suprēmus) |
| multus | plus (plūs) | summit (summus) |

4. (1) a smaller war

(2) the worst (very bad) war

(3) a greater war

(4) former wars

(5) a very similar book

(6) a more difficult book

(7) the smallest boy

(8) the better boy

(9) a very (most) beautiful girl

(10) a more beautiful girl

(11) very many girls

(12) greater faith

(13) very small faith

(14) a smaller sea

(15) in a smaller sea

(16) larger seas

(17) the best fruits

(18) worse fruit

(19) the fiercest (very fierce) men

(20) fiercer men

(21) more men

(22) most (very) difficult labor

(23) the last (supreme) labor

(24) more labor

(25) more labors

(26) the best leaders

(27) greater leaders

(28) better leaders

(29) the smallest gifts

(30) more gifts

(31) the first gifts

(32) more praise

(33) more praises

(34) the worst citizens

(35) better citizens

(36) very free citizens

5. The easiest things often are not the best. 6. The difficult things are often the greatest. 7. The better pursuits are more (rather) difficult. 8. The worst authors write very many books. 9. These books are worse than the books of better authors. 10. The smaller boy received a larger gift. 11. That very small republic had the greatest hopes. 12. More men believe that this war is worse than the first war. 13. A better leader will come with greater forces. 14. Fierce leaders often used to praise the fiercer forces of the fiercest enemy. 15. When the very evil tyrant had been banished, the citizens sought a better and a wiser leader. 16. They gave the better leader greater power and more money. 17. Citizens of the smaller cities are not better than those of the largest cities. 18. We are not better than very many men of former ages. 19. Our ancestors used to call Apollo the god of the sun.

## KEY FOR Capvt XXVIII

1. Something other than a fact; e.g., the jussive and purpose clauses learned in this chapter. See p. 227.

2. See p. 227.

3. (1) ē; (2) ā (except that in the 3rd and 4th conjugations the forms **dūcam** and **audiam** are identical in the future indicative and the present subjunctive).

4. Command, called "jussive."

5. Purpose.

6. Jussive.

7. No. (See p. 229.)

8.   (1) he will send

   (2) subjunct., 3rd sg.

   (3) he is sending

   (4) subjunct., 3rd sg.

   (5) he gives

   (6) subjunct., 3rd pl.

   (7) they believe

   (8) they will believe

   (9) they move

   (10) subjunct., 3rd pl.

   (11) we shall be heard

   (12) subjunct., 1st pl. pass.

   (13) we are heard

   (14) subjunct., 2nd sg.

   (15) you (sg.) are seizing

   (16) you (sg.) will seize

   (17) they are known

   (18) they will be known

   (19) subjunct., 3rd pl. pass.

   (20) you (pl.) are freed

   (21) subjunct., 2d. pl. pass.

   (22) you (pl.) will be freed

(23) they are destroyed

(24) subjunct., 3rd pl. pass.

(25) you (sg.) will be conquered

(26) you (sg.) are conquered

(27) subjunct., 2nd sg. pass.

(28) we say

(29) we shall say

(30) subjunct., 1st pl.

9. Let that leader come. We are awaiting him. 10. Let the base citizens depart from (our) republic so that we may live in peace. 11. If those two men desire friends, let them do real kindnesses. 12. He shows kindnesses to others in order to be loved (so that he may be loved). 13. I say these happy words to you so that you may not depart. 14. Let us do these very difficult things for the sake of our country. 15. Give more money to those unfortunate people so that they may not lack arms against the enemy. 16. He thinks that they will do it to avoid my anger. 17. Let us prepare arms so that our liberty may not be taken away. 18. Will our freedom be rescued from danger by arms alone? 19. Let philosophers not write too difficult books. 20. For (= the truth is) we shall not receive enough wisdom from too difficult books. 21. Let him do better and greater things so that he may not lead a most wretched life. 22. Tell these things to that very famous author so that they may be written in his book. 23. Let us always seek the truth, without which the greatest souls cannot be happy.

| 24. Word | Form | Reason |
|---|---|---|
| (9) veniat | pres. subjunct. | command (jussive) |
| (10) discēdant | pres. subjunct. | command |
| vīvāmus | pres. subjunct. | purpose |
| (11) faciant | pres. subjunct. | command |
| (12) praestat | pres. indic. | statement of fact |
| amētur | pres. subjunct. | purpose |
| (13) discēdātis | pres. subjunct. | purpose |
| (14) faciāmus | pres. subjunct. | command |
| (15) date | imper. | command in 2nd per. |
| armīs | abl. | separation |
| careant | pres. subjunct. | purpose |
| (16) eōs | acc. | subj. of infin. |
| factūrōs esse | fut. act. infin. | indirect statement |
| vītent | pres. subjunct. | purpose |
| (17) parēmus | pres. subjunct. | command |
| tollātur | pres. subjunct. | purpose |
| (18) armīs | abl. | means |
| ēripiētur | fut. indic. | fact |
| (19) scrībant | pres. subjunct. | command |
| (20) accipiēmus | fut. indic. | fact |
| (21) faciat | pres. subjunct. | command |
| agat | pres. subjunct. | purpose |
| (22) nārrā | imper. | command in 2nd per. |
| scrībantur | pres. subjunct. | purpose |
| (23) quaerāmus | pres. subjunct. | command |

**KEY FOR Capvt XXIX**

1. Present active infinitive + personal endings. See p. 236.
2. Yes.
3.

| | |
|---|---|
| (1) impf. subjunct., 3 sg. | (16) pres. subjunct., 3 sg. |
| (2) impf. subjunct., 3 pl. | (17) impf. subjunct., 3 pl. |
| (3) impf. subjunct., 1 pl. | (18) they will depart |
| (4) impf. subjunct., 1 sg. | (19) pres. subjunct., 3 pl. |
| (5) impf. subjunct., 2 sg. | (20) pres. subjunct., 1 pl. |
| (6) pres. subjunct., 3 sg. | (21) pres. subjunct., 1 pl. |
| (7) impf. subjunct., 2 pl. | (22) impf. subjunct., 3 pl. |
| (8) pres. subjunct., 3 sg. | (23) pres. subjunct., 2 sg. |
| (9) you (sg.) will find | (24) you will receive |
| (10) pres. subjunct., 2 sg. | (25) impf. subjunct., 2 sg. |
| (11) pres. subjunct., 3 sg. | (26) you (pl.) will be banished |
| (12) he will say | (27) impf. subjunct., 2 pl. |
| (13) he says | (28) pres. subjunct., 2 pl. |
| (14) pres. subjunct., 3 pl. | (29) impf. subjunct., 3 pl. |
| (15) impf. subjunct., 3 sg. | (30) they are moved |

4. **Ut** or **ut nōn** + subjunctive.
5. See p. 238.
6. See p. 237.

7. They read the best books with such great care that they learned much wisdom. 8. We used to read good books with care so that we might learn wisdom. 9. The best books ought to be read by students in order that they may learn the truth and good character. 10. Let the wisest authors write more books so that they may be able to help all peoples. 11. The souls of very many men are so foolish that they do not wish to learn. 12. But many minds are so keen that they can learn well. 13. Some teachers used to teach their pupils so skillfully (with such great skill) that even the pupils themselves wanted to learn. 14. The power of that tyrant was so great that the senate could not drive him out. 15. Let all citizens dedicate (give) themselves to the country so that the enemy may not take away their liberty. 16. Caesar was such a keen leader that the enemy did not conquer the Roman soldiers. 17. Are we leading other peoples with such great wisdom and courage that liberty is being preserved? 18. You (pl.) used to do such great kindnesses that all loved you. 19. He was so harsh that no one loved him. 20. Thousands of citizens kept fleeing from that land in order not to be oppressed by the tyrant. 21. They so loved liberty that they were never conquered by the enemy.

22.

| Word | Form | Reason |
|---|---|---|
| (7) discerent | impf. subjunct. | result |
| (8) discerēmus | impf. subjunct. | purpose |
| (9) discant | pres. subjunct. | purpose |
| (10) scrībant | pres. subjunct. | command |
| possint | pres. subjunct. | purpose |
| (11) cupiant | pres. subjunct. | result |
| (12) possint | pres. subjunct. | result |
| (13) cuperent | impf. subjunct. | result |

| (14) | posset | impf. subjunct. | result |
|------|--------|-----------------|--------|
| (15) | dent | pres. subjunct. | command |
| | tollant | pres. subjunct. | purpose |
| (16) | vincerent | impf. subjunct. | result |
| (17) | cōnservētur | pres. subjunct. | result |
| (18) | amārent | impf. subjunct. | result |
| (19) | amāret | impf. subjunct. | result |
| (20) | opprimerentur | impf. subjunct. | purpose |
| (21) | vincerentur | impf. subjunct. | result |

## KEY FOR Capvt XXX

1. It is the perfect active infinitive (-**isse**) + personal endings; e.g., **pōnere-m** and **posuisse-m**.
2. It is the perfect passive participle + **essem** (the imperfect subjunctive of **sum**); e.g., **positus eram** and **positus essem**.
3. **Positus sit** is perfect subjunctive passive.
4. The future perfect indicative.
5. (1) impf. pass., 3 sg.
   (2) pluperf. act., 1 sg.
   (3) perf. pass., 3 pl.
   (4) pres. pass., 1 pl.
   (5) perf. act., 3 pl.
   (6) impf. act., 1 pl.
   (7) pluperf. act., 2 pl.
   (8) pluperf. pass., 3 sg.
   (9) impf. act., 3 pl.
   (10) pluperf. pass., 1 pl.
   (11) pres. act., 3 sg.
   (12) perf. pass., 2 sg.
   (13) pluperf. act., 2 sg.
   (14) impf. pass., 3 sg.
   (15) perf. act., 1 pl.
   (16) pluperf. act., 3 pl.
6. (1) Present and future. See p. 247–48.
   (2) Present and perfect.
   (3) The past tenses.
   (4) Imperfect and pluperfect.
7. (1) The same time or time after (contemporaneous or subsequent). See p. 248.
   (2) The same time or time after.
   (3) Time before (prior).
   (4) Time before (prior).

8. Where is (was) the leader? 9. They ask where the leader is (was). 10. They kept asking where the leader was (had been). 11. They will ask where the leader is (was). 12. I do not know where the money was put. 13. Do you (sg.) know where the money is being put? 14. They knew where the money was being put. 15. He did not know where the money had been put. 16. We shall tell you (pl.) why the soldier did (does) this. 17. They told me why the soldier had done (was doing) this. 18. Tell me who came (is coming). 19. The orator asked why the other citizens had not learned these plans. 20. We announced to the leader that the other soldiers were fleeing (had fled) into that land. 21. We announced to the leader into what land the other soldiers were fleeing (had fled). 22. We heard that the citizens were so faithful that they preserved the state. 23. We heard what the citizens had done to preserve the state. 24. They kept inquiring in whose state peace could be found. 25. We learned that peace had not been found in their country. 26. Those foolish men

always ask what is better than power or money. 27. We certainly think that money itself is not bad; but we believe that truth and liberty and friendship are better and greater. 28. These things we desire so that we may live a finer life; for money alone and power can make men harsh, so that they are not happy. 29. Finally, let him explain all things so that you (pl.) may now understand what great crimes have been committed against the republic.

30. *Word*

| | *Word* | *Form* | *Reason* |
|---|---|---|---|
| (15) | posita esset | pluperf. subjunct. | ind. quest. |
| (16) | fēcerit | perf. subjunct. | ind. quest. |
| (17) | fēcisset | pluperf. subjunct. | ind. quest. |
| (18) | vēnerit | perf. subjunct. | ind. quest. |
| (20) | fugere | pres. infin. | ind. state. |
| (21) | fugerent | impf. subjunct. | ind. quest. |
| (22) | esse | pres. infin. | ind. state. |
| | cōnservārent | impf. subjunct. | result |
| (23) | fēcissent | pluperf. subjunct. | ind. quest |
| | cōnservārent | impf. subjunct. | purpose |
| (24) | posset | impf. subjunct. | ind. quest. |
| (25) | inventam esse | perf. infin. | ind. state. |
| (26) | sit | pres. subjunct. | ind. quest. |
| (27) | esse | pres. infin. | ind. state. |
| (28) | agāmus | pres. subjunct. | purpose |
| | sint | pres. subjunct. | result |
| (29) | expōnat | pres. subjunct. | jussive |
| | comprehendātis | pres. subjunct. | purpose |
| | commissa sint | pres. subjunct. | ind. quest. |

## KEY FOR Capvt XXXI

1. When (circumstantial, which is to be distinguished from **cum** temporal), since, although.
2. Although.
3. (1) The 3rd conjugation.
   (2) They lack the connecting vowel **e/i**, which is seen in the corresponding forms of **dūcō**. (See p. 256.)
4. (1) pres. subjunct. act., 3 sg.
   (2) he bears
   (3) impf. subjunct. act., 3 sg.
   (4) he will bear
   (5) to bear
   (6) they bear
   (7) they will bear
   (8) pres. subjunct. act., 3 pl.
   (9) he is borne
   (10) bear (2 pl.)
   (11) you (pl.) bear
   (12) you (sg.) will be borne
   (13) you (sg.) are borne
   (14) bear (2 sg.)
   (15) to be borne
   (16) to have borne
   (17) to be about to bear
   (18) to be borne (gerundive)
   (19) to have been borne
   (20) pluperf. subjunct. act., 3 sg.

5. When we had said this, those twenty men replied that they would offer a just peace. 6. Although he had gone into another country, nevertheless he found new friends. 7. Since they offer us friendship, we shall offer them aid. 8. Since the danger was great, they brought all their troops and arms together in a short time. 9. What do *you* (sg.) bring? What does he bring? Tell me why these gifts are offered. 10. When he had explained what he was seeking, you (sg.) said that such great aid could not be offered. 11. Although they had brought pleasing gifts, I was able nevertheless to recognize their treachery. 12. Since we now understand your plans, we will not endure your treachery. 13. Such great evils are not to be endured. Go (betake yourself) into exile. 14. Finally, let these hundred citizens bear aid to the republic. 15. I kept thinking that they would bring the wine in ships (*lit.,* by ships). 16. Although our soldiers had conquered the enemy, nevertheless they offered them many kindnesses. 17. When he had learned what great benefits the other three men were offering, he himself offered equal benefits. 18. We ought to offer sufficient aid to the unfortunate citizens of small nations. 19. When the consul had spoken these words, the senate replied that money had been brought together for this purpose.

| 20. *Word* | *Form* | *Reason* |
|---|---|---|
| (5) dīxissēmus | pluperf. subjunct. | **cum** circumstantial |
| oblātūrōs esse | fut. infin. | ind. state. |
| (6) contulisset | pluperf. subjunct. | **cum** *although* |
| (7) offerant | pres. subjunct. | **cum** *since* |
| (8) esset | impf. subjunct. | **cum** *since* |
| (9) offerantur | pres. subjunct. | ind. quest. |
| (10) exposuisset | pluperf. subjunct. | **cum** circumstantial |
| peteret | impf. subjunct. | ind. quest. |
| (11) tulissent | pluperf. subjunct. | **cum** *although* |
| (12) comprehendāmus | pres. subjunct. | **cum** *since* |
| (13) cōnfer | imper. 2 sg. | command |
| (14) ferant | pres. subjunct. | jussive (command) |
| (15) nāvibus | abl. pl. | means |
| lātūrōs esse | fut. infin. | ind. state. |
| (16) vīcissent | pluperf. subjunct. | **cum** *although* |
| (17) offerrent | impf. subjunct. | ind. quest. |
| (19) dīxisset | pluperf. subjunct. | **cum** circumstantial |

## KEY FOR Capvt XXXII
1. (1) -ē; (2) -iter (e.g., līberē, celeriter).
2. The ending -*ly* (e.g., freely, quickly).
3. No. For example, see the list on p. 264.
4. (1) -ius (e.g., līberius, celerius).
   (2) It is identical with the nom. and acc. n. sg.
   (3) It is usually formed by using *more* (*too, rather*) with the positive degree of the adverb (e.g., more/too freely, more quickly).
5. The base is the same in both instances.
6. (1) **līberius** = more/too/rather freely.
   (2) **līberrimē** = most/very freely.

7.  (1) pleasantly
    (2) more/too pleasantly
    (3) most/very pleasantly
    (4) better
    (5) very faithfully
    (6) briefly
    (7) very quickly
    (8) worse
    (9) more faithfully
    (10) more easily

    (11) very little, least of all
    (12) more, rather
    (13) longer
    (14) badly
    (15) more wretchedly
    (16) less
    (17) easily
    (18) especially, most of all
    (19) very seriously
    (20) more swiftly

8.  (1) **vol-**; (2) **vel-**. See p. 266.
9.  It is similar to **sum.** See p. 266.
10. (1) you (sg.) will wish
    (2) pres. subjunct., 2 sg.
    (3) you (sg.) wish
    (4) impf. subjunct., 2 sg.
    (5) he prefers
    (6) pres. subjunct., 1 pl.
    (7) impf. subjunct., 1 pl.
    (8) pluperf. subjunct., 2 sg.
    (9) I shall wish
    (10) they kept wishing
    (11) he will wish
    (12) you (pl.) wish

    (13) to have wished
    (14) they wish
    (15) we wished
    (16) to wish
    (17) he had wished
    (18) they wished
    (19) you (sg.) wished
    (20) impf. subjunct., 3 sg.
    (21) they do not wish
    (22) impf. subjunct., 3 sg.
    (23) pres. subjunct., 3 sg.
    (24) he will not wish

11. Certain men prefer to believe that all men are equal. 12. Certain men say that all men's minds at least are not equal. 13. These men obtained wealth very quickly; those will be poor for a very long time. 14. This man wishes to get very many honors as easily as possible. 15. Do not lose this knowledge. 16. The citizens themselves managed the state better than the leader. 17. There the land is more level and is more open. 18. Free men will not wish to keep us from knowledge; but tyrants especially so wish. 19. The tyrant used to oppress his citizens so badly that they always wished to be free. 20. He will offer very many gifts very freely so that the army may be willing to help that tyrant. 21. Since they had very little wish to offer aid, we were unwilling to show them many favors. 22. Since the enemy are coming swiftly against us, we want to call our men to arms as quickly as possible. 23. Although they truly wanted to preserve their liberty and laws, nevertheless the crimes of the tyrant had to be endured very long. 24. He prefers to do these things more wisely so that he may not lose this occasion at least. 25. Do not leave, my friend.

## KEY FOR Capvt XXXIII

1.  (1) The present subjunctive. (2) See p. 274.
2.  (1) (A) Present contrary to fact; (B) past contrary to fact.
    (2) The conditional clause. See p. 274.
3.  **Nisi.**
4.  The future less vivid condition.
5.  See *Vocābula* p. 275.

6. If reason leads, you (sg.) are happy. 7. If reason leads, you will be happy. 8. If reason should lead, you would be happy. 9. If reason were leading, you would be happy. 10. If reason had led, you would have been happy. 11. If you (sg.) love money, you lack wisdom. 12. If you love money, you will lack wisdom. 13. If you should love money, you would lack wisdom. 14. If you were in love with money, you would lack wisdom. 15. If you had loved money, you would have lacked wisdom. 16. If we seek the truth, we find knowledge. 17. If we seek the truth, we shall find knowledge. 18. If we should seek the truth, we would find knowledge. 19. If we were seeking the truth, we would find knowledge. 20. If we had sought the truth, we would have found knowledge. 21. If you do not avoid anger, you will lose your two friends. 22. If you had not avoided anger, you would have lost your five friends. 23. If you should not avoid anger (if you should fail to avoid anger), you would lose many friends. 24. If you were not avoiding anger, you would be losing many friends. 25. If you do not avoid anger, you are losing many friends. 26. If you did not avoid anger, you lost many friends. 27. If anyone has a good character, we praise him. 28. If anyone had had a good character, we would have praised him. 29. If anyone should have a good character, we would praise him. 30. If anyone had a good character, we praised (used to praise) him. 31. If anyone were in possession of a good character, we would praise him. 32. If anyone has a good character, we shall praise him. 33. If those men win, we shall depart. 34. If those men should win, we would depart. 35. If those men had won, we would have departed. 36. If you had read books well, you would have written better. 37. If you read books well, you will write better. 38. If you should read books well, you would write better.

39. (6) simple present                    (21) simple fut.
    (7) simple fut.                        (22) past contrary to fact
    (8) fut. less vivid                    (23) fut. less vivid
    (9) pres. contrary to fact             (24) pres. contrary to fact
    (10) past contrary to fact             (25) simple present
                                           (26) simple past

## KEY FOR Capvt XXXIV

1. See p. 282.

2.

| | Indicative | |
|---|---|---|
| *Pres.* | cōnāmur | loquitur |
| *Impf.* | cōnābāmur | loquēbātur |
| *Fut.* | cōnābimur | loquētur |
| *Perf.* | cōnātī sumus | locūtus est |
| *Pluperf.* | cōnātī erāmus | locūtus erat |
| *Fut. Perf.* | cōnātī erimus | locūtus erit |
| | **Subjunctive** | |
| *Pres.* | cōnēmur | loquātur |
| *Impf.* | cōnārēmur | loquerētur |
| *Perf.* | cōnātī sīmus | locūtus sit |
| *Pluperf.* | cōnātī essēmus | locūtus esset |

3. (1) Participles

| | |
|---|---|
| *Pres.* | patiēns, *suffering* |
| *Perf.* | passus, *having suffered* |
| *Fut.* | passūrus, *about to suffer* |
| *Ger.* | patiendus, *to be endured* |

(2) Infinitives

| | |
|---|---|
| *Pres.* | patī, *to suffer* |
| *Perf.* | passus esse, *to have suffered* |
| *Fut.* | passūrus esse, *to be about to suffer* |

4. (1) illud cōnsilium; (2) illō cōnsiliō; (3) illud cōnsilium
5. Ablative (of means) with special deponent verbs. See p. 285.
6. Pres. partic.; fut. partic.; fut. infin.; e.g., **patiēns, passūrus, passūrus esse** in 3 above.
7. (1) cōnor                    (2) loquor
   2 sg. cōnāre, *try*              loquere, *speak*
   2 pl. cōnāminī, *try*             loquiminī, *speak*
8. (1) locūtus, *having said*          (5) secūtus, *having followed*
   (2) mortuus, *having died*         (6) ēgresssus, *having gone out*
   (3) cōnātus, *having tried*        (7) profectus, *having set out*
   (4) passus, *having suffered*
9. (1) he will use                 (11) to endure
   (2) pres. subjunct., 3 sg.         (12) they endured
   (3) he uses                        (13) to have endured
   (4) impf. subjunct., 3 sg.         (14) enduring
   (5) having used                    (15) pres. subjunct., 3 sg.
   (6) pluperf. subjunct., 3 sg.      (16) he endures
   (7) to be about to use             (17) we shall endure
   (8) you (sg.) will endure          (18) pres. subjunct., 3 sg.
   (9) you (sg.) are enduring         (19) impf. subjunct., 3 sg.
   (10) endure (imper.)               (20) it must be endured

10. He thinks that these evils ought to be endured. 11. We shall try to endure these evils. 12. If you do not wish to die, endure these evils. 13. Having endured the greatest evils, the poor man died. 14. The tyrant thought that those two men would endure these evils a long time. 15. When they had endured three wars, they dared to force that tyrant into exile. 16. If you follow this new leader, you will enjoy liberty and leisure. 17. When these words had been said, we dared to follow him. 18. Having spoken these words, we set out so that we might not die in that miserable place. 19. Although he thought that you had used a bad plan, nevertheless he spoke with you freely. 20. If anyone should dare to use wine of that sort, he would quickly die. 21. His son was born and died on the same day. 22. Let us use all our resources so that our country may be saved. 23. When he tried to set out into another land, he was captured by soldiers. 24. I kept thinking that he would go out of the city with his ten friends. 25. Having set out that night, Caesar came to a certain very famous island. 26. If they had used better books, they would have learned more. 27. If you wish to have many friends, do not be arrogant.

28. (12) simple pres.; (16) simple fut.; (20) fut. less vivid; (26) past contrary to fact.

29. 

| Word | Form | Reason |
|---|---|---|
| (14) passūrōs esse | fut. infin. | ind. state. |
| (17) verbīs | abl. | abl. abs. |
| (18) locūtī | nom. pl. of perf. partic. | agrees with subject of verb |
| morerēmur | impf. subjunct. | purpose |
| (19) cōnsiliō | abl. | special deponents |
| arbitrārētur | impf. subjunct. | **cum** *although* |
| (21) diē | abl. | time when |
| (22) ūtāmur | pres. subjunct. | jussive |
| (25) nocte | abl. | time when |
| (26) librīs | abl. | special deponents |

## KEY FOR Capvt XXXV

1. See p. 295.
2. See p. 296.
3. 
   (1) eum; they recognize him.
   (2) eī; they forgive him.
   (3) eī; they serve him.
   (4) eum; they save him.
   (5) eum; I prepared him.
   (6) eī; I obeyed him.
   (7) eum; they endure him.
   (8) eum; they will find him.
   (9) eī; they injure him.
   (10) eum; they help him.
   (11) eī; they please him.
   (12) eum; they throw him.
   (13) eum; they overcome him.
   (14) eī; they trust him.
   (15) eō; they lack it.
   (16) eī; they study it.
   (17) eum; they urge him.
   (18) eum; they follow him.
   (19) eī; they persuade him.
   (20) eō; they use it (him).
   (21) eum; they strike him.
   (22) eī; they spare him.
   (23) eī; they command him.
   (24) eum; they order him.

4. He saved the leader. 5. He served the leader. 6. Slaves serve other men. 7. Brave men save others. 8. That slave served my son and saved him. 9. If anyone serves himself alone, he will never save the republic. 10. If someone had undertaken this work, he would have saved a thousand men. 11. The gods will pardon me; you, O citizens, pardon the whole army. 12. If we want God to forgive us, we ought to forgive other men. 13. They do not trust me now, and they will never be willing to trust my two sons. 14. Those friends are very dear to me. 15. Since you lacked good faith, they could not trust you. 16. Let us obey this leader so that he may spare us and save the city. 17. If Caesar does not please the citizens, they will not spare his life. 18. I am studying Latin literature, which I like (pleases me) even if I cannot persuade my friends. 19. Let us always study and obey truth and wisdom. 20. Always study the best subjects if you wish to be truly happy. 21. As we study these subjects, let us enjoy both books and life. 22. A good man wishes to harm nobody; he spares all, he helps all. 23. My rewards are very similar to yours.

24. *Word*  *Form*  *Reason*

| | | |
|---|---|---|
| (5) ducī | dat. | special verbs |
| (8) eum | acc. | obj. of **servāvit** |
| (9) sibi | dat. | special verbs |
| (11) exercituī | dat. | special verbs |
| (12) hominibus | dat. | special verbs |
| (13) fīliīs | dat. | special verbs |
| (14) mihi | dat. | dat. with adjs. |
| (15) fidē | abl. | separation |
| (16) ducī | dat. | special verbs |
| pāreāmus | pres. subjunct. | jussive |
| servet | pres. subjunct. | purpose |
| (17) cīvibus | dat. | special verbs |
| vītae | dat. | special verbs |
| (18) litterīs | dat. | special verbs |
| amīcīs | dat. | special verbs |
| (21) rēbus | dat. | special verbs |
| librīs | abl. | special depon. verbs |
| ūtāmur | pres. subjunct. | jussive |
| (22) omnibus | dat. | special verbs |
| (23) tuīs | dat. | dat. with adjs. |

## KEY FOR Capvt XXXVI

1. Indirect command = **ut** (**nē**) + subjunctive. See p. 303.
2. Imperō, dīcō, cūrō, moneō, hortor, persuādeō, petō, quaerō, ōrō, rogō. See p. 303–04.
3. (1) it will be made/done, he will become
   (2) it is made/done, he becomes
   (3) pres. subjunct., 3 sg.
   (4) impf. subjunct., 3 sg.
   (5) to be made/done, to become
   (6) they are made/done, they become
   (7) they were being made/done, they were becoming
   (8) you (sg.) will be made, become
   (9) to have been made/done, become
   (10) impf. subjunct., 3 pl.
   (11) we are made, become
   (12) they will be made, become
   (13) you (sg.) are made, become
   (14) impf. subjunct., 1 sg.
   (15) pres. subjunct., 3 pl.
   (16) gerundive, to be made/done
   (17) pres. subjunct., 1 pl.

4. He said that they were studying Latin literature. 5. He told why they were studying Latin literature. 6. He said that they should study Latin literature (he told them to study . . .). 7. We asked them why they were studying Greek philosophy. 8. Do you ask that we learn (= ask us to learn) the nature of all things? 9. I warn you to spare these wise men. 10. He warned the soldiers not to injure those seeking peace. 11. He will command us not to trust the enemy. 12. He commanded you to obey the leader. 13. I ask you why you did this. 14. I ask you to do this. 15. I beg of you that peace be made. 16. They kept begging me not to make war. 17. I begged him not to obey the disgraceful king. 18. We beg you to become very keen pupils. 19. Do not be like that harsh tyrant. 20. Caesar took care that his power be made greatest in the state. 21. The speaker urged us to serve our free country eagerly. 22. He persuaded us that we should always use just laws. 23. We are

trying to persuade the leader not to harm the arts and laws of the country. 24. A tyrant commands that money be made; and money is made. But that fool does not perceive that this money will be nothing without good faith. 25. Let us urge more students certainly to study the Latin language.

26. | *Word* | *Form* | *Reason* |
|---|---|---|
| (4) studēre | pres. infin. | ind. state. |
| (5) studērent | impf. subjunct. | ind. quest. |
| (6) studērent | impf. subjunct. | jussive noun |
| (7) studērent | impf. subjunct. | ind. quest. |
| (8) cognōscāmus | pres. subjunct. | jussive noun |
| (9) parcās | pres. subjunct. | jussive noun |
| (10) eīs | dat. | special verbs |
| pācem | acc. | obj. **petentibus** |
| (11) hostibus | dat. | special verbs |
| (13) fēceris | perf. subjunct. | ind. quest. |
| (14) faciās | pres. subjunct. | jussive noun |
| (16) facerem | impf. subjunct. | jussive noun |
| (18) fiātis | pres. subjunct. | jussive noun |
| (22) lēgibus | abl. | special depon. verbs |
| (23) lēgibus | dat. | special verbs |
| (24) futūram esse | fut. infin. | ind. state. |
| (25) hortēmur | pres. subjunct. | jussive |

## KEY FOR Capvt XXXVII

1. (1) Present indicative and present subjunctive.
   (2) It is **ī-**.
2. Nom. sg. = **iēns**; nom. pl. = **euntēs.**
3. In writing the synopsis of a verb one should follow the sequence of tenses in the indicative and the subjunctive as given above in #2 of the Key of Capvt XXXIV. If this is done there is no need to label the tenses.
   Eō 2nd sg.: Indicative—īs, ībās, ībis, īstī, ierās, ieris.
       Subjunctive—eās, īrēs, ieris, īssēs.
   Eō 3d pl.: Indicative—eunt, ībant, ībunt, iērunt, ierant, ierint.
       Subjunctive—eant, īrent, ierint, īssent.
4. (1) we went
   (2) we are going
   (3) impf. subjunct., 1 pl.
   (4) we shall go
   (5) pluperf. subjunct., 1 pl.
   (6) pres. subjunct., 1 pl.
   (7) to be about to go
   (8) going (acc. sg.)
   (9) they went
   (10) they are going
   (11) pres. subjunct., 3 pl.
   (12) they will go
   (13) I went
   (14) he was going
   (15) they had gone
   (16) perf. subjunct., 1 sg.
   (17) impf. subjunct., 3 sg.
   (18) to have gone
   (19) going (nom./acc. pl.)
   (20) I shall go
   (21) he went
   (22) we were going
   (23) pluperf. subjunct., 3 sg.
   (24) pres. subjunct., 3 sg.

5. (1) **ab, dē, ex** + abl.; ab (ex) eā terrā.
   (2) **in** + abl.: in eā terrā; in eā īnsulā.
   (3) **in** or **ad** + acc.: in (ad) eam terram.
6. (1) Place from which = abl. without a preposition.
   (2) Place where = locative without a preposition.
   (3) Place to which = accusative without a preposition.
7. The locative is the case which expresses the idea of "place where" when **domus** or the name of a city, town, or small island is used; for Forms, see p. 314.
8. (1) Time when = abl. without a prep.: eōdem diē.
   (2) Time how long = acc. usually without a prep.: multōs diēs.
   (3) Time within which = abl. without a prep.: ūnō diē.
9. Since an impersonal verb lacks the 1st and the 2nd persons sg. and pl., the 1st and the 3rd principal parts are given in the 3rd pers. sg. See p. 315, *Vocābula*, s.v. **licet. Licet tibi īre.**
10. (1) (for) one day
    (2) in one day
    (3) on that day
    (4) from Rome
    (5) at Rome
    (6) to Rome
    (7) in a few days
    (8) on the same night
    (9) (for) many days
    (10) into the ship
    (11) in the ship
    (12) out of the ship
    (13) home (= to home)
    (14) at/from Athens
    (15) at home
    (16) to Athens
    (17) from home
    (18) (for) a few hours

11. In a few hours we shall go to Rome. 12. We are going to the city; they are going home. 13. As we have often admitted, you may not (are not permitted to) go from Rome to Athens (*lit.,* to go is not permitted to you). 14. Why did you leave home (go away from home) so quickly? 15. They are coming to Rome in order to go to Athens with my brother. 16. Do not go away from Rome. 17. When your brother had been killed at Rome, we kept urging you to return to Athens. 18. If he should go into the territory of the enemy at this time, he would perish in a few hours. 19. He said that he did not want to stay in that country of yours many days. 20. You said that you would return home from Athens in one hour. 21. I beg of you to return from the ship to the island in a short time. 22. In those days we were accustomed to be at Athens. 23. If they had injured his friends at Rome, he would have returned to Rome in a very short time. 24. Although my brother stayed at home, I nevertheless went away from home into new lands. 25. The Romans, if they wanted to say something bad, often used to say: "Go to the devil." 26. He is persuading them to study Latin.

27. (11) **hōrīs** = abl.: time within which; **Rōmam** = acc.: place to which; (12) **domum** = acc.: place to which; (13) **Rōmā** = abl.: place from; **Athēnās** = acc.: place to; **īre** = pres. infin.: subject of **licet**; (14) **domō** = abl.: place from; (15) **Rōmam** = acc.: place to; (18) **frātre** = abl.: abl. abs.; (18) **tempore** = abl.: time when; **eat** = pres. subjunct.: fut. less vivid; **hōrīs** = abl.: time within; (19) **velle** = pres. infin.: ind. state.; **diēs** = acc.: time how long; (20) **domum** = acc.: place to; **Athēnīs** = abl.: place from; **hōrā** = abl.: time within; **reditūrum esse** = fut. infin.: ind. state.; (21) **tempore** = abl. time within; **redeās** = pres. subjunct.: jussive noun clause; (22) **diēbus** = abl.: time when; **Athēnīs** = locative: place where; (23) **amīcīs** = dat.: special verbs; **Rōmae** = locative: place where; **redīsset** = pluperf. subjunct.: past contrary to fact condit.; (24) **domī** =

locative: place where; **terrās** = acc.: place to; **domō** = abl.: place from; (26) **studeant** = pres. subjunct.: jussive noun clause.

## KEY FOR Capvt XXXVIII
1. A relative clause with the indicative tells a *fact* about the antecedent.
2. A relative clause with the subjunctive tells a *characteristic* of the antecedent, indicates it to be a person or thing of such a sort. See p. 323.
3. See p. 324.
4. See p. 324.

5. My friend who defended the consul was himself a very famous man. 6. But there was no one who would defend that base fellow. 7. What is there which men fear more than a tyrant? 8. Who is there who would hesitate between liberty and the command of a tyrant? 9. At ancient Rome there were those who loved money more than the state. 10. Let that evil man depart from his country—he who has endured the hatred of all good citizens. 11. Catiline, who had made such a great plot against the state, was driven from the city by Cicero. 12. What life can be pleasant for that leader as he goes off into exile? 13. Who is there who would be able to bear such pain? 14. If a person is not agreeable and good, he will not live a truly happy life, it seems to me. 15. They will not trust a consul who would do base deeds. 16. Do not trust a man who is harsh to his friends. 17. Cicero was a consul who would place the state before his own safety. 18. They knew why we wanted to follow such a brave consul. 19. I know nothing which could be easier for me. 20. I am seeking a leader whom all men would praise. 21. They were going to Rome to ask for freedom. 22. The Romans, who had captured ten Greek republics with their own armies, were themselves—amazing to say—taken captive by the Greek arts! 23. For the ancient men there was nothing which was better than courage and wisdom. 24. Nothing is to be feared which cannot injure the soul.

25. The **quī . . . dēfendit** states a fact about the **amīcus**; it does not describe his character. The subjunctive clause in #6 tells what kind of person the imagined **nēmō** might be.
26. Syntax: (7) **metuat** = pres. subjunct.: characteristic; (8) **dubitet** = pres. subjunct.: characteristic; (9) **Rōmae** = loc.: place where; **amārent** = impf. subjunct.: characteristic; (10) **abeat** = pres. subjunct.: jussive; **passus est** = perf. indic. rel. clause of fact; (11) **fēcerat** = pluperf. indic.: rel. clause of fact; (12) **ducī** = dat.: reference; **potest** = pres. indic.: main verb in a direct question; (13) **possit** = pres. subjunct.: characteristic; (14) **erit** = fut. indic.: simple fut. condit.; **mihi** = dat.: ref.; (15) **cōnsulī** = dat.: special verbs; (16) **amīcīs** = dat.: dat. with adjs.; (17) **salūtī** = dat.: compound verb; **antepōneret** = impf. subjunct.: characteristic; (18) **vellēmus** = impf. subjunct.: ind. quest.; (19) **mihi** = dat.: ref.; **possit** = pres. subjunct.: characteristic; (21) **rogātum** = acc. supine: purpose; (22) **cēperant** = pluperf. indic.: rel. clause of fact; **dictū** = abl. supine: respect; (23) **virīs** = dat.: ref.; (24) **animō** = dat.: special verbs; **possit** = pres. subjunct.: characteristic.

## KEY FOR Capvt XXXIX
1. (1) See p. 332 s.v. "The Gerund."
   (2) See p. 332.

(3) See p. 332.

(4) It is used as a noun is used, except not as a subject or direct object. See p. 332–33.

(5) The infinitive; see p. 332.

2.  (1) See p. 332 s.v. "The Gerundive."

(2) The gerund*ive* is an adjec*tive.*

(3) As an adjective it modifies a noun or pronoun and agrees with that noun or pronoun in gender, number, and case.

(4) The gerundive (e.g., **laudandus**, -a, -um) is declined as **magnus**, -a, -um is. See p. 333.

(5) Since the gerund has only the endings -ī, -ō, -um, -ō, any feminine or any plural ending on an -**nd**- base is bound to indicate a gerundive; and also, if an -**nd**- form agrees with a noun as an adjectival modifier, it must be a gerundive.

3.  (1) The Latin gerund is normally translated by the English gerund in -*ing* with any attending noun constructions or adverbial modifiers.

(2) The gerundive is to be translated as if it were a gerund with an object and any adverbial modifiers. In other words, both the gerund and the gerundive are to be translated in the same way. See p. 333–34.

(3) (A) We learn by reading with care.

(B) We learn by reading books with care.

4. We learn by experiencing. 5. They came to learn (for learning). 6. He gave (devoted) himself to learning. 7. They came to your school to learn (for the sake of learning). 8. The boy went to the school desirous of learning (eager to learn). 9. The fear of dying kept terrifying him. 10. The hope of living after death encourages many people. 11. By thinking (= by using his head) he overcame them.

12. He devoted (gave) himself—(1) to seeking glory. (2) to waging war. (3) to making money. (4) to getting power. (5) to destroying states. (6) to following this leader. (7) to saving his country. (8) to seeking peace. (9) to attacking wrongs. (10) to writing books. (11) to reading books. (12) to learning philosophy. (13) to learning Latin literature. (14) to understanding the truth. (15) to seeking wisdom. (16) to helping human beings.

13. He came to Rome—(1) to undertake this work. (2) to see the Roman games. (3) to see the old buildings. (4) to seek peace. (5) for the sake of undertaking this work (to undertake . . .). (6) for the sake of learning philosophy (to learn . . .). (7) for the sake of reading new books (to read . . .). (8) to see the games.

14. He wrote a book—(1) about enduring pain. (2) about overcoming fear. (3) about living a good life. (4) about managing the state. (5) about waging war. (6) about defending liberty. (7) about conquering the enemy. (8) about giving gifts.

15. We become wiser—(1) by reading Latin literature. (2) by learning philosophy. (3) by experiencing life. (4) by conquering fear. (5) by following truth.

16. We help our very selves—(1) by always reading good books. (2) by freeing unfortunate men from fear. (3) by offering aid. (4) by helping others.

17. He consumed much time—(1) in thinking (speaking, running). (2) in doing these tasks. (3) in finding the way. (4) in preparing an army. (5) in preparing supplies (troops).

18. He had time for writing this book only.

**KEY FOR Capvt XL**

1. See p. 341.
2. Positive fear clauses are introduced by **nē**; negative clauses by **ut.**
3. The noun must itself be modified by an adjective.

4. I greatly fear that the general may not send us enough help. 5. She was a woman of the greatest courage and loyalty and in fact very like her mother. 6. Do not fear that all the men and women of great courage will depart from Rome. 7. This is, indeed, easy to say but difficult to do! 8. They came home to please their parents. 9. You do wish to hear something good, don't you? 10. Do you wish to have much wisdom? Study Latin! 11. He ordered the three soldiers to go to Rome to seek peace. 12. You do not hesitate to say this, do you, my friend? 13. You urge me to be of great courage and to have hope of safety, but I fear that I may be too weak. 14. For my part I place wealth ahead of wisdom. For I do not think that human beings can find a happy life without a great deal of money. 15. However, very many rich men experience much fear. 16. Poor men are often happier and have less fear. 17. Money itself is not bad; but the things of the mind and the soul offer more help for living happily. 18. Nine of the leaders urged us to supply more aid. 19. When five of the guards had been killed, my father fled into that free land with two of his sons and with a large number of friends. 20. Never will he have enough leisure; yet some leisure is better than nothing. 21. In our times we all have too much of fear and too little of hope. 22. Great faith and courage must be found by all men.

# APPENDIX

SOME ETYMOLOGICAL AIDS

    Two Rules of Phonetic Change

    Prefixes

    Suffixes

SUPPLEMENTARY SYNTAX

SVMMĀRIVM FŌRMĀRVM

# SOME ETYMOLOGICAL AIDS

## TWO RULES OF PHONETIC CHANGE

"Phonetic" derives from Greek **phōnḗ**, *sound, voice, speech* (cf. phonograph, phonology, symphony, telephone). Consequently, phonetic change means a change which occurs in original speech sounds for one reason or another. Of the many instances of this in Latin, the following two rules of phonetic change are probably the most important ones for the beginner.

A. *Vowel weakening* usually occurs in the medial syllables of compounds according to the following outline.

    1. ă > ĭ before a single consonant and before **ng**.

       ă > ĕ before two consonants.

       căpiō, căptum: ac-cĭpiō, ac-cĕptum

       făciō, făctum: per-fĭciō, per-fĕctum

       făcilis: dif-fĭcilis

       cădō, cāsum: oc-cĭdō, oc-cāsum (Note that long ā does not change.)

       tăngō, tăctum: con-tĭngō, con-tăctum

2. ĕ > ĭ before a single consonant.

    tĕneō: con-tĭneō (*but* contentum)

    prĕmō: com-prĭmō (*but* compressum)

3. **ae > ī.**

    quaerō, quaesītum: re-quīrō, re-quīsītum

    laedō, laesum: col-līdō, col-līsum

    caedō, caesum: in-cīdō, in-cīsum; oc-cīdō, oc-cīsum

    aestimō: ex-īstimō

4. **au > ū.**

    claudō: in-clūdō, ex-clūdō

    causor: ex-cūsō

B. *Assimilation* of the final consonant of a prefix to the initial consonant of the base word commonly occurs.

| | |
|---|---|
| ad-capiō > ac-cipiō | in-mortālis > im-mortālis |
| dis-facilis > dif-ficilis | in-ruō > ir-ruō |

## PREFIXES

Listed here are important prefixes helpful in the analysis of both Latin words and English derivatives. The Latin prefixes have passed over into English unchanged except where indicated. Incidentally, most Latin prefixes were also used by the Romans as prepositions; but the few labeled "inseparable" appear only as prefixes.

**ā-, ab-,** *away, from.*

    **ā-vocō,** *call away* (avocation)

    **ā-vertō,** *turn away* (avert)

    **ā-mittō,** *send away, let go, lose*

    **ab-sum,** *be away* (absent)

    **ab-eō,** *go away*

    **ab-dūcō,** *lead away* (abduct)

**ad-** (by assimilation **ac-, af-, ag-, al-, an-, ap-, ar-, as-, at-**), *to, towards, in addition.*

    **ad-vocō,** *call to, call* (advocate)

    **ad-dūcō,** *lead to* (adduce)

    **ad-mittō,** *send to, admit*

    **ac-cēdō,** *go to, approach* (accede)

    **ac-cipiō (ad-capiō),** *get, accept*

    **ap-pōnō,** *put to* (apposition)

    **as-sentiō,** *feel towards, agree to, assent*

**ante-,** *before.*

    **ante-pōnō,** *put before, prefer*

    **ante-cēdō,** *go before, precede, excel* (antecedent)

**circum-,** *around.*

    **circum-dūcō,** *lead around*

    **circum-veniō,** *come around, surround* (circumvent)

    **circum-stō,** *stand around* (circumstance)

com- (com = cum; also appears as con-, cor-, col-, co-), *with, together;* intensive force: *completely, very, greatly, deeply, forcibly.*

    con-vocō, *call together* (convoke)

    con-dūcō, *lead together* (conduct)

    com-pōnō, *put together, compose* (component)

    com-mittō, *send together, bring together, entrust* (commit)

    cōn-sentiō, *feel together, agree* (consent)

    cō-gō (co-agō), *drive together, force* (cogent)

    com-pleō, *fill completely, fill up* (complete)

    cōn-servō, *save completely, preserve* (conserve)

    con-cēdō, *go completely, go away, yield, grant* (concede)

    con-tendō, *stretch greatly, strive, hurry* (contend)

    col-laudō, *praise greatly* or *highly*

    cor-rōborō, *strengthen greatly* (corroborate)

contrā-, *against, opposite.* (Not common as a prefix in Latin but fairly common in English, especially in the form *counter-.*)

    contrā-dicō, *speak against* or *opposite, oppose, rely* (contradict)

    contrā-veniō (late Latin), *come against, oppose* (contravene)

dē-, *down, away, aside, out, off;* intensive force: *utterly, completely.*

    dē-dūcō, *lead down* or *away, drawn down* (deduce, deduct)

    dē-pōnō, *put aside, lay aside, entrust* (deponent, deposit)

    dē-mittō, *send down, throw down, let fall* (demit)

    dē-veniō, *come from, arrive at, reach*

    dē-vocō, *call away* or *off*

    dē-cēdō, *go away* (decease)

    dē-mēns, *out of one's mind, demented*

    dē-certō, *fight it out, fight to the finish*

dis- (dif-, dī-; inseparable), *apart, away, not.*

    dis-pōnō, *put apart in different places, arrange* (disposition)

    dis-cēdō, *go away, depart*

    dī-mittō, *send away in different directions, let go* (dismiss)

    dif-ferō, dī-lātus, *bear apart, scatter, put off, differ* (different, dilate)

    dis-similis, *not similar, unlike, dissimilar*

    dif-ficilis, *not easy, difficult*

ē-, ex- (ef-), *from out, forth;* intensive force: *exceedingly, up.*

    ē-dūcō, *lead out* (educe)

    ex-cēdō, *go out, from, away; go beyond* (exceed)

    ē-mittō, *send out, forth* (emit)

    ē-vocō, *call out, forth* (evoke)

    ex-pōnō, *put out, set forth, explain* (exponent, exposition)

    ē-veniō, *come out, forth; turn out, happen* (event)

    ef-ficiō, (ex-faciō), *produce, accomplish, perform* (efficient, effect)

    ex-pleō, *fill up, complete*

    ex-asperō, *roughen exceedingly, irritate* (exasperate)

**in-** (**im-, il-, ir-**; sometimes *en-* or *em-* in Eng.), *in, into, on, upon, against.* (Also see **in-** below.)

　**in-vocō,** *call in, call upon* (invoke)
　**in-dūcō,** *lead in* or *into, introduce, impel* (induce)
　**im-mittō,** *send into, send against, let loose against*
　**im-pōnō,** *put in, lay upon* (impose)
　**in-veniō,** *come upon, find* (invent)
　**in-clūdō,** *shut in, shut* (include, enclose)
　**in-vādō,** *go into, move against* (invade)
　**ir-ruō,** *rush into* or *upon*
　**il-līdō** (**in-laedō**), *strike* or *dash against*
　**in-genium** (**in** + **gen-**, from **gignō,** *beget, give birth to*), *inborn nature, natural capacity, talent, character* (engine, ingenious)

**in-** (**im-, il-, ir-**; inseparable prefix; cognate with Eng. *un-*), *not, un-.*

　**in-certus,** *not certain, uncertain*
　**in-iūstus,** *not just, unjust* (*cf.* injustice)
　**īn-fīnītus,** *not limited, unlimited* (infinite)
　**īn-firmus,** *not firm, weak* (infirm)
　**im-mortālis,** *not mortal, deathless* (immortal)
　**il-litterātus,** *unlearned, ignorant* (illiterate)
　**ir-revocābilis,** *not-call-back-able, unalterable* (irrevocable)

**inter-,** *between, among.*

　**inter-veniō,** *come between; interrupt* (intervene)
　**inter-cēdō,** *go between* (intercede)
　**inter-mittō,** *place between, leave off* (intermittent)
　**inter-pōnō,** *put between, bring forward* (interpose)
　**inter-rēgnum,** *period between two reigns* (interregnum)

**intrō-,** *within, in.* (Also used as adv.)

　**intrō-dūcō,** *lead in* (introduce)
　**intrō-mittō,** *send in*
　**intrō-spiciō,** *look within* (introspect)

**ob-** (**oc-, of-, op-**), *towards, to, opposite, against, over.*

　**ob-dūcō,** *lead toward* or *against*
　**ob-veniō,** *come opposite, meet*
　**oc-currō,** *run to meet, meet* (occur)
　**of-ferō,** *bear towards, furnish* (offer)
　**op-pōnō,** *put opposite, set against, oppose* (opposition)

**per-** (**pel-**), *through;* intensive force: *thoroughly, very, completely.*

　**per-dūcō,** *lead through* or *along*
　**per-veniō,** *come through to, arrive at, reach*
　**per-ferō,** *carry through, bear thoroughly, endure*
　**per-mittō,** *let go through, entrust, allow* (permit)
　**per-ficiō** (**-faciō**), *do thoroughly, accomplish, finish* (perfect)

**per-facilis,** *very easy*
**per-paucus,** *very small*
**pel-lūcidus,** *shining through, transparent*

**post-,** *after.*

**post-pōnō,** *put after, esteem less, disregard* (postpone)
**post-ferō,** *put after, esteem less, disregard* (postpone)
**post-scrībō,** *write after, add* (postscript)

**prae-,** *before, in front, forth;* intensive force: *very.* (In Eng. also spelled *pre-.*)

**prae-moneō,** *warn before, forewarn* (premonition)
**prae-cēdō,** *go before, excel* (precede)
**prae-pōnō,** *put before, place in command of, prefer* (preposition)
**prae-mittō,** *send before* or *forth, set before* (premise)
**prae-scrībō,** *write before, order* (prescribe, prescription)
**prae-ferō,** *bear before, set before, prefer*
**prae-clārus,** *very noble, very famous, excellent*

**prō-,** *before, in front, forth, out, away, instead of, for.* (Sometimes *pur-* in Eng.)

**prō-vocō,** *call forth* or *out, challenge, excite* (provoke)
**prō-videō,** *see ahead, foresee, care for* (provide, provision, purvey)
**prō-dūcō,** *lead before* or *out, bring forth, prolong* (produce)
**prō-cēdō,** *go forward, advance* (proceed)
**prō-pōnō,** *put in front, set forth, declare* (proponent, purpose)
**prō-mittō,** *send forth, assure* (promise)
**prō-cōnsul,** *one who served in place of a consul* (proconsul)

**re- (red-;** inseparable), *back again.*

**re-vocō,** *call back, recall* (revoke)
**re-dūcō,** *lead back* (reduce)
**re-cēdō,** *go back, retire* (recede)
**re-pōnō,** *put back, replace, restore* (repository)
**re-mittō,** *send back, give up* (remit)
**red-dō,** *give back, restore, return*
**red-eō,** *go back, return*

**sē-** (inseparable), *apart, aside, without.*

**sē-dūcō,** *lead aside, separate* (seduce)
**sē-cēdō,** *go apart, withdraw, retire* (secede)
**sē-pōnō,** *put aside, select*
**sē-moveō,** *move aside, separate*
**sē-cūrus,** *without care, untroubled, serene* (secure)

**sub- (suc-, suf-, sug-, sup-, sur-, sus-),** *under, up* (*from beneath*); *rather, somewhat, a little, secretly.*

**sub-dūcō,** *draw from under, withdraw secretly*
**suc-cēdō,** *go under, go up, approach, prosper* (succeed)
**sup-pōnō,** *put under; substitute* (supposition, supposititious)
**sub-veniō,** *come under, help* (subvene, subvention)
**sus-tineō (-teneō),** *hold up, support, endure* (sustain)

super- (also *sur-* in Eng.), *over, above.*

> **super-pōnō,** *place over* or *upon, set over* (superposition)
> **super-sedeō,** *sit above* or *upon, be superior to, be above, refrain from, desist* (supersede)
> **super-sum,** *be over and above, be left, survive*
> **superō,** *be above, surpass, conquer* (insuperable)
> **superbus,** *above others, haughty, proud* (superb)
> **super-vīvō,** *survive*
> **super-ficiēs,** *surface*

trāns- (trā-), *across, over.*

> **trāns-mittō,** *send across, cross over* (transmit)
> **trā-dūcō,** *lead across* (traduce)
> **trāns-eō,** *go across* (transition)
> **trā-dō,** *give over, surrender, hand down* (tradition)

## SUFFIXES

Of the very numerous Latin suffixes only a few of the more important ones are listed here with their English equivalents.

1. Suffix denoting the *agent,* the *doer,* the *one who* (**-tor** or **-sor,** m.; **-trīx,** f.).

-tor *or* -sor (cf. *Eng.* -er)

> **victor** (**vincō, victum,** *conquer*), *conqueror, victor*
> **scrīptor** (**scrībō, scrīptum,** *write*), *writer*
> **lēctor, lēctrīx** (**legō, lēctum,** *read*), *reader*
> **ōrātor** (**ōrō, ōrātum,** [*speak*], *plead*), *speaker, orator*
> **repertor, repertrīx** (**reperiō, repertum,** *discover*), *discoverer*
> **auctor** (**augeō, auctum,** *increase*), *increaser, author*
> **līberātor** (**līberō, līberātum,** *free*), *liberator*
> **tōnsor** (**tondeō, tōnsum,** *shave, clip*), *barber*
> **amātor** (**amō, amātum,** *love*), *lover*

These nouns have the same base as that of the perfect participle.

2. Suffixes denoting *action* or *result of action* (**-or, -ium, -tiō**).

-or (Eng. *-or*)

> **amor** (**amō,** *love*), *love, amour*
> **timor** (**timeō,** *fear*), *fear*
> **dolor** (**doleō,** *suffer pain*), *pain, suffering, grief*
> **error** (**errō,** *go astray, err*), *error*
> **terror** (**terreō,** *frighten, terrify*), *fright, terror*

-ium (Eng. *-y; -ce* when **-ium** is preceded by **c** or **t**)

> **studium** (**studeō,** *be eager*), *eagerness, study*
> **colloquium** (**colloquor,** *talk with*), *talk, conference, colloquy*
> **imperium** (**imperō,** *command*), *command, power*
> **odium** (**ōdī,** *hate*), *hate*

aedificium (aedificō, *build*) *building, edifice*
silentium (silēns, silentis, *silent*), *silence*

**-tiō, -tiōnis,** *or* **-siō, -siōnis** (Eng. *-tion* or *-sion*)

admonitiō (admoneō, admonitum, *admonish*) *admonition*
ratiō (reor, ratum, *reckon, think*), *reckoning, plan, reason* (*ration*)
ōrātiō (ōrō, ōrātum, [*speak*], *plead*), *oration*
nātiō (nāscor, nātum, *be born*), *birth, nation*
occāsiō (occidō, occāsum, *fall down*) *a befalling, occasion, opportunity*

3. Suffixes denoting *quality, state,* or *condition* (**-ia, -tia, -tās, -tūdō**).

**-ia** (Eng. *-y*)

miseria (miser, *miserable*), *misery*
īnsānia (īnsānus, *insane*), *insanity*
victōria (victor, *victor*), *victory*
invidia (invidus, *envious*), *envy*
iniūria (iniūrus, *wrong, unjust*), *injustice, injury*

**-tia** (Eng. *-ce*)

amīcitia (amīcus, *friendly*), *friendship*
sapientia (sapiēns, *wise*), *wisdom, sapience*
scientia (sciēns, *knowing*), *knowledge, science*
iūstitia (iūstus, *just*), *justice*
dīligentia (dīligēns, *diligent*), *diligence*

**-tās, -tātis** (Eng. *-ty*)

lībertās (liber, *free*), *freedom, liberty*
vēritās (vērus, *true*), *truth, verity*
paupertās (pauper, *poor*), *poverty*
cupiditās (cupidus, *desirous, greedy*), *greed, cupidity*
gravitās (gravis, *heavy, grave*), *weight, seriousness, gravity*
celeritās (celer, *swift*), *swiftness, celerity*

**-tūdō, -tūdinis** (Eng. *-tude*)

multitūdō (multus, *much, many*), *multitude*
magnitūdō (magnus, *large, great*), *magnitude*
pulchritūdō (pulcher, *beautiful*), *beauty, pulchritude*
sōlitūdō (sōlus, *alone*), *solitude*
sollicitūdō (sollicitus, *agitated, solicitous*), *solicitude*

4. Adjectival suffix meaning *full of* (**-ōsus**).

**-ōsus, -ōsa, -ōsum** (Eng. *-ous* or *-ose*)

studiōsus (studium, *zeal*), *full of zeal, eager* (*studious*)
imperiōsus (imperium, *command*), *full of command, imperious*
perīculōsus (perīculum, *danger*), *full of danger, dangerous*
vitiōsus (vitium, *fault, vice*), *faulty, vicious*
verbōsus (verbum, *word*), *wordy, verbose*

5.  Adjectival suffix meaning *able to be, worthy to be;* sometimes *able to* (**-bilis**).

**-bilis, -bile** (Eng. *-able, -ible, -ble*)

  **laudābilis** (**laudō,** *praise*), *worthy to be praised, laudable*
  **amābilis** (**amō,** *love*), *worthy to be loved, lovable, amiable*
  **incrēdibilis** (**crēdō,** *believe*), *not worthy to be believed, incredible*
  **mōbilis** (**moveō,** *move*), *able to be moved, movable, mobile*
  **inexpugnābilis** (**expugnō,** *conquer*), *unconquerable*
  **stabilis** (**stō,** *stand*), *able to stand, stable*

6.  Adjectival suffixes denoting *pertaining to* (**-ālis** or **-āris, -ānus, -icus**).

**-ālis, -āle,** *or* **-āris, -āre** (Eng. *-al* or *-ar*)

  **mortālis** (**mors,** *death*), *pertaining to death, mortal*
  **vītālis** (**vīta,** *life*), *pertaining to life, vital*
  **fātālis** (**fātum,** *fate*), *fatal*
  **populāris** (**populus,** *people*), *popular*
  **vulgāris** (**vulgus,** *the common people*), *common, vulgar*

**-ānus, -āna, -ānum** (Eng. *-an* or *-ane*)

  **Rōmānus** (**Rōma,** *Rome*), *pertaining to Rome, Roman*
  **hūmānus** (**homō,** *man*), *pertaining to man, human, humane*
  **urbānus** (**urbs,** *city*), *urban, urbane*
  **mundānus** (**mundus,** *world*), *worldly, mundane*

**-icus, -ica, -icum** (Eng. *-ic*)

  **domesticus** (**domus,** *house*), *pertaining to the house, domestic*
  **pūblicus** (**populus,** *people*), *pertaining to the people, public*
  **rūsticus** (**rūs,** *country*), *rustic*
  **cīvicus** (**cīvis,** *citizen*), *civic*
  **classicus** (**classis,** *class*), *pertaining to the classes, of the highest class; classic*

# SUPPLEMENTARY SYNTAX

The following constructions are listed for the benefit of students who plan to continue their study of Latin beyond the introductory year. A number of these constructions have already been encountered here and there in the 40 formal chapters of this book. However, although often these can be easily translated without benefit of syntactical labels, it seems wise to catalog them here along with the more difficult items.

## GENITIVE OF MATERIAL

The genitive may indicate the material of which a thing is made.

  pōculum **aurī,** *a goblet of gold*
  Numerus **hostium** crēscit, *the number of the enemy is increasing.*

Mōns **aquae** secūtus est et tempestās trēs nāvēs cīnxit aggere **harēnae,** *a mountain of water followed and the storm surrounded three ships with a mound of sand.*

## OBJECTIVE GENITIVE

The objective genitive depends on a noun of verbal meaning and is used as the object of the verbal idea. It is sometimes translated by *for.*

amor **laudis,** *love of praise* (= amat laudem, *he loves praise.*)
cupiditās **pecūniae,** *greed for money* (= cupit pecūniam, *he longs for money.*)
metus **mortis,** *fear of death* (= metuit mortem, *he fears death.*)
spēs **salūtis,** *hope for safety* (= spērat salūtem, *he hopes for safety.*)
Fēmina erat dux **factī,** *a woman was the leader of the enterprise* (= dūxit factum.)
laudātor **temporis** āctī, *a praiser of the past* (= laudat tempus āctum.)

## DATIVE OF PURPOSE

The dative may express the purpose for which a person or thing serves. A dative of reference (Capvt XXXVIII) often appears in conjunction with the dative of purpose, and this combination is called the "double dative" construction.

Petītiō mea **tibi** (dat. of ref.) summae **cūrae** (dat. of purp.) est, *my candidacy is ( for) the greatest concern to you.*
Ea rēs **mihi** (ref.) summae **voluptātī** (purp.) erat, *that matter was for the greatest pleasure to me = gave me the greatest pleasure.*
Illī **nōbīs** (ref.) **auxiliō** (purp.) vēnērunt, *they came as an aid to us.*
Hōs librōs **dōnō** (purp.) mīsit, *he sent these books as a gift.*
Hoc mē iuvat et **mihi** (ref.) **mellī** (purp.) est, *this gratifies me and is (as) honey to me.*
Optant locum **tēctō** (purp.), *they desire a place for a roof (building).*

## DATIVE OF POSSESSION

The dative can be used with **sum** to express the idea of possession.

Liber est **mihi,** *a book is to me = I have a book.*
    (Contrast: liber est **meus,** *the book is mine.*)
Illī maior turba clientium est, *that man has a greater throng of retainers.*
Sunt **tibi** animus et mōrēs, *you have a soul and character.*
Haec **eīs** semper erunt, *they will always have these things.*
Prūdentia est illī **puellae,** *that girl has prudence.*
Ō virgō, nōn **tibi** est vultus mortālis, *O maiden, you do not have the face of a mortal.*
Sī umquam **mihi** fīlius erit . . . , *if I ever have a son. . . .*

## ABLATIVE OF RESPECT OR SPECIFICATION

The ablative may be used to tell in what specific respect a verb or an adjective holds true.

Hī omnēs **linguā, īnstitūtīs, lēgibus** inter sē differunt, *these all differ from one another in language, customs, and laws.*

Illī **virtūte** omnibus (dat.) praestābant, *those men used to excel all in courage.*

Id genus erat intractābile **bellō,** *that race was unmanageable in war.*

Quis est praestantior aut **nōbilitāte** aut **probitāte** aut **studiō** optimārum artium?
*Who is more outstanding in nobility or integrity or the pursuit of the finest arts?*

Ager bene cultus est ūber ūsū et ōrnātus **speciē,** *a field well cultivated is rich in usefulness and beautiful in appearance.*

Asia omnibus terrīs (dat.) antecellit **ūbertāte** agrōrum et **varietāte** frūctuum et **multitūdine** eārum quae exportantur, *Asia excels all lands in richness of fields and variety of fruits and large number of those things which are exported.*

## ABLATIVE OF CAUSE

The ablative can be used to indicate a cause or reason.

Miser **timōre** dēlīrat, *the wretched man is insane with fear.*

Corpora eōrum **metū** dēbilia sunt, *their bodies are weak from fear.*

Aper **dentibus** timētur, *the boar is feared because of his teeth.*

Nihil arduum mortālibus est; caelum ipsum **stultitiā** petimus, *nothing is (too) arduous for mortals; we seek the sky itself in our folly.*

**Odiō** tyrannī in exsilium fūgit, *because of his hatred of the tyrant he fled into exile.*

Bonī **amōre** virtūtis peccāre ōdērunt, *good men because of their love of virtue hate to sin.*

## ABLATIVE OF DEGREE OF DIFFERENCE

With comparatives and adverbs suggesting comparison the ablative can be used to indicate the degree of difference in the comparison.

**Tantō** melius, *the better by so much = so much the better.*

Senex nōn facit ea quae iuvenis, at **multō** maiōra et meliōra facit, *an old man does not do the things which a young man does, but he does much greater and better things (greater by much).*

**Multō** ācrius iam vigilābō, *I shall now watch much more keenly.*

Rōmam **paucīs** post **diēbus** vēnistī, *you came to Rome a few days afterwards (afterwards by a few days).*

Aberat ab eā urbe **tribus mīlibus** passuum, *he was three miles from that city (was away by three miles).*

Bonae Athēnae **paulō** plūs artis adiēcērunt, *good Athens added a little more skill (more by a little).*

## SUBORDINATE CLAUSES IN INDIRECT STATEMENT

In indirect statement, subordinate clauses regularly have verbs in the subjunctive mood, even though they had the indicative in the direct form.

Lēgit librōs quōs mīserās, *he read the books which you had sent.*
Dīxit sē lēgisse librōs quōs **mīsissēs,** *he said that he had read the books which you had sent.*

⎰ Eī malī quī in urbe manent īnfirmī erunt sine duce, *those evil men who remain*
⎨ *in the city will be weak without their leader.*
⎪ Putō eōs malōs quī in urbe **maneant** īnfirmōs futūrōs esse sine duce, *I think that*
⎩ *those evil men who remain in the city will be weak without their leader.*

⎰ Sī id crēdet, errābit. *If he believes this, he will be wrong.*
⎱ Dīcō sī id **crēdat** eum errātūrum esse. *I say that if he believes this he will be wrong.*

## OBJECTIVE INFINITIVE

The complementary infinitive has no subject accusative (see Capvt VI). However, when an infinitive with subject accusative is used as the object of a verb, it is called an objective infinitive.

Volunt venīre, *they wish to come.* (complem. infin.)
Iussit eōs venīre, *he ordered them to come.* (obj. infin.)
Nōn possum loquī, *I cannot speak.* (complem. infin.)
Nōn patitur mē loquī, *he does not permit me to speak.* (obj. infin.)
Nōn audet īre, *he does not dare to go.* (complem. infin.)
Coēgērunt eum īre, *they forced him to go.* (obj. infin.)

# SVMMĀRIVM FŌRMĀRVM

## NOUNS—DECLENSIONS

| First | Second | | | | Third | |
|-------|--------|--|--|--|-------|--|
| porta, -ae | amīcus, -ī | puer, -ī | ager, -grī | dōnum, -ī | rēx, rēgis | corpus, -oris |
| f., *gate* | m., *friend* | m., *boy* | m., *field* | n., *gift* | m., *king* | n., *body* |
| **Sg.** | | | | | | |
| *N.* | port-a | amīc-us[1] | puer | ager | dōn-um | rēx | corpus |
| *G.* | port-ae | amīc-ī | puer-ī | agr-ī | dōn-ī | rēg-is | corpor-is |
| *D.* | port-ae | amīc-ō | puer-ō | agr-ō | dōn-ō | rēg-ī | corpor-ī |
| *A.* | port-am | amīc-um | puer-um | agr-um | dōn-um | rēg-em | corpus |
| *Ab.* | port-ā | amīc-ō | puer-ō | agr-ō | dōn-ō | rēg-e | corpor-e |
| **Pl.** | | | | | | |
| *N.* | port-ae | amīc-ī | puer-ī | agr-ī | dōn-a | rēg-ēs | corpor-a |
| *G.* | port-ārum | amīc-ōrum | puer-ōrum | agr-ōrum | dōn-ōrum | rēg-um | corpor-um |
| *D.* | port-īs | amīc-īs | puer-īs | agr-īs | dōn-īs | rēg-ibus | corpor-ibus |
| *A.* | port-ās | amīc-ōs | puer-ōs | agr-ōs | dōn-a | rēg-ēs | corpor-a |
| *Ab.* | port-īs | amīc-īs | puer-īs | agr-īs | dōn-īs | rēg-ibus | corpor-ibus |

| Third (I-Stems) | | | Fourth | | Fifth |
|-----------------|--|--|--------|--|-------|
| cīvis, -is | urbs, -is | mare, -is | frūctus, -ūs | cornū, -ūs | diēs, -ēī |
| m., *citizen* | f., *city* | n., *sea* | m., *fruit* | n., *horn* | m., *day* |
| **Sg.** | | | | | |
| *N.* | cīv-is | urb-s | mar-e | frūct-us | corn-ū | di-ēs |
| *G.* | cīv-is | urb-is | mar-is | frūct-ūs | corn-ūs | di-ēī |
| *D.* | cīv-ī | urb-ī | mar-ī | frūct-uī | corn-ū | di-ēī |
| *A.* | cīv-em | urb-em | mar-e | frūct-um | corn-ū | di-em |
| *Ab.* | cīv-e | urb-e | mar-ī | frūct-ū | corn-ū | di-ē |
| **Pl.** | | | | | |
| *N.* | cīv-ēs | urb-ēs | mar-ia | frūct-ūs | corn-ua | di-ēs |
| *G.* | cīv-ium | urb-ium | mar-ium | frūct-uum | corn-uum | di-ērum |
| *D.* | cīv-ibus | urb-ibus | mar-ibus | frūct-ibus | corn-ibus | di-ēbus |
| *A.* | cīv-ēs | urb-ēs | mar-ia | frūct-ūs | corn-ua | di-ēs |
| *Ab.* | cīv-ibus | urb-ibus | mar-ibus | frūct-ibus | corn-ibus | di-ēbus |

*Vīs* is irregular: Sg., N., vīs, G. (vīs), D. (vī), A. vim. Ab. vī; Pl., N. vīrēs, G. vīrium, D. vīribus, A. vīrēs, Ab. vīribus.

[1]The vocative singular of nouns like **amīcus** and of masculine adjectives like **magnus** ends in -e. The vocative singular of fīlius and of names in -**ius** ends in a single -ī (**fīlī, Vergilī**); the vocative singular of the masculine adjective **meus** is **mī**; the vocative singular of masculine adjectives in -**ius** ends in -**ie** (**ēgregius; ēgregie**). Otherwise, the vocative has the same form as the nominative in all declensions.

# ADJECTIVES—DECLENSIONS

## First and Second Declensions

| | Adjs. in -us, -a, -um | | | Adjs. in -er, -era, -erum; -er, -ra, -rum | |
|---|---|---|---|---|---|
| M. | F. | N. | M. | F. | N. |
| | **Singular** | | | **Singular[2]** | |
| N. | magnus | magna | magnum | līber | lībera | līberum |
| G. | magnī | magnae | magnī | līberī | līberae | līberī |
| D. | magnō | magnae | magnō | līberō | līberae | līberō |
| A. | magnum | magnam | magnum | līberum | līberam | līberum |
| Ab. | magnō | magnā | magnō | līberō | līberā | līberō |
| | **Plural** | | | **Singular[2]** | |
| N. | magnī | magnae | magna | pulcher | pulchra | pulchrum |
| G. | magnōrum | magnārum | magnōrum | pulchrī | pulchrae | pulchrī |
| D. | magnīs | magnīs | magnīs | pulchrō | pulchrae | pulchrō |
| A. | magnōs | magnās | magna | pulchrum | pulchram | pulchrum |
| Ab. | magnīs | magnīs | magnīs | pulchrō | pulchrā | pulchrō |

## Third Declension

| Two endings | | Three endings | | One ending | | Comparatives[5] | |
|---|---|---|---|---|---|---|---|
| fortis, forte | | ācer, ācris, ācre | | potēns[3] | | fortior, fortius | |
| *brave* | | *keen, severe* | | *powerful* | | *braver* | |
| M. & F. | N. | M. & F. | N. | M. & F. | N. | M. & F. | N. |
| **Sg.** | | | | | | | |
| N. | fortis | forte | ācer ācris | ācre | potēns | potēns | fortior | fortius |
| G. | fortis | | ācris | | potentis | | fortiōris | |
| D. | fortī | | ācrī | | potentī | | fortiōrī | |
| A. | fortem | forte | ācrem | ācre | potentem | potēns | fortiōrem | fortius |
| Ab. | fortī | | ācrī | | potentī | | fortiōre | |
| **Pl.** | | | | | | | |
| N. | fortēs | fortia | ācrēs | ācria | potentēs | potentia | fortiōrēs | fortiōra |
| G. | fortium | | ācrium | | potentium | | fortiōrum | |
| D. | fortibus | | ācribus | | potentibus | | fortiōribus | |
| A. | fortēs[4] | fortia | ācrēs[4] | ācria | potentēs[4] | potentia | fortiōrēs | fortiōra |
| Ab. | fortibus | | ācribus | | potentibus | | fortiōribus | |

[2] The plural follows the pattern of the singular except that it has the plural endings.

[3] Present participles follow the declension of **potēns** except that they have -e in the ablative singular when used as genuine participles.

[4] For -īs (acc. pl.) see Capvt XVI.

[5] For irregular **plūs** see Capvt XXVII.

# PRONOUNS
## Demonstrative

hic, *this*        ille, *that*

| | M. | F. | N. | M. | F. | N. |
|---|---|---|---|---|---|---|
| **Sg.** | | | | | | |
| *N.* | hic | haec | hoc | ille | illa | illud |
| *G.* | huius | huius | huius | illīus | illīus | illīus |
| *D.* | huic | huic | huic | illī | illī | illī |
| *A.* | hunc | hanc | hoc | illum | illam | illud |
| *Ab.* | hōc | hāc | hōc | illō | illā | illō |
| **Pl.** | | | | | | |
| *N.* | hī | hae | haec | illī | illae | illa |
| *G.* | hōrum | hārum | hōrum | illōrum | illārum | illōrum |
| *D.* | hīs | hīs | hīs | illīs | illīs | illīs |
| *A.* | hōs | hās | haec | illōs | illās | illa |
| *Ab.* | hīs | hīs | hīs | illīs | illīs | illīs |

**Relative**        **Interrogative**[6]        **Intensive**

quī, *who, which*      quis, *who?*      ipse, *himself,* etc.

| | M. | F. | N. | M. & F. | N. | M. | F. | N. |
|---|---|---|---|---|---|---|---|---|
| **Sg.** | | | | | | | | |
| *N.* | quī | quae | quod | quis | quid | ipse | ipsa | ipsum |
| *G.* | cuius | cuius | cuius | cuius | cuius | ipsīus | ipsīus | ipsīus |
| *D.* | cui | cui | cui | cui | cui | ipsī | ipsī | ipsī |
| *A.* | quem | quam | quod | quem | quid | ipsum | ipsam | ipsum |
| *Ab.* | quō | quā | quō | quō | quō | ipsō | ipsā | ipsō |
| **Pl.** | | | | | | | | |
| *N.* | quī | quae | quae | (Plural is same as that of | | ipsī | ipsae | ipsa |
| *G.* | quōrum | quārum | quōrum | relative.) | | ipsōrum | ipsārum | ipsōrum |
| *D.* | quibus | quibus | quibus | | | ipsīs | ipsīs | ipsīs |
| *A.* | quōs | quās | quae | | | ipsōs | ipsās | ipsa |
| *Ab.* | quibus | quibus | quibus | | | ipsīs | ipsīs | ipsīs |

[6] The interrogative adjective **quī? quae? quod?** meaning *what? which? what kind of?* has the same declension as that of the relative pronoun.

# PRONOUNS

## Demonstrative

is, *this, that, he, she, it*                    idem, *the same*

|      | M.       | F.       | N.       | M.             | F.        | N.        |
|------|----------|----------|----------|----------------|-----------|-----------|
| **Sg.** |       |          |          |                |           |           |
| *N.* | is       | ea       | id       | īdem           | eadem     | idem      |
| *G.* | eius     | eius     | eius     | eiusdem        | eiusdem   | eiusdem   |
| *D.* | eī       | eī       | eī       | eīdem          | eīdem     | eīdem     |
| *A.* | eum      | eam      | id       | eundem         | eandem    | idem      |
| *Ab.* | eō      | eā       | eō       | eōdem          | eādem     | eōdem     |
| **Pl.** |       |          |          |                |           |           |
| *N.* | eī,iī    | eae      | ea       | eīdem, īdem    | eaedem    | eadem     |
| *G.* | eōrum    | eārum    | eōrum    | eōrundem       | eārundem  | eōrundem  |
| *D.* | eīs, iīs | eīs, iīs | eīs, iīs | eīsdem[7]      | eīsdem    | eīsdem    |
| *A.* | eōs      | eās      | ea       | eōsdem         | eāsdem    | eadem     |
| *Ab.* | eīs     | eīs      | eīs      | eīsdem         | eīsdem    | eīsdem    |

## Irregular Adjectives[8]                    Personal[9]                    Reflexive[9]

sōlus, *alone, only*                                             suī, *himself, herself, itself*

|      | M.       | F.       | N.       | ego, *I*            | tū, *you*           |                 |
|------|----------|----------|----------|---------------------|---------------------|-----------------|
| **Sg.** |       |          |          |                     |                     |                 |
| *N.* | sōlus    | sōla     | sōlum    | ego                 | tū                  | ———             |
| *G.* | sōlīus   | sōlīus   | sōlīus   | meī                 | tuī                 | suī[10]         |
| *D.* | sōlī     | sōlī     | sōlī     | mihi                | tibi                | sibi            |
| *A.* | sōlum    | sōlam    | sōlum    | mē                  | tē                  | sē[11]          |
| *Ab.* | sōlō    | sōlā     | sōlō     | mē                  | tē                  | sē[11]          |
| **Pl.** |       |          |          |                     |                     |                 |
| *N.* | sōlī     | sōlae    | sōla     | nōs                 | vōs                 | ———             |
| *G.* | sōlōrum  | sōlārum  | sōlōrum  | { nostrum / nostrī }| { vestrum / vestrī }| suī             |
| *D.* | sōlīs    | sōlīs    | sōlīs    | nōbīs               | vōbīs               | sibi            |
| *A.* | sōlōs    | sōlās    | sōla     | nōs                 | vōs                 | sē[11]          |
| *Ab.* | sōlīs   | sōlīs    | sōlīs    | nōbīs               | vōbīs               | sē[11]          |

---

[7] Also **īsdem.**

[8] Similarly **ūnus, tōtus, ūllus, nūllus, alius, alter, uter, neuter** (see Capvt IX).

[9] All forms of the pronouns of the first and second persons except the nom. sg. and the nom. pl. may also be used as reflexive pronouns.

[10] These forms are reflexive only. The nonreflexive forms of the third person are supplied by **is, ea, id** (see Capita XI, XIII).

[11] The form **sēsē** is also frequently found.

## COMPARISON OF ADJECTIVES

| Positive | Comparative | Superlative |
|---|---|---|
| **Regular** | | |
| longus, -a, -um (*long*) | longior, -ius | longissimus, -a, -um |
| fortis, -e (*brave*) | fortior, -ius | fortissimus, -a, -um |
| fēlīx, gen. fēlīcis, (*happy*) | fēlīcior, -ius | fēlīcissimus, -a, -um |
| sapiēns, gen. sapientis (*wise*) | sapientior, -ius | sapientissimus, -a, -um |
| facilis, -e (*easy*) | facilior, -ius | facillimus, -a, -um |
| līber, -era, -erum (*free*) | līberior, -ius | līberrimus, -a, -um |
| pulcher, -chra, -chrum (*beautiful*) | pulchrior, -ius | pulcherrimus, -a, -um |
| ācer, ācris, ācre (*keen*) | ācrior, -ius | ācerrimus, -a, -um |
| **Irregular** | | |
| bonus, -a, -um (*good*) | melior, -ius | optimus, -a, -um |
| magnus, -a, -um (*large*) | maior, -ius | maximus, -a, -um |
| malus, -a, -um (*bad*) | peior, -ius | pessimus, -a, -um |
| multus, -a, -um (*much*) | —, plūs | plūrimus, -a, -um |
| parvus, -a, -um (*small*) | minor, minus | minimus, -a, -um |
| (prae, prō) | prior, -ius (*former*) | prīmus, -a, -um |
| superus, -a, -um (*that above*) | superior, -ius | summus (suprēmus), -a, -um |

## COMPARISON OF ADVERBS

| Positive | Comparative | Superlative |
|---|---|---|
| **Regular** | | |
| longē (*far*) | longius | longissimē |
| fortiter (*bravely*) | fortius | fortissimē |
| fēlīciter (*happily*) | fēlīcius | fēlīcissimē |
| sapienter (*wisely*) | sapientius | sapientissimē |
| facile (*easily*) | facilius | facillimē |
| līberē (*freely*) | līberius | līberrimē |
| pulchrē (*beautifully*) | pulchrius | pulcherrimē |
| ācriter (*keenly*) | ācrius | ācerrimē |
| **Irregular** | | |
| bene (*well*) | melius | optimē |
| magnopere (*greatly*) | magis | maximē |
| male (*badly*) | peius | pessimē |
| multum (*much*) | plūs | plūrimum |
| parum (*little*) | minus | minimē |
| (prae, prō) | prius (*before*) | prīmum; prīmō |
| diū (*a long time*) | diūtius | diūtissimē |

# NUMERALS

| Cardinals | Ordinals | Roman Numerals |
|---|---|---|
| 1. ūnus, -a, -um | prīmus, -a, -um | I |
| 2. duo, duae, duo | secundus, alter | II |
| 3. trēs, tria | tertius | III |
| 4. quattuor | quārtus | IIII; IV |
| 5. quīnque | quīntus | V |
| 6. sex | sextus | VI |
| 7. septem | septimus | VII |
| 8. octō | octāvus | VIII |
| 9. novem | nōnus | VIIII; IX |
| 10. decem | decimus | X |
| 11. ūndecim | ūndecimus | XI |
| 12. duodecim | duodecimus | XII |
| 13. tredecim | tertius decimus | XIII |
| 14. quattuordecim | quārtus decimus | XIIII; XIV |
| 15. quīndecim | quīntus decimus | XV |
| 16. sēdecim | sextus decimus | XVI |
| 17. septendecim | septimus decimus | XVII |
| 18. duodēvīgintī | duodēvīcēsimus | XVIII |
| 19. ūndēvīgintī | ūndēvīcēsimus | XVIIII; XIX |
| 20. vīgintī | vīcēsimus | XX |
| 21. vīgintī ūnus, ūnus et vīgintī | vīcēsimus prīmus | XXI |
| 30. trīgintā | trīcēsimus | XXX |
| 40. quadrāgintā | quadrāgēsimus | XXXX, XL |
| 50. quīnquāgintā | quīnquāgēsimus | L |
| 60. sexāgintā | sexāgēsimus | LX |
| 70. septuāgintā | septuāgēsimus | LXX |
| 80. octōgintā | octōgēsimus | LXXX |
| 90. nōnāgintā | nōnāgēsimus | LXXXX; XC |
| 100. centum | centēsimus | C |
| 101. centum ūnus | centēsimus prīmus | CI |
| 200. ducentī, -ae, -a | duocentēsimus | CC |
| 300. trecentī | trecentēsimus | CCC |
| 400. quadringentī | quadringentēsimus | CCCC |
| 500. quīngentī | quīngentēsimus | D |
| 600. sescentī | sescentēsimus | DC |
| 700. septingentī | septingentēsimus | DCC |
| 800. octingentī | octingentēsimus | DCCC |
| 900. nōngentī | nōngentēsimus | DCCCC |
| 1000. mīlle | mīllēsimus | M |
| 2000. duo mīlia | bis mīllēsimus | MM |

## Declension of Numerals

For the declension of **ūnus** see Capvt IX or **sōlus** above.

For **duo, trēs,** and **mīlle** see Capvt XV.

The forms from **trecentī** through **nōngentī** are declined in the plural like **ducentī, -ae, -a.**

The ordinals are declined like **prīmus, -a, -um.**

The other forms are indeclinable.

# CONJUGATIONS 1–4

## Principal Parts

| | | | |
|---|---|---|---|
| 1*st:* laudō | laudāre | laudāvī | laudātum |
| 2*nd:* moneō | monēre | monuī | monitum |
| 3*rd:* agō | agere | ēgī | āctum |
| 4*th:* audiō | audīre | audīvī | audītum |
| 3*rd* (-iō): capiō | capere | cēpī | captum |

## Indicative Active

### Present

| | | | | |
|---|---|---|---|---|
| laudō | moneō | agō | audiō | capiō |
| laudās | monēs | agis | audīs | capis |
| laudat | monet | agit | audit | capit |
| laudāmus | monēmus | agimus | audīmus | capimus |
| laudātis | monētis | agitis | audītis | capitis |
| laudant | monent | agunt | audiunt | capiunt |

### Imperfect

| | | | | |
|---|---|---|---|---|
| laudābam | monēbam | agēbam | audiēbam | capiēbam |
| laudābās | monēbās | agēbās | audiēbās | capiēbās |
| laudābat | monēbat | agēbat | audiēbat | capiēbat |
| laudābāmus | monēbāmus | agēbāmus | audiēbāmus | capiēbāmus |
| laudābātis | monēbātis | agēbātis | audiēbātis | capiēbātis |
| laudābant | monēbant | agēbant | audiēbant | capiēbant |

### Future

| | | | | |
|---|---|---|---|---|
| laudābō | monēbō | agam | audiam | capiam |
| laudābis | monēbis | agēs | audiēs | capiēs |
| laudābit | monēbit | aget | audiet | capiet |
| laudābimus | monēbimus | agēmus | audiēmus | capiēmus |
| laudābitis | monēbitis | agētis | audiētis | capiētis |
| laudābunt | monēbunt | agent | audient | capient |

### Perfect

| | | | | |
|---|---|---|---|---|
| laudāvī | monuī | ēgī | audīvī | cēpī |
| laudāvistī | monuistī | ēgistī | audīvistī | cēpistī |
| laudāvit | monuit | ēgit | audīvit | cēpit |
| laudāvimus | monuimus | ēgimus | audīvimus | cēpimus |
| laudāvistis | monuistis | ēgistis | audīvistis | cēpistis |
| laudāvērunt | monuērunt | ēgērunt | audīvērunt | cēpērunt |

### Pluperfect

| | | | | |
|---|---|---|---|---|
| laudāveram | monueram | ēgeram | audīveram | cēperam |
| laudāverās | monuerās | ēgerās | audīverās | cēperās |
| laudāverat | monuerat | ēgerat | audīverat | cēperat |
| laudāverāmus | monuerāmus | ēgerāmus | audīverāmus | cēperāmus |
| laudāverātis | monuerātis | ēgerātis | audīverātis | cēperātis |
| laudāverant | monuerant | ēgerant | audīverant | cēperant |

### Future Perfect

| | | | | |
|---|---|---|---|---|
| laudāverō | monuerō | ēgerō | audīverō | cēperō |
| laudāveris | monueris | ēgeris | audīveris | cēperis |
| laudāverit | monuerit | ēgerit | audīverit | cēperit |
| laudāverimus | monuerimus | ēgerimus | audīverimus | cēperimus |
| laudāveritis | monueritis | ēgeritis | audīveritis | cēperitis |
| laudāverint | monuerint | ēgerint | audīverint | cēperint |

## Subjunctive Active

**Present**

| | | | | |
|---|---|---|---|---|
| laudem | moneam | agam | audiam | capiam |
| laudēs | moneās | agās | audiās | capiās |
| laudet | moneat | agat | audiat | capiat |
| laudēmus | moneāmus | agāmus | audiāmus | capiāmus |
| laudētis | moneātis | agātis | audiātis | capiātis |
| laudent | moneant | agant | audiant | capiant |

**Imperfect**

| | | | | |
|---|---|---|---|---|
| laudārem | monērem | agerem | audīrem | caperem |
| laudārēs | monērēs | agerēs | audīrēs | caperēs |
| laudāret | monēret | ageret | audīret | caperet |
| laudārēmus | monērēmus | agerēmus | audīrēmus | caperēmus |
| laudārētis | monērētis | agerētis | audīrētis | caperētis |
| laudārent | monērent | agerent | audīrent | caperent |

**Perfect**

| | | | | |
|---|---|---|---|---|
| laudāverim | monuerim | ēgerim | audīverim | cēperim |
| laudāverīs | monuerīs | ēgerīs | audīverīs | cēperīs |
| laudāverit | monuerit | ēgerit | audīverit | cēperit |
| laudāverīmus | monuerīmus | ēgerīmus | audīverīmus | cēperīmus |
| laudāverītis | monuerītis | ēgerītis | audīverītis | cēperītis |
| laudāverint | monuerint | ēgerint | audīverint | cēperint |

**Pluperfect**

| | | | | |
|---|---|---|---|---|
| laudāvissem | monuissem | ēgissem | audīvissem | cēpissem |
| laudāvissēs | monuissēs | ēgissēs | audīvissēs | cēpissēs |
| laudāvisset | monuisset | ēgisset | audīvisset | cēpisset |
| laudāvissēmus | monuissēmus | ēgissēmus | audīvissēmus | cēpissēmus |
| laudāvissētis | monuissētis | ēgissētis | audīvissētis | cēpissētis |
| laudāvissent | monuissent | ēgissent | audīvissent | cēpissent |

## Present Imperative Active

| | | | | |
|---|---|---|---|---|
| laudā | monē | age | audī | cape |
| laudāte | monēte | agite | audīte | capite |

## Indicative Passive

**Present**

| | | | | |
|---|---|---|---|---|
| laudor | moneor | agor | audior | capior |
| laudāris(-re) | monēris(-re) | ageris(-re) | audīris(-re) | caperis(-re) |
| laudātur | monētur | agitur | audītur | capitur |
| laudāmur | monēmur | agimur | audīmur | capimur |
| laudāminī | monēminī | agiminī | audīminī | capiminī |
| laudantur | monentur | aguntur | audiuntur | capiuntur |

**Imperfect**

| | | | | |
|---|---|---|---|---|
| laudābar | monēbar | agēbar | audiēbar | capiēbar |
| laudābāris(-re) | monēbāris(-re) | agēbāris(-re) | audiēbāris(-re) | capiēbāris(-re) |
| laudābātur | monēbātur | agēbātur | audiēbātur | capiēbātur |
| laudābāmur | monēbāmur | agēbāmur | audiēbāmur | capiēbāmur |
| laudābāminī | monēbāminī | agēbāminī | audiēbāminī | capiēbāminī |
| laudābantur | monēbantur | agēbantur | audiēbantur | capiēbantur |

### Future

| | | | | |
|---|---|---|---|---|
| laudābor | monēbor | agar | audiar | capiar |
| laudāberis(-re) | monēberis(-re) | agēris(-re) | audiēris(-re) | capiēris(-re) |
| laudābitur | monēbitur | agētur | audiētur | capiētur |
| laudābimur | monēbimur | agēmur | audiēmur | capiēmur |
| laudābiminī | monēbiminī | agēminī | audiēminī | capiēminī |
| laudābuntur | monēbuntur | agentur | audientur | capientur |

### Perfect

| | | | | |
|---|---|---|---|---|
| laudātus[12] sum | monitus sum | āctus sum | audītus sum | captus sum |
| laudātus es | monitus es | āctus es | audītus es | captus es |
| laudātus est | monitus est | āctus est | audītus est | captus est |
| laudātī sumus | monitī sumus | āctī sumus | audītī sumus | captī sumus |
| laudātī estis | monitī estis | āctī estis | audītī estis | captī estis |
| laudātī sunt | monitī sunt | āctī sunt | audītī sunt | captī sunt |

### Pluperfect

| | | | | |
|---|---|---|---|---|
| laudātus eram | monitus eram | āctus eram | audītus eram | captus eram |
| laudātus erās | monitus erās | āctus erās | audītus erās | captus erās |
| laudātus erat | monitus erat | āctus erat | audītus erat | captus erat |
| laudātī erāmus | monitī erāmus | āctī erāmus | audītī erāmus | captī erāmus |
| laudātī erātis | monitī erātis | āctī erātis | audītī erātis | captī erātis |
| laudātī erant | monitī erant | āctī erant | audītī erant | captī erant |

### Future Perfect

| | | | | |
|---|---|---|---|---|
| laudātus erō | monitus erō | āctus erō | audītus erō | captus erō |
| laudātus eris | monitus eris | āctus eris | audītus eris | captus eris |
| laudātus erit | monitus erit | āctus erit | audītus erit | captus erit |
| laudātī erimus | monitī erimus | āctī erimus | audītī erimus | captī erimus |
| laudātī eritis | monitī eritis | āctī eritis | audītī eritis | captī eritis |
| laudātī erunt | monitī erunt | āctī erunt | audītī erunt | captī erunt |

## Subjunctive Passive

### Present

| | | | | |
|---|---|---|---|---|
| lauder | monear | agar | audiar | capiar |
| laudēris(-re) | moneāris(-re) | agāris(-re) | audiāris(-re) | capiāris(-re) |
| laudētur | moneātur | agātur | audiātur | capiātur |
| laudēmur | moneāmur | agāmur | audiāmur | capiāmur |
| laudēminī | moneāminī | agāminī | audiāminī | capiāminī |
| laudentur | moneantur | agantur | audiantur | capiantur |

### Imperfect

| | | | | |
|---|---|---|---|---|
| laudārer | monērer | agerer | audīrer | caperer |
| laudārēris(-re) | monērēris(-re) | agerēris(-re) | audīrēris(-re) | caperēris(-re) |
| laudārētur | monērētur | agerētur | audīrētur | caperētur |
| laudārēmur | monērēmur | agerēmur | audīrēmur | caperēmur |
| laudārēminī | monērēminī | agerēminī | audīrēminī | caperēminī |
| laudārentur | monērentur | agerentur | audīrentur | caperentur |

---

[12] The participles **laudātus** (-a, -um), **monitus** (-a, -um), etc., are used as predicate adjectives, and so their endings vary to agree with the subject.

**Perfect**

| laudātus sim | monitus sim | āctus sim | audītus sim | captus sim |
|---|---|---|---|---|
| laudātus sīs | monitus sīs | āctus sīs | audītus sīs | captus sīs |
| laudātus sit | monitus sit | āctus sit | audītus sit | captus sit |
| laudātī sīmus | monitī sīmus | āctī sīmus | audītī sīmus | captī sīmus |
| laudātī sītis | monitī sītis | āctī sītis | audītī sītis | captī sītis |
| laudātī sint | monitī sint | āctī sint | audītī sint | captī sint |

**Pluperfect**

| laudātus essem | monitus essem | āctus essem | audītus essem | captus essem |
|---|---|---|---|---|
| laudātus essēs | monitus essēs | āctus essēs | audītus essēs | captus essēs |
| laudātus esset | monitus esset | āctus esset | audītus esset | captus esset |
| laudātī essēmus | monitī essēmus | āctī essēmus | audītī essēmus | captī essēmus |
| laudātī essētis | monitī essētis | āctī essētis | audītī essētis | captī essētis |
| laudātī essent | monitī essent | āctī essent | audītī essent | captī essent |

## Present Imperative Passive

In classical Latin, passive form imperatives are found chiefly in deponent verbs (for forms, see Capvt XXXIV).

## Participles

**Active**

| | | | | | |
|---|---|---|---|---|---|
| *Pres.* | laudāns | monēns | agēns | audiēns | capiēns |
| *Fut.* | laudātūrus | monitūrus | āctūrus | audītūrus | captūrus |

**Passive**

| | | | | | |
|---|---|---|---|---|---|
| *Perf.* | laudātus | monitus | āctus | audītus | captus |
| *Fut.* | laudandus | monendus | agendus | audiendus | capiendus |

## Infinitives

**Active**

| | | | | | |
|---|---|---|---|---|---|
| *Pres.* | laudāre | monēre | agere | audīre | capere |
| *Perf.* | laudāvisse | monuisse | ēgisse | audīvisse | cēpisse |
| *Fut.* | laudātūrus esse | monitūrus esse | āctūrus esse | audītūrus esse | captūrus esse |

**Passive**

| | | | | | |
|---|---|---|---|---|---|
| *Pres.* | laudārī | monērī | agī | audīrī | capī |
| *Perf.* | laudātus esse | monitus esse | āctus esse | audītus esse | captus esse |
| *Fut.* | laudātum īrī | monitum īrī | āctum īrī | audītum īrī | captum īrī |

# DEPONENT VERBS

**Principal Parts**

| | | | |
|---|---|---|---|
| *1st Conj.:* | hortor | hortārī | hortātus sum (*urge*) |
| *2nd Conj.:* | fateor | fatērī | fassus sum (*confess*) |
| *3rd Conj.:* | sequor | sequī | secūtus sum (*follow*) |
| *4th Conj.:* | mōlior | mōlīrī | mōlītus sum (*work at*) |
| *3rd (-iō):* | patior | patī | passus sum (*suffer*) |

## Indicative

### Present

| | | | | |
|---|---|---|---|---|
| hortor | fateor | sequor | mōlior | patior |
| hortāris(-re) | fatēris(-re) | sequeris(-re) | mōlīris(-re) | pateris(-re) |
| hortātur | fatētur | sequitur | mōlītur | patitur |
| hortāmur | fatēmur | sequimur | mōlīmur | patimur |
| hortāminī | fatēminī | sequiminī | mōlīminī | patiminī |
| hortantur | fatentur | sequuntur | mōliuntur | patiuntur |

### Imperfect

| | | | | |
|---|---|---|---|---|
| hortābar | fatēbar | sequēbar | mōliēbar | patiēbar |
| hortābāris(-re) | fatēbāris(-re) | sequēbāris(-re) | mōliēbāris(-re) | patiēbāris(-re) |
| hortābātur | fatēbātur | sequēbātur | mōliēbātur | patiēbātur |
| hortābāmur | fatēbāmur | sequēbāmur | mōliēbāmur | patiēbāmur |
| hortābāminī | fatēbāminī | sequēbāminī | mōliēbāminī | patiēbāminī |
| hortābantur | fatēbantur | sequēbantur | mōliēbantur | patiēbantur |

### Future

| | | | | |
|---|---|---|---|---|
| hortābor | fatēbor | sequar | mōliar | patiar |
| hortāberis(-re) | fatēberis(-re) | sequēris(-re) | mōliēris(-re) | patiēris(-re) |
| hortābitur | fatēbitur | sequētur | mōliētur | patiētur |
| hortābimur | fatēbimur | sequēmur | mōliēmur | patiēmur |
| hortābiminī | fatēbiminī | sequēminī | mōliēminī | patiēminī |
| hortābuntur | fatēbuntur | sequentur | mōlientur | patientur |

### Perfect

| | | | | |
|---|---|---|---|---|
| hortātus sum | fassus sum | secūtus sum | mōlītus sum | passus sum |
| hortātus es | fassus es | secūtus es | mōlītus es | passus es |
| hortātus est | fassus est | secūtus est | mōlītus est | passus est |
| hortātī sumus | fassī sumus | secūtī sumus | mōlītī sumus | passī sumus |
| hortātī estis | fassī estis | secūtī estis | mōlītī estis | passī estis |
| hortātī sunt | fassī sunt | secūtī sunt | mōlītī sunt | passī sunt |

### Pluperfect

| | | | | |
|---|---|---|---|---|
| hortātus eram | fassus eram | secūtus eram | mōlītus eram | passus eram |
| hortātus erās | fassus erās | secūtus erās | mōlītus erās | passus erās |
| hortātus erat | fassus erat | secūtus erat | mōlītus erat | passus erat |
| hortātī erāmus | fassī erāmus | secūtī erāmus | mōlītī erāmus | passī erāmus |
| hortātī erātis | fassī erātis | secūtī erātis | mōlītī erātis | passī erātis |
| hortātī erant | fassī erant | secūtī erant | mōlītī erant | passī erant |

### Future Perfect

| | | | | |
|---|---|---|---|---|
| hortātus erō | fassus erō | secūtus erō | mōlītus erō | passus erō |
| hortātus eris | fassus eris | secūtus eris | mōlītus eris | passus eris |
| hortātus erit | fassus erit | secūtus erit | mōlītus erit | passus erit |
| hortātī erimus | fassī erimus | secūtī erimus | mōlītī erimus | passī erimus |
| hortātī eritis | fassī eritis | secūtī eritis | mōlītī eritis | passī eritis |
| hortātī erunt | fassī erunt | secūtī erunt | mōlītī erunt | passī erunt |

## Subjunctive

### Present

| | | | | |
|---|---|---|---|---|
| horter | fatear | sequar | mōliar | patiar |
| hortēris(-re) | fateāris(-re) | sequāris(-re) | mōliāris(-re) | patiāris(-re) |
| hortētur | fateātur | sequātur | mōliātur | patiātur |
| hortēmur | fateāmur | sequāmur | mōliāmur | patiāmur |
| hortēminī | fateāminī | sequāminī | mōliāminī | patiāminī |
| hortentur | fateantur | sequantur | mōliantur | patiantur |

### Imperfect

| | | | | |
|---|---|---|---|---|
| hortārer | fatērer | sequerer | mōlīrer | paterer |
| hortārēris(-re) | fatērēris(-re) | sequerēris(-re) | mōlīrēris(-re) | paterēris(-re) |
| hortārētur | fatērētur | sequerētur | mōlīrētur | paterētur |
| hortārēmur | fatērēmur | sequerēmur | mōlīrēmur | paterēmur |
| hortārēminī | fatērēminī | sequerēminī | mōlīrēminī | paterēminī |
| hortārentur | fatērentur | sequerentur | mōlīrentur | paterentur |

### Perfect

| | | | | |
|---|---|---|---|---|
| hortātus sim | fassus sim | secūtus sim | mōlītus sim | passus sim |
| hortātus sīs | fassus sīs | secūtus sīs | mōlītus sīs | passus sīs |
| hortātus sit | fassus sit | secūtus sit | mōlītus sit | passus sit |
| hortātī sīmus | fassī sīmus | secūtī sīmus | mōlītī sīmus | passī sīmus |
| hortātī sītis | fassī sītis | secūtī sītis | mōlītī sītis | passī sītis |
| hortātī sint | fassī sint | secūtī sint | mōlītī sint | passī sint |

### Pluperfect

| | | | | |
|---|---|---|---|---|
| hortātus essem | fassus essem | secūtus essem | mōlītus essem | passus essem |
| hortātus essēs | fassus essēs | secūtus essēs | mōlītus essēs | passus essēs |
| hortātus esset | fassus esset | secūtus esset | mōlītus esset | passus esset |
| hortātī essēmus | fassī essēmus | secūtī essēmus | mōlītī essēmus | passī essēmus |
| hortātī essētis | fassī essētis | secūtī essētis | mōlītī essētis | passī essētis |
| hortātī essent | fassī essent | secūtī essent | mōlītī essent | passī essent |

### Present Imperative

| | | | | |
|---|---|---|---|---|
| hortāre | fatēre | sequere | mōlīre | patere |
| hortāminī | fatēminī | sequiminī | mōlīminī | patiminī |

### Participles

| | | | | |
|---|---|---|---|---|
| *Pres.* hortāns | fatēns | sequēns | mōliēns | patiēns |
| *Perf.* hortātus | fassus | secūtus | mōlītus | passus |
| *Fut.* hortātūrus | fassūrus | secūtūrus | mōlītūrus | passūrus |
| *Ger.* hortandus | fatendus | sequendus | mōliendus | patiendus |

### Infinitives

| | | | | |
|---|---|---|---|---|
| *Pres.* hortārī | fatērī | sequī | mōlīrī | patī |
| *Perf.* hortātus esse | fassus esse | secūtus esse | mōlītus esse | passus esse |
| *Fut.* hortātūrus esse | fassūrus esse | secūtūrus esse | mōlītūrus esse | passūrus esse |

## IRREGULAR VERBS

### Principal Parts

| | | | | |
|---|---|---|---|---|
| sum | esse | fuī | futūrum | (*be*) |
| possum | posse | potuī | | (*be able, can*) |
| volō | velle | voluī | | (*wish, be willing*) |
| nōlō | nōlle | nōluī | | (*not to wish, be unwilling*) |
| mālō | mālle | māluī | | (*prefer*) |
| eō | īre | iī | itum | (*go*) |

## Indicative[13]

**Present**

| | | | | | |
|---|---|---|---|---|---|
| sum | possum | volō | nōlō | mālō | eō |
| es | potes | vīs | nōnvīs | māvīs | īs |
| est | potest | vult | nōn vult | māvult | it |
| sumus | possumus | volumus | nōlumus | mālumus | īmus |
| estis | potestis | vultis | nōn vultis | māvultis | ītis |
| sunt | possunt | volunt | nōlunt | mālunt | eunt |

**Imperfect**

| | | | | | |
|---|---|---|---|---|---|
| eram | poteram | volēbam | nōlēbam | mālēbam | ībam |
| erās | poterās | volēbās | nōlēbās | mālēbās | ībās |
| erat | poterat | volēbat | nōlēbat | mālēbat | ībat |
| erāmus | poterāmus | volēbāmus | nōlēbāmus | mālēbāmus | ībāmus |
| erātis | poterātis | volēbātis | nōlēbātis | mālēbātis | ībātis |
| erant | poterant | volēbant | nōlēbant | mālēbant | ībant |

**Future**

| | | | | | |
|---|---|---|---|---|---|
| erō | poterō | volam | nōlam | mālam | ībō |
| eris | poteris | volēs | nōlēs | mālēs | ībis |
| erit | poterit | volet | nōlet | mālet | ībit |
| erimus | poterimus | volēmus | nōlēmus | mālēmus | ībimus |
| eritis | poteritis | volētis | nōlētis | mālētis | ībitis |
| erunt | poterunt | volent | nōlent | mālent | ībunt |

**Perfect**

| | | | | | |
|---|---|---|---|---|---|
| fuī | potuī | voluī | nōluī | māluī | iī |
| fuistī | potuistī | voluistī | nōluistī | māluistī | īstī |
| fuit | potuit | voluit | nōluit | māluit | iit |
| fuimus | potuimus | voluimus | nōluimus | māluimus | iimus |
| fuistis | potuistis | voluistis | nōluistis | māluistis | īstis |
| fuērunt | potuērunt | voluērunt | nōluērunt | māluērunt | iērunt |

**Pluperfect**

| | | | | | |
|---|---|---|---|---|---|
| fueram | potueram | volueram | nōlueram | mālueram | ieram |
| fuerās | potuerās | voluerās | nōluerās | māluerās | ierās |
| etc. | etc. | etc. | etc. | etc. | etc. |

**Future Perfect**

| | | | | | |
|---|---|---|---|---|---|
| fuerō | potuerō | voluerō | nōluerō | māluerō | ierō |
| fueris | potueris | volueris | nōlueris | mālueris | ieris |
| etc. | etc. | etc. | etc. | etc. | etc. |

## Subjunctive

**Present**

| | | | | | |
|---|---|---|---|---|---|
| sim | possim | velim | nōlim | mālim | eam |
| sīs | possīs | velīs | nōlīs | mālīs | eās |
| sit | possit | velit | nōlit | mālit | eat |
| sīmus | possīmus | velīmus | nōlīmus | mālīmus | eāmus |
| sītis | possītis | velītis | nōlītis | mālītis | eātis |
| sint | possint | velint | nōlint | mālint | eant |

[13] Note that the verbs in this list have no passive voice (except for the idiomatic impersonal passive of **eō**, which is not used in this book).

**Imperfect**

| | | | | | |
|---|---|---|---|---|---|
| essem | possem | vellem | nōllem | māllem | īrem |
| essēs | possēs | vellēs | nōllēs | māllēs | īrēs |
| esset | posset | vellet | nōllet | māllet | īret |
| essēmus | possēmus | vellēmus | nōllēmus | māllēmus | īrēmus |
| essētis | possētis | vellētis | nōllētis | māllētis | īrētis |
| essent | possent | vellent | nōllent | māllent | īrent |

**Perfect**

| | | | | | |
|---|---|---|---|---|---|
| fuerim | potuerim | voluerim | nōluerim | māluerim | ierim |
| fuerīs | potuerīs | voluerīs | nōluerīs | māluerīs | ierīs |
| fuerit | potuerit | voluerit | nōluerit | māluerit | ierit |
| fuerīmus | potuerīmus | voluerīmus | nōluerīmus | māluerīmus | ierīmus |
| fuerītis | potuerītis | voluerītis | nōluerītis | māluerītis | ierītis |
| fuerint | potuerint | voluerint | nōluerint | māluerint | ierint |

**Pluperfect**

| | | | | | |
|---|---|---|---|---|---|
| fuissem | potuissem | voluissem | nōluissem | māluissem | īssem |
| fuissēs | potuissēs | voluissēs | nōluissēs | māluissēs | īssēs |
| fuisset | potuisset | voluisset | nōluisset | māluisset | īsset |
| fuissēmus | potuissēmus | voluissēmus | nōluissēmus | māluissēmus | īssēmus |
| fuissētis | potuissētis | voluissētis | nōluissētis | māluissētis | īssētis |
| fuissent | potuissent | voluissent | nōluissent | māluissent | īssent |

**Present Imperative**

| | | | | | |
|---|---|---|---|---|---|
| es | —— | —— | nōlī | —— | ī |
| este | —— | —— | nōlīte | —— | īte |

**Participles**

| | | | | | | |
|---|---|---|---|---|---|---|
| *Pres.* | —— | potēns | volēns | nōlēns | —— | iēns (*gen.* euntis) |
| *Perf.* | —— | —— | —— | —— | —— | itum |
| *Fut.* | futūrus | —— | —— | —— | —— | itūrus |
| *Ger.* | —— | —— | —— | —— | —— | eundus |

**Infinitives**

| | | | | | | |
|---|---|---|---|---|---|---|
| *Pr.* | esse | posse | velle | nōlle | mālle | īre |
| *Pf.* | fuisse | potuisse | voluisse | nōluisse | māluisse | īsse |
| *Fu.* | futūrus esse *or* fore | —— | —— | —— | —— | itūrus esse |

# IRREGULAR: ferō, ferre, tulī, lātum, *to bear, carry*

## Indicative

| Present Act. | Pass. | Imperfect Act. | Pass. | Future Act. | Pass. |
|---|---|---|---|---|---|
| ferō | feror | ferēbam | ferēbar | feram | ferar |
| fers | ferris(-re) | ferēbās | ferēbāris(-re) | ferēs | ferēris(-re) |
| fert | fertur | ferēbat | ferēbātur | feret | ferētur |
| ferimus | ferimur | ferēbāmus | ferēbāmur | ferēmus | ferēmur |
| fertis | feriminī | ferēbātis | ferēbāminī | ferētis | ferēminī |
| ferunt | feruntur | ferēbant | ferēbantur | ferent | ferentur |

| Perfect | | Pluperfect | | Future Perfect | |
|---|---|---|---|---|---|
| **Act.** | **Pass.** | **Act.** | **Pass.** | **Act.** | **Pass.** |
| tulī | lātus sum | tuleram | lātus eram | tulerō | lātus erō |
| tulistī | lātus es | tulerās | lātus erās | tuleris | lātus eris |
| tulit | lātus est | tulerat | lātus erat | tulerit | lātus erit |
| etc. | etc. | etc. | etc. | etc. | etc. |

### Subjunctive

| Present | | Imperfect | | Perfect | |
|---|---|---|---|---|---|
| **Act.** | **Pass.** | **Act.** | **Pass.** | **Act.** | **Pass.** |
| feram | ferar | ferrem | ferrer | tulerim | lātus sim |
| ferās | ferāris(-re) | ferrēs | ferrēris(-re) | tulerīs | lātus sīs |
| ferat | ferātur | ferret | ferrētur | tulerit | lātus sit |
| ferāmus | ferāmur | ferrēmus | ferrēmur | etc. | etc. |
| ferātis | ferāminī | ferrētis | ferrēminī | | |
| ferant | ferantur | ferrent | ferrentur | | |

| Pluperfect | |
|---|---|
| **Act.** | **Pass.** |
| tulissem | lātus essem |
| tulissēs | lātus essēs |
| tulisset | lātus esset |
| etc. | etc. |

| Pres. Imper. | | Participles | | Infinitives | |
|---|---|---|---|---|---|
| **Act.** | **Pass.** | **Act.** | **Pass.** | **Act.** | **Pass.** |
| fer | —— | *Pres.* ferēns | —— | ferre | ferrī |
| ferte | —— | *Perf.* —— | lātus | tulisse | lātus esse |
| | | *Fut.* lātūrus | ferendus | lātūrus esse | lātum īrī |

## IRREGULAR: fīō, fierī, factus sum, *to happen, become; be made, be done*

### Indicative

| Pres. | Impf. | Fut. | Perf. | Pluperf. | Fut. Perf. |
|---|---|---|---|---|---|
| fīō | fīēbam | fīam | factus sum | factus eram | factus erō |
| fīs | fīēbās | fīēs | factus es | factus erās | factus eris |
| fit | fīēbat | fīet | factus est | factus erat | factus erit |
| fīmus | fīēbāmus | fīēmus | factī sumus | factī erāmus | factī erimus |
| fītis | fīēbātis | fīētis | factī estis | factī erātis | factī eritis |
| fīunt | fīēbant | fīent | factī sunt | factī erant | factī erunt |

### Subjunctive

| Pres. | Impf. | Perf. | Pluperf. |
|---|---|---|---|
| fīam | fierem | factus sim | factus essem |
| fīās | fierēs | factus sīs | factus essēs |
| fīat | fieret | factus sit | factus esset |
| fīāmus | fierēmus | factī sīmus | factī essēmus |
| fīātis | fierētis | factī sītis | factī essētis |
| fīant | fierent | factī sint | factī essent |

| Part. | Inf. |
|---|---|
| **Pres.** —— | fierī |
| **Perf.** factus | factus esse |
| **Fut.** faciendus | factum īrī |

**Imperative:** fī, fīte

# VOCĀBVLA: ENGLISH-LATIN

An Arabic (1) in parentheses after a verb shows that this is a regular verb of the 1st conjugation with a sequence of principal parts ending in **-āre, -āvī, -ātum** (or, if deponent, **-ārī, -ātus sum**). For prefixes and suffixes see the lists in the Appendix. For more complete definitions of the Latin words, see the Latin-English **Vocābula.**

## A

**abandon,** relinquō, -ere, -liquī, -lictum
**able (be),** possum, posse, potuī
**about (concerning),** dē + *abl.*
**absolute ruler,** tyrannus, -ī, *m.*
**abundance,** cōpia, -ae, *f.*
**accomplish,** faciō, -ere, fēcī, factum; **be accomplished,**
  fīō, fierī, factus sum
**across,** trāns + *acc.*
**advice,** cōnsilium, -iī, *n.*
**advise,** moneō, -ēre, -uī, -itum
**affect,** adficiō, -ere, -fēcī, -fectum
**afraid (be),** metuō, -ere, -uī
**after,** post + *acc.*
**afterwards,** posteā
**after all,** postrēmum
**again,** iterum
**against,** contrā + *acc.*
**age,** aetās, -tātis, *f.*
**alas,** heu, vae
**all,** omnis, -e
**alone,** sōlus, -a, -um
**also,** quoque
**although,** cum + *subjunct.*
**always,** semper
**among,** inter + *acc.*
**ancestors,** maiōrēs, maiōrum, *m. pl.*
**ancient,** antīquus, -a, -um
**and,** et, -que, ac, atque
**anger,** īra, -ae, *f.*
**angry,** īrātus, -a, -um

**animal,** animal, -mālis, *n.*
**announce,** nūntiō (1)
**another,** alius, -a, -ud
**answer,** respondeō, -ēre, -spondī, -spōnsum
**any,** ūllus, -a, -um; aliquis, aliquid
**any (anyone, anything,** *after* sī, nisi, nē, num), quis, quid
**argument,** argūmentum, -ī, *n.*
**army,** exercitus, -ūs, *m.*
**arms,** arma, -ōrum, *n. pl.*
**arrest,** comprehendō, -ere, -ī, -hēnsum
**arrogant,** superbus, -a, -um
**art,** ars, artis, *f.*
**as,** ut + *indic.*
**as . . . as possible,** quam + *superlative*
**Asia,** Asia, -ae, *f.*
**ask,** rogō (1)
**assure (I assure you, you may be assured),** *use personal*
  *pron. in dat. case (dat. of ref., e.g.,* tibi)
**at** (= *time*), abl. *of time;* (= *place*), *loc. of names of cities*
**Athens,** Athēnae, -ārum, *f. pl.*
**attack,** oppugnō (1)
**author,** auctor, -tōris, *m.*
**avert,** āvertō, -ere, -ī, -versum
**away from,** ab + *abl.*

## B

**bad,** malus, -a, -um
**band,** manus, -ūs, *f.*
**banish,** expellō, -ere, -pulī, -pulsum
**base,** turpis, -e
**be,** sum, esse, fuī, futūrum

**beard,** barba, -ae, *f.*
**beautiful,** pulcher, -chra, -chrum; bellus, -a, -um
**beauty,** fōrma, -ae, *f.*
**because,** quod
**become,** fīō, fierī, factus sum
**before,** ante + *acc.*
**beg,** ōrō (1)
**began,** coepī, coepisse, coeptum (*pres. system supplied by* incipiō)
**begin,** incipiō, -ere, -cēpī, -ceptum (*see* **began** *above*)
**believe,** crēdō, -ere, -didī, -ditum
**benefit,** beneficium, -iī, *n.*
**best,** optimus, -a, -um
**better,** melior, -ius
**blind,** caecus, -a, -um
**body,** corpus, -poris, *n.*
**(be) born,** nāscor, -ī, nātus sum
**book,** liber, -brī, *m.*
**both ... and,** et ... et
**boy,** puer, puerī, *m.*
**brave,** fortis, -e
**brief,** brevis, -e
**bright,** clārus, -a, -um
**bring,** ferō, ferre, tulī, lātum
**bring (back),** referō, -ferre, -ttulī, -lātum
**brother,** frāter, -tris, *m.*
**bull,** bōs, bovis, *m./f.*
**but,** sed, at
**by** (= *agent*), ā *or* ab + *abl.;* (= *means*), *simple abl.*

## C

**Caesar,** Caesar, -saris, *m.*
**call,** vocō (1); appellō (1)
**can,** possum, posse, potuī
**capture,** capiō, -ere, -cēpī, captum
**care,** cūra, -ae, *f.*
**certain (definite, sure),** certus, -a, -um; (*indef.*) quīdam, quaedam, quiddam (*pron.*) *or* quoddam (*adj.*)
**certainly,** certē
**change,** mūtō (1)
**character,** mōrēs, mōrum, *m. pl.*
**cheer,** recreō (1)
**Cicero,** Cicerō, -rōnis, *m.*
**citizen,** cīvis, -is, *m./f.*
**citizenship,** cīvitās, -tātis, *f.*
**city,** urbs, urbis, *f.*
**come,** veniō, -īre, vēnī, ventum
**come back,** reveniō, -īre, -vēnī, -ventum
**comfort,** sōlācium, -iī, *n.*
**command** (*noun*), imperium, -iī, *n.;* (*verb*), imperō (1)

**common,** commūnis, -e
**commonwealth,** rēs pūblica, reī pūblicae, *f.*
**compare,** comparō (1)
**complain,** queror, -ī, questus sum
**concerning,** dē + *abl.*
**confess,** fateor, -ērī, fassus sum
**conquer,** superō (1); vincō, -ere, vīcī, victum
**conspirators,** coniūrātī, -ōrum, *m. pl.*
**constellation,** sīdus, -deris, *n.*
**consul,** cōnsul, -sulis, *m.*
**country,** patria, -ae, *f.;* terra, -ae, *f.*
**courage,** virtūs, -tūtis, *f.*
**create,** creō (1)
**custom,** mōs, mōris, *m.*
**crime,** scelus, -leris, *n.*

## D

**danger,** perīculum, -ī, *n.*
**dare,** audeō, -ēre, ausus sum
**daughter,** fīlia, -ae, *f.* (*dat. and abl. pl.* fīliābus)
**day,** diēs, -ēī, *m.*
**dear,** cārus, -a, -um
**death,** mors, mortis, *f.*
**dedicate,** dēdicō (1)
**deed,** factum, -ī, *n.*
**defend,** dēfendō, -ere, -ī, -fēnsum
**delay,** mora, -ae, *f.*
**delight,** dēlectō (1)
**deny,** negō (1)
**depart,** discēdō, -ere, -cessī, -cessum; abeō, -īre, -iī, -itum
**deprived of (be),** careō, -ēre, -uī, -itūrum
**descendant,** nepōs, -pōtis, *m.*
**desire** (*verb*), cupiō, -ere, -īvī, -ītum; dēsīderō (1); (*noun*), voluptās, -tātis, *f.*
**despise,** contemnō, -ere, -tempsī, -temptum
**destroy,** dēleō, -ēre, -ēvī, -ētum
**destruction,** exitium, -ī, *n.*
**die,** morior, -ī, mortuus sum
**difficult,** difficilis, -e
**dignity,** dignitās, -tātis, *f.*
**dine,** cēnō (1)
**dinner,** cēna, -ae, *f.*
**discover,** reperiō, -īre, -pperī, -pertum
**disgraceful,** turpis, -e
**dissimilar,** dissimilis, -e
**do,** faciō, -ere, fēcī, factum; **be done,** fīō, fierī, factus sum
**doctor,** medica, -ae, *f.;* medicus, -ī, *m.*
**drag,** trahō, -ere, trāxī, tractum
**dread** (*verb*), metuō, -ere, -uī; (*noun*), metus, -ūs, *m.*
**drive out,** expellō, -ere, -pulī, -pulsum

# E

**eagerness,** studium, -iī, *n.*
**ear,** auris, -is, *f.*
**easy,** facilis, -e
**eight,** octō
**either,** uter, utra, utrum
**either . . . or,** aut . . . aut
**eleven,** ūndecim
**emperor,** imperātor, -tōris, *m.*
**end,** fīnis, -is, *m.*
**endure,** ferō, ferre, tulī, lātum; patior, -ī, passus sum
**enemy,** hostis, -is, *m. (usually pl.)*
**enjoy,** ūtor, -ī, ūsus sum + *abl.*
**enjoyment,** frūctus, -ūs, *m.*
**enough,** satis
**entire,** tōtus, -a, -um
**entrust,** committō, -ere, -mīsī, -missum
**envy, (be) envious,** invideō, -ēre, -vīdī, -vīsum + *dat.*
**err,** errō (1)
**esteem,** dīligō, -ere, -lēxī, -lēctum
**even,** etiam; **not even,** nē . . . quidem
**ever,** umquam
**every(one),** omnis, -e
**evil** (*adj.*), malus, -a, -um; (*noun*), malum, -ī, *n.*
**exhibit,** ostendō, -ere, -ī, -tentum
**expect,** exspectō (1)
**expel,** expellō, -ere, -pulī, -pulsum
**eye,** oculus, -ī, *m.*

# F

**face,** vultus, -ūs, *m.*
**faith,** fidēs, -eī, *f.*
**faithful,** fidēlis, -e
**fall,** cadō, -ere, cecidī, cāsūrum
**false,** falsus, -a, -um
**fame,** fāma, -ae, *f.*
**family,** familia, -ae, *f.*
**farmer,** agricola, -ae, *m.*
**father,** pater, -tris, *m.*
**fault,** culpa, -ae, *f.;* vitium, -iī, *n.*
**fear** (*verb*), timeō, -ēre, -uī; (*noun*), metus, -ūs, *m.;* timor, -mōris, *m.*
**feel,** sentiō, -īre, sēnsī, sēnsum
**feeling,** sēnsus, -ūs, *m.*
**ferocious,** ferōx, *gen.* ferōcis
**few,** paucī, -ae, -a (*pl.*)
**fidelity,** fidēs, -eī, *f.*
**fierce,** ācer, ācris, ācre; ferōx, *gen.* ferōcis
**fifth,** quīntus, -a, -um
**finally,** dēnique

**find,** inveniō, -īre, -vēnī, -ventum
**first** (*adj.*), prīmus, -a, -um; (*adv.*) prīmum, prīmō
**five,** quīnque
**flee,** fugiō, -ere, fūgī, fugitūrum
**follow,** sequor, -ī, secūtus sum
**foolish,** stultus, -a, -um
**for** (*conj.*), nam, enim; (= **since, because**), quod, quoniam; (*prep.*), prō + *abl.; often simply the dat. case.*
**force,** vīs, vīs, *f.*
**forces (troops),** cōpiae, -ārum, *f. pl.*
**forgive,** ignōscō, -ere, -nōvī, -nōtum + *dat.*
**former,** prior, prius
**fortunate,** fortūnātus, -a, -um
**fortune,** fortūna, -ae, *f.*
**forum,** forum -ī, *n.*
**four,** quattuor
**free** (*verb*), līberō (1); (*adj.*), līber, -era, -erum
**freedom,** lībertās, -tātis, *f.*
**freely,** līberē
**friend,** amīca, -ae, *f.;* amīcus, -ī, *m.*
**friendly,** amīcus, -a, -um
**friendship,** amīcitia, -ae, *f.*
**frighten,** terreō, -ēre, -uī, -itum
**from (away),** ab; **(out)** ex; **(down)** dē: *all* + *abl.*
**fruit,** frūctus, -ūs, *m.*
**full,** plēnus, -a, -um

# G

**game,** lūdus, -ī, *m.*
**gate,** porta, -ae, *f.*
**general,** dux, ducis, *m.;* imperātor, -tōris, *m.*
**gift,** dōnum, -ī, *n.*
**girl,** puella, -ae, *f.*
**give,** dō, dare, dedī, datum
**(be) glad,** gaudeō, -ēre, gāvīsus sum
**glory,** glōria, -ae, *f.*
**go,** eō, īre, iī, itum
**go astray,** errō (1)
**go away,** abeō, -īre, -iī, -itum
**god,** deus, -ī, *m.* (*voc. sg.* deus, *nom. pl.* deī *or* dī, *dat. and abl. pl.* dīs)
**goddess,** dea, -ae, *f.* (*dat. and abl. pl.* deābus)
**good,** bonus, -a, -um
**gratitude,** grātia, -ae, *f.*
**great,** magnus, -a, -um
**greedy,** avārus, -a, -um
**Greek,** Graecus, -a, -um; **a Greek,** Graecus, -ī, *m.*
**grieve,** doleō, -ēre, -uī, -itūrum
**ground,** humus, -ī, *f.;* terra, -ae, *f.*
**guard,** custōdia, -ae, *f.*

# H

**hand,** manus, -ūs, *f.*
**happy,** beātus, -a, -um; fēlīx, *gen.* fēlīcis
**harm,** noceō, -ēre, -uī, -itum + *dat.*
**harsh,** dūrus, -a, -um; acerbus, -a, -um
**have,** habeō, -ēre, -uī, -itum
**he,** is; *often indicated only by the personal ending of verb*
**head,** caput, -pitis, *n.*
**healthy,** sānus, -a, -um
**hear,** audiō, -īre, -īvī, -ītum
**heart (in one's),** *use personal pron. in dat. case (dat. of ref., e.g.,* mihi, tibi)
**heavy,** gravis, -e
**help** (*verb*), adiuvō, -āre, -iūvī, -iūtum; (*noun*), auxilium, -iī, *n.*
**her** (*possessive*) eius (*not reflexive*); suus, -a, -um (*reflexive*)
**herself,** suī (*reflexive*); ipsa (*intensive*)
**hesitate,** dubitō (1)
**high,** altus, -a, -um
**higher,** altior, -ius; superior, -ius
**himself,** suī (*reflexive*); ipse (*intensive*)
**his,** eius (*not reflexive*); suus, -a, -um (*reflexive*)
**hold,** teneō, -ēre, -uī, tentum
**home,** domus, -ūs, *f.;* **at home,** domī; **(to) home,** domum; **from home,** domō
**honor,** honor, -nōris, *m.*
**hope** (*noun*), spēs, -eī, *f.;* (*verb*), spērō (1)
**horn,** cornū, -ūs, *n.*
**horse,** equus, -ī, *m.*
**hour,** hōra, -ae, *f.*
**house,** casa, -ae, *f.*
**however,** autem (*postpositive*)
**how great,** quantus, -a, -um
**how many,** quot
**human,** hūmānus, -a, -um
**human being,** homō, -minis, *m.*
**humane,** hūmānus, -a, -um
**humble,** humilis, -e
**hundred,** centum
**hurt,** noceō, -ēre, -uī, -itum + *dat.*

# I

**I,** ego, meī; *often expressed simply by the personal ending of verb*
**if,** sī; **if . . . not,** nisi
**ill,** malum, -ī, *n.*
**illustrious,** clārus, -a, -um
**immortal,** immortālis, -e
**in,** in + *abl.*

**infancy,** īnfantia, -ae, *f.*
**injustice,** iniūria, -ae, *f.*
**into,** in + *acc.*
**invite,** invītō (1)
**iron,** ferrum, -ī, *n.*
**it,** is, ea, id; *often indicated only by personal ending of verb.*
**Italy,** Italia, -ae, *f.*
**itself,** suī (*reflexive*); ipsum (*intensive*)

# J

**join,** iungō, -ere, iūnxī, iūnctum
**judge,** iūdex, -dicis, *m.*
**judgment,** iūdicium, -iī, *n.*
**just,** iūstus, -a, -um

# K

**keen,** ācer, ācris, ācre
**keenly,** ācriter
**kindness,** beneficium, -iī, *n.*
**king,** rēx, rēgis, *m.*
**kiss,** bāsium, -iī, *n.*
**knee,** genū, -ūs, *n.*
**know,** sciō, -īre, -īvī, -ītum; **not know,** nesciō, -īre, -īvī, -ītum
**knowledge,** scientia, -ae, *f.*

# L

**labor,** labor, -bōris, *m.*
**lack,** careō, -ēre, -uī, -itūrum + *abl.*
**land,** patria, -ae, *f.;* terra, -ae, *f.*
**language,** lingua, -ae, *f.*
**large,** magnus, -a, -um
**Latin,** Latīnus, -a, -um
**law,** lēx, lēgis, *f.*
**lead,** dūcō, -ere, dūxī, ductum
**leader,** dux, ducis, *m.*
**learn** (*in the academic sense*), discō, -ere, didicī; (*get information*), cognōscō, -ere, -nōvī, -nitum
**leave,** abeō, -īre, -iī, -itum
**left,** sinister, -tra, -trum
**leisure,** ōtium, -iī, *n.*
**let (someone do something),** *express this with jussive subjunct.*
**letter (epistle),** litterae, -ārum, *f. pl.*
**liberty,** lībertās, -tātis, *f.*
**life,** vīta, -ae, *f.*
**light,** lūx, lūcis, *f.*
**listen (to),** audiō, -īre, -īvī, -ītum
**literature,** litterae, -ārum, *f. pl.*

**little,** parvus, -a, -um; **little book,** libellus, -ī, *m.*
**live,** vīvō, -ere, vīxī, vīctum; **live one's life,** vītam agō,
   -ere, ēgī, āctum
**long (for a long time),** diū
**lose,** āmittō, -ere, -mīsī, -missum
**love** (*verb*), amō (1); (*noun*), amor, amōris, *m.*
**loyal,** fidēlis, -e
**luck,** fortūna, -ae, *f.*

**M**
**make,** faciō, -ere, fēcī, factum
**man,** vir, virī, *m.;* homō, -minis, *m.; often expressed by*
   *m. of an adj.*
**many,** multī, -ae, -a
**master,** magister, -trī, *m.;* dominus, -ī, *m.*
**may** (*indicating permission to do something*), licet + *dat.*
   + *infin.*
**me.** *See* **I.**
**memory,** memoria, -ae, *f.*
**mercy,** clēmentia, -ae, *f.*
**method,** modus, -ī, *m.*
**middle,** medius, -a, -um
**mind,** mēns, mentis, *f.*
**mix,** misceō, -ēre, -uī, mixtum
**mob,** vulgus, -ī, *n.* (*sometimes m.*)
**modest,** pudīcus, -a, -um
**money,** pecūnia, -ae, *f.*
**monument,** monumentum, -ī, *n.*
**moon,** lūna, -ae, *f.*
**more,** plūs, plūris; *compar. of adj. or adv.*
**most,** plūrimus, -a, -um; *superl. of adj. or adv.*
**mother,** māter, -tris, *f.*
**mountain,** mōns, montis, *m.*
**move,** moveō, -ēre, mōvī, mōtum
**much,** multus, -a, -um
**murder,** necō (1)
**must,** dēbeō, -ēre, -uī, -itum; *or, for pass., use pass.*
   *periphrastic*
**my,** meus, -a, -um (*m. voc. sg.* mī)
**myself** (*reflexive*), meī, mihi, *etc.;* (*intensive*) ipse, ipsa

**N**
**name,** nōmen, -minis, *n.*
**narrate,** nārrō (1)
**nation,** gēns, gentis, *f.*
**nature,** nātūra, -ae, *f.*
**neglect,** neglegō, -ere, -glēxī, -glēctum
**neighbor,** vīcīna, -ae, *f.;* vīcīnus, -ī, *m.*
**neither . . . nor,** neque . . . neque
**never,** numquam

**nevertheless,** tamen
**new,** novus, -a, -um
**night,** nox, noctis, *f.*
**nine,** novem
**no,** nūllus, -a, -um
**nobody, no one,** nēmō, *m./f.; for decl. see Lat.-Eng.*
   *Vocab.*
**not,** nōn; nē *with jussive, jussive noun, and purp-clauses;*
   ut *with fear clauses*
**nothing,** nihil (*indecl.*), *n.*
**now,** nunc
**number,** numerus, -ī, *m.*

**O**
**obey,** pāreō, -ēre, -uī + *dat.*
**offer,** offerō, -ferre, obtulī, oblātum
**office,** officium, -iī, *n*; honor, honōris, *m.*
**often,** saepe
**old,** antīquus, -a, -um; senex, senis
**old man,** senex, senis, *m.*
**on** (= *place*), in + *abl.;* (= *time*), *simple abl.*
**on account of,** propter + *acc.*
**once,** semel
**one,** ūnus, -a, -um
**only** (*adv.*), tantum; (*adj.*), sōlus, -a, -um
**opinion,** sententia, -ae, *f.;* (**in one's**) **opinion,** *use*
   *personal pron. in dat. case* (*dat. of ref., e.g.,* mihi,
   tibi)
**opportunity,** occāsiō, -ōnis, *f.*
**or,** aut
**oration,** ōrātiō, -ōnis, *f.*
**orator,** ōrātor, -tōris, *m.*
**order,** iubeō, -ēre, iussī, iussum; imperō (1) + *dat.*
**(in) order to,** ut (+ *subjunct.*); **in order not to,** nē (+
   *subjunct.*)
**other, another,** alius, alia, aliud; **the other (of two),** alter,
   -era, -erum; (**all**) **the other,** cēterī, -ae, -a
**ought,** dēbeō, -ēre, -uī, -itum; *or, for pass., use pass.*
   *periphrastic*
**our,** noster, -tra, -trum
**out of,** ex + *abl.*
**overcome,** superō (1)
**overpower,** opprimō, -ere, -pressī, -pressum
**own, his own,** suus, -a, -um; **my own,** meus, -a, -um

**P**
**pain,** dolor, -lōris, *m.*
**part,** pars, partis, *f.*
**passage,** locus, -ī, *m.*
**passion,** cupiditās, -tātis, *f.*

patience, patientia, -ae, *f.*
pay. *See* penalty.
peace, pāx, pācis, *f.*
penalty, poena, -ae, *f.*; pay the penalty, poenās dare
people, populus, -ī, *m.*
perceive, sentiō, -īre, sēnsī, sēnsum
perhaps, fortasse
period (of time), aetās, -tātis, *f.*
perish, pereō, -īre, -iī, -itum
permit, patior, -ī, passus sum; it is permitted, licet, licēre, licuit (*impers.*)
perpetual, perpetuus, -a, -um
persuade, persuādeō, -ēre, -suāsī, -suāsum + *dat.*
philosopher, sapiēns, -entis, *m.*; philosopha, -ae, *f.*; philosophus, -ī, *m.*
philosophy, philosophia, -ae, *f.*
place, locus, -ī, *m.*; *pl.*, loca, -ōrum, *n.*
plan, cōnsilium, -iī, *n.*
pleasant, iūcundus, -a, -um
please, placeō, -ēre, -uī, -itum + *dat.*; with a request, amābō tē
pleasure, voluptās, -tātis, *f.*
plebeians, plēbs, plēbis, *f.*
plot, īnsidiae, -ārum, *f. pl.*
poem, carmen, -minis, *n.*
poet, poēta, -ae, *m.*
point out, dēmōnstrō (1)
(as . . . as) possible (*or* greatest possible, brightest possible, *etc.*), quam + *superl. of adj. or adv.*
poverty, paupertās, -tātis, *f.*
power (command), imperium, -iī, *n.*
powerful, potēns, *gen.* potentis
praise (*verb*), laudō (1); (*noun*), laus, laudis, *f.*
prefer, mālō, mālle, māluī
prepare, parō (1)
preserve, cōnservō (1)
press, premō, -ere, pressī, pressum
pretty, bellus, -a, -um; pulcher, -chra, -chrum
priest, sacerdōs, -dōtis, *m.*
prohibit, prohibeō, -ēre, -uī, -itum
promise, prōmittō, -ere, mīsī, -missum
provided that, dummodo + *subjunct.*
pupil, discipula, -ae, *f.*; discipulus, -ī, *m.*
pursuit, studium, -iī, *n.*
put, pōnō, -ere, posuī, positum

## Q

queen, rēgīna, -ae, *f.*
quick, celer, -eris, -ere
quickly, celeriter, cito

## R

raise, tollō, -ere, sustulī, sublātum
rather: *express this with compar. degree of adj. or adv.*
read, legō, -ere, lēgī, lēctum
real, vērus, -a, -um
reason, ratiō, -ōnis, *f.*
receive, accipiō, -ere, -cēpī, -ceptum
recite, recitō (1)
recognize, recognōscō, -ere, -nōvī, -nitum
refuse, recūsō (1)
regain, recipiō, -ere, -cēpī, -ceptum
region, loca, -ōrum, *n.*
remain, remaneō, -ēre, -mānsī, -mānsum
report, nūntiō (1)
republic, rēs pūblica, reī pūblicae, *f.*
reputation, fāma, -ae, *f.*
rescue, ēripiō, -ere, -uī, -reptum
rest, the rest, cēterī, -ae, -a
restrain, teneō, -ēre, -uī, -tentum
return (go back), redeō, -īre, -iī, -itum
return (in return for), prō + *abl.*
riches, dīvitiae, -ārum, *f. pl.*
right (*noun*), iūs, iūris, *n.*; (*adj.*), dexter, -tra, -trum
road, via, -ae, *f.*
Roman, Rōmānus, -a, -um
Rome, Rōma, -ae, *f.*
rose, rosa, -ae, *f.*
rule (*noun*), regnum, -ī, *n.*; (*verb*), regō, -ere, rēxī, rēctum
rumor, rūmor, -mōris, *m.*
run, currō, -ere, cucurrī, cursum

## S

sad, tristis, -e
safe, salvus, -a, -um
safety, salūs, -lūtis, *f.*
sailor, nauta, -ae, *m.*
sake (for the sake of), *gen.* + causā
salt, sāl, salis, *m.*
same, īdem, eadem, idem
satisfy, satiō (1)
save, servō (1); cōnservō (1)
say, dīcō, -ere, dīxī, dictum
school, lūdus, -ī, *m.*
sea, mare, -is, *n.*
second, secundus, -a, -um; alter, -era, -erum
see, videō, -ēre, vīdī, vīsum
seek, petō, -ere, -īvī, -ītum; quaerō, -ere, -sīvī, -sītum
seem, videor, -ērī, vīsus sum
seize, rapiō, -ere, -uī, raptum

**senate,** senātus, -ūs, *m.*
**send,** mittō, -ere, mīsī, missum
**serious,** gravis, -e
**serve,** serviō, -īre, -īvī, -ītum + *dat.*
**service,** officium, -iī, *n.*
**seven,** septem
**she,** ea; *often indicated only by the personal ending of verb*
**ship,** nāvis, -is, *f.*
**short,** brevis, -e
**show,** ostendō, -ere, -ī, -tentum; dēmōnstrō (1)
**shun,** vītō (1); fugiō, -ere, fūgī, fugitūrum
**sign,** signum, -ī, *n.*
**similar,** similis, -e
**since,** quoniam + *indic.;* cum + *subjunct.; abl. abs.*
**sister,** soror, -rōris, *f.*
**six,** sex
**skill,** ars, artis, *f.*
**slave,** servus, -ī, *m.;* **slavegirl,** serva, -ae, *f.*
**slavery,** servitūs, -tūtis, *f.*
**sleep** (*verb*), dormiō, -īre, -īvī, -ītum; (*noun*), somnus, -ī, *m.*
**slender,** gracilis, -e
**small,** parvus, -a, -um
**so,** ita, sīc (*usually with verbs*), tam (*usually with adjs. and advs.*); **so great,** tantus, -a, -um
**soldier,** mīles, -litis, *m.*
**some, a certain one** (*indef.*), quīdam, quaedam, quiddam; (*more emphatic pron.*), aliquis, aliquid
**some . . . others,** aliī . . . aliī
**son,** fīlius, -iī, *m.*
**soon,** mox
**sort,** genus, -neris, *n.*
**soul,** animus, -ī, *m.*
**sound,** sānus, -a, -um; salvus, -a, -um
**spare,** parcō, -ere, pepercī, parsūrum + *dat.*
**speak,** dīcō, -ere, dīxī, dictum; loquor, -ī, locūtus sum
**spirit,** spīritus, -ūs, *m.*
**stand,** stō, stāre, stetī, statum
**star,** stēlla, -ae, *f.*
**start,** proficīscor, -ī, -fectus sum
**state,** cīvitās, -tātis, *f.;* rēs pūblica, reī pūblicae, *f.*
**story,** fābula, -ae, *f.*
**street,** via, -ae, *f.*
**strength,** vīrēs, -ium, *f. pl.*
**strong,** fortis, -e; **be strong,** valeō, -ēre, -uī, -itūrum
**student,** discipula, -ae, *f.;* discipulus, -ī, *m.*
**study** (*noun*), studium, -iī, *n.;* (*verb*), studeō, -ēre, -uī + *dat.*
**suddenly,** subitō
**summer,** aestās, -tātis, *f.*

**sun,** sōl, sōlis, *m.*
**support,** alō, -ere, -uī, altum
**suppose,** opīnor, -ārī, -ātus sum; putō (1)
**suppress,** opprimō, -primere, -pressī, -pressum
**supreme power,** imperium, -iī, *n.*
**sure,** certus, -a, -um
**surrender,** trādō, -ere, -didī, -ditum
**sweet,** dulcis, -e
**swift,** celer, -eris, -ere
**sword,** ferrum, -ī, *n.;* gladius, -iī, *m.*
**Syracuse,** Syrācūsae, -ārum, *f. pl.*

**T**

**talk,** loquor, -ī, -cūtus sum
**teach,** doceō, -ēre, -uī, doctum
**teacher,** magister, -trī, *m.;* magistra, -ae, *f.*
**tear,** lacrima, -ae, *f.*
**tell,** dīcō, -ere, dīxī, dictum
**ten,** decem
**terrify,** terreō, -ēre, -uī, -itum
**territory,** fīnēs, -ium, *m. pl.*
**than,** quam; *or simple abl.*
**thank,** grātiās agō, -ere, ēgī, āctum + *dat.*
**that** (*demonstrative*), ille, illa, illud; is, ea, id; **that (of yours),** iste, ista, istud
**that** (*subord. conj.*), *not expressed in ind. state.;* ut (*purp. and result*); nē (*fear*)
**that . . . not,** nē (*purp.*); ut . . . nōn (*result*); ut (*fear*)
**that** (*rel. pron.*), quī, quae, quod
**their,** suus, -a, -um (*reflexive*); eōrum, eārum (*not reflexive*)
**them.** *See* **he, she, it.**
**then,** tum, deinde
**there,** ibi
**therefore,** igitur (*postpositive*)
**these.** *See* **this,** *demonstrative.*
**they.** *See* **he, she, it;** *often expressed simply by the personal ending of verb*
**thing,** rēs, reī, *f.; often merely the n. of an adj.*
**think,** putō (1); arbitror, -ārī, -ātus sum
**third,** tertius, -a, -um
**this,** hic, haec, hoc; is, ea, id
**those.** *See* **that,** *demonstrative.*
**thousand,** mīlle (*indecl. adj. sg.*), mīlia, -ium, *n.* (*noun in pl.*)
**three,** trēs, tria
**through,** per + *acc.*
**throughout,** per + *acc.*
**throw,** iaciō, -ere, iēcī, iactum
**thus,** sīc

**time,** tempus, -poris, *n.;* **(period of) time,** aetās, -tātis, *f.*
**to** (*place to which*), ad + *acc.;* (*ind. obj.*), dat.; (*purp.*), ut + *subjunct.,* ad + *gerund or gerundive*
**today,** hodiē
**tolerate,** tolerō (1)
**tomorrow,** crās
**too,** nimis, nimium; *or use compar. degree of adj. or adv.*
**touch,** tangō, -ere, tetigī, tāctum
**travel (abroad),** peregrīnor, -ārī, -ātus sum
**trivial,** levis, -e
**troops,** cōpiae, -ārum, *f. pl.*
**Troy,** Trōia, -ae, *f.*
**true,** vērus, -a, -um
**truly,** vērē
**trust,** crēdō, -ere, -didī, -ditum + *dat.*
**truth,** vēritās, -tātis, *f.*
**try,** experior, -īrī, expertus sum
**turn,** vertō, -ere, -ī, versum
**twenty,** vīgintī
**two,** duo, duae, duo
**type,** genus, -neris, *n.*
**tyrant,** tyrannus, -ī, *m.*

**U**

**unable (be),** nōn possum
**uncertain,** incertus, -a, -um
**under,** sub + *abl.* (= *place where*), + *acc.* (= *place to which*)
**understand,** intellegō, -ere, -lēxī, -lēctum; comprehendō, -ere, -ī, -hēnsum
**unfortunate,** miser, -era, -erum
**unless,** nisi
**unwilling (be),** nōlō, nōlle, nōluī
**urban, urbane,** urbānus, -a, -um
**urge,** hortor, -ārī, -ātus sum
**use,** ūtor, -ī, ūsus sum + *abl.*

**V**

**Vergil,** Vergilius, -iī, *m.*
**verse,** versus, -ūs, *m.*
**very,** *express this by the superl. degree of adj. or adv.*
**vice,** vitium, -iī, *n.*
**virtue,** virtūs, -tūtis, *f.*

**W**

**wage,** gerō, -ere, gessī, gestum
**walls,** moenia, -ium, *n. pl.*
**want,** volō, velle, voluī
**war,** bellum, -ī, *n.*

**warn,** moneō, -ēre, -uī, -itum
**water,** aqua, -ae, *f.*
**we.** *See* **I;** *often expressed simply by the personal ending of verb*
**wealth,** dīvitiae, -ārum, *f. pl.*
**weapons,** arma, -ōrum, *n. pl.*
**well,** bene
**what** (*pron.*), quid; (*adj.*), quī, quae, quod
**whatever,** quisquis, quidquid
**when,** *participial phrase; abl. abs.;* cum + *subjunct.;* (*interrog.*), quandō; (*rel.*), ubi
**whence,** unde, *adv.*
**where,** ubi
**wherefore,** quārē
**which** (*rel. pron. and interrog. adj.*), quī, quae, quod
**while,** dum
**who** (*rel.*), quī, quae, quod; (*interrog.*), quis, quid
**whole,** tōtus, -a, -um
**why,** cūr
**wicked,** malus, -a, -um
**wife,** uxor, uxōris, *f.*
**willing (be),** volō, velle, voluī
**window,** fenestra, -ae, *f.*
**wine,** vīnum, -ī, *n.*
**wisdom,** sapientia, -ae, *f.*
**wise,** sapiēns, *gen.* sapientis
**wisely,** sapienter
**wish,** cupiō, -ere, -īvī, -ītum; volō, velle, voluī
**with,** cum + *abl.; abl. of means* (*no prep.*)
**without,** sine + *abl.*
**woman,** fēmina, -ae, *f.; often expressed by f. of an adj.*
**word,** verbum, -ī, *n.*
**work,** labor, -bōris, *m.;* opus, operis, *n.*
**world,** mundus, -ī, *m.*
**worse,** peior, -ius
**worst,** pessimus, -a, -um
**write,** scrībō, -ere, scrīpsī, scrīptum
**writer,** scrīptor, -tōris, *m.*

**Y**

**year,** annus, -ī, *m.*
**yesterday,** heri
**yield,** cēdō, -ere, cessī, cessum
**you,** tū, tuī; *often expressed simply by the personal ending of verb*
**young man,** adulēscēns, -centis, *m.*
**your** (*sg.*), tuus, -a, -um; (*pl.*), vester, -tra, -trum
**yourself** (*reflexive*), tuī, tibi, *etc.;* (*intensive*), ipse, ipsa
**youth,** iuvenis, -is, *m.*

# VOCĀBVLA: LATIN-ENGLISH

An Arabic numeral after a vocabulary entry indicates the chapter **Vocābula** in which the word is first introduced. Arabic (1) in parentheses after a verb shows that this is a regular verb of the 1st conjugation with a sequence of principal parts ending in **-āre, -āvī, -ātum**. For prefixes and suffixes see the lists in the Appendix.

## A

**ā** *or* **ab**, *prep.* + *abl.*, from, away from; by (*agent*). 14

**abeō, -īre, -iī, -itum**, go away, depart, leave. 37

**absconditus, -a, -um**, hidden, secret

**absēns**, *gen.* **-sentis**, *adj.*, absent, away. 37

**absum, -esse, āfuī, āfutūrum**, be away, be absent

**abundantia, -ae**, *f.*, abundance

**ac.** *See* **atque.**

**accēdō, -ere, -cessī, -cessum**, come near, approach. 36

**accipiō, -ere, -cēpī, -ceptum**, take, receive, accept. 24

**accommodō** (1), adjust, adapt

**accūsātor, -tōris**, *m.*, accuser

**accūsō** (1), accuse

**ācer, ācris, ācre**, sharp, keen, eager, severe, fierce. 16

**acerbitās, -tātis**, *f.*, harshness

**acerbus, -a, -um**, harsh, bitter, grievous. 12

**Achillēs, -is**, *m.*, Achilles, Greek hero, chief character in the *Iliad*

**aciēs, -ēī**, *f.*, sharp edge, keenness, line of battle

**acquīrō, -ere, -quīsīvī, -quīsītum**, acquire, gain

**ācriter**, *adv.*, keenly, fiercely. 32

**ad**, *prep.* + *acc.*, to, up to, near to. 8

**addiscō, -ere, -didicī**, learn in addition

**addūcō, -ere, -dūxī, -ductum**, lead to, induce

**adeō, -īre, -iī, -itum**, go to, approach. 37

**adferō, -ferre, attulī, allātum**, bring to. 31

**adficiō, -ere, -fēcī, -fectum**, affect, afflict, weaken

**adiciō, -ere, -iēcī, -iectum**, add

**adiuvō, -āre, -iūvī, -iūtum**, help, aid, assist; please. 4

**admīror, -ārī, -ātus sum**, wonder at, admire

**admittō, -ere, -mīsī, -missum**, admit, receive, let in. 17

**admoneō = moneō**

**adnuō, -ere, -nuī**, nod assent

**adoptō** (1), wish for oneself, select, adopt

**adsum, -esse, -fuī, -futūrum**, be near, be present, assist

**adūlātiō, -ōnis**, *f.*, fawning, flattery

**adulēscēns, -centis**, *m. and f.*, young man or woman. 12

**adulēscentia, -ae**, *f.*, youth, young manhood; youthfulness. 5

**adultus, -a, -um**, grown up, mature, adult

**adūrō, -ere, -ussī, -ustum**, set fire to, burn, singe

**adveniō, -īre, -vēnī, -ventum**, come (to), arrive

**adversus, -a, -um**, facing, opposite, adverse. 34

**adversus**, *prep.* + *acc.*, toward, facing; against

**advesperāscit, advesperāscere, advesperāvit**, *impers.*, evening is coming on, it is growing dark

**aedificium, -iī**, *n.*, building, structure. 39

**aegrē**, *adv.*, with difficulty, hardly, scarcely

**aequitās, -tātis**, *f.*, justice, fairness, equity

**aequus, -a, -um**, level, even, calm, equal, just, favorable. 22

**aes, aeris**, *n.*, bronze. 40

**aestās, -tātis**, *f.*, summer. 35

**aestus, -ūs**, *m.*, heat, tide

**aetās, -tātis**, *f.*, period of life, life, age, an age, time. 16

**aeternus, -a, -um**, eternal

**Agamemnon, -nonis**, *m.*, Agamemnon, commander-in-chief of the Greek forces at Troy

**ager, agrī**, *m.*, field, farm. 3

**agō, -ere, ēgī, āctum**, drive, lead, do, act; *of time or life*, pass, spend; **grātiās agere** + *dat.*, thank. 8

**agricola, -ae**, *m.*, farmer. 3

**agrīcultūra, -ae**, *f.*, agriculture

**āit, āiunt**, he says, they say, assert. 25

**Alexander, -drī,** *m.,* Alexander the Great, renowned Macedonian general and king, 4th cent., B.C.

**aliēnus, -a, -um,** belonging to another (*cf.* **alius**), foreign, strange, alien

**aliōquī,** *adv.,* otherwise

**aliquī, aliqua, aliquod,** *indef. pronominal adj.,* some

**aliquis, aliquid** (*gen.* **alicuius;** *dat.* **alicui**), *indef. pron.,* someone, somebody, something. 23

**aliter,** *adv.,* otherwise

**alius, alia, aliud,** other, another; **aliī . . . aliī,** some . . . others. 9

**alō, -ere, aluī, altum,** nourish, support, sustain, increase; cherish. 13

**alter, -era, -erum,** the other (of two), second. 9

**altus, -a, -um,** high, deep

**ambitiō, -ōnis,** *f.,* a canvassing for votes; ambition; flattery

**ambulō** (1), walk. 39

**āmēn,** *adv. from Hebrew,* truly, verily, so be it

**amīca, -ae,** *f.,* (female) friend. 3

**amīcitia, -ae,** *f.,* friendship. 10

**amiculum, -ī,** *n.,* cloak

**amīcus, -a, -um,** friendly. 11

**amīcus, -ī,** *m.,* (male) friend. 3

**āmittō, -ere, -mīsī, -missum,** send away; lose, let go. 12

**amō** (1), love, like; **amābō tē,** please. 1

**amor, amōris,** *m.,* love. 7

**āmoveō, -ēre, -mōvī, -mōtum,** move away, remove

**an,** *adv. and conj. introducing the second part of a double question* (*see* **utrum**), or; *used alone,* or, can it be that

**ancilla, -ae,** *f.,* maidservant

**angelus, -ī,** *m.,* angel

**angulus, -ī,** *m.,* corner

**angustus, -a, -um,** narrow, limited

**anima, -ae,** *f.,* air, breath; soul, spirit. 34

**animal, -mālis,** *n.,* a living creature, animal. 14

**animus, -ī,** *m.,* soul, spirit, mind; **animī, -ōrum,** high spirits, pride, courage. 5

**annus, -ī,** *m.,* year. 12

**ante,** *prep. + acc.,* before (*in place or time*), in front of; *adv.,* before, previously. 13

**anteā,** *adv.,* before, formerly

**antepōnō, -ere, -posuī, -positum,** put before, prefer + *dat.* 35

**antīquus, -a, -um,** ancient, old-time. 2

**Apollō, -linis,** *m.,* Phoebus Apollo, god of sun, prophecy, poetry, etc.

**apparātus, -ūs,** *m.,* equipment, splendor

**appellō** (1), speak to, address (as), call, name. 14

**approbō** (1), approve

**appropinquō** (1) + *dat.,* approach, draw near to

**aptus, -a, -um,** fit, suitable

**apud,** *prep. + acc.,* among, in the presence of, at the house of. 31

**aqua, -ae,** *f.,* water. 14

**āra, -ae,** *f.,* altar

**arānea, -ae,** *f.,* spider's web

**arbitror, -ārī, -ātus sum,** judge, think. 34

**arbor, -boris,** *f.,* tree. 38

**arcus, -ūs,** *m.,* bow

**argentum, -ī,** *n.,* silver, money

**argūmentum, -ī,** *n.,* proof, evidence, argument. 19

**arma, -ōrum,** *n.,* arms, weapons. 28

**arō** (1), plow

**ars, artis,** *f.,* art, skill. 14

**arx, arcis,** *f.,* citadel, stronghold. 23

**as, assis,** *m.,* an as (a small copper coin roughly equivalent to a cent). 31

**Asia, -ae,** *f.,* Asia, commonly the Roman province in Asia Minor. 12

**asper, -era, -erum,** rough, harsh. 21

**aspiciō, -ere, -spexī, -spectum,** look at, behold

**assentātor, -tōris,** *m.,* yes-man, flatterer

**astrum, -ī,** *n.,* star, constellation

**at,** *conj.,* but; but, mind you; but, you say; *a more emotional adversative than* **sed.** 19

**āter, ātra, ātrum,** dark, gloomy

**Athēnae, -ārum,** *f. pl.,* Athens. 37

**Athēniēnsis, -e,** Athenian; **Athēniēnsēs, -ium,** the Athenians

**atque** *or* **ac,** *conj.,* and also, and even, and in fact. 21

**atquī,** *conj.,* and yet, still

**auctor, -tōris,** *m.,* increaser; author, originator. 19

**auctōritās, -tātis,** *f.,* authority

**audācia, -ae,** *f.,* daring, boldness, audacity

**audāx,** *gen.* **audācis,** daring, bold

**audeō, -ēre, ausus sum,** dare. 7

**audiō, -īre, -īvī, -ītum,** hear, listen to. 10

**audītor, -tōris,** *m.,* hearer, listener, member of an audience. 16

**auferō, -ferre, abstulī, ablātum,** bear away, carry off

**Augustus, -ī,** *m.,* Augustus, the first Roman emperor

**aureus, -a, -um,** golden

**auris, -is,** *f.,* ear. 14

**aurum, -ī,** *n.,* gold

**aut,** *conj.,* or; **aut . . . aut,** either . . . or. 17

**autem,** *postpositive conj.,* however; moreover. 11

**auxilium, -iī,** *n.,* aid, help. 31

**avāritia, -ae,** *f.,* greed, avarice

**avārus, -a, -um,** greedy, avaricious. 3

**āvehō, -ere, -vexī, -vectum,** carry away

āvertō, -ere, -vertī, -versum, turn away, avert. 23

āvocō (1), call away, divert

# B

balbus, -a, -um, stammering, stuttering

barba, -ae, f., beard

bāsium, -iī, n., kiss. 4

beātus, -a, -um, happy, fortunate, blessed. 10

bellicus, -a, -um, relating to war, military

bellum, -ī, n., war. 4

bellus, -a, -um, pretty, handsome, charming. 4

bene, adv. of bonus, well, satisfactorily, quite. 11 (compar. melius; superl. optimē. 32)

beneficium, -iī, n., benefit, kindness, favor. 19

benevolentia, -ae, f., good will, kindness

bēstia, -ae, f., animal, beast

bibō, -ere, bibī, drink. 30

bis, adv., twice

bonus, -a, -um, good, kind. 4 (compar. melior; superl. optimus. 27)

bōs, bovis, m./f., bull, ox, cow

brevis, -e, short, small, brief. 16

brevitās, -tātis, f., shortness, brevity

breviter, adv., briefly

Britannia, -ae, f., Britain

Brundisium, -iī, n., important seaport in S. Italy

Brūtus, -ī, m., famous Roman name: L. Junius Brutus, who helped establish the Roman republic; M. Junius Brutus, one of the conspirators against Julius Caesar

# C

C., abbreviation for the common name Gāius

cadō, -ere, cecidī, cāsūrum, fall. 12

caecus, -a, -um, blind. 17

caelestis, -e, heavenly, celestial

caelum, -ī, n., sky, heaven. 5

Caesar, -saris, m., Caesar, especially Gaius Julius Caesar. 12

calamitās, -tātis, f., misfortune, disaster

calculus, -ī, m., pebble

campana, -ae, f., bell (late Lat.)

candidus, -a, -um, shining, bright, white; beautiful. 33

canis, -is (gen. pl. canum), m./f., dog

canō, -ere, cecinī, cantum, to sing about

cantō (1), sing

capillus, -ī, m., hair (of head or beard)

capiō, -ere, cēpī, captum, take, capture, seize, get. 10

captō (1), grab, seek to get, hunt for (legacies, etc.)

caput, -pitis, n., head; leader; beginning; life; heading, Capvt XI

carbō, -bōnis, m., coal, charcoal

careō, -ēre, -uī, -itūrum + abl. of separation, be without, be deprived of, want, lack, be free from. 20

cāritās, -tātis, f., dearness, affection

carmen, -minis, n., song, poem. 7

carpō, -ere, carpsī, carptum, harvest, pluck; seize. 36

Carthāgō, -ginis, f., Carthage (city in N. Africa). 24

cārus, -a, -um, dear. 11

casa, -ae, f., house, cottage, hut. 21

cāsus, -ūs, m., accident, chance

catēna, -ae, f., chain

Catilīna, -ae, m., L. Sergius Catiline, leader of the conspiracy against the Roman state in 63 B.C.

Catullus, -ī, m., Gaius Valerius Catullus, 1st cent. B.C. lyric poet

cattus, -ī, m., cat (late word for classical fēlēs, -is)

causa, -ae, f., cause, reason; case, situation; causā with a preceding gen., for the sake of, on account of. 21

caveō, -ēre, cāvī, cautum, beware, avoid

cavus, -ī, m., hole

cēdō, -ere, cessī, cessum, go, withdraw; yield to, submit, grant. 28

celer, -eris, -ere, swift, quick, rapid. 16

celeritās, -tātis, f., speed, swiftness

celeriter, swiftly, quickly

cēna, -ae, f., dinner. 26

cēnō (1), dine. 5

centum, indecl. adj., a hundred. 15

cernō, -ere, crēvī, crētum, distinguish, discern, perceive. 22

certē, adv., certainly

certus, -a, -um, definite, sure, certain, reliable. 19

cervus, -ī, m., stag, deer

cēterī, -ae, -a, the remaining, the rest, the other. 30

Cicerō, -rōnis, m., Marcus Tullius Cicero. 8

cicūta, -ae, f., hemlock (poison)

cinis, -neris, m., ashes

circēnsēs, -ium, m. pl. (sc. lūdī), games in the Circus

cito, adv., quickly. 17

cīvīlis, -e, civil, civic

cīvis, -is, m./f., citizen. 14

cīvitās, -tātis, f., state, citizenship. 7

clārus, -a, -um, clear, bright; renowned, famous, illustrious. 18

claudō, -ere, clausī, clausum, shut, close

clēmentia, -ae, f., mildness, gentleness, mercy. 16

coepī, coepisse, coeptum (defective verb; pres. system supplied by incipiō), began. 17

coërceō, -ēre, -uī, -itum, curb, check, repress

cōgitō (1), think, ponder, consider, plan. 1

cognōscō, -ere, -nōvī, -nitum, become acquainted with, learn, recognize; in perf. tenses, know. 30

**cōgō, -ere, coēgī, coāctum,** drive *or* bring together, force, compel. 36

**colligō, -ere, -lēgī, -lēctum,** gather together, collect

**collocō** (1), place, put, arrange

**collum, -ī,** *n.,* neck

**colō, -ere, coluī, cultum,** cultivate; cherish

**color, -ōris,** *m.,* color

**commemorō** (1), remind, relate, mention

**commisceō, -ēre, -uī, -mixtum,** intermingle, join

**committō, -ere, -mīsī, -missum,** entrust, commit. 15

**commūnis, -e,** common, general, of/for the community. 20

**comparō** (1), compare

**compōnō, -ere, -posuī, -positum,** put together, compose

**comprehendō, -ere, -hendī, -hēnsum,** grasp, seize, arrest; comprehend, understand. 30

**concēdō, -ere, -cessī, -cessum,** yield, grant, concede

**concilium, -iī,** *n.,* council

**condō, -ere, -didī, -ditum,** put together or into, store; build, found, establish. 29

**cōnferō, -ferre, contulī, collātum,** bring together, compare; confer, bestow; **sē cōnferre,** take oneself, *i.e.,* go. 31

**cōnfīdō, -ere, -fīsus sum,** have confidence in, believe confidently, be confident

**cōnfiteor, -ērī, -fessus sum,** confess

**congregō** (1), gather together, assemble

**coniciō, -ere, -iēcī, -iectum,** throw, hurl, put with force; put together, conjecture

**coniūrātiō, -ōnis,** *f.,* conspiracy

**coniūrātī, -ōrum,** *m. pl.,* conspirators. 20

**cōnor, -ārī, -ātus sum,** try, attempt. 34

**cōnscientia, -ae,** *f.,* consciousness, knowledge; conscience

**cōnscius, -a, -um,** conscious, aware of

**cōnservō** (1), preserve, conserve, maintain. 1

**cōnsilium, -iī,** *n.,* counsel, advice, plan, purpose; judgment, wisdom. 4

**cōnsistō, -ere, -stitī + in,** depend on

**cōnstō, -āre, -stitī, -stātūrum + ex,** consist of

**cōnsuēscō, -ere, -suēvī, -suētum,** become accustomed

**cōnsul, -sulis,** *m.,* consul. 11

**cōnsulō, -ere, -suluī, -sultum,** look out for, have regard for

**cōnsultum, -ī,** *n.,* decree

**cōnsūmō, -ere, -sūmpsī, -sūmptum,** use up, consume. 30

**contemnō, -ere, -tempsī, -temptum,** despise, scorn. 36

**contendō, -ere, -tendī, -tentum,** strive, struggle, contend, hasten. 29

**contineō, -ēre, -tinuī, -tentum,** hold together, keep, enclose, restrain, contain. 21

**contingō, -ere, -tigī, -tāctum,** touch closely, befall, fall to one's lot

**contrā,** *prep. + acc.,* against. 19

**contundō, -tundere, -tudī, -tūsum,** beat, crush, bruise, destroy. 36

**conturbō** (1), throw into confusion

**convertō, -ere, -vertī, -versum,** turn around, cause to turn

**convocō** (1), call together, convene

**cōpia, -ae,** *f.,* abundance, supply; **cōpiae, -ārum,** supplies, troops, forces. 8

**cōpiōsē,** *adv.,* fully, at length, copiously

**Corinthus, -ī,** *f.,* Corinth

**cornū, -ūs,** *n.,* horn. 20

**corōna, -ae,** *f.,* crown

**corpus, -poris,** *n.,* body. 7

**corrigō, -ere, -rēxī, -rēctum,** make right, correct

**corrōborō** (1), strengthen

**corrumpō, -ere, -rūpī, -ruptum,** ruin, corrupt

**cōtīdiē,** *adv.,* daily, every day. 36

**crās,** *adv.,* tomorrow. 5

**creātor, -tōris,** *m.,* creator

**creātūra, -ae,** *f.,* creature (*late Lat.*)

**crēber, -bra, -brum,** thick, frequent, numerous

**crēdō, -ere, crēdidī, crēditum,** believe, trust. 25; + *dat.* 35

**creō** (1), create. 12

**crēscō, -ere, crēvī, crētum,** increase. 34

**crūdēlis, -e,** cruel

**crūstulum, -ī,** *n.,* pastry, cookie

**cubiculum, -ī,** *n.,* bedroom, room

**culpa, -ae,** *f.,* fault, blame. 5

**culpō** (1), blame, censure. 5

**cultūra, -ae,** *f.,* cultivation

**cum,** *conj., with subjunct.,* when, since, although; *with indic.,* when. 31

**cum,** *prep. + abl.,* with. 10

**cūnctātiō, -ōnis,** *f.,* delay

**cūnctātor, -tōris,** *m.,* delayer

**cūnctor** (1), delay

**cupiditās, -tātis,** *f.,* desire, longing, passion; cupidity, avarice. 10

**cupīdō, -dinis,** *f.,* desire, passion. 36

**cupidus, -a, -um,** desirous, eager, fond; + *gen.,* desirous of, eager for. 39

**cupiō, -ere, cupīvī, cupītum,** desire, wish, long for. 17

**cūr,** *adv.,* why. 18

**cūra, -ae,** *f.,* care, attention, caution, anxiety. 4

**cūrō** (1), care for, attend to; heal, cure; take care. 36

**currō, -ere, cucurrī, cursum,** run, rush, move quickly. 14

**cursus, -ūs,** *m.,* running, race; course. 28

**curvus, -a, -um,** curved, crooked, wrong

custōdia, -ae, *f.,* protection, custody; *pl.,* guards. 32

custōs, -tōdis, *m.,* guardian, guard

# D

damnō (1), condemn

Dāmoclēs, -is, *m.,* Damocles, an attendant of Dionysius

dē, *prep. + abl.,* down from, from; concerning, about. 3

dea, -ae, *f.* (*dat. and abl. pl.* deābus), goddess. 6

dēbeō, -ēre, -uī, -itum, owe, ought, must, should. 1

dēbilitō (1), weaken

dēcernō, -ere, -crēvī, -crētum, decide, settle, decree. 36

dēcertō (1), fight it out, fight to the finish, contend

decimus, -a, -um, tenth. 15

dēcipiō, -ere, -cēpī, -ceptum, deceive

decor, -cōris, *m.,* beauty, grace

dēcrētum, -ī, *n.,* decree

dēdicō (1), dedicate. 28

dēfendō, -ere, -fendī, -fēnsum, ward off, defend, protect. 20

dēficiō, -ere, -fēcī, -fectum, fail

dēgustō (1), taste

dehinc, *adv.,* then, next. 25

deinde, *adv.,* thereupon, next, then. 18

dēlectātiō, -ōnis, *f.,* delight, pleasure, enjoyment. 27

dēlectō (1), delight, charm, please. 19

dēleō, -ēre, dēlēvī, dēlētum, destroy, wipe out, erase. 17

dēlīberō (1), consider, deliberate

dēmēns, *gen.* -mentis, *adj.,* out of one's mind, insane, foolish

dēmittō, -ere, -mīsī, -missum, let down, lower

dēmōnstrō (1), point out, show, demonstrate. 8

Dēmosthenēs, -is, *m.,* Demosthenes, the most famous Greek orator, 4th cent. B.C.

dēnique, *adv.,* at last, finally. 29

dēns, dentis, *m.,* tooth

dēpōnō, -ere, -posuī, -positum, put down, lay aside

dēportō (1), carry off

dēsīderō (1), desire, long for, miss. 17

dēsidiōsus, -a, -um, lazy

dēsinō, -ere, -sīvī, -situm, cease, leave off

dēsipiō, -ere, act foolishly

dēstinātus, -a, -um, resolved, resolute, firm

dētrīmentum, -ī, *n.,* loss, detriment

deus, -ī, *m.* (*voc. sg.* deus, *nom. pl.* deī or dī, *dat. and abl. pl.* dīs), god. 6

dēvocō (1), call down *or* away

dexter, -tra, -trum, right, right-hand. 20

diabolus, -ī, *m.,* devil

dīcō, -ere, dīxī, dictum, say, tell, speak; call, name. 10

dictāta, -ōrum, *n. pl.,* things dictated, lessons, precepts

dictātor, -tōris, *m.,* dictator

dictō (1), say repeatedly, dictate

diēs, -ēī, *m.,* day. 22

difficilis, -e, hard, difficult, troublesome. 16

digitus, -ī, *m.,* finger, toe. 31

dignitās, -tātis, *f.,* merit, prestige, dignity. 38

dignus, -a, -um + *abl.,* worthy, worthy of. 29

dīligēns, *gen.* -gentis, *adj.,* diligent, careful. 27

dīligenter, *adv.,* diligently

dīligentia, -ae, *f.,* diligence

dīligō, -ere, dīlēxī, dīlēctum, esteem, love. 13

dīmidium, -iī, *n.,* half

dīmittō, -ere, -mīsī, -missum, send away, dismiss

Dionȳsius, -iī, *m.,* Dionysius, tyrant of Syracuse

discēdō, -ere, -cessī, -cessum, go away, depart. 20

discipula, -ae, *f.,* learner, pupil, disciple. 6

discipulus, -ī, *m.,* learner, pupil, disciple. 6

discō, -ere, didicī, learn. 8

disputātiō, -ōnis, *f.,* discussion

disputō (1), discuss

dissimilis, -e, unlike, different. 27

dissimulō (1), conceal

distinguō, -ere, -stīnxī, -stīnctum, distinguish

diū, *adv.,* long, for a long time. 12

dīves, *gen.* dīvitis *or* dītis, *adj.,* rich, wealthy. 32

dīvīnus, -a, -um, divine, sacred

dīvitiae, -ārum, *f. pl.,* riches, wealth. 13

dō, dare, dedī, datum, give, offer. 1

doceō, -ēre, -uī, doctum, teach. 8

doctrīna, -ae, *f.,* teaching, instruction, learning

doctus, -a, -um, taught, learned, skilled. 13

doleō, -ēre, -uī, -itūrum, grieve, suffer; hurt, give pain. 31

dolor, -lōris, *m.,* pain, grief. 38

domesticus, -a, -um, domestic; civil

domina, -ae, *f.,* mistress, lady. 40

dominātus, -ūs, *m.,* rule, mastery, tyranny

dominicus, -a, -um, belonging to a master; the Lord's

dominus, -ī, *m.,* master, lord. 40

domus, -ūs (-ī), *f.,* house, home; domī, at home; domum, (to) home; domō, from home. 37

dōnum, -ī, *n., gift,* present. 4

dormiō, -īre, -īvī, -ītum, sleep. 31

dubitō (1), doubt, hesitate. 30

dubium, -iī, *n.,* doubt

dūcō, -ere, dūxī, ductum, lead; consider, regard; prolong. 8

dulcis, -e, sweet, pleasant, agreeable. 16

dum, *conj.,* while, as long as; at the same time that; until. 8

dummodo, *conj., with subjunct.,* provided that, so long as. 32

duo, duae, duo, two. 15

dūrō (1), harden, last, endure

dūrus, -a, -um, hard, harsh, rough, stern, unfeeling, hardy, tough, difficult. 29

dux, ducis, *m.,* leader, guide, commander, general. 23

## E

ē. *See* ex.

ecclēsia, -ae, *f.,* church (*ecclesiastical Lat.*)

ēducō (1), bring up, educate. 23

ēdūcō, -ere, -dūxī, -ductum, lead out

efferō, -ferre, extulī, ēlātum, carry out; bury; lift up, exalt

efficiō, -ere, -fēcī, -fectum, accomplish, perform, bring about, cause

effugiō, -ere, -fūgī, -fugitūrum, flee from, flee away, escape

egeō, -ēre, eguī + *abl. or gen.,* need, lack, want. 28

ego, meī, I. 11

ēgredior, -ī, -gressus sum, go out, depart. 34

ēiciō, -ere, -iēcī, -iectum, throw out, drive out. 15

elementum, -ī, *n.,* element, first principle

elephantus, -ī, *m.,* elephant. 31

ēloquēns, *gen.* -quentis, *adj.,* eloquent

ēloquentia, -ae, *f.,* eloquence

ēmendō (1), correct, emend

emō, -ere, ēmī, ēmptum, buy

ēmoveō, -ēre, -mōvī, -mōtum, move away, remove

enim, *postpositive conj.,* for, in fact, truly. 9

Ennius, -iī, *m.,* Quintus Ennius, early Roman writer

ēnumerō (1), count up, enumerate

eō, īre, iī (*or* īvī), itum, go. 37

epigramma, -matis, *n.,* inscription, epigram

epistula, -ae, *f.,* letter, epistle

equa, -ae, *f.,* horse. 23

eques, equitis, *m.,* horseman

equidem, *adv. especially common with 1st pers.,* indeed, truly, for my part

equitātus, -ūs, *m.,* cavalry

equus, -ī, *m.,* horse. 23

ergā, *prep.* + *acc.,* toward. 38

ergō, *adv.,* therefore

ēripiō, -ere, -ripuī, -reptum, snatch away, take away, rescue. 22

errō (1), wander; err, go astray, make a mistake, be mistaken. 1

error, -rōris, *m.,* a going astray, error, mistake

et, *conj.,* and; even (= etiam); et . . . et, both . . . and. 2

etiam, *adv.,* even, also. 11

etsī, *conj.,* even if (et-sī), although. 38

ēveniō, -īre, -vēnī, -ventum, come out, turn out, happen

ēventus, -ūs, *m.,* outcome, result

ex *or* ē, *prep* + *abl.,* out of, from within, from; by reason of, on account of; *following cardinal numerals,* of. Ex *can be used before consonants or vowels;* ē, *before consonants only.* 8

excellentia, -ae, *f.,* excellence, merit

excipiō, -ere, -cēpī, -ceptum, take out, except; take, receive, capture. 24

exclāmō (1), cry out, call out

exclūdō, -ere, -clūsī, -clūsum, shut out, exclude

excrusiō (1), torture, torment

excūsātiō, -ōnis, *f.,* excuse

exemplar, -plāris, *n.,* model, pattern, original. 14

exemplum, -ī, *n.,* example, model

exeō, -īre, -iī, -itum, go out, exit. 37

exercitus, -ūs, *m.,* army. 32

exigō, -igere, -ēgī, -āctum (*ex* + *agō*), drive out, force out, extract, drive through, complete, perfect. 36

eximius, -a, -um, extraordinary, excellent

exitium, -iī, *n.,* destruction, ruin. 4

expellō, -ere, -pulī, -pulsum, drive out, expel, banish. 24

experior, -īrī, -pertus sum, try, test; experience. 39

expleō, -ēre, -plēvī, -plētum, fill, fill up, complete. 28

explicō (1), unfold; explain; spread out, deploy. 40

expōnō, -ere, -posuī, -positum, set forth, explain, expose. 30

exquīsītus, -a, -um, sought-out, exquisite, excellent

exsilium, -iī, *n.,* exile, banishment. 31

exspectō (1), look for, expect, await. 15

exstinguō, -ere, -stīnxī, -stīnctum, extinguish

externus, -a, -um, foreign

extorqueō, -ēre, -torsī, -tortum, twist away, extort

extrā, *prep.* + *acc.,* beyond, outside

extrēmus, -a, -um, outermost, last, extreme

## F

Fabius, -iī, *m.,* Roman name; especially Quintus Fabius Maximus Cunctator (the Delayer), celebrated for his delaying tactics (Fabian tactics) against Hannibal

fābula, -ae, *f.,* story, tale; play. 24

facile, *adv.,* easily. 32

facilis, -e, easy; agreeable, affable. 16

faciō, -ere, fēcī, factum, make, do, accomplish, 10; *pass.:* fīō, fierī, factus sum. 36

factum, -ī, *n.,* deed, act, achievement. 13

facultās, -tātis, *f.,* ability, skill, opportunity, means

falsus, -a, -um, false, deceptive

fāma, -ae, *f.,* rumor, report; fame, reputation. 2

familia, -ae, *f.,* household, family. 19

fās (*indecl.*), *n.,* right, sacred duty; fās est, it is right, fitting, lawful

fateor, -ērī, fassus sum, confess, admit. 34

fatīgō (1), weary, tire out. 40

fātum, -ī, *n.*, fate; death; *often pl.,* the Fates. 29

faucēs, -ium, *f. pl.,* jaws; narrow passage.

fēlīciter, *adv.,* happily. 32

fēlīx, *gen.* -līcis, *adj.,* lucky, fortunate, happy. 22

fēmina, -ae, *f.,* woman. 3

fenestra, -ae, *f.,* window. 21

ferē, *adv.,* almost, nearly, generally

ferō, ferre, tulī, lātum, bear, carry, bring; suffer, endure, tolerate; say, report. 31

ferōx, gen. -rōcis, fierce, savage. 25

ferrum, -ī, *n.,* iron, sword. 22

ferus, -a, -um, wild, uncivilized, fierce

festīnātiō, -ōnis, *f.,* haste

festīnō (1), hasten, hurry

fīcus, -ī *and* -ūs, *f.,* fig tree

fidēlis, -e, faithful, loyal. 25

fidēs, -eī, *f.,* faith, trust, trustworthiness, fidelity; promise, guarantee, protection. 22

fīlia, -ae, *f.* (*dat. and abl. pl.* fīliābus), daughter. 3

fīlius, -iī, *m.,* son. 3

fīnis, -is, *m.,* end, limit, boundary; purpose; fīnēs, -ium (boundaries) territory. 21

fīō, fierī, factus sum, occur, happen; become, be made, be done. 36

fīrmus, -a, -um, firm, strong; reliable. 38

flamma, -ae, *f.,* flame, fire

fleō, -ēre, flēvī, flētum, weep

flūctus, -ūs, *m.,* billow, wave

flūmen, -minis, *n.,* river. 18

fluō, -ere, flūxī, flūxum, flow. 18

for, fārī, fātus sum, speak (prophetically), talk, foretell. 40

forīs, *adv.,* out of doors, outside. 37

fōrma, -ae, *f.,* form, shape, beauty. 2

formīca, -ae, *f.,* ant

fōrmō (1), form, shape, fashion

fors, fortis, *f.,* chance, fortune

forsan, *adv.,* perhaps

fortasse, *adv.,* perhaps. 36

fortis, -e, strong, brave. 16

fortiter, *adv.,* bravely. 32

fortūna, -ae, *f.,* fortune, luck. 2

fortūnātē, *adv.,* fortunately

fortūnātus, -a, -um, lucky, fortunate, happy. 13

forum, -ī, *n.,* market place, forum. 26

foveō, -ēre, fōvī, fōtum, comfort, nurture, support. 35

frāter, -tris, *m.,* brother. 8

frōns, frontis, *f.,* forehead, brow, front

frūctus, -ūs, *m.,* fruit; profit, benefit, enjoyment. 20

frūgālitās, -tātis, *f.,* frugality

frūstrā, *adv.,* in vain

fuga, -ae, *f.,* flight

fugiō, -ere, fūgī, fugitūrum, flee, hurry away; escape; go into exile; avoid, shun. 10

fugitīvus, -ī, *m.,* fugitive, deserter, runaway slave

fugō (1), put to flight, rout

fulgeō, -ēre, fulsī, flash, shine

furor, -rōris, *m.,* rage, frenzy, madness

fūrtificus, -a, -um, thievish

fūrtim, *adv.,* stealthily, secretly. 30

## G

Gāius, -iī, *m.,* Gaius, a common praenomen (first name); usually abbreviated to C. in writing

Gallus, -ī, *m.,* a Gaul. The Gauls were a Celtic people who inhabited the district which we know as France.

gaudeō, gaudēre, gāvīsus sum, be glad, rejoice. 23

gaudium, -iī, *n.,* joy, delight

geminus, -a, -um, twin. 25

gēns, gentis, *f.,* clan, race, nation, people. 21

genū, genūs, *n.,* knee. 20

genus, generis, *n.,* origin; kind, type, sort, class. 18

gerō, -ere, gessī, gestum, carry; carry on, manage, conduct, wage, accomplish, perform. 8

gladius, -iī, *m.,* sword

glōria, -ae, *f.,* glory, fame. 5

gracilis, -e, slender, thin. 27

Graecia, -ae, *f.,* Greece. 19

Graecus, -a, -um, Greek; Graecus, -ī, *m.,* a Greek. 6

grātia, -ae, *f.,* gratitude, favor; grātiās agere + *dat.,* to thank. 8

grātus, -a, -um, pleasing, agreeable; grateful. 37

gravis, -e, heavy, weighty; serious, important; severe, grievous. 19

gravitās, -tātis, *f.,* weight, seriousness, importance, dignity

graviter, *adv.,* heavily, seriously

gustō (1), taste

## H

habeō, -ēre, -uī, -itum, have, hold, possess; consider, regard. 3

hāmus, -ī, *m.,* hook

Hannibal, -balis, *m.,* Hannibal, celebrated Carthaginian general in the 2nd Punic War, 218–201 B.C.

hasta, -ae, *f.,* spear. 23

haud, *adv.,* not, not at all (*strong negative*)

heri, *adv.,* yesterday. 5

heu, *interj.,* ah!, alas! (*a sound of grief or pain*). 33

hic, haec, hoc, *demonstrative adj. and pron.,* this, the latter; *at times weakened to* he, she, it, they. 9

hīc, *adv.,* here. 25

hinc, *adv.,* from this place, hence

hodiē, *adv.,* today. 3

Homērus, -ī, *m.,* Homer, the Greek epic poet

homō, hominis, *m.,* human being, man. 7

honor, -nōris, *m.,* honor, esteem; public office. 30

hōra, -ae, *f.,* hour, time. 10

horrendus, -a, -um, horrible, dreadful

hortor, -ārī, -ātus sum, urge, encourage. 34

hortus, -ī, *m.,* garden

hospes, -pitis, *m.,* stranger, guest; host

hostis, -is, *m.,* an enemy (of the state); **hostēs, -ium,** the enemy. 18

hui, *interj., sound of surprise or approbation not unlike our* "whee"

hūmānitās, -tātis, *f.,* kindness, refinement

hūmānus, -a, -um, pertaining to man, human; humane, kind; refined, cultivated. 4

humilis, -e, lowly, humble. 27

humus, -ī, *f.,* ground, earth; soil. 37

hypocrita, -ae, *m.,* hypocrite (*ecclesiastical Lat.*)

I

iaceō, -ēre, -uī, lie; lie prostrate; lie dead. 25

iaciō, -ere, iēcī, iactum, throw, hurl. 15

iaculum, -ī, *n.,* dart, javelin

iam, *adv.,* now, already, soon. 19

iānua, -ae, *f.,* door. 35

ibi, *adv.,* there. 6

īdem, eadem, idem, the same. 11

identidem, *adv.,* repeatedly, again and again

idōneus, -a, -um, suitable, fit, appropriate. 37

igitur, *postpositive conj.,* therefore, consequently. 5

ignārus, -a, -um, not knowing, ignorant

ignis, -is, *m.,* fire. 22

ignōscō, -ere, -nōvī, -nōtum + *dat.,* grant pardon to, forgive, overlook. 35

illacrimō (1) + *dat.,* weep over

ille, illa, illud, *demonstrative adj. and pron.,* that, the former; the famous; *at times weakened to* he, she, it, they. 9

illūdō, -ere, -lūsī, -lūsum, mock, ridicule

imāgō, -ginis, *f.,* image, likeness

imitor, -ārī, -ātus sum, imitate

immineō, -ēre, overhang, threaten

immodicus, -a, -um, beyond measure, immoderate, excessive

immortālis, -e, not subject to death, immortal. 19

immōtus, -a, -um, unmoved; unchanged; unrelenting. 37

impedīmentum, -ī, *n.,* hindrance, impediment

impediō, -īre, -īvī, -ītum, impede, hinder, prevent. 38

impellō, -ere, -pulī, -pulsum, urge on, impel

impendeō, -ēre, hang over, threaten, be imminent

imperātor, -tōris, *m.,* general, commander-in-chief, emperor. 24

imperiōsus, -a, -um, powerful, domineering, imperious

imperium, -iī, *n.,* power to command, supreme power, authority, command, control. 24

imperō (1), give orders to, command + *dat.* + **ut.** 35

impleō, -ēre, implēvī, implētum, fill up, complete

imprīmīs, *adv.,* especially, particularly

imprōvidus, -a, -um, improvident

impudēns, *gen.* -dentis, *adj.,* shameless, impudent

impudenter, *adv.,* shamelessly, impudently

impūnītus, -a, -um, unpunished, unrestrained, safe

in, *prep.* + *abl.,* in, on, 3; + *acc.,* into, toward, against. 9

inānis, -e, empty, vain

incertus, -a, -um, uncertain, unsure, doubtful

incipiō, -ere, -cēpī, -ceptum, begin, commence. 17

inclūdō, -ere, -clūsī, -clūsum, shut in, inclose

incorruptus, -a, -um, uncorrupted, genuine, pure

incrēdibilis, -e, incredible

indicō (1), indicate, expose, accuse

indignus, -a, -um, unworthy

indūcō, -ere, -dūxī, -ductum, lead in, introduce, induce

industria, -ae, *f.,* industry, diligence

industrius, -a, -um, industrious, diligent

ineō, -īre, -iī, -itum, go in, enter; enter into, begin. 37

ineptiō, -īre, play the fool, trifle

inexpugnābilis, -e, impregnable, unconquerable

īnfantia, -ae, *f.,* infancy

īnferī, -ōrum, *m. pl.,* those below, the dead

īnferō, -ferre, intulī, illātum, bring in, bring upon, inflict

īnfīnītus, -a, -um, unlimited, infinite

īnfīrmus, -a, -um, not strong, weak, feeble. 38

īnflammō (1), set on fire, inflame

īnfōrmis, -e, formless, deformed, hideous

īnfortūnātus, -a, -um, unfortunate

ingenium, -iī, *n.,* nature, innate talent. 29

ingēns, *gen.* -gentis, *adj.,* huge. 16

ingrātus, -a, -um, unpleasant, ungrateful

iniciō, -ere, -iēcī, -iectum, throw on *or* into, put on; inspire

inimīcus, -ī, *m.,* (personal) enemy

inīquus, -a, -um, unequal, unfair, unjust

initium, -iī, *n.,* beginning, commencement. 33

iniūria, -ae, *f.,* injustice, injury, wrong. 39

iniūstus, -a, -um, unjust

inops, *gen.* -opis, *adj.,* poor, needy

inquam. *See* inquit.

**inquit,** *defective verb,* he says, *placed after one or more words of a direct quotation; other forms:* **inquam,** I say, **inquis,** you say. 22

**īnsānia, -ae,** *f.,* insanity, folly

**īnsciēns,** *gen.* **-entis,** unknowing, unaware

**īnscrībō, -ere, -scrīpsī, -scrīptum,** inscribe, entitle

**īnsidiae, -ārum,** *f. pl.,* ambush, plot, treachery. 6

**īnsōns,** *gen.* **-sontis,** guiltless, innocent

**īnstituō, -ere, -stituī, -stitūtum,** establish, institute

**īnsula, -ae,** *f.,* island. 23

**īnsurgō, -ere, -surrēxī, -surrēctum,** rise up

**integer, -gra, -grum,** untouched, whole, unhurt

**intellegō, -ere, -lēxī, -lēctum,** understand. 11

**intempestīvus, -a, -um,** untimely

**inter,** *prep.* + *acc.,* between, among. 15

**intercipiō, -ere, -cēpī, -ceptum,** intercept

**interdum,** *adv.,* at times, sometimes

**intereā,** *adv.,* meanwhile

**interficiō, -ere, -fēcī, -fectum,** kill, murder. 37

**interrogātiō, -ōnis,** *f.,* interrogation, inquiry

**intrō** (1), walk into, enter

**intrōdūcō, -ere, -dūxī, -ductum,** lead in, introduce

**intus,** *adv.,* within

**invādō, -ere, -vāsī, -vāsum,** enter on, move against, assail

**inveniō, -īre, -vēnī, -ventum,** come upon, find. 10

**inventor, -tōris,** *m.,* inventor

**invēstīgō** (1), track out, investigate

**invictus, -a, -um,** unconquered; unconquerable

**invideō, -ēre, -vīdī, -vīsum,** be envious; + *dat.,* look at with envy, envy, be jealous of. 31

**invidia, -ae,** *f.,* envy, jealousy, hatred. 31

**invīsus, -a, -um,** hated; hateful

**invītō** (1), entertain; invite, summon. 26

**invītus, -a, -um,** unwilling, against one's will

**iocus, -ī,** *m.,* joke, jest

**ipse, ipsa, ipsum,** *intensive pron.,* myself, yourself, himself, herself, itself, *etc.;* the very, the actual. 13

**īra, -ae,** *f.,* ire, anger. 2

**īrāscor, -ī, īrātus sum,** be angry

**īrātus, -a, -um,** angered, angry. 35

**irrītō** (1), excite, exasperate, irritate

**is, ea, id,** *demonstrative pron. and adj.,* this, that; *personal pron.,* he, she, it. 11

**iste, ista, istud,** *demonstrative pron. and adj.,* that of yours, that; such *(as you have, as you speak of); sometimes with contemptuous force, e.g.,* that despicable, that wretched. 9

**ita,** *adv. used with adjs., verbs, and advs.,* so, thus. 29

**Italia, -ae,** *f.,* Italy. 15

**itaque,** *adv.,* and so, therefore. 15

**iter, itineris,** *n.,* journey; route, road. 37

**iterō** (1), repeat

**iterum,** *adv.,* again, a second time. 21

**iubeō, -ēre, iussī, iussum,** bid, order, command. 21

**iūcunditās, -tātis,** *f.,* pleasure, charm

**iūcundus, -a, -um,** agreeable, pleasant, gratifying. 16

**iūdex, -dicis,** *m.,* judge, juror. 19

**iūdicium, -iī,** *n.,* judgment, decision, opinion; trial. 19

**iūdicō** (1), judge, consider

**iungō, -ere, iūnxī, iūnctum,** join. 13

**Iuppiter, Iovis,** *m.,* Jupiter, Jove

**iūrō** (1), swear

**iūs, iūris,** *n.,* right, justice, law. 14; **iūs iūrandum, iūris iūrandī,** *n.,* oath

**iussū,** *defective noun, abl. sg. only, m.,* at the command of

**iūstus, -a, -um,** just, right. 40

**iuvenis, -is** (*gen. pl.* **iuvenum**), *m./f.,* a youth, young person

**iuvō, -āre, iūvī, iūtum,** help, aid, assist; please. 4

## L

**lābor, -ī, lāpsus sum,** slip, glide

**labor, -bōris,** *m.,* labor, work, toil. 7

**labōrō** (1), labor; be in distress. 21

**labrum, -ī,** *n.,* lip

**lacessō, -ere, -īvī, -ītum,** harass, attack

**lacrima, -ae,** *f.,* tear. 40

**lacūnar, -nāris,** *n.,* paneled ceiling

**laetāns,** *gen.* **-tantis,** *adj.,* rejoicing

**laetus, -a, -um,** happy, joyful

**Latīnus, -a, -um,** Latin. 22

**laudātor, -tōris,** *m.,* praiser

**laudō** (1), praise. 1

**laus, laudis,** *f.,* praise, glory, fame. 8

**lēctor, -tōris,** *m.,* reader. 36

**lēctrīx, -trīcis,** *f.,* reader. 36

**lectus, -ī,** *m.,* bed

**lēgātus, -ī,** *m.,* ambassador, deputy

**legiō, -ōnis,** *f.,* legion

**legō, -ere, lēgī, lēctum,** pick out, choose; read. 18

**lēnis, -e,** smooth, gentle, kind

**lentē,** *adv.,* slowly

**Lentulus, -ī,** *m.,* P. Cornelius Lentulus Sura, chief conspirator under Catiline, left in charge of the conspiracy when Catiline was forced to flee from Rome

**Lesbia, -ae,** *f.,* Lesbia, the name which Catullus gave to his sweetheart

**levis, -e,** light; easy, slight, trivial. 17

**lēx, lēgis,** *f.,* law, statute. 26

**libellus, -ī,** *m.,* little book. 17

libenter, *adv.*, with pleasure, gladly. 38

līber, -era, -erum, free. 5

liber, -brī, *m.*, book. 6

līberālis, -e, of, relating to a free person; worthy of a free man, decent, liberal, generous. 39

līberālitās, -tātis, *f.*, generosity, liberality

līberātor, -tōris, *m.*, liberator

līberē, *adv.*, freely. 32

līberī, -ōrum, *m. pl.*, (one's) children

līberō (1), free, liberate. 19

lībertās, -tātis, *f.*, liberty, freedom. 8

libō (1), pour a libation of, on; pour ritually; sip; touch gently. 39

licet, licēre, licuit, *impers. + dat. and infin.*, it is permitted, one may. 37

ligō (1), bind, tie

līmen, -minis, *n.*, threshold. 26

lingua, -ae, *f.*, tongue; language. 25

linteum, -ī, *n.*, linen, napkin

littera, -ae, *f.*, a letter of the alphabet; litterae, -ārum, a letter (epistle); literature. 7

lītus, -toris, *n.*, shore, coast. 23

locō (1), place, put

locuplētō (1), enrich

locus, -ī, *m.*, place; passage in literature; *pl.*, loca, -ōrum, *n.*, places, region; locī, -ōrum, *m.*, passages in literature. 9

longē, *adv.*, far. 32

longinquitās, -tātis, *f.*, distance, remoteness

longus, -a, -um, long. 16

loquāx, *gen.* -quācis, *adj.*, talkative, loquacious

loquor, -ī, locūtus sum, say, speak, tell, talk. 34

lucrum, -ī, *n.*, gain, profit

lūdō, -ere, lūsī, lūsum, play

lūdus, -ī, *m.*, game, sport; school. 18

lūna, -ae, *f.*, moon. 28

lupus, -ī, *m.*, wolf

lūx, lūcis, *f.*, light. 26

luxuria, -ae, *f.*, luxury, extravagance

## M

Maecēnās, -ātis, *m.*, Maecenas, unofficial "prime minister" of Augustus, and patron and friend of Horace

magis, *adv.*, more, rather

magister, -trī, *m.*, master, schoolmaster, teacher. 4

magistra, -ae, *f.*, mistress, schoolmistress. 4

magnanimus, -a, -um, great-hearted, brave, magnanimous. 23

magnopere, *adv.*, greatly, exceedingly (*compar.* magis; *superl.* maximē). 32

magnus, -a, -um, large, great; important. 2 (*compar.* maior; *superl.* maximus. 27); maiōrēs, -um, *m. pl.*, ancestors. 27

maiestās, -tātis, *f.*, greatness, dignity, majesty

maior. *See* magnus.

maiōrēs, -um, *m. pl.*, ancestors. 27

male, *adv.*, badly, ill, wrongly (*compar.* peius; *superl.* pessimē). 32

mālō, mālle, māluī, to want (something) more, instead; prefer. 32

malum, -ī, *n.*, evil, misfortune, hurt, injury. 30

malus, -a, -um, bad, wicked, evil. 4 (*compar.* peior; *superl.* pessimus. 27)

mandātum, -ī, *n.*, order, command, instruction

maneō, -ēre, mānsī, mānsum, remain, stay, abide, continue. 5

manus, -ūs, *f.*, hand; handwriting; band. 20

Mārcellus, -ī, *m.*, Marcellus, Roman general who captured Syracuse in 212 B.C.

Mārcus, -ī, *m.*, Marcus, a common Roman first name, usually abbreviated to M. in writing

mare, -is, *n.*, sea. 14

marītus, -ī, *m.*, husband

māter, -tris, *f.*, mother. 12

māteria, -ae, *f.*, material, matter

mātrimōnium, -iī, *n.*, marriage

maximus. *See* magnus.

medica, -ae, *f.*, doctor, physician. 12

medicus, -ī, *m.*, doctor, physician. 12

mediocris, -e, ordinary, moderate, mediocre. 31

meditor, -ārī, -ātus sum, reflect upon, practice

medius, -a, -um, middle; *used partitively,* the middle of. 22

mel, mellis, *n.*, honey

melior. *See* bonus.

meminī, meminisse, *defective,* remember

memor, *gen.* -moris, *adj.*, mindful

memoria, -ae, *f.*, memory, recollection. 15

mendōsus, -a, -um, full of faults, faulty

mēns, mentis, *f.*, mind, thought, intention. 16

mēnsa, -ae, *f.*, table; dining; dish, course; mēnsa secunda, dessert. 26

mēnsis, -is, *m.*, month

merces, -cēdis, *f.*, pay, reward, recompense

merīdiānus, -a, -um, of midday, noon; southern

merus, -a, -um, pure, undiluted. 33

mēta, -ae, *f.*, turning point, goal, limit, boundary. 40

metuō, -ere, metuī, fear, dread; be afraid for + *dat.* 38

metus, -ūs, *m.*, fear, dread, anxiety. 20

meus, -a, -um (*m. voc.* mī), my. 2

mīles, mīlitis, *m.*, soldier. 23

mīlitāris, -e, military

mīlle, *indecl. adj. in sg.,* thousand; **mīlia, -ium,** *n., pl. noun,* thousands. 15

minimus. *See* parvus.

minor. *See* parvus.

minuō, -ere, minuī, minūtum, lessen, diminish. 30

mīrābilis, -e, amazing, wondrous, remarkable. 38

mīror, -ārī, -ātus sum, marvel at, admire, wonder. 35

mīrus, -a, -um, wonderful, surprising, extraordinary

misceō, -ēre, miscuī, mixtum, mix, stir up, disturb. 18

miser, -era, -erum, wretched, miserable, unfortunate. 15

miserē, *adv.,* wretchedly

misericordia, -ae, *f.,* pity, mercy

mītēscō, -ere, become *or* grow mild

mītis, -e, mild, gentle; ripe

mittō, -ere, mīsī, missum, send, let go. 11

modo, *adv.,* now, just now, only; **modo . . . modo,** at one time . . . at another

modus, -ī, *m.,* measure, bound, limit; manner, method, mode, way. 22

moenia, -ium, *n. pl.,* walls of a city. 29

molestus, -a, -um, troublesome, disagreeable, annoying

mōlior, -īrī, mōlītus sum, work at, build, undertake, plan. 34

molliō, -īre, -īvī, -ītum, soften; make calm *or* less hostile. 29

mollis, -e, soft, mild, weak

moneō, -ēre, -uī, -itum, remind, warn, advise, 1; **moneō eum ut** + *subjunct.* 36

monitiō, -ōnis, *f.,* admonition, warning

mōns, montis, *m.,* mountain. 20

mōnstrum, -ī, *n.,* portent; monster

monumentum, -ī, *n.,* monument. 40

mora, -ae, *f.,* delay. 4

morbus, -ī, *m.,* disease, sickness. 9

morior, -ī, mortuus sum, die. 34

mors, mortis, *f.,* death. 14

mortālis, -e, mortal. 18

mortuus, -a, -um, dead. 28

mōs, mōris, *m.,* habit, custom, manner; **mōrēs, mōrum,** habits, morals, character. 7

moveō, -ēre, mōvī, mōtum, move; arouse, affect. 18

mox, *adv.,* soon. 30

mulier, -eris, *f.,* woman. 39

multō (1), punish, fine

multum, *adv.,* much (*compar.* **plūs;** *superl.* **plūrimum**). 32

multus, -a, -um, much, many, 2 (*compar.* **plūs;** *superl.* **plūrimus.** 27)

mundus, -ī, *m.,* world, universe. 21

mūnīmentum, -ī, *n.,* fortification, protection

mūniō, -īre, -īvī, -ītum, fortify, defend; build (a road)

mūnus, -neris, *n.,* service, office, function, duty; gift

mūs, mūris, *m./f.,* mouse

Mūsa, -ae, *f.,* a Muse (one of the goddesses of poetry, music, etc.)

mūtātiō, -ōnis, *f.,* change

mūtō (1), change, alter; exchange. 14

**N**

nam, *conj.,* for. 13

nārrō (1), tell, narrate, report. 24

nāscor, -ī, nātus sum, be born, spring forth, arise. 34

nāsus, -ī, *m.,* nose. 40

nāta, -ae, *f.,* daughter. 29

nātālis, -is (*sc.* **diēs**), *m.,* birthday

nātiō, -ōnis, *f.,* nation, people

nātūra, -ae, *f.,* nature. 10

nauta, -ae, *m.,* sailor. 2

nāvigātiō, -ōnis, *f.,* voyage, navigation

nāvigō (1), sail, navigate. 17

nāvis, -is, *f.,* ship. 21

nē, *conj. with subjunct.,* that . . . not, in order that . . . not, in order not to, 28, 36; that, 40; *adv. in* **nē . . . quidem,** not . . . even. 29

-ne, *interrog. suffix attached to the first word of a sent., typically the verb or another word on which the question hinges, to introduce a question whose answer is uncertain.* 5

nec. *See* neque.

necessārius, -a, -um, necessary

necesse, *indecl. adj.,* necessary, inevitable. 39

necō (1), murder, kill. 7

nefās (*indecl.*), *n.,* wrong, sin

neglegō, -ere, -lēxī, -lēctum, neglect, disregard. 17

negō (1), deny, say that . . . not. 25

nēmō, (nūllīus), nēminī, nēminem, (nūllō, -ā), *m./f.,* no one, nobody. 11

nepōs, -pōtis, *m.,* grandson, descendant. 27

neque *or* nec, *conj.,* and not, nor; **neque . . . neque,** neither . . . nor. 11

nesciō, -īre, -īvī, -ītum, not to know, be ignorant. 25

neuter, -tra, -trum, not either, neither. 9

nēve, and not, nor (*used to continue* **ut** *or* **nē** + *subjunct.*)

niger, -gra, -grum, black

nihil (*indecl.*), *n.,* nothing. 1, 4

nihilum, -ī, *n.,* nothing

nimis *or* nimium, *adv.,* too, too much, excessively; *in a positive sense,* exceedingly, very. 9

nisi, if . . . not, unless, except. 19

niveus, -a, -um, snowy, white

noceō, -ēre, nocuī, nocitum + *dat.,* do harm to, harm, injure. 35

nōlō, nōlle, nōluī, not . . . wish, be unwilling. 32

nōmen, nōminis, *n.,* name. 7

nōn, *adv.,* not. 1

nōndum, *adv.,* not yet

nōnne, *interrog. adv. which introduces questions expecting the answer "yes."* 40

nōnnūllus, -a, -um, some, several

nōnnumquam, sometimes

nōnus, -a, -um, ninth

nōs. *See* ego.

nōscō, -ere, nōvī, nōtum, become acquainted with, learn, recognize; *in perf. tenses,* know. 30

noster, -tra, -trum, our, ours. 5

notārius, -iī, *m.,* writer of shorthand, stenographer

novem, *indecl. adj.,* nine. 15

novus, -a, -um, new, strange. 7

nox, noctis, *f.,* night. 26

nūbēs, -is, *f.,* cloud. 14

nūbō, -ere, nūpsī, nūptum, cover, veil; + dat. (*of a bride*) be married to, marry. 35

nūllus, -a, -um, not any, no, none. 9

num, *interrog. adv.:* (1) *introduces dir. questions which expect the answer "no";* (2) *introduces ind. questions and means* whether. 40

numerus, -ī, *m.,* number. 3

numquam, *adv.,* never. 8

nunc, *adv.,* now, at present. 6

nūntiō (1), announce, report, relate. 25

nūntius, -iī, *m.,* messenger, message

nūper, *adv.,* recently. 12

nūtriō, -īre, -īvī, -ītum, nourish, rear

## O

Ō, *interj.,* O!, oh! 2

obdūrō (1), be hard, persist, endure

obeō, -īre, -iī, -itum, go up against, meet; die. 37

obiciō, -ere, -iēcī, -iectum, offer; cite (*as grounds for condemnation*)

oblectō (1), please, amuse, delight; pass time pleasantly. 36

obruō, -ere, -ruī, -rutum, overwhelm, destroy

obsequium, -iī, *n.,* compliance

obstinātus, -a, -um, firm, resolved

occāsiō, -ōnis, *f.,* occasion, opportunity. 28

occidō, -ere, -cidī, -cāsum (cadō, fall), fall down; die; set (*of the sun*). 31

occīdō, -ere, -cīdī, -cīsum (caedō, cut), cut down; kill, slay

occultē, *adv.,* secretly

occupō (1), seize

oculus, -ī, *m.,* eye. 4

ōdī, ōdisse, ōsūrum (*defective verb*), hate. 20

odium, -ī, *n.,* hatred. 38

Oedipūs, -podis, *m.,* Oedipus, Greek mythical figure said to have murdered his father and married his mother

offerō, -ferre, obtulī, oblātum, offer. 31

officium, -iī, *n.,* duty, service. 4

ōlim, *adv.,* once, long ago, formerly; some day, in the future. 13

omittō, -ere, -mīsī, -missum, let go, omit

omnīnō, *adv.,* wholly, entirely, altogether; *with negatives,* at all. 40

omnipotēns, *gen.* -tentis, *adj.,* all-powerful, omnipotent

omnis, -e, every, all. 16

onerō (1), burden, load

onus, oneris, *n.,* burden, load

opera, -ae, *f.,* work, pains, help

opīnor, -ārī, -ātus sum, suppose. 40

oportet, -ēre, oportuit (*impers.*), + *infin.,* it is necessary, proper, right. 39

oppōnō, -ere, -posuī, -positum, set against, oppose

opportūnē, *adv.,* opportunely

opportūnus, -a, -um, fit, suitable, advantageous, opportune

opprimō, -ere, -pressī, -pressum, suppress, overwhelm, overpower, check. 23

opprobrium, -iī, *n.,* reproach, taunt, disgrace

oppugnō (1), fight against, attack, assault, assail. 39

ops, opis, *f.,* help, aid; opēs, opum, power, resources, wealth. 33

optimus. *See* bonus.

optō (1), wish for, desire

opus, operis, *n.,* a work, task; deed, accomplishment. 38

ōrātiō, -ōnis, *f.,* speech. 38

ōrātor, -tōris, *m.,* orator, speaker. 23

orbis, -is, *m.,* circle, orb; orbis terrārum, the world, the earth

ōrdō, ōrdinis, *m.,* rank, class, order

orior, -īrī, ortus sum, arise, begin, proceed, originate

ōrnō (1), equip, furnish, adorn. 39

ōrō (1), speak, plead; beg, beseech, entreat, pray. 36

ōs, ōris, *n.,* mouth, face. 14

ōsculum, -ī, *n.,* kiss. 29

ostendō, -ere, -tendī, -tentum, exhibit, show, display. 23

ōstium, -iī, *n.,* entrance, door

ōtium, -iī, *n.,* leisure, peace. 4

ovis, -is, *f.,* sheep

## P

paedagōgus, -ī, *m.,* slave who attended children (*particularly at school*)

pāgānus, -ī, *m.,* a countryman, peasant; pagan

palam, *adv.,* openly, plainly

palma, -ae, *f.,* palm

pānis, -is, *m.,* bread

pār, *gen.* paris, *adj.,* equal, like. 32

parcō, -ere, pepercī, parsūrum + *dat.,* be lenient to, spare. 35

parēns, -rentis, *m./f.,* parent. 28

pāreō, -ēre, -uī + *dat.,* be obedient to, obey. 35

pariēs, -ietis, *m.,* wall

pariō, -ere, peperī, partum, beget, produce

parmula, -ae, *f.,* little shield

parō (1), prepare, provide; get, obtain. 19

pars, partis, *f.,* part, share; direction. 14

parum, *adv.,* little, too little, not very (much) (*compar.* minus; *superl.* minimē). 32

parvus, -a, -um, small, little, 4 (*compar.* minor; *superl.* minimus. 27)

passer, -seris, *m.,* sparrow

patefaciō, -ere, -fēcī, -factum, make open, open; disclose, expose. 25

pateō, -ēre, -uī, be open, lie open; be accessible; be evident. 32

pater, -tris, *m.,* father. 12

patiēns, *gen.* -entis, *adj.,* patient; + *gen.,* capable of enduring

patientia, -ae, *f.,* suffering; patience, endurance. 12

patior, -ī, passus sum, suffer, endure; permit. 34

patria, -ae, *f.,* fatherland, native land, (one's) country. 2

patrōnus, -ī, *m.,* patron, protector

paucī, -ae, -a, *usually pl.,* few, a few. 3

pauper, *gen.* -peris, *adj.,* of small means, poor. 32

paupertās, -tātis, *f.,* poverty, humble circumstances. 32

pāx, pācis, *f.,* peace. 7

peccō (1), sin, do wrong

pectus, -toris, *n.,* breast, heart. 35

pecūnia, -ae, *f.,* money. 2

peior. *See* malus.

pellō, -ere, pepulī, pulsum, strike, push; drive out, banish. 24

per, *prep.* + *acc.,* through; *with reflexive pron.,* by. 13

percipiō, -ere, -cēpī, -ceptum, gain, learn, perceive

perdō, -ere, perdidī, perditum, destroy, ruin, lose

pereō, -īre, -iī, -itum, pass away, be destroyed, perish. 37

peregrīnor, peregrīnārī, peregrīnātus sum, travel abroad, wander. 37

perfectus, -a, -um, complete, perfect

perferō, -ferre, -tulī, -lātum, bear, endure, suffer

perficiō, -ere, -fēcī, -fectum, do thoroughly, accomplish, bring about

perfugium, -iī, *n.,* refuge, shelter. 24

perīculōsus, -a, -um, dangerous

perīculum, -ī, *n.,* danger, risk. 4

perimō, -ere, -ēmī, -ēmptum, destroy

perītus, -a, -um, skilled, expert

permittō, -ere, -mīsī, -missum, permit, allow

perniciōsus, -a, -um, destructive, pernicious

pernoctō (1), spend *or* occupy the night. 39

perpetuus, -a, -um, perpetual, lasting, uninterrupted, continuous. 6

perscrībō, -ere, -scrīpsī, -scrīptum, write out, place on record

persequor, -ī, -secūtus sum, follow up, pursue, take vengeance on

Persicus, -a, -um, Persian

persuādeō, -ēre, -suāsī, -suāsum, succeed in urging, persuade, convince

perterreō, -ēre, -uī, -itum, frighten thoroughly, terrify

pertineō, -ēre, -uī, -tentum, pertain to, relate to, concern

perturbō (1), throw into confusion, trouble, disturb, perturb

perveniō, -īre, -vēnī, -ventum + ad, come through to, arrive at, reach

pēs, pedis, *m.,* lower leg, foot. 38

pessimus. *See* malus.

pestis, -is, *f.,* plague, pestilence, curse, destruction

petō, -ere, petīvī, petītum, seek, aim at, beg, beseech, 23; petō ab eō ut + *subjunct.* 36

philosopha, -ae, *f.,* philosopher. 33

philosophia, -ae, *f.,* philosophy, love of wisdom. 2

philosophus, -ī, *m.,* philosopher. 33

piger, -gra, -grum, lazy, slow, dull

pīpiō (1), chirp, pipe

piscātor, -tōris, *m.,* fisherman

piscis, -is, *m.,* fish

placeō, -ēre, -uī, -itum + *dat.,* be pleasing to, please. 35

plācō (1), placate, appease

plānē, *adv.,* plainly, clearly

platea, -ae, *f.,* broad way, street

Platō, -tōnis, *m.,* Plato, the renowned Greek philosopher

plēbs, plēbis, *f.,* the common people, populace, plebeians. 33

plēnus, -a, -um, full, abundant, generous. 6

plūrimus. *See* multus.

plūs. *See* multus.

poēma, -matis, *n.,* poem

poena, -ae, *f.,* penalty, punishment; poenās dare, pay the penalty. 2

poēta, -ae, *m.,* poet. 2

pōmum, -ī, *n.,* fruit, apple

pōnō, -ere, posuī, positum, put, place, set. 27

pōns, pontis, *m.,* bridge

populus, -ī, *m.,* the people, a people, nation. 3

porta, -ae, *f.,* gate, entrance. 2
possessiō, -ōnis, *f.,* possession, property
possum, posse, potuī, be able, can, have power. 6
post, *prep. + acc.,* after, behind. 7
posteā, *adv.,* afterwards. 24
postpōnō, -ere, -posuī, -positum, put after, consider
    secondary
postquam, *conj.,* after
postrēmum, *adv.,* after all, finally; for the last time. 40
potēns, *gen.* -tentis, *pres. partic. of* possum *as adj.,* able,
    powerful, mighty, strong. 16
potestās, -tātis, *f.,* power, ability, opportunity
potior, -īrī, potītus sum + *gen.* or *abl.,* get possession of,
    possess, hold
potius, *adv.,* rather, preferably
prae, *prep. + abl.,* in front of, before. 26
praebeō, -ēre, -uī, -itum, offer, provide. 32
praeceptum, -ī, *n.,* precept
praeclārus, -a, -um, noble, distinguished, famous,
    remarkable
praeferō, -ferre, -tulī, -lātum, bear before, display; place
    before, prefer
praeficiō, -ere, -fēcī, -fectum, put in charge of
praemittō, -ere, -mīsī, -missum, send ahead *or* forward
praemium, -iī, *n.,* reward, prize. 35
praesidium, -iī, *n.,* guard, detachment, protection
praestō, -āre, -stitī, -stitum, excel (+ *dat.*); exhibit, show,
    offer, supply. 28
praesum, -esse, -fuī, be at the head of, be in charge of
praeter, *prep. + acc.,* besides, except; beyond, past. 40
praetereō, -īre, -iī, -itum, go by, pass, omit
praeteritus, -a, -um, *perf. partic. of* praetereō *as adj.,* past
premō, -ere, pressī, pressum, press; press hard, pursue. 23
pretium, -iī, *n.,* price, value, reward
prex, precis, *f.,* prayer
prīmō, *adv.,* at first, first, at the beginning. 30
prīmum, *adv.,* first, in the first place; quam prīmum, as
    soon as possible
prīmus. *See* prior. 27
prīnceps, *gen.* -cipis, chief; *m./f. noun,* leader, prince,
    emperor. 28
prīncipium, -iī, *n.,* beginning. 12
prior, prius, *compar. adj.,* former, prior; prīmus, -a, -um,
    first, foremost, chief, principal. 27
prīstinus, -a, -um, ancient, former, previous. 38
prius, *adv.,* before, previously
prīvātus, -ī, *m.,* private citizen
prīvō (1), deprive
prō, *prep. + abl.,* in front of, before, on behalf of, in
    return for, instead of, for, as. 12
probitās, -tātis, *f.,* uprightness, honesty, probity. 18

probō (1), approve; recommend; test. 27
prōcōnsul, -sulis, *m.,* proconsul, governor of a province
prōditor, -tōris, *m.,* betrayer, traitor
proelium, -iī, *n.,* battle
prōferō, -ferre, -tulī, -lātum, bring forward, produce,
    make known, extend
proficīscor, -ī, -fectus sum, set out, start. 34
profor, -ārī, -ātus sum, speak out
prōfundō, -ere, -fūdī, -fūsum, pour forth
prohibeō, -ēre, -uī, -itum, prevent, hinder, restrain,
    prohibit. 20
prōiciō, -ere, -iēcī, -iectum, throw forward *or* out
prōmittō, -mittere, -mīsī, -missum, send forth,
    promise. 32
prōnūntiō (1), proclaim, announce; declaim; pro-
    nounce. 20
prōpōnō, -ere, -posuī, -positum, put forward, propose
proprius, -a, -um, one's own, peculiar, proper, personal,
    characteristic
propter, *prep. + acc.,* on account of, because of. 5
prōtinus, *adv.,* immediately. 22
prōvideō, -ēre, -vīdī, -vīsum, foresee, provide, make
    provision
proximus, -a, -um (*superl. of* propior), nearest, next
prūdēns, *gen.* -dentis, *adj.,* wise, prudent
prūdenter, *adv.,* wisely, discreetly
prūdentia, -ae, *f.,* foresight, wisdom, discretion
pūblicus, -a, -um, of the people, public; rēs pūblica,
    reī pūblicae, *f.,* the state
pudīcus, -a, -um, modest, chaste. 26
pudor, -dōris, *m.,* modesty, bashfulness
puella, -ae, *f.,* girl. 2
puer, puerī, *m.,* boy; *pl.* boys, children. 3
puerīliter, *adv.,* childishly, foolishly
pugna, -ae, *f.,* fight, battle
pugnō (1), fight. 29
pulcher, -chra, -chrum, beautiful, handsome; fine. 5
pulchrē, *adv.,* beautifully, finely. 32
pulchritūdō, -dinis, *f.,* beauty
pūniō, -īre, -īvī, -ītum, punish
pūrgō (1), cleanse
pūrus, -a, -um, pure, free from
putō (1), reckon, suppose, judge, think, imagine. 25
Pȳthagorās, -ae, *m.,* Pythagoras, Greek philosopher and
    mathematician of 6th cent. B.C.

## Q

quā, *adv.,* by which route, where
quadrāgintā, *indecl. adj.,* forty
quaerō, -ere, quaesīvī, quaesītum, seek, look for, strive
    for; ask, inquire, inquire into. 24

**quam**, *adv.*, how, 16; *conj. (after compar.)*, than, 26; as . . . as possible (*before superl.*), 26

**quamvīs**, *adv. and conj.*, however much, however; although

**quandō**, *interrog. and rel. adv. and conj.*, when; **sī quandō**, if ever. 5

**quantus, -a, -um**, how large, how great, how much. 30

**quārē**, *adv.*, because of which thing, therefore, wherefore, why. 6

**quārtus, -a, -um**, fourth. 15

**quasi**, *adv. or conj.*, as if, as it were. 39

**quattuor**, *indecl. adj.*, four. 15

**-que**, *enclitic conj.*, and. *It is appended to the second of two words to be joined.* 6

**quemadmodum**, *adv.*, in what manner, how

**queror, -ī, questus sum**, complain, lament. 38

**quī, quae, quod**, *rel. pron.*, who, which, what, that. 17

**quī? quae? quod?**, *interrog. adj.*, what? which? what kind of?; *sometimes with exclamatory force*, what (a)! what sort of! 19

**quia**, *conj.*, since, because

**quid**, what, why. See **quis**.

**quīdam, quaedam, quiddam** (*pron.*) *or* **quoddam** (*adj.*), *indef. pron. and adj.: as pron.*, a certain one *or* thing, someone, something; *as adj.*, a certain. 26

**quidem**, *postpositive adv.*, indeed, certainly, at least, even; **nē . . . quidem**, not even. 29

**quiēs, -ētis**, *f.*, quiet, rest, peace

**quīn**, *adv.*, indeed, in fact. 40

**quīn etiam**, *adv.*, why even, in fact, moreover

**Quīntus, -ī**, *m.*, Quintus, a Roman praenomen, abbreviated to **Q.** in writing

**quis? quid?**, *interrog. pron.*, who? what? which? 19

**quis, quid**, *indef. pron., after* **sī, nisi, nē**, *and* **num**, anyone, anything, someone, something. 33

**quisquam, quidquam** (*or* **quicquam**), *indef. pron. and adj.*, anyone, anything

**quisque, quidque**, *indef. pron.*, each one, each person, each thing. 13

**quisquis, quidquid**, *indef. pron.*, whoever, whatever. 23

**quō**, *adv.*, to which *or* what place, whither, where

**quod**, *conj.*, because. 11

**quōmodo**, *adv.*, in what way, how

**quondam**, *adv.*, formerly, once. 22

**quoniam**, *conj.*, since, inasmuch as. 10

**quoque**, *adv.*, also, too. 17

**quot**, *indecl. adj.*, how many, as many. 27

**quotiēnscumque**, *adv.*, however often, whenever

## R

**rapiō, -ere, rapuī, raptum**, seize, snatch, carry away. 21

**rārus, -a, -um**, rare

**ratiō, -ōnis**, *f.*, reckoning, account; reason, judgment, consideration; system, manner, method. 8

**recēdō, -ere, -cessī, -cessum**, go back, retire, recede

**recipiō, -ere, -cēpī, -ceptum**, take back, regain; admit, receive. 24

**recitō** (1), read aloud, recite. 17

**recognōscō, -ere, -nōvī, -nitum**, recognize, recollect. 38

**recordātiō, -ōnis**, *f.*, recollection

**recreō** (1), restore, revive; refresh, cheer. 36

**rēctus, -a, -um**, straight, right; **rēctum, -ī**, *n.*, the right, virtue

**recuperātiō, -ōnis**, *f.*, recovery

**recuperō** (1), regain

**recūsō** (1), refuse. 33

**reddō, -ere, -didī, -ditum**, give back, return

**redeō, -īre, -iī, -itum**, go back, return. 37

**redūcō, -ere, -dūxī, -ductum**, lead back, bring back

**referō, -ferre, -ttulī, -lātum**, carry back, bring back; repeat, answer, report. 31

**rēgīna, -ae**, *f.*, queen. 7

**rēgius, -a, -um**, royal

**rēgnum, -ī**, *n.*, rule, authority, kingdom

**regō, -ere, rēxī, rēctum**, rule, guide, direct. 16

**relegō, -ere, -lēgī, -lēctum**, read again, reread

**relevō** (1), relieve, alleviate, diminish

**relinquō, -ere, -līquī, -lictum**, leave behind, leave, abandon. 21

**remaneō, -ēre, -mānsī, -mānsum**, remain, stay behind, abide, continue. 5

**remedium, -iī**, *n.*, cure, remedy. 4

**remissiō, -ōnis**, *f.*, letting go, release; relaxation. 34

**removeō, -ēre, -mōvī, -mōtum**, remove

**repente**, *adv.*, suddenly. 30

**reperiō, -īre, -pperī, -pertum**, find, discover, learn; get. 40

**repetītiō, -ōnis**, *f.*, repetition

**repetō, -ere, -īvī, -ītum**, seek again, repeat

**rēpō, -ere, rēpsī, rēptum**, creep, crawl

**repugnō** (1) + *dat.*, fight against, be incompatible with

**requiēscō, -ere, -quiēvī, -quiētum**, rest. 37

**requīrō, -ere, -quīsīvī, -sītum**, seek, ask for; miss, need, require. 36

**rēs, reī**, *f.*, thing, matter, property, business, affair; **rēs pūblica, reī pūblicae**, state, commonwealth. 22

**resistō, -ere, -stitī**, make a stand, resist, oppose

**respondeō, -ēre, -spondī, -spōnsum**, answer. 29

**restituō, -ere, -stituī, -stitūtum**, restore

**retrahō, -ere, -trāxī, -tractum**, drag *or* draw back

**reveniō, -īre, -vēnī, -ventum**, come back, return

**revertor, -ī, -vertī** (*perf. is act.*), **-versum**, return

**revocō** (1), call back, recall

rēx, rēgis, *m.*, king. 7
rhētoricus, -a, -um, of rhetoric, rhetorical
rīdeō, -ēre, rīsī, rīsum, laugh, laugh at. 24
rīdiculus, -a, -um, laughable, ridiculous. 30
rogō (1), ask, ask for. 30; rogō eum ut + *subjunct.*, 36
Rōma, -ae, *f.*, Rome. 14
Rōmānus, -a, -um, Roman. 3
rosa, -ae, *f.*, rose. 2
rōstrum, -ī, *n.*, beak of a ship; Rōstra, -ōrum, the
    Rostra, speaker's platform
rota, -ae, *f.*, wheel
rotundus, -a, -um, wheel-shaped, round
rūmor, -mōris, *m.*, rumor, gossip. 31
ruō, -ere, ruī, rutum, rush, fall, be ruined
rūs, rūris, *n.*, the country, countryside. 37
rūsticor, -ārī, -ātus sum, live in the country. 34
rūsticus, -a, -um, rustic, rural

S

sabbatum, -ī, *n.*, the Sabbath
sacculus, -ī, *n.*, little bag, purse
sacrificium, -iī, *n.*, sacrifice
sacerdōs, sacerdōtis, *m.*, priest. 23
sacrilegus, -a, -um, sacrilegious, impious
saepe, *adv.*, often. 1
saeta equīna, -ae -ae, *f.*, horse-hair
sagitta, -ae, *f.*, arrow
sāl, salis, *m.*, salt; wit. 33
salsus, -a, -um, salty, witty
salūbris, -e, healthy, salubrious
salūs, salūtis, *f.*, health, safety; greeting. 21
salūtō (1), greet
salveō, -ēre, be well, be in good health. 1
salvus, -a, -um, safe, sound. 6
sānctificō (1), sanctify, treat as holy
sānctus, -a, -um, sacred, holy
sānitās, -tātis, *f.*, health, soundness of mind, sanity
sānō (1), heal
sānus, -a, -um, sound, healthy, sane. 5
sapiēns, *gen.* -entis, *adj.*, wise, judicious; *as a noun, m.*,
    a wise man/woman, philosopher. 25
sapienter, *adv.*, wisely, sensibly. 32
sapientia, -ae, *f.*, wisdom. 3
sapiō, -ere, sapīvī, have good taste; have good sense, be
    wise. 35
satiō (1), satisfy, sate. 3
satis, *indecl. noun, adj., and adv.*, enough, sufficient(ly). 5
sator, -tōris, *m.*, sower, planter; begetter, father. 38
satura, -ae, *f.*, satire. 16
saxum, -ī, *n.*, rock, stone. 40
scabiēs, -ēī, *f.*, the itch, mange

scelerātus, -a, -um, criminal, wicked, accursed
scelestus, -a, -um, wicked, accursed, infamous
scelus, -leris, *n.*, evil deed, crime, sin, wickedness. 19
schola, -ae, *f.*, school
scientia, -ae, *f.*, knowledge, science, skill. 18
sciō, -īre, -īvī, -ītum, know. 21
scrībō, -ere, scrīpsī, scrīptum, write, compose. 8
scrīptor, -tōris, *m.*, writer, author. 8
sēcernō, -ere, -crēvī, -crētum, separate
secundus, -a, -um, second; favorable. 6
sēcūrus, -a, -um, free from care, untroubled, safe
sed, *conj.*, but. 2
sedeō, -ēre, sēdī, sessum, sit. 34
sēductor, -tōris, *m. (ecclesiastical Lat.)*, seducer
semel, *adv.*, a single time, once, once and for all,
    simultaneously. 31
semper, *adv.*, always. 3
senātor, -tōris, *m.*, senator
senātus, -ūs, *m.*, senate. 20
senectūs, -tūtis, *f.*, old age. 10
senex, senis, *adj. and n.*, old, aged; old man. 16
sēnsus, -ūs, *m.*, feeling, sense. 20
sententia, -ae, *f.*, feeling, thought, opinion, vote;
    sentence. 2
sentiō, -īre, sēnsī, sēnsum, feel, perceive, think,
    experience. 11
septem, *indecl. adj.*, seven. 15
sepulchrum, -ī, *n.*, grave, tomb
sequor, -ī, secūtus sum, follow. 34
serēnō (1), make clear, brighten; cheer up, soothe. 36
sēriō, *adv.*, seriously
sērius, -a, -um, serious, grave
sermō, -mōnis, *m.*, conversation, talk
serō, -ere, sēvī, satum, sow
serva, -ae, *f.*, slave. 24
serviō, -īre, -īvī, -ītum + *dat.*, be a slave to, serve. 35
servitūs, -tūtis, *f.*, servitude, slavery. 20
servō (1), preserve, keep, save, guard. 1
servus, -ī, *m.*, slave. 24
sevēritās, -tātis, *f.*, severity, sternness, strictness
sī, *conj.*, if. 1
sīc, *adv. (most commonly with verbs)*, so, thus. 29
sīcut, *adv. and conj.*, as, just as, as it were
sīdus, -deris, *n.*, constellation, star. 29
signum, -ī, *n.*, sign, signal, indication; seal. 13
silentium, -iī, *n.*, silence
silva, -ae, *f.*, forest, wood
similis, -e, similar to, like, resembling. 27
simplex, *gen.* -plicis, *adj.*, simple, unaffected
simulātiō, -ōnis, *f.*, pretense
sine, *prep.* + *abl.*, without. 2

**singulī, -ae, -a**, *pl.*, one each, single, separate

**singultim**, *adv.*, stammeringly

**sinister, -tra, -trum**, left, left-hand; harmful, ill-omened. 20

**sitiō, -īre, -īvī**, be thirsty

**socius, -iī**, *m.*, companion, ally

**Sōcratēs, -is**, *m.*, Socrates

**sōl, sōlis**, *m.*, sun. 27

**sōlācium, -iī**, *n.*, comfort, relief. 24

**soleō, -ēre, solitus sum**, be accustomed. 37

**sōlitūdō, -dinis**, *f.*, solitude, loneliness

**sollicitō (1)**, stir up, arouse, incite

**sollicitūdō, -dinis**, *f.*, anxiety, concern, solicitude

**sollicitus, -a, -um**, troubled, anxious, disturbed

**Solōn, -lōnis**, *m.*, Solon, Athenian sage and statesman of the 7th-6th cent. B.C.

**sōlum**, *adv.*, only, merely; **nōn sōlum . . . sed etiam**, not only . . . but also. 9

**sōlus, -a, -um**, alone, only, the only. 9

**somnus, -ī**, *m.*, sleep. 26

**Sophoclēs, -is**, *m.*, Sophocles, one of the three greatest writers of Greek tragedy

**sopor, -pōris**, *m.*, deep sleep

**sordēs, -dium**, *f. pl.*, filth; meanness, stinginess

**soror, -rōris**, *f.*, sister. 8

**spargō, -ere, sparsī, sparsum**, scatter, spread, strew

**spectāculum, -ī**, *n.*, spectacle, show

**spectō (1)**, look at, see. 34

**speculum, -ī**, *n.*, mirror. 33

**spernō, -ere, sprēvī, sprētum**, scorn, despise, spurn

**spērō (1)**, hope for, hope. 25

**spēs, -eī**, *f.*, hope. 22

**spīritus, -ūs**, *m.*, breath, breathing; spirit, soul. 20

**stabilis, -e**, stable, steadfast

**stadium, -iī**, *n.*, stadium

**statim**, *adv.*, immediately, at once

**statua, -ae**, *f.*, statue

**stēlla, -ae**, *f.*, star, planet. 28

**stilus, -ī**, *m.*, stilus (*for writing*)

**stō, stāre, stetī, statum**, stand, stand still *or* firm. 13

**studeō, -ēre, -uī** + *dat.*, direct one's zeal to, be eager for, study. 35

**studiōsus, -a, -um**, full of zeal, eager, fond of

**studium, -iī**, *n.*, eagerness, zeal, pursuit, study. 9

**stultus, -a, -um**, foolish; **stultus, -ī**, *m.*, a fool. 4

**suāvis, -e**, sweet. 33

**sub**, *prep.* + *abl. with verbs of rest*, + *acc. with verbs of motion*, under, up under, close to, down to/into, to/at the foot of. 7

**subitō**, *adv.*, suddenly. 33

**subitus, -a, -um**, sudden

**subiungō, -ere, -iūnxī, -iūnctum**, subject, subdue

**sublīmis, sublīme**, elevated, lofty; heroic, noble. 38

**subrīdeō, -rīdēre, -rīsī, -rīsum**, smile (down) upon. 35

**succurrō, -ere, -currī, -cursum**, run up under, help

**sufficiō, -ere, -fēcī, -fectum**, be sufficient, suffice

**suī (sibi, sē, sē)**, *reflexive pron. of 3rd pers.*, himself, herself, itself, themselves. 13

**sum, esse, fuī, futūrum**, be, exist. 4; **est, sunt** *may mean* there is, there are. 1

**summa, -ae**, *f.*, highest part, sum, whole

**summus, -a, -um**. See **superus**.

**sūmō, -ere, sūmpsī, sūmptum**, take, take up, assume

**sūmptus, -ūs**, *m.*, expense, cost

**supellex, -lectilis**, *f.*, furniture, apparatus

**superbus, -a, -um**, arrogant, overbearing, haughty, proud. 26

**superior**. See **superus**.

**superō (1)**, be above, have the upper hand, surpass, overcome, conquer. 5

**superus, -a, -um**, above, upper; **superī, -ōrum**, *m.*, the gods (*compar.* **superior, -ius**, higher; *superl.* **suprēmus, -a, -um**, last, *or* **summus, -a, -um**, highest). 27

**supplicium, -iī**, *n.*, punishment

**suprā**, *adv. and prep.* + *acc.*, above

**suprēmus**. See **superus**.

**surculus, -ī**, *m.*, shoot, sprout

**surgō, -ere, surrēxī, surrēctum**, get up, arise. 29

**suscipiō, -ere, -cēpī, -ceptum**, undertake. 25

**suspendō, -ere, -pendī, -pēnsum**, hang up, suspend; interrupt. 38

**sustineō, -ēre, -uī, -tentum**, hold up, sustain, endure

**suus, -a, -um**, *reflexive possessive adj. of 3rd pers.*, his own, her own, its own, their own. 13

**synagōga, -ae**, *f.*, synagogue

**Syrācūsae, -ārum**, *f. pl.*, Syracuse. 37

# T

**tabella, -ae**, *f.*, writing tablet; **tabellae, -ārum**, letter, document

**taceō, -ēre, -uī, -itum**, be silent, leave unmentioned. 28

**tālis, -e**, such, of such a sort. 34

**tam**, *adv. used with adjs. and advs.*, so, to such a degree; **tam . . . quam**, so . . . as. 29

**tamen**, *adv.*, nevertheless, still. 8

**tamquam**, *adv.*, as it were, as if, so to speak. 29

**tandem**, *adv.*, at last, finally

**tangō, -ere, tetigī, tāctum**, touch. 21

**tantum**, *adv.*, only. 26

**tantus, -a, -um**, so large, so great, of such size. 29

**tardus, -a, -um**, slow, tardy

tēctum, -ī, *n.*, roof, house

tegō, -ere, tēxī, tēctum, cover, hide, protect

temeritās, -tātis, *f.*, rashness, temerity

temperantia, -ae, *f.*, moderation, temperance, self-control

tempestās, -tātis, *f.*, period of time, season; weather, storm. 15

templum, -ī, *n.*, sacred area, temple

temptātiō, -ōnis, *f.*, trial, temptation

tempus, -poris, *n.*, time; occasion, opportunity. 7

tendō, -ere, tetendī, tentum *or* tēnsum, stretch, extend; go

teneō, -ēre, -uī, tentum, hold, keep, possess, restrain. 14

terō, -ere, trīvī, trītum, rub, wear out

terra, -ae, *f.*, earth, ground, land, country. 7

terreō, -ēre, -uī, -itum, frighten, terrify. 1

tertius, -a, -um, third. 15

thema, -matis, *n.*, theme

Themistoclēs, -is, *m.*, Themistocles, celebrated Athenian statesman and military leader who advocated a powerful navy at the time of the Persian Wars

timeō, -ēre, -uī, fear, be afraid of, be afraid. 15

timor, -mōris, *m.*, fear. 10

titulus, -ī, *m.*, label, title; placard

toga, -ae, *f.*, toga, the garb of peace

tolerō (1), bear, endure, tolerate. 6

tollō, -ere, sustulī, sublātum, raise, lift up; take away, remove, destroy. 22

tondeō, -ēre, totondī, tōnsum, shear, clip

tōnsor, -sōris, *m.*, barber

tōnsōrius, -a, -um, of *or* pertaining to a barber, barber's

tot, *indecl. adj.*, so many, as many; tot . . . quot, as many . . . as. 40

tōtus, -a, -um, whole, entire. 9

tractō (1), drag about; handle, treat, discuss

trādō, -ere, -didī, -ditum, give over, surrender, hand down, transmit, teach. 33

tragoedia, -ae, *f.*, tragedy

trahō, -ere, trāxī, tractum, draw, drag; derive, acquire. 8

trāns, *prep. + acc.*, across. 14

trānseō, -īre, -iī, -itum, go across, cross; pass over, ignore. 39

trānsferō, -ferre, -tulī, -lātum, bear across, transfer, convey

trānsitus, -ūs, *m.*, passing over, transit; transition. 39

trēdecim, *indecl. adj.*, thirteen. 15

tremō, -ere, tremuī, tremble

trepidē, *adv.*, with trepidation, in confusion

trēs, tria, three. 15

trīgintā, *indecl. adj.*, thirty

trīstis, -e, sad, sorrowful; joyless, grim, severe. 26

triumphus, -ī, *m.*, triumphal procession, triumph

Trōia, -ae, *f.*, Troy. 23

Trōiānus, -a, -um, Trojan

tū, tuī, you. 11

Tullius, -iī, *m.*, Cicero's family name

tum, *adv.*, then, at that time; thereupon, in the next place. 5

tumultus, -ūs, *m.*, uprising, disturbance

tumulus, -ī, *m.*, mound, tomb

tunc, *adv.*, then, at that time

turba, -ae, *f.*, uproar, disturbance; mob, crowd, multitude. 14

turpis, -e, ugly; shameful, base, disgraceful. 26

tūtus, -a, -um, protected, safe, secure

tuus, -a, -um, your, yours (*sg.*). 2

tyrannus, -ī, *m.*, absolute ruler, tyrant. 6

## U

ubi, *rel. adv. and conj.*, where; when; *interrog.*, where? 6

ulcīscor, -ī, ultus sum, avenge, punish for wrong done

ūllus, -a, -um, any. 9

ultimus, -a, -um, farthest, extreme; last, final. 25

ultrā, *adv. and prep. + acc.*, on the other side of, beyond. 22

umbra, -ae, *f.*, shade; ghost

umerus, -ī, *m.*, shoulder, upper arm

umquam, *adv.*, ever, at any time. 23

unde, *adv.*, whence, from what *or* which place; from which, from whom. 30

ūnus, -a, -um, one, single, alone. 9

urbānus, -a, -um, of the city, urban, urbane, elegant. 26

urbs, urbis, *f.*, city. 14

usque, *adv.*, all the way, up (to), even (to), continuously, always. 31

ūsus, -ūs, *m.*, use, experience, skill, advantage

ut, *conj.*; A. *with subjunct., introducing* (1) *purp.*, in order that, that, to (28); (2) *result*, so that, that (29); (3) *jussive noun clauses*, to, that (36); (4) *fear clauses*, that . . . not (40); B. *with indic.*, just as, as, when. 24

uter, utra, utrum, either, which (of two). 9

ūtilis, -e, useful, advantageous. 27

ūtilitās, -tātis, *f.*, usefulness, advantage

ūtor, -ī, ūsus sum + *abl.*, use; enjoy, experience. 34

utrum . . . an, *conj.*, whether . . . or. 30

uxor, -ōris, *f.*, wife. 7

## V

vacō (1), be free from, be unoccupied

vacuus, -a, -um, empty, devoid (of), free (from)

vae, *interj.*, alas, woe to. 34

**valeō, -ēre, -uī, -itūrum**, be strong, have power; be well, fare well; **valē (valēte)**, good-bye. 1

**valētūdō, -dinis**, *f.*, health, good health, bad health

**varius, -a, -um**, various, varied, different

**-ve**, *conj.*, or 33

**vehemēns**, *gen.* **-mentis**, *adj.*, violent, vehement, emphatic, vigorous

**vehō, -ere, vexī, vectum**, carry, convey

**vel**, *conj.*, or (*an optional alternative*)

**vēlōx**, *gen.* **-lōcis**, *adj.*, swift

**vēndō, -ere, vēndidī, vēnditum**, sell. 38

**venia, -ae**, *f.*, kindness, favor, pardon

**veniō, -īre, vēnī, ventum**, come. 10

**ventitō (1)**, come often

**ventus, -ī**, *m.*, wind. 39

**Venus, -neris**, *f.*, Venus, goddess of grace, charm, and love

**verbera, -rum**, *n. pl.*, blows, a beating

**verbum, -ī**, *n.*, word. 5

**vērē**, *adv.*, truly, really, actually, rightly

**vereor, -ērī, veritus sum**, show reverence for, respect; be afraid of, fear. 40

**Vergilius, -iī**, *m.*, Vergil, the Roman epic poet

**vēritās, -tātis**, *f.*, truth. 10

**vērō**, *adv.*, in truth, indeed, to be sure, however. 29

**versus, -ūs**, *m.*, line, verse. 20

**vertō, -ere, vertī, versum**, turn, change. 23

**vērus, -a, -um**, true, real, proper. 4

**vesper, -peris** *or* **-perī**, *m.*, evening; evening star. 28

**vespillō, -lōnis**, *m.*, undertaker

**vester, -tra, -trum**, your, yours (*pl.*). 6

**vestiō, -īre, -īvī, -ītum**, clothe

**vetus**, *gen.* **-teris**, *adj.*, old. 34

**via, -ae**, *f.*, road, street, way. 10

**vīcīna, -ae**, *f.*, neighbor. 21

**vīcīnus, -ī**, *m.*, neighbor. 21

**vicissitūdō, -dinis**, *f.*, change, vicissitude

**victor, -tōris**, *m.*, victor

**victōria, -ae**, *f.*, victory. 8

**vīctus, -ūs**, *m.*, living, mode of life

**videō, -ēre, vīdī, vīsum**, see, observe; understand, 1; **videor, -ērī, vīsus sum**, be seen, seem, appear. 18

**vigilō (1)**, be awake, watch, be vigilant

**vigor, -gōris**, *m.*, vigor, liveliness

**vīlla, -ae**, *f.*, villa, country house

**vincō, -ere, vīcī, victum**, conquer, overcome. 8

**vinculum, -ī**, *n.*, bond, chain. 36

**vīnum, -ī**, *n.*, wine. 31

**vir, virī**, *m.*, man, hero. 3

**virgō, -ginis**, *f.*, maiden, virgin. 7

**virtūs, -tūtis**, *f.*, manliness, courage; excellence, virtue, character, worth. 7

**vīs, vīs**, *f.*, force, power, violence; **vīrēs, vīrium**, strength. 14

**vīta, -ae**, *f.*, life, mode of life. 2

**vitiōsus, -a, -um**, full of vice, vicious

**vitium, -iī**, *n.*, fault, vice, crime. 6

**vītō (1)**, avoid, shun. 14

**vīvō, -ere, vīxī, vīctum**, live. 10

**vīvus, -a, -um**, alive, living. 30

**vix**, *adv.*, hardly, scarcely, with difficulty

**vocō (1)**, call, summon. 1

**volō, velle, voluī**, wish, want, be willing, will. 32

**volō (1)**, fly

**voluntārius, -a, -um**, voluntary

**voluntās, -tātis**, *f.*, will, wish

**voluptās, -tātis**, *f.*, pleasure. 10

**vōs.** *See* **tū.**

**vōx, vōcis**, *f.*, voice, word. 34

**vulgus, -ī**, *n.* (*sometimes m.*), the common people, mob, rabble. 21

**vulnus, -neris**, *n.*, wound. 24

**vultus, -ūs**, *m.*, countenance, face, 40.

## X

**Xenophōn, -phontis**, *m.*, Xenophon, Greek general and author

# ABBREVIĀTIŌNĒS

## AUTHORS AND WORKS CITED

Aug., St. Augustine
    Conf., Confessions
Caes., Caesar
    B Civ., Bellum Civile
    B Gall., Bellum Gallicum
Catull., Catullus
    Carm., Carmina
Cic., Cicero
    Amic., De Amicitia
    Arch., Pro Archia
    Att., Epistulae ad Atticum
    Cat., In Catilinam
    De Or., De Oratore
    Div., De Divinatione
    Fam., Epistulae ad Familiares
    Fin., De Finibus
    Inv. rhet., De Inventione Rhetorica
    Leg., De Legibus
    Marcell, Pro Marcello
    Nat. D., De Natura Deorum
    Off., De Officiis
    Or., Orator
    Phil., Orationes Philippicae
    Pis., In Pisonem
    Planc., Pro Plancio
    Q Fr., Epistulae ad Quintum Fratrem
    Rep., De Republica
    Rosc. Am., Pro Sexto Roscio Amerino
    Sen., De Senectute
    Sull., Pro Sulla
    Tusc., Tusculanae Disputationes
    Verr., In Verrem

Hor., Horace
    Ars.P., Ars Poetica (Epist. 2.3)
    Carm., Carmina or Odes
    Epist., Epistulae
    Epod., Epodi
    Sat., Saturae or Sermones
Juv., Juvenal
    Sat., Saturae
Liv., Livy
    Urbe Cond., Ab Urbe Condita
Lucr., Lucretius
    Rer. Nat., De Rerum Natura
Mart., Martial
    Epig., Epigrammata
Macrob., Macrobius
    Sat., Saturnalia
Nep., Nepos
    Att., Atticus
    Cim., Cimon
    Milt., Miltiades
Ov., Ovid
    Am., Amores
    Ars. Am., Ars Amatoria
    Her., Heroides
    Met., Metamorphoses
Pers., Persius
    Sat., Saturae
Petron., Petronius
    Sat., Satyricon
Phaedr., Phaedrus
    Fab., Fabulae

Plaut., Plautus
   Aul., Aulularia
   Mil., Miles Gloriosus
   Mostell., Mostellaria
   Pers., Persa
   Stich., Stichus
Plin., Pliny (the Elder)
   HN, Naturalis Historia
Plin., Pliny (the Younger)
   Ep., Epistulae
Prop., Propertius
   El., Elegiae
Publil. Syr., Publilius Syrus
   Sent., Sententiae
Quint., Quintilian
   Inst., Institutio Oratoria
Sall., Sallust
   Cat., Bellum Catilinae
Sen., Seneca (the Elder)
   Controv., Controversiae
Sen., Seneca (the Younger)
   Brev. Vit., De Brevitate Vitae
   Clem., De Clementia
   Cons. Polyb., Ad Polybium de Consolatione
   Ep., Epistulae Morales

Suet., Suetonius
   Aug., Divus Augustus
   Caes., Julius Caesar
Tac., Tacitus
   Ann., Annales
   Dial., Dialogus de Oratoribus
Ter., Terence
   Ad., Adelphoe
   An., Andria
   Heaut., Heautontimorumenos
   Hec., Hecyra
   Phorm., Phormio
Veg., Vegetius
   Mil., De Re Militari
Vell., Velleius Paterculus
   Hist. Rom., Historia Romana
Verg., Vergil
   Aen., Aeneid
   Ecl., Eclogues
   G., Georgics
Vulg., Vulgate
   Eccles., Ecclesiastes
   Exod., Exodus
   Gen., Genesis

# OTHER ABBREVIATIONS

| abl. | ablative case |
|---|---|
| abs. | absolute |
| acc. | accusative case |
| act. | active voice |
| A.D. | after Christ (Lat. *annō dominī*, lit., *in the year of the Lord*) |
| adj. | adjective |
| adv. | adverb |
| App. | Appendix |
| B.C. | before Christ |
| ca. | about (Lat. *circā*) |
| cent. | century |
| cf. | compare (Lat. *cōnfer*) |
| Ch(s). | Chapter(s) |
| compar. | comparative (degree) |

| complem. | complementary |
|---|---|
| conj. | conjunction |
| dat. | dative case |
| decl. | declension |
| depon. | deponent |
| dir. obj. | direct object |
| ed. | edition; edited by |
| e.g. | for example (Lat. *exemplī gratiā*) |
| Eng. | English |
| esp. | especially |
| etc. | and others (Lat. *et cētera*) |
| Exerc. | *Exercitātiōnēs* |
| f. | feminine gender |
| ff. | and the following (lines, pages) |
| Fr. | French |

| | | | |
|---|---|---|---|
| fut. | future tense | obj. | object *or* objective |
| fut. perf. | future perfect tense | Occ. | Occitan |
| gen. | genitive case | p. | page(s) |
| Ger. | German | partic. | participle |
| Gk. | Greek | pass. | passive voice |
| ibid. | in the same place (Lat. *ibidem*) | perf. | perfect (present perfect) tense |
| id. | the same (Lat. *idem*) | pers. | person |
| i.e. | that is (Lat. *id est*) | pl. | plural |
| imperat. | imperative mood | pluperf. | pluperfect (past perfect) tense |
| imperf. | imperfect tense | Port. | Portuguese |
| impers. | impersonal | pred. | predicate |
| indecl. | indeclinable | prep. | preposition |
| indef. | indefinite | pres. | present tense |
| indic. | indicative mood | pron. | pronoun |
| ind. obj. | indirect object | purp. | purpose |
| ind. quest. | indirect question | ref. | reference |
| ind. state. | indirect statement | rel. | relative |
| infin. | infinitive | Rom. | Romanian |
| interj. | interjection | Russ. | Russian |
| interrog. | interrogative | S.A. | *Sententiae Antīquae* |
| Introd. | Introduction | sc. | supply, namely (Lat. *scīlicet*) |
| irreg. | irregular | sent. | sentence |
| It. | Italian | sg. | singular |
| Lat. | Latin | Sp. | Spanish |
| lit. | literal(ly) | S.S. | Supplementary Syntax |
| loc. | locative case | subj. | subject |
| Locī Ant. | *Locī Antīquī* | subjunct. | subjunctive mood |
| Locī Im. | *Locī Immūtātī* | superl. | superlative |
| m. | masculine gender | s.v. | under the word (Lat. *sub verbō*) |
| mid. | middle | voc. | vocative case |
| n. | note *or* neuter gender | Vocab. | Vocabulary/*Vocābula* |
| no(s). | number(s) | vs. | as opposed to, in comparison with (Lat. *versus*) |
| nom. | nominative case | | |

# INDEX

*Page references to illustrations are italicized.*

**Ab**
  with ablative of personal agent, 148, 177
  in place constructions, 313
Ablative case
  absolute, 193–94, 196
  of accompaniment, 13, 116–17, 177
  as adverbial case, 13–14
  with cardinal numerals, 125, 177
  of cause, 493
  of comparison, 212
  of degree of difference, 493
  of description, 342
  forms of. *See* Declension
  of manner, 13, 116–17, 177–78
  of means or instrument, 13, 116–17, 178
  of personal agent, 148, 177
  of place from which, 13, 163, 177, 313–14
  of place where 13, 177, 313–14
  with prepositions
    summary of uses, 177
  without prepositions, summary of uses, 178
  of respect or specification, 216, 271, 492–93
  of route, 317, 330
  of separation, 163–64, 177–78
  with special deponent verbs, 285
  of time when or within which, 13–14, 125–26, 178, 314
  usage of, 13–14, 116–17
Accents, xl, 4
Accompaniment, ablative of, 116–17, 177
Accusative case
  as direct object, 13
  of duration of time, 102, 125, 314
  of exclamation, 70
  forms of. *See* Declension

  infinitive in indirect statement with, 203–04
  as object of preposition, 13
  of place to which, 313–14
Achilles, 110–11
Active periphrastic, 247
Active voice, 2
  deponent verbs, 282–85
  infinitive, 201–02
  participles, 184–85
  perfect system. *See* Perfect system, active voice
  personal endings for, 2–3
  present system
    1st and 2nd conjugation, 3–5, 40–42
    3rd conjugation, 63–65, 80–82
    4th conjugation, 80–81
    subjunctive, 228, 236–37
**Ad**
  with gerundive or gerund, 334
  in place constructions, 313
Adjectives
  1st declension, 14–15, 33, 42, 73–74
  2nd declension, 23–25, 32–33, 42, 73–74
  3rd declension, 131–33, 211
  with adverbial force, 189
  agreement of, 15, 33, 56
  attributive, 15, 35, 133
  comparison of, 210–11. *See also* Comparative degree
    and Superlative degree
    declension, 211, 219
    formation, 210–11
    irregular formation, 218–19, 226
    summary of forms, 499
    usage and translation, 211
  dative case with, 294
  definition of, 15

Adjectives (*cont.*)
  demonstrative, 71–73
    **īdem, eadem, idem,** 90
    **is, ea, id,** 90
  with genitive ending in -**īus** and dative ending in -**ī,**
      73–74
  interrogative, 155
  objective complement, 133
  positive degree, 210
  possessive, 89
  predicate, 34–35, 133
  reflexive possessives, 106–07
  substantive, 35, 133
  summary of forms, 33, 496
  UNUS NAUTA, 73–74
  verbal. *See* Gerundive; Participles
  word order and, 15–16, 25–26
Adverbs, 25
  ablative case and, 13
  comparison of, 264–65
    irregular, 265–66
    summary of forms, 499
  definition of, 5, 13
  formation of, 264–65
Aeneas, 190–91, 192, 346–48, 349
Agamemnon, *68*
Agent
  ablative of, 148
  dative of, 195
Agreement
  of adjectives, 15, 33, 56
  of relative pronouns, 139–41
  subject-verb, 15–16
Alexander the Great, 110–*11*, 278
Alliteration, 278, 290, 322
Allobroges, 166, 310
Alma-Tadema, Sir Lawrence, *20, 144*
Alphabet, xxxv–xxxix
Ambiguous forms, 16, 24, 58, 111, 177
Anaphora, 94, 243, 278, 290
Anglo-Saxon language, xxvi–xxix
Antecedent, 109, 139–44, 150, 155, 243, 291, 323, 326,
      328
Antithesis, 137
Antony, Marc, 93, 345
Apex, xxxvii
Apodosis, 273
Aposiopesis, 321
Apposition, 25
Archaic Period of Latin Literature, xxx–xxxi

Archaising Period, xxxiii
Aristotle, 278–*79*
Arria, 337–*38,* 405
Articles, 14, 18, 78
Assimilation, 48, 58, 66, 195
Asyndeton, 137
Athena. *See* Minerva
**Audiō,** conjugation of, 80–81
Augustan Period (of Latin literature), xxxii
Augustine, Saint, xxxiv
Augustus, xxxii, 28, 197, 262

Bacon, Francis, xxxv
Bakalowicz, Stefan, *11, 22*
Base, of nouns and adjectives, 14, 23–24, 32, 42, 50,
      55–56
Bede, Caedmon's Anglo-Saxon Verses and the Difficul-
      ties of Translation, 360–61
Browne, Sir Thomas, xxix
Brutus, Lucius, 101

Caecina Paetus, 337, *338,* 405–06
Caelius (Rufus), 222
Caesar, xxxi, 101, 161, 215, *215,* 318, 327, 329–30
  The Nations of Gaul, *215*–16
Caesar of Heisterbach, The Devil and a Thirteenth-
      Century Schoolboy, 361–62
Calendar, 199–200, 234
Calliope, *84*
**Capiō,** conjugation of, 84
Cardinal numerals, 123–24, 129–30, 500
  ablative with, 125
  genitive with, 124
Carthage, 51, 192, 197, 349
Cases
  definition of, 12
  of nouns, 12–14, 15–16. *See also* Ablative case;
      Accusative case; Dative case; Declension;
      Genitive case; Locative case; Nominative case;
      Vocative case
Catiline (Lucius Sergius Catilina), 93–*94,* 120–21,
      *166*–67, 252, 254, 263, 288, 309–10, 366–74
Catullus, xxxi, *20,* 39, 244, 253, 318, 363–66
  Alley Cat, *22*
  Ask Me if I Care, 330
  Bids a Bitter Farewell to Lesbia, 159–60
  Bids His Girlfriend Farewell, *20*
  B.Y.O.B., etc., etc., 277–78
  Death of a Pet Sparrow, 364–65
  Dedicates His Poetry Book, 60–61

A Dedication, 363–64
Disillusionment, 351–52
Fräter Avē, Atque Valē, 365–66
Give Me a Thousand Kisses!, *260*–61
How Many Kisses?, 364
I Love Her . . . I Love Her Not, 309
On Lesbia's Husband, 290–92
Promises, Promises!, 337
Thanks a Lot, Tully!, 223
**Causā,** with genitive phrase, 334
Cause, ablative of, 493
Chiasmus, 52, 77, 120, 253–54
Characteristic, relative clauses of, 323–24
Cicero, xxxi, xxxiv–xxxv, *38, 94*, 189, 223, 254, 262,
    263, 299, 350, 366–84
    The Aged Playwright Sophocles Holds His Own,
        158–*59*
    Alexander the Great and the Power of Literature,
        110–11
    On Ambition and Literature, Both Latin and Greek,
        182
    anecdotes from, 380–83
    The Arrest and Trial of the Conspirators, 369–74
    The Authority of a Teacher's Opinion, 112
    On Contempt of Death, 377–78
    Cyrus' Dying Words on Immortality, *128*
    Death of a Puppy (Example of an Omen), 380
    Denounces Catiline in the Senate, 93
    Derivation of "Philosophus" and Subjects of Philos-
        ophy, 354
    **Dē Vītā et Morte,** 374–78
    On the Ethics of Waging War, 69
    Evidence and Confession, 252
    Fabian Tactics, 128–29
    Get the Tusculan Country House Ready, 383
    How Demosthenes Overcame His Handicaps, 352
    Imagines the State of Rome Itself Urging Him to
        Punish the Catilinarian Conspirators, 120
    The Incomparable Value of Friendship, 86
    Literature: Its Value and Delight, 378–80
    **Mārcus Quīntō Frātrī S.,** 319–20
    More Examples of Roman Wit, 328–29
    A More Positive View About Immortality, 375–77
    The Nervousness of Even a Great Orator, 242
    On the Pleasures of Love in Old Age, 143
    **Quam Multa Nōn Dēsīderō!,** 381
    The Rarity of Friendship, 38
    Socrates' "Either-Or" Belief, 374–75
    Sorry, Nobody's Home!, 300
    The Sword of Damocles, 353
    Testimony Against the Conspirators, 309–10
    Themistocles; Fame and Expediency, 382–83
    Thermopylae: A Soldier's Humor, 45–46
    Too Conscientious (An Example of Irony), 380
    Two Letters to, *329*–30
    The Tyrant Can Trust No One, 352–53
    Urges Catiline's Departure from Rome, *166*–67
    On the Value and the Nature of Friendship, 354–55
    The Value of Literature, 348
    Vitriolic Denunciation of the Leader of a Conspiracy
        Against the Roman State, 366–69
    On War, 355–56
    What Makes a Good Appetite, 381–82
    Your Loss, My Gain, 279
Ciceronian Period (of Latin literature), xxxi–xxxii
Cimon, 270–71
Cincinnatus, 207
Circus, 150–*51*
Claudius, *289*–90
Clauses
    participial phrases translated as, 186–87
    subjunctive, 227
        conditional sentences, 274
        **cum,** 255–56
        fear, 341–42
        indirect questions, 247
        jussive, 228–29
        jussive noun, 303–04
        proviso, 267–68
        purpose, 229–30, 237–38, 303
        relative clause of characteristic, 323
        result, 237–38
    subordinate, 17, 139–40, 142, 155, 186, 203, 206, 229,
        237, 247, 255–56, 267, 273, 303, 310, 493–94
        in indirect statement, 493–94
Cleopatra, 327
Clodia. *See* Lesbia
Cognate languages, xxvi, xxviii
Cognomen, 30, 69, 113, 138
Collatinus, 59–60
Collective nouns, 108, 149
Commands
    imperative, 2, 5, 64, 65, 81, 229, 256–57, 267, 284–85,
        313
    jussive noun clauses, 303–04
    jussive subjunctive, 228–29
    negative, **nōlō** and, 267
Comparative degree
    of adjectives, 210–11
        declension, 211, 219

Comparative degree (*cont.*)
    formation, 210–11
    summary of forms, 499
    usage and translation, 211
  of adverbs, 264–65
    irregular, 265–66
    summary of forms, 499
Comparison, ablative of, 212
Complementary infinitive, 49
Compound verbs, 195
  dative case with, 298
Conditional sentences, 69, 273–74
  indicative, 273–74
  mixed, 274
  subjunctive, 274
Conjugation. *See also* First conjugation; Fourth
     conjugation; Second conjugation; Third conju-
     gation
  definition of, 2
  of deponent verbs, 282–85
  personal endings for. *See* Personal endings
  summary of forms of, 501–09
Conjunction
  coordinating, 17
  Correlative, 141
  **cum** as, 255
  definition of, 17
  subordinating, 17
Consonantal **i**, xxxviii, 88, 220
Consonants, pronunciation of, xxxvii–xxxix
Consonant stems (3rd declension nouns), 114
Constantine, 113
Contraction, 10, 39, 48, 277, 308
Conversational Latin, 10–11, 138
Cornelius Nepos. *See* Nepos
Correlative adjectives, 249
**Cum,** with ablative case, 116–17, 177
**Cum** clauses, 255–56
Cyrus the Great, *128*

Dante, xxxiv–xxxv
Dative case
  with adjectives, 294
  of agent, 195
  with compound verbs, 296
  forms of. *See* Declension
  general use of, 13
  indirect object, 13
  of possession, 492
  of purpose, 492

  of reference or interest, 260, 324
  of separation, 291
  with special verbs, 295–96
**Dē**
  ablative case with, 125, 177
  in place constructions, 313
Declension, xxxiv
  1st, 14–15
    adjectives, 14–15, 33, 42, 73
  2nd, 23–25
    adjectives, 23–25, 33, 73
    masculines ending in **-er,** 23–24, 42
    masculines ending in **-us,** 23–25
    neuters, 32–33
  3rd, 55–56
    adjectives, 131–33, 211
    i-stem nouns, 114–15, 132
  4th, 162–63
  5th, 176–77
  of adjectives, summary of forms, 498
  definition of, 14
  of gerund, 332
  of participles, 185
  of pronouns
    demonstratives, 71–72, 90
    intensive, 107
    personal, 87–88
    reflexive, 105–06
    relative, 139
  use of term, 14
Decline, 14, 15–16
Defective verbs, 141, 164, 204
Definite article, 14, 78
Degree of difference, ablative of, 493
Demonstratives
  **hic, ille, iste,** 71–73, 75
  **īdem, eadem, idem,** 90
  **is, ea, id,** 90
  usage and translation of, 72–73
Demosthenes, 165, *241*
Deponent verbs, 282–85
  ablative case with, 285
  definition of, 282
  principal parts and conjugation of, 282–85
  semi-deponent, 58, 187, 285
  summary of forms of, 504–06
Derived languages, xxviii
Descartes, 39
Description, genitive and ablative of, 342
Diction, 52

**Diēs Īrae**, 183
Diminutive (form), 21, *53,* 79
Dionysius, 51, 127, 143, 222, 318
Diphthongs, pronunciation of, xxxvii
Dipinti, *182–83, 234–35, 310*–11
Direct address, 14
Direct object, 2, 13, 16, 18, 25–26, 34–35, 88, 140,
      148, 186, 194, 202, 294–96, 324, 333
  accusative case and, 13
Direct questions, **-ne, num,** and **nōnne,** 341
**Domus,** in place constructions, 313–14
Dufresnoy, Charles, *251*
**Dummodo,** 267–68

**Ego/nōs**
  declension of, 87
  usage of, 88–90
Ellipsis, 290
Enclitic, 50
Endings
  1st declension, 14–15, 24–25
  2nd declension, 23–25, 32
  3rd declension, 55–56, 132
  4th declension, 162–63
  5th declension, 176–77
  i-stem, 114–15, 132
  personal, 2–3
    deponent verbs, 282
    perfect system active, 97–99
    present system active, 2–3
    present system passive, 146
English language, xxv–xxx
Ennius, 128, 300
**Eō,** conjugation of, 312–13
**-er** adjectives, 1st and 2nd declension, 42
Erasmus, xxxv
Etymology. *See also last section of several of the*
    *chapters*
  definition of, 21
**Ex**
  ablative case with, 125, 177
  in place constructions, 313–14

Fabius Maximus, Quintus, 128–29, 279
Fear clauses, 341–42, 344
**Ferō,** conjugation of, 256–57
Ficherelli, Felice, *60*
Fifth declension, 176–77
  summary of forms of, 495
Finite verbs, 2

**Fīō,** conjugation of, 304–05
First conjugation
  future indicative
    active, 40–41
    passive, 147
  imperative, 5
  imperfect indicative
    active, 40–41
    passive, 147
  present indicative
    active, 4
    passive, 146
  present infinitive
    active, 3
    passive, 147
  subjunctive, 227–28, 236, 245–46
  summary of forms of, 501–04
First declension, 14–15
  2nd declension compared with, 24–25
  adjectives, 14–15, 33
    ending in **-er,** 42
  summary of forms of, 495–96
Fourth conjugation, 80–81, 169–70
  future indicative
    active, 81
    passive, 169
  imperative, 81
  imperfect indicative
    active, 81
    passive, 170
  present indicative
    active, 80
    passive, 169
  present infinitive
    active, 81
    passive, 170
  subjunctive, 227–28, 236, 245–46
  summary of forms of, 501–04
Fourth declension, 162
  summary of forms of, 495
French (including Old French), *xxvii*–xxix, 30, 39, 54,
    61–62, 78, 82–83, 95, 121–22, 130, 145, 175, 183,
    225–26, 243–44, 331
Fronto, xxxiii
Function (use), grammatical, 16
Future active periphrastic, 247
Future indicative
  deponent verbs, 283
  of **possum,** 49
  of **sum,** 48

Future indicative active
    1st and 2nd conjugation, 40–41
    3rd conjugation, 63, 64
    4th conjugation, 81
Future indicative passive
    1st and 2nd conjugation, 147
    3rd and 4th conjugation, 169
Future passive participle. *See* Gerundive
Future perfect
    active, 98
    deponent verbs, 283
    passive, 153
Future tense, translation of, 41–42

Gaul, 215
Gellius, xxxiii
Gender, 15, 26
    1st declension, 15
    2nd declension, 23–24, 32–33
    3rd declension, 55–56, 115
    4th declension, 162
    5th declension, 176
    definition of, 15
Genitive case
    of description, 342
    forms of. *See* Declension
    general use of, 13
    of indefinite value, 260
    of material, 491–92
    objective, 492
    partitive (of the whole), 124, 345
    possessive, 13
    predicate, 348
Gérôme, Jean-Léon, 293
Gerundive (future passive participle), 184, 332–34, 340
    gerund compared with, 332–34
    in passive periphrastic, 194
    phrases, 333–34
Gerunds, 332–34, 340
    declension of, 332
    gerundive compared with, 333–34
    phrases, 333–34
Gladiators, *53, 280*, 293
Golden Age (of Latin literature), xxx–xxxiii
Graffiti, *9–10, 21, 29–30, 38–39, 47, 53, 61, 69–70, 78, 86, 94, 103, 112, 121, 129, 137–38, 144–45, 152, 160–61, 167, 174, 182, 191, 199, 209, 216–17, 224–25, 234, 243, 253–54, 262–63, 272, 280, 292, 301–02, 310–11, 320–21, 330–31, 339, 349*
Greek alphabet, xxxvi

Greek (language), xxvi–*xxvii*, xxxvi, xxxviii, 3, 16, 17, 21, 30, 47, 54, 68, 82, 104, 108, 121, 160, 174, 181, 208, 222, 226, 233, 243, 261–62, 273, 289–90, 318, 328, 331, 346
Greek literature, xxx–xxxi

Hamilcar, 338–39
Hannibal, 128, 338–39
Head verbs, 203, 206
**Hic**
    declension of, 71–72
    **is** compared with, 90
    use and translation of, 72–73
Historical present, 248
Historical (secondary) tenses, 247–48
Homer, 110, *144*, 180
Horace, xxxii, *8–9*, 226, 350, 394–99
    **Aurea Mediocritās**—The Golden Mean, 396–97
    Autobiographical Notes, 357–58
    **Carpe Diem**, 394
    Contemplates an Invitation, 8–9
    **Dē Cupiditāte**, 197–98
    **Diēs Fēstus**, 399
    The Grass Is Always Greener, 29
    **Integer Vītae**, 395
    **Lābuntur Annī**, 397–98
    Longs for the Simple, Peaceful Country Life on His Sabine Farm, 358–59
    A Monument More Lasting than Bronze, 348, 399
    The Satirist's Modus Operandi, 199
    A Sense of Balance in Life, 398–99
    Who Is Truly Free?, 309
**Humus**, in place constructions, 314

**Īdem, eadem, idem**, 90
**Ille**
    declension of, 71–72
    etymology and, 78
    **is** compared with, 90
    use and translation of, 72–73
Imperative, 229
    1st and 2nd conjugation, 5
    3rd conjugation, 64–65, 81
    4th conjugation, 81
    definition of, 5
    of deponent verbs, 284–85
    future, 292
    **nōlō**, 267
Imperfect indicative
    deponent verbs, 283

of **possum**, 49
of **sum**, 48
Imperfect indicative active
1st and 2nd conjugation, 40–41
3rd conjugation, 64, 81
4th conjugation, 81
Imperfect indicative passive
1st and 2nd conjugation, 147
3rd and 4th conjugation, 170
Imperfect subjunctive, 236–37
deponent verbs, 283
usage and translation of, 237
Imperfect tense
perfect (present perfect) tense compared with, 98–99
translation, 41–42
Impersonal verbs, 315, 325
**In**
with ablative case, 177
in place constructions, 313
Incunabula, xxxv, n. 9
Indeclinable (nouns, adjectives), 35, 42, 123
Indefinite article, 14, 78
Independent clauses, 229
Indicative, xxxiv
definition of, 2
future. *See* Future indicative; Future indicative active; Future indicative passive
imperfect. *See* Imperfect indicative; Imperfect indicative active; Imperfect indicative passive; Imperfect tense
present. *See* Present indicative; Present indicative active; Present indicative passive
subjunctive compared with, 227
Indicative conditional sentences, 273–74
Indirect command (jussive noun clauses), 303–04
Indirect object, 13, 16, 25, 67, 88, 294
Indirect questions, 242, 247–48
Indirect statement
definition of, 202
infinitive in, with accusative subject, 202–03
list of verbs followed by, 205
subordinate clauses in, 493–94
Indo-European languages, xxvi, 178
Infinitive, 201
complementary, 49
definition of, 3
of deponent verbs, 284
to distinguish the conjugations, 3, 64
in indirect statement, with accusative subject, 202–04

irregular verbs
**possum, posse, potuī**, 48
**sum**, 34
objective, 202
present passive, 147, 170
usage of, 202
Infix, 41
Inflected languages, xxvi
Inflections, xxvi, 3, 12
Instrument (means), ablative of, 116–17, 178
Intensive pronouns, 107, 109
Interest, dative of, 260, 324
Interlocked word order, 253
Interrogative adjectives, 155–56
Interrogative pronouns, 154–56
Intertextuality, 223
Intransitive verbs, 34. *See also* **sum**
-**iō** verbs
conjugation of, 80–82
participles, 185
subjunctive, 228, 236
**Ipse, ipsa, ipsum**, 107
Irregular verbs
**eō**, 312–13
**ferō**, 256–57
**fiō**, 304–05
**mālō**, 267
**nōlō**, 267
**possum**, 48–49, 237
**sum**, 34, 48
summary of forms of, 506–09
**volō**, 266
**Is, ea, id**
declension of, 88
as demonstrative, 90
usage of, 88–90
Isidore of Seville, xxxiv
The Days of the Week, 233
**Iste**, declension of, 72
I-stem nouns of 3rd declension, 114–15, 125, 132
Italian, *xxvii*–xxviii, xxxiv, 30, 39, 61–62, 78, 95, 121, 130, 145, 175, 183, 217, 225, 243–44, 331, 340
**Iubeō**, with jussive noun clauses, 304

Jalabert, Charles Francois, *8*
Jerome, Saint, xxviii, xxxiv
Johnson, Samuel, xxxiii
Jussive noun clauses, 277, 303–04
Jussive subjunctive, 228–29

Juvenal, xxxiii, 47, 254, 272, 293
    Explains His Impulse to Satire, 136–37

Latin language, in linguistic history, xxv–xxx
Latin literature
    brief survey of, xxx–xxxv
    "vulgar," xxviii, xxxiii–xxxiv
Lentulus, 252, 310
Leonidas, 45–46
Lepautre, Pierre, *338*
Lesbia (Clodia), xxxi, *20*, 159, 222–23, 242, 260, 290–91
Linking verbs, intransitive, 34. *See also* **sum**
Literacy, 47, *321*
Livy, xxxii, 52, 293
    On the Death of Cicero, 383–84
    Laments the Decline of Roman Morals, 52–*53*
    The Rape of Lucretia, 59–*60*
Locative case, 314
Long marks. *See* Macrons
Lucretia, rape of, 59–60
Lucretius, xxxi

Maccari, Cesare, *94*
Macrobius, Facētiae (Witticisms), 262
Macrons, xxxvii, 4, 17, 50, 64
Maecenas, *8–9, 28*
**Mālō**
    conjugation of, 267
    with jussive noun clauses, 304
Manlius, 167
Manner, ablative of, 13, 116–17, 177–78
Manuscripts, *53, 103,* 145, 160, 291, 322
Martial, xxxiii, 410–11
    A Covered Dish Dinner!, 252
    Diaulus Still Buries His Clients, 102
    Even Though You Do Invite Me—I'll Come!, 410
    Fake Tears, 410
    The Good Life, 216
    To Have Friends One Must Be Friendly, 233
    His Only Guest Was a Real Boar!, 45
    "I Do." "I Don't!," 300
    "I Do Not Love Thee, Doctor Fell," 52
    I Don't Cook for Cooks!, 308
    Issa, 411
    It's All in the Delivery, 143–*44*
    Large Gifts—Yes, but Only Bait, 360
    A Legacy-Hunter's Wish, 253
    Maronilla Has a Cough, 301
    Message from a Bookcase, 160
    Note on a Book by Lucan, 328

Note on a Copy of Catullus' Carmina, 253
Oh, I'd Love to Read You My Poems . . . Not!, 308
The Old Boy Dyed His Hair, 410
**Paete, Nōn Dolet**, 337
Please . . . Don't!, 271
Please Remove My Name from Your Mailing List!,
    232
Pretty Is as Pretty Does, 290
Pro-*cras*-tination, 410–11
The Quality of Martial's Book, 308
The Rich Get Richer, 278
Ringo, *261–62*
Store Teeth, 119–*20*
Summer Vacation, 301
On a Temperamental Friend, 137
Thanks . . . but No Thanks!, 318
A Vacation . . . from You!, 271
And Vice Is Not Nice!, 290
A Visit from the Young Interns, *181*
When I Have . . . Enough!, 76
You're All Just Wonderful!, 242–43
Material, genitive of, 491–92
Matthew, The Lord's Prayer, 360
Means (instrument), ablative of, 13, 116–17, 178
Medieval Period, xxxiv–*xxxv*
Metaphor, 152, 183, 256, 294, 308, 350
Middle English, xxix
Milo, 259
Milton, John, xxxv
Minerva (Athena), 190–91, 207–08, *261*
Mood
    definition of, 2, 227
    imperative, 2, 5, 64–65, 81, 227, 284–85
    indicative, 2, 227
    subjunctive, 2, 227
More, Sir Thomas, xxxv
Morphology, 1
Mycenae, *68*

Names (Roman), 30
-**ne, num, nōnne,** in direct questions, 341
Nepos, xxxii, 60–61, 384–94
    Aristides the Just, 391–92
    The Character of Cimon, 270–71
    Hannibal; The Second Punic War, 356–57
    Hannibal and the Beginnings of the Second Punic
        War, 338–39
    Miltiades and the Battle of Marathon, 384–87
    Themistocles and the Battle of Salamis, 388–90
    Timoleon, 392–94

Newton, Sir Isaac, xxxv
**Nōlō**
  conjugation of, 267
  with jussive noun clauses, 304
  negative commands and, 267
Nomen, 30
Nominative case
  forms of. *See* Declension
  predicate nominative, 13
  as subject, 12
Nouns
  1st declension, 14–15
  2nd declension, 23–24, 32–33
  3rd declension, 55–56, 114–15 *See also* I-stem nouns;
    Consonant stems
  4th declension, 162–63
  5th declension, 176–77
  abstract, 12, 56
  agentive, 56, 70, 86
  in apposition, 25
  cases of, 12. *See also* Ablative case; Accusative case;
    Dative case; Declension; Genitive case; Locative
    case; Nominative case; Vocative case
  common, 12
  concrete, 12
  definition of, 12
  predicate, 34
  proper, 12
  substantive adjectives as, 35
  summary of forms, 495
  verbal. *See* Gerund; Infinitive; Supine
Number, 2
Numerals, 129–30, 500
  cardinal, 123–23
    ablative case, 125
  distributive, 130
  multiplicative, 130
  ordinal, 129

Objective complement, 119, 133
Objective genitives, 492
Objective infinitive, 494
Object of verb
  direct, 2, 13, 25
  indirect, 13, 25
Occitan (including Old Occitan), xxviii, 30, 39, 61–62,
    78, 95, 121, 130, 145, 175, 183, 225–26, 244, 331,
    340
Odo de Cerinton, Who Will Put the Bell on the Cat's
    Neck!, 361

Onomatopoeia, 277
Ordinal numerals, 129, 500
Orestes, 233
Ovid, xi, xxxii
  Asks the Gods to Inspire His Work, 299–300
  On Death and Metamorphosis, 151

Paetus, Caecina, 337–*38*
Paraclausithyron, 320
Paradigms
  meaning and use of, 3
  said aloud, 4
Participles (participial phrases), 184–87. *See also*
    Gerundive
  ablative absolute, 193–94
  declension of, 185
  of deponent verbs, 284
  passive periphrastic, 145, 194–95
  translation of
    as clauses, 186–87
  as verbal adjectives, 185–86
Partitive genitive (genitive of the whole), 124, 345
Parts of speech, 1–2
Passive periphrastic (gerundive + **sum**), 145,
    194–96
Passive voice, 2
  definition of, 146
  infinitive, 147, 170, 201–02
  participles in, 184–85
  perfect system, 153–54
    subjunctive, 245–46
    usage and translation, 157, 246
  present system
    1st and 2nd conjugation, 146–48
    3rd and 4th conjugation, 169–70
    subjunctive, 228, 236
Past perfect. *See* Pluperfect
Past tense (simple past). *See* Perfect
Patristic Period (of Latin literature), xxxiv
Perfect indicative
  active, 96–98
  active stem, 97
  deponent verbs, 282–83
  imperfect tense compared with, 98–99
  passive, 153–54
  translation of, 98–99
Perfect subjunctive
  active, 245–46
  deponent verbs, 283
  passive, 246

Perfect system, 96
  active voice, 96–98
    perfect active stem and, 97
    principal parts, 96–97
    usage, translation and distinction from the
      imperfect, 98–99
  definition of, 96
  passive voice, 153–54
    usage and translation, 154, 157
  subjunctive, 245–46
Periphrasis, definition of, 194. *See also* Future active
    periphrastic; Passive periphrastic
Persia, 35–36, *128*, 165, 259
Persius, 349–50
Person, 2, 16
Personal agent, ablative of, 148, 177
Personal endings
  active voice, 2–3, 97
  passive voice, 146
Personal pronouns, 87–90
  declension of, 87–88
  definition of, 87
  reflexive pronouns compared with, 106
  usage of, 87–90
Personification, 76
Petrarch, xxxv
Petronius, xxxiii
  Trimalchio's epitaph, 318–19
Phaedrus, 400–03
  The Ass and the Old Shepherd, 402
  Dē Cupiditāte, 197–98
  The Fox and the Tragic Mask, 400
  The Fox Gets the Raven's Cheese, 401–02
  The Other Person's Faults and Our Own, 400
  Sour Grapes, 400
  The Stag at the Spring, 401
  The Two Mules and the Robbers, 402–03
Phonetic change, 484–85
Phrases
  gerund and gerundive, 333–34
  participial
    ablative absolute, 193–94
    translation, 193–94
Place constructions
  from which, 163, 177, 313–14
  to which, 313–14
  where, 177, 313–14
Plato, 189
Plautus, xxx–xxxi, xxxiv
Pliny, xxxiii, 403–10
  On Behalf of a Penitent Freedman, 408–09

Concern about a Sick Freedman, 407–08
Delights of the Country, 403
Endows a School, 359–60
Faithful in Sickness and in Death, 405–06
Happy Married Life, 404–05
Selection of a Teacher, 409–10
A Sweet, Brave Girl, 406–07
What Pliny Thinks of the Races, 359
Why No Letters?, 359
Writes to Marcellinus about the Death of Fundanus'
    Daughter, 102–03
Pluperfect (past perfect), usage of, 98–99
Pluperfect indicative
  active, 98
  deponent verbs, 283
  passive, 153
Pluperfect subjunctive, 245–46
  deponent verbs, 283
**Plūs**, declension of, 219
Polyphemus, *135*
Polysyndeton, 290
Pompeii, 9, *321*. *See also* Graffiti
Pompey, *329*
Pontilianus, 232
Portuguese, *xxvii*–xxviii, 30, 39, 61–62, 78, 95, 121, 130,
    145, 175, 183, 217, 225, 244, 331, 340
Positive degree (of adjectives), 210
Possession
  dative of, 492
  genitive of, 13
Possessives
  adjectives, 89
  reflexive, 106–07
  supplying in English translation, 28
**Possum**
  with complementary infinitive, 49
  conjugation of, 49
    subjunctive, 237
Post-Augustan period (of Latin literature), xxxiii
Postpositive word, 42–43
Potential subjunctive, 308
Praenomen, 30
Predicate, definition of, 34
Predicate adjectives, 13, 34
Predicate genitive, 348
Predicate nouns, 13, 34
Prefixes, 18, 27, 36, 57, 66, 75, 78, 82, 100, 108, 117–18,
    126, 151, 195, 213, 296, 342
  Inseparable, 78, 195–96
Prepositions, xxxiv
  with ablative case, 14, 74, 116–17, 148, 177–78, 313

with accusative case, 13, 74, 313
definition of, 13
object of, 13–14
phrases, 13
in place constructions, 313
Present imperative active
1st and 2nd conjugation, 5
3rd conjugation, 64–65, 81
4th conjugation, 81
Present imperative passive, deponent verbs, 284–85
Present indicative
deponent verbs, 282–83
of **possum**, 48–49
of **sum**, 34
Present indicative active
1st and 2nd conjugation, 4
3rd conjugation, 63, 80
4th conjugation, 80
Present indicative passive
1st and 2nd conjugation, 146
3rd and 4th conjugation, 169
Present perfect. *See* Perfect
Present stems. *See* Stems of verbs, present
Present subjunctive
conjugation of, 228
deponent verbs, 283
of **possum**, 236–37
of **sum**, 236–37
translation of, 228
Present system
1st and 2nd conjugation, 40, 43
imperative, 5
indicative, 3–4, 40–41, 146–47
subjunctive, 227–28, 236,
3rd conjugation
imperative, 64–65, 81
indicative, 63–65, 80–82, 169–70
subjunctive, 227–28, 236
4th conjugation
imperative, 81
indicative, 80–81, 169–70
subjunctive, 227–28, 236
definition of, 40, 96
Present tense
emphatic present, 4
progressive present, 4
simple present, 4
Primary tenses, 247–48
Principal parts. *See* Verbs
Prodelision, 328
Programmata, *182*–83, 235, *310–11*

Pronouns
demonstrative
**hic, ille, iste**, 71–73
**īdem, eadem, idem**, 90
**is, ea, id**, 88–90
intensive, 107, 109
interrogative, 154–55
personal, 87–90
declension, 87–88
definition of, 87
reflexive pronouns compared with, 105–06
usage, 88–90
reflexive, 105–07
personal compared with, 105–06
relative, 139–41
declension, 139
interrogative adjectives compared with, 155–56
usage and agreement, 139–141
summary of forms of, 497–98
Pronunciation, xxxv–xl
accent and, xl
of consonants, xxxvii–xxxix, 17, 99, 178, 321, 325, 339
of diphthongs, xxxvii
syllables and, xxxix
of vowels, xxxvi–xxxvii, 52, 57
Propertius, xxxii
Protasis, 69, 85, 273
Provençal. *See* Occitan
Proviso clauses, 267–68
Publilius Syrus, xxxii
Punctum, *86, 292, 310*–11
Purpose, dative of, 492
Purpose clauses, 229–30 , 239–40
jussive noun clauses compared with, 303–04
relative clauses of, 328
Pylades, 233
Pyrrhus, 207
Pythagoras, 112

**Quam**
with comparative and superlative adjectives, 212
with comparative and superlative adverbs, 265
Questions
direct, **-ne, num,** and **nōnne**, 341
indirect, 247
**Quī, quae, quod**
as interrogative adjectives, 154–55
as relative pronouns, 139–41
**Quīdam**, 125

Quintilian, xxxiii
  Aristotle, Tutor of Alexander the Great, 278–79

Reading passages. *See specific authors*
Reference, dative of, 260, 324
Reflexive possessives, 106–07
Reflexive pronouns, 105–07
  personal pronouns compared with, 105–06
Regulus, 336
Relative clause, 139–41
  of characteristic, 323–24, 326
  of purpose, 328
  of result, 328–29
Relative pronouns, 139–41, 145
  declension of, 139
  interrogative adjectives compared with, 155–56
  usage and agreement, 139–40
Result clauses, 237–40
  relative clauses of result, 328–29
Romance languages, xxviii, xxxiv
  etymology and, 30, 39, 62, 78, 95, 121, 129–30, 145,
    175, 183, 217, 225–26, 243–44, 331, 340
Romanian, *xxvii*–xxviii, 30, 39, 61–62, 78, 95, 121,
    130, 145, 175, 183, 225, 331, 340
Rome, *317*
Rubicon river, 161, 330
**Rūs,** in place constructions, 314

Salinator, Marcus Livius, 279
Satire, 136–37, 199
Scipio Nasica, 300
Second conjugation,
  future indicative
    active, 40–41
    passive, 147
  imperative, 5
  imperfect indicative
    active, 40–41
    passive, 147
  present indicative
    active, 4
    passive, 146
  present infinitive
    active, 3
    passive, 147
  subjunctive, 227–28, 236, 245–46
  summary of forms of, 501–04
Second declension, 23–25
  1st declension compared with, 24–25
  adjectives, 32–33
    in **-er,** 42

masculines in **-er,** 24
masculines in **-us,** 23–24
neuters, 32–33
summary of forms of, 495–96
Semi-deponent verbs, 58, 285
Seneca, xxxiii, *77*
  Claudius' Excremental Expiration, 289
  When I Have . . . Enough!, 77
Separation, ablative of, 163–64, 177–78
Shakespeare, William, xxxi
Silver Age (of Latin literature), xxxiii
Simile, 209
Socrates, 189, 207, *251*
Solon, 307
Sophocles, 101, 158–*159*
Spanish, *xxvii*–xxviii, 30, 39, 61–62, 78, 95, 121, 130,
    145, 175, 183, 217, 225, 243–44, 331, 340
Specification, ablative of, 216, 271, 492–93
Spelling errors (in graffiti), 10
Stem vowel, 3, 33, 63, 80, 82
Stems of participles, 184–85
Stems of verbs
  perfect active, 97
  present
    1st and 2nd conjugation, 3–4
    3rd conjugation, 64, 82
    4th conjugation, 80–82
**Sub**
  with ablative case, 177
  in place constructions, 177, 313
Subject, 25
  agreement of with verb, 16
  of indicative, accusative case, 202–04
  nominative case as, 12
Subject-object-verb (SOV) pattern, 7, 25
Subjunctive, xxxiv, 227–30, 236–38, 245–48
  clauses
    by attraction, 310
    conditional sentences, 273–74
    **cum,** 255–56
    fear, 341–42, 344
    indirect questions, 242, 247–48
    jussive, 228–29
    jussive noun, 277, 303–04
    potential, 308
    proviso, 267–68
    purpose, 229–30
    relative clause of characteristic, 323–24, 326
    result, 237–38
  definition of, 2, 227
  of deponent verbs, 283

imperfect, 236–37
  usage and translation, 237
perfect, 245–46
pluperfect, 245–46
of **possum**, 236–37
present
of **sum**, 236–37
translation of, 228, 237, 246
Subordinate clauses, 229
  in indirect statement, 493–94
Substantive adjectives, 35
Suffixes, 489–91
**Sum**
  conjugation of
    future and imperfect indicative, 48
    present indicative, 33–34
    subjunctive, 236–37
  with gerundive, 194–95
  with predicate nouns or adjectives, 34
Superlative degree
  of adjectives
    declension, 211
    irregular formation, 218–19
    regular formation, 210–11
    usage and translation, 211
  of adverbs, 264–66
Supine, 201, 324
Suppletion, 91, 179
Syllables, xxxix
  antepenult, xli
  penult, xli
Syncope, 21, 308
Synopsis, 99, 154, 170, 246, 257, 266, 283–84
Syntax, 1, 16

Tacitus, xxxiii
Tarquinius Superbus, 59–60, 197
Tarquinius, Sextus, 59–*60*
Tense(s)
  definition of, 2
  future, 40–41, 48–49, 63–65, 80–82, 146–48, 169–70
  future perfect, 98, 153
  imperfect
    indicative, 40–41, 48–49, 63–65, 80–82, 146–48, 169–70
    subjunctive, 236–37
  infinitive, 201–04
  participles, 184–85
  perfect
    indicative, 96–98, 153–54
    subjunctive, 245–46

pluperfect
  indicative, 96–98, 153–54
  subjunctive, 245–46
present
  imperative, 5
  indicative, 4, 33–34, 49, 63–65, 80–82, 146–48, 169–70
  subjunctive, 228, 237
sequence of, 247–48
subjunctive, 227
Tense sign, 40
Terence, xxx, 62
  An Uncle's Love for His Nephew and Adopted Son, 223–*24*
Themistocles, 165, 259
Thermopylae, 45–46, 207
Third conjugation
  future indicative
    active, 63–64, 81
    passive, 169
  imperative, 64
  imperfect indicative
    active, 64–65, 81
    passive, 170
  **-iō** verbs, 80–82
  present indicative
    active, 63–64, 80
    passive, 169
  present infinitive
    active, 64, 82
    passive, 170
  subjunctive, 227–28, 236, 245–46
  summary of forms of, 501–04
Third declension
  adjectives, 131–33
    usage, 133
  **i**-stem nouns, 114–15, 132
  summary of forms of, 145–46
Time constructions
  when or within, 125, 178, 314
  duration, 314
Transferred epithet, 291
Transitive verbs
  definition of, 2
  infinitive, 201–02
  participles of, 184–85
  voice and, 2
Translation
  3rd declension and, 56
  of comparative adjectives, 211
  of demonstratives, 72–73

Translation (*cont.*)
 of future tense, 41–42
 of imperfect tense, 41–42
 of **is, ea, id**, 88–90
 of perfect passive system, 154
 of perfect tense, 98–99
 of relative pronouns, 139–40
 of subjunctive, 228, 237, 246
Troy, 189–91, 207–*08*, 232, 346–47
**Tū/vōs**
 declension of, 88
 usage of, 88–90

**Ūnus**, etymology and, 78
UNUS NAUTA adjectives, 73–74
Use (function), grammatical, 16

Verbs. *See also* Conjugation; Mood; Tense(s); Voice
 agreement of with subject, 16
 auxiliary, xxxiv
 characteristics of, 1–2
 dative case with
  compound verbs, 296
  special verbs, 295–96
 definition of, 1
 deponent, 282–85
  summary of forms of, 504–06
 finite, 2
 intransitive, 34. *See also* **sum**
  infinitive, 201
 irregular. *See* Irregular verbs
 principal parts, 5, 70, 86, 96–97, 104, 125, 153, 184, 280

 transitive, 2
  infinitive, 201
  participles, 184
 word order and, 7, 25–26
Vergil, xxxii, *8–9*, *173*–74, 192, 253, 349
 The Death of Laocoon . . . and Troy, 207–*08*
 Jupiter Prophesies to Venus the Future Glory of Rome, 346–48, *347*
 Laocoon Speaks Out Against the Trojan Horse, *189–90*
 Messianic Eclogue, *173*–74
Vesuvius, 9
Vincotte, Thomas, 166
**Vīs**, declension of, 114–15
Vocative case
 forms of. *See* Declension
 usage of, 14
Voice. *See also* Active voice; Passive voice
 definition of, 2
**Volō**
 conjugation of, 266
 with jussive noun clauses, 304
Vowel weakening, 179, 187
Vowels, pronunciation of, xxxvi–xxxvii
*Vulgate*, xxviii, xxxiv

Whole, genitive of the (partitive genitive), 124, 345
Wilson, Thomas, xxix
Word order, 7, 15, 18, 25–26, 72

Xenophon, 173
Xerxes, 46

Zeugma, 347

# LOCATION OF THE SENTENTIAE ANTĪQVAE

1. (1) Pers., Sat. 6.27. (2) Plaut., Mostell. 1.3.30. (3) Suet., Aug. 25 (4) Hor., Sat. 1.2.11. (5) Sen., Clem. 1.2.2. (6) Cic., Sest. 67.141. (7) Cic., Cat. 4.3. (8) Verg., Aen. 3.121 and 4.173 and 184. (9) Ter., Heaut. 190 et passim. (10) Cic., Fam. 2.16.4. (11) Hor., Sat. 1.9.78. (12) Hor., Sat. 1.10.81–83. (13) Cic., Cat. 1.12.30. (14) Cic., Inv. rhet. 1.1.1. (15) Publil. Syr. 321.

2. (1) Plaut., Stich. 5.2.2. (2) Verg., Aen. 3.121. (3) Ter., Ad. 5.8.937. (4) Cic., Marcell. 4.12. (5) Cic., Verr. 2.4.54. (6) Hor., Sat. 2.7.22–24. (7) Sen., Ep. 8.1. (8) Sen., Ep. 17.5. (9) Cic., Fin. 3.1.2. (10) Sen., Ep. 8.5. (11) Sen., Ep. 18.14, De Ira 1.1.2; cf. Capvt XVI S.A.8. (12). Sen., Ep. 18.15. (13) Sen., Ep. 115.16. (14) Hor., Carm. 3.11.45. (15) Cic., Pis. 10.22.

3. (1) Cic., Cat. 4.1. (2) Hor., Sat. 2.6.41. (3) Phaedr., Fab. I. Prologus 4. (4) Cic., Tusc. 5.3.9. (5) Hor., Sat. 2.7.84 and 88. (6) Nep., Cim. 4. (7) Hor., Epist. 1.2.56. (8) Sen., Ep. 94.43. (9) Publil. Syr., 56. (10) Publil. Syr. 697. (11) Sen., Clem. 1.2.2.

4. (1) Cic., Amic. 15.54. (2) Ter., Heaut. 2.3.295–296. (3) Ter., Ad. 5.9.961. (4) Hor., Sat. 1.4.114. (5) Proverbial; cf. Cic., Phil. 12.2.5. (6) Hor., Carm. 2.16.27–28. (7) Sen., De Ira II 18ff. and III init.; cf. Ter., Phor. 1.4.185. (8) Verg., Ecl. 5.61. (9) Hor., Sat. 1.1.25. (10) Ter., Ad. 4.5.701–702. (11) Catull. 5.7. (12) Vulg., Eccles. 1.15. (13) Cic., Amic. 21.79. (14) Pers., Sat. 6.27. (15) Cic., Cat. 1.4.9.

5. (1) Cic., Cat. 1.9.23. (2) Cic., Cat. 1.13.31. (3) Cic., Off. 1.20.68. (4) Ov., Her. 3.85. (5) Cic., Fam. 14.3.1 (6) Ter., Ad. 5.8.937. (7) Ter., Ad. 5.9.992–993. (8) Cic., Att. 2.2. (9) Sen., Cons. Polyb. 9.6. (10) Ter., Ad. 5.8.937. (11) Sen., Ep. 17.5. (12) Verg., Ecl. 5.78. (13) Hor., Epist. 2.3.445–446 (Ars Poetica).

6. (1) Cic., Tusc. 5.20.57. (2) Cic., Tusc. 5.21.61. (3) Cic., Cat. 3.1.3. (4) Cic., Cat. 3.12.29. (5) Cic., Cat. 1.6.13. (6) Liv. 21.1.2. (7) Cic., Arch. 3.5. (8) Sen., Ep. 73.16. (9) Publil. Syr. 302. (10) Publil. Syr. 282.

7. (1) Ter., Heaut. 1.1.77. (2) Vulg., Eccles. 1.10. (3) Hor., Carm. 3.1.2–4. (4) Hor., Sat. 2.7.22–23. (5) Hor., Epist. 1.16.52. (6) Mart. 12.6.11–12. (7) Hor., Sat. 1.6.15–16. (8) Cic.; cf. graffiti. (9) Sen., Ep. 82.2. (10) Cic., Phil. 10.10.20. (11) Hor., Sat. 1.9.59–60. (12) Cic., Cat. 3.12.29. (13) Vulg., Luke 2.14.

8. (1) Ter., Ad. 5.4.863. (2) Ter., Heaut. 3.1.432. (3) Laberius; see Macrob. 2.7. (4) Cic., Cat. 3.1.3. (5) Publil. Syr. 507; also Macrob. 2.7. (6) Sen., Ep. 8.3. (7) Catull. 49. (8) Liv. 26.50.1. (9) Cic., Tusc. 1.42.98. (10) Cic., Arch. 11.26. (11) Cic., Marcell. 5.15. (12) Hor., Epist. 2.2.65–66. (13) Hor., Epist. 1.2.1–2. (14) Sen., Ep. 106.12. (15) Sen., Ep. 7.8. (16) Liv. 22.39.21.

9. (1) Ter., Phor. 4.5.727. (2) Ter., Phor. 4.3.670. (3) Ter., Heaut. 4.3.709. (4) Cic., Amic. 27.102. (5) Ter., Phor. 3.3.539. (6) Cic., Cat. 1.13.31. (7) Cic., Cat. 1.4.9. (8) Mart. 10.72.4. (9) Liv. 22.39.10.

10. (1) Cic., Off. 1.20.68. (2) Ter., Ad. 4.3.593. (3) Ter., Ad. 3.2.340. (4) Mart. 6.70.15. (5) Cic., Clu. 18.51. (6) Lucr. 6.93–95. (7) Pers. 5.153. (8) Hor., Epod. 13.3–4. (9) Cic., Sen. 19.67. (10) Verg., Georg. 3.284. (11) Verg., Aen. 3.395. (12) Publil. Syr. 764. (13) Cic., Amic. 24.89.

11. (1) Hor., Sat. 2.5.33. (2) Ter., Ad. 1.1.49. (3) Plin., Ep. 1.11.1. (4) Plin., Ep. 5.18.1. (5) Ter., Hec. 1.2.197. (6) Cic., Cat. 1.8.20. (7) Cic., Marcell. 11.33. (8) Cic., Fam. 1.5.b.2. (9) Liv. 120. (10) Hor., Epist. 2.2.58. (11) Mart. 12.47. (12) Cic., Amic. 21.80.

12. (1) Vulg., Gen. 1.1 and 27. (2) Suet., Caes. 37. (3) Ter., Hec. 3.5.461. (4) Cic., Sen. 19.68. (5) Sen., Brev. Vit.; see Duff, Silver Age p. 216. (6) Ter., Phor. 2.1.302. (7) Cic., Sen. 7.22. (8) Cic., Off. 1.24.84. (9) Tac., Ann. 1.1.1. (10) Laber. in Macrob. 2.7.

13. (1) Caes., B Gall. 1.21. (2) Cic., Sull. 24.67. (3) Cic. Cat. 3.10. (4) Cic., Amic. 21.80. (5) Publil. Syr. 206. (6) Sen., Ep. 7.8. (7) Sen., Ep. 80.3. (8) Phaedr. 4.21.1.

14. (1) Vulg., Gen. 1.10. (2) Lucr. 5.822–823. (3) Verg., Ecl. 2.33. (4) Hor., Sat. 1.1.33–34. (5) Ter., Phor. 3.2.506. (6) Hor., Carm. 3.1.13. (7) Ennius in Cic., Rep. 3.3.6. (8) Sall., Cat. 3.4. (9) Hor., Carm. 3.30.6–7. (10) Hor., Epist. 2.3.268–269. (11) Cic., Sen. 6.17. (12) Hor., Epist. 1.11.27.

15. (1) Ter., Hec. 3.4.421–422. (2) Cic., Fam. 16.9.2. (3) Cic., Arch. 3.5. (4) Tac., Ann. 12.32. (5) Cic., Cat. 3.2.3. (6) Cic., Verr. 2.5.62. (7) Catull. 3.5 and 10. (8) Ter., Ad. 5.4 passim. (9) Cic., Tusc. 5.20.58.

16. (1) Phaedr., 3.7.1. (2) Verg., G. 1.145. (3) Ter., Phor. 1.4.203. (4) Cic., Or. 59.200. (5) Verg., Aen. 3.657–658. (6) Verg., Aen. 4.569–570. (7) Mart. 7.85.3–4. (8) Hor.,

Epist. 1.2.62; cf. Capvt II S.A. 11. (9) Servius on Aen. 1.683. (10) Hor., Carm. 2.16.27–28. (11) Phaedr., Fab. 1. Prologus 3–4. (12) Cic., Leg. 1.22.58. (13) Sen., Clem. 1.19.6. (14) Sen. Brev. Vit. (15) Cic., Sen. 19.70. (16) Vell. 2.66.3 (cf. Duff., Silver Age p. 91).

17. (1) Ter., Phor. 2.1.287–288. (2) Cic., N.D. 3.34.83. (3) Cic., Cat. 1.12.30. (4) Publil. Syr. 321. (5) Hor., Epist. 1.2.40–41. (6) Publil. Syr. 353. (7) Publil. Syr. 232. (8) Cic., Amic. 15.54. (9) Publil. Syr. 86. (10) Cic., Amic. 25.92. (11) Cic., Amic. 27.102. (12) Sen., Ep. 7.1 and 8.

18. (1) Verg., Aen. 5.231. (2) Tac., Ann. 15.59. (3) Cic., Cat. 1.3.6. (4) Publil. Syr. 393. (5) Ov., Met. 4.428. (6) Plin., Ep. 9.6.1. (7) Cic., Fam. 9.20.3. (8) Lucr. 3.830–831. (9) Publil. Syr. 37. (10) Cic., Marcell. 2.7. (11) Ennius (See Duff, Golden Age p. 148.) (12) Hor., Sat. 1.2.11. (13) Juv. 1.74.

19. (1) Lucr. 1.112. (2) Cic., Cat. 3.5.13. (3) Cic., Sest. 67.141. (4) Ter., Hec. 1.2.132. (5) Cic., Cat. 1.4.9. (6) Cic., Planc. 33.80. (7) Cic., Amic. 15.55.

20. (1) Mart. 13.94.1. (2) Cic., Fin. 5.29.87. (3) Cic., Amic. 12.42. (4) Cic., De Or. 1.61.261. (5) Hor., Carm. 1.38.1. (6) Hor., Sat. 1.3.66. (7) Cic., Sen. 5.15. (8) Sen., Clem. 1.6.2–3. (9) Cic., Off. 1.2.4. (10) Quint., Inst. 8.3.41. (11) Hor., Carm. 1.22.1–2. (12) Cic., Fam. 16.9.3. (13) Cic., Cat. 3.5.10.

21. (1) Publil. Syr. 507. (2) Mart. 1.86.1–2. (3) Cic., Cat. 1.11.27. (4) Hor., Epod. 16.1–2. (5) Cic., Amic. 6.22. (6) Cic., Sen. 19.69. (7) Cic., N.D. 2.62.154. (8) Cic., Sen. 17.59. (9) Phaedr., App. 27. (10) Vulg., Job 28.12. (11) Liv., 22.39.19.

22. (1) Cic., Att. 9.10.3. (2) Hor., Carm. 2.3.1–2. (3) Cic., Rep. 3.31. (4) Cic., Cat. 1.1.3. (5) Cic., Marcell. 10.32. (6) Cic., Cat. 1.12.30. (7) Cic., Cat. 3.1.1. (8) Liv. 32.33.10. (9) Plaut., Aul. 4.10.772. (10) Cic., Amic. 17.64. (11) Hor., Epist. 2.3.148–149. (12) Verg., Georg. 2.490 and 493. (13) Sen., Ep. 17.12. (14) Hor., Epist. 1.1.19. (15) Hor., Sat. 1.1.106–107. (16) Mart. 10.76.1

23. (1) Cic., Cat. 1.2.6. (2) Liv. 44.42.4. (3) Hor., Sat. 1.1.68–69. (4) Cic., N.D. 2.4.12. (5) Hor., Epist. 2.1.156. (6) Nep., Att. 4. (7) Quint., Inst. Praef. 5. (8) Hor., Sat. 1.10.72. (9) Quint., Inst. 11.3.157. (10) Cic., N.D. 3.33.82. (11) Cic., Sen. 3.9. (12) Hor., Epist. 1.16.66. (13) Sen., Ep. 61.3. (14) Hor., Epist. 1.18.71.

24. (1) Cf. Plutarch, Cato ad fin. (2) Plin., HN 33.148. (3) Caes., B Civ. 2.43. (4) Cic., Rosc. Am. 1.3. (5) Cic., Marcell. 8.24. (6) Hor., Carm. 3.14.14–16. (7) Cic., Rep. 2.30. (8) Tac., Dial. 5. (9) Caes., B. Gall. 2.20

25. (1) Ter., Heaut. Prolog. 18. (2) Cic., 1.11.27. (3) Cic., Cat. 1.11.27. (4) Cic., Cat. 3.2.4. (5) Cic., Cat. 4.10.22. (6) Cic., Off. 1.1.1. (7) Ter., Phor. 4.1.581–582. (8) Cic., Sen. 16.56. (9) Ennius in Cic., Div. 2.56.116. (10) Cic., Tusc. 1.42.101. (11) Cic., Tusc. 5.37.108. (12) Cic., quoted in Dumesnil's Lat. Synonyms s.v. abnuere. (13) Cic., Tusc., 5.40.118. (14) Cic., Sen. 21.77. (15) Cic., Sen. 19.68. (16) Plin., Ep. 7.9.15.

26. (1) Cic., Sen. 16.55. (2) Cic., Cat. 1.3.6. (3) Sen., Controv. 6.7.2; Publil. Syr. 253. (4) Cic., Cat. 3.1.5. (5) Sen., Ep. 61.3. (6) Ov., Her. 17.71–72. (7) Hor., Epod. 2.1,7,8. (8) Cic.,

Amic. 26.99. (9) Cic., Sen. 19.68. (10) Mart. 1.107.1–2. (11) Mart. 14.208. (12) Cic., Off. 1.22.74. (13) Catull. 12.

27. (1) Ov., Met. 7.21–22. (2) Mart. 1.16.1. (3) Ter., Ad. 5.5.884, 5.7.922. (4) Plin., Ep. 10.88. (5) Cic., Sen. 6.19. (6) Cic., Off. 1.22.78. (7) Cic., Off. 1.22.77. (8) Cic., Sen. 2.5. (9) Sen., Ep. 17.9. (10) See Capvt IV S.A.7. (11) Cic., Marcell. 3.8. (12) Cic., Tusc. 5.20.57–5.21.62. (13) Verg., Aen. 7.312.

28. (1) Liv. 22.39.21. (2) Cic., Off. 1.22.77. (3) Cic., Cat. 1.7.18. (4) Ter., Phor. 5.5.831. (5) Hor., Epod. 13.3–4. (6) Sen., Ep. 80.3. (7) Sen. (8) Diog. Laert.: a Latin translation from his Greek. (9) Quint., Inst. 2.2.5. (10) Cic., Amic. 24.89. (11) Ov., Ars Am. 1.97. (12) Verg., Aen. 1.1–2.

29. (1) Verg., Ecl. 10.69. (2) Verg., Aen. 4.653, 655 (3) Ter., Phor. 3.2.497–498. (4) Hor., Epist. 1.1.40. (5) Juv. 1.30. (6) Cic., Cat. 1.1.3. (7) Cic., Phil. 10.10.20. (8) Cic., Phil. 4.5.9. (9) Nep., Milt. 5. (10) Cic., De Or. 1.61.260. (11) Hor., Ars. P. (Epist. 2.3) 335–336. (12) Ter., Heaut. 4.2.675. (13) Cic., Off. 1.23.80. (14) Cic., Amic. 9.29.

30. (1) Cic., Cat. 4.3.6. (2) Phaedr. 3.7.1. (3) Hor., Sat. 1.5.67–68. (4) Verg., Ecl. 8.43. (5) Hor., Sat. 1.4.16. (6) Cic., Marcell. 10.30. (7) Lucr. 1.55–56. (8) Lucr. 2.4. (9) Hor., Epist. 1.2.1–4. (10) Hor., Epist. 1.18.96–97, 100–101. (11) Sen., Ep. 115.14. (12) Prop. 2.15.29–30. (13) Cic., Tusc. 1.41.99.

31. (1) Cic., Cat. 1.6.15. (2) Cic., Amic. 12.42. (3) Cic., Cat. 1.5.10 and 1.9.23. (4) Hor., Carm. 1.14.1–2. (5) Cic., Marcell. 7.22. (6) Cic., Q. Fr. 1.2.4.14. (7) Cic., Cat. 3.5.12. (8) Cic., Sen. 10.33. (9) Liv. 45.8. (10) Ter., Ad. 2.1.155. (11) Ter., Phor. 1.2.137–138. 12. Cic., Cluent. 53.146.

32. (1) Publil. Syr. 512. (2) Cic., Cat. 1.5.10. (3) Hor., Epist. 1.6.29. (4) Ter., Ad. 5.9.996. (5) Ter., Heaut. 4.1.622. (6) Cic., Sen. 3.7. (7) Ter., Ad. 4.5.701. (8) Caes., B Gall. 3.18. (9) Plaut., Trin. 2.2.361. (10) Publil. Syr. 129. (11) Sall., Cat. 8. (12) Cic., Fin. 3.7.26. (13) See Capvt XVIII S.A. 11. (14) Sen., Ep. 80.6. (15) Hor., Sat. 1.1.25–26. 16. Hor., Epist. 2.3.102–103 (Ars Poetica).

33. (1) Veg., Mil. Prolog. 3. (2) Cic., Off. 1.22.76. (3) Cic., Sull. 31.87. (4) Cic., Q. Fr. 1.3.5. (5) Phaedr. App. 18. (6) Hor., Sat. 2.7.22–24. (7) Publil. Syr. 412. (8) Hor., Carm. 4.10.6. (9) Juv. 3.152–153. (10) Cic., Cat. 1.5.10. (11) Quint., Inst. 4.5.13.

34. (1) Verg., Aen. 3.188. (2) Hor., Sat. 1.3.68–69. (3) Cic., N.D. 2.62.154. (4) Cf. Sen., De Ira 2.9.1 and Cic., Tusc. 3.9.19. (5) Cic., Cat. 1.5.10. (6) Hor., Carm. 3.16.17. (7) Cic., Fam. 7.10.1. (8) Publil. Syr. 350. (9) Mart. Bk. I Praef. 1–2. (10) Cic., Sen. 19.69. (11) Ter., Heaut. 1.2.239–240. (12) Cic., Amic. 6.22. (13) Cic., De Or. 2.67.274. (14) Verg., Aen. 1.199.

35. (1) Sen., cf. Ep. 8.7; and Hor., Sat. 2.7.83 ff. and Epist. 1.16.66. (2) Publil. Syr. 290. (3) Publil. Syr. 99. (4) Hor., Sat. 1.1.86–87. (5) Cic., Fin. 1.18.60, 4.24.65; De Or. 1.3.10 et passim. (6) Publil. Syr. 767 and 493. (7) Vulg., Gen. 1.26. (8) Cic., Rep. 2.24.59. (9) Caes., B Gall. 4.23 and 5.45. (10) Quint., Inst. 10.1.112. (11) Hor., Epist. 2.2.41–42. (12) Publil. Syr. 687. (13) Hor., Sat. 2.2.135–136. (14) Verg., Aen. 1.630. (15) Publil. Syr. 288. (16) Aug., Conf. 10.20.29. (17) Plaut. Pers. 3.1.332.

36. (1) Vulg., Gen. 1.3. (2) Lucr. 1.205. (3) Ter., Heaut. 2.3.314. (4) Caes., B Civ. 2.43. (5) Ter., Ad. 3.4.505. (6) Ter., Heaut. 5.5.1049 and 1067. (7) Hor., Carm. 1.11.7–8. (8) Pers. 5.151–152. (9) Sen., Ep. 61.2. (10) Cic., Sen. 8.26. (11) Hor., Epist. 2.2.206–211. (12) Hor., Carm. 1.24.19–20. (13) Ov., Am. 1.2.10. (14) Cic., Amic. 5.7. (15) Cic., Arch. 2.3. (16) Pseudo-Sen., Proverbs 104. (17) Publil. Syr. 107.

37. (1) Hor., Epist. 2.3.68. (2) Verg., Aen. 6.127. (3) Ov., Ars Am. 3.62–65. (4) Ter., Hec. 1.2.132; Ad. 1.1.26. (5) Ter., Ad. 5.5.882. (6) Ter., Ad. 4.1.517, 4.2.556. (7) Hor., Sat. 1.9.1. (8) Cic., Tusc. 5.21.62. (9) Cic., Verr. 2.4.54.120. (10) Ter., Hec. 3.4.421 and 423. (11) Cic., Cat. 1.9.23. (12) Nep., Att. 8; Cic., Phil. 2.12.28, Tusc. 5.37.109 (names changed). (13) Cic., Att. 12.50. (14) Cic., Sen. 7.24. (15) Prop., 2.15.23–24. (16) Ter., An. 64–65.

38. (1) Caes., B Gall. 1.31. (2) Cic., Cat. 1.4.9. (3) Cat., 4.7.16. (4) Cic., Amic. 7.23. (5) Cic., Cat. 1.6.13. (6) Cic., Amic. 15.53. (7) Cic., Cat. 1.7.18. (8) Cic., Cat. 4.11.24. (9) Verg., Ecl. 1.7. (10) Cic., Fam. 4.5.6. (11) Sen., Ep. 17.11. (12) Cic., Marcell. 4.11. (13) Plin., Ep. 5.16.4–5. (14) Hor., Carm. 1.37.1–2. (15) Ov., Am. 1.11.18. (16) Plaut., Stich. 139.

39. (1) Cic., Cat. 1.12.30. (2) Cic., Cat. 1.13.32. (3) Cic., Off. 1.22.74. (4) Publil. Syr. 762. (5) Cic., Off. 1.25.89. (6) Cic., Verr. 2.4.54. (7) Cic., Off. 3.32.113. (8) Cic., Sest. 2.5 (9) Cic., Sen. 5.15. (10) Cic., Att. 2.23.1. (11) Publil. Syr. 704. (12) Cic., Leg. 1.23.60. (13) Verg., Aen. 4.175. (14) Cic., Fam. 5.12.4. (15) Cic., De Or. 2.87.3.

40. (1) Cic., Cat. 4.7.14. (2) Hor., Carm. 3.30.6–7. (3) Cic., Tusc. 1.41.97. (4) Ter., Ad. 5.4.856. (5) Sen., Ep. 7.7. (6) Plin., Ep. 9.6.2. (7) Lucr. 4.1286–87. (8) Cic., Fam. 14.12. (9) Liv.: see Locī Im. XVII. (10) Cic., Marcell. 10.32. (11) Catull. 43.1–3. (12) Ter., Heaut. 1.1.77. (13) Cic., Amic. 21.81. (14) Vulg., Exod. 20.11. (15) Caes., B Gall. 1.47. (16) Cic., Cat. 1.4.8. (17) Cic., Planc. 42.101.

# ABOUT THE AUTHORS

Frederic M. Wheelock (1902–1987) received the A.B., A.M., and Ph.D. degrees from Harvard University. His long and distinguished teaching career included appointments at Haverford College, Harvard University, the College of the City of New York, Brooklyn College, Cazenovia Junior College (where he served as Dean), the Darrow School for Boys (New Lebanon, NY), the University of Toledo (from which he retired as full Professor in 1968), and a visiting professorship at Florida Presbyterian (now Eckerd) College. He published a number of articles and reviews in the fields of textual criticism, palaeography, and the study of Latin; in addition to *Wheelock's Latin* (previously titled *Latin: An Introductory Course Based on Ancient Authors*), his books include *Wheelock's Latin Reader* (previously titled *Latin Literature: A Book of Readings*) and *Quintilian as Educator* (trans. H. E. Butler; introd. and notes by Prof. Wheelock). Professor Wheelock was a member of the American Classical League, the American Philological Association, and the Classical Association of the Atlantic States. Biographies of Dr. Wheelock authored by Professor Ward Briggs appear in his book, *A Biographical Dictionary of American Classicists* (Westport, CT: Greenwood Press, 1994), as well as in the Winter, 2003, issue of *The Classical Outlook*. Frederic retired to Amherst, New Hampshire, and then to Kent, Connecticut with his beloved wife of 50 years, Dorothy Rathbone Wheelock. He is survived by his two daughters, Martha Wheelock and Deborah Wheelock Taylor, who have continued his tradition as teachers, and by his two grandchildren, Vanessa Taylor Sands and Ian Taylor.

Richard A. LaFleur received the B.A. and M.A. in Latin from the University of Virginia and the Ph.D. in Classical Studies from Duke. He has taught since 1972 at the University of Georgia, where he served for 21 years as head of one of the largest Classics programs in North America and was appointed in 1998 to the chair of Franklin Professor of Classics. He has numerous publications in Latin language, literature, and pedagogy, including the books *The Teaching of Latin in American Schools: A Profession in Crisis, Latin Poetry for the Beginning Student, Love and Transformation: An Ovid Reader, Latin for the 21st Century: From Concept to Classroom, A Song of War: Readings from Vergil's Aeneid* (with Alexander G. McKay), *Scribblers, Scvlptors, and Scribes,* and the revised editions of *Wheelock's Latin, Wheelock's Latin Reader,* and (with Paul Comeau) *Workbook for Wheelock's Latin.*

Professor LaFleur served as editor of *The Classical Outlook* for nearly 25 years and is a past President of the American Classical League. He has been recipient of more than a million dollars in grants from the National Endowment for the Humanities and other agencies, and of state, regional, and national awards for teaching and professional service, including the American Philological Association's award for Excellence in the Teaching of Classics. He has three children (Jean-Paul, Caroline, and Kimberley) and five grandchildren (Zachary, Jackson, Lucas, Anna Caroline, and Charlotte), and joyfully resides with his wife Alice in the home she designed for them on the banks of Lake Oglethorpe, near Athens, Georgia.

# CREDITS

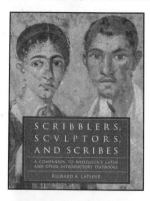
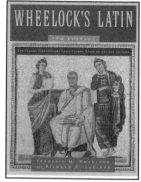
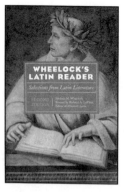